29th Pacific Asia Conference on Language, Information and Computation (PACLIC 2015)

Shanghai, China
30 October – 1 November 2015

ISBN: 978-1-5108-1756-2

Printed from e-media with permission by:

Curran Associates, Inc.
57 Morehouse Lane
Red Hook, NY 12571

Some format issues inherent in the e-media version may also appear in this print version.

Printed by Curran Associates, Inc. (2015)

Association for Computational Linguistics
209 N. Eighth Street
Stroudsburg, Pennsylvania 18360

Phone: 1-570-476-8006
Fax: 1-570-476-0860

acl@aclweb.org

Additional copies of this publication are available from:

Curran Associates, Inc.
57 Morehouse Lane
Red Hook, NY 12571 USA
Phone: 845-758-0400
Fax: 845-758-2634
Email: curran@proceedings.com
Web: www.proceedings.com

Sponsors

Department of Computer Science and Engineering, Shanghai Jiao Tong University
Chinese Information Processing Society of Chine (CIPS)
LY Education Technology
Shanghai Computer Federation Artificial Intelligence Committee (SCFAIC)

Preface

Distinguished scholars and colleagues:

The 29th Pacific Asia Conference on Language, Information and Computation (PACLIC 29) is organized by the Department of Computer Science and Engineering, Shanghai Jiao Tong University, October 30 - November 1, 2015. The PACLIC series of conferences emphasize the synergy of theoretical analysis and processing of language, and provide a forum for researchers in different fields of language study in the Pacific-Asia region to share their findings and interests in the formal and empirical study of languages. For the past years since its establishment, the PACLIC conferences have gained more and more interests and participations from linguistic researchers, as evidenced by the increasing number of papers and by the wider range of topics. Organized under the auspices of the PACLIC Steering Committee, it is the latest installment of our long standing collaborative efforts among theoretical and computational linguists in the Pacific-Asia region.

PACLIC conference has received an overwhelming response of 221 papers from 104 countries or regions namely China, Japan, Korea, Hong Kong, Taiwan, France, Israel, New Zealand, Thailand, Tunisia, UK, Vietnam, Algeria, Egypt, Germany, India, Ireland, Singapore (87.50% from 10 regions in Asia, 6.73% from 4 regions in Europe, 3.85% from Africa, 1.92% from New Zealand). To ensure that all accepted papers meet the high quality standard of the PACLIC conference, each submission was reviewed by 2-4 reviewers. As a result, only approximately 63 (28.5%) of top-notch academic papers were accepted for oral presentations and 41 (18.5%) for poster sessions. From these accepted papers, 104 (47.0%) papers were presented and published in this proceedings.

PACLIC-29 thanks for tremendous efforts and contributions from several parties. We congratulate the Department of Computer Science and Engineering, Shanghai Jiao Tong University, Chinese Information Processing Society of Chine (CIPS), LY Education Technology and Shanghai Computer Federation Artificial Intelligence Committee (SCFAIC) for their collaboration towards this significant achievement. We would like to take this opportunity to thank our keynote and invited speakers, namely Dr. Sumita Eiichiro from the National Institute of Information and Communications Technology (NICT, Japan), Professor Guodong Zhou from Soochow University, Dr. Philippe Blache from National Center for Scientific Research (CNRS, France), Professor Renqiang Wang from Sichuan International Studies University and Assistant Professor Yao Yao from Hong Kong Polytechnic University. We are also overwhelmed with a sense of gratitude for the presenters and colleagues for donating your valuable time to attend and enrich this conference.

PC Chair
Hai Zhao

Program Committee:

Wirote Aroonmanakun	Chulalongkorn University
Hailong Cao	HIT
Hee-Rahk Chae	Hankuk University of Foreign Studies
Wanxiang Che	Harbin Institute of Technology
Doris Chen	National Taiwan Normal University
Kuang-Hua Chen	National Taiwan University
Wenliang Chen	Soochow University
Eng-Siong Chng	Nanyang Technological University
Siaw-Fong Chung	National Chengchi University
Beatrice Daille	Laboratoire d'Informatique de Nantes Atlantique
Jing Ding	The Hong Kong Polytechnic University
Amanda Ding	
Chen-Chun E	The Hong Kong Polytechnic University
Guohong Fu	Heilongjiang University
Helena Hong Gao	Nanyang Technological University
Wei Gao	Qatar Computing Research Institute
Yasunari Harada	Waseda University
Choochart Haruechaiyasak	National Electronics and Computer Technology Center (NECTEC)
Munpyo Hong	Sungkyunkwan Univ.
Shu-Kai Hsieh	National Taiwan Normal University
Jong-Bok Kim	Kyung Hee University
Richard Kim	Fudan University
Valia Kordoni	Humboldt University Berlin
Oi-Yee Kwong	The Chinese University of Hong Kong
Huei-Ling Lai	National Chengchi University
Gina-Anne Levow	University of Washington

Rui Wang	Shanghai Jiao Tong University
Jiajuan Xiong	The University of Hong Kong
Ruifeng Xu	Harbin Institute of Technology
Hongzhi Xu	The Hong Kong Polytechnic University
Cheng-Zen Yang	Dept. of Computer Science and Engineering, Yuan Ze University
Kei Yoshimoto	Tohoku University
Liang-Chih Yu	Yuan Ze University
Jiajun Zhang	Institute of Automation Chinese Academy of Sciences
Qi Zhang	Fudan University
Yu Zhou	CIP, NLPR, CASIA
Ming Zhou	Microsoft
Conghui Zhu	Harbin Institute of Tecnology, China
Michael Zock	CNRS-LIF

Keynote talk

Sumita Eiichiro (NICT, Japan)

Talk Title:Research Activities for Translating Asian Languages

Abstract: This talk will introduce automatic translation projects for Asian languages, wherein we intend to seek greater cooperation.

First, a worldwide speech translation consortium, Universal Speech Translation Advanced Research (U-STAR), is introduced. Speech translation involves the integration of three elements: speech recognition, machine translation, and speech synthesis; therefore, to build a speech translation system that includes many languages including Asian languages, it is a good idea to cooperate with other laboratories that specialize in the languages concerned. The consortium now comprises 32 institutes from 27 different countries/regions. The collaboration has improved the accuracy of the integrated systems and has created new forms of integration. U-STAR is always open and welcomes new participants.

Second, we introduce two projects related to the translation of Asian languages: the Workshop on Asian Translation (WAT) and the Asian Language Treebank (ALT). WAT is an open evaluation campaign focusing on translation among Asian languages. We will outline the workshops conducted in past two years' and touch on our plan for next year. ALT is currently a start-up project that will undertake the task of building a treebank of Asian languages. This will be a valuable language resource, not only as a parser for each language but also as an accurate translation system from one language to another.

Third, we discuss the Global Communication Program (GCP), a Japanese government project announced in April 2014 to develop a multi-lingual speech translation system to bridge the language barrier during the Olympic Games in 2020. It aims to provide real-time machine translation services, by using National Institute of Information and Communications Technology's (NICT) translation technology, in day-to-day situations to help foreigners who may feel hesitant about coming to Japan. It will cover 10 languages, including Asian ones, e.g., Thai, Vietnamese, Indonesian, and Myanmar. At NICT, public and private entities have already begun working together as part of a nationwide collaboration. This talk will explain the current status and future vision.

Finally, we touch on NICT's recent research topics, including an approach to high-quality patent translation and new ideas on neural translation.

Zhou Guodong (Soochow University)

Talk: Building Chinese Discourse Corpus with Connective-driven Dependency Tree Structure

Abstract: It is well-known that interpretation of a text requires understanding of its rhetorical relation hierarchy since discourse units rarely exist in isolation. Such discourse structure is fundamental to discourse understanding and many text-based applications. In this talk, we propose a Connective-driven Dependency Tree (CDT) scheme to represent the discourse rhetorical structure in Chinese language, with elementary discourse units as leaf nodes and connectives as non-leaf nodes, largely motivated by the Penn Discourse Treebank and the Rhetorical Structure Theory. In particular, connectives are employed to directly represent the hierarchy of the tree structure and the rhetorical relation of a discourse, while the nuclei of discourse units are globally determined with reference to the dependency theory. Guided by the CDT scheme, we manually annotate a Chinese Discourse Treebank (CDTB) of 500 documents. Preliminary evaluation justifies the appropriateness of the CDT scheme to Chinese discourse analysis and the usefulness of our manually annotated CDTB corpus.

Guodong Zhou is a distinguished professor (Grade II) and a member of the university academic committee in Soochow University, China. He obtained his Ph.D. degree from National University of Singapore in 1999. He joined the Institute of Infocomm Research, Singapore in 1999 and Soochow University in 2006. His research interests include natural language processing and artificial intelligence with more and more focus on fundamental language issues.

Prof Zhou has published over 100 papers in leading NLP and AI conferences and journals such as ACL/EMNLP/COLING/AAAI/IJCAI with over 4000 citations (Google Scholar). He was/is on the editorial board of several international journals, such as Computational Linguistics, ACM TALIP and Chinese Journal of Software, and is a regular PC member of the major conferences in NLP and AI.

Since 2006, Prof Zhou has established the Suda NLP lab with now 16 staff members, including 7 full professors and 7 associate professors.

Philippe Blache (CNRS)

Talk Title:New approaches to sentence processing: a cognitive perspective

Abstract: Sentence processing is usually considered as an incremental mechanism: each new word is integrated into a structure under construction that can be interpreted compositionally. In this architecture, understanding a sentence comes to a step-by-step building of the meaning. I will present in this talk different elements challenging this approach. Starting from works in linguistics, psycholinguistics and natural language processing, we will see that language processing by human can be, depending on the situation, very superficial and incomplete. A more realistic language processing architecture would therefore have to integrate into a unique model different levels of processing: one which is superficial, relying on the recognition of large units with a strong cohesion; and another consisting in a classical incremental word by word integration. This organization corresponds to a double level shallow-and-deep parsing process.

Table of Contents

PACLIC 2015

29th Pacific Asia Conference on Language, Information and Computation

Proceedings of PACLIC 2015: Oral Papers

Program chair:

Hai Zhao

30 October - 1 November, 2015

Shanghai, China

Two-level Word Class Categorization Model in Analytic Languages and Its Implications for POS Tagging in Modern Chinese Corpora

Renqiang Wang
Graduate School,
Sichuan International Studies University,
Chongqing 40031
wangrenqiang@sisu.edu.cn

Changning Huang
Department of Computer Science and Technology, Tsinghua University,
Beijing 100084
cnhuang0908@126.com

Abstract

The study of word classes has a history of over 4000 years, and the word class problem in over 1000 analytic languages like Modern Chinese can be seen as the Goldbach Conjecture in linguistics. This paper first outlines the existing problems in the POS tagging of Modern Chinese corpora with a case study of 自信. Then it introduces the Two-level Word Class Categorization Model in analytic languages, which is based on the perspectives of language as a complex adaptive system and the nature of major parts of speech as propositional speech act functions. Finally, the implications of Two-level Word Class Categorization Model for POS tagging in Modern Chinese corpora are explored.

1 Introduction

Categorization is a fundamental task in linguistics, and linguistic categories like word classes or parts of speech were considered as the study of "god particles" in language in the 36th Annual Conference of the German Linguistic Society held at the University of Marburg, Germany, in March, 2014. In natural language processing, part-of-speech tagging plays a key role. As pointed out by Rabbi (2012), "It is a significant pre-requisite for putting a human language on the engineering track." The study of word classes has a history of over 4000 years, but the word class problem in over one thousand analytic languages like Modern Chinese, Modern English and Tongan can be seen as the Goldbach Conjecture in linguistics, which has witnessed several upsurges over the last century.

Let's take the example of 自信 in Chinese. The first five editions of *The Contemporary Chinese Dictionary* (hereinafter called CCD) have almost the same treatment of 自信 with the only definition of 相信自己, which is obviously a verbal usage according to the definition metalanguage, though it is only in CCD5 published in 2005 that the lexeme is explicitly labeled as VERB:

【自信】 zìxìn 动 相信自己：～心｜～能够完成这个任务。

In CCD6 published in 2012, however,

29th Pacific Asia Conference on Language, Information and Computation pages 1 - 10
Shanghai, China, October 30 - November 1, 2015

we can see that 自信 is labeled as a multi-category lexeme belonging to VERB, NOUN and ADJECTIVE:

【自信】zìxìn ❶ 动 相信自己：～心 ｜ ～能够完成这个任务。❷ 名 对自己的信心：不能失去～ ｜ 工作了几年之后，他更多了几分～。❸ 形 对自己有信心：他做事总是很～。

In the second edition of *The Grammatical knowledge-base of Contemporary Chinese — A Complete Specification* (Yu et al., 2003), 自信 is specified only as VERB with the following examples, which illustrate its typical usages:

～心 ｜ 他～自己能考取北京大学/我～能完成任务/～地说/在困难面前，需要～

Then what about the POS tagging of 自信 in Chinese corpora? We downloaded all the concordance lines from the Modern Chinese Corpus developed by the China National Language and Character Working Committee (hereinafter called CN CORPUS, http:// cncorpus.org/ CCindex. aspx). There are altogether 187 downloadable concordance lines of 自信. As shown in Table 1, the most frequent usages of 自信 are as VERB and ADJECTIVE, with only one occurrence as NOUN.

	parts of speech	frequency	percentage
1	VV	142	75.94%
2	JJ	43	22.99%
3	NN	1	0.53%
4	word-formation morpheme	1	0.53%
total		187	100.00%

Table 1: POS Tagging of 自信 in CN CORPUS

However, through careful analysis, we find that 117 of them (accounting for 62.54%) seem to have problems in their POS tagging. Though the usages of 自信 in the corpus are respectively tagged as VERB, ADJECTIVE and NOUN, which seems to be consistent with the word class labeling in CCD6, we have found the following five types of problematic POS tagging in CN CORPUS:

First, usages of reference when used as subjects or objects of the sentences are tagged differently with the parts of speech of NOUN as in (1), ADJECTIVE as in (2), (3), (8), (9) and (12), and VERB as in (4), (5), (6), (7), (10), (11), (13), (14) and (15). Admittedly, not all of them are correct tagging. Moreover, usages of 自信 classified by 一种 are all tagged as VERB as in (5), (6) and (7), which are typical nominal usages. Interestingly, juxtaposed words as objects of the sentences are obviously NOUN like 激情 and 力量 while 自信 are still tagged as VERB, as in (11) and (12).

(1) 话/n 虽/c 这么说/v ，/w 织云/nh 也/d 并/c 没有/v 多少/m 自信/n

(2) /w 声音/n 里/nd 没有/v 一点/m 自信/a ，/w 连/p 她/r 自己/r 也/d 感觉/v 到了/v 。/w

(3) 他/r 那/r 种/q 到/v 哪儿/r 、/w 永远/d 吃/v 得/u 开/v 的/u 自信/a 从/p 何/r 而/c 来/vd ？/w

(4) 聪明/a 、/w 好学/v 、/w 自信/v 是/vl 王惠莹/nh 的/u 突出/a 特点/n 。/w

(5) w 在/p 中国/ns 模特/n 身上/nl 有/v 一/m 种/q 发自/v 内心/n 的/u 自信/v …/w …/w

(6) 他/r 笑/v 了/u ，/w 眸子/n 里/nd 透出/v 一/m 种/q 自信/v 。/w

(7) 但/c 她/r 时时/d 表现/v 出/vd 一/m 种/q 能/vu 战胜/v 危险/a 的/u 自信/v 。/w

(8) 雷嘉/nh 帮助/v 她/r 获得/v 了/u 冷静/a 和/c 自信/a 。/w

(9) 他/r 充满/v 了/u 对/p 自己/r 这/r 一代/nt 人/n 的/u 骄傲/a 和/c 自信/a 。/w

(10) 口气/n 充满/v 了/u 自信/v 。/w

(11) 一/m 个/q 人/n 只要/vu 真正/a 树立/v 了/u 对/p 祖国/n 、/w 对/p 人民/n 、/w 对/p 社会/n 的/u 责任感/n ，/w 就/d 会/vu 自觉/a 地/u 对/p 生活/n 充满/v 激情/n 和/c 自信/v

(12) 他/r 又/d 恢复/v 了/u 自信/a 和/c 力量/n 。/w

(13) /w 他/r 怔怔/a 地/u 看/v 着/u 我/r ，/w 但/c 很快/a 又/d 恢复/v 了/u 自信/v

(14) 她/r 的/u 笑容/n 中/nd 蕴含/v 着/u 对/p 改革/v 的/u 无限/d 自信/v 。/w

(15) 我/r 仔细/a 想/v 着/u ，/w 把/p 花/n 角儿/n 的/u 动作/n 合理化/v ，/w 使/v 自己/r 增加/v 自信/v

Secondly, usages of modification of entities are tagged differently with the parts of speech of ADJECTIVE as in (16) to (18), and VERB as in (19) to (24) , even when juxtaposed words like 平静, 刚愎, 愉快 and 自大 are tagged as ADJECTIVE as in (19), (21), (22) and (23).

(16) /w 吉明/nhs 本来/d 是/vl 个/q 坚强/a 自信/a 的/u 青年/n

(17) /w 她/r 的/u 眼睛/n 不如/v 水子/nh 灵气/n ，/w 透出/v 刚毅/a 自信/a 的/u 光芒/n ；

(18) 渐渐/a 他/r 的/u 脸色/n 恢复/v 了/u 常态/n ，/w 又/d 浮上/vd 了/u 他/r 平日/n 那/r 种/q 自信/a 和/c 冷漠/a 的/u 神气/n

(19) /w 一个/mq 平静/a 而/c 又/d 自信/v 的/u 声音/n ，/w 在/p 我们/r 身后/nl 响起/v 。

(20) /w 当/p 他/r 年轻/a 的/u 时候/n 他/r 是/vl 非常/d 自信/v 的/u 人/n 。/w

(21) 刚才/d 还/d 刚愎/a 自信/v 的/u 斐烈/nh ，/w 这时候/nt 抓耳挠腮/i ，/w 无可奈何/i 地/u 摇/v 了/u 摇头/v 。/w

(22) 他/r 那/r 愉快/a 的/u 自信/v 的/u 调子/n ，/w 好象是/v 他/r 在/p 指挥/v 着/u 它们/r 似的/u 。

(23) 在/p 他们/r 这/r 种/q 自信/v 的/u 心理/n ，/w 也/d 可/vu 说/v 是/vl 自大/a 的/u 心理/n ，/w 这/r 种/q 精神/n 胜利/v 便/d 成为/v 绝对/a 不可/vu 缺/v 之/u 物/n 。/w

(24) 看/v 着/u 王惠莹/nh 领奖/v 时/nt 自信/v 的/u 面容/n ，/w 许多/a 体操/n 行家/n 和/c 新闻记者/n 都/d 预言/v

Thirdly, usages of predicative adjectives of 自信 are tagged differently: some are tagged as ADJECTIVE as in (25) to (28), whereas others as VERB as in (29) to (33), even when juxtaposed words like 精干, 果断 and 平静 are tagged as ADJECTIVE as in (30), (32) and (33).

(25) /w 他/r 的/u 口气/n 倔强/a 而/c 自信/a 。/w

(26) 中国人/n 哟/u ，/w 是/vl 大胆/a 、/w 自信/a 的/u ，/w 有时/d 甚至/d 是/vl 执拗/a 的/u 。

(27) /w 他/r 的/u 神色/n 显得/v 更/d 庄严/a 、/w 更/d 高傲/a 和/c 更/d 自信/a 了/u 。/w

(28) 但/c 那时/nt 你/r 年轻/a ，/w 自信/a ，/w 浑身/n 洋溢/v 着/u 青春/n 的/u 活力/n

(29) 也许/d 他/r 太/d 过于/d 自信/v ，/w 命运/n 竟/d 捉弄/v 了/u 他/r —/w

(30) /w 模样/n 儿/k 很/d 精干/a ，/w 也/d 很/d 自信/v 。

(31) 灰灰/nh 可/d 自信/v 啦/u ，/w 他/r 说/v ：/w "/w 是/vl 红海/ns ！/w

(32) 白脖黑/n 她/r 从来/d 都/d 是/vl 走/v 在/p 鸭/n 群/n 队伍/n 的/u 第/h 一个/mq ：/w 挺/v 着/u 胸脯/n ，/w 自信/v 而/c 又/d 果断/a

(33) 王/nhf 所长/n 用/p 疑惑/v 的/u 目光/n 望/v 着/u 冯/nhf 教授/n ，/w 教授/n 还是/d 那么/r 平静/a 而/c 自信/v ：/w

Fourthly, usages of 自信 plus 地 in adverbial constructions are tagged differently: ADJECTIVE in (34) and (35) while VERB in (36) to (38).

(34) 戈华/nh 非常/d 自信/a 地/u 判断/v 说/v 。

(35) 高福源/nh 很/d 自信/a 地/u 表示/v ：/w "/w 我/r 自己/r 既然/c 要求/v 回去/v ，/w 就/d 有/v 这个/r 把握/v 。/w

(36) 黑仔/nh 作/v 了/u 一下/mq 深呼吸/v ，/w 十分/d 自信/v 地/u 说/v 。

(37) 盟军/n 总参谋长/n 自信/v 地/u 用/p 指示/n 棍/n 指点/v 着/u 墙上/nl 的/u 军用地图/n

(38) 我/r 自信/v 地/u 说/v ：/w "/w 我/r 要/vu 发明/v 一/m 种/q 更/d 理想/a 的/u 东西/n ，/w 是/vl 给/p 人/n 吃/v 的/u ！/w

Lastly, word-formation usages of 自信 are tagged differently: no tagging in (39) while VERB in (40) to (42), the latter of which seems somewhat awkward .

(39) /w 提高/v 全/a 民族/n 的/u 自信心/n 更有/v 其/r 伟大/a 意义/n 。/w

(40) 鲁迅/nh 先生/n 曾/d 对/p "/w 不/d 失掉/v 自信/v 力/n 的/u 中国人/n "/w 给予/v 热烈/a 的/u 赞颂/v

(41) 一个/mq 国家/n ，/w 一个/mq 民族/n ，/w 如果/c 没有/v 自信/v 力/n 就/d 不/d 可能/vu 振兴/v 社稷/n

(42) /w 使/v 人/n 在/p 认知/v 上/nd 建立/v 了/u 极/d 大/a 的/u 安全感/n 与/c 稳定/a 感/n ，/w 以及/c 对/p 自己/r 的/u 自信/v 感/n 。

To sum up, we have the following questions: (1) Both the first five editions of CCD and the second edition of *The Grammatical knowledge-base of Contemporary Chinese — A Complete Specification* seem to have adhered to the Principle of Parsimony (namely fewest possible multi-category words), as advocated by Lü Shuxiang (1979), Zhu Dexi (1985), Guo Rui (2002), Lu Jianming (1994, 2013), Yu Shiwen et al (2003) and Shen Jiaxuan (2009, 2012), but then is the word class labeling of 自信 as VERB, NOUN and ADJECTIVE in CCD6 correct? (2) What's the relationship between the word class labeling of lexemes in Chinese dictionaries and the part-of-speech tagging in Chinese corpora? (3) How to improve the part-of-speech tagging in Chinese corpora? To properly answer the above questions, we will first introduce the Two-level Word Class Categorization Model (TLWCCM) in analytic languages and then discuss its implications for the part-of-speech tagging in Chinese corpora.

2 Two-level Word Class Categorization Model (TLWCCM)

2.1 The Theoretical Model

The multifunctionality / heterosemy / multiple class membership of lexemes in many languages has remained a contentious issue ever since linguistics emerged as an independent discipline in the 19th century. And van Lier & Rijkhoff (2013: 1) considers it as "[c]urrently one of the most controversial topics in linguistic typology and grammatical theory".

Based on the perspectives of language as a complex adaptive system (Beckner et al, 2009; Larsen-Freeman & Cameron, 2008; Lee et al, 2009; Bybee, 2010) and the nature of major parts of speech as propositional speech act functions proposed by Croft (1991, 2001) and Croft & van Lier (2012) on the basis of Searle (1969), Wang (2014a) argues in his Two-level Word Class Categorization Model in Analytic Languages that just as there are two states of existence of word at the two levels of *langue* (i.e. word type or lexeme in lexicon in a communal language) and *parole* (i.e. word token in syntax), word class categorization also happens at the two levels: (1) The word token categorization in syntax at *parole* is the speaker's expression of propositional speech act functions like reference, predication and modification, whereas the word type categorization in lexicon at *langue* is the conventionalized propositional speech act function(s) of a word type resulted from self-organization or collective unconscious; (2) The class membership of a word type does not have *a priori* existence, nor is it precategorial, but is liable to change through recurrent use in various propositional speech act constructions in syntax at *parole*; (3) The multifunctionality or multiple class membership of word types in synchrony derives from diachronic change and is closely related to frequency of use, which reveals the competing motivations of economy and iconicity in communication; (4) The class membership (either single or multiple class membership) of a word type is its meaning potential(s) at *langue*, which is to be discovered by descriptive linguists through corpus-based usage pattern surveys, as is done by dictionary compilers in word class labeling, whereas the class membership of a word token is its meaning as an event as expressed in a certain context, which normally has a single part of speech; (5) With regard to the class membership of a word token, there are prototypical correlations between propositional speech act functions and semantic classes.

2.2 Empirical Studies

Four empirical studies have been conducted with regard to the Two-level Word Class Categorization Model.

Wang (2013) surveys the multiple class membership in Modern Chinese based on CCD5. It is found that 2778 lexemes (accounting for 5.40%) in CCD5 are multi-category words, that multiple class membership exists typically between the major word classes of NOUN, VERB, ADJECTIVE and ADVERB, and that CCD5 has basically labeled with more accuracy the typical parts-of-speech for the headwords and the typical members of the relevant word classes but it is somewhat conservative in dealing with multiple class membership. More importantly, the description of the headwords in the dictionary is partially consistent with the reality of language use in the Chinese community, which reveals the invalid theoretical basis for multiple class membership: the so-called "Principle of Simplicity" in grammar analysis which sticks to the principle of "fewest possible multi-category words" is proved to be problematic.

Wang (2014b) investigates the current status of multiple class membership in Modern English based on *Oxford Advanced Learner's English Dictionary* (7th ed.) (hereinafter called OALD7). It has been found that 4861 lexemes (accounting for10.48%) in OALD7 are multi-category words, that there are 81 different types of multiple class membership, the most typical of which are those between the major word classes of NOUN, VERB, ADJECTIVE and ADVERB, and that multiple class membership is characteristic of analytic languages like Modern English and Modern Chinese in lexicon at *langue*. Interestingly, the types of multiple class membership in Modern Chinese is similar to that of Modern English, though CCD5 minimized the number of multi-category lexemes by following the Principle of Parsimony/Simplicity, creating a false impression that the percentage of multi-category lexemes in Modern Chinese is far lower than that in Modern English. It is found that this false impression results to some degree from the ban of multiple class membership especially for self-reference lexemes advocated by leading scholars like Zhu (1985), Guo (2002), and Shen (2009), who argue for multifuntionality of Chinese word classes rather than Chinese lexemes. However, this has obviously led to indeterminacy of Chinese word classes.

Wang & Chen (2014) makes a corpus-based study of the relationship between verbs and constructions and proposes four criteria to measure conventionalization of a word's usage (namely, type frequency, token frequency, time span and register variation). It is shown that lexicon and syntax form a continuum with two ends, and that the relationship between verbs and constructions is interdependent in that the verb itself is liable to change through repetitive use in constructions. It is found that the erroneous conclusions in previous studies result from not adopting the corpus-based bottom-up approach, leading to the difficulty of distinguishing the class membership of word types in lexicon at *langue* and that of word tokens in syntax at *parole*, and from committing the logical fallacy of overgeneralization.

Wang & Zhou (2015) makes an empirical study of the correlation between multiple class membership and frequency on the basis of the CN CORPUS and the DIY Word Class Labeling Database of CCD5. The findings of both studies have verified the positive correlation between heterosemy and frequency, but there is a significant difference between them. It is found that the correlation between heterosemy and frequency in analytic languages like Modern Chinese and Modern English results from the competing motivations of economy and iconicity in communication, and that CCD5 minimized the number of multi-category lexemes by following the Principle of Parsimony, creating a false impression that the percentage of heterosemy in Modern Chinese is far lower than that in Modern English.

3 Implications of TLWCCM for POS Tagging in Modern Chinese Corpora

Part-of-speech tagging is the process of assigning a part of speech to each word token in a corpus. From the perspective of TLWCCM, POS tagging is the word class categorization at the level of *parole* in syntax, in which propositional speech act functions (i.e., reference, predication and modification) correlate in markedness patterns with semantic types (i.e., objects, actions , and properties) in contexts.

Accordingly, we can make some

corrections in the above problematic POS tagging in CN CORPUS: 自信 in concordances lines like (12) "他/r 又/d 恢复/v 了/u 自信/a 和/c 力量/n " should be retagged as NOUN instead of ADJECTIVE; 自信 in concordances lines like (13) "他/r 怔怔/a 地/u 看/v 着/u 我/r ，/w 但/c 很快/a 又/d 恢复/v 了/u 自信/v " should be retagged as NOUN instead of VERB; 自信 in concordances lines like (19) "一个/mq 平静/a 而/c 又/d 自信/v 的/u 声音/n ，/w 在/p 我们/r 身后/nl 响起/v " should be retagged as ADJECTIVE instead of VERB; and 自信 in concordances lines like (30) "/w 模样/n 儿/k 很/d 精干/a ，/w 也/d 很/d 自信/v " should be retagged as ADJECTIVE (i.e. predicative adjective) instead of VERB.

Thus, multi-category lexemes like 自信 can cause tag ambiguity in POS tagging in corpora. But how hard is the tagging problem? Or how common is tag ambiguity? Jurafsky & Martin (2009: 135) describes the situation in English:

> It turns out that most words in English are umambiguious; that is, they have only a single tag. But many of the most common words in English are ambiguous...... In fact, DeRose (1988) reports that while only 11.5% of English word types in the Brown corpus are ambiguous, over 40% of Brown tokens are ambiguous.

From the perspective of TLWCCM, tag ambiguity in POS tagging can be removed easily in context (namely in syntax at *parole*). As pointed out in Section 1, many leading scholars in Chinese grammar and Chinese natural language processing adhere to the Principle of Parsimony so as to minimize the scope of multiple class membership or tag ambiguity, and instead argue for multifunctionality of word classes rather than that of lexemes, which is theoretically invalid and practically unnecessary. As verified by Wang Renqiang & Zhou Yu (2015), there is positive correlation between heterosemy and frequency in Modern Chinese. Harbsmeier (1998: 138) correctly pointed out that, in English as in Chinese, the context “painlessly removes the ambiguity of constructions which, taken in isolation, would have been ambiguous”.

This observation has its positive effects on POS tagging in Modern Chinese corpora. According to Bakeoff (2008), among the 5 POS tagged corpora in the survey, 3 are based on the word class information in dictionaries while 2 are token-based. Huang and Huang (2014) found out that the machine learnability of the latter 2 corpora is 2-4 percent higher than the former 3, which indicates that the accuracy of automatic POS tagging can be improved dramatically if we tag the class membership of word tokens in syntax.

Now, if we retag all the problematic concordance lines of 自信 from CN CORPUS from the perspective of TLWCCM, we can get the following results as shown in Table 2. Compared with the original results in Table 1, the number of nominal tags of 自信 has risen dramatically while the number of verbal tags of 自信 has dropped sharply. From Table 2, we can also reach a conclusion that the verbal, nominal and adjectival usages of 自信 are conventionalized, and that CCD6 is right to label 自信 as a multi-category lexeme belonging to VERB, NOUN and ADJECTIVE. According to *Lexicon of Common Words in Contemporary Chinese* released by the

China National Language and Character Working Committee in 2008, 自信 is ranked 3904, which implies that 自信 is a relatively higher frequency lexeme. This obviously explains why it has a higher chance to become a multi-category lexeme and why the accuracy rate POS tagging of 自信 is so low in CN CORPUS.

	parts of speech	frequency	percentage
1	VV	30	16.04%
2	JJ	84	44.92%
3	NN	64	34.22%
4	word-formation morpheme	9	4.81%
total		187	100.00%

Table 2: Results of Revised POS Tagging of 自信

It must be admitted that compared with CCD5, some improvements have been made in CCD6 with regard to word class labeling, but not so much. Our recent survey reveals that for many of the most common words, similar problems still remain: The Principle of Parsimony is still blindly followed. For example, there are still problems in CCD6 in treating lexemes like 研究,方便, 男性, 女性, 自燃, 自杀, 他杀, 拔河, 滑雪, 突变, 渐变, and so on. That's why Huang & Jin (2013: 187) maintains the criteria of POS tagging based on X-Bar Theory, which is to some extent similar to TLWCCM with regard to the word class categorization in syntax at *parole*. And that's also why Huang & Wang (2015) argues that lifting the ban on self-reference senses of multi-category words is an important way out of the Chinese word class dilemma. Since many tagging algorithms require a dictionary that lists all the conventionalized parts-of-speech of every lexeme (Jurafsky & Martin, 2009: 160), the problem now is not that dictionaries are not helpful in POS tagging in analytic languages like Modern Chinese, but that current Chinese dictionaries like the authoritative CCD6 are yet to be the reliable basis for POS tagging in Modern Chinese corpora.

4 Conclusion

To summarize, there is urgent need to improve both the word class labeling in Chinese dictionaries and the POS tagging in Chinese corpora, in which the former often serves as the basis for the latter. And the Two-level Word Class Categorization Model has proved to be effective in providing the guidance for both.

References

Changning Huang and Guangjin Jin. 2013. Three problems of Chinese grammar observed from the Penn Chinese Treebank. *Language Sciences*, (2): 178-192.

Changning Huang and Renqiang Wang. 2015. Lifting the ban on self-reference senses of multi-category words is an important way out of the Chinese word class dilemma. In Proceedings of The 16th Chinese Lexical Semantic Workshop, held in May 2015 at Beijing Normal University.

Changning Huang and Wanmei Huang. 2014. Learnability – A quantititative index of comparative tagsets. *Proceedings of the International Conference on Chinese Word Classes*, Central China Normal University, Wuhan, October 10-10-11.

Christoph Harbsmeier. 1998. *Science and Civilization in China, Volume 7, Part I: Language and Logic*. Cambridge University Press, Cambridge, UK.

Clay Beckner, et al. 2009. Language is a complex adaptive system: Position paper. *Language Learning*, 59(s1): 1-26.

Daniel Jurafsky and James H. Martin. 2009. *Speech and Language Processing: An Introduction to Natural Language Processing, Computational Linguistics, and Speech Recognition (Second Edition)*. Pearson Education Inc.

Deborah A. Coughlin. 1996. Deriving part of speech probabilities from a machine-readable dictionary. In *Proceedings of the Second International Conference on New Methods in Natural Processing*. Ankara, Turkey: 37-44.

Dexi Zhu. 1985. *The Questions and Answers on Grammar*. The Commercial Press, Beijing, China.

Diane Larsen-Freeman and Lynne Cameron. 2008. *Complex Systems and Applied Linguistics*. Oxford University Press, Oxford.

Guangjin Jin and Xiao Chen. 2008. The Fourth International Chinese Language Processing Bakeoff : Chinese Word Segmentation, Named Entity Recognition and Chinese POS Tagging. In *Proceedings of SIGHAN-2008*, Vol. 1 (pp.69-81). Hyderabad, India, January 8-10.

Ihsan Rabbi. 2012. Part of Speech Tagging for Pashto. LAP LAMBERT Academic Publishing.

Jan Rijkhoff and Eva van Lier. 2013. *Flexible Word Classes: A Typological Study of Underspecified Parts-of-speech*. Oxford: Oxford University Press.

Jianming Lu. 2013. *A Course Book of Modern Chinese Grammar Research (4th edition)*. Peking University Press, Beijing, China.

Jiaxuan Shen. 2009. My view of word classes in Chinese. *Language Sciences*, (1): 1-12.

Jiaxuan Shen. 2012. Reflections on "nouny verbs": Problems and solutions. *Chinese Teaching in the World*, (1): 3-17.

Joan Bybee. 2010. *Language, Usage and Cognition*. Cambridge University Press, Cambridge, UK.

John Searle. 1969. *Speech Acts: An Essay in the Philosophy of Language*. Cambridge University Press, Cambridge, UK.

Namhee Lee, et al. 2009. *The Interactional Instinct: The Evolution and Acquisition of Language*. Oxford University Press, Oxford, UK.

Patrick Hanks. 2013. Lexical Analysis: Norms and Exploitations. The MIT Press, Cambridge, US.

R. H. Robins. 1989. *General Linguistics: An Introductory Survey*. Longman, London.

Renqiang Wang and Hemin Chen. 2014. A corpus-based study of the relationship between verbs and constructions: The conventionalization of transitive *sneeze* [J]. *Foreign Language Teaching and Research*, (1): 19-31.

Renqiang Wang and Yu Zhou. 2015. A study of the correlation between heterosemy and frequency in Modern Chinese: A note on the validity of the Principle of Parsimony. *Foreign Language and Literature*, (2): 61-69.

Renqiang Wang. 2006. *An Empirical Study of Word Class Labeling in Chinese-English Dictionaries from the Cognitive Perspective*. Shanghai Translation Publishing House, Shanghai, China.

Renqiang Wang. 2009. Grammatical metaphor and the entry of self-designation senses into Chinese dictionaries: A corpus-based study. *Foreign Language and Literature*, (1): 100-108.

Renqiang Wang. 2010. A validity study of the word class system in Modern Chinese as seen from the

Contemporary Chinese Dictionary (5th edition). Foreign Language Teaching and Research, (5): 380-386.

Renqiang Wang. 2013. A study of multiple class membership in Modern Chinese with a comment on the significance of the linguistic theories of Ferdinand de Saussure [J]. *Foreign Language and Literature*, (1): 12-20.

Renqiang Wang. 2014a. Two-level word class categorization in analytic languages: A comparative study of multiple class membership in Modern Chinese and Modern English. In *Proceedings of Workshop of Grammatical categories in macro- and microcomparative linguistics in 36th Annual Conference of the German Linguistic Society*, March 5th-7th 2014, University of Marburg, Germany: 345~347.

Renqiang Wang. 2014b. Multiple class membership in Modern English: A study based on *Oxford Advanced Learner's Dictionary (7th ed.). Journal of Foreign Languages*, (4): 50-59.

Rui Guo. 2002. *A Study of Chinese Word Classes*. The Commercial Press, Beijing, China.

Shiwen Yu, et al. 2003. *The Grammatical knowledge-base of Contemporary Chinese - A Complete Specification*. Tsinghua University, Beijing, China.

William Croft and Eva van Lier. 2012. Language universals without universal categories. *Theoretical Linguistics*, 38(1-2): 57~72.

William Croft. 1991. Syntactic Categories and Grammatical Relations: The Cognitive Organization of Information. The University of Chicago Press, Chicago.

William Croft. 2001. *Radical Construction Grammar: Syntactic Theory in Typological Perspective*. Oxford University Press, Oxford.

A Review of Corpus-based Statistical Models of Language Variation

Yao Yao
Department of Chinese and Bilingual Studies
The Hong Kong Polytechnic University
Hong Kong
ctyaoyao@polyu.edu.hk

Abstract

This paper is a brief review of the research on language variation using corpus data and statistical modeling methods. The variation phenomena covered in this review include phonetic variation (in spontaneous speech) and syntactic variation, with a focus on studies of English and Chinese. The goal of this paper is to demonstrate the use of corpus-driven statistical models in the study of language variation, and discuss the contribution and future directions of this line of research.

1 Introduction

Human language is inevitably variable. The same meaning may be wrapped in different sentence forms without losing the semantic content; the same word or the same sound could be pronounced slightly differently by different speakers, or even by the same speaker but in different linguistic or non-linguistic contexts. Sometimes we can come up with an explanation for the observed differences (e.g. men and women talk differently), but more often than not, variation seems so ubiquitous and random. In fact, variation used to be considered as noise in the signal – something that needs to be filtered out before the signal can be processed. In recent years, however, the value of 'random' variation has been gradually uncovered in linguistic research.

What has changed to cause the rising interest in variation? In our view, the change is largely due to the availability of large-scale linguistic datasets – often extracted from big corpora – and sophisticated statistical tools that allow researchers to look for patterns in a sea of seemingly random and unpredictable data. Thus, variation is no longer viewed as noise but a gold mine of information about how language is produced and used in communication. For instance, examining patterns of pronunciation variation in spontaneous speech can help us understand what factors (e.g. word frequency, contextual predictability, information status) may play a role in the speech production process, what is the relative importance of these factors, and how they interact with each other. Furthermore, a variation model also makes it possible to examine the effect of some particular factor by statistically controlling for other factors that are also active. By comparison, in an experimental study, it is often hard to completely balance all relevant factors when creating experimental stimuli and conditions.

In the remaining of this paper, we will first introduce the general methodology of building corpus-based statistical models of language variation; we will then briefly discuss several previous studies on phonetic variation and syntactic variation that cover a few different languages (English, French, Chinese). Finally, we will briefly discuss the contribution and future directions of this line of research.

29th Pacific Asia Conference on Language, Information and Computation pages 11 - 15
Shanghai, China, October 30 - November 1, 2015

2 General Methodology

The general methodology of a corpus-based variation study consists of two major stages: dataset compilation and model building. A dataset contains observations of the linguistic phenomenon under investigation (e.g. pronunciation of function words in English). The observations are extracted from some corpora and are annotated with a set of linguistic properties. To use the modeling approach, it is necessary that the linguistic variation under investigation is encoded in some quantifiable (or categorical) measures. For instance, variation in word pronunciation may be encoded in the duration of a word, which is a quantitative measure. Such measures will be used as the outcome variable in the statistical model. Furthermore, each observation will be annotated – either manually or automatically – with a number of features that are hypothesized to be predictors of the linguistic variation (e.g. usage frequency of a word might predict the duration of a word in natural production). Variation models typically include thousands or tens of thousands of observations, in order to ensure enough statistical power. Thus, it is critical to choose an appropriate data source that contains enough relevant observations and adequate representation of the predictor variables.

After the dataset is prepared, it will be fed into the statistical model. Currently, the most popular and widely used model in the field is the mixed-effects regression model (Baayen et al., 2008). Compared to a simple regression model, mixed-effects models have the advantage of allowing two levels of predictors: random-effects predictors and fixed-effects predictors. The inclusion of random-effects predictors is particularly useful for modeling linguistic variation, because we know that part of the variation will be truly random and cannot be predicted by any annotated feature. For example, different speakers will pronounce the word *to* slightly differently, and ultimately, some individual differences are beyond the predicting power of speaker sex, age, height, weight, etc. and will have to be random. Similarly, the differences among individual words (e.g. *to* and *too*) could also be idiosyncratic and unpredictable. In a mixed-effects model, random effects may co-exist with fixed-effects, which means that, for example, both gender differences (i.e. sex as a fixed-effects predictor) and true individual differences (i.e. speaker as a random-effects predictor) may both be represented in a model of pronunciation variation.

Depending on the type of the outcome variable, one may use either mixed-effects linear regression model (for numerical outcome variables) or mixed-effects generalized regression model (for categorical outcome variables). Research on modeling language variation

2.1 Modeling phonetic variation

This vein of corpus-based language variation research first started with studies on phonetic variation – probably because phonetic features are readily quantifiable. Some of the pioneering works on English pronunciation variation were completed around the turn of the century (Bell et al. 2009; Fosler-Lussier and Morgan 1999; Gregory, et al. 1999; Jurafsky et al. 1998, 2001a, among others), with phonetic data from the Switchboard corpus of telephone conversations (Godfrey et al. 1992), which contains 240 hours of speech (of which 4 hours are phonetically transcribed and used in the statistical models).

The studies above mostly examined word duration and vowel pronunciation (full vs. reduced) as parameters of pronunciation variation. In addition to describing the general picture of variation, these studies were also deeply interested in the effects of probabilistic factors (e.g. word frequency, contextual probability, etc) on pronunciation variation. The results presented in these studies are cited as empirical support for the general claim that probabilistic relations have profound influence on the representation and production of words in speech (Jurafsky et al., 2001b)

Later on, with the completion of the Buckeye corpus (Pitt et al., 2007), which contains 40 hours of phonetically transcribed conversational speech, another batch of corpus-based phonetic variation studies appeared (Johnson, 2004; Gahl et al., 2012; Yao, 2009, 2011, etc). Since the Buckeye corpus is recorded in a studio, the recording quality is high enough to warrant automatic measurement of VOT (Yao, 2009) and vowel formants (Yao et al., 2010). This allows for modeling of gradient vowel dispersion, measured by the distance between a specific vowel token from the center of the vowel space on a F1-F2 plane (Bradlow et al., 1996).

Furthermore, some of the variation studies based on the Buckeye corpus (Gahl et al., 2012; Yao, 2011) focused on the effects of a particular lexical measure called phonological neighborhood density. Phonological neighborhood density refers to the number of similar-sounding words given a specific target word. Thus, the models built in these studies had one critical predictor (i.e. phonological neighborhood density), and all the other non-neighborhood predictors were included as control variables. Results from these studies revealed the effects of phonological neighborhood structure in word production when all other factors that could also influence word production were statistically controlled.

In addition to English, corpus-based pronunciation variation research has also been conducted in other languages (Dutch: Pluymaekers et al., 2005, among others; French: Meunier and Espesser, 2011; Yao and Meunier, 2014; Taiwan Southern Min: Myers and Li, 2009).

2.2 Modeling syntactic variation

The work on modeling syntactic variation started later than the work on modeling phonetic variation. Most of the pioneering works were done by Bresnan and her colleagues at Stanford (Bresnan, 2007; Bresnan et al., 2007; Bresnan and Ford, 2010; Tily et al., 2009; Wolk et al. 2011, etc) on dative variation (e.g. *I gave John a book* vs. *I gave a book to John*) and genitive variation (e.g. *John's book* vs. *the book of John*) in English. For the American English data, Bresnan and colleagues also used the Switchboard corpus. Since syntactic variation has a discrete set of variants (i.e. different sentence forms), the phenomenon is modelled by generalized regression models. Bresnan and colleagues' work showed that the choice of the surface form under investigation was predictable from a set of factors relating to different components in the local sentence (e.g. semantic type of the verb, NP accessibility, pronominality, definiteness, syntactic complexity, etc) and the context (e.g. presence of parallel structures). When taking all the factors into consideration, Bresnan et al.'s models can correctly predict the surface dative/gentive form in more than 90% of the cases (compare with a baseline accuracy around 79%). Variation patterns revealed in Bresnan et al.'s works were later confirmed in behavioral experiments (e.g. Bresnan and Ford, 2010).

Inspired by Bresnan and colleagues' work on English syntactic variation, there have also been a few studies that apply a similar modeling approach to the study of syntactic variation in Chinese languages (Cantonese: Starr, 2015; Mandarin: Yao, 2014; Yao and Liu, 2010).

In particular, Yao and colleagues (Yao, 2014; Yao and Liu, 2010) investigated both dative variation and BA-form variation in written Mandarin using data from the Academia Sinica corpus (Chen et al., 1996). Sentence patterns involved in Mandarin dative-variation (e.g. 我送小张一本书 'I gave Xiaozhang a book' vs. 我送一本书给小张 'I gave a book to Xiaozhang' vs. 我把一本书送给小张 'I (BA) a book gave to Xiaozhang') are more complicated than those in English. In addition to the two dative constructions similar to those in English, Mandarin Chinese also allows the direct object to be preposed before the verb. Yao and Liu' work showed that the three-way dative variation in Mandarin Chinese can be modeled by a hierarchy of two models: one on the upper level for the pre-verbal vs. post-verbal distinction and the other on the lower level for the dative vs. double object distinction. Yao and Liu' models raise the prediction accuracy by 27% (upper level) and 7% (lower level) compared to the baseline accuracy levels.

Furthermore, to understand the general properties of the pre-verbal vs. post-verbal word order variation, Yao also built general models on syntactic variation between BA and non-BA sentences. The results from this study showed that the surface word order in Mandarin Chinese is most significantly influenced by the prominence (accessibility, definiteness, etc) and length of the NP, as well as the presence of a similar word order in the nearby context (i.e. parallel structure).

3 Discussion

In this paper, we have briefly reviewed some previous studies that use corpus-based statistical models to investigate language variation phenomena. The focus of this review is on studies of phonetic variation (in spontaneous speech) and syntactic variation in English and Chinese. As discussed above, corpus-based research on linguistic variation is still dominated by studies on

English; by comparison, there is much less research on linguistic variation – especially phonetic variation – in Chinese. One possible reason for the lack of Chinese phonetic variation research is the unavailability of large annotated conversational speech Chinese corpora (to linguists). In our view, the lack of resources may in fact indicate a potential opportunity of collaboration between theoretical linguists and speech engineers (computational linguists). We discuss this in more detail in our next point.

We have observed that so far, the researchers who work on corpus-based language variation studies are mostly linguists who are interested in the general variation patterns or the effects of particular factors that are critical to some linguistic theories. One may say that these researchers are doing 'computational linguistics' in the sense that they use computational (modeling) methods to investigate linguistic questions. In reality, of course, the term 'computational linguistics' refers to the area of study that aims to develop language-related (or text-related) applications in computer science. However, despite the seemingly disparate research interest, we must recognize that these two lines of research do share some common features – mostly in the corpus-based and computational nature of the work – and that people working in these areas may benefit from collaborating with each other. Among other things, computational linguists can help theoretical linguists develop tools for automatically annotating a corpus, and theoretical linguists' work can provide generalizations of variation patterns that may in turn inform computational linguistic applications.

To conclude, while we believe that the research on corpus-based variation research has made significant contribution to the study of language, we are convinced that greater success can be achieved if theoretical and computational linguists will work jointly on these topics.

Acknowledgments

Research reported in this paper was supported by the Early Career Scheme of Hong Kong RGC (Grant No. 558913) and the Newly Recruited Junior Academic Staff funding of the Hong Kong Polytechnic University (Grant Account A-PL27).

References

Baayen, R. H., Davidson, D. J., and D. M. Bates. 2008. Mixed-effects modeling with crossed random effects for subjects and items. *Journal of Memory and Language*, 59(4):390–412.

Bell, A., J. M. Brenier, M. Gregory, C. Girand, and D. Jurafsky. 2009. Predictability effects on durations of content and function words in conversational english. *Journal of Memory and Language* 60 (1):92–111.

Bradlow, A. R., G. Torretta, and D. Pisoni. 1996. Intelligibility of normal speech I: Global and fine-grained acoustic-phonetic talker characteristics. *Speech Communication,* 20(3–4):255–272.

Bresnan, J. 2007. Is syntactic knowledge probabilistic? Experiments with the English dative alternation. In Sam Featherston and Wolfgang Sternefeld (eds) *Roots: Linguistics in search of its evidential base*, pp 77-96. Series: Studies in Generative Grammar. Berlin: Mouton de Gruyter.

Bresnan, J., Cueni, A., Nikitina, T. and H. Baayen. 2007. Predicting the dative alternation. In G. Boume et al. (eds) *Cognitive foundations of interpretation*, pp 69-94. Amsterdam: Royal Netherlands Academy of Science.

Bresnan, J., and M. Ford. 2010. Predicting syntax: Processing dative constructions in American and Australian varieties of English. *Language*, 86(1):168–213.

Chen, K.-j., Huang, C.-r., Chang, L.-p., and H.-L. Hsu. 1996. Sinica Corpus: Design Methodology for Balanced Corpora. In B.-S. Park and J.B. Kim (eds) *Proceeding of the 11th Pacific Asia Conference on Language, Information and Computation,* pp.167–176. Seoul: Kyung Hee University.

Fosler-Lussier, E., and N. Morgan. 1999. Effects of speaking rate and word frequency on pronunciations in conversational speech. *Speech Communication*, 29(2):137–158.

Gahl, S., Yao, Y., and Johnson, K. 2012. Why reduce? Phonological neighborhood density and phonetic reduction in spontaneous speech. *Journal of Memory and Language*, 66(4):789–806.

J. Godfrey, E. Holliman, and J. McDaniel. 1992. SWITCHBOARD: Telephone speech corpus for research and development. In *Proceedings of the International Conference on Acoustics, Speech and Signal Processing* (*ICASSP-92*), pp. 517–520.

Gregory, M. L., W. D. Raymond, A. Bell, E. Fosler-Lussier, and D. Jurafsky. 1999. The effects of collocational strength and contextual predictability in lexical production. In *Proceedings of the Chicago Linguistic Society,* 35, pp. 151–166.

Johnson, K. 2004. Massive reduction in conversational American English. In K. Yoneyama and K. Maekawa (Eds.), *Spontaneous speech: Data and analysis. Proceedings of the 1st session of the 10th International Symposium*, pp. 29–54. Tokyo: The National International Institute for Japanese Language.

Jurafsky, D., A. Bell, E. Fosler-Lussier, C. Girand, and W. Raymond. 1998. Reduction of English function words in Switchboard. In *Proceedings of the 5th International Conference on Spoken Language Processing (ICSLP '98)*, Volume 7, pp. 3111–3114. Sydney, Australia.

Jurafsky, D., A. Bell, M. Gregory, and W. Raymond. 2001a. The effect of language model probability on pronunciation reduction. In *Proceedings of the IEEE International Conference on Acoustics, Speech, and Signal Processing (ICASSP'01)*, Volume 2, pp. 801–804. Salt Lake City, Utah.

Jurafsky, D., A. Bell, M. Gregory, and W. Raymond 2001b. Probabilistic relations between words: Evidence from reduction in lexical production. In J. Bybee and P. Hopper (Eds.), *Frequency and the Emergence of Linguistic Structure*, pp. 229–254. Amsterdam: John Benjamins.

Meunier, C., and R. Espesser. 2011. Vowel reduction in conversational speech in French: The role of lexical factors. *Journal of Phonetics,* 39(3):271–278.

Myers, J., and Y. Li. 2009. Lexical frequency effects in Taiwan Southern Min syllable contraction. *Journal of Phonetics,* 37 (2):212–230.

Pitt, M. A., L. Dilley, K. Johnson, S. Kiesling, W. Raymond, E. Hume, and E. Fosler-Lussier. 2007. Buckeye Corpus of Conversational Speech (2nd release). Department of Psychology, Ohio State University. http://www.buckeyecorpus.osu.edu.

Starr, Rebecca L. 2015. Predicting NP Forms in Vernacular Written Cantonese. *Journal of Chinese Linguistics,* 43.1A.

Pluymaekers, M., M. Ernestus, and R. H. Baayen. 2005. Lexical frequency and acoustic reduction in spoken Dutch. *Journal of Acoustical Society of America*, 118(4):2561–2569.

Tily, H., Gahl, S., Arnon, I., Snider, N., Kothari, A., and J. Bresnan. 2009. Syntactic probabilities affect pronunciation variation in spontaneous speech. *Language and Cognition*, 1(2):147–165.

Wolk, C., Bresnan, J., Rosenbach, A., and B. Szmrecsányi. 2011. Dative and genitive variability in Late Modern English: Exploring cross-constructional variation and change. *Diachronica*, 30(3):382–419.

Yao, Y. 2009. An Exemplar-based approach to automatic burst detection in spontaneous speech. In *Proceedings of the 18th International Congress of Linguists (CIL XVIII).* Seoul: Korea University.

Yao, Y. 2011. *The effects of phonological neighborhoods on pronunciation variation in conversational speech.* Unpublished PhD dissertation. University of California, Berkeley.

Yao, Y. 2014. Predicting the use of BA construction in Mandarin Chinese discourse: A modeling study with two verbs. In *Proceedings of the 28th Pacific Asia Conference on Language, Information and Computing (PACLIC28).* December 12-14, 2014. Phuket, Thailand.

Yao, Y., and F.-h. Liu. 2010. A working report on statistically modeling dative variation in Mandarin Chinese. In *Proceedings of the 23rd International Conference on Computational Linguistics (COLING 2010).* Beijing, China.

Yao, Y., and C. Meunier. 2014. Effects of phonological neighborhood density on phonetic variation: The curious case of French. *The 14th Laboratory Phonology Conference*, Tokyo, July 25-27, 2014.

Yao, Y., Tilsen, S., Sprouse, R.L., and K. Johnson. 2010. Automated measurement of vowel formants in the Buckeye Corpus. *言語研究 Gengo Kenkyu (Journal of the Linguistic Society of Japan)*, 138:99–113.

Translation of Unseen Bigrams by Analogy Using an SVM Classifier

Hao Wang **Lu Lyu** **Yves Lepage**
Graduate School of Information, Production and Systems
Waseda University
2-7 Hibikino, Wakamatsu-ku, Kitakyushu, Fukuoka 808-0135, Japan
{oko_ips@ruri., lulv90@ruri., yves.lepage@}waseda.jp

Abstract

Detecting language divergences and predicting possible sub-translations is one of the most essential issues in machine translation. Since the existence of translation divergences, it is impractical to straightforward translate from source sentence into target sentence while keeping the high degree of accuracy and without additional information. In this paper, we investigate the problem from an emerging and special point of view: bigrams and the corresponding translations. We first profile corpora and explore the constituents of bigrams in the source language. Then we translate unseen bigrams based on proportional analogy and filter the outputs using an Support Vector Machine (SVM) classifier. The experiment results also show that even a small set of features from analogous can provide meaningful information in translating by analogy.

1 Introduction

Over the last decade, phrase-based statistical machine translation (Koehn et al., 2003) systems have demonstrated that they can produce reasonable quality when ample training data is available, especially for language pairs with similar word order. However, the PB-SMT model has not yet been capable of satisfying the various translation tasks for very different languages (Isozaki et al., 2010). The existence of translation divergences makes the straightforward transfer from source sentences into target sentences hard. Though many previous pieces of work (Dorr, 1994; Habash et al., 2002; Dorr et al., 2004) have attempted to take account for divergences and to deal with this linguistic problem using various translation approaches. This paper further inquires the topic.

Since sentence consists of bigrams, instead of analysing the syntactic structures of the whole sentence or part of the sentence as in (Ding and Palmer, 2005), we explore the possibilities of translating unseen bigrams based on an analogy learning method. We investigate the coverage of translated bigrams in the test set and inspect the probability of translating a bigram using analogy. Analogical learning has been investigated by several authors. To cite a few, Lepage et al. (2005) showed that proportional analogy can capture some syntactic and lexical structures across languages. Langlais et al. (2007) investigated the more specific task of translating unseen words. Bayoudh et al. (2007) explored generating new learning examples from very scarce original learning data using analogy to train an SVM classifier. Dandapat et al. (2010) performed transliteration by analogical learning for English-to-Hindi.

In the issue of translation using analogy, one of the main drawbacks should be addressed is the problem of "over-generative". Analogy is able to capture the most divergences of translation in the most cases, yet it generates a great number of solutions that are ungrammatical and incorrect. In this paper, we propose to translate useen bigrams as reconstructing with the principle of analogy learning. In machine learning, SVMs have been shown that it is efficient in performing a non-linear classification. By specifying features used in experiment, we employ an SVM classifier to fast filter the solutions output by the analogy solver. The final goal of this research is to explore the possibility of translation

29th Pacific Asia Conference on Language, Information and Computation pages 16 - 25
Shanghai, China, October 30 - November 1, 2015

using analogy and point out a feasible way to solve the problem of "over-generative".

The remainder of this paper is organized as follows: Section 2 describes basic notions in alignment and analogy. In Section 3, we explore the classification of bigrams and their contributions to the whole corpus and report some profiling results. Section 4 presents our approach, depending on the analogous, and describes how to processing the data and extract examples for training an SVM classifier. We also evaluate the result using the some standard measures. Finally, in Section 5, conclusions and perspectives are presented.

2 Basic notions

2.1 Alignment classification

In this section, from a theoretical point of view, we study the categories of word alignment in translating. Given a sentence, various alignments of bigram exist. The following is an example of non-monotonic alignments where alignment links are crossing between parallel sentences (Japanese and English):

e: *He*$_1$ *saw*$_2$ *a cat*$_3$ *with a long*$_4$ *tail*$_5$.
j: *Kare_ha*$_1$ *nagai*$_4$ *sippo_no*$_5$ *neko_wo*$_3$ *mita*$_2$.
$\tilde{e}$: *He long tail_of cat saw*

In this example, e means an original English sentence in parallel texts, j means a Japanese sentence, and $\tilde{e}$ means an amended English sentence which is better for translation parameter training with j. The phrases with the same index are aligned. Based on these two sentences, different categories of alignments have been identified. For each category, examples are given:

According to whether the translation is continuous or not, we divide the alignments into 2 categories: 1. both the n-gram and its translation in the target language are continuous. 2. the translation in the target language contains gaps because of *syntactic divergence* (Dorr et al., 2004). We define "[X]" to stand for gaps in the target side as denoted by (Chiang, 2005) in syntax-based MT and we can have the following classifications:

- **Continuous Alignment**
  - **Bigram-to-ngram** the translation in the target language is continuous ngram, e.g., (1) *long tail* to *nagai sippo*.
  - **Bigram-to-unigram** the bigram corresponds to a unigram, e.g., (3) *a cat* to *neko*.
  - **Crossing-N-gram** the translation is continuous, but in a different order, e.g., (2) *cat with* to *no neko*.

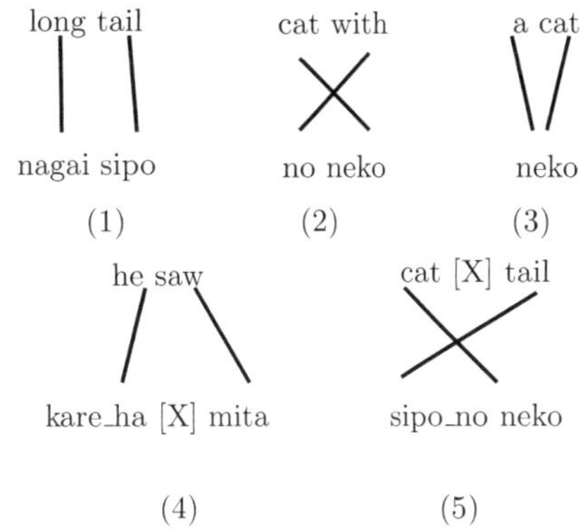

Figure 1: Various Alignments found in the experiment corpus, "[X]" stands gaps between words.

- **Discontinuous Alignment**
  - **Bigram-to-N-gram-with-gaps** a large number of translations in the target language are not continuous. This is a common phenomenon is illustrated by (4). *he saw* to *kara_wa [X] mita*.
  - **Crossing-N-gram-with-gaps** the bigram was aligned with dis-continuous words with gaps in the middle, at same time, the translation is in a different order, e.g., (5). *sipo_no neko* to *cat [X] tail*.

2.2 Proportional analogy

In this section, we describe employing analogy to deal with diverse alignments for bigram translation. We follow (Turney, 2006) to describe the basic notions of proportional analogy used in this work. Verbal analogies are often written $A : B :: C : D$. They meaning A is to B as C is to D. For example:

annual taxes : *annual statistics* :: *the taxes* : *the statistics*

The above example can be understood as follows: we reconstruct an unseen bigram *annual taxes* by a triple of known bigrams. All the elements in the unseen bigram is taken by similarity from the second (*annual statistics*) and third (*the taxes*) known bigrams and put together by difference with the fourth known bigram (*the statistics*). The definition of proportional analogy that we use in this paper is drawn from (Lepage, 1998) and we focus in this study on formal proportional analogies. A 4-tuple of n-grams *A, B, C* and D is said to be a proportional analogy if the following 3 constraints are verified. The lengths of the n-grams may be different, but should meet the following constraints:

1. $|A|_a + |D|_a = |C|_a + |B|_a, \forall a$
2. $d(A, B) = d(C, D)$
3. $d(A, C) = d(B, D)$

where d is the edit distance that counts the minimal number of insertions and deletions that are necessary to transform a string into another string. $|A|_a$ is the number of occurrences of the word a in the n-gram A. This approach still works well on different length of n-grams in fact. However, this method is a necessary condition but not sufficient when applying to translation issue.

As for bilingual translation using analogy, Denoual et al. (2007) presented a parallelopiped view on translating unknown words using analogy, we expand it to bigrams (see Figure 2). Suppose that we want to translate the following bigram (English): *annual taxes* into French, in order to translate the unknown bigram, bilingual proportional analogy requires a triple of source bigrams and corresponding translations. This procedure can be splitted into 2 steps:

1. reconstruct unseen bigram with a triple of source bigrams
2. translate using analogy

2.3 Bigram reconstruction

Given a bigram, it can be reconstructed using other n-grams via different reconstruction patterns. For instance, we can rebuild the bigram: *annual taxes* in following several ways:

Pattern 1: *ab* : *ac* :: *db* : *dc*

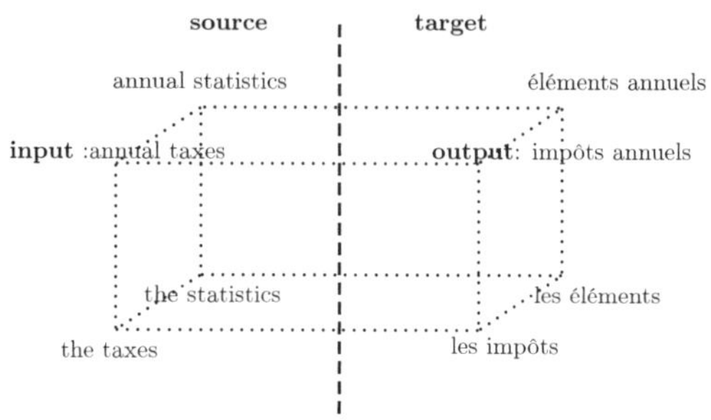

Figure 2: View of the harmonization parallelopiped: four terms in each language form a monolingual proportional analogy.

annual taxes : *annual statistics* :: *the taxes* : *the statistics*

Pattern 2: *ab* : *b* :: *ac* : *c*

annual taxes : *taxes* :: *annual statistics* : *statistics*

Pattern 3: *ab* : *a* :: *db* : *d*

annual taxes : *annual* :: *the taxes* : *the*

Pattern 4: *ab* : *db* :: *ac* : *dc*

annual taxes : *the taxes* :: *annual statistics* : *the statistics*

Pattern 5: *ab* : *aeb* :: *ac* : *aec*

annual taxes : *annual income taxes* :: *annual statistics* : *annual income statistics*

annual taxes is reconstructed with different n-grams extracted from the training corpus. Beside these 5 Patterns, analogy in general can capture other various patterns in natural language.

We restrict to Pattern 1 in reconstructing of source bigrams because this Pattern contains more information of context and crossing-language alignment. On the contrary, we allow all Patterns in the target side as we want to collect as many translations as possible.

2.4 Translation by analogy

The problem that we define is, given an unseen bigram A in the source languages, supposing we have known an alignment between n-gram and its translation which is represented by a, we want to find the appropriate template T_i, to adapt the synchronous analogy and finally generate the target $\tilde{A}'$ successfully. We formalize analogical deduction as following:

$$A : B_i :: C_j : x \quad (1)$$

Assume the previous analogical equation has a solution x. We define the case when x belongs to the training set as "*reconstructible*". $\varphi(.)$ is the translation function, bidirectional analogical deduction also requires to repeat this operation with all target translations corresponding to the source bigrams in the opposite direction. In other words, satisfies following equation:

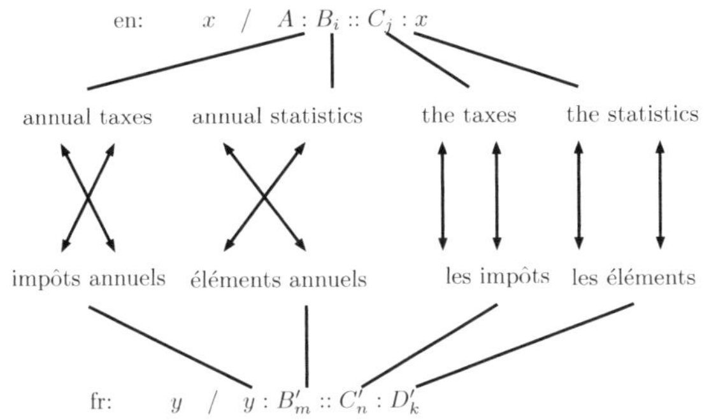

Figure 3: Bilingual analogical reduction for the bigram from the input *annual taxes* (English) to the output *impôts annuels* (French), the related analogous and its translation are indicated in the figure.

$$\exists(B'_m, C'_n, D'_k) \in \varphi(B_i) \times \varphi(C_i) \times \varphi(x) / \quad (2)$$

$$\exists y / y : B'_m :: C'_n : D'_k \quad (3)$$

We define "*bidirectional reconstructible*" as when input an unseen bigram and finally it outputs the solution as y. In this model, a stands alignment between source language bigram and its translation in target language, $a \Leftrightarrow (X, X')$, if the alignment (A, y) appears in the test set (as $\exists y \in \varphi(A)$), we recognize the output as the translation, called "*attested translation*".

The Figure 3 describes this procedure and Figure 4 shows the details about constituents of bigrams. Since the proceeding of the whole produce of analogical derivation is very time-consuming, in order to evaluate the ceiling coverage of "*attested translation*", we conduct the synchronous parsing for fast obtaining the examples. It is easy to obtain the alignments between A and A' in the test set with some automatic aligners. From a bigram A and its translation A', for each elements in source side and with all relevant of bigrams $\widehat{B}, \widehat{C}$ from the source part of the bicorpus, if there also exists the translations $\widehat{B'}$, $\widehat{C'}$, we can reduce the remaining D and D' which is described as following formula:

$$(A, A'):(B_i, B'_m)::(C_j, C'_n) \Rightarrow (D, D')$$

If finally we find D and D' at the end of this equation are linked, we consider that from A it can arrive to A' successfully.

3 Data profiling

We first profile the test set by exploring the proportion of unseen bigrams in the source language. Then we investigate the reconstructiblility/bidirectional reconstructibility of unseen bigrams in the source language. Finally, we estimate the maximum of attested translation bigrams using this analogy-based approach.

3.1 Data preprocessing

We use the Europarl Corpora[1] (Koehn, 2005) to prepare the classification examples used to train and test the SVM classifier. We split the corpus into two parts: a training set and a test set. A set of 100,000 sentences which lengths less than 30 with the French translation are extracted as the training set. We also sample a set of 10,000 sentences from the remaining corpus not contained in training set as the test set. This corpus only offers aligned texts, however, it does not provide word alignment information for each language pair. Table 1 shows some statistic of bigrams and the proportion of unseen bigrams in the experiment data.

3.2 Word-to-word alignment

Before reconstructing, we preprocess to obtain word-to-word alignments. Our work is based on the dominant method to obtain word alignment, which trained from the Expectation Maximization (EM) algorithm. To extract the word alignment, EM algorithm will be utilized to train the bilingual corpus for several iterations, and then phrase pairs that are consistent with this word alignment will be extracted. We align the words automatically relying on the

[1]http://www.statmt.org/europarl/archives.html#v3

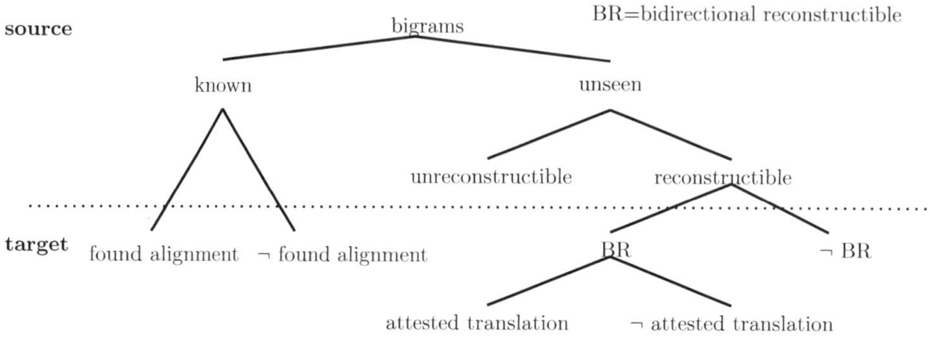

Figure 4: Logic binary tree for the problem of analogy and bidirectional analogy in the source language, "not found alignment" means the known bigrams that have not been aligned in the training set.

		English	**French**
Test	sentences	10k	10k
	words	177,890	202,418
	avg.(words/sentence)	17.79	20.24
	stdev.(words/sentence)	±6.24	±7.17
	bigrams (unique)	68,600	73,126
Training	sentences	100k	100k
	words	1,780,128	2,027,369
	avg.(words/sentence)	17.80	20.27
	stdev.(words/sentence)	±6.25	±7.16
	bigrams (unique)	345,384	336,995
Unseen	bigrams	22,078	23,251
	Proportion	32.18%	31.80%

Table 1: Statistics on the English-French parallel corpus used for the training and test sets, it also indicates the statistics of unseen bigrams in the test set.

		bigrams	**proportion**
Test	aligned	63,537	92.68%
	unaligned	5,063	7.38%
Training	aligned	320,983	92.94%
	unaligned	24,401	7.06%

Table 2: Statistics on the aligned and unaligned bigrams in data, it also indicates GIZA++ can not align all words in the source language after grow-diag-final-and.

		bigrams	**proportion**
known	¬ found alignment	995	1.45%
	found alignment	45,527	66.37%
unseen	reconstructible	20,056	29.14%
	unreconstructible	2,022	2.95%
Total		68,600	100.00%

Table 3: Distribution of bigrams, e.g., unaligned and aligned in the training data. More than 90% of unseen bigrams can be reconstructed.

GIZA++[2] (Ochet al., 2003) implementation of the IBM Models in Moses toolkit (Koehn et al., 2007), running the algorithm in both directions, source to target and target to source.

The heuristics applied to obtain a symmetrized alignment in this step is *grow-diag-final-and*, it starts with the intersection of directional word alignments and enrich it with alignment points from the union. We employ this algorithm to obtained alignment, and from that we extract the continuous bigrams and their aligned targets directly from the alignment files. At same time, an aligned test set was build as the golden reference using the same approach. "aligned" means it is aligned by GIZA++.

3.3 Reconstructiblity

Though the most of bigrams are reconstructible, not all bigrams belonging to this set can really generate a solution (case of BR) as same as the aligned translations in the target language. That is a quiet interesting and rifeness phenomenon in the most cases (case of $\neg BR$). We implement bilingual synchronizing parsing to quickly search the reusable and useful templates (case of *attested translation*). As the matter of fact, though not all final solution are acceptable, we are aiming at to bound the mount of successful analogy in total. The statistics are provided in the following.

[2]http://www.statmt.org/moses/giza/GIZA++.html

	Negative Examples	Templates T_s: (B_i, B'_m) ,(C_j, C'_n), (D, D')		
Input:	joint development	joint talks	the development	the talks
Output:	débattues [X] codes	débattues [X] pourparlers	des codes	des pourparlers
ref:	développement communautaire			
Input:	rates within	rates will	areas within	areas will
Output:	des taux [X] au sein [X]	des taux [X] permettra	domaines [X] au sein	domaines permettra
ref:	des taux de [X] au sein de			
Input:	military security	military interests	our security	our interests
Output:	[X] de sécurité [X] militaires	intérêts [X] militaires	nos [X] de sécurité	nos intérêts
ref:	militaires [X] sécurité			
Input:	common set	common institutions	the set	the institutions
Output:	limites communes	institutions communes	les limites	les institutions
ref:	une série			
	Positive Examples	Templates T_s: (B_i, B'_m) ,(C_j, C'_n), (D, D')		
Input:	this renegotiation	this transition	the renegotiation	the transition
Output:	cette renégociation	cette transition	la renégociation	la transition
ref:	cette renégociation			
Input:	accounts procedure	accounts for	voting procedure	voting for
Output:	procédure [X] comptes	comptes de	procédure [X] vote	vote de
ref:	procédure [X] comptes			
Input:	efficient legal	efficient european	of legal	of european
Output:	judiciaire [X] efficace	européen efficace	judiciaire [X] de	européen de
ref:	judiciaire [X] efficace			
Input:	bold measures	bold proposals	various measures	various proposals
Output:	des mesures audacieuses	des propositions audacieuses	diverses mesurese	diverses propositions
ref:	des mesures audacieuses			

Table 5: Samples of bigrams and related analogical templates, according $(B_i, B'_m), (C_j, C'_n), (D, D')$, the translation A' is produced. Both positive and negative examples are presented in the table.

	reconstructible			
	BR			$\neg BR$
	attested	unattested	total	
bigrams	7,659	10,347	18,006	2,050
proportion	11.16%	15.09%	26.25%	2.99%

Table 4: Distribution of bigrams, e.g., attested translation and unattested translation using analogy, it means more than 3/4 $(66.37\%+11.16\%)$ of bigrams are attested translation only referring to the training data.

3.4 SVM Classifier

Since the proportional analogy for translation mapping is the necessary condition but not sufficient, identifying the correct translation via proportional analogy with some machine learning approaches is very necessary. In the following, we will describe how we collect the examples and from them to extract the features to train the SVM classifier. It implements the estimating-processing by using the specified features: independent features from (A, A') as well as relative features from analogical templates of (B_i, B'_m), (C_j, C'_n), (D, D').

3.4.1 Features

For classifying the outputs as correct translation or not, the software LIBSVM[3] (Chang et al., 2012) in used, which is an integrated software comes with scripts that automate normalization of the features and optimization of the γ and C parameters. We still need to restrict the features to feed it for training.

- **Independent Features**

  Lexical Weighting: the direct lexical weighting $P_{lex}(e|f)$ and inverse lexical weighting $P_{lex}(f|e)$ for (A, A'). Given a word alignment a, we apply the formula of IBM Model 1 to compute the lexical translation probability of a phrase e given the foreign phrase f as (Koehn

[3]https://www.csie.ntu.edu.tw/ cjlin/libsvm/

et al., 2003):

$$P_{lex}(e|f,a) = \prod_{i=1}^{I} \frac{1}{\{j|(i,j) \in a\}} \sum_{\forall(i,j)\in a} w(e_i|f_j) \quad (4)$$

Here, we compute the score as the following equation without the word alignment:

$$P_{lex}(e|f) = \frac{1}{I}\sum_{i=1}^{I} \log \max_{\{j|\forall(i,j)\in a\}} \{w(e_i|f_j)\} \quad (5)$$

Length: the lengths of A' in words, '[X]' should not be recognized as a word, because it can be ε.

Frequency: we compile the data with the suffix array for fast searching (Lopez, 2007). We calculate the frequency of occurrence for each n-gram generated by analogy in French (with/without gaps). The complete French subset of Europarl corpus is used as the reference.

	Reference (French)
sentences	386,237
words	12,175,424
avg.(words/sentence)	31.52
stdev.(words/sentence)	±6.24

Table 6: Statistics on the French monolingual corpus used as reference.

MutualInformation: It is considered as the most widely used measure in extraction of collocations. We only compute the score only for A' as following:

$$I(X) = \log \frac{p(w_1, w_2, .., w_m)}{\prod_{i=1}^{m} p(w_i)} \quad (6)$$

- **Relative Features**

LexicalWeight: the lexical weightings of (B_i, B'_m), (C_j, C'_n) and (D, D') in both directions (direct lexical weighting $P_{lex}(e|f)$ and inverse phrase translation probabilities $P_{lex}(f|e)$. Blue triangles stand positive examples and red circles stand negative examples. We found that the output with the balanced template in lexical weighting does not mean it has the larger probability to be a positive examples.

Length: the lengths of B'_m, C'_n and D' in words, "[X]" should not be recognized as a word, because it can be ε.

Frequency: the occurrences of B_i, C_j and D and same to targets.

Dice's coefficient: Dice coefficient measures the presence/absence of data between to phrases, where $|X|$ and $|Y|$ are the number of words in set X and Y, respectively, and $|X \cap Y|$ is the number of words shared by the two set. We import the following formula to compute the score of Dice coefficient among B', C' and D', e.g.:

$$Dice(X,Y) = \frac{2|X \cap Y|}{|X| + |Y|} \quad (7)$$

MutualInformation: This measures the co-occurrence phrases mutual dependence. x stands the word in source bigram and y stands the word in the solution of analogy. $p(x, y)$ is the word-to-word translation probability. $p(.)$ is the probability distribution function.

$$I(X,Y) = \sum_{x,y} p(x,y) \log \frac{p(x,y)}{p(x)p(y)} \quad (8)$$

3.4.2 Problem formulation

As we treat verifying analogy output as a binary classification problem, we obtained various outputs from analogy engine for each bigram. $\varphi(.)$ is the translation function, we label the training examples as in (5):

$$y = \begin{cases} 1, & if\ A' \in \varphi(A) \\ 0, & if\ A' \notin \varphi(A) \end{cases} \quad (9)$$

Each instance is associated with a set of features that have been discussed in the previous section.

3.4.3 Experimental settings

The bilingual-crossing examples are generated by the previous script depends on the alignment output by GIZA++. During training of the SVM classifier, positive and negative instances of examples are generated from the subset of *attested translation* and unusable templates in the middle of analogy proceeding. We also build a test set to validate the accuracy of such a classifier.

	Negative	Positive	Total
Test	1k	1k	2k
Training	5k	5k	10k

Table 7: Size of the examples used as the test set and training set in the experiment.

3.4.4 Evaluation

To test the performance of our approach we focus on the accuracy of the results. We first sample 2k examples as test data (as in Table 7). During training the SVM classifier determines a maximum margin hyperplane between the positive and negative examples. We measure the quality of the classification by precision and recall. Let C be the set of output predictions. We standardly define precision P, recall R and F-measure as in (10):

$$P = \frac{C_{tp}}{C_{tp} + C_{fp}}, R = \frac{C_{tp}}{C_{tp} + C_{fn}}, F = \frac{2PR}{P + R} \quad (10)$$

It should be noted that the number of examples for training are different for the systems of different language pairs. Because we are interested in the possibilities of found translation, we used the standard accuracy measure to evaluate the performance of classifier on the test set:

$$accuracy = \frac{C_{tp} + C_{tn}}{C} \quad (11)$$

where C_{tp} is the counts of true-positive and C_{tn} is the counts of true-negative. C is the total counts of candidates. We show the details of evaluation scores in Table 8.

4 Conclusion and Future works

In this paper we have performed an investigation on translating unseen bigrams in MT by employing an analogy-based method empirically, which has never been explored. We investigated the maximum possible coverage of bilingual reconstructible bigrams in the test and the probabilities when a bigram is attested translation by using the analogy.

As can be noticed from the presented results, after importing the features of templates which are used in analogy diveration, the performance of SVM classifier improves. In other words, it means that the analogous information has the positive effects on classification.

Though the accuracy is not as high as we expected, there are some reason can explain it, first, even the alignment output by GIZA++ is still so far from completely correct, and second, the used features are very simple. Moreover, without the contextual information, this result should be acceptable. The results suggest lexical weighting and mutual information contribute most to identifying the correct translation.

Another should be addressed that bigrams translation is the most difficult in analogy-based machine translation. If a bigram is attested translation, unquestionable, it will help the longer n-grams translation.

The future works should focus on identifying the proper longer chunk/phrase translations using the similar approach.

Acknowledgments

This work is supported in part by China Scholarship Council (CSC) under the CSC Grant No.201406890026 is acknowledged. We also thank the anonymous reviewers for their insightful comments.

References

Dice, L.R. 1945. Measures of the amount of ecologic association between species. *Ecology*, Vol.26, No.3, pp.297–302.

Bonnie J. Dorr. 1994. Machine translation divergences: A formal description and proposed solution. *Computational Linguistics*.20.4: pp.597–633.

Philippe Langlais and Alexandre Patry 2007. Translating unknown Words by Analogical Learning. *In EMNLP/CoNLL'07*, pages 877–886, Prague, Czech Republic.

Sandipan Dandapat, Sara Morrissey, Sudip Kumar Naskar, and Harold Somers. 2010. Mitigating problems in analogy-based ebmt with smt and vice versa: a case study with named entity transliteration. *In 24th Pacific Asia Conference on Language Information and Computation (PACLIC'10)*, pages 365–372, Sendai, Japan.

Ron Bekkerman and James Allan. Using bigrams in text categorization. Department of Computer Science, University of Massachusetts, Amherst 1003 (2004): 1-2.

Features Used		Precision	Recall	F-measure	Accuracy
Independent Features	Length	65.51%	71.60%	68.42%	66.95%
	LexicalWeight	68.32%	81.11%	**74.47%**	71.75%
	Freq	**82.76%**	2.40%	4.66%	50.95%
	MutualInfo	62.74%	**86.90%**	72.87%	67.65%
	Length+LexicalWeight+Freq+MutualInfo	69.92%	78.92 %	74.15%	**72.48%**
Relative Features	Length	65.64%	72.60%	68.95%	67.30%
	LexicalWeight	64.97%	71.60%	68.13%	66.50%
	Freq	**71.90%**	21.50%	33.10%	56.55%
	Dice	65.52%	72.20%	68.70%	67.10%
	MutualInfo	63.28%	85.30%	72.66%	**67.90%**
	Length+LexicalWeight+Freq+MutualInfo	62.74%	**86.90%**	**72.87%**	67.65%
Independent Features + Relative Features	Length	65.54%	73.40%	69.25%	67.40%
	LexicalWeight	68.71%	79.70%	73.80%	71.70%
	Dice+Length	65.10%	58.20%	61.46%	63.50%
	LexicalWeight+Length	63.18%	80.15%	70.66%	66.73%
	LexicalWeight+Length+Dice	70.01%	85.80%	77.10%	74.52%
	LexicalWeight+Length+Freq+MutualInfo	71.83%	86.20%	78.36%	76.20%
	LexicalWeight+Length+Dice+Freq+MutualInfo	**73.32%**	**87.33%**	**79.71%**	**77.78%**

Table 8: Classifier's performance on identification the successes of bigram translation.

Dekai Wu. 1997. Stochastic inversion transduction grammars and bilingual parsing of parallel corpora. *Computational linguistics*.23.3: pp.377–403.

Yves Lepage. 1998. Solving analogies on words: an algorithm. *Proceedings of the 36th Annual Meeting of the Association for Computational Linguistics and 17th International Conference on Computational Linguistics-Volume 1*. Association for Computational Linguistics.

Philip Resnik, Douglas Oard and Gina Levow. 2001. Improved cross-language retrieval using backoff translation. *In Proceedings of the Proceedings of the First International Conference on Human Language Technology Research (HLT)*.

Nizar Habash and Bonnie Dorr. 2002. Handling translation divergences: Combining statistical and symbolic techniques in generation-heavy machine translation. *Springer Berlin Heidelberg*.

Franz Josef Och and Hermann Ney. 2003. A systematic comparison of various statistical alignment models. *Computational linguistics*29.1, pp.19–51.

Arul Menezes and Stephen D. Richardson. 2003. A best-first alignment algorithm for automatic extraction of transfer mappings from bilingua corpora. *Recent advances in example-based machine translation*. Springer Netherlands. pp.421–442.

Bonnie Dorr, Necip Fazil Ayan and Nizar Habash. 2004. Divergence Unraveling for Word Alignment of Parallel Corpora. *Natural Language Engineering*, 1 (1), pp.1–17.

Philipp Koehn, Franz Josef Och and Daniel Marcu 2003. Statistical phrase-based translation. *Proceedings of the 2003 Conference of the North American Chapter of the Association for Computational Linguistics on Human Language Technology-Volume 1*.Association for Computational Linguistics

Michel Simard, Nicola Cancedda, Bruno Cavestro, Marc Dymetman, Eric Gaussier, Cyril Goutte, Kenji Yamada, Philippe Langlais and Arne Mauser. 2005. Translating with non-contiguous phrases *In Proceedings of the Human Language Technology Conference and Conference on Empirical Methods in Natural Language Processing (HLT-EMNLP)*. Association for Computational Linguistics, pp.755–762.

Chris Callison-Burch, Colin Bannard and Josh Schroeder. 2005. Scaling phrase-based statistical machine translation to larger corpora and longer phrases. *Proceedings of the 43rd Annual Meeting on Association for Computational Linguistics*. Association for Computational Linguistics.

Yuan Ding and Martha Palmer. 2005. Machine translation using probabilistic synchronous dependency insertion grammars. *Proceedings of the 43rd Annual Meeting on Association for Computational Linguistics*. Association for Computational Linguistics.

Peter D. Turney and Michael L. Littman. 2005. Corpus-based learning of analogies and semantic relations. *Machine Learning*60.1-3 (2005): pp.251–278.

Philipp Koehn. 2005. Europarl: A parallel corpus for statistical machine translation. *MT summit*. Vol. 5

J. M. Crego, M. R. Costa-Jussa, J. B. Mariño and J. A. Fonollosa. 2005. N-gram-based versus phrasebased statistical machine translation *In Proceedings of the International Workshop on Spoken Language Technology (IWSLT'05)*.

Josep M. Crego, José B. Mariño and Adrià de Gispert. 2005. An Ngram-based statistical machine translation decoder. *Proc. of the 9th European Conference on Speech Communication and Technology (Interspeech'05).*

David Chiang. 2005. A hierarchical phrase-based model for statistical machine translation *Proceedings of the 43rd Annual Meeting on Association for Computational Linguistics.*Association for Computational Linguistics

Peter D. Turney 2006. Similarity of semantic relations *Computational Linguistics.*32(2):pp.379–416.

Adam Lopez and Philip Resnik. 2006. Word-based alignment, phrase-based translation: What's the link. *Proc. of AMTA.*

Etienne Denoual. 2007. Analogical translation of unknown words in a statistical machine translation framework. *Proceedings of Machine Translation Summit XI.* Copenhagen

Philipp Koehn, Hieu Hoang, Alexandra Birch, Chris Callison-Burch, Marcello Federico, Nicola Bertoldi, Brooke Cowan, Wade Shen, Christine Moran, Richard Zens, et al. 2007. Moses: Open source toolkit for statistical machine translation. *In Proceedings of the 45th Annual Meeting of the ACL on Interactive Poster and Demonstration Sessions.* Association for Computational Linguistics, pp.177–180

Sabri Bayoudh, Harold Mouchère, Laurent Miclet and E. Anquetil. 2007. Learning a classifier with very few examples: analogy based and knowledge based generation of new examples for character recognition. *Machine Learning: ECML 2007*, pp.527–534.

Adam Lopez. 2007. Hierarchical Phrase-Based Translation with Suffix Arrays. *EMNLP-CoNLL*, pp.976–985

Peter D Turney. 2008. A uniform approach to analogies, synonyms, antonyms, and associations. *Proceedings of the 22nd International Conference on Computational Linguistics (Coling 2008)*, pp.527–534.

Maike Erdmann, Kotaro Nakayama, Takahiro Hara and Shojiro Nishio . 2009. Using an SVM Classifier to Improve the Extraction of Bilingual Terminology from Wikipedia. *User-Contributed Knowledge and Artificial Intelligence: An Evolving Synergy*, pp.15.

Yves Lepage and Etienne Denoual. 2005. The 'purest' EBMT system ever built: no variables, no templates, no training, examples, just examples, only examples. *Proceedings of the MT Summit X, Second Workshop on Example-Based Machine Translation*, pp.81–90.

Yves Lepage, Julien Gosme and Adrien Lardilleux. 2010. The structure of unseen trigrams and its application to language models: A first investigation. *Universal Communication Symposium (IUCS), 2010 4th International.* IEEE. pp.944–952.

Hideki Isozaki, Tsutomu Hirao, Kevin Duh, Katsuhito Sudoh, and Hajime Tsukada. 2010. Automatic evaluation of translation quality for distant language pairs. Proceedings of the 2010 Conference on Empirical Methods in Natural Language Processing *Association for Computational Linguistics.* pp.944–952.

Ahmet Aker, Yang Feng and Robert J. Gaizauskas. 2012. Automatic Bilingual Phrase Extraction from Comparable Corpora. *COLING.* pp.23–32.

Chang, C. C., and C. J. Lin. 2012. LIBSVM: a library for support vector machines. *ACM transactions on intelligent systems and technology.* 2: 27: 1-27: 27.

Machine Translation Experiments on PADIC: A Parallel Arabic DIalect Corpus

Karima Meftouh
Badji Mokhtar
University
Annaba, Algeria

Salima Harrat
Ecole Supérieure
d'Informatique (ESI), ENSB*
Algiers, Algeria

Salma Jamoussi
MIRACL†
Pole Technologique
de Sfax, Tunisia

Mourad Abbas
CRSTDLA‡
Algiers, Algeria

Kamel Smaili
Campus Scientifique LORIA
Nancy, France

Abstract

We present in this paper PADIC, a Parallel Arabic DIalect Corpus we built from scratch, then we conducted experiments on cross-dialect Arabic machine translation. PADIC is composed of dialects from both the Maghreb and the Middle-East. Each dialect has been aligned with Modern Standard Arabic (MSA). Three dialects from Maghreb are concerned by this study: two from Algeria, one from Tunisia, and two dialects from the Middle-East (Syria and Palestine). PADIC has been built from scratch because the lack of dialect resources. In fact, Arabic dialects in Arab world in general are used in daily life conversations but they are not written. At the best of our knowledge, PADIC, up to now, is the largest corpus in the community working on dialects and especially those concerning Maghreb. PADIC is composed of 6400 sentences for each of the 5 concerned dialects and MSA. We conducted cross-lingual machine translation experiments between all the language pairs. For translating to MSA we interpolated the corresponding Language Model (LM) with a large Arabic corpus based LM. We also studied the impact of language model smoothing techniques on the results of machine translation because this corpus, even it is the largest one, it still very small in comparison to those used for translation of natural languages.

* Ecole Normale Supérieure Bouzareah.

† Multimedia, InfoRmation systems and Advanced Computing Laboratory.

‡ Centre de Recherche Scientifique et Technique pour le Développement de la Langue Arabe.

1 Introduction

Recently, in addition of translating MSA (Modern Standard Arabic), a new challenging issue emerges: How to deal with the translation of Arabic dialects? Few years ago, some works have been proposed to process Arabic dialects and more specifically those of Middle-East. These works concerned building lexicon, analyzing text morphology, POS tagging, diacritization, etc, (Kilany et al., 2002; Kirchhoff et al., 2003; Habash and Rambow, 2006; Chiang et al., 2006; Habash et al., 2013; Elfardy and Diab, 2013; Pasha et al., 2014; Harrat et al., 2014). In the context of Machine Translation some Arabic dialects have started receiving increasing attention (Sawaf, 2010; Zbib et al., 2012; Salloum and Habash, 2013).

Number of researchers have exploited the NLP tools dedicated to MSA to develop their Machine Translation (MT) systems for Arabic dialects, considered as under-resourced languages. Ridouane and Karim (2014) used tools designed for MSA and adapted them to Moroccan dialect in order to build a translation system from MSA to Moroccan, by combining a rule-based approach and a statistical approach. Sawaf (2010) built a hybrid AD-English MT system that uses a MSA pivot approach. In this approach, AD is transferred into MSA using character-based AD normalization rules. In addition an AD normalization decoder that relies on language models, an AD morphological analyzer, and a lexicon were employed to achieve the translation task. Similarly, Salloum and Habash (2012) presented Elissa , an MT system from AD to MSA which employed a rule-based approach that relies on morphological analy-

29th Pacific Asia Conference on Language, Information and Computation pages 26 - 34
Shanghai, China, October 30 - November 1, 2015

sis, morphological transfer rules and dictionaries in addition to language models to produce MSA paraphrases of dialectal sentences. Elissa handles Levantine, Egyptian, Iraqi, and to a lesser degree Gulf Arabic. Zbib et al. (2012) used crowdsourcing to build Levantine-English and Egyptian-English parallel corpora. They selected dialectal sentences from a large corpus of Arabic web text, and translated them using Amazon's Mechanical Turk platform. They used this data to build dialectal Arabic MT systems, and find that small amounts of dialectal data have a dramatic impact on translation quality.

Multidialectal Arabic parallel corpora do not exist, the first and the unique such corpus was presented in (Bouamor et al., 2014). It is a collection of 2000 sentences in MSA, Egyptian, Tunisian, Jordanian, Palestinian and Syrian, in addition to English. The sentences were selected from the Egyptian part of the Egyptian-English corpus built by Zbib et al. (2012).

In this paper, we present PADIC, a corpus composed of 5 Arabic dialects, each of them contains 6400 sentences. Each dialect is aligned at the sentence level with the four other dialects and also with MSA. In this paper, we highlight machine translation results obtained for all the pairs of dialects contained into PADIC. The reminder of this paper is organized as follows, in section 2 we give some differences that distinguish MSA from its dialects. Section 3 describes the processes we used to build PADIC. Finally, we present in section 4 experiments of machine translation between several pairs of dialects and MSA. We also show the impact of the smoothing techniques over the BLEU scores due to the size of the training corpora.

2 Main differences between modern standard Arabic and its dialects

MSA is characterized by a complex morphology and a rich vocabulary. It is an inflexional and agglutinative language. We recall that, compared to English, an Arabic word (or more rigorously a lexical entry) can sometimes correspond to a whole English sentence.

The differences that distinguish dialects from MSA are at the morphological, lexical and syntactical levels. Because it is difficult for a non-Arabic to understand these differences, let us give some examples. In Maghreb, the phrase ما نكتبش "*mā nktbš*" (*I dont write*) is the negation of the word نكتب (*I write*). While in MSA, the negation form is expressed by one of the two function words لا "*lā*" or ما "*mā*" . Consequently, *I don't write* ما نكتبش is written as follows in MSA: لا أكتب "*lā ˀktb*" . For the Maghrebian dialect, such as in the previous example, the morpheme ش /*š*/ is added to the end of the stem نكتب, and the negation marker "ما *mā*" is inserted in the beginning of the phrase[1]. Between MSA and the above dialect, morphologically, we have the same stem كتب "*ktb*" , however for the Maghrebian dialects, the affixes have been changed and a new one has been added. Lexically, most dialectal words are taken from MSA, however many foreign words (verbs and nouns) have been introduced in the daily spoken communications. Maghrebian dialect speakers often use foreign verbs with some modifications; the expressions: شرجاها "*šarǧāhā*" and يشرجيها "*yšarǧīhā*" for respectively *he charged it* and *he charges it* are noticed as two single words but in reality are two sentences, formed by concatenating the morphemes ها /*hā*/ (the object) and ي /*y*/ (the subject) to the verb شرجا "*šarǧā*" *to charge* .

Syntactically, the Verb-Subject-Object order (VSO) is common in MSA and so is (SVO), but (OVS) and (OSV) are also correct even they are not widely used. Nevertheless, in some dialects (SVO) is more used than (VSO) such as in Levantine Arabic. In other dialects as Maghrebian, (VSO) is more preferred. Up to now, no one is able to give an answer to: *which is the closest dialect to MSA?*. It is then necessary to go through a comparative study of these dialects to objectively answer this question. In fact, some old expressions of classical Arabic are still used by Maghrebian people and no longer used in the Arabian Peninsula. Inversely, other aspects of MSA are preserved in the Arabian Peninsula, such as Tanween (to mark indefiniteness) but not used in North Africa at all.

[1]The morpheme ش "*š*" is the abridged dialectal form of the MSA word شيء "*šayˀ*" "thing". Ex: the origin of the word ما نكتبش "*mā nktbš*" is ما نكتب شيء for لا أكتب شيئا "I dont write anything".

Necessity of adopting writing rules

MSA is a natural language with linguistic rules and a typographic system of writing, dialects do not have any standardized set of rules. In fact, there is no reason to write dialects which are usually spoken in daily conversations. But a new phenomenon arises with social networks: people are free to write whatever they want and express their opinions such as they speak, it means in their dialect. Accordingly, they write dialectal words just as they are pronounced. For instance, to write *tell him*, one would write it, just as he heard it: "*qūllu*" قولّو while the right expression is "*qūl lū*" قول لو (original expression in MSA is قل له).

This freedom of writing pushed us to adopt some writing rules for standardizing our corpus. In our work each dialectal word is written by adopting MSA rules, that means if a dialectal word does exist in MSA, it must be written such as in MSA, otherwise the word is written as it is uttered. In this last case, we could extract the phonetic directly form from its orthographic representation, which will be necessary in the frame of the ultimate goal of this study which is Speech-To-Speech translation.

In Arabic dialects, some foreign words contain non Arabic phonemes, such as /g/ which could be written either with /غ/ or /ج/ such as for the English words *English* and *Ghana* which are respectively written انجليزي and غانا.

However, the few dialectal texts retrieved from the web constitute a big challenge to researchers. This is not only because of the non standardization of orthographies, but also due to the absence of diacritics as it is the case for MSA and all its dialects (Harrat et al., 2013). In social networks, Arabic dialects are written in different ways, sometimes in Arabic script, sometimes in Latin one and in some cases such as a mixture of letters and some specific numbers. For example, the number 3 is used to represent the phoneme /ع/ because of the similarity between 3 and /ع/. In Table 1, we address some Arabic letters and the adopted Arabic numbers used to represent them. Note the similarity in the form between the letters and the numbers.

To illustrate the different ways of writing dialects in social networks, in Table 2, some examples of Algerian sentences are given.

Table 1: Numbers adopted to represent some Arabic letters when Latin grapheme are used to write Arabic

Example	Arabic number	Arabic letter
tbarra3	3	/ع/
fra7	7	/ح/
sou9	9	/ق/

3 Building a parallel corpus

It is well known that parallel corpora are the foundation stone of several natural language processing tasks, particularly cross-language applications such as machine translation, bilingual lexicon extraction and multilingual information retrieval. Building this kind of resources is a challenging task especially when it deals with under-resourced languages (Skadiņa et al., 2010). The problem is much deeper with the Arabic dialects which are used by a huge number of people only in daily oral communication. Moreover, they are not taught in schools and are absent from formal written communications. This makes building dialectal resources automatically almost impossible. The few available texts in social networks, usually produced by less educated Arab people are not homogeneous and suffer from the varieties in orthography, due to the absence of writing rules. In addition, some Arabic dialects are written by using Latin graphemes by a slice of Arabic societies. The reason is that Arabic language was not widely supported by devices. Consequently, Arab people have been used to this situation by using Latin graphemes.

For all the aforementioned reasons, crawling the web is not a solution to build a parallel corpus, thus, we decided to build it from scratch.

PADIC: A New Parallel Arabic Dialect Corpus

The approach we used to build PADIC is almost similar to that of Bouamor et al. (2014) except that in our case, we started from scratch and we are still working on the development of all the necessary tools. We should note that the particularity of our corpus is that it is composed also of Maghrebian dialects that present difficulties to collect and process since they are mixture of several languages (Arabic,

Table 2: Different ways of writing dialects on Facebook.

Cases of writing dialects	Dialectal sentences	Equivalent in English
Written with Arabic letters	واش راك خويا	How do you do my brother?
Written only with Latin letters	Wachrak khouya?	How do you do my brother?
Written with a mixture of Latin letters and Arabic numbers	rabi ya7fedek	God protect you
A sentence that contain both Arabic and French words	*Et bien* hakda rak f9edt'houm *les deux*	So you have lost both of them

French, Berber, ...). Also, because they are not much used on the Web and when it is the case, people use generally Latin script for writing, as we mentioned it in section 2.

A preliminary study of the PADIC corpus was given in (Harrat et al., 2015). The goal of this work is to focus more on Statistical Machine Translation experiments from MSA to dialectal Arabic and vice versa. This work in turn is part of a big and challenging project, a Speech to Speech Translation system that we are working on. Challenging not only because speech recognition and speech synthesis are involved, but also because of the lack of dialectal Arabic parallel corpora.

Five dialects, in addition to MSA, are concerned by this study: Annaba's dialect (ANB), spoken in the east of Algeria, Algiers's dialect (ALG), used in the capital of Algeria, Sfax's dialect (TUN) spoken in the south of Tunisia, Syrian and Palestinian dialects (SYR) and (PAL) which are spoken in Damascus and Gaza respectively. [2]

ANB corpus was created by recording different conversations from every day life, whereas, for ALG, we used the recordings corresponding to movies and TV shows which are often expressed in the dialect of Algiers. Then we transcribed both of them by hand. To increase the size of the two corpora, we translated each of them into the other. Afterwards, these two corpora have been translated into MSA.

MSA was then used as a pivot language to get other dialectal corpora. To do that, we translated the MSA corpus to TUN, SYR and PAL. The Tunisian corpus was produced by 20 native speakers. Each one was responsible of translating almost 320 sentences from MSA to TUN. Speakers have very slight differences in their spoken languages. All of them are from the south of Tunisia where people tend to use Arabic words rather than French words as it is the case in the north of the country. In fact, the dialect used in the south is closer to MSA than that used in the north of Tunisia. Syrian and Palestinian corpora were created in the same way by respectively two native speakers. Finally, we get a multi-dialectal parallel corpus PADIC composed of the five aforementioned dialects, in addition to MSA. PADIC is made of 6400 parallel sentences, for which we present some statistics in Table 3.

Table 3: PADIC statistics

Corpus	#Distinct words	#Words
ALG	8966	38707
ANB	9060	38428
TUN	10215	36648
SYR	9825	37259
PAL	9196	39286
MSA	9131	40906

The MSA part contains 40906 words including 9131 different words. PADIC includes an average of 37500 words for one a dialect with a vocabulary which does not exceed 10250 words. The average number of words in a dialectal sentence is of 6 while it is of 7 for MSA. The shortest sentence in the corpus is composed of 4 words and the longest one contains 25 words.

We give in Table 4 examples of parallel sentences from PADIC. Even if we do not read Arabic at all, we can notice that some words have the same form in several dialects, while others are completely dif-

[2]The only argument in the choice of these dialects and not others is that the authors of this paper are from Algeria and Tunisia and for the two others we asked kindly colleagues from Syria and Gaza to help us to translate a MSA corpus into these two dialects without any financial compensation. Translating the corpus into Moroccan dialect is under work.

Table 4: Examples of parallel sentences from PADIC

Lang.	Sentence
ALG	جوزت ايامات روعة ما ننساهاش طول حياتي
ANB	عقبت ايامات على الكيف ما ننساهاش طول عمري
TUN	عديت ايامات حلوة ما ننساهاش طول عمري
SYR	مضيت أيام حلوة عمري ما بنساها
PAL	قضيت أيام جميلة مش حانساها طول عمري
MSA	أمضيت أيام جميلة لن أنساها طول عمري
EN	I spent beautiful days I will never forget throughout my life.
ALG	خدمت في وحد السبيطار قريب من دارنا الحمد لله راني لاباس و عايش مع بابا
ANB	خدمت في وحد السبيطار ڨريب من دارنا الحمد لله أموري مليحة و عايش مع بابا
TUN	خدمت في سبيطار قريب من الدار الحمد لله أموري باهية و عايش مع بابا
SYR	إشتغلت بمشفى قريب من بيتي الحمد لله أموري ميسرة و عايش مع أهلي
PAL	إشتغلت في واحد من المستشفيات القريبة من بيتي الحمد لله أموري متيسرة و عايش مع أبوي
MSA	عملت في أحد المستشفيات القريبة من بيتي الحمد لله أموري متيسرة و أعيش مع والداي
EN	I worked in a hospital near my home. Praise be to God, everything is fine and I live with my parents

ferent.

4 Experiments on Machine Translation of Arabic dialects

In the following, we present several experiments in machine translation in both sides between all the combinations of dialect pairs. We conduct also experiments of machine translation between these dialects and MSA also in both sides.

All the MT systems we used are phrase-based (Koehn et al., 2007) with default settings: bidirectional phrase and lexical translation probabilities, distortion model, a word and a phrase penalty and a trigram language model. We have not used a larger language model because PADIC is not suitable for large ngrams. We used GIZA++ (Och and Ney, 2003) for alignment and SRILM toolkit (Stolcke, 2002) to compute trigram language models. Since the parallel corpus is small, we experimented the Kneser-Ney and Witten-Bell smoothing techniques hoping to identify the one which best fits. The results conducted on a test set of 500 sentences are presented in terms of BLEU, TER and METEOR in Tables 5, 6 and 7 respectively.

Because it is difficult to increase the size of PADIC, we decided to interpolate the corresponding language models by larger Arabic corpora when the target language is MSA. For this purpose, we used two MSA corpora: Tashkeela[3] and LDC Arabic Treebank (Part3,V1.0) (Maamouri et al., 2004). Unfortunately, the results of the interpolation did not outperform those of Table 5.

5 Discussion

5.1 Impact of the smoothing techniques on BLEU

Several conclusions can be presented regarding results of the Table 5. First of all, for a small parallel corpus, it seems that the smoothing technique has an impact on the BLEU scores. A difference of almost 2 points has been observed for translating from ANB to ALG. But, we can not generalize by affirming that one smoothing technique is definitely better than another. We have not calculated the significance of this difference because our corpus is too small, consequently we can not have several small test corpora in order to perform significance tests. In order to have an idea about the impact of the smoothing technique on the results and to have a scale comparison of the BLEU for small corpora we did some

[3] A collection of classical Arabic books from an online library available on `http://sourceforge.net/project/tashkeela`

Table 5: BLEU score of Machine Translation on different pairs of languages using two smoothing techniques

	Target											
	ALG		ANB		TUN		SYR		PAL		MSA	
Source	KN	WB	KN	WB	KN	WB	KN	WB	KN	WB	KN	WB
ALG	-	-	61.06	60.81	9.67	9.36	7.29	7.95	10.61	10.14	15.1	14.64
ANB	67.31	65.55	-	-	9.08	8.64	7.52	7.95	10.12	9.84	14.44	13.95
TUN	9.89	9.48	9.34	9.01	-	-	13.05	12.93	22.55	22.21	25.99	25.21
SYR	7.57	7.50	7.50	7.64	13.67	13.23	-	-	26.60	25.74	24.14	22.96
PAL	11.28	10.67	9.53	9.15	17.93	16.64	23.29	23.07	-	-	40.48	39.76
MSA	13.55	13.05	12.54	11.72	20.03	20.44	21.38	20.32	42.46	41.37	-	-

Table 6: TER score (in %) of Machine Translation on different pairs of languages using two smoothing techniques

	Target											
	ALG		ANB		TUN		SYR		PAL		MSA	
Source	KN	WB	KN	WB	KN	WB	KN	WB	KN	WB	KN	WB
ALG	-	-	21.41	21.75	75.17	76.37	79.54	79.51	69.63	70.75	65.63	66.85
ANB	17.12	17.81	-	-	74.83	75.62	79.13	79.13	69.10	70.26	67.40	68.47
TUN	71.10	71.76	73.13	73.71	-	-	66.03	66.55	51.20	51.57	50.85	51.30
SYR	76.89	77.67	76.89	77.67	66.54	67.91	-	-	32.28	33.24	52.81	53.59
PAL	71.43	72.51	72.25	73.47	58.51	59.65	32.44	33.86	-	-	36.74	36.87
MSA	67.02	67.91	68.94	70.16	57.18	57.28	56.60	57.08	34.00	34.66	-	-

Table 7: METEOR score of Machine Translation on different pairs of languages using two smoothing techniques

	Target											
	ALG		ANB		TUN		SYR		PAL		MSA	
Source	KN	WB	KN	WB	KN	WB	KN	WB	KN	WB	KN	WB
ALG	-	-	0.452	0.450	0.181	0.178	0.161	0.164	0.202	0.199	0.222	0.218
ANB	0.472	0.464	-	-	0.172	0.172	0.156	0.159	0.196	0.194	0.200	0.200
TUN	0.186	0.183	0.182	0.182	-	-	0.203	0.203	0.261	0.260	0.268	0.266
SYR	0.155	0.154	0.159	0.157	0.195	0.190	-	-	0.359	0.356	0.259	0.256
PAL	0.189	0.185	0.187	0.183	0.229	0.225	0.365	0.360	-	-	0.341	0.339
MSA	0.205	0.203	0.201	0.199	0.242	0.245	0.247	0.247	0.359	0.356	-	-

experiments on a small parallel Arabic-English corpus extracted from WMT. We took small corpora in order to be approximatively in the same context such as with PADIC. We used several small training parallel corpora of $20K$, $50K$, $120K$ and $150K$ parallel sentences which will be denoted respectively S_2, S_5, S_{12} and S_{15}. For each training corpus we performed 20 experiments on 20 different small test corpora (500 sentences such as for the dialects). The results are presented in Table 8.

In Table 8, *Min*, *Max*, *E[X]*, σ^2 represent respectively the *minimum*, *maximum*, *mean* and *variance* of the corresponding distribution of BLEU according to the used smoothing technique. While σ_{XY} and *p-value* correspond respectively to the *covariance* and the *p-value* of the two distributions. The statistical test used is T-test after checking that the two distributions follow a Gaussian law. The hypothesis H_0 is that the two distributions are similar (in terms of mean).
According to these different results, it seems that the results obtained by the first or the second smoothing techniques are not distinguishable since for each training corpus and for 20 different tests, the results are equivalent in terms of *minimum*, *maximum*, *mean* and *variance* BLEU values. Furthermore, the covariance is positive for all the experiments which would mean that the two distributions are linearly dependent. The *p-value* whatever the training corpus is greater than the α risk set to 0.05 which means that there is at least a risk of 33% to accept the alternative hypothesis H_1. In conclusion, unfortunately even if there is a difference between the results of BLEU according to the used smoothing techniques, the difference is not significant.

5.2 Cross-translation results comparison

High score of translation has been achieved between ANB and ALG in both sides. This result is natural since these two dialects are spoken in the same country and share up to 60% of words. Almost the same observation is made for the pair SYR and PAL since these two dialects belong to the same language family (Levantine).
Another interesting and expected result is BLEU score between MSA and dialects. In fact, the highest one is related to PAL (for both sides) showing that this dialect is the closest to MSA. Most surprising results are those relative to SYR and TUN. It seems that it is easier to translate TUN to MSA than SYR to MSA. Also, translating from MSA to TUN gives better results than from MSA to the Algerian dialects. In the symmetric side of translation we get the same scale of results. This definitely shows the closeness of TUN dialect to MSA in comparison to the Algerian dialects. The same conclusions can be inferred from the results in terms of TER or METEOR. Also, it seems that the smoothing technique has no impact on both scores. The differences are almost negligible.
We can notice that the values of BLEU are weak in comparison to what the community get usually for large training corpora. This is obviously due to the weak size of the training corpora. But when we compare the scale values of BLEU for dialects to those achieved for English-Arabic (Table 8) which have been performed with small training corpus, we notice that those obtained for dialects are higher. This is probably due to the fact that, even if dialects are very different, nevertheless there is a strong relationship between them. For instance the experiment performed on the corpus S_2, the smallest value of BLEU is 4.25 and the highest is 9.56 while for the worst results of translation (from Syrian to Algerian) the minimum value is 7.57. Knowing that for this comparison, the training corpus S_2 (English-Arabic) is 3 times larger than the one used for the dialect.

6 Conclusion

In this paper, we first presented PADIC a parallel corpus containing five dialects from Maghreb and middle-east. PADIC has been built from scratch because there is no standard resources due to the kind of theses languages which are only used for conversations and not for writing. Then, we presented experiments on cross-dialectal Arabic machine translation. In the best of our knowledge, this is the first work on machine translation of dialects from both Maghreb and Middle-East and also the largest existing parallel Arabic dialect corpora. On the limited corpora of 6400 parallel sentences we built, we achieved some interesting results.
Due to the small size of the corpus, we analyzed the impact of the language model on the process

Table 8: Statistics on machine translation with small training corpus and by varying the smoothing techniques of the language model.

	KN				**WB**					
Corpus	Min	Max	$E[X]$	σ^2	Min	Max	$E[X]$	σ^2	σ_{XY}	*p-value*
S_2	4.25	9.56	6.64	2.47	4.1	8.97	6.43	2.23	2.33	0.33
S_5	5.15	11.75	8.15	3.26	5.18	11.32	7.99	2.92	3.16	0.35
S_{12}	5.94	14.38	9.58	4.62	5.95	14.13	9.35	4.32	4.45	0.36
S_{15}	6.13	14.39	9.91	4.85	6.19	14.27	9.74	4.72	4.75	0.39

of machine translation by varying the smoothing techniques and by interpolating it with a larger one trained on well known corpora. Unfortunately the results are not significant even if in some cases we get some improvements.

The best results of translation are achieved between the dialects of Algeria. This is not a surprising result since they share a large part of the vocabulary. And even if the size of the training corpus is weak, we noticed that the BLEU is very high. The performance of machine translation between Palestinian and Syrian are relatively high in accordance to the size of the corpus. This could be explained by the closeness of the two regions. The worst result is achieved between Syrian and Algerian dialects which are, in fact, very different since the Algerian borrowed a lot of French words which do not exist obviously in the Syrian dialect. Concerning MSA, the best results of machine translation have been achieved with Palestinian dialect. This means that the two languages are very close since they share a large number of words.

Our future work consists in extending PADIC to other dialects such as Moroccan in order to have the dialects of the three countries of Maghreb and then we will work on using the large existing corpora of MSA to rewrite part of them into dialects.

Acknowledgement This work has been supported by PNR (Projet National de Recherche of Algerian research Ministry).

References

Houda Bouamor, Nizar Habash, and Kemal Oflazer. 2014. A Multidialectal Parallel Corpus of Arabic. In *Proceedings of the Language Resources and Evaluation Conference, LREC-2014*, pages 1240–1245.

David Chiang, Mona Diab, Nizar Habash, Owen Rambow, and Safiullah Shareef. 2006. Parsing Arabic Dialects. In *Proceedings of the European Chapter of ACL (EACL)*.

Heba Elfardy and Mona Diab. 2013. Sentence Level Dialect Identification in Arabic. In *ACL (2)*, pages 456–461.

Nizar Habash and Owen Rambow. 2006. Magead: A Morphological Analyzer and Generator for the Arabic Dialects. In *Proceedings of the 21st International Conference on Computational Linguistics and 44th Annual Meeting of the Association for Computational Linguistics*, pages 681–688.

Nizar Habash, Ryan Roth, Owen Rambow, Ramy Eskander, and Nadi Tomeh. 2013. Morphological analysis and disambiguation for dialectal arabic. In *Proceedings of NAACL-HLT*, pages 426–432, Atlanta, Georgia.

Salima Harrat, Mourad Abbas, Karima Meftouh, and Kamel Smaili. 2013. Diacritics restoration for arabic dialect texts. In *Proceedings of 14th Annual Conference of the International Communication Association (Interspeech)*, pages 125–132.

Salima Harrat, Karima Meftouh, Mourad Abbas, and Kamel Smaili. 2014. Building resources for algerian arabic dialects. In *Proceedings of 15th Annual Conference of the International Communication Association (Interspeech)*, pages 2123–2127.

Salima Harrat, Karima Meftouh, Mourad Abbas, Salma Jamoussi, and Kamel Smaili. 2015. Cross-dialectal arabic processing. In *Computational Linguistics and Intelligent Text Processing, 16th International Conference, CICLing 2015 proceeding, part 1*, pages 620–632, April.

Hanaa Kilany, H. Gadalla, Howaida Arram, A. Yacoub, Alaa El-Habashi, and C. McLemore. 2002. Egyptian Colloquial Arabic Lexicon. In *LDC catalog number LDC99L22*.

Katrin Kirchhoff, Jeff Bilmes, Sourin Das, Nicolae Duta, Melissa Egan, Gang Ji, Feng He, John Hopkins, Daben Liu, Mohamed Noamany, Pat Schone, Richard Schwartz, and Dimitra Vergyri. 2003. Novel Approaches to Arabic Speech Recognition: Report from the 2002 Johns-Hopkins Summer Workshop. In *Proc.*

IEEE Intl. Conf. on Acoustics, Speech, and Signal Processing, pages 344–347.

Philipp Koehn, Hieu. Hoang, Alexandra Birch, Chris Callison-Burch, Marcello Federico, Nicola Bertoldi, Brooke Cowan, Wade Shen, Christine Moran, Richard Zens, Chris Dyer, Ondrej Bojar, Alexandra Constantin, and Evan Herbst. 2007. Moses: Open Source Toolkit for Statistical Machine Translation. *Proceedings of the Annual Meeting of the Association for Computational Linguistics, demonstation session*, pages 177–180.

Mohamed Maamouri, Ann Bies, Tim Buckwalter, and Hubert Jin. 2004. Arabic treebank: Part 3 v 1.0. In *Linguistic Data Consortium.*

Franz Josef Och and Hermann Ney. 2003. A Systematic Comparison of Various Statistical Alignment Models. *Computational Linguistics, Volume 29, No 1*, pages 19–51.

Arfath Pasha, Mohamed Al-Badrashiny, Ramy Kholy Ahmed El Eskander, Mona Diab, Nizar Habash, Manoj Pooleery, Owen Rambow, and Ryan Roth. 2014. Madamira: A fast, comprehensive tool for morphological analysis and disambiguation of arabic. In *LREC 2014, Language Resources and Evaluation Conference*, Reykjavik, Iceland.

Tachicart Ridouane and Bouzoubaa Karim. 2014. A hybrid approach to translate moroccan arabic dialect. In *SITA'14, 9th International Conference on Intelligent Systems.*

Wael. Salloum and Nizar. Habash. 2012. Elissa: A dialectal to standard arabic machine translation system. In *Coling'2012, 24th International Conference on Computational Linguistics*, pages 385–392.

Wael Salloum and Nizar Habash. 2013. Dialectal Arabic to English Machine Translation: Pivoting through Modern Standard Arabic. In *Proceedings of the 2013 Conference of the North American Chapter of the Association for Computational Linguistics: Human Language Technologies*, NAACL HLT 13, pages 348–358.

Hassan. Sawaf. 2010. Arabic dialect handling in hybrid machine translation. In *AMTA'2010, 9th Conf. of the Association for Machine Translation in the Americas.*

Inguna Skadiņa, Ahmet Aker, Voula Giouli, Dan Tufis, Robert Gaizauskas, Madara Mieriņa, and Nikos Mastropavlos. 2010. A Collection of Comparable Corpora for Under-resourced Languages. In *Proceedings of the 2010 Conference on Human Language Technologies – The Baltic Perspective: Proceedings of the Fourth International Conference Baltic HLT 2010*, pages 161–168.

Andreas Stolcke. 2002. Srilm – an Extensible Language Modeling Toolkit. In *ICSLP*, pages 901–904, Denver, USA.

Rabih Zbib, Erika Malchiodi, Devlin Jacob, David Stallard, Spyros Matsoukas, Richard Schwartz, John Makhoul, Omar Zaidan, and Chris Callison-Burch. 2012. Machine Translation of Arabic Dialects. In *Proceedings of the 2012 Conference of the North American Chapter of the Association for Computational Linguistics: Human Language Technologies*, NAACL HLT 12, pages 49–59.

Surrounding Word Sense Model for Japanese All-words Word Sense Disambiguation

Kanako KOMIYA [1] **Yuto SASAKI** [2] **Hajime MORITA** [3]
Minoru SASAKI [1] **Hiroyuki SHINNOU** [1] **Yoshiyuki KOTANI** [2]
[1]Ibaraki University [2]Kyoto University [3]Tokyo University of Agriculture and Technology
kanako.komiya.nlp@vc.ibaraki.ac.jp, 50010268030@st.tuat.ac.jp
morita@nlp.ist.i.kyoto-u.ac.jp, minoru.sasaki.01@vc.ibaraki.ac.jp
hiroyuki.shinnou.0828@vc.ibaraki.ac.jp, kotani@cc.tuat.ac.jp

Abstract

This paper proposes a surrounding word sense model (SWSM) that uses the distribution of word senses that appear near ambiguous words for unsupervised all-words word sense disambiguation in Japanese. Although it was inspired by the topic model, ambiguous Japanese words tend to have similar topics since coarse semantic polysemy is less likely to occur than that in Western languages as Japanese uses Chinese characters, which are ideograms. We thus propose a model that uses the distribution of word senses that appear near ambiguous words: SWSM. We embedded the concept dictionary of an Electronic Dictionary Research (EDR) electronic dictionary in the system and used the Japanese Corpus of EDR for the experiments, which demonstrated that SWSM outperformed a system with a random baseline and a system that used a topic model called Dirichlet Allocation with WORDNET (LDAWN), especially when there were high levels of entropy for the word sense distribution of ambiguous words.

1 Introduction

This paper proposes a surrounding word sense model (SWSM) for unsupervised Japanese all-words Word Sense Disambiguation (WSD). SWSM assumes that the sense distribution of surrounding words varies according to the sense of a polysemous word.

For instance, a word "可能性" (possibility) has three senses according to the Electronic Dictionary Research (EDR) electronic dictionary (Miyoshi et al., 1996):

(1) The ability to do something well

(2) Its feasibility

(3) The certainty of something happenings

Although sense (3) is the most frequent in the prior distributions, sense (1) will be more likely when the local context includes some concepts like "人間" (man) or "誰々の" (someone's). It is challenging in practice to accurately learn the difference in the senses of surrounding words in an unsupervised manner, but we developed an approximate model that took conditions into consideration.

SWSM is a method for all-words WSD inspired by the topic model (Section 2). It treats the similarities of word senses using WORDNET-WALK and it generates word senses of ambiguous words and their surrounding words (Section 3). First, SWSM abstracted the concepts of the concept dictionary (Section 4) and calculated the transition probabilities for priors (Section 5). Then it estimated the word senses using Gibbs Sampling (Section 6) . Our experiments with an EDR Japanese corpus and a Concept Dictionary (Section 7) indicated that SWSM was effective for Japanese all-words WSD (Section 8) . We discuss the results (Section 9) and concludes this paper (Section 10) .

2 Related Work

There are many methods of all-words WSD. Pedersen et al. (2005) proposed calculation of the semantic relatedness of the word senses of ambiguous words and their surrounding words. Some papers have reported that methods using topic models (Blei et al., 2003) are most effective. Boyd-Graber et al. (2007) proposed a model, called Latent Dirichlet Allocation with WORDNET (LDAWN), which was a model where the probability distributions of words that the topics had were replaced with a word generation process on WordNet: WORDNET-WALK. They ap-

29th Pacific Asia Conference on Language, Information and Computation pages 35 - 43
Shanghai, China, October 30 - November 1, 2015

plied the topic model to unsupervised English all-words WSD. Although Guo and Diab (2011) also used the topic model and WordNet, they also used WordNet as a lexical resource for sense definitions and they did not use its conceptual structure. They reported that the performance of their system was comparable with that reported by Boyd-Graber et al.

There has been little work, on the other hand, on unsupervised Japanese all-words WSD. As far as we know, there has only been one paper (Baldwin et al., 2008) and there have been no reported methods that have used the topic model. We think this is because ambiguous words in Japanese tend to have similar topics since coarse semantic polysemy is less likely to occur compared to that with Western languages as Japanese uses Chinese characters, which are ideograms. In addition, Guo and Diab (2011) reported that *in word sense disambiguation (WSD), an even narrower context was taken into consideration*, as Mihalcea (2005) had reported. Therefore, we assumed that the word senses of the local context are differentiated depending on the word sense of the target word like that in supervised WSD. SWSM was inspired by LDAWN, it thus uses WORDNET-WALK and Gibbs sampling but it does not use the topics but the word senses of the surrounding words. We propose SWSM as an approach to unsupervised WSD and carried out Japanese all-words WSD.

3 Surrounding Word Sense Model

SWSM uses the distribution of word senses that appear near the target word in WSD to estimate the word senses assuming that the word senses of the local context are differentiated depending on the word sense of the target word. In other words, SWSM estimates the word sense according to $p(\boldsymbol{s}|\boldsymbol{w})$, which is a conditional probability of a string of senses, $\boldsymbol{s}$, given a string of words $\boldsymbol{w}$.

SWSM involves three assumptions. First, each word sense has a probability distribution of the senses of the surrounding words. Second, when c_i denotes the sense string of the surrounding words of the target word w_i, the conditional probability of c_i given w_i is the product of the those of the senses in c_i given w_i. For example, when w_i is “可能性” (possibility) and its surrounding words are “両者” (both sides) and “人間” (human), $c_i = (s_{both}, s_{human})$ and $P(c_i|s_{possibility}) = P(s_{both}|s_{possibility})P(s_{human}|s_{possibility})$ are defined where $s_{possibility}$, s_{both}, and s_{human} denote word senses of “可能性” (possibility), “両者” (both sides), and “人間” (human). Finally, each polyseme has a prior distribution of the senses. Given these assumptions, SWSM calculates the conditional probability of $\boldsymbol{s}$ that corresponds to $\boldsymbol{w}$, under the condition where $\boldsymbol{w}$ is observed as:

$$P(\boldsymbol{s}, \boldsymbol{c}|\boldsymbol{w}) = \prod_{i=1}^{N} P(s_i|w_i)P(c_i|s_i, \boldsymbol{w}), \quad (1)$$

where $\boldsymbol{c}$ denotes the string of c_i and N denotes the number of all the words in the text. The initial part on the right is the probability distribution of the word sense of each word and the last part is that of the senses of the surrounding words for each word sense. We set the Dirichlet distribution as their prior.

The final equation considering prior is described using the following parameters:

$$P(\boldsymbol{s}, \boldsymbol{c}, \boldsymbol{\theta}, \boldsymbol{\phi}|\boldsymbol{w}, \gamma_k, \tau_j) =$$

$$\prod_{k=1}^{W} P(\theta_k|\gamma_k) \prod_{j=1}^{S} P(\phi_j|\tau_j) \prod_{i=1}^{N} P(s_i|\theta_{w_i})P(c_i|\phi_{s_j}, \boldsymbol{w}), \quad (2)$$

where W denotes the number of words, S denotes the number of senses, θ_k denotes the probability distribution of the senses of word k, and ϕ_j denotes the probability distribution of the word senses surrounding word sense j. θ_k and ϕ_j are the parameters of the multinomial distribution. γ and τ are the parameters of the Dirichlet distribution.

Eq. (2) is the basic form. We replace ϕ, the probability distribution of each sense, with the generation process by using the WORDNET-WALK of the concept dictionary. The WORDNET-WALK in this work does not generate words but word senses using a hyper-transition probability parameter, $S\alpha$. We set α according to the senses to differentiate the sense distribution of the surrounding words before training. By doing this, we can determine which sense in the model corresponds to the senses in the dictionary.

SWSM estimates the word senses using Gibbs sampling as:

(1) Pre-processing

1 Abstract the concepts in the concept dictionary

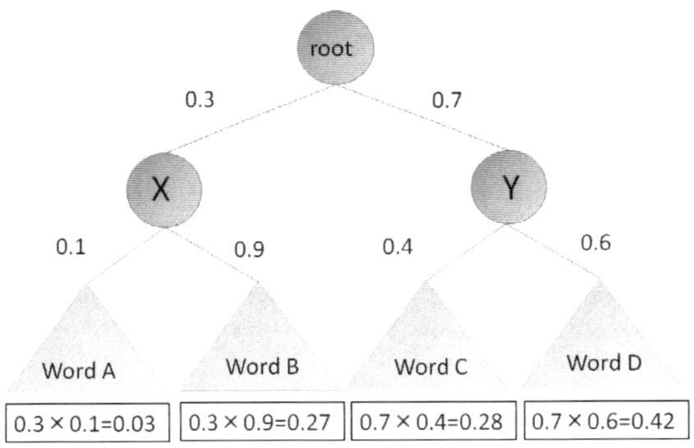

Figure 1: Example of WORNET-WALK

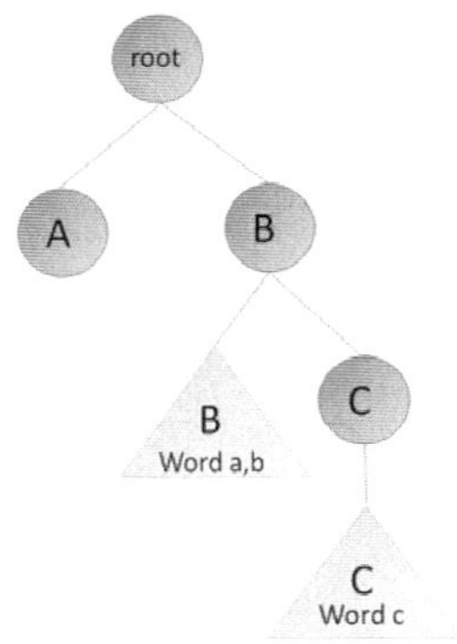

Figure 2: Addition of Word Sense Nodes

2 Calculate the transition parameters using the sense frequencies

(2) Training: Gibbs sampling to estimate the word senses

4 Concept Abstraction

SWSM obtains the sense probability of the surrounding words using WORDNET-WALK. WORDNET-WALK involves the generation process, which represents the probabilistic walks over the hierarchy of conceptual structures like WordNet. Figure 1 shows the easy example of the generation probabilities of words by WORDNET-WALK. When circle nodes represent concepts and triangle nodes represent words of leaf concepts ,i.e., X and Y, and numbers represent the transition probabilities, the generation probabilities of words A, B, C, and D are 0.03, 0.27, 0.28, and 0.42. LDAWN calculated the probabilities of word senses using the transition probability from the root node in a concept dictionary. WORDNET-WALK generated words in (Boyd-Graber et al., 2007) but our WORDNET-WALK generates word senses. However, the word senses sometimes do not correspond to leaf nodes but to internal nodes in our model and that causes a problem: the sum of the probabilities is not one. Thus, we added leaf nodes of the word senses directly below the internal nodes of the concept dictionary (c.f. Figure 2).

Concept abstraction involves the process by which hyponym concepts map onto hypernym concepts. Most concepts in a very deep hierarchy are fine grained like the "Tokyo University of Agriculture and Technology" and "Ibaraki University" and they should be combined together like "university" to avoid the zero frequency problem. Thus, SWSM combines semantically similar concepts in the concept dictionary.

Hirakawa and Kimura (2003) reported that they compared three methods for concept abstraction, i.e, flat depth, flat size, and flat probability methods, by using the EDR concept dictionary, and the flat probability method was the best. Therefore, we used the flat probability method for concept abstraction.

The flat probability method consists of two steps. First, there is a search for nodes from the root node in depth first order. Second, if the concept probability calculated based on the corpus is less than a threshold value, the concept and its hyponym concepts are mapped onto its hypernym concept.

We employed the methods of (Ribas, 1995) and (McCarthy, 1997) to calculate the concept probability. Ribas (1995) calculated the frequency of sense s as:

$$freq(s) = \sum_{w} \frac{|senses(w) \in U(s)|}{|senses(w)|} count(w), \tag{3}$$

where $senses(w)$ denotes the possible senses of a word w, $U(s)$ denotes concept s and its hyponym concepts, and $count(w)$ denotes the frequency of word w. This equation weights $count(w)$ by the ratio of concept s and its hyponym concepts in all the word senses of w. probability $P(s_i)$ was calculated as:

$$P(s_i) = \frac{freq(s_i)}{N}, \tag{4}$$

where N denotes the number of word tokens.

Figure 3 demonstrates the example of the conceptual structure[1]. The nodes A∼F represent the

[1]The leaf concepts below C, D, E, and F are omitted.

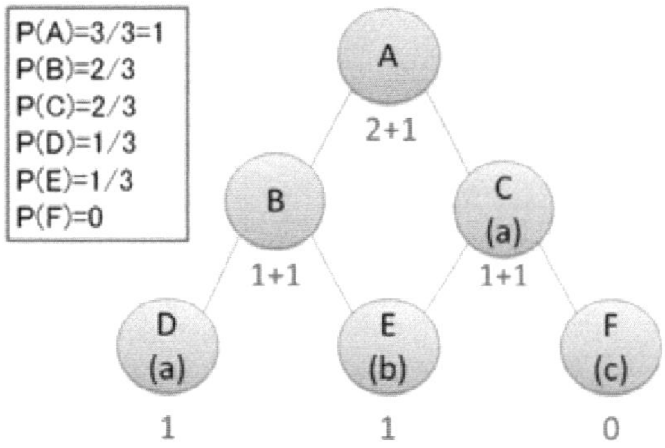

Figure 3: Example of Concept Structure

concepts and (a)∼(c) represent the words, which indicates that word (a) is a polyseme that have two word senses, i.e., C and D. When word (a) appeared twice and word (b) appeared once, the probabilities are as illustrated in Figure 3. Note that C and D share the frequencies of word (a).

A Turing estimator (Gale and Sampson, 1995) was used for smoothing with rounding of the weighted frequencies.

Concept abstraction sometimes causes a problem where some word senses of a polyseme are mapped onto the same concept. The most frequent sense in the corpus has been chosen for the answer in these cases.

5 Transition Probability

SWSM differentiates the sense distribution of the surrounding words of each target word before training using α : the transition probability parameter. As our method is an unsupervised approach, we cannot know the word senses in the corpus. Therefore, SWSM counts the frequencies of all the possible word senses of the surrounding words in the corpus. That is, if there are polysemes A and B in the corpus and B is a surrounding word of A, SWSM counts the frequencies of the senses by considering that all the senses of B appeared near all the senses of A. That makes no difference in the sense distributions of A; however, if there is another polyseme or a monosemic word, C, and a sense of C is identical with a sense of A, the sense distributions of A will be differentiated by counting the frequencies of the senses of C. As this example indicates, SWSM expects that words that have an identical sense, like A and C, have similar local contexts.

SWSM uses these counted frequencies to calculate the transition parameter α so that the transition probabilities to each concept are proportional to the word sense frequencies of the surrounding words. We calculate α_{s_i,s_j}, i.e., the transition probability from hypernym s_i to hyponym s_j, like that in (Jiang and Conrath, 1997) as:

$$\alpha_{s_i,s_j} = P(s_j|s_i) = \frac{P(s_i,s_j)}{P(s_i)} = \frac{P(s_j)}{P(s_i)}. \quad (5)$$

In addition, probability $P(s_i)$ is calculated as:

$$P(s_i) = \frac{freq(s_i)}{N}, \quad (6)$$

where $freq(s_i)$ denotes the frequency of sense s_i.

Moreover, $freq(s_i)$ is calculated like that in (Resnik, 1995):

$$freq(s_i) = \sum_{w \in words(s_i)} count(w). \quad (7)$$

Here, $words(s_i)$ denotes a concept set that includes s_i and its hyponyms, and N denotes the number of the word tokens in the corpus. However, the probability that Eq. (7) will have a problem, i.e., the sum of the transition probabilities from a concept to its hyponyms is not one. Thus, we calculate the probability by considering that the same concept that follow a different path is different:

$$freq(s_i) = \sum_{s_j \in L(s_i)} path(s_i,s_j) \sum_{w \in words(s_i)} count(w), \quad (8)$$

where $path(s_i, s_j)$ denotes the number of the paths from concept s_i to its hyponym s_j and $L(s_i)$ denotes the leaf concepts below s_i. Consequently, the transition probability can be calculated by dividing the frequencies of the hyponym by that of its hypernym.

When word (a) appeared twice and word (b) appeared once, the transition probability from A to B, i.e., $\alpha_{A,B}$ is 1/2 because the frequencies of A and B are six [2] and three in Figure 3.

Here, $p(path_{s_l})$, i.e., a transition probability of an arbitrary path from the root node to a leaf concept, $path_{s_l}$, is:

$$p(path_{s_l})$$

[2]It is sum of twice from path ABD (a), twice from path AC (a), once from path ABE (b), and once from path ACE (b).

$$= \frac{freq(c_1)}{freq(s_{root})} \frac{freq(c_2)}{freq(c_1)} \cdots \frac{freq(c_n)}{freq(c_{n-1})} \frac{freq(s_l)}{freq(c_n)}$$

$$= \frac{freq(s_l)}{freq(s_{root})}, \quad (9)$$

where $c_1 c_2 \ldots c_n$ denote the concepts in $path_{s_l}$. Therefore, when we set the frequency of the word sense frequencies of s_l, the surrounding words, as $freq(s_l)$, $p(path_{s_l})$ are proportional to the frequency.

We eventually used the following transition probability parameter to avoid the zero frequency problem:

$$S_a \alpha_a + S_b \alpha_b^s, \quad (10)$$

where α_a denotes a transition probability parameter where all the leaf nodes have the same amount probability and α_b^s denotes the transition probability parameter that is pre-trained using the above equations. S_a and S_b are constant numbers to control the effect of pre-processing.

The transition probability parameter where all the leaf nodes have the same amount probability, α_a, is calculated by assuming that the frequencies of all the leaf nodes are as follows. [3]

$$freq(s_l) = \frac{1}{path(s_{root}, s_l)} \quad (11)$$

6 Sense Estimation using Gibbs Sampling

SWSM estimates the word sense, s, using Gibbs sampling (Liu, 1994). As described in Section 3, the conditional probability of the model is in Eq. (12).

$$P(\boldsymbol{s}, \boldsymbol{c}, \boldsymbol{\theta}, \boldsymbol{\phi} | \boldsymbol{w}) =$$

$$\prod_{k=1}^{W} P(\theta_k|\gamma_k) \prod_{j=1}^{S} P(\phi_j|\tau_j) \prod_{i=1}^{N} P(s_i|\theta_{w_i}) P(c_i|\phi_{s_j}, \boldsymbol{w}) \quad (12)$$

We calculate the conditional distribution that is necessary for sampling. We regard variants except those for word w_i as constant numbers. The probability distribution, $\boldsymbol{\phi}$, of the word sense is actually replaced by WORDNET-WALK in the word sense generation process and it will have plural multinomial distributions of the transitions to the hyponym concepts.

We calculated the conditional distribution $P(s_i, c_i | \boldsymbol{s_{-i}}, \boldsymbol{c_{-i}}, \boldsymbol{w})$ as:

$$P(s_i = x, c_i = \boldsymbol{y} | \boldsymbol{s_{-i}}, \boldsymbol{c_{-i}}, \boldsymbol{w})$$

$$\propto (n_{w_i,x}^{-i} + \gamma) \cdot \prod_{j=1}^{|\boldsymbol{y}|} \frac{(n_{x,y_j}^{-i} + m_y(j, y_i) + \tau_{x,y_j})}{\sum_{sen} (n_{x,sen}^{-i} + \tau_{x,sen}) + (j-1)}, \quad (13)$$

where x and $\boldsymbol{y}$ correspond to the real values of word sense s_i and the vector of the word senses of the surrounding words, c_i. $n_{w_i,x}^{-i}$ denotes the number of x, i.e., the word senses that are assigned to word w_i except for the i_{th} variate, which is the sampling target now. n_{x,y_i}^{-i} denotes the frequency where y_j appears around word sense x except for the i_{th} variate. $m_y(j, y_j)$ is the frequency where word sense y_j appear before the j_{th} surrounding word sense in $\boldsymbol{y}$ and it can be ignored if y_j appeared once in $\boldsymbol{y}$. We approximately and determinately assign the sequence of the word senses to $\boldsymbol{y}$, calculate each probability of s_i, and determine s_i, i.e., the word sense that corresponds to word w_i.

If the probability distributions of word senses are replaced with WORDNET-WALK, the last part of the right side of Eq. (13) will also be replaced. When $r_{j,0}, r_{j,1}, \ldots, r_{j,l}$ denotes the path from the root concept of word sense y_j in $\boldsymbol{y}$, we obtain Eq. (14) by calculating the following values of all combinations from the root concept for all word senses, and summing them.

$$\prod_{j=1}^{|y|} \prod_{p=1}^{l-1} \{ T_{x,r_{j,p},r_{j,p+1}}^{-i} + m_y(j, r_{j,p}, r_{j,p+1})$$
$$+ S_a \alpha_{a,r_{j,p},r_{j,p+1}} + S_b \alpha_{b,r_{j,p},r_{j,p+1}}^{x} \}$$
$$/ \{ \sum_r (T_{x,r_{j,p},r}^{-i} + m_y(j, r_{j,p}, r) + S_b \alpha_{b,r_{j,p},r}^{x}) + S_a \}, \quad (14)$$

where $T_{x,r_{j,p},r_{j,p+1}}^{-i}$ denotes the frequency where the word sense of the surrounding words of word sense x pass the link from concept $r_{j,p}$ to concept $r_{j,p+1}$ except for the i_{th} variate. $m_y(j, r_{j,p}, r_{j,p+1})$ denotes the frequency where the link from concept $r_{j,p}$ to concept $r_{j,p+1}$ is passed before the j_{th} path. The value of T_{s_i} should be updated after word sense s_i is assigned. Thus, the paths of the word senses of the surrounding words are necessary. This time, we assign values proportional to each probability to each path. When $path_1$,$path_2$,

[3]The reason we did not set the frequencies of all the leaf nodes to one ($freq(s_l) = 1$) is as follows. If so, all the probabilities of all the paths from the root node to each leaf node would have been the same. However, the more paths from the root node a leaf node has, the higher the probability the leaf node will have. We used Eq.(11) so that all the leaf nodes would have the same probability.

$\cdots$,$path_n$ denote the paths from the root concept to word sense $c_{i,j}$, i.e., a word sense of surrounding words c_i of word sense s_i, we added following value to $T_{s_i,path_k}$, which is the frequency where a link in $path_k$ is passed, for each word sense $c_{i,j}$.

$$\frac{P(path_k|s_i)}{\sum_{l=1}^{n} P(path_l|s_i)} \tag{15}$$

The probability $p(path_k|s_i)$ is as follows, when $r_1, r_2, \cdots, r_l$ denote the concepts that $path_k$ follows.

$$P(path_k|s_i) = \sum_{p=1}^{l-1} \frac{T_{s_i,r_p,r_{p+1}}^{-i} + S_a \alpha_{a,r_p,r_{p+1}} + S_b \alpha_{b,r_p,r_{p+1}}^{s_i}}{\sum_r (T_{s_i,r_p,r}^{-i} + S_b \alpha_{b,r_p,r}^{s_i}) + S_a} \tag{16}$$

Concepts that have many paths from the root concept are concepts that have many properties. Thus, we can view these cases as that of an appearance of word sense $c_{i,j}$ that was assigned to multiple properties.

Algorithm 1 demonstrates the algorithm of one iteration in Gibbs Sampling of SWSM. Note that x and $\boldsymbol{y}$ are sampled according to Eq. (13) where the last part on the right side is replaced with Eq. (14) and each $T_{s_i,path_k}$ is updated with Eq. (15).

Algorithm 1 Processes of One Iteration in Gibbs Sampling of SWSM

Require: Disambiguate the word sense s_i in text
for each word w_i in text **do**
$n_{w_i,s_i} \Leftarrow n_{w_i,s_i} - 1$
for each word sense $c_{i,j}$ in c_i **do**
for each path $path_k$ for $c_{i,j}$ **do**
$T_{s_i,path_k} \Leftarrow T_{s_i,path_k} - \frac{P(path_k|s_i)}{\sum_{l=1}^{n} P(path_l|s_i)}$
end for
end for
$c_i \Leftarrow \boldsymbol{y}$
$s_i \Leftarrow x$
$n_{w_i,s_i} \Leftarrow n_{w_i,s_i} + 1$
for each word sense $c_{i,j}$ in c_i **do**
for each path $path_k$ for $c_{i,j}$ **do**
$T_{s_i,path_k} \Leftarrow T_{s_i,path_k} + \frac{P(path_k|s_i)}{\sum_{l=1}^{n} P(path_l|s_i)}$
end for
end for
end for

7 Data

We used the Japanese word dictionary, the concept dictionary, and the Japanese corpus of the second version of the EDR electronic dictionary. All the nouns and verbs that could be followed from the root node in the concept dictionary were used for the experiments. In addition, we added some nouns by deleting "する (suru, the suffix that means do)" from nominal verbs, to the concept dictionary. Consequently, the concept dictionary included 263,757 words and 406,710 leaf concepts, and 199,430 leaf concepts in them were used for the experiments. The internal nodes that were used for the experiments were 203,565 concepts. Most of the concepts that were not used were those that had no links to Japanese words. In addition, the concept dictionary included 13,846 concepts and 6,905 leaf concepts after concept abstraction. The threshold value we used was 5.0×10^{-5}.

The Japanese corpus consisted of seven sub-corpora: the Nikkei, the Asahi Shimbun, AERA, Heibonsha World Encyclopedia, Encyclopedic Dictionary of Computer Science, Magazines, and Collections. They were annotated with word sense tags that were the concepts in the concept dictionary. Table 1 summarizes the numbers of documents and word tokens according to the type of text. The documents in this corpus only consisted of one sentence.

Type of Text	Docs	Word tokens
The Nikkei	5,018	121,301
The Asahi Shimbun	91,400	2,272,555
AERA	49,589	1,183,897
Heibonsha World Encyclopedia	10,072	284,059
Encyclopedic Dictionary of Computer Science	13,578	357,607
Magazines	21,199	528,452
Collections	16,946	368,285

Table 1: Summary of Sub-corpora.

We used the Nikkei for evaluation. The other six sub-corpora were used for pre-processing in an unsupervised manner. The EDR Japanese corpus did not include the basic forms of words. Thus we used a morphological analyzer, Mecab[4], to identify the basic forms of words in the corpus.

Shirai (2002) set up the three difficulty classes listed in Table 2. Tables 7 and 3 indicate the number of word types, noun tokens, and verb tokens according to difficulty and the average polysemy

[4]https://github.com/jordwest/mecab-docs-en

of target words according to difficulty. Only words that appeared more than four times in the corpus were classified based on difficulty.

Difficulty	Entoropy
Easy	$E(w) < 0.5$
Normal	$0.5 \leq E(w) < 1$
Hard	$1 \leq E(w)$

Table 2: Difficulty of disambiguation

Difficulty	Word types	Tokens(N)	Tokens(V)
All	4,822	12,149	6,199
Easy	399	3,630	1,723
Normal	337	2,929	1,541
Hard	105	1,028	1,196

Table 3: Types and tokens of words according to difficulty

Difficulty	Noun polysemy	Verb polysemy
All	4.2	5.5
Easy	3.9	4.0
Normal	4.4	5.3
Hard	8.6	10.3

Table 4: Average polysemy of target words according to difficulty

8 Result

We used nouns and independent verbs in a local window whose size was $2N$ except for marks, as the surrounding words. We set $N = 10$ in this research. In addition, we deleted word senses that appeared only once through pre-processing.

We performed experiments using the nine settings of the transition probability parameters: $S_a = \{1.0, 5.0, 10.0\}$ and $S_b = \{10.0, 15.0, 20.0\}$ in Eq.(10). We set the hyper-parameter $\gamma = 0.1$ in Eq.(2) for all experiments. Gibbs sampling was iterated 2,000 times and the most frequent senses of 100 samples in the latter 1,800 times were chosen for the answers. We performed experiments three times per setting for the transition probability parameters and calculated the average accuracies.

Table 4 summaries the results. It includes the micro- and macro-averaged accuracies of SWSM for the nine settings of the parameters, those of the random baseline, and those of LDAWN [5]. The experiments for the random baseline were performed 1,000 times. The best results are indicated in boldface.

S_a	S_b	micro	macro
1	10	38.91%	**42.58%**
5	10	38.67%	42.42%
10	10	37.62%	42.37%
1	15	39.20%	42.43%
5	15	38.23%	42.29%
10	15	38.41%	42.17%
1	20	37.78%	42.26%
5	20	**39.60%**	42.09%
10	20	36.67%	42.04%
Random baseline		30.97%	36.63%
LDAWN		36.12%	42.51%

Table 5: Summary of result

The table indicates that our model, SWSM, was better than both the random baseline and LDAWN. Although the macro-averaged accuracies of LDAWN were better than those of SWSM except when $S_a = 1$ and $S_b = 10$, both the micro- and macro-averaged accuracies of SWSM outperformed those of LDAWN when $S_a = 1$ and $S_b = 10$.

Tables 5 and 6 summarize the micro-averaged accuracies of all words and the macro-averaged accuracies of all words. SWSM1 and SWSM2 in these tables denote the SWSMs with the setting when the best macro-averaged accuracy for all words was obtained ($S_a = 1$ and $S_b = 10$) and with the setting when the best micro-averaged accuracy for all words was obtained ($S_a = 5$ and $S_b = 20$). The best results in each table are indicated in boldface. These tables indicate that SWSM1 or SWSM2 was always better than both

[5] The best results for the 13 settings. We changed the number of topics and the scale parameters according to (Boyd-Graber et al., 2007). In addition, we tested that the effect of the size of a text, a sentence, or a whole daily publication because a document only consisted of a sentence in our Japanese corpus and there was no clues that indicated to what article the sentence belonged. Furthermore, we tested two kinds of transition probabilities, those that used priors and those where all the leaf nodes had the same amount probability. The best was the setting where there were 32 topics, scale parameter S was 10, the text size was a sentence, and the transition probabilities were those where all the leaf nodes had the same amount probability. The details are similar to those in (Sasaki et al., 2014). However, we performed the experiments three times and calculated the accuracies but they only performed the experiments twice.

the random baseline and LDAWN.

Method	All	Easy	Normal	Hard
Random	30.97	33.01	29.35	13.47
LDAWN	36.12	42.06	30.66	13.52
SWSM1	38.91	46.87	**33.44**	19.92
SWSM2	**39.60**	**48.90**	32.85	**23.95**

Table 6: Micro-averaged accuracies for all words (%)

Method	All	Easy	Normal	Hard
Random	36.63	36.91	32.09	16.03
LDAWN	42.51	44.65	34.83	17.80
SWSM1	**42.58**	**44.78**	**36.38**	**21.06**
SWSM2	42.09	43.68	36.01	20.44

Table 7: Macro-averaged accuracies for all words (%)

Table 6 indicates that the macro averaged accuracies of LDAWN (42.51%) outperformed those of SWSM2 (42.09%) when all the words were evaluated. However, the same table reveals that the reason is due to the results for the easy class words, i.e., the words that almost always had the same sense. In addition, Tables 5 and 6 indicate that SWSM clearly outperformed the other systems for words in the normal and hard classes.

9 Discussion

The examples"可能性 (possibility)" and "洗う (wash)" were cases where most senses were correctly predicted. "可能性 (possibility)" is a hard-class word and it appeared 18 times in the corpus. SWSM correctly predicted the senses of ~70% of them. It had three senses as described in Section 1: (1) the ability to do something well, (2) its feasibility, and (3) the certainty of something happenings. First, SWSM could correctly predict the first sense. The words that surrounded them were, for instance, "両者 (both sides)" and "人間 (human)", and "研究 (research)", "コンビナート (industrial complex)", and "今後 (hereafter)". Second, SWSM could correctly predict almost none of the words that had the second sense. The words surrounding an example were "毎日 (every day)", "違う (various)", "直面する (to face)", and "人々 (people)", and SWSM predicted the sense as sense (1). We think that "人々 (people)" misled the answer. The words surrounding another example were "破る (break through)", "音楽 (music)", and "広げる (spread)", and SWSM predict the sense as sense (1). We think that "広げる (spread)" could be a clue to predict the sense, but "音楽 (music)" misled the answer because it appeared many times in the corpus. Finally, SWSM could correctly predicted the last sense. The words surrounded them were, for instance, (1) "事態 (situation)", "生ずる (arise)", and "出る (appear)", (2) "円高 (appreciation)", "進む (escalate)", and "出る (appear)", and (3) "読む (read)" and"否定する (deny)".

"洗う (wash)" is a normal-class word and it appeared five times in the corpus. SWSM correctly predicted the senses of ~80%, viz., four of them. It has two senses in the corpus: (1) sanctify (someone's heart) and (2) wash out a stain with water. The words surrounding the example that were incorrectly predicted were "今夜 (tonight)", "体 (body)", and "否 (not)", and SWSM answered the sense as (1) even though it was (2). The words surrounding the examples that were correctly predicted were (1) "島民 (islander)", "涙 (tear)", and "石 (stone)", (2) "見る (look at)" and "心 (heart)", (3) "手足 (limb)", "顔 (face)", "私 (I)", and "風呂 (bath)", (4) "体 (body)", "水 (water)", and "抜く (drain)".

These examples demonstrate that the surrounding words were good clues to disambiguate the word senses.

10 Conclusion

We proposed the surrounding word sense model (SWSM), which used the word sense distribution around ambiguous words, and performed unsupervised all-words word sense disambiguation in the Japanese language. The system incorporated the EDR concept dictionary and we performed experiments using the EDR Japanese corpus. We evaluated the performance of the model using difficulty classes based on the entropy of senses in the corpus: easy, normal, and hard. We performed experiments with SWSM in nine settings for the transition probability parameters. The experiments revealed that SWSM outperformed the random baseline and LDAWN, which is a system that uses the topic model. The SWSM model clearly outperformed the other systems for senses in the normal and hard classes. Some examples that correctly predicted senses indicated that the surrounding words were good clues to disambiguate word senses even if we used unsupervised WSD.

References

Timothy Baldwin, Su Nam Kim, Francis Bond, Sanae Fujita, David Martinez, and Takaaki Tanaka. 2008. Mrd-based word sense disambiguation: Further extending lesk. In *Proceedings of the 2008 International Joint Conference on Natural Language Processing*, pages 775–780.

David Blei, Andrew Ng, and Michael Jordan. 2003. Latent dirichlet allocation. *Journal of Machine Learning Research*, 1(3):993–1022.

Jordan Boyd-Graber, David M. Blei, and Xiaojin Zhu. 2007. A topic model for word sense disambiguation. In *Proceedings of the 2007 Joint Conference on Empirical Methods in Natural Language Processing and Computational Natural Language Learning*, pages 1024–1033.

W. Gale and G. Sampson. 1995. Good-turing smoothing without tears. *Journal of Quantitative Linguistics*, 2(3):217–237.

Weiwei Guo and Mona Diab. 2011. Semantic topic models: Combining word distributional statistics and dictionary definitions. In *Proceedings of the 2011 Conference on Empirical Methods in Natural Language Processing*, pages 552–561.

Hideki Hirakawa and Kazuhiro Kimura. 2003. Concept abstraction methods using concept classification and their evaluation on word sense disambiguation task. *IPSJ Journal*, 2(44):421–432, (In Japanese).

Jay J. Jiang and David W. Conrath. 1997. Semantic similarity based on corpus statistics and lexical taxonomy. In *Proceedings of International Conference Research on Computational Linguistics*, pages 19–33.

Jun S Liu. 1994. The collapsed gibbs sampler in bayesian computations with applications to a gene regulation problem. *Journal of the American Statistical Association*, 427(40):958–966.

Diana McCarthy. 1997. Estimation of a probability distribution over a hierarchical classification. In *The Tenth White House Papers COGS - CSRP*, pages 1–9.

Rada Mihalcea. 2005. Unsupervised large-vocabulary word sense disambiguation with graph-based algorithms for sequence data labeling. In *Proceedings of the 2005 Conference on Empirical Methods in Natural Language Processing*, pages 411–418.

Hideo Miyoshi, Kenji Sugiyama, Masahiro Kobayashi, and Takano Ogino. 1996. An overview of the edr electronic dictionary and the current status of its utilization. In *Proceedings of the COLING 1996 Volume 2: The 16th International Conference on Computational Linguistics*, pages 1090–1093.

Ted Pedersen, Satanjeev Banerjee, and Siddharth Patwardhan. 2005. Maximizing semantic relatedness to perform word sense disambiguation. In *Research Report UMSI*.

Philip Resnik. 1995. Using information content to evaluate semantic similarity in a taxonomy. In *International Joint Conferences on Artificial Intelligence*, pages 448–453.

Francesc Ribas. 1995. On learning more appropriate selectional restrictions. In *Proceedings of the Seventh Conference of the European Chapter of the Association for Computational Linguistics*, pages 112–118.

Yuto Sasaki, Kanako Komiya, and Yoshiyuki Kotani. 2014. Word sense disambiguation using topic model and thesaurus. In *Proceedings of the fifth corpus Japanese workshop*, pages 71–80 (In Japanese).

Kiyoaki Shirai. 2002. Construction of a word sense tagged corpus for senseval-2 japanese dictionary task. In *Proceedings of the third International Conference on Language Resources and Evaluation*, pages 605–608.

Computing Semantic Text Similarity Using Rich Features

Yang Liu[1], Chengjie Sun[1], Lei Lin[1], Yuming Zhao[2] and Xiaolong Wang[1]
[1] Harbin Institute of Technology, Harbin Heilongjiang 150001, China
[2] Northeast Forestry University, Harbin Heilongjiang 150040, China
{yliu,cjsun,linl,ymzhao,wangxl}@insun.hit.edu.cn

Abstract

Semantic text similarity (STS) is an essential problem in many Natural Language Processing tasks, which has drawn a considerable amount of attention by research community in recent years. In this paper, our work focused on computing semantic similarity between texts of sentence length. We employed a Support Vector Regression model with rich effective features to predict the similarity scores between short English sentence pairs. Our model used WordNet-Based features, Corpus-Based features, Word2Vec-based features, Alignment-Based feature and Literal-Based features to cover various aspects of sentences. And the experiment conducted on SemEval 2015 task 2a shows that our method achieved a Pearson correlation: 80.486% which outperformed the wining system (80.15%) by a small margin, the results indicated a high correlation with human judgments. Specially, among the five test sets which come from different domains used in the estimation, our method got better results than the top team on two of them whose domain-related data is available for training, while comparable results were achieved on the rest three unseen test sets. The experiments results indicated that our solution is more competitive when the domain-specific training data is available and our method still keeps good generalization ability on novel data.

1 Introduction

Semantic text similarity is a fundamental challenge in many Natural Language Processing tasks, such as Machine Reading, Deep Question Answering (Narayanan & Harabagiu, 2004), Automatic Machine Translation Evaluation (Papineni, Roukos et al., 2002), Automatic Text Summarization (Fattah & Ren, 2008) and Query Reformulation (Metzler, Dumais et al., 2007), etc. Previous researches on semantic text similarity have been focused on documents and paragraphs, while comparison objects in many NLP tasks are texts of sentence length, such as Video descriptions, News headlines and beliefs, etc. In this paper, we study semantic similarity between sentences. Given two input text segments, we need to automatically determine a score that indicates their semantic similarity. The difficulties of this task lie on several aspects. First, there were no existing effective measures to represent sentences which could be understood by computers without losing any information. Second, even with good representations, it's very hard to find a metric which can fully compare the equivalence between two sentence representations. Third, similarity itself is a very complex concept, and semantic space is also hard to define and quantize. Given the same pair of sentences, different people may mark different similarity scores; this inconsistency is derived from people's judgments of difference. Although with these difficulties ahead, a lot of methods have been proposed to handle this problem in recent years. And our efforts mainly focused on trying to combine different existing approaches to represent a sentence, and hope to cover as many aspects of sentence as possible on semantic level.

In this paper, we exploited WordNet-Based, Corpus-Based, Word2Vec-based, Alignment-Based and Literal-Based features to measure semantic equivalence between short English sentences. We used a SVR model to combine all of these similarities and predict a final score between 0~5 to denote the magnitude of semantic similarity. And the experiment conducted on SemEval 2015 task 2a shows that our method achieved a Pearson correlation: 80.486% which outperformed the wining system (80.15%) by a small margin. Experimental results demonstrate the effectiveness of our approach.

29th Pacific Asia Conference on Language, Information and Computation pages 44 - 52
Shanghai, China, October 30 - November 1, 2015

Feature Category	Feature Name
WordNet-Based	Path_similarity, Res_similarity, Lin_similarity, Wup_similarity
Corpus-Based	LSA_similarity, IDF_LSA_similarity, Freq_LSA_similarity, Text_LSA_similarity, LDA_similarity, RIC_Difference
Word2Vec-Based	W2V_similarity, IDF_W2V_similarity, S2V_similarity, Text_W2V_similarity
Alignment-Based	Alignment_similarity
Literal-Based	EditDistance_similarity, ShallowSyntatic_similarity, DifferLen_Rate, Digit_similarity, Digit_in_Fea, No_overlap_Fea, Neg_Sentiment_Fea

Table 1 Feature sets of our system configuration

2 Related Work

Previous efforts have focused on computing semantic similarity between documents, concepts or phrases. Recent natural language processing applications show a stronger demand of finding effective methods to measure semantic similarity between texts of variable length, and extensive method have been proposed in these years. Related work could roughly be divided into five major categories: Word co-occurrence methods, Corpus-based and Knowledge-based methods, String similarity methods, Descriptive feature-based methods and Alignment-based methods.

Word co-occurrence methods are usually used in Information Retrieval (IR) systems (Manning, Raghavan et al., 2008). This method is based on the hypothesis that more similar documents would have more words in common. This method has some drawbacks when used in sentence. As sentences are relatively short compared to documents, they would share fewer words in common; moreover, IR systems often exclude function words in their method while these words carry structural information in sentences (Li, McLean et al., 2006), which eventually may lead to unsatisfactory results.

Many methods combined both corpus-based and knowledge-based measures to reach a better result. Two well-known corpus-based methods are Latent Semantic Analysis (LSA) (Dumais, 2004) and Hyperspace analogues to Language (HAL) (Burgess, Livesay et al., 1998). Another effective corpus-based measure is Explicit Semantic Analysis (ESA) (Gabrilovich & Markovitch, 2007). ESA is a method that represents the meaning of texts in a high-dimension space of concepts derived from Wikipedia. As this methodology explicitly uses the knowledge collected and organized by humans, common-sense and domain-specific world knowledge are considered in it which leads to substantial improvements in measure semantic similarity between sentences, and it is also easy to interpret by human. Knowledge-based methods are often based on semantic networks such as WordNet. Some well-known knowledge-based measures include: S&P's Measure, Wu&Palmer Measure, Leakcock&Chodorow's Measure, Renik's Measure, Lin's Measure and Jiang's Measure.

As to String-based similarity, Islam et al. proposed a normalized and modified version of the Longest Common Subsequence (LCS) string matching algorithm to measure text similarity (Islam & Inkpen, 2008). Combined with a corpus-based measure, their methods achieved a very competing result.

Descriptive feature-based methods uses predefined features to capture information contained in the sentence. Then feed these features into the classifier, this supervised method achieved best in SemEval 2012 (Šarić, Glavaš et al., 2012).

For alignment-based methods, Sultan et al. (Sultan, Bethard et al., 2014a) proposed an effective solution to align words in monolingual sentences which achieved state-of-the-art performance while relying on almost no supervision and a very small number of external. Based on the output of word aligner, they taking the proportion of their aligned content words as the semantic degree of the two sentences. This simple unsupervised method leads to state-of-art results for sentence level semantic similarity in SemEval 2014 STS task.

Specially, SemEval has hold STS for four years in a row, and many wining methods have been published (Bär, Biemann et al., 2012; Han, Kashyap et al., 2013; Sultan, Bethard et al., 2014b).

3 Feature Generation

The core idea of our method is to use the combination of word similarities to estimate sentence similarity, as lots of effective methods have been proposed to measure word-to-word similarity in recent years. Our features could roughly be divided into five categories: WordNet-Based features, Corpus-Based features, Word2Vec-based features, Alignment-Based feature and Literal-Based features. Generally, Word2Vec-Based methods also can be regarded as Corpus-Based methods, to explore the effectiveness of deep learning based methods, in our paper, we separately classified Word2Vec-Based features into a category. Features used in our model are shown in Table 1.

After combination of these features, we got a very competitive result, which indicated that different features capture different aspects of semantics in sentences. We will look into these features in detail in the following sections.

3.1 WordNet-Based Features

WordNet (Miller, 1995) is a widely used semantic net of English, and it is an effective tool to find synonyms of nouns, verbs, adjectives and adverbs. WordNet is particularly well suited for similarity and relatedness measures, since it organizes nouns and verbs into hierarchies of *is-a* relations (Pedersen, Patwardhan et al., 2004). In this paper, these similarity measures were tried in our experiments. After selection, four of them were kept in our final model: Path_similarity, Res_similarity, Lin_similarity, and Wup_similarity. We provided below a short description for each of these metrics first, and then explain how these measures were used in our evaluation of sentence semantic similarity.

The main idea of the Path_similarity measure (The Shortest Path based Measure) is that the similarity between two concepts can be derived from the length of the path linking the concepts and the position of the concepts in the WordNet taxonomy (Meng, Huang et al., 2013). Formally, the Path_similarity between concepts c_1 and c_2 is defined as following formula:

$$Sim_{path}(c_1, c_2) = 2 * deep\_\max - len(c_1, c_2) \quad (1)$$

where the deep_max is the maximum depth of the taxonomy and $len(c_1, c_2)$ is the length of the shortest path from synset c_1 to synset c_2 in WordNet.

Res_similarity (Resnik's Measure) is a similarity measure based on information content. It assumes that similarity is dependent on the corpus that generates the information content.

$$Sim_{res}(c_1, c_2) = -logp\left(lso(c_1, c_2)\right) = IC\left(lso(c_1, c_2)\right) \quad (2)$$

where $lso(c_1, c_2)$ is the lowest common subsume of c_1 and c_2.

Lin_similarity (Lin's Measure) (Lin, 1998) is a similarity measure based on the Resnik measure, which adds a normalization factor consisting of the information content of the two input concepts:

$$Sim_{lin}(c_1, c_2) = \frac{2*IC(LCS)}{IC(c_1)+IC(c_2)} \quad (3)$$

Wup_similarity (Wu & Palmer's Measure) (Wu & Palmer, 1994) measure is based on the depth of two given concepts in the WordNet taxonomy and that of their Least Common Subsumer (LCS), the similarity score of two concepts is defined as following formula(Resnik, 1999):

$$Sim_{wup}(c_1, c_2) = \frac{2*depth(LCS)}{depth(c_1)+depth(c_2)} \quad (4)$$

In our experiment, we used the NLTK[1] toolkit (Bird, 2006) WordNet APIs to calculate WordNet-based similarities. Based on WordNet and Brown corpus (to obtain IC through statistical analysis of Brown corpus), we generated the four WordNet-based features following the same steps proposed in (Liu, Sun et al.).

Issues that required attention is that the results of Res_similarity measure needs to process normalization to make sure the value lies in the interval [0.0, 1.0].

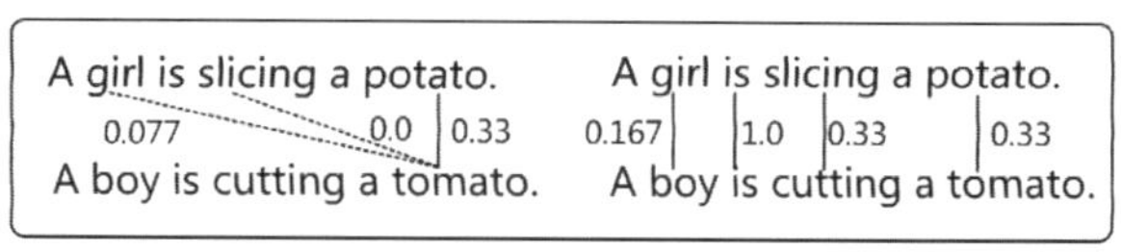

Figure 1 A simple example of word alignment using knowledge-based similarity measures

[1] http://www.nltk.org/

Parameters	num_topics	passes	update_every	alpha	eval_every
Values	400	10	1	'auto'	10

Table 2 Parameter setting of LDA model

Figure 1 is an example of how we find the most probable sense in second sentence which has the maximum WordNet similarity with word in first sentence.

3.2 Corpus-Based Features

Latent semantic analysis (LSA) is a technique for comparing texts using a vector-based representation learned from a corpus. A term-document ma trix describes the occurrences of terms in document. The matrix is decomposed by singular value decomposition (SVD). SVD is a factorization of a SVD decompose the term-by-document matrix into three smaller matrixes like follows:

$$X = U\Sigma V^T \quad (5)$$

real or complex matrix in linear algebra. In LSA, where U and V are column-orthogonal matrixes and Σ is a diagonal matrix containing singular values. Now, columns in U could be preserved as the semantic representations of words. Similarity is then measured by the cosine distance between their corresponding row vectors. To make full use of the semantic information in LSA model, we proposed several methods to compute the sentence similarity based on LSA. These features incude: LSA_similarity,Text_LSA_similarity, IDF_LSA_similarity and Freq_LSA_similarity.

In our experiment, we directly use the LSA model provided by SEMILAR [2] (Ştefănescu, Banjade et al., 2014). The model was decomposed from the whole 2014 Wikipedia articles. One word is represented as a 200-dimension real value vector. We call it "LSA vector" in the rest of the paper. LSA_similarity represent a sentence by summing all LSA vectors of words appeared in the sentence and then averaged it with the length of the sentence. Thus we can get vector representations V_1 and V_2 of the two sentences. The LSA_similarity could be measured with cosine similarity between the two vectors.

The Cosine similarity is defined as follows:

$$Cos\_Dis(V_1, V_2) = \frac{V_1 \cdot V_2}{\|V_1\|\|V_2\|} \quad (6)$$

[2] http://www.semanticsimilarity.org/

Text_LSA_similarity measures similarity between two sentences S_1 and S_2 using the following scoring function (Mihalcea, Corley et al., 2006):

$$\mathrm{Sim}(S_1, S_2) = \frac{1}{2}\left(\frac{\sum_{w\in\{S_1\}}(maxSim(w, S_2) * idf(w))}{\sum_{w\in\{S_1\}} idf(w)} + \frac{\sum_{w\in\{S_2\}}(maxSim(w, S_1) * idf(w))}{\sum_{w\in\{S_2\}} idf(w)}\right) \quad (7)$$

$$maxSim(w, S) = \mathrm{MAX}\{Cos\_Dis(LSA(w), LSA(w\_s))\}, w\_s \in S \quad (8)$$

This similarity score has a value between 0 and 1, with a score 1 indicating identical text segments, and a score 0 indicating no semantic overlap between two texts.

We also generated two weighted features: IDF_LSA_similarity and Freq_LSA_similarity.

$$IDFV(S) = \sum_{w\in S \,\&\, w\notin StW} IDF(w) * \frac{LSA(w)}{norm(LSA(w))} \quad (9)$$

where *StW* is the predefined stop words list, *LSA(w)* is LSA vector of w and IDF(w) is the inverse document frequency of w.

$$WFSV(S) = \sum_{w\in S \,\&\, w\notin StW} WF(w) * \frac{LSA(w)}{norm(LSA(w))} \quad (10)$$

where $WF(w)$ is the word frequency of w. In our experiment, the inverse document frequency and word frequency of each word is computed on Wikipedia corpus dumped in December of 2013.

After got the vector representations of sentences, the cosine distance between two vectors is the value of two features.

Latent Dirichlet Allocation (LDA) (Blei, Ng et al., 2003) is a widely used topic model, typically used to find topics distribution in documents; we tried this technology in our model. The LDA model is trained on the training set of SemEval 2015.

In our experiments, we use the gensim[3] toolkit (Řehůřek & Sojka, 2010) to find the topic distribution of each sentence, and the cosine distance of the vectors could be regarded as the topic similarity of the sentence pair. The parameter setting in the experiment is shown in Table 2.

RIC_Difference measures difference of information content the sentences bearing. In information theory, the information content of a concept can be quantified as negative the log likelihood -logp(c). In our work, the information content of a word w is defined as:

$$ic(w) = \ln\frac{\sum_{w' \in C} freq(w')}{freq(w)} \quad (11)$$

where C is the set of words in the corpus and $freq(w)$ is the frequency of the word w in the corpus. We use the Wikipedia to obtain word frequency. And the Information Content difference between two sentences S_1 and S_2 could be quantified as:

$$RIC(S_1, S_2) = \frac{\left|\sum_{w \in S_1} ic(w) - \sum_{w \in S_2} ic(w)\right|}{MAX(\sum_{w \in S_1} ic(w)\,,\ \sum_{w \in S_2} ic(w))} \quad (12)$$

3.3 Word2Vec-Based Features

Word2Vec (Mikolov, Chen et al., 2013) is a language modeling technique that maps words from vocabulary to continuous vectors (usually 200 to 500 dimensions). Recently, word embedding has shown its ability to boost the performance in NLP tasks such as syntactic parsing and sentiment analysis. In our work, we employ this technology to represent a word and use several different methods to combine these word vectors to represent a sentence. These generated features include: W2V_similarity, IDF_W2V_similarity, Text_W2V_similarity and S2V_similarity. Similar to generation of LSA-based features, we generate W2V_similarity Text_W2V_similarity is similar to Text_LSA_similarity, computed using the same formula. Only replace the maxSim with the following formula:

$$maxSim(w, S) = \mathrm{MAX}\,\{Cos\_Dis(W2V(w), W2V(w_s)), w_s \in S\} \quad (13)$$

Furthermore, to improve our performance, we also used the recently proposed-Sent2Vec (also known as paragraph vector) (Le & Mikolov, 2014) to represent a sentence. Paragraph Vector is an unsupervised learning algorithm that learns vector representations for variable length pieces of texts such as sentences and documents. In our experiment, we use the open source code Sentence2vec[4] to train paragraph vectors on Wikipedia. And the cosine distance between two paragraph vectors denote the sentence semantic similarity. This feature is called S2V_similarity. In our development stage, we observed that if more corpora were given to train Sent2Vec, this feature could be more effective.

3.4 Alignment-Based Features

Alignment_similarity is a similarity measure based on monolingual alignment. We first align related words across the two input sentences. And the proportion of aligned content words is regarded as their semantic similarity. In our model, we directly used the monolingual word aligner provided by (Sultan et al., 2014). The aligner is based on the hypothesis that words with similar meanings represent potential pairs for alignment if located in similar contexts. More details about the aligner may refer to the paper, we didn't discuss here. Based on the alignment results, we can compute the similarity using the following formula:

$$sts(S_1, S_2) = \frac{n_c^a(S_1) + n_c^a(S_2)}{n_c(S_1) + n_c(S_2)} \quad (14)$$

where $n_c^a(S_i)$ and $n_c(S_i)$ are the number of content words and the number of aligned content words in S_i. We didn't achieve as good results as in the paper, the reason may because that we didn't consider some stopwords in that filed.

In our experiments, we also used plenty of style-related features, we call it "literal-based" features. Here, we give a short description to each of them.

3.5 Literal-Based Features

EditDistance_similarity is based on the hypothesis: two sentences that look more similar are closer in semantics. So we use the Levenshtein Distance

[3] http://radimrehurek.com/gensim/

[4] https://github.com/klb3713/sentence2vec

over characters to measure the similarity between two sentences.

DifferLen_Rate measures the difference of length of two sentences which can be regarded as evidence of comparing the similarity between sentences.

Shallow Syntactic Similarity considers the similarity in terms of English voices. After Part-Of-Speech tagging to each sentence, we use the Jaccard Distance to compute the syntactic constituent overlap.

Neg_Sentiment_Fea is feature measures shallow sentiment of sentences, we manually chose a list NEG_SENTIMENT = {'no', 'not', 'never', 'little', 'few', 'nobody', 'neither', 'seldom' 'hardly', 'rarely', 'scarcely'} to judge the sentiment, the appearance of word in this list indicating an opposed meaning, if only one word in the list appeared only once in this pair of sentences, we think that this pair of sentences expressing opposite meaning.

Digit_in_Fea is a binary feature which cares about whether there is digit numbers appeared in only sentence in the pair. To our intuitive, if only one sentence obtain numbers in it and another contains only text, then human annotators tend to give a lower score to this pair. So, if Digit_in_Fea of a pair of sentences was set to '1', this can be interpreted to give classifier a signal to give a lower similarity score.

Digit_similarity could be regarded as complement to feature Digit_in_Fea. We implemented a simple algorithm to extract numbers from text.and then compares the difference of numbers appeared in two sentences.

No_overlap_Fea measures whether two sentences are totally different in terms of words appeared in the sentences. Although this hypothesis is not always true, but we observed that this assumption is correct under most cases and this feature still contributes to our overall performance.

4 Experiments

We conduct our experiments on the SemEval 2015 STS English subtask. Given two sentences of English text, S_1andS_2, we need to compute how similar S_1 and S_2 are, returning a similarity score between 0.0 (no relation) to 5.0 (semantic equivalence), indicating the semantic similarity between two sentences.

4.1 Datasets

In SemEval 2015 2a, the trial dataset comprises the 2012, 2013 and 2014 datasets, which can be used to develop and train models. The details of the dataset refer to (Agirre & Banea, 2015).

4.2 Evaluation Metrics

The official estimation is based on the average of Pearson correlation. This metric is determined as:

$$\rho_{X,Y} = \frac{\sum XY - \frac{\sum X \sum Y}{N}}{\sqrt{\left(\sum X^2 - \frac{(\sum X)^2}{N}\right)\left(\sum Y^2 - \frac{(\sum Y)^2}{N}\right)}} \tag{15}$$

where X is the golden-standard scores vector, and Y is the output of SVRs.

4.3 Results and Discussion

To achieve a better result, we trained three Support Vector Regression models to predict similarity scores on different test sets, we used all the datasets (except SMT of 2013, we got worse performance after added it, so we exclude SMT in our final model) before 2015 as training set for the first three test sets which are unseen data for the classifier. This classifier was denoted as Clf-1. For headlines and images, all headlines / images data sets appeared before were used as training sets. The trained classifier was denoted as Clf-2 and Clf-3 respectively.

In terms of implementation, we used Scikit-learn[5] toolkit(Pedregosa, Varoquaux et al., 2011) to do the classification and the parameter settings for three SVR models are shown in the following table, we chose these parameters by experiences, Clf-2 and Clf-3 used the same setting, and a better result may be achieved through fine tuning:

Classifier	kernel	Gamma	C	epsilon
Clf-1	'rbf'	0.1	1.8	0.1
Clf-2	'rbf'	0.16	100	0.1
Clf-3	'rbf'	0.16	100	0.1

Table 3 Parameter settings of our three classifiers

After the prediction of the similarity scores of sentences, we conducted a post-processing step to boost and correct results, we truncate at the extre-

[5] http://scikit-learn.org/stable/

Data Set	Ans-for	Ans-stu	Belief	Hdlines	Images	Mean
All features	0.7381	0.7644	0.7377	**0.8521**	**0.8650**	**0.8049**
w/o WordNet-based	0.7356	0.7516	0.7260	0.8450	0.8560	0.7959
w/o Corpus-based	0.7150	**0.7850**	0.7389	0.8387	0.8620	0.8032
w/o Word2Vec-based	**0.7460**	0.7498	0.7366	0.8510	0.8536	0.7989
w/o Alignment-based	0.7278	0.7551	0.7168	0.8355	0.8614	0.7926
w/o Literal-based	0.7175	0.7320	**0.7501**	0.8240	0.8618	0.7879

Table 4 Performance of different feature combinations (exclude one kind each time)

Feature Set	Ans-for	Ans-stu	Belief	Hdlines	Images	Mean
All features	**0.7381**	**0.7644**	**0.7377**	**0.8521**	**0.8650**	**0.8049**
WordNet-based	0.6813	0.7252	0.7289	0.7509	0.8352	0.7541
Corpus-based	0.6182	0.6245	0.6652	0.7257	0.8254	0.7043
Word2Vec-based	0.6065	0.7305	0.6904	0.7365	0.8369	0.7381
Alignment-based	0.6675	0.7789	0.6699	0.7891	0.7872	0.7560
Literal-based	0.6666	0.5725	0.5235	0.5493	0.3326	0.5123

Table 5 Results of comparing the importance of different kinds of features on SemEval 2015

mes to keep the score in [0.0, 5.0], and an additional step similar to the details in (Bär et al., 2012). The post-processing step contributed a 0.1% improvement in our overall performance.

Test Set	Winning team	Our System
answers-forums	0.7390	0.7381
answers-students	0.7725	0.7644
belief	0.7491	0.7377
headlines	0.8250	**0.8521**
images	0.8644	**0.8650**
Weight Mean	0.8015	**0.8049**

Table 6 Performances of our model and winning system on SemEval 2015 STS test sets

Table 4 reported the results of our method on SemEval 2015 Task 2a, from which we can know that our method outperformed the winning system by a big margin on the headlines, but only slightly better on the images. The reason may because that in the winning system, images was already achieved a very high accuracy, but due to the incomplete use of the semantic information, didn't perform as well as in headlines. As our method used more sufficient features, our approach achieved both state-of-the-art results on headlines and images. The winning system mainly based on word alignment, which guaranteed very good generalization ability, but much of the semantic information contained in the training set was not used, while these information can also contribute to the system performance, especially for domain-specific test set, in other word, our method can be used to verify this idea. For the first three datasets, our method may achieve much better performance if more domain-specific data was given for learning. Overall, our system performed slightly better than the wining system in terms of average Pearson correlation.

To compare the importance of each kind of feature, we separately exclude one kind of them in our model and compare new model's performance.

The results are shown in Table 5. And the performance of using only one kind of feature showed in Table 6.

The experiment results demonstrated the effectiveness of our generated features, except Liter-based features, each kind of other features alone could lead to a relatively good performance. Although Literal-based features didn't perform well on its own, exclude it from our model leads to the biggest decrease in Mean correlation, which indicated it is an important complement to other features. We also observed that corpus-based features seem less effective compared to other features as they didn't perform as well as other semantic related features and the absence of it has little impact on the overall performance. The different combinations of them boosted the results to achieve a higher correlation. Also, SVR model played an important role in our approach, it provide a good out-of-sample generalization as the loss function typically leads to a sparse representation of the decision rule which makes our model more robust on novel data. And we think that the appropriate choice of kernel function in SVR may also help a lot in the model.

5 Conclusion

In this paper, we presented our approach to evaluate semantic similarity between short English sentences. We employed a Support Vector Regression model combined with WordNet-Based features, Corpus-Based features, Word2Vec-based features, Binary Features and some other features to predict the semantic similarity score between sentence pairs. Our experiment results showed a high correlation with human annotations which outperformed the top system in SemEval 2015 task 2a. We also observed that our method performed much better compared to winning system on two test sets whose domain-specific data is available for training, results also indicated that our solution still maintains good generation ability on novel datasets which means this technique could be well generalized to other data domains. While the context of the sentence is unavailable and the information about the tone of sentence was eliminated by us (most modal particles and punctuations appeared in sentences were treated as stop words in our process), our model could not distinguish the tone of sentence, for example we may give a high similarity score to a sentence pair consists of a declarative and an imperative if they shared many words. This situation was not considered in feature generation stage, but will be researched latter. Our future work will include the refinements of training effective representations for words and sentences on corpus (LSA, Word2Vec and Sent2Vec), the expansion of stop word list through adding proper selected domain-specific stop words and the re-implementation of a well-designed feature selection process to simplify our model. We hope that these measures could be helpful for improvement, make our model more robust and improve our method's generalization ability as well.

Acknowledgments

The authors would like to thank the anonymous reviewers for their helpful suggestions and comments. This work is supported by the National Natural Science Foundation of China (61300114 & 61572151) and Natural Science Foundation of Heilongjiang Province (F201132).

References

Agirre Eneko, & Banea Carmen. (2015). *SemEval-2015 task 2: Semantic textual similarity, English, S-panish and pilot on interpretability.* Paper presented at the Proceedings of the 9th International Workshop on Semantic Evaluation (SemEval 2015), June.

Bär Daniel, Biemann Chris, Gurevych Iryna, & Zesch Torsten. (2012). *Ukp: Computing semantic textual similarity by combining multiple content similarity measures.* Paper presented at the Proceedings of the First Joint Conference on Lexical and Computational Semantics-Volume 1: Proceedings of the main conference and the shared task, and Volume 2: Proceedings of the Sixth International Workshop on Semantic Evaluation.

Bird Steven. (2006). *NLTK: the natural language toolkit.* Paper presented at the Proceedings of the COLING/ACL on Interactive presentation sessions.

Blei David M, Ng Andrew Y, & Jordan Michael I. (2003). Latent dirichlet allocation. *the Journal of machine Learning research, 3*, 993-1022.

Burgess Curt, Livesay Kay, & Lund Kevin. (1998). Explorations in context space: Words, sentences, discourse. *Discourse Processes, 25*(2-3), 211-257.

Dumais Susan T. (2004). Latent semantic analysis. *Annual review of information science and technology, 38*(1), 188-230.

Fattah Mohamed Abdel, & Ren Fuji. (2008). Automatic text summarization. *World Academy of Science, Engineering and Technology, 37*, 2008.

Gabrilovich Evgeniy, & Markovitch Shaul. (2007). *Computing Semantic Relatedness Using Wikipedia-based Explicit Semantic Analysis.* Paper presented at the IJCAI.

Han Lushan, Kashyap Abhay, Finin Tim, Mayfield James, & Weese Jonathan. (2013). UMBC EBIQUITY-CORE: Semantic textual similarity systems. *Atlanta, Georgia, USA, 44*.

Islam Aminul, & Inkpen Diana. (2008). Semantic text similarity using corpus-based word similarity and string similarity. *ACM Transactions on Knowledge Discovery from Data (TKDD), 2*(2), 10.

Le Quoc V, & Mikolov Tomas. (2014). *Distributed representations of sentences and documents.* Paper presented at the Proceedings of NIPS 2013

Li Yuhua, McLean David, Bandar Zuhair, O'shea James D, & Crockett Keeley. (2006). Sentence similarity based on semantic nets and corpus statistics. *Knowledge and Data Engineering, IEEE Transactions on, 18*(8), 1138-1150.

Lin Dekang. (1998). *An information-theoretic definition of similarity.* Paper presented at the ICML.

Liu Yang, Sun Chengjie, Lin Lei, & Wang Xiaolong. yiGou: A Semantic Text Similarity Computing System Based on SVM. Paper presented at the Proceedings of the 9th International Workshop on Semantic Evaluation, pages 80-84, Denver, Colorado, USA.

Manning Christopher D, Raghavan Prabhakar, & Schütze Hinrich. (2008). *Introduction to information retrieval* (Vol. 1): Cambridge university press Cambridge.

Meng Lingling, Huang Runqing, & Gu Junzhong. (2013). A review of semantic similarity measures in wordnet. *International Journal of Hybrid Information Technology, 6*(1), 1-12.

Metzler Donald, Dumais Susan, & Meek Christopher. (2007). *Similarity measures for short segments of text*: Springer.

Mihalcea Rada, Corley Courtney, & Strapparava Carlo. (2006). *Corpus-based and knowledge-based measures of text semantic similarity.* Paper presented at the AAAI.

Mikolov Tomas, Chen Kai, Corrado Greg, & Dean Jeffrey. (2013). *Efficient estimation of word representations in vector space.* Paper presented at the ICLR, 2013.

Miller George A. (1995). WordNet: a lexical database for English. *Communications of the ACM, 38*(11), 39-41.

Narayanan Srini, & Harabagiu Sanda. (2004). *Answering questions using advanced semantics and probabilistic inference.* Paper presented at the Proceedings of the Workshop on Pragmatics of Question Answering, HLT-NAACL, Boston, USA.

Papineni Kishore, Roukos Salim, Ward Todd, & Zhu Wei-Jing. (2002). *BLEU: a method for automatic evaluation of machine translation.* Paper presented at the Proceedings of the 40th annual meeting on association for computational linguistics.

Pedersen Ted, Patwardhan Siddharth, & Michelizzi Jason. (2004). *WordNet:: Similarity: measuring the relatedness of concepts.* Paper presented at the Demonstration papers at hlt-naacl 2004.

Pedregosa Fabian, Varoquaux Gaël, Gramfort Alexandre, Michel Vincent, Thirion Bertrand, Grisel Olivier, . . . Dubourg Vincent. (2011). Scikit-learn: Machine learning in Python. *the Journal of machine Learning research, 12*, 2825-2830.

Řehůřek Radim, & Sojka Petr. (2010). Software framework for topic modelling with large corpora. Paper presented at the Proceedings of the LREC 2010 Workshop on New Challenges for NLP Frameworks, pages 45–50, Valletta, Malta, May 2010. ELRA

Resnik Philip. (1999). Semantic similarity in a taxonomy: An information-based measure and its application to problems of ambiguity in natural language. *J. Artif. Intell. Res.(JAIR), 11*, 95-130.

Šarić Frane, Glavaš Goran, Karan Mladen, Šnajder Jan, & Bašić Bojana Dalbelo. (2012). *Takelab: Systems for measuring semantic text similarity.* Paper presented at the Proceedings of the First Joint Conference on Lexical and Computational Semantics-Volume 1: Proceedings of the main conference and the shared task, and Volume 2: Proceedings of the Sixth International Workshop on Semantic Evaluation.

Ştefănescu Dan, Banjade Rajendra, & Rus Vasile. (2014). Latent semantic analysis models on wikipedia and tasa. The 9th Language Resources and Evaluation Conference (LREC 2014).

Sultan Md Arafat, Bethard Steven, & Sumner Tamara. (2014a). Back to basics for monolingual alignment: Exploiting word similarity and contextual evidence. *Transactions of the Association for Computational Linguistics, 2*, 219-230.

Sultan Md Arafat, Bethard Steven, & Sumner Tamara. (2014b). DLS@CU: Sentence Similarity from Word Alignment. Paper presented at the Proceedings of the 8th International Workshop on Semantic Evaluation, pages 241-246, Dublin, Ireland

Wu Zhibiao, & Palmer Martha. (1994). *Verbs semantics and lexical selection.* Paper presented at the Proceedings of the 32nd annual meeting on Association for Computational Linguistics.

Mechanical Turk-based Experiment vs Laboratory-based Experiment: A Case Study on the Comparison of Semantic Transparency Rating Data

Shichang Wang, Chu-Ren Huang, Yao Yao, Angel Chan
Department of Chinese and Bilingual Studies
The Hong Kong Polytechnic University
Hung Hom, Kowloon, Hong Kong
shi-chang.wang@connect.polyu.hk
{churen.huang, y.yao, angel.ws.chan}@polyu.edu.hk

Abstract

In this paper, we conducted semantic transparency rating experiments using both the traditional laboratory-based method and the crowdsourcing-based method. Then we compared the rating data obtained from these two experiments. We observed very strong correlation coefficients for both overall semantic transparency rating data and constituent semantic transparency data ($rho > 0.9$) which means the two experiments may yield comparable data and crowdsourcing-based experiment is a feasible alternative to the laboratory-based experiment in linguistic studies. We also observed a scale shrinkage phenomenon in both experiments: the actual scale of the rating results cannot cover the ideal scale $[0, 1]$, both ends of the actual scale shrink towards the center. However, the scale shrinkage of the crowdsourcing-based experiment is stronger than that of the laboratory-based experiment, this makes the rating results obtained in these two experiments not directly comparable. In order to make the results directly comparable, we explored two data transformation algorithms, z-score transformation and adjusted normalization to unify the scales. We also investigated the uncertainty of semantic transparency judgment among raters, we found that it had a regular relation with semantic transparency magnitude and this may further reveal a general cognitive mechanism of human judgment.

1 Introduction

In experimental linguistic studies, researchers are frequently frustrated by the problem of linguistic data bottleneck which constantly limits the feasibility, efficiency, and reliability of various research projects. It's caused by the practical difficulties of conducting traditional laboratory-based linguistic experiments. Firstly, it's very difficult to obtain large samples using laboratory-based experiments for they are usually very time-consuming and expensive. In order to solve this problem, we need to find a more efficient and economic way to conduct linguistic experiments. Secondly, what's more difficult is to recruit highly diverse subjects due to the difficulties in subject recruitment and the spacial limitations of laboratory-based experiments. As a result, researchers heavily and even blindly rely on relatively small sample size which is 30 or so (Sprouse, 2011) and the undergraduate subject pool. From the point of view of sampling, this is not a good practice, since it raises the concern of external validity, i.e., the extent to which the experimental results can be generalized, because a small and homogeneous sample usually cannot be representative enough. In fact the external validity problem that results from using mainly undergraduate subjects is a typical one and has a dedicated term called the college sophomore problem (Stanovich, 2007; Jackson, 2012). Although there are several responses to this criticism (Stanovich, 2007), the really convincing way to resolve this problem is to use a more diverse subject pool.

Mechanical Turk (MTurk) has emerged in recent years to be a promising solution to the problem of linguistic data bottleneck by providing a new paradigm for linguistic experiments, i.e., the MTurk-based experiment (Mason and Suri, 2012; Horton et al., 2011;

29th Pacific Asia Conference on Language, Information and Computation pages 53 - 62
Shanghai, China, October 30 - November 1, 2015

Paolacci et al., 2010; Schnoebelen and Kuperman, 2010; Buhrmester et al., 2011; Sprouse, 2011; Berinsky et al., 2012), which can hopefully address all the problems mentioned above. MTurk is qualified as a genre of both crowdsourcing which refers to the activities to outsource tasks to undefined and generally large crowds on the web via open call (Howe, 2006; Estellés-Arolas and González-Ladrón-de Guevara, 2012; Wang et al., 2013; Schenk and Guittard, 2011; Howe, 2009), and human computation (Quinn and Bederson, 2009; von Ahn, 2005; Quinn and Bederson, 2011). MTurk needs to be implemented through a website, or more precisely, an MTurk platform. An MTurk platform is an on-line crowdsourcing labor marketplace where requesters post small tasks (conventionally called Human Intelligence Tasks, or HITs) and workers undertake tasks for small pay (Mason and Suri, 2012; Sprouse, 2011). The most famous MTurk platform is Amazon's Mechanical Turk (AMT, www.mturk.com) which was lunched publicly in November 2005; it started early and is so popular in the academic world that it is the de facto standard of MTurk implementation, and the genre name MTurk actually originated from its name and is used by some writers to refer to AMT specially. There are other MTurk implementations, for example another well known MTurk platform is Crowdflower (www.crowdflower.com). Relevant demographics shows that the workers on either AMT (Ross et al., 2010; Pavlick et al., 2014; Ipeirotis, 2010) or Crowdflower[1] are come from all over the world, so both can be treated as international MTurk platforms.

In the early stage of the development of MTurk, it's potential to be an efficient and economic tool for linguistic data collection (e.g., annotation, transcription, translation, etc.) and behavioral research (e.g., survey and experimentation) for social sciences has already been recognized and attempted (Snow et al., 2008; Kittur et al., 2008; Chen et al., 2009). Especially since around 2010, there have been more and more reports on conducting experimental research using MTurk (Mason and Suri, 2012; Rand, 2012; Buhrmester et al., 2011; Horton et al., 2011; Paolacci et al., 2010; Schmidt, 2010; Munro et al., 2010; Schnoebelen and Kuperman, 2010; Sprouse, 2011; Enochson and Culbertson, 2015; Kuperman et al., 2012) and several of them focus on linguistic experiments (Munro et al., 2010; Schnoebelen and Kuperman, 2010; Sprouse, 2011; Enochson and Culbertson, 2015; Kuperman et al., 2012). Experiments conducted on MTurk platforms are usually survey-based and use web questionnaires composed using the GUI toolkits provided by the platforms, and advanced users can make use of HTML, CSS, JavaScript, Adobe Flash (Simcox and Fiez, 2014; Enochson and Culbertson, 2015), etc., to realize additional elements, customized appearance, special control, and apparatus they need. Compared to laboratory-based experiment, the MTurk-based experiment has many attractive merits: 1) the recruitment and compensation of subjects is automatic, painless, on demand, and 24x7 based; 2) MTurk workers are willing to take part in experiments with much less pay than subjects of laboratory-based experiments; 3) it is a lot easier to obtain very large samples; 4) MTurk worker pool is far more diverse than typical undergraduate subject pool widely used in laboratory-based experiment; 5) the anonymous nature of MTurk-based experiment can largely help to avoid experimenter effect, subject crosstalk (Paolacci et al., 2010) and the problem of socially desirable responses.

Data quality is the key concern in conducting research using MTurk-based experiments because the MTurk setting is not so controllable as the laboratory setting, a host of studies have been carried out to address this concern. The comparison between the data obtained from MTurk-based experiments and laboratory-based experiments suggests that MTurk-based experiments can provide comparable or even better data (Munro et al., 2010; Schnoebelen and Kuperman, 2010; Sprouse, 2011; Horton et al., 2011). And a large set of classic effects discovered previously in laboratory-based experiments have been successfully replicated using MTurk-based experiments even in the case of the experiments which require millisecond accuracy timing (Enochson and Culbertson, 2015; Simcox and Fiez, 2014; Crump et al., 2013; Horton et al., 2011). These positive results repeatedly confirm that MTurk is a reliable tool to conduct experimental research which not only yields

[1]For the demographics of Crowdflower's worker pool, see https://success.crowdflower.com/hc/en-us/articles/202703345-Contributors-Crowd-Demographics, retrieved on Apr. 22, 2015.

valid data but also minimizes the cost in time, effort, and expense. Conducting research using MTurk-based experiments lets researchers concentrate on data analysis, creative thinking, and writing instead of being disturbed by various administrative tasks of laboratory-based experiments from time to time, therefore increases their academic productivity. Although, this methodology has not been completely established, its future seems to be guaranteed (Horton et al., 2011).

In order to evaluate a new method, it is a common strategy to compare the results yield by the new method with the results yield by the established method to see their agreement. Although neither method is perfect or completely reliable, since the established method is well acceptable, if the new method agrees well enough with it, then the new method is also acceptable to be an alternative. We conducted two similar semantic transparency rating experiments using the Mechanical Turk-based method and the traditional laboratory-based method. We will compare the results from these two experiments to see their agreement hence we can further evaluate the Mechanical Turk-based experimentation.

2 Method

2.1 MTurk-based Semantic Transparency Rating Experiment[2]

2.1.1 Materials

We selected a total of $1,176$ disyllabic Chinese nominal compounds which have mid-range word frequencies and appear in both Sinica Corpus 4.0 (Chen et al., 1996) and the "Lexicon of Common Words in Contemporary Chinese 现代汉语常用词表", see Wang et al. (2014) for details.

2.1.2 Experimental Design

Normally, a crowdsourcing experiment should be reasonably small in size. We randomly divide these 1,176 words into 21 groups, G_i $(i = 1, 2, 3, ..., 21)$; each group has 56 words.

Questionnaires We collect overall semantic transparency (OST) and constituent semantic transparency (CST) data of these words. In order to avoid interaction, we designed two kinds of questionnaires to collect OST data and CST data respectively. So G_i $(i = 1, 2, 3, ..., 21)$ has two questionnaires, one OST questionnaire for OST data collection and one CST questionnaire for CST data collection. Besides titles and instructions, each questionnaire has 3 sections. Section 1 is used to collect identity information includes gender, age, education and location. Section 2 contains four very simple questions about the Chinese language; the first two questions are open-ended Chinese character identification questions, the third question is a close-ended homophonic character identification question, and the fourth one is a close-ended antonymous character identification question; different questionnaires use different questions. Section 3 contains the questions for semantic transparency data collection. Suppose AB is a disyllabic nominal compound, we use the following question to collect its OST rating scores: "How is the sum of the meanings of A and B similar to the meaning of AB?" And use the following two questions to collect its CST rating scores of its two constituents: "How is the meaning of A when it is used alone similar to its meaning in AB?" and "How is the meaning of B when it is used alone similar to its meaning in AB?". 7-point scales are used in section 3; 1 means "not similar at all" and 7 means "almost the same".

In order to evaluate the data received in the experiments, we embedded some evaluation devices in the questionnaires. We mainly evaluated intra-group and inter-group consistency; and if the data have good intra-group and inter-group consistency, we can believe that the data quality is good. In each group we choose two words and make them appear twice, we call them intra-group repeated words and we can use them to evaluate the intra-group consistency. We insert into each group two same extra words, w_1"地步", w_2"高山", to evaluate the inter-group consistency.

Quality Control Measures On a crowdsourcing platform like Crowdflower, the participants are anonymous, they may try to cheat and submit invalid data, and they may come from different countries and speak different languages rather than the required one. There may be spammers who continuously submit invalid data at very high speed and

[2]We have reported this experiment in Wang et al. (2014).

they may even bypass the quality control measures to cheat for money. In order to ensure that the participants are native Chinese speakers and to improve data quality, we use the following measures, (1) a participant must correctly answer the first two Chinese character identification questions in the section 2s of the questionnaires, and he/she must correctly answer at least one of the last two questions in these section 2s; (2) If a participant do not satisfy the above conditions, he/she will not see Section 3s; (3) each word stimulus in section 3s has an option which allows the participants to skip it in case he/she does not recognize that word; (4) all the questions in the questionnaires must be answered except the ones which allow to be skipped and are explicitly claimed to be skipped; (5) we wrote a monitor program to detect and resist spammers automatically; (6) after the experiment is finished, we will analyze the data and filter out invalid data, and we will discuss this in detail in section 2.1.3.

	OST		CST	
G_i	n	%	n	%
G_1	62	68.89	70	77.78
G_2	60	66.67	64	71.11
G_3	61	67.78	58	64.44
G_4	57	63.33	58	64.44
G_5	51	56.67	59	65.56
G_6	55	61.11	54	60
G_7	54	60	55	61.11
G_8	60	66.67	48	53.33
G_9	52	57.78	55	61.11
G_{10}	58	64.44	59	65.56
G_{11}	52	57.78	56	62.22
G_{12}	55	61.11	63	70
G_{13}	52	57.78	57	63.33
G_{14}	56	62.22	54	60
G_{15}	54	60	53	58.89
G_{16}	58	64.44	56	62.22
G_{17}	52	57.78	50	55.56
G_{18}	53	58.89	51	56.67
G_{19}	53	58.89	50	55.56
G_{20}	53	58.89	51	56.67
G_{21}	52	57.78	51	56.67
Min	51	56.67	48	53.33
Max	62	68.89	70	77.78
Median	54	60	55	61.11
Mean	55.24	61.38	55.81	62.01
SD	3.4	3.78	5.32	5.91

Table 1: Amount of valid response in the OST and CST datasets of each group.

Experimental Platform and Procedure We choose Crowdflower as our experimental platform, because according to our previous experiments, it is a feasible crowdsourcing platform to collect Chinese language data. We create one task for each questionnaire on the platform; there are 21 groups of word and each group has one OST questionnaire and one CST questionnaire, so there are a total of 42 tasks T_i^{ost}, T_i^{cst} $(i = 1, 2, 3, ..., 21)$. We publish these 42 tasks successively, and for each task we create a monitor program to detect and resist spammers. All of these tasks use the following parameters: (1) each task will collect 90 responses; (2) we pay 0.15USD for each response of OST questionnaire and pay 0.25USD for each response of CST questionnaire; (3) each worker account of Crowdflower can only submit one response for each questionnaire and each IP address can only submit one response for each questionnaire; (4) we only allow the workers from the following regions (according to IP addresses) to submit data: Mainland China, Hong Kong, Macau, Taiwan, Singapore, Malaysia, USA, UK, Canada, Australia, Germany, France, Italy, New Zealand, and Indonesia; and we can dynamically disable or enable certain regions on demand in order to ensure both data quality and quantity.

2.1.3 Data Cleansing and Result Calculation

The OST dataset produced by the OST task T_i^{ost} $(i = 1, 2, 3, ..., 21)$ is D_i^{ost}. The CST dataset produced by the CST task T_i^{cst} is D_i^{cst}. Each dataset contains 90 responses. Because of the nature of crowdsourcing environment, there are many invalid responses in each dataset; so firstly we need to filter them out in order to refine the data. A response is invalid if (1) its completion time is less than 135 seconds (for OST responses); its completion time is less than 250 seconds (for CST responses); or (2) it failed to correctly answer the first two questions of section 2s of the questionnaires; or (3) it wrongly answered the last two questions of section 2s of the questionnaires; or (4) it skipped more than six words in section 3s of the questionnaires; or (5) it used less than three numbers on the 7-point scales in section 3s of the questionnaires. We also filtered out the responses from the workers who appeared in more than one countries/regions according to their IP addresses. The statistics of valid response are shown in Table 1.

The OST dataset D_i^{ost} $(i = 1, 2, 3, ..., 21)$ contains n_i valid responses; it means word w in the OST dataset of the ith group has n_i OST rating scores; the arithmetic mean of these n_i OST rating scores is the OST result of word w. The CST results of the two constituents of word w are calculated using the same algorithm.

2.2 Laboratory-based Semantic Transparency Rating Experiment

2.2.1 Material

The Mechanical Turk-based semantic transparency rating experiment is a large-scale experiment, it collected the overall and constituent semantic transparency rating data for $1,176$ compounds. This scale is beyond the capacity of common laboratory-based experiment given the time and resource limitations. So it is impossible for us the conduct a completely parallel semantic transparency rating experiment in the laboratory setting. As a practically and statistically feasible alternative, we extracted a representative sample of reasonable size for laboratory-based experiment from the $1,176$ compound stimuli of the Mechanical Turk-based experiment. Then the method comparison will be conducted on the basis of the sample.

The compound stimuli of the Mechanical Turk-based semantic transparency rating experiment belong to three structural categories, i.e., NN, AN, VN, the sample should cover all these category types. According the overall semantic transparency value and constituent semantic transparency value of compound, compounds are usually divided into four categories: 1) TT, the compounds with the largest overall semantic transparency values and the most balanced constituent semantic transparency values, 2) TO, the compounds with the mid-range overall semantic transparency values and the most unbalanced constituent semantic transparency values and the CST of the first morpheme is larger than that of the second, 3) OT, the compounds with the mid-range overall semantic transparency values and the most unbalanced constituent semantic transparency values and the CST of the second morpheme is larger than that of the first, and 4) OO, the compounds with the lowest overall semantic transparency values and the most balanced constituent semantic transparency values. The sample should also cover all these four semantic transparency types. A total of 152 compounds were selected; all of the compounds have the modifier-head structure.

2.2.2 Questionnaire

The questionnaire is divided into three parts. Part I is the demographic questions, we ask the subjects to provide their demographic information on 1) gender, 2) age, 3) language background, 4) native place, and 5) email address (optional). Part II is the overall semantic transparency rating task, the subjects are asked to rate the overall semantic transparency of the compound stimuli one by one, and we use the same questions and rating scales as the Mechanical Turk-based experiment. Part III is the constituent semantic transparency rating task, the subjects are asked to rate the constituent semantic transparency of the compound stimuli one by one, and we also use the same questions and rating scales as the Mechanical Turk-based experiment. We make “笑脸”, “蓝本”, “火灾”, “脾气” appear twice in the questionnaire, so we can use them to check the consistency of ratings. The questionnaire has a simplified Chinese character version and a traditional Chinese character version. And the questionnaires are implemented using Google Form, the whole questionnaire is divided into pages, each page contains six stimuli. At the end of each quarter of the questionnaire, we show the subjects a notice to tell them that they can take a short break (three to five minutes) if they feel tired. It takes about 45 minutes to fill out the questionnaire.

2.2.3 Subjects

We recruited a total of 78 students at the Hong Kong Polytechnic University. Seventy-four of them are undergraduates, and four of them are postgraduates. Thirty-nine of them are from mainland China and the other 39 are Hong Kong local. The subjects from mainland China came from 19 different provinces: Anhui 安徽, 3; Chongqing 重庆, 3; Fujian 福建, 2; Gansu 甘肃, 1; Guangdong 广东, 3; Guizhou 贵州, 2; Hebei 河北, 1; Heilongjiang 黑龙江, 2; Henan 河南, 1; Hubei 湖北, 1; Jiangsu 江苏, 2; Jilin 吉林, 1; Liaoning 辽宁, 1; Neimenggu 内蒙古, 3; Shandong 山东, 5; Shanghai 上海, 1; Shanxi 陕西, 5; Tianjin 天津, 1; Zhejiang 浙江, 1. Fourty-one subjects are 16 to 20 years old; 33 are 21 to 25; 4 are 26 to 30. Twenty-two of them are male, the other 56 are female. Their mother tongue is Chinese and all of them can speak Putonghua.

2.2.4 Procedure

The subjects were invited into the laboratories. Because the subjects from mainland China and Hong Kong would use different versions of questionnaire, two laboratories were prepared for the experiment, one was for the subjects from mainland China and the simplified character version questionnaire would be used, and the other laboratory was for the subjects from Hong Kong and the traditional character version questionnaire would be used. Each subject was assigned a unique code (or seat number). When the subjects arrived, they were guided to their desks according to their codes. On each desk there was a computer which was displaying a brief introduction to the experiment and at the bottom of the introduction, there were two buttons: "I Agree" and "I Disagree" respectively. We briefly explained the experiment to the subjects orally, and then asked them to sign the consent forms on their desks first if they agreed to participate in our experiment. After they signed the consent forms, they could then read the introduction on the screen and press "I Agree" to start to fill in the questionnaire. Once a subject finished the experiment, he/she would get an allowance of 100 Hong Kong dollars. All the 78 subjects finished the experiment, so we collected 78 responses.

2.2.5 Data Cleansing and Result Calculation

We firstly checked the responses one by one and filtered out invalid ones. A response is considered invalid if 1) more than 15 words were skipped (i.e., the subject claimed that he/she didn't know these words), or 2) less than three numbers of the 7-point rating scale were used. Only two invalid responses were identified, one was from a mainland subject, the other was from a Hong Kong subject. So there are a total of 76 valid responses, this means each word was rated by 76 subjects. The OST and CST results of these words were calculated based on these 76 responses, the calculation method was the same as the Mechanical Turk-based experiment.

3 Results and Discussion

3.1 Correlation

We can evaluate the semantic transparency rating results from the Mechanical Turk-based experiment by examining to what extent they correlates with the results from the laboratory-based experiment. This is a commonly used practice in psycholinguistics.

Strictly speaking, the distributions of the overall and constituent semantic transparency of compound are not normal and do not satisfy the requirement of Pearson's product-moment correlation coefficient, so the Spearman's rank-order correlation coefficient is used. We calculated three correlation coefficients, 1) the correlation coefficient between the normalized OST results from the two experiments: 0.94, 2) the correlation coefficient between the normalized CST results of the first morphemes of the compounds from the two experiments: 0.93, and 3) the correlation coefficient between the normalized CST results of the second morphemes of the compounds from the two experiments: 0.92. All of the correlation coefficients are larger than 0.9 which indicates that the results from the Mechanical Turk-based experiment correlate strongly with the results from the laboratory-based experiment. From the scatter plots (see Figure 1), we can see that although these two kinds of results correlates strongly with each other, we cannot say that they agree with each other very well, because the dots do not distribute around the line of equality (the dashed line).

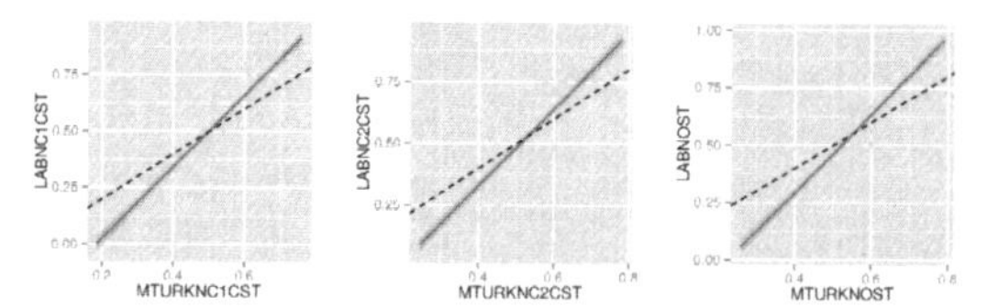

Figure 1: Correlations between normalized OST and CST results from the MTurk-based experiment and the lab-based experiment.

3.2 Scale Shrinkage Issue

We also checked and compared the distributions of the semantic transparency rating results from the Mechanical Turk- and laboratory- based experiments, see Figure 2. We can see that the distributions of the results from the two experiments have

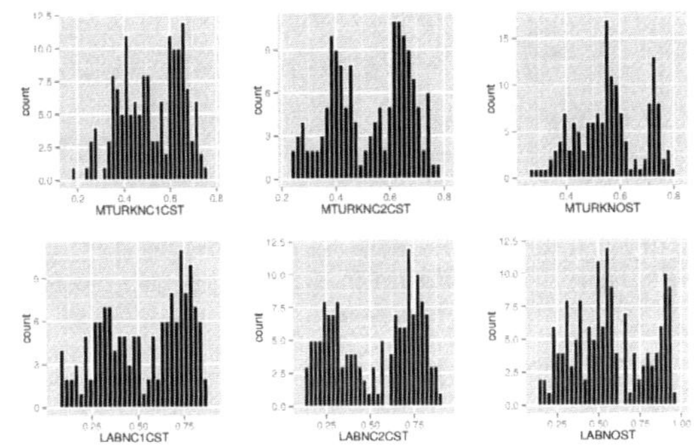

Figure 2: Distributions of semantic transparency rating results from the MTurk-based experiment and the lab-based experiment.

the similar overall forms, but the two kinds of results distribute on different scales. The scale of the Mechanical Turk OST results is from 0.26 to 0.79, however the scale of the laboratory OST results is from 0.14 to 0.95; the scale of the Mechanical Turk C1CST results is from 0.19 to 0.76, while the scale of the laboratory C1CST results is from 0.08 to 0.86; the scale of the Mechanical Turk C2CST results is from 0.24 to 0.78, but the scale of the laboratory C2CST results is from 0.14 to 0.89. Since in our compound stimuli, there are completely transparent compounds and completely opaque compounds, so ideally, two kinds of results should share and cover the same scale from 0 to 1. But virtually, for this kind of subjective rating tasks, subjects rarely totally agree with each other and there is always some noise or errors of varied degrees. Consequently, the distributions of the results of subjective rating tasks rarely cover the whole scale. The actual scales usually shrink towards the center. The scale shrinkage of the results from the Mechanical Turk-based experiment is larger than that of the results from the laboratory-based experiment; this is perhaps because that the Mechanical Turk-based experiment has higher noise level than the laboratory-based experiment.

3.3 Data Transformation

Because the semantic transparency results from the Mechanical Turk- and laboratory-based experiments use different scales and have different units, they are not directly comparable. In order to make the kinds of results comparable, we need to transform the results so that they will use the same scale. We are going to examine two kinds of data transformation methods: 1) Z-score transformation (standardization), 2) adjusted normalization; next we are going to discuss them one by one.

Z-score Transformation

The z score is calculated by the following formula:

$$z\ score = \frac{raw\ score - mean}{standard\ deviation}$$

The raw scores (normalized OST and CST results) from Mechancial Turk- and laboratory-based experiments are transformed into z scores according to the above formula; we call the z-score transformed normalized OST and CST results the standardized OST and CST results. After z-score transformation, the standardized semantic transparency results from the two experiments will share the same scale.

Then we can further examine the agreement of the standardized semantic transparency results from the two experiments, see Figure 3. On these scatter plots, we can see that now all the dots distribute around the line of equality (the dashed line) and the regression line basically coincides with the line of equality; compared with the scatter plots based on the raw scores (see Figure 1), the standardized results agree with each other better which makes the results from the two experiments comparable.

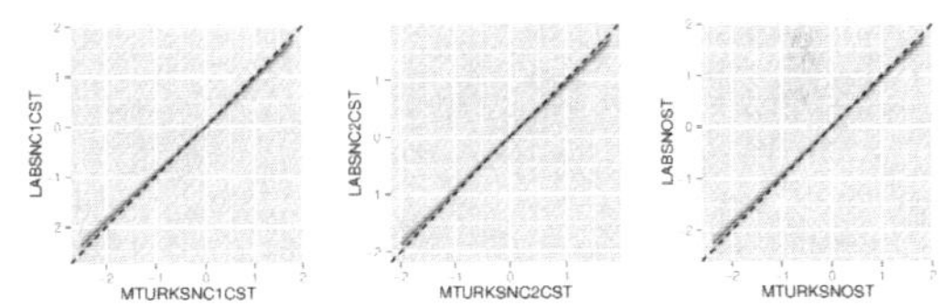

Figure 3: Correlations between standardized OST and CST results from the MTurk-based experiment and the lab-based experiment.

Adjusted Normalization

The adjusted normalized score is calculated according to the following formula:

$$ANscore = \frac{raw\ score - min\ raw\ score}{max\ raw\ score - min\ raw\ score}$$

Since the actual scales of the raw scores shrink towards the center, we can use the above formula to stretch the scales to $[0, 1]$ again. When using this formula, we need to make sure that the maximum and minimum raw scores are not outliers, otherwise this transformation will fail. The results from the two experiments are both transformed using this formula, after this, they will again share the same scale. See Figure 4 for the relations between the adjusted normalized semantic transparency results from both experiments.

Compared with the raw scores (see Figure 1), the adjusted normalized results from the Mechanical Turk- and laboratory-based experiments agree with each other better, but the agreement is not as good as the standardized results (see Figure 3). However the adjusted normalization method has an advantage over the standardization method, that is the adjusted normalization will yield results from 0 to 1 and this scale is accord with the definition of semantic transparency value.

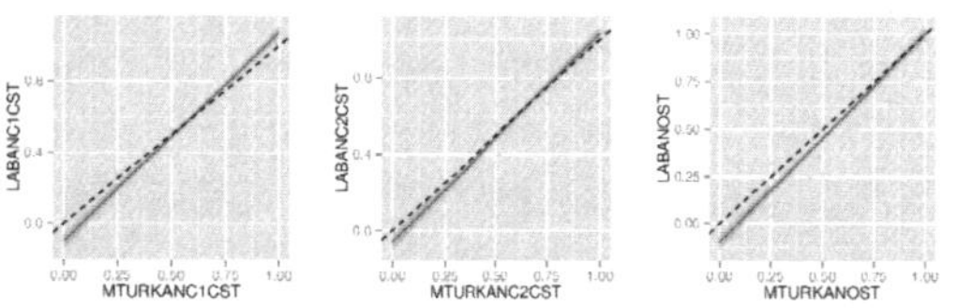

Figure 4: Correlations between adjusted normalized OST and CST results from the MTurk-based experiment and the lab-based experiment.

3.4 Uncertainty of Semantic Transparency Judgment among Raters

Semantic transparency rating task is a subjective rating task. In such a task, the subjects rarely totally agree with each other and there are usually errors of varied degrees. So we can say that there is usually some uncertainty or inconsistency of judgment among raters. Next we are going to measure the uncertainty of judgment among raters and to examine its relationship with the semantic transparency value.

In our semantic transparency rating tasks, 7-point scales are used as the measurement instrument. For a di-morphemic word ab, suppose that m raters rated its overall semantic transparency (OST) and constituent semantic transparency (CST), so ab has m OST ratings scores and also has m C1CST rating scores and m C2CST rating scores; each rating score can only be one of $\{1, 2, 3, 4, 5, 6, 7\}$. For the m OST rating scores, suppose the possibilities of the numbers on the 7-point scale to be chosen are $p_1, p_2, ..., p_7$ respectively, the resultant OST value is the mean of these m rating scores and the uncertainty of judgment among raters can be calculated using the formula of information entropy:

$$OSTRIE = -\sum_{i=1}^{7} p_i \log_2 p_i$$

using the same formula, C1CSTRIE and C2CSTRIE can also be calculated. See Figure 5 for the relationship between semantic transparency value and uncertainty of judgment among raters; both Mechanical Turk data and laboratory data are used to draw the figures. We can observe a very strong and regular relation between them. In terms of this relationship, laboratory data show stronger and more regular relationship than Mechanical Turk data. This kind of curve may reveal some kind of general cognitive mechanism of human subjective judgment.

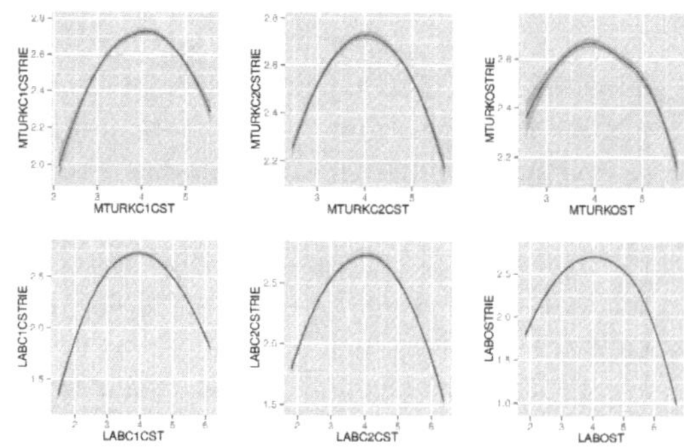

Figure 5: Uncertainty of semantic transparency judgments among the raters of the MTurk-based experiment and the lab-based experiment.

Acknowledgments

The work described in this paper was supported by a grant from the Research Grants Council of the Hong Kong Special Administrative Region, China (Project No. 544011).

References

Adam J Berinsky, Gregory A Huber, and Gabriel S Lenz. 2012. Evaluating online labor markets for experimental research: Amazon. com's mechanical turk. *Political Analysis*, 20(3):351–368.

Michael Buhrmester, Tracy Kwang, and Samuel D Gosling. 2011. Amazon's mechanical turk a new source of inexpensive, yet high-quality, data? *Perspectives on Psychological Science*, 6(1):3–5.

Keh-Jiann Chen, Chu-Ren Huang, Li-Ping Chang, and Hui-Li Hsu. 1996. Sinica corpus: Design methodology for balanced corpora. In B.-S. Park and J.B. Kim, editors, *Proceeding of the 11th Pacific Asia Conference on Language, Information and Computation*, pages 167–176. Seoul:Kyung Hee University.

Kuan-Ta Chen, Chen-Chi Wu, Yu-Chun Chang, and Chin-Laung Lei. 2009. A crowdsourceable qoe evaluation framework for multimedia content. In *Proceedings of the 17th ACM international conference on Multimedia*, pages 491–500. ACM.

Matthew JC Crump, John V McDonnell, and Todd M Gureckis. 2013. Evaluating amazon's mechanical turk as a tool for experimental behavioral research. *PLoS ONE*, 8(3):e57410.

Kelly Enochson and Jennifer Culbertson. 2015. Collecting psycholinguistic response time data using amazon mechanical turk. *PLoS ONE*, 10(3):e0116946, 03.

Enrique Estellés-Arolas and Fernando González-Ladrónde Guevara. 2012. Towards an integrated crowdsourcing definition. *Journal of Information science*, 38(2):189–200.

John J Horton, David G Rand, and Richard J Zeckhauser. 2011. The online laboratory: Conducting experiments in a real labor market. *Experimental Economics*, 14(3):399–425.

Jeff Howe. 2006. The rise of crowdsourcing. *Wired magazine*, 14(6):1–4.

Jeff Howe. 2009. *Crowdsourcing: Why the Power of the Crowd Is Driving the Future of Business*. Three Rivers Press.

Panagiotis G Ipeirotis. 2010. Demographics of mechanical turk.

Sherri Jackson. 2012. *Research methods and statistics: A critical thinking approach*. Cengage Learning.

Aniket Kittur, Ed H Chi, and Bongwon Suh. 2008. Crowdsourcing user studies with mechanical turk. In *Proceedings of the SIGCHI conference on human factors in computing systems*, pages 453–456. ACM.

Victor Kuperman, Hans Stadthagen-Gonzalez, and Marc Brysbaert. 2012. Age-of-acquisition ratings for 30,000 english words. *Behavior Research Methods*, 44(4):978–990.

Winter Mason and Siddharth Suri. 2012. Conducting behavioral research on amazon ' s mechanical turk. *Behavior research methods*, 44(1):1–23.

Robert Munro, Steven Bethard, Victor Kuperman, Vicky Tzuyin Lai, Robin Melnick, Christopher Potts, Tyler Schnoebelen, and Harry Tily. 2010. Crowdsourcing and language studies: the new generation of linguistic data. In *Proceedings of the NAACL HLT 2010 Workshop on Creating Speech and Language Data with Amazon's Mechanical Turk*, pages 122–130. Association for Computational Linguistics.

Gabriele Paolacci, Jesse Chandler, and Panagiotis G Ipeirotis. 2010. Running experiments on amazon mechanical turk. *Judgment and Decision making*, 5(5):411–419.

Ellie Pavlick, Matt Post, Ann Irvine, Dmitry Kachaev, and Chris Callison-Burch. 2014. The language demographics of amazon mechanical turk. *Transactions of the Association for Computational Linguistics*, 2:79–92.

Alexander J Quinn and Benjamin B Bederson. 2009. A taxonomy of distributed human computation. *Human-Computer Interaction Lab Tech Report, University of Maryland*.

Alexander J Quinn and Benjamin B Bederson. 2011. Human computation: a survey and taxonomy of a growing field. In *Proceedings of the SIGCHI conference on human factors in computing systems*, pages 1403–1412. ACM.

David G Rand. 2012. The promise of mechanical turk: How online labor markets can help theorists run behavioral experiments. *Journal of theoretical biology*, 299:172–179.

Joel Ross, Lilly Irani, M Silberman, Andrew Zaldivar, and Bill Tomlinson. 2010. Who are the crowdworkers?: shifting demographics in mechanical turk. In *CHI'10 Extended Abstracts on Human Factors in Computing Systems*, pages 2863–2872. ACM.

Eric Schenk and Claude Guittard. 2011. Towards a characterization of crowdsourcing practices. *Journal of Innovation Economics & Management*, 7(1):93–107.

L Schmidt. 2010. Crowdsourcing for human subjects research. *Proceedings of CrowdConf.*

Tyler Schnoebelen and Victor Kuperman. 2010. Using amazon mechanical turk for linguistic research. *Psihologija*, 43(4):441–464.

Travis Simcox and Julie A Fiez. 2014. Collecting response times using amazon mechanical turk and adobe flash. *Behavior research methods*, 46(1):95–111.

Rion Snow, Brendan O'Connor, Daniel Jurafsky, and Andrew Y Ng. 2008. Cheap and fast—but is it good?: evaluating non-expert annotations for natural language tasks. In *Proceedings of the conference on empirical methods in natural language processing*, pages 254–263. Association for Computational Linguistics.

Jon Sprouse. 2011. A validation of amazon mechanical turk for the collection of acceptability judgments in linguistic theory. *Behavior research methods*, 43(1):155–167.

Keith E Stanovich. 2007. *How to think straight about psychology*. HarperCollins Publishers.

Luis von Ahn. 2005. *Human Computation*. Ph.D. thesis, School of Computer Science, Carnegie Mellon University, Pittsburgh, PA 15213 USA, 12.

Aobo Wang, Cong Duy Vu Hoang, and Min-Yen Kan. 2013. Perspectives on crowdsourcing annotations for natural language processing. *Language Resources and Evaluation*, 47:9–31.

Shichang Wang, Chu-Ren Huang, Yao Yao, and Angel Chan. 2014. Building a semantic transparency dataset of chinese nominal compounds: A practice of crowdsourcing methodology. In *Proceedings of Workshop on Lexical and Grammatical Resources for Language Processing*, pages 147–156, Dublin, Ireland, August. Association for Computational Linguistics and Dublin City University.

Discourse Relation Recognition by Comparing Various Units of Sentence Expression with Recursive Neural Network

Atsushi Otsuka, Toru Hirano, Chiaki Miyazaki, Ryo Masumura, Ryuichiro Higashinaka, Toshiro Makino and **Yoshihiro Matsuo**
NTT Media Intelligence Laboratories
NTT Corporation
{otsuka.atsushi, hirano.tohru, miyazaki.chiaki, masumura.ryo, higashinaka.ryuichiro, makino.toshiro, matsuo.yoshihiro}@lab.ntt.co.jp

Abstract

We propose a method for implicit discourse relation recognition using a recursive neural network (RNN). Many previous studies have used the word-pair feature to compare the meaning of two sentences for implicit discourse relation recognition. Our proposed method differs in that we use various-sized sentence expression units and compare the meaning of the expressions between two sentences by converting the expressions into vectors using the RNN. Experiments showed that our method significantly improves the accuracy of identifying implicit discourse relations compared with the word-pair method.

1 Introduction

Discourse relation recognition is a technique to identify the type of discourse relation between two sentences. Because discourse relation contributes to the coherence of sentences, it has potential applications in many natural language processing (NLP) tasks. For example, in text summarization, it makes summary documents more consistent by using discourse relations and structures (Gerani et al., 2014). Similarly, in conversational systems (Higashinaka et al., 2014), discourse relations can help the system select contextually appropriate system utterances.

Discourse relations are categorized into explicit and implicit relations. Explicit relations have a discourse marker such as a connective, making them easy to identify with a high degree of accuracy (Pitler and Nenkova, 2009). Implicit discourse relations, in contrast, have no discourse marker between sentences. Previous studies have proposed many methods for implicit discourse recognition, among them reasoning-based (Sugiura et al., 2013) and pattern-based (Saito et al., 2006) methods. Many of these earlier studies (Marcu and Echihabi, 2002; Lin et al., 2009; Pitler et al., 2009; Wang et al., 2012; Lan et al., 2013; Biran and McKeown, 2013; Rutherford and Xue, 2014) focused on using word pairs or their derivative features. For example, take the two following sentences:

$A1$: *I like summer.*
$B1$: *I prefer winter.*

In this case, we can easily identify the relation as "comparison" by focusing on the word pair "*summer - winter*". However, there is emerging evidence that word pairs may no longer have a role to play in implicit discourse relation recognition (Park and Cardie, 2012). This is because identification is not always possible by using just word pairs. When we consider the following sentences,

$A2$: *I got soaked by the sudden rain yesterday.*
$B2_1$: *Did you forget your umbrella at the office?*
$B2_2$: *The rain was so heavy that my umbrella was useless.*

discourse $A2 - B2_1$ and $A2 - B2_2$ have different relations. discourse $A2 - B2_1$ is causal relation: $B2_1$ explains the reason for $A1$, and $A2 - B2_2$ is expansion relation: $B2_2$ is a supplemental explanation about the "*sudden rain*" in $A2$. Nevertheless, the same word pair "*soaked - umbrella*" can be ex-

29th Pacific Asia Conference on Language, Information and Computation pages 63 - 72
Shanghai, China, October 30 - November 1, 2015

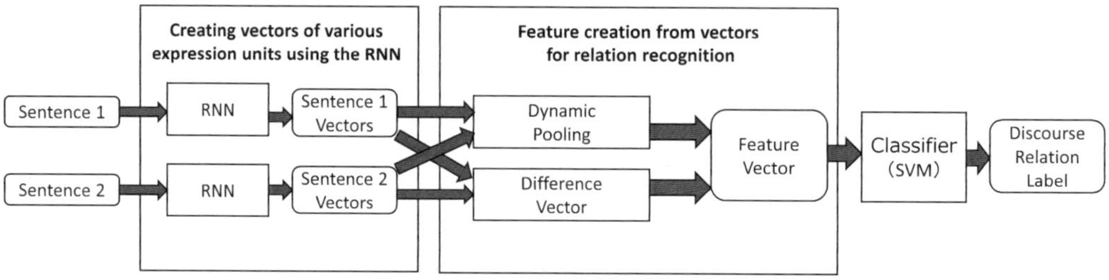

Figure 1: Overview of proposed discourse relation recognition.

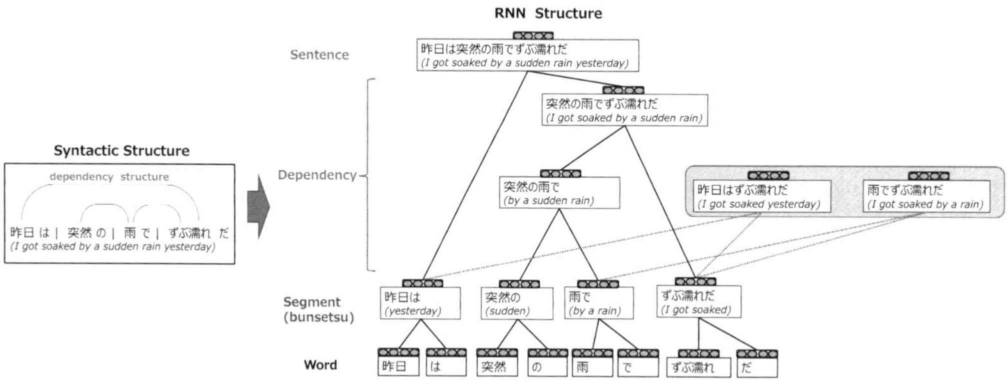

Figure 2: RNN structure in Japanese dependency structure.

tracted for both cases, making little contribution to relation recognition. If we can use pairs of longer expressions such as "*I got soaked - forget your umbrella*" and "*I got soaked by the sudden rain - so heavy that my umbrella was useless* ", it will be easier to perform relation recognition because the units employed are more specific and distinguishing of discourse relations.

This paper proposes a novel method for implicit discourse relation recognition that compares various expression units between two sentences. The smallest units of a sentence expression are words, and the largest are the entire sentence. To consider various expression units, we turn to a recursive neural network (RNN) based approach. The RNN is the neural network based method to create vectors of various expression units on the basis of the syntactic structure of a sentence and has been applied to various NLP tasks (Socher et al., 2011; Li et al., 2014; Liu et al., 2014). Here, we employ the RNN based approach for implicit discourse recognition and show that our proposed method significantly outperforms the word pair based approach.

In this paper, we demonstrate through experiments using Japanese conversational data that our method can improve the estimation performance of implicit discourse relation recognition more than the conventional word pair method. In the following sections, we first describe our proposed method using the RNN with Japanese sentences in Section 2. Section 3 explains the experiments we performed on implicit discourse recognition in Japanese dialogue, and we discuss the results in Section 4. Finally, we conclude in Section 5.

2 Discourse relation recognition by comparing various units of sentence expressions

Figure 1 shows an overview of the proposed method using various units of expressions in a sentence to identify implicit discourse relations. First, we input sentences to the RNN. The RNN then creates vectors of various expression units on the basis of the input syntactic structures in a bottom-up fashion. Next, we create a feature vector by comparing vectors of various units of expression. The discourse relation is identified by a discriminative classifier such as a support vector machine (SVM). In this section, we explain how the RNN works, describe how the vectors are created by the RNN, and show how to create the feature for the classifier from vectors.

2.1 Recursive neural network

The RNN is a kind of deep neural network created by applying the same set of weights recursively over a structure. The RNN has a binary tree structure, and its framework computes the representation for each parent iteratively in a bottom-up fashion on the basis of its children. We assume that word vectors c_1, c_2, and c_3 have N dimensions. Each word is given vectors in advance by word embeddings (e.g., *word2vec* (Mikolov et al., 2013a)). Segment vectors are created by combining word vectors from left to right in each segment. The c_1 and c_2's parent representation vector p_1 is computed as

$$p_1 = f(W_e[c_1; c_2] + b_e) \qquad (1)$$

where $[c_1; c_2]$ is the $2N$-dimension concatenation vector of c_1 and c_2, W_e is the $N \times 2N$ encoding matrix, b_e is the N-dimension encode bias vector, and f denotes an element-wise activation function (we use tanh). The next parent representation vector p_2, which has children p_1 and c_3, is computed in the same way by an input concatenation vector $[p_1; c_3]$ and encoding parameters W_e and b_e.

2.2 Creating vectors of various expression units using the RNN

The RNN creates vectors of various expression units during the process of creating a sentence vector. Our approach compares the meaning of two sentences by using these interim vectors. In this subsection, we introduce a method for extracting vectors of various expression units by the RNN for Japanese sentences.

Figure 2 shows the RNN structure based on Japanese dependency structure. Japanese sentences have dependency structures made up of bunsetsu segments (bunsetsu is a Japanese expression unit comprising one or more content words with zero or more function words). We obtain the syntactic structures of sentences by Japanese dependency parsing. Refer to (Kudo and Matsumoto, 2003) for how Japanese dependency parsing works in general.

We create segment vectors by combining word vectors. The sentence vector is the root vector of the RNN created at the end of the combining process. In this paper, we construct an RNN tree structure on top of the Japanese dependency structure. In Japanese, dependency relationships are generally directed from left to right, so we constantly combine segment vectors from the right-most segment to obtain the segment vector, as in the example shown in Fig. 2.

Because Japanese dependency structures are not a binary tree, there are some vectors that are not used in the process of creating the sentence vector. For example, the vectors of the expressions "*I got soaked yesterday*" and "*I got soaked by rain*" are not created in the process of creating the sentence vector in Fig. 2. Since these vectors have an independent meaning and can be useful, in our proposed method, we use all the vectors (including ones that do not lead to the sentence vector) in the RNN structure for discourse relation recognition as we describe in the following section.

2.3 Feature creation from vectors for discourse relation recognition

If sentences 1 and 2 have n and m vectors, respectively, we have to create a feature vector considering $n \times m$ patterns. However, the feature vector for the classifier must be fixed-length although the number of vectors extracted from a sentence changes dynamically depending on the number of words and on the syntactic structure. Therefore, we need to create a fixed-length feature vector without dependence on the number of vectors. The simplest approach to do this is to use a concatenation of sentence vectors as the feature vector. However, this way does not allow us to directly compare the meaning of intermediate expression units. Here, we create fixed-length feature vectors by dynamic pooling and difference vectors as follows:

Dynamic Pooling

Dynamic Pooling (DP) (Socher et al., 2011) is a method to create fixed-length features using the similarity between two vectors (Fig. 3). First, we create a similarity matrix between the vectors within the two sentences. The similarity between two vectors is computed with cosine

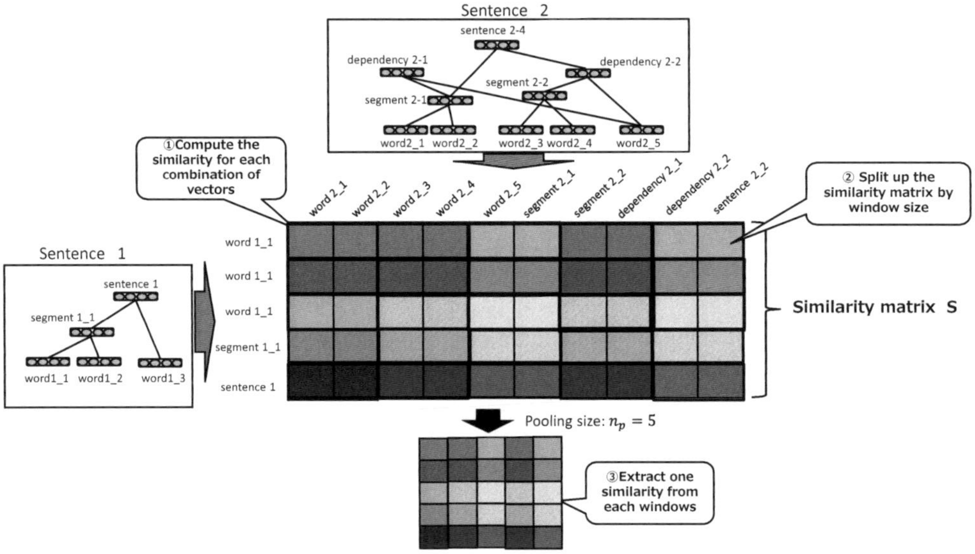

Figure 3: Overview of Dynamic Pooling.

similarity, as follows:

$$sim(v_1, v_2) = \frac{v_1 \cdot v_2}{|v_1||v_2|} \tag{2}$$

where v_1 and v_2 denote vectors extracted from sentences 1 and 2, respectively. The row and column order of the matrix is placed depth-first in the RNN tree, right-to-left. Specifically, matrix element s_{00}, which is the first element of similarity matrix S, is the degree of similarity between the left-most word vectors in each sentence.

In DP, the similarity matrix is split up into a sub-matrix by a grid window. The size of the grid window is computed depending on pooling size n_p. If sentences 1 and 2 have N and M vectors, respectively, the grid window size is $[\frac{N}{n_p}] \times [\frac{M}{n_p}]$. We extract a maximum similarity value element in each sub-matrix to create a pooled matrix. This pooled matrix is consistently fixed-length because the grid window size dynamically varies depending on sentence length. Similarity information between two sentences is consolidated into a fixed-length feature by the DP.

Difference vectors

Recent studies of word embeddings such as word2vec (Mikolov et al., 2013b) have revealed that difference vectors are meaningful. In the well-known word2vec example, the vector operation "*king - man + woman = queen*" holds. That is, the difference vector "*king - man* " represents the information of kingship. Following this insight, we use the difference vector in the hope that it can capture some relations between sentences. The difference vector is computed by subtracting two vectors, v_1 and v_2,

$$diff(v_1, v_2) = \frac{v_1 - v_2}{|v_1 - v_2|} \tag{3}$$

where vectors v_1 and v_2 denote vectors created by the RNN. In this paper, we utilize the mean vector of all difference vectors created by a combination of all the vectors (i.e., vectors that correspond to all the cells in the matrix S in Fig. 3) of two sentences as a feature vector.

3 Experiment

We performed experiments using a Japanese conversational corpus. First, we explain the dataset used

```
<s line = "1" speaker= "A">
  普段はお酒を飲まれますか？  ( Do you drink alcoholic beverages in your daily life? )
</s>

<s line = "2" speaker = "B">
  <connective category="Implicit"  class="EXPANSION"  type="Instantiation"  rel="1" marker="たとえば(For example)" />
  スミノフアイスをよく飲みます。  ( I often drink Smirnoff-ice. )
</s>

<s line = "3" speaker = "A">
  <connective category="Implicit"   class="CONTINGENCY"   type="Cause"   rel="2" marker ="なぜなら(Because)" />
  スッキリしますよね。(It has a refreshing taste. )
</s>

<s line = "4" speaker = "A">
  日本酒は飲みますか？( Do you drink Japanese Sake? )
</s>

<s line = "5" speaker = "B">
  <connective category="Implicit"   class="COMPARISON"   type="Contrast"    rel="2" marker ="でも (But)" />
  日本酒はあまり飲みません。( I rarely drink Japanese Sake. )
</s>

<s line = "6" speaker = "B">
  独特の味がする (its taste is so unique.)
   <connective category="Explicit"   class="CONTINGENCY"   type="Cause"   rel="5" >
     ので。(Because )
   </connective>
</s>
```

Figure 4: Discourse relation corpus from Japanese dialogue.

Utterance 1	Utterance 2	Relation	Connective
普段はお酒を飲まれますか？ (*Do you drink alcoholic beverages in your daily life?*))	スミノフアイスをよく飲みます。(*I often drink Smirnoff Ice.*)	Implicit EXPANSION Instantiation	例えば (*For example*)
スミノフアイスをよく飲みます。(*I often drink Smirnoff Ice.*)	スッキリしますよね。(*It has a refreshing taste.*)	Implicit CONTINGENCY Cause	なぜなら (*Because*)
スミノフアイスをよく飲みます。(*I often drink Smirnoff Ice.*)	日本酒はあまり飲みません。(*I rarely drink Japanese sake.*)	Implicit COMPARISON Contrast	でも (*But*)
日本酒はあまり飲みません。(*I rarely drink Japanese sake.*)	独特の味がするので。(*Because I think its taste is so unique.*)	Explicit CONTINGENCY Cause	ので (*Because*)

Table 1: Examples of utterance pairs and discourse relations extracted from Fig. 4.

for the experiment. Next, we describe our experimental methodology and comparative methods. Finally, we present the experimental results.

3.1 Dataset

In this paper, we focus on conversational dialogue because we want sophistication of dialogue analysis by using discourse relations.

The annotation framework follows the Penn Discourse Treebank (PDTB), a corpus of English texts from the Wall Street Journal in which the relations between abstract objects in discourse are annotated (Prasad et al., 2008). The PDTB has four classes (CONTINGENCY, COMPARISON, EXPANSION, and TEMPORAL) and 16 types of discourse relation within its hierarchical structure. In the PDTB, the discourse relations are decided with connectives: "*because*", "*and*", "*but*", and so on. If a discourse marker (e.g., a connective) is written clearly in either target sentence, the discourse relation is categorized as *Explicit*. Discourse relations without any discourse marker are called *Implicit*.

We annotated PDTB-style discourse relations to the Japanese conversational dialogue corpus created by Higashinaka et al. (2014). Figure 4 shows the annotated Japanese conversational dialogue corpus. We provide connective tags to each utterance if they have a connective. Connective elements have five attributes: *category*, which denotes discourse relation category and can be either explicit or implicit; *class*, which includes the four discourse relations; *type*, which denotes detailed relation types; *rel*, which denotes an utterance line number that has a discourse relation; and *marker*, which denotes the connective appropriate for discourse relation if the relation is *Implicit*. Table 1 gives a tabular view of the utterance pairs from Fig. 4.

Note that there is another dialogue corpus annotated with PDTB-style discourse relations (Tonelli et al., 2010); however, they focus on the design of the corpus and do not tackle the problem of discourse relation recognition.

3.2 Experimental method and results

We evaluate our proposed approach using the annotated conversational dialogue corpus. We created an implicit discourse relation classifier using an SVM with training data consisting of utterance pairs that have an explicit discourse relation. Explicit relations are more certain than implicit relations, so explicit relational data have been used as training data (Pitler and Nenkova, 2009).

We performed the evaluation by classifying three discourse relations (CONTINGENCY, COMPARISON , and EXPANSION) using classifiers. Here, we do not use the TEMPORAL relation class because far fewer utterance pairs have a relation to TEMPORAL than the other relations. Training data consisted of 5,000 utterance pairs for each relation. Test data were utterance pairs that have an implicit discourse relation, with each relation containing 500 utterance pairs by random sampling.

We evaluated our proposed method along with several comparative methods. All the methods derive features for two sentences to be classified by the SVM. The features used by the methods are described as below.

- Comparative methods

  Word pair
  The word pair feature is a basic feature for discourse recognition. Input sentences are split into words by a morphological analyzer MeCab[1] (we used this analyzer throughout the paper). We create word pair tokens from the combination of words between two sentences. Finally, the word pair feature is created by creating word-pair appearance frequency vectors.

  Vector centroid
  We create a sentence vector by computing the centroid of all word vectors in the sentence and use the vector as a feature. Here, word vectors are given by the word2vec model created using Japanese Wikipedia data. Note that the word centroid vector reflects the whole meaning of the sentence without syntactic structure or word order.

  RNN sentence
  The RNN sentence feature is the root node vector of the RNN structure. Parameters of the RNN are trained with data consisting of 100,000 utterances from the aforementioned dialogue corpus. The sentence vector differs from the word centroid vector in that it includes the information of syntactic structure.

- Proposed methods

  RNN + DP
  The RNN+DP feature is a concatenation vector with the RNN sentence vector and Dynamic Pooling vector (window size: 5).

  RNN + DP + diff
  The RNN+DP+diff feature is a concatenation vector with the RNN sentence vector, Dynamic Pooling, and a difference vector.

Figure 5 shows the results of the overall classification accuracy and McNemar's testing, and Table 2 shows the implicit discourse classification performance for each discourse relation by using precision, recall, and F-score. As can be seen in Fig. 5, our proposed method **(RNN + DP + diff)** had the

[1] `http://taku910.github.io/mecab/`

	CONTINGENCY			COMPARISON			EXPANSION		
	Precision	Recall	F-score	Precision	Recall	F-score	Precision	Recall	F-score
Word pair	0.38	**0.60**	**0.46**	0.41	0.32	0.36	0.37	0.22	0.28
Vector centroid	0.39	0.38	0.38	0.40	**0.40**	**0.40**	**0.41**	0.43	0.42
RNN sentence	0.42	0.26	0.32	0.47	0.26	0.34	0.36	**0.66**	0.47
RNN + DP	0.41	0.41	0.41	0.46	0.29	0.36	0.39	0.53	0.45
RNN + DP + diff	**0.45**	0.41	0.43	**0.48**	0.30	0.37	**0.41**	0.60	**0.49**

Table 2: Implicit discourse classification scores.

Utterance 1	Utterance 2	Predicted relation
Example of correct classification by all methods		
私もスキー得意です！(*I'm good at skiing too!*)	ボードは難しくて (*Snowboarding is hard for me.*)	COMPARISON
好きな番組のジャンルありますか (*What type of TV programs do you like?*)	バラエティですかね (*I like variety shows.*)	EXPANSION
Example of correct classification by **RNN + DP + diff**		
昨日遊園地に行きました (*I went to an amusement park yesterday.*)	好きなバンドのライブがそこであったんです (*My favorite band performed played a live show there.*)	CONTINGENCY
メイクの仕方ってどこで学ぶんでしょね？(*Where do you learn your makeup techniques?*)	私は雑誌を見ながらですね (*I learn them by reading magazines.*)	EXPANSION

Table 3: Examples of discourse relation recognition between two utterances.

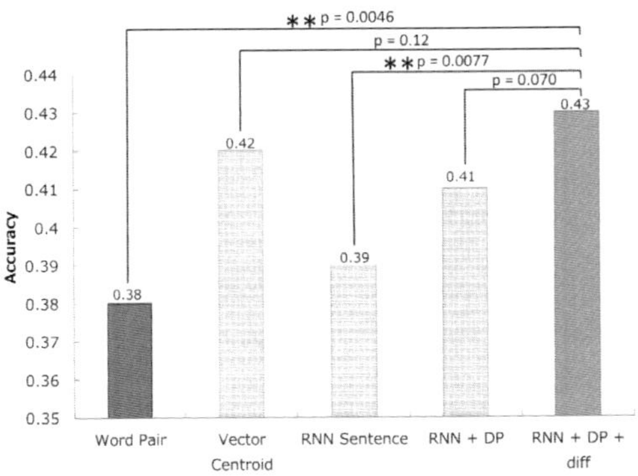

Figure 5: Comparison of classification accuracy.

highest accuracy ($accuracy = 0.43$), and the results of McNemar's testing reveal a significant difference between the **(Word pair)** and **(RNN + DP + diff)** methods ($p = 0.0046$, $p < 0.001$) and between the **(RNN sentence)** and **(RNN + DP + diff)** methods ($p = 0.0077$, $p < 0.001$). In contrast, the difference between the **(Vector centroid)** and **(RNN + DP + diff)** methods was only marginally significant ($p = 0.12$).

The accuracy of the baseline method **Word pair** (0.38) is very close to that of pure chance (0.33). We separately checked the inter-annotator agreement of discourse relation relation annotation and found that the accuracy of human (taking another annotator's annotation as gold standard) is 0.67. If the upper bound is 0.67, then our proposed method (0.43) achieves 64% accuracy relative to human performance, which is a lot higher than 57% accuracy (0.38) of **Word pair**, showing our contribution to implicit discourse relation recognition.

We show examples of the discourse relation recognition results between two Japanese utterances in Table 3. The upper two examples show utterance pairs that were classified correctly by all methods, while the two examples at the bottom were correctly classified by only the **(RNN + DP + diff)** method.

4 Discussion

The accuracy and McNemar's testing results indicate that our proposed approach **(RNN + DP + diff)** outperformed the word-pair and sentence vector approach, demonstrating that our approach, with its use of various units of expression, is more effective than the approach based on word pair and sentences.

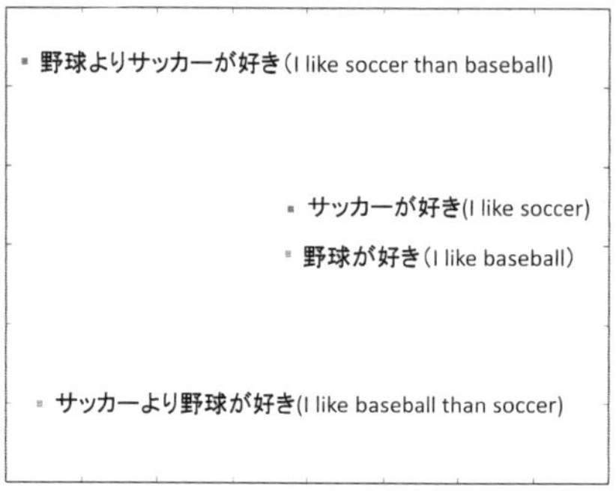

Figure 6: Visualization of RNN sentence vectors.

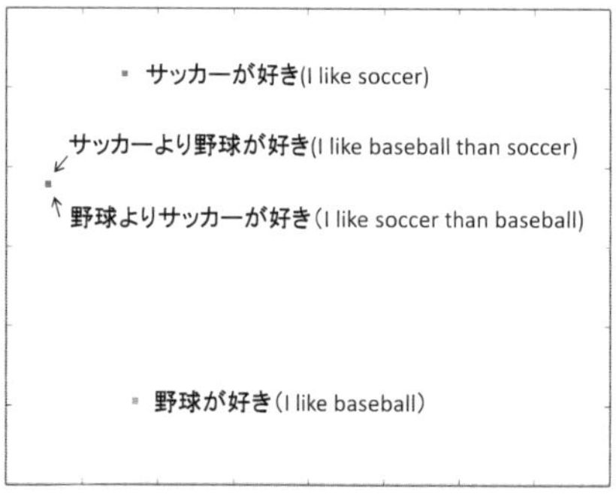

Figure 7: Visualization of word centroid vectors. Note that the vector "*I like soccer more than baseball*" overlaps with the vector "*I like baseball more than soccer.*".

In the example in Table 3, the inputs classified correctly by all methods were identified by extracting the characteristic content words from each utterance. For example, in the first example, the relation is identified as COMPARISON by extracting the pair "*skiing - snowboarding*". In contrast, in the last example, while the relation is difficult to identify as EXPANSION by extracting the pairs "*makeup - magazine*" or "*makeup - learn*", we can identify the relation by extracting the expression pairs "*your makeup techniques - by reading a magazine*". By taking advantage of the various units of expression in a sentence, our approach appropriately identifies the discourse relation between two sentences.

Our experimental results show that the RNN vectors are not always superior to word centroid vectors because there are cases where it is not necessary to consider syntax. Sometimes, word pairs are better suited for obtaining the generic topic of a sentence. However, we also found that implicit discourse relation recognition requires to detect slight differences in expressions in sentences. For example, Figs. 6 and 7 compare RNN vectors and word-centroid vectors in the visualization of vector space. The sentences "*I like baseball more than soccer.*" and "*I like soccer more than baseball.*" are in different places in Fig. 6. If the first sentence is "*I like soccer.*" and the second sentence is "*I like soccer more than baseball.*", the discourse relation between two sentences is EXPANSION (*I like soccer. Moreover, I like soccer more than baseball.*). However, if the second sentence is "*I like baseball more than soccer.*", the most appropriate discourse relation is COMPARISON (*I like soccer. But I like baseball more than soccer.*). The RNN vectors are able to capture these different structures, enabling our proposed method to recognize discourse relations more precisely.

5 Conclusion

We proposed an implicit discourse relation detection method using various units of expressions between two sentences. All expressions are converted into vectors by the RNN and then applied to Japanese dependency structures. Experimental results showed that our approach performs better than the conventional word-pair features method. This paper is the first to show that various expression units in sentences are effective for implicit discourse relation recognition.

Our future work is to enable more feature selection using intermediate expression vectors and to consider applications for dialogue systems. Current dialogue systems have problems that they choose a contextually inappropriate utterance for the user input. Since two utterances with a discourse relation can be coherent, we expect the quality of utterance selection to be increased by selecting an utterance that has a discourse relation with the user utterance.

References

Or Biran and Kathleen McKeown. 2013. Aggregated word pair features for implicit discourse relation disambiguation. *Proc of the 51st Annual Meeting of the Association for Computational Linguistics (ACL 2013)*, pages 69–73.

Shima Gerani, Yashar Mehdad, Giuseppe Carenini, Raymond T. Ng, and Bita Nejat. 2014. Abstractive summarization of product reviews using discourse structure. *Proc of the 2014 Conference on Empirical Methods in Natural Language Processing (EMNLP 2014)*, pages 1602–1613.

Ryuichiro Higashinaka, Kenji Imamura, Toyomi Meguro, Chiaki Miyazaki, Nozomi Kobayashi, Hiroaki Sugiyama, Toru Hirano, Toshiro Makino, and Yoshihiro Matsuo. 2014. Towards an Open Domain Conversational System Fully Based on Natural Language Processing. *Proc of the 25th International Conference on Computational Linguistics (COLING 2014)*, pages 928–939.

Taku Kudo and Yuji Matsumoto. 2003. Fast methods for kernel-based text analysis. *Proc of the 41st Annual Meeting of the Association for Computational Linguistics (ACL 2003)*, pages 24–31.

Man Lan, Yu Xu, and Zhengyu Niu. 2013. Leveraging Synthetic Discourse Data via Multi-task Learning for Implicit Discourse Relation Recognition. *Proc of the 51st Annual Meeting of the Association for Computational Linguistics(ACL 2013)*, pages 476–485.

Jiwei Li, Rumeng Li, and Eduard Hovy. 2014. Recursive deep models for discourse parsing. *Proc of the 2014 Conference on Empirical Methods in Natural Language Processing (EMNLP 2014)*, pages 2061–2069.

Ziheng Lin, Min-Yen Kan, and Hwee Tou Ng. 2009. Recognizing Implicit Discourse Relations in the Penn Discourse Treebank. *Proc of the 2009 Conference on Empirical Methods in Natural Language Processing (EMNLP 2009)*, pages 343–351.

Shujie Liu, Nan Yang, Mu Li, and Ming Zhou. 2014. A recursive recurrent neural network for statistical machine translation. *Proc of the 52nd Annual Meeting of the Association for Computational Linguistics (ACL 2014)*, pages 1491–1500.

Daniel Marcu and Abdessamad Echihabi. 2002. An Unsupervised Approach to Recognizing Discourse Relations. *Proc of the 40th Annual Meeting on Association for Computational Linguistics (ACL 2002)*, pages 368–375.

Tomas Mikolov, Kai Chen, Greg Corrado, and Jeffrey Dean. 2013a. Efficient Estimation of Word Representations in Vector Space. *Proc of the Workshop at International Conference on Learning Representations (ICLR 2013)*.

Tomas Mikolov, Wen-tau Yih, and Geoffrey Zweig. 2013b. Linguistic regularities in continuous space word representations. *Proc of the 2013 Conference of the North American Chapter of the Association for Computational Linguistics: Human Language Technologies (NAACL-HLT 2013)*, pages 746–751.

Joonsuk Park and Claire Cardie. 2012. Improving implicit discourse relation recognition through feature set optimization. *Proc of the 13th Annual Meeting of the Special Interest Group on Discourse and Dialogue (SIGDIAL 2012)*, pages 108–112.

Emily Pitler and Ani Nenkova. 2009. Using Syntax to Disambiguate Explicit Discourse Connectives in Text. *Proc of the Joint Conference of the 47th Annual Meeting of the ACL and the 4th International Joint Conference on Natural Language Processing of the AFNLP Short Papers (ACL-IJCNLP 2009)*, pages 13–16.

Emily Pitler, Annie Louis, and Ani Nenkova. 2009. Automatic Sense Prediction for Implicit Discourse Relations in Text. *Proc of the Joint Conference of the 47th Annual Meeting of the ACL and the 4th International Joint Conference on Natural Language Asian Federation of Natural Language Processing (AFNLP 2009)*, pages 683–691.

Rashmi Prasad, Nikhil Dinesh, Alan Lee, Eleni Miltsakaki, Livio Robaldo, Aravind Joshi, and Bonnie Webber. 2008. The Penn Discourse TreeBank 2.0. *Proc of the sixth international conference on Language Resources and Evaluation (LREC 2008)*.

Attapol Rutherford and Nianwen Xue. 2014. Discovering implicit discourse relations through brown cluster pair representation and coreference patterns. *Proc of the 14th Conference of the European Chapter of the Association for Computational Linguistics (EACL 2014)*, pages 645–654, April.

Manami Saito, Kazuhide Yamamoto, and Satoshi Sekine. 2006. Using phrasal patterns to identify discourse relations. *Proc of the 2006 Conference of the North American Chapter of the Association for Computational Linguistics: Human Language Technologies (NAACL-HLT 2006)*, pages 133–136.

Richard Socher, Eric H. Huang, Jeffrey Pennin, Christopher D Manning, and Andrew Y. Ng. 2011. Dynamic Pooling and Unfolding Recursive Autoencoders for Paraphrase Detection. *Proc of Advances in Neural Information Processing Systems (NIPS 2011)*, pages 801–809.

Jun Sugiura, Naoya Inoue, and Kentaro Inui. 2013. Recognizing Implicit Discourse Relations through Abductive Reasoning with Large-scale Lexical Knowledge. *Proc of the 1st Workshop on Natural Language and Automated Reasoning (NLPAR 2013)*, pages 76–87.

Sara Tonelli, Giuseppe Riccardi, Rashmi Prasad, and Aravind Joshi. 2010. Annotation of Discourse Relations for Conversational Spoken Dialogs. *Proc of the Seventh International Conference on Language Resources and Evaluation (LREC 2010)*, pages 19–21.

Xun Wang, Sujian Li, Jiwei Li, and Wenjie Li. 2012. Implicit discourse relation recognition by selecting typical training examples. *Proc of the 24th International Conference on Computational Linguistics (COLING 2012)*, pages 2757–2772.

Bidirectional Long Short-Term Memory Networks for Relation Classification

Shu Zhang[1], Dequan Zheng[2], Xinchen Hu[2] and Ming Yang[1]
[1] Fujitsu Research and Development Center, Beijing, China
{zhangshu, yangming}@cn.fujitsu.com
[2] School of Computer Science and Technology, Harbin Institute of Technology, Harbin, China
{dqzheng, xchu}@mtlab.hit.edu.cn

Abstract

Relation classification is an important semantic processing, which has achieved great attention in recent years. The main challenge is the fact that important information can appear at any position in the sentence. Therefore, we propose bidirectional long short-term memory networks (BLSTM) to model the sentence with complete, sequential information about all words. At the same time, we also use features derived from the lexical resources such as WordNet or NLP systems such as dependency parser and named entity recognizers (NER). The experimental results on SemEval-2010 show that BLSTM-based method only with word embeddings as input features is sufficient to achieve state-of-the-art performance, and importing more features could further improve the performance.

1 Introduction

The automatic classification of semantic relations is an important task, which could offer useful information for many applications, such as question answering, information extraction, the construction and completion of semantic or relational knowledge base.

In this work, we focus on the classification of semantic relations between pairs of nominals (Hendrickx et al., 2010). Given a sentence S with annotated pairs of nominal e_1 and e_2, the task is to classify which of the following nine semantic relations holds between the nominals: *Cause-Effect*, *Instrument-Agency*, *Product-Producer*, *Content-Container*, *Entity-Origin*, *Entity-Destination*, *Component-Whole*, *Member-Collection*, *Message-Topic*, or *Other* if it does not belongs to any of the nine annotated relations.

For example, *News* and *commotion* are connected in a *Cause-Effect* relation in the sentence "The *news* brought about a *commotion* in the office." In this instance, the relation between *news* and *commotion* could be inferred by the meaning of the two nominals and the context of "brought about" around them. Therefore, how to grasp and represent the lexical and context information are the key research points for semantic relation classification.

Supervised methods with carefully handcrafted features from lexical and semantic resources have achieved high performance (Hendrickx *et al.*, 2010; Rink and Harabagiu, 2010). However, the selection of features and the effective integration of knowledge sources into relation classification seem to be difficult.

Recently, deep neural networks has been applied with the aim of reducing the number of handcrafted features, and getting effective features from lexical and sentence level (Socher et al., 2012; Zeng et al., 2014; Yu et al., 2014).

Different from previous work, we propose bidirectional long short-term memory networks (BLSTM) to solve the relation classification. For every word in a given sentence, BLSTM has complete, sequential information about all words before and after it. Long distance relationship may be solved in some extent in this networks. At the same time, we also use features derived from the lexical resources such as WordNet or NLP tools such as dependency parser and named entity recognizers (NER). The experimental results show that only using word embedding as input features is enough to achieve state-of-the-art results. Importing more features could further improve the performance of the relation classification.

29th Pacific Asia Conference on Language, Information and Computation pages 73 - 78
Shanghai, China, October 30 - November 1, 2015

2 Related Work

SemEval-2010 task 8 focused on semantic relation classification, it provides a standard testbed to evaluate and compare the performance of different approaches.

SVM (Rink and Harabagiu, 2010): Using SVM classifier and a number of features derived from NLP tools and many external resources, it achieves the highest performance among the participating systems (10 teams, 28 runs).

Neural network has got great achievement in many applications, it has also been utilized in relation classification as shown in the followings:

MV-RNN (Socher et al., 2012): They propose a recursive neural network model to learn compositional vector representations for phrases and sentences of arbitrary syntactic type and length.

CNN (Zeng et al. (2014): Sentence level features are learned using a convolutional model, and concatenated with lexical features to form the final extracted feature vector.

FCM (Yu et al., 2014): They decompose the sentence into substructures, and extract features for each substructure. Finally they combine these features with the embeddings of words in this substructure to form a substructure embedding.

CR-CNN (Santos et al., 2015): They propose network to learn a distributed vector representation for each relation class. A ranking loss function is proposed to reduce the impact of artificial classes.

DepNN (Liu et al., 2015): Using a recursive neural network to model the subtrees, and a convolutional neural network to capture the most important features on the shortest path.

From the above works, we can see that many different neural network models have been applied to solve relation classification recently. The main target is to learn the effective features in lexical and sentence level to represent the latent relation between the given nominals.

Our work has the same target, and we try to apply BLSTM to mine the sentence level features with its advantage of capturing long distance relationship in a sentence. We also study the influence of adding features obtained from NLP tools and resources on the final classification performance.

3 Long Short Term Memory

The Long Short Term Memory architecture was proposed and extended (Hochreiter and Schmidhuber, 1997; Gers et al., 2002) with the motivation on an analysis of Recurrent Neural Nets (Hochreiter et al., 2001), which found that long time lags were inaccessible to existing architectures, because backpropagated error either blows up or decays exponentially.

A LSTM layer consists of a set of recurrently connected blocks, known as memory blocks. Each one contains one or more recurrently connected memory cells and three multiplicative units - the input, output and forget gates - that provide continuous analogues of write, read and reset operations for the cells. LSTM has achieved the best known results in handwriting recognition (Graves et al., 2009) and speech recognition (Graves et al., 2013).

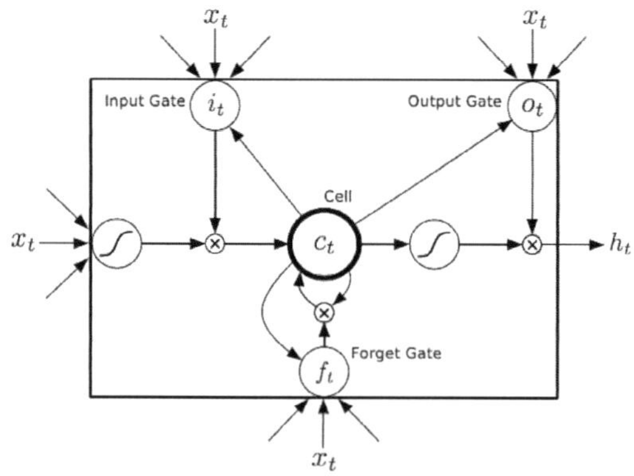

Fig. 1. LSTM memory block with one cell

Figure 1 shows one cell of LSTM memory block. More precisely, the input x_t to the cells is multiplied by the activation of the input gate, the output to the net is multiplied by that of the output gate, and the previous cell values are multiplied by the forget gate. The net can only interact with the cells via the gates.

The basic idea of bidirectional LSTM is to present each training sequence forwards and backwards to two separate recurrent nets, both of which are connected to the same output layer. This means that for every point in a given sequence, the network has complete, sequential information about all points before and after it. The structure of BLSTM is shown in Figure 2.

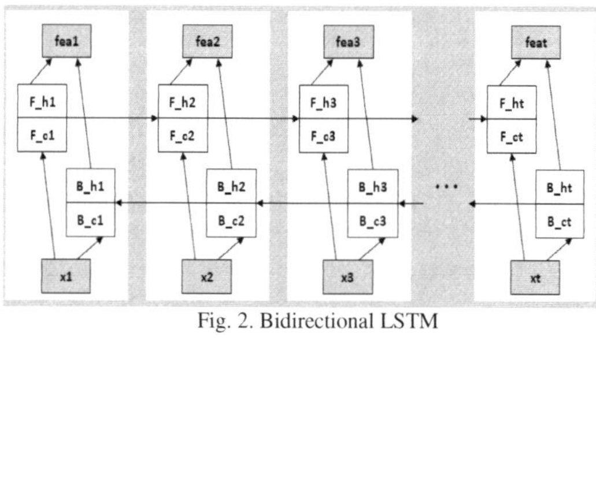

Fig. 2. Bidirectional LSTM

4 Methodology

We propose bidirectional long short-term memory networks (BLSTM) to solve the relation classification. It includes the following parts:

(1) Initial feature extraction: extract from the input sentence.

(2) Features embedding: transform all initial features into real-valued vector representation.

(3) BLSTM-based sentence level representation: get high level feature representation from step (2).

(4) Constructing feature vector: get lexical level and sentence level features from step (2) and step (3), and concatenate them to form the final feature vector.

(5) Classifying: feed final feature vector into a multilayer perceptron (MLP) and softmax layer to get the probability distribution of relation labels.

4.1 Initial Feature Extraction

Besides word and position features, we utilize NLP tools and resources to get POS, NER, dependency parse and hypernyms features. We aim to grasp more features which may indicate the relationship of the pair of two nominals. All these features could be classified into two types: lexical features and relative position relationship features.

We extract word, POS, NER and hypernyms as lexical features. The WordNet hypernyms are adopted as MVRNN (Socher et al., 2012).

Three different relative position relationship features are extracted and shown in Figure 3.

In this work we also utilize the relative word position proposed by Zeng et al. (2014). The position feature (**PF**) is derived from the relative distances of the current word to the target nominals e_1 and e_2. For instance, the word *sat* in the sentence shown in Figure 3, its relative distance to the target nominal *cat* (e_1) and *mat* (e_2) are 1 and -3.

We also chose the Stanford dependency parser to capture long distance relationships between two nominals in a sentence. Our dependency features are based on paths in the dependency tree. Here, we extract two types of features:

Relative dependency features:

- Relative root feature: *r_r* (root node), *r_c* (child node of root), *r_o* (others)
- Relative e_1 feature: e_1_e_1 (e_1 node), e_1_*c* (child node of e_1), e_1_*p* (parent node of e_1), e_1_*o* (others)
- Relative e_2 feature: e_2_e_2 (e_2 node), e_2_*c* (child node of e_2), e_2_*p* (parent node of e_2), e_2_*o* (others)

Dep features: the tag of the current word to its parent node on the dependency tree

The above features represent the relationship between the current word and the target node, including the root, e_1, e_2 and their parent node. Figure 4 gives an example of dependency parser results.

	The	cat(e1)	sat	on	the	mat(e2
Relative root	r_o	r_c	r_r	r_o	r_o	r_c
Relative e1 feature	e1_c	e1_e	e1_p	e1_o	e1_o	e1_o
Relative e2 feature	e2_o	e2_o	e2_p	e2_c	e2_c	e2_e
dep	det	nsubj	root	case	det	nmo
PF	-1 -5	0 -4	1 -3	2 -2	3 -1	4 0

Fig. 3. Example of relative position relationship features

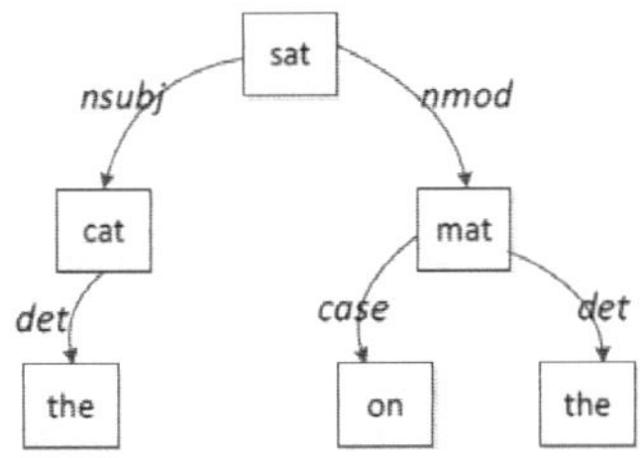

Fig. 4. Example of dependency parser results

4.2 Feature Embedding

Word Embedding is to map each word into a real-valued vector to represent syntactic and semantic information about the words.

Given an embedding matrix $W^{wrd} \in \mathbf{R}^{d^w \times |V|}$, where V is the size of word vocabulary. Each word w has its embedding by using the matrix-vector product:

$$r^w = W^{wrd} v^w$$

where v^w is one-hot represenation, to get one column of the matrix W^{wrd}.

The size of the word embedding d^w is a hyperparameter, which is usually set 50 or 100.

For other kinds of initial features, we also transform them into a vector representation r^{kj}, where j means the *jth* type of feature, the dimension is d^{kj}. The initial value of the vector is random generated with the method proposed by Glorot and Bengio (2010).

Given a sentence $x=\{w_1,w_2,...,w_n\}$, all the initial feature embeddings are concatenated according to the following format to represent each word:

$$x_i = [r_i^w, r_i^{k1}, r_i^{k2} ..., r_i^{km}]$$

where r_i^w is the word embedding of word x_i, r_i^{kj} is embedding of the *jth* types of features.

The parameter *m* is the size of features. Its value is 6 in this paper, because we choose the following six kinds of features: POS, NER, hypernyms(WNSYN), position feature (PF), dependency feature (Dep), relative-dependency feature (Relative-Dep).

4.3 BLSTM-based Sentence Level Representation

It is well known that humans can exploit longer context to mine the relationship of two nominals in a sentence. LSTM has shown its merit on capturing long distance relationship in different fields. With this motivation, we adopt BLSTM to get the sentence level representation.

The LSTM equations are given for a single memory block.

Input Gates:

$$i_t = \sigma(W_{xi}x_t + W_{hi}h_{t-1} + W_{ci}c_{t-1} + b_i)$$

Forget Gates:

$$f_t = \sigma(W_{xf}x_t + W_{hf}h_{t-1} + W_{cf}c_{t-1} + b_f)$$

Cells:

$$c_t = f_t c_{t-1} + i_t \tanh(W_{xc}x_t + W_{hc}h_{t-1} + b_c)$$

Output gates:

$$o_t = \sigma(W_{xo}x_t + W_{ho}h_{t-1} + W_{co}c_t + b_o)$$

Cell Outputs:

$$h_t = o_t \tanh c_t$$

where σ is the activation function, and *i*, *f*, *o* and *c* are respectively the input gate, forget gate, output gate and memory cell.

As shown in Figure 2, the network contained two sub-networks for the left and right sequence context. The outputs of these subnets for the *ith* word are integrated in the following way:

$$F_i = [F\_h_i, F\_c_i, B\_h_i, B\_h_i]$$

where F and B refer to forward and backward directions.

4.4 Constructing Feature Vector

Inspired by the work from Zeng et al. (2014), we extract and concatenate sentence level features and lexical level features to form the finally extracted feature vector.

Lexical level features are focused on the two target nominals $e_1$and e_2. We concatenate the vector got from feature embeddings and BLSTM layer to represent the two nominals as [x_{e1}, F_{e1}, x_{e2}, F_{e2}].

Sentence level features are focused on the context information, which are constructed from the output of BLSTM layer. As shown in Figure 5, the matrix got from BLSTM could be divided into A, B and C parts by e_1 and e_2. Max pooling operation is adopted to extract the vector from A and B parts, B and C parts respectively. The vector m_1 and m_2 is concatenated to form the sentence level representation.

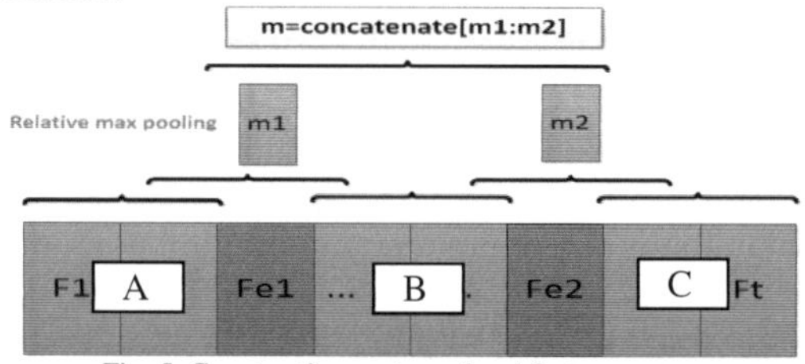

Fig. 5. Constructing sentence level feature vector

The motivation of constructing sentence level in this way is to strengthen the influence of the context between two entities, which are usually contained more information for indicating the relationship.

4.5 Classifying

A multilayer perceptron (MLP) will be used for combining sentence level feature and lexical feature into the final extracted feature vector. Finally, the final extracted features are fed into a softmax classifier to predict the sematic relation labels.

5 Experiments

5.1 Data and metrics

Experiments are conducted on the SemEval-2010 task 8 dataset (Hendrickx *et al.*, 2010). It includes 8,000 training instances and 2,717 test instances. There are 9 relation types, and each type has two directions. If the instance could not refer to any of 9 relation types, there is a type *Other*.

We adopt the official evaluation metric to evaluate our systems, which is based on macro-averaged F1-score for the nine proper relations and others.

5.2 Experiments setting

The dimension of feature embeddings used in the experiments are listed in the following.

Features	Embedding Dimension
WF	50, 100
PF	2*5
POS	20
NER	20
WNSYN	20
DEP	20
RELATIVE-DEP	3*10

Table 1. Embedding dimension

We select two available trained word embeddings to see its influence to the classification performance. One is from Turian et al. (2010), the dimension of word embedding is 50. The other is from Jeffrey Pennington et al. (2014), the dimension of word embedding is 100.

As shown in the above, position feature (PF) contains two elements, and relative-dependency feature (Relative-Dep) contains three elements. Therefore, embedding dimension of PF is 2*5, that of RELATIVE-DEP is 3*10.

The BLSTM layer contains 400 units for each direction, and MLP layer contains 1000 units.

5.3 Results and Analysis

Firstly, we testify the performance of proposed BLSTM-based method with two feature set. One only uses word embedding as input, the other uses all features shown in section 4.1. We also list the results of CNN and CR-CNN methods as reference.

Model	Feature Set	F1
CNN (Zeng et al., 2014)	Only word embeddings	69.7
	word embeddings, word position embeddings,word pair, words around word pair, WordNet	82.7
CR-CNN (Santos et al., 2015)	Only word embeddings	82.8
	word embeddings, word position embeddings	84.1
BLSTM	Only word embedding (100)	82.7
	All features	84.3

Table 2. Comparison with previously published results

In table 2, only using word embedding as input features, BLSTM-based method achieves F1 of 82.7, which is similar to the results of CNN with multiple features, and CR-CNN with only word embedding features. However, CR_CNN use word embeddings of size 400, our method use word embeddings of size 100. It proves that BLSTM-based method is effective to mine the relationship between two nominals. With more features, the performance achieves F1 of 84.3, which testifies general features gotten from NLP tools could improve the classification performance.

Secondly, we testify the influence of different features for the classification by removing one type of features from feature set in each time.

From Table 3, we see that the performance has very slight change by removing position and NER features. It shows that BLSTM has better representation on sentence level relationship without position features. The information of position features is already contained in BLSTM networks. The whole features are considered from lexical and sentence level. The performances of removing PF or NER feature don't change obviously, maybe the information they contained is represented by other features.

Removed Feature	F1
PF	84.2
POS	83.9
NER	84.2
WNSYN	83.2
DEP	83.5

Table 3. Results of removing one kind of feature

Finally, we compare the results in different word embedding size. In Table 4 we give the result with using word embedding of size 50. It achieves a F1 of 83.6, about 0.7% less than that with using word embedding of size 100, which shows larger size of dimension of word embedding may contain more information, and it could improve the performance.

We also compare the LSTM based method with only one direction such as forward or backward. The results shows BLSTM has a slight advantage over unidirectional LSTM.

Compared with proposed constructing sentence level feature vector in figure 5, we use Max pooling operation directly from A+B+C parts. The result shows F1 of 83.1, which is lower than our method with F1 of 83.6. It proves that our proposed method is effective.

Model (word embedding 50)	F1
BLSTM	83.6
Forward-LSTM	82.1
Backward-LSTM	82.4
Single-max model	83.1

Table 4. Results of removing one kind of feature

6 Conclusion

In this paper, we propose bidirectional long short-term memory networks (BLSTM) to solve the relation classification. BLSTM is proposed to mine the sentence level representation. The experiment results show that only using word embedding as input features is enough to achieve state-of-the-art results. Importing more features could further improve the performance of the relation classification.

Reference

Bryan Rink and Sanda Harabagiu. 2010. UTD: Classifying Semantic Relations by Combining Lexical and Semantic Resources. In Proceedings of 5th International Workshop on Semantic Evaluation, pages 256–259.

Daojian Zeng, Kang Liu, Siwei Lai, Guangyou Zhou, and Jun Zhao. 2014. Relation Classification via Convolutional Deep Neural Network. In Proceedings of the 25th International Conference on Computational Linguistics (COLING), pages 2335–2344.

Iris Hendrickx, Su Nam Kim, Zornitsa Kozareva, Preslav Nakov, Diarmuid Ó Séaghdha, Sebastian Padó, Marco Pennacchiotti, Lorenza Romano, and Stan Szpakowicz. 2010. Semeval-2010 Task 8: Multi-way Classification of Semantic Relations Between Pairs of Nominals. In Proceedings of the 5th International Workshop on Semantic Evaluation, pages 33–38.

Richard Socher, Brody Huval, Christopher D. Manning, and Andrew Y. Ng. 2012. Semantic Compositionality through Recursive Matrix-Vector Spaces. In Proceedings of the Joint Conference on Empirical Methods in Natural Language Processing and Computational Natural Language Learning, pages 1201–1211.

Yang Liu, Furu Wei, Sujian Li, Heng Ji, Ming Zhou, and Houfeng Wang. 2015. A Dependency-based Neural Network for Relation Classification. In Proceedings of the 53rd Annual Meeting of the Association for Computational Linguistics and the 7th International Joint Conference on Natural Language Processing (Short Papers), pages 285-290.

Cícero Nogueira dos Santos, Bing Xiang, and Bowen Zhou. 2015. Classifying Relations by Ranking with Convolutional Neural Networks. In Proceedings of the 53rd Annual Meeting of the Association for Computational Linguistics and the 7th International Joint Conference on Natural Language Processing, pages 626–634.

Alex Graves, Marcus Liwicki, Santiago Fernández, Roman Bertolami, Horst Bunke, Jürgen Schmidhuber. 2009. A Novel Connectionist System for Improved Unconstrained Handwriting Recognition. IEEE Transactions on Pattern Analysis and Machine Intelligence, 31(5): 855-868.

Alex Graves, Abdel-rahman Mohamed, and Geoffrey Hinton. 2013. Speech Recognition with Deep Recurrent Neural Networks. IEEE International Conference on Acoustics, Speech and Signal Processing (ICASSP), pages 6645–6649.

Joseph Turian, Lev Ratinov, and Yoshua Bengio. 2010. Word Representations: A Simple and General Method for Semi-Supervised Learning. In Proceedings of the 48th annual meeting of the association for computational linguistics, pages 384-394.

Jeffrey Pennington, Richard Socher, and Christopher Manning. 2014. GloVe: Global Vectors for Word Representation. In Proceedings of the Empirical Methods in Natural Language Processing, pages 1532-1543.

Xavier Glorot and Yoshua Bengio. 2010. Understanding the Difficulty of Training Deep Feedforward Neural Networks. International conference on artificial intelligence and statistics, pages 249-256.

Mo Yu, Matthew R. Gormley, and Mark Dredze. 2014. Factor-based Compositional Embedding Models. In NIPS Workshop on Learning Semantics.

Sepp Hochreiter and Jürgen Schmidhuber. 1997. Long Short-Term Memory. Neural Computation, 9(8):1735–1780.

Sepp Hochreiter, Yoshua Bengio, Paolo Frasconi, and Jürgen Schmidhuber. 2001. Gradient Flow in Recurrent Nets: the Difficulty of Learning Long-Term Dependencies. In Kremer, S. C.and Kolen, J. F., editors, A Field Guide to Dynamical Recurrent Neural Networks. IEEE Press.

Felix A. Gers, Nicol N. Schraudolph, and Jürgen Schmidhuber. 2002. Learning Precise Timing with LSTM Recurrent Networks. Journal of Machine Learning Research, 3:115–143.

Distant Supervision for Entity Linking

Miao Fan*, **Qiang Zhou and Thomas Fang Zheng**
CSLT, Division of Technical Innovation and Development
Tsinghua National Laboratory for Information Science and Technology
Department of Computer Science and Technology,
Tsinghua University, Beijing, 100084, China
*fanmiao.cslt.thu@gmail.com

Abstract

Entity linking is an indispensable operation of populating knowledge repositories for information extraction. It studies on aligning a textual entity mention to its corresponding disambiguated entry in a knowledge repository. In this paper, we propose a new paradigm named distantly supervised entity linking (DSEL), in the sense that the disambiguated entities that belong to a huge knowledge repository (Freebase) are automatically aligned to the corresponding descriptive webpages (Wiki pages). In this way, a large scale of weakly labeled data can be generated without manual annotation and fed to a classifier for linking more newly discovered entities. Compared with traditional paradigms based on solo knowledge base, DSEL benefits more via jointly leveraging the respective advantages of Freebase and Wikipedia. Specifically, the proposed paradigm facilitates bridging the disambiguated labels (Freebase) of entities and their textual descriptions (Wikipedia) for Web-scale entities. Experiments conducted on a dataset of 140,000 items and 60,000 features achieve a baseline F1-measure of 0.517. Furthermore, we analyze the feature performance and improve the F1-measure to 0.545.

1 Introduction

To build the "Digital Alexandria Library" for our human race, researchers in the NLP community have dedicated themselves to *Information Extraction* (Sarawagi, 2008) over the past decades. Information extraction focuses on processing natural language text to produce structured knowledge, which is usually represented as triples (two entities and their relation) for the convenience of storage in a database, retrieval, or even automatic reasoning. For example, if we send a natural language sentence, *Michael Jordan visited CMU yesterday*, to the pipeline of information extraction machine, it will be processed by three operations in advance, i.e.,

- **Named Entity Recognition** (Nadeau and Sekine, 2007): Entities should firstly be identified and classified into predefined categories, such as person (PER), location (LOC) and organization (ORG). The sentence will be annotated as *[Michael Jordan]/PER visited [CMU]/ORG yesterday*, after being processed by this operation.

- **Coreference Resolution** (Ng, 2010): Some entities may have alias or abbreviations. It is well known that *CMU* is the abbreviation for *Carnegie Mellon University*. The knowledge repository may only store the regularized name, e.g., *Carnegie Mellon University*, for this named entity, so coreference resolution is indeed necessary.

- **Relation Extraction** (Bach and Badaskar, 2007): After both of the named entities (*[Michael Jordan]/PER* and *[Carnegie Mellon University]/ORG*) are recognized and regularized, we begin to study on the relation between them. In this case, we extract the verb *visited* and map it to the relation *visit*. Then the output will be a triple, i.e., (*Michael Jordan [PER], visit, Carnegie Mellon University [ORG]*).

So far, we only abstract the triple as the structured knowledge from the natural language sentence. However, it devotes nothing to increasing the scale of the knowledge repository such as Free-

29th Pacific Asia Conference on Language, Information and Computation pages 79 - 86
Shanghai, China, October 30 - November 1, 2015

base (Bollacker et al., 2007) which is a huge[1], public[2], collaborative[3](Bollacker et al., 2008) and online knowledge base with billions of triples and millions of disambiguated entities, and is primarily maintained by Google Inc., because we even do not know which exact *Michael Jordan* the triple (*Michael Jordan [PER], visit, Carnegie Mellon University [ORG]*) refers to in Freebase. As illustrated in Figure 1, there are three different persons named *Michael Jordan* in Freebase and each of them may be the protagonist of that news. Therefore, to populate knowledge repositories (Ji and Grishman, 2011), we need the *fourth operation*:

- **Entity Linking** (Rao et al., 2013): It concerns about the study of aligning a textual entity mention to the corresponding disambiguated entry in a knowledge repository. More specifically, since there are several *Michael Jordan* disambiguated by different MIDs (machine identifiers) as illustrated in Figure 1, we may build a classifier that can help assign the *Michael Jordan* in the extracted triplet *(Michael Jordan [PER], visit, Carnegie Mellon University [ORG])* to the exact named entity in Freebase or find out that this *Michael Jordan* is a newly discovered named entity (NIL).

Hachey et al. (2013) and Rao et al. (2013) elucidate that most of the literatures (Bunescu and Pasca, 2006; Mihalcea and Csomai, 2007; Cucerzan, 2007; Milne and Witten, 2008; Ratinov et al., 2011) and the entity linking tracks[4] in TAC-KBP (McNamee and Dang, 2009; Ji et al., 2010) concentrate on linking ambiguous entities to the entries in Wikipedia, whereas our ultimate goal is to populate the structured knowledge repository, e.g., Freebase. However, to the best of our knowledge, few works (Zheng et al., 2012) concern about disambiguating named entities using Freebase which contains much more entries but less text information for each entry than Wikipedia.

Overall, Hachey et al. (2013) and Zheng et al. (2012) represent two research directions leveraging Wikipedia and Freebase, respectively. As both of the two collaborative web resources have their respective superiorities, i.e., more context information and more disambiguated entities, we begin to study a new paradigm that could bridge the gap between those two separated repositories and benefit from their respective advantages. From the perspective of supervised learning, entity linking can be naturally regarded as a classification problem. To build a training dataset for disambiguating a set of entities with the same name, we can firstly collect the sentences that mention that name from webpages, such as Wiki pages[5], and then manually annotate each entity mention with its unique machine identifier (MID) in Freebase given the contexts of sentences that it occurs in. However, hand-labeled data is time consuming and usually applicable to some specific classes of entities, such as person (*PER*), location (*LOC*) and organization (*ORG*). Therefore, we look forward to an approach that averts the tedious and laborious work.

Inspired by the idea of weak labeling (Fan et al., 2014; Craven et al., 1999), we contribute a new paradigm called distantly supervised entity linking (DSEL) without manual annotation in this paper. More specifically, we take advantage of a heuristic alignment assumption based on crowd sourcing to connect a certain disambiguated entity in Freebase with its related webpages. In these webpages, feature vectors can be extracted from the sentence-level textual contexts of that entity mention, and be labeled by its corresponding MID in

Figure 1: The disambiguated entities with the same name *Michael Jordan* in Freebase. The entities in Freebase are disambiguated by a unique machine identifier, e.g., the famous basketball player, Michael Jordan labeled by 054c1 (MID).

[1]According to the statistics released on 10th March, 2014 by Google Inc., there are about 1.9 billion Freebase triples and 43 million entities.

[2]The whole dump of Freebase can be downloaded from `https://developers.google.com/freebase/data`

[3]One can access to Freebase and contribute more knowledge.

[4]`http://www.nist.gov/tac/2013/KBP/EntityLinking/index.html`

[5]The Wiki page for the famous basketball player, Michael Jordan, is `http://en.wikipedia.org/wiki/Michael_jordan`.

Figure 2: The topic equivalent webpages of the famous basketball player, *Michael Jordan* in Freebase.

Freebase. Then we can produce a large scale of weakly labeled[6] dataset in this way. Moreover, it is unrealistic to learn a specific classifier for each entity, as there are about 43 million disambiguated entities in Freebase. To tackle with those challenges, we propose a strategy of training a general classifier for disambiguating multiple entities and select a well known classifier, i.e., *liblinear* (Fan et al., 2008) to self-learn the weights among the high-dimensional sparse and noisy features. Experiments are conducted on a dataset of 140,000 items and 60,000 features. DSEL achieves a baseline F1-measure of 0.517. Furthermore, we analyze the performance influenced by other different features, and finally the F1-measure is improved to 0.545.

2 Paradigm

Traditional supervised learning methods for entity disambiguation require tedious labor on manual annotation to build training datasets. Manual annotation costs a lot, and can only cover some specific category, e.g., person names (Christen, 2006) as well. Therefore, we look forward to exploring a paradigm that could automatically generate large scale of open-category training datasets without manual annotation. Based on the dataset, we aim to build a practical classifier and generalize it to disambiguate more unlinked entity mentions in free texts.

Freebase contains 43 million disambiguated entities falling into 76 categories. Each entity is assigned by a unique machine identifer (MID). Those MIDs are the natural labels for the newly identified entity mentions linking to. However, there are inadequate free texts *locally* for extracting features, as Freebase is a well-structured knowledge repository with billions of triples. Therefore, we resort to other free-text corpus that could be *distantly supervised* by Freebase and the key challenge is to find the bridge of supervision.

Fortunately, every entity in Freebase maintains a list of links to its topic equivalent webpages via crowd sourcing (Howe, 2006) as shown in Figure 2. These links will guide us to find the description webpages for that entity. Even though those links involves in different languages, we only choose the English Wiki pages to conduct experiments. Overall, we jointly exploit Freebase and Wikipedia to automatically construct the data for training a classifier.

3 Feature

For each entity in Freebase, we find its topic-equivalent Wiki page and extract the contextual features of its mention at sentence level.

Generally, we simultaneously choose K ($K = 1, 2, 3$) open-class words (Van Petten and Kutas, 1991), namely nouns, verbs, adjectives and adverbs, in front and behind the given entity mention. If we ignore the sequence of these words, we can gain the bag-of-words feature, whereas the word sequence feature. Furthermore, we use Stanford NLP core[7] and add the part-of-speech tagging feature which may help disambiguate those contextual words. Therefore, for each K size window surrounding the entity mention, we could extract four kinds of different features, i.e., bag of words (BOW), word sequence (WS), bag of words plus part-of-speech tagging (BOW + POS) and word sequence plus part-of-speech tagging (WS + POS). In total, there are twelve kinds of lexical features.

To elucidate the various kinds of contextual features, we randomly pick up a sentence from the Wiki page of the famous basketball player as example, i.e.,

His biography on the National Basketball Association (NBA) website states, "By acclamation, **Michael Jordan** *is the greatest basketball player of all time."*

The twelve kinds of lexical features for the sentence above are listed in Table 1. We will compare the performance among these features in Section 5.

[6]Auto-labeling via crowd sourcing may naturally bring about noise. Therefore, we regard the dataset weakly labeled.

[7]`http://nlp.stanford.edu/software/corenlp.shtml`

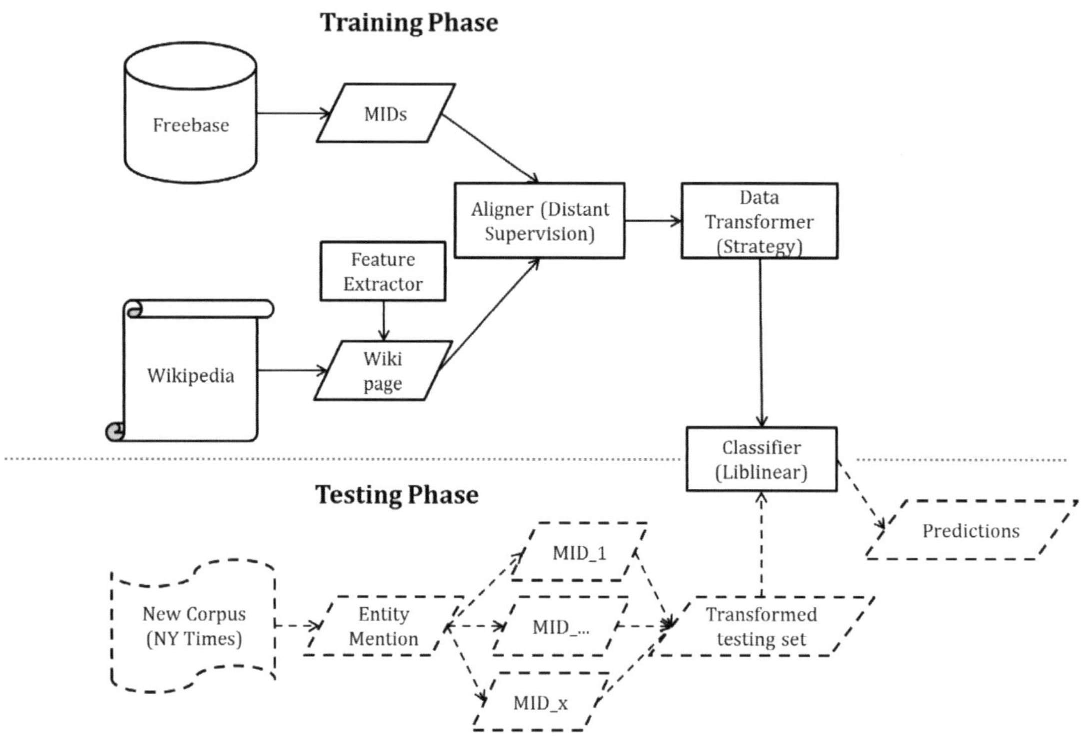

Figure 3: The architecture of DSEL system.

Sentence	*His biography on the National Basketball Association (NBA) website states, "By acclamation,* **Michael Jordan** *is the greatest basketball player of all time."*
BOW ($K = 1$) **BOW** ($K = 2$) **BOW** ($K = 3$)	<{acclamation}, {is}> <{states}, {acclamation}, {is}, {greatest}> <{website}, {states}, {acclamation}, {is}, {greatest}, {basketball}>
WS ($K = 1$) **WS** ($K = 2$) **WS** ($K = 3$)	<{acclamation}, {is}> <{states-acclamation}, {is-greatest}> <{website-states-acclamation},{is-greatest-basketball}>
BOW + POS ($K = 1$) **BOW + POS** ($K = 2$) **BOW + POS** ($K = 3$)	<{acclamation/NN}, {is/VBZ}> <{states/NNS}, {acclamation/NN}, {is/VBZ} {greatest/JJS}> <{website/NN}, {states/NNS}, {acclamation/NN}, {is/VBZ}, {greatest/JJS}, {basketball/NN}>
WS + POS ($K = 1$) **WS + POS** ($K = 2$) **WS + POS** ($K = 3$)	<{acclamation/NN}, {is/VBZ}> <{states/NNS-acclamation/NN}, {is/VBZ-greatest/JJS}> <{website/NN-states/NNS-acclamation/NN},{is/VBZ-greatest/JJS-basketball/NN}>

Table 1: Twelve kinds of lexical features for the given sentence. A pair of angle brackets stands for a feature vector, e.g., <{*states*}, {*acclamation*}, {*is*} {*greatest*}>. A feature item is marked by a pair of braces, e.g., {*states-acclamation*}.

# of MIDs with the same name	# of names	# of MIDs with the same name	# of names	# of MIDs with the same name	# of names
2	4,467,216	**5**	180,489	**8**	60,273
3	740,530	**6**	134,012	**9**	41,256
4	440,261	**7**	76,459	**10**	33,628

Table 2: The distribution of ambiguous entities in Freebase.

4 Implementation

As we have already automatically produced a training dataset based on the proposed distant supervision paradigm, an intuitive idea is to feed a specific classifier for each ambiguous name with its unambiguous MIDs and the corresponding feature vectors. However, Table 2 shows that there are at least 5.5 million names that denominate more than one entity (MID) in Freebase. Therefore, it is infeasible to build 5.5 million specific classifiers. To train a general classifier that does not restrict itself to disambiguating a certain name, we adopt a strategy that merges those specific classifiers. Concretely, we transform MIDs, the original labels into features and use 1/0 to indicate whether the contextual features from Wiki pages and MIDs in Freebase match or not with each other. If we choose the BOW ($K = 3$) feature in Table 1 for instance, one positive training sample will contain a new feature vector ($<${website}, {states}, {acclamation}, {is}, {greatest}, {basketball}, {MID:054c1}$>$) labeled by 1. To balance the training dataset, we randomly pick up features from other entities uniformly named to generate negative samples. For example, another well-known *Michael Jordan* (MID:0bby3vs) is an English mycologist. We can extract a BOW ($K = 3$) feature vector, i.e., $<${is}, {English}, {mycologist}$>$, and it concatenates {MID:054c1} to construct a negative sample labeled by 0.

The distant supervision paradigm and the strategy of building the training set for a general classifier lead to high-dimensional noisy and sparse features. Moreover, given the millions of training samples produced by aligning Freebase and Wikipedia, we choose a linear classifier that is based on logistic regression approach, i.e., Liblinear (Fan et al., 2008), to rapidly self-learn the weights among the high-dimensional sparse and noisy features.

For a newly discovered entity mention in the testing corpus, we firstly extract its contextual feature, e.g., bag of words as above. Then the feature concatenates all the candidate MIDs that share the same name with that entity mention. Each testing sample within the same name collection will predict a score indicating the strength of linking. For each collection, the Top-N predictions with higher probabilities are selected for evaluation.

We summarize the procedures of implementing our proposed paradigm and use Figure 3 to demonstrate the architecture of DSEL system.

5 Experiments

In this section ,we report the experimental results following the procedures described in Section 4. To evaluate the performance of different features, we adopt three widely used metrics (Meij et al., 2013), namely precision, recall and F1-measure.

5.1 Dataset

We randomly select 20,000 ambiguous names (collections) in Freebase. About 82,000 sentences that contain at least one entity mention are extracted from the topic-equivalent Wiki pages. For each collection, 80% sentences are randomly picked up for constructing the training set and 20% remains are for held-out evaluation. Following the procedures of building training samples described in Section 4, we gain a dataset including around 140,000 items and 60,000 features.

5.2 Evaluation metrics

Precision and recall are widely used metrics to evaluate different rank-based approaches on entity linking. F1-measure synthetically measures precision and recall by calculating the harmonic mean of them. Suppose that C denotes the whole collection set for testing. $C_{i,j}$ represents the set of Top-j predictions with higher probabilities in the i-th collection. G_i stands for the set of gold standards of the i-th collection. $\#(S)$ is the function that counts the entries in set S. Then the formulae to calculate precision, recall and F1-measure are as follows,

Feature type	Avg. F1-measure	Feature type	Avg. F1-measure
BOW ($K = 1$)	**0.539**	**WS** ($K = 1$)	**0.544**
BOW ($K = 2$)	0.531	**WS** ($K = 2$)	0.532
BOW ($K = 3$)	0.529	**WS** ($K = 3$)	0.518
BOW + POS ($K = 1$)	**0.540**	**WS + POS** ($K = 1$)	**0.545**
BOW + POS ($K = 2$)	0.532	**WS + POS** ($K = 2$)	0.531
BOW + POS ($K = 3$)	0.529	**WS + POS** ($K = 3$)	0.517

Table 3: The F1-measure comparison among different features.

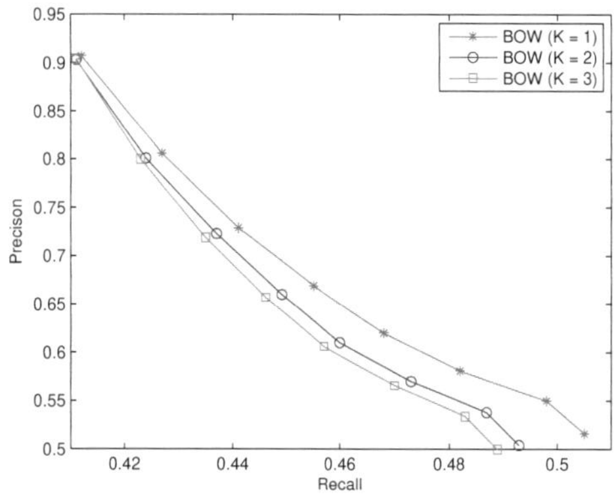

(a) Precision-Recall curves for BOW features.

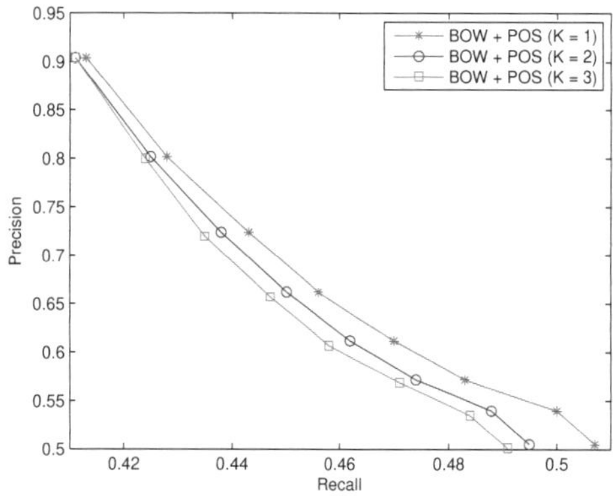

(b) Precision-Recall curves for BOW + POS features.

Figure 4: Precision-Recall curves for the BOW-class lexical features.

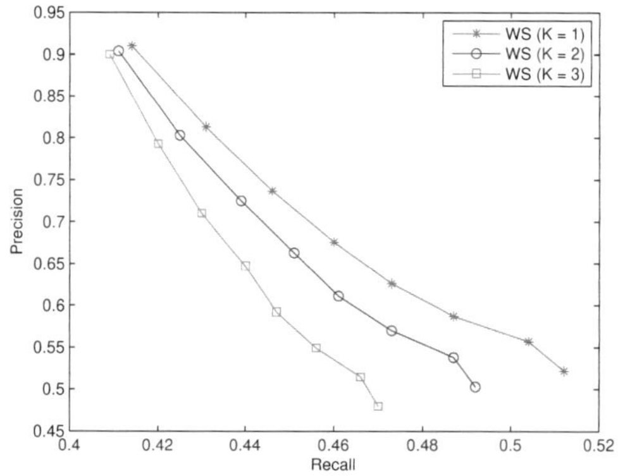

(a) Precision-Recall curves for WS features.

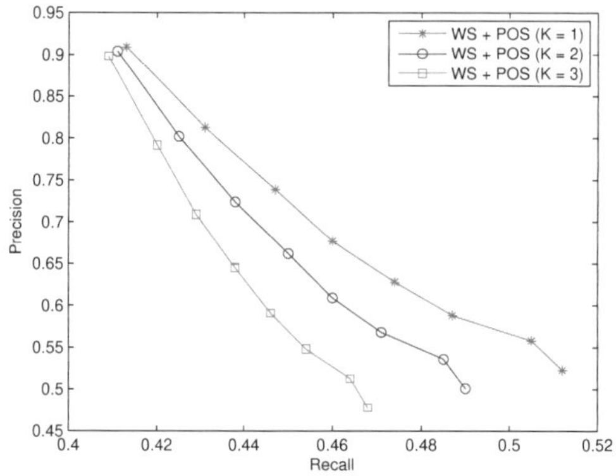

(b) Precision-Recall curves for WS + POS features.

Figure 5: Precision-Recall curves for the WS-class lexical features.

$$\text{Precision} = \sum_i \sum_j \frac{\#(C_{i,j} \bigwedge G_i)}{\#(C_{i,j})},$$

$$\text{Recall} = \sum_i \sum_j \frac{\#(C_{i,j} \bigwedge G_i)}{\#(C)},$$

$$\text{F1-measure} = \frac{2 \times Precision \times Recall}{Precision + Recall}.$$

5.3 Feature comparison

For each type of feature, we conduct one trial and tune the parameters for the logistic classifier using 5-fold cross validation. Then we adopt held-out testing taking advantage of the 20% sentences left.

Figure 4 and Figure 5 show the precision-recall curves for the twelve lexical features, and Table 3 displays the average F1-measure comparison among different features. We find out that the WS-class features generally outperform the BOW-class features, and the short-distance contextual features ($K = 1$) are more effective than the long-distance ones ($K = 2, 3$).

6 Conclusion and Future Work

As far as we know, it is the first attempt to deal with the task of entity linking based on the idea of distant supervision. We leverage a heuristic alignment assumption, i.e., the topic equivalent pages, to bridge the gap between Freebase and Wikipedia and jointly use those two knowledge bases to automatically produce training data without manual annotation. Moreover, we propose a strategy that transforms labels into features and feed them to a general classifier, rather than building an individualized classifier for each ambiguous name for millions of entities.

For the future work, we believe that this new paradigm leaves several open questions:

- Besides the entities (MIDs) that have already been stored in knowledge repositories (Freebase), new entity instances (NIL) with the same name need to be discovered. Therefore, further study could focus on extending paradigm to identify unknown entities.
- The link for many other webpages in different languages are also provided in Freebase, as illustrated in Figure 2. It may facilitate the research of cross-lingual entity linking.
- The alignment assumption is simple and heuristic. Further studies may dedicate on discovering other reasonable alignment principles.
- Even though the strategy for generating training data that fits a general classifier, it rises the problem that high-dimensional sparse and noisy features impact the effectiveness and efficiency of the proposed paradigm.

Generally speaking, the experiments prove that our new proposed paradigm is promising and it is worthy of being further studied.

Acknowledgements

This work is mainly supported by National Program on Key Basic Research Project (973 Program) under Grant 2013CB329304, National Science Foundation of China (NSFC) under Grant No.61433018 and No.61373075, and China Scholarship Council. Thanks to Yulong Gu, Yingnan Xiao and anonymous reviewers for their insightful comments.

References

Nguyen Bach and Sameer Badaskar. 2007. A review of relation extraction. *Literature review for Language and Statistics II.*

Kurt Bollacker, Robert Cook, and Patrick Tufts. 2007. Freebase: A shared database of structured general human knowledge. In *Proceedings of the national conference on Artificial Intelligence*, volume 22, page 1962. Menlo Park, CA; Cambridge, MA; London; AAAI Press; MIT Press; 1999.

Kurt Bollacker, Colin Evans, Praveen Paritosh, Tim Sturge, and Jamie Taylor. 2008. Freebase: a collaboratively created graph database for structuring human knowledge. In *Proceedings of the 2008 ACM SIGMOD international conference on Management of data*, pages 1247–1250. ACM.

Razvan C Bunescu and Marius Pasca. 2006. Using encyclopedic knowledge for named entity disambiguation. In *EACL*, volume 6, pages 9–16.

Peter Christen. 2006. A comparison of personal name matching: Techniques and practical issues. In *Data Mining Workshops, 2006. ICDM Workshops 2006. Sixth IEEE International Conference on*, pages 290–294. IEEE.

Mark Craven, Johan Kumlien, et al. 1999. Constructing biological knowledge bases by extracting information from text sources. In *ISMB*, volume 1999, pages 77–86.

Silviu Cucerzan. 2007. Large-scale named entity disambiguation based on wikipedia data. In *EMNLP-CoNLL*, volume 7, pages 708–716.

Rong-En Fan, Kai-Wei Chang, Cho-Jui Hsieh, Xiang-Rui Wang, and Chih-Jen Lin. 2008. Liblinear: A library for large linear classification. *The Journal of Machine Learning Research*, 9:1871–1874.

Miao Fan, Deli Zhao, Qiang Zhou, Zhiyuan Liu, Thomas Fang Zheng, and Edward Y Chang. 2014. Distant supervision for relation extraction with matrix completion. In *Proceedings of the 52nd Annual Meeting of the Association for Computational Linguistics*, volume 1, pages 839–849.

Ben Hachey, Will Radford, Joel Nothman, Matthew Honnibal, and James R Curran. 2013. Evaluating entity linking with wikipedia. *Artificial intelligence*, 194:130–150.

Jeff Howe. 2006. The rise of crowdsourcing. *Wired magazine*, 14(6):1–4.

Heng Ji and Ralph Grishman. 2011. Knowledge base population: Successful approaches and challenges. In *Proceedings of the 49th Annual Meeting of the Association for Computational Linguistics: Human Language Technologies-Volume 1*, pages 1148–1158. Association for Computational Linguistics.

Heng Ji, Ralph Grishman, Hoa Trang Dang, Kira Griffitt, and Joe Ellis. 2010. Overview of the tac 2010 knowledge base population track. In *Third Text Analysis Conference (TAC 2010)*.

Paul McNamee and Hoa Trang Dang. 2009. Overview of the tac 2009 knowledge base population track. In *Text Analysis Conference (TAC)*, volume 17, pages 111–113.

Edgar Meij, Krisztian Balog, and Daan Odijk. 2013. Entity linking and retrieval. In *Proceedings of the 36th international ACM SIGIR conference on Research and development in information retrieval*, pages 1127–1127. ACM.

Rada Mihalcea and Andras Csomai. 2007. Wikify!: linking documents to encyclopedic knowledge. In *Proceedings of the sixteenth ACM conference on Conference on information and knowledge management*, pages 233–242. ACM.

David Milne and Ian H Witten. 2008. Learning to link with wikipedia. In *Proceedings of the 17th ACM conference on Information and knowledge management*, pages 509–518. ACM.

David Nadeau and Satoshi Sekine. 2007. A survey of named entity recognition and classification. *Lingvisticae Investigationes*, 30(1):3–26.

Vincent Ng. 2010. Supervised noun phrase coreference research: The first fifteen years. In *Proceedings of the 48th annual meeting of the association for computational linguistics*, pages 1396–1411. Association for Computational Linguistics.

Delip Rao, Paul McNamee, and Mark Dredze. 2013. Entity linking: Finding extracted entities in a knowledge base. In *Multi-source, multilingual information extraction and summarization*, pages 93–115. Springer.

Lev Ratinov, Dan Roth, Doug Downey, and Mike Anderson. 2011. Local and global algorithms for disambiguation to wikipedia. In *Proceedings of the 49th Annual Meeting of the Association for Computational Linguistics: Human Language Technologies-Volume 1*, pages 1375–1384. Association for Computational Linguistics.

Sunita Sarawagi. 2008. Information extraction. *Foundations and trends in databases*, 1(3):261–377.

Cyma Van Petten and Marta Kutas. 1991. Influences of semantic and syntactic context on open- and closed-class words. *Memory & Cognition*, 19(1):95–112.

Zhicheng Zheng, Xiance Si, Fangtao Li, Edward Y Chang, and Xiaoyan Zhu. 2012. Entity disambiguation with freebase. In *Proceedings of the The 2012 IEEE/WIC/ACM International Joint Conferences on Web Intelligence and Intelligent Agent Technology-Volume 01*, pages 82–89. IEEE Computer Society.

Toward Algorithmic Discovery of Biographical Information in Local Gazetteers of Ancient China

Chao-Lin Liu[†] **Chih-Kai Huang**[§] **Hongsu Wang**[‡] **Peter K. Bol**[!]

[†§]Department of Computer Science, National Chengchi University, Taiwan
[‡!]Institute for Quantitative Social Science, Harvard University, USA
[†]Graduate Institute of Linguistics, National Chengchi University, Taiwan
{[†]chaolin,[§]102753029}@nccu.edu.tw, {[‡]hongsuwang, [!]pkbol}@fas.harvard.edu

Abstract[1]

Difangzhi (地方志) is a large collection of local gazetteers complied by local governments of China, and the documents provide invaluable information about the host locality. This paper reports the current status of using natural language processing and text mining methods to identify biographical information of government officers so that we can add the information into the China Biographical Database (CBDB), which is hosted by Harvard University. Information offered by CBDB is instrumental for human historians, and serves as a core foundation for automatic tagging systems, like MARKUS of the Leiden University. Mining texts in *Difangzhi* is not easy partially because there is litter knowledge about the grammars of literary Chinese so far. We employed techniques of language modeling and conditional random fields to find person and location names and their relationships. The methods were evaluated with realistic *Difangzhi* data of more than 2 million Chinese characters written in literary Chinese. Experimental results indicate that useful information was discovered from the current dataset.

1 Introduction

Person and location names are two crucial ingredients for studying historical documents. Knowing the participants and locations provides a solid foundation for detecting and reasoning about the developments of historical events. Detecting temporal markers is also very important for historical studies, yet, for Chinese history, it is relatively easier to spot the temporal markers because the names of the dynasties and reign periods (年號, nian2 hao4) are known and stable.

We apply techniques of natural language processing and machine learning to find person names, location names, and their relationships in *Difangzhi* (**地方志, DFZ** henceforth) in the present work, aiming to enrich the contents of the China Biographical Database (Bol, 2012). DFZ is a general name for a large number of local gazetteers that were compiled by local governments of different levels in China since as early as the 6th century AD (cf. Hargett, 1996). DFZ contain a wide range of information about their host locations, and the biographical information about the government officers is our current focus.

The main barrier for achieving our goals is that there is little completed work in the literature about the grammars for literary Chinese, while grammars are central for extracting named entities like person and location names from texts with computational methods (Gao et al., 2005; Nadeau and Sekine, 2007).

Figure 1 shows the image of a sample DFZ page. In the old days, Chinese texts were written from top to bottom and from right to left on a page. Most linguists know that there are no word boundaries in modern Chinese. It might be quite surprising for researchers outside of the Chinese community that there were even no punctuations in literary Chinese. Without clear delimiters between words and sentences, it is very challenging even for people to read literary Chinese, so it takes a serious research to find ways not just for segmenting words but also for splitting sentences in literary Chinese (Huang et al., 2010).

Grammar induction (de la Higuera, 2005) is a general name for enabling computers to learn the grammars of natural languages. Some researchers worked on the grammars for selected sources of Chinese. Huang et al. (2001) ex-

[1] An extended version of this paper appears in the proceedings of the Third Big Humanities Data Workshop in the 2015 IEEE Int'l Conf. on Big Data (Liu et al., 2015). The main contents of this paper and the workshop paper are the same, while the workshop paper is an extended version.

29th Pacific Asia Conference on Language, Information and Computation pages 87 - 95
Shanghai, China, October 30 - November 1, 2015

Figure 1. A page of DFZ

plored the induction problem with about a thousand sentences that were extracted from Hanfeizi (韓非子) and Xunzi (荀子), both of which are classics that are more than two thousand years old. Kuo (2009) tried to find phrase-structure rules for modern Chinese texts, and Lee and Kong (2012) built treebanks for Tang poems. Although these researchers worked on grammars for Chinese texts, they encountered Chinese patterns that are quite different from the ones that we need to handle in DFZ.

Previous works for inducing grammars of literary Chinese employed some forms of pre-existing information to begin the induction procedures. Given that literary Chinese texts consisted of just long sequences of characters, the needs for external information for grammar induction should be expected. Hwa (1999) assumed that the training corpus was partially annotated with high-level syntactic labels. Lü et al. (2002) started with bilingual corpora. Yu et al. (2010) embarked with a sample treebank, and Boonkwan and Steedman (2011) began with some syntactic prototypes.

We tackle the NER tasks in literary Chinese from two unexplored perspectives. First, we employ the biographical information in the China Biographical Database (**CBDB**, henceforth) to annotate the DFZ texts, learn language models (**LMs**, henceforth) from the annotated texts, and extract biographical information based on the learned models. Alternatively, we train conditional-random-field (Sutton and McCallum, 2011) models with a set of labeled DFZ data that were achieved in (Bol et al., 2012; Pang et al., 2014), and use the conditional-random-field (**CRF**, henceforth) models to extract candidate names from the test data, which is another set of DFZ texts. We have verified the findings of the LM-based and the CRF-based methods. Both show very good results for NER in DFZ.

We present the sources of our data, define our target problems, and discuss the motivation for our work in Section 2. We then provide details about our main approaches in two long sections. In Sections 3 and 4, we look into details about the LM-based and CRF-based methods, respectively, including the designs of the classification models and results of several evaluation tasks. In Section 5, we wrap up this paper with a brief summary and discussions about some technical issues.

2 Data Sources, Problem Definitions, and Motivation

We provide information about the sources of our data, define the problems that we wish to solve, and explain the rationality of our approaches in this section.

2.1 Unlabeled Data

Currently, we have two sets of DFZ text files. The unlabeled part has more than 900 thousand of characters that were extracted from 83 volumes of local gazetteers (Bol et al., 2015). The labeled part will be presented in Section 2.4.

These 83 volumes were compiled between the middle of the Ming dynasty (1368-1644AD) and the early Min-Guo period (since 1912AD). These books were produced by governments of different levels at 65 locations in China.

Figure 1 shows a sample page from this collection. It is hard to count the number of columns on this page. Typically, we consider that a column, in this case, consists of two thinner columns. A person name is emphasized by occupying the width of a column, and details about this person are recorded in the thin columns. Therefore, we would say that the leftmost three columns of text in Figure 1 would read like the passage shown in Figure 2.

The DFZ texts may contain characters that are not or seldom used in modern Chinese. If these characters have modern counterparts, they will be substituted by their modern replacements; otherwise, spaces will take their positions. As an example for the former case, the eleventh character on the second column from the right in

不知勞洪武元年楊璟取廣西吉尼堅壁不下城破
執送京師不屈死郡人感其德立廟祀之陳瑜字仲
庸雷州人廣西中書省都事城破以佩刀自刎有劉
永錫者潭州人與瑜同事率妻子溺於白龍池死焉
曾尚賓江西人為義兵千户洪武元年明兵圍靜江
尚賓守西城城陷身中數鎗知不敵

Figure 2. A partial DFZ passage from Figure 1

Figure 1 is "裏" (li3), which may be written as "裡" (li3) in our files. When the latter cases occur, understanding the original DFZ records will become even more challenging.

2.2 Problem Definitions

We wish to build a system that can extract biographical information from DFZ to enrich the contents of CBDB. The current contents of CBDB were extracted from sources other than DFZ (Pang et al., 2014). Hence, we are interested in spotting all types biographical information in DFZ.

In this paper, we focus on issues about finding person names and location names, and extend to some relevant topics, such as checking whether the locations were native places. In the longer run, we will expand our attention to find information about social networks and personal careers as well.

2.3 More on Motivation

For a text passage as illustrated in Figure 2, it is very challenging for people to find useful information without assistive information, even for modern generations of native speakers of Chinese. In the text file, it is not easy to find the name "陳瑜" (chen2 yu2) that was written in larger characters in the original DFZ.

The grammars of literary and modern Chinese are not exactly the same, and reading literary Chinese is a lot harder than reading modern Chinese, especially when there are no boundary markers between sentences. In addition, historical knowledge is also required for correct word segmentation and lexical disambiguation, which are important for understanding and extracting desired information from the texts.

To achieve our goals, we need some informative sources for the work of information extraction. The importance of these informative sources for our methods for extracting information is just like that of the machine-readable dictionaries for the methods for handling modern natural languages.

Our approaches are innovative because we utilize the biographical information in CBDB to provide semantic information about the DFZ texts. In contrast, the literature that we reviewed in Section 1 carried out grammar induction with such linguistic knowledge as part-of-speech tags and syntactic structures.

2.4 Labeled Data

We have a set of labeled DFZ data. This set of data was collected from 143 volumes of DFZ, which contained more than 1498 thousand of characters.

The DFZ texts were labeled with regular expressions (**REs**, henceforth) that were compiled by domain experts (Bol et al., 2012; Pang et al. 2014), and the REs were designed to extract biographical information. The labeled data were then saved as records in a large table with 113,784 records in total.

Each record has many fields, and the fields were designed to contain a wide variety of factoids about the individuals. Major fields contain information about an individual's legal name, style name (字, zi4), pen name (號, hao4), dynasty, native place (籍貫, ji2 guan4), serving office (官職, guan1 zhi2), entry method (入仕方法, ru4 shi4 fang1 fa3), service time, service location, and reign period (年號, nian2 hao4).

Due to the nature of the original DFZ data and the limited expressiveness of REs, a non-negligible portion of the fields do not have values (i.e., have missing values), and, sometimes, the values are not correct. Nevertheless, these labeled data remain to be valuable and prove to be useful from the perspectives of historical studies (Pang et al., 2014) and of building machine-learning models.

3 Language-Model-based Approach

We annotate the DFZ with the biographical information available in CBDB, and find the frequent and *consistent* n-grams for locating candidate strings from which we may extract legal names and style names.

3.1 Labeling and Disambiguation

Figure 3 lists the steps of our main procedure, **Constrained N-Grams** (**CNGRAM**), for NER. First, we label the text with information in CBDB. Five types of labels are in use now: **name** for a legal or a style name, **address** for locations, **entry** for entry methods, **office** for

Procedure CNGRAM (txt, idbs, cc)
txt: DFZ texts
idbs: information databases
cc: chosen conditions for checking consistency
Steps
1. Label the text based on the given ***idbs***. Prefer the labels that cover longer strings, all else being equal.
2. For contexts of chosen conditions, ***cc***, remove the inconsistent labels.
3. Find the frequent consistent *n*-gram patterns, and use them as filter patterns
4. Try to extract named entities from strings that conform to the filter patterns

Figure 3. The CNGRAM procedure

service office, and **nianhao** for reign periods.

In reality, some strings may be labeled in more than one ways. For instance, "陽朔" (yang1 shuo4) can be a reign period of the Han dynasty or a location name, and "王臣" (wang2 chen2) is a very popular person name that was used in many dynasties. Before we try to disambiguate the labeling, we will keep all possible labels for a string.

We will use the following short excerpt of Figure 2 to explain the execution of CNGRAM.

T1: 陳瑜字仲庸雷州人廣西中書省都事

Identifying T1 from its context is possible because this string begins and ends with words that have corresponding labels. We will find out that there was a person named "陳瑜" (chen2 yu2) in Yuan, Ming, and Qing dynasties and that both "雷州" (lei2 zhou1) and "廣西" (guang3 xi1) were addresses.

At the first step of CNGRAM, we prefer longer matches for the same type of labels, as a heuristic principle for disambiguation. The principle of preferring longer words is very common for Chinese word segmentation. In T1, both "中書省都事" (zhong1 shu1 sheng3 dou1 shi4) and "中書省" can be labeled as office names in the Yuan dynasty, but we would choose the former because "中書省都事" is a longer string. In contrast, we do not have "中書省都事" for the Ming dynasty, so will use "中書" and "都事" for Ming.

We also assume that named entities in a passage should be ***consistent*** in some senses, as another heuristic principle for disambiguation. This consistent principle should be reminiscent of the "**one sense per discourse**" principle for word sense disambiguation (Yarowsky, 1995).

Currently, we presume that named entities in a context of six labels should be referring to something of the same dynasty, where six is an arbitrary choice and can be varied. We have not used addresses to check consistency because we are still expanding our list of addresses. Therefore, we do not accept a "陳瑜" of the Qing dynasty because neither "中書省都事" nor "中書" is an entity in Qing. Using the consistent principle, we will keep labels only for the Song and Ming dynasties for the sample passage, thereby achieving some disambiguation effects.

Hence, we have two consistent sequences: [name("陳瑜", Yuan), address("雷州"), address ("廣西"), office("中書省都事", Yuan)] and [name("陳瑜", Ming), address("雷州"), address("廣西"), office("中書", Ming), office("都事", Ming)].

3.2 Extracting Unknown Style Names

Aiming at extracting person and style names for government officers, we focus on the consistent sequences that have at least one **name** label. We then identify and prefer strings that are associated with more different labels. We show four such ***filter patterns*** below.

P1: name-address-nianhao-entry
P2: name-address-entry-nianhao
P3: name-name-address-address
P4: name-address-address-office

These patterns shed light on how person names were presented in DFZ texts. We can now examine the DFZ strings that are labeled with these patterns to judge whether these patterns indeed carry useful information. Usually, we find regularities in these statements, and can implement specific programs for extracting target information from such patterns.

Our running example, T1, contains the P4 pattern in two different ways, and we list the substrings.

T2: 陳瑜字仲庸雷州人廣西中書
T3: 陳瑜字仲庸雷州人廣西中書省都事

In both T2 and T3, we see that a key signal "字" (zi4), which is a typical prefix for style names, follows a **name** label. "字" is followed by two unlabeled characters which are then followed by an **address**, an unlabeled character, another **address**, and an **office**. Thus, T2 and T3 are examples of pattern P5, where <name> and <address> represent labeled strings and Z1 and Z2 are two unlabeled characters.

P5: <name> 字 Z1 Z2 <address>

The unlabeled characters, Z1 and Z2, can be extracted as style names because practical statistics indicate that over 98% of style names contain exactly two characters. Therefore, we embody this finding with actions in our programs.

The third step in CNGRAM is thus an interactive step[2], and requires human participation. Notice that the work for domain experts is quite minimal and that the results are worthwhile. A human expert does not have to read 83 books to find the candidate patterns. Using CNGRAM to locate string patterns that contain useful information, we are able process a large amount of data both efficiently and effectively.

With the extracted style name "仲庸" (zhong4 yong1), we can create two records, i.e., (Yuan, 陳瑜, 仲庸) and (Ming, 陳瑜, 仲庸). "仲庸" is unknown to CBDB, and can be added to CBDB with the approval of domain experts.

The CNGRAM procedure actually helps us learn the language models that were used in DFZ. By inspecting frequent and consistent patterns that actually contain biographical information, we can gather more knowledge about grammar rules in DFZ and then implement NER procedures based on the observations.

3.3 Empirical Evaluations

We compared the extracted records with the records in CBDB (2014 version) to evaluate the CNGRAM procedure, and show the results in Table 1, where the circles and crosses, respectively, indicate matches and mismatches between the extracted and CBDB records.

The matching results are categorized into types, e.g., type 1 is the group that we had perfect matches in dynasty, legal name, and style name. We have 609 such instances in the current experiment, and the proportion of type-1 instances is 28.3% of the 2152 extracted records.

The two records that we obtained in the previous subsection belong to type 2, because "仲庸" is not known to CBDB. All extracted records of type 2 provide opportunities of finding unknown style names for CBDB. However, they should be confirmed by historians. The experts may check the original texts for this approval procedure, which is an operation facilitated by our software platform.

Table 1. Analysis of 2152 extracted records

Type	Dynasty	Name	Style N.	Quan.	Prop.
1	○	○	○	609	28.30%
2	○	○	×	665	30.90%
3	×	○	○	117	5.44%
4	○	×	○	262	12.17%
5	×	○	×	220	10.22%
6	×	×	○	45	2.09%
7	○/×	×	×	234	10.87%

Records of types 3 and 4 are similar to records of type 2. They offer opportunities of adding extra information to CBDB. Records of types 5, 6, and 7 provide some opportunities for adding information about new persons in CBDB. After inspecting the original text segments, we will be able to tell whether these mismatches are new discoveries or just incorrect extractions.

3.4 Further Extensions

We are more ambitious than verifying whether CNGRAM can help us find correct biographical information. Type-1 records can be instrumental for advanced applications. They help us find the beginnings of the descriptions that contain information about the owners of type-1 records.

If we can determine the beginnings of two consecutive segments, then we can find persons who have relationships. T1 is the beginning of a major segment in Figure 1. The string "也兒吉尼字尚文唐兀氏人" is the beginning of a segment for a person named "也兒吉尼" (ye3 er2 ji2 ni2). The person mentioned between "也兒吉尼字尚文唐兀氏" and T1, e.g., "楊璟" (yang2 jing3), should have some relationships with "也兒吉尼".

In addition, it is quite intriguing to apply pattern P5, in Section 3.2, in an extreme way. Figure 4 shows the raw data for the text in Figure 2. If we compare Figure 4 and the image in Figure 1 carefully, we can find that the circles were added to signify (1) changes between major columns and thin columns or (2) changes of lines. The semantics of the circles are ambiguous, but they are potentially useful.

If "字" is really a strong indicator that connects legal names and style names, P6 and P7 may lead us to find pairs of legal and style names. Here, we use C1, C2, and C3 to denote Chinese characters.

P6: ○ C1 C2 C3 字 Z1 Z2

P7: ○ C1 C2 字 Z1 Z2

[2] Using computers to select the patterns is possible if we are willingly to set a frequency threshold to determine "frequent" patterns, which may not be a perfect choice for historical studies.

〇不知勞洪武元年楊璟取廣西吉尼堅壁不下〇
城破執送京師不屈死郡人感其德立廟祀之〇陳
瑜〇字仲庸雷州人廣西中書省都事城破以佩刀
自刎〇有劉永錫者潭州人與瑜同事率妻子溺於
白龍池〇死〇焉〇曾尚賓〇江西人為義兵千户
洪武元年明兵圍靜〇江尚賓守西城城陷身中數
鎗知不敵自〇

Figure 4. A partial DFZ passage with circles

When we find substrings that conform to P6 or P7 in the raw data, we may want to check whether C1-C2-C3 (or C1-C2) is a legal name, Z1-Z2 is a style name, and their combination is for a real person.

We evaluated this heuristic approach with the unlabeled data of Section 2.1, and found 3765 pairs of (legal_name, style_name). We checked these pairs with CBDB (2014 version), and achieved Table 2. Note that strings conforming to P6 and P7 have very short contexts, so we could not judge the dynasties of these names, so Table 2 is simpler than Table 1.

Table 2 shows that 31% of the pairs have corresponding records in CBDB. Although we cannot guarantee the correctness of these matched records, the statistics are promising and encouraging. 1192 type-1 records matched the legal and style names of certain CBDB records. This amount is more than the number of type-1 records in Table 1. Some of the pairs that we identify with the current heuristic did not appear in filter patterns that we discussed in Section 3.2, suggesting that a hybrid approach might be worthy of trying in the future.

4 CRF-based Approach

CRF-based models (Sutton and McCallum, 2011) are very common for handling NER with machine learning methods (Nadeau and Sekine, 2007). We employed MALLET (McCallum, 2002) tools for building linear-chain CRF models, and trained and tested our models with the labeled data that we discussed in Section 2.4.

4.1 Features

Given the training data (cf. Section 2.4) and the biographical information in CBDB, we can create a feature set for each Chinese character in DFZ for training and testing a CRF model. We consider four types of features: original characters, relative positions of named entities in CBDB, whether the character was used in person or location names in DFZ, and whether the characters belong to a named entity.

Table 2. Analysis of 3765 extracted records

Type	Name	Style Name	Quan.	Prop.
1	○	○	1192	31.66%
2	○	×	885	23.51%
3	×	○	1104	29.32%
4	×	×	584	15.51%

We explain our features listed in Table 3, using T3, in Section 3.2, as a running example.

The original Chinese characters are basic features, summarized in groups 1 and 2 in Table 3. For the position of "州" (zhou1), "州" is an obvious feature for itself. The surrounding *k* characters can be included in the feature set as well. If we set *k* to three, the three characters before and after "州", i.e., "仲" (zhong4), "庸" (yong1), "雷" (lei2), "人" (ren2), "廣" (guang3), and "西"(si1), are included in the feature set.

Relative positions of the closest named entities (NEs) are summarized in group 3 in Table 3. We consider four types of NEs: office names, entry methods, reign periods, and time markers, and will record NEs on both sides of the current position. The first three types are just like the office, entry, and nianhao labels that we discussed in Section 3.1. The time markers refer to a special way of counting years in China, i.e., Chinese sexagenary cycle (干支, gan1 zhi1), and names of months when they were used. We consider NEs that are within 30 characters on either side of the current position, so a position can have up to eight features of group 3.

In T3, there are three characters between "州" and "中書省都事", so **officeRight@3** would be used as a feature for "州". The label name consists of three parts: the type of NEs, the direction respective to the current position (i.e., Right or Left), and the number of characters between the current position and the NE.

Group 4 is about the usage of the current position. It would be helpful to know the probability of the current character being used in a person name or in a location name. Equation (1) shows the basic formula.

$$\Pr(x \text{ in person names}) = \frac{freq(x \text{ in person names})}{freq(x \text{ in } DFZ)} \quad (1)$$

In T3, "雷" is used as a character in a location name. We calculated the frequency of "雷" being used in location names, and divided this frequency by the total frequency of "雷" in DFZ. We discretized the probability measure into five equal ranges: [0, 0.2), [0.2, 0.4), [0.4, 0.6), [0.6,

Table 3. Features for CRF models

Group	Types	Description
1	Chinese characters	self
2	Chinese characters	surrounding *k* characters
3	relative positions of selected named entities	office, entry, reign period, and time
4	usage	used in person or location name
5	usage	family name?
6	named entities	office, entry, reign period, and time

0.8), and [0.8, 1.0]. If the probability of "雷" was used in a location name was 0.45, we would add probLoc@3 for "雷", where 3 means the third interval in the discretized ranges.

Group 5 is also about the usage of the current position. There is a list of well-known Chinese family names, that is commonly called Hundred Family Names (百家姓, bai3 jia1 xing4)[3]. We add a feature to the current position if it is in the list. In T3, "陳" (chen2) is such a character. If a family name has two characters, the features will indicate the positions of the characters, e.g., "歐" (ou1) and "陽" (yang2) in "歐陽" will, respectively, have surename@1 and surename@2 as their features.

Features in group 6 are for four types of the named entities, i.e., **office**, **entry**, **nianhao** (for reign period), and **time** (as we discussed for the features in group 3). In general, historians have more complete information about these key types of NEs in Chinese history, so using specific tags for these NEs may offer stronger signals for nearby person and location names.

When we used group 6 along with other groups, we would not annotate a position with features in groups 1 through 5, if the position is part of certain named entities of group 6. Instead, we would use only the values for group 6. For example, at the beginning of the text in Figure 2, we have "洪武元年楊璟" (hong2 wu3 yuan2 nian2 yang2 jing3), where "洪武" represented a reign period, so both characters would be annotated only by **nianhao**. "楊璟" did not belong to any types of NEs in group 6, so would be annotated with other features.

Features of groups 3 and 6 are related in nature. We will see that using group 6 in places of group 3 led to better performance in the next section.

4.2 Evaluation: Labeled Data

We evaluated the effectiveness of using linear-chain CRF models for recognizing person and location names in DFZ with the labeled data that was discussed in Section 2.4. Given the original labels, we could create feature sets for all characters, and then ran 5-fold cross validations.

We classified the characters into seven categories: NB, NI, NE, AB, AI, AE, and O. We use N and A to denote name and location, respectively. B, I, and E denote beginning, internal, and ending, respectively. O means others. Hence, for example, NB is for the first character of a person name and AE is the last character of a location name.

We ran several experiments for CRF models that considered different combinations of the features that we discussed in Section 4.1. The classification results were measured by standard metrics, i.e., precision, recall, and F_1 measure that are very common for information retrieval.

Table 4 shows the experimental results for four such combinations. The results improved gradually for the experiments listed from the left to the right side. The first row of Table 4 lists the combinations of features used in the experiments. The second row shows the abbreviated names of the performance measures. The leftmost column shows the seven categories of the classification results.

The experiments that used only group 1 as the feature provided results that were better than we thought. Identifying categories of individual characters in the dataset of Section 2.4 did not seem to be a very challenging task. We added the second group of features by setting *k* to five. Then, we added group 4, group 5, and group 6, one by one for the listed experiments.

We did add group 3 in some of our experiments, but adding this group generally made the experimental results worse than not having them, so we do not show those results.

We also set *k* to three and seven, but we did not observe significant differences in the results. Setting *k* to seven provided a bit better results, but the improvement was not statistically significant.

Recognizing the categories of individual

[3] http://baike.baidu.com/subview/6559/15189786.htm

Table 4. Performances of selected CRF models

	Group 1			Groups 1+2			Groups 1+2+4+5			Groups 1+2+4+5+6		
	Prec.	Recall	F_1	Prec.	Recall	F_1	Prec.	Recall	F_1	Prec.	Recall	F_1
O	0.96	0.90	0.93	0.97	0.94	0.95	0.97	0.96	0.96	0.97	0.97	0.97
NB	0.76	0.91	0.83	0.85	0.94	0.89	0.91	0.94	0.93	0.93	0.95	0.94
NI	0.78	0.85	0.82	0.86	0.91	0.88	0.91	0.92	0.91	0.93	0.93	0.93
NE	0.72	0.87	0.79	0.82	0.92	0.87	0.89	0.92	0.90	0.91	0.93	0.92
AB	0.78	0.83	0.80	0.85	0.86	0.86	0.89	0.88	0.88	0.91	0.89	0.90
AI	0.48	0.73	0.57	0.71	0.84	0.77	0.80	0.86	0.83	0.83	0.89	0.86
AE	0.79	0.83	0.81	0.85	0.86	0.86	0.89	0.88	0.88	0.91	0.89	0.90

characters was just a basic task for our system. Our goal was to identify person names and location names. Hence, we really care about whether a sequence of NB, NI, and NE, for instance, indeed represented a person name.

We conducted such an integrated verification with the best performing model in Table 4, i.e., using groups 1, 2, 4, 5, and 6 as features. A name, either for a person or for a location, must exactly match the original labels, to be considered as a correct classification. For person names, the precision and recall rates are 92.0% and 93.9%, respectively. For location names, the precision and recall rates are 91.0% and 89.5%, respectively. Fining location names is harder than finding person names.

4.3 Evaluation: Unlabeled Data

We trained a CRF model, employing feature groups 1, 2, 4, 5, and 6, with all of the labeled data (Section 2.4), and evaluated the model with the task of identifying person and location names in the unlabeled data (Section 2.1). Due to the page limit, we cannot report the results.

5 Discussions and Concluding Remarks

We reported our work for mining biographical information from *Difangzhi* with techniques of language models and conditional random fields. Results observed in practical evaluations proved the effectiveness of these technologies for named entities recognition in literary Chinese.

As illustrated in Figures 1 and 2, processing texts of literary Chinese with computer programs is challenging. We approach this problem with gradually more complex methods. Building our current work on the data that were labeled in previous work (Bol, 2012; Pang et al., 2014) and CBDB, we were able to apply LM and CRF based models. The CNGRAM (Section 3.1) is an interactive procedure that was designed to guide researchers to find useful patterns.

For practical applications, the LM and CRF models may be integrated with an online tagging service, MARKUS (Ho, 2015)[4], of the Leiden University. As we collect more information about person names, style names, pen names, location names, and native places, we become more competent to separate the continuous Chinese strings into meaningful paragraphs (cf. Section 3.4) and find social networks of the government officers (Bol et al., 2015).

In the near future, we will consider more domain-dependent knowledge and contextual constraints to recognize and disambiguate named entities. People of different dynasties may have the same name, for instance. In a *Difangzhi* book, records about government officers of the same dynasty usually appeared close to each other. Many times, the records were ordered chronically. Considering these constrains for disambiguation can make our annotations about a person more precise.

In the longer run, mining the grammar rules of literary Chinese is a bigger and rewarding challenge. It was found that the language models and CRF models worked better for some of the 83 *Difangzhi* books but not as well for others (Bol et al., 2015). People who compiled these books adopted different styles of writing, and the styles varied from time to time and from place to place. Knowing the grammar rules that govern these language patterns will enable us to find more precise information from *Difangzhi* and perhaps other historical documents written in literary Chinese.

Acknowledgements

This work was supported in part by the Ministry of Science and Technology of Taiwan under grants MOST-102-2420-H-004-054-MY2 and MOST-104-2221-E-004-005-MY3. We thank the reviewers for their valuable comments, with which we can strengthen our work in the future.

[4] http://chinese-empires.eu/analysis/tools/

References

Bol, Peter K. 2012. Historical research in a digital environment, keynote speech in the 3rd International Conference on Digital Archives and Digital Humanities, <http://isites.harvard.edu/fs/docs/icb.topic1080143.files/Historical%20Research%20in%20Dig%20Env.ppt>.

Bol, Peter K., Jieh Hsiang, and Grace Fong. 2012. Prosopographical databases, text-mining, GIS and system interoperability for Chinese history and literature, *Proceedings of the 2012 International Conference on Digital Humanities*.

Bol, Peter K., Chao-Lin Liu, and Hongsu Wang. 2015. Mining and discovering biographical information in *Difangzhi* with a language-model-based approach, Presented in the 2015 International Conference on Digital Humanities.

Boonkwan, Prachya and Mark Steedman. 2011. Grammar induction from text using small syntactic prototypes, *Proceedings of the 5th International Joint Conference on Natural Language Processing*, 438–446.

de la Higuera, Colin. 2005. A bibliographical study of grammatical inference, *Pattern Recognition*, 38: 1332–1348.

Gao, Jianfeng, Mu Li, Andi Wu, and Chang-Ning Huang. 2005. Chinese word segmentation and named entity recognition: A pragmatic approach, *Computational Linguistics*, 31(4): 531–574.

Hargett, James M. 1996. Song dynasty local gazetteers and their place in the history of Difangzhi writing, *Harvard Journal of Asiatic Studies*, 56(2):405–442.

Ho, Hou Ieong. 2015. MARKUS: A fundamental semi-automatic markup platform for classical Chinese, Presented in the 2015 International Conference on Digital Humanities.

Huang, Hen-Hsen, Chuen-Tsai Sun, and Hsin-Hsi Chen. 2010. Classical Chinese sentence segmentation, *Proceedings of CIPS-SIGHAN Joint Conference on Chinese Language Processing*, 15–22.

Huang, Liang, Yinan Peng, Huan Wang, and Zhenyu Wu. 2001. PCFG parsing for restricted classical Chinese texts, *Proceedings of the 1st SIGHAN Workshop on Chinese Language processing*, 1–6.

Hwa, Rebecca. 1999. Supervised grammar induction using training data with limited constituent information, *Proceedings of the 37th Annual Meeting of the Association for Computational Linguistics*, 73–79.

Kuo, Yu-Chen. 2009. *Using Reinforcement Learning to Learn Phrase Structure Parsing in Mandarin Chinese*, Master's Thesis, National Tsing Hua University, Taiwan. (in Chinese)

Lee, John and Yin Hei Kong. 2012. A dependency treebank of classical Chinese poems, *Proceedings of 2012 Conference of the North American Chapter of the Association for Computational Linguistics: Human Language Technologies*, 191–199.

Lü, Yajuan, Sheng Li, Tiejun Zhao, and Muyun Yang. 2002. Learning Chinese bracketing knowledge based on a bilingual language model, *Proceedings of the 19th International Conference on Computational Linguistics*, 1–7.

Liu, Chao-Lin, Chih-Kai Huang, Hongsu Wang, and Peter K. Bol. 2015. Mining local gazetteers of literary Chinese with CRF and pattern based methods for biographical information in Chinese history, *Proceedings of the 3rd Big Humanities Data Workshop* in 2015 IEEE International Conference on Big Data, accepted.

McCallum, Andrew Kachites. 2002. MALLET: A Machine Learning for Language Toolkit. <http://mallet.cs.umass.edu>

Nadeau, David and Satoshi Sekine. 2007. A survey of named entity recognition and classification, *Linguisticae Investigationes*, 30(1):3–26.

Pang, Wai-him, Shih-pei Chen, and Hui Cheng. 2014. From text to data: Extracting posting data from Chinese local monographs, *Proceedings of the 5th International Conference on Digital Archives and Digital Humanities*, 93–116.

Sutton, Charles and Andrew McCallum. 2011. An introduction to conditional random fields, *Foundations and Trends in Machine Learning*, 4(4):267–373.

Yarowsky, David. 1995. Unsupervised word sense disambiguation rivaling supervised methods, *Proceedings of the 33rd Annual Meeting of the Association for Computational Linguistics*, 189–196.

Yu, Kun, Yusuke Miyao, Xiangli Wang, Takuya Matsuzaki, and Junichi Tsujii. 2010. Semi-automatically developing Chinese HPSG grammar from the Penn Chinese Treebank for deep parsing, *Proceedings of the 23rd International Conference on Computational Linguistics*: posters, 1417–1425.

Fast and Large-scale Unsupervised Relation Extraction

Sho Takase[†] **Naoaki Okazaki**[†‡] **Kentaro Inui**[†]
Graduate School of Information Sciences, Tohoku University[†]
Japan Science and Technology Agency (JST)[‡]
{takase, okazaki, inui}@ecei.tohoku.ac.jp

Abstract

A common approach to unsupervised relation extraction builds clusters of patterns expressing the same relation. In order to obtain clusters of relational patterns of good quality, we have two major challenges: the semantic representation of relational patterns and the scalability to large data. In this paper, we explore various methods for modeling the meaning of a pattern and for computing the similarity of patterns mined from huge data. In order to achieve this goal, we apply algorithms for approximate frequency counting and efficient dimension reduction to unsupervised relation extraction. The experimental results show that approximate frequency counting and dimension reduction not only speeds up similarity computation but also improves the quality of pattern vectors.

1 Introduction

Semantic relations between entities are essential for many NLP applications such as question answering, textual inference and information extraction (Ravichandran and Hovy, 2002; Szpektor et al., 2004). Therefore, it is important to build a comprehensive knowledge base consisting of instances of semantic relations (e.g., authorOf) such as *authorOf* ⟨*Franz Kafka, The Metamorphosis*⟩. To recognize these instances in a corpus, we need to obtain patterns (e.g., "X write Y") that signal instances of the semantic relations.

For a long time, many researches have targeted at extracting instances and patterns of specific relations (Riloff, 1996; Pantel and Pennacchiotti, 2006; De Saeger et al., 2009). In recent years, to acquire a wider range knowledge, Open Information Extraction (Open IE) has received much attention (Banko et al., 2007). Open IE identifies relational patterns and instances automatically without predefined target relations (Banko et al., 2007; Wu and Weld, 2010; Fader et al., 2011; Mausam et al., 2012). In other words, Open IE acquires knowledge to handle open domains. In Open IE paradigm, it is necessary to enumerate semantic relations in open domains and to learn mappings between surface patterns and semantic relations. This task is called unsupervised relation extraction (Hasegawa et al., 2004; Shinyama and Sekine, 2006; Rosenfeld and Feldman, 2007).

A common approach to unsupervised relation extraction builds clusters of patterns that represent the same relation (Hasegawa et al., 2004; Shinyama and Sekine, 2006; Yao et al., 2011; Min et al., 2012; Rosenfeld and Feldman, 2007; Nakashole et al., 2012). In brief, each cluster includes patterns corresponding to a semantic relation. For example, consider three patterns, "X write Y", "X is author of Y" and "X is located in Y". When we group these patterns into clusters representing the same relation, patterns "X write Y" and "X is author of Y" form a cluster representing the relation *authorOf*, and the pattern "X is located in Y" does a cluster for *locatedIn*. In order to obtain these clusters, we need to know the similarity between patterns. The better we model the similarity of patterns, the better a clustering result correspond to semantic relations. Thus, the similarity computation between patterns is crucial for unsupervised relation extraction.

29th Pacific Asia Conference on Language, Information and Computation pages 96 - 105
Shanghai, China, October 30 - November 1, 2015

We have two major challenges in computing the similarity of patterns. First, it is not clear how to represent the semantic meaning of a relational pattern. Previous studies define a feature space for patterns, and express the meaning of patterns by using such as the co-occurrence statistics between a pattern and an entity pair, e.g., co-occurrence frequency and pointwise mutual information (PMI) (Lin and Pantel, 2001). Some studies employed vector representations of a fixed dimension, e.g., Principal Component Analysis (PCA) (Collins et al., 2002) and Latent Dirichlet Allocation (LDA) (Yao et al., 2011; Riedel et al., 2013). However, the previous work did not compare the effectiveness of these representations when applied to a collection of large-scaled unstructured texts.

Second, we need design a method scalable to a large data. In Open IE, we utilize a large amount of data in order to improve the quality of unsupervised relation extraction. For this reason, we cannot use a complex and inefficient algorithm that consumes the computation time and memory storage. In this paper, we explore methods for computing pattern similarity of good quality that are scalable to huge data, for example, with several billion sentences. In order to achieve this goal, we utilize approximate frequency counting and dimension reduction. Our contributions are threefold.

- We build a system for unsupervised relation extraction that is practical and scalable to large data.
- Even though the proposed system introduces approximations, we demonstrate that the system exhibits the performance comparable to the one without approximations.
- Comparing several representations of pattern vectors, we discuss a reasonable design for representing the meaning of a pattern.

2 Methods

2.1 Overview

As mentioned in Section 1, semantic representations of relational patterns is key to unsupervised relation extraction. Based on the distributional hypothesis (Harris, 1954), we model the meaning of a relational pattern with a distribution of entity pairs co-occurring with the pattern. For example, the meaning of a relational pattern "X write Y" is represented by the distribution of the entity pairs that fills the variables (X, Y) in a corpus. By using vector representations of relational patterns, we can compute the semantic similarity of two relational patterns; for example, we can infer that the patterns "X write Y" and "X is author of Y" present the similar meaning if the distribution of entity pairs for the pattern "X write Y" is similar to that for the pattern "X is author of Y".

Researchers have explored various approaches to vector representations of relational patterns (Lin and Pantel, 2001; Rosenfeld and Feldman, 2007; Yao et al., 2011; Riedel et al., 2013). The simplest approach is to define a vector of a relational pattern in which an element in the vector presents the co-occurrence frequency between a pattern and an entity pair. However, the use of raw frequency counts may be inappropriate when some entity pairs co-occur with a number of patterns. A solution to this problem is to use a refined co-occurrence measure such as PMI (Lin and Pantel, 2001). In addition, we may compress a vector representation with a dimensionality reduction method such as PCA because pattern vectors tend to be sparse and high dimensional (Yao et al., 2011; Riedel et al., 2013).

Meanwhile, it may be difficult to implement the above procedures that can handle a large amount of data. Consider the situation where we find 1.1 million entity pairs and 0.7 million relational patterns from a corpus with 15 billion sentences. Even though the vector space is sparse, we need to keep a huge number of frequency counts that record co-occurrences of the entity pairs and relational patterns in the corpus.

In order to acquire pattern vectors from a large amount of data, we explore two approaches in this study. One approach is to apply an algorithm for approximate counting so that we can discard unimportant information in preparing pattern vectors. Another approach is to utilize distributed representations of words so that we can work on a semantic space of a fixed and compact size. In short, the former approach reduces the memory usage for computing statistics, whereas the latter compresses the vector space beforehand.

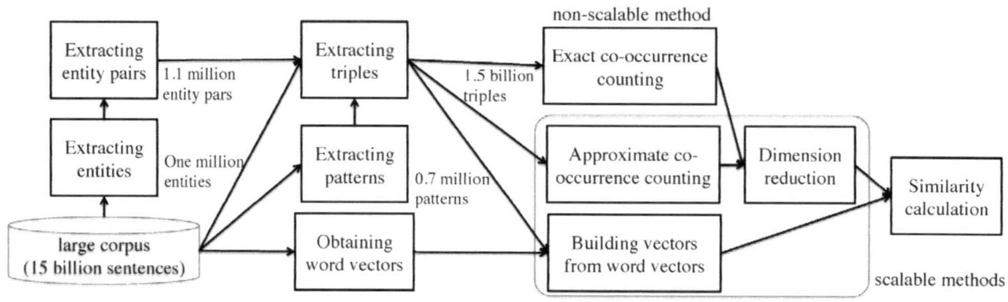

Figure 1: Overview of the system for unsupervised relation extraction

Figure 1 illustrates the overview of the system of unsupervised relation extraction presented in this paper. We extract a collection of triples each of which consists of an entity pair and a relational pattern (Section 2.2). Because this step may extract meaningless triples, we identify entity pairs and relational patterns occurring frequently in the corpus. We compute co-occurrence statistics of entity pairs and relational patterns to obtain pattern vectors. Section 2.3 describes this process, followed by an online variant of PCA in Section 2.4. Furthermore, we present two approaches that improve the scalability to large data in Section 2.5.

2.2 Extracting triples

In this study, we define a triple as a combination of an entity pair and a relational pattern that connects the two entities. In order to extract meaningful triples from a corpus, we mine a set of entities and relational patterns in an unsupervised fashion.

2.2.1 Extracting entities

We define an entity mention as a sequence of nouns. Because quite entity mentions consist of two or more nouns (e.g., "Roadside station" and "Franz Kafka"), we adapt a simple statistical method (Mikolov et al., 2013) to recognize noun phrases. Equation 1 computes the score of a noun bigram $w_i w_j$,

$$\mathrm{score}(w_i, w_j) = \mathrm{cor}(w_i, w_j) * \mathrm{dis}(w_i, w_j), \quad (1)$$

$$\mathrm{cor}(w_i, w_j) = \log \frac{f(w_i, w_j) - \delta}{f(w_i) \times f(w_j)}, \quad (2)$$

$$\mathrm{dis}(w_i, w_j) = \frac{f(w_i, w_j)}{f(w_i, w_j)+1} \frac{\min\{f(w_i), f(w_j)\}}{\min\{f(w_i), f(w_j)\}+1}. \quad (3)$$

Here, $f(w_i)$ denotes the frequency of the noun w_i, and $f(w_i, w_j)$ does the frequency of the noun bigram $w_i w_j$. The parameter δ is a constant value to remove infrequent noun sequences. Consequently, $\mathrm{cor}(w_i, w_j)$ represents the degree of the connection between w_i and w_j. However, $\mathrm{cor}(w_i, w_j)$ becomes undesirably large if either $f(w_i)$ or $f(w_j)$ is small. We introduce the function $\mathrm{dis}(w_i, w_j)$ to 'discount' such sequences.

We form noun phrases whose scores are greater than a threshold. In order to obtain noun phrases longer than two words, we run the procedure four times, decreasing the threshold value[1]. In this way, we can find, for example, "Franz Kafka" as an entity in the first run and "Franz Kafka works" in the second run. After identifying a set of noun phrases, we count the frequency of the noun phrases in the corpus, and extract noun phrases occurring no less than 1,000 times as a set of entities.

2.2.2 Extracting entity pairs

After determining a set of entities, we discover entity pairs that may have semantic relationships in order to locate relational patterns. In this study, we extract a pair of entities if the entities co-occur in more than 5,000 sentences. We denote the set of entity pairs extracted by this procedure E.

2.2.3 Extracting patterns

As a relational pattern, this study employs the shortest path between two entities in a dependency tree, following the previous work (Wu and Weld, 2010; Mausam et al., 2012; Akbik et al., 2012). Here, we introduce a restriction that a relational pattern must include a predicate in order to reject semantically-

[1] The threshold values are 10 (first time), 5 (second time), and 0 (third and fourth times).

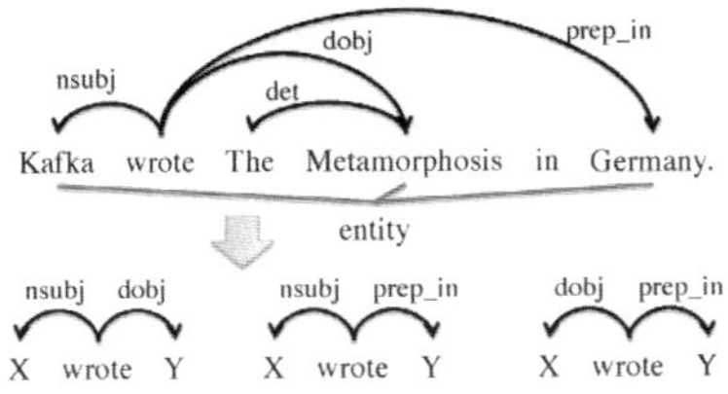

Figure 2: Example of parsed sentence and extracting patterns

ambiguous patterns such as "X of Y". Additionally, we convert an entity into a variable (i.e., X or Y). Consider the sentence shown in Figure 2 as an example. An arrow between words expresses a dependency relationship. This sentence contains three entities: "Kafka", "The Metamorphosis" and "German". Therefore, we obtain three patterns, "X $\xleftarrow{nsubj}$ wrote $\xrightarrow{dobj}$ Y", "X $\xleftarrow{nsubj}$ wrote $\xrightarrow{prep\_in}$ Y" and "X $\xleftarrow{dobj}$ wrote $\xrightarrow{prep\_in}$ Y"[2]. Counting the frequency of a pattern, we extract one appearing no less than 1,500 times in the corpus. We denote the set of relation patterns P hereafter.

2.3 Building pattern vectors

We define a vector of a relational pattern as the distribution of entity pairs co-occurring with the pattern. Processing the whole collection of the corpus, we extract mentions of triples $(p, e), p \in P, e \in E$. For example, we obtain a triple,

$$\begin{aligned} p = &\quad \text{X} \xleftarrow{nsubj} \text{wrote} \xrightarrow{dobj} \text{Y}, \\ e = &\quad \langle\text{"Franz Kafka"}, \text{"The Metamorphosis"}\rangle, \end{aligned}$$

from the sentence "Franz Kafka wrote The Metamorphosis." The meaning of the pattern p is represented by the distribution of the entity pairs co-occurring with the pattern.

In this study, we compare two statistical measures of co-occurrence: the raw frequency (FREQ) and PMI (PMI). In FREQ setting, a relational pattern p is represented by a vector whose elements present the frequency of co-occurrences $f(p, e)$ of every entity pair $e \in E$. PMI refines the strength of co-occurrences with this equation,

$$\text{PMI}(p, e) = \log \frac{\frac{f(p,e)}{M}}{\frac{\Sigma_{i \in P} f(i,e)}{M} \frac{\Sigma_{j \in E} f(p,j)}{M}} \times \text{dis}(p, e). \tag{4}$$

Here, $f(p, e)$ presents the frequency of co-occurrences between a pattern p and an entity pair e; and $M = \sum_i^P \sum_j^E f(i, j)$. The discount factor $\text{dis}(p, e)$ is defined similarly to Equation 3. In PMI setting, we set zero to the value for an entity pair e if $\text{PMI}(p, e) < 0$.

2.4 Dimensionality reduction for pattern vectors

The vector space defined in Section 2.3 is extremely high dimensional and sparse, encoding all entity pairs as separate dimensions. The space may be too sparse to represent the semantic meaning of relational patterns; for example, entity pairs ("Franz Kafka", "the Metamorphosis") and ("Kafka", "the Metamorphosis") present two different dimension even though "Franz Kafka" and "Kafka" refer to the same person. In addition, we need an associative array to compute the similarity of two sparse vectors.

In order to map the sparse and high dimensional space into a dense and compact space, we use *Principal Component Analysis* (PCA). In essence, PCA is a statistical procedure that finds principal components and scores of a matrix. PCA is closely related to *Singular Value Decomposition* (SVD), which factors an $m \times n$ matrix $\mathbf{A}$ with,

$$\mathbf{A} = \mathbf{U}\mathbf{\Sigma}\mathbf{V}^t. \tag{5}$$

Here, $\mathbf{U}$ is an $m \times m$ orthogonal matrix, $\mathbf{V}$ is an $n \times n$ orthogonal matrix and $\mathbf{\Sigma}$ is an $m \times n$ diagonal matrix storing singular values. Each column of $\mathbf{V}$ corresponds to a principal component, and each column of $\mathbf{U\Sigma}$ corresponds to a score of a principal component of $\mathbf{A}$.

However, a full SVD requires heavy computations while we only need principal components corresponding to the top r singular values of $\mathbf{A}$. This hinders the scalability of the system, which obtains a huge co-occurrence matrix between patterns and entity pairs. We solve this issue by using the randomized algorithm proposed by Halko et al. (2011).

[2] In the experiments, we use a collection of Japanese Web pages. However, we explain the procedure with an English sentence because the procedure for extracting patterns is universal to other languages.

Algorithm 1 Space saving for each pattern

Input: N: counter size for each pattern
Input: D: a set of triples (p, e)
Output: $c_{p,e}$: counter for each pattern p
1: **for all** $(p, e) \in D$ **do**
2:   **if** T_p does not exist **then**
3:     $T_p \leftarrow \emptyset$
4:   **end if**
5:   **if** $e \in T_p$ **then**
6:     $c_{p,e} \leftarrow c_{p,e} + 1$
7:   **else if** $|T_p| < N$ **then**
8:     $T_p \leftarrow T \cup \{e\}$
9:     $c_{p,e} \leftarrow 1$
10:   **else**
11:     $i \leftarrow \text{argmin}_{i \in T_p} c_{p,i}$
12:     $c_{p,e} \leftarrow c_{p,i} + 1$
13:     $T_p \leftarrow T \cup \{e\} \setminus \{i\}$
14:   **end if**
15: **end for**

The goal of this algorithm is to find an $r \times n$ matrix $\mathbf{B}$ storing the compressed information of the rows of $\mathbf{A}$. We first draw an $n \times r$ Gaussian random matrix $\mathbf{\Omega}$. Next, we derive the $m \times r$ matrix $\mathbf{Y} = \mathbf{A\Omega}$. We next construct an $m \times r$ matrix $\mathbf{Q}$ whose columns form an orthonormal basis for the range of $\mathbf{Y}$. Here, $\mathbf{QQ}^t\mathbf{A} \approx \mathbf{A}$ is satisfied. Finally, we obtain the matrix $\mathbf{B} = \mathbf{Q}^t\mathbf{A}$, in which $\mathbf{Q}^t$ compresses the rows of $\mathbf{A}$.

We compute principal component scores for r dimensions by applying SVD to $\mathbf{B}$. The computation is easy because $r \ll m$. In this study, we used redsvd[3], an implementation of Halko et al. (2011). We represents the meaning of a pattern with the scores of r principle components.

2.5 Improving the scalability to large data

As described previously, it may be difficult and inefficient to count the exact numbers of co-occurrences from a large amount of data. In this study, we explore two approaches: approximate counting (Section 2.5.1) and distributed representations of words (Section 2.5.2).

2.5.1 Approximate counting

We may probably not need exact counts of co-occurrences for representing pattern vectors because a small amount of elements in a pattern vector greatly influence the similarity computation. In other words, it may be enough to find top-k entity pairs with larger counts of co-occurrences for each pattern, and to ignore other entity pairs with smaller counts. The task of finding top-k frequent items has been studied extensively as *approximate counting algorithms*.

We employ *Space Saving* (Metwally et al., 2005), which is the most efficient algorithm to obtain top-k frequent items. Algorithm 1 outlines the Space Saving algorithm adapted for counting frequencies of co-occurrences. The space saving algorithm maintains at most N counters of co-occurrences for each pattern p.

For each triple (p, e), where p and e present a pattern and an entity pair, respectively, the algorithm checks if the co-occurrence count for the triple (p, e) is available or not. If it is available (Line 5), we increment the counter as usual (Line 6). If it is unavailable but the number of counters kept for the pattern is less than N (Line 7), we initialize the counter with one (Lines 8 and 9). If the count is unavailable and if the pattern has already maintained N counters, the algorithm removes a counter $c_{p,i}$ with the least value, and creates a new counter for the entity pair e with the approximated count $c_{p,i} + 1$ (Lines 11–13).

This algorithm has the nice property that the error of the frequency count of a frequent triple is within a range specified by the number of counters N. In addition, Metwally et al. (2005) describes a data structure for finding the least frequent triple efficiently in Line 11. We can obtain the frequency counts of the top-k frequent triples if we set the number of counters N much larger than k. In this way, we can find the frequency count of the top-k frequent triple $f(p, e)$ approximately, and assume frequency counts of other triples zero.

2.5.2 Building pattern vectors from word vectors

A number of NLP researchers explored approaches to representing the meaning of a word with fixed-length vectors (Bengio et al., 2003; Mikolov et al., 2013). In particular, word2vec[4], an implementation of Mikolov et al. (2013), received much attention in the NLP community.

[3] `https://code.google.com/p/redsvd/wiki/English`

[4] `https://code.google.com/p/word2vec/`

Switching our attention to the pattern feature vector, our goal is to express the semantic meaning of a relational pattern with a distribution of entity pairs. Here, we explore the use of low-dimensional word vectors learned by word2vec from the large corpus: the meaning of a pattern is represented by the distribution of entity vectors. Thus, we obtain the vector representation of a relational pattern p,

$$\boldsymbol{p} = \sum_{e \in E} f(p, e) \begin{bmatrix} \boldsymbol{v}_{e_0} \\ \boldsymbol{v}_{e_1} \end{bmatrix}. \quad (6)$$

Here, $\boldsymbol{v}_{e_0}$ denotes the vector for an entity e_0 in the entity pair e, and $\boldsymbol{v}_{e_1}$ does the vector for another entity e_1 in the pair e.

3 Experiments

3.1 Data

For our experimental corpus, we collected 15 billion Japanese sentences by crawling web pages. To remove noise such as spam and non-Japanese sentences, we apply a filter that checks the length of a sentence, determines whether the sentence contains a specific character in Japanese (*hiragana*), and then checks the number of symbols. As a result of filtering, we obtained 6.3 billion sentences. We then parsed these sentences using Cabocha[5], a Japanese dependency parser. For preprocessing, we extracted 1 million entities, 1.1 million entity pairs, and 0.7 million patterns. Finally, we extracted about 1.5 billion triples from the corpus.

We then manually checked some of the pattern pairs extracted from Wikipedia that were also contained within the 6.3 billion sentence corpus. Specifically, we first extracted frequent patterns from some domains in Wikipedia for obtaining the patterns representing a specific relation. We selected patterns referring to an illness, an author, and an architecture as target domains. Next, we gathered patterns sharing many entity pairs because these patterns may represent the same relation. We obtained 527 patterns and 4,531 pattern pairs. Four annotators classified these pairs into the same relation or not. We then randomly sampled 90 pairs and found an average of 0.63 for the Cohen's kappa value for two annotators. We annotated the 4,531 pairs by two or more annotators. Therefore, if two or more annotators labeled a pair with the same relation, we regarded the pair as the same relation. Finally, we acquired 720 pairs expressing the same relation. We applied each method to 4,531 pairs and we identified patterns with higher than threshold. We investigated whether the pair is included in the same relation pairs.

[5]`https://code.google.com/p/cabocha/`

3.2 Experimental settings

We evaluated the quality of pattern vectors build by the proposed approaches on the similarity calculation. Concretely, we investigated the impact on accuracy and computation time. For the evaluation, we computed the cosine similarity based on the feature vectors obtained by each method. We compared the following methods.

Exact counting (baseline): We counted the co-occurrence frequency between an entity pair and a pattern in triples using a machine with 256GB of memory (EXACT-FREQ). In addition, we calculated PMI defined in equation 4 based on the co-occurrence frequency (EXACT-PMI).

Exact counting + PCA: Using PCA, we converted EXACT-FREQ and EXACT-PMI into the fixed dimensional vector EXACT-FREQ+PCA and EXACT-PMI+PCA. We determined the number of dimensions as 1,024 based on comparisons[6] between 256, 512, 1,024, and 2,048.

Approximate counting: We counted the co-occurrence frequency using approximate counting explained in Section 2.5.1 (APPROX-FREQ). The counter size N was 10,240 and we used the top 5,120 frequent entity pairs as a feature. Moreover, we obtained PMI based on the result of approximate counting (APPROX-PMI).

Approximate counting + PCA: Using PCA, we converted APPROX-FREQ and APPROX-PMI into the fixed dimensional vector APPROX-FREQ+PCA and APPROX-PMI+PCA. Similar to Exact counting + PCA, we selected the dimension of feature vectors as 1,024.

Exact counting + word2vec: We obtained pattern feature vectors using the result of word2vec (EXACT-FREQ+WORD2VEC). Moreover, instead of calculating the feature vector by co-occurrence frequency, we weight the entity vector with PMI

[6]The result of 1,024 dimensional vector is close to the one of 2,048. We selected 1,024 since the smaller the number of feature dimensions are, the faster we calculate similarity.

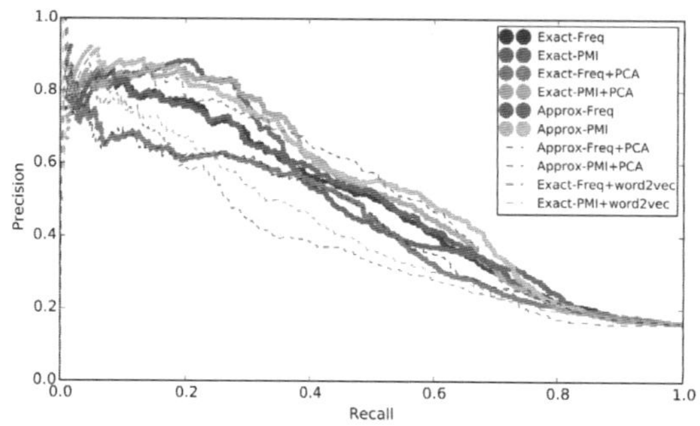

Figure 3: Precision and recall of each method

(EXACT-PMI+WORD2VEC). We trained word2vec using all entities, verbs, and adverbs in the corpus on four AMD Opteron 6174 processors (12-core, 2.2GHz). It took about 130 hours to train word2vec (the number of threads was 42 and window size was 5). Similar to PCA, we selected the dimension of each word vector as 512: namely, the dimension of pattern vectors was 1,024 because of concatenating.

3.3 Evaluating accuracy of each method

Figure 3 shows the precision and recall of each method. We illustrated this graph by changing the threshold value. We focus attention on the difference between exact counting and approximate counting. These results of EXACT-FREQ and APPROX-FREQ were about the same. On the other hand, APPROX-PMI outperformed EXACT-PMI in most areas. These results demonstrated that approximate counting is enough to compute co-occurrence frequency between a pattern and an entity pair. The results also suggest that approximate counting possibly improves the performance.

Comparing the results with PCA and without PCA, the figure shows that PCA does not always improve the performance. However, APPROX-PMI+PCA achieved the best performance in most areas. For computation time, we verify that PCA is important in this aspect.

In contrast, feature vectors based on word2vec worsened the performance against not only approximate counting but also exact counting. Although we expected that the vector formed by word2vec was appropriate for representing the meaning of a pattern, EXACT-FREQ+WORD2VEC was worse than all the other methods in Figure 3. We suspect that this result was caused by separating entity pairs into entities in feature generation. Concretely, for obtaining pattern feature vectors using word2vec, we concatenate the sum of vectors assigned to one side of entity pairs and the ones assigned to the other side. Therefore, there is a possibility that we obtain pattern pairs with a high similarity when both of the patterns contain one of the same entity types. In other words, we need to encode not entities separately but maintaining entity pair as a pattern feature vector.

From Figure 3, approximate counting is effective for the similarity calculation. In addition, PCA is useful for representing the meaning of a pattern in the compact space.

Method	10k	100k	all (664k)
EXACT-PMI	55m	121hr	8,499hr
APPROX-PMI	38m	110hr	7,441hr
APPROX-PMI+PCA	4m	7hr	785hr

Table 1: Similarity calculation time of each method with one thread

3.4 Evaluating computation time

Table 1 demonstrates the similarity calculation time of EXACT-PMI, APPROX-PMI and APPROX-PMI+PCA for processing 10k patterns, 100k patterns, and 664k patterns (the maximum). We executed a program written in C++ on four AMD Opteron 6174 processors (12-core, 2.2GHz) with 256GB of the memory. We measured the calculation time using a single thread. Note that, we split the calculation targets and predicted computation time based on the result of division and split number, because much time is required to complete the calculation for 100k and 664k patterns. For 100k patterns, we split the calculation targets into 48 groups. For 664k pattern, we split the calculation targets into 4,096 groups.

APPROX-PMI executed quicker than EXACT-PMI because APPROX-PMI decreased the number of non-zero features for each pattern. Nevertheless, APPROX-PMI took a large amount of time for the similarity calculation. On the other hand, the computation time of APPROX-PMI+PCA was much smaller than that of EXACT-PMI and APPROX-PMI. As a result, it is necessary to reduce the amount of dimensions because APPROX-PMI would take 7,441 hours (about a year) to calculate all pattern similarity with one thread. We conclude that it is necessary to prepare low dimensional feature vectors using dimension reduction or word vectors for completing similarity calculation in a realistic time.

4 Related work

Unsupervised relation extraction poses three major challenges: extraction of relation instances, representing the meaning of relational patterns, and efficient similarity computation. A great number of studies proposed methods for extracting relation instances (Wu and Weld, 2010; Fader et al., 2011; Fader et al., 2011; Akbik et al., 2012). We do not describe the detail of these studies, which are out of the scope of this paper.

Previous studies explored various approaches to represent the meaning of relational patterns (Lin and Pantel, 2001; Yao et al., 2012; Mikolov et al., 2013). Lin and Pantel (2001) used co-occurrence statistics of PMI between an entity and a relational pattern. Even though the goal of their research is not on relation extraction but on paraphrase (inference rule) discovery, the work had a great impact to the research on unsupervised relation extraction. Yao et al. (2012) modeled sentence themes and document themes by using LDA, and represented the meaning of a pattern with the themes together with the co-occurrence statistics between patterns and entities. Recently, methods inspired by neural language modeling received much attentions for representation learning (Bengio et al., 2003; Mikolov et al., 2010; Mikolov et al., 2013). In this study, we compared the raw frequency counts, PMI, and word embeddings (Mikolov et al., 2013).

In order to achieve efficient similarity computation, some researchers used entity types, for example, "Franz Kafka" as a co-referent of *writer* (Min et al., 2012; Nakashole et al., 2012). Min et al. (2012) obtained entity types by clustering entities in a corpus. When computing the similarity values of patterns, they restricted target pattern pairs to the ones sharing the same entity types. In this way, they reduced the number of similarity computations. Nakashole et al. (2012) also reduced the number of similarity computations by using entity types obtained from existing knowledge bases such as Yago (Suchanek et al., 2007) and Freebase (Bollacker et al., 2008). However, it is not so straightforward to determine the semantic type of an entity in advance because the semantic type may depends on the context. For example, "Woody Allen" stands for an actor, a movie director, or a writer depending on the context. Therefore, we think it is also important to reduce the computation time for pattern similarities by simplifying the semantic representation of relational patterns.

The closest work to ours is probably Goyal et al. (2012). Their paper proposes to use algorithms of count-min sketch (approximate counting) and approximate nearest neighbor search for NLP tasks. They applied these techniques for obtaining feature vectors, reducing the dimension of the vector space, and searching similar items to a query. Even though they demonstrated the efficiency of the algorithms, they did not demonstrate the effectiveness of the approach in a specific NLP task.

5 Conclusion

In this paper, we presented several approaches to unsupervised relation extraction on a large amount of data. In order to handle large data, we explored three approaches: dimension reduction, approximate counting, and vector representations of words. The experimental results showed that approximate frequency counting and dimension reduction not only speeds up similarity computation but also improved the quality of pattern vectors.

The use of vector representation of words did not show an improvement. This is probably because we need to learn a vector representation specialized for patterns that encode the distributions of entity pairs. A future direction of this research is to establish a method to learn the representations of patterns jointly with the representations of words. Furthermore, it would be interesting to incorporate the meaning of constituent words of a pattern into the representation.

Acknowledgments

This work was supported by JSPS KAKENHI Grant Numbers 26 · 5820, 15H05318 and Japan Science and Technology Agency (JST).

References

Alan Akbik, Larysa Visengeriyeva, Priska Herger, Holmer Hemsen, and Alexander Löser. 2012. Unsupervised discovery of relations and discriminative extraction patterns. In *Proceedings of the 24th International Conference on Computational Linguistics (COLING2012)*, pages 17–32.

Michele Banko, Michael J Cafarella, Stephen Soderland, Matt Broadhead, and Oren Etzioni. 2007. Open information extraction from the web. In *Proceedings of the 20th International Joint Conference on Artifical Intelligence (IJCAI2007)*, pages 2670–2676.

Yoshua Bengio, Réjean Ducharme, Pascal Vincent, and Christian Janvin. 2003. A neural probabilistic language model. 3:1137–1155.

Kurt Bollacker, Colin Evans, Praveen Paritosh, Tim Sturge, and Jamie Taylor. 2008. Freebase: A collaboratively created graph database for structuring human knowledge. In *Proceedings of the 2008 ACM SIGMOD International Conference on Management of Data (SIGMOD '08)*, pages 1247–1250.

Michael Collins, Sanjoy Dasgupta, and Robert E. Schapire. 2002. A generalization of principal components analysis to the exponential family. In *Advances in Neural Information Processing Systems 14 (NIPS2002)*, pages 617–624.

Stijn De Saeger, Kentaro Torisawa, Jun'ichi Kazama, Kow Kuroda, and Masaki Murata. 2009. Large scale relation acquisition using class dependent patterns. In *Proceedings of the 2009 Ninth IEEE International Conference on Data Mining (ICDM2009)*, pages 764–769.

Anthony Fader, Stephen Soderland, and Oren Etzioni. 2011. Identifying relations for open information extraction. In *Proceedings of the 2011 Conference on Empirical Methods in Natural Language Processing (EMNLP2011)*, pages 1535–1545.

Amit Goyal, Hal Daumé, III, and Raul Guerra. 2012. Fast large-scale approximate graph construction for nlp. In *Proceedings of the 2012 Joint Conference on Empirical Methods in Natural Language Processing and Computational Natural Language Learning (EMNLP-CoNLL2012)*, pages 1069–1080.

Nathan Halko, Per Gunnar Martinsson, and Joel A. Tropp. 2011. Finding structure with randomness: Probabilistic algorithms for constructing approximate matrix decompositions. *SIAM Review*, 53(2):217–288.

Zellig Harris. 1954. Distributional structure. *Word*, 10(23):146–162.

Takaaki Hasegawa, Satoshi Sekine, and Ralph Grishman. 2004. Discovering relations among named entities from large corpora. In *Proceedings of the 42nd Annual Meeting on Association for Computational Linguistics (ACL2004)*, pages 415–422.

Dekang Lin and Patrick Pantel. 2001. Dirt - discovery of inference rules from text. In *Proceedings of the Seventh ACM SIGKDD International Conference on Knowledge Discovery and Data Mining (KDD2001)*, pages 323–328.

Mausam, Michael Schmitz, Robert Bart, Stephen Soderland, and Oren Etzioni. 2012. Open language learning for information extraction. In *Proceedings of the 2012 Joint Conference on Empirical Methods in Natural Language Processing and Computational Natural Language Learning (EMNLP2012)*, pages 523–534.

Ahmed Metwally, Divyakant Agrawal, and Amr El Abbadi. 2005. Efficient computation of frequent and top-k elements in data streams. In *Proceedings of the 10th International Conference on Database Theory (ICDT2005)*, pages 398–412.

Tomas Mikolov, Martin Karafiát, Lukas Burget, Jan Cernocký, and Sanjeev Khudanpur. 2010. Recurrent neural network based language model. In *INTERSPEECH*, pages 1045–1048.

Tomas Mikolov, Ilya Sutskever, Kai Chen, Gregory S. Corrado, and Jeffrey Dean. 2013. Distributed representations of words and phrases and their compositionality. In *Proceedings of the Neural Information Processing Systems Conference and Workshops (NIPS2013)*, pages 3111–3119.

Bonan Min, Shuming Shi, Ralph Grishman, and Chin-Yew Lin. 2012. Ensemble semantics for large-scale unsupervised relation extraction. In *Proceedings of the 2012 Joint Conference on Empirical Methods in Natural Language Processing and Computational Natural Language Learning (EMNLP-CoNLL2012)*, pages 1027–1037.

Ndapandula Nakashole, Gerhard Weikum, and Fabian Suchanek. 2012. Patty: A taxonomy of relational patterns with semantic types. In *2012 Joint Conference on Empirical Methods in Natural Language Processing and Computational Natural Language Learning (EMNLP-CoNLL2012)*, pages 1135–1145.

Patrick Pantel and Marco Pennacchiotti. 2006. Espresso: Leveraging generic patterns for automatically harvesting semantic relations. In *Proceedings of the 21st International Conference on Computational Linguistics and the 44th Annual Meeting of the Association for Computational Linguistics (ACL2006)*, pages 113–120.

Deepak Ravichandran and Eduard Hovy. 2002. Learning surface text patterns for a question answering system. In *Proceedings of the 40th Annual Meeting on Association for Computational Linguistics (ACL2002)*, pages 41–47.

Sebastian Riedel, Limin Yao, Andrew McCallum, and Benjamin M. Marlin. 2013. Relation extraction with matrix factorization and universal schemas. In *Proceedings of the Main Conference on Human Language Technology Conference of the North American Chapter of the Association of Computational Linguistics (HLT-NAACL2013)*, pages 74–84.

Ellen Riloff. 1996. Automatically generating extraction patterns from untagged text. In *Proceedings of the 13th National Conference on Artificial Intelligence - Volume 2 (AAAI96)*, pages 1044–1049.

Benjamin Rosenfeld and Ronen Feldman. 2007. Clustering for unsupervised relation identification. In *Proceedings of the Sixteenth ACM Conference on Conference on Information and Knowledge Management (CIKM2007)*, pages 411–418.

Yusuke Shinyama and Satoshi Sekine. 2006. Preemptive information extraction using unrestricted relation discovery. In *Proceedings of the Main Conference on Human Language Technology Conference of the North American Chapter of the Association of Computational Linguistics (HLT-NAACL2006)*, pages 304–311.

Fabian M. Suchanek, Gjergji Kasneci, and Gerhard Weikum. 2007. Yago: A core of semantic knowledge. In *Proceedings of the 16th International Conference on World Wide Web (WWW 2007)*, pages 697–706.

Idan Szpektor, Hristo Tanev, Ido Dagan, and Bonaventura Coppola. 2004. Scaling web-based acquisition of entailment relations. In *Proceedings of the 2004 Conference on Empirical Methods in Natural Language Processing (EMNLP2004)*, pages 41–48.

Fei Wu and Daniel S. Weld. 2010. Open information extraction using wikipedia. In *Proceedings of the 48th Annual Meeting of the Association for Computational Linguistics (ACL2010)*, pages 118–127.

Limin Yao, Aria Haghighi, Sebastian Riedel, and Andrew McCallum. 2011. Structured relation discovery using generative models. In *Proceedings of the 2011 Conference on Empirical Methods in Natural Language Processing (EMNLP2011)*, pages 1456–1466.

Limin Yao, Sebastian Riedel, and Andrew McCallum. 2012. Unsupervised relation discovery with sense disambiguation. In *Proceedings of the 50th Annual Meeting of the Association for Computational Linguistics (ACL2012)*, pages 712–720.

Reducing Lexical Features in Parsing by Word Embeddings

Hiroya Komatsu, Ran Tian, Naoaki Okazaki and **Kentaro Inui**
Tohoku University, Japan
{h-komatsu, tianran, okazaki, inui}@ecei.tohoku.ac.jp

Abstract

The high-dimensionality of lexical features in parsing can be memory consuming and cause over-fitting problems. We propose a general framework to replace all lexical feature templates by low-dimensional features induced from word embeddings. Applied to a near state-of-the-art dependency parser (Huang et al., 2012), our method improves the baseline, performs better than using cluster bit string features, and outperforms a recent neural network based parser. A further analysis shows that our framework has the effect hypothesized by Andreas and Klein (2014), namely (i) connecting unseen words to known ones, and (ii) encouraging common behaviors among in-vocabulary words.

1 Introduction

Lexical features are powerful machine learning ingredients for many NLP tasks, but the very high-dimensional feature space brought by these features can be memory consuming and cause over-fitting problems. Is it possible to use low-dimensional word embeddings to reduce the high-dimensionality of lexical features? In this paper, we propose a general framework for this purpose. As a proof of concept, we apply the framework to dependency parsing, since this is a task where lexical features are essential.

Our approach is illustrated in Figure 1. Consider a transition-based dependency parser (Yamada and Matsumoto, 2003; Nivre et al., 2006; Zhang and Clark, 2008; Huang and Sagae, 2010; Zhang and Nivre, 2011), in which the words on top of the stack and the queue (denoted by $s_0\mathtt{w}$ and $q_0\mathtt{w}$, respectively) are typically used as features to calculate scores of transitions. When $s_0\mathtt{w}$ is used as a feature template, the features in this template (e.g. $s_0\mathtt{w}_{saw}$ and $s_0\mathtt{w}_{look}$) can be viewed as one-hot vectors of a dimension of the lexicon size (Figure 1). Corresponding to $s_0\mathtt{w}$, a weight is assigned to *each word* (e.g. $W(s_0\mathtt{w}_{saw})$ and $W(s_0\mathtt{w}_{look})$) for calculating a transition score. Instead, we propose to utilize a d-dimensional word embedding, and replace the feature template $s_0\mathtt{w}$ by d features, namely $s_0e_1, \ldots, s_0e_d$. Given the vector representation of a word (e.g., $\mathsf{e}_{saw} = (0.6, \ldots, 0.2)$), we replace the lexical feature (e.g. $s_0\mathtt{w}_{saw}$) by a linear combination of the d features (e.g., $s_0\mathsf{e}_{saw} := 0.6 s_0 e_1 + \ldots + 0.2 s_0 e_d$). Then, instead of the weights in a number of lexicon size assigned to $s_0\mathtt{w}$, now we use d

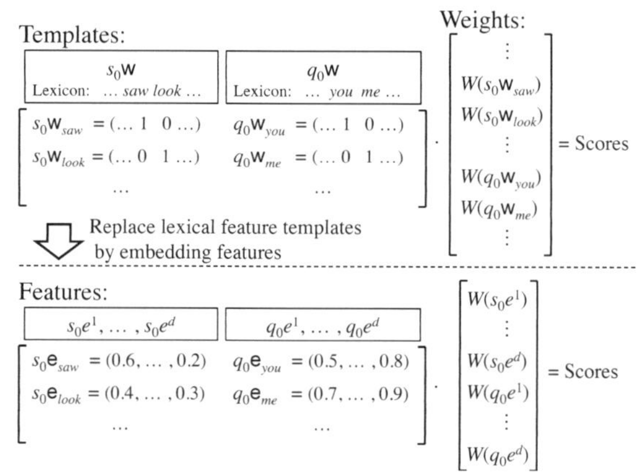

Figure 1: Each lexical feature template is replaced by a small number of embedding features.

29th Pacific Asia Conference on Language, Information and Computation pages 106 - 113
Shanghai, China, October 30 - November 1, 2015

weights (i.e., $W(s_0e_1), \ldots, W(s_0e_d)$) to calculate a transition score. In this work, we reduce feature space dimensionality by *replacing all lexical features*, including combined features such as $s_0\mathtt{w}q_0\mathtt{w}$, by the word embedding features.

In experiments, we applied the framework to a near state-of-the-art dependency parser (Huang et al., 2012), evaluated different vector operations for replacing combined lexical features, and explored different word embeddings trained from unlabeled or automatically labeled corpora. We expect word embeddings to augment parsing accuracy, by the mechanism hypothesized in Andreas and Klein (2014), namely (i) to connect unseen words to known ones, and (ii) to encourage common behaviors among in-vocabulary words. In contrast to the negative results reported in Andreas and Klein (2014), we find that our framework indeed has these effects, and significantly improves the baseline. As a comparison, our method performs better than the technique of replacing words by cluster bit strings (Koo et al., 2008; Bansal et al., 2014), and the results outperform a neural network based parser (Chen and Manning, 2014).

2 Related Work

A lot of recent work has been done on training word vectors (Mnih and Hinton, 2009; Mikolov et al., 2013; Lebret and Collobert, 2014; Pennington et al., 2014), and utilizing word vectors in various NLP tasks (Turian et al., 2010; Andreas and Klein, 2014; Bansal et al., 2014). The common approach (Turian et al., 2010; Koo et al., 2008; Bansal et al., 2014) is to use vector representations in *new features*, added to (near) state-of-the-art systems, and make improvement. As a result, the feature space gets even larger. We instead propose to *reduce lexical features* by word embeddings. To our own surprise, though the feature space gets much smaller, the resulted system performs better.

Another stream of research is to use word embeddings in whole neural network architectures (Collobert et al., 2011; Socher et al., 2013; Chen and Manning, 2014; Weiss et al., 2015; Dyer et al., 2015; Watanabe and Sumita, 2015). Though this is a promising direction and has brought breakthroughs in the field, the question is left open on what exactly

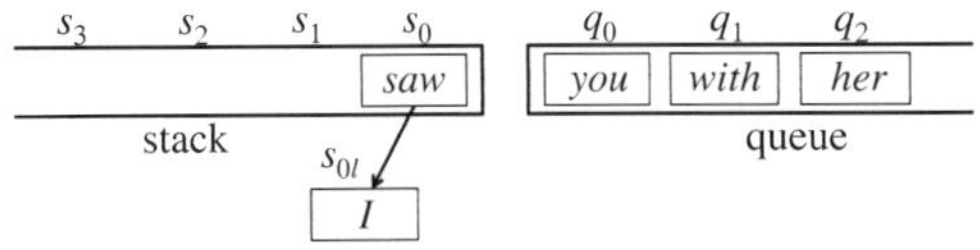

Figure 2: An internal state of a dependency parser.

has contributed to the power of neural based approaches. In this work, we conjecture that the power may partly come from the low-dimensionality of word embeddings, and this advantage can be transferred to traditional feature based systems. Our experiments support this conjecture, and we expect the proposed method to help more mature, proven-to-work existing systems.

Machine learning techniques have been proposed for reducing model size and imposing feature sparsity (Suzuki et al., 2011; Yogatama and Smith, 2014). Compared to these methods, our approach is simple, without extra twists of objective functions or learning algorithms. More importantly, by using word embeddings to reduce lexical features, we explicitly exploit the inherited syntactic and semantic similarities between words.

Another technique to reduce features is dimension reduction by matrix or tensor factorization (Argyriou et al., 2007; Lei et al., 2014), but typically applied to supervised learning. In contrast, we use word embeddings trained from unlabeled or automatically labeled corpora, bringing the aspects of semi-supervised learning or self-training.

3 Formalization

In this section, we formalize the framework of reducing lexical features. We take transition-based parsing as an example, but the framework can be applied to other systems using lexical features.

3.1 Transition-based Parsing

In typical transition-based parsing, input words are put into a queue and partially built parse trees are cached in a stack (Figure 2). At each step, a shift-reduce action is selected, which consumes words from the queue and/or build new structures in the stack. For the set of actions, we adopt the arc-standard system (Yamada and Matsumoto, 2003; Nivre, 2008; Huang and Sagae, 2010), in which the actions are:

1. `Shift`, which pops the top of the queue and pushes it to the stack;
2. `Reduce-Left`, which replaces the top two trees in the stack by their consolidated tree, left as child;
3. `Reduce-Right`, which replaces the top two trees in the stack by their consolidated tree, right as child.

Following Huang et al. (2012), we use the max-violation perceptron for global learning and beam-search for decoding.

In order to select the appropriate action, a set of features are used for calculating transition scores of each action. The features are typically extracted from internal states of the queue and the stack. For example, if we denote the elements in the stack by $s_0, s_1, \ldots$ from the top, and elements in the queue by $q_0, q_1, \ldots$ from the front; then, the words such as $s_0\mathtt{w}$ and $q_0\mathtt{w}$, the POS-tags such as $s_0\mathtt{t}$, and the combined word and POS-tags such as $s_0\mathtt{wt}$ are used as features. Other features include the POS-tag $s_{0l}\mathtt{t}$ (where s_{0l} denotes the leftmost child of s_0, and s_{0r} denotes the rightmost child of s_0), and the combined feature $s_0\mathtt{w}q_0\mathtt{w}$, *etc.*

If the corresponding words and POS-tags are specified in a concrete state, we use subscripts of `w` and `t` to denote the concrete feature. For example, from the state illustrated in Figure 2, we can extract features such as $s_0\mathtt{w}_{saw}$, $q_0\mathtt{w}_{you}$, $s_0\mathtt{t}_{\text{VBD}}$, $s_0\mathtt{w}_{saw}\mathtt{t}_{\text{VBD}}$, $s_{0l}\mathtt{t}_{\text{PRP}}$, and $s_0\mathtt{w}_{saw}q_0\mathtt{w}_{you}$, *etc.*

For the purpose of this work, we mainly focus on the words (e.g., $\mathtt{w}_{saw}$, $\mathtt{w}_{you}$) in the above features. Other parts, including positions such as s_0 and q_0, and POS-tags such as $\mathtt{t}_{\text{VBD}}$, are regarded as formal symbols.

3.2 Reducing Lexical Features

Formally, we define **lexial features** as the features comprising one or more words, possibly in combination with other symbols. We propose to replace lexical features as follows, and leaving other features (e.g. $s_0\mathtt{t}_{\text{VBD}}$) unchanged in the system.

Lexical Feature of One Word Let $s\mathtt{w}$ be a one word lexical feature, where `w` is the word and s is an arbitrary symbol. Let $\mathsf{e} = (v_i)_{1\leq i \leq d}$ be a d-dimensional vector representation of the word `w`, where v_i is the i-th entry. Then, we replace $s\mathtt{w}$ by $s\mathsf{e}$, a linear combination of $se_1, \ldots, se_d$:

$$s\mathsf{e} := \sum_{i=1}^{d} v_i \cdot (se_i).$$

For example, assume that the word "*saw*" has a vector representation $\mathsf{e}_{saw} = (0.6, \ldots, 0.2)$. Then, the feature $s_0\mathtt{w}_{saw}$ is replaced by

$$s_0\mathsf{e}_{saw} := 0.6 s_0 e_1 + \ldots + 0.2 s_0 e_d.$$

In the above, $s_0e_1, \ldots, s_0e_d$ are introduced to replace the feature template $s_0\mathtt{w}$. Note that, instead of using a different feature $s_0\mathtt{w}_x$ for each different word x, now we only have d features, $s_0e_1, \ldots, s_0e_d$, commonly used by all words, across the feature template $s_0\mathtt{w}$.

As another example, in the case of features combining a word and its POS tag, such as $s_0\mathtt{t}_{\text{VBD}}\mathtt{w}_{saw}$, we treat $s_0\mathtt{t}_{\text{VBD}}$ as a formal symbol and replace the feature as the following:

$$s_0\mathtt{t}_{\text{VBD}}\mathsf{e}_{saw} := 0.6 s_0\mathtt{t}_{\text{VBD}} e_1 + \ldots + 0.2 s_0\mathtt{t}_{\text{VBD}} e_d.$$

Lexical Feature of Two or More Words For lexical features of two or more words, such as $s_0\mathtt{w}q_0\mathtt{w}$, we replace the words by a combination of the two or more corresponding word vectors. More precisely, for a two-word lexical feature $s\mathtt{w}_1\mathtt{w}_2$, assume that the vectors $\mathsf{e}_1 = (u_i)_{1\leq i\leq d}$ and $\mathsf{e}_2 = (v_i)_{1\leq i\leq d}$ represent $\mathtt{w}_1$ and $\mathtt{w}_2$, respectively. Then, we propose the following operations[1] to replace $s\mathtt{w}_1\mathtt{w}_2$:

- OUTER PRODUCT ($\otimes$):

$$s(\mathsf{e}_1 \otimes \mathsf{e}_2) := \sum_{i=1}^{d}\sum_{j=1}^{d} u_i v_j \cdot (se_i\tilde{e}_j),$$

For example, if $\mathsf{e}_{saw} = (0.6, \ldots, 0.2)$ and $\mathsf{e}_{you} = (0.5, \ldots, 0.8)$, then $s_0\mathtt{w}_{saw}q_0\mathtt{w}_{you}$ is replaced by:

$$s_0q_0(\mathsf{e}_{saw} \otimes \mathsf{e}_{you}) := (0.6 \times 0.5) s_0q_0e_1\tilde{e}_1 + \ldots + (0.6 \times 0.8) s_0q_0e_1\tilde{e}_d + \ldots + (0.2 \times 0.8) s_0q_0e_d\tilde{e}_d.$$

Here, $\tilde{e}_1, \ldots, \tilde{e}_d$ are copies of $e_1, \ldots, e_d$.

[1]Operations for more than three word vectors are similar.

- SUM (+):

$$s(\mathsf{e}_1 + \mathsf{e}_2) := \sum_{i=1}^{d} (u_i + v_i) \cdot (se_i).$$

Following the previous example, $s_0\mathtt{w}_{saw}q_0\mathtt{w}_{you}$ is replaced by:

$$s_0q_0(\mathsf{e}_{saw} + \mathsf{e}_{you}) := (0.6 + 0.5)s_0q_0e_1 + \dots + (0.2 + 0.8)s_0q_0e_d.$$

- CONCATENATION ($\oplus$):

$$s(\mathsf{e}_1 \oplus \mathsf{e}_2) := \sum_{i=1}^{d} u_i \cdot (se_i) + \sum_{j=1}^{d} v_j \cdot (s\tilde{e}_j).$$

Following the example, replace $s_0\mathtt{w}_{saw}q_0\mathtt{w}_{you}$ by

$$s_0q_0(\mathsf{e}_{saw} \oplus \mathsf{e}_{you}) := 0.6s_0q_0e_1 + \dots + 0.2s_0q_0e_d + 0.5s_0q_0\tilde{e}_1 + \dots + 0.8s_0q_0\tilde{e}_d.$$

Theoretically, OUTER PRODUCT is the natural operation, because if $s_0\mathtt{w}_x$ and $q_0\mathtt{w}_y$ are regarded as high-dimensional one-hot vectors (Figure 1), the feature combination $s_0\mathtt{w}_xq_0\mathtt{w}_y$ corresponds to the outer product of $s_0\mathtt{w}_x$ and $q_0\mathtt{w}_y$ (i.e., $s_0\mathtt{w}_xq_0\mathtt{w}_y$ fires when $s_0\mathtt{w}_x$ *and* $q_0\mathtt{w}_y$ fire). Empirically, we find that OUTER indeed performs the best among the three operations; however, the outer product also introduces d^2 embedding features, many more than the d features in SUM or $2d$ features in CONCATENATION. We also find that SUM performs better than CONCATENATION, being both effective and low-dimensional (Section 4.1).

4 Experiments

We reimplemented the parser of Huang et al. (2012) and replaced all lexical feature templates by embedding features, according to our framework. We set beam size to 8, and report unlabeled attachment scores (UAS) on the standard Penn Treebank (PTB) split, using the data attached to Huang et al. (2012)'s system[2]. POS-tags are assigned by Stanford Tagger[3]. To highlight the effect of word embeddings on unseen words, we also report UAS on 148 sentences in the Dev. set which contain words in vocabulary of the embeddings but unseen in PTB training data (Unseen).

	Dev	Test	Unseen
Huang et al. (2012)	91.93	91.68	89.01
Different Operations, using STATE embedding:			
OUTER	**92.57***	**92.20***	**90.27***
SUM	92.25*	91.85	90.10*
CONCATENATION	92.18	91.86	89.96
Different Embeddings, using OUTER operation:			
PLAIN	92.33*	91.78	90.08*
TREE	92.37*	92.09*	89.82
STATE	**92.57***	**92.20***	**90.27***
Cluster Bit String:			
PLAIN	91.71	91.20	89.18
TREE	90.38	90.07	88.00
STATE	91.31	90.96	89.04
Bansal et al. (2014)	92.06	91.75	90.13
Neural Network (Chen and Manning, 2014):			
Random	86.37	86.19	81.06
PLAIN	90.68	90.48	87.02
TREE	91.06	90.82	87.38
STATE	91.03	90.57	87.88

Table 1: Parsing Results (UAS). Numbers marked by asterisk (*) are statistically significant ($p < 0.05$), compared to the baseline (Huang et al., 2012) under a paired bootstrap test.

We built 300 dimensional word embeddings from 6 months articles in New York Times Corpus[4] (01/2007-06/2007, 1.5M sentences), for words of frequencies greater than 50. Word vectors are obtained from singular value decomposition (SVD) of the PPMI matrices (Levy and Goldberg, 2014b), for co-occurrence matrices of target words with various types of contexts (Levy and Goldberg, 2014a), to be specified later. We choose SVD for training word vectors because it is fast; and recent research suggests that SVD can perform as well as other embedding methods (Levy et al., 2015).

We investigated the following types of contexts for training word vectors: PLAIN, which uses words within a window of 3 to each side of the target word as contexts; TREE, which uses words within 3 steps of the target in the dependency trees, obtained from applying Huang et al. (2012)'s parser to the corpus; and STATE, which records the internal states of

[2] http://acl.cs.qc.edu/~lhuang/

[3] http://nlp.stanford.edu/software/corenlp.shtml

[4] https://catalog.ldc.upenn.edu/LDC2008T19

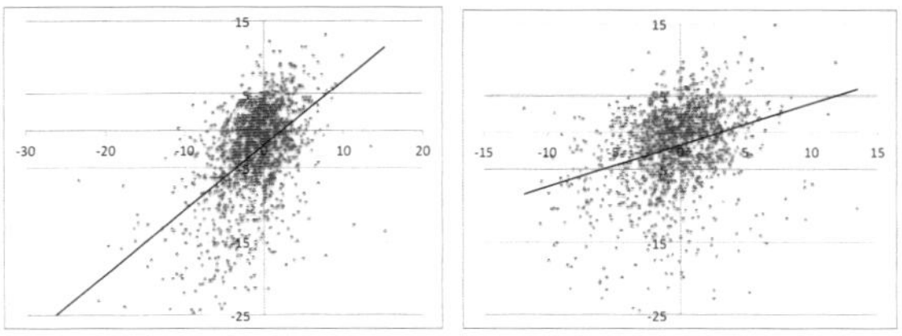

Figure 3: We plot X by the weight of the feature $s_0\mathtt{w}_x$, and Y by the weight of $s_0\mathtt{e}_x$, for x of high (Left) and middle (Right) frequency words.

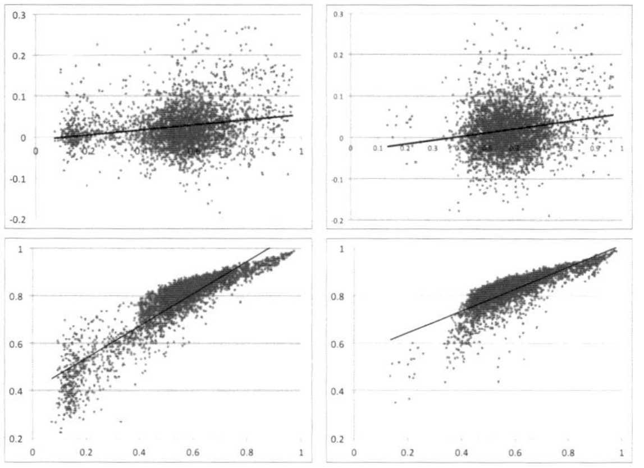

Figure 4: We plot X by cosine similarities between words, and Y by cosine similarities of weights, learned for lexical features (Upper) and embedding features (Lower). Words are of high (Left) and middle (Right) frequencies.

Huang et al. (2012)'s parser, and uses words at positions $\{s_1, s_2, s_3, s_{0l}, s_{0r}, s_{1l}, s_{1r}, q_0, q_1, q_2\}$ as contexts for a target s_0. These positions are where parsing features are extracted from. We expect TREE and STATE to encode more syntactic related information.

4.1 Parsing Results

The parsing results are shown in Table 1. We find that, the OUTER operation used for combined features and the STATE contexts for training word vectors perform the best for transition-based parsing, but other settings also improve the baseline (Huang et al., 2012), especially for sentences containing unseen words. We conducted paired bootstrap test to compare our proposed method with the baseline, and find out that most improvements are statistically significant.

We also compared with the method of replacing words in lexical features by cluster bit strings (Koo et al., 2008; Bansal et al., 2014). We use bit strings constructed from hierarchical clusters induced from the previous word embeddings; as well as the the bit strings constructed in Bansal et al. (2014)[5]. Lengths of the bit strings are set to 4, 6, 8, 12, 16, and 20. It turns out that the performance gains are not as significant as our proposed method.

For reference, we report results by a neural network based parser (Chen and Manning, 2014), since our method shares a similar motivation with Chen and Manning's work, i.e. to use low-dimensional dense features instead of high-dimensional sparse features in parsing, aiming to obtain better generalization. For initializing word embeddings in the neural network, we tried 300 dimensional random vectors and the PLAIN, TREE, STATE vectors as described previously. We find that pre-trained word embeddings can improve performance, with TREE and STATE slightly better than PLAIN, suggesting that TREE and STATE may contain more information useful to parsing. However, the STATE vector is not as powerful as used with Huang et al. (2012)'s parser, suggesting that for a given baseline, it may be more helpful to train word vectors from contexts specific to that baseline. Chen and Manning's parser generally performs worse than Huang et al. (2012)'s baseline, suggesting that we cannot immediately obtain a better parser by switching to neural networks; other factors, such as global optimization and carefully selected features may still have merits, which makes our method useful for improving existing mature parsers.

4.2 Analysis

Is our modified parser really a feature reduction of the baseline system, i.e. is the parsing model trained for embedding features actually correlated to the baseline parsing model using lexical features? In Figure 3, we plot weights learned for the feature $s_0\mathtt{w}_x$ as X, and weights for $s_0\mathtt{e}_x$ as Y, where x ranges over high or middle frequency words. The weight for $s_0\mathtt{e}_x$ is calculated by taking inner product of the vector $s_0\mathtt{e}_x$ and the weight vector $(W(s_0e_1), \ldots, W(s_0e_d))$. As the direction of

[5]http://ttic.uchicago.edu/~mbansal/

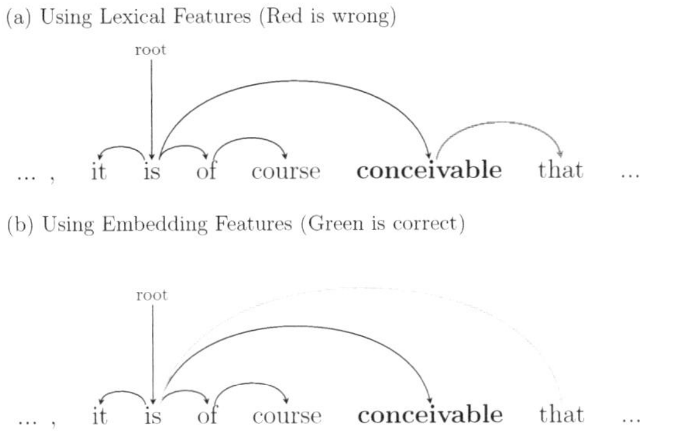

"While it is possible that the Big Green initiative will be ruled unconstitutional, it is of course conceivable that in modern California it could slide through."

Figure 5: Improved parsing results with unseen (bold) words.

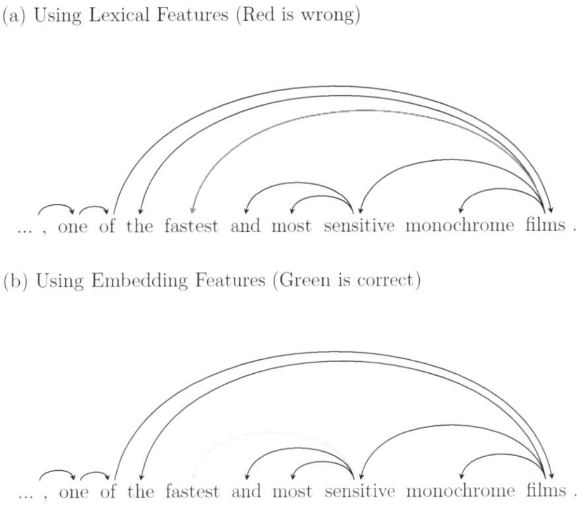

"The Rochester, N.Y., photographic giant recently began marketing T-Max 3200, one of the fastest and most sensitive monochrome films."

Figure 6: Improved parsing results on parallel structure of adjectives.

the regression lines show, weights learned for $s_0\mathtt{e}_x$ are positively correlated to weights learned for $s_0\mathtt{w}_x$. It suggests that the parsing model trained for embedding features is indeed correlated to the parsing model of the baseline, which implies that the baseline parser and our modified parser would have similar behaviors. This may explain the significance results reported in Table 1: though our improvements against the baseline is fairly moderate, they are still statistically significant because our modified parser behaves similarly as the baseline parser, but would correct the mistakes made by the baseline while preserving most originally correct labels. Such improvements are easier to achieve statistical significance (Berg-Kirkpatrick et al., 2012), and are arguably indicating better generalization.

So how does our modified parser improve from the baseline? In Figure 4, we plot cosine similarities between word vectors as X, and cosine similarities between weight vectors of all one-word lexical features as Y, compared to the similarities of weights of the corresponding embedding features. The plots show that, for similar words, the learned weights for the corresponding lexical features are only slightly similar; but after the lexical features are reduced to low-dimensional embedding features, the learned weights for the corresponding features are more strongly correlated. In other words, weights for embedding features encourage similar behaviors between similar words, due to a much lower dimensionality. This property may have two favorable effects on parsing, as hypothesized in Andreas and Klein (2014): (i) to connect unseen words to known ones, and (ii) to encourage common behaviors among in-vocabulary words.

The effects on unseen words have been observed in the Unseen column in Table 1, and we present a concrete example in Figure 5. In this example, "*conceivable*" is unseen in the training data, thus cannot be recognized by the baseline parser; however, its word vector is similar to "*subjective*" and "*undeniably*", whose behaviors are learned and generalized to "*conceivable*", by our modified parser using embedding features.

To illustrate the effects on in-vocabulary words, we take a specific parallel structure of adjectives. More precisely, we consider an internal state of the parser such that: $s_1\mathtt{t}$ and $s_0\mathtt{t}$ have POS-tags JJ, JJS or JJR; and $s_{0\ell}\mathtt{t}$ has a POS-tag CC or Comma. Then, in 98.8% instances of such a state in the training data, the golden label action is `Reduce-Left`, suggesting a strong tendency of the state to become a parallel structure of adjectives, such as "*black and white*". However, when we parse New York Times data using the baseline parser, the proportion of `Reduce-Left` action when facing the state decreases to 96.7%, suggesting that this tendency is

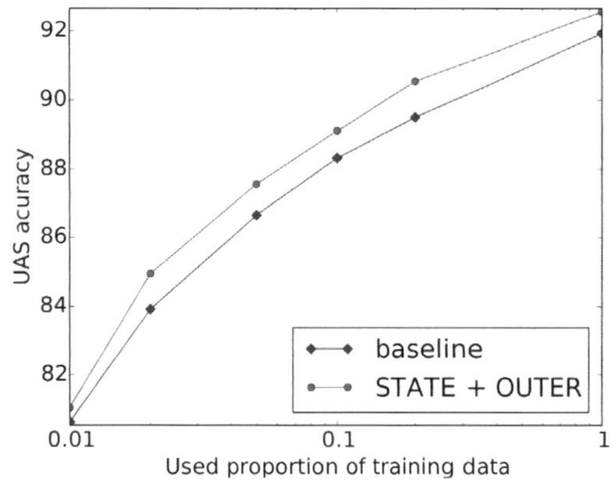

Figure 7: UAS on Dev. set, of models trained on less data.

not fully generalized as a rule for parallel structure of adjectives. This is not astonishing, because POS-tags and surface forms of lexical features are diverse in the training data. However, when we use our modified parser, the proportion of `Reduce-Left` action turns out to be 99.4%, significantly higher than using the baseline parser according to a permutation test. It suggests that our modified parser generalizes and strengthens the rule of parallel structure, by enforcing similar behaviors among similar adjectives. A concrete example of improvement is presented in Figure 6.

In Figure 7, we vary the size of training data and plot UAS of the obtained parsing models. As the figure shows, our modified parser using embedding features constantly outperforms the baseline. However, the performance of both settings decrease as the training data size decreases, suggesting that there may not be much syntactic information encoded in the word embeddings, even though the word embeddings are trained on internal states of the baseline parser, which is trained on full training data. We believe this graph indicates that, word embeddings can help parsing, but not because they encode extra syntactic information; rather, it is because word embeddings bring better generalization.

5 Conclusion

We have proposed a framework for reducing lexical features by word embeddings, and applied the framework to transition-based dependency parsing. A near state-of-the-art parser is improved, even though the features are reduced. This work is still preliminary, as we have only tested on one parser; however, our results are promising and our analysis suggests that the proposed method may indeed bring better generalization. We believe our framework can help more systems to reduce lexical features and alleviate the risk of overfitting, thanks to its generality.

References

Jacob Andreas and Dan Klein. 2014. How much do word embeddings encode about syntax? In *Proceedings of ACL*.

Andreas Argyriou, Theodoros Evgeniou, and Massimiliano Pontil. 2007. Multi-task feature learning. In *Advances in NIPS*.

Mohit Bansal, Kevin Gimpel, and Karen Livescu. 2014. Tailoring continuous word representations for dependency parsing. In *Proceedings of ACL*.

Taylor Berg-Kirkpatrick, David Burkett, and Dan Klein. 2012. An empirical investigation of statistical significance in nlp. In *Proceedings of EMNLP-CoNLL*.

Danqi Chen and Christopher D Manning. 2014. A fast and accurate dependency parser using neural networks. In *Proceedings of EMNLP*.

Ronan Collobert, Jason Weston, Léon Bottou, Michael Karlen, Koray Kavukcuoglu, and Pavel Kuksa. 2011. Natural language processing (almost) from scratch. *J. Mach. Learn. Res.*, 12.

Chris Dyer, Miguel Ballesteros, Wang Ling, Austin Matthews, and Noah A. Smith. 2015. Transition-based dependency parsing with stack long short-term memory. In *Proceedings of ACL-IJCNLP*.

Liang Huang and Kenji Sagae. 2010. Dynamic programming for linear-time incremental parsing. In *Proceedings of ACL*.

Liang Huang, Suphan Fayong, and Yang Guo. 2012. Structured perceptron with inexact search. In *Proceedings of NAACL-HLT*.

Terry Koo, Xavier Carreras, and Michael Collins. 2008. Simple semi-supervised dependency parsing. In *Proceedings of ACL*.

Rémi Lebret and Ronan Collobert. 2014. Word embeddings through Hellinger PCA. In *Proceedings of EACL*.

Tao Lei, Yu Xin, Yuan Zhang, Regina Barzilay, and Tommi Jaakkola. 2014. Low-rank tensors for scoring dependency structures. In *Proceedings of ACL*.

Omer Levy and Yoav Goldberg. 2014a. Dependency-based word embeddings. In *Proceedings of ACL*.

Omer Levy and Yoav Goldberg. 2014b. Neural word embedding as implicit matrix factorization. In *Advances in NIPS*.

Omer Levy, Yoav Goldberg, and Ido Dagan. 2015. Improving distributional similarity with lessons learned from word embeddings. *Trans. ACL*, 3.

Tomas Mikolov, Ilya Sutskever, Kai Chen, Greg Corrado, and Jeffrey Dean. 2013. Distributed representations of words and phrases and their compositionality. In *Advances in NIPS*.

Andriy Mnih and Geoffrey E. Hinton. 2009. A scalable hierarchical distributed language model. In *Advances in NIPS*.

Joakim Nivre, Johan Hall, Jens Nilsson, Gülşen Eryiğit, and Svetoslav Marinov. 2006. Labeled pseudo-projective dependency parsing with support vector machines. In *Proceedings of CoNLL*.

Joakim Nivre. 2008. Algorithms for deterministic incremental dependency parsing. *Comput. Linguist.*

Jeffrey Pennington, Richard Socher, and Christopher Manning. 2014. Glove: Global vectors for word representation. In *Proceedings of EMNLP*.

Richard Socher, John Bauer, Christopher D. Manning, and Ng Andrew Y. 2013. Parsing with compositional vector grammars. In *Proceedings of ACL*.

Jun Suzuki, Hideki Isozaki, and Masaaki Nagata. 2011. Learning condensed feature representations from large unsupervised data sets for supervised learning. In *Proceedings of ACL-HLT*.

Joseph Turian, Lev-Arie Ratinov, and Yoshua Bengio. 2010. Word representations: A simple and general method for semi-supervised learning. In *Proceedings of ACL*.

Taro Watanabe and Eiichiro Sumita. 2015. Transition-based neural constituent parsing. In *Proceedings of ACL-IJCNLP*.

David Weiss, Chris Alberti, Michael Collins, and Slav Petrov. 2015. Structured training for neural network transition-based parsing. In *Proceedings of ACL-IJCNLP*.

Hiroyasu Yamada and Yuji Matsumoto. 2003. Statistical dependency analysis with support vector machines. In *In Proceedings of IWPT*.

Dani Yogatama and Noah A. Smith. 2014. Linguistic structured sparsity in text categorization. In *Proceedings of ACL*.

Yue Zhang and Stephen Clark. 2008. A tale of two parsers: Investigating and combining graph-based and transition-based dependency parsing. In *Proceedings of EMNLP*.

Yue Zhang and Joakim Nivre. 2011. Transition-based dependency parsing with rich non-local features. In *Proceedings of ACL*.

High-order Graph-based Neural Dependency Parsing

Zhisong Zhang[1,2] **and Hai Zhao**[1,2,*,†]
[1]Center for Brain-Like Computing and Machine Intelligence,
Department of Computer Science and Engineering,
Shanghai Jiao Tong University, Shanghai, 200240, China
[2]Key Laboratory of Shanghai Education Commission for Intelligent Interaction
and Cognitive Engineering, Shanghai Jiao Tong University, Shanghai, 200240, China
zzs2011@sjtu.edu.cn, zhaohai@cs.sjtu.edu.cn

Abstract

In this work, we present a novel way of using neural network for graph-based dependency parsing, which fits the neural network into a simple probabilistic model and can be furthermore generalized to high-order parsing. Instead of the sparse features used in traditional methods, we utilize distributed dense feature representations for neural network, which give better feature representations. The proposed parsers are evaluated on English and Chinese Penn Treebanks. Compared to existing work, our parsers give competitive performance with much more efficient inference.

1 Introduction

There have been two classes of typical approaches for dependency parsing: transition-based parsing and graph-based parsing. The former parses sentences by making a series of shift-reduce decisions (Yamada and Matsumoto, 2003; Nivre, 2003), while the latter searches for a tree through graph algorithms by decomposing trees into factors. This paper will focus on graph-based methods, which are based on dynamic programming strategies (Eisner, 1996; McDonald et al., 2005; McDonald and Pereira, 2006). In this recent decade, extensions have been made to use high-order factors (Carreras, 2007; Koo and Collins, 2010) in graph models and the highest one considers fourth-order (Ma and Zhao, 2012). However, all those methods usually use sparse indicator features as inputs and linear models to get the scores for later inference process. They are easy to suffer from the problem of sparsity, and linear models can be insufficient to effectively integrate all the sparse features in spite of various rich context that can be potentially exploited.

Distributed representations and neural network provide a way to alleviate such a drawback (Bengio et al., 2003; Collobert et al., 2011). Instead of high-dimensional sparse indicator feature vectors, distributed representations use low-dimensional dense vectors (also known as embeddings) to represent the features, and then they are usually used in a neural network. For example, in the traditional methods, a word is usually expressed by a one-hot vector; while distributed representations use a dense vector. By appropriate representation learning (usually by back-propagations in neural network), these embeddings can replace traditional sparse features and perform quite well together with neural network.

In recent years, using distributed representations and neural network has gradually gained popularity in natural language processing (NLP) since the pioneer work of (Bengio et al., 2003). Several neural network language models have reported exciting results for the tasks of machine translation and speech recognition (Schwenk, 2007; Mikolov et al., 2010;

*Correspondence author.

†This work was partially supported by the National Natural Science Foundation of China (No. 61170114, and No. 61272248), the National Basic Research Program of China (No. 2013CB329401), the Science and Technology Commission of Shanghai Municipality (No. 13511500200), the European Union Seventh Framework Program (No. 247619), the Cai Yuanpei Program (CSC fund 201304490199 and 201304490171), and the art and science interdiscipline funds of Shanghai Jiao Tong University, No. 14X190040031, and the Key Project of National Society Science Foundation of China, No. 15-ZDA041.

29th Pacific Asia Conference on Language, Information and Computation pages 114 - 123
Shanghai, China, October 30 - November 1, 2015

Wang et al., 2013; Wang et al., 2014; Wang et al., 2015). Many other tasks of NLP have also been reconsidered using neural network, the SENNA system[1] (Collobert et al., 2011) solved the tasks of part-of-speech (POS) tagging, chunking, named entity recognition and semantic role labeling.

In this work, we utilize neural network for first-order, second-order and third-order graph-based dependency parsing, with the help of the existing graph-based parsing algorithms. For high-order parsing, it is performed after the first-order parser prunes unlikely parts of the parsing tree. We use neural network to learn dense representations for word, POS and distance information, and predict how likely the dependency relationships are for a sub-tree factor in the dependency tree. For unlabeled projective dependency parsing, we have put a free distribution of our implementation on the Internet[2].

The remainder of the paper is organized as follows: Section 2 discusses related work, Section 3 gives the background for graph-based dependency parsing, Section 4 describes our neural network model and how we utilize it with graph-based parsing and Section 5 presents our experiments, results and some discussions. We summarize this paper in Section 6.

2 Related Work

There has been a few of attempts to parse with neural network. For dependency parsing, (Chen and Manning, 2014) uses neural network for greedy transition-based dependency parsing. We explore graph-based methods in this work, which might be difficultly utilized with neural network. (Le and Zuidema, 2014) implements a generative dependency model with a recursive neural network, but the model is used for re-ranking which needs k-best candidates.

For constituency parsing, (Collobert, 2011) uses a convolutional neural network and solves the problem with a hierarchical tagging process. (Socher et al., 2010) and (Socher et al., 2013) use recursive neural network to model phrase-based parse trees, but their methods might be unlikely generalized to dependency parsing because a dependency parse tree has no non-terminal nodes while constituency parse trees are derived from the phrases structure.

[1]http://ronan.collobert.com/senna/

[2]https://github.com/zzsfornlp/nngdparser

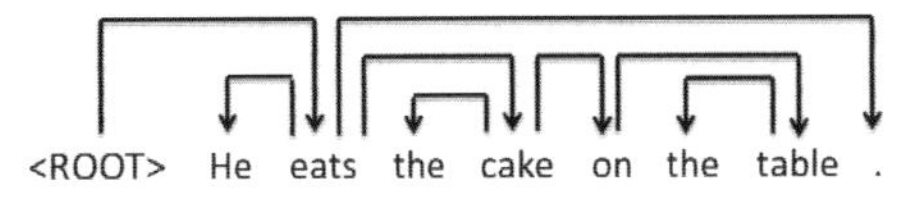

Figure 1: An example dependency tree.

Semi-supervised methods usually incorporate word representations as the embeddings for words in the projection layer in neural network; they usually make use of lots of unlabeled data to find the patterns in natural languages. If we utilize pre-trained word vectors (see in Section 5.1), our models can be regarded as semi-supervised to some extent. (Koo et al., 2008) uses Brown clustering algorithm to obtain word representations, but then transforms them into sparse features as additional features and again uses the traditional methods; while in neural network models including this work, the embeddings directly replace sparse features for inputs.

3 Graph-based Dependency Parsing

3.1 Background of Dependency Parsing

Syntax information is important for many other tasks (Zhang and Zhao, 2013; Chen et al., 2015). As a classic syntactic problem, dependency parsing aims to predict a dependency tree, which directly represents head-modifier relationships between words in a sentence. Figure 1 shows a dependency tree, in which all the links connect head-modifier pairs. By enforcing that all the nodes must have one and only one parent and the resulting graphs should be acyclic and connected, we can get a directed dependency tree for a sentence (we usually add a dummy node $\langle root \rangle$ for the sentence as the highest level node).

Labels or dependency category can also be defined for the links in the dependency tree, however, this work will focus on unlabeled dependency parsing, because once the parsing tree has been built, labeling can be very effectively performed. Most dependency trees for most treebanks follow a useful constrain that is called projectiveness, i.e., no cross links exist in the tree. In treebanks for major languages such as English, nearly all sentences are pro-

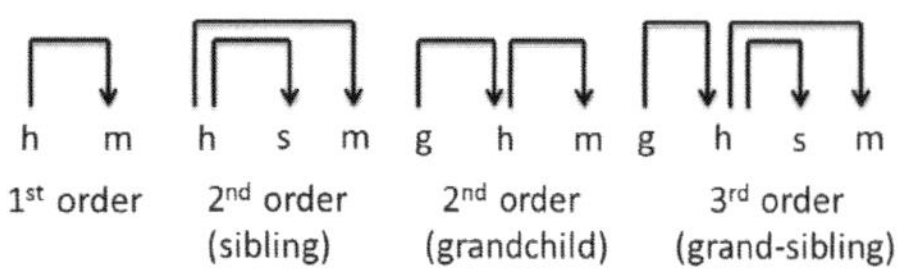

Figure 2: The decompositions of factors.

jective. Therefore this work also considers projective dependency parsing only.

3.2 Graph-based Methods and their Decompositions

In graph-based methods, dependency trees are decomposed into specific factors that do not influence with each other. Each factor, usually represented by a sub-tree, is given a score individually based on its features. The score for a whole dependency tree T is the summation of the scores of all the factors:

$$Score_{tree}(T) = \sum_{p \in factors(T)} Score_{factor}(p)$$

According to the sub-tree size of the factors, we can define the order of the graph model, some of the decomposition methods are shown in Figure 2. As the simplest case, the first-order model just considers sub-tree factor of single edge and its score is obtained by adding all the scores of the edges. For second-order models, another node is added into the factor, which can be either sibling or grandparent. For third-order models, the simplest form is the grand-sibling decomposition, which adds both sibling and grandparent nodes. Existing work also applied various decompositions, such as third-order tri-sibling (Koo and Collins, 2010) which considers two siblings of the modifier and fourth-order grand-tri-sibling (Ma and Zhao, 2012) which adds a grandparent node on tri-siblings.

For the sake of simplicity and the convenient use of neural network, we only consider four models discussed above (the sub-tree patterns of their factors are also shown in Figure 2). The notations for the four models are defined as follows:

- $o1$, first-order model
- $o2sib$, second-order model with sibling nodes
- $o2g$, second-order model with grandparent nodes
- $o3g$, third-order model with both sibling and grandparent nodes

3.3 Parsing Algorithms

Graph-based methods usually need to use dynamic programming based parsing algorithms, which make use of the scores of sub-trees for larger sub-trees in a bottom-up way. These algorithms solve the inference problem, that is, how to get an optimal tree given the scores for the parts. Our proposed parsers also take these algorithms as backbones and use them for inference.

In the traditional methods, scores are usually obtained directly from a linear model. In the learning phase, parameter estimation methods for structured linear models may adopt averaged perceptron (Collins, 2002; Collins and Roark, 2004) and max-margin methods (Taskar et al., 2004).

Still using all the existing parsing algorithms, this work focuses on improving scoring for the factors. In detail, our work uses neural network to determine the scores. Nevertheless the traditional methods might be difficultly extended to neural network because of the non-linearity. Therefore, we do not directly obtain scores from neural network. Instead we utilize a probabilistic model and obtain scores by some transformations, and then use these existing parsing algorithms for inference.

4 Neural Network Parsers

4.1 The Probabilistic Model

For graph-based dependency parsing, it is not straightforward to extend the linear models to the more powerful nonlinear neural network, because we need to figure out the scores for the factors of the tree, which are not specified in the original treebank. That is, we only know which factors are in the correct parsing tree, but there are no natural ways to indicate how they are scored; the only intuition is to give high scores to the right factors and low scores to the wrong ones.

In this work, a simple probabilistic model is adopted for the neural network parsers. It is one of Eisner's models (Eisner, 1996). Precisely, Eisner's model A is chosen and slightly modified for scoring. The model describes bi-gram lexical affinities, and it gives each possible link an affinity probability. The final probability of drawing a parsing tree for a sentence is the product of all the affinity probabilities. The original model also considers probabilities of words and tags and its formula is given as follows:

$$
\begin{aligned}
& Pr(words, tags, links) \\
&= Pr(words, tags) \cdot Pr(links\ present\ or\ not | words, tags) \\
&\approx Pr(words, tags) \cdot \prod_{1 \le h,m \le n} Pr(L_{hm} | tword(h), tword(m))
\end{aligned}
$$

Unlike the original model, we determine only the probability for the parsing tree (the existence of the links):

$$
Pr(T|S) = \prod_{\substack{0 \le h \le length(S) \\ 0 < m \le length(S)}} Pr(L_{hm} | context(h, m))
$$

Here L_{hm} is a binary variable with Bernoulli distribution which means whether node h is the head of node m and $context(h, m)$ means the context of the two nodes which includes words, POS tags and distance.

When looking for the best tree, we simply find the tree with highest probability (we use logarithmic form for more convenient computations). Considering the single-headed constrain for dependency tree construction, if we assign 1 to L_{Hm}, which makes H the parent of m, we must assign 0 to all other L_{hm}, h means all the nodes that are not equal to H. The logarithmic probability can be rewritten as follows:

$$
\begin{aligned}
\log(Pr(T|S)) = & \sum_{0 < m \le length(S)} \Big(\log(Pr(L_{Hm} = 1)) \\
& + \sum_{\substack{0 \le h \le length(S) \\ h \ne H, h \ne m}} \log(Pr(L_{hm} = 0)) \Big)
\end{aligned}
$$

Here H represents the real parent node of node m. The formula is in the form of summation of the factor scores, which are defined as:

$$
\begin{aligned}
Score(H, m) = & \log(Pr(L_{Hm} = 1)) \\
& + \sum_{\substack{0 \le h \le length(S) \\ h \ne H, h \ne m}} \log(Pr(L_{hm} = 0))
\end{aligned}
$$

After defining the score of each dependency factor, we can apply the scores to the existing parsing algorithms (Eisner, 1996; McDonald et al., 2005).

4.2 High-Order Parsing

We now generalize the model to high-order parsing. In the first-order model, we define probabilities for the head-modifier pair, which is the factor for first-order parsing. Naturally, we can define probabilities for high-order factors. The probability of a parse tree is the product of all its factors (either existing ones or wrong ones), the probability for one factor is again a binary value which means whether the factor exists in the dependency tree.

Using single-headed constraint again, for all the factors with the same node as the children, only one can exist in a legal parsing tree. The similar transformations can be performed and then again we will take the transformed scores as inputs to the corresponding parsing algorithms.

We describe the high-order extension by taking the $o2g$ model as an example and other models can be handled in a similar way. We will use the similar notations: L_{ghm} is the binary variable that indicates the factor with node g as grandparent, node h as head and node m as modifier exists in the parse tree. We continuously use H as the parent of m and G as its grandparent so that L_{GHm} is 1 (representing an existing factor) in the parser tree. The logarithmic probability can be given by the following equation:

$$
\begin{aligned}
\log(Pr(T|S)) &= \sum_{g,h,m} Pr(L_{ghm} | context(g, h, m)) \\
&= \sum_{0 < m \le length(S)} \Big(\log(Pr(L_{GHm} = 1)) \\
&\quad + \sum_{\substack{h,g \\ h \ne H, g \ne G \\ h \ne m, g \ne m}} \log(Pr(L_{ghm} = 0)) \Big)
\end{aligned}
$$

4.3 Neural Network Model

Now we adopt feed-forward neural network to learn and compute the probability for a factor. The inputs for the network are features for a factor such as word forms, POS tags and distance, and the output will be the probability that the factor exists in the parse tree. Figure 3 shows the structure of our neural network for the $o2g$ model, the networks for other models will be similar.

For the architecture of the neural network, as usual, the first layer is the projection layer or the embedding layer, which performs the concatenation for the embeddings. All features are treated equally and mapped to embeddings of the same dimension. So, the embedding or projection matrix $E \in \mathbb{R}^{d \times N}$ in-

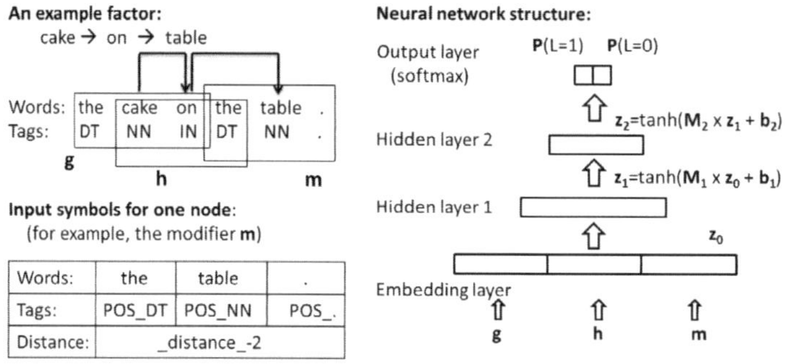

Figure 3: The structure of neural network for *o2g* model for an example input factor "*cake* → *on* → *table*". Here we only demonstrate the case of a three-word window.

cludes the embeddings for features, where d is the dimension for the embedding, N is total number of possible features.

For the rest of the network, it can be viewed as a fully-connected feed-forward neural network with two hidden layers and a probabilistic output layer (we use a two-way softmax output unit to compute the probability). For the hidden layers, we use hyperbolic tangent as activation function.

The training objective is to maximize the logarithmic probability of parse trees with an L2-regularization term to avoid over-fitting, which equals to minimizing the cross-entropy loss with L2-regularization:

$$L(\theta) = -\sum_{S} \log(Pr(T|S)) + \frac{\lambda}{2} \cdot \|\theta\|^2$$

Here θ means parameters of the neural network and λ is the hyper-parameter for weight decay. We initialize all the weights with random values and use mini-batch stochastic gradient descent for training.

4.4 Feature Sets

We utilize three kinds of features:

- Word forms (inside a specified sized window)
- POS tags (for each word)
- Distance (to the node's parent in the factor)

Using embeddings and neural network, we only need to provide unigram features, which will be mapped to embeddings in the neural network. The connections between features will be exploited by the non-linear computations of the neural network. Those three kinds of features are treated in the same way as strings in the vocabulary, and special prefix strings are added to POS and distance features to differ them from word features ("POS_" and "_distance_" respectively).

Features for the head node:
w_{h-1}, w_h, w_{h+1}; t_{h-1}, t_h, t_{h+1}; $d_{g,h}$
Features for the modifier node:
w_{m-1}, w_m, w_{m+1}; t_{m-1}, t_m, t_{m+1}; $d_{h,m}$
Features for the grandparent node:
w_{g-1}, w_g, w_{g+1}; t_{g-1}, t_g, t_{g+1}

Table 1: Features for the *o2g* model (with three-word windows). w: words, t: POS tags, d: distance. +1 and -1 means neighboring indexes.

Again, take the situation for *o2g* model as an example, there are three nodes in a factor: g for grandparent, h for head and m for modifier. We show the features in Table 1 when considering three-word window, there will be three word forms and three tags for each node, h and m both have one distance feature while g does not have one because its parent is unknown at this time. In fact, larger-sized context can be included and a seven-word window is actually considered for later experiments.

4.5 Integrating Lower-order Models for Higher-order Parsing

Following standard practice for high-order models (McDonald and Pereira, 2006; Carreras, 2007; Koo and Collins, 2010), we integrate the lower-order scores into the higher order parsing for better performance. For *o2sib* and *o2g* models in this work, we integrate the scores computed from the first-order model into second order factors. And for *o3g* model, two lower-order scores are integrated. Specifically, the score for the factor (g, h, s, m) will include the lower-order scores of $o1$ and *o2sib* in addition to the third-order score $o3gScore(g, h, s, m)$ from $o3g$ model. The integration of the scores can be shown by the following equation:

$$\begin{aligned} Score(g, h, s, m) &= o1Score(h, m) \\ &+ o2sibScore(h, s, m) \\ &+ o3gScore(g, h, s, m) \end{aligned}$$

More importantly, we may let the first-order model to serve as an edge-filter for high-order parsing. This type of pruning has been used by many graph-based models (Koo and Collins, 2010; Rush and Petrov, 2012) to avoid too expensive operations in high-order parsing. For our model, we utilize our own first-order neural network model which will produce the probabilities for all the edges in the graph. We simply set a pruning threshold so that all edges whose probabilities are under the threshold will be discarded for high-order parsing.

4.6 Efficient Neural Network Computation

This subsection introduces two techniques to speed up neural network computation.

Efficient computation strategies have been explored extensively for neural network language models (Morin and Bengio, 2005; Mnih and Hinton, 2008; Vaswani et al., 2013). These models consider speeding up the output softmax layer which contains thousands of neurons. However, it is not the case for our neural network as the output layer of our network only has two neurons. Main computation cost in our network is from the first hidden layer, which needs matrix multiplications and the hyperbolic tangent activation calculations for the hidden neurons.

Similar to some previous work (Devlin et al., 2014; Chen and Manning, 2014), we apply the pre-calculation strategy to speed up the most concerned computation. This can be implemented as calculating a lookup table for the first hidden layer (values before computing activation function), which can replace the operations of the looking-up for embedding layer and the matrix multiplication for second layer (first hidden layer after). With the pre-calculation table, we only need to look up the corresponding matrix multiplication results for each position's input and add them together to get the values for the first hidden layer.

Another technique is to pre-calculate a hyperbolic tangent table, which will replace the computation for the activation function with a table looking-up process.

#Number of sentences			
Corpus	Train	Dev	Test
PTB	39832	1700	2416
CTB	16091	803	1910
#Number of tokens			
Corpus	Train	Dev	Test
PTB	950348	40121	56702
CTB	437990	20454	50315

Table 2: Statistics for the data sets for dependency parsing.

5 Experiments and Discussions

The proposed parsers are evaluated on English Penn Treebank (PTB3.0) and Chinese Penn Treebank(CTB7.0). For all the results, we report unlabeled attachment scores (UAS) excluding punctuations[3] as in previous work (Koo and Collins, 2010; Zhang and Clark, 2008). In Table 2, we show statistics of both treebanks.

For English, we follow the splitting conventions, using sections 2-21 for training, 22 for developing and 23 for test. We patch the Treebank using Vadas' NP bracketing[4] (Vadas and Curran, 2007) and use the LTH Converter[5] (Johansson and Nugues, 2007) to get the dependency treebank. We use Stanford POS tagger (Toutanova et al., 2003) to get predicted POS tags for development and test sets, and the accuracies for their tags are 97.2% and 97.4%, respectively.

For Chinese, we follow the convention described in (Zhang and Clark, 2008). The dependencies are converted with Penn2Malt tool[6]. As in previous work, we use gold segmentation and POS tags.

For both treebanks, all the graph-based parsers

[3] Punctuations are the tokens whose gold POS tag is one of {“ ” : , .} for PTB and *PU* for CTB.

[4] http://sydney.edu.au/engineering/it/~dvadas1

[5] http://nlp.cs.lth.se/software/treebank_converter

[6] http://stp.lingfil.uu.se/ nivre/research/Penn2Malt.html

Initialize	Source	UAS
random	–	91.79
SENNA[7]	Collobert et al. (2011)	91.75
GloVe[8]	Pennington et al. (2014)	91.73
word2vec[9]	Mikolov et al. (2013)	91.81

Table 3: Accuracies for different initializations, with first-order models on dev set.

Threshold	W_t	W_d	*#inst(M)*	*Time(min.)*	*Acc.*
0.01	0.47	1.41	315	29	92.41
0.001	0.13	0.58	764	65	92.47
0.0001	0.02	0.13	2591	220	92.43

Table 4: Effects of pruning methods with different thresholds (on English dev set with the *o2sib* model).

run on the same machine with Intel Xeon 3.47GHz CPU using single core.

5.1 Different Embedding Initializations

We initialize the embedding matrix (only the parts for the embeddings of words) with some trained word embeddings or word vectors as shown in Table 3. Compared to the random initialization method, using pre-trained embeddings does not bring too significant improvements. We contribute this mostly to already large enough training set. In fact, the number of the training samples fed to the network is over 20 million. Another possible reason is that the embedding initialization only works for word form features and other features such as POS tags and distance will have to be initialized with random values. Those two types of initializations existing in the same space may cause possible inconsistence. Based on the above empirical results and comparison, we will only use random initialization for our parsers.

5.2 Pruning

For high-order models, their full training can be computationally expensive or even impossible, so we must prune unlikely dependencies as we stated before in Section 4.5. We use a simple strategy by setting a fixed probability threshold and the results of different thresholds are shown in Table 4. In this table, the notations are defined as the following:

- W_t = %edges wrongly pruned in training set
- W_d = %edges wrongly pruned in dev set
- *#inst* = number of instances for one iteration
- *Time* = time for one iteration
- *Acc.* = UAS on dev set

With a large threshold, we might prune some correct dependencies, but if the threshold is set smaller, more incorrect dependencies will remain and the training will be more expensive. Even though those wrongly pruned dependencies are allowed, their scores are also too low to influence the inference. A threshold of 0.001 is finally chosen for other experiments in this work.

5.3 Main Results

As for detailed neural network setting, we use embeddings of 50 dimensions, and the size of the two hidden layers are 200 and 40, respectively. We initialize the learning rate as 0.1. After each iteration, the parser is tested on the development set and if the accuracy decreases, the learning rate will be halved. We train the models for 10 iterations and select the ones that perform best on the development set.

For the inputs, we consider a seven-word window. Notice that only with distributed representations, can we incorporate such very-long-context features. We ignore the words that occur less than 3 times in the training treebank and use a default token to represent unknown words.

Our evaluations will follow the setting in (Chen and Manning, 2014), which reported results of the transition-based neural network parser. For graph-based parsers, in order to get exact comparisons between traditional methods and neural network methods, we run the traditional graph-based parsers under the same executing environment as our parsers. In detail, MSTParser[10] for *o1* and *o2sib* models and MaxParser[11] (Ma and Zhao, 2012) for *o2g* and *o3g* models are respectively used for comparison. Notice that in recent years, there have been plenty of graph-based parsers which utilize various techniques and obtain state-of-art results (Rush and Petrov, 2012; Zhang and McDonald, 2012), however, they will not be included in the comparisons for the reason that we only concern about basic graph-based parsing al-

[10]http://sourceforge.net/projects/mstparser/

[11]http://sourceforge.net/projects/maxparser/, this is a C++ implementation for several high-order graph-based parsers

Parser	UAS	Root	CM	Speed
o1-nn	91.77	96.61	35.89	150
o2sib-nn	92.35	96.40	39.86	109
o2g-nn	92.18	96.85	38.45	89
o3g-nn	92.52	96.81	41.10	38
o1-Mst	91.31	95.12	36.67	18
o2sib-Mst	91.99	95.90	39.74	14
o2g-Max	92.12	96.03	40.11	2
o3g-Max	92.60	96.31	42.63	0.3
transition	92.0	–	–	1013

Table 5: Results on PTB, the English treebank.

Parser	UAS	Root	CM	Speed
o1-nn	83.59	76.86	26.60	112
o2sib-nn	86.00	77.59	31.94	70
o2g-nn	84.13	77.75	27.59	49
o3g-nn	86.01	78.06	31.88	11
o1-Mst	83.31	71.57	27.49	9
o2sib-Mst	85.34	75.60	32.98	8
o2g-Max	84.96	76.32	31.94	1
o3g-Max	86.41	78.22	34.82	0.1
transition	83.9	–	–	936

Table 6: Results on CTB, the Chinese treebank.

gorithms.

We report three accuracy metrics, UAS, Root (percentage of the root words correctly identified), CM (complete rate, percentage of sentences for which the whole tree is correct) and Speed (number of sentences per second). For Chinese, the UAS and CM both consider root words.

Tables 5 and 6 show the results for PTB and CTB. As for name suffix in the tables, *nn* means our neural network graph-based parsers, *Mst* means MstParser, *Max* means MaxParser, *transition* means the transition-based neural network parser (Chen and Manning, 2014).

From the results, we can see that our parsers can get similar or even better results compared to the traditional graph-based models of the corresponding orders. In addition, our speed is faster (notice that even our *o3g* parser is faster than the traditional first-order graph-based parser). Compared to the transition-based neural network parser, although our parsers are not that fast (transition-based parsers usually have O(n) time complexity), they give better performance in accuracies.

5.4 Discussions

We find that integrating lower-order models into high-order parsing leads to better results. Although the high-order factors already include the lower-order parts, it might be hard for the neural network to decide whether the whole factor is correct. During training, we specify a factor as a positive sample only if all the dependencies in it are correct because we only do a binary classification. This might be the limitation for our high-order model and might explain the reason why some of our high-order parsers do not surpass traditional ones in accuracy, we might need more appropriate object functions to improve its learning.

Compared to the features of traditional methods, the only information beyond the proposed feature set is the words that fall out of the windows between the nodes in the factor (previously called in-between features) because so far we only use fixed-size inputs for the feed-forward neural network. Extra operations for embedding vectors (like adding embedding vectors) and other forms of neural networks (such as convolutional neural network which can consider the context of a whole sentence) might be explored in the future.

6 Conclusions

In this paper, we show a way to use neural network for graph-based dependency parsing and the method is also suitable for high-order parsing. We show that using distributed representations for neural network to replace traditional sparse features in traditional graph models can be suitable for dependency parsing, even though only using a feed-forward network. From the evaluation results and comparison with existing models, we show that the proposed parsers get good results with quite efficient inference even though graph-based models usually need at least cubic-time for inference.

References

Yoshua Bengio, Réjean Ducharme, Pascal Vincent, and Christian Janvin. 2003. A neural probabilistic language model. *Journal of Machine Learning Research (JMLR)*, 3:1137–1155, March.

Xavier Carreras. 2007. Experiments with a higher-order projective dependency parser. In *Proceedings of the*

CoNLL Shared Task Session of EMNLP-CoNLL 2007, pages 957–961, Prague, Czech Republic, June. Association for Computational Linguistics.

Danqi Chen and Christopher Manning. 2014. A fast and accurate dependency parser using neural networks. In *Proceedings of the 2014 Conference on Empirical Methods in Natural Language Processing (EMNLP)*, pages 740–750, Doha, Qatar, October. Association for Computational Linguistics.

Changge Chen, Peilu Wang, and Hai Zhao. 2015. Shallow discourse parsing using constituent parsing tree. In *Proceedings of the Nineteenth Conference on Computational Natural Language Learning - Shared Task*, pages 37–41, Beijing, China, July. Association for Computational Linguistics.

Michael Collins and Brian Roark. 2004. Incremental parsing with the perceptron algorithm. In *Proceedings of the 42nd Meeting of the Association for Computational Linguistics (ACL'04), Main Volume*, pages 111–118, Barcelona, Spain, July.

Michael Collins. 2002. Discriminative training methods for hidden markov models: Theory and experiments with perceptron algorithms. In *Proceedings of the 2002 Conference on Empirical Methods in Natural Language Processing*, pages 1–8. Association for Computational Linguistics, July.

Ronan Collobert, Jason Weston, Léon Bottou, Michael Karlen, Koray Kavukcuoglu, and Pavel Kuksa. 2011. Natural language processing (almost) from scratch. *Journal of Machine Learning Research (JMLR)*, 12:2493–2537, August.

Ronan Collobert. 2011. Deep learning for efficient discriminative parsing. In *AISTATS*.

Jacob Devlin, Rabih Zbib, Zhongqiang Huang, Thomas Lamar, Richard Schwartz, and John Makhoul. 2014. Fast and robust neural network joint models for statistical machine translation. In *Proceedings of the 52nd Annual Meeting of the Association for Computational Linguistics (Volume 1: Long Papers)*, pages 1370–1380, Baltimore, Maryland, June. Association for Computational Linguistics.

Jason M. Eisner. 1996. Three new probabilistic models for dependency parsing: An exploration. In *Proceedings of the 16th International Conference on Computational Linguistics*, pages 340–345, Copenhagen, August.

Richard Johansson and Pierre Nugues. 2007. Extended constituent-to-dependency conversion for english. In *Proceedings of NODALIDA 2007*.

Terry Koo and Michael Collins. 2010. Efficient third-order dependency parsers. In *Proceedings of the 48th Annual Meeting of the Association for Computational Linguistics*, pages 1–11, Uppsala, Sweden, July. Association for Computational Linguistics.

Terry Koo, Xavier Carreras, and Michael Collins. 2008. Simple semi-supervised dependency parsing. In *Proceedings of ACL-08: HLT*, pages 595–603, Columbus, Ohio, June. Association for Computational Linguistics.

Phong Le and Willem Zuidema. 2014. The inside-outside recursive neural network model for dependency parsing. In *Proceedings of the 2014 Conference on Empirical Methods in Natural Language Processing (EMNLP)*, pages 729–739, Doha, Qatar, October. Association for Computational Linguistics.

Xuezhe Ma and Hai Zhao. 2012. Fourth-order dependency parsing. In *Proceedings of COLING 2012: Posters*, pages 785–796, Mumbai, India, December. The COLING 2012 Organizing Committee.

Ryan McDonald and Fernando Pereira. 2006. Online learning of approximate dependency parsing algorithms. In *Proceedings of the 11th Conference of the European Chapter of the ACL (EACL 2006)*, pages 81–88. Association for Computational Linguistics.

Ryan McDonald, Koby Crammer, and Fernando Pereira. 2005. Online large-margin training of dependency parsers. In *Proceedings of the 43rd Annual Meeting of the Association for Computational Linguistics (ACL'05)*, pages 91–98, Ann Arbor, Michigan, June. Association for Computational Linguistics.

Tomas Mikolov, Martin Karafiát, Lukas Burget, Jan Cernockỳ, and Sanjeev Khudanpur. 2010. Recurrent neural network based language model. In *Proceedings of INTERSPEECH-2010*, pages 1045–1048.

Tomas Mikolov, Ilya Sutskever, Kai Chen, Greg S Corrado, and Jeff Dean. 2013. Distributed representations of words and phrases and their compositionality. In *NIPS*.

Andriy Mnih and Geoffrey Hinton. 2008. A scalable hierarchical distributed language model. In *NIPS*.

Frederic Morin and Yoshua Bengio. 2005. Hierarchical probabilistic neural network language model. In *AISTATS05*, pages 246–252.

Joakim Nivre. 2003. An efficient algorithm for projective dependency parsing. In *Proceedings of the 8th International Workshop on Parsing Technologies (IWPT)*, pages 149–160, April.

Jeffrey Pennington, Richard Socher, and Christopher Manning. 2014. Glove: Global vectors for word representation. In *Proceedings of the 2014 Conference on Empirical Methods in Natural Language Processing (EMNLP)*, pages 1532–1543, Doha, Qatar, October. Association for Computational Linguistics.

Alexander Rush and Slav Petrov. 2012. Vine pruning for efficient multi-pass dependency parsing. In *Proceedings of the 2012 Conference of the North American Chapter of the Association for Computational Lin-*

guistics: Human Language Technologies, pages 498–507, Montréal, Canada, June. Association for Computational Linguistics.

Holger Schwenk. 2007. Continuous space language models. *Computer Speech and Language*, 21(3):492–518.

Richard Socher, Christopher D. Manning, and Andrew Y. Ng. 2010. Learning continuous phrase representations and syntactic parsing with recursive neural networks. In *Proceedings of the NIPS-2010 Deep Learning and Unsupervised Feature Learning Workshop*.

Richard Socher, John Bauer, Christopher D. Manning, and Ng Andrew Y. 2013. Parsing with compositional vector grammars. In *Proceedings of the 51st Annual Meeting of the Association for Computational Linguistics (Volume 1: Long Papers)*, pages 455–465, Sofia, Bulgaria, August. Association for Computational Linguistics.

Ben Taskar, Dan Klein, Mike Collins, Daphne Koller, and Christopher Manning. 2004. Max-margin parsing. In Dekang Lin and Dekai Wu, editors, *Proceedings of EMNLP 2004*, pages 1–8, Barcelona, Spain, July. Association for Computational Linguistics.

Kristina Toutanova, Dan Klein, Christopher D. Manning, and Yoram Singer. 2003. Feature-rich part-of-speech tagging with a cyclic dependency network. In *PROCEEDINGS OF HLT-NAACL*, pages 252–259.

David Vadas and James Curran. 2007. Adding noun phrase structure to the penn treebank. In *Proceedings of the 45th Annual Meeting of the Association of Computational Linguistics*, pages 240–247, Prague, Czech Republic, June. Association for Computational Linguistics.

Ashish Vaswani, Yinggong Zhao, Victoria Fossum, and David Chiang. 2013. Decoding with large-scale neural language models improves translation. In *Proceedings of EMNLP-2013*, pages 1387–1392, Seattle, Washington, USA, October. Association for Computational Linguistics.

Rui Wang, Masao Utiyama, Isao Goto, Eiichro Sumita, Hai Zhao, and Bao-Liang Lu. 2013. Converting continuous-space language models into n-gram language models for statistical machine translation. In *Proceedings of the 2013 Conference on Empirical Methods in Natural Language Processing*, pages 845–850, Seattle, Washington, USA, October. Association for Computational Linguistics.

Rui Wang, Hai Zhao, Bao-Liang Lu, Masao Utiyama, and Eiichiro Sumita. 2014. Neural network based bilingual language model growing for statistical machine translation. In *Proceedings of the 2014 Conference on Empirical Methods in Natural Language Processing (EMNLP)*, pages 189–195, Doha, Qatar, October. Association for Computational Linguistics.

Rui Wang, Hai Zhao, Bao-Liang Lu, Masao Utiyama, and Eiichiro Sumita. 2015. Bilingual continuous-space language model growing for statistical machine translation. *IEEE/ACM Transactions on Audio, Speech, and Languange Processing*, 23:1209–1220.

Hiroyasu Yamada and Yuji Matsumoto. 2003. Statistical dependency analysis with support vector machines. In *Proceedings of the 8th International Workshop on Parsing Technologies (IWPT)*, pages 195–206, April.

Yue Zhang and Stephen Clark. 2008. A tale of two parsers: Investigating and combining graph-based and transition-based dependency parsing. In *Proceedings of the 2008 Conference on Empirical Methods in Natural Language Processing*, pages 562–571, Honolulu, Hawaii, October. Association for Computational Linguistics.

Hao Zhang and Ryan McDonald. 2012. Generalized higher-order dependency parsing with cube pruning. In *Proceedings of the 2012 Joint Conference on Empirical Methods in Natural Language Processing and Computational Natural Language Learning*, pages 320–331, Jeju Island, Korea, July. Association for Computational Linguistics.

Jingyi Zhang and Hai Zhao. 2013. Improving function word alignment with frequency and syntactic information. In *IJCAI-2013*, pages 2211–2217, Beijing, China, August.

A Dynamic Syntax Modelling of Postposing in Japanese Narratives

Tohru Seraku
Dept. of Japanese Interpretation and Translation
Hankuk University of Foreign Studies
seraku@hufs.ac.kr

Abstract

Japanese is prescriptively said to be verb-final, but it exhibits postposing in colloquial register, where an element is placed after a verb. Based on narrative data, we show that the syntactic type of postposed element is quite diverse and that, contrary to the prevalent, opposing view, Japanese postposing is not restricted to a matrix clause. These issues are addressed in Dynamic Syntax, with the outcome of developing some formal aspects of the framework.

1 Introduction[1]

Japanese is prescriptively verb-final as in (1)a, but elements may be placed after a verb in colloquial register. In (1)b, *sushi-o* appears after *tabe* 'eat.'

(1)a. *Ken-ga* *sushi-o* *tabe-ta-yo*
K-NOM sushi-ACC eat-PAST-FP
'Ken ate sushi.'
b. *Ken-ga* Δ *tabe-ta-yo*, *sushi-o*
K-NOM eat-PAST-FP sushi-ACC

The postposed item *sushi-o* is underlined in (1)b, and the gap is notated as Δ without any theoretical implications. Finally, *yo* is a final particle (FP) that appears in colloquial register.

Japanese postposing has been explored in formal syntax (Takano 2014, Takita 2014) as well as in dialogue/discourse studies (Nomura 2008, Ono 2006). Except for Fujii (1995: 169), grammatical properties of Japanese postposing have not been examined based on naturally-occurring materials. We provide narrative data to set out an empirical ground of a grammatical study of postposing:

- It seems postposing may occur at an embedded level, contrary to the prevalent, opposing view.
- A wider variety of syntactic element may be postposed than has been held in the literature.

These syntactic flexibilities pose a challenge for grammar modelling, and we propose a solution in Dynamic Syntax (DS) (Cann et al. 2005). DS has been employed for postposing in several languages (Section 4); still, no analysis has been developed for Japanese presumably because it allows a wider range of items to be postposed. The application to Japanese advances formal aspects of the theory and broadens empirical coverage.

2 Narrative Data

Several works have extracted postposing data from spontaneous resources (Nomura 2008), but they tend to avoid the syntactic facets of postposing. In this section, we shed light on grammatical aspects of the phenomenon based on narrative data.

Firstly, since Kuno (1978), it has been held that Japanese postposing is restricted to a matrix level ("root-phenomenon"). Whitman (2000: 465) offers data suggesting otherwise. Our narrative data like (2) may also suggest that Japanese postposing is not a root-phenomenon, although it is possible that (2) is a case of indirect speech.

(2) [*yappari* Δ *wakatten-na* *kono-hito*]-*to*
[as.expected know-FP this-person]-COMP
watashi-wa *omou*
I-TOP think
'I think this person knows the thing.'
(adapted from {kirishima, p.74})

[1] This work was supported by Hankuk University of Foreign Studies Research Fund of 2015.

29th Pacific Asia Conference on Language, Information and Computation pages 124 - 132
Shanghai, China, October 30 - November 1, 2015

The postposed element *kono-hito* 'this person' is a subject of the embedded verb *wakaru* 'know' (< *wakatten*). Together with Whitman's (2000) data, it is then assumed that Japanese postposing is not a root-phenomenon.

Second, a range of syntactic elements may be at a postposed position. Fujii (1995: 169) reports that in spontaneous speech, a postposed element may be: NPs (2), PPs (3), AdvPs (4), connectives (5), and noun-modifiers (see (9)-(11) below).

(3) *mainichi-noyouni* Δ *oaishitemasu-yo*
everyday-like meet.POL-FP
yonjukkai-de
40th.floor-at
'We meet almost everyday at the 40th floor.'
{mikeneko, p.119}

(4) *tsumasaki-ga* Δ *itai* *sukoshi-dake*
toe-NOM ach little-only
'My toe is aching a little.' {kirishima, p.55}

(5) Δ *'kekkoudesu' jya-nai-ndatte* *dakara*
'ok' COP-NEG-FP as.I.said
'As I said, it's not 'ok'.' {roll, p.71}

To this Fujii's list we add: the Adv clause (6) and the complement clause (7).

(6) Δ *daijyoubu-desu* *[hitori-jya-nai]-kara*
all.right-COP [alone-COP-NEG]-because
'It's all right as I'm not alone.' {roll, p.101}

(7) *tomodachi-kara* Δ *kii-ta-mon*
friend-from hear-PAST-FP
Mei-to-Satsuki-wa mou kono-yo-ni
M-and-S-TOP already this-world-in
inai-nda-to
absent-FP-COMP
'I heard Mei and Satsuki were not in this world any longer.' (adapted from {kirishima, p.100})

Our narrative data also confirm the existence of "multiple postposing" (Abe 1999).

(8) Δ Δ Δ *fuman-toka* *aru-wake-nee-daro*
complaint-like exist-reason-NEG-FP
yorinimoyotte *ore-kara* *Nozomi-ni*
of.all.things I-from N-to
'Of all things, it's never the case that I have a complaint for Nozomi.' {yuunou, p.172}

In (8), the adverb *yorinimoyotte* 'of all things,' the PP *ore-kara* 'from me,' and the PP *Nozomi-ni* 'to Nozomi' are postposed.

As for the postposing of a noun-modifier, Kuno (1978) notes that it is a unique feature of Japanese postposing. In (9)-(10), the relative clause and the genitive are postposed, respectively (adapted from Kuno (1978: 75)). In our data (11), the coordinated adjectives are postposed.

(9) *nanika* Δ *daikenkyuu-o* *nasatta-*
something great.resarch- ACC do.POL-
nodesu-ka *[gaikoku-de nasarete-nai]*
POL- Q [foreign.country-in done-NEG]
'Have you done any great research which has not been conducted in foreign countries?'

(10) *kimi* *Δ-imouto-to* *kekkon-shitekurenaika*
you sister-with marriage-do.please
boku-no
I-GEN
'Can you please marry my sister?'

(11) Δ *futari-no-himitsu-ga* *fueta*
two.person-GEN-secret-NOM increased
sasayakana demo kanbina
tiny but sweet
'We've had another tiny but sweet secret of us.' (adapted from {Tokyo, p.69})

The issue of noun-modifiers, though it is a unique property of Japanese postposing, has been largely neglected except for a few works (Takano 2014).[2]

In sum, Japanese postposing is flexible in that it is not restricted to a root clause and that it allows a wide array of syntactic items to be postposed.

3 Dynamic Syntax (DS)

DS models knowledge of language as a reflection of language use (Cann et al. 2005, Kempson et al. 2001), with the two fundamental assumptions:

- Structure building proceeds as a string is parsed word-by-word.[3]

[2] Takano (2014: 150) claims that, when there are multiple postposed items, a noun-modifier cannot co-occur with the other types of syntactic element. This generalisation, however, is challenged by a spontaneous example of Fujii (1995: 171).
[3] See Purver et al. (2014) for the DS modelling of production.

- A DS structure is semantic; a string is mapped onto a semantic tree without any separate level of syntactic representation.

3.1 The Basic Formalism

The DS structure is semantic, represented in a tree-format. For instance, (12) is mapped onto (13).

(12) *Ken-ga* *hashi-tta*
K-NOM run-PAST
'Ken ran.'

(13) Parsing the string (12) (ignoring tense)

Fo(*hashi'*(*Ken'*)), *Ty*(t), ◇

Fo(*Ken'*), *Ty*(e) *Fo*(*hashi'*), *Ty*(e→t)

Each non-terminal node is binary-branched, with the left daughter being an argument node and the right daughter being a functor node. Each node is decorated with various types of statement.

- Fo(X): *Fo* is a "formula" predicate that takes a content X as argument. *Fo*(*Ken'*) declares that the content denoted at this node is *Ken'*.
- Ty(X): *Ty* is a "type" predicate that takes a type X as argument. *Ty*(e) declares that the content denoted at this node is of type e.

The top node in (13) is also annotated with ◇ , a pointer. This highlights a node under development.

More decorations on a node are illustrated if we see a "partial" tree. For instance, if *Ken-ga* alone is parsed in (12), the corresponding tree is (14).

(14) Parsing *Ken-ga* in (12)

?*Ty*(t), ◇

Fo(*Ken'*), *Ty*(e)

The parse of *Ken-ga* creates a subject node. (The term "subject" is used for presentation purposes.) ? is used to form a requirement. For instance, ?*T*(t) in (14) requires that *Ty*(t) will hold at this node.

Let us turn to the structure-building process. The initial state of DS tree-update is (15).

(15) AXIOM (= the initial state)

?*Ty*(t), ◇

The initial state is progressively updated by two types of action: "general" and "lexical" actions.

General actions are not lexically triggered and are optional (as long as an execution condition holds). LOCAL *ADJUNCTION posits a structurally-unfixed node. In the left-hand tree of (16), the unfixed node (shown by a dashed line) may be a subject node, an object node, etc., at a later stage.

(16) LOCAL *ADJUNCTION ⇒ Parsing *Ken*

?*Ty*(t) ?*Ty*(t)

?*Ty*(e), ◇ *Fo*(*Ken'*), *Ty*(e), ◇

Lexical actions are those encoded in each lexical item. *Ken* encodes the action to decorate a ?*Ty*(e)-node with *Fo*(*Ken'*) and *Ty*(e), as in the right-hand tree (16). The nominative case marker *ga* encodes the action to resolve an unfixed node as a subject node, as in (14). (A solid line visually shows that a structural uncertainty has been fixed.) As another example of lexical action, the parse of *hashi* 'run' provides a predicate node with the *Fo*-statement involving the content *hashi'* and the *Ty*-statement involving the type e→t.

(17) Parsing *Ken-ga hashi-tta* (ignoring tense)

?*Ty*(t)

Fo(*Ken'*), *Ty*(e) *Fo*(*hashi'*), *Ty*(e→t), ◇

What remains to be done in (17) is to conduct functional application and type deduction. This is formulated as the general action of ELIMINATION, which engenders the final state (13).

The tree (13) is "well-formed" in the sense that requirements like ?*Ty*(t) are not in place any more. A string is "grammatical" iff there exists a parse-route that leads to a well-formed tree.

3.2 The LINK Machinery

The formalism is enriched with LINK, a formal pairing of two distinct trees. Consider (18).

(18) [[*Ken-ga* *tabe-ta*] *sushi*]-*ga* *oishii*
[[K-NOM eat-PAST] sushi]-NOM tasty
'Sushi which Ken ate is tasty.'

The parse of the relative clause *Ken-ga tabe-ta* projects a propositional structure where an object node is decorated with a variable x (representing a gap). This propositional tree is associated with an emergent tree by being LINKed to a ?*Ty*(e)-node. (A LINK relation is expressed as a curved arrow.)

(19) Parsing *Ken-ga tabe-ta*

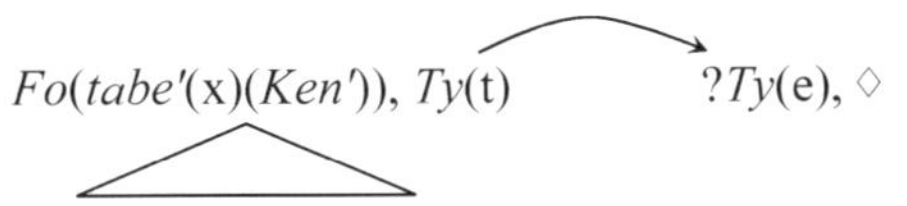

The current node is decorated by the parse of the head noun *sushi* in (18). This node will be part of the propositional structure for the matrix clause.

4 The DS Account

The DS framework is used to model postposing in several languages: English (Cann et al. 2004), Greek (Chatzikyriakidis 2011, Gregoromichelaki 2013), and Mandarin (Wu 2005). These studies are primarily concerned with NP postposing, but our data confirm that a wider range of syntactic items may be postposed in Japanese. In this section, we propose a DS account of Japanese postposing by advancing formal aspects of the framework. For brevity, the analysis is based on artificial examples which preserve the essence of the narrative data.

4.1 The Baseline

Let us start with the basic example (20), where the postposed item is the NP *sushi-o*.

(20) *Ken-ga* Δ *tabe-ta-yo*, <u>*sushi-o*</u>
K-NOM eat-PAST-FP sushi-ACC
'Ken ate sushi.'

The parse of the preceding clause *Ken-ga tabe-ta-yo* gives rise to (21). (The gap is notated with x.)

(21) Parsing *Ken-ga tabe-ta-yo*

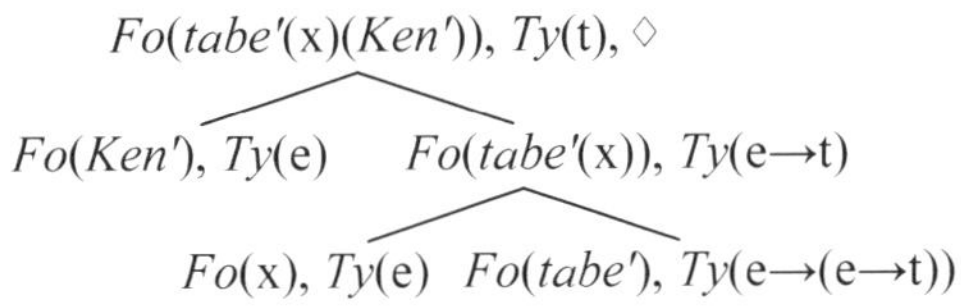

To parse the postposed element *sushi-o*, a ?*Ty*(e)-node must be present. In the previous DS studies on postposing (Cann et al. 2004, Chatzikyriakidis 2011, Gregoromichelaki 2013, Wu 2005), a LINK relation is launched to introduce a ?*Ty*(e)-node. A postposed element is then parsed at this LINKed ?*Ty*(e)-node. But this LINK-strategy cannot be applied to the postposed item *sushi-o* in (20) as the parse of a case marker at a LINKed node aborts a tree-update. (The case marker *-o* may be dropped (Tanaka & Kizu 2007), in which case the LINK-strategy is available (Seraku & Ohtani fthc.).)

A ?*Ty*(e)-node can also be introduced by LOCAL *ADJUNCTION (Section 3.1). This action, however, cannot be run here because it is allowed to be run only if a root node is decorated with ?*Ty*(t) (Cann et al. 2005). This restriction is indeed essential for ensuring verb-finality of non-colloquial register of Japanese. On the other hand, postposing is attested colloquially. In order to solve this ambivalence, we propose to extend the formalism with (22).

(22) <u>Proposal</u>: LOCAL *ADJUNCTION is subject to the ?*Ty*(t)-restriction in usual register. But this restriction is relaxed in colloquial register.

The intuitive idea behind is that some grammatical rules are "not observed" in casual register, though it may be prescriptively regarded as the "wrong use of language."

Once LOCAL *ADJUNCTION is allowed to fire at a *Ty*(t)-node, it may induce an unfixed ?*Ty*(e)-node for the postposed item *sushi*.

(23) Parsing *Ken-ga tabe-ta-yo, sushi*

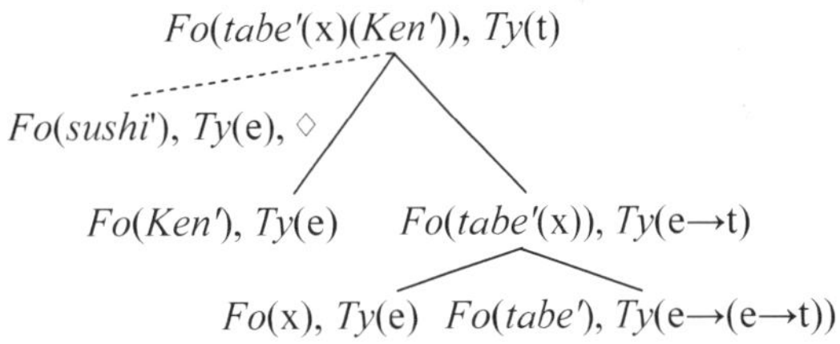

The unfixed node is resolved as an object node by the parse of the accusative case marker *o*. Since the two nodes collapse, the node description is updated, with the variable being saturated as *sushi'*. After ELIMINATION is run, the final state (24) emerges.

(24) ELIMINATION (twice)

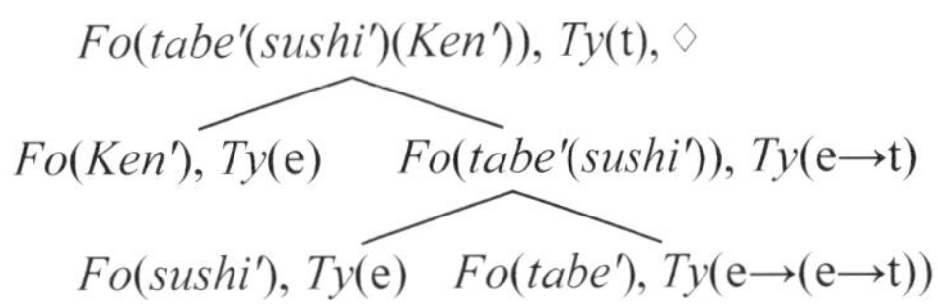

The above analysis readily solves our first set of the data on the syntactic flexibility of postposing. That is, postposing may take place at an embedded level. With the proposal (22), the general action of LOCAL *ADJUNCTION can be run at any *Ty*(t)-node of any subordinate structure.

Another advantage of the analysis is that it deals with multiple postposing straightforwardly.

(25) Δ Δ *tabe-ta-yo*, <u>*Ken-ga*</u> <u>*sushi-o*</u>
eat-PAST-FP K-NOM sushi-ACC
'Ken ate sushi.'

In DS, only a single unfixed node can be present at a time due to the tree logic (Cann et al. 2005). This constraint is met in our account. In (25), an unfixed node is introduced for *Ken*, but it is immediately resolved as a subject node by the parse of the nominative case marker *ga* as in (26).

(26) Parsing *tabe-ta-yo*, *Ken-ga*

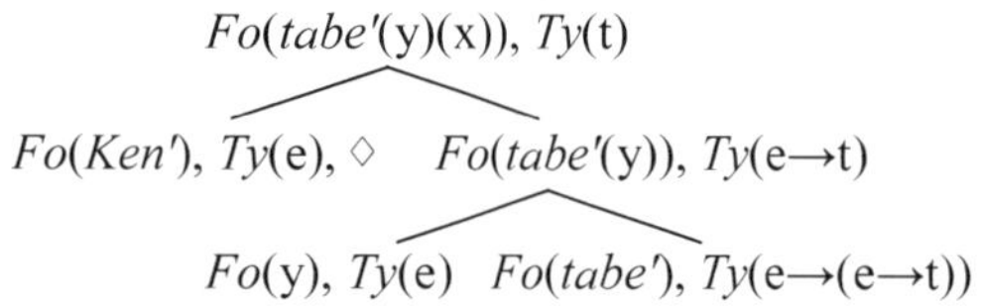

As no unfixed node remains in the tree, the parser can safely posit an unfixed node, this time for the second postposed item *sushi*. In this tree-update, there is only a single unfixed node at a time. Thus, the parse of the multiple postposed items is licit. It also follows from the analysis that the order of the postposed items may be swapped:

(27) Δ Δ *tabe-ta-yo*, <u>*sushi-o*</u> <u>*Ken-ga*</u>
eat-PAST-FP sushi-ACC K-NOM
'Ken ate sushi.'

In the tree-update for (27), too, there is a single unfixed node at a time: the unfixed node for the first postposed item *sushi* has been resolved by the parse of the accusative marker *o* before an unfixed node is posited for the second item *Ken*.

It is not clear whether a LINK-based strategy in the past DS works deals with multiple postposing. This is because multiple LINK relations launched from the same node collapse and inconsistency of descriptions occurs. For instance, consider (28).

(28) Two LINK relations (schematic display)

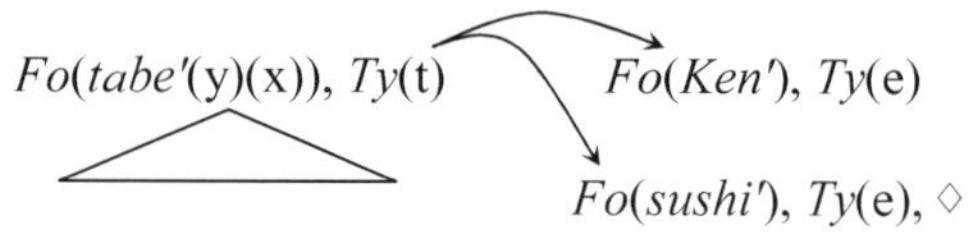

This tree appears to have two LINKed nodes, but these nodes collapse. The collapsed single node is decorated with distinct statements: *Fo*(*Ken'*) and *Fo*(*sushi'*). This leads to inconsistency. By contrast, our underspecification-based strategy is extendable to multiple postposing straightforwardly.

4.2 Noun-Modifiers

This section explicates how a noun-modifier can be postposed in Japanese (but not other languages). To this end, two formal ingredients are introduced.

First, in addition to the *Fo* and *Ty* predicates, we introduce the *Tn* predicate (Cann et al. 2005):

- <u>*Tn*(X)</u>: *Tn* is a "tree-node" predicate that takes a numeral X assigned to the node as argument.

Each node in a tree is assigned a unique numerical value to designate a node position. The root node is assigned "0." If a mother is assigned "α," the left-daughter "α 0" and the right-daughter "α 1." This numerical value is taken as an argument for *Tn*.

(29) Illustration of *Tn*-statements

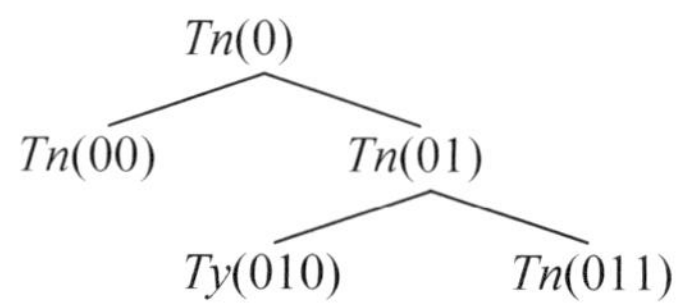

Second, there is a variant of the general action LOCAL *ADJUNCTION (LA), called GENERALISED ADJUNCTION (GA). Whilst LA induces an unfixed node that must be resolved in a local structure, GA induces an unfixed node which could be resolved anywhere (Cann et al. 2005). This globally unfixed node is visually shown by a dotted line in (30).

(30) GENERALISED ADJUNCTION

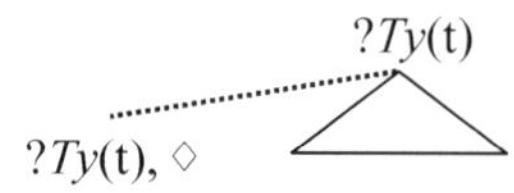

In (30), an unfixed node is decorated with ?*Ty*(t), but the action can introduce a ?*Ty*(e)-node as well.

Further, we propose, as with (22), that GA can fire at a *Ty*(t)-node in colloquial register.

Based on these additional mechanisms, we shall examine (i) the relative clause, (ii) the adjective, and (iii) the genitive in turn.

Relative Clause. Consider example (31).

(31) *Ken-ga* Δ *sushi-o* *tabe-ta-yo*,
K-NOM sushi-ACC eat-PAST-FP
[*Mari-ga tsuku-tta*]
[M-NOM make-PAST]
'Ken ate sushi which Mari made.'

After the preceding clause is parsed, GENERALISED ADJUNCTION introduces a globally unfixed ?*Ty*(t)-node, where the relative clause is parsed.

(32) Parsing the string (31)

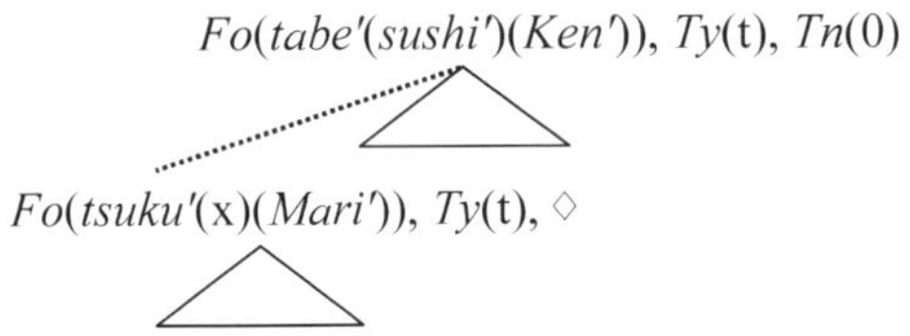

The parser runs the general action of introducing a LINK relation for relatives (Cann et al. 2005).

(33) Launching a LINK relation

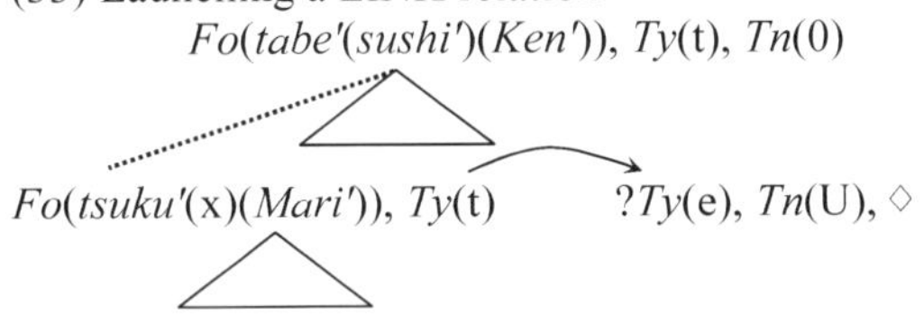

U in *Tn*(U) is a metavariable, a place-holder which is in need of saturation. If the parser identifies the address of the LINKed node with that of the node for *sushi*, *Tn*(U) is then updated into *Tn*(010). (This is the "tree-node identification" in Seraku (2013).) *Ty*-statements are omitted for brevity in (34).

(34) Tree-node identification

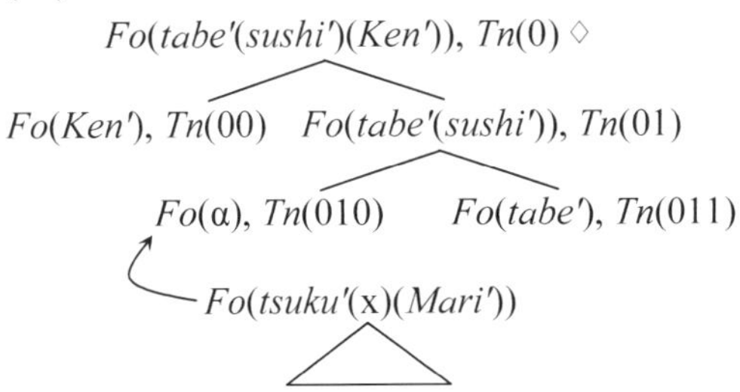

Here, α is a term denoting sushi which Mari made. (Formally, α is represented in the epsilon calculus.) Due to the node-identification process, the node for the relative clause has now been resolved as a node which is LINKed to the *Tn*(010)-node.

In the analysis above, the relative clause modifies *sushi*. It is also formally allowed to modify *Ken* but this modification is blocked on semantic grounds. (This remark applies to the analysis of adjectives and genitives to be presented below.)

Adjective. Consider example (35).

(35) *Ken-ga* Δ *sushi-o* *tabe-ta-yo*, *oishii*
K-NOM sushi-ACC eat-PAST-FP tasty
'Ken ate tasty sushi.'

A DS account of adjectives is underway (Cann et al. 2005). Setting aside non-predicative adjectives, we assume that the "predicative" adjective *oishii* 'tasty' constitutes a relative clause. Then, the tree-update is essentially the same as that detailed for the relative clause example in (32)-(34).

Genitive. In DS, genitives have not been seriously investigated either. Consider (36).

(36) *Ken-ga* Δ-*sushi-o* *tabe-ta-yo*, *Mari-no*
K-NOM sushi-ACC eat-PAST-FP M-GEN
'Ken ate Mari's sushi.'

The parse of the preceding clause gives rise to a propositional tree. GENERALISED ADJUNCTION is run to introduce an unfixed ?*Ty*(e)-node for *Mari*.

(37) Parsing *Ken-ga sushi-o tabe-ta-yo, Mari*

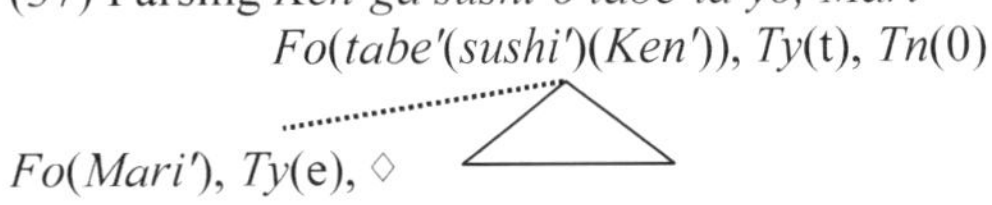

Here, we propose that the genitive *no* encodes the action to launch a LINK relation, as in (38).[4]

(38) Proposal: Parsing the genitive *no*

Two remarks are in order. First, the LINKed node is inhibited by a metavariable U. This is because *no* may stand alone, as in (39). In such cases, U is

[4] See Seraku (2013) for the DS analysis of other kinds of *no*.

contextually saturated. If *no* is followed by a noun, U is updated into the content of the noun.

(39) *Mari-no*
M-GEN
'Mari's'

Second, *R*(α, U) is a "presupposition" for U, and it declares that α is in relation *R* to U. This is also important as the relation described by the genitive *no* is vastly context-dependent (Nishiyama 2003), as in (40). *R* is saturated as a salient relation.

(40) *Mari-no-hon*
M-GEN-book
'Mari's book' (= 'a book which Mari bought,' 'a book which Mari loves,' etc.)

With the proposal (38), the genitive *no* is parsed at the tree (37), which outputs (41). (*R* is simply taken as *POS(session)* in the present context.)

(41) Parsing *Ken-ga sushi-o tabe-ta-yo, Mari-no*

Fo(*tabe'*(*sushi'*)(*Ken'*)), *Ty*(t), *Tn*(0)

Fo(*Mari'*), *Ty*(e)

$Fo(\mathrm{U}_{POS(Mari',\,\mathrm{U})})$, *Ty*(e), *Tn*(V), ◇

The parser then identifies the current node with the node for *sushi* by saturating V in *Tn*(V) as 010. This process also saturates U in *Fo*(U) as *sushi'*.

(42) Tree-node identification

Fo(*tabe'*(*sushi'*)(*Ken'*)), *Tn*(0)

Fo(*Ken'*), *Tn*(00) *Fo*(*tabe'*(*sushi'*)), *Tn*(01)

$Fo(sushi'_{POS(Mari',\,sushi')})$, *Tn*(010), ◇ *Fo*(*tabe'*), *Tn*(011)

Fo(*Mari'*), *Ty*(e)

Our account makes further predictions. Firstly, a genitive phrase may be multiplied, as in (43).

(43) *Ken-ga* Δ-*sushi-o tabe-ta-yo,*
K-NOM sushi-ACC eat-PAST-FP
<u>*Mari-no-tomodachi-no-kareshi-no*</u>
M-GEN-friend-GEN-boyfriend-GEN
'Ken ate Mari's friend's boyfriend's sushi.'

In this case, every time *no* is parsed, it induces a LINK relation. The LINKed node posited by the final *no* is identified with the node for *sushi*.

Secondly, due to the use of a metavariable in a *Fo*-statement, (44) is predicted to be ambiguous.

(44) *musuko-ga ka-tta-yo,* <u>*Ken-no*</u>
son-NOM buy-PAST-FP K-GEN
(i) e.g., 'Ken's son bought something.'
(ii) e.g., 'My son bought Ken's book.'

If the LINKed node introduced by *no* is identified with the node for *musuko* 'son,' U in *Fo*(U) at the LINKed node is saturated as *musuko'*, which yields the reading (i). If the LINKed node is identified with the internal-argument node for *ka* 'buy,' U in *Fo*(U) is pragmatically saturated as a content that denotes a contextually-salient entity such as a book. This gives rise to the reading (ii).

So far, the DS modelling of the postposing of a noun-modifier has been articulated. The heart of the analysis is GENERALISED ADJUNCTION. In DS, this action was formulated for Japanese relatives (Cann et al. 2005: Ch.6). It is speculated that the availability of this action is a necessary (if not a sufficient) condition on the postposing of a noun-modifier. This accounts for why such postposing is impossible in, say, English where we assume that the action is unavailable. It needs to be worked out what other conditions may be, so that the account is extendable to other languages.

4.3 Other Syntactic Elements

Our account applies to the other syntactic elements (though the analysis of connectives requires some stipulation), as briefly mentioned below.

PP/AdvP. PPs and AdvPs are adjuncts (excluding PPs in ditransitive verbs). In DS, Marten (2002) hypothesises that these adjuncts are of type e. We could apply Marten's analysis to the PP data (45).

(45) *Ken-ga* Δ *hashi-tta-yo* <u>*kouen-de*</u>
K-NOM run-PAST-FP park-in
'Ken ran in a park.'

After the parse of the preceding clause engenders a propositional tree, LOCAL *ADJUNCTION creates an unfixed ?*Ty*(e)-node. This node is decorated by the parse of *kouen* 'park' and resolved by the parse of the postposition *de* 'in.'

The same analysis extends to AdvP. In this case, we need to assume that an adverb itself encodes the action to resolve an unfixed node because an AdvP does not involve a postposition.

Marten's analysis, however, blurs the distinction between arguments and adjuncts. If one would like to maintain the distinction, we could make use of Davidson's (1967) analysis of adjuncts by utilising a situation term (Gregoromichelaki 2006).

Adv Clause. For an Adv clause, a LINK relation starts from a *Ty*(t)-node to a ?*Ty*(t)-node, as in (47) for the example (46). The postposed Adv clause will then be parsed at the LINKed ?*Ty*(t)-node.

(46) Δ *Ken-ga waratta-yo* <u>*[Mari-ga kita]-toki*</u>
K-NOM smiled-FP [M-NOM came]-when
'When Mari came, Ken smiled.'

(47) Launching a LINK relation

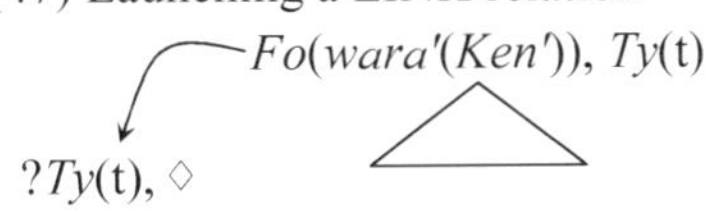

Comp Clause. A complement clause is of type t, and cannot be modelled by LOCAL *ADJUNCTION, which creates a ?*Ty*(e)-node. DS defines a variant of this action: *ADJUNCTION, which introduces a ?*Ty*(t)-node. Cann et al. (2005) assume that this action cannot fire at a *Ty*(t)-node; we stipulate that in colloquial register, this restriction is relaxed (cf., (22)). A complement clause is processed under the unfixed ?*Ty*(t)-node, and this node is resolved by the parse of a complementiser.

For instance, the underlined part in (48) is parsed at a ?*Ty*(t)-node introduced by *ADJUNCTION. The node is resolved as the object node in the main tree by the parse of the complementiser *to*.

(48) *tomodachi-kara* Δ *kii-ta-mon*
friend-from hear-PAST-FP
<u>*Mei-to-Satsuki-wa mou kono-yo-ni*</u>
M-and-S-TOP already this-world-in
<u>*inai-nda-to*</u>
absent-FP-COMP
'I heard Mei and Satsuki were not in this world any longer.' (adapted from {kirishima, p.100})

A bonus of this analysis is that it explains why postposing exhibits a "long-distance dependency" (Kuno 1978: 74). An unfixed node introduced by *ADJUNCTION can be fixed at any embedding level (but not across a LINK relation). In the case of the long-distance postposing of an NP, the parser first executes *ADJUNCTION to introduce a non-locally unfixed ?*Ty*(t)-node and LOCAL *ADJUNCTION to introduce a locally unfixed ?*Ty*(e)-node under the unfixed ?*Ty*(t)-node. See Seraku (2013) for details of the successive applications of these actions.

Yet, there is a problem. Since general actions are optional, GENERALISED ADJUNCTION can be used to parse a postposed complement clause. This is problematic because an unfixed node introduced by this action can be fixed anywhere (even across a LINK relation, DS equivalence of an "island"). We then tentatively stipulate that the complementiser *to* encodes the action to abort a tree-update if the unfixed node is hung from a *Ty*(t)-node.

Connective. Discourse connectives are generally taken to contribute to a non-truth-conditional level of meaning, one theoretical conception of which is "higher explicature," a dimension of meaning that represents a speech-act, a propositional attitude, etc. (Blakemore 2002). For example, (49) remains the same truth-conditionally when *dakara* is taken out. Rather, *dakara* encode some non-truth-conditional content roughly glossed as 'as I said.'

(49) Δ *'kekkoudesu' jya-nai-ndatte* <u>*dakara*</u>
'ok' COP-NEG-FP as.I.said
'As I said, it's not 'ok'.' {roll, p.71}

Purver et al. (2010) represent this "higher-level" meaning on top of the usual DS tree. We assume that *dakara* encodes the action to place a content decoration relating to a propositional attitude at the "higher-level" representation.

5 Conclusion

This article has provided narrative data, revealing the syntactic flexibilities of Japanese postposing. The postposing of a noun-modifier especially sets a challenge for grammar analysis. We have offered a DS solution with the consequence of advancing the formalism and broadening empirical coverage.

Acknowledgments

I thank Akira Ohtani and the anonymous PACLIC reviewers for their helpful comments on the earlier versions of the present article.

References

Abe, J. 1999. On directionality of movement. Ms., Nagoya University.

Blakemore, D. 2002. *Relevance and Linguistic Meaning*. Cambridge University Press, Cambridge.

Cann, R., Kempson, R., and Marten, L. 2005. *The Dynamics of Language*. Elsevier, Oxford.

Cann, R., Kempson, R., Marten, L., Otsuka, M., and Swinburne, D. 2004. On the left and on the right. In Adger, D. et al. (eds.) *Peripheries*, pp. 19-47. Kluwer, Dordrecht.

Chatzikyriakidis, S. 2011. Right dislocations in Greek. Ms., CNRS.

Davidson, D. 1967. The logical form of action sentences. In Rescher, N. (ed.) *The Logic of Decision and Action*, pp. 81-95. University of Pittsburg Press, Pittsburg.

Fujii, Y. 1995. Nihongo-no-gojyun-no gyakuten-nitsuite. (On the reversed word orders in Japanese) In Takami, K. (ed.) *Nichieigo-no Uhou Teni Koubun*, pp. 167-98. Hituzi Publishing, Tokyo.

Gregoromichelaki, E. 2006. *Conditionals in Dynamic Syntax*. PhD thesis, King's College London.

Gregoromichelaki, E. 2013. A dynamic perspective on left-right asymmetries. In Webelhuth, G. et al. (eds.) *Rightward Movement in a Comparative Perspective*, pp. 321-68. John Benjamins, Amsterdam.

Kempson, R., Meyer-Viol, W., and Gabbay, D. 2001. *Dynamic Syntax*. Blackwell, Oxford.

Kuno, S. 1978. *Danwa-no Bunpou*. (Grammar of Discourse) Taishukan, Tokyo.

Marten, L. 2002. *At the Syntax-Pragmatics Interface*. Oxford University Press, Oxford.

Nishiyama, Y. 2003. *Nihongo Meishiku-no Imiron-to-Goyouron*. (The Semantics and Pragmatics of Noun Phrases in Japanese) Hituzi Publishing, Tokyo.

Nomura, J. 2008. *Japanese Postposing*. PhD thesis, University of Hawaii.

Ono, T. 2006. Postpredicate-elements in Japanese conversation. In Vance, T. & Jones, K. (eds.) *Japanese/Korean Linguistics 14*, pp. 381-91. Stanford: CSLI Publications.

Purver, M., Gregoromichelaki, E., Meyer-Viol, W., and Cann, R. 2010. Splitting the 'I's and crossing the 'you's. In Łupkowski, P. & Purver, M. (eds.) *Aspects of Semantics and Pragmatics of Dialogue*, pp. 43-50. Polish Society for Cognitive Science, Poznań

Purver, M., Hough, J., and Gregoromichelaki, E. 2014. Dialogue and compound contributions. In Stent, A. & Bangalore, S. (eds.) *Natural Language Generation in Interactive Systems*, pp. 63-92. Cambridge University Press, Cambridge.

Seraku, T. 2013. *Clefts, Relatives, and Language Dynamics*. DPhil thesis, University of Oxford.

Seraku, T. & Ohtani, A. fthc. The *wh*-licensing in Japanese right dislocations. Paper to be presented at Colloque de Syntaxe et Sémantique à Paris 2015. Université Paris Diderot, France

Takano, Y. 2014. A comparative approach to Japanese postposing. In Saito, M. (ed.) *Japanese Syntax in Comparative Perspective*, pp. 139-80. Oxford University Press, Oxford.

Takita, K. 2014. Pseudo-right dislocation, the bare-topic construction, and hanging topic constructions. *Lingua* 140: 137-57.

Tanaka, H. & Kizu, M. 2007. Island insensitive constructions in Japanese. *York Papers in Linguistics* 2: 219-34.

Whitman, J. 2000. Right dislocation in English and Japanese. In Takami, K. et al. (eds.) *Syntactic and Functional Explorations in Honor of Susumu Kuno*, pp. 445-70. Kuroshio Publishers, Tokyo.

Wu, Y. 2005. *The Dynamic Syntax of Left and Right Dislocation*. PhD thesis, University of Edinburgh.

Appendix: Citation Information

{kirishima} [ISBN: 978-4-08-74681705]
Asai, Ryo. *Kirishima Bukatsu Yamerutteyo*
Tokyo: Shueisha Publishing. (2012)

{mikeneko} [ISBN: 978-4-334-76865-2]
Akagawa, Jiro. *Mikeneko Homuzu-no Yumekikou*
Tokyo: Kobunsha. (2015)

{roll} [ISBN: 978-4-04-389804-6]
Arikawa, Hiro. 'Roll Out' in *Kujira-no Kare*.
Tokyo: Kadokawa Shoten Publishing. (2010)

{tokyo} [ISBN: 4-10-133921-X]
Ekuni, Kaori. *Tokyo Tower*
Tokyo: Shinchosha Publishing. (2006)

{yunou} [ISBN: 978-4-04-389804-6]
Arikawa, Hiro. 'Yunouna Kanojo' in *Kujira-no Kare*.
Tokyo: Kadokawa Shoten Publishing. (2010)

Unsupervised and Lightly Supervised Part-of-Speech Tagging Using Recurrent Neural Networks

Othman Zennaki [1,2] **Nasredine Semmar** [1] **Laurent Besacier** [2]

[1]CEA, LIST, Vision and Content Engineering Laboratory, Gif-sur-Yvette, France
{othman.zennaki, nasredine.semmar}@cea.fr
[2]Laboratory of Informatics of Grenoble, Univ. Grenoble-Alpes, Grenoble, France
laurent.besacier@imag.fr

Abstract

In this paper, we propose a novel approach to induce automatically a Part-Of-Speech (POS) tagger for resource-poor languages (languages that have no labeled training data). This approach is based on cross-language projection of linguistic annotations from parallel corpora without the use of word alignment information. Our approach does not assume any knowledge about foreign languages, making it applicable to a wide range of resource-poor languages. We use Recurrent Neural Networks (RNNs) as multilingual analysis tool. Our approach combined with a basic cross-lingual projection method (using word alignment information) achieves comparable results to the state-of-the-art. We also use our approach in a weakly supervised context, and it shows an excellent potential for very low-resource settings (less than 1k training utterances).

1 Introduction

Nowadays, Natural Language Processing (NLP) tools (part-of-speech tagger, sense tagger, syntactic parser, named entity recognizer, semantic role labeler, etc.) with the best performance are those built using supervised learning approaches for resource-rich languages (where manually annotated corpora are available) such as English, French, German, Chinese and Arabic. However, for a large number of resource-poor languages, annotated corpora do not exist. Their manual construction is labor intensive and very expensive, making supervised approaches not feasible.

The availability of parallel corpora has recently led to several strands of research work exploring the use of unsupervised approaches based on linguistic annotations projection from the (resource-rich) *source* language to the (under-resourced) *target* language. The goal of cross-language projection is, on the one hand, to provide all languages with linguistic annotations, and on the other hand, to automatically induce NLP tools for these languages. Unfortunately, the state-of-the-art in unsupervised methods, is still quite far from supervised learning approaches. For example, Petrov et al. (2012) obtained an average accuracy of 95.2% for 22 resource-rich languages supervised POS taggers, while the state-of-the-art in the unsupervised POS taggers achieved by Das and Petrov (2011) and Duong et al. (2013) with an average accuracy reaches only 83.4% on 8 European languages. Section 2 presents a brief overview of related work.

In this paper, we first adapt a similar method than the one of Duong et al. (2013) [1], to build an unsupervised POS tagger based on a simple cross-lingual projection (Section 3.1). Next, we explore the possibility of using a recurrent neural network (RNN) to induce multilingual NLP tools, without using word alignment information. To show the potential of our approach, we firstly investigate POS tagging.

In our approach, a parallel corpus between a resource-rich language (having a POS tagger) and a lower-resourced language is used to extract a common words representation (cross-lingual words representation) based only on sentence level alignment. This representation is used with the source side of the parallel corpus (tagged corpus) to learn a neural network POS tagger for the source language. No

[1]We did not use incremental training (as Duong et al. (2013) did).

29th Pacific Asia Conference on Language, Information and Computation pages 133 - 142
Shanghai, China, October 30 - November 1, 2015

word alignment information is needed in our approach. Based on this common representation of source and target words, this neural network POS tagger can also be used to tag target language text (Section 3.2).

We assume that these two models (baseline cross-lingual projection and RNN) are complementary to each other (one relies on word-alignment information while the other does not), and the performance can be further improved by combining them (linear combination presented in Section 3.3). This unsupervised RNN model, obtained without any target language annotated data, can be easily adapted in a weakly supervised manner (if a small amount of annotated target data is available) in order to take into account the target language specificity (Section 4).

To evaluate our approach, we conducted an experiment, which consists of two parts. First, using only parallel corpora, we evaluate our unsupervised approach for 4 languages: French, German, Greek and Spanish. Secondly, the performance of our approach is evaluated for German in a weakly supervised context, using several amounts of target adaptation data (Section 5). Finally, Section 6 concludes our study and presents our future work.

2 Related Work

Several studies have used cross-lingual projection to transfer linguistic annotations from a resource-rich language to a resource-poor language in order to train NLP tools for the target language. The projection approach has been successfully used to transfer several linguistic annotations between languages. Examples include POS (Yarowsky et al., 2001; Das and Petrov, 2011; Duong et al., 2013), named entity (Kim and Lee, 2012), syntactic constituent (Jiang et al., 2011), word senses (Bentivogli et al., 2004; Van der Plas and Apidianaki, 2014), and semantic role labeling (Padó , 2007; Annesi and Basili, 2010).

In these approaches, the source language is tagged, and tags are projected from the source language to the target language through the use of word alignments in parallel corpora. Then, these partial noisy annotations can be used in conjunction with robust learning algorithms to build unsupervised NLP tools. One limitation of these approaches is due to the poor accuracy of word-alignment algorithms, and also to the weak or incomplete inherent match between the two sides of a bilingual corpus (the alignment is not only a one-to-one mapping, it can also be one-to-many, many-to-one, many-to-many or some words can remain unaligned). To deal with these limitations, recent studies have proposed to combine projected labels with partially supervised monolingual information in order to filter out invalid label sequences. For example, Li et al. (2012), Täckström et al. (2013b) and Wisniewski et al. (2014) have proposed to improve projection performance by using a dictionary of valid tags for each word (coming from Wiktionary [2]).

In another vein, various studies based on cross-lingual representation learning methods have proposed to avoid using such pre-processed and noisy alignments for label projection. First, these approaches learn language-independent features, across many different languages (Al-Rfou et al., 2013). Then, the induced representation space is used to train NLP tools by exploiting labeled data from the source language and apply them in the target language. To induce interlingual features, several resources have been used, including bilingual lexicon (Durrett et al., 2012; Gouws and Søgaard, 2015a) and parallel corpora (Täckström et al., 2013a; Gouws et al., 2015b). Cross-lingual representation learning have achieved good results in different NLP applications such as cross-language POS tagging and cross-language super sense (SuS) tagging (Gouws and Søgaard, 2015a), cross-language named entity recognition (Täckström et al., 2012), cross-lingual document classification and lexical translation task (Gouws et al., 2015b), cross language dependency parsing (Durrett et al., 2012; Täckström et al., 2013a; Xiao and Guo, 2014) and cross language semantic role labeling (Titov and Klementiev, 2012). Our approach described in next section, is inspired by these works since we also try to learn a common language-independent feature space. Our common (multilingual) representation is based on the occurrence of source and target words in a parallel corpus. Using this representation, we learn a cross-lingual POS tagger (multilingual POS tagger if a multilingual parallel corpus is used) based on a recurrent neural network (RNN) on the source

[2] http://www.wiktionary.org/

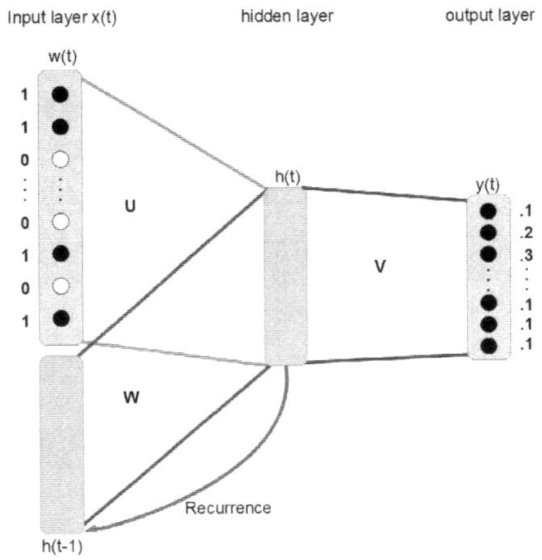

Figure 1: Architecture of the recurrent neural network.

labeled text and apply it to tag target language text. We also show that the architecture proposed is well suited for lightly supervised training (adaptation).

Finally, several works have investigated how to apply neural networks to NLP applications (Bengio et al., 2006; Collobert and Weston, 2008; Collobert et al., 2011; Henderson, 2004; Mikolov et al., 2010; Federici and Pirrelli, 1993). While Federici and Pirrelli (1993) was one of the earliest attempts to develop a part-of-speech tagger based on a special type of neural network, Bengio et al. (2006) and Mikolov et al. (2010) applied neural networks to build language models. Collobert and Weston (2008) and Collobert et al. (2011) employed a deep learning framework for multi-task learning including part-of-speech tagging, chunking, named-entity recognition, language modelling and semantic role-labeling. Henderson (2004) proposed training methods for learning a statistical parser based on neural network.

3 Unsupervised Approach Overview

To avoid projecting label information from deterministic and error-prone word alignments, we propose to represent the bilingual word alignment information intrinsically in a neural network architecture. The idea consists in implementing a neural network as a cross-lingual POS tagger and show that, in combination with a simple cross-lingual projection method, this achieves comparable results to state-of-the-art unsupervised POS taggers.

Our approach is the following: we assume that we have a POS tagger in the source language and a parallel corpus. The key idea is to learn a bilingual neural network POS tagger on the pre-annotated *source* side of the parallel corpus, and to use it for tagging *target* text. Before describing our bilingual neural network POS tagger, we present the simple cross-lingual projection method, considered as our baseline in this work.

3.1 Unsupervised POS Tagger Based on a Simple Cross-lingual Projection

Our simple POS tagger (described by Algorithm 1) is close to the approach introduced in Yarowsky et al. (2001). These authors were the first to use automatic word alignments (from a bilingual parallel corpus) to project annotations from a *source* language to a *target* language, to build unsupervised POS taggers. The algorithm is shortly recalled below.

Algorithm 1 : Simple POS Tagger

1: Tag source side of the parallel corpus.
2: Word align the parallel corpus with Giza++ (Och and Ney, 2000) or other word alignment tools.
3: Project tags directly for 1-to-1 alignments.
4: For many-to-one mappings project the tag of the middle word.
5: The unaligned words (target) are tagged with their most frequent associated tag in the corpus.
6: Learn POS tagger on target side of the bi-text with, for instance, TNT tagger (Brants, 2000).

3.2 Unsupervised POS Tagger Based on Recurrent Neural Network

There are two major architectures of neural networks: Feedforward (Bengio et al., 2006) and Recurrent Neural Networks (RNN) (Mikolov et al., 2010). Sundermeyer et al. (2013) showed that language models based on recurrent architecture achieve better performance than language models based on feedforward architecture. This is due to the fact that recurrent neural networks do not use a context of limited size. This property led us to use, in our experiments, a simple recurrent architecture (Elman, 1990).

In this section, we describe in detail our method for building an unsupervised POS tagger for a target language based on a recurrent neural network.

3.2.1 Model description

The RNN consists of at least three layers: input layer in time t is $x(t)$, hidden layer $h(t)$ (also called context layer), and output layer is denoted as $y(t)$. All neurons of the input layer are connected to every neuron of hidden layer by weight matrix U and W. The weight matrix V connects all neurons of the hidden layer to every neuron of output layer, as it can be seen in Figure 1.

In our RNN POS tagger, the input layer is formed by concatenating vector representing current word w, and the copy of the hidden layer at previous time. We start by associating to each word in both the source and the target vocabularies a common vector representation, namely $V_{wi}, i = 1, ..., N$, where N is the number of parallel sentences (bi-sentences in the parallel corpus). If w appears in i-th bi-sentence of the parallel corpus then $V_{wi} = 1$. Therefore, all input neurons corresponding to current word w are set to 0 except those that correspond to bi-sentences containing w, which are set to 1. The idea is that, in general, a source word and its target translation appear together in the same bi-sentences and their vector representations are close.We can then use the RNN POS tagger, initially trained on source side, to tag the target side (because of our *common vector representation*).

We also use two hidden layers (our preliminary experiments have shown better performance than one hidden layer), with variable sizes (usually 80-1024 neurons) and sigmoid activation function. These hidden layers inherently capture word alignment information. The output layer of our model contains 12 neurons, this number is determined by the POS tagset size. To deal with the potential mismatch in the POS tagsets of source and target languages, we adopted the Petrov et al. (2012) universal tagset (12 tags common for most languages): NOUN (nouns), VERB (verbs), ADJ (adjectives), ADV (adverbs), PRON (pronouns), DET (determiners and articles), ADP (prepositions and postpositions), NUM (numerals), CONJ (conjunctions), PRT (particles), . (punctuation marks) and X (all other categories, e.g., foreign words, abbreviations). Therefore, each output neuron corresponds to one POS tag in the tagset. The softmax activation function is used to normalize the values of output neurons to sum up to 1. Finally, the current word w (in input) is tagged with most probable output tag.

3.2.2 Training the model

The first step in our approach is to train the neural network, given a parallel corpus (training corpus), and a validation corpus (different from train data) in the source language. In typical applications, the source language is a resource-rich language (which already has an efficient POS tagger). Before training the model, the following pre-processing steps are performed :

- Source side of training corpus and validation corpus are annotated (using the available supervised POS tagger).
- Using a parallel corpus, we build the common vector representations for source and target side words.

Then, the neural network is trained through several epochs. Algorithm 2 below describes one training epoch.

Algorithm 2 : Training RNN POS Tagger

1: Initialize weights with Normal distribution.
2: Set time counter t = 0, and initialize state of the neurons in the hidden layer h(t) to 1.
3: Increase time counter t by 1.
4: Push at the input layer w(t) the vector representation of the current (source) word of training corpus.
5: Copy the state of the hidden layer h(t-1) to the input layer.
6: Perform a forward pass to obtain the predicted output y(t).
7: Compute the gradient of the error in the output layer $e_o(t) = d(t) - y(t)$ (difference between the predicted *y(t)* and the desired output *d(t)*).
8: Propagate the error back through the network and update weights with stochastic gradient descent using Back-Propagation *(BP)* and Back-Propagation-through-time *(BPTT)* (Rumelhartet al., 1985).
9: If not all training inputs were processed, go to 3.

After each epoch, the neural network is used to tag the validation corpus, then the result is compared with the result of the supervised POS tagger, to calculate the *per-token* accuracy. If the per-token accuracy increases, training continues in the new epoch. Otherwise, the learning rate is halved at the start of the new epoch. After that, if the per-token accuracy does not increase anymore, training is stopped to prevent over-fitting. Generally convergence takes 5–10 epochs, starting with a learning rate $\alpha = 0.1$.

After learning the model, step 2 simply consists in using the trained model as a target language POS tagger (using our common vector representation). It is important to note that if we train on a multilingual parallel corpus with N languages ($N > 2$), the same trained model will be able to tag all the N languages.

Hence, our approach assumes that the word order in both source and target languages are similar. In some languages such as English and French, word order for contexts containing nouns could be reversed most of the time. For example, *the European Commission* would be translated into *la Commission europenne*. In order to deal with the word order constraints, we combined the RNN model with the cross-lingual projection model, and we also propose Light Supervision (adaptation) of RNN model where a few amount of target data will help to learn the word order (and consequently POS order) in the target language.

3.3 Combining Simple Cross-lingual Projection and RNN Models

Since the simple cross-lingual projection model *M1* and RNN model *M2* use different strategies for POS tagging (TNT is based on Markov models while RNN is a neural network), we assume that these two models are complementary. In addition, model *M2* does not implement any out-of-vocabulary (OOV) words processing yet. So, to keep the benefits of each approach, we explore how to combine them with linear interpolation. Formally, the probability to tag a given word *w* is computed as

$$P_{M12}(t|w) = (\mu P_{M1}(t|w, C_{M1}) + (1-\mu) P_{M2}(t|w, C_{M2})) \tag{1}$$

where, C_{M1} and C_{M2} are, respectively the context of w considered by *M1* and *M2*. The relative importance of each model is adjusted through the interpolation parameter μ.

The word w is tagged with the most probable tag, using the function f described as

$$f(w) = \arg\max_t (P_{M12}(t|w)) \tag{2}$$

4 Light Supervision (adaptation) of RNN model

While the unsupervised RNN model described in the previous section has not seen any annotated data in the target language, we also consider the use of a small amount of adaptation data (manually annotated in target language) in order to capture target language specificity. Such an adaptation is performed on top of the unsupervised RNN model without retraining the full model. The full process is the following (steps 1 and 2 correspond to the unsupervised case):

1. Each word in the parallel corpus is represented by a binary occurrence vector (same initial common vector representation).
2. The source side of the parallel corpus (using the available supervised POS tagger) and common vector representation of words are combined to train the RNN (Algorithm 2).
3. The RNN trained is adapted in a light supervision manner, using a small monolingual target corpus (manually annotated) and the common vector representation of words (extracted from the initial parallel corpus).

Such an approach is particularly suited for an iterative scenario where a user would post-edit (correct) the unsupervised POS-tagger output in order to produce rapidly adaptation data in the training language (light supervision).

5 Experiments and Results

5.1 Data and tools

Initially, we applied our method to the English–French language pair. French was considered as the target language here. French is certainly not a resource-poor language, but it was used as if no tagger was available (in fact, TreeTagger (Schmid, 1995), a supervised POS tagger exists for this language and helps us to obtain a ground truth for

Lang. / Model	French		German		Greek		Spanish	
	All words	OOV	All words	OOV	All words	OOV	All words	OOV
Simple Projection	80.3%	77.1%	78.9%	73%	77.5%	72.8%	80%	79.7%
RNN-640-160	78.5%	70%	76.1%	76.4%	75.7%	70.7%	78.8%	72.6%
Projection+RNN	**84.5%**	**78.8%**	81.5%	**77%**	78.3%	**74.6%**	83.6%	**81.2%**
(Das, 2011)	—	—	82.8%	—	**82.5%**	—	**84.2%**	—
(Duong, 2013)	—	—	**85.4%**	—	80.4%	—	83.3%	—
(Gouws, 2015a)	—	—	84.8%	—	—	—	82.6%	—

Table 1: Unsupervised model : token-level POS tagging accuracy for Simple Projection, RNN [4], Projection+RNN and methods of Das & Petrov (2011), Duong et al (2013) and Gouws & Søgaard (2015).

evaluation). To train the RNN POS tagger, we used a training set of $10,000$ parallel sentences extracted from the ARCADE II English–French corpus (Veronis et al., 2008). Our validation corpus contains 1000 English sentences (these sentences are not in the train set) extracted from the ARCADE II English corpus. The test corpus is also extracted from the ARCADE II corpus, and it contains 1000 French sentences (which are obviously different from the train set) tagged with the French *TreeTagger* Toolkit (Schmid, 1995) and manually checked.

Encouraged by the results obtained on the English–French language pair, and in order to confirm our results, we run additional experiments on other languages, we applied our method to build RNN POS taggers for three more target languages — German, Greek and Spanish — with English as the source language, in order to compare our results with those of (Das and Petrov, 2011; Duong et al., 2013; Gouws and Søgaard, 2015a). Our training and validation (English) data extracted from the Europarl corpus (Koehn, 2005) are a subset of the training data of (Das and Petrov, 2011; Duong et al., 2013). The sizes of the data sets are: $65,000$ (train) and $10,000$ (dev) bi-sentences. For testing, we used the same test corpora (from CoNLL shared tasks on dependency parsing (Buchholz and Marsi, 2006)) as (Das and Petrov, 2011; Duong et al., 2013; Gouws and Søgaard, 2015a). The evaluation metric (*per-token* accuracy) and the Universal Tagset are the same as before. The source sides of the training corpora (ARCADE II and Europarl) and the validation corpora are tagged with the English *TreeTagger* Toolkit. Using the matching provided by Petrov et al. (2012) we map the TreeTagger and the CoNLL tagsets to a common Universal Tagset.

In order to build our unsupervised tagger based on a Simple Cross-lingual Projection (Algorithm 1), we tag the target side of the training corpus, with tags projected from English side through word-alignments established by GIZA++. After tags projection we use TNT Tagger to induce a target language POS Tagger (see Algorithm 1 described in Section 3.1).

Also, our proposed approach implements Algorithm 2 described before. We had to slightly modify the Recurrent Neural Network Language Modeling Toolkit (RNNLM) provided by Mikolov et al. (2011), to learn our Recurrent Neural Network Based POS Tagger[5]. The modifications include: (1) building the cross-lingual word representations automatically; and (2) learning and testing models with several hidden layers (common representation as input and universal POS tags as output).

The combined model is built for each considered language using cross-validation on the test corpus. First the test corpus is split into 2 equal parts and on each part, we estimate the interpolation parameter μ (Equation 1) which maximizes the *per-token* accuracy score. Then each part of test corpus is tagged using the combined model tuned (Equation 2) on the other part, and vice versa (standard cross-validation procedure).

Finally, we investigate how the performance of the adapted model changes according to target adaptation corpus size. We choose German as target adaptation language, because we dispose of a large German annotated data set (from CoNLL shared

[4]For RNN a single system is used for German, Greek and Spanish

[5]The modified source code is Available from the following URL `https://github.com/othman-zennaki/RNN_POS_Tagger.git`

tasks on dependency parsing). Then, we generate German adaptation sets of 7 different sizes (from 100 to 10,000 utterances). Each adaptation set is used to adapt our unsupervised RNN POS tagger. As contrastive experiments, we also learn supervised POS Taggers based on RNN, TNT or their linear combination.

5.2 Results and discussion

5.2.1 Unsupervised model

In table 1 we report the results obtained for the unsupervised approach. Preliminary RNN experiments used one hidden layer, but we obtained lower performance compared to those with two hidden layers. So we report here RNN accuracy achieved using two hidden layers, containing respectively 640 and 160 neurons (RNN-640-160). As shown in the table, this accuracy is close to that of the simple projection tagger, the difference coming mostly from out-of-vocabulary (OOV) words. As OOV words are not in the training corpus, their vector representations are empty (they contain only 0), therefore the RNN model uses only the context information, which is insufficient to tag correctly the OOV words in the test corpus. We also observe that both methods seem complementary since the best results are achieved using the linearly combined model Projection+RNN-640-160. It achieves comparable results to Das and Petrov (2011), Duong et al. (2013) (who used the full Europarl corpus while we used only a 65,000 subset of it) and Gouws and Søgaard (2015a) (who in addition used Wiktionary and Wikipedia) methods. It is also important to note that a single RNN tagger applies to German, Greek and Spanish; so this is a truly multilingual POS tagger! Therefore, as for several other NLP tasks such as language modelling or machine translation (where standard and NN-based models are combined in a log-linear model), the use of both standard and RNN-based approaches seems necessary to obtain optimal performances.

In order to know in what respect using RNN improves combined model accuracy, and vice versa, we analyzed the French test corpus. In the example provided in table 2, RNN information helps to resolve the French word *"précise"* tag ambiguity: in the Simple Projection model it is tagged as a verb

English	a precise breakdown of spending
French	une répartition précise des dépenses
Simple Projection	une/DET répartition/NOUN précise/**VERB** des/ADP ...
Projection + RNN	une/DET répartition/NOUN précise/**ADJ** des/ADP ...

Table 2: Improved tagged example for french target language.

(VERB), whereas it is an adjective (ADJ) in this particular context. We hypothesize that the context information is better represented in RNN, because of the recurrent connections.

In case of word order divergence, we observed that our model can still handle some divergence, notably for the following cases:

- Obviously if the current tag word is unambiguous (case of ADJ and NOUN order from English to French - see table 3), then the context (RNN history) information has no effect.
- When the context is erroneous (due to the fact that word order for the target test corpus is different from the source training corpus), the right word tag can be recovered using the combination (RNN+Cross-lingual projection - see table 4).

EN Supervised Treetagger	... other/ADJ specific/ADJ groups/NOUN ...
FR Unsupervised RNN	... autres/ADJ groupes/NOUN spcifiques/ADJ ...

Table 3: Word order divergence -unambiguous tag word-.

EN Supervised Treetagger	... two/NUM local/ADJ groups/NOUN ...
FR Unsupervised RNN	... deux/NUM groupes/NOUN locaux/**NOUN** ...
Projection + RNN	... deux/NUM groupes/NOUN locaux/ **ADJ** ...

Table 4: Word order divergence -ambiguous tag word-.

5.2.2 Lightly supervised model

In table 5 we report the results obtained after adaptation with a gradually increasing amount of

DE Corpus Size / Model	0	100	500	1k	2k	5k	7k	10k
Unsupervised RNN + DE Adaptation	76.1%	**82.1%**	**87.3%**	**90.4%**	90.7%	91.2%	91.4%	92.4%
Supervised RNN DE only	—	71%	76.4%	82.1%	90.6%	93%	94.2%	95.2%
Supervised TNT DE only	—	80.5%	86.5%	89%	92.2%	94.1%	95.3%	95.7%
Supervised RNN + Supervised TNT DE	—	81%	86.7%	90.1%	**94.2%**	**95.3%**	**95.7%**	**96%**

Table 5: Lightly supervised model : effect of German adaptation corpus (manually annotated) size on method described in Section 4 (Unsupervised RNN + DE Adaptation trained on EN Europarl and adapted to German). Contrastive experiments with German supervised POS taggers using same data (RNN, TNT and RNN+TNT). 0 means no German corpus used during training.

target language data annotated (from 100 to $10,000$ utterances). We focus on German target language only. It is compared with two supervised approaches based on TNT or RNN. The supervised approaches are trained on the adaptation data only. For supervised RNN, it is important to mention that the input vector representation has a different dimension for each amount of adaptation data (we recall that the vector representation is $V_{wi}, i = 1, ..., N$, where N is the number of sentences; and N is growing from 100 to $10,000$). The results show that our adaptation, on top of the unsupervised RNN is efficient in very low resource settings ($<$ 1000 target language utterances). When more data is available ($>$ 1000 utterances), the supervised approaches start to be better (but RNN and TNT are still complementary since their combination improves the tag accuracy).

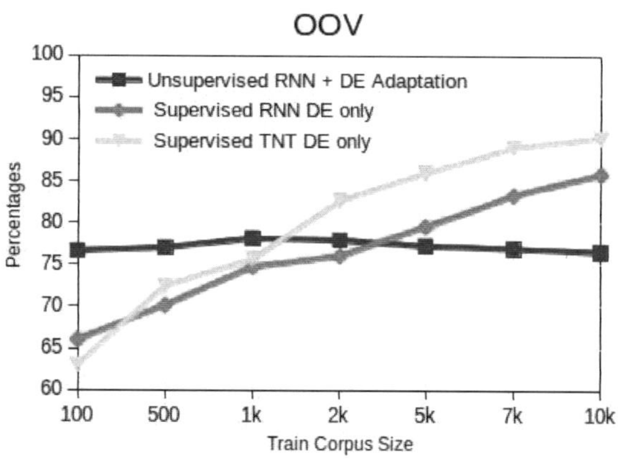

Figure 2: Accuracy on OOV according to German training corpus size for Unsupervised RNN + DE Adaptation, Supervised RNN DE and Supervised TNT DE.

Figure 2 details the behavior of the same methods for OOV words. We clearly see the limitation of the Unsupervised RNN + Adaptation to handle OOV words, since the input vector representation is the same (comes from the initial parallel corpus) and does not evolve as more German adaptation data is available. Better handling OOV words in unsupervised RNN training is our priority for future works.

Finally, these results show that for all training data sizes, RNN brings complementary information on top of a more classical approach such as TNT.

6 Conclusion

In this paper, we have presented a novel approach which uses a language-independent word representation (based only on word occurrence in a parallel corpus) within a recurrent neural network (RNN) to build multilingual POS tagger. Our method induces automatically POS tags from one language to another (or several others) and needs only a parallel corpus and a POS tagger in the source language (without using word alignment information).

We first empirically evaluated the proposed approach on two unsupervised POS taggers based on RNN : (1) English–French cross-lingual POS tagger; and (2) English–German–Greek–Spanish multilingual POS tagger. The performance of the second model is close to state-of-the-art with only a subset $(65,000)$ of Europarl corpus used.

Additionally, when a small amount of supervised data is available, the experimental results demonstrated the effectiveness of our method in a weakly supervised context (especially for very-low-resourced settings).

Although our initial experiments are positive, we believe they can be improved in a number of ways. In future work, we plan, on the one hand, to better manage OOV representation (for instance using Cross-lingual Word Embeddings), and, on the other hand, to consider more complex tasks such as word senses projection or semantic role labels projection.

References

R. Al-Rfou, B. Perozzi and S. Skiena. 2013. Polyglot: Distributed word representations for multilingual nlp, In *Proceedings of the Seventeenth Conference on Computational Natural Language Learning*:183–192.

P. Annesi and R. Basili. 2010. Cross-lingual alignment of FrameNet annotations through Hidden Markov Models, In *Proceedings of CICLing* :12–25.

Y. Bengio, H. Schwenk, J. Senécal, F. Morin and J. Gauvain. 2006. Neural probabilistic language models, In *Innovations in Machine Learning*:137–186.

L. Bentivogli, P. Forner and E. Pianta. 2004. Evaluating cross-language annotation transfer in the MultiSemCor corpus, In *Proceedings of the 20th international conference on Computational Linguistics*:364–370. Association for Computational Linguistics.

S. Buchholz and E. Marsi. 2006. CoNLL-X shared task on multilingual dependency parsing, In *Proceedings of the Tenth Conference on Computational Natural Language Learning*:149–164. Association for Computational Linguistics.

T. Brants. 2000. TnT: a statistical part-of-speech tagger, In *Proceedings of the sixth conference on Applied natural language processing*:224–231.

R. Collobert and J. Weston. 2008. A unified architecture for natural language processing: Deep neural networks with multitask learning, In *Proceedings of the International Conference on Machine Learning (ICML)*:160–167.

R. Collobert, J. Weston, L. Bottou, M. Karlen, K. Kavukcuoglu, and P. Kuksa. 2011. Natural language processing (almost) from scratch, In *Journal of Machine Learning Research (JMLR)*, volume 12:2493–2537.

D. Das and S. Petrov. 2011. Unsupervised Part-of-Speech Tagging with Bilingual Graph-Based Projections, In *Proceedings of the 49th Annual Meeting of the Association for Computational Linguistics: Human Language Technologies*, volume 1:600–609. Association for Computational Linguistics.

L. Duong, P.Cook, S. Bird and P. Pecina. 2013. Simpler unsupervised POS tagging with bilingual projections, In *ACL (2)* :634–639.

G. Durrett, A. Pauls and D. Klein. 2012. Syntactic transfer using a bilingual lexicon, In *Proceedings of the 2012 Joint Conference on Empirical Methods in Natural Language Processing and Computational Natural Language Learning*:1–11. Association for Computational Linguistics.

J.L. Elman. 1990. Finding structure in time, In *Cognitive science*:179–211.

J. Henderson. 2004. Discriminative training of a neural network statistical parser, In *Proceedings of the Annual Meeting of the Association for Computational Linguistics (ACL)*:95–102.

S. Federici and V. Pirrelli. 1993. Analogical modelling of text tagging, *unpublished report*, Istituto diLinguistica Computazionale, Pisa, Italy.

S. Gouws and A. Søgaard 2015. Simple task-specific bilingual word embeddings, In *The 2015 Conference of the North American Chapter of the Association for Computational Linguistics: Human Language Technologies, NAACL'15*:1386–1390.

S. Gouws, Y. Bengio and G. Corrado 2015. BilBOWA: Fast Bilingual Distributed Representations without Word Alignments, In *Proceedings of the 32nd International Conference on Machine Learning, ICML 2015*:748–756.

W. Jiang, Q. Liu and Y. Lü, 2011 Relaxed cross-lingual projection of constituent syntax, In *Proceedings of the Conference on Empirical Methods in Natural Language Processing*:1192–1201. Association for Computational Linguistics.

S. Kim, K. Toutanova and H. Yu, 2012 Multilingual named entity recognition using parallel data and metadata from wikipedia, In *Proceedings of the 50th Annual Meeting of the Association for Computational Linguistics: Long Papers-volume 1*:694–702. Association for Computational Linguistics.

S. Li, J.V Graça and B. Taskar. 2012 Wiki-ly supervised part-of-speech tagging, In *Proceedings of the 2012 Joint Conference on Empirical Methods in Natural Language Processing and Computational Natural Language Learning*:1389–1398. Association for Computational Linguistics.

T. Mikolov, M. Karafiát , L. Burget, J. Cernocký and S. Khudanpur. 2010. Recurrent neural network based language model, In *INTERSPEECH*:1045–1048.

T. Mikolov, S. Kombrink , A. Deoras, L. Burget and J. Cernocky. 2011. RNNLM-Recurrent neural network language modeling toolkit, In *Proc. of the 2011 ASRU Workshop*:196–201.

F.Och and H.Ney. 2000. Improved Statistical Alignment Models, In *ACL00*:440–447.

S. Padó. 2007. Cross-Lingual Annotation Projection Models for Role-Semantic Information, In *German Research Center for Artificial Intelligence and Saarland University*, volume 21.

S. Petrov, D. Das and R. McDonald. 2012. A Universal Part-of-Speech Tagset, In *Proceedings of the 8th International Conference on Language Resources and Evaluation (LREC '12)*:2089–2096.

P. Koehn 2005. Europarl: A parallel corpus for statistical machine translation, In *MT summit*, volume 5 :79–86.

D. Rumelhart, E. Hinton and R.J. Williams . 1985. Learning internal representations by error propagation,

In *Learning internal representations by error propagation* .

H. Schmid. 1995. TreeTagger— a Language Independent Part-of-speech Tagger, In *Institut für Maschinelle Sprachverarbeitung, Universität Stuttgart*, volume 43 :28.

M. Sundermeyer, I. Oparin, J. Gauvain, B. Freiberg, R. Schluter and H.Ney. 2013. Comparison of feedforward and recurrent neural network language models, In *Acoustics, Speech and Signal Processing (ICASSP), 2013 IEEE International Conference*:8430–8434.

O. Täckström, R. McDonald and J. Uszkoreit. 2012. Cross-lingual word clusters for direct transfer of linguistic structure, In *Proceedings of the 2012 Conference of the North American Chapter of the Association for Computational Linguistics: Human Language Technologies*:477–487. Association for Computational Linguistics.

O. Täckström, R. McDonald, J. Nivre. 2013. Target language adaptation of discriminative transfer parsers, In *Proceedings of the Conference of the North American Chapter of the Association for Computational Linguistics: Human Language Tech-nologies (NAACL).*

O. Täckström, D. Das, S. Petrov, R. McDonald and J. Nivre. 2013. Token and type constraints for cross-lingual part-of-speech tagging, In *Transactions of the Association for Computational Linguistics*: volume 1 :1–12. Association for Computational Linguistics.

I. Titov and A. Klementiev. 2012. Crosslingual induction of semantic roles, In *Proceedings of the 50th Annual Meeting of the Association for Computational Linguistics: Long Papers-volume 1*:647–656. Association for Computational Linguistics.

L. Van der Plas and M. Apidianaki. 2014. Cross-lingual Word Sense Disambiguation for Predicate Labelling of French, In *Proceedings of the 21st TALN (Traitement Automatique des Langues Naturelles) conference* :46–55.

J. Veronis, O. Hamon, C. Ayache, R. Belmouhoub, O. Kraif, D. Laurent, T.M.H. Nguyen, N. Semmar, F. Stuck and Z. Wajdi. 2008. Arcade II Action de recherche concerte sur l'alignement de documents et son valuation, Chapitre 2, *Editions Hermés* .

L. Van der Maaten and G. Hinton 2008 Visualizing data using t-SNE, In *Journal of Machine Learning Research (JMLR),* 9:2579–2605.

G. Wisniewski, N. Pécheux, S. Gahbiche-Braham and F. Yvon. 2014. Cross-Lingual Part-of-Speech Tagging through Ambiguous Learning, In *EMNLP'14*:1779–1785.

M. Xiao and Y. Guo. 2014. Distributed Word Representation Learning for Cross-Lingual Dependency Parsing, In *CoNLL-2014*:119–129.

D. Yarowsky, G. NGAI and R. Wicentowski. 2001. Inducing multilingual text analysis tools via robust projection across aligned corpora, In *Proceedings of the first international conference on Human language technology research*:1–8. Association for Computational Linguistics.

Identifying Prepositional Phrases in Chinese Patent Texts with Rule-based and CRF Methods

Hongzheng Li and Yaohong Jin
Institute of Chinese Information Processing, Beijing Normal University
19, Xinjiekou Wai St., Haidian District, Beijing, 100875, China
lihongzheng@mail.bnu.edu.cn, jinyaohong@bnu.edu.cn

Abstract

Identification of prepositional phrases (PP) has been an issue in the field of Natural Language Processing (NLP). In this paper, towards Chinese patent texts, we present a rule-based method and a CRF-based method to identify the PPs. In the rule-based method, according to the special features and expressions of PPs, we manually write targeted formal identification rules; in the CRF approach, after labelling the sentences with features, a typical CRF toolkit is exploited to train the model for identifying PPs. We then conduct some experiments to test the performance of the two methods, and final precision rates are over 90%, indicating the proposed methods are effective and feasible.

1 Introduction

In recent years, patent text information processing (such as patent machine translation) has gradually become an important application field of natural language processing (NLP), and has aroused widespread attention.

Prepositional phrases (PPs), as an important type of phrase, are widely distributed in Chinese patent text, in which the vast majority serve as adverbial components. According to (Li, et al., 2014), in a random sample of 500 Chinese patent sentences, the number of sentences containing PPs are 226, accounting for 45.2% of the total sample, indicating the high proportion of PPs.

In the sentence $S = W_1, W_2, W_3 ...... W_n$, assuming the string W_i, $W_{i+1} ...... W_j$ is the PP to be identified, the main task of identifying PP is to recognize the word W_i and W_j as left and right boundaries of PP, and identify the whole string as PP chunk. Since W_i is the preposition itself, thus the key issue is to determine the position of W_j.

There exists some following difficulties in identifying PP of Chinese patent texts:

(1) Different with other domain texts, PPs in the patent texts are much longer, with more characters. According to (Gan, et al., 2005; Hu, 2015), the average length of PPs in news texts has 4.9 characters, while 12.3 characters in patent texts. On the other hand, PPs tend to have much more complex structures, which can be composed of prepositions and various kinds of phrases, or even clauses.

(2) Prepositions in Chinese are usually multi-category words, they can also serve as nouns, quantifiers, adjectives, conjunctions and verbs in different contexts.

(3) Several parallel or nested PPs can appear in the same sentence.

Here is an example sentence in the patent texts:

本发明[PP1 在条件允许的情况下][PP2 通过 [PP3 为不同区域]提供预测信息]而提出了许多更加准确的结果。

(The invention has proposed more accurate results [PP1 under the permitted condition] {PP2 by providing forecast information [PP3 for various regions.]})

As shown, two parallel PP1 and PP2 appear together in the same sentence, where PP2 also includes a nested PP3.

29th Pacific Asia Conference on Language, Information and Computation pages 143 - 149
Shanghai, China, October 30 - November 1, 2015

Note that, correct identification of PPs is significant to many tasks and applications in NLP. Take patent machine translation for example, PPs have direct impacts on a plurality of processing modules such as source language parsing, transformation and word reordering.

Considering the wide distribution of PPs and significance of correct identification, we propose a rule-based method and Conditional Random Field (CRF) method to recognize the PPs. Although facing difficulties, patent text processing still have its advantages: from words to sentences, patent texts possess kinds of common and fixed structures and expressions, which are more suitable for rule-based approach to describe and process. That's why we try to use the rule-based approach to identify the special PP chunks.

We test and compare the performances of the two approaches by designing some experiments. Final precision rates were over 90%, indicating that the approaches perform well in our task.

The rest of the paper are organized as follow: Section 2 discusses some related work. Section 3 introduces some structural and semantic analysis of PP in Chinese patent texts. Section 4 and 5 present the rule-based and CRF methods. Section 6 conducts some experiments and analysis, and the last section comes with the conclusion and future work.

2 Related Work

Identification of Chinese prepositional phrases has been an issue in the field of Chinese language processing. Many effective methods, including rule-based and statistical approaches, were proposed in past several years.

(Zhu, 2013; Hu, 2015) studied the identification of PPs towards Chinese-English patent machine translation by using a rule-based method. (Yu, 2006) applied the Maximum Entropy Model to the task of identifying PPs. Based on Hidden Markov Model, (Xi, et al., 2007) presented a novel method to identify PP chunks with dependency grammar, achieving good performance. (Jian, et al., 2009) tried to identify PP from two directions (left-right and right-left) by using the classical SVM classifier.

As a powerful sequence modeling framework that combines the advantages of both generative model and classification model, CRF was first introduced into language processing in (Lafferty, et al., 2001). Since then, the model has been successfully applied to various NLP tasks such as word segmentation (Tseng, et al., 2005), Semantic Role Labelling (Cohn and Blunsom, 2005) and parsing (Finkel, et al., 2008; Yoshimasa, et al., 2009).

(Hu, 2008; Song, 2011 and Zhang, 2013) proposed linear-CRF models to identify PPs in Chinese news corpus, aiming to identify the nested PPs.

Note that, most previous works focus on identifying PPs in news corpus, there exists few research in other domains. In this paper, we want to study some unique features of PP chunks in Chinese patent texts, and try to identify them with two different approaches.

3 Structural Analysis of PP

In this part, we need to introduce some structural and semantic analysis of PP in Chinese patent texts, which are the basis of the rule-based method in the following sections.

3.1 Types of Prepositions

After analyzing considerable Chinese patent texts, we divide the prepositions into two basic types. Some prepositions, such as "把(BA)", "由(YOU)", "将(JIANG)" and "被(BEI)", usually introduce semantic components like agent, patient in the sentence, these can be marked as P0; Other prepositions which can lead the time, manner etc. are marked as P1, including "按/按照/根据 (according to)", "通过 (by/through)" and so on. A significant difference between the two types is, components behind the P0 prepositions must be NPs, while components behind P1 are not just limited to NPs, and they can be other kinds of phrases or even clauses. Generally, the number of P1 is much more than that of P0.

3.2 Boundaries of PP

PP chunk has left and right boundary words, and the left boundary is preposition. Some right boundary words often appear together with some specific prepositions, forming fixed collocation structures. For example, in the strings "当……时 (when……)" and "在……中(in……)", the word "时" is the collocation of preposition "当", and the word "中" is the collocation of preposition "在". Such PPs with collocation structures are called *explicit PP*. Clearly, prepositions in explicit PP usually belong to P1 type, correspondingly, the right boundary words can be marked as P1H. On the contrary, *implicit PP*, refer to those PPs whose right boundary words have no specific linguistic features and cannot form collocation with the prepositions. The number of implicit PPs are also much more than that of explicit ones.

3.3 Positions of PP

PP in Chinese usually located between the subject and core predicate, forming the "(NP) + PP + VP" format, which is the most common form. Meanwhile, in order to highlight the prepositional phrases, PP can also be separated from subject and predicate by commas, alone as an independent structural unit, forming "PP +, + (NP) + VP" format.

Both the two structures have something in common: Subjects in the sentences can sometimes be omitted; several parallel PPs can exist simultaneously; and the PPs can be either explicit or implicit. But the difference is that prepositions in first format can be either P0 or P1 type, while prepositions of the second format generally can only be P1 type, because PPs introduced by P0 type have much closer relationship with the predicate structures and cannot be separated from them.

3.4 Syntactic levels of PP

For the sake of parsing, it is necessary to distinguish the PPs according to their syntactic levels in the sentences. We define two levels: LEVEL1 and LEVEL2. From the point of syntax tree, the level of PP, whose upper node is the root node of sentence, should belong to LEVEL1, indicating that PPs are direct components of the sentences; and level of other PPs, whose nodes are non-terminals, should belong to LEVEL2. In the example sentence of section 1, for instance, the levels of PP1 and PP2 are LEVEL1, and PP3 belongs to LEVEL2.

4 Rule-based Method

Based on the Chinese patent corpus provided by *State Intelligent Property Office of China* (SIPO), we build a considerable knowledge base and artificially write numerous formal rules. In the knowledge base, all words extracted from the texts are labelled with several syntactic and semantic attributes. According to the P0 and P1 types of preposition, different rules are specially designed to identify the PPs. After integrating the knowledge base and rules into the system, the rules can use information shown in the knowledge base. We will discuss the identification progress by selecting some rules and examples.

4.1 Identifying PP Introduced by P0

As mentioned, PPs introduced by prepositions of P0 types have direct relationship with the predicate structure. We have found that such PPs always appear with two-valence or three-valence verbs. Thus in the rules, it is necessary to take the valence attributes of verb into consideration to help identify the PPs. The valence attributes have already been labelled in the knowledge base.

Rule1:
(0){CHN[与]}+(1)NP+(f){(2)Verb&Valence[2] &END%}=>(PP,0,1)&PUT(PP,LEVEL,1)
Rule2:
(0){CHN[与]}+(1)NP+(f){(2)Verb&Valence[2]} +(3)CHN[的]=>(PP,0,1)&PUT(PP,LEVEL,2)

The meaning of rule 1 is that, if there exists a two-valence verb behind the Chinese character (CHN) "与(with)", and located at the end of the sentence (END%), then the string from node(0) to node (1) will be identified as PP, and its level should be LEVEL1.

Rule2 is similar to rule1, but since the verb is followed by the common auxiliary word "的(DE)", the PP is just a modifier, and its level will be LEVEL2 instead of LEVEL1.

E.g.1:本发明的结果可以[PP ***与***样本指数]***匹配***。(The results of the present invention can be matched [PP with the sample index].)

E.g.2: [NP[PP ***与***样本指数]***匹配***的结果]表明了实验的有效性。(The results matched [PP with the sample index] has proved the effectiveness of the experiment.)

4.2 Identifying PP Introduced by P1

PPs introduced by P1 actually include explicit and implicit PPs. For explicit PPs, since the left and right boundary words are collocation, they can be labelled with special marks in the knowledge base and can be first identified. As a result, after identifying them as the boundary words of PP, the whole PP chunk will be recognized easily.

Rule3:

(0)CHN[当]+(f){(1)CHN[时]}=>(PP,0,1)$

The rule means that, if the character "时" is located behind the character "当" in the same sentence, then the string between the two characters will be identified as PP chunk.

E.g.3: [PP ***当***产品的性能超过一定阈值***时***]可以出现下图所示的现象。(The phenomenon, as shown in the following figure, can occur [PP when the performance of products exceeds a certain threshold].)

For implicit PPs, since the right boundary words are not collocations of the preposition and have no specific features, it is much difficult to determine the proper positions of the right boundaries. However, we can employ other contextual information and expressions to help recognize them. For example, in many patent sentences, PPs are usually followed by some special conjunctions such as "以(Yi),来(Lai) and 而(Er)". In this case, the word in front of the conjunction will be identified as right boundary. In another case, as mentioned above, if the PP is separated by comma, then it is clearly that the comma can be used to identify the PP chunk.

Rule4:

(0){CHN[通过,经由,经过,基于,根据,藉由]}+(f){(2)CHN[以,而,来]}+(1)! CHK[，]=>(ABK,0,2]&PUT(PP,LEVEL,1)

Rule5:

(0)P1+(f){(1)CHN[，]}=>(ABK,0,1]&PUT(PP,LEVEL,1)

Rule4 indicates that if there exists Chinese conjunctions behind the prepositions at node 0, then the whole string before the conjunctions (not included) will be recognized as PP chunk (ABK). Rule5 means that the string, which begins with the preposition of P1 type and ends with the comma, will be recognized as PP chunk.

E.g.4: [PP1 根据本发明的实施例]，可[PP2 通过提供动态图像]***来***扩大方法的应用范围。([PP1 According to the embodiment of the present invention], the scope of application of the method can be expanded [PP2 by providing a dynamic image].)

Sum up, the identification rules try to take full advantages of the boundary words and contextual information around to identify PPs. The targeted rules only need to pay attention to local rather than global information in the sentence, thus they are more efficient and effective.

5 CRF Method

In this paper, we will use the CRF++ toolkit (V0.53)[1] to train the model for identifying the PP chunks and test the effects of the method.

5.1 Sequential Labelling

Chunking based on CRF method is usually recognized as sequential labelling issue. Input X is a data sequence to be labelled, and Output Y is a corresponding labelled sequence, which is taken from a specific tag set.

We adopt the B-I-E-O scheme as tag sets to label PP chunks in the sentence. B-I-E refers to Beginning, Intermediate and End elements of PP structure, and O for Outsides of the chunk.

5.2 Features

After analyzing the structural and linguistic features of patent sentences in the corpus, we defined following five effective and representative features for the model. Each feature, as shown below, is composed of feature name and its value.

Feature	Value
Token	Each token in the sentence.
POS	Marks only one proper POS of each word and punctuations (marked as "punc") according to context in the sentence.
Candidate left boundary (CLB)	From the current position of each word, find forward to find the preposition. If the preposition exists, the value is the preposition itself; otherwise marks "N".
Candidate right boundary (CRB)	If current word can be RBW of PP, marks "Y"; otherwise "N".
Candidate last word (CLW)	The word behind the RB, which is also helpful in the identification, is defined as last word (LW). If

[1] http://crfpp.googlecode.com/

	current word is LW, then marks "Y"; otherwise "N".

Table 1. Feature Sets of the CRF Model

After word segmentation, we manually label each sentence sequence including PP chunks with above features.Table2 shows a tagged sequence example.

Words	POS	CLB	CRB	CLW	Tag Set
本发明	n	N	N	N	O
通过	prep	通过	N	N	B
采用	v	通过	N	N	I
先进	a	通过	N	N	I
技术	n	通过	Y	N	E
而	conj	通过	N	Y	O
提高	v	通过	N	N	O
生产力	n	通过	N	N	O
。	punc	通过	N	N	O

Table 2. A Tagged Sentence Example

The first five columns are designed features, and the last column represents tag set of the sequences. According to the format of the CRF toolkit, each column is separated by a separator, and each sentence sequence is separated by a line break.

6 Experiments

In this section, we conducted some experiments to test the performance of the two methods mentioned above, and compared their results. Precision rate (P), Recall rate (R) and F1 are three evaluation metrics of the experiments.

6.1 Data

1000 sentences containing PPs, which were randomly selected from the patent corpus provided by SIPO, were considered as test set of the methods. In the CRF test, we chose another different 5000 sentences as training set from the same corpus to train the model in the toolkit.

6.2 Results

The experimental results of the two methods are shown in the following table.

	P (%)	R (%)	F1 (%)
Rule-based	96.86	74.67	84.33
CRF	92.65	90.07	91.33

Table 3. Experimental Results of the Two Methods

In order to observe the effects that the two methods identified different individual prepositions, we further tested identification precision and recall rates of 10 most frequently appeared prepositions in the test set. Following table and line chart showed the results.

No.	Prep.	RB Method		CRF Method	
		P (%)	R (%)	P (%)	R (%)
1	在(ZAI)	100	90.19	95.63	95.63
2	将(JIANG)	100	61.67	95.95	95.95
3	通过 (TONGGUO)	100	52.27	86.84	86.84
4	由(YOU)	90.67	68.00	69.57	66.67
5	从(CONG)	94.74	85.71	70.00	63.63
6	当(DANG)	100	90.48	87.50	87.50
7	与(YU)	92.6	25.00	88.89	88.89
8	对(DUI)	91.37	70.59	80.00	70.59
9	对于(DUIYU)	100	93.75	100	100
10	向(XIANG)	96.12	55.56	75.00	60.00

Table 4. Identification Results of 10 Most Frequently Appeared Prepositions (in descending order)

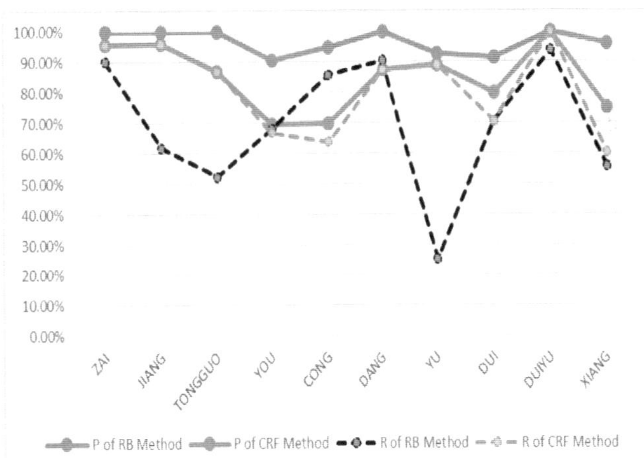

Figure 1. Line Chart of Identification Results

6.3 Analysis

As shown in Table 3, the overall precision rates of the two methods reached over 90%, indicating that the methods are feasible and effective for identifying prepositional phrases, showing a good performance.

Precision of rule-based method were higher than those of CRF in the overall test and identification of 10 prepositions. Identification precision of some individual prepositions even reached 100%, indicating that the rules can describe the linguistic information of PPs more accurately, especially for those PP chunks with long distance and collocations. However, recall rates of rule-based method were much lower than CRF, which were also clearly reflected in the line chart, there exists significant differences between the recall rates of various prepositions, what's more, fluctuation ranges of recall rates of rule-based method were greater than CRF. From the results, we can come to the conclusion that, as a statistical approach, CRF method does have better stability and adaptability.

On the other hand, the recall rates were lower than precision rates in the two approaches. And, fluctuation ranges between precision and recall of rule-based method were greater than CRF. These are inevitable results of rule-based approaches in NLP.

Despite the methods performed well, we still found some reasons accounting for error identification after analyzing the experimental results.

For the rule-based method, the reasons included:

(1) Because of the performance of the current system itself, sometimes it has difficulties in processing sentences with much longer and complex structures.

(2) Word segmentation ambiguities resulted in error identification. For example, in the sentence "[PP ***将来自***前一步骤的溶液]加入到实验装置中。"(The solution from the previous step was added to the test device.), the word "来自(from)" was behind the preposition "将(Jiang)", since the word "将来" is already in the word list, the system will first segment the word "将来" from the sentence, thus the monosyllabic word "将(Jiang)" cannot be identified as preposition, as a result, the PP chunk will not be identified at last.

(3) In some cases, it is harder for the system to recognize ambiguous strings caused by multi-category prepositions. For example, in the sentence "应用程序可以使用 SIM 工具包接口与移动设备通信" (The applications can use the SIM toolkit interface to communicate with mobile devices.), the preposition "与(YU, with)" can also serve as conjunction(equivalent to the word "and" in English) in Chinese. Thus, when chunking the sentence, the string "与移动设备(with mobile devices)" may not be identified as PP chunk, instead, the string "SIM 工具包接口与移动设备" is recognized as NP (the SIM toolkit interface *and* mobile devices).

For the CRF method, the possible reasons included:

(1) Some prepositions had little or no occurrences in the training set, and CRF model cannot study the features of these prepositions, thus it is difficult to identify them correctly when they appear in the test set.

(2) Some strings led by the prepositions were ambiguous. Under this condition, it was not easy to determine the right boundaries of PP chunks. For example, in the sentence "通过本发明的*墨水着色剂*可以有效地使实验产品沉淀", the italic noun "墨水(ink)" is followed by another noun "着色剂(colorants)", it is not really clear which noun should actually be right boundary of the PP chunk. If the two nouns represent a compound noun, then the boundary should be the second noun; but if they are independent of each other, then the boundary should be the first noun, and the second noun will serve as subject of the sentence.

(3) The model is quite sensitive to features in the sequences, during the label process, error and improper manually tagged information is inevitable, which can also result in error identifications.

7 Conclusion and Future Work

In this paper, we proposed a rule-based and CRF method for identifying PP chunks in Chinese patent texts. In the rule-based method, we built the knowledge base and designed various targeted rules for different types of PPs, in the CRF method, we employed the effective CRF toolkit to train the identification models by labelling the sentences with several features. We also conducted several tests to justify the performance of the two approaches and compared the experimental results.

Which have proved the methods performed well in identifying the PPs, although there still existed some error identifications.

In the future, we will try to combine the two method together, and pay more attention to the reasons resulting in the error identification, hoping to improve the performance further.

Acknowledgments

This work was supported by the National Hi-Tech Research and Development Program of China (2012AA011104), we also want to express our sincere thanks to the anonymous reviewers of this article.

References

Guizhe Song. 2011. Research on Identification of Chinese Preposition Phrases.

Guodong Zhou, Jian Su and Tongguan Tey. 2000. Hybrid Text Chunking. In: *Proceeding of CoNLL2000 and LLL*, 163-165.

Hongqiao Li, Chang-Ning Huang, Jianfeng Gao and Xiaozhong Fan. 2004. Chinese Chunking with another Type of Spec. In: *Proceeding of 42nd Association for Computational Linguistics SIGHAN workshop*, 41-48.

Hongzheng Li, Yun Zhu, Yang Yang and Yaohong Jin. 2014. Reordering Adverbial Chunks in Chinese-English Patent Machine Translation. In: *Proceedings of 2014 3rd International Conference on Cloud Computing and Intelligence Systems*, 375-379.

Jenny Rose Finkel, Alex Kleeman and Christopher D. Manning. 2008. Efficient, Feature-based, Conditional Random Field Parsing. In *Proceedings of the Annual Meeting of the Association for Computational Linguistics: HLT*, 959-967.

Jianqing Xi and Qiang Luo. 2009. Research on Automatic Identification for Chinese Prepositional Phrase Based on HMM. *Computer Engineering*, 33(3):172-173,182.

Jie Zhang. 2013. Research on Chinese Prepositional Phrase Identification based on Multi-Layer Conditional Random Fields.

Juntao Yu. 2006. Identification of Preposition Phrases Based on Maximum Entropy Model.

Junwei Gan and Degen Huang. 2005. Automatic Identification of Preposition Phrases in Chinese. *Journal of Chinese Information Processing*, 19(4):17-23.

Lafferty J., Mccallum A. and Pereira F. 2001. Conditional random fields: probabilistic models for segmenting and labeling sequence data. In: *Proceedings of the International Conference on Machine Learning*. 282-289.

Mengjie Liang, Yu Song, Yingjie Han and Hongying Zan. 2013. Automatic Annotation Research on Preposition Usage Based on Sorting Rules. *Journal of Henan Normal University (Natural Science Edition)*, 41(3):152-155.

Ping Jian and Chengqing Zong. 2009. A New Approach to Identifying Chinese Maximal Phrases Using Bidirectional Labelling. *CAAI Transaction on Intelligence Systems*, 4(5):406-413.

Renfen Hu. 2015. on the Methods of Auto-Identifying Prepositional Phrases in Chinese-English Patent Machine Translation. *Applied Linguistics*, (1):136-144.

Silei Hu. 2008. Automatic Identification of Chinese Prepositional Phrase Based on CRF.

Trevor Cohn and Philip Blunsom. 2005. Semantic Role Labelling with Tree Conditional Random Fields. In *Proceedings of the 9th Conference on Computational Natural Language Learning (CoNLL)*, 169–172.

Huihsin Tseng, Pichuan Chang, Galen Andrew, Daniel Jurafsky and Christopher Manning. 2005. A Conditional Random Field Word Segmenter for SIGHAN Bakeoff 2005. In *Proceedings of the fourth SIGHAN workshop on Chinese language Processing*.

Wenliang Chen, Yujie Zhang and Hitoshi Isahara. 2006. An Empirical Study of Chinese Chunking. In: *Proceeding of the COLING/ACL 2006*, 97–104.

Yoshimasa Tsuruoka, Jun'ichi Tsujii and Sophia Ananiadou. 2009. Fast Full Parsing by Linear-Chain Conditional Random Fields. In *Proceedings of the 12th Conference of the European Chapter of the Association for Computational Linguistics*, 790–798.

Yun Zhu and Yaohong Jin. 2012. A Chinese-English Patent Machine Translation System based on the Theory of Hierarchical Network of Concepts. *The Journal of China Universities of Posts and Telecommunications*, 19(Suppl. 2): 140-146.

Japanese Sentiment Classification with Stacked Denoising Auto-Encoder using Distributed Word Representation

Peinan Zhang
Graduate School of System Design
Tokyo Metropolitan University
zhang-peinan@ed.tmu.ac.jp

Mamoru Komachi
Graduate School of System Design
Tokyo Metropolitan University
komachi@tmu.ac.jp

Abstract

Traditional sentiment classification methods often require polarity dictionaries or crafted features to utilize machine learning. However, those approaches incur high costs in the making of dictionaries and/or features, which hinder generalization of tasks. Examples of these approaches include an approach that uses a polarity dictionary that cannot handle unknown or newly invented words and another approach that uses a complex model with 13 types of feature templates. We propose a novel high performance sentiment classification method with stacked denoising auto-encoders that uses distributed word representation instead of building dictionaries or utilizing engineering features. The results of experiments conducted indicate that our model achieves state-of-the-art performance in Japanese sentiment classification tasks.

1 Introduction

As the popularity of social media continues to rise, serious attention is being given to review information nowadays. Reviews with positive/negative ratings, in particular, help (potential) customers with product comparisons and to make purchasing decisions. Consequently, automatic classification of the polarities (such as positive and negative) of reviews is extremely important.

Traditional approaches to sentiment analysis utilize polarity dictionaries or classification rules. Although these approaches are fairly accurate, they depend on languages that may require significant amounts of manual labor. Further, dictionary-based methods have difficulty dealing with new or unknown words.

Machine learning-based methods are widely adopted in sentiment classification in order to mitigate the problems associated with the making of dictionaries and/or rules. One of the most basic features used in machine learning-based sentiment classification is the bag-of-words feature (Wang and Manning, 2012; Pang et al., 2002). In machine learning-based frameworks, the weights of words are automatically learned from a training corpus instead of being manually assigned.

However, the bag-of-words feature cannot take syntactic structures into account. This leads to mistakes such as "a great design but inconvenient" and "inconvenient but a great design" being deemed to have the same meaning, even though their nuances are different; the former is somewhat negative whereas the latter is slightly positive. To solve this syntactic problem, Nakagawa et al. (2010) proposed a sentiment analysis model that used dependency trees with polarities assigned to their subtrees. However, their proposed model requires specialized knowledge to design complicated feature templates.

In this study, we propose an approach that uses distributed word representation to overcome the first problem and deep neural networks to alleviate the second problem. The former is an unsupervised method capable of representing a word ' s meaning without using hand-tagged resources such as a polarity dictionary. In addition, it is robust to the data sparseness problem. The latter is a highly expressive model that does not utilize complex engineering features or models.

Our research makes the following two main contributions:

29th Pacific Asia Conference on Language, Information and Computation pages 150 - 159
Shanghai, China, October 30 - November 1, 2015

- We show that distributed word representation learned from a large-scale corpus and multiple layers (more than three layers) contributes significantly to classification accuracy in sentiment classification tasks.
- We achieve state-of-the-art performance in Japanese sentiment classification tasks without designing complex features and models.

2 Related Works

In this section, we discuss related works from two areas: sentiment classification and deep learning (distributed word representation and multi-layer neural networks).

2.1 Sentiment classification

Sentiment classification has been researched extensively in the past decade. Most of the previous approaches in this area rely on either time-consuming hand-tagged dictionaries or knowledge-intensive complex models.

Ikeda et al. (2008) proposed a method that classifies polarities by learning them within a window around a word. Their proposed method works well with words registered in a dictionary. However, building a polarity dictionary is expensive and their approach is not able to cope with unknown words. In contrast, our proposed approach does not use a polarity dictionary and works robustly even when there are infrequent words in the test data.

In a similar manner, Choi et al. (2008) proposed a method in which rules are manually built up and polarities are classified considering dependency structures. However, the rules are based on English, which cannot be applied directly to other languages. This is unlike our method, which does not employ any language-specific rules.

Nakagawa et al. (2010) proposed a supervised model that uses a dependency tree with polarity assigned to each subtree as hidden variables. The proposed approach further classifies sentiment polarities in English and Japanese sentences with Conditional Random Field (CRF), considering the interactions between the hidden variables. The dependency information enables them to take syntactic structures into account in order to model polarity flip. However, their proposed method is so complex that it has to create multiple feature templates. In contrast, our model is quite simple and does not require the engineering of such features.

2.2 Deep learning

One of the great advantages of deep learning is that it reduces the need to hand-design features. Instead, it automatically extracts hierarchical features and enhances the end-to-end classification performance learned through backpropagation. As a consequence, it avoids the engineering of task-specific ad-hoc features using copious amounts of prior knowledge. Further, it sometimes surpasses human-level performance (He et al., 2015). Two of the most actively studied areas in deep learning for NLP applications are representation learning and deep neural networks.

Representation learning Several studies have attempted to model natural language texts using deep architectures. Distributed word representations, or word embeddings, represent words as vectors. Distributed representations of word vectors are not sparse but dense vectors that can express the meaning of words. Sentiment classification tasks are significantly influenced by the data sparseness problem. As a result, distributed word representation is more suitable than traditional 1-of-K representation, which only treats words as symbols.

In our proposed method, to learn the word embeddings, we employ a state-of-the-art word embedding technique called word2vec (Mikolov et al., 2013b; Mikolov et al., 2013a), which we discuss in Section 3.1. Although several word embedding techniques currently exist (Collobert and Weston, 2008; Pennington et al., 2014), word2vec is one of the most computationally efficient and is considered to be state-of-the-art. Collobert et al. (2008) presented a model that learns word embedding by jointly performing multi-task learning using a deep convolutional architecture. Their method is considered to be state-of-the-art as well, but it is not readily applicable to Japanese.

Multi-layer neural networks A stacked denoising auto-encoder (SdA) is a deep neural network that extends a stacked auto-encoder (Bengio et al., 2007) with denoising auto-encoders (dA). Stacking multiple layers and introducing noise to the input layer adds high generalization ability to auto-encoders. This method is used in speech recognition (Dahl et al., 2011), image processing (Xie et al., 2012) and domain adaptation (Chen et al., 2012); further, it exhibits high representation ability.

Glorot et al. (2011) used SdAs to perform domain adaptation in sentiment analysis. After learning sentiment classification in four domains of the reviews of products on Amazon, they tested each model with different domains. Although the task and method are similar to those of our proposed approach, they only use the most frequent verbs as input.

Dos Santos et al. (2014) and Tang et al. (2014) researched sentiment classification of microblogs such as Twitter using the distributed representation learned by the methods of Collobert et al. (2008) and Mikolov et al. (2013b; 2013a). Those two tasks are the same task as ours, but the former generats sentence vectors using string-based convolution networks while the latter utilizes a model that treats the distributed word representation itself as polarities. Our proposed approach makes sentence vectors by simply averaging the distributed word representation, yet achieves state-of-the-art performance in Japanese sentiment classification tasks.

Kim (2014) classified the polarities of sentences using convolutional neural networks. He built a simple CNN with one layer of convolution, whereas our model uses multiple hidden layers.

Socher et al. (2011; 2013) placed common auto-encoders recursively (recursive neural networks) and concatenated input vectors to take syntactic information such as the order of words into account. In addition, they arranged auto-encoders (AEs) to syntactic trees to represent the polarities of each phrase. Recursive neural networks construct sentence vectors differently from our approach. Compared to their model, our distributed sentence representation is quite simple yet effective for Japanese sentiment classification.

3 Sentiment Classification with Stacked Denoising Auto-Encoder using Distributed Word Representation

In this study, we treated the task of classifying the polarity of a sentence as a binary classification.

Our proposed approach makes a sentence vector from the input sentence, and then inputs the sentence vector to a classifier. The sentence vector is computed from the average of word vectors in the sentence, based on distributed word representation.

In Section 3.1 we introduce distributed representation of words and sentences, and in Section 3.2 we explain multi-layer neural networks.

3.1 Distributed representation

1-of-K representation is a traditional word vector representation for making bag-of-words. The dimension of a word vector in 1-of-K is the same as the size of the vocabulary, and the elements of a dimension correspond to words. 1-of-K treats different words as discrete symbols. However, 1-of-K representation fails to model the shared meanings of words. For example, the word vectors "dog" and "cat" should share "animal" or "pet" meanings to a certain degree, but 1-of-K representation is not able to capture this similarity. Consequently, we propose distributed word representation.

The task of learning distributed representation is called representation learning and has been of significant interest in the NLP literature in the last few years. Distributed word representation learns a low-dimension dense vector for a word from a large-scale text corpus to capture the word's features from its context.

3.1.1 Distributed word representation

Let the number of vocabularies be $|V|$, the dimension of a vector representing words be d, 1-of-K vector be $\boldsymbol{b} \in \mathbb{R}^{|V|}$ and the matrix of all word vectors be $\boldsymbol{L} \in \mathbb{R}^{d \times |V|}$. The kth target word vector $\boldsymbol{w}_k$ is consequently represented as in Equation 1.

$$\boldsymbol{w}_k = \boldsymbol{L}\boldsymbol{b}_k \quad (1)$$

Continuous Bag-of-Words (CBOW) and Skip-gram models in word2vec (Mikolov et al., 2013b; Mikolov et al., 2013a) have attracted tremendous attention as a result of their effectiveness and efficiency. The former is a model that predicts the target word using contexts around the word, whereas the latter is a model that predicts the surrounding context from the target word. According to Mikolov's work, skip-gram shows higher accuracy than CBOW[1]. Therefore, we used skip-gram in our experiments.

[1] We carried out a preliminary experiment using CBOW representation and found that skip-gram considerably outper-

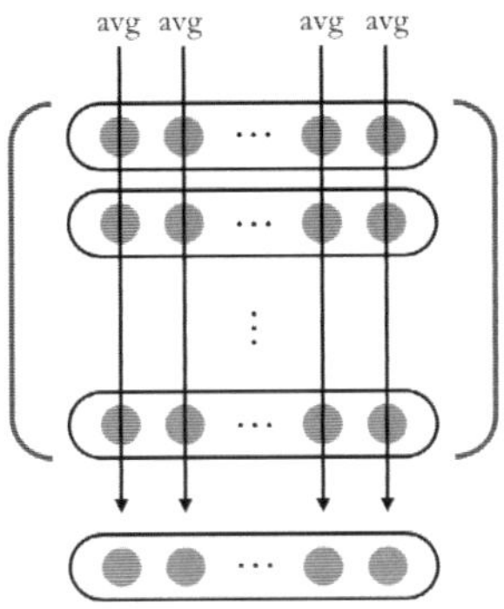

Figure 1: The sentence vector construction method.

3.1.2 Distributed sentence representation

In our approach, we construct a sentence matrix $\boldsymbol{S} \in \mathbb{R}^{|M| \times d}$ from the corpus containing $|M|$ sentences.

First, we describe how to create a sentence vector from word vectors. The ith ($1 \leq i \leq M$) input sentence composed of $|N^{(i)}|$ words is used to make a sentence vector $\boldsymbol{S}^{(i)} \in \mathbb{R}^d$ with the word vectors.

The jth ($1 \leq j \leq d$) element of sentence vector $\boldsymbol{S}^{(i)}$ is calculated by averaging the corresponding element of the word vectors in the sentence as expressed in Equation 2 (Figure 1).

$$\boldsymbol{S}_j^{(i)} = \frac{1}{N^{(i)}} \sum_{n=1}^{N^{(i)}} \boldsymbol{w}_n^{(i)} \tag{2}$$

Finally, the sentence matrix $\boldsymbol{S}$ is defined by Equation 3.

$$\boldsymbol{S} = \begin{bmatrix} \boldsymbol{S}^{(1)T} \\ \boldsymbol{S}^{(2)T} \\ \vdots \\ \boldsymbol{S}^{(M)T} \end{bmatrix} \tag{3}$$

3.2 Auto-Encoder

An auto-encoder is an unsupervised learning method devised by Hinton and Salakhutdinov (2006) that uses neural networks. It learns shared features of the input at the hidden layer. By restricting the dimension of the hidden layer to be smaller than that of an input layer, it reduces the dimension of the input layer. The encode function that calculates a hidden layer from an input is shown in Equation 4, and the

formed it. Therefore, we present only the experiments conducted using skip-gram in this paper.

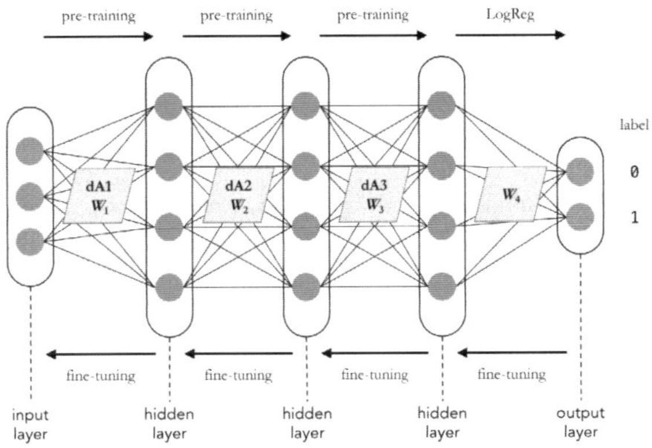

Figure 2: The learning process of a four layer stacked denoising auto-encoder.

decode function that calculates an output layer from the hidden layer is shown in Equation 5 below.

$$\boldsymbol{y} = s(\boldsymbol{W}\boldsymbol{x} + \boldsymbol{b}) \tag{4}$$

$$\boldsymbol{z} = s(\boldsymbol{W}'\boldsymbol{y} + \boldsymbol{b}') \tag{5}$$

$s(*)$ represents nonlinear functions such as $\tanh$ or sigmoid, $\boldsymbol{W}, \boldsymbol{W'}$ are weight matrices and $\boldsymbol{b}, \boldsymbol{b'}$ are bias terms, respectively.

The parameters of auto-encoders are learned by minimizing the following loss functions. The loss function measures the difference between input vector $\boldsymbol{x}$ and output vector $\boldsymbol{z}$ using the cross entropy (Equation 6). We use Stochastic Gradient Descent (SGD) to minimize the loss function.

$$L_H(\boldsymbol{x}, \boldsymbol{z}) = -\sum_{k=1}^{d} [\boldsymbol{x_k} \log \boldsymbol{z_k} + (1 - \boldsymbol{x_k}) \log(1 - \boldsymbol{z_k})] \tag{6}$$

3.2.1 Denoising Auto-Encoder

Regularization is usually used in the loss function in traditional multi-layer perceptrons. Denoising techniques play the same role as regularization in auto-encoders.

A denoising auto-encoder is a stochastic extension of a regular auto-encoder that adds noise randomly to the input during training to obtain higher generalization ability. Because the loss function of denoising auto-encoders evaluates the input without adding noise, denoising auto-encoders can be expected to extract better representations than auto-encoders (Vincent et al., 2008). DropOut (Hinton et al., 2012) achieves similar regularization objectives by ignoring the hidden nodes, not input, with a uniform probability.

3.2.2 Stacked Denoising Auto-Encoder

A stacked denoising auto-encoder piles dAs into multiple layers and improves representation ability. The deeper the layers go, the more abstract features will be extracted (Vincent et al., 2010). The training procedure used for SdAs comprises two steps. Initially, dAs are used to pre-train each layer via unsupervised learning, after which the entire neural network is fine-tuned via supervised learning. In the pre-training phase, feature extraction is carried out by the dAs from input A_i, and the extracted hidden representation is treated as the input to the next hidden layer. After the final pre-training process, the last hidden layer is classified with softmax and the resulting vector is passed to the output layer. The fine-tuning phase backpropagates supervision to each layer to update weight matrices (Figure 2).

In Figure 2, the input vector is obtained from Equation 2 and dA1 is applied with the weight matrix of the first layer $\boldsymbol{W}_1$ to calculate the first hidden layer. Note that the numbers of hidden layers and hidden nodes are hyperparameters. We define n_i to be the number of hidden nodes of the ith layer. Therefore, using Equation 4 the dimension of weight matrix $\boldsymbol{W}_1$ will be $n_1 \times d$. Similarly, the weight matrices up to the $l-1$th layer will be $\boldsymbol{W}_i \in \mathbb{R}^{n_i \times n_{i-1}}$ ($i > 2$). At the final lth layer, we need to convert the dimension of the hidden layer into d_{label}, the dimension of the label, so the dimension of weight matrix $\boldsymbol{W}_l$ should become $d_{label} \times n_{l-1}$.

4 Experiments

4.1 Methods

To demonstrate the effectiveness of a nonlinear SdA, we compared it with a linear classifier (logistic regression, LogRes-w2v).[2] In addition, to investigate the usefulness of distributed word representation, we compared methods using bag-of-features (LogRes-BoF, SdA-BoF). We constructed sentence vectors $\boldsymbol{S} \in \mathbb{R}^{|V|}$ with 1-of-K representation in the same manner as Equation 2, and performed dimension reduction to $d = 200$ using Principal Component Analysis (PCA).[3]

We introduce a weak baseline (most frequent sense) and a strong baseline (state-of-the-art). The latter is a method by Nakagawa et al. (2010), which uses the same corpus.

MFS. The most frequent sense baseline. It always selects the most frequent choice (in this case, negative).

Tree-CRF. The state-of-the-art baseline with hidden variables learned by tree-structured CRF (Nakagawa et al., 2010).

LogRes-BoF. Performs sentiment classification using bag-of-features with a linear classifier (logistic regression).

SdA-BoF. Classifies polarity with the same input vectors as LogRes-BoF.

LogRes-w2v. Classifies polarity with a linear classifier (logistic regression) using the sentence vector computed by distributed word representation.

SdA-w2v. Our proposed method that classifies polarity with a SdA using the same input as LogRes-w2v.

SdA-w2v-neg. Similar to Nakagawa et al. (2010), we pre-processed negation before creating distributed word representation as in SdA-w2v.

We adjusted the noise rate, the numbers of hidden layers and hidden nodes, as follows.

To demonstrate the denoising efficiency, we varied the noise rate (0%, 10%, 20%, 30%, 40% and 50%) for SdAs. We then performed denoising by zeroing a vector with binomial distribution at a specified rate.

To show the effect of stacking, we increased the number of hidden layers (from 1 to 6).

To examine the representation ability of the network, we varied the number of hidden nodes (100, 300, 500, and 700).

[2]Both SdA and logistic regression were implemented using Theano version 0.6.0.

[3]We used scikit-learn version 0.10.

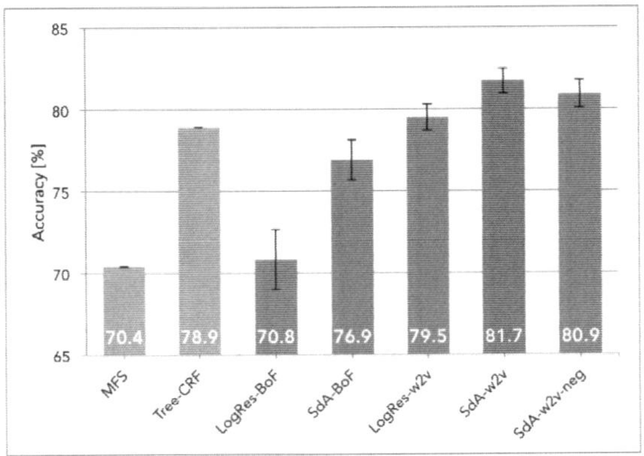

Figure 3: Accuracy of each method with standard error.

4.2 Corpus and tools

We obtained distributed word representations using word2vec[4] with Skip-gram (Mikolov et al., 2013b; Mikolov et al., 2013a). We used Japanese Wikipedia's dump data (2014.11) to learn the 200 dimension distributed representation with word2vec after word-segmentation with MeCab [5]. The vocabulary of the models contains 426,782 words (without processing negation) and 431,782 words (with processing negation).

The corpus used in the experiment was the Japanese section of NTCIR-6 OPINION (Seki et al., 2007). The data used in our research were the sentences from The Mainichi Newspaper and The Japan News articles with polarities annotated by three annotators. For each sentence, we took the union of the annotations of the three annotators. When the annotations were split to both positive and negative, we always used the annotation of the specific annotator. The resulting corpus contained 2,599 sentences. The positive instances comprised 765 sentences whereas the negative instances comprised 1,830 sentences. Although a neutral polarity existed, we ignored it because our task is binary classification.

We performed 10-fold cross validation with 10 threads of parallel processing and evaluated the performance of binary classification with accuracy.

4.3 Results

First, Figure 3 shows the accuracy and standard errors of each method for the NTCIR-6 corpus.

It can be clearly seen that our method is superior to all baselines, including the state-of-the-art Nakagawa et al. (2010)'s method by up to 11.3 points. This result shows that the distributed word representation is sufficiently effective on the Japanese sentiment classification task, even though only a simple word embedding model, not a complex tuned representation learning model such as dos Santos et al. (2014)'s, is used.

Note that the parameters of the SdAs above are the best combination of noise rate, number of hidden layers, and number of hidden nodes (noise rate: 10%, four layers, and 500 dimensions). [6]

Table 1: Accuracies of SdA models with different hyperparameters.

Parameters		Accuracy
Noise rate	0%	81.1%
	10%	81.5%
	20%	81.4%
	30%	80.9%
	40%	81.1%
	50%	**81.6%**
Number of hidden layers	1	80.6%
	2	80.4%
	3	81.1%
	4	**81.6%**
	5	81.4%
	6	81.1%
Number of hidden nodes	100	81.1%
	300	81.2%
	500	**81.3%**
	700	81.2%

Table 1 contrasts the various hyperparameters. We changed one parameter at a time, while leaving all other parameters fixed. The upper row compares the accuracy of the system with changing noise rate. The best result was obtained when the noise rate was set to 50%. Compared with the standard stacked auto-encoder (noise rate: 0%, accuracy: 81.1%), an SdA with a noise rate of 50% exhibits better accuracy (81.6%). In the middle of the table, we changed the number of hidden layers. It turned out that, the classifier worked best with four layers. As can be seen, the stacked auto-encoder is superior to the unstacked one by 1.0 accuracy point. At the bottom of the table, we changed the dimension of hidden nodes. We changed hidden nodes in intervals of 200 dimensions, but the accuracy only fluctuated by ± 0.1 point. The accuracy was highest when the dimension was 500.

[4] `https://code.google.com/p/word2vec/`

[5] MeCab version-0.996, IPADic version-2.7.0

[6] We carried out 10-fold cross validation without using the development set.

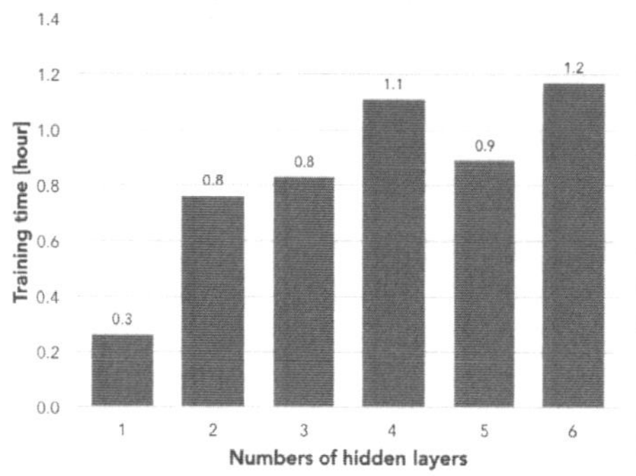

Figure 4: Learning time with varying numbers of hidden layers.

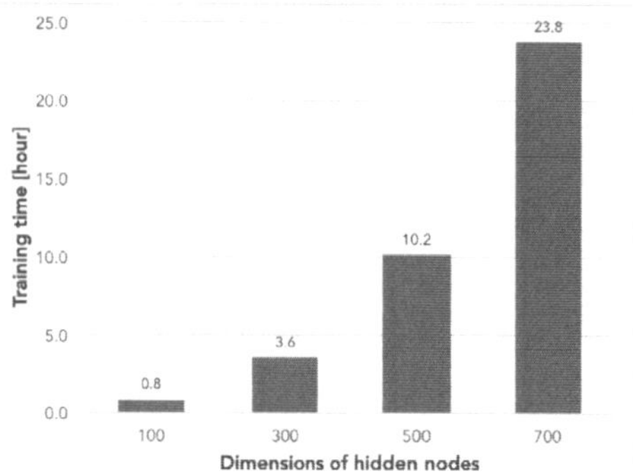

Figure 5: Learning time with varying dimensions of hidden nodes.

5 Discussion

In this section, we discuss the results of the models (Figure 3), parameter tuning (Table 1), and examples (Table 2).

5.1 Methods

BoF vs. Distributed word representation. When the model was fixed to a linear classifier (logistic regression), the accuracies with Bag-of-Features and distributed word representation were 70.8% and 79.5%, respectively. In contrast, using an SdA, the result for Bag-of-Features was 76.9% and that of distributed word representation was 81.7%. Considering these outcomes, it can be seen that a 4.8 to 8.7 point increase in accuracy occurred when distributed word representation was used. Hence, the contribution of distributed word representation is the largest among the different experimental settings.

Linear classifier vs. SdA. The accuracies of logistic regression and SdAs with the same word vectors made from Bag-of-Features were 70.8% and 76.9%, respectively. With distributed word representation, the accuracy of the linear classifier was 79.6% and that of SdA was 81.7%. Thus, a 2.2 to 6.1 point improvement was obtained using SdAs over a traditional linear classifier.

Negation handling. As can be seen in Figure 3, the accuracy of SdA-w2v-neg decreased by 0.8 point compared with SdA-w2v. This differs from Nakagawa et al. (2010)'s report. The reason for this phenomenon may be the data sparseness problem caused by the negation process. We checked the number of negations in the corpus and found that the numbers of types and tokens are 326 (3.8%) and 1,239 (1.0%), respectively. Thus, the negation process may have little influence on the accuracy.

5.2 Parameters

Figures 4 and 5 show the total training time obtained with 10 parallel processes by changing the numbers of hidden layers and hidden nodes.

Figure 4 shows that the training time grew gradually as the number of hidden layers increased. In contrast, Figure 5 shows that the training time doubled when the number of hidden nodes was increased by 200. These results originate from the structure of SdAs. The nodes of the two adjacent hidden layers are fully connected. Hence, if the network has l layers and n dimensional nodes, the number of connections will be $l \times n \times n = ln^2$. That indicates the relationship between the number of layers and connections is linear, but the number of connections grows exponentially with the number of nodes. Consequently, a small increase in the number of nodes results in a long training time. In contrast, as can be seen from Table 1, the number of nodes has little or no effect on accuracy, whereas changing the number of layers helps to improve the performance.

5.3 Examples

Several examples are presented in Table 2. The values P and N represent the prediction of positive and negative, respectively.

Looking at the top of the correct answer, it can be seen that our model classified polarity robustly

Table 2: Correct and incorrect examples. BoF, LR, AE, Neg, SdA and Gold represent Bag-of-Features, LogRes, Auto-Encoder (one layer SdA without stacking), Negation Processed, Proposal and the Gold answer, respectively.

Correct examples						
BoF	LR	AE	Neg	SdA	Gold	Examples
N	N	N	N	P	P	同２５日の毎日新聞との単独会見では，貧困率などの細かい数字を挙げて１０年間の政権の成果を強調し「フジモリズムはペルー全土に根付いている」と胸を張った． In the exclusive interview with The Mainichi Newspaper in the same month on the 25th, he lined up small numbers such as poverty rate and stressed the result of the regime in the decade, thrusting out his chest saying "Fujimorism is rooted in Peru throughout".
N	P	N	N	P	P	牛で成功したクローン技術を人へ応用するのは難しいことではない． It is not difficult to adapt the clone technology succeed with cows to humans.
Incorrect examples						
BoF	LR	AE	Neg	SdA	Gold	Examples
N	N	N	N	P	N	もう少し配慮した書き方があったかなとも思う」と反省を口にした． He regrets "there must be other ways of writing that should be more thoughtful".
N	N	N	N	N	P	教育省の談話は「歴史教科書は歴史の真相を反映すべきであり，そうしてこそ若い世代に正しい歴史観をもたせ，悲劇の再演を防止できる」と批判した． In the discourse of Ministry of Education, he criticized "History textbooks should reflect the truth of history, and only that can make the younger to have the correct view of history so that it can prevent to playing the tragedy again".
P	N	N	P	N	P	同市は圧力に屈せず，この宣言を守り抜いてもらいたい． I would like him not to yield to the pressure and to keep his declaration to the end.

against the data sparseness problem, such as with the coined word "フジモリズム (Fujimorism)" with which the BoF model is weak. Further, linear classifiers and the unstacked AE fail to handle double negative sentences such as at the bottom. Regardless of the difficulties, our model copes well with the situation.

Moving on to the wrong answers, it can be seen that our proposed model made human-like mistakes. For example, it mistook the top one containing the word "反省 (thinking over, reflection, regret)," but it is an ambiguous sentence that might be labeled as positive. Similarly, it failed to classify the middle sentence containing the phrase "悲劇の再演を防止する (prevent to replay the tragedy)," which ends with "批判した (criticize)." The annotations of the above two examples were divided into both positive and negative[7]. At the bottom, the proposed method did not successfully identify the polarity flipping with the phrase "圧力に屈せず (not yield to the pressure)." Because the model with negation handling answered it correctly, there remains much room for improvement on how to deal with interactions between syntax and semantics (Tai et al., 2015; Socher et al., 2013).

[7]As explained in Section 4.2, we arbitrarily determined the polarity of a sentence when the annotations were split.

6 Conclusion

In this study, we presented a high performance Japanese sentiment classification method that uses distributed word representation learned from a large-scale corpus with word2vec and a stacked denoising auto-encoder. The proposed method requires no dictionaries, complex models, or the engineering of numerous features. Consequently, it can easily be adapted to other tasks and domains without the need for advanced knowledge from experts. In addition, due to the nature of learning with vectors, our system does not depend on languages.

As our future works, we will try to create the distributed sentence representation using the Recurrent Neural Networks (Irsoy and Cardie, 2014) and Recursive Neural Networks (Socher et al., 2011; Socher et al., 2013) to capture global information.

References

Yoshua Bengio, Pascal Lamblin, Dan Popovici, and Hugo Larochelle. 2007. Greedy layer-wise training of deep networks. In *Advances in Neural Information Processing Systems*, pages 153–160.

Minmin Chen, Zhixiang Xu, Kilian Weinberger, and Fei Sha. 2012. Marginalized denoising autoencoders for domain adaptation. In *Proceedings of The 29th International Conference on Machine Learning*, pages 767–774.

Yejin Choi and Claire Cardie. 2008. Learning with compositional semantics as structural inference for subsentential sentiment analysis. In *Proceedings of the 2008 Conference on Empirical Methods in Natural Language Processing*, pages 793–801.

Ronan Collobert and Jason Weston. 2008. A unified architecture for natural language processing: Deep neural networks with multitask learning. In *Proceedings of the 25th International Conference on Machine Learning*, pages 160–167.

George E Dahl, Dong Yu, Li Deng, and Alex Acero. 2011. Context-dependent pre-trained deep neural networks for large-vocabulary speech recognition. In *Audio, Speech, and Language Processing, IEEE Transactions*, volume 20, pages 30–42.

Cıcero Nogueira dos Santos and Maıra Gatti. 2014. Deep convolutional neural networks for sentiment analysis of short texts. In *Proceedings of the 25th International Conference on Computational Linguistics*, pages 69–78.

Xavier Glorot, Antoine Bordes, and Yoshua Bengio. 2011. Domain adaptation for large-scale sentiment classification: A deep learning approach. In *Proceedings of the 28th International Conference on Machine Learning*, pages 513–520.

Kaiming He, Xiangyu Zhang, Shaoqing Ren, and Jian Sun. 2015. Delving deep into rectifiers: Surpassing human-level performance on imagenet classification. *CoRR*, abs/1502.01852.

Geoffrey E. Hinton and Ruslan R. Salakhutdinov. 2006. Reducing the dimensionality of data with neural networks. *Science*, 313(5786):504–507.

Geoffrey E. Hinton, Nitish Srivastava, Alex Krizhevsky, Ilya Sutskever, and Ruslan R Salakhutdinov. 2012. Improving neural networks by preventing co-adaptation of feature detectors. *arXiv preprint arXiv:1207.0580*.

Daisuke Ikeda, Hiroya Takamura, Lev-Arie Ratinov, and Manabu Okumura. 2008. Learning to shift the polarity of words for sentiment classification. In *Proceedings of the 3rd International Joint Conference on Natural Language Processing*, pages 296–303.

Ozan Irsoy and Claire Cardie. 2014. Opinion mining with deep recurrent neural networks. In *Proceedings of the 2014 Conference on Empirical Methods in Natural Language Processing*, pages 720–728.

Yoon Kim. 2014. Convolutional neural networks for sentence classification. In *Proceedings of the 2014 Conference on Empirical Methods in Natural Language Processing (EMNLP)*, pages 1746–1751.

Tomas Mikolov, Kai Chen, Greg Corrado, and Jeffrey Dean. 2013a. Efficient estimation of word representations in vector space. In *International Conference on Learning Representations Workshop*.

Tomas Mikolov, Ilya Sutskever, Kai Chen, Greg S Corrado, and Jeff Dean. 2013b. Distributed representations of words and phrases and their compositionality. In *Advances in Neural Information Processing Systems 26*, pages 3111–3119.

Tetsuji Nakagawa, Kentaro Inui, and Sadao Kurohashi. 2010. Dependency tree-based sentiment classification using crfs with hidden variables. In *Proceedings of Human Language Technologies: The 2010 Annual Conference of the North American Chapter of the Association for Computational Linguistics*, pages 786–794.

Bo Pang, Lee Lillian, and Vaithyanathan Shivakumar. 2002. Thumbs up?: sentiment classification using machine learning techniques. In *Proceedings of the Conference on Empirical Methods in Natural Language Processing*, pages 79–86.

Jeffrey Pennington, Richard Socher, and Christopher D Manning. 2014. GloVe: Global vectors for word representation. In *Proceedings of the Empiricial Methods in Natural Language Processing*, pages 1532–1543.

Yohei Seki, David Kirk Evans, Lun-Wei Ku, Hsin-Hsi Chen, Noriko Kando, and Chin-Yew Lin. 2007. Overview of opinion analysis pilot task at NTCIR-6. In *Proceedings of NTCIR-6 Workshop Meeting*, pages 265–278.

Richard Socher, Jeffrey Pennington, Eric H. Huang, Andrew Y. Ng, and Christopher D. Manning. 2011. Semi-supervised recursive autoencoders for predicting sentiment distributions. In *Proceedings of the 2011 Conference on Empirical Methods in Natural Language Processing*, pages 151–161.

Richard Socher, Alex Perelygin, Jean Wu, Jason Chuang, Christopher D. Manning, Andrew Y. Ng, and Christopher Potts. 2013. Recursive deep models for semantic compositionality over a sentiment treebank. In *Proceedings of the 2013 Conference on Empirical Methods in Natural Language Processing*, pages 1631–1642.

Sheng Kai Tai, Richard Socher, and D. Christopher Manning. 2015. Improved semantic representations from tree-structured long short-term memory networks. In *Proceedings of the 53rd Annual Meeting of the Association for Computational Linguistics and the 7th International Joint Conference on Natural Language Processing*, pages 1556–1566.

Duyu Tang, Furu Wei, Nan Yang, Ming Zhou, Ting Liu, and Bing Qin. 2014. Learning sentiment-specific word embedding for twitter sentiment classification. In *Proceedings of the 52nd Annual Meeting of the Association for Computational Linguistics*, volume 1, pages 1555–1565.

Pascal Vincent, Hugo Larochelle, Yoshua Bengio, and Pierre-Antoine Manzagol. 2008. Extracting and composing robust features with denoising autoencoders. In *Proceedings of the 25th International Conference on Machine Learning*, pages 1096–1103.

Pascal Vincent, Hugo Larochelle, Isabelle Lajoie, Yoshua Bengio, and Pierre-Antoine Manzagol. 2010. Stacked denoising autoencoders: Learning useful representations in a deep network with a local denoising criterion. *The Journal of Machine Learning Research*, 11:3371–3408.

Sida Wang and Christopher D. Manning. 2012. Baselines and bigrams: Simple, good sentiment and topic classification. In *Proceedings of the 50th Annual Meeting of the Association for Computational Linguistics*, pages 90–94.

Junyuan Xie, Linli Xu, and Enhong Chen. 2012. Image denoising and inpainting with deep neural networks. In *Advances in Neural Information Processing Systems 25*, pages 341–349.

Is Wikipedia Really Neutral? A Sentiment Perspective Study of War-related Wikipedia Articles since 1945

Yiwei Zhou, Alexandra I. Cristea and Zachary Roberts
Department of Computer Science
University of Warwick
Coventry, United Kingdom
{Yiwei.Zhou, A.I.Cristea, Z.L.Roberts}@warwick.ac.uk

Abstract

Wikipedia is supposed to be supporting the "Neutral Point of View". Instead of accepting this statement as a fact, the current paper analyses its veracity by specifically analysing a typically controversial (negative) topic, such as war, and answering questions such as "Are there sentiment differences in how Wikipedia articles in different languages describe the same war?". This paper tackles this challenge by proposing an automatic methodology based on *article level* and *concept level* sentiment analysis on multilingual Wikipedia articles. The results obtained so far show that reasons such as people's feelings of involvement and empathy can lead to sentiment expression differences across multilingual Wikipedia on war-related topics; the more people contribute to an article on a war-related topic, the more extreme sentiment the article will express; different cultures also focus on different concepts about the same war and present different sentiments towards them. Moreover, our research provides a framework for performing different levels of sentiment analysis on multilingual texts.

1 Introduction

Wikipedia is the largest and most widely used encyclopaedia in collaborative knowledge building (Medelyan et al., 2009). Since its start in 2001, it contains more than 33 million articles in more than 200 languages, while only about 4 million articles are in English[1]. Possible sources for the content include books, journal articles, newspapers, webpages, sound recordings[2], etc. Although a "Neutral point of view" (NPOV)[3] is Wikipedia's core content policy, we believe sentiment expression is inevitable in this user-generated content. Already in (Greenstein and Zhu, 2012), researchers have raised doubt about Wikipedia's neutrality, as they pointed out that "Wikipedia achieves something akin to a NPOV across articles, but not necessarily within them". Moreover, people of different language backgrounds share different cultures and sources of information. These differences have reflected on the style of contributions (Pfeil et al., 2006) and the type of information covered (Callahan and Herring, 2011). Furthermore, Wikipedia webpages actually allow to contain opinions, as long as they come from reliable authors[4]. Due to its openness to multiple forms of contribution, the articles on Wikipedia can be viewed as a summarisation of thoughts in multiple languages about specific topics. *Automatically detecting and measuring the differences* can be crucial in many applications: public relation departments can get some useful suggestions from Wikipedia about topics close to their hearts; Wikipedia readers can get some insights about what people speaking other languages think about the same topic; Wikipedia administrators can quickly locate the Wikipedia articles that express extreme sentiment, to better apply the NPOV policy, by eliminating some edits.

[1] http://meta.wikimedia.org/wiki/List_of_Wikipedias

[2] http://en.wikipedia.org/wiki/Wikipedia:Citing_sources

[3] http://en.wikipedia.org/wiki/Wikipedia:Neutral_point_of_view

[4] http://en.wikipedia.org/wiki/Wikipedia:Identifying_reliable_sources

29th Pacific Asia Conference on Language, Information and Computation pages 160 - 168
Shanghai, China, October 30 - November 1, 2015

In order to further gain insight on these matters, and especially, on the degree of neutrality on given topics presented in different languages, we explore an approach that can perform *multiple levels of sentiment analysis on multilingual Wikipedia articles*. We generate *graded sentiment analysis* results for multilingual articles, and attribute sentiment analysis to concepts, to analyse the sentiment that one*specific named entity* is involved in. For the sake of simplicity, we restrict our scenario within the war-related topics, although our approach can be easily applied on other domains. Our results show that even though the overall sentiment polarities of multilingual Wikipedia articles on the same war-related topic are consistent, the strengths of sentiment expression vary from language to language.

The remainder of the paper is structured as follows. In Section 2, we present an overview of different approaches of sentiment analysis. Section 3 describes the approach selected in this research to perform article level and concept level sentiment analysis on multilingual Wikipedia articles. In Section 4, experimental results are presented and analysed, and in Section 5, we conclude the major findings and remarks for further research.

2 Related Research

Researchers have been addressing the problem of sentiment analysis of user-generated content mainly at three levels of granularity: *sentence level* sentiment analysis, *article level* sentiment analysis and *concept level* sentiment analysis.

The most common level of sentiment analysis is the *sentence level*, which has laid the ground for the other two. Its basic assumption is that each sentence has only one target concept.

Article level (or *document level*) sentiment analysis is often used on product reviews, news and blogs, where it is believed there is only one target concept in the whole article. Our research performs article level sentiment analysis of Wikipedia articles. We believe this is applicable here, as the Wikipedia webpages' structure is that with a topic as the title, the body of the webpage is the corresponding description of the topic. There are mainly two directions for article level sentiment analysis: *analysis towards the whole article*, or *analysis towards the subjective parts* only. Through extracting the subjective sentences of one article, a classifier can not only achieve higher efficiency, because of the shorter length, but can also achieve higher accuracy, by leaving out the 'noises'. We thus choose to extract the possible subjective parts of the articles first.

More recently, many researchers have realised that multiple sentences may express sentiment about the same concept, or that one sentence may contain sentiment towards different concepts. As a result, the *concept level* (or *aspect level*) sentiment analysis has attracted more and more attention. Researchers have proposed two approaches to extract concepts. The first approach is to manually create a list of interesting concepts, before the analysis (Singh et al., 2013). The second approach is to extract candidate concepts from the object content, automatically (Mudinas et al., 2012). As in Wikipedia different articles will mention different concepts, it is impossible to pre-create the concepts list without reading all the articles. We thus choose to automatically extract the named entities in the subjective sentences as concepts.

3 Methodology

3.1 Overview

We employ war-related topics in Wikipedia as counter-examples to refute the statement that 'Wikipedia is neutral'.

Based on our choice of approaches (see Section 2), we build a straightforward processing pipeline (Figure 1) as briefly sketched below (with details in the subsequent sub-sections).

First, we retrieve the related topic name based on some input keywords. After that, the Wikipedia webpages in *all* available languages on this topic are downloaded. Because of the diversity of the content in Wikipedia webpages, some data pre-processing, as described in Section 3.2, is needed, in order to acquire plain descriptive text. We further translate the plain descriptive text into English (see notes in Section 3.2 on accuracy and the estimated errors introduced), for further processing. To extract the subjective contents from each translated article, we tokenise the article into sentences, and then perform subjective analysis, as is described in Section 3.3, on each sentence. As mentioned already, based on prior

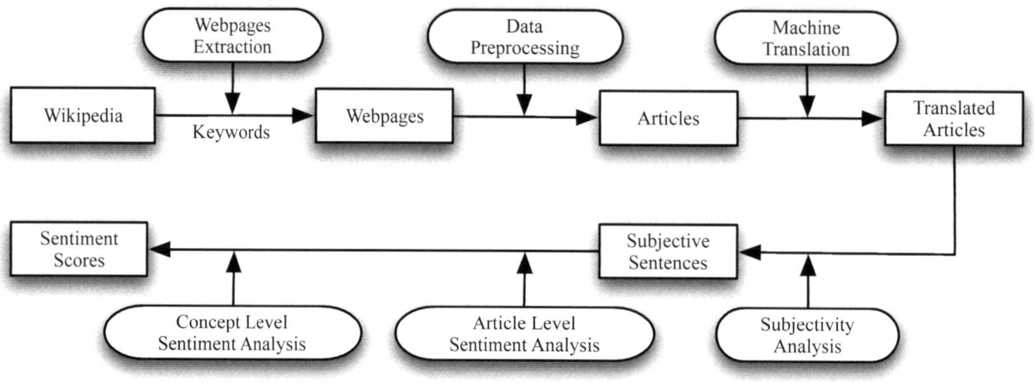

Figure 1: Processing Pipeline

research (Pang and Lee, 2004), only the subjective sentences are retained, while the rest are discarded. We then leverage the English sentiment analysis resources to measure the sentiment score for each subjective sentence, and utilise named entity extraction tools to extract the named entities as target concepts in this subjective sentence. We calculate the article level sentiment scores, as is described in Section 4.1, as well as the concept level sentence scores, as is described in Section 3.5, with both being based on the sentence level sentiment scores. In the final step, all the absolute sentiment scores of multilingual Wikipedia articles on the same topic are normalised within a range of [0, 1], for better visualisation and comparison.

3.2 Data Acquisition and Pre-processing

All the data of Wikipedia can be accessed through its official MediaWiki web API[5]. However, the downloaded webpages contain multiple kinds of information — such as references, external links, and the infobox, rather than simple plain descriptive text. Thus, the first step of data pre-processing is to discard all the parts that contain no sentiment information from the downloaded webpages . Moreover, we use the lxml[6] HTML parser, in order to remove all the HTML tags.

Whilst there are plenty of sentiment analysis tools and methods with satisfying performance for English, many of them are free, or easy to be implemented, not the same can be said for other languages. To close the gap between other languages and English sentiment analysis resources, we apply machine translation on the texts in other languages. To date, machine translation techniques are well developed; products such as Google Translate[7] and Bing Translator [8] are widely used in academic (Bautin et al., 2008; Wan, 2009) and business context. In (Balahur and Turchi, 2014), researchers pointed out that the machine translation techniques have reached a reasonable level of maturity, which could be applied in multilingual sentiment analysis. We choose Google Translate, because of its extensive use and excellent reputation. We also are able to more confidently use machine translation, after performing the following test: we translate English articles to all the other available languages for the target topic and then back to English, and we evaluate the resulting sentiment scores' changes. This test will be further discussed in Section 4.

3.3 Subjectivity Analysis

Conforming with the NPOV policy, we couldn't find clear sentiment expression in the greatest proportion of the content of the translated articles, it is the subjective parts of the content that we really care about. By extracting these parts of the content, we can compress the long Wikipedia articles into much shorter texts, with the sentiment information retained (Pang and Lee, 2004). This greatly simplifies the next pro-

[5] `http://www.mediawiki.org/wiki/API:Main_page`

[6] `http://lxml.de/index.html`

[7] `https://translate.google.com/`

[8] `http://www.bing.com/translator/`

cessing step and saved memory usage. Moreover, reliable subjectivity analysis can make the article "cleaner", by eliminating the possible errors introduced by objective sentences.

As in the next step, we will apply another more accurate tool to grade the sentiment scores of the sentences, in this stage, it is the *recall* that we focus on, rather than the *precision*.

Our proposed method thus first performs subjectivity analysis at sentence level. Since extracting as many sentences that may contain sentiment expression as possible is our first consideration, we use sentiment-bearing words' occurrences as indicators of sentiment expression in Wikipedia sentences. The detailed rule is: if one sentence contains any word from a sentiment-bearing words lexicon, then this sentence is classified as a subjective sentence; otherwise this sentence is discarded. Our method for subjectivity is based on an assumption that for a sentence, if it contains sentiment-bearing words, it may or may not be a subjective sentence; if it contains no sentiment-bearing words at all, then it is definitely not a subjective sentence. This method can greatly reduce the level of computational complexity and maintain a high recall.

Liu et al. (Liu et al., 2005) created a list of positive and negative opinion words for English, which has about 6800 words, including most of the adjectives, adverbs and verbs that contain sentiment information used on the web. This list fully satisfies all our needs, thus is used in our subjectivity analysis.

3.4 Article Level Sentiment Analysis

It is the overall sentiment score of each Wikipedia article rather than the separate sentiment scores of sentences in the article that we care about in this research. For example, if *Article A* has 10 positive sentences and 2 negative sentences, and *Article B* has 5 positive sentences and 3 negative sentences, we assume that *Article A* is more positive than *Article B*, thus will have a higher absolute sentiment score. It should be noted that we do not normalise the article level sentiment scores by the numbers of sentences here because the numbers of positive/negative sentences can also reflect the sentiment levels of different articles. Similar to (Ku et al., 2006) and (Zhang et al., 2009), we calculate the sentiment score $S(a)$ of an article a, by aggregating the sentiment scores of the subjective sentences in it, as follows:

$$S(a) = \sum_{i=1}^{m} S(s_i, a) \tag{1}$$

where: $S(s_i, a)$ denotes the sentiment score of the ith subjective sentence s_i in article a, and m denotes the number of subjective sentences in article a.

There are a lot of applicable sentence level sentiment analysis tools, and it is essential to choose the one most suits for this context. As different sentences will express different levels of sentiment, it is better to use the sentiment analysis tool that can estimate such a difference, rather than only classifies the sentences as positive or negative. Moreover, the chosen sentiment analysis tool should have acceptable performance in measuring the sentiment levels of sentences on war-related topics.

The Stanford CoreNLP sentiment annotator in Stanford natural language processing toolkit(Manning et al., 2014) can reach an accuracy of 80.7% on movie reviews (Socher et al., 2013). The annotator will classify the sentiment of each sentence into five classes, including very negative, negative, neutral, positive and very positive. To verify its performance on war-related sentences, we generate a list of English sentences randomly selected from war-related Wikipedia articles. After manually labelling 200 sentences, we use Stanford CoreNLP sentiment annotator to generate graded results for our labelled data. Its accuracy on war-related sentences is 72%, which satisfies our needs for this application. For calculation convenience, we assign each class a sentiment score from -2 to 2, where -2 represents very negative, -1 represents negative, 0 represents neutral, 1 represents positive and 2 represents very positive. The sentiment scores of sentences will be aggregated later into the overall sentiment score of each translated article according to Equation 1. In short, if S_a is greater than 0, it means this is a positive article; if S_a is equal to 0, it means this is a neutral article; otherwise this is a negative article. Besides that, the scores also give account of the levels of sentiment involved.

3.5 Concept Level Sentiment Analysis

After computing the sentiment scores of articles on the same topic in multiple languages, we expand our research to finer granularity, the concept level sentiment analysis. By exploring what concepts are mentioned and their corresponding sentiment scores in one article, we expect to locate the underlying reasons of why articles show different levels of sentiment. Inspired by (Mudinas et al., 2012), we extract the named entities from the subjective sentences, as the concepts mentioned in the article. In (Atdag and Labatut, 2013), Atdag and Labatut compared different named entity recognition tools' performance, and the Stanford NER[9] showed the best results. Thus we apply Stanford NER to extract the concepts. We use the sentences that one concept occurs in as its opinionated context (as in (Singh et al., 2013; Mudinas et al., 2012)).

The sentiment score $S(c, a)$ of each concept c in article a is calculated as follows:

$$S(c, a) = \sum_{j=1}^{n} S(s_j, c, a) \quad (2)$$

where: $S(s_j, c, a)$ denotes the sentiment score of the jth subjective sentence s_j in article a which mentions the concept c, and n denotes the number of subjective sentences in article a which mentions the concept c. As mentioned in Section 4.1, if $S(c, a)$ is greater than 0, it means concept c is more involved in positive sentiment; if $S(c, a)$ is equal to 0, it means concept c has a overall neutral context; otherwise the concept is more involved in a negative sentiment. Similar to article level sentiment score, we do not apply normalisation here either because the number of positive/negative sentences that mention this concept can also reflect the level of sentiment this concept involved in.

4 Evaluation

We choose war-related topics as a start for the neutrality analysis of multilingual Wikipedia for the following reasons. First, Wikipedians have different sentiment expression patterns for topics from different domains. While it is not possible to perform the multilingual Wikipedia sentiment differences analysis for all these domains, we choose one domain as a start. If the the NPOV of Wikipedia cannot hold for this domain, by providing these topics as counterexamples , Wikipedia is not neutral in general (although there exist many neutral articles). Second, war-related topics are controversial in the first place. For different belligerents of the wars, they often use different official languages, and have different interpretations towards the same incidents, which makes the detection of sentiment differences possible. Third, as illustrated in Section 4.1, Stanford CoreNLP sentiment annotator has acceptable performance on the sentences from the domain of wars, but its performance on the sentences from other domains remains unknown.

To analyse sentiment differences in the perception of war-related topics, we compare sentiment scores of multilingual Wikipedia articles, perform concept level sentiment analysis and explore the relationship between the sentiment scores and numbers of words/concepts in the articles, as described below.

4.1 Article Level Sentiment Differences in Multilingual Wikipedia Articles on War-related Topics

We have performed article level analysis on all the wars with clear belligerents and a certain level of popularity since the ending of the *Second World War*. There are 30 of them satisfy our demands from the list of wars provide by Wikipedia[10]. Due to page limitation, the results of 7 of them can be found in Table 1.

There are 666 Wikipedia pages in 68 languages on these 30 war-related topics, 100% of them have an overall negative sentiment. This shows consistency of sentiment polarity of multilingual Wikipedia articles on war-related topics. In Table 1, a ranked list is given, starting from the most neutral language to the most negative language, thus the languages in the first half of the ranked list have articles more neutral than the languages in the second half of the ranked list on a specific war-related topic; the official languages of belligerents are marked in *italic* characters.

To measure the influence of Google Translate on the final results, we design one test: for each one the 30 war-related topics, we translate its English edi-

[9] http://nlp.stanford.edu/software/CRF-NER.shtml

[10] http://en.wikipedia.org/wiki/Category:Lists_of_wars_by_date

Table 1: Sentiment Differences in Multilingual Wikipedia on War-related topics.

War-related topics	Languages' ranked list (from most neutral to most negative)
Korean War	Japanese, Nepali, Hindi, Afrikaans, Malay, Macedonian, Esperanto, Armenian, Tamil, Welsh, Bengali, Swahili, Belarusian, Azerbaijani, Basque, Persian, Latin, Serbian, Arabic, Hungarian, Greek, Romanian, Norwegian, Turkish, Lithuanian, Slovak, Filipino, Icelandic, Thai, Danish, Bosnian, Croatian, Estonian, Galician, Dutch, Latvian, Polish, Swedish, Czech, Spanish, Mongolian, Finnish, Bulgarian, Ukrainian, Slovenian, Portuguese, German, Indonesian, Telugu, Kannada, *Russian*, Italian, French, Vietnamese, *Korean*, *Chinese*, *English*
Algerian War	Greek, Romanian, Malay, Bengali, Persian, Esperanto, Irish, Basque, Portuguese, Spanish, Swedish, Vietnamese, Welsh, *Arabic*, Lithuanian, Korean, Chinese, Croatian, Catalan, Turkish, Polish, Hungarian, Serbian, Norwegian, Dutch, Finnish, Japanese, Czech, Latvian, Russian, Italian, Ukrainian, German, *French*, English
Turkish invasion of Cyprus	Serbian, Arabic, Polish, Czech, Romanian, Norwegian, Persian, Korean, German, Chinese, Portuguese, Hungarian, French, Spanish, Russian, *Turkish*, Swedish, Finnish, Italian, *Greek*, English
Dirty War	Esperanto, Finnish, Swedish, Tamil, Korean, Welsh, Ukrainian, Georgian, Polish, Russian, Malay, Portuguese, Bosnian, Persian, Chinese, Japanese, Czech, Serbian, Croatian, Italian, Indonesian, German, Dutch, French, Galician, *Spanish*, English
Romanian Revolution of 1989	Basque, Indonesian, Irish, Croatian, Arabic, Thai, Norwegian, Czech, Japanese, Swedish, Slovak, Korean, Chinese, Russian, Turkish, Serbian, Portuguese, French, Ukrainian, Bulgarian, Filipino, Finnish, Dutch, Polish, Catalan, Spanish, Galician, Italian, Hungarian, English, *Romanian*, German
Civil war in Tajikistan	Bosnian, Italian, Portuguese, Serbian, Norwegian, Catalan, Bulgarian, Welsh, Polish, German, Ukrainian, Spanish, Japanese, French, English, Czech, *Russian*
War in North-West Pakistan	Korean, *Urdu*, Czech, Portuguese, Spanish, Croatian, Welsh, Hungarian, German, Russian, Japanese, French, *English*, Polish

tion Wikipedia article to all its other available languages on Wikipedia, then we translate the translated articles back to English. Then we calculate the sentiment scores of these translated-then-back articles and get the new ranks of them. After this process, we find that all these 30 war-related topics satisfy: if the English edition Wikipedia article is in the first/second half of the ranked list, all its translated-then-back articles remains in the first/second half of the ranked list. This test shows Google Translate's impact on our final result is quite limited.

People from the belligerents usually suffer the most from the wars, so we expect the official languages of belligerents have the most negative sentiment towards the wars. Our results show: of these war-related topics we tested, 80% share a common characteristic, which is the official languages of the belligerents have relatively more negative sentiment towards the wars (rank in the second half of the ranked list) than other non-relevant languages. The results we get are quite consistent with our expectations, which also prove the effectiveness of our method. For example, Russian is one of the belligerents of Civil war in Tajikistan; it has the most negative sentiment towards this topic. US, China and Korea are greatly involved in the Korean War, and the corresponding Wikipedia editions are most negative on this topic. This is the same as in the case of French on the Algerian War, Greek on the Turkish invasion of Cyprus, Spanish on the Dirty War and Romanian on the Romanian Revolution of 1989. On the contrary, the most neutral Wikipedia articles about Civil war in Tajikistan are in Bosnian, Italian and Portuguese. This may be caused by the following reasons: first, Bosnian Wikipedia is not as widely used as some other languages (ranked 69 in number of Wikipedia articles[11]), which will result in a limited number of edits on these articles; second, the Civil war in Tajikistan has little relevance to the people speaking, e.g., Italian or Portuguese, because of the geographical distance, which may result in limited attention to this topic. Our findings, besides corroborating our method, also present some other interesting patterns that are worth exploring. For example, on the topic of Korean War, we can also see that Vietnamese, a language used among only 75 millions people[12], also holds very negative senti-

[11] `http://meta.wikimedia.org/wiki/List_of_Wikipedias`

[12] `http://en.wikipedia.org/wiki/`

ment. This may due to the geographical distance between Vietnam and Korea, but also because the Korean War is very close in time to the Vietnam War. Thus, the extreme sentiment of Vietnamese people towards the Korean War may not be surprising at all. On the topic of the Romanian Revolution of 1989, German and Hungarian Wikipedia hold very negative sentiment. This is because during the period of the Romanian Revolution of 1989, there are also similar revolutions in Hungary and East Germany. Some kind of empathy makes German and Hungarian Wikipedia users have similar sentiment as the Romanian Wikipedia users. On the topic of War in North-West Pakistan, Polish pages have the most negative sentiment. We can speculate that Polish people feel involved in this war, as a Polish engineer was kidnapped and killed by Pakistani extremists.

However, some official languages of belligerents seems to be not that negative towards the wars they were involved in. For example, the sentiment of Arabic Wikipedia on the Algerian War and the sentiment of Urdu Wikipedia on the War in North-West Pakistan. The possible reasons can be summarised as follows. First, according to the statistics provided by Wikipedia [13], the Arabic Wikipedia and Urdu Wikipedia is far less active than some other languages, such as English and German. Second, these languages' sentiment expression patterns may be largely different from English, thus the sentiment analysis resources for English may not work well on these languages' translated articles. A detailed analysis of sentiment expression patterns on linguistic level is beyond the scope of this work.

4.2 Concept Level Sentiment Analysis on English Wikipedia and Russian Wikipedia on the Civil war in Tajikistan

Table 2 lists the concepts extracted from French Wikipedia on Civil war of Tajikistan. For comparison, Table 3 lists the concepts extracted from the Russian Wikipedia on the same topic. To add readability, we only keep the concepts with absolute sentiment scores no less than 2. The method of calculating the sentiment scores of concepts can be found in Section 3.5.

From Table 2 and Table 3, concepts that are involved in negative sentiment in both French Wikipedia and Russian Wikipedia on the topic of Civil war in Tajikistan are marked in *italic* characters. Obviously there are more concepts involved in negative sentiment in Russian Wikipedia than French Wikipedia, which is understandable since Russian is the the most widely used language among the countries that are involved in the war. People from these Russian speaking countries have more detailed information about the war, and rich sentiment towards the war, thus will mention more concepts in its corresponding Wikipedia article and express stronger sentiment in the contexts of these concepts.

There are some concepts that occur only in French Wikipedia, but not in Russian Wikipedia. For example, Abdullo Nazarov, Rasht Vally and Movement for Islamic Revival of Tajikistan. Similarly, a lot more concepts occur only in the Russian Wikipedia but not in the French Wikipedia. Concepts occurring only in specific languages editions of Wikipedia may point to people's variances in preference and focus.

Table 4: Pearson correlation coefficient between sentiment scores and articles' features

Results	p_1	p_2
Average	0.971	0.948
Standard deviation	0.020	0.025

4.3 Relationship Between Sentiment Scores and Number of Words/Concepts in Multilingual Wikipedia Articles

To analyse the underlying reasons leading to the differences in sentiment level, we calculate the Pearson correlation coefficient between the article level sentiment scores and some features of the articles. The article features we choose are the number of words in the article and the number of concepts mentioned in subjective sentences in the article. The statistical summary of results of 30 war-related topics we test is displayed in Table 4. In the table, p_1 is the Pearson correlation coefficient between sentiment scores and numbers of words; p_2 is the Pearson correlation coefficient between sentiment scores and numbers of concepts.

Vietnamese_language

[13]http://meta.wikimedia.org/wiki/List_of_Wikipedias

Table 2: Concept Level Sentiment Analysis of French Wikipedia about the Civil war in Tajikistan.

Concept Type	**Concepts involved in Negative Sentiment**
Person	Abdullo Nazarov, Tolib Ayombekov, *Mullah Abdullah*
Location	*Afghanistan*, *Dushanbe*, *Garmi*, *Gorno-Badakhshan*, Rasht Valley, Samsolid, *Tajikistan*, Taloqan, *Uzbekistan*
Organisation	Movement for Islamic Revival of Tajikistan, Taliban, *United Tajik Opposition*

Table 3: Concept Level Sentiment Analysis of Russian Wikipedia about the Civil war in Tajikistan.

Concept Type	**Concepts involved in Negative Sentiment**
Person	Dawlat Khudonazarov, Emomali Rahmon, Karim Yuldashev, Mahmoud Khudayberdiev, Mirzo Ziyoyev, Mukhiddin Olimpur, *Mullah Abdullah*, Nozim Vahidov, Otakhon Latifi, Rahmon Nabiyev, Rahmon Sanginova, Safarali Kenjayev, Saifullo Rakhimov, Victor Khudyakov, Yusuf Iskhaki
Location	*Afghanistan*, Darwaz, *Dushanbe*, *Garmi*, *Gorno-Badakhshan*, Hissar, Iran, Karategin, Kazakhstan, Khujand, Kofarnihon, Kulyab, Kulob Oblast, Kurgan-Tube, Kyrgyzstan, Leninabad, Lomonosov, Majlisi Oli, Nurek Dam, Ozodi, Pakistan, Shakhidon, *Tajikistan*, Tavildara, *Uzbekistan*, Vakhsh
Organisation	Afghan Mukahideen, CIS, Communist Party, Democratic Party of Tajikistan, Islamic Renaissance Party, Lali Badakhshan, Rastokhez, National Guard, Tajikistan Interior Ministry, *United Tajik Opposition*

The Pearson correlation coefficient measures the strength of linear correlation between the articles' features and the sentiment scores of these articles from different Wikipedia editions. A Pearson correlation coefficient of nearly 1 means there is strong positive correlation between the two variables. 100% of the Pearson correlation coefficients between sentiment scores and numbers of words of multilingual Wikipedia articles (p_1), and 96.7% of the Pearson correlation coefficients between sentiment scores and numbers of named entities of multilingual Wikipedia articles (p_2) are above 0.9. This illustrates that for the war-related articles in Wikipedia, the more words in one negative article, the more negative the article will be; the more concepts in subjective sentences in one negative article, the more negative the article will be. Both the number of words and the number of concepts in one translated article reflect the degree of concern of people speaking that language about this topic. A higher degree of concern will drive people to add more contents to the Wikipedia article about that topic in their language, which will lead to stronger sentiment expression in corresponding article.

5 Conclusion

Is Wikipedia really neutral? By using war-related topics as proof by counter-examples, we find the short answer to this question: no.

Our results demonstrate that, while multilingual Wikipedia articles on one war-related topic have a consistent sentiment polarity, there are differences on levels of sentiment expression. People's degree of concern about one war-related topic will influence the number of words, and the number of subjective concepts, which in turn determine the levels of sentiment expression. The subjective concepts mentioned and their frequencies also reflect the fact that people speaking different languages have different focuses and interests about the same war-related topic. For some languages, there is no obvious connection between them and the belligerent countries at first glance; nevertheless, they often have more extreme sentiment towards the war than other irrelevant languages. When discrepancies happen, some underlying reasons can always be found by thoroughly researching into the war history. Since it is not possible to ask people to read all the Wikipedia articles in different languages on the same topic and rank them based on their sentiment expression levels, we validate our results through qualitative analysis, by locating the underlying reasons that lead to such results.

While our findings only apply to war-related topics on Wikipedia, our approaches can be further applied on various topics and domains to explore the sentiment differences of multilingual Wikipedia.

References

Samet Atdag and Vincent Labatut. 2013. A comparison of named entity recognition tools applied to biographical texts. In *Systems and Computer Science (ICSCS), 2013 2nd International Conference on*, pages 228–233. IEEE.

Alexandra Balahur and Marco Turchi. 2014. Comparative experiments using supervised learning and machine translation for multilingual sentiment analysis. *Computer Speech & Language*, 28(1):56–75.

Mikhail Bautin, Lohit Vijayarenu, and Steven Skiena. 2008. International sentiment analysis for news and blogs. In *ICWSM*.

Ewa S. Callahan and Susan C. Herring. 2011. Cultural bias in wikipedia content on famous persons. *Journal of the American Society for Information Science and Technology*, 62(10):1899–1915.

Shane Greenstein and Feng Zhu. 2012. Collective intelligence and neutral point of view: The case of wikipedia.

Lun-Wei Ku, Yu-Ting Liang, and Hsin-Hsi Chen. 2006. Opinion extraction, summarization and tracking in news and blog corpora. In *AAAI Spring Symposium: Computational Approaches to Analyzing Weblogs*, volume 100107.

Bing Liu, Minqing Hu, and Junsheng Cheng. 2005. Opinion observer: Analyzing and comparing opinions on the web. In *Proceedings of the 14th International Conference on World Wide Web*, WWW '05, pages 342–351. ACM.

Christopher D Manning, Mihai Surdeanu, John Bauer, Jenny Finkel, Steven J Bethard, and David McClosky. 2014. The stanford corenlp natural language processing toolkit. In *Proceedings of 52nd Annual Meeting of the Association for Computational Linguistics: System Demonstrations*, pages 55–60.

Olena Medelyan, David Milne, Catherine Legg, and Ian H. Witten. 2009. Mining meaning from wikipedia. *International Journal of Human-Computer Studies*, 67(9):716–754.

Andrius Mudinas, Dell Zhang, and Mark Levene. 2012. Combining lexicon and learning based approaches for concept-level sentiment analysis. In *Proceedings of the First International Workshop on Issues of Sentiment Discovery and Opinion Mining*, WISDOM '12, pages 5:1–5:8. ACM.

Bo Pang and Lillian Lee. 2004. A sentimental education: Sentiment analysis using subjectivity summarization based on minimum cuts. In *Proceedings of the 42Nd Annual Meeting on Association for Computational Linguistics*, ACL '04. Association for Computational Linguistics.

Ulrike Pfeil, Panayiotis Zaphiris, and Chee Siang Ang. 2006. Cultural differences in collaborative authoring of wikipedia. *Journal of Computer-Mediated Communication*, 12(1):88–113.

V.K. Singh, R. Piryani, A Uddin, and P. Waila. 2013. Sentiment analysis of movie reviews: A new feature-based heuristic for aspect-level sentiment classification. In *2013 International Multi-Conference on Automation, Computing, Communication, Control and Compressed Sensing (iMac4s)*, pages 712–717.

Richard Socher, Alex Perelygin, Jean Y Wu, Jason Chuang, Christopher D Manning, Andrew Y Ng, and Christopher Potts. 2013. Recursive deep models for semantic compositionality over a sentiment treebank. In *Proceedings of the conference on empirical methods in natural language processing (EMNLP)*, volume 1631, page 1642.

Xiaojun Wan. 2009. Co-training for cross-lingual sentiment classification. In *Proceedings of the Joint Conference of the 47th Annual Meeting of the ACL and the 4th International Joint Conference on Natural Language Processing of the AFNLP: Volume 1 - Volume 1*, ACL '09, pages 235–243. Association for Computational Linguistics.

Changli Zhang, Daniel Zeng, Jiexun Li, Fei-Yue Wang, and Wanli Zuo. 2009. Sentiment analysis of chinese documents: From sentence to document level. *Journal of the American Society for Information Science and Technology*, 60(12):2474–2487.

A Comprehensive Filter Feature Selection for Improving Document Classification

Le Nguyen Hoai Nam
School of Information Technology
VNUHCM - University of Science
Ho Chi Minh City, Vietnam
lnhnam@fit.hcmus.edu.vn

Ho Bao Quoc
School of Information Technology
VNUHCM - University of Science
Ho Chi Minh City, Vietnam
hbquoc@fit.hcmus.edu.vn

Abstract

High dimension of bag-of-words vectors poses a serious challenge from sparse data, overfitting, irrelevant features to document classification. Filter feature selection is one of effective methods for dimensionality reduction by removing irrelevant features from feature set. This paper focuses on two main problems of filter feature selection which are the feature score computation and the imbalance in the feature selection performance between categories. We propose a novel filter feature selection method, named ExFCFS, to comprehensively resolve these problems. We experiment on related filter feature selection methods with two benchmark datasets - Reuters-21578 dataset and Ohsumed dataset. The experimental results show the effectiveness of our solutions in terms of both Micro-F1 measure and Macro-F1 measure.

Keywords— bag-of-words vector, filter feature selection, document classification

1 Introduction

Document classification is to assign documents to predefined categories based on their text contents (Sebastiani 2002). It is a useful tool for managing the organization of a large set of documents. In the document classification, a bag-of-words vector is usually used for presenting a document (Yang et al. 2012), (Joachims 1996). Concretely, a document is shown in the form of a vector in which each term appearing in the document is considered as a feature.

However, with a large set of documents, the dimension of a bag-of-words vector can reach thousands (Fragoudis et al. 2005), (Yang et al. 2012). Therefore, it poses a serious challenge from sparse data, overfitting, irrelevant features to document classification (Fragoudis et al. 2005), (Sebastiani 2002). In (Bellman 1961), the author referred it to as "the curse of dimensionality". Thus, dimensionality reduction is a major research area.

The aim of dimensionality reduction is to decrease the number of features without degrading the performance of the system (Sebastiani 2002). An efficient approach for dimension reduction is Feature Selection (FS) (Yang and Pedersen 1997). Feature selection eliminates irrelevant features to select a good subset of the original feature set. A strong point of FS is that the interpretation of the important features in the original set is not altered in dimensionality reduction process.

Two main types of FS are wrapper methods (Bermejo et al. 2014) and filter methods (Yang and Pedersen 1997). Wrapper methods select a subset of features which is the most suitable with a specific classification algorithm. Conversely, filter methods do not depend on any classification algorithms. It relies on a function for evaluating the importance of a feature in the classification process. A subset of features is selected by simply ranking the value of every feature on the evaluation function. Therefore, it is commonly used in document classification (Fragoudis et al. 2005), (Yang et al. 2012).

29th Pacific Asia Conference on Language, Information and Computation pages 169 - 177
Shanghai, China, October 30 - November 1, 2015

In this paper, we focus on filter feature selection methods. Table 1 shows their general structure.

Input: Bag-of-words vectors; L: the number of selected features.
Output: S_L: a subset of features with predefined size L
Step 1: For each term t_k (k = 1 ...$\|T\|$)
Step 2: For each category C_i (i = 1 ...$\|C\|$)
Step 3: Compute the importance of term t_k for the prediction of category C_i: $catScore(t_k, C_i)$.
Step 4: End for
Step 5: Compute global score of term t_k for the prediction of all categories from $catScores$ of term t_k: $globalScore(t_k)$.
Step 6 : End for
Step 7: Select L terms from top L highest $globalScores$: S_L.

Table 1: The general structure of filter FS methods

Specifically, filter feature selection methods compute the importance of term t_k for the prediction of category C_i, noted by $catScore(t_k, C_i)$. Then, the importance of term t_k for the prediction of all categories, noted by $globalScore(t_k)$, is calculated by using the average or maximum value of category-specific scores of term t_k over the different categories (Yang and Pedersen 1997). The terms from top highest $globalScore$ are selected to the final set. Next, we present main methods for computing $catScore(t_k, C_i)$ as following:

1.1 Information Gain

The basic idea of Information Gain (Quinlan 1986) is to measure predictable bits of category value if we know in advance the occurrence of a term. With IG, the score of term t_k with respect to a specific category C_i is as following:

$$catScore_{IG}(t_k, C_i) = \sum_{C \in \{C_i, \overline{C_i}\}} \sum_{t \in \{t_k, \overline{t_k}\}} P(t, C) \log \frac{P(t,C)}{P(t).P(C)}$$

where $P(t, C)$ is the probability of a document belonging to category C and containing term t; $P(C)$ is the probability of a document belonging to category C; $P(t)$ is the probability of a document containing term t. However, it is impossible to determine a set of features whose IG is maximal. It is NP problem (Yan et al. 2005). Therefore, IG formula is applied for each feature and the final set consists of the features from the top global scores. With this greedy characteristic, Information Gain is a non-optimal method (Yan et al. 2005).

1.2 Chi-square

Similar to IG, Chi-square (Yang and Pedersen 1997) (CHI) is a greedy algorithm. It measures the independence of category value and feature value. The formula of CHI is as following:

$$catScore_{CHI}(t_k, C_i) = \frac{n.P(t_k)^2.(P(C_i|t_k) - P(C_i))^2}{P(t_k).(1 - P(t_k)).P(C_i)(1 - P(C_i))}$$

Where n is the number of documents, $|C|$ is the number of categories, $P(t_k)$ is the probability of a document containing term t_k, $P(C_i)$ is the probability of a document belonging to category C_i, $P(C_i|t_k)$ is the conditional probabilities of a document belonging to category C_i given that it contains term t_k.

1.3 Frequency-based approach

This approach only focuses on the term-category frequency matrix for computing $catScore(t_k, C_i)$ as Document Frequency (DF) (Yang and Pedersen 1997), DIA association factor (DIF) (Sebastiani 2002), Comprehensively Measure Feature Selection (CMFS) (Yang et al. 2012). In CMFS, term t_k is important in the prediction of category C_i if term t_k largely appears in category C_i and the frequency of term t_k in the training set focuses much on category C_i. Therefore, $catScore_{CMFS}(t_k, C_i)$ is computed as following:

$$catScore_{CMFS}(t_k, C_i) = P(t_k|C_i).P(C_i|t_k) \quad (1)$$

Where $P(t_k|C_i)$ is the conditional probabilities of term t_k given that it occurred in category C_i; $P(C_i|t_k)$ is the conditional probabilities of category C_i given the occurrence of term t_k. In $catScore_{CMFS}(t_k, C_i)$, $P(t_k|C_i)$ presents a intra-category condition for the frequency of terms in category C_i, while $P(C_i|t_k)$ indicates a inter-category condition related to the frequency of term t_k not only in category C_i but also in various categories.

1.4 Cluster-based approach

This approach aims at selecting a subset of features in order to optimize objective functions for clustering where each cluster is corresponding to a predefined document category. Orthogonal Centroid Feature Selection (OCFS) is a well-known method of this approach (Yan et al. 2005). It optimizes the separation of categories (clusters) in the filter FS process. It is implemented into $global\ Score$ of a term as following:

$$globalScore_{OCFS}(t_k) = \sum_{i=1}^{|C|} \frac{n_{C_i}}{n} \left(m^{(t_k)} - m_{C_i}^{(t_k)}\right)^2 \quad (2)$$

Where n is the number of documents in training set; m is the mean vector of all documents in training set; n_{C_i} is the number of documents in category C_i; m_{C_i} is the mean vector of all documents in C_i; $m^{(t_k)}$ denotes the feature value of term t_k in global centroid vector m; $m_{C_i}^{(t_k)}$ denotes the feature value of term t_k in category centroid vector m_{C_i}

According to (Yang and Pedersen 1997), a way for computing the global score of term t_k for the category prediction, $globalScore(t_k)$, is the average of the category-specific scores of term t_k over the different categories as following:

$$globalScore(t_k) = \sum_{i=1}^{|C|} P(C_i) catScore(t_k, C_i) \quad (3)$$

From Eq. (2) and Eq. (3), $catScore_{OCFS}(t_k, C_i)$ can be presented as following:

$$catScore_{OCFS}(t_k, C_i) = \left(m^{(t_k)} - m_{C_i}^{(t_k)}\right)^2 \quad (4)$$

2 Approach

In this section, we analyze two filter feature selection approaches which are the frequency-based approach and the cluster-based approach. Our aim is to point out their weak points and strong points to propose a filter feature selection method for improving the performance of document classification.

For the frequency-based approach, $catScore_{CMFS}(t_k, C_i)$ is a comprehensive combination of the frequency-based intra-category condition, which is $P(t_k|C_i)$, and the frequency-based inter-category condition, which is $P(C_i|t_k)$. Regarding the frequency-based inter-category condition, $P(C_i|t_k)$ is rewritten according to conditional probability theory as following:

$$P(C_i|t_k) = \frac{tf(t_k, C_i) + 1}{tf(t_k) + |C|}$$

Where $tf(t_k, C_i)$ is the frequency of term t_k in category C_i; $tf(t_k)$ is the frequency of term t_k in the training set; $|C|$ is the number of categories. For $P(C_i|t_k)$, the greatness of the proportion of the frequency of term t_k in category C_i to the frequency of term t_k in the other categories is utilized to present the contribution of term t_k for discriminating category C_i from the other categories. However, this is not really perfect because a term t_k almost never showed in category C_i but often appearing in the other categories is still useful for classifying a document into category C_i.

Therefore, an inter-category condition in $catScore(t_k, C_i)$ is presented more clearly under the view point of clustering. Concretely, this is the deviation of the representative of term t_k in category/cluster C_i, which is the centroid value of term t_k in C_i ($m_{C_i}^{(t_k)}$), to the representative of term t_k in the training set, which is the centroid value of term t_k in the training set ($m^{(t_k)}$) as shown in $catScore_{OCFS}(t_k, C_i)$. In the other hand, $catScore_{OCFS}(t_k, C_i)$ presents such a good inter-category condition but does not mention any conditions of term t_k for intra-category C_i. Therefore, according to the conclusion of CMFS (Yang et al. 2012), this is not good for a filter FS process.

Based on this observation, we propose a novel filter feature selection approach for the combination of the cluster-based inter-category condition, which is $catScore_{OCFS}(t_k, C_i)$ as Eq. (4), and the frequency-based intra-category condition, which is the first part of Eq. (1). The formula of FCFS is as following:

$$catScore_{FCFS}(t_k, C_i) = P(t_k|C_i).\left(m^{(t_k)} - m_{C_i}^{(t_k)}\right)^2 = \frac{tf(t_k, C_i) + 1}{tf(t, C_i) + |T|}.\left(m^{(t_k)} - m_{C_i}^{(t_k)}\right)^2$$

Where $tf(t, C_i)$ is the sum of the frequency of all terms in category C_i; $|T|$ is the number of terms in the bag-of-words vector.

Furthermore, FCFS does not consider the imbalance in the classification performance between categories after the filter feature selection process. This problem is caused by two factors.

Firstly, classification algorithms tend to focus on categories containing more training documents than the others. This is a big challenge of data mining field. Secondly, the computation of $catScore_{FCFS}(t_k, C_i)$ does not mention the separation degree of the category C_i from the others. Concretely, if the separation degree of category C_n is greater than that of category C_m from the other categories, presented terms of category C_n obviously have higher score compared with those of category C_m. Therefore, after the term score ranking, there are a large number of terms supporting category C_n to be selected into the final set, while it does not contain enough terms for classifying category C_m.

To solve this problem, we propose an Extended version of FCFS, named ExFCFS, with aim of strengthening the score of a term with respect to rare categories and poor separation categories, and weakening the score of a term with respect to abundant categories and great separation categories. Therefore, in ExFCFS, we modify $catScore_{FCFS}(t_k, C_i)$ in inverse proportion to the number of training document of category C_i (n_{C_i}) and the separation degree of category C_i from the other categories as following:

$$catScore_{ExFCFS}(t_k, C_i) = \frac{\frac{tf(t_k, C_i) + 1}{tf(t, C_i) + |T|} \cdot \left(m^{(t_k)} - m_{C_i}^{(t_k)}\right)^2}{n_{C_i} . catSep(C_i)}$$

Where $catSep(C_i)$ is the separation degree of category C_i from the other categories. According to (Friedman et al. 2001), (Chakraborti et al. 2007), (Howland and Park 2004), under the view point of clustering where each cluster is considered as a predefined document category, $catSep(C_i)$ is computed using the "within-cluster" (W) and "between-cluster" (B) factor of cluster (category) C_i as following:

$$catSep(C_i) = \frac{B(C_i)}{W(C_i)} = \frac{\|m_{C_i} - \mathrm{m}\|^2}{\frac{\sum_{j \in C_i} \|d_j - m_{C_i}\|^2}{n_{C_i}}}$$

To compute the importance of a term globally, the maximum value of the category-specific term scores of a term over the different categories is particularly useful according to (Aggawal and Zhai 2012):

$$globalScore(t_k) = \max_{i=1..|C|} catScore(t_k, C_i) \quad (5)$$

Therefore, in this paper, we apply Eq. (5) for computing the global score of ExFCFS as following:

$$globalSocre_{ExFCFS}(t_k) = \max_{i=1..|C|} \left\{ \frac{\frac{tf(t_k, C_i) + 1}{tf(t, C_i) + |T|} \cdot \left(m^{(t_k)} - m_{C_i}^{(t_k)}\right)^2}{n_{C_i} . catSep(C_i)} \right\}$$

For the feature selection, the final set consists of the terms from the top L highest global term scores where L is a predefined size of the selected feature set. The detail of ExFCFS is presented in Table 2.

Input: Bag-of-words vectors; L: the number of selected features
Output: S_L: the subset of features with the predefined size L
Step 1: For each category C_i ($i = 1 \ldots |C|$)
Step 2: Compute the sum of term frequency of all terms in category C_i: $tf(t, C_i)$.
Step 3: Compute the centroid vector of all documents in category C_i: m_{C_i}.
Step 4: End for
Step 5: Compute the centroid vector of all documents: m.
Step 6: For each term t_k ($k = 1 \ldots |T|$)
Step 7: Get the value of term t_k in global centroid vector m: $m^{(t_k)}$.
Step 8: For each category C_i ($i = 1 \ldots |C|$)
Step 9: Get the value of term t_k in category centroid vector m_{C_i}: $m_{C_i}^{(t_k)}$.
Step 10: Compute the frequency of term t_k in category C_i: $tf(t_k, C_i)$.
Step 11: Get the number of training documents in category C_i: n_{C_i}.
Step 12: Compute the score of term t_k with category C_i from $tf(t, C_i), tf(t_k, C_i), m^{(t_k)}, m_{C_i}^{(t_k)}$, n_{C_i}, m_{C_i}, m: $catScore_{ExFCFS}(t_k, C_i)$.
Step 13: Compute the maximum of $catScore_{ExFCFS}(t_k, C_i)$: $globalScore_{ExFCFS}(t_k)$
Step 14: End for
Step 15: End for
Step 16: Select L terms from the top L highest $globalScore_{ExFCFS}$: S_L

Table 2: The description of ExFCFS

3 Experiment

3.1 Experimental steps

In the experiment, we compare the performance of the proposed filter FS method with that of related filter feature selection methods as CMFS (Yang et al. 2012), OCFS (Yan et al. 2005), IG (Quinlan 1986), CHI (Yang and Pedersen 1997). The experimental steps are as following:

- For preprocessing, stop words are removed by using a set of 659 stop words. The stemming process is executed with Porter Stemming algorithm (Porter 1997). For text representation, we use TF-IDF of every term as well as bag-of-words technique.
- The training bag-of-words vectors are reduced by a filter FS method. Then, they are used for building a leaning model using SVM classifier by SMO (Platt 1999) with default setting of WEKA tool (Hall et al. 2009).
- The testing bag-of-words vectors are created only based on the selected terms from the filter feature selection process. The classification system is evaluated on these bag-of-words vectors.

3.2 Dataset

In this paper, we use two benchmark datasets for evaluating the performance of filter feature selection methods. The first dataset is the top-10 categories of Reuters-21578 ModApte's split (Asuncion and Newman 2007). They consist of stories collected from the Reuters news. The second dataset is top-10 categories of medical abstracts of year 1991 from U.S National Library of Medicine, named Ohsumed collection. A standard training and testing split of Ohsumed collection is Joachim's split (Joachims 1998). The detailed description of these datasets is presented in Table 3-4.

3.3 Measure

Two standard measures for evaluating the performance for multi categories classification are Macro-F1 and Micro-F1 (Sebastiani 2002). Macro-F1 measure considers all categories equally including rare categories (Tascı and Güngör 2013). Concretely, Macro-F1 is computed as following:

$$P_{macro} = \frac{\sum_{i=0}^{|C|} P_i}{|C|} \quad R_{macro} = \frac{\sum_{i=0}^{|C|} R_i}{|C|}$$

$$F1_{macro} = \frac{2R_{macro}P_{macro}}{R_{macro} + P_{macro}}$$

Where P_i and R_i are precision and recall measure on category C_i, $|C|$ is the number of categories. Contrary to Macro-F1, Micro-F1 measure ignores the category discrimination. The Micro-F1 measure is computed globally as following:

$$P_{micro} = \frac{\sum_{i=0}^{|C|} TP_i}{\sum_{i=0}^{|C|}(TP_i + FP_i)} \quad R_{micro} = \frac{\sum_{i=0}^{|C|} TP_i}{\sum_{i=0}^{|C|}(TP_i + FN_i)}$$

$$F1_{micro} = \frac{2R_{micro}P_{micro}}{R_{micro} + P_{micro}}$$

To explicitly compare the performance of filter feature selection methods, (Gunal & Edizkan 2008) relies on the above measures to propose dimension reduction rate as following:

$$S = \frac{1}{k}\sum_{i=1}^{k} \frac{Dim_N}{Dim_i} R_i \qquad (10)$$

where k is the number of tests in the experiment, Dim_i is the number of selected features in i^{th} test, R_i is the accuracy measure in i^{th} test, and Dim_N is the maximum feature size which is tested.

Category	Train Docs	Test Docs
C01	423	506
C04	1163	1467
C06	588	632
C08	473	600
C10	621	941
C12	491	548
C14	1249	1301
C20	525	695
C21	546	717
C23	1799	777
The number of features in bag-of-words vector: 17756		

Table 3: The description of Ohsumed dataset

Category	Training Docs	Testing Docs
Corn	181	56
Wheat	212	71
Ship	197	89
Trade	369	117
Interest	347	131
Grain	433	149
money-fx	538	179
Crude	389	189
Acq	1650	719
Earn	2877	1087
The number of features in bag-of-words vector: 16684		

Table 4: The description of Reuters-21578dataset

3.4 Experimental Result and Discussion

Table 5-8 show the experimental results of the filter feature selection methods in our study. It can be noted from these tables as following:

- In terms of Macro-F1, the best filter selection methods are FCFS and ExFCFS. In comparison between them, ExFCFS products better result than FCFS.
- Regarding Micro-F1, ExFCFS attains the most favourable result. FCFS is often superior to IG, CHI, OCFS, CMFS, but at the large number of selected features, their differences are rather small.

An exact explanation for the goodness of FCFS and ExFCFS is the effective combination of the clustered-based inter-category condition and frequency-based intra-category condition in the computation of their term score. This lends support to the theory of CMFS (Yang et al. 2012).

To observe detailed performance of filter feature selection methods, we present F1-measure of each category with CMFS, IG, FCFS, and ExFCFS at 60 features in Fig. 1-2. Specifically, FCFS and ExFCFS show the effectiveness with rare categories as "Ship, Trade, Grain, Interest, Money-Fx, Crude" of Reuters-21578 dataset and "C01, C06, C08, C10, C12, C20, C21" of Ohsumed dataset in comparison with IG and CMFS. This occurs due to the reason that in case of IG, CMFS, the score of a term with respect to a category is based on the greatness of the frequency of a term in the entire category, while the frequency of a term in rare categories is very low. Conversely, FCFS and ExFCFS only use the centroid value of a term in every category and in the training set for term score computation. Therefore, they preliminarily improve the feature selection performance of rare categories.

Next, we consider the correlation between performance of FCFS and ExFCFS. ExFCFS is actually an extended version of FCFS for radically overcoming the imbalance of classification performance between categories after filter feature selection process. As analyzed in this paper, this problem is directly caused by the imbalance of the number of training documents between categories and the imbalance of the separation degree between categories. Therefore, in ExFCFS, we adjust FCFS score of a term with respect to a category in inverse proportion to these factors in order to improve the classification performance of rare categories and poor separation categories after filter feature selection process. Especially, both of these two factors are occurred in Reuters-21578 datset and Ohsumed dataset. Under these properties of two experimental datasets, the performance of ExFCFS is superior to that of FCFS. This accounts for the effectiveness of our adjustments in ExFCFS formula.

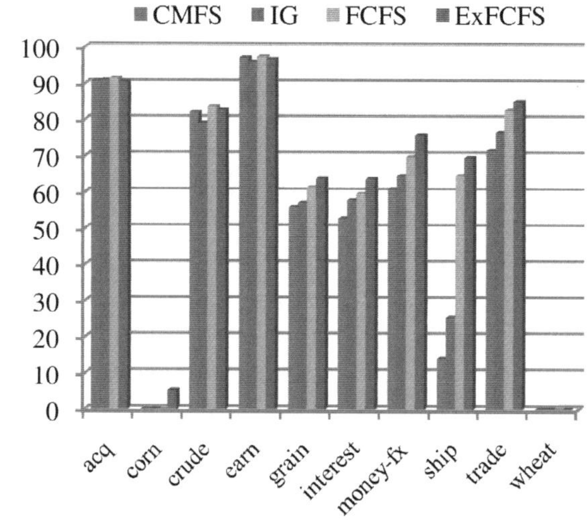

Fig. 1: F1-measure of CMFS, IG, FCFS, and ExFCFS on Reuter dataset at 60 features

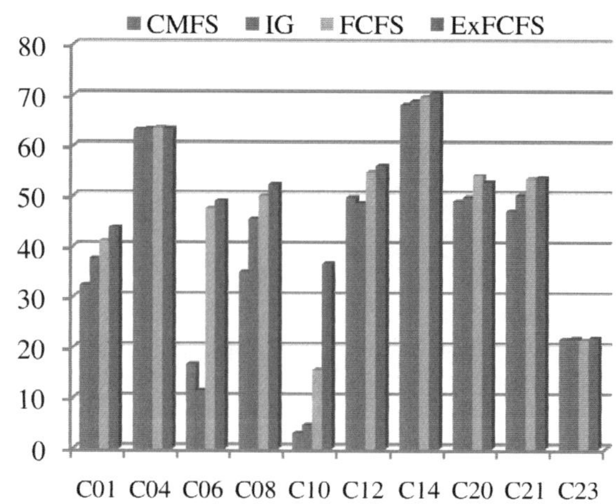

Fig. 2: F1-measure of CMFS, IG, FCFS, and ExFCFS on Ohsumed dataset at 60 features

Table 9 shows the performance of dissimilar terms and similar terms selected by filter FS methods. For the comparison between two FS methods, similar terms are terms selected by both of them, while dissimilar terms are terms selected by only one of them. Clearly, dissimilar terms are the most important for considering two FS methods. The result listed in Table 9 shows that at top-60 selected terms, dissimilar terms of FCFS are superior to those of CHI, IG, CMFS, and OCFS but is inferior to those of ExFCFS. This is one of strong evidences for the superiority of ExFCFS and FCFS over the other methods.

Regarding dimension reduction rate, due to the best Micro-F1 and Macro-F1 results of ExFCFS, it produces better dimension reduction rate than the other methods in all two datasets as shown in Fig. 3-4. FCFS is superior to CHI, IG, CMFS and OCFS at the small number of selected features and they show the competition at the larger number of features. However, based on dimension reduction rate formula presented in Eq. (10), FS methods having better performance at smaller number of selected features are preferred. Therefore, dimension reduction rate of FCFS is better than that of CHI, IG, CMFS, and OCFS as presented in Fig. 3-4.

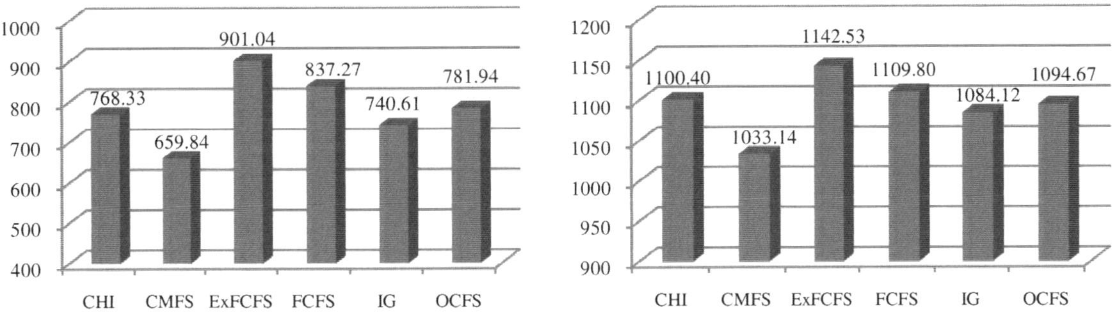

(a) (b)

Fig. 3. Dimension Reduction Rate on Reuters-21578 dataset: (a) for Macro-F1; (b) for Micro-F1

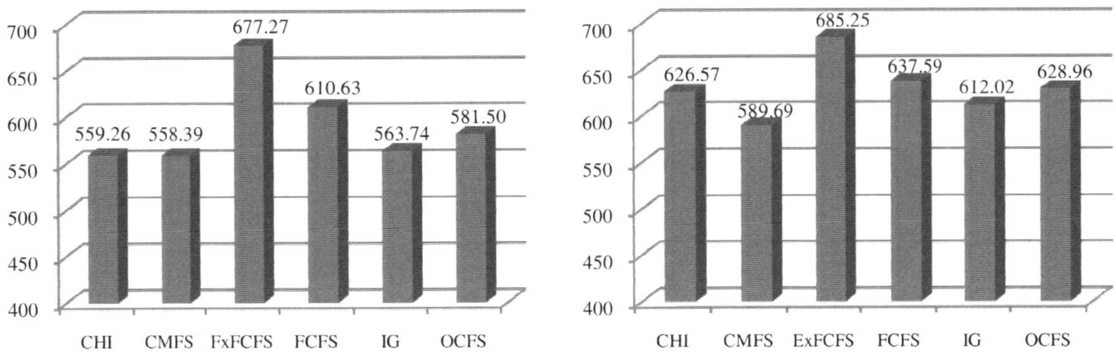

(a) (b)

Fig. 4. Dimension Reduction Rate on Ohsumed dataset: (a) for Macro-F1; (b) for Micro-F1

FS	20	60	100	200	400	600	800	1000	1200	1400	1600	1800	2000
CHI	48.88	58.12	62.21	64.91	64.22	65.03	66.24	67.97	65.95	66.53	67.32	66.91	66.67
CMFS	35.82	55.83	61.3	63.44	64.56	65.92	67.53	66.01	65.85	67.78	67.53	66.43	66.46
ExFCFS	**58.89**	**67.08**	**73.83**	**72.57**	**73.35**	**70.72**	**71.53**	**71.15**	**71.75**	**71.64**	**71.86**	**71.67**	**71.18**
FCFS	**53.55**	**62.00**	**70.12**	**71.75**	**71.85**	**67.74**	**68.9**	**68.58**	**68.24**	**70.62**	**69.8**	**69.52**	**69.37**
IG	45.45	58.56	61.23	63.99	64.18	64.6	65.48	66.7	67.39	66.8	67.3	67.39	66.36
OCFS	49.66	60.00	63.02	64.43	67.36	66.65	66.97	67.13	67.86	67.18	66.95	66.88	66.87

Table 5: Macro-F1 result on Reuters-21578 dataset. Bold numbers are the top 2 performances

FS	20	60	100	200	400	600	800	1000	1200	1400	1600	1800	2000
CHI	72.95	81.93	86.13	86.73	87.14	87.51	88.05	**88.23**	87.73	87.69	87.76	87.55	87.48
CMFS	65.14	80.45	84.79	85.8	85.91	86.16	88.2	88.05	87.94	**88.27**	**88.05**	87.59	**87.69**
ExFCFS	**76.48**	**85.74**	**87.15**	**88.23**	**89.23**	**89.94**	**89.05**	**88.94**	**89.20**	**89.05**	**89.23**	**89.09**	**88.76**
FCFS	**73.12**	**84.1**	**87.06**	**87.82**	87.82	87.97	88.07	88.11	87.11	87.23	87	**87.89**	87.61
IG	70.88	81.98	85.89	86.41	87.09	87.87	88.02	87.94	87.98	87.66	87.69	87.8	87.33
OCFS	71.36	83.89	86.11	87.73	**88.30**	**88.05**	**88.23**	88.16	**88.2**	87.94	87.73	87.48	87.51

Table 6: Micro-F1 result on Reuters-21578 dataset. Bold numbers are the top 2 performances

FS	20	60	100	200	400	600	800	1000	1200	1400	1600	1800	2000
CHI	32.59	44.59	49.83	50.71	53.52	54.32	53.82	52.96	52.34	51.59	51.08	50.98	50.37
CMFS	33.72	43.08	47.4	49.69	51.76	51.96	52.65	52.44	52.74	52.5	52.27	51.91	51.66
ExFCFS	**43.93**	**51.66**	**53.33**	**54.33**	**56.40**	**56.75**	**56.15**	**56.51**	**55.97**	**55.02**	**54.79**	**54.36**	**54.29**
FCFS	**37.26**	**49.21**	**50.82**	**51.8**	**54.07**	**54.49**	54.2	**54.13**	53.47	53.28	**52.78**	**52.37**	52.23
IG	33.07	45.34	48.8	51.28	53.43	54.44	53.82	52.98	52.34	51.6	51.1	50.98	50.36
OCFS	34.53	46.68	49.8	51.88	53.77	54.2	**54.54**	54.03	**53.59**	**53.46**	52.65	52.02	**52.3**

Table 7: Macro-F1 result on Ohsumed dataset. Bold numbers are the top 2 performances

FS	20	60	100	200	400	600	800	1000	1200	1400	1600	1800	2000
CHI	39.69	**48.8**	**50.71**	**51.8**	52.88	**54.04**	53.43	52.79	52.44	51.94	51.37	51.45	50.88
CMFS	38.23	43.91	44.9	48.01	50.68	51.56	51.63	52.69	53.15	53.04	52.94	52.57	52.39
ExFCFS	**45.22**	**51.60**	**52.97**	**53.06**	**55.54**	**56.22**	**55.96**	**56.67**	**56.09**	**55.43**	**55.37**	**55.21**	**54.99**
FCFS	**41.35**	47.97	50.51	50.97	**53.2**	53.85	53.87	**54.24**	53.75	**54.76**	53.35	**53.19**	**52.9**
IG	39.79	44.31	48.78	50.65	52.99	**54.15**	53.42	52.81	52.43	51.93	51.39	51.45	50.87
OCFS	40.66	47.24	49.83	50.61	53.02	53.63	**54.39**	54.12	**53.97**	54.08	**53.4**	52.96	52.34

Table 8: Micro-F1 result on Ohsumed dataset. Bold numbers are the top 2 performances

DataSet	Measure	Type	CHI	CMFS	IG	OCFS	ExFCFS	Measure	Type	CHI	CMFS	IG	OCFS	ExFCFS
Reuters	Micro-F1	A	54.64	58.08	52.90	51.31	65.21	Macro-F1	A	31.42	18.92	30.57	18.60	32.47
		B	56.30	63.94	60.28	51.67	62.42		B	32.51	49.62	40.77	38.61	24.18
		C	80.98	78.70	80.93	82.96	83.07		C	57.31	55.27	58.01	59.31	60.51
Ohsumed	Micro-F1	A	19.62	16.69	14.42	10.92	23.93	Macro-F1	A	16.89	11.68	19.72	12.04	22.15
		B	12.26	20.15	19.90	12.98	17.58		B	20.78	23.54	21.37	15.99	18.82
		C	48.70	47.61	45.00	47.05	47.31		C	44.38	44.59	45.77	46.50	47.03

Table 9: Micro-F1 and Macro-F1result of similar terms and dissimilar terms selected by FCFS and the other FS methods at top-60 selected terms. A, B, and C indicate dissimilar terms of the corresponding FS, dissimilar terms of FCFS, and their similar terms respectively.

4 Conclusion

This paper propose a comprehensive filter FS method, named ExFCFS, for computing feature score and overcoming the imbalance of FS performance between categories. In ExFCFS, the feature score with respect to a specific category is the combination of the cluster-based inter-category condition and the frequency–based intra-category condition to exploit the strong point of two related approaches. Then, we adjust this combination in inverse proportion to the number of training document of the category and the separation degree of the category. The experimental results show the effectiveness of our solutions in terms of both Micro-F1 measure and Macro-F1 measure.

References

Aggarwal, C. C., & Zhai, C. (2012). A survey of text classification algorithms. In Mining text data (pp. 163-222). Springer US.

Asuncion, A., & Newman, D. (2007). UCI machine learning repository.

Bermejo, P., Gámez, J. A., & Puerta, J. M. (2014). Speeding up incremental wrapper feature subset selection with Naive Bayes classifier. Knowledge-Based Systems, 55, 140-147.

Bellman, R., (1961). Adaptive control processes: a guided tour (Vol. 4). Princeton: Princeton university press.

Chakraborti, S., Mukras, R., Lothian, R., Wiratunga, N., Watt, S. N., & Harper, D. J. (2007, January). Supervised Latent Semantic Indexing Using Adaptive Sprinkling. In IJCAI (pp. 1582-1587).

Friedman, J., Hastie, T., & Tibshirani, R. (2001). The elements of statistical learning (Vol. 1). Springer, Berlin: Springer series in statistics

Fragoudis, D., Meretakis, D., & Likothanassis, S. (2005). Best terms: an efficient feature-selection algorithm for text categorization. Knowledge and Information Systems, 8(1), 16-33.

Gomez, J. C., & Moens, M. F. (2012). PCA document reconstruction for email classification. Computational Statistics & Data Analysis, 56(3), 741-751.

Gunal, S., & Edizkan, R. (2008). Subspace based feature selection for pattern recognition. Information Sciences, 178(19), 3716-3726.

Hall, M., Frank, E., Holmes, G., Pfahringer, B., Reutemann, P., & Witten, I. H. (2009). The WEKA data mining software: an update. ACM SIGKDD explorations newsletter, 11(1), 10-18.

Howland, P., & Park, H. (2004). Generalizing discriminant analysis using the generalized singular value decomposition. Pattern Analysis and Machine Intelligence, IEEE Transactions on, 26(8), 995-1006.

Joachims, T. (1996). A Probabilistic Analysis of the Rocchio Algorithm with TFIDF for Text Categorization (No. CMU-CS-96-118).

Joachims, T. (1998). Text categorization with support vector machines: Learning with many relevant features (pp. 137-142). Springer Berlin Heidelberg.

Liu, H., & Motoda, H. (Eds.). (1998). Feature extraction, construction and selection: A data mining perspective. Springer Science & Business Media.

Platt, J. (1999). Fast training of support vector machines using sequential minimal optimization. Advances in kernel methods—support vector learning, 3.

Porter, M. F. (1980). An algorithm for suffix stripping. Program, 14(3), 130-137.

Quinlan, J. R. (1986). Induction of decision trees. Machine learning, 1(1), 81-106.

Sebastiani, F. (2002). Machine learning in automated text categorization. ACM computing surveys, 34(1), 1-47.

Taşcı, Ş., & Güngör, T. (2013). Comparison of text feature selection policies and using an adaptive framework. Expert Systems with Applications, 40(12), 4871-4886.

Yan, J., Liu, N., Cheng, Q., ... & Ma, W. Y. (2005, August). OCFS: optimal orthogonal centroid feature selection for text categorization. In Proceedings of the 28th annual international ACM SIGIR conference on Research and development in information retrieval (pp. 122-129). ACM.

Yang, J., Liu, Y., Zhu, X., Liu, Z., & Zhang, X. (2012). A new feature selection based on comprehensive measurement both in inter-category and intra-category for text categorization. Information Processing & Management, 48(4), 741-754.

Yang, J., Liu, Z., Qu, Z., & Wang, J. (2014, June). Feature selection method based on crossed centroid for text categorization. In Software Engineering, Artificial Intelligence, Networking and Parallel/Distributed Computing (SNPD), 2014 15th IEEE/ACIS International Conference on (pp. 1-5). IEEE.

Yang, Y., & Pedersen, J. O. (1997, July). A comparative study on feature selection in text categorization. In ICML (Vol. 97, pp. 412-420)

Sentiment Analyzer with Rich Features for Ironic and Sarcastic Tweets

Piyoros Tungthamthiti[1], **Enrico Santus**[2], **Hongzhi Xu**[2], **Chu-Ren Huang**[2], **and Kiyoaki Shirai**[1]

[1]Japan Advanced Institute of Science and Technology
1-1, Asahidai, Nomi City, Ishikawa, Japan 923-1292
{s1320204,kshirai}@jaist.ac.jp

[2]Dept. of Chinese and Bilingual Studies
The Hong Kong Polytechnic University, Hong Kong
{e.santus,hongzhi.xu}@connect.polyu.hk
{churen.huang}@polyu.edu.hk

Abstract

Sentiment Analysis of tweets is a complex task, because these short messages employ unconventional language to increase the expressiveness. This task becomes even more difficult when people use figurative language (e.g. irony, sarcasm and metaphors) because it causes a mismatch between the literal meaning and the actual expressed sentiment. In this paper, we describe a sentiment analysis system designed for handling ironic and sarcastic tweets. Features grounded on several linguistic levels are proposed and used to classify the tweets in a 11-scale range, using a decision tree. The system is evaluated on the dataset released by the organizers of the SemEval 2015, task 11. The results show that our method largely outperforms the systems proposed by the participants of the task on ironic and sarcastic tweets.

1 Introduction

Whenever a message is encoded into linguistic form for being communicated – either in a spoken or written text[1] – information revealing judgments, evaluations, attitudes and emotions is also encoded (Martin and White, 2005). This is true for both informal and formal texts, independently of how much attention the writer pays in cleaning such information out. This is also true for texts posted on social networks (i.e. Facebook, Twitter, etc.), where judgments, evaluations, attitudes and emotions constitute an important part of the message (Pak and Paroubek, 2010).

Sentiment analysis (also known as opinion mining and subjectivity analysis) is a Natural Language Processing (NLP) task that focuses on identification of such judgments, evaluations, attitudes and emotions. It can be compared to other classification tasks, as it consists in associating the analyzed texts with a label that represents the sentiment of the message or the affective state of the writer (Hart, 2013).

In its earliest incarnations, sentiment analysis was limited to the identification of the polarity of the texts, and the classification label was either positive or negative. Later on, the task was extended to address more challenging and complex goals, such as the identification of the sentiment of the messages or the writer's affective state in a more fine scale, with labels including anger, happiness or depression.

Such extension could not avoid considering one of the most pervasive tools used in communication, namely figurative language. In fact, this expressive tool is not only very frequent in various kinds of texts, but it also strongly affects the sentiment expressed in the text, often completely reversing its polarity (Xu et al., 2015; Ghosh et al., 2015).

Because figurative language is used in unpredictable ways in communication (i.e. either in crystallized forms or in creative ways) and it can involve several linguistic and extra-linguistic levels (i.e. from syntax to concepts and pragmatics), its identification and understanding is often difficult, even for human beings. If humans are able to rely on prosody (e.g. stress or intonation), kinesis (e.g. facial gestures), co-text (i.e. immediate textual environment) and context (i.e. wider environment), as well as cultural background, machines cannot access the same type of information. These difficulties pose a major challenge in sentiment analysis.

Currently, a large number of studies have been devoting to the problem. Most of them focus on microblogging, especially Twitter, because i) social networks are rich of spontaneous public messages written by several users in different styles; ii)

[1]In this paper we will mainly refer to written texts, but most of what is said is also applicable to spoken ones.

29th Pacific Asia Conference on Language, Information and Computation pages 178 - 187
Shanghai, China, October 30 - November 1, 2015

tweets are short (i.e. a tweet can contain maximum 140 characters) and containing a lot of unconventional textual elements (e.g. emoticons, abbreviations, slang, emphasized capitalization and punctuation, etc.), which pose another interesting challenge; iii) social networks provide a precise picture of peoples' sentiments about a topic or product in a specific moment. This third point, in particular, is relevant for companies, political parties and other public entities in order to adapt and improve their marketing strategies and decisions (Medhat et al., 2014; Pang and Lee, 2008).

In this paper, we introduce a sentiment analysis system created with a particular focus on the identification and proper elaboration of irony and sarcasm in tweets. The system is developed by combining and improving two previous algorithms (Tungthamthiti et al., 2014; Xu et al., 2015). In particular, we propose a new method for coherence identification across sentences, some additional features indicating the strong emotion of the Twitter user, and several features of punctuations & special symbols that contribute to the final sentiment score.

2 Related work

Figurative language has been studied since the ancient Greece and Rome. It was, in fact, a part of the basic rhetorical background that every politician, lawyer and military officer should have had, in order to be able to persuade and convince his/her audience. Already in the first century CE, Quintilian (1953) defined irony as "saying the opposite of what you mean". This rhetorical figure violates the expectations of the listener, flouting the maxim of quality (Stringfellow, 1994; Grice, 1975). In a similar way, sarcasm is generally understood as the use of irony to mock or convey contempt (Stevenson, 2010). According to Haiman (1998), the main difference between sarcasm and irony is that sarcasm requires the presence of the intention to mocks. Irony, instead, can exist independently (e.g. there are ironic situations, but not sarcastic ones).

Although irony and sarcasm are well studied in linguistics and psychology, algorithms for their recognition and proper processing in sentiment analysis and other NLP tasks are still novel and far from perfect (Pang and Lee, 2008). In the last several years, however, such studies have attracted a lot of attention due to the availability of data. The simple use of hashtags on Twitter (e.g. #irony, #sarcasm or #not) allows the immediate collection of thousands of tweets. For example, 40,000 tweets were easily collected in four categories (i.e. irony, education, humour and politics) by Reyes et al. (2013).

Among the several approaches to irony and sarcasm in NLP, Carvalho et al. (2009) investigate the accuracy of a set of surface patterns (i.e. emoticons, onomatopoeic expressions for laughter, heavy punctuation marks, quotation marks and positive interjections) in comments at newspaper's articles. They show that surface patterns are much more accurate (from 45% to 85%) than deeper linguistic information.

Hao and Veale (2010) propose a nine steps algorithm to automatically distinguish ironic similes from non-ironic ones, without relying of any sentiment dictionary.

Tsur et al. (2010) propose a semi-supervised method for the automatic recognition of sarcasm in Amazon product reviews. Their method, which was compared to a strong heuristic baseline built by exploiting the star rating meta-data provided by Amazon (i.e. strongly positive reviews associated to low star rates were considered sarcastic), exploited syntactic and pattern-based features. A similar method, achieving high precision, was then applied to tweets (Davidov et al., 2010).

In Reyes and Rosso (2012), verbal irony is represented in terms of six kinds of features: n-grams, POS-grams, funny profiling, positive/negative profiling, affective profiling, and pleasantness profiling. They use Naive Bayesian, Support Vector Machine and Decision Tree classifiers, achieving an acceptable level of accuracy. Moreover, they built a freely available data set with ironic reviews from news articles, satiric articles and customer reviews, collected from Amazon.

More recently, a new complex model for identifying sarcasm was defined to extend the method far beyond the surface of the text and took into account features on four levels: signatures, degree of unexpectedness, style, and emotional scenarios (Reyes et al., 2013). They demonstrate that these features do not help the identification of irony and sarcasm in isolation. However, they do when they are combined in a complex framework.

Barbieri and Saggion (2014) use several lexical and semantic features, such as frequency of the words in reference corpora, their intensity, their written/spoken nature, their length and the number of related synsets in WordNet (Miller, 1995).

Buschmeier et al. (2014) provided an important baseline for irony detection in English by assessing the impact of features used in previous studies and evaluating them with several classifiers. They reach an F1-measure of up to 74% using logistic regression.

Finally, in the very recent Task 11 of SemEval 2015 (Ghosh et al., 2015), fifteen participants proposed systems to address the sentiment analysis of tweets employing figurative language (i.e. irony, sarcasm and metaphor). Those systems mainly relied on supervised learning methods (i.e. Support Vector Machines (SVMs) and regression models over carefully engineered features). The best of them for ironic and sarcastic tweets achieved respectively a precision of 0.918 (Xu et al., 2015) and 0.904 (Gimenez et al., 2015) on a test set containing 4,000 tweets.

3 Methodology

Our method is divided into two main modules as shown in Figure 1. Each module generates various kinds of features, which will be used to classify the ironic and sarcastic tweets on an 11 points scale ranging from -5 to +5. The regression tree algorithm RepTree (Thaseen and Kumar, 2013) implemented in Weka (Hall et al., 2009) is used for training and predicting the sentiment intensity of figurative data.

3.1 Data pre-processing

Before extracting the features, the tweets were preprocessed using the Stanford Lemmatizer[2] in order to transform the words in the tweets into lemmas. Then, a set of heuristic rules was created to handle the unregulated and arbitrary nature of the texts that cannot be recognized by the Stanford Lemmatizer. Words in tweets may contain repeated vowels (e.g. "loooove") or unexpected capitalization (e.g. "LOVE") to emphasize certain sentiments or emoticons. Thus, the repeated vowels are removed (e.g. from "loooove" to "love") and the capitalization is normalized (e.g. from "LOVE" to "love") to improve the lemmatization and parsing accuracy. The emphasized words are saved in a special feature bag as they are important indicators of sentiments, especially when they are in sentiment lexicons. The heavy punctuation is also handled. The use of combination of exclamation and question marks (e.g. "?!?!!") will be replaced with only a single mark (e.g. "?!"). Another step we also consider is the segmentation of the words. The segmentation is, in fact, often lost in tweets (e.g. "yeahright"). Therefore, the maximal matching algorithm is applied to segment the words (e.g. "yeah right"). In addition, all usernames, URLs and hashtags are removed from tweets as they do not provide any information about the sentiments and they might become noise for the classification process. Finally, the Stanford parser[3] was used to generate the POS tags and dependency structures of the normalized tweets.

3.2 Module 1

The overview of the module 1 is shown in Figure 1. It is based on the algorithm presented in SemEval 2015 task 11 (Xu et al., 2015). In the feature extraction sub-module, eight kinds of features are extracted.

- Token based features:
  - The "UniToken" refers to uni-grams of tokens.
  - The "BiToken" refers to bi-grams of tokens.
  - The "DepTokenPair" refers to "parent-child" pairs in the dependency structures of the tweets.
  - The "additional features" refers to the emphatic features capturing four ways twitter users express their emotions: *duplicate_vowel* ("loooove"), *capitalized* ("LOVE"), *heavy_punctuation* ("?!?!?"), and *emoticon* (":-D").
- Polarity dictionary based features:
  - The "PolarityWin" stores the sum of the polarity values of all the tokens in a tweet. A window size of five is used to verify whether negations are present. If a negation is present, the resulting value is set to zero. Besides, the sum of the polarity values of the tokens of the same POS tags are also stored in a different dimension. This is to measure the contributions on polarity values by different POS tags.
  - The "PolarityDep" is similar to "PolarityWin", but it differs in that the negation is checked based on the dependency structure.
  - The "PolarShiftWin" measures the difference between the most positive item and the most negative item in a window of size 5.
  - The "PolarShiftDep" measures the polarity difference of "parent-child" pairs in the dependency structures of the tweets.

Four sentiment dictionaries were used: Opinion Lexicon (Hu and Liu, 2004), Afinn (Nielsen, 2011), MPQA (Wiebe et al., 2005), and SentiWordnet (Baccianella et al., 2010). The union and intersection of the four dictionaries are also used as two additional dictionaries. Formally, the polarity feature can be represented as a (*key, val*) pair, where the key is <*pos, dict*>, or <*dict*>. For example, (<*adj, mpqa*>, 1.0) means that according to the dictionary MPQA, adjectives contribute to the polarity value

[2] http://nlp.stanford.edu/software/corenlp.shtml

[3] http://nlp.stanford.edu/software/lex-parser.shtml

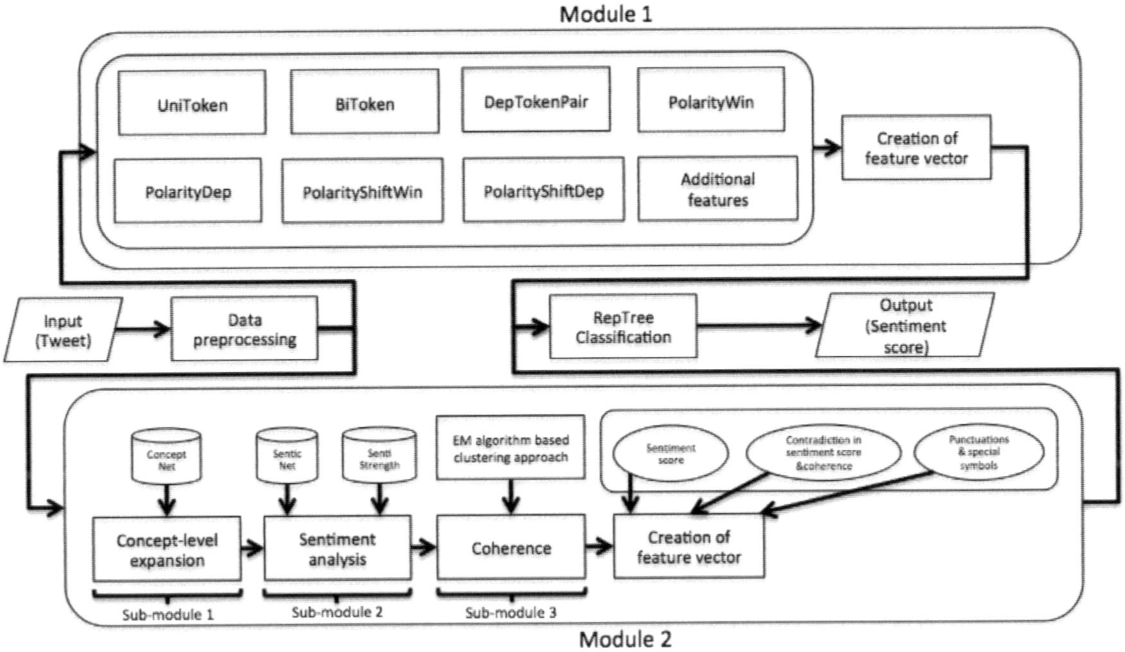

Figure 1: Flowchart of overall process of our method

for 1.0. Finally, features that occur less than three times are excluded.

In feature normalization, all the feature values are normalized within [-1, 1] based on Equation 1, where $f_{i,j}$ is the value of feature j in the ith example, and N is the sample size.

$$norm(f_{i,j}) = \frac{f_{i,j}}{\max\limits_{1 \leq k \leq N} |f_{k,j}|} \quad (1)$$

We perform feature selection through the correlative coefficient measure (Pearson's r score). A threshold value of r is used to rule out less important features. In the experiment, the correlative coefficient threshold is set to $r = 0.035$.

3.3 Module 2

The second module, described in Figure 1, relies on features that were proven to be effective in Tungthamthiti et al. (2014). These features include sentiment polarity score, coherence and punctuation features. Their identification and usage have been improved to become more suitable for the sentiment prediction rather than the sarcasm identification task. Note that weights of all features in the module 2 are binary.

3.3.1 Sentiment analysis

In this subpart of module 2, we create features that rely on sentiment analysis as well as the semantic analysis of tweets using concepts and commonsense knowledge.

The algorithm consists of two main steps. In the first subpart, ConceptNet[4] is used to expand the concepts for the words whose sentiment score are unknown in the SentiStrength lexicon (Cambria et al., 2010). The expanded concepts provide effective information that would benefit the task of sentiment analysis. In the second subpart of module 2, the sentiment polarity scores are calculated for each word and its expanded concepts within a tweet. Then, we create seven features. Six of them are created as an indicator of positive and negative phrases according to three possible classes (*low*, *medium* and *high*). In addition, sarcasm can be recognized as a contrast between a positive sentiment referring to a negative situation (Ellen et al., 2013). Thus, another feature is created as a contradiction in sentiment score feature. This feature is activated when there exists both a positive and a negative polarity word within a tweet.

[4] http://conceptnet5.media.mit.edu

3.3.2 Coherence identification

A new method for coherence identification is proposed. As explained earlier, the contradiction of the polarity in a tweet is a useful clue. However, if positive and negative sentences mention different topics (i.e. they are incoherent), conflict of the polarity may not indicate the sarcasm or irony. Therefore, the module 2 identifies coherence in a tweet and uses it as a feature.

There are several studies related to coherence identification. A set of heuristic rules based on grammatical relations was proposed to identify coherence in tweets (Tungthamthiti et al., 2014). A more complex method, based on machine learning, was presented by Soon et al. (2001) to link coreferring noun phrases both within and across sentences. However, such method would not be appropriate for our scope, because it focuses specifically on coreference resolution, rather than identifying the coherence relationship. Nevertheless, it provides some useful insights, which can be exploited in our method.

The proposed method is based on unsupervised learning approach. Below, eleven features are created for the clustering task, in order to divide the tweets into coherence and non-coherence class. Let us suppose that sentence s_1 precedes s_2, and word w_1 and w_2 are the subject, noun or pronoun of s_1 and s_2, respectively.

1. Pronoun feature 1 – w_1 includes reflexive pronouns, personal pronouns or possessive pronouns.
2. Pronoun feature 2 – w_2 includes reflexive pronouns, personal pronouns or possessive pronouns.
3. String match feature – w_1 and w_2 are identical.
4. Definite noun phrase feature – w_2 starts with the word "the".
5. Demonstrative noun phrase feature – w_2 starts with the "this", "that", "these" and "those".
6. Both proper names feature – w_1 and w_2 are both the name entities. Two or more sentences contain proper names recognized by the Stanford Named Entity Recognizer (NER)[5].
7. Coreference resolution – two or more sentences contain coreference resolution property recognized by Stanford Deterministic Coreference Resolution System[6].
8. Semantic class agreement feature – w_1 and w_2 are semantically similar. In order to identify the word similarity, the method consists of three steps:
   - First, we create lists of synsets for both w_1 and w_2. SenseLearner 2.0[7] is used to disambiguate the meaning of the words, which allows only the suitable synsets of w_1 and w_2 to make similarity comparison.
   - Then, all possible combinations of synsets that belong to each w_1 and w_2 are compared to evaluate the similarity between them. A method proposed by Resnik (1995) is used to define the similarity between two synsets based on the information content of their lowest super-ordinate (most specific common subsumer).
   - The feature is activated when the similarity of one of synset pairs is greater than a threshold. It is set to 1.37 by our intuition.
9. Number agreement feature – w_1 and w_2 agree in number (i.e., they are both singular or plural)
10. Acronyms and abbreviation – A tweet contains an acronym or abbreviation (i.e., "lol", "ynwa").
11. Emoticons – A tweet contains an emoticon (i.e., ":-)", "☺").

After conducting a preliminary experiment, we found that the EM (expectation maximization) algorithm outperforms other approaches, including hierarchical, k-mean and DBScan, in the identification of coherence in tweets. Therefore, EM algorithm is used to cluster the tweets into two groups, one for coherent and one for non-coherent tweets. Then, a cluster label is used as the feature.

3.3.3 Punctuations and special symbols

In addition, features for punctuations and special symbols are also included in our research. The following 7 indicators are considered to determine the weights for punctuation features: number of emoticons, number of repetitive sequence of punctuations, number of repetitive sequence of characters, number of capitalized words, number of slang and booster words, number of exclamation marks and number of idioms. We use *low*, *medium* and *high* as possible scores to describe the frequency of punctuations and symbols in a tweet. These features amount to $7 \times 3 = 21$.

4 Experiment

In this section, we describe how the experiments were conducted to evaluate the performance of our method.

[5] http://nlp.stanford.edu/ner/

[6] http://nlp.stanford.edu/projects/coref.shtml

[7] http://web.eecs.umich.edu/~mihalcea/downloads.html#senselearner

4.1 Data

In our experiment, we used the training and test data distributed for SemEval-2015 Task 11 on "Sentiment Analysis of Figurative Language in Twitter"[8]. The data set consists of tweets containing sarcasm, irony, metaphor and non-figurative tweets. The training set contains 7,952 tweets, while the test set contains 4,000 tweets. All tweets are manually annotated with a fine-grained sentiment scale value in 11 points (between -5 to +5).

4.2 Task

The task is to estimate a degree of fine-grained sentiment score for each tweet in the dataset. There are two subtasks. One is to predict the sentiment score by 5-fold cross validation on the training set (reported in Subsection 5.1). In this task, the effectiveness of individual features is mainly investigated. The other is to predict the sentiment intensity of the test set using the model learned from the training data (reported in Subsection 5.2). The performance of the proposed method is analyzed considering several types of tweets (sarcastic, ironic, metaphorical and non-figurative ones).

4.3 Baselines

In this study, two baselines are created. One was developed as a naive prediction using the average polarity value of the training data, while the other one uses supervised machine learning (RepTree) with UniToken (uni-gram) features to train classifier for sentiment classification.

4.4 Evaluation measures

Cosine similarity and root mean squared error (RMSE) are used as the evaluation criteria of sentiment intensity estimation. They illustrate how similar the predicted values and the actual annotated values are. They can be calculated by using equation 2 and 3, respectively.

$$Cosine[a,b] = \frac{\sum_{i=1}^{n} a_i \times b_i}{\sqrt{\sum_{i=1}^{n}(a_i)^2} \times \sqrt{\sum_{i=1}^{n}(b_i)^2}} \quad (2)$$

$$RMSE = \sqrt{\frac{1}{n}\sum_{i=1}^{n}(a-b)^2} \quad (3)$$

- i refers to the value of tweet index.
- n refers to the number of tweets.
- a refers to the human-annotated sentiment score of tweet i.
- b refers to the predicted sentiment score of tweet i by our system.

[8]http://alt.qcri.org/semeval2015/task11/

5 Results and discussion

5.1 Results on the training data

Table 1: Results of the module 1 of 5-fold cross validation on the training data

Method	Cosine	RMSE
Avg. polarity (Baseline1)	0.818	1.985
UniToken (Baseline 2)	0.851	1.682
UniToken		
+BiToken	0.849	1.700
+DepTokenPair	0.851	1.673
+PolarityWin	0.852	1.657
+PolarityDep	0.854	1.643
+PolarityShiftWin	0.854	1.640
+PolarityShiftDep	0.854	1.640

Table 1 shows the results of the two baselines and those of module 1, trained with UniToken and one additional feature on the training data. Surprisingly, the average polarity value (baseline 1) and the classification based on UniToken features (baseline 2) were powerful predictor of the sentiment. Both methods achieved relatively high cosine values (i.e. 0.818 and 0.851, respectively). In particular, it is interesting to notice that baseline 1 can achieve such results because the majority of the tweets are annotated with moderate negative values, varying from -2 to -3. Accordingly, the average polarity value of words computed by our baseline system also indicates the moderate negative range. Thus, baseline 1 achieved a high accuracy and also became competitive with other methods.

BiToken and DepTokenPair. As can be seen, the result shows that all features have taken part in the method to enhance the accuracy, except for BiToken. Thus, we can easily conclude that BiToken is not a relevant feature for sentiment prediction of figurative tweets.

PolarityWin and PolarityDep features. The features contributed some improvements to the overall result. The reason is that these features handle the negations, which often occurs within the figurative tweets.

PolarityShiftWin and PolarityShiftDep features. The result also indicates that PolarityShiftWin and

PolarityShiftDep features contributed to some improvement towards the overall result. The difference between the most positive and negative items can represent the strength of the overall polarity and also indicate if there exists a conflict in a tweet, which may reveal either irony or sarcasm. As a result, we can conclude that the shift in polarity value has an impact on the sentiment prediction for figurative tweets.

Table 2: Results of the module 2 of 5-fold cross validation on the training data

Method	Cosine	RMSE
All features (module 2)	0.825	1.376
– Sentiment contradiction	0.821	1.384
– Sentiment score	0.803	1.511
– Punctuations + symbols	0.820	1.402
– Coherence	0.817	1.425
– Concept level knowledge	0.781	1.658

Table 2 shows the overall result of the module 2 and also how the results change as the features are removed. Cosine value and RMSE of the module 2 were 0.825 and 1.376, which were better than baseline 1 but worse than baseline 2.

Punctuations and special symbols. The feature contributed to some improvement to the overall method. The cosine value is reduced by 0.005 (from 0.825 to 0.803) when the feature is removed. Figurative tweets often contain emoticons and heavy punctuation marks to simulate the gestural signs, onomatopoeic expressions and also boosting the intensity of emotion. Therefore, the feature can be used to capture this particular characteristic.

The concept-level knowledge. Expansion of the concepts implemented in the first subpart can also enhance the performance of the sentiment score. Tweets are considered as unstructured and context free data. There are many words and slangs, which cannot be compiled in any dictionaries. Concept-level and common-sense knowledge are applied to compensate to such lack with related concepts, which allows the system to compute the sentiment score more accurately.

Coherence identification. In our experiment, it is clearly shown that coherence feature has an impact on the improvement of the result. This is a proof that it is necessary to verify whether there are terms referring to each other across the sentences, in order to make the contradiction identification more effective.

Table 3: Results of the integrated system of 5-fold cross validation on the training data

Method	Cosine	RMSE
Module 1	0.859	1.256
Module 2	0.825	1.376
Integrated module 1 & 2	0.882	1.154

Table 3 shows the results comparison of the module 1, module 2 and integration of them. The results show that the integration of the module 1 and 2 performs significantly better than the baseline 2 that uses uni-gram feature. It is also clearly shown that the cosine value of the integrated system outperforms each module 1 and 2 by 0.023 and 0.057, respectively.

5.2 Results on the test data

Table 4: Results of the module 1 on the test dataset

Category	Cosine	RMSE
Sarcasm	0.896	0.997
Irony	0.918	0.671
Metaphor	0.535	3.917
Non-figurative	0.290	4.617
Overall	0.687	2.602

Table 5: Results of the module 2 on the test dataset

Category	Cosine	RMSE
Sarcasm	0.948	0.732
Irony	0.912	0.851
Metaphor	0.389	4.165
Non-figurative	0.207	4.682
Overall	0.542	2.030

Table 4 shows the results of sentiment prediction of the module 1 on the test data. The performance is effective on sarcastic and ironic data, since the module 1 achieved the cosine value of 0.896 and 0.918, respectively. However, the performance is rather poor when we attempted to predict the sentiment score for metaphor and non-figurative tweets. In Table 5, the results of the module 2 seem to be very competitive to the module 1 in all categories. The cosine value was higher for sarcasm tweets and comparable for irony tweets. The major differences in the module 1 and 2 are the use of the concept expansion and coherence feature. They seem especially work well for guessing the sentiment score of the sarcasm tweets.

Table 6: Results of the integrated system on the test dataset

Category	Cosine	RMSE
Sarcasm	0.953	0.718
Irony	0.921	0.821
Metaphor	0.561	3.899
Non-figurative	0.297	4.520
Overall	0.736	1.382

Table 6 shows the results of the integrated system, clearly indicating that the overall result of the proposed method is much better than both the module 1 and 2. Thus, it is obvious that the feature sets of both modules complement each other when they are integrated into a single method. Table 7 shows the comparison of the cosine measure among our system and the five top systems participated in SemEval 2015 Task 11. Note that our system largely outperformed all the other 15 participating systems on the ironic and sarcastic tweets, although achieved second in the overall dataset.

Table 7: Comparison of the our result against five top peer systems participated in SemEval 2015 Task 11

System	All	S	I	M	N
ClaC	**0.758**	0.892	0.904	**0.655**	**0.584**
UPF	0.711	0.903	0.873	0.520	0.486
LLT_PolyU	0.687	0.896	0.918	0.535	0.290
LT3	0.658	0.891	0.897	0.443	0.346
elirf	0.658	0.904	0.905	0.411	0.247
Our system	0.736	**0.953**	**0.921**	0.561	0.297

Note: S = sarcasm, I = irony, M = metaphor, N = non-figurative
ClaC = Concordia university; UPF = Universitat Pompeu Fabra; LLT_PolyU = Hong Kong Polytechnic University; LT3 = Ghent University; elirf = Universitat Politecnica de Valencia

The performance of our system as well as the participating systems in SemEval 2015 was much better for the sarcasm and irony than metaphor and non-figurative. It may be worthy noticing here that most of the mentioned models were developed keeping in mind that sarcasm and irony mostly rely on incongruity (i.e. logical inconsistency), while metaphor and non-figurative texts rely on congruity[9]. Therefore, the systems designed to identify incongruity poorly perform on the congruous texts. It suggests that the sarcasm/irony and metaphor/non-figurative are needed to be handled differently.

[9]In metaphor, a concept in a target domain is expressed by terms from a source domain, but there is no incongruity among the used terms and concepts.

5.3 Paired t-Test

Table 8: Paired t-test results between the module 1 or the module 2 and the integration of module 1 and 2

Pair 1: Module 1 - integrated modules 1 & 2	
$P(T <= t)$ one-tail	0.069
$P(T <= t)$ two-tail	0.098
Pair 2: Module 2 - integrated modules 1 & 2	
$P(T <= t)$ one-tail	0.029
$P(T <= t)$ two-tail	0.047

A paired t-test was conducted to see whether there was a statistical significant difference between the module 1 or module 2 and the integration of them. Table 8 shows two results of paired t-test: 'pair 1' between the module 1 and the integrated system, and 'pair 2' between the module 2 and the integrated system. α value was 0.029 (one-tail) and 0.047 (two-tail) for the pair 1 and also 0.069 and 0.098 for the pair 2. Since the α values of both pairs are less than 0.1, we can conclude that there was a significant difference in the mean scores between both pairs with 90% confident interval.

6 Conclusion

In this research, we present a model for the prediction of fine-grained sentiment score for sarcastic and ironic tweets. The method consists of two modules that are refined from the previous methods, also introducing some new features. The results of the experiments indicate that our proposed method is better than the strong baselines, and integration of two modules achieves the best result among the participating systems in SemEval-2015 for the sarcastic and ironic tweets. On top of the features derived from two previous well performing systems, we enriched the feature set with several new implemented ones. In particular, the "additional features" is added to the module 1, while the counters of several punctuations & special symbols and a new method to identify "coherence feature" is proposed in the module 2. The contribution of each feature has been carefully analyzed and reported.

In the near future, we intend to apply the feature set to different tasks. One of them is to predict whether a tweet contains irony or sarcasm, rather than calculating the sentiment score. Other applications will be explored.

References

Baccianella S., Esuli A., and Sebastiani F.. 2010. Sentiwordnet 3.0: An enhanced lexical resource for sentiment analysis and opinion mining. In *LREC*, volume 10, pages 2200–2204.

Barbieri F. and Saggion H. 2014, Modelling irony in twitter, *In Proceedings of the Student Research Workshop at the 14th Conference of the European Chapter of the Association for Computational Linguistics*, pages 56–64

Buschmeier K., Cimiano P., and Klinger R. 2014, An impact analysis of features in a classification approach to irony detection in product reviews

Cambria E., Speer R., Havasi C. and Hussain A. 2010, SenticNet: A Publicly Available Semantic Resource for Opinion Mining, *Commonsense Knowledge: Papers from the AAAI Fall Symposium*

Carvalho P., Sarmento L., Silva J. M. and Oliveira D. E. 2009, Clues for detecting irony in user-generated contents: oh...!! its so easy;-), *In Proceedings of the 1st international CIKM workshop on Topic-sentiment analysis for mass opinion*, pages 53–56

Davidov D., Tsur O., and Rappoport A. 2010, Semi-supervised recognition of sarcastic sentences in twitter and amazon, *In Proceedings of the Fourteenth Conference on Computational Natural Language Learning*, pages 107–116, Association for Computational Linguistics

Ellen R., Ashequl Q., Prafulla S., Lalindra S., Gilbert D. S., Gilbert N., Ruihong H. 2013, Sarcasm as Contrast between a Positive Sentiment and Negative Situation, *In Proceedings of the Conference on Empirical Methods on Natural Language Processing (EMNLP)*, pages 704–714, Seattle, Washington

Finn Årup Nielsen. 2011, A new anew: Evaluation of a word list for sentiment analysis in microblogs, In *Proceedings of the ESWC2011 Workshop on 'Making Sense of Microposts': Big things come in small packages.*

Ghosh A., Li G., Veale T., Rosso P., Shutova E., Reyes A., and Barnden J. 2015, Semeval-2015 task 11: Sentiment analysis of figurative language in twitter, *In Proceedings of the International Workshop on Semantic Evaluation (SemEval-2015), Co-located with NAACL and *SEM*, Denver, Colorado, USA

Gimenez M., Pla F. and Hurtado L.F. 2015, ELiRF: A Support Vector Machine Approach for Sentiment Analysis Tasks in Twitter at SemEval-2015, *In Proceedings of the 9th International Workshop on Semantic Evaluation (SemEval 2015)*, Association for Computational Linguistics, pages 673–678, Denver, Colorado

Grice H. P. 1975, Logic and conversion, *Syntax and semantics 3: Speech arts*, pages: 41–58

Haiman J. 1998, Talk is cheap: Sarcasm, alienation, and the evolution of language, *Language Arts & Disciplines*, Oxford, Oxford University Press

Hall M., Frank E., Holmes G., Pfahringer B., Reutemann P., and Witten I.H. 2009, The weka data mining software: An update, *SIGKDD Explorations*

Hao Y. and Veale T. 2010, An ironic fist in a velvet glove: Creative mis-representation in the construction of ironic similes, *Minds and Machines*, 20(4):635–650

Hart L. 2013, The Linguistics of Sentiment Analysis, Portland State University, PDX Scholar 2013, http://pdxscholar.library.pdx.edu/honorstheses/20

Martin J. R. and White P. R.R. 2005, The Language of Evaluation: Appraisal in English, *Palgrave*, London, UK

Miller A. G. 1995 WordNet: A Lexical Database for English *Communications of the ACM*

Hu M. and Liu B., 2004. Mining and summarizing customer reviews, In *Proceedings of the tenth ACM SIGKDD international conference on Knowledge discovery and data mining*, pages 168–177, ACM.

Pak E. and Paroubek P. 2010, Twitter as a corpus for sentiment analysis and opinion mining, *In Proceedings of the Seventh Conference on International Language Resources and Evaluation*

Pang B. and Lee L. 2008, Opinion mining and sentiment analysis, *Foundations and Trends in Information Retrieval* Vol. 2, pages 1–135

Quintilian 1953, The institutio Oratoria of Quintilian. With an English Translation by Harold Edgeworth Butler. London: William Heinemann

Resnik P. 1995, Using Information Content to Evaluate Semantic Similarity in a Taxonomy, *CoRR*

Reyes A., Rosso P. 2012, Making objective decisions from subjective data: detecting irony in customer reviews, *Decision Support System 2012*, 53:754–760.

Reyes A., Rosso P., and Veale T. 2013, A multidimensional approach for detecting irony in twitter, *Language Resources and Evaluation*, 47(1):239–268.

Soon W. M., Ng H. T, Lim D. C. Y. 2001 A Machine Learning Approach to Coreference Resolution of Noun Phrases *Computational Linguistics*, pages 521–544, Cambridge, MA, USA

Stevenson A. 2010, Oxford dictionary of English, Oxford University Press

Stringfellow, F. J. 1994. *The Meaning of Irony* NewYork: State University of NY.

Thaseen S. and Kumar C. A. 2013, An analysis of supervised tree based classifiers for intrusion detection system, *Pattern Recognition, Informatics and Mobile Engineering (PRIME), 2013 International Conference on*, pages 294–299, Salem, MA, USA

Tsur O., Davidov D. 2010 ICWSM - a great catchy name: Semi-supervised recognition of sarcastic sentences in product reviews *In International AAAI Conference on Weblogs and Social*

Tungthamthiti P., Kiyoaki S., and Masnizah M. 2014, Recognition of Sarcasm in Tweets Based on Concept Level Sentiment Analysis and Supervised Learning Approaches, *In Proceedings of the 28th Pacific Asia Conference on Language, Information and Computation*, pages 404–413, Phuket, Thailand

Wiebe J., Wilson T., and Cardie C. 2005. Annotating expressions of opinions and emotions in language, *Language resources and evaluation*, 39(2-3):165–210.

Xu, Hongzhi and Santus, Enrico and Laszlo, Anna and Huang, Chu-Ren 2015, LLT-PolyU: Identifying Sentiment Intensity in Ironic Tweets, *In Proceedings of the 9th International Workshop on Semantic Evaluation (SemEval 2015)*, Association for Computational Linguistics, pages 673–678, Denver, Colorado

Thai Stock News Sentiment Classification using Wordpair Features

Apinan Chattupan
Knowledge Management and Knowledge Engineering Laboratory (KMAKE Lab)
Faculty of Information Technology
King Mongkut's Institute of Technology Ladkrabang, Bangkok, Thailand
S7606151@kmitl.ac.th

Ponrudee Netisopakul
Knowledge Management and Knowledge Engineering Laboratory (KMAKE Lab)
Faculty of Information Technology
King Mongkut's Institute of Technology Ladkrabang, Bangkok, Thailand
ponrudee@it.kmitl.ac.th

Abstract

Thai stock brokers issue daily stock news for their customers. One broker labels these news with plus, minus and zero sign to indicate the type of recommendation. This paper proposed to classify Thai stock news by extracting important texts from the news. The extracted text is in a form of a 'wordpair'. Three wordpair sets, manual wordpairs extraction (ME), manual wordpairs addition (MA), and automate wordpairs combination (AC), are constructed and compared for their precision, recall and f-measure. Using this broker's news as a training set and unseen stock news from other brokers as a testing set, the experiment shows that all three sets have similar results for the training set but the second and the third set have better classification results in classifying stock news from unseen brokers.

Keywords: Thai stock news, sentiment classification, text classification, wordpair features.

1 Introduction

Thai stock news are daily issued from many stock brokers. Thai stock news is an important source of information for stock traders to make a decision on stock trading. However, a usual Thai stock news has a long message and sometimes not easily to interpret or conclude. One stock broker makes it easier by labeling each news with plus (+), minus (-) and zero (0) sign, to indicate the type of news as positive, negative and neutral. This automatically classifies the news into three classes.

In this research, we assume that 'features' that can be used for classifying the news must be presented as text in the news. Although this assumption could be too strong in general, for our sole purpose of investigation, our focus here is on text form of the news. Therefore, we proposed to construct a set of these 'texts' to be used as features in order to classify Thai stock news into three sentiments: positive, negative and neutral classes, using known sentiment news as a training set and unseen news as a testing set.

Each feature is called a *wordpair*, since it is a pair of a keyword and a polarity word. A keyword is a word that signifies upcoming information. A polarity word is a word associated with a keyword and signifies a sentiment that related to the keyword. Following the classification from one broker, there are three sentiments: positive, negative, and neutral.

However, due to the flexibility of Thai language, the order of a keyword, a polarity word and a stock symbol may not be the same in the news. That is - a keyword may come before or after a polarity word. In addition, they may come before, after or between the stock symbols they intend to recommend.

29th Pacific Asia Conference on Language, Information and Computation pages 188 - 195
Shanghai, China, October 30 - November 1, 2015

There are two objectives of this paper. First, describing methods to construct these wordpairs collection. Second, utilizing them for constructing automatic classification models for classifying Thai stock news into three corresponding classes. This method can be very useful for general investors because investors can quickly obtain the information and make a decision in stock trading by following the trend of Thai stock news from the classification model.

The outline of this paper is as follows. Section 2 reviews related work. Section 3 describes stock news collection and wordpair construction. In subsection 3.1, we show an example stock news, signs, and stock symbols and compare the frequency of stock symbols in the training and testing set. In subsection 3.2, we propose three sets of wordpairs, which are used to classify Thai stock news sentiments. Section 4 gives details of two experimental designs. We also discuss an effect of varying window sizes for extracting wordpairs features. The results of stock news sentiment classification are also shown in this section. Section 5 analyzes misclassified stock news from the testing set. The last section gives a conclusion and our plan for imminent future work.

2 Related Work

There are two involving areas related to our work. First, the research involved language structure and processing research. Second, the research involved analyzing the stock and classification.

Tongtep and Theeramunkong (2010) mentioned the structural model for extracting patterns from Thai news documents. They focus on a pattern of unique name or noun such as person name, organization name, location, date and time. In addition, Sutheebanjard and Premchaiswadi (2010); Lertcheve and Aroonmanakun (2009) mentioned a similar extracting pattern. They extracted only the person name and only the product name respectively.

Taboada et al. (2011); Lertsuksakda et al. (2014) mentioned the types of word; such as a noun, a verb, an adjective and adverb; and polarity of the word. Taboada et al. (2011) discussed the types of word that have an emotional level and the negation of word that will affect to an emotional level. Lertsuksakda et al. (2014) discussed Thai sentiment terms by using the hourglass of emotion. They assigned an emotional level of a Thai word using two-way translation from English word corpus to Thai word. These techniques will be applied to extract wordpairs from Thai stock news.

Mittermayer (2004); Schumaker and Chen (2009); Chattupan and Netisopakul (2014) demonstrated stock trends prediction using text in the stock news. In addition, Lertsuksakda et al. (2015) discussed text mining techniques in Thai children stories. We will take above techniques and apply them to our work.

3 Stock News and Wordpairs

Section 3.1 describes data preparation including stock news collection and preliminary analysis. Section 3.2 describes wordpairs construction for stock news sentiment classification experiments.

3.1 Stock News Collection

The experiment collects Thai stock news from several brokers such as Bualuang securities (BLS), Thanachart securities (TNS), Krungsri securities (KSS), and so on. In this paper, we tag wordpairs from BLS stock news, hence, we use news from this set as a training set. Stock news from other brokers are combined and used as a testing set. Another important reason for using BLS as a training set is that the broker recommendation includes sentiment signs, such as +, 0, -, *. Therefore, wordpairs sentiments from this broker can be directly tagged using the sign sentiment. The example of stock news published by BLS with their signs are shown in Table 1. Note that some news contain more than one stock symbols.

Thai stock news from BLS (Bualuang Securities, 2015) was collected between 04/04/2014 to 27/05/2015. There are 1,381 stock news with totally 6,596 paragraph news containing stock symbols. Paragraph length is from 200 to 500 letters. Furthermore, Thai stock news under investigation was selected with the following condition. First, the selected stock news must have a stock symbol. This is used for obtaining stock statistics; percent price changes and trading volume. Second, stock news must contain at least one wordpairs. Hence, the stock news contains only a stock symbol and recommended price will not be selected.

Date	Stock news	Sign	Symbol
17/02/2015	MAKRO กำไรดีกว่าคาด คงกำไรปีนี้ / คงคำแนะนำถือ makro-kum-rai-dee-kwa-kard-kong-kum-rai-pee-nee-/-kong-kum-nae-num-thux 'Makro earn better than expected. This year continued profit. / Recommend hold.'	0	MAKRO
06/10/2014	กลุ่มโรงแรมท่องเที่ยวรายงาน... เรายังคงแนะนำซื้อ MINT CENTEL และ ERW koom-rong-ram-tong-tiew-rai-ngan-…-rao-young-kong-nae-num-shux-mint-centel-lae-erw 'The hotel and travel report… We recommend buy Mint, Centel and Erw.'	+	MINT CENTEL ERW
17/02/2015	เช้านี้เกาหลีใต้ คงดอกเบี้ย 2% Shao-nee-kao-lee-tai-kong-dok-bia-song-per-cent 'This morning, south korea fixed interest rate 2%.'	+	No

Table 1: The example of Thai stock news published by BLS

Thai stock news from other brokers (Stock News Online, 2015) were collected between 10/03/2015 to 03/07/2015 and has totally 3,489 paragraphs news. We used the same selecting criteria as the training set. However, we notice that this set has longer paragraph length from 500 to 1000 letters. We prepare this testing set from unseen data set in order to support for future unseen stock news.

Industry	BLS		Other Brokers	
	Freq.	Rank	Freq.	Rank
Agro	780	3	303	5
Consump	310	8	139	8
Fincial	514	5	345	3
Indus	359	7	189	7
Propcon	2512	1	1356	1
Resourc	629	4	265	6
Service	1094	2	562	2
Tech	398	6	330	4

Table 2: Comparing frequency of stock symbols grouped by types of industry in training and testing set

Table 2 shows the preliminary investigation of stock symbols frequencies grouped by types of industry, comparing the training set (BLS) and the testing set (other brokers). Notice that for both sets, the most and second most frequent stock symbols are in industry: Propcon and Service; while the least and second least frequent symbols are in industry: Consump and Indus, respectively. The total number of unique symbols in the training set is 296 comparing to 219 in the testing set. Hence, the average mentioned frequency for each symbol in the training and testing set are 51.74% and 38.28%, respectively. The total numbers of symbols grouped by types of industry are shown in Table 3.

Industry	Unique symbols in SET	Unique symbols in training set	Unique symbols in testing set
Agro	54	32	29
Consump	42	12	8
Fincial	61	32	27
Indus	87	32	17
Propcon	152	76	53
Resourc	36	28	20
Service	99	57	41
Tech	41	27	23
Summary	572	296	219

Table 3: The total number of unique symbols grouped by types of industry in SET, training set, and testing set

3.2 Wordpairs Construction

This paper proposed to use stock sentiment wordpairs to classify stock news into the positive, negative and neutral news. A wordpairs is a tuple of size 3, consists of a keyword, a polarity word and a sentiment. A keyword usually is a noun or a verb indicating characteristics of stock or business, such as *"profit, recommend, income, price, growth ..."* and so on. A polarity word is a verb or an adjective or an adverb for the keyword above, such as *"good profit, recommend buy, steady income ..."* and so on. In this paper, we have only three sentiments: positive (1) if the news has + sign, negative (-1) if the news has – sign, and neutral (0) if the news has 0 sign. The examples of wordpairs are shown in Table 4.

Keyword	Polarity word	Sentiment
กำไร kum-rai 'profit'	ดี dee 'good'	+
คาด kard 'forecast'	กำไร kum-rai 'profit'	+
ปัจจัย pud-jai 'factor'	หนุน nun 'support'	+
แนะนำ nae-num 'recommend'	ถือ thux 'hold'	0
รายได้ rai-dai 'income'	ทรงตัว song-tua 'steady'	0
ราคา ra-ka 'price'	พักตัว puk-tua 'dormancy'	0
ผลกระทบ pon-kra-tob 'effect'	เชิงลบ chung-lop 'negative'	-
เศรษฐกิจ set-ta-kit 'economy'	ชะลอ cha-loor 'slow down'	-
ราคาหุ้น ra-ka-hoon 'stock price'	เสี่ยง seiyng 'risky'	-

Table 4: An example of wordpairs with a pattern {keyword, polarity word, sentiment}

We obtain the first set of wordpairs by hand – called *manual extraction* set (ME). Next, we add new wordpairs into the first set by duplicating the same keyword augmented with an opposite and a neutral polarity words. The second set is called manual wordpairs addition set or *manual addition* (MA), for short. For example, a keyword and polarity word ราคาหุ้น,ขึ้น ra-ka-hoon-,-khun 'stock price, up', the negation polarity word ราคาหุ้น,ลง ra-ka-hoon-,-lng 'stock price, down' and a neutral polarity word ราคาหุ้น,คงที่ ra-ka-hoon-,-kong-thi 'stock price, unchanged'. The MA set has only the positive and negative sense and does not have the neutral sense of 'stock price'. Therefore, this sense is added in the second set. Other examples are shown in Table 5.

The third set of wordpairs is automatically generated from the second set. Wordpairs with partial common keywords are assigned with the same polarity words and signs. For instance, the keywords ราคาหุ้น ra-ka-hoon 'stock price' and ราคา ra-ka 'price' have a common word 'ราคา – stock price'; hence, they will share the same set of polarity words and sentiments.

Keyword	Polarity word	Sentiment
กำไร kum-rai 'profit'	ทรงตัว song-tua 'settled'	0
	ขึ้น khun 'up'	+
	ลง lng 'down'	-
การลงทุน karn-lng-thun 'investment'	ฟื้นตัว fun-taw 'recover'	+
	ซบเซา sob-sea 'stagnant'	-
	คงที่ khong-thi 'stable'	0
แนะนำ nae-num 'recommend'	ขาย khai 'sell'	-
	ซื้อ sux 'buy'	+
	ถือ thux 'hold'	0

Table 5: The manual wordpairs addition with opposite and neutral polarity words

Keyword	Polarity word	Existing wordpairs	New wordpairs
ราคาหุ้น ra-ka-hoon 'stock price'	ขึ้น khun 'up'	ราคาหุ้น, ขึ้น ra-ka-hoon-,-khun 'stock price, up'	ราคา, ขึ้น ra-ka-,-khun 'price, up'
ราคาหุ้น ra-ka-hoon 'stock, price'	บวก bawk 'positive'	ราคาหุ้น, บวก ra-ka-hoon-,-bawk 'stock price, positive'	ราคา, บวก ra-ka-,-bawk 'price, postive'
ราคา ra-ka 'price'	ปรับลด prub-rod 'diluted'	ราคา, ปรับลด ra-ka-,-prub-rod 'price, diluted'	ราคาหุ้น, ปรับลด ra-ka-hoon-,-prub-rod 'stock price, diluted'

Table 6: The automate wordpairs combination

Examples of these crossovers are shown in Table 6. We called the third set automate wordpairs combination or *automate combination*

(AC), for short. The numbers of wordpairs for the three sets are 133, 277 and 331 respectively.

4 Experimental Design and Result

We hypothesized that wordpairs affecting the stock news sentiment can be located near the stock symbol. Hence, we design experiments, using the stock symbol as a center, with different window sizes varying from 20, 40, 60 and 80 letters. Figure 1 demonstrates effects of varying window sizes when extracting wordpairs features.

เรายังคงแนะนำซื้อ MINT CENTEL และ ERW

←←10→MINT←10→

←←←←←←20→CENTEL←20→→→

←←←←←←←←←←←←←30→ERW←30→→→

range 20 extracts:
[แนะนำ][ซื้อ][MINT] → '[recommend][buy][MINT]'

range 40 extracts:
[แนะนำ][ซื้อ][MINT] → '[recommend][buy][MINT]'
[แนะนำ][ซื้อ][CENTEL] →
'[recommend][buy][CENTEL]'

range 60 extracts:
[แนะนำ][ซื้อ][MINT] → '[recommend][buy][MINT]'
[แนะนำ][ซื้อ][CENTEL] →
'[recommend][buy][CENTEL]'
[แนะนำ][ซื้อ][ERW] → '[recommend][buy][ERW]'

Figure 1: Effects of varying window sizes for extracting wordpairs features

We found that the optimal window size for extracting wordpairs features is 60, with average 1-3 wordpairs for each stock symbol, as shown in Figure 2. We also found that 80-letter window size sometimes extracts irrelevant wordpairs, such as wordpairs of the next symbol. For example, the stock news on Figure 2 has a stock symbol (1) and three wordpairs. Notice that a keyword and a polarity word of the second wordpairs (3) (forecast and profit) are not immediately adjacent to each other.

(1)MAKRO กำไร(2)ดี(2)กว่าคาด(3) คงกำไร(3)ปีนี้ / คงคำแนะนำ(4) ถือ(4)	
(1)MAKRO	→ symbol
(2)กำไร, ดี kum-rai-dee 'profit, good'	→ wordpairs
(3)คาด, กำไร kard-kum-rai 'forecast profit'	→ wordpairs
(4)แนะนำ, ถือ nae-num-thux 'recommend, hold'	→ wordpairs

Figure 2: An example of wordpair features for a stock

In short, there are 6 combinations of {symbol (S), keyword (K), polarity (P)} as shown in Table 7. In the training set, the most frequent patterns found is pattern#3 (K-P-S) with 335, 387, and 387 occurrences when extracted by ME, MA and AC set, respectively. The second most frequent is pattern#5 (P-K-S) with 215, 254, and 257 occurrences when extracted by ME, MA and AC set, respectively. The least frequent pattern found is pattern#4 with 47, 55 and 57 occurrences.

The most and the second most frequent patterns in the testing set found are similar to the training set with 599, 674, and 675 occurrences in pattern#3 and 577, 669, 669 occurrences in pattern#5.

There are two main experiments. The first experiment is designed to examine the effects of the three sets of wordpairs, manual extraction (ME), manual addition (MA) and automate combination (AC), as described in section 3 in training and testing set.

The second experiment is designed to examine the effects of S-K-P patterns on training and testing set. We use an open source software 'Weka' (Weka, 2013) to build classification model using decision tree and support vector machine.

For the first experiment, the results of decision tree and SVM classification models using ME, MA and AC wordpairs sets as features are shown in Table 8. We found that, for the training set, there are no significant differences for all three sets of wordpairs features.

Pattern#	{Symbol, keyword, polarity} combinations
1: SKP	[RATCH][แนะนำ] [ถือ] ราคาเป้าหมาย 64 บาท... [Symbol] [Keyword][Polarity] 'RATCH hold with a target price of 64 Thai baht...'
2: SPK	[SAMTEL] SAT [กำไร] ตาม [คาด]... [Symbol] [Polarity][Keyword] 'SAMTEL and SAT profit as expected...'
3: KSP	รายงานกลุ่ม Small Cap [คาด] [UNIQ] และ TRC มีโอกาสทำ [กำไร]... [Keyword][Symbol] [Polarity] 'small cap segment reported UNIQ and TRC are expected profitable opportunities...'
4: KPS	คงคำ [แนะนำ] [ซื้อ] [TP] 24 บาท... [Keyword][Polarity][Symbol] 'maintain buy with TP 24 Thai baht...'
5: PSK	เรา[ลด] [ราคา]เป้าหมาย และคำแนะนำ [SIM] และ SAMTEL ลงเหลือถือจากซื้อ... [Polarity] [Keyword] [Symbol] 'we lower our target price and recommendation SIM and SAMTEL to hold from buy'
6: PKS	เดือน สค. พบว่า[ปรับสูงขึ้น] 0.5% และ +4.3% โดย [BBL] BAY TMB KBANK SCB รายงาน[สินเชื่อ]เติบโต [Polarity] [Symbol] [Keyword] 'In august, showed a rise of 0.5% and +4.3% BBL BAY TMB KBANK SCB loan growth...'

Table 7: The types of structure matching with the real Thai stock news

The first set – ME, gives a slightly better precision of 0.741 for decision tree model comparing to MA and AC with the precision of 0.722 and 0.721. The same is hold for SVM model, where ME give a slightly better precision result of 0.723 comparing to 0.712 for MA and AC. Every model has the same recall and F-measure of approximately 0.75 and 0.66 respectively. This is not surprising because wordpairs in the first set – ME – are extracted from the training set. Therefore, the first set of wordpairs, when use to classify the training set, should be the most accurate features.

Set	Decision tree		SVM	
ME	Precision	0.741	Precision	0.723
	Recall	0.758	Recall	0.755
	F-Measure	0.669	F-Measure	0.663
MA	Precision	0.722	Precision	0.712
	Recall	0.757	Recall	0.755
	F-Measure	0.669	F-Measure	0.665
AC	Precision	0.721	Precision	0.712
	Recall	0.757	Recall	0.754
	F-Measure	0.669	F-Measure	0.664

Table 8: The result of decision tree and SVM classification of each pattern

The resulting decision tree is partially shown in Figure 3.

Since the precision results of decision tree are better than SVM, we use these training models to classify the testing set. We found that, from 3,489 stock news (# of rows) in the testing set, ME, MA, and AC models predict the same outcome for 3,457 rows or 99.08%; predict the same outcomes two out of three times for 32 rows or 0.91%. There is no totally different outcome prediction – all three models predict different outcomes 0%.

We assume that if three classification models predict the same outcome, then there is no need to verify more. Now, we examine the 32 rows (same two out of three) by comparing the classification models outcomes with solutions provided by a human. The majority outcomes (two same outcomes) is correct for 12 times; while the minority outcome (one out of three) is correct for 16 times. The leftover 4 rows are those outcomes not matched to the solutions. These will be analyzed in section 5.

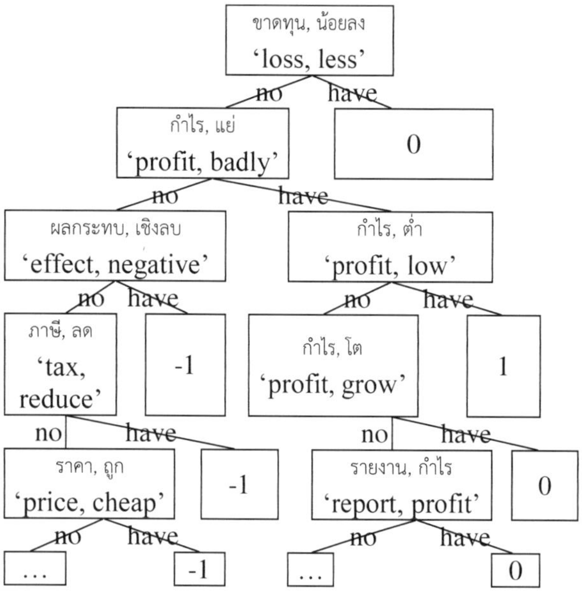

Figure 3: Partial decision tree model built from ME wordpairs features

Wordpair Features		ME			MA			AC		
		Precision	Recall	F-Measure	Precision	Recall	F-Measure	Precision	Recall	F-Measure
Decision tree	P#1:SKP	0.68	0.69	0.66	0.77	0.80	0.77	0.77	0.80	0.77
	P#2:SPK	0.93	0.92	0.91	0.90	0.91	0.90	0.90	0.91	0.90
	P#3:KSP	0.63	0.64	0.62	0.58	0.61	0.58	0.58	0.61	0.58
	P#4:KPS	0.75	0.76	0.74	0.74	0.75	0.72	0.74	0.75	0.72
	P#5:PSK	0.65	0.74	0.69	0.63	0.69	0.66	0.68	0.71	0.69
	P#6PKS	0.75	0.76	0.75	0.79	0.80	0.79	0.76	0.77	0.76
	average	**0.73**	**0.75**	**0.73**	**0.74**	**0.76**	**0.74**	**0.74**	**0.76**	**0.74**
SVM	P#1:SKP	0.70	0.71	0.70	0.81	0.83	0.81	0.79	0.81	0.80
	P#2:SPK	0.96	0.96	0.96	0.95	0.95	0.95	0.95	0.95	0.95
	P#3:KSP	0.70	0.71	0.70	0.69	0.70	0.70	0.69	0.70	0.69
	P#4:KPS	0.70	0.71	0.70	0.71	0.73	0.71	0.71	0.73	0.72
	P#5:PSK	0.77	0.78	0.77	0.72	0.72	0.72	0.75	0.77	0.76
	P#6PKS	0.69	0.71	0.69	0.74	0.76	0.75	0.73	0.75	0.74
	average	**0.75**	**0.76**	**0.75**	**0.77**	**0.78**	**0.77**	**0.77**	**0.79**	**0.78**

Table 9: The result of decision tree and SVM classification of each pattern

For the second experiment, the result is shown in Table 9. Overall, the SVM models give a slightly better results than the decision tree models for all three wordpairs sets. Comparing among the SVM models, the first set – ME, gives the least average recall of 0.76. The second set – MA and the last set – AC give the second best average result of 0.78 and the best average result of 0.79, respectively. However, the result of pattern#2 (S-P-K) obtains very high results above 0.90 for all models. We will discuss insights for this pattern in the next section. The second best result is pattern#1 (S-K-P). It obtains recall of 0.83 and 0.81 when uses with MA and AC set respectively. The other patterns give the similar average results of 0.7 in SVM models.

5 Error Analysis and Discussion

In the first experiment, there are 4 stock news where no machine classification matches the human solutions. The investigation found that these 4 news appear during adjacent business days and have exact same text messages as shown in Figure 4.

กลุ่มรับเหมา... คาดกำไรในไตรมาส 2/58 เติบโตดีอย่าง PTTGC koom-rab-mao-…-kard-kum-rai-nai-tri-mart-song-/-ha-sib-pad-teib-to-dee-yang-pttgc 'Contractor group… Earning expected in the quarter 2/58 growth as PTTGC'	
The wordpairs should be extracted.	เติบโต, ดี teib-to-dee 'growth, good'
The wordpairs is in the ME, MA, and AC sets.	การเติบโต, ดี karn-teib-to-dee 'growth, good'

Figure 4: Error analysis for stock news classification

From the figure 4, the wordpairs เติบโต, ดี teib-to-dee 'growth, good' and การเติบโต, ดี karn-teib-to-dee 'growth, good' have the same meaning. However, in all three wordpair sets, there is no เติบโต, ดี teib-to-dee 'growth, good' as a wordpair feature. Hence, the keyword is not extracted as a feature. The type of เติบโต tieb-to 'growth' is a verb, but การเติบโต karn-tieb-to 'growth' is a noun. In Thai language, the addition prefix of the word การ karn or ความ kwarm will change a type of a word from a verb to a noun. This investigation suggests that this factor should be considered in order to construct a better set of wordpair features for Thai language in the future.

In the second experiment, pattern#2 (S-P-K) has the highest precision, recall and f-measure. An investigation of the training set for pattern#2 (S-P-K) found that the set has only two sentiments: positive (1) and negative (-1). The training set contains no neutral sentiment. Therefore, there will be only two classes of classification results instead of three. The results suggest that the stock news sentiments classification for this pattern – (S-P-K) can be performed with more accuracy than other patterns because it has only two polarities instead of three polarities.

6 Conclusion and Future Work

This paper proposes to classify stock news into three classes: positive, negative and neutral using only text in the news called wordpairs. Three sets of wordpairs are constructed. The first set is manually extracted from 1,381 stock news. It contains 133 wordpairs. The second set is manually added with opposite and neutral polarities and contains 277 wordpairs. The third set is automatically generated using partial keyword combined with existing polarities and contains 331 wordpairs.

Two experiments are conducted to test the effects of three wordpair sets. The result found no significant differences in the training set but found slightly improvement, for the second the third wordpair sets, when they are applied to unseen stock news (a testing set) from other brokers. Moreover, we found six combination patterns of a stock symbol, a keyword and a polarity (S-K-P) in stock news. The result from the second experiment shows that some pattern (S-P-K) has only two polarities, instead of three and therefore achieved the highest correct classification results.

For the future work, we will resolve the problem found and discussed in the error analysis section by consider adding and deleting a keyword's prefix.

References

Apinan Chattupan and Ponrudee Netisopakul. 2014. Stock sentiment analysis model using data mining (In Thai). In Knowledge and Smart Technology (KST), 2014. Proceeding of 6th National Conference on. Chonburi, Thailand.

Maite Taboada, Julian Brooke, Milan Tofiloski, Kimberly Voll and Manfred Stede. 2011. Lexicon-based methods for sentiment analysis. Computational Linguistics, 37(2):267-307.

Marc-André Mittermayer. 2004. Forecasting intraday stock price trends with text mining techniques. In System Sciences, 2004. Proceeding of the 37th Annual Hawaii International Conference on. IEEE.

Nattadaporn Lertcheva and Wirote Aroonmanakun. 2009. A linguistic study of product names in Thai economic news. In Natural Language Processing, 2009. SNLP'09. Eight International Symposium on, 26-29. IEEE.

Nattapong Tongtep and Thanaruk Theeramunkong. 2010. Pattern-based extraction of named entities in thai news documents. Thammasat International Journal of Science and Technology, 15(1):70-81.

Phaisarn Sutheebanjard and Wichian Premchaiswadi. 2010. Disambiguation of Thai personal name from online news articles. In Computer Engineering and Technology (ICCET), 2010 2nd International Conference on, 3:302-306. IEEE.

Rathawut Lertsuksakda, Kitsuchart Pasupa and Ponrudee Netisopakul. 2015. Sentiment analysis of Thai children stories on support vector machine. In Artificial Life and Robotics (AROB), 2015. Proceeding of the Twentieth International Symposium on. Beppu, Japan.

Rathawut Lertsuksakda, Ponrudee Netisopakul and Kitsuchart Pasupa. 2014. Thai sentiment terms construction using the Hourglass of Emotions. In Knowledge and Smart Technology (KST), 2014 6th International Conference on, 46-50. IEEE.

Robert P. Schumaker and Hsinchun Chen. 2009. Textual analysis of stock market prediction using breaking financial news: The AZFin text system. ACM Transactions on Information System (TOIS), 27(2).

Bualuang Securities. Retrieved February 15, 2015. http://www.bualuang.co.th/th/index.php

Stock News Online. Retrieved May 15, 2015. http://www.kaohoon.com/online/content/category/13/ภาวะเศรษฐกิจและตลาดหุ้นในประเทศ

Weka 3.7.1. Retrieved October 1, 2013. http://www.cs.waikato.ac.nz/ml/weka

Sentiment Classification of Arabic Documents: Experiments with multi-type features and ensemble algorithms

Amine Bayoudhi
ANLP Group, MIRACL
FSEGS, Sfax University
3018, Sfax, TUNISIA
bayoudhi.amine@gmail.com

Lamia Hadrich Belguith
ANLP Group, MIRACL
FSEGS, Sfax University
3018, Sfax, TUNISIA
l.belguith@rnu.fsegs.tn

Hatem Ghorbel
ISIC Lab, HE-Arc
Applied Science University
CH-2610, Switzerland
hatem.ghorbel@he-arc.ch

Abstract

Document sentiment classification is often processed by applying machine learning techniques, in particular supervised learning which consists basically of two major steps: feature extraction and training the learning model. In the literature, most existing researches rely on n-grams as selected features, and on a simple basic classifier as learning model. In the context of our work, we try to improve document classification findings in Arabic sentiment analysis by combining different types of features such as opinion and discourse features; and by proposing an ensemble-based classifier to investigate its contribution in Arabic sentiment classification. Obtained results attained 85.06% in terms of macro-averaged F-measure, and showed that discourse features have moderately improved F-measure by approximately 3% or 4%.

1 Introduction

With the expanding growth of social networks services, user generated content web has emerged from being a simple web space for people to express their opinions and to share their knowledge, to a high value information source for business companies to discover consumer feedbacks about their products or even to decide future marketing actions. Therefore, opinion mining is becoming a potential research domain interesting more and more researchers who attempt to improve current results and to solve more advanced and complex issues in the domain. Typically, mining opinions is viewed as a classification problem called sentiment classification. Sentiment classification aims to determine whether the semantic orientation of a text is positive, negative or neutral. It can be tackled at many levels of granularity: expression or phrase level, sentence level, and document level. Expression sentiment classification aims to determine the prior sentiment class or valence of an expression. As for sentence level, the objective is to calculate the contextual polarity of a sentence. Concerning document level, which is our focus in this research, the main goal is to mine the overall polarity of a document with the hypothesis that is expressed by a single author towards a single target.

Document sentiment classification is often processed by applying machine learning techniques, in particular supervised learning which consists basically of two major steps: feature extraction and training the learning model. In the literature, most existing researches rely on n-grams as selected features, and on a simple basic classifier as learning model. The limit of these two choices is revealed when shifting from one domain to another. As a matter of fact, in one hand, each domain has generally his specific vocabulary. So, n-grams features produced from one domain fail to be discriminative in another. In the other hand, numerous studies showed that the performance of classification algorithms is domain dependent (Xia et al., 2011).

In the context of our work, we try to improve document classification findings in Arabic sentiment analysis by (*i*) combining different types of features such as opinion and discourse features; and by (*ii*) proposing an ensemble-based classifier consisting of a set of accurate basic classifiers to investigate its contribution in Arabic sentiment classification similarly to some other languages such as Chinese (Wang et al., 2014).

29th Pacific Asia Conference on Language, Information and Computation pages 196 - 205
Shanghai, China, October 30 - November 1, 2015

The rest of the paper is organized as follows. In section 2, we review a selection of related work to document sentiment classification for English and Arabic languages. In section 3, we detail our proposed approach and focus on the feature extraction and the classification model selection steps. In section 4, we describe the conducted experiments and discuss the obtained results. Finally, we summarize our conclusions and provide some perspectives.

2 Related Work

2.1 English Sentiment classification

In English sentiment classification, various strategies have been proposed, (Liu, 2012). The most effective ones are related to machine-learning paradigm, viewing the opinion and polarity detection as text classification tasks. These techniques vary from supervised to unsupervised learning, typically probabilistic methods such as Naïve Bayes (NB) and Maximum Entropy (MaxEnt), and linear discrimination methods such as Support Vector machine (SVM). As other possible classification schemes, we mention non-parametric classifiers such as k-Nearest Neighbor (KNN), as well as similarity scores methods (i.e. phrase pattern matching, distance vector, frequency counts and statistical weight measures).

Nevertheless, to get a good accurate classifier, we need to select the most effective set of textual predictors (Liu and Motoda, 2008). In sentiment classification, n-grams (Pang et al., 2002) are the most used features, however, there are some researches where other semantic features are tested such us opinion words and phrases, opinion operators such as negation (Mejova et al., 2011), parts of speech (Wang et al., 2014), and syntactic dependencies (Nakagawa et al., 2010). Some other researches attempt to integrate discourse features and report a significant added value of rhetorical roles in sentiment classification (Chardon et al., 2013). For instance, Somasundarun et al. (Somasundarun et al., 2009) proposed a supervised and unsupervised methods employing Discourse relations to improve sentiment classification. This is performed by adopting relational feature that exploit discourse and neighbor opinion information.

In general, most of adopted features tend to be domain specific (e.g., the term *television* has a negative polarity in a movie review, but may have a positive one in a book review). This problem can be solved by the second approach: the lexicon based approach.

Lexicon-based approach relies on a sentiment lexicon to calculate orientation for a document from the semantic orientation of words or phrases in the document (Taboada et al., 2011). Sentiment lexicon is a collection of classified opinion terms that can be compiled according to three approaches: dictionary-based approach, corpus-based approach, or combined approach.

In dictionary based approach, we attempt to find a set of opinion seed words and then enrich them by retrieving their synonyms and antonyms from dictionaries such WordNet and Thesaurus. For instance, Hu and Liu (Hu and Liu, 2004) and Esuli and Sebastiani (Esuli and Sebastiani, 2005) classify polarity using emotion words and semantic relations from WordNet, WordNet Gloss, WordNet-Affect and SentiWordNet respectively.

However, in corpus-based approach, we use patterns in particular syntactic ones to mine large domain specific corpora and extract opinion terms. Among well-known researches in lexicon-based approach, we mention those of Taboada et al. (Taboada et al., 2011) who developed a semantic orientation calculator called SO-CAL. They started by manually creating a sentiment lexicon by annotating a large corpus of reviews extracted from *Epinions* website. The lexicon was enhanced by positive and negative words from the General Inquirer dictionary. To calculate the semantic orientation of each review, the authors took in consideration intensification by multiplying intensifier words by a percentage, and they incorporated Negation by shifting the semantic orientation toward the opposite polarity by a fixed amount.

Note that some researches combined the machine learning and the lexicon based approaches by exploiting a sentiment lexicon in the framework of a supervised learning method (Mejova et al., 2011) (Maynard et al., 2011).

2.2 Arabic Sentiment Classification

Most of the work in sentiment analysis was devoted to the English language, an important number of resources and tools have been elaborated accordingly. When addressing the same issue to other target languages such as Arabic, several difficulties come out as potential challenges, including the lack of standard lexical and sentiment resources and of good accurate linguistic analyzers and parsers. That's why, we consider that Arabic sentiment classification is still limited compared to English.

Nevertheless, there are many published research papers focusing on sentiment classification of Arabic documents. These researches have been the object of some surveys (Korayem et al., 2012) (Al-Twairesh et al., 2014). For example, we cite Abbasi et al. (Abbasi et al., 2008) who proposed a machine learning method based on entropy weighted genetic algorithms to classify movie reviews and forum comments in English and Arabic. Conducted experiments based mainly on stylistic features yielded an accuracy of 93.62% but with a high computational cost.

Rushdi-Saleh et al. (Rushdi-Saleh et al., 2011) have introduced in their research a new collected corpus of movie reviews called OCA (Opinion Corpus for Arabic). They reported as well as some experiments based on n-grams words and carried out with SVM and NB classifiers. The best F-measure attained 90.73% with SVM classifier.

Mountassir et al. 2013 (Mountassir et al., 2013) investigated three classification settings in an n-grams framework based on three classifiers namely NB, SVM and KNN. The tested settings are stemming type, term frequency thresholding and term weighting. Experiments are performed on two data collections: OCA and ACOM (collected by the authors). Best results in terms of F-measure attained 93% on OCA with KNN classifier and 87.5% and 76.4% respectively on ACOM DS1 and ACOM DS2 with NB classifier.

El-Halees (El-Halees, 2011) followed an hybrid sequential approach by applying lexicon-based method with a seed word list enriched from online dictionaries. Classified documents were then used to train a MaxEnt based classifier. Classified documents of the two previous steps were finally used to train a KNN based classifier. Experiments were conducted on a multi-domain corpus consisting of 1143 documents. Achieved accuracy was around of 80%.

3 Proposed Approach

In this section, we present our approach proposed for the sentiment classification of Arabic documents. This approach, based on multi-type features, is using a set of publicly available linguistic resources and tools. It takes as input an Arabic review about a given target and predicts its polarity which can be Positive or Negative. The approach consists chiefly of three sequential phases which are composed of one or more steps. The three phases are: document pre-processing, feature extraction, and sentiment classification.

3.1 Data Description

In Arabic language, sentiment resources are in general rare. However, in the task of document sentiment classification, there are many used data collections since they are easy to collect and to annotate. In fact, we remark that each researcher has collected his own datasets and used in the evaluation of his classification approach, which does not allow comparing properly the obtained results. Therefore, we have decided to use in our experiments existent datasets that have been widely used by the NLP research community.

According to the literature, there are few publicly available sentiment corpora for document sentiment classification. They are derived from different domain such as social networks (Abdullah et al., 2013), product reviews (Abbasi et al., 2008) (Rushdi-Saleh et al., 2011) (Mountassir et al., 2013) and news (Ahmad et al., 2006) (Almas et al., 2007). Among these corpora, the most used one is OCA (Rushdi-Saleh et al., 2011) and the largest one is ACOM (Mountassir et al., 2013). That's why, we have chosen these two corpus to evaluate our approach and to compare our results.

OCA (Opinion Corpus for Arabic) consists of 500 documents divided equally into positive and negative (Table 1). The corpus was collected by extracting reviews about movies from Arabic web pages and blogs. After that, many processing steps on each review were carried out in order to obtain a formatted document. The main steps were removing HTML tags and special characters, correcting spelling mistakes, filtering out nonsense and nonrelated comments, fixing Romanized comments and comments in different languages. The classification of documents into positive and negative were automatically performed by exploiting the review rating score given by the user. This annotation strategy avoids wasting time in manual annotation, but, it does not always succeed to assign the right class to the annotated review. In fact, reviewers can mention much more negative feedbacks than positive ones, but give a weak positive rating score to the movie.

Property	Neg.	Pos.
Total documents	250	250
Total tokens	94,556	121,392
Avg. tokens in each file	378	485
Total sentences	4,881	3,137
Avg. sentences in each file	20	13

Table 1: Statistics on OCA

ACOM (Arabic Corpus for Opinion Mining) is a multi-genre corpus collected from Aljazeera polls and forums. It consists of three datasets of different domains. The first dataset DS1 consists of 594 documents and falls within movie review domain. The second dataset DS2 is sport-specific dataset and consists of 1492 comments about 18 sport topics. The third dataset DSP2 is a collection of 1082 comments about a political issue titled "Arab support for the Palestinian affair". ACOM were manually annotated according to four classes: positive, negative, neutral and dialectal. Then, neutral and dialectal categories were eliminated since the authors were interested in classification by polarity of documents written only in Modern Standard Arabic (Table 2).

Dataset	Positive	Negative	Total
DS1	184	284	468
DS2	486	517	1003
DS3	149	462	611
Total	819	1263	2082

Table 2: Statistics on the collected ACOM

In addition, the authors proceeded to eliminate a number of negative comments from each dataset in a way to equalize the number of documents for each category (Mountassir et al., 2013). The final number of documents used in experiments is 1368 documents: 698 negative and 670 positive (Table 3).

Property	Negative	Positive
Total documents	698	670
Total tokens	45697	38819
Avg. tokens in each file	65.46	57.93

Table 3: Statistics on the datasets of ACOM used in experiments

3.2 Document preprocessing

Before going on with the classification task, some preprocessing steps are necessary to prepare the raw documents to the feature extraction step. This step requires to search and to identify a set of lexical cue words and markers. To this end, three main steps are required: segmentation, stemming and stop-word removal.

Segmentation: This step, which we carried out using Stanford word segmenter (Monroe et al. , 2014), includes text normalization and word segmentation. Normalization aims to normalize the spelling of some Arabic characters which can be written in different ways. Arabic text can be vowelized, non-vowelized, or even partially vowelized. To ensure the detection and extraction of all orthographic word forms, we decided to eliminate discretization from the reviews. Normalization is also applied to some characters such as alef by transforming all his forms (Alef Hamza above "أ" and Alef Hamza below "إ") into bare Alef "ا". This process is applied because many reviewers omit or confuse these similar letters and use them interchangeably.

Stemming: MADAMIRA (Pasha et al., 2014) is used to apply a light stemming on the reviews. Light stemming aims, to transform nouns in singular and to conjugate verbs with the third personal pronoun. In fact, stemming, which reduces words to their roots, is not convenient in Arabic language, because it may affect the word sense. Light stemming will be helpful to detect all morphological variations of the word.

Stop-word removal: To accelerate the detection process of the lexical cues, we have profited from the stop-word list of Khoja stemmer tool (Khoja and Garside, 1999) and revised it. In fact, this Stop-word list was established to serve information retrieval applications. However, in sentiment classification task, a more reduced list is required, because many non-informative bearing words (such as negation operators and discourse markers) can be helpful cues in sentiment classification.

3.3 Extraction of classification features

In English language, several features ranging from lexical to deep analysis features were tested in the sentiment classification task. However, in Arabic, research works were focused on lexical or statistical features in particular n-grams. This is due to many reasons basically the lack of sentiment resources (i.e. lexicons, standard annotated corpora) and high accurate linguistic tools (i.e. syntactic parser, segmenter). That's why, we propose to adopt a set multi-type features. Our selected features are: opinion features, discourse markers, stylistic features, domain dependent features and morpho-lexical features. In feature extraction step, a set of linguistic resources and tools are required.

Opinion features: include opinion bearing words and opinion operators. Opinion bearing words were detected using a sentiment lexicon called LAP (Bayoudhi et al., 2014). It is an Arabic lexicon that contain over than 8,000 entries, semi-automatically constructed from the MPQA Arabic translated lexicon (Elarnaoty et al., 2012). It is also fed by mapping synonyms from Arabic Wordnet (Boudabous et al., 2013), by manual annotation of sentiment corpora and by entries from multilingual sentiment lexicons. Statistics on this lexicon are illustrated in Table 4.

Regarding Opinion operators, they are linguistic elements which do not intrinsically bear opinions, but they are altering the characteristics of opinion words located in their scope (Chardon, 2013).

Class	Number of entries
Negative Strong	2,281
Negative Weak	2,689
Positive Strong	1,726
Positive Weak	1,437
Total	8,133

Table 4: Statistics on the lexicon LAP

In the course of our research, we propose to classify opinion operators in three categories: intensifiers, negation operators, and epistemic modality operators. A list of each opinion operator is prepared by a linguistic expert.

- *Intensifiers*: they are operators altering the intensity of the opinion expression. We distinguish two types of intensifiers: *(i)* amplifiers (i.e. very, much, extremely) strengthen the intensity of the opinion expression, *(ii)* attenuators (i.e. little, less) weaken the intensity of the opinion expression.

- *Negation operators*: affect the polarity of the opinion expression (i.e. not, never, neither). This effect is handled at the sentence level by following different strategies such as switch polarity (Sauri, 2008) and linear shift polarity (Taboada et al., 2011) and angular shift polarity (Chardon, 2013).

- *Epistemic modality operators*: Epistemic modality serves to reveal how confident writers are about the truth of the ideational material they convey (Palmer, 1986). There are two types of epistemic modality operators: hedges and boosters. Hedges (i.e. perhaps, I guess) are words employed by the speaker to reduce the degree of his liability or responsibility towards the expression. Boosters (i.e. definitely, I assure that and of course) are elements used by the speaker to emphasize the expression. Both hedges and boosters modify polarity of the opinion expression, either strengthen or weaken it (Abdul-Mageed et al., 2012).

Discourse features: In document sentiment classification, many research studies have investigated the integration of deep analysis techniques through syntactic parsing and dependency relations, or through discourse analysis and role relation detection. Accordingly, we propose in our research to follow the same approach by adopting discourse features. In fact, compared to dependencies relations, discourse relations contain, in addition to the structural aspect, a semantic aspect which can be exploited in the sentiment classification. However, unfortunately, discourse processing researches in Arabic are very limited. It focuses on either annotating corpus with discourse information (Al-saif and Market, 2010) or proposing taxonomies of discourse relations (Khalifa et al., 2012). Therefore, it is not possible to profit, in Arabic language, from an automatic generated discourse structure or an automatic recognition of discourse relations to improve sentiment classification. Hence, discourse analysis can be exploited only through discourse markers called also discourse connectives (DC) (Asher, 1993). To use these discourse markers, we have adopted the list of Arabic Text Segmenter (Keskes, 2015), an Arabic tool that segments text into elementary Discourse Units. This list is structured in a discourse relation hierarchy containing 24 relations categorized in four main classes: thematic, temporal, causal and structural. In the context of this work, we started by exploiting only the structural class. This class contains 7 relations illustrated in Table 5.

Relation	Sample of DCs
Contrast	في المقابل، إلا أن، بينما
Antithetic	في حين أن، ليس،
Concession	غير أن، لكن، بيد أن
Correction	لا بل، كلا، إنما
Alternation	سواء، أم، أو
Parallel	كذلك، كما، مع
Conditional	لو، شرط أن، إذا

Table 5: Discourse relation hierarchy that we used in sentiment classification

To exploit these DCs in our classification model, we have grouped them according to their effect in opinion expressions into three feature categories: polarity propagation, polarity switch, conditional polarity (Figure 1).

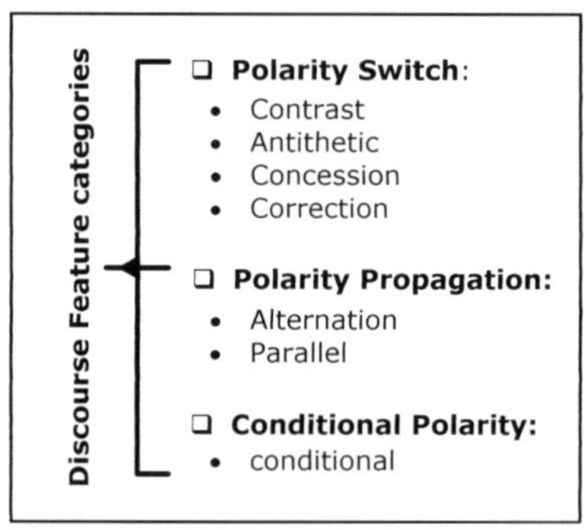

Figure 1: Proposed discourse features for the sentiment classification

Stylistic features: consist mainly of:

- Punctuation marks: three punctuation marks are considered in our research: period (full stop), question mark and exclamation mark. Comma is not taken into account since it is not often used in Arabic writing.
- Number of words per document.
- Polarities of the first and last expressed opinion words: based on the assumption that the first and last sentences of a document are the most informative sentences, we added to our stylistic features the polarity of the first expressed opinion word and the polarity of the last expressed opinion word.

Domain dependent features: n-grams are widely used as features in text classification and sentiment classification for their capacity to encode word order information and substantially the context of the document (Pang et al., 2002). However, these features are domain dependent; they cause a big decrease in the performance of the classifier when testing it with other data collections. Therefore, we have decided to minimize the effect of domain dependent features by excluding unigrams and relying only on bigrams and trigrams. Choosing bigrams and trigrams is explained also by the fact that the lexicon LAP does not contain compound words. Hence, to feed the classifier with compound words, we selected a set of bigrams and trigrams based on their frequency.

Morpho-lexical features: Since adjectives and adverbs are the most morphological forms expressing opinions, and since the lexicon LAP do not include Part-of-speech information, we propose to consider, as additional features, the number of positive adjectives and adverbs and also the number of negative adjective and adverbs in each document.

3.4 Feature transformation

Feature transformation step determines the numerical representation used in the classification process. It's performed by applying a weighting scheme on the extracted textual data of the corpus. We distinguish three weighting schemes: binary, term frequency and TF-IDF representation. Binary schema takes into account presence or absence of a term in a document. Term frequency considers the number of times a term occurs in a document (Li et al., 2009). TF-IDF (Term Frequency - Inverse Document Frequency) considers not only term frequencies in a document, but also the relevance of a term in the entire collection of documents (Manning et al., 2008).

Many researches confirm that the most suitable representation for sentiment classification is binary since overall sentiment may not usually be highlighted through repeated use of the same terms. In fact, Pang et al. (Pang et al., 2002) showed in their experiments that better performance is obtained using presence rather than frequency, that is, binary-valued feature vectors in which the entries merely indicate whether a term occurs or not formed a more effective basis for review polarity classification. Whereas, Mountassir et al. (Mountassir et al., 2013) point out that TF-IDF is also a suitable weighting for SVM and KNN.

3.5 Attribute selection

Attribute selection aims to evaluate the effectiveness of features by identifying relevant features ones to be considered in the learning process. This is allows performing an intense dimensionality reduction without losing on the classifier accuracy.

There are many algorithms for attribute selection such as information gain (Abbasi et al., 2008), mutual information, and chi-square (Li et al., 2009). None of them has been widely accepted as the best feature selection method for sentiment classification, despite the fact that information gain has often been competitive: it ranks terms by considering their presence and absence in each class (Moraes et al., 2013).

3.6 Learning Algorithm

Apart from classification features, Sentiment classification task depends highly on the used learning algorithm. According to the literature, the most popular algorithms are NB, SVM, MaxEnt, Artificial Neural Networks (ANN). Many studies were interested in evaluating and comparing these learning techniques and experimental findings confirm that a given learning algorithm can outperform all others only for a specific problem or an exact subset of the input data, it is abnormal to find a single algorithm achieving the best results on the overall problem domain (Kuncheva, 2004). For instance, a lot of authors reported that they achieved the best performance with SVM in their experiments (liu et al., 2011) (Rushdi Saleh, 2011). Moraes et al. (Moraes et al., 2013) affirm that ANN produce superior or at least comparable results to SVM. Other researchers claim that they yield the best performance by applying KNN and NB (Mountassir et al., 2013).

The proposed solution for this problem is adopting the ensemble technique. This technique consists in combining, in an efficient way, the outputs of several classification models to form an integrated output. We distinguish in the literature many combination types such as sum, voting, weighted combination and meta-classifier (Xia et al., 2011). In the context of our research, we are focusing on four well-known ensemble algorithms namely Bagging (Breiman, 1996), Boosting (Schapire et al., 1998), Voting (Kuncheva, 2004) and Stacking (Syarif et al., 2012).

4 Experiments and discussion

In this section, we carried out two types of experiments. The first type of experiments focus on evaluating a set of base learning algorithms versus a set of ensemble based classifiers. The objective is to find the combination configuration that ensures the best and stable performance across different domains. The second type of experiments concentrates on the feature set used in the classification process. The objective is to evaluate, in particular, the effectiveness of discourse features in Arabic sentiment classification.

All results reported in this section are obtained by applying an evaluation method based on 10-folds cross validation. Attribute transformation, attribute selection and learning algorithms are applied using the Weka data mining software (Hall et al., 2009). Binary representation is used for opinion features, and the TF-IDF representation for bigrams and trigrams.

4.1 Base Classifier evaluation

In this first type of experiments, we conducted a comparative evaluation of three well-known classification algorithms namely SVM, MaxEnt and ANN. The objective is to determine the best accurate base algorithm in each dataset. Many attempts with different parameters are made to achieve the best performance. These experiments were performed on the following data collections: OCA, ACOM DS1, ACOM DS2, ACOM DS3, ACOMB (ACOM Balanced data), ACOMA (ACOM All data).

Obtained results are expressed in terms of F-measure (Table 6). But, since we are applying our model to several sets of data, we need an averaging evaluation metric to get an idea about the best performance in the overall experiments. There are two types of averaging methods: macro-averaged and micro-averaged. Macro-averaging gives equal weight to each dataset, whereas micro-averaging gives equal weight to each document. Because the F-measure ignores true negatives and is mostly determined by the number of true positives, large datasets dominate small datasets in micro-averaging. Micro-averaged results are therefore really a measure of effectiveness on the large datasets in a test collection (Van Asch, 2013). Hence, we have used in Table 6 macro-averaged F-measure to compare the performance of the three algorithms on the different datasets.

Compared to earlier work, our results overstep state of the art existing performances. Indeed, MaxEnt classifier tested in OCA has achieved 95% of F-measure, which exceed 93% reported by Mountassir et al. with KNN classifier (Mountassir et al., 2013) and 90.73% reported by Rushdi-Saleh et al. with SVM classifier (Rushdi-Saleh et al., 2011). Similarly, our obtained results in ACOM DS1 and ACOM DS2 which are respectively 89.3% and 80.1% exceed Mountassir et al. reported results (87.5% and 76.4%). Concerning ACOM DS3, ACOMA and ACOM, these data collections are not yet evaluated by any earlier work.

Dataset	SVM	MaxEnt	ANN
OCA	91.8	95	90.6
ACOM DS1	86	87.5	89.3
ACOM DS2	80.1	80	76.2
ACOM DS3	89.5	86.2	86.8
ACOMB	80.5	80.1	77.8
ACOMA	79.6	75.7	76.1
Macro-avg	84.58	84.08	82.8

Table 6: Results of the base classifiers

According to our experiments, SVM seems to be the most stable classifier among the three classifiers. In fact, it achieved the best results on ACOM DS2, ACOM DS3, ACOMB and on ACOMA.

Regarding OCA and ACOM DS1, the best performance was yielded respectively by MaxEnt and ANN, although these two datasets are derived from the same domain (movie review) and have a relatively close size. The difference in terms of F-measure between the two classification results is considered significant since it exceeds 5.5%. As for DS2, results were less good than the other datasets. In fact, although the documents are in the same domain, they talk about 18 different sports, which make the dataset relatively heterogeneous. On the other hand, DS3 is derived from political specific domain which is a very large domain, but all documents discuss only one political issue, which explain why the classification results were good. Concerning ACOMA and ACOMB, as expected, results were better in ACOMB in which the number of documents is much less than ACOMA.

4.2 Ensemble classifier evaluation

In addition to the evaluation of base classifiers, we conducted another set of experiments to evaluate ensemble classifiers with the same datasets and evaluation metrics. The combination of the classifiers is performed according to the four methods: boosting, bagging, voting and stacking. Several experiments are performed to choose the base classifiers and the combination method that reach the best performance. At the end, we have maintained these four experiments: *(i)* bagging MaxEnt, *(ii)* boosting MaxEnt, *(iii)* majority voting with SVM, MaxEnt and ANN as base classifiers, *(iiii)* stacking SVM and MaxEnt with Linear regression as meta-classifier. The results achieved in each experiment are illustrated in terms of F-measure and macro-averaged F-measure in Table 7.

Dataset	Bag.	Boost.	Vot.	Stack.
OCA	95	94	93.2	94.8
ACOM DS1	92.9	89.4	90.4	87.8
ACOM DS2	80.3	79.6	80.6	79.7
ACOM DS3	88.2	84	90.3	88.2
ACOM B	79.4	79.9	81.4	80
ACOM A	75.9	74	79.7	79
M. Avg	84.7	83.38	85.06	84.26

Table 7: Results of ensemble based classifiers

Compared to Table 6, Table 7 indicates that most of the selected ensemble classifiers have exceeded the results yielded by base classifiers in terms of macro-averaged F-measure. In particular, majority voting of MaxEnt, SVM and ANN has achieved the best results with a macro-averaged F-measure of 85.06%. In five among six datasets, this ensemble classifier has performed better results than the best base classifiers.

4.3 Discourse feature evaluation

In order to evaluate the effectiveness of the discourse features, we have reapplied the best accurate base algorithms on our datasets with removing discourse features. This was performed with respecting all pre-mentioned constraints of attribute transformation and attribute selection steps. Table 8 presents the new achieved F-measure in each dataset with the best accurate algorithm obtained according to the experiments described in section 4.1.

Dataset	Best classifier	F-meas. (%)	Diff (%)
OCA	MaxEnt	92.6	-2.4
ACOM DS1	ANN	85.3	-4
ACOM DS2	SVM	79.7	-0.4
ACOM DS3	SVM	89.2	-0.3
ACOMB	SVM	80.5	0
ACOMA	SVM	79.82	0

Table 8: Discourse feature evaluation

Obtained results show that discourse features are more efficient with OCA and ACOM DS1 derived from movie review domain. In fact, removing discourse features with OCA and ACOM DS1 has respectively decreased F-measure by 2.4% and 4%. This can be explained by the fact that in movie review domain in particular, discourse markers are frequently employed.. Nevertheless, regarding ACOM DS2 and ACOM DS3, the results were not very altered by removing discourse features since F-measure has decreased only by 0.3% and 0.4%. So, this type of features is not very efficient for sport or political domain. Concerning the two last experiments, removing discourse features while evaluating ACOMA and ACOMB has not revealed any impact on the classification results.

5 Conclusion

In this paper, we have proposed a supervised classification approach of Arabic documents. The proposed approach is based on multi-type feature set including opinion features, discourse markers, stylistic features, domain dependent features and morpho-lexical features. In addition, we have carried out a comparative study between some well-known base classifiers and some ensemble-based classifier with different combination methods. Obtained results showed that MaxEnt, SVM and ANN combined with majority voting rules have achieved the best results with a macro-averaged F1-mesaure of 85.06%. Furthermore, experiments showed that discourse features have improved F-measure by approximately 3% or 4%.

As perspectives, we intend to integrate discourse structure and relations as features. This is can be performed by exploiting cross lingual discourse parsing of parallel sentiment corpora, since there is no Arabic discourse parser. In addition, following the same approach, we intend to adopt also syntactic information and dependency relations as classification features.

References

Abbasi A., Chen H., Salem A. 2008. Sentiment analysis in multiple languages: Feature selection or opinion classification in Web forums. ACM Transactions on Information Systems 26(3):12.

Abdul-Mageed M., Diab M. 2012. AWATIF: A Multi-Genre Corpus for Modern Standard Arabic Subjectivity and Sentiment Analysis. In Proc LREC 2012, pp. 3907-3914.

Ahmad K., Cheng D., Almas Y. 2006. Multi-lingual sentiment analysis of financial news streams. In Proc. of the 1st International Conference on Grid in Finance.

Almas Y., Ahmad K. 2007. A note on extracting sentiments in financial news in English, Arabic & Urdu. In Proc of Workshop on Computational Approaches to Arabic Script-based Languages.

Al-Saif A., Markert K. 2010. The Leeds Arabic discourse treebank: Annotating discourse connectives for Arabic. In Proc of LREC, 17-23 May, Malta.

Al-Twairesh N., Al-Khalifa H., Al-Salman A. 2014. Subjectivity and Sentiment Analysis of Arabic: Trends and Challenges. In Proc. Of the 11th ACS/IEEE International Conference on Computer Systems and Applications (AICCSA' 2014), Doha, Qatar, 10-13 November.

Asher N. 1993. Reference to Abstract Objects in Discourse. Kluwer Dordrecht.

Bayoudhi A., Koubaa H., Ghorbel H., Hadrich Belguith L. 2014. Vers un lexique arabe pour l'analyse des opinions et des sentiments, In Proc of the 5th International Conference on Arabic Language Processing CITALA'14, Oujda, Morocco, 26 – 27 November.

Boudabous M.M., Chaâben Kammoun N., Khedher N., Hadrich Belguith L., Sadat F. 2013. Arabic WordNet semantic relations enrichment through morpho-lexical patterns, in Proc. of the First International Conference on Communications, Signal Processing, and their Applications (ICCSPA'13), Sharjah, UAE, February 12-14.

Breiman L. 1994. Bagging predictors. Technical Report 421, Department of Statistics, University of California, Berkeley.

Chardon B. 2013. Chaîne de traitement pour une approche discursive de l'analyse d'opinion. Phd dissertion UPS France.

Elarnaoty M., AbdelRahman S., Fahmy A. 2012. A machine learning approach for opinion holder extraction in Arabic, International Journal of Artificial Intelligence & Applications; March 2012, Vol. 3 Issue 2, p45.

El-Halees A. 2011. Arabic Opinion Mining Using Combined Classification Approach. In Proc of the international Arab Conference on Information Technology, 11-14 December, Riyadh, Saudi Arabia.

Esuli A., Sebastiani F. 2006. SentiWordNet: A Publicly Available Lexical Resource for Opinion Mining. In Proc of the fifth international conference on Language Resources and Evaluation, 22-28 May, Genoa, Italy.

Hall M., Frank E., Holmes G., Pfahringer B., Reutemann P., Witten I.H. 2009. The WEKA data mining software: an update, ACM SIGKDD Explorations Newsletter, Volume 11 Issue 1, pp 10-18, June 2009.

Hu M., Liu B. 2004. Mining Opinions Features in Customer Reviews. Proc of 19th international conference on Artificial Intelligence AAAI, 25-29 July, San Jose, California, pp. 755-760.

Keskes I. 2015. Discourse Analysis of Arabic Documents and Application to Automatic Summarization. PhD dissertion, UPS France.

Khoja S. and Garside R. 1999. Stemming Arabic Text, UK: Computing Department, Lancaster University.

Khalifa I., Feki Z., Farawila A. 2011. Arabic discourse segmentation based on rhetorical methods. In Electric Computer Sciences 11.

Korayem M., Crandall D., Abdul-Mageed M. 2012. Subjectivity and Sentiment Analysis of Arabic: A Survey. in Advanced Machine Learning Technologies and Applications AMLTA, 322.

Kuncheva L. 2004. Combining pattern classifiers: methods and algorithms. John Wiley & Sons.

Li S., Xia R., Zong C., Huang C.-R. 2009. A framework of feature selection methods for text categorization. In Proc of the 47th Annual Meeting of the Association for Computational Linguistics, 2-7 August, suntec, Singapore.

Liu B. 2009. Sentiment Analysis and Opinion Mining. Boca Raton: Morgan & Claypool Publishers.

Liu B. 2011. Web data mining: Exploring hyperlinks, New York: Springer, Lovins, J. B. (1968). Development of a stemming algorithm. Mechanical Translation and Computational Linguistic.

Liu H., Motoda H. 2008. Computational Methods of Feature Selection, Boca Raton: Chapman & Hall.

Manning C.D., Raghavan P., Schtze H. 2008. Introduction to information retrieval. Cambridge University Press.

Maynard D., Funk A. 2011. Automatic detection of political opinions in tweets. In Proc of the 10th International semantic web conference, 23-27 October, Bonn, Germany.

Medhat W., Hassan A., Korashy A. 20140. Sentiment analysis algorithms and applications: A survey. Ain Shams Engineering Journal 5, pp. 1093–1113.

Mejova Y., Srinivasan P. 2011. Exploring Feature Definition and Selection for Sentiment Classifiers. In Proc of the Fifth International AAAI Conference on Weblogs and Social Media ICWSM, 17-21 July, Barcelona, Spain.

Monroe W., Green S., Manning C.D. 2014. Word Segmentation of Informal Arabic with Domain Adaptation. In Proc of the 52nd Annual Meeting of the Association for Computational Linguistics, 22-27 June, Baltimore, USA.

Moraes R., Francisco Valiati J., Gavião Neto W.P. 2013. Document-level sentiment classification: An empirical comparison between SVM and ANN. Expert Systems with Applications 40, pp. 621-633.

Mountassir A., Benbrahim H., Berrada I. 2013. Sentiment classification on Arabic corpora: A preliminary cross-study. Document Numérique 16(1): 73-96.

Nakagawa T., Inui K., Kurohashi S. 2010. Dependency Tree-based Sentiment Classification using CRFs with Hidden Variables, Human Language Technologies, The 2010 Annual Conference of the North American Chapter of the ACL NAACL HLT, pp 786–794, 1-6 June, Los Angeles, California.

Palmer F. 1986. Mood and Modality. Cambridge University Press.

Pang B., Lee L., Vaithyanathan S. 2002. Thumbs up? Sentiment Classification using Machine Learning Techniques, In Proc of the Conference on Empirical Methods in Natural Language Processing EMNLP, 6-7 July, Philadelphia, PA, USA.

Pasha A., Al-Badrashiny M., Diab M.T., El-Kholy A., Eskander R., Habash N., Pooleery M., Rambow O., Roth R. 2014. MADAMIRA: A Fast, Comprehensive Tool for Morphological Analysis and Disambiguation of Arabic. In Proc of the The 9th edition of the Language Resources and Evaluation Conference LREC, 26-31 May, Reykjavik, Iceland.

Rushdi-Saleh M., Martın-Valdivia M., Urena-Lopez L., Perea-Ortega J. 2011. OCA: Opinion corpus for Arabic. Journal of the American Society for Information Science and Technology 62(10).

Saurı R. 2008. A Factuality Profiler for Eventualities in Text. PhD dissertation.

Schapire R. E., Freund Y., Bartlett P., Lee W.S. 1998. Boosting the margin: A new explanation for the effectiveness of voting methods. Annals of Statistics.

Somasundaran S., Namata G., Wiebe J., Getoor L. 2009. Supervised and unsupervised methods in employing discourse relations for improving opinion polarity classification. In Proc of the conference on Empirical Methods in Natural Language Processing EMNLP, 6-7 August, Suntec, Singapore.

Syarif I, Zaluska E., Prugel-Bennett A., Wills G. 2012. Application of bagging, boosting and stacking to intrusion detection. In Proc of the 8th International Conference on Machine Learning and Data Mining MLDM, 13-20 Jul, Berlin, DE.

Taboada M., Brooke J, Tofiloski M., Voll K., Stede M. 2011. Lexicon-based methods for sentiment analysis. Computational Linguistics 37, pp 267 -307.

Van Asch V. 2013. Macro- and micro-averaged evaluation measures [[basic draft]].

Wang G., Sun J., Ma J., Xue K., Gud J. 2014. Sentiment classification: The contribution of ensemble learning. Decision Support Systems 57, pp. 77–93.

Xia R., Zong C., Li S. 2011. Ensemble of feature sets and classification algorithms for sentiment classification, Information Sciences 181, pp 1138–1152.

The Invertible Construction in Chinese

Yan Cong
Dept. of Chinese and Bilingual Studies
Hong Kong Polytechnic University
stella.cong@polyu.edu.hk

Chu-Ren Huang
Dept. of Chinese and Bilingual Studies
Hong Kong Polytechnic University
churen.huang@polyu.edu.hk

Lian-Hee Wee
Dept. of English Language and Literature
Hong Kong Baptist University
lianhee@hkbu.edu.hk

ABSTRACT

This paper argues that the Invertible Construction (IC) in Chinese is a kind of distributive construction. What appears to be an inversion of word order is best understood as the division of the theme NP to be acted upon by a number of agents for an embedded event. This analysis best captures a number of otherwise intractable properties of the IC including the necessarily quantitative interpretation of the NPs and the incompatibility with adverbs of volition.

1 Introduction

The paper revisits the so-called Invertible Construction in Chinese (henceforth IC); see also (Li & Thompson, 1981:377-395; Li, 1996, 1998; Wee, 2008). Among them, one highly relevant work was a semantic constraint oriented Constructional Grammar account for the IC in Chinese (Huang et al., 1999). Adopting an LFG framework, this paper offers an arguably more comprehensive account of IC through mapping an event structure containing three participants to a dyadic argument structure, thereby producing IC's signature inversion effect as well as other characteristics that otherwise appear to be unrelated.

Traditionally, the IC, or the Flip-flop construction has been described as having the canonical NP_1 V NP_2 being inverted to produce NP_2 V NP_1, (1).

(1) Invertible Construction in Chinese (IC)
NP_1 V $NP_2 \leftrightarrow NP_2$ V NP_1
a. 八个人吃三碗饭
ba-ge-ren chi san-wan-fan
8-CL-person eat 3-CL-rice
Eight people to eat three bowls of rice
b. 三碗饭吃八个人
san-wan-fan chi ba-ge-ren
3-CL-rice eat 8-CL-person
Three bowls of rice to eat eight people

In (1a, b), the English glosses are provided in the infinitive since the Chinese expression is neutral with regard to the specification of tense and aspect. We shall continue to do so throughout the rest of this paper to maintain a faithful translation to the original language's grammar rather than the literary content. The sentence in (1a) has the canonical order of the noun phrases in terms of agenthood and patienthood. In contrast, (1b) is "inverted" or "flip-flopped". The "inverted" form (1b) is more marked than (1a) in that speakers are sometimes stunned by the apparently weird interpretation of the rice being human-eaters before they draw upon the intended reading[1]. It should however be noted that the markedness of (1b) is not due to ungrammaticality, as will be evident when compared with the anomalous reading of (2b) below.

(2) Non-invertability
a. 八个人砸三只碗
ba-ge-ren za san-zhi-wan
8-CL-person break 3-CL-bowls
Eight people to break three bowls
b. * 三只碗砸八个人
san-zhi-wan za ba-ge-ren
3-CL-bowls break 8-CL-person

[1] Note that any possible metaphorical inferences derived from (1b) are excluded from this paper. The present study is confined to the grammatical content of data.

29th Pacific Asia Conference on Language, Information and Computation pages 206 - 211
Shanghai, China, October 30 - November 1, 2015

Reading A: three bowls to break 8 people
Reading B: *three bowls to be broken by 8 people

As presented in (1), the IC appears to be a curious case of a freer word order in a language like Chinese that has no overt case marking, thus the label "IC" refers to both orders i.e., NP_1 V NP_2 (canonical order) and NP_2 V NP_1 (flip-flopped order) that share the same semantic interpretation, which is as shall be explained in Sections 3 and 4, a distributive reading.

It is important to recognize the incompatibility of the IC with expressions of volition (3).

(3) Incompatibility of the IC with volition

a. 八个人故意吃三碗饭 (cf. (1a))
ba-ge-ren guyi chi san-wan-fan
8-CL-person intentionally eat 3-CL-rice
8 people intentionally to eat three bowls of rice

b.* 三碗饭故意吃八个人 (cf. (1b))
san-wan-fan guyi chi ba-ge-ren
3-CL-rice intentionally eat 8-CL-person
3 bowls of rice intentionally to eat 8 people

If the IC is a case of simple inversion, one would expect (3b) to be acceptable given the acceptability of (3a). Incompatibility with expressions of volition demonstrates that the IC does not involve agenthood.

Another property of the IC is the constraint on the quantity readings of the participant NPs, (4) and (5).

(4) Quantity reading of NP_1

a. 张三吃三碗饭
Zhangsan chi san-wan-fan
Zhangsan eat 3-CL-rice
Zhangsan to eat three bowls of rice

b.* 三碗饭吃张三
san-wan-fan chi Zhangsan
3-CL-rice eat Zhangsan
Three bowls of rice to eat Zhangsan

(5) Quantity reading of NP_2

a. 八个人吃饭
ba-ge-ren chi fan
8-CL-people eat rice
Eight people to eat rice

b.* 饭吃八个人
fan chi ba-ge-ren
Rice eat 8-CL-people
Rice to eat eight people

The acceptability of (4a, 5a) in contrast with (4b, 5b) points to the constraint that the participant NPs in the IC must be quantities and non-referential, a point also noted in Li (1996) and Wee (2008).

A third important observation about the IC is the stability of valence. As may be seen with how the IC interacts with monadic or triadic verbs. As shown in (6), *gei* "give" is triadic; *san-ge-xiaofendui* "three teams" is the SOURCE/ AGENT, *wu-ge-shequ* "five communities" is the GOAL/ BENEFICIARY, and *shi-tai-dianshiji* "ten TVs" the THEME.

(6) IC with triadic verbs

a. 三个小分队给五个社区十台电视机
san-ge-xiaofendui geiwu-ge-shequ shi-tai-dianshiji
3-CL-team give 5-CL-community 10-CL-TV
Three teams to give ten TVs to five communities

b.? 五个社区给三个小分队十台电视机
wu-ge-shequ gei san-ge-xiaofendui shi-tai-dianshiji
5-CL-community give 3-CL-team 10-CL-TV
Ten TVs to be given to three teams by five communities

c.? 十台电视机给五个社区三个小分队
shi-tai-dianshiji gei wu-ge-shequ san-ge-xiaofendui
10-CL-TV give 5-CL-community 3-CL-team
Ten TVs to be given to five communities and three teams

d.? 五个社区三个小分队给十台电视机
wu-ge-shequ san-ge-xiaofendui gei shi-tai-dianshiji
5-CL-community 3-CL-team give 10-CL-TV
Five communities and three teams to be given ten TVs

e.* 十台电视机五个社区给三个小分队
shi-tai-dianshiji wu-ge-shequ gei san-ge-xiaofendui
10-CL-TV 5-CL-community give 3-CL-team
Ten TVs and five communities to be given to three teams

f. 十台电视机给五个社区

shi-tai-dianshiji gei wu-ge-shequ
10-CL-TV give 5-CL-community
Ten TVs to give five communities

g. 五个社区给三个小分队
wu-ge-shequ gei san-ge-xiaofendui
5-CL-community give 3-CL-team
Five communities to give three teams

As shown in the acceptability of (6f, g) but the marginality of (6b-d) and the unacceptability of (6e), the IC appears to prefer the expression of two NPs. In (7), we see how an otherwise monadic verb triggers the overt expression of another NP.

(7) <u>IC with monadic verbs</u>

a. 八个人哭了
ba-ge-ren ku le
8-CL-people cry ASP-LE
Eight people cried

b.* 八个人哭
ba-ge-ren ku
8-CL-people cry
Eight people to cry

c.* 三口棺材哭
san-kou-guancai ku
3-CL-coffin cry
Three coffins to cry

d. 八个人哭三口棺材
ba-ge-ren ku san-kou-guancai
8-CL-people cry 3-CL-coffin
Eight people to cry beside three coffins

e. 三口棺材哭八个人
san-kou-guancai ku ba-ge-ren
3-CL-coffin cry 8-CL-people
Three coffins to cry eight people

Whether the verb in the IC is triadic or monadic verbs, the data above suggest the dyadic valence of the IC.

In view of above observations, any account of the IC must take into consideration the characteristics listed (8).

(8) <u>Central characteristics of the IC</u>

a. The license in ordering the theme/patient NPs before the Agent NPs (i.e. the impression of inversion)
b. The unavailability of the IC with certain verbs
c. The incompatibility of the IC with volition
d. The quantity readings of the participant NPs
e. The dyadic valence of the IC

This paper argues that capturing all the above aspects of the IC is best done by understanding the IC as a kind of distributive construction that expresses the divisibility of the theme NP. This captures under a single analytical umbrella the apparently unrelated set of puzzles involving the inverted word order, the incompatibility with volition, as well as the dyadicity of the construction without resorting to very complex structures that might be necessary in a purely syntactic account. The analysis is fleshed out using the conceptual framework of Mohanan's (1994) multi-dimensional syntax, where interface between semantics and syntax can be explicitly expressed and elaborated in the ensuing sections.

2 The Dimensions of Syntax

Regardless of the theoretical framework to which one may subscribe, any syntactic theory must relate (a) the grouping of words, i.e. the constituencies of a given word string; (b) the grammatical function of substrings of words in a sentence, i.e. subjecthood and objecthood against which case and concord are manifest; (c) the valence of predicates, e.g. the transitivity of the main verbs; and (d) the semantic roles played by the participants expressed in the sentence, i.e. thematic roles.

In Government and Binding frameworks, these four "dimensions" of syntax are captured via the movement of syntactic constituents, the binding of traces and the assignment of various properties projected from lexical and/or functional heads (Chomsky, 1981; Haegeman, 1991). Subsequent frameworks such as Minimalism adopt essentially the same strategy (Radford, 1997), also for more alternative frameworks like that of Van Valin and La Polla (1997). Lexical-Functional Grammar (Bresnan, 1982, 2001) relates various dimensions in (a-d) by mapping across different levels.

Consider for example a Chinese sentence such as (9), and a syntactic representation of its constituents as given in Figure 1.

(9) 八个人骑三匹马
Ba-ge-ren qi san-pi ma
8-CL-people ride 3-CL horses

Eight people to ride three horses.

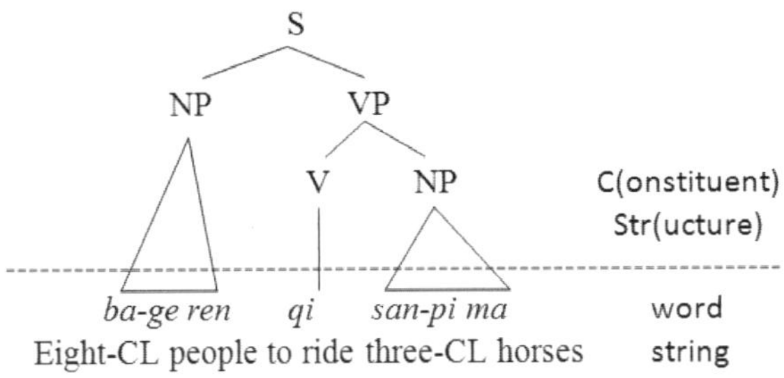

Figure 1. Constituent Structure of (9)

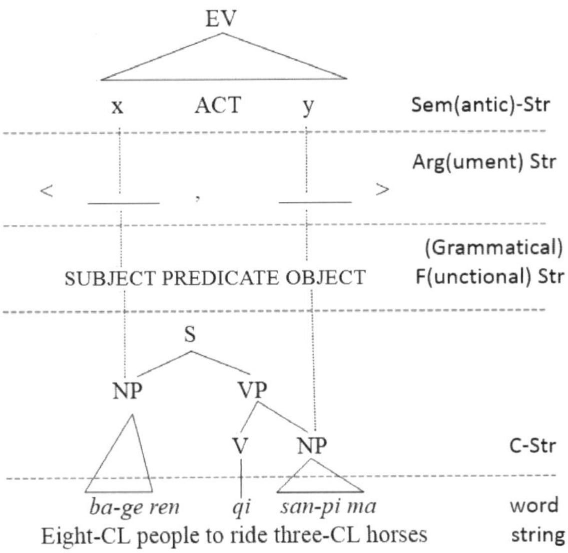

Figure 2. A multi-dimensional model of (9)

Figure 2 is an extension of Figure 1 and captures the various aspects of the (9) sentence in terms of the different parallel dimensions. The C-Str provides the constituencies of the word string. The grammatical roles are expressed in F-Str. These grammatical roles in turn fulfill the valence requirements of the predicate as expressed in the Arg-Str. The Sem-Str informs us that the sentence involves two participants, an actor and a patient, as related by the semantic predicate ACT and its two participants. In Figure 2, the first participant "x" is Agent/actor, which is associated with the first argument slot, the subject grammatical role and the constituent NP. The mapping relations are similarly read for the second semantic participant "y". Encoding thematic information requires a more elaborate Sem-Str than simply saying a NP is assigned a particular thematic role. Mohanan's (1994) conception of the Sem-Str is an adaptation of Dowty's (1970) formalization of Vendler's (1957) verb classification. Vendler recognizes four classes of verbs, (a) state, (b) activity, (c) achievement, and (d) accomplishment, adapted and formalized in Dowty (1979: 159-163). From these, the basic types of thematic roles may be inferred. More elaborate models of Sem-Str can be found in Jackendoff (2002) and various papers in Mohanan (1994) and Wee (1995).

3. The Syntax-Semantics Interface

This section focuses on spelling out why IC licenses two different word orders. This will be most obvious when the semantics of the IC are fully fleshed. The effects will is most transparent when this is presented using Mohanan's (1994) multidimensional model.

We might recall from Section 1 that the IC requires the NPs to have a quantificational reading and is incompatible with expressions of volition. These two properties together suggest that the IC is in fact a construction that expresses the distribution of the theme NP. This implies that at the semantics level there is a complexity of predication, offering the license of word order inversion. Further, as noted in Section 1, the IC is dyadic, hence it must be stipulated that the construction has a valence of two. To this end, we propose the representation in Figure 3 for IC.

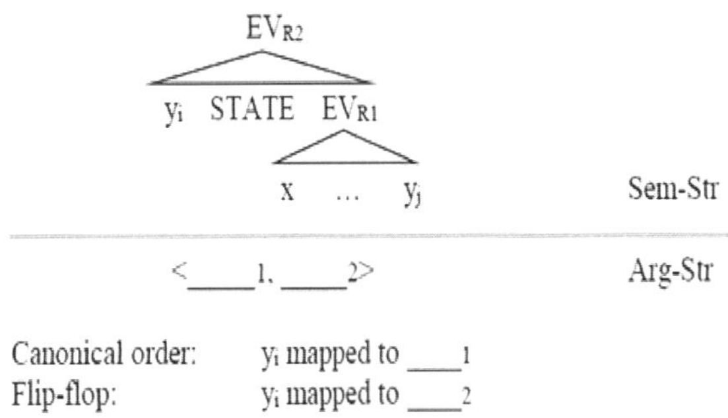

Figure 3. Model of the IC

Figure 3 captures the intended reading that the IC is a stative, and not an activity or an accomplishment as might otherwise been assumed when one sees verbs like *ride* or *eat*. The stative here is that of "distributivity" with the interpretation that y_i is to be the dividend. This explains why the NPs in ICs are necessarily numeral NPs that do not bear referentiality are non-volitional (Li, 1998; Wee, 2001).

The IC contains a sub-event EV_{R1} that corresponds to the verb, but that is not what the IC is. The IC is the whole structure, with the semantics corresponding to EV_{R2}. There is therefore a third and higher semantic participant corresponding to y_i, which is co-referent with the embedded y_j, the former being the theme of the matrix stative event EV_{R2} and the latter the theme/patient of the embedded event EV_{R1}.

From Figure 3, there are two options of mapping the semantic participants to the arguments in the Arg-Str. Notice that there are only two argument positions. If mapping lines are not allowed to cross (more on this in relation to the Uniformity of Theta Assignment Hypothesis later), there are exactly two possible mappings: either y_i maps to the first argument slot and x to the second, or x could map to the first and y_j the second. This effectively produces two possible word orders for the same semantic representation. The impression of inversion is thus illusory of what is in our account the optionality of mapping between the semantic participants and the argument positions.

The account squares nicely with the Uniformity of Theta Assignment Hypothesis (UTAH, Baker, 1997) where semantic prominence aligns with the linear order of the arguments. UTAH militates against possibilities of cross mappings between the Sem-Str and the Arg-Str, which therefore predicts that there will only be two possible orders for the IC and would also ensure that all semantic participants will surface (recall that y_i and y_j are co-referent).

Returning to the example in (1), we now offer the following explanations. Firstly, given that there are two orders in the IC, one of the orders will be coincidental to the canonical expression that would have an agentive reading. That agentive reading would correspond to EV_{R1} but crucially there is no higher matrix EV_{R2} bearing the stative predicate. Secondly, since the IC has a distributive reading due to the presence of EV_{R2}, there will be three semantic participants which must be mapped into the Arg-Str that has only two slots. With UTAH, this produces exactly two word orders. Thirdly, the stativity of EV_{R2} predicts incompatibility of expressions of volition. Finally, the dyadicity of the IC is accounted for by the Arg-Str that has only two slots, and is therefore oblivious to the valence of the verb. In IC, it is the valence of the construction. In the case of (1) where the verb is *eat*, the solution is largely the same as that given in Figure 3, except that here the EV_{R1} is an accomplishment, shown in Figure 4.

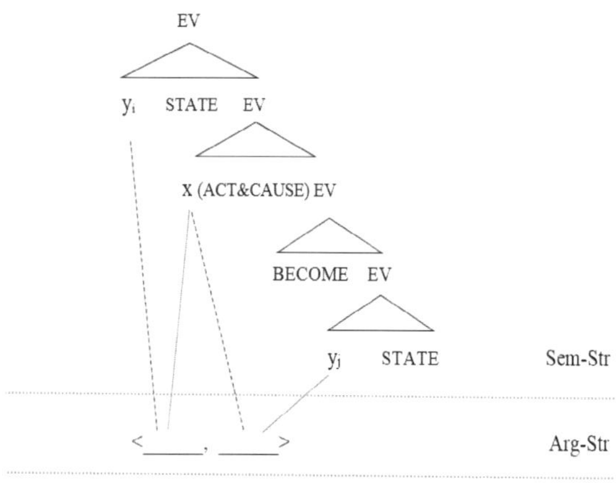

Figure 4. IC with accomplishment verbs

In summary, the hypothesized model in Figure 3 works well in that it explains the puzzles put forward in Section 1, successfully predicting all the main characteristics of the IC:

i. the dyadic valence of the IC;
ii. the quantity reading of the IC;
iii. the incompatibility of the IC with volition; and
iv. the unavailability of the IC with certain verbs

There is only one issue has not been explored in this paper regarding the IC. We have not attempted to sort out which verbs are compatible with IC, as evidently not attested with the example in (2), and also probably not with the verb *ride* in (9). It is certainly an important issue for a comprehensive grasp of the IC and presumably some kind of constraint must be at work. Wee (2008) suspects that the issue may not be syntactic or semantic at all, but rather due to pragmatic factors. We shall have to leave this area unexplored for now.

4. Concluding Remarks

This paper explains the IC as essentially a kind of

distributive construction (calculation formula), with dyadic valences, i.e., the dividend and the divisor. This divisibility nature of the IC determines that the participant roles must be quantity denoting. In explaining the syntax-semantics interface that is so central to how the IC works, this paper adopted an LFG based multi-dimensional framework. However, it must be noted that any other framework that is capable of expressing this interface would be compatible with the analysis advocated here.

ACKNOWLEDGMENT

We would like to thank HK PolyU-PKU Research Centre for Chinese Linguistics for the support to present this paper at PACLIC-29. First author would also like to thank the Phonology Lab at the Hong Kong Baptist University under the directorship of Dr. Wee for the stimulating discussion that led to the idea of this paper. All remaining errors are ours.

REFERENCES

Baker, Mark. 1997. Thematic roles and syntactic structure, Haegeman, Lilianne. (ed.), *Elements ofGrammar.*, 73-137, Kluwer Academic Publishers.

Bresnan, Joan. 1982. *The mental representation of Grammatical Relations*. Cambridge, Mass: the MIT Press.

Bresnan, Joan. 2001. *Lexical-Functional Syntax*. Oxford: Blackwell Publishers.

Chomsky, Noam. 1981. *Lectures on Government and Binding*. Dordrecht: Foris.

Dowty, David. 1979. *Word Meaning and Montague grammar—the Semantics of Verbs and Times in Generative Semantics and in Montague's PTQ*. Holland: D. Reidel Publishing Company.

Dowty, David. 1991. Thematic Proto-Roles and Argument Selection. *Language*. 67: 547-619.

Haegeman, Lilianne. 1991. *Introduction to Government and Binding Theory*. Oxford: Blackwell Publishers.

Huang, Chu-Ren and Lin, Fu-Wen. 1992. Composite Event Structure and Complex Predicates: A Template-based Approach to Argument Selection. In *Proceedings of the Third Annual Meeting of the Formal Linguistics Society of Mid-America*, Indiana University Linguistics Club, Bloomington, Indiana, pp.90-108.

Huang, Chu-Ren, Li-Ping Chang, Kathleen Ahrens, and Chao-Ran Chen. 1999. 詞彙語意和句式語意的互動關係。(The Interaction of Lexical Semantics and Constructional Meanings). In Y. Yin et al. Eds. *Chinese Language and Linguistics V: Interactions in Language*. Pp.413-438. Taipei: Institute of Linguistics, Academia Sinica.

Jackendoff, Ray. 2002. *Foundations of Language*. Oxford University Press.

Li, Audrey Yen-Hui. 1996. *A Number Projection. Unpublished manuscript*, University of Southern California at Los Angeles.

Li, Audrey Yen-Hui. 1998. Argument determiner phrases and number phrases. *Linguistic Inquiry* 29: 693-702.

Li, Charles N. and Thompson, Sandra. A. 1981. *Mandarin Chinese: A Functional Reference Grammar*. Berkeley, California: University of California Press.

Mohanan, Tara. 1994. *Arguments in Hindi*. Stanford: CSLI Publications.

Mohanan, Tara and Wee, L. 1999. *Grammatical Semantics: evidence for structure in meanging*. Stanford: CSLI.

Radford, Andrew. 1997. *Syntax: A minimalist introduction*. London: Cambridge University Press.

Van Valin, Robert D. and Randy La Polla. 1997. *Syntax: structure, meaning and function*. Cambridge University Press.

Vendler, Zeno. 1957. Verbs and Times. *The Philosophical Review*. 66:143-160.

Wee, Lian-Hee. 2008. "The rice ate four people" and such Flip-Flops. *The Chinese Language Teachers Association* 43: 33-58.

ABBREVIATIONS & SYMBOLS IN THE CONTENT

Activity: ACT
Argument structure: Arg-Str
ASP: aspect marker
Classifier(s): CL
Determiner: Det
Determiner Phrase: DP
Event: EV
Lexical Functional Grammar: LFG
Grammatical Constituent Structure: C-Str
Grammatical Function Structure: F-Str
Invertible Construction: IC
Le: LE (aspectual marker)
Number: Num
Numeral phrase: NumP
Particle: Prt
Semantic Structure: Sem-Str
Syntactically unacceptable: *
Semantically odd: ?

Pan's (2001) puzzle revisited

Hyunjun Park
City University of Hong Kong
tudorgepark@gmail.com

Abstract

The notion of logophoricity has long played a crucial role in understanding the co-referential relations between certain anaphoric expressions cross-linguistically, especially for long-distance anaphors violating a locality constraint and syntactic prominence conditions within the framework of pure syntactic accounts. However, Pan (2001) has shown that the long-distance binding of Chinese *ziji* should not be treated with the logophoric accounts in some aspects. This paper revisits Pan's (2001) puzzle, which arises from the ability of *ziji* to serve as a logophor, in order to call attention to what the alternative to this view might be, and proposes a solution to it through the notion of empathy, in Kuno and Kaburaki's (1977) sense of the term, so that long-distance anaphors, which are not fully covered in terms of logophoricity, can be reconciled with other East Asian languages, such as Japanese *zibun* and Korean *caki*, in terms of a unified treatment.

1 Introduction

It has been widely noted that what licenses the long-distance binding is closely related to the logophoric property of reflexives. More specifically, since Sells' (1987) logophoric approach on Icelandic and Japanese, many researchers (Yoon 1989, Huang and Liu 2001, among others) have argued that the binding behaviors of long-distance anaphors, such as those in Korean and Chinese, are attributed to the logophoric use of reflexives and that they carry the de facto identical function.

Huang and Liu (2001) point out that the three distinct roles in discourse, which are **source**, **self**, and **pivot** originally coined by Sells (1987), for the logophoric use of the Chinese long-distance *ziji* are a necessary but not a sufficient condition for long-distance anaphors. For this reason, they suggest that the notion of attitude *de se* be introduced to the long-distance anaphor *ziji*.[1]

However, despite a close link between the long-distance anaphor and logophoricity as a licensing condition for the referent it refers to, it has been repeatedly observed that logophoric accounts of long-distance anaphors have not been fully successful, facing a variety of counterexamples. In addition, in contrast to logophoric accounts for *ziji* binding, Pan (2001) strongly argues that the long-distance anaphor *ziji* should not be treated with logophoric accounts since some properties of *ziji* are not compatible with logophoricity. Pan's view is not incorrect. Indeed, the definition that lies at the heart of logophoricity is not satisfactory to cover every aspect of long-distance anaphors, especially in Chinese, since they are used as a versatile tool.

This paper revisits Pan's (2001) puzzle, which arises from the ability of *ziji* to serve as a logophor, in order to call attention to what the alternative to this view might be, and proposes a solution to it through the notion of empathy, in Kuno and Kaburaki's (1977) sense of the term, so that the long-distance anaphors, which are not fully covered in terms of logophoricity, can be reconciled with other East Asian languages, such as Japanese *zibun* and Korean *caki*, in terms of a unified treatment.

The structure of this paper is as follows. We discuss Pan's puzzle in Section 2, describing which kinds of binding behaviors in Chinese are not compatible with the properties of logophoricity. Section 3 argues that the term empathy should be accepted in order to complement the logophoric accounts of

[1] Pan (1997) first proposed that the Chinese long-distance anaphor *ziji* can be treated as a *de se* anaphor, resulting in an obligatory *de se* construal.

29th Pacific Asia Conference on Language, Information and Computation pages 212 - 220
Shanghai, China, October 30 - November 1, 2015

the long-distance bound anaphor *ziji*. Section 4 revisits Pan's puzzle and describes that his claim is partly the case in certain environments, and that it can be accounted for with the empathic accounts. Thus, we argue that the long-distance anaphor *ziji* in Chinese should be divided into two categories of logophor and empathy. Finally, we conclude our work in Section 5.

2 Pan's (2001) puzzle

Following logophoric analysis, many scholars have tried to account for the peculiar phenomena of long-distance anaphors cross-linguistically. It has been observed in the literature (Clements 1975, Sells 1987, Kuno 1987, Stirling 1993, Pearson 2013, among others) that a logophoric pronoun commonly manifests the three properties listed in (1).

(1) a. It can always have the **source** as its antecedent.
b. It cannot have the first person pronoun as its antecedent.
c. It does not exhibit the blocking effect.
(Pan 2001: 290)

Interestingly, Pan (2001) proposes the above properties as evidence against the treatment of *ziji* as a logophor. More specifically, if *ziji* functions as a logophor in a certain reported discourse context, it should exhibit the three properties which are the characteristics of a logophoric pronoun. However, it genuinely seems to be the case that the binding behaviors of *ziji* do not show any of them. To illustrate this point, this section reviews Pan's puzzle for logophoric *ziji*.

2.1 Source

According to Pan (2001), *ziji* co-referential with the long-distance antecedent cannot always have the noun phrase carrying the role of **source** as its antecedent, though logophoric pronouns can. The following examples illustrate this point.

(2) a. Ama$_i$ se tso Kofi$_j$ gbɔ be
Ama hear from Kofi side that
yè$_{i/j}$-xɔ nunana.
Log-receive gift
'Ama$_i$ heard from Kofi$_j$ that she$_i$/he$_j$ had received a gift.'
b. Me$_i$-se tso Kofi$_j$ gbɔ be yè$_{*i/j}$-xɔ
Pro-hear from Kofi side that Log-receive
nunana.
gift
'I$_i$ heard from Kofi$_j$ that *I/he$_j$ had received a gift.' (Clements 1975: 158-9)

(3) a. Lisi$_i$ shuo Zhangsan$_j$ de shu
Lisi say Zhangsan DE book
hai-le ziji$_{i/j}$.
hurt-Perf self
'Lisi says that Zhangsan's book hurt him/himself.'
b. Zhangsan$_i$ cong Lisi$_j$ nar tingshuo
Zhangsan from Lisi there hear
naben shu hai-le ziji$_{i/*j}$.
that-CL book hurt-Perf self
'Zhangsan heard from Lisi that that book hurt himself.' (Pan 2001: 291)

While the logophoric pronoun *yè* in Ewe, one of the West African languages, in (2a) can be co-referential with either the matrix subject *Ama* or oblique *Kofi*, which functions as the **source** of the given reportive context, that in (2b) can only refer to *Kofi* with the thematic function of **source**, but not the first person pronoun *me* 'I'. That is, the sentence in (2b) is unacceptable when the first person pronoun *me* 'I' is an antecedent of the logophoric pronoun *yè* because the referent of a logophoric pronoun should be in the third person. Similarly, the matrix subject *Lisi* in (3a) is understood as the **source** of the reported speech and thus can be a candidate for the possible antecedents of *ziji* as well as possessive *Zhangsan* in the complement clause. In contrast to (2a), on the other hand, the oblique *Lisi* in (3b) cannot be the antecedent of *ziji* in spite of its **source** role in the reported discourse. The following sentence is compatible with this idea.

(4) Wo$_i$ cong Lisi$_j$ nar tingshuo laoshi
I from Lisi there hear teacher
ma-le ziji$_{i/*j}$.
criticize-Perf self
'I heard from Lisi that the teacher criticized me.'

Ziji in (4) is co-referential with the first person pronoun *wo* 'I' rather than with the **source** *Lisi*. Therefore, the long-distance bound *ziji* cannot always refer to a **source** of communication, as in Sells' (1987) system, and thus in this case logophoric *ziji* does not seem to be a sufficient condition to independently license its antecedent, unlike logophoric pronouns.

2.2 First person pronoun

Pan (2001) recognizes that *ziji* can refer to the first person pronoun *wo* 'I' at a long-distance with ease in a given discourse context, but this is an entirely different property from that which logophoric pronouns exhibit, as exemplified in (5).

(5) a. Wo$_i$ zhidao Lisi$_j$ bu xihuan ziji$_{?i/j}$.
I know Lisi not like self
'I knew that Lisi did not like me/himself.'

b. Wo$_i$ yizhi yiwei Zhangsan$_j$ xihuan ziji$_{i/j}$,
I so-far think Zhangsan like self
keshi wo cuo le.
but I wrong Perf
'I always thought that Zhangsan liked me/himself, but I was wrong.'

c. Wo$_i$ bu xihuan Lisi$_j$ guan ziji$_{i/j}$ de
I not like Lisi interfere self DE
shi.
Matter
'I don't like Lisi interfering in my/his (own) business.'

d. Ni$_i$ xihuan Lisi$_j$ guan ziji$_{i/j}$ de shi
You like Lisi interfere self DE matter
ma?
Q
'Do you like Lisi interfering in your (own) business?' (Pan 2001: 283)

According to Pearson (2013), the logophoric pronoun *yè* in Ewe preferentially refers to a third person as its antecedent, whereas referring to a first or second person antecedent is degraded, as illustrated in (6) and (7).

(6) a. *M xɔse be yè nyi sukuvi nyoe de.
Pro believethat Log Cop student good Art
'I believe that I am a good student.'

b. M xɔse be m nyi sukuvi nyoe de.
Pro believe that Pro Cop student good Art
'I believe that I am a good student.'

(7) a. *O xɔse be yè nyi sukuvi nyoe de.
Pro believethat Log Cop student good Art
'You believe that you are a good student.'

b. O xɔse be o nyi sukuvi nyoe de.
Pro believethat Pro Cop student good Art
'You believe that you are a good student.'
(Pearson 2013:449-50)

Clements (1975) also claims that logophoric pronouns in Ewe mainly appear to introduce indirect speech when referring to the attitude holder with respect to the propositional complement clause, though they can be replaced by the first person pronoun *I* in direct discourse. Moreover, the logophoric pronouns are complementary with first person pronouns in direct speech, which means that the logophoric pronouns are restricted to having third person antecedents, and cannot have first person pronoun antecedents. This point can be illustrated by the following sentences.

(8) Kofi gblɔ na wo be yè-a-dyi ga-a
Kofi speak to Pro that Log-T-seek money-D
na wo.
for Pro
'Kofi$_i$ said to them that he$_i$ would seek the money for them.'

(9) Kofi gblɔ na wo be: ma-dyi ga-a
Kofi speak to Pro that I-seek money-D
na mi.
for Pro
'Kofi$_i$ said to them: "I'll seek the money for you."' (Clements 1975: 152)

The sentences in (8) and (9) have shown that the Ewe language makes a sharp distinction between indirect speech and direct speech. In other words, the logophoric pronoun *yè* is exclusively used in the reportive context, as in (8), and the first person pronoun *ma*, which is the complex form consisting of the first person pronoun *me* and tense marker *a-*, as in (9), is normally used to refer to the external speaker in direct speech.

2.3 Blocking effect

The long-distance binding of *ziji* exhibits the blocking effect in which first and second person elements block the long-distance binding of *ziji* by all the possible third person antecedents, while the long-distance anaphors in the other languages, such as Japanese[2] and Korean respectively, do not, as exemplified in (10) through (12).

(10) a. Zhangsan$_i$ renwei Lisi$_j$ neiyang zuo
Zhangsan think Lisi that-way do
dui ziji$_{i/j}$ buli.
to self not-beneficial
'Zhangsan$_i$ felt that Lisi's$_j$ acting that way didn't do him$_{i/j}$ any good.'

[2] It has long been noted that there is no blocking effect in Japanese *zibun* binding. However, Nishigauchi (2014) indicates that the blocking effect can be observed even in Japanese, when the addition of a first person pronoun results in conflicting Empathy Foci.

b. Zhangsan$_i$ renwei wo/ni$_j$ neiyang zuo
Zhangsan think I/you that-way do
dui ziji$_{*i/j}$ buli.
to self not-beneficial
'Zhangsan$_i$ felt that my/your$_j$ acting that way didn't do him$_{*i}$/me/you$_j$ any good.'
(Pan 2001: 281)

(11) a. Taroo$_i$-wa boku-ga zibun$_i$-o but-ta
Taroo-Top I-Nom self-Acc hit-Past
koto-o mada urande-i-ru.
fact-Acc still resent-Asp-Pres
'Taroo$_i$ still resents that I hit him$_i$.'

b. Taroo$_i$-wa boku-ga zibun$_i$-ni okane-o
Taroo-Top I-Nom self-Dat money-Acc
kasi-ta koto-o sukkari
lend-Past that-Acc completely
wasure-ta rasii.
forget-Past seem
'Taroo seems to have completely forgotten that I had loaned self money.'
(Kuno 1978: 212-213)

(12) a. Chelswu$_i$-nun nay$_j$-ka caki$_{i/*j}$-lul
Chelswu-Top I-Nom self-Acc
Piphanhay-ess-tako sayngkakha-n-ta.
criticize-Past-Comp think-Pres-Decl
'Chelswu thinks that I criticized him/*myself.'

b. Na$_i$-nun Chelswu$_j$-ka caki$_{*i/j}$-lul
I-Top Chelswu-Nom self-Acc
Piphanhay-ess-tako sayngkakha-n-ta.
criticize-Past-Comp think-Pres-Decl
'I think that Chelswu criticized *me/himself.'

As a matter of fact, the blocking effect is not the property of logophoric pronouns, since logophoric pronouns are necessarily construed as referring to the reported speaker who is the attitude holder and this attitude holder is preferentially occupied by a third person. The key evidence from Ewe is shown in (13).

(13) a. Kofi$_i$ xɔ agbalẽ tso gbɔ-nye$_j$ be
Kofi receive letter from side-Pro that
yè$_{i/*j}$-a-va me kpe na m.
Log-T-come cast block for Pro
'Kofi$_i$ got a letter from me saying that he$_i$ should come cast blocks for me.'

b. Me$_i$-xɔ agbalẽ tso Kofi$_j$ gbɔ be
Pro-receive letter from Kofi side that
ma$_i$-va me kpe na yè$_j$.
Pro/T-come cast block for Pro
'I$_i$ got a letter from Kofi$_j$ saying that he$_i$ should come cast blocks for me$_i$.'
(Clements 1975: 159)

In addition, the notion of logophoricity cannot account for the long-distance bound *ziji* observed in extensional contexts, though it can partly explain the occurrences of *ziji* in intensional contexts such as attitude reports or reported propositions, as shown in (14).

(14) Zhangsan$_i$ mingling Lisi$_j$ [s PRO gei ziji$_{i/j}$
Zhangsan order Lisi to self
guahuzi].
shave
'Zhangsan ordered Lisi to shave him/himself.'
(Pan 2001: 291)

Based on the evidence of the above example, Pan (2001) strongly argues that the long-distance bound *ziji* cannot be fully covered in terms of logophoricity. The next section is devoted to resolving this puzzle.

3 Solution through empathy

We consider that the theory of empathy plays an important role in many aspects of the interpretation of long-distance anaphors observed in Chinese. The underlying assumption is that linguistic expression may capture the speaker's attitude toward its participants in describing a state of affairs. The concept of empathy was first introduced into linguistic analysis by Kuno and Kaburaki (1977), and the notion has been developed to account for a host of linguistic phenomena that otherwise defy unified explanation within the framework of formal linguistics (Kuno 1978, 1987, Yokoyama 1980, Oshima 2004, 2007, Wang and Pan 2014, 2015, among others).

3.1 Notion of empathy

Kuno and Kaburaki (1977) vividly describe the term empathy with respect to the camera angle chosen by a director when shooting a scene. Similarly, a speaker makes the same kind of decision when s/he describes an event or state. For instance, in describing a hitting situation involving a man named *John* and his wife *Mary*, the speaker can say it in numerous ways, depending on the different positions which s/he takes, some of which are shown in (15).

(15) a. John hit Mary.
b. John hit his wife.
c. Mary's husband hit her.
(Kuno and Kaburaki 1977: 627)

According to Kuno and Kaburaki (1977), these sentences differ from each other in reference to the speaker's view point or camera angle, though all the examples have the same logical content. In other word, in (15a), the event is being described objectively. That is, the camera is placed at equal distance from both *John* and *Mary*. However, the speaker is describing the event with his standpoint closer to *John* in (15b) and closer to *Mary* in (15c), respectively.

Kuno (1987) defines the notion of empathy, as illustrated in (16).

(16) Empathy is the speaker's identification, which may vary in degree, with a person/thing that participates in the event or state that he describes in a sentence.
Degree of Empathy: The degree of the speaker's empathy with x, E(x), ranges from 0 to 1, with E(x)=1 signifying his total identification with x, and E(x)=0 signifying a total lack of identification.
(Kuno 1987: 206)

To see how the empathy works in the sentence, consider the following examples in Japanese.

(17) Taroo-wa Hanako-ni hon-o yat-ta.
Taroo-Top Hanako-Dat book-Acc give-Past
'Taroo gave Hanako a book.'

(18) Taroo-wa Hanako-ni hon-o kure-ta.
Taroo-Top Hanako-Dat book-Acc give-Past
'Taroo gave Hanako a book.'

As noted by Kuno (1987), Japanese has a built-in mechanism for overtly specifying what the speaker's standpoint is when an event is described, which includes special verbs such as giving verbs *yaru* and *kureru* which express the empathy relationship. The speaker describes (17) from *Taroo*'s standpoint and (18) from *Hanako*'s point of view. In other words, the agent-centered verb *yaru* is used when the speaker empathizes more with the referent of the subject, whereas the beneficiary-centered verb *kureru* is used when the speaker empathizes more with the referent of the dative object rather than with that of the subject object.

Assuming that the verbs such as *hear from* and *receive from* in English require that the speaker's empathy be placed on the referent as the goal occurring in subject position, rather than the agent in object position of the preposition *from*, the sentences in (19) and (20) seem highly compatible with empathy-based accounts.

(19) John told Mary that Bill was sick.
(20) Mary heard from John that Bill was sick.
(Kuno and Kaburaki 1977: 645)

The two sentences in (19) and (20) fundamentally deliver identical situations in their logical content, but they seem to differ from each other in the standpoint from which the speaker has intentionally chosen to describe the events, and empathize more with a specific person. Thus, it can be easily presupposed that the speaker empathizes more with *John* than with *Mary* in (19), while the speaker empathizes more with *Mary* than with *John* in (20).

3.2 Japanese *zibun* as an empathy locus

Given the fundamental notion of empathy we have discussed so far, Kuno (1987) has further formalized some possible empathy relationships within a sentence, based on semantic or pragmatic scales, where a higher ranked participant tends to be much more empathized with than a lower ranked one, as shown below.

(21) Surface Structure Empathy Hierarchy: It is easier for the speaker to empathize with the referent of the subject than with the referent of other NPs in the sentence.
E(subject) > E(other NPs)

(22) Speech Act Empathy Hierarchy: The speaker cannot empathize with someone else more than with himself/herself.
E(speaker) > E(others)

(23) Ban on Conflicting Empathy Foci: A single sentence cannot contain logical conflicts in empathy relationships.

(24) Animacy Empathy Hierarchy: It is easier for the speaker to empathize with animate objects than with inanimate objects.[3]
(Kuno 1987: 207-212)

Kuno and Kaburaki (1977) remark that Japanese reflexive pronoun *zibun* can be characterized as an empathy expression, namely an empathy locus referring to the participant with which the speaker represents his or her high degree of empathy, as shown in (25) and (26).

(25) *Taroo$_i$-wa Hanako-ga zibun$_i$-ni
Taroo-Top Hanako-Nom self-Dat
yat-ta hon-o yon-da.
give-Past book-Acc read-Past

[3] This is the revised version offered by Oshima (2006: 169).

'Taroo$_i$ read the book Hanako gave to him$_i$.'

(26) Taroo$_i$-wa Hanako-ga zibun$_i$-ni kure-ta
Taroo-Top Hanako-Nom self-Dat give-Past
hon-o yon-da.
book-Acc read-Past
'Taroo$_i$ read the book Hanako gave to him$_i$.'
(Oshima 2006: 174)

As mentioned earlier, according to the Ban on Conflicting Empathy Foci, proposed by Kuno and Kaburaki (1977), the empathy relationships within a single sentence must be consistent with each other. We have observed that the giving verbs, such as *yaru* and *kureru*, in Japanese can overtly specify the speaker's empathy with different participants in his or her description of events or states produced in a given context. Hence, the use of *kureru* indicates the relatively higher degree of the speaker's empathy with the recipient, but the use of *yaru* represents empathy with the agent. The reflexive form *zibun*, on the other hand, can also function as representing the empathy locus by empathizing with its referent. More specifically, the speaker is allowed to use *zibun* to refer to its antecedent *Taroo* as his or her empathy locus in both (25) and (26). In this connection, the speaker's empathy locus of *zibun* in (26) is compatible with that of *kureru*, but not that of *zibun* in (25). Based on this fact, (26) is acceptable, but (25) is unacceptable. Eventually, the conflicting empathy foci in a single sentence yield the contrast between (25) and (26).

At this point, it is necessary to mention that the speaker's empathy can play a leading role in the way that it provides a lucid explanation of the long-distance anaphors, especially in East Asian languages such as Chinese *ziji*, Japanese *zibun*, and Korean *caki*. Moreover, Oshima (2004, 2006, 2007) claims that the concepts between logophor and empathy should, strictly speaking, be distinguished in terms of the licensing conditions of each use. Such a subtle distinction could be explained by the following expression.

(27) ɖɛvi-a$_i$ xɔ tohehe be
child-Det receive punishment so.that
yè$_i$-a-ga-da alakpa ake o.
Log-T-P-tell lie again not
'The child$_i$ received punishment so that he$_i$ wouldn't tell lies again.'
(Clements 1975: 160)

Clements (1975) accounts for the use of logophoric pronoun *yè* in (27) with an extended logophoric use such that *yè* represents the intention of its antecedent. That is to say that the child voluntarily received punishment to prevent future wrongdoing. However, it is worth noting that there is no attitude predicate in (27). Consider the related examples in East Asian languages, repeated here in (29) from (26).

(28) Zongtong$_i$ qing wo$_j$ zuo zai ziji$_{i/*j}$ de
president ask I sit at self DE
shenbian. (Chinese)
side
'The president$_i$ asked me$_j$ to sit beside him$_i$/myself$_{*j}$.' (Xu 1993: 136)

(29) Taroo$_i$-wa Hanako-ga zibun$_i$-ni kure-ta
Taroo-Top Hanako-Nom self-Dat give-Past
hon-o yon-da. (Japanese)
book-Acc read-Past
'Taroo$_i$ read the book Hanako gave to him$_i$.'

(30) Chelswu$_i$-nun Younghee$_j$-ka caki$_i$-eykey
Chelswu-Top Younghee-Nom self-Dat
cwu-n chayk-ul ilk-ess-ta. (Korean)
give-Abn book-Acc read-Past-Decl
'Chelswu$_i$ read the book Younghee gave to him$_i$.'

Considering the notion of logophoric pronouns, which are always co-referential with the author of a secondary discourse associated with an intensional context, the reason that the expressions observed in (28) through (30) are accounted for, in terms of a linguistic device similar to logophoricity, is not a proper explanation. These expressions are more empathy-loaded than logophoric.

4 Pan's (2001) puzzle revisited

This section revisits Pan's (2001) puzzle, which arises from the ability of *ziji* to serve as a logophor and proposes a solution to it through the notion of empathy.

Given the semantic nature and discourse effects of the empathy relation in a given discourse context, it is expected that languages other than Japanese may make use of similar mechanisms to encode linguistic representation of the empathy relation, though in what domains and how they are postulated in syntax may differ within and between languages. Recall that the logophoric pronouns can show up only in the scope of an attitude predicate, since the expressions in question are a sort of variable that is obligatorily bound by the attitude holder associated with such a predicate. However, in reality, the behaviors of the long-distance anaphor *ziji* are much more extensive than expected.

4.1 Source

As we saw earlier, *ziji* bound by a long-distance antecedent cannot always have the noun phrase carrying the role of **source** as its antecedent, though logophoric pronouns can.

(31) a. Zhangsan$_i$ cong Lisi$_j$ nar tingshuo
Zhangsan from Lisi there hear
naben shu hai-le ziji$_{i/*j}$.
that-CL book hurt-Perf self
'Zhangsan heard from Lisi that that book hurt himself.' (Pan 2001: 291)

b. Wo$_i$ cong Lisi$_j$ nar tingshuo
Zhangsan from Lisi there hear
laoshi ma-le ziji$_{i/*j}$.
teacher criticize-Perf self
'I heard from Lisi that the teacher criticized me.'

While the logophoric pronoun *yè* in (2a) can be coreferential with either *Ama* or *Kofi,* that in (2b) may refer only to *Kofi* with the thematic function of **source**, but not the first person pronoun *me* 'I'. On the other hand, Chinese *ziji*, as shown in (31a) and (31b), can only refer to the matrix subject other than the **source** of the reported discourse regardless of person. In this regard, we can employ the Surface Structure Empathy Hierarchy, which shows that the speaker's empathy with the referent of the subject is ranked higher than any other individual, to account for this sort of behavior of *ziji*. In addition, another advantage is that the use of long-distance anaphors in extensional contexts may be compatible with the empathic interpretation, as shown in (14).

The logophoricity account for *ziji* cannot be postulated here because the distribution of the logophoric pronoun is strictly restricted to the scope of attitude predicates, as exemplified in (32).

(32) a. *Kofi wɔ be Marie yè dzo.
Kofi do that Mary Log leave
'Kofi caused Mary to leave.'

b. Kofi wɔ be Marie dzo.
Kofi do that Mary leave
'Kofi caused Mary to leave.'
(Pearson 2013: 445)

The sentence in (32a) shows that when the verb which subcategorizes a clause complement is not an attitude predicate, the logophoric pronoun such as *yè* cannot be used to refer to the referent as an attitude holder. Thus, (32a) is unacceptable, but (32b) is acceptable because there is no logophoric pronoun in the sentence.[4]

4.2 First person pronoun

Accounting for the distribution of logophoric pronouns may be able to offer a vital clue in solving the puzzle of the qualification of *ziji* to perform as a logophor, posed by Pan (2001). It has generally been noted that logophoric pronouns always refer to the agent of reported utterance or thought. In addition, as Yoon (1989) points out, the use of a logophor to indirectly report the thoughts or feelings of a first person, who is the speaker, or a second person, who is the addressee, seems to be highly unnatural.[5] For this reason, logophoric pronouns in Ewe mainly appear to introduce indirect speech when referring to the attitude holder with respect to the propositional complement clause, though they can be replaced by the first person pronoun *I* in direct discourse, as shown in (8) and (9).

As we can see from the examples above, the role of logophoric pronouns and first person pronouns somewhat resemble each other with respect to being used as first person forms except that while first person pronouns refer to the actual speaker in direct discourse, logophoric pronouns refer to the reported speaker in indirect discourse. If this is correct, it can be said that logophoric pronouns are in complementary distribution with first person pronouns and thus the two forms never occur in exactly the same environment, but in mutually-exclusive environments.

Given the properties of the distribution of logophors observed so far, it seems unreasonable to conclude that the following sentences can be correctly predicted according to the licensing condition on logophoricity. Consider the examples of (5c) and (5d).

[4] A reviewer points out how we can explain the ambiguity in the co-referential relations: given the distinction between logophoric and empathic use, we assume that the long-distance *ziji* refers to either the internal speaker as the attitude holder or the external speaker's empathy locus in the discourse context.

[5] Yoon further argues that the binding behaviors of Korean *caki* fit nicely into the notion of logophoricity since *caki* is not compatible with first or second person antecedents.

In these examples, *ziji* can take the matrix subjects *wo* 'I' and *ni* 'you' at a long-distance as its antecedents. However, note that they are not construed as referring to the attitude holder because the verb such as *like* is not an attitude predicate. Rather, these sentences seem to be more readily accounted for in terms of empathy relation rather than logophoricity. If the empathy locus is anchored to the speaker, then *ziji* can be co-referential with the first person pronoun *wo* 'I' referring to the external speaker, as in (5c). If the empathy locus is anchored to the addressee, then *ziji* can refer to the second person pronoun *ni* 'you' referring to the addressee, as in (5d). Therefore, this empathy relation is compatible with the Speech Act Empathy Hierarchy.

4.3 Blocking effect

Recall that Pan (2001) claims that there is no reasonable way to explain the blocking effect of the long-distance binding *ziji* by means of the property of logophoric use. This is because what appears to be the blocking effect in Chinese is due to the presence of a first person pronoun in the sentence. From the discussion thus far, however, it can be said that the logophoric pronoun is not used to refer to a first person pronoun in the reported discourse. The incompatibility with the blocking effect in the logophoric environment is confirmed by the sentences in (13). There are no blocking effects though first person pronouns, referring to the external speaker, occur either in the complement clause or in the matrix clause, since the logophoric pronoun *yè* only refers to the third person rather than the first person pronoun.

Moreover, it is worth making a contrast between the logophoric and empathic use of Japanese *zibun*, as exemplified in (33) and (34).

(33) Taroo$_i$-wa boku-ga zibun$_i$-o but-ta
Taroo-Top I-Nom self-Acc hit-Past
koto-o mada urande-i-ru.
fact-Acc still resent-Asp-Pres
'Taroo$_i$ still resents that I hit him$_i$.'

(34) *Taroo$_i$-wa boku-ga zibun$_i$-ni kasi-ta
Taroo-Top I-Nom self-Dat lend-Past
okane-o nakusite-simat-ta rasii.
money-Acc lose-end.up-Past it.seems
'It seems that Taroo$_i$ lost the money I lent to him$_i$.' (Kuno 1978: 212-3)

Kuno (1978) points out that *zibun* occurring in the scope of the purely logophoric environment, as in (33), can be construed as referring to the attitude holder, even though it conflicts with what empathy locus constraints require within the propositional complement clause. In contrast to (33), on the other hand, the sentence in (34) does not occur in the logophoric environment. Thus, the unacceptability of (34) is not due to the presence of the first person pronoun but due to the conflicting empathy foci. In other words, there are two empathy loci in a single sentence. One is the first person *boku* 'I' by using an agent-centered verb *kasu* 'lend' and the other is *zibun* referring to the matrix subject *Taroo*. According to the Ban on Conflicting Empathy Foci, a single sentence cannot contain logical conflicts in empathy relationships.

Conflicting empathy foci trigger the blocking effect in Chinese as well. In other words, the blocking effect is not attributed to the person feature mismatch, but to the empathy relationship between the participants in a given discourse context. Therefore, we propose that the blocking effect of *ziji* does not exist in logophoric environments, but occurs in empathy environments. This analysis can unify the blocking effect observed not only in Chinese but also in Japanese and Korean, and more clearly accounts for why there is a blocking effect in these languages.

5 Conclusion

Adopting the view from Oshima (2004, 2007) and Wang and Pan's (2014, 2015) arguments, we propose that the long-distance anaphor *ziji* should be divided into two categories: logophor and empathy. By doing so, we can properly reconcile the seemingly different binding behaviors in East Asian languages, such as Chinese *ziji*, Japanese *zibun*, and Korean *caki*, with a unified treatment through the empathy theory.

Acknowledgments:

We appreciate the valuable suggestions and comments of the anonymous reviewers of the PACLIC 29 conference.

References:

Clements, George N. 1975. The logophoric pronoun in Ewe: Its role in discourse. *Journal of West African Languages* 2: 141-177.

Huang, C.-T. James and C.-S. Luther Liu. 2001. Logophoricity, attitudes, and *ziji* at the interface, In *Long-distance reflexives:Syntax and semantics 33*, ed. by Peter Cole, Gabriella Hermon, and C.-T. James Huang, 141-195. New York: Academic Press.
Kuno, Susumu and Etsuko Kaburaki. 1977. Empathy and syntax. *Linguistic Inquiry* 8: 627-672.
Kuno, Susumu. 1978. *Danwa no bunpoo* [grammar of discourse]. Tokyo: Taishukan.
Kuno, Susumu. 1987. *Functional syntax: Anaphora, discourse and empathy*. Chicago: University of Chicago Press.
Nishigauchi, Taisuke. 2014. Reflexive binding: awareness and empathy from a syntactic point of view. *Journal of East Asian Linguistics* 23: 157-206.
Oshima, David Y. 2004. *Zibun* revisited: empathy, logophoricity, and binding. *University of Washington Working Papers in Linguistics* 22: 175-190.
Oshima, David Y. 2006. Perspectives in reported discourse. PhD Dissertation, Stanford University.
Oshima, David Y. 2007. On empathic and logophoric binding. *Research on Language and Computation* 5: 19-35.
Pan, Haihua. 2001. Why the blocking effect? In *Long-distance reflexives:Syntax and semantics 33*, ed. by Peter Cole, Gabriella Hermon, and C.-T. James Huang, 279-316. New York: Academic Press.
Park, Hyunjun. 2015. Logophor, empathy, and long-distance anaphors in East Asian languages. PhD Dissertation, City University of Hong Kong.
Pearson, Hazel. 2013. The sense of self: Topics in the semantics of *de se* expressions. PhD Dissertation, Harvard University.
Sells, Peter. 1987. Aspects of logophoricity. *Linguistic Inquiry* 18: 445-479.
Stirling, Lesley. 1993. *Switch reference and discourse representation*. Cambridge; Cambridge University Press.
Wang, Yingying and Haihua Pan. 2014. A note on the non-de se interpretation of attitude reports. *Language* 90: 746-754.
Wang, Yingying and Haihua Pan. 2015. Empathy and Chinese long-distance reflexive *ziji*-remarks on Giorgi (2006, 2007). *Natural Language and Linguistic Theory*.
Xu, Liejiong. 1993. The long-distance binding of *ziji*. *Journal of Chinese Linguistics* 21: 123-142.
Yokoyama, Olga T. 1980. Studies in Russian functional syntax. in *Harvard Studies in Syntax and Semantics* 3, ed. by S. Kuno, 451-774. Cambridge.
Yoon, Jeong-Me. 1989. Long-distance anaphors in Korean and their cross-linguistic implications. In *Papers from the 25th Annual Meeting of the Chicago Linguistic Society*, ed. by Caroline Wiltshire, Randolph Graczyk, & Music Bradley, 479-495. Chicago: Chicago Linguistic Society.

English Right Dislocation

Kohji Kamada
Chiba University
1-33, Yayoicho, Inage Ward, Chiba-shi, Chiba, 263-8522 Japan
k-kamada@L.chiba-u.ac.jp/k-kamada@chiba-u.jp

Abstract

A number of researchers claim that the derivation of the Right Dislocation Construction (RDC) involves movement (e.g., Chung, 2012, for Korean; Ott & de Vries, 2012, 2015, for Dutch and German; Tanaka, 2001 and Abe, 2004, for Japanese; Whitman, 2000, for English, Japanese, and Korean). However, the RDC in English does not obey movement constraints such as the Coordinate Structure Constraint and the Left Branch Condition; that is, there are acceptable sentences that seem to violate these movement constraints. This suggests that the derivation of the English RDC should not involve movement. The present paper demonstrates that some syntactic properties of the English RDC can be explained instead through the interaction of independently motivated parsing strategies with a licensing condition for adjoined elements.

1 Introduction

The Right Dislocation Construction (RDC) is a construction in which a dislocated NP appearing in sentence-final position refers to a pronoun, as observed in example (1), with the relevant pronoun in italics and the dislocated NP in boldface.

(1) *He* is real smart, **John**.

As (2) shows, the dislocated NP cannot occur outside the embedded clause that contains the relevant pronoun. This seems to suggest that the dislocated NP is derived by movement, because a violation of a movement constraint—namely, the Right Roof Constraint (RRC)—appears to be present (Ross, 1986: 179). [1]

(2) *That *they* spoke to the janitor about that robbery yesterday is terrible, **the cops**. (Ross, 1986: 258)

However, there is a construction that violates the RRC but is still acceptable, as seen in (3).

(3) [That *they* spoke to the janitor about that robbery yesterday] is terrible, I mean, **the cops**. (Whitman, 2000: 450)

The sentence in (3) differs from that in (2) only in that it has *I mean* inserted between the preceding clause and the dislocated element. This suggests that the derivation of the RDC should at least not involve rightward movement. [2] Note that the relevant pronoun is not a "resumptive" pronoun that repairs an island violation; it would otherwise be difficult to account for the unacceptability of the example in (2), in which the pronoun seems to play no role in repairing the violation of the RRC. [3]

Further acceptable examples that appear to violate movement constraints exist, as in (4).

(4) a. I saw Mary and *him* downtown yesterday, **your friend from Keokuk**. (Ross, 1986: 260)
b. I noticed *his* car in the driveway last night, **your friend from Keokuk**. (*ibid.*)

In (4), it is possible to connect the dislocated NPs with *him* and *his*, respectively. If the dislocated NP in (4a) were extracted from the position occupied by the pronoun *him*, a conjunct could be moved. Likewise in (4b), if the dislocated NP were extracted from the position occupied by *his*, an

[1] Another possibility is a violation of the Sentential Subject Constraint.

[2] An example of the type in (3) was originally provided by Tsubomoto (1995), who argues against a movement analysis for the RDC and accounts for some of its properties in terms of information structure.

[3] If movement were involved in the derivation of the RDC and the relevant pronoun were a resumptive pronoun, the RRC would be a condition on a representation.

29th Pacific Asia Conference on Language, Information and Computation pages 221 - 230
Shanghai, China, October 30 - November 1, 2015

element could be moved out of the specifier position of the NP.

Irrespective of whether an element moves rightward or leftward, however, English observes the Coordinate Structure Constraint (CSC) and the Left Branch Condition (LBC), as shown in (5) and (6), respectively.

(5) a. ***What sofa**$_i$ will he put the chair between some table and t_i? (*ibid.*: 97)

b. *I saw Mary and t_i downtown yesterday, **your friend from Keokuk**$_i$. (*ibid.*: 260)

(6) a. ***Whose**$_i$ did you steal t_i money? (McCawley, 1998: 526)

b. *I noticed t_i car in the driveway last night, **your friend from Keokuk**$_i$. (Ross, 1986: 260)

If the derivation of the RDC involved rightward movement in any way, the examples in (4) would violate the movement constraints, resulting in unacceptability—contrary to the actual situation. Furthermore, the examples in (4) suggest that the derivation of the RDC involves no rightward movement.[4]

This paper is structured as follows. In section 2, I argue that the derivation of the RDC involves no movement, by pointing out empirical problems with the argument by Whitman (2000), who claims that the derivation of the RDC in English involves the operation of deletion after leftward movement. In section 3, I first set out a number of independently motivated principles, such as parsing principles and a licensing condition for adjoined elements, and then I demonstrate that the interaction of the licensing condition with these principles can account for the cases with which movement analyses fail to cope. Section 4 concludes the paper.

2 Problems with a Biclausal + Deletion Analysis

In the previous section, I discussed certain empirical problems with rightward movement analyses. In this section, I take up Whitman (2000) as an example of leftward movement analyses, and demonstrate that it fails to account for several properties of the English RDC.

Whitman (2000) follows Kayne (1994) in claiming that a sentence like that in (1) is derived from the biclausal structure shown in (7), as in (8).

(7)

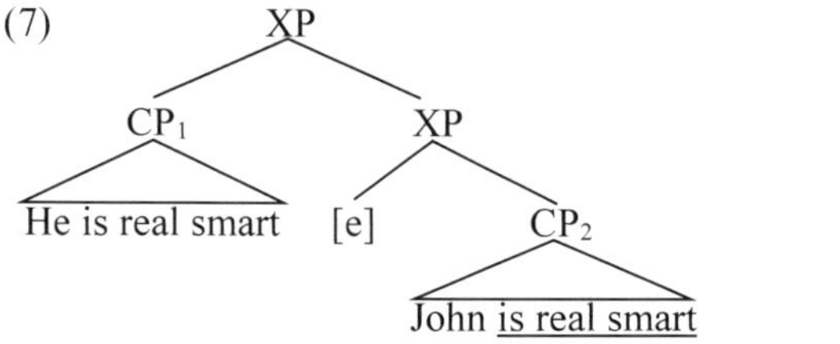

(adapted from Whitman, 2000: 452)

(8) [$_{CP1}$He is real smart], John$_i$, [$_{CP2}$ t_i ~~is real smart~~]

As (8) shows, *John* is left-adjoined/dislocated to CP$_2$, and the remaining elements (i.e., the underlined parts) are deleted under an identity condition, thereby generating (1).[5,6]

According to Whitman (2000), the RRC effect displayed in (2) is explained as follows: As in (1), (2) is formed by first conjoining two clauses, and then, as shown in (9), *the cops* is extracted from the sentential subject in CP$_2$ to adjoin to the left side of CP$_2$. This extraction, however, violates the Sentential Subject Constraint, resulting in the RRC effect.

(9) *[$_{CP1}$That they spoke to the janitor about that robbery yesterday] is terrible, [the cops]$_i$, [$_{CP2}$ [that t_i spoke to the janitor about that robbery yesterday] is terrible]. (Whitman, 2000: 458)

However, the analysis above is empirically problematic, because (3) would be excluded in the

[4] It is assumed that the CSC and the LBC are regarded as conditions on movement rather than on representations.

[5] Whitman (2000) claims that his analysis is also applicable to the RDC in Japanese and Korean. Similar proposals are made by, e.g., Chung (2012) for Korean, Ott and de Vries (2012, 2015) for Dutch and German, and Endo (1996), Tanaka (2001) and Abe (2003) for Japanese. What these proposals have in common is that the RDC has a biclausal structure and undergoes left-adjoinment to the second clause before deletion under an identity condition. Hence, the application of these approaches to English RDCs will face similar sorts of empirical problems to those Whitman (2000) does.

[6] The identity condition is not clearly defined in Whitman (2000). Incidentally, Ott and de Vries (2012) follow Merchant (2001) in assuming that "the deleted domain in CP$_2$ and its antecedent domain in CP$_1$ must be semantically equivalent…."

same way as (2) is.[7] Furthermore, the analysis is not adequate to account for the examples in (4). That is, *your friend from Keokuk('s)* would be extracted from the respective second clauses [*I saw Mary and **your friend from Keokuk** downtown yesterday*] and [*I noticed **your friend from Keokuk's** car in the driveway last night*]. These extractions, however, violate the CSC and the LBC, as discussed in section 1. Thus, the biclausal + deletion analysis also cannot account for the acceptability of the examples in (4) (see footnote 4).[8]

Moreover, the biclausal + deletion analysis faces another empirical problem.

(10) The girl who ate *it*, **the potato salad**, was rushed to the hospital.[9] (Gundel, 1988: 132)

The example in (10) shows that the RDC is possible inside an embedded clause.[10] There are at least two possible ways for (10) to be derived under the analysis in question. The relevant possible structures corresponding to that in (8) before deletion takes place would be those in (11), with the content of CP_1 in (11a) ignored.

(11) a. [$_{CP1}$ ...], **the potato salad**$_i$ [$_{CP2}$ the girl who ate t_i was rushed to the hospital]
b. (the girl who) [[$_{CP1}$ ate it], **the potato salad**$_i$ [$_{CP2}$ ate t_i]]

In (11a), ***the potato salad*** moves out of a relative clause. This movement violates the Complex NP Constraint, and so this possibility should be excluded. As for (11b), ***the potato salad*** moves leftward inside a relative clause. As Gundel (1988: 151) points out, however, leftward movement in a relative clause is not permitted, as illustrated by (12).

(12) *The one who [topic-comment structure$_i$ doesn't understand t_i] is me. (adapted from Gundel, 1988: 151)

Hence, the structure in (11b) would not be appropriate either.

The biclausal + deletion analysis might claim that the internal structure of the embedded clause in (10) is different from that of the relative clause in a sentence like (12). If so, the analysis would be unable to cope with an unacceptable example such as (13), in which the embedded clause appears to have the same structure as that in (10).

(13) *Bill gave the girl who [ate *it*, **the potato salad**], a dollar.

Thus, biclausal + deletion analyses such as that of Whitman (2000) have empirical problems. On the basis of the discussion in sections 1 and 2 here, it seems safe to say that the derivation of the English RDC does not involve movement (i.e., that the RDC is base-generated).

3 A Base-Generation Analysis

3.1 Parsing strategies

Concerning a parsing strategy, I follow Pritchett (1992b) in adopting the Generalized Theta Attachment (GTA) strategy, formulated in (14).

(14) Generalized Theta Attachment (GTA):
Every principle of the Syntax attempts to be maximally satisfied at every point during processing. (Pritchett, 1992b: 138)

Despite the presence of "theta attachment" in the name, Pritchett (1992b) notes that the GTA strategy should be understood to denote that the parser attempts to maximally satisfy all syntactic principles—not just the theta-attachment principle. To instantiate (14), consider a simple English sentence like that in (15), the parsing of which is set out in (16).

In (15), *John* is identified as an NP with no assigned theta-role, and the GTA strategy is attempted. However, as no theta-role assigner has been encountered, theta-roles are unavailable. *John* is therefore stored (i.e., left unattached to anything) until a theta-role assigner is encountered; otherwise,

[7] Although Whitman (2000) provides (3) in his paper, it is unclear how he accounts for its acceptability as he does not elaborate on this type of example.
[8] One of the reviewers of this paper has mentioned that if island constraints are a PF-phenomenon, as Merchant (2001, 2003) claims, the argument based on islands becomes moot. As the reviewer points out, however, the example in (2) would challenge Whitman's analysis.
[9] Left dislocation is not permitted in an embedded clause.
(i) *The woman who **that book**, wrote *it* is a well-known linguist. (Gundel, 1988: 84)
[10] The RDC in an embedded clause is not always possible. See (13) in this regard.

the theta-criterion would not be locally satisfied (see 16a).

(15) John saw Mary.

(16) a. NP *John* b. *saw*, V, [θ_1, θ_2]

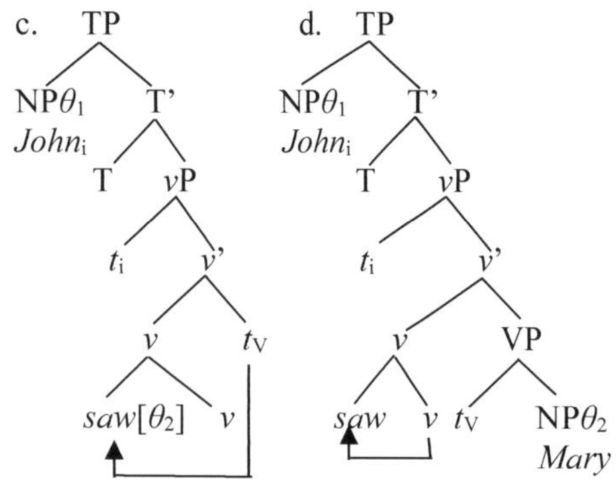

When *saw* is encountered, it is identified as a transitive verb (see 16b). The GTA strategy is again attempted, and this time, a potential argument (i.e., *John*) and a theta-role assigner (i.e., *saw*) are available. At this point, the strategy may be successfully applied: The parser integrates *John* as a subject, postulating a trace in the specifier position of the *v*P such that the trace can be assigned a theta-role by the verb *saw*, the theta-role being transmitted through a chain to the subject *John*. Consequently, the parser contains a structure like (16c). [11] Note that the theta-criterion is maximally satisfied here, although *saw* still has a theta-role to discharge (see Mulders, 2002: 187). The structure in (16c) therefore does not contain a node that might be predicted to exist as an object of *saw* on the basis of the lexical information (argument structure).

When *Mary* is encountered, it is identified as an argument, and the GTA strategy is attempted once again to assign *Mary* a theta-role. *Mary* is merged with the trace of *saw*, and is then assigned a theta-role through the chain. The parser finishes successfully, yielding the parse tree in (16d).

In addition to the GTA in (14), I adopt the Right Association Principle (RAP) proposed by Kimball (1973), presented in a slightly modified form in (17).

[11] CP and C are omitted for reasons of space.

(17) Right Association Principle (RAP):
Terminal symbols optimally associate to the lowest non-terminal node. (Kimball, 1973: 24)

The RAP can account, for example, for (18)'s having a preference for the reading in (18'a) rather than that in (18'b).

(18) Joe figured that Susan wanted to take the train to New York out. (*ibid.*)

(18') a. Joe figured that Susan wanted to [take the train to New York out].
b. Joe [figured that Susan wanted to take the train to New York] out.

In (18'a), the particle *out* is associated with [*take the train to New York*], whereas in (18'b), *out* is linked to [*figured that Susan wanted to take the train to New York*]. The RAP requires *out* to be linked to the lower verb phrase. [12] Thus, the preferred interpretation is (18'a), where *take the train to New York out* forms a constituent.

3.2 Garden path phenomena

In addressing garden path phenomena, I propose the reanalysis condition in (19), which is adapted from the On-Line Locality Constraint originally proposed by Pritchett (1992b).[13]

(19) Unconscious Reanalysis Condition (URC):
It is possible for the human parser to make a syntactic reanalysis (i.e., reanalysis is low-cost) only if the final attachment site β c-commands the original attachment site α, and every phase (i.e., *v*P, CP) containing α contains β.[14]

[12] The reason that the particle *out* is not associated with the "real" lowest node [$_{NP}$ New York] may be that, even if it is associated with the NP, this combination of the NP and *out* is not permitted in English. Thus, I assume tentatively that the lowest node to which an element must attach should be construed as the lowest among the nodes to which the element attaches to get a permissible combination of items in a relevant language.

[13] On-Line Locality Constraint (OLLC):
The target position (if any) assumed by a constituent must be governed or dominated by its source position (if any), otherwise attachment is impossible for the automatic Human Sentence Processor. (Pritchett, 1992b: 101)

[14] "Node A c-commands node B if neither A nor B dominates the other and the first branching node which dominates A dominates B." (Reinhart, 1976: 32)

Note that the URC includes the notion of the "phase" introduced within the minimalist framework (see Chomsky, 2001; cf. Citko, 2014).[15] To see how the URC works, let us compare the sentences in (20).[16]

(20) a. John gave her books to Mary.
b. #I put the candy in the jar into my mouth.
(Pritchett, 1992b: 101, 104)

In (20a), *her* is initially identified as an object of *gave*. On reaching *books*, the parser analyzes it as the second complement of the verb. The parse tree at this point is as in (21a), with CP and C omitted for reasons of space.[17]

(21) a.

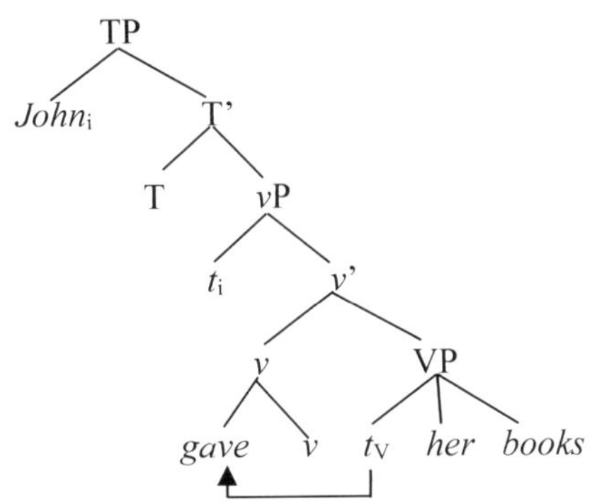

b.

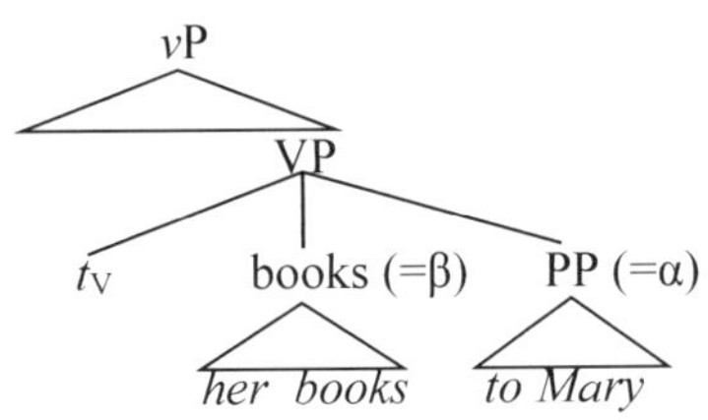

Upon encountering *to Mary*, the parser can reanalyze *her* and *books* respectively as a determiner and the head of the first (rather than the second) internal argument; the subsequent parse tree will be that in (21b), with only the relevant parts illustrated for reasons of space. In (21b), the element in the final attachment site *books* (=β) c-commands the original attachment site *to Mary* (=α) (i.e., the second internal argument position), and every phase (i.e., *v*P) containing *to Mary* (=α) also contains *books* (=β). According to the URC in (19), this is a low-cost reanalysis; thus, (20a) is easily comprehensible.[18]

Now, let us turn to (20b). When *into my mouth* is encountered, *the candy* and *in the jar* must undergo reanalysis. The resulting parse tree would be that in (22), again with CP and C omitted for reasons of space. Here, however, the final attachment site *in the jar* (=β) does not c-command the original attachment site *into my mouth* (=α); this results in a high-cost reanalysis. Thus, (20b) requires conscious processing.

(22)

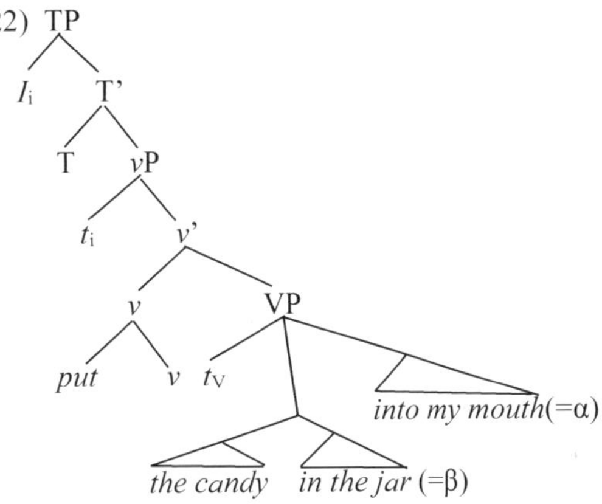

Next, let us consider the sentence in (23).

(23) #After Susan drank the water evaporated.
(Pritchett, 1992b: 101, 104)

In (23), *the water* is initially identified as the direct object of *drank*. As soon as *evaporated* is encountered, *the water* is reinterpreted as the subject of *evaporated*; *drank* is simultaneously reinterpreted as an intransitive verb. This yields a parse tree like that in (24), with the final attachment site in bold italics. In (24), the final attachment site β cannot c-command the original attachment site α. The reattachment of *the water* to the specifier position of the matrix TP is thus

[15] It is assumed here that syntactic structures are constructed by *Merge* (Chomsky, 1995).

[16] # indicates that the relevant sentence is grammatical but unacceptable.

[17] Chomsky (2005: 12) points out that "[w]ithout further stipulations, external Merge yields n-ary constituents." I therefore assume that VP constituents can have more than two branches.

[18] To complete the URC, it is necessary to add the disjunctive statement "or α contains β," which accounts for the ability of *her* to undergo reanalysis (cf. Pritchett, 1992a; Siloni, 2014).

costly, and the sentence in (23) is therefore difficult to comprehend.

(24)

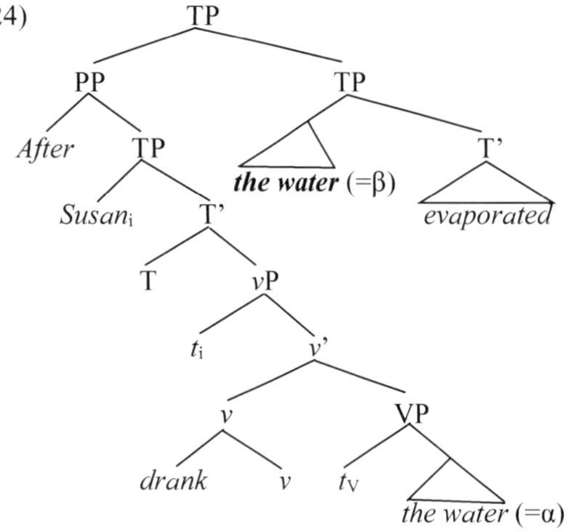

3.3 An Analysis

Before discussing how the RRC effect in the RDC follows from the above parsing strategies, I adopt the licensing condition (LC) for adjoined elements proposed by Kamada (2009, 2010, 2013a,b) in a slightly amended form, as presented in (25).

(25) The licensing condition for adjoined phrases (where X=any syntactic category):
A phrase α adjoined to XP is licensed only if α is associated with an element β such that
(i) α c-commands β, and
(ii) α is non-distinct from β in terms of φ-features and Case features.[19]

Furthermore, I have revised the Interpretive Rules originally proposed by Kamada (2009, 2010, 2013a,b), given in revised form in (26)

(26) Interpretive rules for adjoined phrases
Suppose that a phrase α is adjoined to XP (where X=any syntactic category) and is associated with an element β; then,
(i) α is construed as an element sharing properties with β[20] only if
a. α is an NP or a CP and
b. α is non-distinct from β in terms of semantic features and semantic types.[21]
(ii) α is construed as a potential modifier of β only if α cannot be construed as an element sharing properties with β (cf. Heim & Kratzer, 1998: 65).

Let us first reconsider (1) in order to illustrate how (25) and (26) interact with the parsing strategies. In (1), upon encountering ***John***, the parser realizes that there are no following elements, and starts to find a relevant element to license ***John***, at the same time adjoining ***John*** to the preceding element. The RAP in (17) mandates that ***John*** should adjoin to the lowest AP node. The parse tree existing at this point is given in (1'), again with only the relevant parts illustrated for reasons of space.

(1')

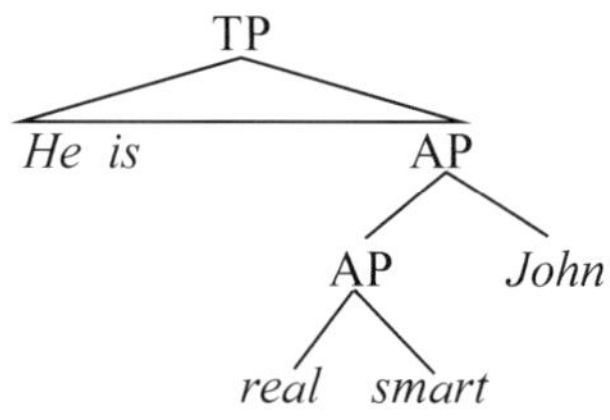

In (1'), ***John*** c-commands AP (i.e., *real smart*), and they are non-distinct from each other with respect to φ- and Case features.[22] ***John*** can thus be associated with *real smart*, thereby being licensed. ***John*** and *real smart* cannot be construed as elements sharing properties with each other,

[19] Adger and Harbour (2008: 16) point out that in German, when *Mädchen* 'girl', which is grammatically neuter, is referenced by a pronoun, the feminine is used but not the neuter. Hence, the neuter could be non-distinct from the feminine somehow.

[20] α and β share properties including theta-roles (if any), referentiality, and semantic features/types unless semantic conflicts occur.

[21] Concerning semantic types, if *α* is an NP, its semantic type may be <e> or < <e, t> t>, and if *α* is a CP, its semantic type may be <t> or <e, t>.

[22] If the right-dislocated NPs had Case features, uninterpretable Case features would remain unchecked, yielding a violation of the principle of Full Interpretation. This point is supported by the observation that fronted NPs can appear in nonargument positions without Case features being checked, as show in (i.b) and (i.d):
(i) a. *I assured you John to be a nice guy.
b. John$_i$, I assure you t_i to be a nice guy. (Rizzi, 1990: 60)
c. *He alleged Melvin to be a pimp.
d. Who$_i$ did he allege t_i to be a pimp? (Postal, 1974: 304-5)
The above observation falls under the generalization that overt NPs in peripheral positions do not have to have Case features. This generalization may extend to the case of RDCs.

because their semantic types are different (i.e., <e> for *John* and <e, t> for *real smart*). Furthermore, semantic deviance excludes the possibility of ***John***'s being construed as a modifier of *real smart*. The parser will therefore attempt to reattach ***John*** to *v*' in order to obtain an appropriate interpretation. The parse tree after the reanalysis is that in (1''), where the final attachment site of the dislocated NP is indicated by bold italics.

(1'')

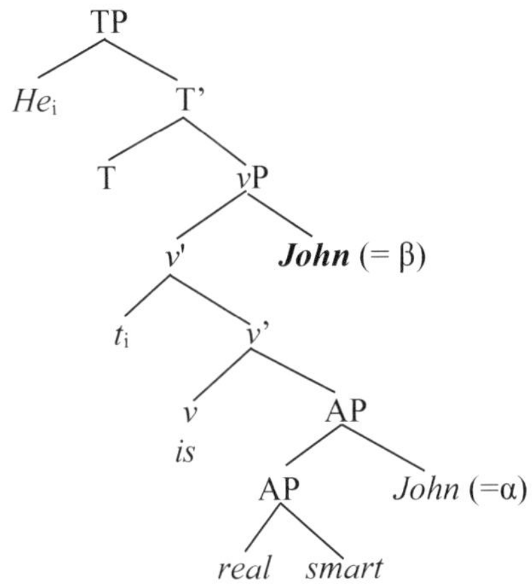

The URC in (19) allows the parser to reattach *John* to the *v*P, because the final attachment site ***John*** (=β) c-commands the original attachment site *John* (=α), and every phase (i.e., *v*P) containing *John* (=α) contains ***John*** (=β). ***John*** thus c-commands the trace of *he* (i.e., t_i), and they are non-distinct in terms of φ- and Case features (see footnote 21). According to (25), ***John*** is thus associated with the trace, thereby being licensed. Then, ***John*** is non-distinct from the trace of *he* in terms of semantic features and semantic type. Thus, (26) allows ***John*** to be construed as an element sharing properties with the trace (i.e., *he*).[23] The sentence in (1) is therefore acceptable.

Next, let us return to the sentence in (2), in which the RRC effect is observed. In accordance with the RAP in (17), as in the case of (1), when ***the cops*** is encountered, it is adjoined to the lowest AP node. The parse tree at this point is that in (2'), where the relevant pronoun *they*/its trace is within the sentential subject that moves to the specifier position of the main TP, leaving its trace in the specifier position of the main *v*P.

(2')

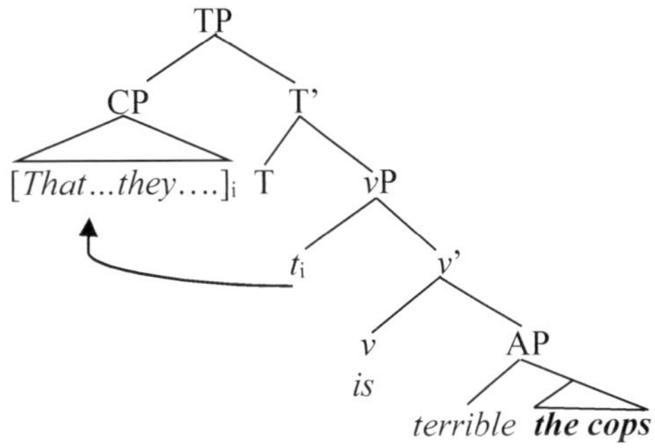

In (2'), ***the cops*** c-commands *terrible*, and they are non-distinct from each other in terms of φ- and Case features. ***The cops*** can therefore be associated with *terrible*, thereby being licensed. ***The cops***, however, cannot be construed as modifying *terrible*, because of semantic deviance. ***The cops*** must thus be reattached to the *v*' in the main clause, as shown in (2''). This reattachment is low-cost for the same reason as in (1'').

(2'')

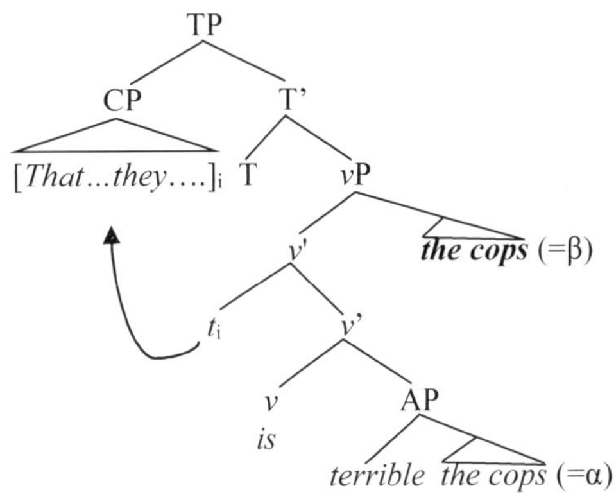

However, ***the cops*** (=β) in (2'') still fails to c-command the pronoun *they* or its trace inside the sentential subject [*they spoke to the janitor about that robbery yesterday*]. Thus, ***the cops*** cannot be associated with *they* or its trace, and is not licensed. An alternative analysis would reattach ***the cops*** to the matrix TP or CP, where ***the cops*** could c-command *they*. However, this syntactic reanalysis would be banned, as the final attachment site is not contained in the phase *v*P that contains the original attachment site. Example (2), therefore, displays the RRC effect.

[23] As Fiengo and May (1994) point out, noncoindexing does not mean noncoreference. Hence, the binding principle (C) precludes the coindexing of *John* and *he* in (1''), but they can still become coreferential through (26).

The claim that the RRC effect is not a grammatical phenomenon is supported by the example in (3), which is acceptable. Suppose that, when *I mean* is encountered, it should be adjoined to the main clause CP, as shown in (3').[24] Then, the dislocated NP is adjoined to the main clause. As a result, ***the cops*** c-commands the pronoun *they*; ***The cops*** can thus be associated with *they*, and is properly licensed. The interpretive rules in (26) allow ***the cops*** to be construed as an element sharing properties with *they*, because they are non-distinct in terms of semantic features and semantic type. Thus, (3) is acceptable.

(3')

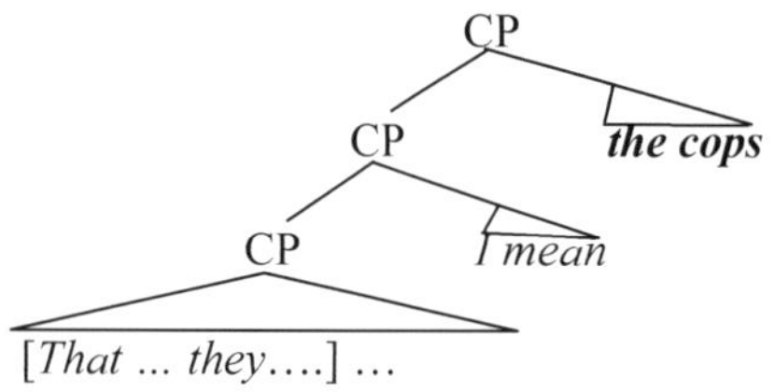

Let us now consider the examples in (4), which respectively appear to violate the CSC and the LBC. When the dislocated NPs are encountered, they adjoin to the VP. As a result, they c-command the relevant pronouns (*him* and *his*, respectively). In (4a), *him* is associated with the dislocated NP because they are non-distinct in terms of φ- and Case features. Hence, the dislocated NP is properly licensed. According to (26), *him* and the dislocated NP are non-distinct in terms of semantic features and semantic type. The dislocated NP can therefore be construed as an element sharing properties with *him*.

Likewise in (4b), the dislocated NP is associated with the genitive pronoun *his* and is properly licensed, because they are non-distinct in terms of φ- and Case features (see footnote 22). *His* and the dislocated NP are non-distinct in terms of semantic features and semantic type. Thus, the dislocated NP and *his* can be construed as sharing properties.

Now, let us return to the cases in (10) and (13), where RDCs may or may not appear in embedded clauses. In (10), when ***the potato salad*** is encountered, it is identified as an NP that has no theta-role assigned. At this point there is no theta-role assigner, and hence the NP is held in store. Upon encountering *rushed*, the parser attaches ***the potato salad*** to the preceding element based on the RAP; otherwise, the complex NP (i.e., *the girl who ate it*) would not be assigned a theta-role. In order to license ***the potato salad***, the application of the LC in (25) is attempted. Within the structure [$_{VP}$ [$_{VP}$ t$_{V}$ *it*] **the potato salad**], ***the potato salad*** c-commands the pronoun *it*, and is therefore associated with the pronoun and licensed. Then, the complex NP [$_{NP}$ the girl who ate *it*, **the potato salad**] is attached to the matrix T to receive a theta-role and have its Case checked. ***The potato salad*** is non-distinct from *it* in terms of semantic features and semantic type, and can thus be construed as sharing properties with *it*. Thus, example (10) is acceptable.

As for (13), when ***the potato salad*** is encountered, it is identified as an NP that has no theta-role assigned. At this point, *gave*, which is a theta-role assigner, is available. Thus, the GTA strategy in (14) is attempted, and ***the potato salad*** is attached to the object position to which *gave* assigns its theta-role, resulting in local satisfaction of the theta criterion. When *a dollar* is reached, ***the potato salad*** is reattached to a constituent inside the embedded clause. According to the URC in (19), however, this reattachment is impossible: the final attachment site fails to c-command the original attachment site of ***the potato salad***. Thus, (13) is difficult to comprehend.

4 Conclusion

This paper claims that the derivation of the English RDC involves no movement and that the (un)acceptability of the RDC can be accounted for through the interaction of the licensing condition with parsing strategies. In this way, certain syntactic phenomena receiving a formal grammatical account are better explained in terms of independently motivated properties of language processing mechanisms.

Acknowledgements

This work was supported by JSPS KAKENHI Grant Number 26370439. I would like to thank Masahiro Akiyama and Ryoya Okabe as well as the two PACLIC 29 reviewers for their valuable comments.

[24] It seems that the permissible combination of an interjection or a discourse marker such as *I mean* with elements in English is only the attachment of the former (e.g., *I mean*) to a main clause (see footnote 12).

References

Abe, Jun. 2003. On Directionality of Movement: A Case of Japanese Right Dislocation. Proceedings of the 58th Conference, The Tohoku English Literary Society: 54-61.

Adger, David and Daniel Harbour. 2008. Why Phi? In Daniel Harbour, David Adger, and Susan Béjar, (eds.) Phi Theory: Phi-Features across Modules and Interfaces. Oxford: Oxford University Press. pp. 1-34.

Chomsky, Noam. 1995. The Minimalist Program. Cambridge, Mass.: MIT Press.

Chomsky, Noam. 2001. Derivation by Phase. In Michael Kenstowicz, (ed.) Ken Hale: A life in language. Cambridge, Mass: MIT Press. pp. 1-52.

Chomsky, Noam. 2005. Three Factors in Language Design. Linguistic Inquiry 36: 1-22.

Chung, Daeho, 2012. Pre-vs. Post-verbal Asymmetries and the Syntax of Korean RDC. Proceedings of the 26th Pacific Asia Conference on Language, Information and Computation: 219-228.

Citko, Barbara, 2014. Phase Theory: An Introduction. Cambridge: Cambridge University Press.

Endo, Yoshio.1996. Right Dislocation. In Masatoshi Koizumi, Masayuki Oishi and Uli Sauerland, (eds.) Formal Approaches to Japanese Linguitics 2, MIT Working Papers in Linguistics 29. Cambridge: Department of Linguistics, MIT: 1-20.

Fiengo, Robert and Robert May. 1994. Indices and Identity. Cambridge, MA: MIT Press.

Gundel, Jeanette K. 1988. The role of topic and comment in linguistic theory. New York: Garland.

Heim, Irene and Angelika Kratzer. 1998. Semantics in Generative Grammar. Oxford: Blackwell.

Kamada, Kohji. 2009. Rightward Movement Phenomena in Human Language. Doctoral dissertation, the University of Edinburgh.

Kamada, Kohji. 2010. Eigo-no Uhoten-i Koubun [The Right Dislocation Construction in English]. Sophia Linguistica 57: 131-153.

Kamada, Kohji. 2013a. The Island Effect in Postverbal Constructions in Japanese. Proceedings of the 27th Pacific Asia Conference on Language, Information and Computation: 459-466.

Kamada, Kohji. 2013b. Nihongo Kouchi Koubun to Gengo Shori [Japanese Postverbal Constructions and Language Processing]. Sophia Linguistica 61: 165-185.

Kayne, Richard. 1994. The Antisymmetry of Syntax. Cambridge, Mass: MIT Press.

Kimball, John. 1973. Seven principles of surface structure parsing in natural language. Cognition, 2 (1): 15-47.

Merchant, Jason. 2001. The Syntax of Silence: Sluicing, Islands, and the Theory of Ellipsis. Oxford: Oxford University Press.

Merchant, Jason. 2003. Sluicing. Ms. Available from http://home.uchicago.edu/merchant/pubs/SynCom.sluicing.pdf.

Mulders, Iris, 2002. Transparent parsing: Head-driven processing of verb-final structures. Doctoral dissertation, Utrecht University. LOT Dissertation Series 56.

Ott, Dennis and Mark de Vries. 2012. A biclausal analysis of right-dislocation. Ms.

Ott, Dennis and Mark de Vries. 2015. Right-dislocation as deletion. Natural Language and Linguistic Theory 33.

Postal, Paul. 1974. On Raising. Cambridge, Mass.: MIT Press.

Pritchett, Bradley. 1992a. Parsing with grammar: islands, heads, and garden paths. In Helen Goodluck and Michael Rochemont (eds.), Island Constraints: Theory, Acquisition and Processing. Dordrecht: Kluwer Academic Publishers. pp. 321-349.

Pritchett, Bradley. 1992. Grammatical Competence and Parsing Performance, Chicago: University of Chicago Press.

Reinhart, Tanya. 1976. The Syntactic Domain of Anaphora. Doctoral dissertation, MIT.

Rizzi, Luigi. 1990. Relativized Minimality, Cambridge, MA: MIT Press.

Ross, John, R. 1986. Infinite Syntax!. New Jersey: Ablex.

Siloni, Tal. 2014. Grammatical Processing. In Enoch Oladé Aboh, Maria Teresa Guasti, and Ian Roberts (eds.), Locality. Oxford: Oxford University Press. pp. 274-302.

Tanaka, Hidekazu. 2001. Right-Dislocation as scrambling. Journal of Linguistics 37: 551-579.

Tsubomoto, Atsuro. 1995. Gojun to Ten-i Bun [Word Order and Dislocation Sentences]. In Takeo Saito, Shosuke Haraguchi, and Hidekazu Suzuki (eds.), Eibunpou eno Sasoi [An Invitation to English Grammar]. Tokyo: Kaitakusha. pp. 182-197.

Whitman, John. 2000. Right Dislocation in English and Japanese. In Ken-ichi Takami, Akio Kamio and John Whitman (eds.), Syntactic and Functional Explorations in Honor of Susumu Kuno. Tokyo: Kurosio Publishers. pp. 445-470.

A Comparative Study on Mandarin and Cantonese Resultative Verb Compounds

Helena Yan Ping Lau
Department of Chinese and Bilingual Studies
The Hong Kong Polytechnic University
Hong Kong
helena.lau@connect.polyu.hk

Sophia Yat Mei Lee
Department of Chinese and Bilingual Studies
The Hong Kong Polytechnic University
Hong Kong
ym.lee@polyu.edu.hk

Abstract

This paper explores the conditions where Mandarin RVCs can be preserved in their Cantonese counterparts. Six types of Mandarin RVCs – ergatives, unergatives, accusatives, causatives, pseudo-passives and object-fronting – have been examined. Modifications have been made for certain kinds of RVCs that are usually misclassified. The analysis has been done at both the lexical and syntactic levels. At the lexical level, the concept of 'strong resultative' and 'weak resultative' has been adduced to support the idea that indirect causation cannot be expressed by RVC in Cantonese. At the syntactic level, the presentations of the same RVCs falling into different sentence types are illustrated. Since the structure of Mandarin RVCs are often restricted in Cantonese, three substitutive constructions have been introduced for presenting the same resultatives in Cantonese.

1 Introduction

Resultative verb compound (RVC) has been a well-ventilated topic in Modern Chinese linguistics due to its ubiquitous occurrence in Chinese especially Mandarin. A resultative verb compound in Chinese is composed of two elements, with the second element (V2) denoting the result of the action indicated by the first element (V1) (Thompson 1973, Lu 1977, Li and Thompson 1981, Shi 2002)[1]. As one of the main varieties of Chinese, Cantonese seems to be closely-related to Mandarin. There are, however, some remarkable differences between them in terms of the usage. An example of Mandarin RVC construction is shown in (1), with a syntactically parallel yet ill-formed sentence in Cantonese illustrated in (2).

(1) 我 跑丟-了 車票
1.SG run lost-ASP ticket
'I lost the ticket as I ran.'

(2) *我 跑跌-咗 張 車飛
1.SG run lost-ASP CL ticket

Since RVCs in Cantonese are found to be less productive than they are in Mandarin, most of the previous works have been dedicated to the study of Mandarin Chinese, neglecting numerous concerns regarding Cantonese RVCs. Under what circumstances can the Mandarin RVCs be preserved in their Cantonese counterparts? What are the factors of prohibition of RVCs in Cantonese? What methods will be used when RVCs are not allowed in the corresponding sentences in Cantonese? These are the questions that motivate the current research.

In this study, we attempt to provide a systematic pattern of how resultatives are presented when the corresponding Mandarin RVCs are not allowed in

[1] Since 'V1' and 'V2' are widely used as the first and the second predicates of RVCs in previous studies, these terms are adopted in this paper.

29th Pacific Asia Conference on Language, Information and Computation pages 231 - 239
Shanghai, China, October 30 - November 1, 2015

Cantonese, by examining six types of Mandarin RVCs, namely ergatives, unergatives, accusatives, causatives, pseudo-passives, and object-fronting.

2 Related Work

With regard to Chinese RVCs, numerous studies have examined them concerning the headedness. There are four approaches proposed: a) V1 being the head (Li 1990, 1995, Cheng & Huang 1994, Wang 2001), b) V2 being the head (Tai 2003), c) neither V1 nor V2 being the head (Huang & Lin 1992), and d) both V1 and V2 being the heads (Gu 1992). The formation of RVCs also intrigued many researchers. Li (1990, 1995) suggested that RVCs are formed in the lexicon. Gu (1992) further pointed out that they are occasionally formed in the lexicon through theta-identification. Huang (1992) proposed that they are derived syntactically.

While most previous studies focus on Mandarin Chinese, little work has been done in investigating Cantonese RVCs. Cheng et al. (1997) compared the properties of verbal compounds in Cantonese, Mandarin, and Taiwanese, proposing that Cantonese and Mandarin are similarly formed in the lexicon, whereas Taiwanese is formed in the syntax. Chow (2012) investigated the interface between the semantic and syntactic realizations of RVCs in Mandarin and Cantonese, suggesting that most RVCs in Mandarin have parallel syntactic realizations with their corresponding Cantonese sentences. However, the prevailing use of ill-formed Cantonese RVCs produced by non-native speakers will be unexplained if RVCs in Mandarin and Cantonese share the same structure.

3 Types of RVC Constructions

Drawing on the insight of earlier works, particularly Cheng & Huang (1994) and Wang (2001), this study classifies RVCs into six types, namely ergatives, unergatives, accusatives, causatives, pseudo-passives and object-fronting. It should be noted that it is possible for the same RVC to fall into different types due to the transitivity[2] and canonicality[3] of the RVC.

[2] Transitivity is a property of the RVC that indicates if the RVC can take objects or not

[3] Canonicality concerns with the ordinary word order of a language. For example, a Chinese canonical sentence order would be: "SUBJ+ V+ (OBJ)", of which the subject is the AGENT.

3.1 Ergatives

Ergatives are intransitive verbs that contain only one argument. V1 of an ergative is a non-active verb that indicates a state or a passive action. A THEME/ EXPERIENCER/ CAUSER is selected obligatorily by a non-active RVC (Cheng & Huang 1994). V1 and V2 are referring to the same entity which occupies the subject position of the sentence.

(3) 他　　嚇呆-了
3.SG　　scared stupefy-ASP
'He is shocked.'

3.2 Unergatives

Unergatives involve an intransitive frame. They contain AGENTS as the grammatical subjects who take the actions denoted in V1 and eventually undergo changes of state (Cheng & Huang 1994, Huang 2008). The subject is the AGENT of V1 and the EXPERIENCER/ THEME of V2. V1 and V2 are referring to the same entity, as in (4):

(4) 張三　　吃飽-了
Zhangsan　　eat full-ASP
'Zhangsan ate and he is full.'

3.3 Accusatives

Accusative predicates[4], consisted of active V1 and state-denoting V2, are transitive verbs that obligatorily take two theta roles including an AGENT and a THEME. The AGENT role is assigned to the subject whereas the THEME role is appointed to the object. As the accusative RVCs may differ in their referential properties, accusative RVCs can be divided into two types, namely co-referential and cross-referential.

Co-referential Accusatives

The grammatical subject must be the logical subject of both V1 and V2 but the grammatical object may have three types, we name them Type 1, 2 and 3. According to Wang (2001), it can be (a) the logical object of the whole RVC **(Type 1)**, (b) the logical object of V1 **(Type 2)** or (c) the logical object of V2 **(Type 3)**. The typical examples of the three types are shown as in (5) – (7):

[4] 'Accusatives' is termed 'transitives' in the work of Cheng & Huang (1994).

(5) 他 看懂-了 說明書 (Wang 2001: 66)
3.SG read understand-ASP user guide
'He read the user guide and understood it.'

(6) 張三 打累-了 籃球
Zhangsan play tired-ASP basketball
'Zhangsan played basketball (for a long time) and then he became tired.'

(7) 大黑 跑贏-了 對手 (Wang 2001: 66)
Dahei run win-ASP competitor
'Dahei won in a running competition.'

Cross-referential Accusatives

The grammatical subject must be the logical subject of V1 but the grammatical object may also have three types, we name them Type 4, 5 and 6. If there are only two arguments in the sentence, the grammatical object can be (a) the logical object of V1 and the logical subject of V2 **(Type 4)** or (b) the logical subject of V2 **(Type 5)**. If there are three arguments, the direct object must be the logical object of both the V1 and V2 **(Type 6)**. They are demonstrated as in (8)-(10):

(8) 她 擦乾-了 眼淚
3.SG wipe dry-ASP tears
'She dried her eyes.'

(9) 他 咬碎-了 牙齒
3.SG bite broken-ASP tooth
'He broke his tooth by biting something.'

(10) 老師 教會 我 游泳
teacher teach know 1.SG swim
'The teacher taught me how to swim.'

3.4 Causatives

Causatives are transitive verbs whose grammatical subject is a cause in terms of thematic relations. The event structure proposed by Cheng & Huang (1994) is shown in (11):

(11) $[_{RV}\ V1_{\text{Non-active}}\ [\ V2_{\text{State/ Change-of-State}}]]$
<Causer, Theme/ Experiencer/ Causee>

According to Wang (2001), there are three semantic patterns of causatives, of which one of them needs to be revised. In this paper, all patterns are renamed and two new patterns are introduced.

Co-referential

Type 1 Causatives

"Type 1 causative" is derived from a canonical sentence (i.e. accusatives) simply by switching the positions of the subject and object. The subject is the CAUSER which is the THEME before the deriving from accusatives. In Type 1 causative, V1 denotes an activity taken by the object and the subject is the logical object of V1 as in 大餐吃膩了夫人 (Wang 2001: 63) 'The woman was sick of having the big meal.'

Type 2 Causatives

"Type 2 causative" is sentences with the original AGENTs becoming the CAUSERs. This can be done by verbs that can either be an active verb or an state-denoting verb such as 嚇 'scare', 氣 'irritate'. For example, in 他嚇呆了我 'he scared me', the subject "他" is regarded as the AGENT who takes the action of scaring the object "我". It can also be understood as "He caused me to be scared". The latter one will be referred to in causatives. Thus, the statement "V1 and V2 are cross-referential" suggested by Wang (2001) is incorrect. It is proposed that Type 2 causative RVCs are object-oriented (i.e. co-referential) with an active V1 used in a non-active sense. Since the property of the V1 contains two readings, this kind of sentence involves structural ambiguities.

Type 3 Causatives

"Type 3 causative" is combined with Type 2 in the work of Wang (2001). They are, however, different in their semantic patterns. Thus, we propose "Type 3 causatives" as one of the new sub-category in causatives. "Type 3 causative" is a sentence containing an independent CAUSER, meaning that the CAUSER (i.e. the subject) has no logical connection with the predicates. Both predicates refer to the same entity which is the object, with V1 being an intransitive verb. For example, 夢裡的那件事哭醒了他 'He woke up in tears for the event he dreamt (in his dream).'

Type 4 Causatives

"Type 4 causative" contains a suppressed AGENT of the action stated in V1. The subject is the logical object of V1 while the object is a body part of the one who takes the action denoted by V1. For example, 那些資料看花了眼睛, 'The information made (his) eyes blurred (from reading it).'

Cross-referential
Type 5 Causatives
"Type 5 causative" is a sentence with three arguments in its deep structure. Only two of them appear on the surface and the V1 AGENT is covert. The grammatical subject is the logical object of V1, while V2 denotes the state which is object-oriented. Consider: 這首歌唱哭了觀眾 'The audiences were moved by the song'.

3.5 Pseudo-Passives

"Pseudo-passives", termed "surface ergatives", show the pattern of ergativity. They indeed differ in their properties as pseudo-passives entail the existence of some implicit agent that pure ergatives do not. Pseudo-passive can be divided into two types, namely "1-argument pseudo-passive" as in 桌子擦乾了 'The table is wiped dry' and "2-argument pseudo-passive" as in 花瓶擺錯了地方 (Wang 2001: 70) 'Someone put the vase in a wrong place'. The latter is often neglected by many linguists and was misclassified as "object-fronting" in Wang (2001). Due to its cross-referentiality, we re-categorize and name it "2-argument pseudo-passive". The sole difference between "2-argument pseudo-passives" and "1-argument pseudo-passives" is that the former contains two arguments while the latter comprises only one argument on the surface. They both have a suppressed agent in their deep structures.

3.6 Object-Fronting

Similar to pseudo-passives, the logical object of "object-fronting" is in the subject position. Therefore, many often confuse "object-fronting" with "pseudo-passive". Although it has been mentioned in some works before, the distinguishability is not accurately proposed. We clearly distinguish "object-fronting" from "pseudo-passives" by examining the passivizability of the sentences. This is demonstrated as in (12) and (13):

Pseudo-passives:
(12) a. 飯 吃完-了
rice eat finish-ASP
'The rice was eaten up.'

b. 飯 被 他 吃完-了 (Thompson 1973: 367)
rice by 3.SG eat all-ASP
'The rice was eaten up by him.'

Object-fronting:
(13) a. 飯 吃飽-了
rice eat full-ASP
'(Someone) has had enough rice.'

b. * 飯 被 他 吃飽-了 (Thompson 1973: 367)
rice by 3.SG eat full-ASP

4 Comparison between Mandarin and Cantonese

While some researchers suggest that almost all resultative constructions in Mandarin have a parallel structure with their corresponding Cantonese sentences, we find that sentences containing different types of RVCs in Mandarin may use various methods in re-producing corresponding sentences in Cantonese. As observed, some RVCs could be preserved in Cantonese while some were restricted and presented by means of V-*dou3* (V-到), V-copying and '*gau2-dou3*' (攪到) constructions. Although the selection process seems to be arbitrary, it is believed that there must be a rule governing the interpretation process for the sentences to be produced in a correct and natural way.

Moreover, it should be noted that it is possible for the same RVC in Mandarin to be categorized into different types due to the transitivity and canonicality of the RVC. For examples, 他寫累了 'He wrote himself tired' is an unergative, 他寫累了論文 'He is tired for he has been writing his essay' is an accusative, and 論文寫累了他 'He is tired for he has been writing his essay' is a causative. The same RVC 寫累 'write-tired' falls into different categories. The alternation in the examples of unergative and accusative shows that canonical intransitive RVC can be presented in a canonical transitive way. It is also instantiated in the examples of accusative and causative that RVC may have both canonical and non-canonical transitive use. Thus, whether or not sentence types affect the presentation of the sentences in Cantonese will be investigated in Section 4.2.

4.1 At the Lexical Level

There are four ways for the resultatives to be expressed in Cantonese, namely RVC, V-*dou3* (V-到), V-copying and '*gau2-dou3*' (攪到) constructions. Similar to Cantonese, RVCs and V-*de* (V-得)/ V-*dao* (V-到) constructions are the most common ways of presenting resultatives in Mandarin. Consider (14):

(14) a. 他 踢破-了 鞋子
3.SG kick broken-ASP shoes
'He has ruined his shoes.'

b. 他 踢-到/得 鞋子 破-了
3.SG kick-dao/de shoes broken-ASP
'He has ruined his shoes.'

c. 佢 踢爛-咗 對 鞋
3.SG kick broken-ASP CL shoes
'He has ruined his shoes.'

d. 佢 踢-到 對 鞋 爛-咗
3.SG kick-dou3 CL shoes broken-ASP
'He has ruined his shoes.'

In (14), (a) and (b) are in Mandarin, while (c) and (d) are in Cantonese. RVC and V-*dou3* are interchangeable in both Mandarin and Cantonese as shown in these examples. It should also be noted that "V-*dou3*" in Mandarin can also be substituted by "V-*de*". In Mandarin, "V-*de*" marks either a degree complement or a state complement whereas "V-*de*" in Cantonese can only be used in marking degree complement and "V-*dou3*" is used to mark state complement. Thus, it can be concluded that V-*de* in Mandarin corresponds to V-*dou3* in Cantonese.

The morpheme *de* 得 in "V-*de*" is regarded as a dummy *de* which makes no difference between the semantic meaning of the same sentence presented by RVCs (Huang 1992, Sybesma 1999, Tang 2002). This practice may be true in Mandarin but it is not the case in Cantonese. The alternation between RVCs and V-*dou3* in these two Chinese varieties are different. Consider (15):

(15) a. 他 的 眼睛 哭紅-了
3.SG POSS eye cry red-ASP
'He cried and his eyes turned red as a result.'

b. 他 的 眼睛 哭-得 紅-了
3.SG POSS eye cry-de red-ASP
'He cried and his eyes turned red as a result.'

c. * 佢 對 眼 喊紅-咗
3.SG CL eye cry red-ASP

d. 佢 對 眼 喊-到 紅-咗
3.SG CL eye cry-dou3 red-ASP
'He cried and his eyes turned red as a result.'

As shown in (15a) and (15b), RVCs and V-*dou3*/ V-*de* in Mandarin are interchangeable whereas RVCs and V-*dou3* are not in Cantonese sometimes as in (15c) and (15d). Two questions are raised here: (a) How should one explain why (14c) and (14d) are interchangeable while (15c) and (15d) are not?, and (b) Do the sentences (14c) and (14d), presented by different methods, possess the same meaning? Such incompatibility could confuse Cantonese learners on the usage of RVCs and V-*dou3*. Misbelieving the two Chinese varieties are the same, learners might produce ill-formed sentences like (15c) on the basis of their prior knowledge in Mandarin RVCs. Thus, a rule governing the alternation of RVCs and V-*dou3* in Cantonese must be proposed to avoid ungrammaticality.

"Strong resultatives" vs. "weak resultatives"
According to Washio (1997:7, 1999: 685-686), "resultatives in which the meaning of the verb and the meaning of the adjective are completely independent of each other will be referred to as STRONG resultatives". For example, 張三跑丟了車票 'Zhangsan has lost his ticket' is a strong resultative since that *Zhang-san* has lost something is not implicated by the running event. Combined with Washio (1997), we define WEAK resultatives as resultatives in which the result denoted by V2 is either the purpose or the conventional result of the action stated in V1. There are two types of weak resultatives. The first type is that the result (V2) entailed in V2 (i.e. 短 'short') is repeating what the V1 already contain in its semantics. For example, 他剪短了頭髮 'He had a haircut'. The second type is that the "restricted" result (V2) can be inferred

by the logical object. For example, in 我跑贏了比賽 'I won the running competition', the result can only be "win", "lose" or "draw" as restricted by the logical object *competition*.

"RVC" vs. "V-*dou3*" Constructions

By examining different RVCs, we observe that it is ordinarily possible for RVCs to be substituted freely by V-*dou3* in Cantonese as in ergatives, unergatives, accusatives (Type 3, 4, 5), pseudo-passives and object-fronting. It is, therefore, important to know under what circumstances that RVCs and V-*dou3* are not interchangeable. We will investigate those resultatives that can never appear as a RVC (V1 and V2 are adjacent) and the RVC that *dou3* 到 can never be inserted, under all six types of sentences in Cantonese.

First of all, it is not the properties of V2 that determines the methods but the semantic relations between V1 and V2 that matter. Resultatives with a verbal V2 such as *唱喊 (唱哭) 'sing-cry'、*聽瞓 (聽睡) 'listen-asleep' and *跑跌 (跑丟) 'run-lose' are prohibited. Those V2 are obviously indicating another activity which should be regarded as "strong resultatives". However, even RVCs with an adjectival V2 are not allowed to appear in a RVC pattern in Cantonese, such as *寫攰 (寫累) 'write-tired'、*跑攰 (跑累) 'run-tired'、*追攰 (追累) 'chase-tired'、*喊紅 (哭紅) 'cry-red'、*睇花 (看花) 'read-blurred'、*聽怕 (聽怕) 'listen-afraid' etc.. In Cantonese, RVC-pattern is not used when the result (V2) is not unique to a particular action. For example, the result 累 'tired' can be triggered by many action such as 寫'write',跑 'run' and 追 'chase' as shown in the examples, these examples in RVC-patterns are therefore prohibited. However, it is not applicate to the cases of Mandarin RVCs.

Without the aid of the logical objects, unergatives select the presentation method based on the uniqueness of V2 to V1. For example, in 我飽了 'I'm full', the action 吃/食 'eat' is probably predictable simply because the adjectival predicate 飽 ought to be fulfilled by the eating event. Thus, the weak resultative can be re-structured in a RVC-pattern as 我食飽喇 in Cantonese.

Apart from those V-*dou3*-only compounds, there are some RVC-only compounds such as 我跑贏咗場比賽 'I won the running competition' and 我訓醒喇 'I woke up'. In the two examples mentioned here, the Cantonese morpheme *dou3* 到 is not allowed to be inserted in between the two predicates in Cantonese. As V1 and V2 are closely related in semantics, this kind of RVC should be considered a "weak resultative".

To sum up, the concept of "strong/ weak resultative" is critical to the method selection. There are three factors determining whether RVCs and V-dou3 is interchangeable. Firstly, "weak resultatives" in Cantonese may be presented by means of RVC or V-*dou3* whereas "strong resultatives" can only be demonstrated in V-*dou3* constructions. It should be noted that if a resultative compound is presented as an RVC, that compound must be regarded as a "weak resultative" only. However, a weak resultative is not necessarily a RVC. Secondly, when more than two arguments are found in a sentence (i.e. Type 6 accusative), only RVC-patterns can be allowed. Lastly, non-canonical sentences (i.e. all types of causatives) can only be presented in V-*dou3* constructions.

Exceptional cases

Without the presence of an active verb, ergatives with both V1 and V2 denoting states should not be categorized as "weak resultative". However, they can still be presented in both RVCs and V-*dou3* constructions in Cantonese. For examples, 佢嚇呆咗/佢嚇到呆咗 (嚇呆) 'He is shocked'.

"V-copying" Constructions

項 (1997) and 趙 (2001) propose that V-copying is used to stress the action taken or the unexpected result. 張 (2002) suggests that the construction is used to give expression to long-distance cause and effect. V-copying construction is not permitted normally if V1 and V2 are semantically-closed. If RVC is not allowed in Cantonese, V-copying construction is used to stress the long distance of the cause and result. If RVC is allowed in Cantonese, V-copying construction is then used to emphasize the unexpected result denoted by V2. It is found that V-copying construction can only be used if the object is the logical object of V1 in canonical sentences (i.e. Type 1, 2 and 4 accusatives). For Type 1 and 2, some of them may be presented in the form of RVC in Cantonese if the RVC is a weak one. For Type 4, it is possible for them to be presented in V-*dou3* and RVC.

"Gau2-dou3" Constructions

"*Gau2-dou3*" construction is only used for Type 2 and Type 3 causatives. For Type 2, this construction is used to separate the CAUSER from the predicate and object so as to avoid ambiguity. For Type 3, since the SUBJ of the sentence is an independent causer that can neither be the logical object of V1 nor V2, "*gau2-dou3*" appears to indicate that causer and predicate are not closely related. "*Gau2-dou3*" (攪到) is actually equal to "*ling6*" (令) in Cantonese, but the former is more frequently used by Cantonese speakers.

4.2 At the Syntactic Level

It is common to have the same RVCs belonging to different sentence types, and therefore, analyzing RVCs at the syntactic level could be prominent in uncovering the logic behind. In this section, we will analyze the method selected for the same RVC in different sentence types.

"Accusatives" and "Causatives"

Both accusatives and causatives have all these three elements: subject, verb and object in each of their sentences. The same RVC sometimes belongs to both of them as shown in (16) and (17).

Accusatives:

(16) a. 張三 寫累-了 論文
Zhangsan write tired-ASP essay
'Zhangsan is tired for he has been writing his essay.'

b. 張三 **寫論文 寫-到 好攰**
Zhangsan write essay write-dou3 very tired
'Zhangsan is tired for he has been writing his essay.'

Causatives:

c. 論文 寫累-了 張三
essay write tired-ASP Zhangsan
'Zhangsan is tired for he has been writing his essay.'

d. 篇 論文 **寫-到 張三 好攰**
CL essay write-dou3 Zhangsan very tired
'Zhangsan is tired for he has been writing his essay.'

In (16), (a) and (c) are Mandarin examples whereas (b) and (d) are Cantonese. As we can see in (a) and (c), the only difference between accusatives and causatives in Mandarin is the word order of the sentences. The subject and the object in (a) switched their positions as in (c). The co-referential RVC "寫累" should be regarded as a strong resultative since 累 'tired' is a state that takes a long period of time to achieve. RVC pattern is therefore not used in Cantonese corresponding sentences. Different methods are selected for accusatives and causatives. V-copying is used in accusatives while V-*dou3* construction is used in causatives. In (16a) and (16b), the AGENTs are in the subject positions. (16b) is re-structured as "張三寫論文", with the complement "寫到好攰" added to indicate the state of the AGENT. In (16c) and (16d), the THEMEs are in the subject positions. Since V-copying construction can only deal with canonical sentences, adopting it in causative would end up producing an ill-formed sentence as "*篇論文寫張三寫到好攰". Thus, if the same RVCs belong to both causatives and accusatives while predicates of each RVC are not semantically related, V-copying is used in accusatives while V-*dou3* is used in causatives. If a Mandarin RVC belonging to causatives and accusatives is a weak one, would different methods be used in Cantonese? Consider (17), where (a) and (d) are in Mandarin, and (b), (c) and (e) are in Cantonese:

Accusatives:

(17) a. 他 吃膩-了 蛋糕
3.SG eat bored-ASP cake
'He was sick of eating the cake.'

b. 佢 **食厭**-咗 蛋糕
3.SG eat bored-ASP cake
'He was sick of eating the cake.'

c. 佢 **食蛋糕 食-到 厭**
3.SG eat cake eat-dou3 bored
'He was sick of eating the cake.'

Causatives:

d. 那 個 蛋糕 吃膩-了 他
That CL cake eat bored-ASP 3.SG
'He was sick of eating the cake.'

e. 個 蛋糕 **食-到** **佢** **厭-咗**
CL cake eat-dou3 3.SG bored-ASP
'He was sick of eating the cake.'

In (17), "吃膩" is a weak resultative since the result can be predicted if we have "SUBJ + V1___ + OBJ" (他吃___了蛋糕). Since 吃 and 膩 are semantically related, its RVC pattern is preserved in a Cantonese accusative sentence as in (17b). V-copying construction is also accepted as in (17c). It should be noted that (17b) and (17c) have different readings where (17b) is simply making a statement while (17c) is to stress the boredom of eating that cake which is an unexpected state.

It can be concluded that even if the RVC is a weak resultative, causative RVCs in Cantonese are not allowed due to the non-canonical word order.

"Unergatives", "Accusatives", "Causatives" and "Object-fronting"

As mentioned in Section 4, the same RVC in Mandarin may belong to different types due to the transitivity and canonicality. 吃膩 'eat-bored' is found to be fell into the categories of "unergatives", "accusatives", "causatives", and "object-fronting". The structures of their corresponding sentences in Cantonese are shown below:

Mandarin	Cantonese
Unergatives: (18) 他吃膩了	a. 佢**食厭**咗喇 b. 佢**食到厭**喇
Accusatives: (19) 他吃膩了這款蛋糕	a. 佢**食厭**咗呢款蛋糕喇 b. 佢**食呢款蛋糕食到厭**喇
Causatives: (20) 這款蛋糕吃膩了他	a. *呢款蛋糕**食厭**咗佢喇 b. 呢款蛋糕**食到佢厭**喇
Object-fronting: (21) 這款蛋糕吃膩了	a. 呢款蛋糕**食厭**咗喇 b. 呢款蛋糕**食到厭**喇

As shown in (18) - (21), the weak resultative 吃膩 'eat-bored' is allowed in unergatives, accusatives and object-fronting since RVCs are not allowed in causatives. However, RVC-patterns in causatives are strictly prohibited. It is also observed that only accusatives use V-copying construction instead of V-*dou3* construction. Hence, it is assumed that V-copying construction can only be used in a canonical sentence which has at least two arguments on the surface of the sentence.

5 Conclusion

In this paper, we introduced different types of resultative verb compounds, re-defined the properties of ergatives, re-categorized the accusatives based on their referentiality, and proposed to add two new sub-types (i.e. Type 3 and Type 5) to causatives and clearly distinguished object-fronting constructions from pseudo-passives based on the frameworks of Cheng & Huang (1994) and Wang (2001).

We also discussed how the presentation of RVCs is affected at the lexical level and syntactic level. V-*de* and V-*dao* have been proved to be equal in certain situations. RVC and V-*dou3*/ V-*de* are always interchangeable in Mandarin, while they are sometimes restricted in Cantonese. Thus, V-*dou3* in Cantonese should not be deemed as a dummy like V-*de* in Mandarin. Other methods used to present resultatives in Cantonese, namely V-copying and "*gau2-dou3*" constructions, are introduced as well. The method-selection for each sentence type is also suggested. The analyses of the factors affecting the method-selection are illustrated at both the lexical and syntactic levels with the help of the concepts of 'strong resultative' and 'weak resultative' (not applicable to ergatives and causatives).

Ubiquitously found in Chinese, 'V-R compounding is a rich source of new verbs in Mandarin Chinese…' (Lin 1998). This work is meant to provide a systematic way of how resultatives are presented in Cantonese to the non-native speakers of Cantonese, especially those of a Mandarin-speaking background.

Acknowledgments

This work is supported by an Early Career Scheme (ESC) sponsored by the Research Grants Council of Hong Kong (Project No. 559313).

References

Cheng, Lai-Shen Lisa and Huang, Cheng-Teh James. 1994. On the Argument Structure of Resultative Compounds. In Matthew Y. Chen and Ovid J. L. Tzeng (eds.), *In Honor of William S.-Y. Wang: Interdisciplinary Studies in Language and Language Change*. 187-221. Taipei, Taiwan: Pyramid.

Cheng, L., Huang, C. T. J., Li, Y. H. A., and Tang, C. C. J. 1997. Causative Compounds across Chinese dialects: A study of Cantonese, Mandarin and Taiwanese. *Chinese Languages and Linguistics*, 4, 199-224.

Chow, Pui-lun. 2012. The syntax-semantics interface of resultative constructions in Mandarin Chinese and Cantonese. M.Phil Thesis, The University of Hong Kong.

Gu, Yang. 1992. The Syntax of Resultative and Causative Compounds in Chinese. Ph.D. Dissertation, Cornell University.

Gu, Yang and Virginia Yip. 2004. On the Cantonese Resultative Predicate V-can*. *Concentric: Studies in Linguistics*, 30.2: 35-67.

Huang, Cheng-Teh James. 1992. Complex Predicates in Control. In R. K. Larson, S. Iatridou, U. Lahiri and J. Higginbotham (eds.), *Control and Grammar*. Springer Netherlands. 109-147.

Huang, Chu-ren and Lin, Fu-wen. 1992. Composite event structure and complex predicates: A template-based approach to argument selection. In *Proceedings of the 3rd annual meetings of the Formal Linguistics Society of Mid-America*.

Huang, Han-chun. 2008. Resultative Verb Compounds in Mandarin Chinese: A Constructional Approach. Ph.D. Dissertation. National Tsing Hua University.

Kaufmann, Ingrid & Dieter Wunderlich. 1998. Cross-linguistic patterns of resultatives. *Working papers of the SFB282 'Theorie des Lexikins' 109*. Univeristy of Düsseldorf.

Keung, Sau-ching. 2007. The development of resultative and directional verb compounds in Cantonese-speaking preschool children. M.Phil Thesis, The University of Hong Kong.

Li, Charles N. and Thompson, Sandra A. 1981. *Mandarin Chinese: A Functional Reference Grammar*. Berkeley: University of California Press.

Li, Kin-ling Michelle. 2002. On Cantonese causative constructions: iconicity, grammaticalization and semantic structures. M.Phil Thesis, The University of Hong Kong.

Li, Ya-fei. 1990. On VV compounds in Chinese. *Natural Language & Linguistic Theory*, 8:2, 177-207.

Li, Ya-fei. 1995. The thematic hierarchy and causativity. *Natural Language & Linguistic Theory*, 13, 255-282.

Lin, Fu-wen. 1989. The Verb-Complement (V-R) Compounds in Mandarin Chinese. In Huang, Chu-ren and Chen, Keh-jiann (eds), *Proceedings of ROCLING II*. Taipei: Academia Sinica. 253-276.

Lu, Hsiao-tung John. 1977. Resultative verb compounds vs. directional verb compounds in Mandarin. *Journal of Chinese Linguistics* 5: 276-313.

Shi, Yu-zhi. 2002. The resultative construction in modern Chinese. In *The Establishment of Modern Chinese Grammar: The Formation of the Resultative Construction and its Effects*. Amsterdam, Philadelphia: John Benjamins Publishing.

Sybesma, Rint. 1999. *The Mandarin VP*. Dordrecht: Kluwer Academic Publishers.

Thompson, Sandra Annear. 1973. Resultative verb compounds in Mandarin Chinese: a case for lexical rules. *Language* 49: 361-379.

Tai, James H-Y. 2003. Cognitive relativism: resultative construction in Chinese. *Language and Linguistics* 4: 301-316.

Tang Ting-Chi. 2002. The Causative-Inchoative Alternation in Chinese Compound Verbs. *Language and Linguistics* 3:3, 615-644.

Wang, Ling-ling. 2001. A Study of Resultative Constructions in Mandarin Chinese. Ph.D. Dissertation, The Hong Kong Polytechnic University.

Washio, Ryuichi. 1997. Resultatives, compositionality and language variation. *Journal of East Asian Linguistics* 6: 1-49.

Washio, Ryuichi. 1999. Some comparative notes on resultatives. In Masatake Muraki and Enoch Iwamoto (eds.), *Linguistics: In Search of the Human Mind*. 674-707. Tokyo: Kaitakusha.

沈陽、魏航：《動結式中動作 V1 和結果 V2 隱現的句法和語義條件》。《對外漢語研究》，2011 年 00 期。

項開喜：《漢語重動句式的功能研究》。《中國語文》1997 年第 4 期: 260-267。

趙新：《試論重動句的功能》。《語言研究》。2001 年第 46 期。

張旺熹：《重動結構的遠距離因果關係動因》。載徐烈炯、邵敬敏主編《漢語語法研究的新拓展》(一)，杭州：浙江教育出版社，2002 年。

Complex-NP Islands in Korean: An Experimental Approach

Yong-hun Lee
Chungnam National University
99 Daehak-ro, Yuseong-gu
Daejeon 305-764, Korea
yleeuiuc@hanmail.net

Yeonkyung Park
Hannam University
70 Hannamro, Daedeok-gu
Daejeon 306-791, Korea
withbyk@hanmail.net

Abstract

This paper took an experimental approach and examined island constraints in Korean. Among many island constraints, this study took a Complex NP island constraint, and the experiment was designed with 3 related factors: presence vs. absence of island, matrix clause vs. embedded clause, and scrambling. The analysis results illustrated that the presence/absence of complex NP island did not play a role by itself in Korean but that it made distinctions through the interactions with other factor such as matrix vs. embedded clause.

1 Introduction

Since Ross's identifications of island constraints in English (Ross, 1967), there have been a lot of debates on the existence of island constraints in other languages. For example, Nishigauchi (1990) and Watanabe (1992) claimed that there were island constraints in Japanese, but Ishihara (2002) and Sprouse et al. (2011) mentioned that this language had no island constraint. Likewise, there have been controversies on the existence of island constraints in Korean. Some have argued for the presence of island effects (Lee 1982, Han 1992, Hong 2004), while others have argued against it (Sohn 1980, Kang 1986, Suh 1987, Hwang 2007).

This paper investigated the island constraints in Korean. Our questions were (i) if Korean also has the Complex NP island constraints and (ii) if there are, why there have been so many controversies on the existence of island constraints.

In order to answer these questions, this paper took an experimental approach and examined the island properties in Korean. The target sentences were constructed with three factors, and native speakers' intuition was measured with Magnitude Estimation (ME). After the experiment, all the data for the target sentences were extracted and they were statistically analyzed with R.

Through the analysis, it was found that that the presence/absence of Complex NP island did not play a role by itself in Korean but that it made distinctions through the interactions with other factor such as matrix vs. embedded clause. These examples provided an account for why there have been so many controversies on the existence of island constraints in Korean.

This paper is organized as follows. In Section 2, previous studies were reviewed especially focused on the experimental approaches. Section 3 includes the accounts for experimental design (research materials and research methods), and Section 4 enumerates the analysis results. Section 5 contains discussions, and Section 6 summarizes this paper.

2 Previous Studies

2.1 Island Effects in Korean

Since Ross (1967) identified the island constraints in English, there have been lots of studies on the existence of island constraints in other languages. Those studies primarily focused on examining if the island constraints exist in their languages and why the language escaped the island constraints when the language did not demonstrate the island phenomena.

Korean is no exception. There have been lots of studies on the island constraints in Korean. Earlier studies were primarily focused on the basic island properties in Korean. Choi (1989)

29th Pacific Asia Conference on Language, Information and Computation pages 240 - 249
Shanghai, China, October 30 - November 1, 2015

tried to explain the island phenomena with LF-movements. Song (1995) investigated the relationship between the island constraints and *wh*-in-situ property. On the other hand, Lee (1999) studied negative islands in Korean.

There are two opposite positions in the previous approaches. Some claimed that Korean has island constraints (Lee 1982; Han 1992; Hong 2004; Park, 2001, 2009). Hong (2004) proposed 2 diagnostics for syntactic movements: island and intervention effects. The study mentioned that Korean has an island effects and that no intervention effects were observed in the *wh*-movements. Park (2001) and Park (2009) examined sluicing constructions in Korean. Through the investigation, it was found that matrix sluicing in Korean was island-sensitive. The study argued that the island sensitivity arose because the *wh*-phrase did not move to CP in overt syntax. Park (2009) also proposed accounts for the contrast between matrix sluicing and fragment answers in Korean with respect to island sensitivity.

On the other hand, other scholars claimed that there is no island effect in Korean (Sohn, 1980; Kang, 1986; Suh, 1987; Hwang, 2007; Chung, 2005; Yoon, 2011, 2012; Kim, 2013). Chung (2005) mentioned that Korean *ettehkey* (how) did not show island effects. Given the revised nominal analysis, the scope of *ettehkey* (how) in Korean had to be licensed via binding, since there was no island effect. Yoon (2011, 2012) identified two novel environments where *wh*-phrases showed no island effects: the declarative intervention context and the embedded context. Then, the question was why the in-situ *wh*-phrases were not identical to the standard *wh*-phrases in English. The study also mentioned that the standard *wh*-island effects corresponded to the misinterpretation judgment and argued for it by showing that there was a strong correlation between the *wh*-islands and the possibility that *wh*-in-situ questions would be misinterpreted as Yes/No-questions. Kim (2013) investigated *wh*-islands in the relative clauses. The study claimed that the fact that Korean escaped the island constraint can be explained by a semantico-pragmatic constraint, which is based on the notion of coherence and the construction-specific factors that cause processing difficulty.

2.2 Experimental Approaches to Islands

Recently, as computer technology and statistics develop, many researchers have had an interest in measuring native speakers' intuition on syntactic data objectively and scientifically (Bard, Robertson, and Sorace, 1996; Schütze, 1996; Cowart, 1997; Keller, 2000). This research method was also applied into the study of islands, and lots of fruitful facts have been discovered through experimental approaches.

Sprouse et al. (2012) adopted an experimental approach and examined native speakers' intuition. They employed 2×2 factor combinations in (1) and investigated four types of island constraints using the following sentences (Sprouse et al., 2012:87-8).

(1) Factor Combinations
- a. NON-ISLAND | MATRIX
- b. NON-ISLAND | EMBEDDED
- c. ISLAND | MATRIX
- d. ISLAND | EMBEDDED

(2) Whether islands
- a. Who __ thinks that John bought a car?
- b. What do you think that John bought __ ?
- c. Who __ wonders whether John bought a car?
- d. What do you wonder whether John bought __ ?

(3) Complex NP islands
- a. Who __ claimed that John bought a car?
- b. What did you claim that John bought __?
- c. Who __ made the claim that John bought a car?
- d. What did you make the claim that John bought __?

(4) Subject islands
- a. Who __ thinks the speech interrupted the TV show?
- b. What do you think __ interrupted the TV show?
- c. Who __ thinks the speech about global warming interrupted the TV show?
- d. What do you think the speech about __ interrupted the TV show?

(5) Adjunct islands
- a. Who __ thinks that John left his briefcase at the office?
- b. What do you think that John left __ at the office?
- c. Who __ laughs if John leaves his briefcase at the office?
- d. What do you laugh if John leaves __ at the office?

Along with these target sentences, they examined the intuition of 173 native speakers. Through the experiments, they obtained the following results (Sprouse et al. 2012:100).

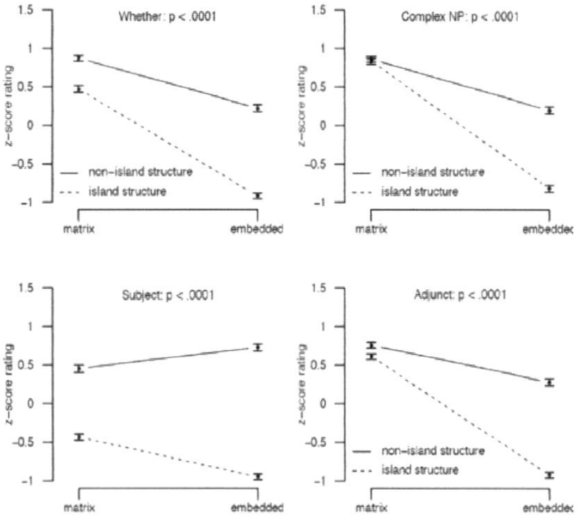

Figure 1. Analysis Results in Sprouse et al. (2012)

These analysis results illustrated (i) that native speakers showed more acceptability for non-island structures than island structures both in matrix and embedded causes and (ii) that the differences of acceptability became greater in embedded clauses rather than matrix clauses. These observations demonstrated that there were clearly island effects in English.

Kim and Goodall (2014) employed a similar method in their experiments and examined the island constraints in Korean. They designed four experiment sets to test the existence of *wh*-island (*whether* island) and adjunct island effects in Korean. Since Korean is a *wh*-in-situ language, another factor (canonical order vs. scrambled) was taken into consideration and their experiments had a 2×2×2 design: Location of *wh*-word (in matrix vs. embedded clause), Embedded clause type (non-island vs. island) and Answer type (appropriate for direct *wh*-question vs. yes/no question).

They made use of question-answer pairs along with appropriate contexts in order to examine native speakers' intuition. They made the questions in the stimuli ambiguous so that *wh*-words might be interpreted either as *wh*-words or as existential, as in Hong (2004).

A total of 48 native speakers participated in the experiments and the intuition was measured with a 7-point Likert scale. The following figures showed us the analysis results.

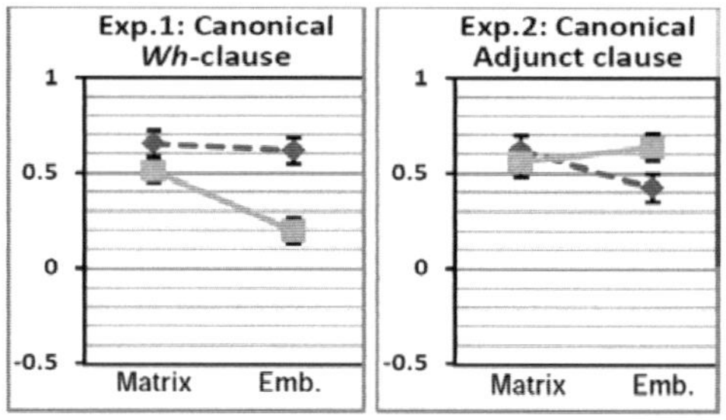

Figure 2. Canonical Order in Korean

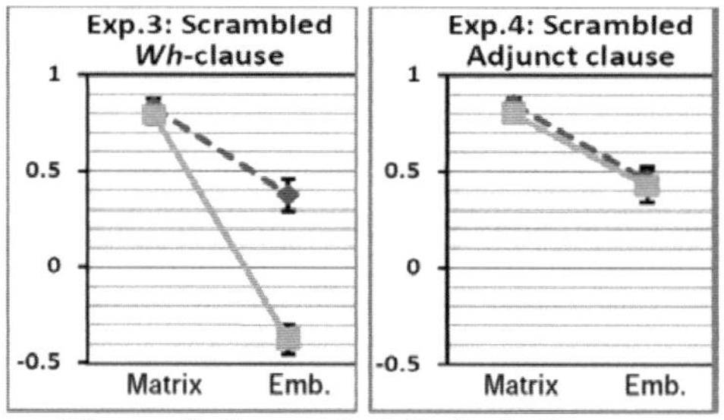

Figure 3. Scrambled Order in Korean

They found that there were a significant interaction between Location (matrix or embedded clause) and Embedded clause type (non-island or island) in Exp. 1 and Exp. 3, but that there was no such interaction in Exp. 2 and Exp. 4. This implies that there is an island effect with *wh*-clauses (Exp. 1 and Exp. 3) but that no island effect exists with adjunct clauses (Exp. 2 and Exp. 4).

Along with these results, they obtained another interesting observation. For the ambiguous questions contained in the question-answer pairs, they observed that one reading or the other was encouraged. Furthermore, they found that the presence or absence of an appropriate context made the *wh*-reading pragmatically plausible or implausible, even in the cases where an island constraint was violated.

3 Research Method

3.1 Research Question and Hypothesis

Among the island constraints proposed in Ross (1967), this paper tried to investigate the Complex NP island constraint in Korean.

Our research questions are as follows.

(6) Research Questions

a. Is there a Complex NP island effect in Korean?

b. If there is an island effect, why are there so many controversies on the existence of island effects?

For these questions, we made the following hypotheses.

(7) Hypothesis

a. If there is no Complex NP island effect in Korean, the acceptability scores of all the types in the target sentences will not be distinguishable from one another.

b. If there is a Complex NP island effect in Korean, the acceptability scores of all the types in the target sentences may be distinguishable from one another or the patterns that the Korean data illustrated may be different from English Complex NP islands.

To examine these hypotheses, an experiment was designed as follows.

3.2 Materials

In order to closely examine the island constraints in Korean, the first thing to be done was to make target sentences. This paper basically followed the factor combinations in (1) à la Sprouse et al. (2012), but another factor Scrambling was also taken into consideration as in Kim and Goodall (2014). That is, the following three factors were employed in the experiment: Island constraint (Absence vs. Presence), Location of *wh*-word (Matrix clause vs. Embedded clause), and Scrambling (Canonical vs. Scrambled). Since three factors were adopted and each factor had two values, the experiment had a 2×2×2 design.

First of all, basic target sentences were made with the sentences in (3) and the sentences in Pearl and Sprouse (2014). The following sentences are basic target sentences for Complex NP constraints in Korean.[1]

(7) a. *Nwu-ka Younghee-ka mok.keli-lul*
Who.NOM Younghee.NOM necklace.ACC
ilhepeli-ess-ta-ko cwucangha-ni?
lose.PAST.DECL.COMP claim.Q
'Who claimed that Younghee lost the necklace?'

b. *Chelsoo-nun Younghee-ka mues-lul*
Chelsoo.TOP Younghee.NOM what.ACC
ilhepeli-ess-ta-ko/nun cwucangha-ni?
lose.PAST.DECL.COMP claim.Q
'What did Chelsoo claim that Younghee lost?'

c. *Nwu-ka Younghee-ka mok.keli-lul*
Who.NOM Younghee.NOM necklace.ACC
ilhepeli-ess-ta-ko cwucang-ul
lose.PAST.DECL.COMP claim..ACC
ha-yss-ni?
do.PAST.Q
'Who made a claim that Younghee lost the necklace?'

d. *Chelsoo-nun Younghee-ka mues-lul*
Chelsoo.TOP Younghee.NOM
what.ACC
ilhepeli-ess-ta-ko cwucang-ul
lose.PAST.DECL.COMP claim..ACC
ha-yss-ni?
do.PAST.Q
'What did Chelsoo made a claim that Younghee lost?'

These four sentences match with the corresponding sentences in (3), and they contained the factor combinations in (1). Four sentences in (7) have a canonical order, and the sentences with scrambled orders were constructed by interchanging the subject and object of these basic target sentences.[2]

Along with these target sentences, the double number of filler sentences were made. The half of the filler sentences (8 sentences) were constructed based on the structure of the target items. However, they was not related with the Complex NP island constraints. The others of the filler sentences (8 sentences) were composed of the sentences that had no relation with the purpose of the experiment. Among them, 4 sentences were grammatical one and the others were ungrammatical one.

After all the target and filler sentences were constructed, a random numbers were generated with the R function (from 1 to 24; 8 target sentences and 16 fillers), and each sentence was given the generated random numbers. Then, the sentences were given to the participants after the sentences were sorted based on the random number.

[1] In fact, the basic target sentences in the experiment were constructed primarily based on Pearl and Sprouse (2014) and Sprouse et al. (2014), rather than based on the sentences in Sprouse et al. (2012), since the Korean translations of the sentences in these studies were more natural.

[2] A reviewer pointed out that the sentences in (7c) and (7d) must contain *ilhepeli-ess-ta-nun*, not *ilhepeli-ess-ta-ko*. In fact, this verb form was also included in the data sets, since it is desirable to avoid the lexicalization effects. However, the differences between the sentences with *ilhepeli-ess-ta-nun* and those with *ilhepeli-ess-ta-ko* were not statistically significant. In addition, these two types of sentences demonstrated the same pattern in Figure 4.

3.3 Procedure

The data for a total of 50 native speakers were collected from the experiment. All the participants (ages ranging between 19 and 27) resided in and around Daejeon area, South Korea. They were either current university students or graduates of universities in Korea.

All the participants were first asked to fill out a simple one-page survey that contains biographical information such as age, gender, and dialect(s), together with the consent form for participating in the experiment. Then they were asked to proceed to take the main task.

The main task used in the experiment was an acceptability judgment task using Magnitude Estimation (ME; Lodge, 1981; Johnson, 2008), not the Likert scale as in Kim and Goodall (2014).

There are several reasons why this paper took an ME in the acceptability judgment task, rather than the Likert scale.[3] First, the Likert scale has limited resolution. For example, if native speakers may feel that a sentence is somewhere between 4 and 5 (something like 4.5), gradient ratings are not available in the latter method. However, the former permits as much resolution as the raters wish to employ. Second, the latter method uses an ordinal scale, and there is no guarantee that the interval between * and ** represent the same difference of impressions as that between ? and ??. The former method, on the other hand, provides judgments on an interval scale for which averages (mean value, *m*) and standard deviations (*sd*) can be more legitimately used. Third, the latter limits our ability to compare results across the experiments. The range of acceptability for a set of sentences has to be fitted to the scale, and what counts as ?? for one set of sentences may be quite different from what counts as ?? for another set of sentences.

There are two types of ME methods: numerical estimates and line drawing. However, as Bard et al. (1996) pointed out, the participants sometimes think of numeric estimates as something like academic test scores, and so they limit their responses to a somewhat categorical scale (e.g. 70, 80, 90, 100), rather than using a ratio scale as intended in the magnitude estimation.

Accordingly, the current study adopted a line drawing method in which the participants were asked to draw different lengths of lines to indicate the naturalness (acceptability) of a given sentence (after reading the sentence). An acceptability judgment task (also known as native speakers' intuition test) was used in the study since this method is known to be a psychological experiment which can be used to get the subconscious knowledge of native speakers in a given language (Carnie, 2012). In the main task, participants were required to draw a line for each sentence, according to the degree of acceptability/naturalness of the given sentence.

4 Statistical Analysis

4.1 Normality Tests and Regression

After all the data were collected from acceptability judgment tasks, the values were extracted for target sentences by measuring the length of lines. Then, the normality tests (Baayen, 2008; Gries, 2013) were performed to check whether parametric tests were available or not. If the distributions of the data follow the normal distribution, the parametric tests are available, such as *t*-tests, ANOVAs, or (ordinary) linear regression tests. However, if the distributions do not follow the normal distribution, the non-parametric tests must be applied such as Wilcoxon tests, Friedman tests, or generalized linear regression tests.

When the normality tests were performed, it was found that all the data sets did not follow the normal distribution. Some were positively skewed, and others showed a slightly bimodal distribution. Accordingly, non-parametric tests had to be applied in the analysis of our data.

After the normality tests, the collected data were descriptively analyzed. Then, in order to closely examine how each factor affects the acceptability of the target sentences, a (generalized) regression test was performed. According to Agresti (2007), a generalized regression test is available when the distribution does not follow the normal distribution. Thus, the test was adopted to examine how each factor affects the acceptability of the sentences.

After we performed a regression analysis, it is necessary to choose the most appropriate model among the several possible models. According to

[3] Lee (2013) contained a detailed discussion on the differences between ME and Likert scales in the acceptability judgment task (intuition tests). Lodge (1981) mentioned that this ME had several advantages over the category scaling (the Likert scale). Although there are some claims that the Likert scales are available in the acceptability judgment task, this paper follows previous studies (Lodge, 1981; Johnson, 2008) and adopted ME in the experiment.

Gries (2013), there are two types of model selection parameters. One is based on the direction of the analysis and the other is the criterion determining whether or not a predictor gets to be in the model. On the direction of the analysis, most analyses have adopted a backward selection, and this paper also took this method. There are two types of approaches to the selection of relevant models: significance-based approaches and criterion-based approaches. This paper took a significance-based approach. That is, the analysis would start from the maximally saturated model, and continued to remove predictors (backward) until the analysis reached the significant differences in the *p*-value (significant-based).

4.2 Descriptive Statistics

Before a regression test was conducted, a basic descriptive analysis was performed to the data. Although all the data sets did not follow the normal distribution, since the *p*-values of the tests were *marginal*, the mean values and their 95% confidence intervals (CIs) were adopted in the descriptive analysis. The following figures show us the overall tendency of the data.

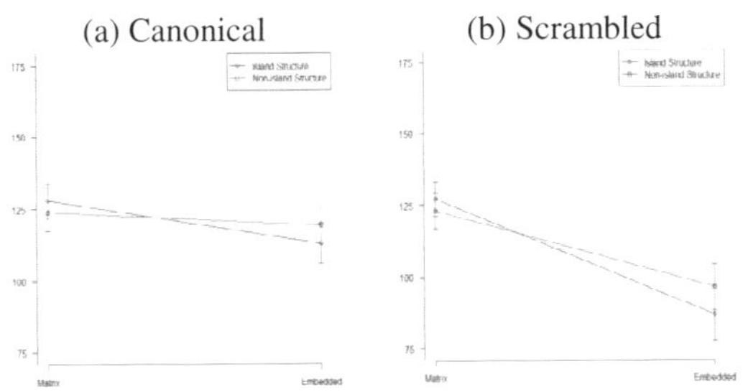

Figure 4. Descriptive Analysis of the Data

As you can observe in these plots, two lines in the plots are crossed. This tendency is similar to that of Exp. 2 (Figure) in Kim and Goodall (2014), but it is different from the Complex NP constraints in English (Figure 1).

Note that the 95% CIs of all of the four pairs overlap. This demonstrates that two data sets are not statistically distinguished, which implies that there is no (Complex NP) island effect in Korean. Also note that the scores for matrix clause in the Scrambled sentences are higher than the values for the embedded sentences. This implies that the matrix vs. embedded distinctions play an important role also in Korean.

4.3 Inferential Statistics

Since it is difficult to visually examine how the three factors play a role in the Complex NP islands in Korean data, a (generalized) linear regression test was performed. [4] This method was taken, since the data set did not follow the normal distribution. The following table illustrates the analysis results. Here, the following abbreviations were used: I for Island constraint (Absence vs. Presence), C (Clause Type) for the location of *wh*-word (Matrix clause vs. Embedded clause), and S for Scrambling (Canonical vs. Scrambled).

	Estimate	*sd*	*t*	*p*
(Intercept)	114.638	1.236	92.751	<<<.001
I	0.988	1.236	0.799	.425
C	-10.858	1.236	-8.785	<<<.001
S	6.288	1.236	5.087	<<<.001
I:C	3.043	1.236	2.462	.014
I:S	-0.413	1.236	-0.334	.739
C:S	6.003	1.236	4.856	<<<.001
I:C:S	-0.428	1.236	-0.346	.730

Table 1. Regression Analysis Results of the Data

As observed in this table, both factors C and S were *highly* significant ($p<.001$), but the factor I was not significant ($p=.425$).

There were interactions between the factors. The factor C has a strong interaction with the factor S ($p<.001$), but a weak but significant interaction with the factor I ($p=.014$). All the other interactions (I:S and I:C:S) were statistically insignificant ($p>.05$).

These results implied that the factor I (the absence vs. presence of Complex NP island constraint in Korean) did not play a role by itself, but played a marginal role through the interaction with the factor C. The factor I did not play a role in the other interactions (I:S and I:C:S).

4.4 Analysis with Effect Plots

Since a (generalized) linear regression test was performed, let's examine how three factors and their interactions influenced the acceptability of the sentences. Figure 5 illustrates the effect plots for each factor.

[4] Someone might ask why a (generalized) mixed effect model was not used here, as in Sprouse et al. (2012). It may be possible to use the model. However, in our experiment, the only random factor was speaker variations. Though speaker variation is also an important factor, a generalized (fixed) linear regression model was applied here to make the statistical process simple.

As observed in these figures, the 95% CIs overlaps in the factor Island, while two groups are clearly distinguished in the other factors Clause Type and Scrambling. This implies that the factor Island by itself is insignificant in the Korean data (p=.425), while the other factors Clause Type and Scrambling are statistically significant in Korean (p<.001 in both factors).

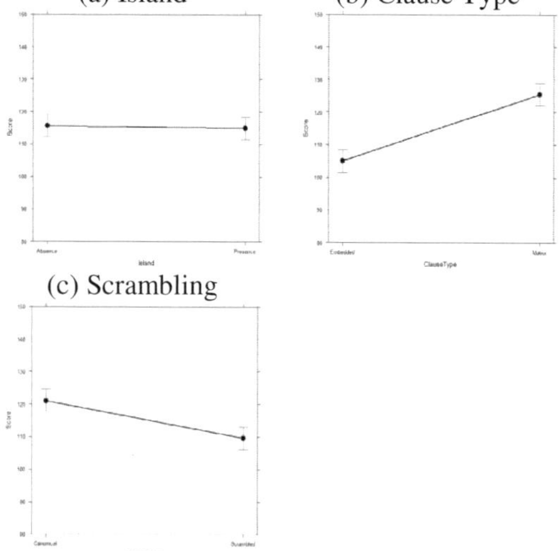
(a) Island (b) Clause Type (c) Scrambling

Figure 5. Effect Plots for 3 Factors

Now, let's move to the interactions among the factors. The following plot shows the interactions between the factor Island and the factor Clause Type.

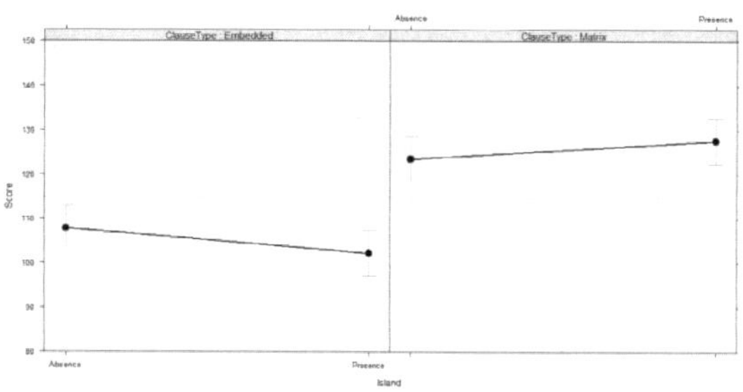

Figure 6. Effect Plot for Island:Clause Type

If there is no interaction between two factors, the lines are parallel. If there is an interaction between two factors, however, the lines are not parallel. As observed in these plots, two lines are not parallel. This implies that there is an interaction between two factors (p=.014).

The following plot shows us the interactions between two factors Island and Scrambling.

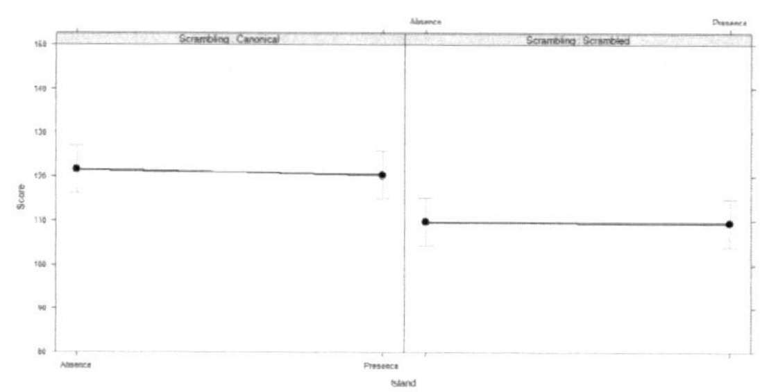

Figure 7. Effect Plot for Island:Scrambling

As observed in these plots, two lines are nearly parallel. This implies that there is no interaction between two factors (p=.739).

The following plot shows us the interactions between the factor Clause Type and the factor Scrambling.

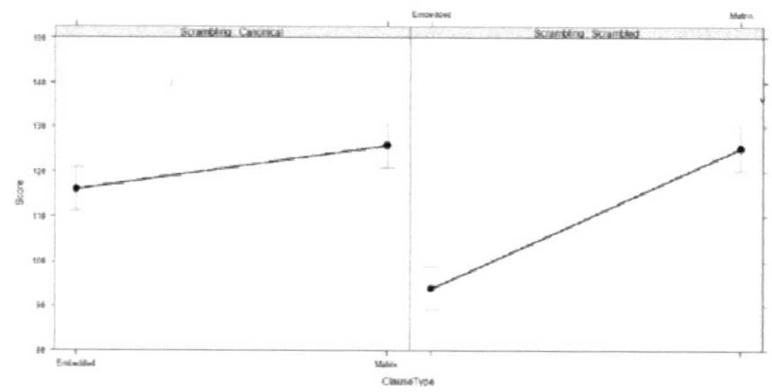

Figure 8. Effect Plot for Clause Type:Scrambling

As observed in these plots, two lines are not parallel. Furthermore, the slopes of two lines are clearly different. This implies that there is a strong interaction between two factors (p<.001).

The last plot shows us the interactions among the three factors: Island, Clause Type, and Scrambling.

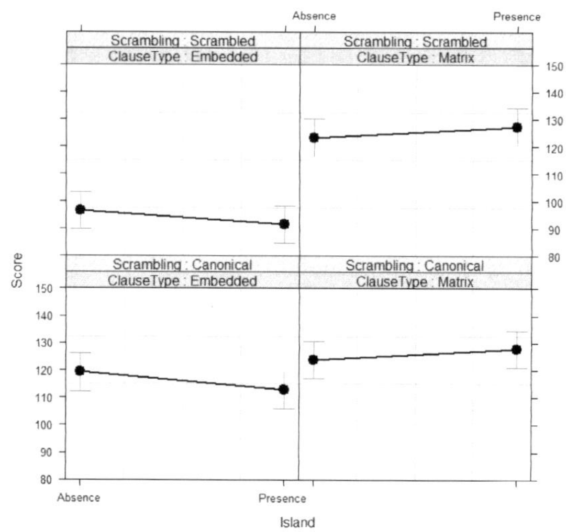

Figure 9. Effect Plot for Interactions

As observed in these plots, all the lines are not parallel. However, the slopes of the lines are not clearly different. This implies that there is little interaction between two factors (p=.730).

5 Discussion

Now, let's see what answers can be provided to the research questions in (6) and Hypothesis in (7) along with the analysis results.

For the first question, the analysis results in Table 1 demonstrated that Korean clearly had a Complex NP island constraint, like English. These results experimentally supported the claims that Korean also HAD island constraints as in English (Lee 1982; Han 1992; Hong 2004; Park, 2001, 2009), though the island types of this paper was different from those of the previous studies.

The second research question is related with two hypotheses in (7). Since it was observed Korean had a Complex NP island constraint in Table 1, the hypothesis in (7a) cannot be maintained anymore. The comparison of the second graph in Figure 2 (Complex NP) and two graphs in Figure 4 clearly demonstrated that the general tendency in Korean was different from that of English, which supports the second hypothesis in (7b). As two graphs in Figure 4 demonstrated, two lines in the graphs for Korean Complex NP island were crossed. It is hard to say that the tendency was made by chance, because two lines were crossed in both cases (both in Canonical order and in Scrambled order). An interesting fact was that the sentences with island structures had higher acceptability than those with non-island structures in the matrix clauses. It is difficult to say that the tendency was made by chance, because this tendency appeared in both cases environments. A similar pattern was also observed in the Exp. 2 (Figure 2) of Kim and Goodall (2014). Therefore, the exact properties for this tendency have to be investigated through the further research.

From theses analysis results, it is possible to guess why there have been so many controversies on the existence of island constraints in Korean. As mentioned in Section 2.1, some claimed that Korean has island constraints (Lee 1982; Han 1992; Hong 2004; Park, 2001, 2009), and others claimed that there is no island effect in Korean (Sohn, 1980; Kang, 1986; Suh, 1987; Hwang, 2007; Chung, 2005; Yoon, 2011, 2012; Kim, 2013). Our analysis results provide a partial answer why there have been so many controversies on the existence of island constraints in Korean. As Table 1 demonstrates, the statistical analysis results in Table 1 contain the supporting evidences of both claims. The p-value of the factor Island (p=0.425) and the effect plot in Figure 8 illustrated that this factor is statistically insignificant. This implies that Korean may have no Complex NP island effects. However, the p-value of the interaction between two factors Island and Clause Type (p=0.014) and the effect plot in Figure 6 illustrated that the interaction between these two factors was statistically significant. This implies that Korean may have Complex NP island effects through the interaction with other factors. That is, though the factor Island itself does not have statistically significant influence on the acceptability of the Korean sentences, if this factor interacts with other factor(s), it may have a statistically significant influence. If no such interaction exists, the factor Island does not have a statistically significant influence. Whether the factor has an interaction with other factors or not depends on the environment of corresponding island constructions. These dual facets of island properties of Korean have made so many controversies on the existence of island constraints in Korean.

6 Conclusion

In this paper, the Complex NP island constraint was closely examined in Korean. Three elements (Island, Clause Type, and Scrambling) were taken as factors which may influence the acceptability of sentences in Korean, and the experiment had a 2×2×2 design.

Based on this design, an experiment (an acceptability judgment task) was performed, where the data for 50 Korean native participants were collected. In the experiment, ME was adopted to measure the acceptability of the native speakers. After the experiments, all the values were extracted for target sentences and they were analyzed with R.

Through the experiments, the following facts were found. First, the factor Island (the absence vs. presence of Complex NP island constraint in Korean) did not play a role by itself, but played a marginal role through the interaction with the factor Clause Type (Matrix vs. Embedded). Second, the factors Clause Type and Scrambling played statistically significant roles in Korean and that there is a strong interaction between two factors.

References

Alan Agresti. 2007. An Introduction to Categorical Data Analysis. 2nd edition. Hoboken, NJ: John Wiley & Sons.

Harald Baayen. 2008. Analyzing Linguistic Data: A Practical Introduction to Statistics Using R. Cambridge: Cambridge University Press.

Ellen Bard, Dan Robertson, and Antonella Sorace, 1996. Magnitude Estimation of Linguistic Acceptability. Language, 72:32-68.

Andrew Carnie. 2012. Syntax: A Generative Introduction. 3rd Edition. Oxford: Blackwell.

Kiyong Choi. 1989. LF Movement: the Wh-island Constraint. Harvard Studies in Korean Linguistics, 3:213-234.

Daeho Chung. 2005. Why is HOW in Korean Insensitive to Islands?: A Revised Nominal Analysis. Studies in Modern Grammar, 39:115-131.

Wayne Cowart. 1997. Experimental Syntax: Applying Objective Methods to Sentence Judgments. Thousands Oaks, CA: Sage Publications.

Stephan Th. Gries. 2013. Statistics for Linguistics with R: A Practical Introduction. Berlin: Guyter.

Jong-Im Han. 1992. Syntactic Movement Analysis of Korean Relativization. Language Research, 28:335–357.

Sun-Ho Hong. 2004. On the Lack of Syntactic Effects in Korean WH-Questions. The Linguistic Association of Korea Journal, 12(3):43-57.

Heeju Hwang. 2007. Wh-Phrase Questions and Prosody in Korean. Proceedings of 17th Japanese/Korean Linguistics. Stanford, CA: CSLI.

Shinichiro Ishihara. 2002. Invisible but Audible Wh-scope Marking: Wh-constructions and Deaccenting in Japanese. Proceedings of the Twenty-first West Coast Conference on Formal Linguistics, 180-193

Keith Johnson. 2008. Quantitative Methods in Linguistics. Oxford: Blackwell.

Young-Se Kang. 1986. Korean Syntax and Universal Grammar. Doctoral dissertation, Harvard University.

Frank Keller. 2000. Gradient in Grammar: Experimental and Computational Aspects of Degrees of Grammaticality. Doctoral dissertation. University of Edinburgh.

Boyoung Kim and Grant Goodall. 2014. An Experimental Investigation of Island Effects in Korean. To appear in Japanese/Korean Linguistics.

Ilkyu Kim. 2013. Rethinking 'Island Effects' in Korean Relativization. Language Sciences, 38:59–82

Doo-Won Lee. 1999. Remarks on Negative Islands in Korean. Harvard Studies in Korean Linguistics, 8: 457-471.

Hyo-Sang Lee. 1982. Asymmetry in Island Constrains in Korean, ms., University of California at Los Angeles

Yong-hun Lee. 2013. Experimental Approach to Multiple Case Constructions in Korean. Language and Information, 17(2): 29-50.

Milton Lodge. 1981. Magnitude Scaling: Quantitative Measurement of Opinions. Beverley Hills, CA: Sage Publications.

Taisuke Nishigauchi. 1990. Quantification in the Theory of Grammar. Dordrecht: Kluwer Academic Publishers.

Bum-Sik Park. 2001. Island-insensitive Sluicing. Harvard Studies in Korean Linguistics, 9: 669-682.

Bum-Sik Park. 2009. Island Sensitivity in Ellipsis and Its Implications for Movement. Studies in Generative Grammar, 19(4):599- 620 .

Lisa Pearl and Jon Sprouse. 2014. Computational Models of Acquisition for Island. In Sprouse, Jon and Norbert Hornstein (eds.), Experimental Syntax and Island Effects, 109-131. Cambridge: Cambridge University Press.

John Ross. 1967. Constraints on Variables in Syntax. Doctoral dissertation, Massachusetts Institute of Technology.

Carson Schütze. 1996. The Empirical Base of Linguistics: Grammaticality Judgments and Linguistic Methodology. Chicago, IL: University of Chicago Press.

Ho-Min Sohn. 1980. Theme-prominence in Korean. Korean Linguistics, 2:2-19.

Jae-Gyun Song. 1995. Wh-in-situ and Island Phenomena in Korean. Harvard Studies in Korean Linguistics, 6: 402-412.

Sanghoun Song, Jae-Woong Choe, and Eunjeong Oh. FAQ: Do Non-linguists Share the Same Intuition as Linguists?. Language Research. 50(2):357-386.

Jon Sprouse, Mathews Wagers, and Colin Phillips. 2012. A Test of the Relation between Working Memory Capacity and Syntactic Island Effects. Language, 88:82–123

Jon Sprouse, Matthew Wagers, and Colin Phillips. 2014. Deriving Competing Predictions from Grammatical Approaches and Reductionist Approaches to Island Effects. In Sprouse, Jon and Norbert Hornstein (eds.), Experimental Syntax and Island Effects, 21-41. Cambridge: Cambridge University Press.

Jon Sprouse, Shin Fukuda, Hajime Ono, and Robert Kluender. 2011. Reverse Island Effects and the Backward Search for a Licensor in Multiple Wh-questions. Syntax 14:179–203.

Chungmok Suh. 1987. WH-constructions in Korean. Seoul: Top Press.

Akira Watanabe. 1992. Wh-in-situ, Subjacency, and Chain Formation, MIT Occasional Papers in Linguistics 2. Cambridge, MA: MIT Press.

Jeong-Me Yoon. 2011. Wh-island Effects of Wh-in-situ Questions in Korean. Studies in Generative Grammar, 21(4): 763-778.

Jeong-Me Yoon. 2012. Wh-island Effects in Korean Wh-in-Situ Questions. Korean Journal of Linguistics, 37(2):357-382.

Two Types of Multiple Subject Constructions (MSCs) in Korean

Ji-Hye Kim
Baird University College
Soongsil University
Seoul, Korea
psychlg@gmail.com

Eunah Kim
College English Program
Seoul National University
Seoul, Korea
eakim2@gmail.com

James Hye-Suk Yoon
Department of Linguistics
University of Illinois,
Urbana-Champaign
U.S.A.

Abstract

Although Multiple Subject Constructions in Korean have received significant attention in theoretical literature, few experimental investigations of various syntactic and semantic properties of these constructions have been conducted. In this study, we administered a Magnitude Estimation (ME) experiment in order to compare the acceptability of Multiple Subject and related Single Subject Constructions (MSCs vs. SSCs) and that of two types of MSCs (Possessor-type vs. Adjunct-type MSCs). The results showed that MSCs received lower acceptability than SSCs. In addition, the Adjunct-type MSCs received higher acceptability scores than the Possessor-type MSCs. Possible reasons for these results are discussed.

1 Introduction

Korean has a type of sentence where more than one nominative-marked NP occurs in a single clause, as shown in (1). These sentences are called Multiple Nominative Constructions (MNCs) or Multiple Subject Constructions (MSCs): (1a) and (1c) show a sentence with two nom-marked NPs, and (1b) and (1d) show a sentence with more than two nom-marked NPs.

(1) a. Cheli-**ka** kho-**ka** khu-ta
Cheli-nom nose-nom is-big-decl
'It is Cheli whose nose is big.'

b. Cheli-**ka** apeci-**ka** kho-**ka** khu-ta
Cheli-nom father-nom nose-nom is-big-decl
'It is Cheli whose father's nose is big.'

c. Yelum-**i** maykcwu-**ka** coh-ta
summer-nom beer-nom good-decl
'In summer, beer is good.'

d. I cip-**i** kyewul-**i** ohwu-**ka** ttattusha-ta
this house-nom winter-nom afternoon-nom is-warm- decl
'This house is warm in winter afternoon.'

In the literature, MSCs have been classified according to certain interpretive relationships between the multiple nom-marked NPs. For example, the two NPs in (1a, b) stand in a Possessor-Possessee (Part-Whole relation) as indicated by the paraphrases (2a, b), whereas the first NP in (1c, d) functions as a scene-setting or temporal Adjunct with respect to which the event denoted by the second NP and its predicate is interpreted.

(2) a. Cheli-**ka/uy** kho-**ka** khu-ta
Cheli-nom/gen nose-nom is-big-decl
'It is Cheli whose nose is big.'

b. Cheli-**ka/uy** apeci-**ka/uy** kho-**ka** khu-ta
Cheli-nom/gen father-nom/gen nose-nom is-big-decl
'It is Cheli whose father's nose is big.'

c. Yelum-**i/ey** maykcwu-**ka** coh-ta
summer-nom/gen beer-nom good-decl
'In summer, beer is good.'

29th Pacific Asia Conference on Language, Information and Computation pages 250 - 258
Shanghai, China, October 30 - November 1, 2015

d. I cip-**i/eyse(-nun)** kyewul-**i/ey**
this house-nom/loc(-top) winter-nom/loc
ohwu.sikan-**i** ttattusha-ta
afternoon-nom is-warm- decl
'This house is warm in winter afternoon.'

Based on the possible paraphrases, the first type of MSCs (cf. 1a, b) is called 'Possessor-type MSCs', while the second (cf. 1c, d) is dubbed 'Adjunct-type MSCs'. Whether or not this classification is theoretically significant depends on a host of interrelated questions.[1]

In this paper, we follow the view on MSCs that Yoon (2004, 2007, 2009, 2015) endorsed, where MSCs are viewed as containing multiple Subjects, with the rightmost NP functioning as the Grammatical Subject that takes the VP as predicate, and the outer NPs functioning as Major Subjects that take a Sentential Predicate (SP) constituted of the Grammatical Subject and its predicate (Teng, 1974; B-S Park, 1973, 2001; I-H Lee, 1987; Heycock and Lee, 1989; Chae and Kim, 2008[2]; Yoon, 2004, 2007, 2009, 2015).

According to Yoon (2004, 2007, 2009, 2015), the licensing conditions on MSCs are as follows:

(3) Properties of MSCs
a. Outer nom-marked NPs in MSCs are licensed syntactically by being assigned nominative case, as multiple Case assignment is possible in Korean.
b. Outer nom-marked NPs in MSCs are licensed semantically through predication from the Sentential Predicate (SP) as Major Subject (MS), by binding a predicate variable within the SP.
c. MS and SP in MSCs have restricted interpretive properties compared to Grammatical Subjects (GS) and VP.
d. Sentential Predicates (SPs) are felicitous if they can be construed as denoting a salient characteristic property of the referent of the MS.
e. MSs are felicitous if they can be construed denoting a newsworthy entity.

In particular, the properties (3c-e) distinguish MSCs from single subject constructions (SSCs).[3] In this approach to MSCs, all MSCs are licensed in the same way. Thus, classificatory distinctions such as P-type vs. A-type do not carry theoretical significance. This is an important point that we return to in the discussion.

Though there is a great deal of previous research on MSCs in Korean and other languages (Teng, 1974; B-S Park, 1973, 2001; I-H Lee, 1987; Heycock and Lee, 1989; Heycock, 1993; Chae and Kim, 2008; Yoon, 2004, 2007, 2009, 2015; Ryu, 2010, 2013, 2014, etc.), they were based on the intuition of researchers, and not validated through experimental investigation. The current study is one of the few studies that adopt experimental methods to investigate the properties of MSCs. In particular, this study focuses on two different types of MSCs mentioned in the literature – Possessor-type and Adjunct-type MSCs. Using Magnitude Estimation (ME), we examined native Korean speakers' knowledge of these two types of constructions.

The organization of the paper is as follows. The next section will introduce some relevant previous studies done on the matter. The following section will explain the methodology of our experiment and present the results. Finally, we will discuss the results and conclude with the future direction of the study.

2 Previous Studies

One reason we decided to distinguish P-type vs. A-type MSCs is because many previous studies have posited different analyses for the two. As mentioned in footnote 1, many researchers assume that P-type MSCs can be explained through the Possessor Raising (PR) (Chun, 1985; Youn, 1990). The idea is that the P-type MSC in (4b) is derived

[1] Possessor vs. adjunct classification is theoretically meaningful if one derives the first NP in a P-type MSC through Possessor Raising (Chun, 1985; Youn, 1990). Under this analysis, P-type MSCs have a unique subject (1st) NP, while in A-type MSCs, the unique subject is the 2nd NP, with the 1st NP functioning as topic/focus (Chun, 1985; Youn, 1990). The distinction is without significance if the two types are licensed in the same way.

[2] Chae & Kim (2008) admitted the clausal analysis of MSCs, but did not agree on the distinct functions of MS and GS in MSCs.

[3] Most subjects in SSCs are nom-marked, so nom-marking of subjects does not differentiate MSCs from SSCs. The external argument of V in VP is the predicate variable in SSCs, so that the requirement of a predicate variable does not distinguish the two either, though the MSCs the predicate variable is not the external argument.

by PR from a single subject construction (SSC) where the first NP is licensed as a Possessor (cf. 4a).

(4) a. [Cheli-**uy** khi-**ka**] khu-ta
Cheli-gen height-nom is-tall-decl
'Cheli is tall.'
b. Cheli-**ka** khi-**ka** khu-ta
Cheli-nom height-nom is-tall-decl
'(It is) Cheli (who) is tall.'

The effect of PR is to demote the NP *Cheli-uy khi-ka* from subject status and create a new subject *Cheli-ka*.

PR cannot extend to A-type MSC in (5a, c), in which the first NP cannot be expressed as a Possessor of the second. Therefore, these MSCs must be licensed differently. Youn (1990) proposes that in A-type MSCs, the second NP is the subject, while the 1st NP is topic/focus, under the additional assumption that the nominative particle doubles as topic/focus particles (see also Yoon 1989; Schutze 2001).

(5) a. ?*Yelum-**uy** maykcwu-ka coh-ta
summer-gen beer-nom good-decl
?'It is during the summer that beer is good.'
b. Yelum-**i** maykcwu-**ka** coh-ta
summer-nom beer-nom good-decl
'In summer, beer is good. (=It is during the summer that beer is good.)'
c. ?*Pihayngki-**uy** 747-**i** khu-ta
airplane-gen 747-nom big-decl
?'It is747 that airplane is big.'
d. Pihayngki-**ka** 747-**i** khu-ta
airplane-nom 747-nom big-decl
'As for airplanes, 747 is big.
(=/=?It is airplane that 747 is big)'

Since the analyses of the two types of MSCs are quite different, we examined whether native speakers distinguish between the two types in their acceptability judgments.

There have been only a few experimental studies conducted on various syntactic and semantic properties of MSCs. Kim (2015) conducted an acceptability judgment of MSC sentences, testing whether the two interpretive conditions[4] mentioned above – characteristic property predication by SPs (cf. 3d) and the newsworthiness requirement on MSs (cf. 3e) – play a role in native speakers' judgments. The results demonstrated that the native speakers of Korean are sensitive to the two interpretive conditions. However, Kim (2015) focused on the Possessor-type MSCs only and did not examine the Adjunct-type MSCs in her study.

Lee (2014) tested the acceptability of different types of MSCs, adopting Ryu (2013)'s classifications of semantic relations which hold between the two nominative NPs in MSCs.[5] Although the focus of Lee (2014) was not the distinction between P-type vs. A-type MSCs, either, the materials of his study included both types of MSCs. Among his data sets, sentences such as (6b) are P-type MSCs, since (6b) can be paraphrased as (6a).

(6) a. Thokki-**uy** kwi-**ka** kil-ta.
Rabbit-gen ear-nom long-decl
'The ears of rabbits are long.'
b. Thokki-**ka** kwi-**ka** kil-ta.
Rabbit-nom ear-nom long-decl
'The ears of rabbits are long.'

On the other hand, (7b) are A-type MSCs. Unlike (6b), (7b) cannot be analyzed as derived from a sentence with possessed-NP subject.

(7) a. ?Yelum-**ey** maykcwu-ka
summer-loc beer-nom
masiss-ta
tasty-decl
'In summer, beer is tasty.'
b. Yelum-**i** maykcwu-**ka** masiss-ta
summer-nom beer-nom tasty-decl
'It is during the summer that beer is tasty.'

Lee's (2014) results for P-type and A-type MSCs are as follows. He used line-drawing Magnitude Estimation in his experiment, and the range of score was 0mm-170mm.

[4] See Yoon (2004, 2007, 2009, 2015) and Kim (2015) for more detailed discussions of characteristic/characterizing properties of SP and newsworthiness of MS.
[5] Ryu (2013) proposed a unified analysis of Multiple Subject Constructions (MSCs) and Multiple Accusative Constructions (MACs) into Multiple Case Constructions (MCCs).

P-type MSCs	A-type MSCs
(6b), *m*=128.20	(7b), *m*=101.50
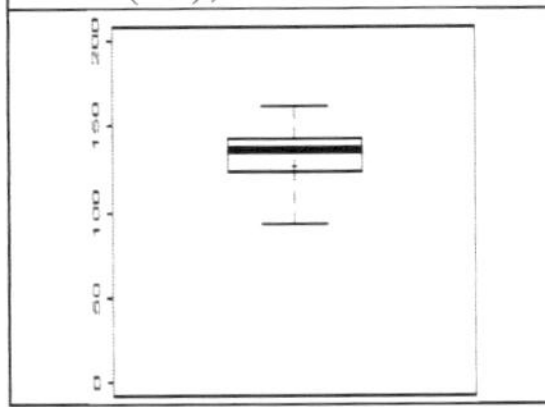	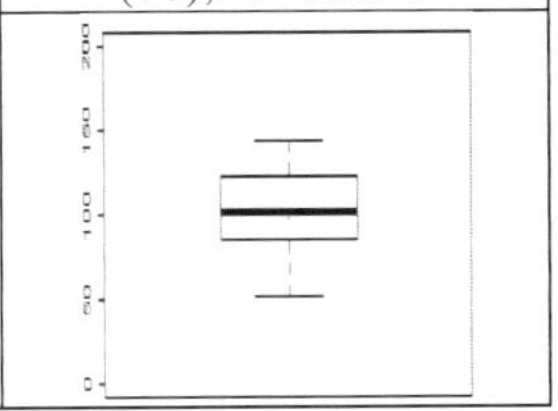

Table 1. P-type vs. A-type in Lee (2014)

As shown in this table, the acceptability of P-type MSCs was higher than that of A-type MSCs. Lee's (2014) results suggest that P-type MSCs and A-type MSCs are judged differently by native speakers, perhaps because they are licensed in different ways, as posited under the theoretical analyses sketched in the previous section. It also seems that P-type MSCs are judged better than A-type MSCs. However, Lee's (2014) study had different classification in the type of MSCs and there were not enough tokens for the clear division of the two types of MSCs. We therefore investigated whether the two types of MSCs are accepted differently by native speakers based on a larger data set.

3 Research Method

3.1 Research Questions and Hypothesis

We conducted an experimental study investigating Korean native speakers' acceptability of P-type and A-type MSCs, as well as the differences in acceptability between MSCs and closely related SSCs. The research question and hypothesis of this study are as follows:

Research Question: Between the Possessor-type (P-type) and the Adjunct-type (A-type) MSCs, which type is more acceptable?

Hypothesis: Korean speakers will regard P-type MSCs as more acceptable than A-type MSCs.

Our hypothesis was based on Lee's (2014) results. This hypothesis is also not improbable given the theoretical analyses reviewed earlier: While P-type MSCs have been treated in terms of PR, A-type MSCs have been treated mostly as having a focused (or topic-like) initial NP. Since interpreting focused/topical NPs in a sentence presented without a context is not easy, it is plausible that A-type MSCs would be considered as less acceptable than P-type MSCs.

The following sections will be dedicated to explanation of the methodology of our experiment. Presentation of the results and discussion will then follow.

3.2 Participants

Seventy Korean native speakers (age range=21~45) residing in and near Seoul, who were either current university students or graduates of universities in Korea, participated in the experiment.

3.3 Task, Materials & Procedures

The main task used in the experiment was an acceptability judgment task using Magnitude Estimation (ME) in which the participants were asked to draw different lengths of lines to indicate the naturalness (acceptability) of a given sentence (after reading the sentence).[6]

Test materials were composed of 80 Korean sentences: There were 40 target MSC sentences divided into 20 P-type MSCs and 20 A-type MSCs. The other 40 sentences were SSCs (single subject constructions), which were identical to the 40 target MSCs except for having a single subject. This was done to compare the acceptability ratings of SSC sentences and related MSC sentences. Examples of the experimental sentences are shown in (8). (8a) shows an example of P-type MSC, whereas (8b) shows an example of A-type MSC. (8c, d) are the examples of SSC sentences that are the counterparts of (8a, b).

(8) a. Cheli-**ka** apeci-**ka** pwuca-ita.
Cheli-nom father-nom rich-decl
'It is Cheli whose father is rich.'
b. Chicago-**ka** kenmwultul-**i** nop-ta
Chicago-nom buildings-nom high-decl
'In Chicago, buildings are tall. '
c. Cheli-**uy** apeci-**ka** pwuca-ita.
Cheli-gen father-nom rich-decl
'Cheli's father is rich.'
d. Chicago-**uy** kenmwultul-**i** nop-ta
Chicago-gen/loc buildings-nom high-decl
'Chicago's buildings are tall. '

[6] For more information about the Magnitude Estimation task used in this experiment and its rationale, see Kim, Lee and Kim (2015).

Participants were first given a brief questionnaire about biographical information such as age, gender and dialect(s) together with a consent form. They were then asked to take the main task. In the main task, participants were required to draw a line for each sentence, according to the degree of acceptability/naturalness of the given sentence.

3.4 Statistical Analysis

After the data collection, normality tests were first performed in order to check if the values followed normal distribution, so as to determine the applicability of parametric tests. If the distributions of the data follow normal distribution, parametric tests are applicable, such as a *t*-test, an ANOVA, or (ordinary) linear regression tests. However, if the distributions do not follow normal distribution, non-parametric tests must be applied such as a Wilcoxon test, a Friedman test, or generalized linear regression tests.

When normality tests were performed, it was found that most of the data sets did not follow normal distribution. Some were positively skewed, and others had a slightly bimodal distribution. Thus, a non-parametric test – a generalized linear regression test – was performed with a Gaussian distribution, in order to examine how the Possessor/Adjunct distinctions affected the acceptability of sentences.

4 Results

4.1 Descriptive Analysis

In our data set, two factors tested (SSC/MSC and Possessor/Adjunct). SentenceType is the variable which indicates whether the sentence is a Single Subject Construction (SSC) or a Multiple Subject Construction (MSC), and ConstType is the variable which indicates whether the sentence corresponds to a Possessor type (P-type) or an Adjunct type (A-type).

We first compared the acceptability of SSC with that of MSC. Figure 1 below illustrates the degree of acceptability of SSCs and MSCs.

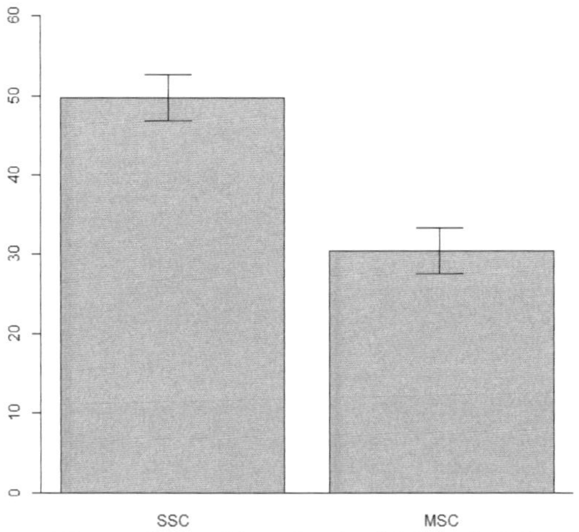

Figure 1. Bar Plots for the SSC vs. MSC

Figure 1 demonstrates that the mean values for SSCs are much higher than those of MSCs. That is, the participants considered MSCs less acceptable than SSCs.

Secondly, we compared the acceptability of P-type MSCs with that of A-type MSCs. The pattern of results is shown in Figure 2.

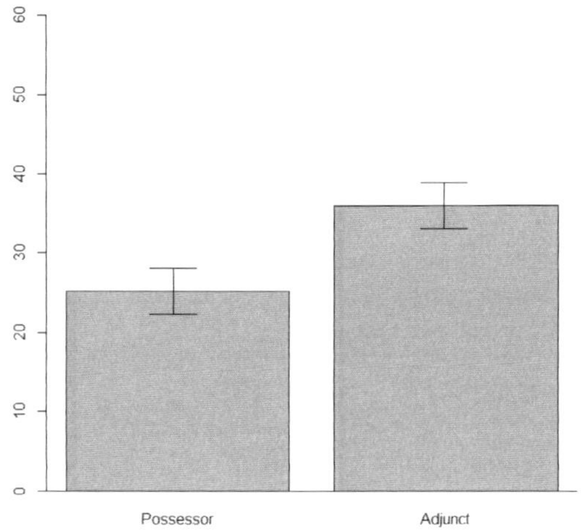

Figure 2. Bar Plots for the P-type vs. A-type MSC

As shown in this figure, among the MSC sentences, A-type MSCs received higher acceptability than P-type MSCs. This pattern of results is different from Lee (2014).

4.2 Inferential Analysis

In order to examine how two factors (SentenceType and ConstType) affected the acceptability of sentences, a generalized regression test was performed. The following table illustrates the results.

	Estimate	*sd*	*t*	*p*
(Intercept)	40.058	0.3073	130.364	<<<.001
SentenceType	-9.634	0.3073	-31.353	<<<.001
ConstType	3.988	0.3073	12.977	<<<.001
SentenceType: ConstType	2.243	0.3073	7.298	<<<.001

Table 2. Results of Regression Tests

As this table shows, both factors (SentenceType and ConstType) significantly influenced the acceptability of the sentences ($p<.001$, *highly* significant). There is also an interaction between two factors, as the *p*-value of SentenceType:ConstType indicates ($p<.001$).

To graphically examine the effects of the factors and their interactions, the effect plots were drawn for the data set. Figure 3 has the effect plot for the factor SentenceType.

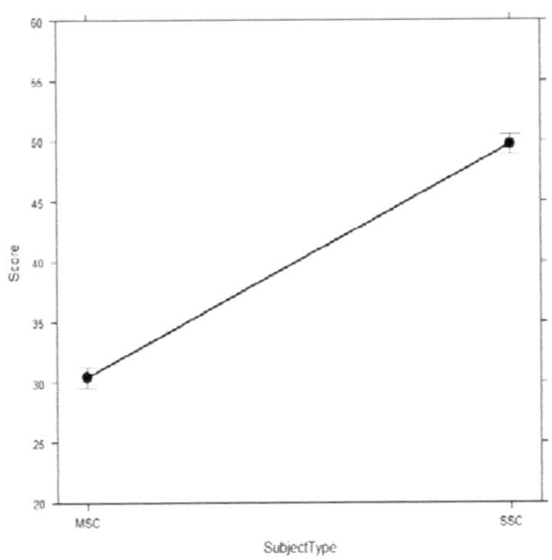

Figure 3. Effect Plot for SentenceType

In this figure, the mean score of SSCs is much higher than that of MSCs. Furthermore, 95% CIs (Confidence Interval) are clearly distinguished. This implies that native speakers clearly prefer SSC to MSC.

Figure 4 has the effect plot for the factor ConstType.

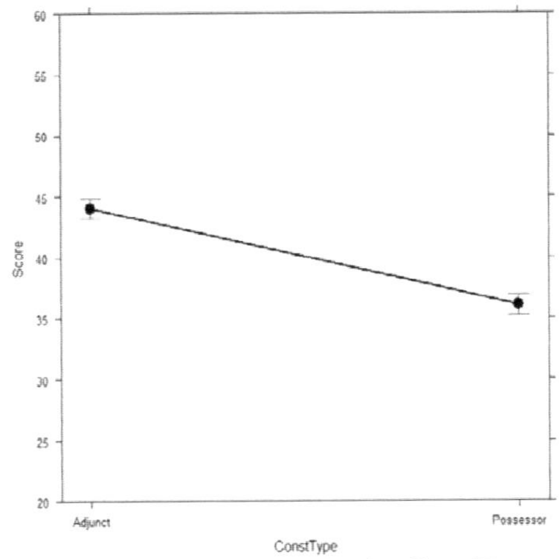

Figure 4. Effect Plot for ConstType

As shown earlier in Figure 2, the average score of Adjunct is much higher than that of Possessor, and the 95% CIs do not overlap, suggesting that native speakers prefer the A-type MSCs to P-type MSCs.

Figure 5 has the effect plot for the interactions between two factors SentenceType and ConstType.[7]

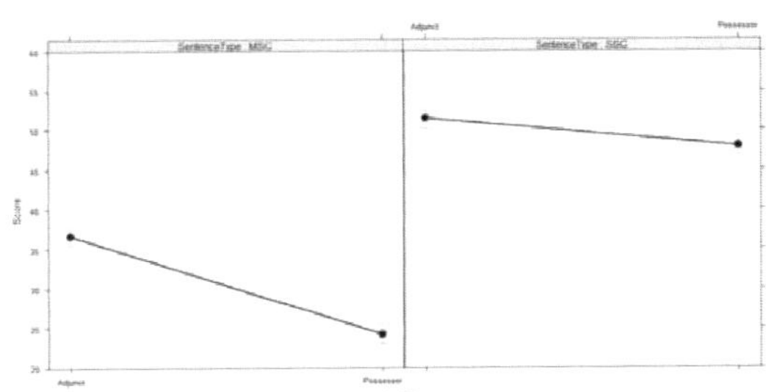

Figure 5. Effect Plot for SentenceType:ConstType

The effect plot in this figure demonstrates that there is an interaction between the two factors SentenceType and ConstType. If there is no interaction between two factors, the two lines in MSC and SSC have to be parallel. If there is an interaction, however, the two lines will not be parallel. Note that the two lines in Figure 5 are not parallel. This means that there is an interaction between two factors SentenceType and ConstType.

In this figure, note that the differences in MSCs are much bigger than those in SSCs. This suggests

[7]Since the comparison of the two types of MSCs is meaningful in MSC sentences rather than SSC sentences, we can focus on the pattern of the results represented on the left side.

that the Possessor vs. Adjunct distinction plays a more important role in determination of the acceptability of MSCs than SSCs.

5 Discussion

While we hypothesized that Korean native speakers would give higher acceptability scores for P-type MSCs than A-type MSCs, based on Lee (2014), the results did not support the hypothesis. Since both Lee (2014) and the current study used line-drawing Magnitude Estimation and were administered to similar groups of native speakers, we need to explain the inconsistency in the results. We speculate that the characteristics of the experimental sentences used in this study may explain the inconsistency. And this in turn casts doubt the theoretical utility of classifications such as P vs. A-type MSCs.

First, a close look at the test sentences suggests that many of the P-type sentences used as stimuli may not be fully optimal semantically and pragmatically as MSCs, whereas many of the A-type sentences satisfy such constraints. The contrast between (9a) a P-type MSC and (9c) an A-type MSC is illustrative.

(9) a. Cheli-**ka** emeni-**ka** mwusep-ta.
Cheli-nom mother-nom scary-decl
'Cheli's mother is scary.'
b. Cheli-**ka** khi-**ka** khu-ta
Cheli-nom height-nom tall-decl
'It is Cheli whose height is tall.'
c. Chicago-**ka** kenmwultul-**i** nop-ta
Chicago-nom buildings-nom high-decl
'In Chicago, buildings are high. '

Recall that an optimal MSC has a characteristic property-denoting SP and a newsworthy MS, as Kim (2015) demonstrated experimentally.

Let us look at (9a), which was used in the experiment as an example of MSC. In this MSC, the newsworthiness condition is met, since the MS is referentially more salient than GS (MS is a name and GS is a relational noun). However, the SP '(someone's) mother is scary' cannot be construed as expressing a characteristic property of MS *Cheli*, and hence, the SP in this MSC is not optimal.[8] This becomes clear when (9a) is compared to (9b), where the SP '(someone's) height is tall', can be understood easily as a characteristic property of an individual. Notice that the difference between (9a) and (9b), which are both P-type MSCs, is the nature of the possession relationship between the MS and GS. In (9b), it is inalienable possession, while in (9a) it is an alienable relation.

Because of the characteristic property condition on SPs, optimal P-type MSCs are those with an inalienable possession relation between the MS and the GS. However, most P-type MSCs used in the experiment had an alienable possessor relation, which possibly reduced the felicity of P-type MSCs. On the other hand, the P-type stimuli used in Lee (2014) contained mostly inalienable possession, which probably contributed to the increased felicity of the MSCs overall. We suspect this is the reason why our subjects gave lower ratings to P-type MSCs, compared to Lee's (2014) subjects.

By contrast, if we examine examples of A-type MSCs in (9c), both the MS and the SP satisfy the interpretive conditions easily. The MS *Chicago* is more referentially salient than the GS 'building'. The SP may be considered a characterizing property of MS: 'having lots of buildings (and hence, a large, metropolitan city)' could be construed as a characteristic property of cities. Many of our A-type sentences had a salient MSs and characterizing SPs as in (9c). Therefore, this could have contributed to participants' higher ratings of naturalness of the MSC sentences.

Also, we should note that in some cases the boundary between the P-type and A-type MSC seems not very clear, as shown in (10). Though the basic structure looks the same between (10a) and (10c), with the same MS and characteristic SPs, the relation between the two NPs – as shown in the contrast between (10a, b) and (10c, d) - can make different type of MSCs. While (10a) represents A-type MSC, (10c) stands for P-type MSC, respectively.

(10) a. Boston-**i** kwankwangkyayk-**i**
Boston-nom tourists-nom

[8] If given a specific context, this property can characterize an individual, becoming what Yoon (2007, 2009, etc.) dub a characterizing (contextually characteristic) property. However, the sentences were not given with an appropriate context, so speakers gave a rating assuming a null context, where only SPs denoting properly characteristic properties are judged optimal.

nul pwumpin-ta.
always bustle-decl
'As for Boston, tourists bustle all the time.'

b. Boston-**ey(-nun)** kwankwangkyayk-**i**
Boston-loc(-top) tourists-nom
nul pwumpin-ta.
always bustle-decl
'As for Boston, tourists bustle all the time.'

c. Boston-**i** wichi-**ka** acwu
B-nom location-nom very
coh-ta.
good-decl
'Boston has a very good location.'

d. Boston-**uy** wichi-**ka** acwu
Boston-gen location-nom very
coh-ta.
good-decl
'Boston has a very good location.'

These sentences show that the boundary between P-type and A-type is not clear and that there are some sentences which can be either P-type MSCs or A-type MSCs. Likewise, the A-type MSC we used in the experiment (cf. 9c) could be interpreted as both A-type MSC ('In Chicago, buildings are tall') and P-type MSC ('The buildings of Chicago are tall') to some individuals.

In a way, though, the contradictory results of this study and Lee (2014) or the difficulty of classifying an MSC as P or A-type is not important, if we adopt the analysis proposed by Yoon (2004, 2007, 2009, 2015) and others (Chae & Kim, 2008; Park, 2010; Kim, 2015, etc.). This is because in this analysis, all MSCs are licensed the same way. Classificatory labels such as P-type, A-type, or for that matter, sub-types within a type (inalienable vs. alienable P-type) are mere descriptive labels and carry little theoretical weight, unlike analyses that view different MSCs to be licensed in different ways. What matters is whether and how the MSCs come to satisfy the licensing conditions—in particular, the interpretive conditions. What we have seen is that even within the same type (P-type), different MSCs may satisfy the licensing conditions in different ways, and this is what explains native speakers' judgments of acceptability of MSCs.

6 Conclusion

The current experimental study investigated how Korean native speakers rate the acceptability of MSCs and related SSCs, and of two different types of MSCs: P-type MSCs vs. A-type MSCs. The overall results showed that Korean native speakers regarded MSCs less acceptable than SSCs, but clearly better than ungrammatical sentences.

As for the two types of MSCs, A-type MSCs received higher acceptability scores than P-type MSCs, contrary to our expectations and the results of previous studies. We speculated that the reason may stem from the fact that many experimental P-type MSCs used in the current study did not satisfy the interpretive properties of MSCs in an optimal way, which also allows us to make sense of the differences between our results and Lee (2014).

Spectrum of appropriateness as MSCs may not be narrow within each type of MSC, and this warns of possible danger of making a categorical statement about P-type vs. A-type MSCs, or taking this distinction seriously in one's theoretical analysis of MSCs. A follow-up study with more strictly controlled experimental sentences with various divisions of properties that contribute to the overall felicity of MSCs is necessary.

Acknowledgments

References

Hee-Rahk Chae and Ilkyu Kim. 2008. A Clausal Predicate Analysis of Korean Multiple Nominative Constructions. Korean Journal of Linguistics, 33(4):869-900.

Sun-Ae Chun. 1985. Possessor Ascension for Multiple Case Sentences. Harvard Studies in Korean Linguistics I:30-39. Hanshin Publishing, Seoul.

Caroline Heycock and Young-suk Lee. 1989. Subjects and Predication in Korean and Japanese. Language Research, 25(4): 755-792.

Ji-Hye Kim. 2015. An Experimental Study on Interpretive Properties of Multiple Nominative/Subject Constructions (MNCs/MSCs) in Korean. Linguistic Research,32(2).(To appear on August 30, 2015)

Ji-Hye Kim, Yong-hun Lee and Eunah Kim. 2015. Obligatory Control and Coordinated Deletion as Korean Subject Diagnostics: An Experimental Approach. Language and Information, 19(1):75-101.

Ik-Hwan Lee. 1987. Double Subject Constructions in GPSG. Harvard Studies in Korean Linguistics II:287-296.

Yong-hun Lee. 2014. Semantic Relations and Multiple Case Constructions: An Experimental Approach. Linguistic Research 31(2): 213-247.

Byung-Soo Park. 1973. On the Multiple Subject Constructions in Korean. Linguistics, 100: 63-76.

Byung-Soo Park. 2001. Constraints in Multiple Nominative Constructions in Korean: A Constraint-based Lexicalist Approach. The Journal of Linguistic Science, 20:147-190.

Chongwon Park. 2010. The Role of Metonymy in the Interpretation of Korean Multiple Subject Constructions. Language Sciences, 33(1): 206-228.

Byong-Rae Ryu. 2010. Licensing Nominals in the Multiple Nominative Constructions in Korean: A Mereological Perspective. Proceedings of the 24th Pacific Asia Conference on Language, Information and Computation (PACLIC 24).Tohoku University, Sendai, Japan..

Byong-Rae Ryu. 2013.Multiple Case Marking Constructions in Korean Revisited. Language and Information, 17(2):1-27.

Byong-Rae Ryu. 2014. Semantic Constraints on Multiple Case Marking in Korean. In Doris Gerland, Christian Horn, Anja Latrouite and Albert Ortmann (eds.),Meaning and Grammar of Nouns and Verbs:77-112. dup, Düsseldorf.

Carson Schütze. 2001. On Korean 'Case Stacking': The Varied Functions of the Particles -ka and -lul. The Linguistic Review, 18:193-232.

Shou-Hsin Teng. 1974. Double Nominatives in Chinese. Language, 50: 455-473.

James Hye-Suk Yoon. 2004. Non-nominative (Major) Subjects and Case-stacking in Korean. In Peri Bhaskararao and Karumuri VenkataSubbarao (eds.), Non-nominative Subjects, volume 2:265-314.Mouton de Gruyter, Berlin.

James Hye-SukYoon. 2007. Raising of Major Arguments in Korean and Japanese. Natural Language and Linguistic Theory, 25:615-653.

James Hye-Suk Yoon. 2009. The Distribution of Subject Properties in Multiple Subject Constructions. Proceedings of Japanese/Korean Linguistics, 64-83. CSLI, Stanford, CA.

James Hye-Suk Yoon. 2015. Double Nominative and Double Accusative Constructions. In Lucien Brown and Jaehoon Yeon (eds.), The Handbook of Korean Linguistics, First Edition. 79-97. John Wiley & Sons, Inc.

Jong-Yurl Yoon. 1989. On the Multiple *-ka* and *-lul* Constructions in Korean. Harvard Studies in Korean Linguistics III:383-394. Hanshin Publishing Company, Seoul.

Cheong Youn. 1990. A Relational Analysis of Korean Multiple Nominative Constructions. Ph.D dissertation, State University of New York at Buffalo.

A Large-scale Study of Statistical Machine Translation Methods for Khmer Language

Ye Kyaw Thu†, Vichet Chea‡, Andrew Finch†, Masao Utiyama † and Eiichiro Sumita†

†Advanced Speech Translation Research and Development Promotion Center, NICT, Kyoto, Japan
‡Research and Development Center, NIPTICT, Cambodia
{yekyawthu, andrew.finch, multiyama, eiichiro.sumita}@nict.go.jp
vichet.chea@niptict.edu.kh

Abstract

This paper contributes the first published evaluation of the quality of automatic translation between Khmer (the official language of Cambodia) and twenty other languages, in both directions. The experiments were carried out using three different statistical machine translation approaches: phrase-based, hierarchical phrase-based, and the operation sequence model (OSM). In addition two different segmentation schemes for Khmer were studied, these were syllable segmentation and supervised word segmentation. The results show that the highest quality machine translation was attained with word segmentation in all of the experiments. Furthermore, with the exception of very distant language pairs the OSM approach gave the highest quality translations when measured in terms of both the BLEU and RIBES scores. For distant languages, our results showed a hierarchical phrase-based approach to be the most effective. An analysis of the experimental results indicated that Kendall's tau may be directly used as a means of selecting an appropriate machine translation approach for a given language pair.

1 Introduction

Natural language processing for the Khmer language is currently at an early stage and linguistic resources for the language are scarce. As far as the authors are aware there has been only one published work on Khmer statistical machine translation (Surabaya Jabin and Sokphyrum, 2013). In the paper a step-by-step procedure for implementing an English-to-Khmer machine translation system using the Do Moses Yourself (DoMY) Community Edition[1] was described. The system was developed using a small parallel corpus of 5,734 sentence pairs of English-Khmer. The paper mentions that the system obtained good performance compared with Google Translate for in-domain sentences, however, no numerical evaluation of the system was given.

The main contribution of this paper, is the first large-scale study of Khmer statistical machine translation. 40 language pairs was used in the experiments, and translation quality was evaluated using both the BLEU and RIBES evaluation metrics. We developed the SMT systems using a parallel corpus of 162,121 sentence pairs for each language pair and studied the machine translation performance using three different SMT techniques (phrase-based SMT, hierarchical phrase-based SMT, and the operation sequence model), using two different segmentation schemes for Khmer.

The structure of the paper is as follows. In the next section we briefly introduce the Khmer language, outline the approaches taken so far to Khmer word segmentation, and describe the two approaches we have chosen to examine in this study. These are a simple approach that divides Khmer into its component syllables, and a more sophisticated supervised word segmen-

[1] http://www.precisiontranslationtools.com/?option=com_content&view=article&id=1&Itemid=22

29th Pacific Asia Conference on Language, Information and Computation pages 259 - 269
Shanghai, China, October 30 - November 1, 2015

tation approach. Then we describe the methodology used in the machine translation experiments, present the results of these experiments, and finally conclude and offer possible avenues for future research.

2 Segmentation

2.1 Khmer Language

The official language of Cambodia is Khmer, also known as Cambodian. It is the native language of the approximately 16 million speakers. It is also spoken in the Mekong Delta area of South Vietnam and in northeastern Thailand (Ehrman, 1972). It is also the earliest recorded and earliest written language of the Mon–Khmer language family[2]. Khmer is primarily an analytic, isolating language, which means it makes most of its grammatical distinctions by means of word-order rather than by means of affixes and changes within words (Ehrman, 1972). General grammatical word order is Subject-Verb-Object (SVO). Khmer language differs from neighbouring languages Lao, Myanmar, Thai and Vietnamese in that it is non-tonal. In Khmer texts, words composed of single or multiple syllables are usually not separated by white space. Spaces are used for easier reading and generally put between phrases, but there are no clear rules for using spaces in Khmer language. Therefore, some form of segmentation is a necessary prerequisite for machine translation involving Khmer.

2.2 Prior Research

The first Khmer word segmentation scheme was proposed by a research group of Cambodia PAN Localisation (Huor et al., 2007). A word bigram model and an orthographic syllable bigram model approaches were investigated. Their results showed that the word bigram approach outperformed the orthographic syllable bigram approach and achieved 91.56 (Precision), 92.14 (Recall) and 91.85 (F-Score) on test data drawn from the news and novel domains.

(Van and Kameyama, 2013) proposed a rule-based Khmer word segmentation approach based on statistical analysis using in combination with specific linguistic rules of Khmer. The rule learning algorithm based on SEQUITUR (the Nevill-Manning algorithm (Nevill-Manning and Witten, 1997)) was applied to their 3 million word raw corpus in order to detect out-of-vocabulary words (OOV) words without using any predefined information such as the part-of-speech (POS) tags. Linguistic rules were also applied in the final word extraction step to improve the OOV detection performance. Their approach was shown to outperform that of (Huor et al., 2007) in terms of precision and f-score, but with lower recall.

(Bi and Taing, 2014) studied Bi-directional Maximal Matching (BiMM), Forward Maximum Matching (FMM) and Backward Maximum Matching (BMM) word segmentation methods for Khmer languages. Here, BiMM is the combination of FMM and BMM, using both forward and backward directions of scanning input text. The results showed that BiMM achieving the highest level of accuracy (98.13%). FMM and BMM results are almost same and outperformed Maximum Matching (Chanveasna, 2012).

2.3 Syllable Segmentation

As we mentioned in Section 2.1, there are no clear word boundaries between Khmer words. In SMT, word segmentation is a necessary step in order to yield a set of tokens upon which the alignment and indeed the whole machine learning process can operate. One simple method to get consistent units of Khmer text is break it into syllables. This section describes our method of syllable breaking based on the orthography of the Khmer language.

There are only 2 rules required to break Khmer syllables if the input text is encoded in Unicode where dependent vowels and other signs are encoded after the consonant to which they apply. Rule one is applied first, to the whole input sequence, followed by Rule 2. The rules are:

Rule 1: Put a break point after a consonant (but not between consonant and stacked consonant), vowels, independent vowels, numbers, divination numbers (astrology), upper signs and punctuation signs.

[2]https://en.wikipedia.org/wiki/Khmer_language

Consonant	⟨*break*⟩	◌័ (Samyok Sannya)	⟨*break*⟩	Consonant
Character	⟨*break*⟩	Consonant	⟨*break*⟩	◌៍ (Toandakhiat)
Consonant	⟨*break*⟩	◌៏ (Ashda)		
Character	⟨*break*⟩	Consonant	⟨*break*⟩	◌់ (Bantok)
Character	⟨*break*⟩	Consonant	⟨*break*⟩	◌៌ (Robat)
Consonant	⟨*break*⟩	◌៊ (Triisap)		
Consonant	⟨*break*⟩	◌៉ (Muusikatoan)		

Figure 1: Syllable breaking heuristics.

Rule 2: Remove one or two break points for some character combinations or patterns as in Figure 1. If any of the patterns in Figure 1 match, all of the ⟨*break*⟩'s in the patterns are removed.

Using these heuristics, the segmentation into syllables can be made perfectly accurate with full coverage of the language.

An example of the syllable segmentation of a Khmer sentence (meaning: A Japanese company has a very successful experience) is as follows:

Input:
ក្រុមហ៊ុនជប៉ុនមានពិសោធន៍ជោគជ័យណាស់

Output:
ក្រុ ម ហ៊ុ ន ជ ប៉ុ ន មា ន ពិ សោ ធ ន៍ ជោ គ ជ័ យ ណា ស់

2.4 Conditional Random Fields

This section describes a supervised approach to Khmer work segmentation based on conditional random fields.

To created the training corpus, manual word segmentation was performed on 5,000 randomly selected Khmer sentences from the general web domain. Manual word segmentation was based on four types of Khmer words, these are: single words, compound words, compound words with a prefix, and compound word with a suffix. We used the CRF++ toolkit [3] to build the CRF model. We used a bootstrapping approach to create a large manually segmented corpus.

[3]http://taku910.github.io/crfpp/

First, we trained a CRF model from 5,000 manually segmented Khmer sentences. Then we used the trained CRF model to segment new raw (unsegmented) and manually corrected the segmentation. This data was then used to train an improved CRF model. In this way iteratively increased the quantity of manually segmented training data. The process was terminated when the manually annotated data set size reached 103,694 sentences. This final training corpus was broad in scope and included 3,445 sentences from the agriculture domain, 791 sentences from biology domain, 71,296 sentences from BTEC corpus, 2,916 sentences from the Buddhism religious domain, 1,256 sentences from the economic domain, 99 sentences from history domain, 8,374 sentences from the Khmer story domain, 665 sentences from law, 747 sentences from the management domain, 9,817 sentences from the news domain, 3,286 sentences from the research and science domain and 1,002 sentences from other domains.

The feature set used in the CRF model (character uni-grams) was as follows (where t is the index of the character being labeled):

Character unigrams:
$\{w_{t-2}, w_{t-1}, w_t, w_{t+1}, w_{t+2}\}$

These features were combined with label unigrams to produce the feature set for the model. The word CRF segmentation was done from character segmented Khmer. The characters were annotated with tags indicting their character class, and also with the word boundary tags to be predicted. For example, CRF training format of a word segmented Khmer sentence តើ អ្នក ឈ្មោះ អ្វី ? is shown in Table 1.

ត	C	0
ើ	V	1
អ	C	0
្	SUB	0
ន	C	0
ក	C	1
ឈ	C	0
្	SUB	0
ម	C	0
ោ	V	0
ះ	V	1
អ	C	0
្	SUB	0
វ	C	0
ី	V	1
?	UNK	1

Table 1: The annotation of a Khmer sentence used for training the CRF segmenter.

We used 11 tags for tagging Khmer characters (also considering English within Khmer text) and these were C (Consonant), V (Vowel), IV (Independent Vowel), US (Upper Sign), AN (Atak Number), SUB (Subscript Sign), END (End of Sentence), ZS (Zero Space), NS (No Space), UNK (Unknown). Two simple segmentation tags (0 and 1, for non-boundary and boundary respectively) were used for word boundary information.

The final CRF model was evaluated with using unseen test data consisting of 12,462 sentences randomly selected from agriculture, BTEC, news, Khmer story, history and others domains. The CRF segmenter achieved 99.15 Precision, 95.72 Recall and 97.31 F-Score. This CRF word segmenter was used to segment the Khmer BTEC data for the experiments in the next section.

3 Experimental Methodology

3.1 Corpus Statistics

We used twenty one languages from the multilingual Basic Travel Expressions Corpus (BTEC), which is a collection of travel-related expressions (Kikui et al., 2003). The languages were Arabic (ar), Chinese (zh), Danish (da), Dutch (nl), English (en), French (fr), German (de), Hindi (hi), Indonesian (id), Italian (it), Japanese (ja), Khmer (km), Korean (ko), Malaysian (ms), Myanmar (my), Portuguese (pt), Russian (ru), Spanish (es), Tagalog (tl), Thai (th) and Vietnamese (vi). 155,121 sentences were used for training, 5,000 sentences for development and 2,000 sentences for evaluation.

In all experiments, the Khmer language was segmented using syllable and word segmentation methods described in Sections 2.3 and 2.4.

3.2 Phrase-based Statistical Machine Translation (PBSMT)

We used the phrase based SMT system provided by the Moses toolkit (Koehn and Haddow, 2009) for training the phrase-based machine statistical translation system. The Khmer was aligned with the word segmented target languages (except for the Myanmar language that was syllable segmented) using GIZA++ (Och and Ney, 2000). The alignment was symmetrized by grow-diag-final-and heuristic (Koehn et al., 2003). The lexicalized reordering model was trained with the msd-bidirectional-fe option (Tillmann, 2004). We use SRILM for training the 5-gram language model with interpolated modified Kneser-Ney discounting (Stolcke, 2002; Chen and Goodman, 1996). Minimum error rate training (MERT) (Och, 2003) was used to tune the decoder parameters and the decoding was done using the Moses decoder (version 2.1) (Koehn and Haddow, 2009).

3.3 Hierarchical Phrase-based Machine Translation (HPBSMT)

The hierarchical phrase-based SMT approach (Chiang, 2007) is a model based on synchronous context-free grammar. The models are able to be learned from a corpus of unannotated parallel text. The advantage this technique offers over the phrase-based approach is that the hierarchical structure is able to represent the word re-ordering process. The re-ordering is represented explicitly rather than encoded into a lexicalized re-ordering model (commonly used in purely phrase-based approaches). This makes the approach particularly applicable to languages pairs that require long-distance re-ordering during the translation process (Braune et al., 2012). For

Source-Target	Syllable			Word		
	PBSMT	HPBSMT	OSM	PBSMT	HPBSMT	OSM
km-ar	29.87	23.33	30.08	**42.74**	42.46	42.60
km-da	41.53	23.68	40.88	52.22	52.05	**52.66**
km-de	35.03	19.44	35.03	48.79	47.58	**48.99**
km-en	49.07	36.79	49.20	59.51	57.83	**60.02**
km-es	42.17	30.82	41.14	52.97	52.45	**53.53**
km-fr	40.85	34.00	40.96	50.79	49.76	**51.63**
km-hi	26.30	8.82	26.22	40.53	**42.05**	40.87
km-id	43.26	32.18	43.78	53.26	52.14	**53.65**
km-it	37.60	29.15	37.03	47.27	46.87	**47.79**
km-ja	23.46	16.06	23.43	34.27	**36.42**	33.78
km-ko	21.37	22.57	21.53	32.21	**33.61**	32.13
km-ms	42.90	33.55	43.03	**53.85**	52.52	53.56
km-my	27.43	24.40	28.24	38.08	35.47	**38.87**
km-nl	38.84	32.60	39.03	**51.13**	50.07	51.07
km-pt	40.02	28.34	39.48	50.16	**50.54**	50.51
km-ru	30.52	19.76	30.82	**44.17**	42.49	43.38
km-th	45.60	33.08	45.56	50.27	47.83	**51.46**
km-tl	33.21	18.52	32.80	46.95	**46.97**	46.95
km-vi	45.67	27.20	46.91	53.39	52.57	**53.86**
km-zh	23.72	8.14	23.87	32.09	**32.99**	32.22

Table 2: BLEU scores for translating from Khmer.

the experiments in this paper we used the implementation of hierarchical model provided by the Moses machine translation toolkit (both the hierarchical decoder and training procedure provided by the experiment management system), using the default settings.

3.4 Operation Sequence Model (OSM)

The operation sequence model is a model for statistical MT that combines the benefits of two state-of-the-art SMT frameworks, namely n-gram-based SMT and phrase-based SMT (Durrani et al., 2015). It is a generative model that performs the translation process as a linear sequence of operations that jointly generate the source and target sentences. The operation types are (i) generation of a sequence of source and/or target words (ii) insertion of gaps as explicit target positions for reordering operations, and (iii) forward and backward jump operations which perform the actual reordering. The probability of a sequence of operations is given by an n-gram model. The OSM integrates translation and reordering into a single model which provides a natural reordering mechanism that is able to correctly re-order words across long distances. We used Moses (Koehn and Haddow, 2009) for training the OSM, with n-gram model order 5. Other settings such as those used to build the language model and lexicalized reordering model were the same as the default PBSMT system (refer to Section 3.2 for details).

Source-Target	Syllable			Word		
	PBSMT	HPBSMT	OSM	PBSMT	HPBSMT	OSM
ar-km	37.84	38.12	38.72	50.56	50.32	**51.21**
da-km	43.70	42.40	44.13	52.80	52.35	**53.43**
de-km	42.75	40.92	42.60	52.36	53.21	**53.34**
en-km	49.86	49.07	51.12	58.85	58.29	**59.82**
es-km	45.61	44.70	45.95	54.19	54.23	**54.78**
fr-km	42.33	42.98	43.77	51.70	51.11	**52.89**
hi-km	41.41	38.85	41.13	49.90	**51.04**	50.29
id-km	44.89	45.17	45.62	53.17	52.90	**54.28**
it-km	43.77	43.17	44.12	52.78	53.26	**53.52**
ja-km	32.57	22.47	32.58	38.49	**39.03**	38.62
ko-km	32.02	31.68	31.36	36.70	**38.88**	36.76
ms-km	45.72	45.26	46.66	54.54	54.72	**55.26**
my-km	33.82	25.84	33.94	**38.25**	31.83	38.15
nl-km	44.85	43.05	45.22	53.51	**53.98**	53.96
pt-km	44.89	44.13	45.55	53.78	53.78	**54.39**
ru-km	39.22	38.28	40.00	50.30	50.02	**51.34**
th-km	46.19	46.46	47.59	53.16	52.40	**53.27**
tl-km	43.93	42.66	44.06	53.34	**53.39**	52.76
vi-km	47.93	47.80	48.60	54.26	54.45	**55.07**
zh-km	32.21	31.16	32.66	39.20	**39.49**	39.05

Table 3: BLEU scores for translating into Khmer.

4 Results

4.1 Evaluation Criteria

We used two automatic criteria for the evaluation of the machine translation output. One was the de facto standard automatic evaluation metric Bilingual Evaluation Understudy (BLEU) (Papineni et al., 2001) and the other was the Rank-based Intuitive Bilingual Evaluation Measure (RIBES) (Isozaki et al., 2010). The BLEU score measures the precision of n-grams (over all $n \leq 4$ in our case) with respect to a reference translation with a penalty for short translations (Papineni et al., 2001). Intuitively, the BLEU score measures the adequacy of the translations and large BLEU scores are better. RIBES is an automatic evaluation metric based on rank correlation coefficients modified with precision and special care is paid to word order of the translation results. The RIBES score is suitable for distant language pairs such as Khmer and English, Khmer and Korean, Khmer and Myanmar (Isozaki et al., 2010). Large RIBES scores are better. We calculated the Pearson product-moment correlation coefficient (PMCC) between BLEU score and Kendall's tau distance (Kendall, 1938) to assess the strength of the linear relationship between the amount of reordering required during the translation process and the translation quality.

4.2 BLEU Score

The BLEU score results for machine translation experiments with PBSMT, HPBSMT and OSM are shown in Table 2 and Table 3. Bold numbers indicate the highest BLEU scores of the three different approaches. Most of the highest BLEU scores were achieved with the OSM approach translating both to and from Khmer.

4.3 RIBES Score

The RIBES score results for machine translation experiments with PBSMT, HPBSMT and OSM are shown in Appendix A in Table 4 and Table 5. Bold numbers indicate the highest RIBES scores of the three different approaches. Similar to the evaluation using the BLEU score, most of the highest RIBES scores were achieved with the OSM approach.

5 Analysis and Discussion

5.1 Kendall's Tau Distance

Kendall's tau distance is based on the number of transpositions of adjacent symbols necessary to transform one permutation into another (Kendall, 1938), and is one method to gauge the amount of re-ordering that would be required during the translation process between two languages. In this paper we use the version defined in (Birch, 2011) in which maximally close permutations have a distance of 1 and maximally distant permutations have a distance of 0.

Figure 2 shows a scatter plot of all of the PBSMT experiments with word segmented Khmer, plotting BLEU score against Kendall's tau distance. The points show a strong correlation (coefficient: 0.75). From this figure, we can clearly see English, Indonesian, Malaysian, Vietnamese, Spanish, Portuguese and Thai are close distance languages with Khmer in terms of word reordering and able to achieve higher machine translation performance. Note that although we plot points for all language pairs on this graph, the BLEU scores are only directly comparable in the cases where Khmer is the target language.

It is clear from the results in the experiments, that syllable segmentation is a far worse segmentation strategy for SMT than word segmentation. This is not always the case, and for languages such as Myanmar it has been shown (Thu et al., 2013) that syllable segmentation can give rise to machine translation scores that are competitive with other approaches. However, for Khmer the proposed word segmentation strategy gave rise to considerable gains in performance and is therefore to be preferred in all cases. Statistical significance tests using bootstrap resampling (Koehn, 2004) were run for all experiments involving the two segmentation schemes. For all experiments the differences were significant ($p < 0.01$).

For most languages combinations the OSM approach gave the highest scores. It is not surprising that is was able to exceed the performance of the phrase-based approach which it extends. However, in all-but-one of the evaluations involving Japanese and Korean the HPBSMT approach gave rise to the highest scores. Looking at the Kendall's tau distances in Figure 2 it can be seen that Japanese and Korean are the two most distant languages from Khmer in terms of this measure of word order difference. Overall therefore, we would recommend using the OSM approach to translate to and from Khmer except for languages that are very distant in terms of word order, in which cases a hierarchical phrase-based approach is likely to give better performance.

6 Conclusion

This paper has presented the first large-scale evaluation of the application of statistical machine translation techniques to the Khmer language. The paper provides a study of translation systems based on phrase-based, hierarchical phrase-based and operation sequence model-based methods. Our experiments show that the approaches based on the operation sequence model tended to give rise to the highest quality translations, measured both in terms of the BLEU and RIBES scores. The exceptions to this were the language pairs (such as those involving Japanese and Korean) where long distance re-ordering was required. For these language pairs, the hierarchical phrase-based method gave the highest scores. We believe that Kendall's tau distance may be used as a means of selecting an appropriate SMT technique for a given lan-

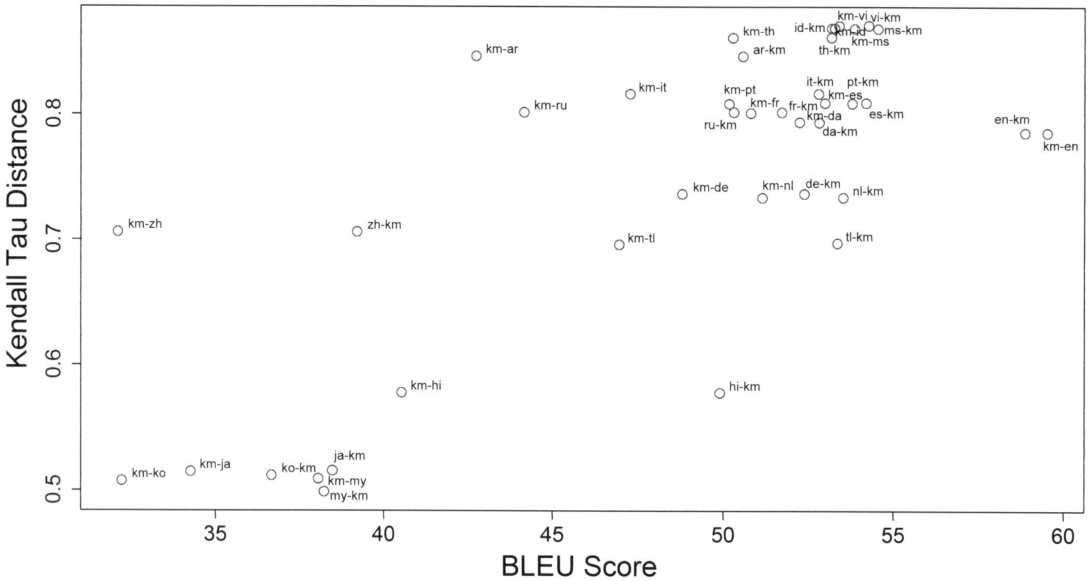

Figure 2: Plot of the Kendall's tau distance against BLEU score.

guage pair. The paper also evaluated the effect of using two different methods of segmentation for Khmer: heuristic syllable-based and a supervised method of word segmentation using CRFs. Our results showed that the word segmentation method to be the substantially more effective in every experiment.

In future work, we would like to improve the quality of the word segmenter, and extend the scope of the translation system to cover a broader domain.

Acknowledgments

We thank Mr. Mech Nan, Mr. Sorn Kea and Mr. Tep Raksa from National Institute of Posts, Telecommunications and Information Communication Technology, Cambodia for their help in segmenting 103,694 sentences of BTEC Khmer Corpus and General Domain Corpus manually.

References

Narin Bi and Nguonly Taing. 2014. Khmer word segmentation based on bi-directional maximal matching for plaintext and microsoft word document. In *Asia-Pacific Signal and Information Processing Association Annual Summit and Conference, APSIPA 2014, Chiang Mai, Thailand, December 9-12, 2014*, pages 1–9.

Alexandra Birch. 2011. *Reordering Metrics for Statistical Machine Translation.* Ph.D. thesis, University of Edinburgh.

Fabienne Braune, Anita Gojun, and Alexander Fraser. 2012. Long-distance reordering during search for hierarchical phrase-based smt. In *EAMT 2012: Proceedings of the 16th Annual Conference of the European Association for Machine Translation, Trento, Italy*, pages 177–184. Citeseer.

Pen Chanveasna. 2012. Khmer unicode text segmentation using maximal matching. Master's thesis, Royal University of Phnom Penh.

Stanley F Chen and Joshua Goodman. 1996. An empirical study of smoothing techniques for language modeling. In *Proceedings of the 34th annual meeting on Association for Computational Linguistics*, pages 310–318. Association for Computational Linguistics.

David Chiang. 2007. Hierarchical phrase-based translation. *Computational Linguistics*, 33(2):201–228.

Nadir Durrani, Helmut Schmid, Alexander Fraser, Philipp Koehn, and Hinrich Schütze. 2015. The Operation Sequence Model – Combining

N-Gram-based and Phrase-based Statistical Machine Translation. *Computational Linguistics*, 41(2):157–186.

Madeline Elizabeth Ehrman. 1972. Foreign Service Institute, Dept. of State.

Chea Sok Huor, Top Rithy, Ros Pich Hemy, and Vann Navy. 2007. Word bigram vs orthographic syllable bigram in khmer word segmentation.

Hideki Isozaki, Tsutomu Hirao, Kevin Duh, Katsuhito Sudoh, and Hajime Tsukada. 2010. Automatic evaluation of translation quality for distant language pairs. In *Proceedings of the 2010 Conference on Empirical Methods in Natural Language Processing*, EMNLP '10, pages 944–952, Stroudsburg, PA, USA. Association for Computational Linguistics.

M. G. Kendall. 1938. A new measure of rank correlation. *Biometrika*, 30(1/2):81–93.

G. Kikui, E. Sumita, T. Takezawa, and S. Yamamoto. 2003. Creating corpora for speech-to-speech translation. In *Proceedings of EUROSPEECH-03*, pages 381–384.

Philipp Koehn and Barry Haddow. 2009. Edinburgh's Submission to all Tracks of the WMT2009 Shared Task with Reordering and Speed Improvements to Moses. In *Proceedings of the Fourth Workshop on Statistical Machine Translation*, pages 160–164.

Philipp Koehn, Franz Josef Och, , and Daniel Marcu. 2003. Statistical phrase-based translation. In *In Proceedings of the Human Language Technology Conference*, Edmonton, Canada.

Philipp Koehn. 2004. Statistical significance tests for machine translation evaluation.

Craig G. Nevill-Manning and Ian H. Witten. 1997. Identifying hierarchical structure in sequences: A linear-time algorithm. *CoRR*, cs.AI/9709102.

F. J. Och and H. Ney. 2000. Improved statistical alignment models. In *ACL00*, pages 440–447, Hong Kong, China.

Franz J. Och. 2003. Minimum error rate training for statistical machine translation. In *Proceedings of the 41st Meeting of the Association for Computational Linguistics (ACL 2003)*, Sapporo, Japan.

K. Papineni, S. Roukos, T. Ward, and W.J. Zhu. 2001. *Bleu: a Method for Automatic Evaluation of Machine Translation.* IBM Research Report rc22176 (w0109022), Thomas J. Watson Research Center.

Andreas Stolcke. 2002. SRILM - An Extensible Language Modeling Toolkit. In *Proceedings of the International Conference on Spoken Language Processing*, volume 2, pages 901–904, Denver.

Suos Samak Surabaya Jabin and Kim Sokphyrum. 2013. How to translate from english to khmer using moses. *IJEI.*

Ye Kyaw Thu, Andrew Finch, Yoshinori Sagisaka, and Eiichiro Sumita. 2013. A study of myanmar word segmentation schemes for statistical machine translation. *Proceeding of the 11th International Conference on Computer Applications*, pages 167–179.

Christoph Tillmann. 2004. A unigram orientation model for statistical machine translation. In *Proceedings of HLT-NAACL 2004: Short Papers*, HLT-NAACL-Short '04, pages 101–104, Stroudsburg, PA, USA. Association for Computational Linguistics.

Channa Van and Wataru Kameyama. 2013. Khmer word segmentation and out-of-vocabulary words detection using collocation measurement of repeated characters subsequences. *GITS/GITI Research Bulletin 2012-2013.*

Appendix A. RIBES Scores

Source-Target	Syllable			Word		
	PBSMT	HPBSMT	OSM	PBSMT	HPBSMT	OSM
km-ar	0.672	0.617	0.681	**0.766**	0.760	**0.766**
km-da	0.841	0.778	0.835	0.889	0.885	**0.893**
km-de	0.831	0.748	0.827	**0.883**	0.874	0.880
km-en	0.887	0.847	0.886	**0.920**	0.911	**0.920**
km-es	0.832	0.785	0.830	0.887	0.879	**0.889**
km-fr	0.810	0.774	0.810	0.852	0.850	**0.854**
km-hi	0.760	0.554	0.765	**0.833**	0.829	0.829
km-id	0.853	0.819	0.855	**0.892**	0.890	0.891
km-it	0.779	0.743	0.778	0.839	0.840	**0.842**
km-ja	0.710	0.598	0.707	0.783	**0.790**	0.785
km-ko	0.640	0.679	0.647	0.734	**0.750**	0.737
km-ms	0.849	0.814	0.853	**0.896**	0.890	0.895
km-my	0.755	0.743	0.751	0.820	0.820	**0.826**
km-nl	0.836	0.811	0.834	**0.893**	0.886	0.891
km-pt	0.805	0.734	0.794	**0.863**	0.861	**0.863**
km-ru	0.762	0.707	0.749	**0.828**	0.811	0.820
km-th	0.817	0.767	0.821	0.855	0.835	**0.856**
km-tl	0.775	0.687	0.774	0.852	0.850	**0.856**
km-vi	0.872	0.810	0.871	0.894	0.893	**0.897**
km-zh	0.698	0.586	0.703	0.509	**0.767**	0.766

Table 4: RIBES scores for translating from Khmer.

Source-Target	Syllable			Word		
	PBSMT	HPBSMT	OSM	PBSMT	HPBSMT	OSM
ar-km	0.826	0.824	0.825	0.870	0.866	**0.876**
da-km	0.846	0.839	0.844	0.875	0.870	**0.876**
de-km	0.838	0.832	0.846	0.873	**0.875**	**0.875**
en-km	0.875	0.869	0.880	0.905	0.899	**0.907**
es-km	0.849	0.845	0.852	0.880	0.877	**0.881**
fr-km	0.840	0.838	0.839	**0.874**	0.865	0.871
hi-km	0.821	0.809	0.823	0.854	**0.861**	0.853
id-km	0.845	0.847	0.848	0.879	0.877	**0.881**
it-km	0.843	0.842	0.850	0.874	0.873	**0.878**
ja-km	0.744	0.650	0.737	0.771	0.764	**0.773**
ko-km	0.734	0.735	0.734	0.770	**0.781**	0.767
ms-km	0.851	0.849	0.856	0.883	0.882	**0.884**
my-km	0.730	0.687	0.730	**0.755**	0.740	0.750
nl-km	0.851	0.846	0.855	0.882	0.882	**0.886**
pt-km	0.852	0.849	0.856	**0.881**	0.879	0.880
ru-km	0.826	0.816	0.825	0.864	0.862	**0.868**
th-km	0.850	0.849	0.851	**0.867**	0.865	**0.867**
tl-km	0.840	0.829	0.840	0.875	0.875	**0.877**
vi-km	0.860	0.860	0.865	0.879	0.880	**0.882**
zh-km	0.751	0.748	0.755	0.788	**0.791**	0.782

Table 5: RIBES scores for translating into Khmer.

English to Chinese Translation: How Chinese Character Matters?

Rui Wang[1,2], **Hai Zhao**[1,2 *†] **and Bao-Liang Lu**[1,2]
[1]Center for Brain-Like Computing and Machine Intelligence,
Department of Computer Science and Engineering,
Shanghai Jiao Tong University, Shanghai, 200240, China
[2]Key Laboratory of Shanghai Education Commission for Intelligent Interaction
and Cognitive Engineering, Shanghai Jiao Tong University, Shanghai, 200240, China
wangrui.nlp@gmail.com and {zhaohai, blu}@cs.sjtu.edu.cn

Abstract

Word segmentation is helpful in Chinese natural language processing in many aspects. However it is showed that different word segmentation strategies do not affect the performance of Statistical Machine Translation (SMT) from English to Chinese significantly. In addition, it will cause some confusions in the evaluation of English to Chinese SMT. So we make an empirical attempt to translation English to Chinese in the character level, in both the alignment model and language model. A series of empirical comparison experiments have been conducted to show how different factors affect the performance of character-level English to Chinese SMT. We also apply the recent popular continuous space language model into English to Chinese SMT. The best performance is obtained with the BLEU score 41.56, which improve baseline system (40.31) by around 1.2 BLEU score.

*Correspondence author.

†Thank all the reviewers for valuable comments and suggestions on our paper. This work was partially supported by the National Natural Science Foundation of China (No. 61170114, and No. 61272248), the National Basic Research Program of China (No. 2013CB329401), the Science and Technology Commission of Shanghai Municipality (No. 13511500200), the European Union Seventh Framework Program (No. 247619), the Cai Yuanpei Program (CSC fund 201304490199 and 201304490171), and the art and science interdiscipline funds of Shanghai Jiao Tong University, No. 14X190040031, and the Key Project of National Society Science Foundation of China, No. 15-ZDA041.

1 Introduction

Word segmentation is necessary in most Chinese language processing doubtlessly, because there are no natural spaces between characters in Chinese text (Xi et al., 2012). It is defined in this paper as character-based segmentation if Chinese sentence is segmented into characters, otherwise as word segmentation.

In Statistical Machine Translation (SMT) in which Chinese is target language, few work have shown that better word segmentation will lead to better result in SMT (Zhao et al., 2013; Chang et al., 2008; Zhang et al., 2008). Recently Xi et al. (2012) demonstrate that Chinese character alignment can improve both of alignment quality and translation performance, which also motivates us the hypothesis whether word segmentation is not even necessary for SMT where Chinese as target language.

From the view of evaluation, the difference between the word-based segmentation methods will also makes the evaluation of SMT where Chinese as target language confusing. The automatic evaluation methods (such as BLEU and NIST BLEU score) in SMT are mostly based on n-gram precision. If the segmentation of test sets are different, the elements of the n-gram of test sets will also be different, which means that the evaluation is made on different test sets. To evaluate the quality of Chinese translation output, the International Workshop on Spoken Language Translation in 2005 (IWSLT'2005) used the word-level BLEU metric (Papineni et al.,2002). However, IWSLT'08 and NIST'08 adopted character-level evaluation metrics

29th Pacific Asia Conference on Language, Information and Computation pages 270 - 280
Shanghai, China, October 30 - November 1, 2015

to rank the submitted systems. Although there are also a lot of other works on automatic evaluation of SMT, such as METEOR (Lavie and Agarwal, 2007), GTM (Melamed et al., 2003) and TER (Snover et al., 2006), whether word or character is more suitable for automatic evaluation of Chinese translation output has not been systematically investigated (Li et al., 2011). Recently, different kinds of character-level SMT evaluation metrics are proposed, which also support that character-level SMT may have its own advantage accordingly (Li et al., 2011; Liu and Ng, 2012).

Traditionally, Back-off N-gram Language Models (BNLM) (Chen and Goodman, 1996; Chen and Goodman, 1998; Stolcke, 2002) are being widely used for probability estimation. For a better probability estimation method, recently, Continuous-Space Language Models (CSLM), especially Neural Network Language Models (NNLM) (Bengio et al., 2003; Schwenk, 2007; Le et al., 2011) are being used in SMT (Schwenk et al., 2006; Son et al., 2010; Schwenk et al., 2012; Son et al., 2012; Wang et al., 2013). These works have shown that CSLMs can improve the BLEU scores of SMT when compared with BNLMs, on the condition that the training data for language modeling are in the same size. However, in practice, CSLMs have not been widely used in SMT mainly due to high computational costs of training and using CSLMs. Since the using costs of CSLMs are very high, it is difficult to use C-SLMs in decoding directly. A common approach in SMT using CSLMs is the two pass approach, or n-best reranking. In this approach, the first pass uses a BNLM in decoding to produce an n-best list. Then, a CSLM is used to rerank those n-best translations in the second pass (Schwenk et al., 2006; Son et al., 2010; Schwenk et al., 2012; Son et al., 2012). Nearly all of the previous works only conduct CSLMs on English, we conduct CSLM on Chinese in this paper. Vaswani et al. propose a method for reducing the training cost of CSLM and apply it into SMT decoder (Vaswani et al., 2013). Some other studies try to implement neural network LM or translation model for SMT (Gao et al., 2014; Devlin et al., 2014; Zhang et al., 2014; Auli et al., 2013; Liu et al., 2013; Sundermeyer et al., 2014; Cho et al., 2014; Zou et al., 2013; Lauly et al., 2014; Kalchbrenner and Blunsom, 2013).

The remainder is organized as follows: In Section 2, we will review the background of English to Chinese SMT. The character based SMT will be proposed in Section 3. In Section 4, the experiments will be conducted and the results will be analyzed . We will conclude our work in the Section 5.

2 Background

The ancient Chinese (or Classical Chinese, 文言文) can be conveniently split into characters, for most characters in ancient Chinese still keep understood by one who only knows modern Chinese (or Written Vernacular Chinese, 白话文) words. For example, "三人行，则必有我师焉。" is one of the popular sentences in the Analects (论语), and its corresponding modern Chinese words and English meaning are shown in TABLE 1. From the table, we can see that the characters in ancient Chinese have independent meaning, but most of the characters in modern Chinese do not, and they must combine together into words to make sense. If we split modern Chinese sentences into characters, the semantic meaning in the words will partially lose. Whether or not this semantic function of Chinese word can be partly replaced by the alignment model and Language Model (LM) of character-based SMT will be shown in this paper.

Ancient Chinese	**Modern Chinese**	**English Meaning**
三	三个	three
人	人	people
行	走路	walk
，	，	,
则	那么	so
必	一定	must
有	存在	be
我	我的	my
师	老师	teacher/tutor
焉	在其中	there
。	。	.

Table 1: Ancient Chinese and Modern Chinese

SMT as a research domain started in the late 1980s at IBM (Brown et al., 1993), which maps individual words to words and allows for deletion and insertion of words. Lately, various researches have shown better translation quality with phrase translation. Phrase-based SMT can be traced back to Och's alignment template model (Och and Ney, 2004), which can be re-framed as a phrase translation system. Other researchers augmented their systems with phrase translation, such as Yamada and Knight (Yamada and Knight, 2001), who used phrase translation in a syntax-based model.

The phrase translation model is based on the noisy channel model. Bayes rule is mostly used to reformulate the translation probability for translating a foreign sentence f into target e as:

$$argmax_e p(e|f) = argmax_e p(f|e)p(e) \quad (1)$$

This allows for the probabilities of an LM $p(e)$ and a separated translation model $p(f|e)$. During decoding, the foreign input sentence f is segmented into a sequence of phrases f_1^i. It is assumed a uniform probability distribution over all possible segmentations. Each foreign phrase f_i in f_1^i is translated into an target phrase e_i. The target phrases may be reordered. Phrase translation is modeled by a probability distribution $\Omega(f_i|e_i)$. Recall that due to the Bayes rule, the translation direction is inverted.

Reordering of the output phrases is modeled by a relative distortion probability distribution $d(start_i, end_{i-1})$, where $start_i$ denotes the start position of the foreign phrase that is translated into the ith target phrase, and end_{i-1} denotes the end position of the foreign phrase that was translated into the $(i-1)-th$ target phrase. A simple distortion model $d(start_i, end_{i-1}) = \alpha^{|start_i - end_{i-1} - 1|}$ with an appropriate value for the parameter α is set.

In order to calibrate the output length, a factor ω (called word cost) for each generated English word in addition to the tri-gram LM p_{LM} is proposed. This is a simple means to optimize performance. Usually, this factor is larger than 1, biasing toward longer output. In summary, the best output sentence given a foreign input sentence f according to the model is:

$$argmax_e p(e|f) = argmax_e p(f|e)p_{LM}(e)\omega^{length(e)}, \quad (2)$$

where $p(f|e)$ is decomposed into:

$$p(f_1^i|e_1^i) = \phi_1^i \Omega(f_i|e_i) d(start_i, end_{i-1}). \quad (3)$$

In this paper, the f stands for English and the e stands for Chinese. In short, there are three main parts both in the English to Chinese and Chinese to English SMT: the alignment $p(f|e)$, the LM $p(e)$ and the parameters training (tuning). When Chinese is the foreign language, there is only the alignment model $p(f|e)$ containing Chinese language processing. Contrarily, when Chinese is the target language, both the the alignment part $p(f|e)$ and the LM $p(e)$ will help retrieve the sematic meaning in the characters which is originally represented by words. So it is possible that we can process the English to Chinese in character level without word segmentation, which may also avoid the confusion in the evaluation part as proposed above.

3 Character-based versus Word-based SMT

The standards of segmentation between word-based and character-based English to Chinese translation are different, as well as the standard of the evaluation of them. That is, the test data contains words as the smallest unit for word-based SMT, and characters for character-based SMT. So the translated sentences of word-based translation will be converted into character-based sentence, and evaluated together with character-based translation BLEU score for fair comparison. We select two popular segmentation segmenters, one of which is based on Forward Maximum Matching (FMM) algorithm with the lexicon of (Low et al., 2005), and the other is based on Conditional Random Fields (CRF) with the same implementation of (Zhao et al., 2006). Because most Chinese words contains 1 to 4 characters, so we set the word-based LM as default trigram in SRILM, and character-based LM for 5-gram. All the different methods share the same other default parameters in the toolkits which will be further introduced in Section 4.

There seems to be no ambiguity in different character segmentations, however English characters, numbers and other symbols are also contained in the corpus. If they are split into "characters" like "年 增 长 百 分 之 2 0 0" (200 % increment per year) or "J o r d a n 是 伟 大 的 篮 球 运 动 员" (Jordan is a great basketball player), they will cause a lot of misunderstanding. So the segmentation is only used for Chinese characters, and the foreign letters, numbers and other symbols in Chinese text are still kept consequent.

Shown in Table 2, the BLEU score of SMT system with character-based segmenter is much higher than both FMM and CRF segmenters. The word-based English to Chinese SMT system is trained and tuned in word level and evaluated in character level, so we use the character-based LM to re-score the nbest-list of the results of the FMM and CRF segmenters. Firstly we convert the translated 1000-best candidates for each sentence into characters. Then calculate their LM scores by the character-based LM, and replace the word-based LM score with character-based LM score. At last we re-calculate the global score to get the new 1-best candidate with the same tuning weight as before. The BLEU score of re-ranked method is slightly higher than before, but still much less than the result of character segmenter. Although we can not conclude the character-based segmenter is better simply according to this experiment, this result gives us the confidence that our approach is reasonable and feasible at least.

4 Comparison Experiment

We use the patent data for the Chinese to English patent translation subtask from the NTCIR-9 patent translation task (Goto et al., 2011). The parallel training, development, and test data consists of 1 million (M), 2,000, and 2,000 sentences, respectively[1].

The basic settings of the NTCIR-9 English to Chinese translation baseline system (Goto et al., 2011) was followed[2]. The Moses phrase-based SMT system was applied (Koehn et al., 2007), together with GIZA++ (Och and Ney, 2003) for alignment and MERT (Och, 2003) for tuning on the development data. 14 standard SMT features were used: five translation model scores, one word penalty score, seven distortion scores and one LM score. The translation performance was measured by the case-insensitive BLEU on the tokenized test data[3].

4.1 The Alignment

In this subsection we investigate two factors in the phrase alignment. Four different kinds of methods for heuristics and three kinds of maximum length of phrases in phrase table are used for word alignment, with other default parameters in the toolkits. The results are shown in Table 3. The $grow-diag-final-and$, which will be set as default without special statement in the following sections, is shown better than other settings, and the BLEU score do not increase as the maximum length of phrases increases.

Alignment Parameters	**BLEU (dev)**	**BLEU (test)**
union	42.24	39.33
intersect	40.64	38.08
grow-diag-final	42.70	39.78
grow-diag-final-and	42.80	**40.31**
Maximum Length	**BLEU (dev)**	**BLEU (test)**
7	42.80	**40.31**
10	42.78	40.04
13	42.85	40.30

Table 3: Different Heuristics Used for Word Alignment

4.2 The N-gram Language Model

In this part, we will investigate how the factors in the n-gram LM influence the whole system.

The scale of the training corpus is one of the most important factors to LM. And *"more data is better data"* (Brants and Xu, 2009) has been proved to be one of the most important rules for constructing a LMs. First we randomly divide the whole training sets into 4 parts equally. We build the LM with 1, 2 and 4 parts (i.e. for 1/4, 1/2 and the whole corpus respectively), with other setting as default. Then, we add the dictionary information to the LM. The pr stands for the size of the dictionary and the pf stands for the characters' frequency in the dictionary. The results in Table 4 show that using the whole corpus

[1] Since we are the participants of NTCIR-9, so we have the bilingual sides of the evaluation data.

[2] We are aware that the original NTCIR patentMT baseline is designed for Chinese-English translation. In this paper, we follow the same setting of the baseline system, only convert the source language and the target language.

[3] It is available at http://www.itl.nist.gov/iad/mig/tests/mt/2009/

Segmentation Methods	BLEU
FMM Segmenter	34.56
FMM Segmenter + Character-based LM Re-rank	35.08
CRF Segmenter	38.28
CRF Segmenter + Character-based LM Re-rank	38.78
Character Segmenter	**40.31**

Table 2: Comparison Between Word-based Translation and Character-based Translation

for language training is necessary and using the dictionary information does not improve the translation performance.

Size of The Corpus	BLEU (dev)	BLEU (test)
1/4 Corpus	42.30	39.76
1/2 Corpus	42.51	40.19
the whole Corpus	42.80	**40.31**
Dictionaries		
pr=10k pf=5	42.63	40.01
pr=10k pf=10	42.60	40.17
pr=20k pf=10	42.73	40.02
No Dictionary	42.80	**40.31**

Table 4: Scale of Corpus for LM

We select the three most popular smoothing algorithms, Witten-Bell, Kneser-Ney (KN), and improved Kneser-Ney (improved KN), and compare their performance in the character-level English to Chinese SMT task. As shown in Table 5, when n is too small , the result is less satisfactory, and the BLEU score continues increase as n increases. However, the BLEU score begins to decrease when the LM becomes too *long*. The best 9-gram LM with Witten-Bell smoothing, corresponding to 5-gram to 7-gram in word-based LM, which is the widestly used in word-bases English to Chinese SMT.

4.3 The Tuning

We have shown that the different lengths of n-gram LMs make a significant influence in the English to Chinese translation. The 4-gram BLEU score is broadly accepted as the evaluate standard when we tune the other parameters using the minimum error rate training, which means that the MERT stage will not stop until it reaches the highest 4-gram BLEU on the development set. However, the same sentence

Smoothing Method	n-gram LM	BLEU (dev)	BLEU (test)
Kneser-Ney	9	42.55	39.91
Improved KN	7	42.95	40.30
Improved KN	9	42.84	40.55
Improved KN	11	42.44	40.07
Witten-Bell	7	42.72	40.10
Witten-Bell	9	42.71	**40.62**
Witten-Bell	11	42.44	39.67

Table 5: Different Smoothing Methods for LM

becomes longer if the character based segmentation is applied. That is, four words may be segmented into around 10 characters. Will the system gain a better performance if the n-gram of BLEU score in the MERT convergence standard increases as the n-gram in the LM increases?

To evaluate this hypothesis, the alignment model is set the same as the best performance in Table 3, and 5-gram LM with improved KN smoothing is set for LM. The results in Table 6 show that singly increasing the n-gram of MERT can not improve the performance of SMT.

n-gram MERT	n-gram BLEU (dev)	4-gram BLEU (test)
4	42.80	**40.31**
7	25.45	40.30
10	15.02	40.17

Table 6: Different Setting on MERT

4.4 Parameter Combinations

We have investigated how different factors affect the performance of English to Chinese SMT. However, most of the other factors are fixed when we discuss one single factor. So in this subsection, we analyze how the combined factors perform in the whole system.

Firstly, we combine the parameters of the smoothing methods and the maximum length of phrases together. The LM is set to 9-gram and $grow - diag - final - and$ is set for alignment, which has the best BLEU score in n-gram LM experiments. Other factors is set as default in the toolkits. The results are shown in Table 7.

Smoothing Method (LM)	**Maximum Length (align)**	**BLEU (dev)**	**BLEU (test)**
KN	7	42.55	39.91
KN	10	42.80	40.49
KN	13	42.89	39.93
Improved KN	7	42.84	40.55
Improved KN	10	43.00	40.24
Improved KN	13	40.07	40.56
Witten-Bell	7	42.71	**40.62**
Witten-Bell	10	42.85	40.06
Witten-Bell	13	42.85	40.09

Table 7: Parameter Combinations of Smoothing Methods and Maximum Length of Phrase Alignment

Then, the length of n-gram MERT and the different order n-gram LM are tuned together. We set the Improved KN as the smoothing method, and others as default in the toolkits. The results are shown in Table 8.

n-gram LM	**n-gram MERT**	**BLEU (dev)**	**4-gram BLEU (test)**
7	4	42.95	40.30
7	7	25.54	39.91
9	4	42.84	40.55
9	7	25.93	**40.75**
9	10	15.82	40.37
13	7	25.41	40.47

Table 8: Parameter Combinations of n-gram LM and n-gram MERT

At last, the length of n-gram MERT and the smoothing methods are tuned together. The LM is set as 9-gram, the best BLEU score in n-gram LM experiments, and other factors set as default in the toolkits. The results are shown in Table 9.

Among different parameters-combined setting,

Smoothing Method	**n-gram MERT**	**BLEU (dev)**	**BLEU (test)**
KN	4	42.55	39.91
KN	7	25.33	40.65
Improved KN	4	42.84	40.55
Improved KN	7	25.93	**40.75**
Improved KN	10	15.82	40.37
Witten-Bell	4	42.71	40.62
Witten-Bell	7	25.45	40.30

Table 9: Parameter Combinations of n-gram MERT and Smoothing Methods

BLEU score is from 38.08 to 40.75, and the best performance is not gained when all the factors which singly perform best are put together. The highest BLEU score occurs when the 9-gram LM, the 7-gram MERT method and the improved KN smoothing algorithm. This BLEU score is about one percent higher than our baseline. At last, we show three parameter combinations with their NIST scores that bring the best performance up to now in Table 10.

4.5 Continues Space Language Model

Traditional Backoff N-gram LMs (BNLMs) have been widely used in many NLP tasks (Jia and Zhao, 2014; Zhang et al., 2012; Xu and Zhao, 2012).

Recently, Continuous-Space Language Models (CSLMs), especially Neural Network Language Models (NNLMs) (Bengio et al., 2003; Schwenk, 2007; Mikolov et al., 2010; Le et al., 2011), are actively used in SMT (Schwenk et al., 2006; Schwenk et al., 2006; Schwenk et al., 2012; Son et al., 2012; Niehues and Waibel, 2012). These models have demonstrated that CSLMs can improve BLEU scores of SMT over n-gram LMs with the same sized corpus for LM training. An attractive feature of CSLMs is that they can predict the probabilities of n-grams outside the training corpus more accurately.

A CSLM implemented in a multi-layer neural network contains four layers: the input layer projects all words in the context h_i onto the projection layer (the first hidden layer); the second hidden layer and the output layer achieve the non-liner probability estimation and calculate the LM probability $P(w_i|h_i)$ for the given context (Schwenk, 2007).

The CSLM calculates the probabilities of al-

Factors vs BLEU	(1) 40.75	(2) 40.65	(3) 40.62
Maximum Length of Phrases	7	10	10
Heuristic for Alignment	grow-diag-final-and	grow-diag-final-and	grow-diag-final-and
Scales of LM	whole	whole	whole
Dictionary of LM	none	none	none
n-gram of LM	9	9	9
Smoothing of LM	Improved KN	Kneser-Ney	Witten-Bell
n-gram MERT	7	7	4
NIST Score	9.32	**9.40**	9.23

Table 10: Parameters for TOP Performance

Methods vs BLEU	(1) 40.75	(2) 40.65	(3) 40.62
CSLM Re-rank	41.15	**41.27**	41.18
CSLM Decoding	41.34	41.34	**41.57**

Table 11: CSLM Re-rank and decoding for TOP Performance

l words in the vocabulary of the corpus given the context at once. However, due to too high computational complexity, the CSLM is only used to calculate the probabilities of a subset of the whole vocabulary. This subset is called a *short-list*, which consists of the most frequent words in the vocabulary. The CSLM also calculates the sum of the probabilities of all words not in the short-list by assigning a neuron. The probabilities of other words not in the short-list are obtained from an Backoff N-gram LM (BNLM) (Schwenk, 2007; Schwenk, 2010; Wang et al., 2013; Wang et al., 2015).

Let w_i, h_i be the current word and history, respectively. The CSLM with a BNLM calculates the probability of w_i given h_i, $P(w_i|h_i)$, as follows:

$$P(w_i|h_i) = \begin{cases} \frac{P_c(w_i|h_i)}{\sum_{w \in V_0} P_c(w|h_i)} P_s(h_i) & \text{if } w_i \in V_0 \\ P_b(w_i|h_i) & \text{otherwise} \end{cases} \quad (4)$$

where V_0 is the short-list, $P_c(\cdot)$ is the probability calculated by the CSLM, $\sum_{w \in V_0} P_c(w|h_i)$ is the summary of probabilities of the neuron for all the words in the short-list, $P_b(\cdot)$ is the probability calculated by the BNLM, and

$$P_s(h_i) = \sum_{v \in V_0} P_b(v|h_i). \quad (5)$$

We may regard that the CSLM redistributes the probability mass of all words in the short-list, which is calculated by using the n-gram LM.

Due to too high computational cost, it is difficult to use CSLMs in decoding directly. As mentioned in the introduction, a common approach in SMT using CSLMs is a two-pass procedure, or n-best re-ranking. In this approach, the first pass uses a BNLM in decoding to produce an n-best list. Then, a CSLM is used to re-rank those n-best translations in the second pass (Schwenk et al., 2006; Son et al., 2010; Schwenk et al., 2012; Son et al., 2012).

Because CSLM outperforms BNLM in probability estimation accuracy and BNLM outperforms CSLM in computational time. To integrate CSLM more efficiently into decoding, some existing approaches calculate the probabilities of the n-grams before decoding and store them (Wang et al., 2013; Wang et al., 2014; Arsoy et al., 2013; Arsoy et al., 2014) in n-gram format. That is, n-grams from BNLM are used as the input of CSLM, and the output probabilities of CSLM together with the corresponding n-grams of BNLM constitute *converted CSLM*. The converted CSLM is directly used in SMT, and its decoding speed is as fast as the n-gram LM.

From the above tables, we find the most important parameter for character-based English to Chinese translation is the LM, and other parameters just have a minor influence. To verify this observation, we use 9-gram character based CSLM (Schwenk et al., 2006), with 4096 characters in the short list, the projection layer of dimension 256 and the hidden layer of dimension 192 are set in the CSLM experiments. (1) We add the CSLM score as the additional feature to re-rank the 1000-best candidates in the top three performance In Table 10. The weight parameters were tuned by using Z-MERT (Zaidan, 2009). This method is called *CSLM Re-rank*. (2) We follow (Wang et al., 2013)'s method and convert CSLM into *n*-gram LM. This converted CSLM can be directly applied to SMT decoding and called *CSLM-decoding*.

It is shown in Table 11 that the BLEU score nearly improve by 0.4 point to 0.6 point (CSLM Re-rank) and 0.6 point to 0.9 point (CSLM-decoding). This indicates that the CSLMs affect the performance of character based SMT in a significant way. This may indicate that the LM can take part place of the segmentation for character based English to Chinese SMT. A better character-based English to Chinese translation can be obtained by building a better LM.

5 Conclusion

Because the role of word segmentation in English to Chinese translation is arguable, an attempt of character-based English to Chinese translation seems to be necessary. In this paper, we have shown why character-based English to Chinese translation is necessary and feasible, and investigated how different factors perform in the system from the alignment, LM and the tuning aspects. Several empirical studies, including recent popular CSLM, have been done to show how to determine a optimal parameters for better SMT performance, and the results show that the LM is the most important factor for character-based English to Chinese translation.

Acknowledgments

We appreciate the anonymous reviewers for valuable comments and suggestions on our paper. Rui Wang, Hai Zhao and Bao-Liang Lu were partially supported by the National Natural Science Foundation of China (No. 60903119, No. 61170114, and No. 61272248), the National Basic Research Program of China (No. 2013CB329401), the Science and Technology Commission of Shanghai Municipality (No. 13511500200), the European Union Seventh Framework Program (No. 247619), the Cai Yuanpei Program (CSC fund 201304490199 and 201304490171), and the art and science interdiscipline funds of Shanghai Jiao Tong University (A study on mobilization mechanism and alerting threshold setting for online community, and media image and psychology evaluation: a computational intelligence approach).

References

Ebru Arsoy, Stanley F. Chen, Bhuvana Ramabhadran, and Abhinav Sethy. 2013. Converting neural network language models into back-off language models for efficient decoding in automatic speech recognition. In *Proceeding of International Conference on Acoustics, Speech and Signal Processing*, Vancouver, Canada, May.

Ebru Arsoy, Stanley F. Chen, Bhuvana Ramabhadran, and Abhinav Sethy. 2014. Converting neural network language models into back-off language models for efficient decoding in automatic speech recognition. *IEEE/ACM Transactions on Audio, Speech, and Language Processing*, 22(1):184–192.

Michael Auli, Michel Galley, Chris Quirk, and Geoffrey Zweig. 2013. Joint language and translation modeling with recurrent neural networks. In *Proceedings of the 2013 Conference on Empirical Methods in Natural Language Processing*, pages 1044–1054, Seattle, Washington, USA, October.

Yoshua Bengio, Réjean Ducharme, Pascal Vincent, and Christian Janvin. 2003. A neural probabilistic language model. *Journal of Machine Learning Research (JMLR)*, 3:1137–1155, March.

Thorsten Brants and Peng Xu. 2009. Distributed language models. In *Proceedings of Human Language Technologies: The 2009 Annual Conference of the North American Chapter of the Association for Computational Linguistics, Companion Volume: Tutorial Abstracts*, NAACL-Tutorials '09, pages 3–4, Boulder, Colorado, USA. Association for Computational Linguistics.

Peter F. Brown, Vincent J. Della Pietra, Stephen A. Della Pietra, and Robert L. Mercer. 1993. The mathematics of statistical machine translation: parameter estimation. *Comput. Linguist.*, 19(2):263–311, June.

Pi-Chuan Chang, Michel Galley, and Christopher D. Manning. 2008. Optimizing Chinese word segmentation for machine translation performance. In *Proceedings of the Third Workshop on Statistical Machine Translation*, StatMT '08, pages 224–232, Columbus, Ohio, USA. Association for Computational Linguistics.

Stanley F. Chen and Joshua Goodman. 1996. An empirical study of smoothing techniques for language modeling. In *Proceedings of the 34th annual meeting on*

Association for Computational Linguistics, ACL '96, pages 310–318, Santa Cruz, California, USA. Association for Computational Linguistics.

Stanley F. Chen and Joshua Goodman. 1998. An empirical study of smoothing techniques for language modeling. Technical report, Computer Science Group, Harvard Univ.

Kyunghyun Cho, Bart van Merrienboer, Caglar Gulcehre, Dzmitry Bahdanau, Fethi Bougares, Holger Schwenk, and Yoshua Bengio. 2014. Learning phrase representations using rnn encoder–decoder for statistical machine translation. In *Proceedings of the 2014 Conference on Empirical Methods in Natural Language Processing (EMNLP)*, pages 1724–1734, Doha, Qatar, October.

Jacob Devlin, Rabih Zbib, Zhongqiang Huang, Thomas Lamar, Richard Schwartz, and John Makhoul. 2014. Fast and robust neural network joint models for statistical machine translation. In *Proceedings of the 52nd Annual Meeting of the Association for Computational Linguistics*, pages 1370–1380, Baltimore, Maryland, June.

Jianfeng Gao, Xiaodong He, Wen-tau Yih, and Li Deng. 2014. Learning continuous phrase representations for translation modeling. In *Proceedings of the 52nd Annual Meeting of the Association for Computational Linguistics*, pages 699–709, Baltimore, Maryland, June.

Isao Goto, Bin Lu, Ka Po Chow, Eiichiro Sumita, and Benjamin K. Tsou. 2011. Overview of the patent machine translation task at the NTCIR-9 workshop. In *Proceedings of NTCIR-9 Workshop Meeting*, pages 559–578, Tokyo, Japan, December.

Zhongye Jia and Hai Zhao. 2014. A joint graph model for pinyin-to-chinese conversion with typo correction. In *Proceedings of the 52nd Annual Meeting of the Association for Computational Linguistics*, pages 1512–1523, Baltimore, Maryland, June.

Nal Kalchbrenner and Phil Blunsom. 2013. Recurrent continuous translation models. In *Proceedings of the 2013 Conference on Empirical Methods in Natural Language Processing*, pages 1700–1709, Seattle, Washington, USA, October.

Philipp Koehn, Hieu Hoang, Alexandra Birch, Chris Callison-Burch, Marcello Federico, Nicola Bertoldi, Brooke Cowan, Wade Shen, Christine Moran, Richard Zens, Chris Dyer, Ondrej Bojar, Alexandra Constantin, and Evan Herbst. 2007. Moses: Open source toolkit for statistical machine translation. In *Proceedings of the 45th Annual Meeting of the Association for Computational Linguistics Companion Volume Proceedings of the Demo and Poster Sessions*, pages 177–180, Prague, Czech Republic, June. Association for Computational Linguistics.

Stanislas Lauly, Hugo Larochelle, Mitesh Khapra, Balaraman Ravindran, Vikas C Raykar, and Amrita Saha. 2014. An autoencoder approach to learning bilingual word representations. In *Advances in Neural Information Processing Systems*, pages 1853–1861.

Alon Lavie and Abhaya Agarwal. 2007. Meteor: an automatic metric for mt evaluation with high levels of correlation with human judgments. In *Proceedings of the Second Workshop on Statistical Machine Translation*, StatMT '07, pages 228–231, Prague, Czech Republic. Association for Computational Linguistics.

Hai-Son Le, I. Oparin, A. Allauzen, J. Gauvain, and F. Yvon. 2011. Structured output layer neural network language model. In *Acoustics, Speech and Signal Processing (ICASSP), 2011 IEEE International Conference on*, pages 5524–5527, Prague, Czech Republic, May. IEEE.

Maoxi Li, Chengqing Zong, and Hwee Tou Ng. 2011. Automatic evaluation of Chinese translation output: Word-level or character-level? In *Proceedings of the 49th Annual Meeting of the Association for Computational Linguistics: Human Language Technologies*, pages 159–164, Portland, Oregon, USA, June. Association for Computational Linguistics.

Chang Liu and Hwee Tou Ng. 2012. Character-level machine translation evaluation for languages with ambiguous word boundaries. In *Proceedings of the 50th Annual Meeting of the Association for Computational Linguistics: Long Papers - Volume 1*, ACL '12, pages 921–929, Jeju Island, Korea, USA. Association for Computational Linguistics.

Lemao Liu, Taro Watanabe, Eiichiro Sumita, and Tiejun Zhao. 2013. Additive neural networks for statistical machine translation. In *Proceedings of the 51st Annual Meeting of the Association for Computational Linguistics*, pages 791–801, Sofia, Bulgaria, August.

Jin Kiat Low, Hwee Tou Ng, and Wenyuan Guo. 2005. A Maximum Entropy Approach to Chinese Word Segmentation. In *Proceedings of the 4th SIGHAN Workshop on Chinese Language Processing*, Jeju Island, Korea, October. Association for Computational Linguistics.

I. Dan Melamed, Ryan Green, and Joseph P. Turian. 2003. Precision and recall of machine translation. In *Proceedings of the 2003 Conference of the North American Chapter of the Association for Computational Linguistics on Human Language Technology: companion volume of the Proceedings of HLT-NAACL 2003–short papers - Volume 2*, NAACL-Short '03, pages 61–63, Edmonton, Canada. Association for Computational Linguistics.

Tomas Mikolov, Martin Karafiát, Lukas Burget, Jan Cernockỳ, and Sanjeev Khudanpur. 2010. Recurrent neural network based language model. In *INTER-SPEECH*, pages 1045–1048.

Jan Niehues and Alex Waibel. 2012. Continuous space language models using restricted boltzmann machines. In *Proceedings of the International Workshop for Spoken Language Translation*, IWSLT 2012, pages 311–318, Hong Kong.

Franz Josef Och and Hermann Ney. 2003. A systematic comparison of various statistical alignment models. *Comput. Linguist.*, 29(1):19–51, March.

Franz Josef Och and Hermann Ney. 2004. The alignment template approach to statistical machine translation. *Comput. Linguist.*, 30(4):417–449, December.

Franz Josef Och. 2003. Minimum error rate training in statistical machine translation. In *Proceedings of the 41st Annual Meeting of the Association for Computational Linguistics*, pages 160–167, Sapporo, Japan, July. Association for Computational Linguistics.

Holger Schwenk, Daniel Dchelotte, and Jean-Luc Gauvain. 2006. Continuous space language models for statistical machine translation. In *Proceedings of the COLING/ACL on Main conference poster sessions*, COLING-ACL '06, pages 723–730, Sydney, Australia. Association for Computational Linguistics.

Holger Schwenk, Anthony Rousseau, and Mohammed Attik. 2012. Large, pruned or continuous space language models on a gpu for statistical machine translation. In *Proceedings of the NAACL-HLT 2012 Workshop: Will We Ever Really Replace the N-gram Model? On the Future of Language Modeling for HLT*, WLM '12, pages 11–19, Montreal, Canada, June. Association for Computational Linguistics.

Holger Schwenk. 2007. Continuous space language models. *Computer Speech and Language*, 21(3):492–518.

Holger Schwenk. 2010. Continuous-space language models for statistical machine translation. *The Prague Bulletin of Mathematical Linguistics*, pages 137–146.

Matthew Snover, Bonnie Dorr, Richard Schwartz, Linnea Micciulla, and John Makhoul. 2006. A study of translation edit rate with targeted human annotation. In *In Proceedings of Association for Machine Translation in the Americas*, pages 223–231.

Le Hai Son, Alexandre Allauzen, Guillaume Wisniewski, and François Yvon. 2010. Training continuous space language models: some practical issues. In *Proceedings of the 2010 Conference on Empirical Methods in Natural Language Processing*, EMNLP '10, pages 778–788, Cambridge, Massachusetts, October. Association for Computational Linguistics.

Le Hai Son, Alexandre Allauzen, and François Yvon. 2012. Continuous space translation models with neural networks. In *Proceedings of the 2012 Conference of the North American Chapter of the Association for Computational Linguistics: Human Language Technologies*, NAACL HLT '12, pages 39–48, Montreal, Canada, June. Association for Computational Linguistics.

Andreas Stolcke. 2002. Srilm-an extensible language modeling toolkit. In *Proceedings International Conference on Spoken Language Processing*, pages 257–286, Seattle, USA, November.

Martin Sundermeyer, Tamer Alkhouli, Joern Wuebker, and Hermann Ney. 2014. Translation modeling with bidirectional recurrent neural networks. In *Proceedings of the 2014 Conference on Empirical Methods in Natural Language Processing (EMNLP)*, pages 14–25, Doha, Qatar, October.

Ashish Vaswani, Yinggong Zhao, Victoria Fossum, and David Chiang. 2013. Decoding with large-scale neural language models improves translation. In *Proceedings of the 2013 Conference on Empirical Methods in Natural Language Processing*, pages 1387–1392, Seattle, Washington, USA, October.

Rui Wang, Masao Utiyama, Isao Goto, Eiichro Sumita, Hai Zhao, and Bao-Liang Lu. 2013. Converting continuous-space language models into n-gram language models for statistical machine translation. In *Proceedings of the 2013 Conference on Empirical Methods in Natural Language Processing*, pages 845–850, Seattle, Washington, USA, October. Association for Computational Linguistics.

Rui Wang, Hai Zhao, Bao Liang Lu, Masao Utiyama, and Eiichiro Sumita. 2014. Neural network based bilingual language model growing for statistical machine translation. In *Proceedings of the 2014 Conference on Empirical Methods in Natural Language Processing*, pages 189–195, Doha, Qatar, October.

Rui Wang, Hai Zhao, Bao-Liang Lu, M. Utiyama, and E. Sumita. 2015. Bilingual continuous-space language model growing for statistical machine translation. *Audio, Speech, and Language Processing, IEEE/ACM Transactions on*, 23(7):1209–1220, July.

Ning Xi, Guangchao Tang, Xinyu Dai, Shujian Huang, and Jiajun Chen. 2012. Enhancing statistical machine translation with character alignment. In *Proceedings of the 50th Annual Meeting of the Association for Computational Linguistics (Volume 2: Short Papers)*, pages 285–290, Jeju Island, Korea, July. Association for Computational Linguistics.

Qiongkai Xu and Hai Zhao. 2012. Using deep linguistic features for finding deceptive opinion spam. In *Proceedings of 24th International Conference on Computational Linguistics*, pages 1341–1350, Mumbai, India, December.

Kenji Yamada and Kevin Knight. 2001. A syntax-based statistical translation model. In *Proceedings of the*

39th Annual Meeting on Association for Computational Linguistics, ACL '01, pages 523–530, Toulouse, France. Association for Computational Linguistics.

Omar F. Zaidan. 2009. Z-MERT: A fully configurable open source tool for minimum error rate training of machine translation systems. *The Prague Bulletin of Mathematical Linguistics*, 91:79–88.

Ruiqiang Zhang, Keiji Yasuda, and Eiichiro Sumita. 2008. Improved statistical machine translation by multiple Chinese word segmentation. In *Proceedings of the Third Workshop on Statistical Machine Translation*, StatMT '08, pages 216–223, Columbus, Ohio, USA. Association for Computational Linguistics.

Xiaotian Zhang, Hai Zhao, and Cong Hui. 2012. A machine learning approach to convert CCGbank to Penn treebank. In *Proceedings of 24th International Conference on Computational Linguistics*, pages 535–542, Mumbai, India, December.

Jingyi Zhang, Masao Utiyama, Eiichiro Sumita, and Hai Zhao. 2014. Learning hierarchical translation spans. In *Proceedings of the 2014 Conference on Empirical Methods in Natural Language Processing*, pages 183–188, Doha, Qatar, October.

Hai Zhao, Chang-Ning Huang, and Mu Li. 2006. An improved Chinese word segmentation system with conditional random field. In *Proceedings of the Fifth SIGHAN Workshop on Chinese Language Processing*, pages 162–165, Sydney, Australia, July. Association for Computational Linguistics.

Hai Zhao, Masao Utiyama, Eiichiro Sumita, and Bao-Liang Lu. 2013. An empirical study on word segmentation for Chinese machine translation. In *Proceedings of the 14th international conference on Computational Linguistics and Intelligent Text Processing - Volume 2*, CICLing'13, pages 248–263, Berlin, Heidelberg. Springer-Verlag.

Will Y. Zou, Richard Socher, Daniel Cer, and Christopher D. Manning. 2013. Bilingual word embeddings for phrase-based machine translation. In *Proceedings of the 2013 Conference on Empirical Methods in Natural Language Processing*, pages 1393–1398, Seattle, Washington, USA, October.

Well-Formed Dependency to String translation with BTG Grammar

Xiaoqing Li[†], **Kun Wang**[†], **Dakun Zhang**[‡], **Jie Hao**[‡]
[†] National Laboratory of Pattern Recognition, Institute of Automation,
Chinese Academy of Sciences
[‡] Toshiba (China) R&D Center
{xqli,kunwang}@nlpr.ia.ac.cn
{zhangdakun,haojie}@toshiba.com.cn

Abstract

This paper proposes a well-formed dependency to string translation model with BTG grammar. By enabling the usage of well-formed sub-structures and allowing flexible reordering of them, our approach is effective to relieve the problems of parsing error and flatness in dependency structure. To utilize the well-formed dependency rules during decoding, we adapt the tree traversal decoding algorithm into a bottom-up CKY algorithm. And a lexicalized reordering model is used to encourage the proper combination of two neighbouring blocks. Experiment results demonstrate that our approach can effectively improve the performance by more than 2 BLEU score over the baseline.

1 Introduction

Due to the merits of holding shallow semantic information and cross-lingual consistency (Fox, 2002), dependency grammar has attracted much attention in the field of machine translation (Lin, 2004; Quirk et al., 2005; Ding and Palmer, 2005; Shen et al., 2008; Xie et al., 2011).

The dependency-to-string model (Xie et al., 2011) falls into the paradigm of "translation after understanding", which tries to understand the structure and meaning of source text. However, there are two typical problems for this approach. One is that the model is prone to be affected by parsing errors. Dependency-to-string model adopts a unique source side tree structure as fixed input and constructs the output by converting each sub-structure into target side. If there is some errors in the source dependency tree, for example, a prepositional subtree is attached to a wrong head, the model can hardly recover the error. Figure 1(a) shows another parsing error, in the correct parsing result, "与北韩...国家" should forms a subtree with "国家" as the head, and then this subtree is dominant by "之一".

The other problem is that dependency structure is too flat for the translation task. Since dependency-to-string model requires a head and all its dependents to be translated as a whole, the flatness of the structure will make rules difficult to be matched during decoding. Furthermore, it will also lower the robustness of translation rules, since many giant and low-frequency rules will be extracted. Figure 1(b) shows an example of the flat structure. The head word "提供" has five dependents in the structure. If no rule can be matched, only the glue rule can be applied. As a result, the prepositional subtree "为了...义务" cannot be correctly reordered to the end in the target side.

Existing solutions for the above problems include (Meng et al., 2013; Xie et al., 2014). The former incorporates phrasal nodes of constituency trees in the source side of translation rules, and the latter modifies translation rules during decoding to allow the usage of phrases which are compatible with well-formed structures. Since these two approaches still adopt head-dependent structure as the backbone of the translation rule, the freedom of generating translation candidates is limited.

On the contrary, we propose to use BTG grammar to combine the translations of two adjacent well-formed structures. To incorporate the BTG rules

29th Pacific Asia Conference on Language, Information and Computation pages 281 - 288
Shanghai, China, October 30 - November 1, 2015

(a) (b)

Figure 1: Examples of parsing error (a) and flatness (b)

into the model, we adapt the tree traversal decoding algorithm into a bottom-up CKY algorithm. Large scale experiments show that our approach can improve the performance by more than 2 BLEU score over the baseline, and it is also superior to the two approaches mentioned above.

2 Background

We briefly review the dependency to string model and the BTG grammar in this section, which are the bases of our proposed model.

2.1 Dependency-to-String Model

The dependency-to-string model proposed by (Xie et al., 2011) translates a source dependency tree by applying head-dependents translation rule at each head node in a recursive way. A head-dependents translation rule consists of a head-dependents fragment in the source side and its translation correspondence in the target side. The rule $r1$ in Figure 2 is an example of their translation rule. This rule specifies the translation of the head node "提供" and leaf nodes "布什", and also the reordering relation of the non-terminal nodes, including the internal node "为" and the generalized internal node "优惠". The word or POS tag at each non-terminal node in the rule describes its matching condition. For example, $X2$:NN in $r1$ means the second non-terminal must be a noun while matching this rule. In principle, all nodes, i.e., head, internal and leaf nodes in the dependency tree, can be generalized to their POS tags (or other categories) to relieve data sparsity.

By including a head and all its dependents into one rule, the dependency-to-string model is good at long distance reordering. However, this structure is not robust enough due to parsing errors and flatness.

2.2 BTG Grammar

Bracketing transduction grammar (BTG) (Wu, 1997) is a special case of synchronous context free grammar. There are only two types of rules in this grammar:

$$X \rightarrow [X^1, X^2] \,|X \rightarrow < X^1, X^2 >$$

$$X \rightarrow x/y$$

The first type of rule is used to merge the translations of two neighbouring blocks X^1 and X^2 with monotone or swap order, and the second type of rule is used to translate source phrase x in to target phrase y. Due to its simplicy and effectiveness of modeling bilingual correspondence, BTG grammar is widely used translation modeling (Xiong et al., 2006; Li et al., 2013), word alignment (Zhang and Gildea, 2005; Haghighi et al., 2009; Pauls et al., 2010), translation system combination (Karakos et al., 2008), etc.

3 Well-Formed Dependency to String Model

In this section, we describe our well-formed dependency to string model with BTG grammar, and explain how it relieves the problems of parsing error and flatness.

3.1 Modified Well-formed structure

Similar to (Shen et al., 2008), we define two kinds of well-formed dependency structures, i.e., fixed structure and floating structure. Fixed structure consists of the heads of a sequence of sibling trees and the common head of these trees; and floating structure consists of the heads of a sequence of sibling trees without their common head. The difference between

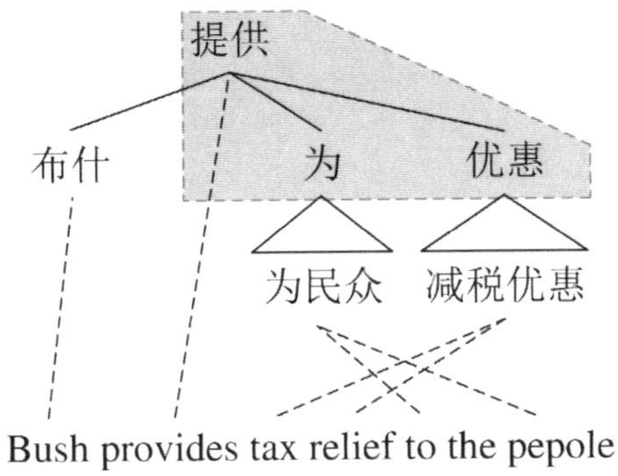

$r1$: 布什 $X1$:为 **提供** $X2$:NN ||| Bush provides $X2$ $X1$
$r2$: $X1$:为 **提供** $X2$:NN ||| provides $X2$ $X1$
Head node in the rules are marked with bold face. NN is the POS tag of the source word "优惠".

Figure 2: examples of dependency to string rule ($r1$) and well-formed dependency to string rule ($r2$)

our definition and that in Shen et al., 2008 is that we only include the heads of subtrees in our structure, while they include the whole subtrees. The shadowed part with red box in Figure 1(b) is an example of fixed structure, which consists of a head "提供" and the heads of two continuous sibling trees "为了" and "报酬". And the shadowed part with green box in Figure 1(b) is an example of floating structure, which consists of the heads of three continuous sibling trees "美国", "不" and "会".

Given a sentence $w_1 w_2 ... w_n$, let d_i denote the head index of w_i, our fixed and floating structure can be formally defined as follows,

Definition 1

A fixed structure $f_{h,C}$ with head h and children C, where $h \in [1, n]$ and $C \subseteq \{1, ..., n\}$, is a two-level tree fragment which satisfies the following conditions:

– $\forall k \in C,\ d_k = h$

– $\forall \min(C) \leq k \leq \max(C),\ d_k \neq h$

Definition 2 A floating structure f_C with children C, where $C \subseteq \{1, ..., n\}$, is a one level tree fragment which satisfies the following conditions:

– $\exists h,\ \forall k \in C,\ d_k = h$

– $\forall \min(C) \leq k \leq \max(C),\ d_k \neq h$

3.2 Well-Formed Dependency-to-String Rule

Our well-formed dependency to string translation rule consists of a well-formed dependency structure in the source side and its translation correspondence in the target side. This definition extends the rule proposed in (Xie et al., 2011) to cover all well-formed dependency structures in the source side, rather than using complete head-dependents structures only. The rule $r2$ is an examples of our translation rule. Compared with $r1$, this rule does not contain "布什" in the source side (and its translation in the target side). Since it contains less context, this rule is more flexible to be applied during decoding. For example, if "布什" is replaced with a pronoun "他" in a testing sentence, this rule can still be applied. However, $r1$ cannot be applied in this case even if it is generalized, since the POS tag of "他" does not match that of "布什".

Our translation rules can be extracted from aligned dependency tree and string pair by traversing the tree and enumerating the well-formed structure at each node. Following previous work(Koehn et al., 2003; Galley et al., 2004; Chiang, 2005), we impose alignment constraint for rule extraction. The intuition is that words in the one side (source/target) cannot be aligned to words outside the other side, and the word alignment within non-terminals also need to satisfy this constraint.

Formally, for a non-terminal node n, we define node span $nsp(n)$ as the closure of the indexes of those words that n is alinged to, and sub-tree span $ssp(n)$ as the closure of node spans of all the nodes in the subtree rooted with n. These two spans are set to ϕ for terminals. In addition, we use N_s to denote the set of all the terminal indexes in the source side, and N_t to denote the set of all the terminal indexes in the target side. Function $a(\cdot)$ is used to get the indexes of the aligned words for a give word. Then the alignment constraint can be described as follows,

– $\forall k \in N_s,\ a(k) \in N_t$

– $\forall k \in N_t,\ a(k) \in N_s$

– $nsp(head) \cap_{n \in children} ssp(n) = \Phi$

A minor difference in our constraint with (Xie et al., 2011) is that we allow the alignment of terminals to be overlaped. For example, in Figure 1(b), if the two terminals "不" and "会" align to a single target word "won't", we consider the alignment constraint is satisfied, while they consider it as invalid.

3.3 Apply Dependency to String Rules with BTG Rules

We use the examples in Figure 1 to illustrate how the well-formed dependency to string rules together with BTG rules can be used to overcome the problems of parsing error and flatness. A plausible derivation for the example in Figure 1(a) is shown in Figure 3, in which the subtree "与...的", the floating structure "少数国家" and the head node is translated first, then the translations of the first two parts can be combined with a BTG rule of swap order. The final translation can be achieved by applying another BTG rule of swap order to the translation just obtained and the translation of "之一". Note that this is not the only derivation that can lead to a correct translation. We can also combine the translation of floating structure "少数国家" and the head node first, then combine with the translation of the first subtree. Similarly, for the example in Figure 1(b), we can first translate the floating structure "美国不会" and the fixed structure "为了...提供...报酬", then combine them with an BTG rule of monotone order to produce the final translation.

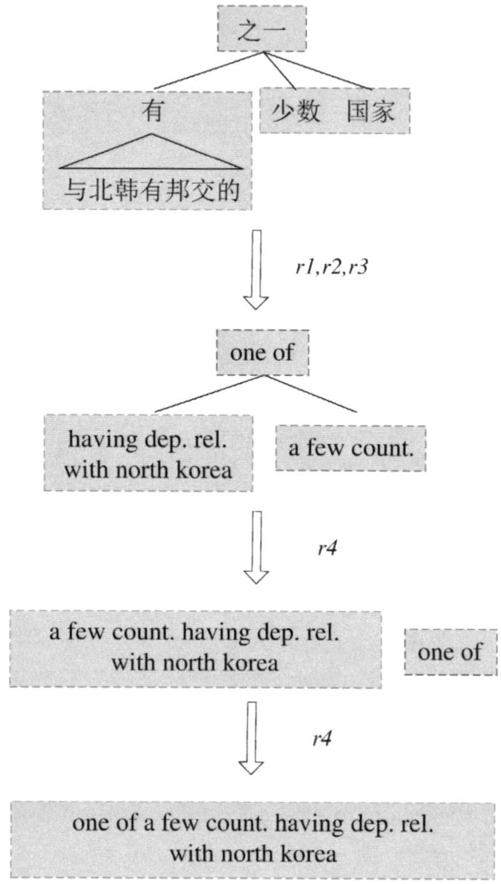

r1: 之一 ||| one of
r2: 与北韩有邦交的 ||| having dep. rel. with north korea
r3: 少数国家 ||| a few countries
r4: *X1 X2* ||| *X2 X1*

Figure 3: a plausible derivation with well-formed dependency to string and BTG grammar for the example in Figure 1(a)

4 Decoding

4.1 Model

We use the standard log-linear model (Och and Ney, 2002) to score the translation hypothesis during decoding. For a specific derivation d that converts a source dependency tree T into a target string s, the score of d will be,

$$P(d) \propto \prod_i \phi_i(d)^{\lambda_i}$$

where ϕ_i are features defined on derivations and λ_i are corresponding weight for each feature. The features adopted in this paper include bidirectional translation probabilities, bidirectional lexical weights, language model, rule penalty, word penalty and reordering probability for BTG rules.

For the last feature, we use a maximum entropy model to estimation the probability and the same features in (Xiong et al., 2006) are adopted, including beginning and ending words in the two blocks to be reordered, from both the source and target side. So there are eight activated features in total for each instance.

4.2 Decoding Algorithm

The decoding algorithm is described in Algorithm 1. The algorithm begins by translating each word in the sentence, then proceed to translate larger spans

Algorithm 1: CKY decoding algorithm with well formed dependency to string rules

```
Input: Source dependency tree T with N words
Output: Target translation
for span:1 → N do
    for start:1 → N+1-span do
        generate initial candidates with well formed dependency to string rule;
        for span_lhs:1 → span-1 do
            if {span_lhs,span_rhs,span} ⊆ well-formed structure then
                generate initial candidates with BTG rules;
            end
        end
        generate KBEST candidates with cube pruning;
    end
end
return the top candidate over the whole sentence as output;
```

in an bottom up manner. When translating a span compatible with a well-formed structure, there are two ways to generate translation candidates. One is based on fixed or floating rules which covers the whole span, and the other is combining the translation candidates in two sub-spans with BTG rule of monotone or swap order. The two sub-spans also need to be compatible with well-formed structure. The cube prunning algorithm (Chiang, 2007; Huang and Chiang, 2007) is used to expand the initial candidates until Kbest candidates have been generated. Finally, the top candidate over the whole sentence will be returned as output.

5 Experiments

We evaluate the performance of our model on Chinese to English translation. And we re-implement the dependency to string model for performance comparison.

5.1 Data preparation

Two sets of training data are adopted in our experiments. The smaller one consists of 270k sentence pairs, and the larger one consists of 2.1M sentence pairs. All the training data comes from the LDC corpus[1]. And we use NIST 02 test set as our development set, NIST 03 and 04 test set as our test set. The case insensitive NIST BLEU-4 metric (Papineni et al., 2002) is adopted for evaluation. We use the SRILM toolkit to train a 5-gram language model with Kneser-Ney smoothing on the Xinhua portion of the Gigaword corpus.

The source side of the training and dev/test set are segmented with our in house segmentation tool (Wang et al., 2010).And they are parsed with Stanford Parser (De Marneffe et al., 2006), which also generates POS tag for each word. The dependency relations on edges are not used in this work.

Word alignments are obtained with our in house tool (Wang and Zong, 2013), which takes dependency cohesion constraints into consideration while doing word alignments. And we use the MaxEnt toolkit[2] to to estimate the context sensitive reordering probability for BTG rules. The weights of the features are tuned with MERT (Och, 2003) to maximize the BLEU score on the development set.

5.2 Results

The strength of our model lies in two aspects. First, our translation unit is more fine-grained than that in the original dependency to tree model, which enables the translation of many linguistically plausible phrases; second, we allow flexible reorderings for adjacent blocks under the guide of context information. To check whether these two points hold, two sets of experiments are conducted in line. Initially,

[1]Including LDC2000T50, LDC2002E18, LDC2003E07, LDC2003E14, LDC200407, LDC2005T06, LDC2002L27, LDC2005T10 and LDC 2005T34.

[2]https://github.com/lzhang10/maxent

System	02 (dev)	03	04	Average
dep2str	33.50	31.92	32.59	32.67
wf-d2s (mono)	35.03	33.31	34.50	34.28
wf-d2s	**35.86**	**34.04**	**35.20**	**35.03**

Table 1: Effects of applying well-formed dependency to string rules and allowing flexible reordering. The system wf-d2s (mono) denotes our well-formed dependency to string model with monotone reordering, and wf-d2s denotes our model with flexible reordering of two directions.

System	02 (dev)	03	04	Average
dep2str	35.24	34.45	34.50	34.73
wf-d2s	**37.07***	**36.38***	**37.01***	**36.82**

Table 2: Experiment results with small and large training data. The "*" denotes that the results are significantly better than the baseline (dep2str) system (p<0.01).

we only allow BTG rule with monotone order, i.e. translation of each well-formed structure are concatenated sequentially, which is equivalent to glue rule. Then BTG rules with both orders are enabled, with context sensitive reordering module. We conduct the experiments with the small training data set. The results are shown in Table 1. Compared with dependency to string rules, applying well-formed dependency to string rules significantly improves the performance by more than 1.5 BLEU score on average. If flexible reordering is further allowed, additional improvement of 0.7 BLEU score can be achieved.

Table 2 shows the performance of our model with large training set. Experiment results show that our model keeps its edge even with large training data. On average, more than 2 point in BLEU score are gained over the baseline. This improvement is much larger than (Meng et al., 2013) and (Xie et al., 2014). Both of them report improvement of about 0.9 point in BLEU score over the baseline on their dataset.

6 Related Work

The work that is most similar to ours is (Xie et al., 2014). However, there are several significant differences between these two work. First They incorporate well-formed dependency rules during decoding by modify the matched dependency rules "on the fly". For example, assume there is a matched rule "$X1$:NR $X2$:AD $X3$:VV $X1$:为了提供 $X2$:报酬||| X1 X2 X3 provide X5 X4" for the head-dependents structure in Figure 1 (b). in order to use the phrase "美国不会||| us won't" during decoding, they will compress the three nodes into one pseudo node "NR_AD_VV". Then the above rule will become "$X1$:NR_AD_VV $X2$:为了* 提供 $X3$:报酬||| $X1$ provide $X3$ $X2$". This new rule will inherit the translation probabilities from the original rule. In the case that there is no matched rule or the probability estimation is unreliable due to sparsity, this method won't work well. Another difference is that they only use phrasal rules corresponding to well formed dependency structures, while we allow variables to be contained in the well-formed dependency rules.

The two problems of parsing error and flatness also exist in constituency tree . In order to make full use of the sub-structures, there have been a lot of work, including tree sequence to string translation (Liu et al., 2007), tree binarization (Zhang et al., 2006), forest-based translation (Mi et al., 2008) and fuzzy rule matching (Zhang et al., 2011).

7 Conclusion and Future Work

In this work, we propose a well-formed dependency to string model to address the problems of parsing error and flatness. By introducing translation rules corresponding to well-formed sub-structures, we are able to learn more reliable translation equivalents. During decoding, we propose to use BTG grammar with lexicalized reordering to combine translations of two neighbouring well-formed structures, which is more flexible than previous work. Experiment results demonstrate that our model can significantly improve translation performance.

Although our model is more flexible to generate translation candidates, it also brings more challenges to model translation quality. In the future, we will explore more powerful features to better score the translation candidates.

Acknowledgments

This research work was funded by the Natural Science Foundation of China under Grant No. 61402478. The authors would like to thank Keh-Yih Su for insightful discussions.

References

David Chiang. 2005. A hierarchical phrase-based model for statistical machine translation. In *Proceedings of the 43rd Annual Meeting of the Association for Computational Linguistics (ACL'05)*, pages 263–270, Ann Arbor, Michigan, June. Association for Computational Linguistics.

David Chiang. 2007. Hierarchical phrase-based translation. *computational linguistics*, 33(2):201–228.

Marie-Catherine De Marneffe, Bill MacCartney, and Christopher Manning. 2006. Generating typed dependency parses from phrase structure parses. In *Proceedings of LREC*, volume 6, pages 449–454.

Yuan Ding and Martha Palmer. 2005. Machine translation using probabilistic synchronous dependency insertion grammars. In *Proceedings of the 43rd Annual Meeting of the Association for Computational Linguistics (ACL'05)*, pages 541–548, Ann Arbor, Michigan, June. Association for Computational Linguistics.

Heidi Fox. 2002. Phrasal cohesion and statistical machine translation. In *Proceedings of the 2002 Conference on Empirical Methods in Natural Language Processing*, pages 304–3111. Association for Computational Linguistics, July.

Michel Galley, Mark Hopkins, Kevin Knight, and Daniel Marcu. 2004. What's in a translation rule? In Daniel Marcu Susan Dumais and Salim Roukos, editors, *HLT-NAACL 2004: Main Proceedings*, pages 273–280, Boston, Massachusetts, USA, May 2 - May 7. Association for Computational Linguistics.

Aria Haghighi, John Blitzer, John DeNero, and Dan Klein. 2009. Better word alignments with supervised itg models. In *Proceedings of the Joint Conference of the 47th Annual Meeting of the ACL and the 4th International Joint Conference on Natural Language Processing of the AFNLP*, pages 923–931, Suntec, Singapore, August. Association for Computational Linguistics.

Liang Huang and David Chiang. 2007. Forest rescoring: Faster decoding with integrated language models. In *Proceedings of the 45th Annual Meeting of the Association of Computational Linguistics*, pages 144–151, Prague, Czech Republic, June. Association for Computational Linguistics.

Damianos Karakos, Jason Eisner, Sanjeev Khudanpur, and Markus Dreyer. 2008. Machine translation system combination using itg-based alignments. In *Proceedings of ACL-08: HLT, Short Papers*, pages 81–84, Columbus, Ohio, June. Association for Computational Linguistics.

Philipp Koehn, Franz Josef Och, and Daniel Marcu. 2003. Statistical phrase-based translation. In *Proceedings of the 2003 Conference of the North American Chapter of the Association for Computational Linguistics on Human Language Technology-Volume 1*, pages 48–54. Association for Computational Linguistics.

Peng Li, Yang Liu, and Maosong Sun. 2013. Recursive autoencoders for ITG-based translation. In *Proceedings of the 2013 Conference on Empirical Methods in Natural Language Processing*, pages 567–577, Seattle, Washington, USA, October. Association for Computational Linguistics.

Dekang Lin. 2004. A path-based transfer model for machine translation. In *Proceedings of Coling 2004*, pages 625–630, Geneva, Switzerland, Aug 23–Aug 27. COLING.

Yang Liu, Yun Huang, Qun Liu, and Shouxun Lin. 2007. Forest-to-string statistical translation rules. In *Proceedings of the 45th Annual Meeting of the Association of Computational Linguistics*, pages 704–711, Prague, Czech Republic, June. Association for Computational Linguistics.

Fandong Meng, Jun Xie, Linfeng Song, Yajuan Lü, and Qun Liu. 2013. Translation with source constituency and dependency trees. In *Proceedings of the 2013 Conference on Empirical Methods in Natural Language Processing*, pages 1066–1076, Seattle, Washington, USA, October. Association for Computational Linguistics.

Haitao Mi, Liang Huang, and Qun Liu. 2008. Forest-based translation. In *Proceedings of ACL-08: HLT*, pages 192–199, Columbus, Ohio, June. Association for Computational Linguistics.

Franz Josef Och and Hermann Ney. 2002. Discriminative training and maximum entropy models for statistical machine translation. In *Proceedings of 40th Annual Meeting of the Association for Computational Linguistics*, pages 295–302, Philadelphia, Pennsylvania, USA, July. Association for Computational Linguistics.

Franz Josef Och. 2003. Minimum error rate training in statistical machine translation. In *Proceedings of the 41st Annual Meeting of the Association for Computational Linguistics*, pages 160–167, Sapporo, Japan, July. Association for Computational Linguistics.

Kishore Papineni, Salim Roukos, Todd Ward, and Wei-Jing Zhu. 2002. Bleu: a method for automatic evaluation of machine translation. In *Proceedings of 40th*

Annual Meeting of the Association for Computational Linguistics, pages 311–318, Philadelphia, Pennsylvania, USA, July. Association for Computational Linguistics.

Adam Pauls, Dan Klein, David Chiang, and Kevin Knight. 2010. Unsupervised syntactic alignment with inversion transduction grammars. In *Human Language Technologies: The 2010 Annual Conference of the North American Chapter of the Association for Computational Linguistics*, pages 118–126, Los Angeles, California, June. Association for Computational Linguistics.

Chris Quirk, Arul Menezes, and Colin Cherry. 2005. Dependency treelet translation: Syntactically informed phrasal SMT. In *Proceedings of the 43rd Annual Meeting of the Association for Computational Linguistics (ACL'05)*, pages 271–279, Ann Arbor, Michigan, June. Association for Computational Linguistics.

Libin Shen, Jinxi Xu, and Ralph Weischedel. 2008. A new string-to-dependency machine translation algorithm with a target dependency language model. In *Proceedings of ACL-08: HLT*, pages 577–585, Columbus, Ohio, June. Association for Computational Linguistics.

Zhiguo Wang and Chengqing Zong. 2013. Large-scale word alignment using soft dependency cohesion constraints. *Transactions of the Association for Computational Linguistics*, 1:291–300.

Kun Wang, Chengqing Zong, and Keh-Yih Su. 2010. A character-based joint model for chinese word segmentation. In *Proceedings of the 23rd International Conference on Computational Linguistics (Coling 2010)*, pages 1173–1181, Beijing, China, August. Coling 2010 Organizing Committee.

Dekai Wu. 1997. Stochastic inversion transduction grammars and bilingual parsing of parallel corpora. *Computational linguistics*, 23(3):377–403.

Jun Xie, Haitao Mi, and Qun Liu. 2011. A novel dependency-to-string model for statistical machine translation. In *Proceedings of the 2011 Conference on Empirical Methods in Natural Language Processing*, pages 216–226, Edinburgh, Scotland, UK., July. Association for Computational Linguistics.

Jun Xie, Jinan Xu, and Qun Liu. 2014. Augment dependency-to-string translation with fixed and floating structures. In *Proceedings of COLING 2014, the 25th International Conference on Computational Linguistics: Technical Papers*, pages 2217–2226, Dublin, Ireland, August. Dublin City University and Association for Computational Linguistics.

Deyi Xiong, Qun Liu, and Shouxun Lin. 2006. Maximum entropy based phrase reordering model for statistical machine translation. In *Proceedings of the 21st International Conference on Computational Linguistics and 44th Annual Meeting of the Association for Computational Linguistics*, pages 521–528, Sydney, Australia, July. Association for Computational Linguistics.

Hao Zhang and Daniel Gildea. 2005. Stochastic lexicalized inversion transduction grammar for alignment. In *Proceedings of the 43rd Annual Meeting of the Association for Computational Linguistics (ACL'05)*, pages 475–482, Ann Arbor, Michigan, June. Association for Computational Linguistics.

Hao Zhang, Liang Huang, Daniel Gildea, and Kevin Knight. 2006. Synchronous binarization for machine translation. In *Proceedings of the Human Language Technology Conference of the NAACL, Main Conference*, pages 256–263, New York City, USA, June. Association for Computational Linguistics.

Jiajun Zhang, Feifei Zhai, and Chengqing Zong. 2011. Augmenting string-to-tree translation models with fuzzy use of source-side syntax. In *Proceedings of the 2011 Conference on Empirical Methods in Natural Language Processing*, pages 204–215, Edinburgh, Scotland, UK., July. Association for Computational Linguistics.

Large-scale Dictionary Construction via Pivot-based Statistical Machine Translation with Significance Pruning and Neural Network Features

Raj Dabre[1], **Chenhui Chu**[2], **Fabien Cromieres**[2], **Toshiaki Nakazawa**[2], **Sadao Kurohashi**[1]
[1]Graduate School of Informatics, Kyoto University
[2]Japan Science and Technology Agency
prajdabre@gmail.com, (chu,fabien,nakazawa)@pa.jst.jp, kuro@i.kyoto-u.ac.jp

Abstract

We present our ongoing work on large-scale Japanese-Chinese bilingual dictionary construction via pivot-based statistical machine translation. We utilize statistical significance pruning to control noisy translation pairs that are induced by pivoting. We construct a large dictionary which we manually verify to be of a high quality. We then use this dictionary and a parallel corpus to learn bilingual neural network language models to obtain features for reranking the n-best list, which leads to an absolute improvement of 5% in accuracy when compared to a setting that does not use significance pruning and reranking.

1 Introduction

Pivot-based statistical machine translation (SMT) (Wu and Wang, 2007) has been shown to be a possible way of constructing a dictionary for the language pairs that have scarce parallel data (Tsunakawa et al., 2009; Chu et al., 2015). The assumption of this method is that there is a pair of large-scale parallel data: one between the source language and an intermediate resource rich language (henceforth called pivot), and one between that pivot and the target language. We can use the source-pivot and pivot-target parallel data to develop a source-target term[1] translation model for dictionary construction.

Pivot-based SMT uses the log linear model as conventional phrase-based SMT (Koehn et al., 2007) does. This method can address the data sparseness problem of directly merging the source-pivot and pivot-target terms, because it can use the portion of terms to generate new terms. Small-scale experiments in (Tsunakawa et al., 2009) showed very low accuracy of pivot-based SMT for dictionary construction.[2]

This paper presents our study to construct a large-scale Japanese-Chinese (Ja-Zh) scientific dictionary, using large-scale Japanese-English (Ja-En) ($49.1M$ sentences and $1.4M$ terms) and English-Chinese (En-Zh) ($8.7M$ sentences and $4.5M$ terms) parallel data via pivot-based SMT. We generate a large pivot translation model using the Ja-En and En-Zh parallel data. Moreover, a small direct Ja-Zh translation model is generated using small-scale Ja-Zh parallel data. ($680k$ sentences and $561k$ terms). Both the direct and pivot translation models are used to translate the Ja terms in the Ja-En dictionaries to Zh and the Zh terms in the Zh-En dictionaries to Ja to construct a large-scale Ja-Zh dictionary (about $3.6M$ terms).

We address the noisy nature of pivoting large phrase tables by statistical significance pruning (Johnson et al., 2007). In addition, we exploit linguistic knowledge of common Chinese characters (Chu et al., 2013) shared in Ja-Zh to further improve the translation model. Large-scale experiments on scientific domain data indicate that our proposed method achieves high quality dictionaries which we manually verify to have a high quality.

Reranking the n-best list produced by the SMT decoder is known to help improve the translation quality given that good quality features are used (Och et al., 2004). In this paper, we use bilingual neural network language model features for reranking the n-best list produced by the pivot-based system which uses significance pruning, and achieve a 2.5% (absolute) accuracy improvement. Compared to a setting which uses neither significance pruning nor n-best list reranking the improvement in accu-

[1] In this paper, we call the entries in the dictionary terms. A term consists of one or multiple tokens.

[2] The highest accuracy evaluated based on the 1 best translation is 21.7% in (Tsunakawa et al., 2009).

29th Pacific Asia Conference on Language, Information and Computation pages 289 - 297
Shanghai, China, October 30 - November 1, 2015

racy is about 5% (absolute). We also use character based neural MT to eliminate the out-of-vocabulary (OOV) terms, which further improves the quality.

The rest of this paper is structured as follows: Section 2 reviews related work. Section 3 presents our dictionary construction using pivot-based SMT with significance pruning. Section 4 describe the bilingual neural language model features using a parallel corpus and the constructed dictionary for reranking the n-best list. Experiments and results are described in Section 5, and we conclude this paper in Section 6.

2 Related Work

Many studies have been conducted for pivot-based SMT. Utiyama and Isahara (2007) developed a method (sentence translation strategy) for cascading a source-pivot and a pivot-target system to translate from source to target using a pivot language. Since this results in multiplicative error propagation, Wu and Wang (2009) developed a method (triangulation) in which they combined the source-pivot and pivot-target phrase tables to obtain a source-target phrase table. They then combine the pivoted and direct tables (using source-target parallel corpora) by linear interpolation whose weights were manually specified. There is a method to automatically learn the interpolation weights (Sennrich, 2012) but it requires reference phrase pairs which are not easily available. Work on translation from Indonesian to English using Malay and Spanish to English using Portuguese (Nakov and Ng, 2009) as pivot languages worked well since the pivots had substantial similarity to the source languages. They used the multiple decoding paths (MDP) feature of the phrase-based SMT toolkit Moses (Koehn et al., 2007) to combine multiple tables which avoids interpolation. The issue of noise introduced by pivoting has not been seriously addressed and although statistical significance pruning (Johnson et al., 2007) has shown to be quite effective in a bilingual scenario, it has never been considered in a pivot language scenario.

(Tsunakawa et al., 2009) was the first work that constructs a dictionary for language pairs that are resource poor using pivot-based SMT, however the experiments were performed on small-scale data. Chu et al. (2015) conducted large-scale experiments and exploited the linguistic knowledge of common Chinese characters shared in Japanese-Chinese (Chu et al., 2013) to improve the translation model.

N-best list reranking (Och et al., 2004; Sutskever et al., 2014) is known to improve the translation quality if good quality features are used. Recently, (Cho et al., 2014) and (Bahdanau et al., 2014) have shown that recurrent neural networks can be used for phrase-based SMT whose quality rivals the state of the art. Since the neural translation models can also be viewed as bilingual language models, we use them to obtain features for reranking the n-best lists produced by the pivot-based system.

3 Dictionary Construction via Pivot-based SMT

Figure 1 gives an overview of our construction method. Phrase-based SMT (Koehn et al., 2007) is the basis of our method. We first generate Ja-Zh (source-target), Ja-En (source-pivot) and En-Zh (pivot-target) phrase tables from parallel data respectively. The generated Ja-Zh phrase table is used as the direct table. Using the Ja-En and En-Zh phrase tables, we construct a Ja-Zh pivot phrase table via En. The direct and pivot tables are then combined and used for phrase-based SMT to the Ja terms in the Ja-En dictionaries to Zh and the Zh terms in the Zh-En dictionaries to Ja to construct a large-scale Ja-Zh dictionary. In addition, we use common Chinese characters to generate Chinese character features for the phrase tables to improve the SMT performance.

3.1 Pivot Phrase Table Generation

We follow the phrase table triangulation method (Wu and Wang, 2007) to generate the pivot phrase table. This method generates a source-target phrase table via all their shared pivot phrases in the source-pivot and pivot-target tables. The formulae for generating the inverse phrase translation probabilities and direct lexical weightings, $\phi(f|e)$ and $lex(f|e)$ are given below. Inverting the positions of **e** and **f** give the formulae for the direct probabilities and weightings, $\phi(e|f)$ and $lex(e|f)$.

$$\phi(f|e) = \sum_{p_i} \phi(f|p_i) * \phi(p_i|e) \tag{1}$$

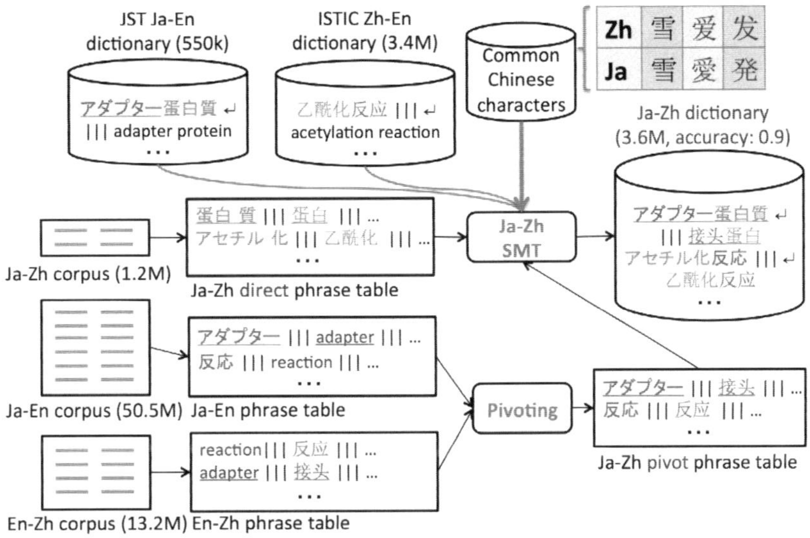

Figure 1: Overview of our dictionary construction method.

$$lex(f|e,a) = \sum_{p_i} lex(f|p_i, a_1) * lex(p_i|e, a_2) \quad (2)$$

where a_1 is the alignment between phrases f (source) and p_i (pivot), a_2 is the alignment between p_i and e (target) and a is the alignment between e and f. Note that the lexical weightings are calculated in the same way as the phrase probabilities. Our results might be further improved if we used more sophisticated approaches like the cross-language similarity method or the method which uses pivot induced alignments (Wu and Wang, 2007).

As pivoting induces a very large number of phrase pairs, we prune all pairs with inverse phrase translation probability less than 0.001. This manually specified threshold is simple, and works in practice but is not statistically motivated.

3.2 Combination of the Direct and Pivot Phrase Tables

To combine the direct and pivot phrase tables, we make use of the MDP method of the phrase-based SMT toolkit Moses (Koehn et al., 2007), which has been shown to be an effective method (Nakov and Ng, 2009). MDP, which uses all the tables simultaneously while decoding, ensures that each pivot table is kept separate and translation options are collected from all the tables.

3.3 Exploiting Statistical Significance Pruning for Pivoting

Consider a source-pivot phrase pair (X,Y) and a pivot-target phrase pair (Y,Z). If Y is a bad translation of X and Z is a bad translation of Y, then the induced pair (X,Z) will also be a bad pair. The phrase pair extraction processes in phrase-based SMT often result in noisy phrase tables, which when pivoted give even noisier tables. Statistical significance pruning (Johnson et al., 2007) is known to eliminate a large amount of noise and thus we used it to prune our tables before pivoting. We used the $\alpha + \epsilon$ threshold which is based on the parallel corpus size and shown to be optimal.

Although the optimal thresholds for a pivot based MT setting might be different, currently we consider only the $\alpha + \epsilon$ threshold which is determined to be the best by (Johnson et al., 2007). Exhaustive testing using various thresholds will be performed and reported in the future. The negative log probability of the p-value (also called significance value) of the phrase pair is computed and the pair is retained if this exceeds the threshold. It is possible that all phrase pairs for a source phrase might be pruned leading to an out-of-vocabulary (OOV) problem. To remedy this we retain the top 5 phrase pairs (according to inverse translation probability) for such a phrase. We tried 3 different settings: Prune source-pivot table only (labeled "Pr:S-P"), Prune pivot-target table only (labeled "Pr:P-T") and Prune both tables (labeled "Pr:Both"). We discuss the effects of each setting in Section 5.2.4.

3.4 Chinese Character Features

Ja-Zh shares Chinese characters. Because many common Chinese characters exist in Ja-Zh, they have been shown to be very effective in many Ja-Zh natural language processing (NLP) tasks (Chu et al., 2013). In this paper, we compute Chinese character features for the phrase pairs in the translation models, and integrate these features in the log-linear model for decoding. In detail, we compute following two features for each phrase pair:

$$CC\_ratio = \frac{Ja\_CC\_num + Zh\_CC\_num}{Ja\_char\_num + Zh\_char\_num} \quad (3)$$

$$CCC\_ratio = \frac{Ja\_CCC\_num + Zh\_CCC\_num}{Ja\_CC\_num + Zh\_CC\_num} \quad (4)$$

where $char\_num$, CC_num and CCC_num denote the number of characters, Chinese characters and common Chinese characters in a phrase respectively. The common Chinese character ratio is calculated based on the Chinese character mapping table in (Chu et al., 2013). We simply add these two scores as features to the phrase tables and use these tables for tuning and testing.

A combination of pivoting, statistical significance pruning and Chinese character features is used to construct the high quality large scale dictionary. One can use this dictionary as an additional component in an MT system. In our case we use it to generate features for N-best list reranking (next section).

4 N-best List Reranking using Neural Features

The motivation behind n-best list reranking is simple: It is quite common for a good translation candidate to be ranked lower than a bad translation candidate. However, it might be possible to use additional features to rerank the list of candidates in order to push the good translation to the top of the list. Figure 2 gives a simple description of the n-best list reranking procedure using neural features. Using the Ja-Zh dictionary constructed using the methods specified in Section 3 and the Ja-Zh ASPEC corpus we train

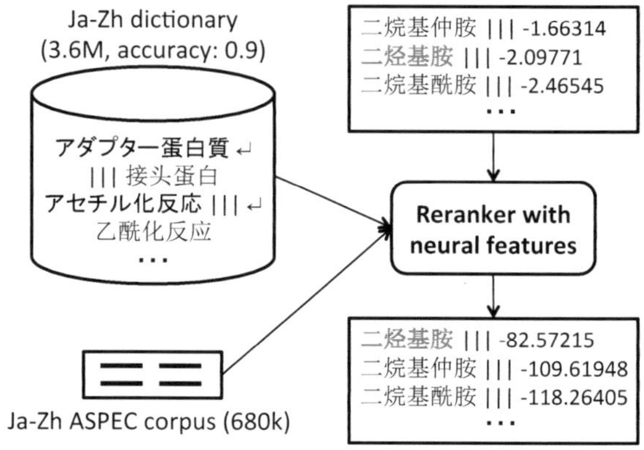

Figure 2: Using neural features for reranking.

4 neural translation models. For each translation direction we train a character based model using the dictionary and corpus separately (2 directions and 2 corpora lead to 4 models). It is important to note that although the dictionary is automatically created and is noisy, neural networks are quite robust and can regulate the noise quite effectively. This claim will be validated by our results (see Section 5.2.4). We use the freely available toolkit for neural MT, GroundHog[3], which contains an implementation of the work by (Bahdanau et al., 2014). After training a neural translation model it can be used either to translate an input sentence or it can be used to produce a score given an input sentence and a candidate translation. In the latter case, the neural translation model can be viewed as a **bilingual language model**.

One major limitation of neural network based models is that they are very slow to train in case of large vocabularies. It is possible to learn character based models but such models are not suited for extremely long sequences. In the case of Japanese and Chinese, however, since both languages use Chinese characters the character sequences are not too long and thus it makes sense to use character based MT here. Since the number of characters is quite smaller compared to the number of words, the training is quite fast. Ultimately, character based MT is always worse than word based MT and so, in this work we only use the character based neural MT models to obtain features for n-best list reranking. We also use

[3]https://github.com/lisa-groundhog/GroundHog

these models to perform character based translation of untranslated words and avoid OOVs.
The procedure we followed to perform reranking is given below. A decoder always gives n-best lists when performing tuning and testing. To learn reranking weights, we use the n-best list, for the tuning/development set, corresponding to the run with the highest evaluation metric score (BLEU in our case).

1. For each input term in the tuning set:
   (a) Obtain 4 neural translation scores for each translation candidate.
   (b) Append the 4 scores to the list of features for the candidate.
2. Use **kbmira**[4] to learn feature weights using the modified n-best list and the references for the tuning set.
3. Charater level BLEU as well as word level BLEU are used as reranking metric.
4. For each input term in the test set:
   (a) Obtain 4 neural translation scores for each translation candidate and append them to the list of features for that candidate.
   (b) Perform the linear combination of the learned weights and the features to get a model score.
5. Sort the n-best list for the test set using the calculated model scores (highest score is the best translation) to obtain the reranked list.

We also try another reranking method by treating it as a classification task using the support vector machine (SVM) toolkit.[5] When evaluating dictionaries, the translation is either correct or incorrect which is unlike sentence translation evaluation. We thus learn a SVM using the development set n-best list and the references to learn a classifier which is able to differentiate between a correct and an incorrect translation. The method we used for reranking is:

[4]We used the K-best batch MIRA in the Moses decoder to learn feature weights.

[5]https://www.csie.ntu.edu.tw/cjlin/libsvm/

1. For each input term in the tuning set:
   (a) Obtain 4 neural translation scores for each translation candidate.
   (b) Append the 4 scores to the list of features for the candidate.
   (c) Generate classification label for candidate by comparing it with the reference.
2. Learn SVM classifier using the constructed training set.
3. For each input term in the test set:
   (a) Obtain 4 neural translation scores for each translation candidate and append them to the list of features for that candidate.
   (b) Use the SVM model to perform classification but give the probability scores instead of labels.
4. Sort the n-best list for the test set using the calculated probability scores (highest score is the best translation) to obtain the reranked list.

If there are any OOVs in the reranked n-best list then we replace them with the translation obtained using the above mentioned character based neural models (in the Ja-Zh direction).

5 Experiments

We describe the data sets, experimental settings and evaluations of the results below.

5.1 Training data

We used following two types of training data:

- Bilingual dictionaries: we used general domain Ja-En, En-Zh and Ja-Zh dictionaries (i.e. Wikipedia title pairs and EDR[6]), and the scientific dictionaries provided by the Japan Science and Technology Agency (JST)[7] and the Institute of Science and Technology information of China (ISTIC)[8] (called the JST dictionary and ISTIC dictionary hereafter), containing $1.4M$, $4.5M$ and $561k$ term pairs respectively. Table 1

[6]https://www2.nict.go.jp/out-promotion/techtransfer/EDR/J_index.html

[7]http://www.jst.go.jp

[8]http://www.istic.ac.cn

Language	Name	Domain	Size
Ja-En	wiki_title	general	361,016
	med_dic	medicine	54,740
	EDR	general	491,008
	JST_dic	science	550,769
En-Zh	wiki_title	general	151,338
	med_dic	medicine	48,250
	EDR	general	909,197
	ISTIC_dic	science	3,390,792
Ja-Zh	wiki_title	general	175,785
	med_dic	medicine	54,740
	EDR	general	330,796

Table 1: Statistics of the bilingual dictionaries used for training.

Language	Name	Size
Ja-En	LCAS	3,588,800
	abst_title	22,610,643
	abst_JICST	19,905,978
	ASPEC	3,013,886
En-Zh	LCAS	6,090,535
	LCAS_title	1,070,719
	ISTIC_pc	1,562,119
Ja-Zh	ASPEC	680,193

Table 2: Statistics of the parallel corpora used for training (All the corpora belong to the general scientific domain, except for ISTIC_pc that is a computer domain corpus).

shows the statistics of the bilingual dictionaries used for training.

- Parallel corpora: the scientific Ja-En, En-Zh and Ja-Zh corpora we used were also provided by JST and ISTIC, containing $49.1M$, $8.7M$ and $680k$ sentence pairs respectively. Table 2 shows the statistics of parallel corpora used for training. Among which ISTIC_pc was provided by ISTIC, and the others were provided by JST.

5.2 Evaluation

5.2.1 Tuning and Testing data

We used the terms with two reference translations[9] in the Ja-Zh Iwanami biology dictionary (5,890 pairs) and the Ja-Zh life science dictionary (4,075 pairs) provided by JST. Half of the data in each dictionary was used for tuning (4,983 pairs), and the other half for testing (4,982 pairs). The evaluation scores on the test set give an idea of the quality of the constructed dictionary.

5.2.2 Settings

In our experiments, we segmented the Chinese and Japanese data using a tool proposed by Shen et al. (2014) and JUMAN (Kurohashi et al., 1994) respectively. For decoding, we used Moses (Koehn et al., 2007) with the default options. We trained a word 5-gram language model on the Zh side of all the En-Zh and Ja-Zh training data ($14.4M$ sentences) using the SRILM toolkit[10] with interpolated Keneser-Ney discounting. Tuning was performed by minimum error rate training which also provides us with the n-best lists used to learn reranking weights.

As a baseline, we compared following three methods for training the translation model:

- Direct: Only use the Ja-Zh data to train a direct Ja-Zh model.
- Pivot: Use the Ja-En and En-Zh data for training Ja-En and En-Zh models, and construct a pivot Ja-Zh model using the phrase table triangulation method.
- Direct+Pivot: Combine the direct and pivot Ja-Zh models using MDP.

We further conducted experiments using different significance pruning methods described in Section 3.3 and compared the following:

- Direct+Pivot (Pr:S-P): Pivoting after pruning the source-pivot table.
- Direct+Pivot (Pr:P-T): Pivoting after pruning the pivot-target table.
- Direct+Pivot (Pr:Both): Pivoting after pruning both the source-pivot and pivot-target tables.

We also conducted additional experiments using the Chinese character features (labeled +CC) (described in 3.4), but we only report the scores on Direct+Pivot (Pr:P-T), which is the best setting (thus labeled BS) for constructing the dictionary. Finally, using the

[9]Different terms are annotated with different number of reference translations in these two dictionaries.

[10]http://www.speech.sri.com/projects/srilm

BS, we translated the Ja terms in the JST ($550k$) dictionary to Zh and the Zh terms in the ISTIC ($3.4M$) dictionary to Ja, and constructed the Ja-Zh dictionary. The size of the constructed dictionary is $3.6M$ after discarding the overlapped term pairs in the two translated dictionaries. We then used this dictionary along with the Ja-Zh ASPEC parellel corpus to rerank the n-best list of the BS using the methods mentioned in Section 4. The following scores are reported:

- BS+RRCBLEU: Using character BLEU to rerank the n-best list.
- BS+RRWBLEU: Using word BLEU to rerank the n-best list.
- BS+RRSVM: Using SVM to rerank the n-best list.

This is followed by substituting the OOVs with the character level translations using the learned neural translation models (which we label as +OOVsub).

5.2.3 Evaluation Criteria

Following (Tsunakawa et al., 2009), we evaluated the accuracy on the test set using three metrics: 1 best, 20 best and Mean Reciprocal Rank (MRR)(Voorhees, 1999). In addition, we report the BLEU-4 (Papineni et al., 2002) scores that were computed on the word level.

5.2.4 Results of Automatic Evaluation

Table 3 shows the evaluation results. We also show the percentage of OOV terms,[11] and the accuracy with and without OOV terms respectively. In general, we can see that Pivot performs better than Direct, because the data of Ja-En and En-Zh is larger than that of Ja-Zh. Direct+Pivot shows better performance than either method.

Different pruning methods show different performances, where Pr:P-T improves the accuracy, while the other two not. To understand the reason for this, we also investigated the statistics of the pivot tables produced by different methods. Table 4 shows the statistics. We can see that compared to the other two pruning methods, Pr:P-T keeps the number of source phrases, which leads a lower OOV rate. It also prunes the number of average translations for each source phrase to a more reasonable number, which allows the decoder to make better decisions. Although the average number of translations for the Pr:Both setting is the smallest, it shows worse performance compared to Pr:P-T method. We suspect the reason for this is that many pivot phrases are pruned by Pr:Both, leading to fewer phrase pairs induced by pivoting. Augmenting with +CC leads to further improvements, and substituting the OOVs using their character level translation gives slightly better performance.

Method	Size	# src phrase	# avg trans
w/o pruning	29G	24,228	10,451
Pr:S-P	16G	19,502	7,058
Pr:P-T	5.5G	24,226	1,744
Pr:Both	2.8G	19,502	1,069

Table 4: Statistics of the pivot phrase tables (for tuning and test sets combined).

The most noteworthy results are obtained when reranking is performed using the bilingual neural language model features. BS+RRCBLEU, which uses character BLEU as a metric, performs almost as well as BS+RRWBLEU which uses word BLEU. There might be a difference in the BLEU scores of these 2 settings but the crucial aspect of dictionary evaluation is the accuracy regarding which there is no notable difference between them. We expected that since reranking using SVM, which focuses on accuracy and not BLEU, would yield better results but it might be the case that the training data obtained from the n-best lists is not very reliable. Finally, substuting the OOVs from the reranked lists further boosts the accuracies and although the increment is slight the OOV rate goes down to 0%. It is important to understand that the 20 best accuracy is 73% in the best case which means that if reranking is proper then it is possible to boost the accuracies by approximately 15%.

5.2.5 Results of Manual Evaluation

We manually investigated the terms, whose top 1 translation was evaluated as incorrect according to our automatic evaluation method. Based on our investigation, nearly 75% of them were actually correct translations. They were undervalued because

[11] An OOV term contains at least one OOV word.

Method	BLEU-4	OOV term	Accuracy w/ OOV			Accuracy w/o OOV		
			1 best	20 best	MRR	1 best	20 best	MRR
Direct	40.64	26%	0.3697	0.5255	0.4258	0.4978	0.7082	0.5736
Pivot	52.32	8%	0.4938	0.7258	0.5730	0.5361	0.7880	0.6220
Direct+Pivot	53.69	8%	0.5088	0.7360	0.5902	0.5522	0.7987	0.6405
Direct+Pivot (Pr:S-P)	52.30	12%	0.4944	0.6881	0.5649	0.5589	0.7779	0.6386
Direct+Pivot (Pr:P-T)	55.44	8%	0.5267	0.7278	0.5990	0.5716	0.7898	0.6500
Direct+Pivot (Pr:Both)	49.71	12%	0.4591	0.6766	0.5391	0.5189	0.7649	0.6094
Direct+Pivot (Pr:P-T)+CC = [BS]	55.86	8%	0.5303	0.7260	0.6005	0.5755	0.7878	0.6517
BS+OOVsub	55.38	0%	0.5325	0.7300	0.6033	0.5325	0.7300	0.6033
BS+RRCBLEU	57.78	8%	0.5568	0.7260	0.6222	**0.6042**	**0.7878**	**0.6752**
BS+RRWBLEU	**58.55**	8%	0.5566	0.7260	0.6218	0.6040	**0.7878**	0.6748
BS+RRSVM	55.28	8%	0.5472	0.7260	0.6147	0.5938	**0.7878**	0.6670
BS+RRCBLEU+OOVsub	57.25	0%	**0.5590**	**0.7300**	**0.6249**	0.5590	0.7300	0.6249
BS+RRWBLEU+OOVsub	58.00	0%	0.5588	**0.7300**	0.6246	0.5588	0.7300	0.6246
BS+RRSVM+OOVsub	54.85	0%	0.5494	**0.7300**	0.6174	0.5494	0.7300	0.6174

Table 3: Evaluation results.

they were not covered by the reference translations in our test set. Taking this observation into consideration, the actual 1 best accuracy is about 90%. Automatic evaluation tends to greatly underestimate the results because of the incompleteness of the test set.

5.3 Evaluating the Large Scale Dictionary

As mentioned before the setting Direct+Pivot (Pr:P-T)+CC was used to translate the Ja terms in the JST ($550k$) dictionary to Zh and the Zh terms in the ISTIC ($3.4M$) dictionary to Ja so as to construct the Ja-Zh dictionary. The size of the constructed dictionary is $3.6M$ after discarding the overlapped term pairs in the two translated dictionaries. Since we had no references to automatically evaluate this massive dictionary, we evaluated its accuracy by humans. We asked 4 Ja-Zh bilingual speakers to evaluate 100 term pairs, which were randomly selected the constructed dictionary. Figure 3 shows the web interface used for human evaluation. It allows the evaluators to correct errors and well as leave subjective comments, which can be used to refine our methods. The evaluation results indicate that the 1 best accuracy is about 90%, which is consistent with the manual evaluation results on the test set.

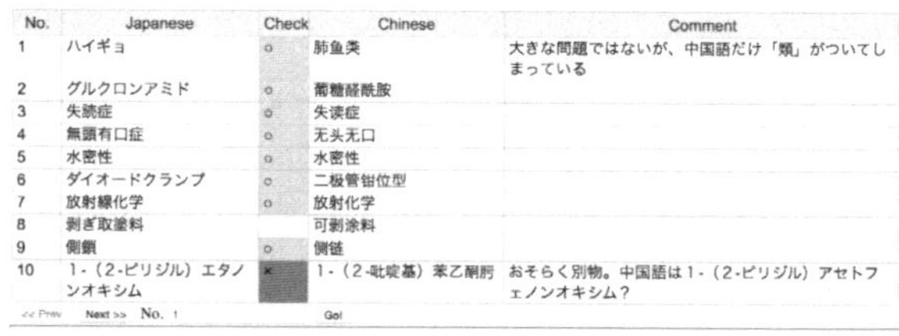

Figure 3: Human evaluation web interface.

6 Conclusion and Future Work

In this paper, we presented a dictionary construction method via pivot-based SMT with significance pruning, chinese character knowledge and bilingual neural network language model based features reranking. Large-scale Ja-Zh experiments show that our method is quite effective. Manual evaluations showed that 90% of the terms are correctly translated, which indicates a high practical utility value of the dictionary. We plan to make the constructed dictionary available to the public in near future, and hope that crowdsourcing could be further used to improve it.

We observed that the weights learned for the neural features and found out that the highest weight was assigned to the feature obtained using the model learned using this dictionary. And since reranking did improve the accuracies on the test set, it is quite evident that this dictionary is of a fairly high quality. In the future we plan to try an iterative process, where we rerank the n-best list of this massive dictionary to get an improved dictionary on which we learn a better neural bilingual language model for reranking.

References

Dzmitry Bahdanau, Kyunghyun Cho, and Yoshua Bengio. 2014. Neural machine translation by jointly learning to align and translate. *CoRR*, abs/1409.0473.

Kyunghyun Cho, Bart van Merrienboer, Çaglar Gülçehre, Fethi Bougares, Holger Schwenk, and Yoshua Bengio. 2014. Learning phrase representations using RNN encoder-decoder for statistical machine translation. *CoRR*, abs/1406.1078.

Chenhui Chu, Toshiaki Nakazawa, Daisuke Kawahara, and Sadao Kurohashi. 2013. Chinese-japanese machine translation exploiting chinese characters. *ACM Transactions on Asian Language Information Processing (TALIP)*, 12(4):16:1–16:25.

Chenhui Chu, Raj Dabre, Toshiaki Nakazawa, and Sadao Kurohashi. 2015. Large-scale japanese-chinese scientific dictionary construction via pivot-based statistical machine translation. In *Proceedings of the 21st Annual Meeting of the Association for Natural Language Processing (NLP 2015)*, pages 99–102, Kyoto, Japan, Match.

Howard Johnson, Joel Martin, George Foster, and Roland Kuhn. 2007. Improving translation quality by discarding most of the phrasetable. In *Proceedings of the 2007 Joint Conference on Empirical Methods in Natural Language Processing and Computational Natural Language Learning (EMNLP-CoNLL)*, pages 967–975, Prague, Czech Republic, June. Association for Computational Linguistics.

Philipp Koehn, Hieu Hoang, Alexandra Birch, Chris Callison-Burch, Marcello Federico, Nicola Bertoldi, Brooke Cowan, Wade Shen, Christine Moran, Richard Zens, Chris Dyer, Ondrej Bojar, Alexandra Constantin, and Evan Herbst. 2007. Moses: Open source toolkit for statistical machine translation. In *Proceedings of ACL*, pages 177–180.

Sadao Kurohashi, Toshihisa Nakamura, Yuji Matsumoto, and Makoto Nagao. 1994. Improvements of Japanese morphological analyzer JUMAN. In *Proceedings of the International Workshop on Sharable Natural Language*, pages 22–28.

Preslav Nakov and Hwee Tou Ng. 2009. Improved statistical machine translation for resource-poor languages using related resource-rich languages. In *Proceedings of the 2009 Conference on Empirical Methods in Natural Language Processing: Volume 3 - Volume 3*, EMNLP '09, pages 1358–1367, Stroudsburg, PA, USA. Association for Computational Linguistics.

Franz Josef Och, Daniel Gildea, Sanjeev Khudanpur, Anoop Sarkar, Kenji Yamada, Alex Fraser, Shankar Kumar, Libin Shen, David Smith, Katherine Eng, Viren Jain, Zhen Jin, and Dragomir Radev. 2004. A smorgasbord of features for statistical machine translation. In Daniel Marcu Susan Dumais and Salim Roukos, editors, *HLT-NAACL 2004: Main Proceedings*, pages 161–168, Boston, Massachusetts, USA, May 2 - May 7. Association for Computational Linguistics.

Kishore Papineni, Salim Roukos, Todd Ward, and Wei-Jing Zhu. 2002. Bleu: a method for automatic evaluation of machine translation. In *Proceedings of ACL*, pages 311–318.

Rico Sennrich. 2012. Perplexity minimization for translation model domain adaptation in statistical machine translation. In *Proceedings of the 13th Conference of the European Chapter of the Association for Computational Linguistics*, EACL '12, pages 539–549, Stroudsburg, PA, USA. Association for Computational Linguistics.

Mo Shen, Hongxiao Liu, Daisuke Kawahara, and Sadao Kurohashi. 2014. Chinese morphological analysis with character-level pos tagging. In *Proceedings of ACL*, pages 253–258.

Ilya Sutskever, Oriol Vinyals, and Quoc V. Le. 2014. Sequence to sequence learning with neural networks. *CoRR*, abs/1409.3215.

Takashi Tsunakawa, Naoaki Okazaki, Xiao Liu, and Jun'ichi Tsujii. 2009. A chinese-japanese lexical machine translation through a pivot language. *ACM Transactions on Asian Language Information Processing (TALIP)*, 8(2):9:1–9:21, May.

Masao Utiyama and Hitoshi Isahara. 2007. A comparison of pivot methods for phrase-based statistical machine translation. In *in Proceedings of the conference on Human Language Technology Conference of the North American Chapter of the Association of Computational Linguistics (NAACL-HLT*, pages 484–491.

Ellen M. Voorhees. 1999. The TREC-8 question answering track report. In *Proceedings of the Eighth TExt Retrieval Conference (TREC-8)*, pages 77–82.

Hua Wu and Haifeng Wang. 2007. Pivot language approach for phrase-based statistical machine translation. *Machine Translation*, 21(3):165–181, September.

Hua Wu and Haifeng Wang. 2009. Revisiting pivot language approach for machine translation. In *Proceedings of the Joint Conference of the 47th Annual Meeting of the ACL and the 4th International Joint Conference on Natural Language Processing of the AFNLP: Volume 1 - Volume 1*, ACL '09, pages 154–162, Stroudsburg, PA, USA. Association for Computational Linguistics.

Annotation and Classification of French Feedback Communicative Functions

Laurent Prévot
Aix-Marseille Université
Laboratoire Parole et Langage
Aix-en-Provence, France
laurent.prevot@lpl-aix.fr

Jan Gorisch
Institut für Deutsche Sprache
Mannheim, Germany
gorisch@ids-mannheim.de

Sankar Mukherjee
Istituto Italiano di Tecnologia
Genova, Italy
sankar1535@gmail.com

Abstract

Feedback utterances are among the most frequent in dialogue. Feedback is also a crucial aspect of all linguistic theories that take social interaction involving language into account. However, determining communicative functions is a notoriously difficult task both for human interpreters and systems. It involves an interpretative process that integrates various sources of information. Existing work on communicative function classification comes from either dialogue act tagging where it is generally coarse grained concerning the feedback phenomena or it is token-based and does not address the variety of forms that feedback utterances can take. This paper introduces an annotation framework, the dataset and the related annotation campaign (involving 7 raters to annotate nearly 6000 utterances). We present its evaluation not merely in terms of inter-rater agreement but also in terms of usability of the resulting reference dataset both from a linguistic research perspective and from a more applicative viewpoint.

1 Introduction

Positive feedback tokens (*yeah, yes, mhm ...*) are the most frequent tokens in spontaneous speech. They play a crucial role in managing the common ground of a conversation. Several studies have attempted to provide a detailed quantitative analysis of these tokens in particular by looking at the form-function relationship (Allwood et al., 2007; Petukhova and Bunt, 2009; Gravano et al., 2012; Neiberg et al., 2013). About form, they looked at lexical choice, phonology and prosody. About communicative function, they considered in particular grounding, attitudes, turn-taking and dialogue structure management.

Despite the previous attempts to quantify that form-function relationship of feedback, we think that more work needs to be done on the conversational part of it. For example, Gravano et al. (2012) used automatic classification of *positive cue words*, however the underlying corpus consists of games, that are far off being "conversational" and therefore do not permit to draw any conclusions on how feedback is performed in conversational talk or talk-in-interaction. What concerns the selection of the feedback units, i.e. utterances, more work that clarifies what consists of feedback is also needed, as an approach that purely extracts specific lexical forms ("okay", "yeah", etc.) is not sufficient in order to account for feedback in general. Also, the question of what features to extract (acoustic, prosodic, contextual, etc.) is far from being answered. The aim of this paper is to shed some more light on these issues by taking data from real conversations, annotating communicative functions, extracting various features and using them in experiments to classify the communicative functions.

The study reported in this paper takes place in a project (Prévot and Bertrand, 2012) that aims to use, among other methodologies, quantitative clues to decipher the form-function relationship within feedback utterances. More precisely, we are interested in the creation of (large) datasets composed of feedback utterances annotated with communicative

29th Pacific Asia Conference on Language, Information and Computation pages 298 - 306
Shanghai, China, October 30 - November 1, 2015

functions. From these datasets, we conduce quantitative (statistical) linguistics tests as well as machine learning classification experiments.

After presenting feedback phenomena and reviewing the relevant literature (Section 2), we introduce our dataset (Section 3), annotation framework and annotation campaign (Section 4). After discussing the evaluation of the campaign (Section 5), we turn to the feature extraction (Section 6) and our first classification experiments (Section 7).

2 Feedback utterances

Definition and illustration Concerning the definition of the term *feedback utterance*, we follow Bunt (1994, p.27): *"Feedback is the phenomenon that a dialogue participant provides information about his processing of the partner's previous utterances. This includes information about perceptual processing (hearing, reading), about interpretation (direct or indirect), about evaluation (agreement, disbelief, surprise,...) and about dispatch (fulfillment of a request, carrying out a command, ...)."*

As a working definition of our class *feedback*, we could have followed Gravano et al. (2012), who selected their tokens according to the individual word transcriptions. Alternatively, Neiberg et al. (2013) performed an acoustic automatic detection of potential feedback turns, followed by a manual check and selection. But given our objective, we preferred to use perhaps more complex units that are closer to *feedback utterances*. We consider that feedback functions are expressed overwhelmingly through short utterances or fragments (Ginzburg, 2012) or in the beginning of potentially longer contributions. We therefore automatically extracted candidate feedback utterances of these two kinds. Utterances are however already sophisticated objects that would require a specific segmentation campaign. We rely on a rougher unit: the Inter-Pausal Unit (IPU). IPUs are stretches of talk situated between silent pauses of a given duration, here 200 milliseconds. An example of an *isolated feedback IPU* is illustrated in Figure 1a. In addition to isolated items, we added sequences of feedback-related lexical items situated at the very beginning of an IPU (see section 3 for more details and Figure 1b for an example).

Related work The study of feedback is generally associated with the study of *back-channels* (Yngve, 1970), the utterances that are not produced on the *main* communication channel in a way not to interfere with the flow of the main speaker. In the seminal work by Schegloff (1982), back-channels have been divided into *continuers* and *assessments*. While *continuers* are employed to make a prior speaker continue with an ongoing activity (e.g. the telling of a story), *assessments* are employed to evaluate the prior speaker's utterance.

A formal model for feedback items was proposed by Allwood et al. (1992). It includes four dimensions for analysing feedback: (i) Type of reaction to preceding communicative act; (ii) Communicative status; (iii) Context sensitivity to preceding communicative act; (iv) Evocative function. The first dimension roughly corresponds to the functions on the grounding scale as introduced by Clark (1996): *(contact / perception / understanding / attitudinal reaction)*. The second dimension corresponds to the way the feedback is provided *(indicated / displayed / signalled)*. The third dimension, *Context sensitivity*, is divided into three aspects of the previous utterance: mood *(statement / question / request / offer)*, polarity and information status of the preceding utterance in relation to the person who gives feedback. The fourth dimension, *Evocative function*, is much less developed but relates to what the feedback requires / evokes in the next step of the conversation.

Grounded in this previous work but more concerned with annotation constraints, especially in the context of multi-modal annotations, Allwood et al. (2007) use a much simpler framework that is associated with the annotation of turn management and discourse sequencing. The feedback analysis is split into three dimensions: (i) basic *(contact, perception, understanding)*; (ii) acceptance; (iii) emotion / attitudes that do not receive an exhaustive list of values but include *happy, surprised, disgusted, certain,* etc.

Muller and Prévot (2003; Muller and Prévot (2009) have focused on more contextual aspects of feedback: function of the feedback target and feedback *scope*.The work relies on a full annotation of communicative functions for an entire corpus. The annotations of feedback-related functions and of feedback scope are reported to be reliable. However, the dataset analysed is small. and the guide-

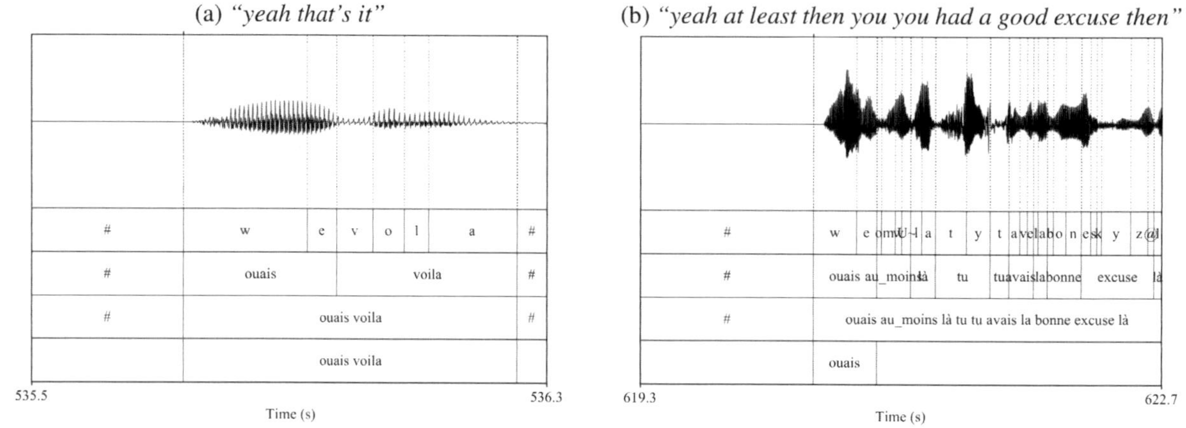

Figure 1: Approximation of feedback items. Isolated feedback (left); Initial feedback item sequence (right).

lines are genre-specific (route instruction dialogues) while we intend here a generalisable approach.

More recent frameworks include work by Gravano et al. (2012) who propose a flat typology of affirmative cue word functions. This typology mixes *grounding* functions with *discourse sequencing* and other unrelated functions. It includes for example *Agreement, Backchannel*, discourse segment *Cue-Beginning* and *Cue-Ending* but also a function called *Literal modifier*. The reason for such a broad annotation is that every instance of an affirmative cue word is extracted following a completely form-driven simple rule. Such an approach allows to create high-performance classifiers for specific token types but hardly relates to what is known about feedback utterances in general. Their dataset is therefore much more homogeneous than ours in terms of lexical forms but more diverse in terms of position since we did not extract feedback related tokens occurring for example in a medial or final position of an IPU. A token-based approach forbids to give justice to complex feedback items such as reduplicated positive cue words, and obvious combinations such as *ah ouais (=oh yeah), ok d'accord (=okeydoke)*. Their strategy is simply to annotate the first token and ignore the other. Our strategy is to capture potential compositional or constructional phenomena within feedback utterances. Moreover, even within a word-based approach, it is debatable to use space from a transcription to delineate the units of analysis. Some of these sequences could already be lexicalized within the actual spoken system. A final point concerns reduplicated words. It is often difficult to determine whether an item is *mh, mh mh* or *mh + mh*. While treating IPUs does not completely resolve this issue, it is more precise than only annotating the first token.

The form-driven approach by Neiberg et al. (2013) also combines automatic data selection with lexical and acoustic cues. As for the function annotation, they identify five scalar attributes related to feedback: *non-understanding – understanding, disagreement – agreement, uninterested – interested, expectation – surprise, uncertainty – certainty*. This scalar approach is appealing because many of these values seem to have indeed a scalar nature. We adopt this two tier approach to characterize communicative functions. We first identify a BASE function and when this function is taken to hold some deeper evaluative content such as agreement or the expression of some attitude, a second level EVALUATION is informed. Moreover, our approach considers that a crucial aspect of feedback utterances is their contextual adequacy and dependence. To test this hypothesis, we included an annotation for the *previous utterance* in our annotation framework (more detail in section 4).

3 Dataset

All data used in this study come from corpora including conversational interactions (CID) and task oriented dialogues (Aix-MapTask). Both corpora include native French speaking participants.

CID Conversation Interaction Data (CID) are audio and video recordings of participants having a conversational interaction with the mere instruction of talking about strange things to kick-off the conversation (Bertrand et al., 2008; Blache et al., 2010). The corpus contains 8 hours of audio recordings[1].

Aix-MapTask Remote The Aix-MapTask (Bard et al., 2013; Gorisch et al., 2014) is a reproduction of the original HCRC MapTask protocol (Anderson et al., 1991) in the French language. It involves 4 pairs of participants with 8 maps per pair and turning roles of giver and follower. The remote condition (MTR) contains audio recordings that sum up to 2h30 with an average of 6 min. 52 sec. per map[2].

Data extraction Our objective is to obtain a dataset that covers as completely as possible feedback utterances. We exploited our rather precise transcriptions (aligned with the signal at the phone level with the tool SPPAS (Bigi, 2012)) that include laughter, truncated words, filled pauses and other speech events. We started from the observation that the majority of feedback utterances are IPUs composed of only a few tokens. We first identified the small set of most frequent lexical items composing feedback utterances by building the lexical tokens distribution for IPUs made of three tokens or less. The 10 most frequent lexical forms are : *ouais / yeah (2781), mh (2321), d'accord / agree-right (1082), laughter (920), oui / yes (888), euh / uh (669), ok (632), ah (433), voil / that's it-right (360)*. The next ones are *et / and (360), non / no (319), tu / you (287), alors / then (151), bon / well (150)* and then follow a series of other pronouns and determiners with frequency dropping quickly. We excluded *tu, et* and *alors* as we considered their presence in these short isolated IPUs were not related to feedback. We then selected all isolated utterances in which the remaining items were represented and treated now each IPU as an instance of our dataset. As mentioned in the introduction, we also extracted feedback related token sequences situated at the beginning of IPUs. This yielded us a total of more than 7000 candidate feedback utterances.

In terms of coverage, given our heuristics for selecting feedback utterances, we miss most of the short utterances that are uniquely made of repetitions or reformulations (not including feedback related tokens). Our recall of feedback utterances is therefore not perfect. However, our final goal is to combine lexical items with prosodic and acoustic features. Therefore, our heuristics focus on these tokens. About lexical items, our coverage is excellent. Although there are some extra items that are not in our list, such as (*vachement* (a slang version of *'a lot'*) or *putain* (a swear word that is used as a discourse marker in rather colloquial French), these items remain relatively rare and moreover, they tend to co-occur with the items of our list. Therefore, most of their instances are part of our dataset in the *complex* category.The plus sign in *ouais+* and *mh+* stands for sequences of 2 or more *ouais* or *mh*. The token *complex* corresponds to all other short utterances extracted that did not correspond to any item from the list, e.g. *ah ouais d'accord, ah ben @ ouais,...*). For more details on the dataset, see Prévot et al. (2015).

4 Annotation of communicative functions

We ended up with 5473[3] cross-annotated candidate utterances from CID and MTR corpora. Although the initial annotation schema was fairly elaborate, not all the dimensions annotated yielded satisfactory inter-annotator agreement[4]. In this paper we focus on two articulated dimensions: the BASE, which is the base function of the feedback utterance *(contact, acknowledgment, evaluation-base, answer, elicit, other)*, and EVALUATION, which was informed when the *evaluation-base* value was selected as the BASE function (evaluations could be: *approval, unexpected, amused, confirmation*). The details for these two dimensions are provided in Table 1. We also asked annotators to rate what the function of the previous utterance of the interlocutor was *(assertion, question, feedback, try, request, incomplete, uninterpretable)*. Although circular, this last annotation was gathered to tell us how useful this kind of contextual information was for our task.

[1]The CID corpus is available online for research: http://www.sldr.org/sldr000027/en/.

[2]The description of MTR is available online: http://www.sldr.org/sldr000732.

[3]The difference from the original data points comes from missing annotation values and technical problems on some files.

[4]Dimensions related to feedback scope and the structure of the interaction were not consistently annotated by our naive annotators and will not be discussed here further.

To conduct the annotation campaign, seven undergraduate and master students were recruited. The campaign was realized on a duration of 2 months for most annotators. Annotating one feedback instance took on average 1 minute. We made sure that every instance received 3 concurrent annotations in order to be able to set-up a voting procedure for building the final dataset.

5 Evaluation

5.1 Inter-rater agreement

Concerning BASE value annotations, the average κ value for the best pair of raters for all the sub-datasets with enough instances to compute this value was around 0.6 for both corpora: MTR (min: 0.45; max: 0.96) and CID (min: 0.4; max: 0.85). Multi-κ yielded low values suggesting some raters were not following correctly the instructions (which was confirmed by closer data inspection). However, we should highlight that the task was not easy. There is a lot of ambiguity in these utterances and lexical items are only part of the story. For example, the most frequent token *ouais* could in principle be used to reach any of the communicative functions targeted. Even after close inspection by the team of experts, some cases are extremely hard to categorize. It is not even sure that the dialogue participants fully determined their meaning as several functions could be accommodated in a specific context.

While best pair's κ seems to be a very favorable evaluation measure, most of our samples received only 3 concurrent annotations. Moreover, aside a couple of exceptions, always the same two raters are excluded. As a result, what we call "best-pair kappa" is actually simply the removal of the annotation of the worse two raters from the dataset, which is a relatively standard practice. There could be a reason for these raters to behave differently from others. Because of timing issues, one annotator could not follow the training sessions with the others and had to catch up later. The other annotator did the training with the others but had to wait almost 2 months before performing the annotation.

Concerning EVALUATION values annotations, it is more complex to compute reliably an agreement to the sporadic nature of the annotation (evaluation values are only provided if the rater used this category in the BASE function). Since the set of raters that annotate a given sample varies, in most cases of MTR the number of instances annotated by a given set of raters is too small to compute reliably agreement. On the CID corpus, which has much larger samples, κ-measures of EVALUATION can be computed but exhibit huge variations with a low average of 0.3. This is indeed a difficult task since raters have to agree first on the BASE value and then on the value of the EVALUATION category. But, as we will see later, our voting procedure over cross-annotated datasets still yielded an interesting annotated dataset.

5.2 Quality of the reference dataset

In order to better understand the choice we have about data use and selection, we evaluated several datasets built according to different confidence thresholds.

For the `base` level, we started with the whole dataset and then built sub-datasets made of the same data but restricted to a certain threshold based on the number of raters that employ this category (threshold values: $\frac{1}{3}, \frac{1}{2}, \frac{2}{3}, \frac{3}{4}, 1$). More precisely, we computed a confidence score for each annotated instance. We then use these different datasets to perform two related tasks: classifying the functions of the whole dataset (using a `None` category for instances that did not reach the threshold) and classifying the functions within a dataset restricted to the instances that received an annotated category of a given threshold. In the case of the classification of `eval`, we first restricted the instances to the ones that received the `evaluation` value as value for the `base` category.

These datasets are ranging from noisy datasets (low threshold, full coverage) to cleaner ones but without full coverage. They correspond to two main objectives of an empirical study: (i) more linguistic / foundational studies would probably prefer to avoid some of the noise in order to establish more precise models to match their linguistic hypotheses, (ii) natural language engineering has no other choice than to work with the full dataset.

Composition of the dataset As for the BASE category distributions, the CID dataset is made of bit more than 40% of *ack* and *eval*, almost 15% of *others* and only 2% of *answer* ($\sim$2%). The MTR

Table 1: Annotated categories of communicative functions and their paraphrases.

Base Function	Paraphrase
contact	I am still here listening.
acknowledgment	I have heard / recorded what you said but nothing more.
evaluation-base	I express something more than mere acknowledgement (approval, expression of an attitude,...).
answer	I answer to your question / request.
elicit	Please, provide some feedback.
other	This item is not related to feedback.
Evaluation	
approval	I approve vs. disapprove / agree vs. disagree with what you said.
expectation	I expected vs. did not expect what you said.
amusement	I am amused vs. annoyed by what you said.
confirmation / doubt	I confirm what you said vs. I still doubt about what you said.

dataset, has a similar amount of *ack*, about 20% of *eval* and *answer*, 10% of *others* and 5% of the *elicit* category (that was basically absent from CID).

As for the EVALUATION category, CID is mostly made of *approbation* (46%) and *amused* (38%), then *confirmation* (8%) and *unexpected* (6%) while MTR has over 60% *confirmation*, only 13% *amused* feedback and 17% *approbation*.

6 Feature extraction

For our experiments, we focused on speech data and our dimensions include properties of items themselves: lexical content (LEX), acoustics (ACO); and properties of their context: apparition, timing and position (POS). We also use three more dimensions: contextual information extracted automatically (CTX-AUT), supplied manually by our annotators (MAN)[5] and meta-data (META). Some details about these features are provided here:

LEX transcription string + presence vs. absence of frequent lexical markers (16 features before binarization)

ACO pitch (min/max/stdev/height/span/steepness/ slope/NaN-ratio[6]), intensity (quartiles Q1, Q2, Q3), avg aperiodicity, formants (F1, F2, F3) and duration (16 features)

POS speech environment in terms of speech/pause duration before/after the item for both the speaker and the interlocutor; including overlap information (10 features)

CTX-AUT first/last tokens and bigrams of previous utterance and interlocutor previous utterance (18 features before binarization)

MAN function of the interlocutor's previous utterance, a circular information providing a kind of topline (1 feature)

META Corpus, Speaker, Session, Role (4 features)

For the classification experiments, all textual and nominal features have been binarized. All numeric features have been attributed min max threshold values and then normalized within these thresholds.

7 Classification experiments

7.1 Classification of the Base function

Our first task was to classify the BASE function. The dataset we used most intensively was the one in which we retain only the base functions proposed by at least $\frac{2}{3}$ of the annotators[7]. This is computationally difficult because none of the levels involved is enough to perform this task. As we will see, only a combination of dimensions allows us to reach interesting classification scores.

We first compared the impact of the classifier choice on the dataset. We set-up a *baseline* consisting of the majority class for each frequent lexical item. For example, all single *'mh'* are classified as *ack* because the majority of them are annotated

[5]This corresponds to the annotation of the previous utterance of the interlocutor within this list of labels: *assert, question, feedback, try (confirmation request), unintelligible, incomplete*.

[6]The ratio of unvoiced parts (NaN = Not a Number) and voiced parts of the F0 contour.

[7]The majority of the instances have been cross-annotated by three annotators.

with this function. Then, we took our full set of features (LEX+ACO+CTX-AUT) and ran many classification experiments with various estimators (Naive Bayes, Decision Tree, SVM and Ensemble classifiers - Ada Boost and Random Forest) that are part of the SCI-KIT LEARN Python library (Pedregosa et al., 2011) and several parameter sets. The *Random Forest* method performed best. One explanation for this can be that *Tree-based* classifiers have no problem handling different categories of feature sets and are not confused by useless features. A nice consequence is that it becomes easy to trace which features contribute the most to the classification. This point is indeed crucial for us who intend to clarify the combination of the different linguistic domains involved. For this reason, and because all the experiments (varying various parameters) always ended up with an advantage for *Random Forest*, we used this classifier (with 50 estimators and minimum size of leaves of 10 instances) for the rest of the study in this paper.

We also checked the learning curve with this classifier and we have seen that it brings already interesting results with only one third of the dataset.

Our second task was to vary the sets of features used. We wanted however to refine this experiment by looking separately at each corpus. In figures 2a and 2b, the feature sets tested are the BASELINE described above, only LEXical, ACOustic or POSitional featues, the combination of the three (LPA), ALL automatically extracted features and ALL + MANually annotated previous utterance function. All experiments have been conducted with 10-fold cross-validation providing us the standard deviations allowing significance comparison as can be seen with the error bars in the figures (typically these deviations range between 1% to 2% for BASE and from 3% to 4% with some deviations going up to 10% for EVALUATION).

The results illustrated in Figure 2a, once we know what our features are good at, can be largely explained by the distribution of the categories across the corpora. There are therefore not many *answer* instances (~2%) in this corpus, a category that is not well caught by our features yet. But LEX, POS and ACO are good to separate precisely *ack, eval* and *other*. The MTR dataset has much more *answers*, which explains the jump in f-measure if we add the manual annotation of the interlocutor's previous utterance (MAN). We simply did not manage to catch this contextual information with our features yet and this has a much stronger impact on MTR than on CID.

7.2 Classification of the evaluation function

We ran the same experiments for the EVALUATION category as presented in Figure 2b. The features used by the classifier are different. Within *evaluation cases*, POS becomes less informative while LEX and ACO retain their predictive power. Corpora differences explain the results. CID has much more AMUSED feedback that are well caught by lexical features. MTR has more *confirmations* that can be signalled by a specific lexical item *(voilà)* but that is also strongly dependent on which participant is considered to be competent about the current question under discussion.

7.3 Individual features contribution

A close inspection of some of the trees composing the Random Forest allows us to understand some of the rules used by the classifier across linguistic domains. Here are some of the most intuitive yet interesting rules:

- if acoustic values `pitch span` and `F1` increase, attitudinal (EVAL) values are more likely than mere `acknowledgment (ack)` and this on various situations.
- `aperiodicity` seems to have been used to catch `amused` values that would not be associated with a *laughter* in the transcription.
- the presence of *mh* and *laughter* in the transcription is a very good predictor of `ack` (in the BASE task) and `amused` (in the EVAL task).
- with an increase of `opb` *(silence duration of the interlocutor channel before the classified utterance)*, `other` than feedback is more likely.

7.4 Impact of the dataset's quality

We checked what happens when one varies the threshold used for proposing a label on the instances and the different results if one uses the whole dataset or only the instances that received a label at a given confidence score (lower score means more labelled

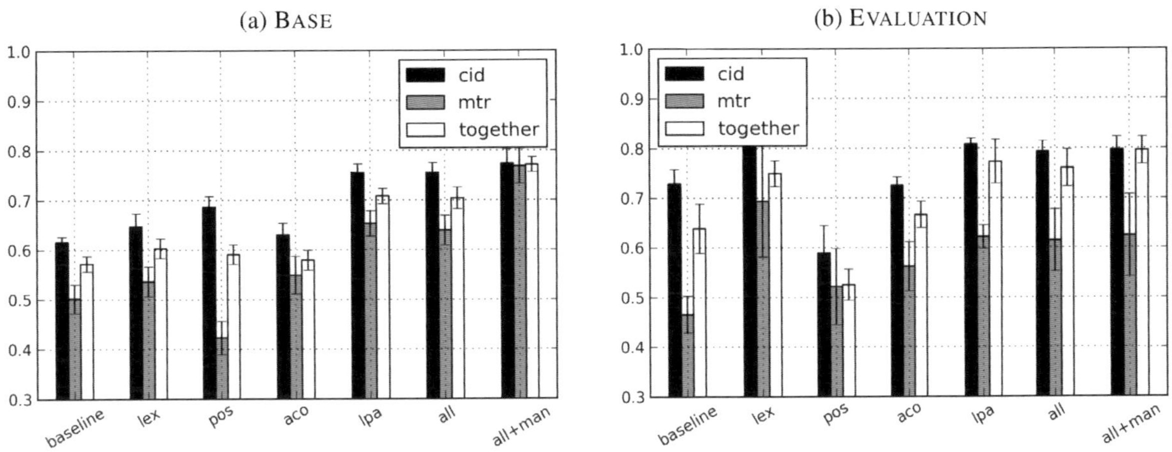

Figure 2: Classification results: f-measure (y-axis) per feature set (x-axis).

data but more noise, higher score means less noise but also less labelled data).

Unsurprisingly, the accuracy on the filtered dataset increases with the employed threshold. We note however that on the `eval` category that has a high score even with a low threshold, the accuracy gain is not fantastic.

About the non-filtered dataset, in the case of `eval` and at threshold $> \frac{3}{4}$, the classifier is focusing on the *None* category to reach a high score (since this category becomes dominant). As for `base`, we note that the changes in threshold have a complex effect on the accuracy. Accuracy is stable for the $\frac{1}{3}$ to $\frac{1}{2}$ shift (reliability on instances is better and coverage still very high), then decrease (with significant decrease of coverage). The shift from $\frac{3}{4}$ to 1 shows a slight increase in accuracy (due to a better recognition of the *None* category).

8 Conclusions

In this paper, the focus was on communicative functions, as they are performed by conversational participants. For everybody who is not directly engaged in the conversation, it is difficult to distinctly categorise such behaviour. In fact, our classification results are getting close to the error rate of the naive raters themselves. On the one hand, we note that some basic important distinctions (in particular the *ack* vs. *eval* divide that can be related to Bavelas et al. (2000) generic vs. specific listener responses) can be fairly efficiently caught by automatic means. This is done thanks to the importance of lexical, positional and acoustic features in determining these differences. On the other hand, our system has to improve as soon as contextual information becomes more important like for identifying *answer* or *confirmation*.

This methodology is almost completely data-driven and can be therefore applied easily to other languages, given that the corresponding annotation campaign is realized. More precisely, the creation of our feature sets and extractions can be fully automated. The main processing step is the forced-alignment. Most of the lexical features can be derived by extracting token frequency from short IPUs (here 3 tokens or less). The real bottleneck is the annotation of communicative functions. But now that the general patterns are known, it becomes possible to design more efficient campaigns.

Acknowledgements

This work is supported by French ANR (ANR-12-JCJC-JSH2-006-01). The second author also benefits from a mobility from Erasmus Mundus Action 2 program MULTI of the European Union (GRANT 2010-5094-7). We would like to thank Roxane Bertrand for the help on the selection of feedback utterances, Brigitte Bigi for help with the automatic processing of the transcriptions and Emilien Gorene for help with recordings and annotation campaigns. Finally, we would like to thank all recruited students who performed the annotations.

References

J. Allwood, J. Nivre, and E. Ahlsen. 1992. On the semantics and pragmatics of linguistic feedback. *Journal of Semantics*, 9:1–26.

J. Allwood, L. Cerrato, K. Jokinen, C. Navarretta, and P. Paggio. 2007. The MUMIN coding scheme for the annotation of feedback, turn management and sequencing phenomena. *Language Resources and Evaluation*, 41(3):273–287.

A. H. Anderson, M. Bader, E. G. Bard, E. Boyle, G. Doherty, S. Garrod, S. Isard, J. Kowtko, J. McAllister, J. Miller, C. Sotillo, H. S. Thompson, and R. Weinert. 1991. The HCRC map task corpus. *Language and Speech*, 34(4):351–366.

E. G. Bard, C. Astésano, M. D'Imperio, A. Turk, N. Nguyen, L. Prévot, and B. Bigi. 2013. Aix Map-Task: A new French resource for prosodic and discourse studies. In *Proceedings of Tools and Resources for the Analysis of Speech Prosody (TRASP)*, Aix-en-Provence, France.

J.B. Bavelas, L. Coates, and T. Johnson. 2000. Listeners as co-narrators. *Journal of Personality and Social Psychology*, 79(6):941–952.

R. Bertrand, P. Blache, R. Espesser, G. Ferré, C. Meunier, B. Priego-Valverde, and S. Rauzy. 2008. Le CID-Corpus of interactional data-annotation et exploitation multimodale de parole conversationnelle. *Traitement Automatique des Langues*, 49(3):1–30.

B. Bigi. 2012. SPPAS: a tool for the phonetic segmentation of speech. In *Proceedings of the Eighth International Conference on Language Resources and Evaluation (LREC'12)*, pages 1748–1755, ISBN 978-2-9517408-7-7, Istanbul, Turkey.

P. Blache, R. Bertrand, B. Bigi, E. Bruno, E. Cela, R. Espesser, G. Ferré, M. Guardiola, D. Hirst, E. Muriasco, J.-C. Martin, C. Meunier, M.-A. Morel, I. Nesterenko, P. Nocera, B. Palaud, L. Prévot, B. Priego-Valverde, J. Seinturier, N. Tan, M. Tellier, and S. Rauzy. 2010. Multimodal annotation of conversational data. In *Proceedings of the Fourth Linguistic Annotation Workshop (LAW IV '10)*, Uppsala, Sweden.

H. Bunt. 1994. Context and dialogue control. *Think Quarterly*, 3(1):19–31.

H.H. Clark. 1996. *Using Language*. Cambridge: Cambridge University Press.

J. Ginzburg. 2012. *The Interactive Stance: Meaning for Conversation*. Oxford University Press.

J. Gorisch, C. Astésano, E. Bard, B. Bigi, and L. Prévot. 2014. Aix Map Task corpus: The French multimodal corpus of task-oriented dialogue. In *Proceedings of The Ninth International Conference on Language Resources and Evaluation (LREC'14)*, Reykjavik, Iceland.

A. Gravano, J. Hirschberg, and Š. Beňuš. 2012. Affirmative cue words in task-oriented dialogue. *Computational Linguistics*, 38(1):1–39.

P. Muller and L. Prévot. 2003. An empirical study of acknowledgement structures. In *Proceedings of 7th workshop on semantics and pragmatics of dialogue (DiaBruck)*, Saarbrücken, Germany.

P. Muller and L. Prévot. 2009. Grounding information in route explanation dialogues. In *Spatial Language and Dialogue*. Oxford University Press.

D. Neiberg, G. Salvi, and J. Gustafson. 2013. Semi-supervised methods for exploring the acoustics of simple productive feedback. *Speech Communication*, 55:451–469.

F. Pedregosa, G. Varoquaux, A Gramfort, V. Michel, B. Thirion, O. Grisel, M. Blondel, P. Prettenhofer, R. Weiss, V. Dubourg, J. Vanderplas, A. Passos, D. Cournapeau, M. Brucher, M. Perrot, and É. Duchesnay. 2011. Scikit-learn: Machine learning in Python. *The Journal of Machine Learning Research*, 12:2825–2830.

V. Petukhova and H. Bunt. 2009. The independence of dimensions in multidimensional dialogue act annotation. In *Proceedings of Human Language Technologies: The 2009 Annual Conference of the North American Chapter of the Association for Computational Linguistics, Companion Volume: Short Papers*, pages 197–200, Boulder, Colorado, USA.

L. Prévot and R. Bertrand. 2012. Cofee-toward a multidimensional analysis of conversational feedback, the case of french language. In *Proceedings of the Workshop on Feedback Behaviors*. (poster).

L. Prévot, J. Gorisch, R. Bertrand, E. Gorene, and B. Bigi. 2015. A SIP of CoFee: A Sample of Interesting Productions of Conversational Feedback. In *16th Annual Meeting of the Special Interest Group on Discourse and Dialogue (SIGdial)*, pages 149–153.

E. A. Schegloff. 1982. Discourse as an interactional achievement: Some use of uh-huh and other things that come between sentences. *Georgetown University Round Table on Languages and Linguistics, Analyzing discourse: Text and talk*, pages 71–93.

V. H. Yngve. 1970. On getting a word in edgewise. In *Papers from the Sixth Regional Meeting of the Chicago Linguistic Society*, pages 567–578.

Automatic conversion of sentence-end expressions for utterance characterization of dialogue systems

Chiaki Miyazaki Toru Hirano Ryuichiro Higashinaka
Toshiro Makino Yoshihiro Matsuo
NTT Media Intelligence Laboratories
1-1 Hikarinooka, Yokosuka, Kanagawa, Japan
{miyazaki.chiaki, hirano.tohru, higashinaka.ryuichiro, makino.toshiro, matsuo.yoshihiro}@lab.ntt.co.jp

Abstract

Building characters for dialogue agents is important in making the agents more friendly and human-like. To build such characters, utterances suitable for the designated characters are usually manually prepared. However, it is expensive to do this for a large number of utterances for various types of characters. We propose a method for automatically converting system utterances into those that are characteristic of designated personal attributes, such as gender, age and area of residence, to characterize agents. In particular, we focus on converting sentence-end expressions, which are considered to greatly affect personal attributes in Japanese. Conversion is done by (i) automatically collecting conversion candidates from various utterances on the Web (e.g., Twitter postings), and (ii) using syntactic and semantic filters to suppress the generation of ill-formed utterances. Experimental results show that our method can convert approximately 95% of utterances into those that are grammatically and semantically acceptable and approximately 90% of utterances into those that are perceived to be acceptable for designated personal attributes.

1 Introduction

Dialogue agents, which can carry out various tasks according to user demand, have been gaining in popularity due to their convenience and potential in casual conversations with humans. To make the agents more attractive as conversation partners, characterization is important since it makes the agents more friendly and human-like. *Characterization* here means adding particular personal characteristics to agent utterances; for example, adding the characteristics of a particular person (Mizukami et al., 2015), Big Five personalities (Mairesse and Walker, 2007), or personal attributes such as gender, age and area of residence (which is closely related to dialects). To characterize agents, utterances suitable for the designated characteristics are usually manually prepared. However, it is expensive to do this for a large number of utterances.

To reduce this cost, we propose a method for automatically converting utterances into those that are suitable for various characters. In particular, the method automatically modifies 'how to say it' (i.e., linguistic expressions) without changing 'what to say' (i.e., contents of the utterances). Conversion is done by (i) collecting conversion candidates from various utterances on the Web (e.g., Twitter postings), which are annotated with their authors' personal attributes (this paper deals especially with gender, age, and area of residence), and (ii) using syntactic and semantic filters to suppress the generation of ill-formed utterances.

The rest of the paper is organized as follows. Section 2 introduces studies related to characterization, Section 3 discusses the features of Japanese sentence-end expressions, Section 4 presents our method for converting sentence-end expressions, Section 5 shows our experimental results, and Section 6 concludes the paper and refers to future work.

2 Related work

Studies related to characterization of dialogue agent utterances have been conducted. For example, a

29th Pacific Asia Conference on Language, Information and Computation pages 307 - 314
Shanghai, China, October 30 - November 1, 2015

method for transforming individual characteristics in dialogue agent utterances (Mizukami et al., 2015) and a language generator that can control parameters related to speakers' Big Five personalities (PERSONAGE) (Mairesse and Walker, 2007) have been proposed. There is also a method for automatically adjusting the language generation parameters of PERSONAGE by using movie scripts (Walker et al., 2011) and a method for automatically adjusting the parameters so that they suit characters or stories of role playing games (Reed et al., 2011).

These studies, including ours, share the same motivation to control personal characteristics of utterances. However, there have not been any studies on converting utterances from the viewpoint of personal attributes. This is mainly because there has been few resources containing utterances together with the personal attributes of interlocutors. The novelty of our work lies in using Twitter as such a resource to mine sentence-end expressions anchored to particular personal attributes.

3 Sentence-end expressions in Japanese

We focus on sentence-end expression since, in Japanese, it is a core element of *role language* (Kinsui, 2003), which relates to stereotypical or characteristic wordings of particular personal attributes such as *feminine language* and *youth language*. We assume that converting sentence-end expressions can be effective in modifying the characteristics of agent utterances. For example, though the utterances shown below differ only in sentence-end expressions, Japanese native speakers can detect the differences in assumed writer/speaker personal attributes.

- gakkoo -ni iki **-tai -no -kayo** [masculine]
- gakkoo -ni iki **-tai -no -kashira** [feminine]
- gakkoo -ni iki **-tai -n -kaina** [western dialect-like]

In these utterances, function words are marked with '-' and those that correspond to sentence-end expressions are in bold. These utterances all convey the meaning that corresponds to 'Do you want to go to school?' in English.

We define a sentence-end expression as a sequence of function words that occurs at the end of a sentence. Function words are those except for content words, such as nouns, verbs, adjectives, and adverbs. The basic role of function words is to denote relations between words, phrases, and clauses, such as case markers (e.g., subject markers and object markers) and connectives (i.e., conjunctions and conjunctive particles).

Japanese sentence-end expressions also play an important role in interaction. Japanese sentence-end expressions contain *interactional particles* (Maynard, 1997), which express speaker judgment and attitude toward the message and the hearer. For instance, 'ne' (a marker of the speaker's assumption that he/she has less information than the hearer; an English counterpart would be "isn't it?") occurs at the end of utterances. In addition, Japanese sentence-end expressions contain auxiliary verbs (e.g., 'mitai' (like) and 'souda' (it seems)), which express speaker attitudes.

4 Method for converting sentence-end expressions

We propose a method for converting sentence-end expressions to characterize dialogue agent utterances. Figure 1 shows the process of the sentence-end expression conversion. First, as preparation, sentence-end expressions, which are characteristic of target characters, are collected through processes (1) and (2) shown in Figure 1 (details are given in Section 4.1). Second, each input utterance is processed in process (1) to find a sentence-end expression to be converted. Here, sequences of function words at the end of sentences are detected as sentence-end expressions according to the part-of-speech (POS) tags obtained using a morphological analyzer (Fuchi and Takagi, 1998). Third, through process (3), appropriate candidates to be substituted for the original sentence-end expression are selected using two filters: POS adjacency and semantic label. Finally, a converted utterance whose sentence-end expression is substituted with one of the candidates is generated as an output.

4.1 Extracting characteristic sentence-end expressions

This section explains a corpus from which the characteristic sentence-end expressions are extracted and the method for extracting the expressions.

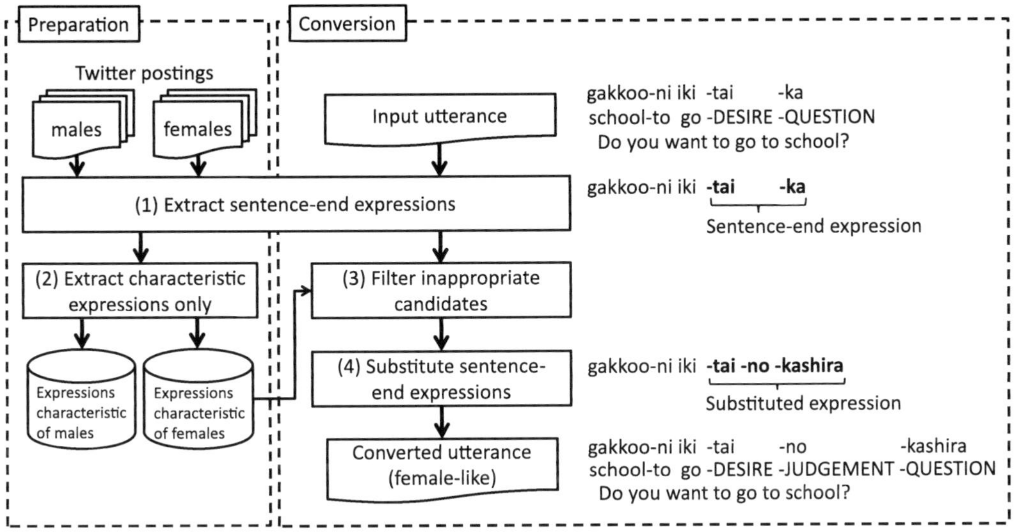

Figure 1: Flow of sentence-end conversion

Attribute	Value	# of authors
gender	female	810
	male	870
age	under 40	1070
	40 and over	610
area of residence	eastern Japan	979
	western Japan	701

Table 1: Author attributes and number

4.1.1 Twitter corpus

For collecting sentence-end expressions, which are characteristic of targeted characters, we use a corpus consisting of Twitter postings that are annotated with their authors' personal attributes (Hirano et al., 2013). The corpus includes two million postings written by 1680 authors. The annotation of the authors' personal attributes to the postings was done based on the self-declarations by the authors. The number of authors for each personal attribute-value is shown in Table 1.

4.1.2 Method for extracting characteristic sentence-end expressions

From each posting of the Twitter corpus, we extract the sequences of function words at the end of the sentences as sentence-end expressions (sentences are period-delimited sequences of words). Then, for each expression, we count the numbers of authors who used them. The numbers of authors are counted separately according to their gender, age, and area of residence. Table 2 lists examples of sentence-end expressions and number of authors who used the corresponding expressions. Then, to extract characteristic sentence-end expressions, the numbers of authors who used each expression are compared. For example, when extracting expressions that are characteristic of female authors, the number of female and male authors who used the expression are compared. With our method, this comparison is done using the G-test. We regard a sentence-end expression as being characteristic of a specific attribute-value if (i) the p-value for the expression is less than a significance level of 5%, which means the number of authors who use the expression is not independent of their attribute, and (ii) if the proportion of authors who used the expression for the specific attribute-value is larger than that for the other value. For example, the expression 'いのだー (i-no-da)' in Table 2 is listed in Table 3 as a characteristic expression of females because its p-value is less than a significant level of 5% and the proportion of female authors who used the expression (14/810) is larger than that for male authors (1/870). Table 3 lists the examples of characteristic sentence-end expressions of females, western Japan, and under 40. In Table 3, some of the characteristic sentence-end expressions of females include the

Expressions	# of authors			
	female		male	
	used	not used	used	not used
いのだー (i-no-da)	14	796	1	869
いのだが (i-no-da-ga)	64	746	132	738
いのだけれど (i-no-da-keredo)	14	796	38	832
いのだし (i-no-da-shi)	0	810	4	866
いのだなぁ (i-no-da-naa)	0	810	4	866

Table 2: Examples of sentence-end expressions and number of authors who used corresponding expressions

	Expressions	G
females	いのよー (i-no-yo)	26.10
	いのよ (i-no-yo)	22.88
	いのー (i-no)	18.37
	いのよね (i-no-yo-ne)	16.20
	いのだー (i-no-da)	14.50
western Japan	いんやけど (i-n-ya-kedo)	19.24
	いんや (i-n-ya)	15.49
	いんやね (i-n-ya-ne)	9.93
	いんやけどね (i-n-ya-kedo-ne)	8.89
	いんやけどな (i-n-ya-kedo-na)	8.83
under 40	いんじゃね (i-n-ja-ne)	23.15
	いよなー (i-yo-na)	16.11
	いよぉー (i-yoo)	7.24
	いよ (i-yo)	6.59
	いよぅ (i-you)	6.53

Table 3: Examples of sentence-end expressions characteristic of females, western Japan, and under 40

expression 'のよ (no-yo)', which is a stereotypical feminine conversational wording in Japanese. In addition, all of the characteristic sentence-end expressions of western japan include the expression 'や (ya)', which is used as a copula in western dialect.

4.2 Part-of-speech adjacency filter

The POS adjacency filter is one of the filters that are used in process (3) in Figure 1. This filter works as a constraint for suppressing the conversion into ungrammatical utterances. This filter removes candidates that are not allowed to be adjacent to a content word on the left of the original sentence-end expression. In particular, the filter removes the candidates whose left adjacent POS is different from that of the original sentence-end expression. The left adjacent POSs of the candidate sentence-end expressions are also extracted and stored together with the candidates, as shown in Table 4.

Adjacent POS on left	Expressions
noun	だからな (da-kara-na)
noun	だからなぁ (da-kara-naa)
noun	だが (da-ga)
verb	ないが (nai-ga)
verb	ないし (nai-shi)
verb	ないじゃないか (nai-ja-nai-ka)
adjective	いです (i-desu)
adjective	いでした (i-deshi-ta)
adjective	いですか (i-desu-ka)

Table 4: Examples of adjacent content word's part-of-speech (POS)

Category	Sub-category	Semantic labels	Examples
factuality	polarity	negation	ない (nai)
	degree of certainty	question	か (ka)
		guess	だろう (darou)
	tense (aspect)	completion	た (ta)
		continuation	ている (te-iru)
intention		desire	たい (tai)
		volition	う (u)
		invitation	うか (u-ka)
		request	てください (te-kudasai)

Table 5: Semantic labels that should be consistent before and after conversion

4.3 Semantic label filter

The semantic label filter is another type of filter that is used in process (3) in Figure 1. We define a set of semantic elements that must be included in both sentence-end expressions before and after conversion. To this end, we use the nine semantic labels listed in Table 5, which were selected from 435 labels corresponding to the meaning categories for functional expressions (Matsuyoshi et al., 2006). From these, we select nine labels regarding the following two aspects: (i) factuality and (ii) intention, since we regard them as the key components of dialogue content.

(i) Semantic labels related to factuality Event factuality refers to the distinction whether event-denoting expressions are presented as corresponding to real-world situations, situations that have not occurred, or situations of uncertain status (Saurí and Pustejovsky, 2007). According to them, event factuality is impacted by polarity (positive vs. negative) and degree of certainty of what is asserted (e.g., possible vs. certain). Tense (aspect) is also often discussed in relation to the meaning of an event (Izumi et al., 2010). Taking these into account, we select five semantic labels, *negation* for polarity, *question* and *guess* for degree of certainty, and *completion* and *continuation* for tense (aspect) to keep the factuality consistent before and after conversion.

(ii) Semantic labels related to intention

Intentions are defined here as what a speaker wants (Sidner and Israel, 1981) or as a discourse purpose (Grosz and Sidner, 1986). To keep the intention consistent before and after conversion, we select four labels, namely, *desire*, *volition*, *invitation*, and *request*. These labels are important for expressing what a speaker wants (to do) or wants his/her hearer to do.

The input utterances and postings in the Twitter corpus, from which the candidates are extracted, are automatically tagged with the semantic labels by using a method that selects the best sequence of semantic labels by a discriminative model (Imamura et al., 2011).

4.4 Conversion of sentence-end expressions

A sentence-end expression of the input utterance is converted through the steps shown in Table 1. First, the input utterance is processed to find a sentence-end expression along with the POS of its adjacent content word and the semantic labels included in it. Second, the pool of sentence-end expressions that are characteristic of a designated personal attribute is filtered with the syntactic and semantic filters (See Sections 4.2 and 4.3). Finally, the sentence-end expression of the input utterance is substituted with the conversion candidates that passed the filters.

When filtering the candidates, the POS of the last content word (the adjacent content word of the sentence-end expression) in the input utterance is used for removing the candidates whose left adjacent POS is different from the last content word of the input utterance. In addition, the semantic labels, which are included in the sentence-end expression of the input utterance, and those of the candidates are compared. If a candidate contains exactly the same set of labels, it remains a candidate; otherwise, the candidate is abandoned.

Adjacent POS	Semantic labels	Expressions	G
verb	DESIRE, JUDGMENT, QUESTION	たいのかしら (tai-no-kashira)	33.00
verb	DESIRE, QUESTION	たいかしら (tai-kashira)	31.19
verb	DESIRE, JUDGMENT, QUESTION, EXCLAMATION	たいのかなあー (tai-no-kanaa)	13.15
verb	DESIRE, QUESTION	たいですかっ (tai-desu-ka)	6.45
verb	DESIRE, QUESTION, EXCLAMATION	たいかなあー (tai-kanaa)	5.90

Table 6: Examples of candidates that passed filters

Consider the following utterance as an example of an input.

gakkoo -ni iki -tai -ka
school -GOAL go -DESIRE -QUESTION
N Particle V Aux Particle
'Do you want to go to school?'

In this utterance, the first line is the alphabetical transcription of the input utterance, and the second line is the semantic denotation that corresponds to the first line. In the semantic denotation, the meanings of content words are denoted in English counterparts and those of function words are denoted with semantic labels written in uppercase. The third line shows the POS of each word, and the fourth line shows the English translation of the input utterance.

In this utterance, a sequence of function words at the end of the utterance 'tai ka' is the sentence-end expression, which is to be converted. Since the sentence-end expression is adjacent to a verb, only the candidates that are also capable of being adjacent to verbs can pass the POS adjacency filter. In addition, the input sentence-end expression includes two kinds of semantic labels, DESIRE and QUESTION. Therefore, only the candidates that also include both labels can pass the semantic label filter. Table 6 lists the examples of the surviving candidates that are characteristic of the female attribute.

In the example in Table 6, there are some semantic labels that are not included in the original sentence-end expression, such as JUDGMENT and EXCLAMATION. Since these labels are not considered with the semantic label filter, it does not matter if they are included in the candidates.

5 Experiments

We conducted two experiments to investigate the performance of our proposed method of converting sentence-end expressions. In particular, we asked a subject to score the converted utterances from the two perspectives of (i) grammatical and semantic acceptability, and (ii) appropriateness for desired personal attributes. The subject was a person who had been working as a linguistic annotator for more than three years. To evaluate inter-rater agreement, we also asked another subject to rate half the utterances.

5.1 Data for collecting conversion candidates and testing

For collecting candidates to be used for conversion, we used the Twitter corpus introduced in Section 4.1.1. The target personal attributes (and values) were gender (male/female), age (under 40/40 and over), and area of residence (eastern/western Japan), and the number of authors for each attribute-value is shown in Table 1.

As input utterances, we used 100 Japanese utterances, which were randomly extracted from a database consisting of manually created utterances (in the form of text) for a dialogue system, which we created. Examples of input utterances are shown below.

水族館が大好きです
suizokukan-ga daisuki-desu
'I like aquariums very much.'

占いって信じますか？
uranai-tte shinji-masu-ka?
'Do you believe in astrology?'

あなたの部屋から星が見えますか？
anata-no heya-kara hoshi-ga mie-masu-ka?
'Can you see stars from your window?'

These utterances were converted so that they would be characterized with six different personal attributes, i.e., male, female, under 40, 40 and over, living in eastern Japan, and living in western Japan. Though various sentence-end expressions were collected as the conversion candidates, we used only one expression whose G-value was the highest among the candidates.

5.2 Procedure and evaluation indices

We randomly presented the converted utterances and the original input utterances to the subjects and asked them to score the utterances regarding the following two aspects.

Grammatical and semantic acceptability Whether an utterance is acceptable in Japanese with respect to grammar and meaning (1: very unacceptable - 5: very acceptable).

Character acceptability Whether an utterance is acceptable regarding a desired characteristic (1: very unacceptable - 5: very acceptable).

Since it is difficult to clearly separate acceptability of grammar from semantics, we evaluated them together. We calculated the inter-rater agreement rate as the percentage of utterances for which the two subjects gave identical judgments.

5.3 Results

Figures 2 and 3 show the average scores of 100 utterances for each personal attribute. In the figures, ***, ** and * indicate statistical significance at the 0.001, 0.01 and 0.05 levels, respectively, and n.s. indicates "not significant". The average scores of characteristic acceptability of the converted utterances were significantly higher than those of the original utterances (paired samples t-test; $p<0.05$) except for the case of 40 and over. In particular, the scores for the cases of under 40, male, female, and western Japan drastically improved (by approximately 0.8-2.0 points) due to the conversion.

Moreover, for the cases of female and western Japan, there were no significant differences in the average scores of grammatical and semantic acceptability between before and after conversion according to paired samples t-test. For the cases of the other attributes, the average scores of grammatical and semantic acceptability of the converted utterances were significantly lower than those of the original utterances (paired samples t-test; $p<0.05$). However, the average scores exceeded 4 (acceptable) except for the case of male. Therefore, we argue that our proposed method can convert utterances without severe malformation of grammar and semantics.

Tables 7 and 8 show the breakdown of scores of the two evaluation indices. For the evaluation of grammatical and semantic acceptability, unacceptable utterances scored 1 (very unacceptable) or 2 (unacceptable) were only 5% or less (The inter-rater agreement rate was 95% when distinguishing unacceptable utterances (2 or below) from acceptable ones) except for the case of male. For the evaluation of characteristic acceptability, the average percentage of unacceptable utterances scored 1 or 2 was 10%, which we believe is good (the inter-rater agreement rate was 85% when distinguishing unacceptable utterances (2 or below) from acceptable ones). However, unacceptable utterances of 40 and over and western Japan scored 1 or 2 exceeded 20%. Considering the practical use in dialogue systems, the results suggest that utterances that are not appropriate for a designated attribute are generated in approximately one in five utterances. Thus, we believe that the characterization is still not sufficient for certain personal attributes, and further investigation and improvement are needed.

6 Conclusion and future work

To build characters for dialogue agents, we proposed a method for automatically converting sentence-end expressions. Our contributions are as follows:

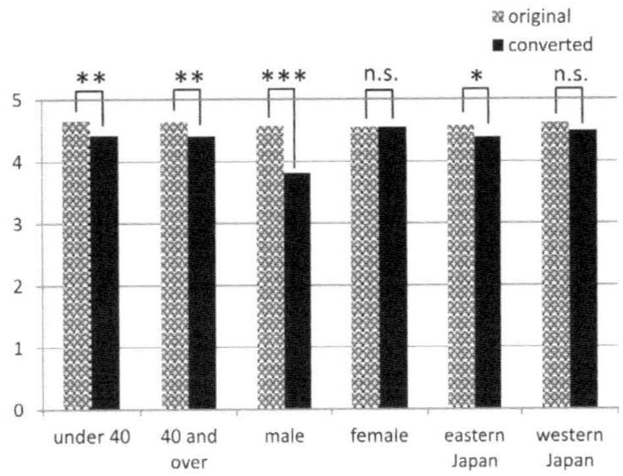

Figure 2: Average scores of grammatical and semantic acceptability

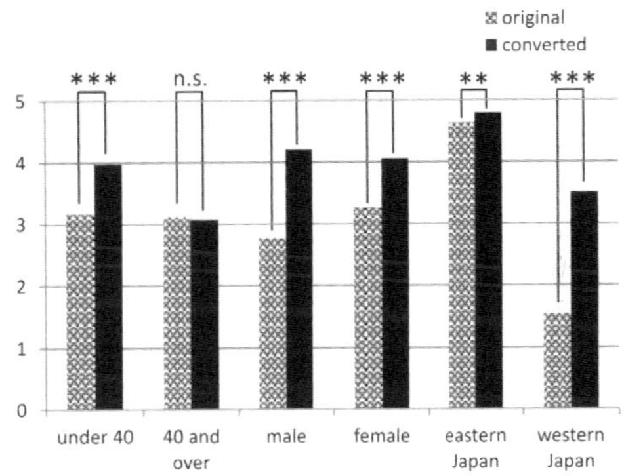

Figure 3: Average scores of character acceptability

	% of utts. for each score				
	1	2	3	4	5
under 40	**3%**	**2%**	1%	38%	56%
40 and over	**2%**	**1%**	8%	32%	57%
male	10%	13%	7%	26%	44%
female	**2%**	**0%**	4%	29%	65%
eastern Japan	**3%**	**1%**	7%	32%	57%
western Japan	**2%**	**3%**	4%	26%	65%

Table 7: Breakdown of scores of grammatical and semantic acceptability

	% of utts. for each score				
	1	2	3	4	5
under 40	**1%**	**3%**	9%	71%	16%
40 and over	2%	28%	31%	39%	0%
male	**0%**	**2%**	16%	41%	41%
female	**0%**	**0%**	21%	52%	27%
eastern Japan	**0%**	**0%**	3%	15%	82%
western Japan	12%	11%	34%	0%	43%

Table 8: Breakdown of scores of character acceptability

- We introduced an effective way of characterization for dialogue agent utterances in Japanese, i.e., conversion of sentence-end expressions.
- We presented a method for converting the sentence-end expressions with limited risk of being syntactically or semantically ill-formed.

These contributions are supported by the experimental results, which show that our method can, except for the case of male, convert approximately 95% of utterances into those that are grammatically and semantically acceptable, and approximately 90% of the converted utterances are perceived to be acceptable for designated personal attributes.

There are still limitations to our proposed method. For instance, conversion of content words is not possible. Since we assume that lexical choice of content words would also be an important component of characterization, we would like to investigate this as future work. In addition, the attributes dealt with in this study were limited to gender, age, and area of residence. The values for each of the attributes were also limited to binary distinctions, such as male/female, under 40/40 and over, and eastern/western Japan. As far as these attributes are concerned, characteristic expressions were successfully extracted from Twitter postings, but this might not be in the case of other attributes and values. Investigating how our proposed method works on different types of attributes and different sizes of data will also be necessary.

References

Takeshi Fuchi and Shinichiro Takagi. 1998. Japanese morphological analyzer using word co-occurrence - JTAG. In *Proceedings of the 36th Annual Meeting of the Association for Computational Linguistics and 17th International Conference on Computational Linguistics*, volume 1, pages 409–413.

Barbara J Grosz and Candace L Sidner. 1986. Attention, intentions, and the structure of discourse. *Computational linguistics*, 12(3):175–204.

Toru Hirano, Toshiro Makino, and Yoshihiro Matsuo. 2013. Inferring user profile from text using markov logic. In *Proceedings of the 27th Annual Conference of the Japanese Society for Artificial Intelligence (in Japanese)*.

Kenji Imamura, Tomoko Izumi, Genichiro Kikui, and Satoshi Sato. 2011. Semantic label tagging to functional expressions in predicate phrases. In *Proceedings of the 17th Annual Meeting of Association for Natural Language Processing (in Japanese)*, pages 308–311.

Tomoko Izumi, Kenji Imamura, Genichiro Kikui, and Satoshi Sato. 2010. Standardizing complex functional expressions in Japanese predicates: Applying theoretically-based paraphrasing rules. In *Proceedings of the 2010 Workshop on Multiword Expressions: from Theory to Applications*, pages 64–72.

Satoshi Kinsui. 2003. Vaacharu nihongo: Yakuwarigo no nazo (in japanese) [Virtual Japanese: The mystery of role language]. *Iwanami Shoten*.

François Mairesse and Marilyn Walker. 2007. PERSONAGE: Personality generation for dialogue. In *Proceedings of the 45th Annual Meeting of the Association of Computational Linguistics*, pages 496–503.

Suguru Matsuyoshi, Satoshi Sato, and Takehito Utsuro. 2006. Compilation of a dictionary of Japanese functional expressions with hierarchical organization. In *Proceedings of the 21st International Conference on Computer Processing of Oriental Languages*, pages 395–402.

S. K. Maynard. 1997. *Japanese Communication: language and thought in context*. University of Hawai'i Press.

Masahiro Mizukami, Graham Neubig, Sakriani Sakti, Tomoki Toda, and Satoshi Nakamura. 2015. Linguistic individuality transformation for spoken language. In *Proceedings of the 6th International Workshop On Spoken Dialogue Systems*.

Aaron A Reed, Ben Samuel, Anne Sullivan, Ricky Grant, April Grow, Justin Lazaro, Jennifer Mahal, Sri Kurniawan, Marilyn A Walker, and Noah Wardrip-Fruin. 2011. A step towards the future of role-playing games: The SpyFeet Mobile RPG Project. In *Proceedings of the 7th Conference on Artificial Intelligence and Interactive Digital Entertainment*, pages 182–188.

Roser Saurí and James Pustejovsky. 2007. Determining modality and factuality for text entailment. In *Proceedings of the 1st IEEE International Conference on Semantic Computing*, pages 509–516.

Candace L Sidner and David J Israel. 1981. Recognizing intended meaning and speakers' plans. In *Proceedings of 7th International Joint Conference on Artificial Intelligence*, pages 203–208.

Marilyn A Walker, Ricky Grant, Jennifer Sawyer, Grace I Lin, Noah Wardrip-Fruin, and Michael Buell. 2011. Perceived or not perceived: Film character models for expressive NLG. In *Proceedings of the 4th International Conference on Interactive Digital Storytelling*, pages 109–121.

Auditory Synaesthesia and Near Synonyms: A Corpus-Based Analysis of sheng1 and yin1 in Mandarin Chinese

Qingqing Zhao[1] **Chu-Ren Huang**[2] **Hongzhi Xu**[3]

The Department of Chinese and Bilingual Studies
The Hong Kong Polytechnic University

[1]zhaoqingqing0611@163.com
[2]churen.huang@polyu.edu.hk
[3]hongz.xu@gmail.com

Abstract

This paper explores the nature of linguistic synaesthesia in the auditory domain through a corpus-based lexical semantic study of near synonyms. It has been established that the near synonyms 聲 sheng "sound" and 音 yin "sound" in Mandarin Chinese have different semantic functions in representing auditory production and auditory perception respectively. Thus, our study is devoted to testing whether linguistic synaesthesia is sensitive to this semantic dichotomy of cognition in particular, and to examining the relationship between linguistic synaesthesia and cognitive modelling in general. Based on the corpus, we find that the near synonyms exhibit both similarities and differences on synaesthesia. The similarities lie in that both 聲 and 音 are productive recipients of synaesthetic transfers, and vision acts as the source domain most frequently. Besides, the differences exist in selective constraints for 聲 and 音 with synaesthetic modifiers as well as syntactic functions of the whole combinations. We propose that the similarities can be explained by the cognitive characteristics of the sound, while the differences are determined by the influence of the semantic dichotomy of production/perception on synaesthesia. Therefore, linguistic synaesthesia is not a random association, but can be motivated and predicted by cognition.

1 Introduction

Synaesthesia is a phenomenon of one sensation connecting to another, which has been studied in two distinct disciplines. One is neuroscience, which characterizes synaesthesia as a neural disorder (Cytowic, 1993), and the other one is linguistics that widely describes synaesthesia as a metaphor (Williams, 1976; Geeraerts, 2010). This paper is focused on the linguistic synaesthesia.

Synaesthesia occurs commonly and naturally in languages (Huang, 2015), such as "sweet voice" in English and 高音 gao-yin "high pitch" in Chinese, of which "sweet" and 高 gao "high" are normally perceived through gustation and vision respectively, while "voice" and 音 yin "sound" both belong to the auditory domain, therefore, the whole combinations exhibit an association of different sensations, namely synaesthesia.

In terms of research on linguistic synaesthesia, most previous studies are concentrated on the directionality of synaesthetic transfers, that is, which sensation usually acts as the source domain and which sensation is the target domain. For instance, Ullmann (1957) studied creative usages of synaesthesia on 2000 examples from poems in the 19th century, and proposed a tendency of hierarchical distribution for synaesthesia. He concluded that synaesthetic transfers are usually from much "lower domains" (such as touch and taste) to much "higher domains" (such as vision and hearing)[1], and the acoustic field emerges as the main recipient. Williams (1976) also claimed that the diachronic meaning change of synaesthetic adjectives in ordinary English obeys a strict rule that can be universal for all human languages, as shown in Figure1.

[1]The terms, "lower domains" and "higher domains", are copied from Ullmann (1957), where the former refers to touch, taste and smell, and the later includes hearing and vision.

29th Pacific Asia Conference on Language, Information and Computation pages 315 - 322
Shanghai, China, October 30 - November 1, 2015

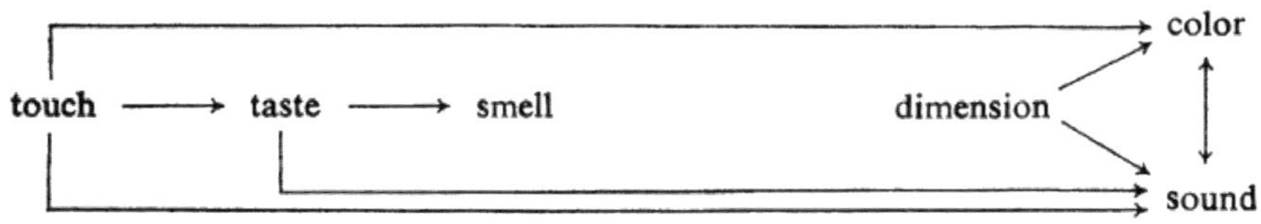

Figure 1: The Meaning Change of Synaesthetic Adjectives (Source: Williams, 1976).

In response to Williams (1976), Zhao and Huang (2015) carried out a study on synaesthesia in the Chinese language and demonstrated that the hierarchy proposed based on English is not applicable to Chinese. Similarly, Strik Lievers (2015) also pointed out that the "directionality principle" reflects the frequency of association types, rather than representing universal constraints on synaesthetic transfers. Thus, linguistic synaesthesia should be investigated specifically for different languages in depth. Unfortunately, fine-grained studies on synaesthesia in Chinese are still scarce.

Given the gap on synaesthesia in Chinese, we think that it could be a good way to start off with examining synaesthesia in near synonyms, because the interaction between synaesthesia and subtle semantic differences in near synonyms could provide much deeper and more fine-grained clues for synaesthesia. The benefits of studies on near synonyms to explain and predict linguistic phenomena have been widely recognized. For example, Chief et al. (2000) suggested that some semantic features obtained by comparing near synonyms can be useful on the prediction of syntactic performances. Similarly, Hong and Huang (2004), Hong and Huang (2005) also pointed that semantic/cognitive features embedded in perceptual near synonyms can influence their usages in the language.

As previous studies show that the auditory domain is the main target of synaesthetic transfers (Ullmann, 1957; Williams, 1976), the near synonyms, 聲 sheng "sound" and 音 yin "sound" in Mandarin Chinese, should be good candidates for our research, which have been established to represent different semantic/cognitive focuses on the sound. Specifically speaking, 聲 is concentrated on the auditory production, while 音 is focused on the auditory perception, although both can refer to the sound (Hong and Huang, 2004; Hong and Huang, 2005). Therefore, through studying the synaesthetic usages of this pair of near synonyms, not only can we test whether synaesthesia is sensitive to the semantic dichotomy of production and perception, but also we can examine the relationship between synaesthesia and cognition.

The present paper is organized as follows: we will introduce the methods of collecting and annotating data in Section 2, and figure out the similarities as well as differences between 聲 and 音 on synaesthesia in Section 3, which will be followed by some explanations in Section 4. In the last Section, we will summarize our main findings and propose our future work.

2 Methodology: Corpus Selection and Data Annotation

2.1 Corpus Selection and Measurement Criteria

In order to make our study more tenable, we attempt to exhaust the data as possible as we can, and hence rely on the corpus for data collection. We select four widely-used huge corpora as our data sources, of which Sinica Corpus [2] (Chen et al., 1996) is the main corpus and other three corpora, including Chinese GigaWord 2 Corpus (Mainland, simplified)[3]; Chinese GigaWord 2 Corpus (Taiwan, traditional)[4] ; and the journal corpus of BCC Corpus[5] , act as the complement.

The reason for giving the priority to Sinica Corpus is on the consideration that the corpus is a well-recognized balanced and high-quality corpus with

[2]Accessed at: `http://app.sinica.edu.tw/kiwi/mkiwi/`

[3]Accessed at: `https://the.sketchengine.co.uk/bonito/run.cgi/first_form?corpname=preloaded/cgw2_sc`

[4]Accessed at: `https://the.sketchengine.co.uk/bonito/run.cgi/first_form?corpname=preloaded/cgw2_tc;`

[5]Accessed at: `http://bcc.blcu.edu.cn/index.php?corpus=2`

tagging information (Chen et al., 1996), which we think can facilitate our research.

Besides, usages in newspapers are normally well-established and the controversial issues about grammaticality for some specific examples could be decreased to a degree, and we hence select three journal corpora as the complement (Refer to Hong and Huang, 2006 for the introduction of two GigaWord corpora).

Regarding the data from different corpora, we set some measurement criteria to make them comparable. To be specific, we depend on the statistical information, which includes the frequency information of examples per million word tokens in their respective corpora and also percentage information of each example in its source corpus. For instance, 大聲 da-sheng "loudly" occurs 407 times in Sinica Corpus (4.0 edition) as a "stative and intransitive verb"[6] and word tokens in the corpus is around 10 million, so its calculated frequency is 40.7 and the percentage is 0.00407% for the analysis in this paper. For some complementary examples, which do not appear in Sinica Corpus, we also utilize the criterion to calculate its frequency in their relevant corpora.[7] For example, the calculated frequency of 長聲 chang-sheng "in prolonged voice" is 0.01 and hence its percentage is 0.000001%, because it occurs 10 times in the journal corpus of BCC with around 1000 million word tokens.

2.2 Data Collection and Annotation

We exhaust all the examples with two characters in the modifier-head relation in Sinica Corpus, whose heads are either 聲 or 音. If the modifier does not belong to audition but can be classified into any of four other sensations, including touch, gustation, olfaction and vision, we think that this example involves synaesthesia.

In terms of determining the sensory domain of modifiers, we refer to its original meaning in 說文解字 shuo-wen-jie-zi and 漢典 han-dian[8] . Take the meaning of 雜 za "mixed" in 說文解字 for example, it is paraphrased as 五彩相會 wu-cai-xiang-hui "five colors mixing together", therefore, we classify it into the visual domain.

Moreover, we divide some sensory domains further into several sub-domains. For instance, we distinguish vision into size, dimension and so on.

All the synaesthetic examples we find in Sinica Corpus are words[9] with the information of part of speech, so we calculate the frequency of each example according to different part of speech labels. For some examples that do not appear in Sinica Corpus, we annotate them manually with the part of speech information compared to Sinica Corpus, and utilize the measurement rule mentioned above to obtain their frequencies and percentages for discussion. If one complementary example has different frequencies and percentages in additional corpora, we take the most frequent one and the respective corpus into consideration.

Therefore, our data is summarized as follows in Table 1 and Table 2, with the part of speech[10], frequency and percentage information[11].

3 Similarity and Difference on Synaesthesia

3.1 Synaesthetic Similarity for the Near Synonyms

As shown in Table 1 and Table 2, we can see that there are some similarities on synaesthesia between the near synonyms.

General speaking, as 聲 and 音 both belong to the auditory sensation, other modalities can transfer frequently to describe these two near synonyms, of which morphemes from both visual and tactile domains can be used to modify 聲 and 音. Therefore, hearing is also a productive target domain of synaesthetic transfers in Mandarin Chinese. This is in line with the observation for English (Ullmann, 1957; Williams, 1976).

[6]The term is used in Sinica Corpus, and marked as VH.

[7]For more detailed information about the size and design of these corpora, please refer to the websites mentioned above.

[8]Accessed at: `http://www.zdic.net/`

[9]We do not plan to involve the controversial issue about how to determine a sequence is a word or not, for the discrimination will not influence the discussion below.

[10]Word/POS/Freq/Perc in Table 1 and Table 2 refers to word, part of speech, frequency and percentage. Please note that we group VH and D, although VH denotes "stative and intransitive verbs" and D denotes "adverbs" in Sinica Corpus, for both of them are related to events, rather than referring to an entity.

[11]Please also note that although there are some polysemous examples in our data, some senses are irrelevant to synaesthesia, such as 美音 mei-yin "pronunciation in American English". We exclude this type of usages.

Source Domain		聲 sheng1 "sound"		音 yin1 "sound"
		Word/POS/Freq/Perc	Word/POS/Freq/Perc	Word/POS/Freq/Perc
VISION	size	大聲/VH/40.7/0.00407% "loudly" 小聲/VH/4.3/0.00043% "in a low voice"		
	dimension	高聲/D/5.4/0.00054% "loudly" 低聲/D/6.3/0.00063% "lowly"		高音/Na/4.6/0.00046% "high pitch" 低音/Na/4.6/0.00046% "low pitch" 中音/Na/2.9/0.00029% "mediant"
	light	朗聲/D/0.1/0.00001% "in a clear voice" 陰聲/D/0.1/0.00001% "in a deep voice"		
	shape	尖聲/D/1.2/0.00012% "in a sharp voice"	平聲/Na/0.4/0.00004% "level tone"	尖音/Na/0.2/0.00002% "sharp sound"
	evaluation	齊聲/D/4/0.0004% "in chorus"	美聲/Na/0.4/0.00004% "bel canto"	美音/Na/0.2/0.00002% "beautiful sound"
	length	長聲/D/0.01/0.000001% "in a prolonged voice"	長聲/Na/0.03/0.000003% "prolonged sound" 短聲/Na/0.013/0.0000013% "short sound"	長音/Na/0.2/0.00002% "prolonged sound" 短音/Na/0.018/0.0000018% "short sound"
	color	雜聲/Na/0.014/0.0000014% "noise"		雜音/Na/3.5/0.00035% "noise"
	transparency	清聲/D/0.001/0.0000001% "in a clear voice"	清聲/Na/0.002/0.0000002% "clear sound"	清音/Na/0.3/0.00003% "voiceless sound" 濁音/Na/0.01/0.000001% "voiced sound"

Table 1: Synaesthetic Examples of 聲 and 音 from Vision in Mandarin Chinese

Specifically, for 聲 and 音, different modalities have different transferability. Vision transfers more frequently to the auditory domain than touch, which can be reflected in both types and frequencies. There are 14 morphemes from the visual domain that can modify 聲 and 10 morphemes from the tactile domain. Similarly, 10 morphemes from the vision can be used to describe 音 and only 6 morphemes from touch. In terms of frequencies of synaesthetic examples, the most frequent modifier for 聲 is 大 da "big"

Source Domain		聲 sheng1 "sound"		音 yin1 "sound"
		Word/POS/Freq/Perc	Word/POS/Freq/Perc	Word/POS/Freq/Perc
TOUCH	weight	輕聲/D/8/0.0008% "in a soft voice" 沉聲/VH/1.4/0.00014% "in a heavy voice"	輕聲/Na/0.4/0.00004% "light tone"	輕音/Na/0.006/0.0000006% "light tone" 重音/Na/0.6/0.00006% "stress"
	texture	粗聲/VH/0.5/0.00005% "raucously" 細聲/D/0.4/0.00004% "in a soft voice" 柔聲/D/2/0.0002% "in a soft voice" 軟聲/VH/0.001/0.0000001% "in a soft voice" 硬聲/D/0.001/0.0000001% "in a hard voice"		細音/Na/0.001/0.0000001% "tiny sound" 柔音/Na/0.002/0.0000002% "soft sound" 軟音/Na/0.001/0.0000001% "soft sound" 滑音/Na/1/0.0001% "smooth sound"
	temperature	寒聲/VH/0.1/0.00001% "in a cold voice" 温聲/D/0.007/0.0000007% "in a warm voice" 冷聲/D/0.003/0.0000003% "in a cold voice"	温聲/Na/0.001/0.0000001% "warm sound"	
TASTE	taste	甜聲/D/0.001/0.0000001% "in a sweet voice"		

Table 2: Synaesthetic Examples of 聲 and 音 from Touch and Taste in Mandarin Chinese

from the visual domain. Similarly, 高 gao "high" and 低 di "low" modify 音 most frequently with the same frequency, which are both from vision. If we calculate the ratio of all the frequencies of morphemes from vision to those from touch, the ration for 聲 is around 5 times and that for 音 is about 10 times. It seems that vision is much easier to transfer into hearing than touch in Mandarin Chinese, which has not been mentioned in previous research yet.

In summary, the similarities on synaesthesia between 聲 and 音 exist in two aspects. The first one is that both 聲 and 音 can be productive recipients of synaesthetic transfers, which can be described by visual words and tactile words. The other similar property is concerned with the priority of vision to touch when modifying these two synonyms. In other words, vision is used more frequently to characterize 聲 and 音 than touch.

3.2 Synaesthetic Difference for the Near Synonyms

Besides similarities, there are also two differences on synaesthesia for 聲 and 音, one of which is reflected in selective constraints and the other exists in the syntactic function of the whole combinations.

3.2.1 Selective Constraints

As we see in Table 1 and Table 2, there are more domains and more modifiers that can be used for 聲 than 音. 聲 can be naturally described by gustation, but 音 cannot. There are totally 25 morphemes modifying 聲, including 14 from vision, 10 from touch and 1 from taste, while only 16 morphemes modifying 音, including 10 from vision and 6 from touch. In terms of the frequencies of words, words containing 聲 occur more frequently in corpora than those containing 音. Therefore, 聲 seems to be much easier and more common to be described than 音 through synaesthesia.

Interestingly, there is another difference between 聲 and 音 on synaesthesia about the selection constraint. That can be instantiated in the symmetry of modifiers selection for sub-domains. Polar items in gradable antonymous relations (Lyons, 1977) in each sub-domain are usually selected for synaesthetic usages, such as 大 da "big" and 小 xiao "small" for the size and 清 qing "clear" and 濁 zhuo "turbid" for the transparency. For some sub-domains, there exists the symmetry between modifiers selection. For examples, in terms of the dimension domain for 聲, the modifiers selection is symmetrical, because the polar items 高 gao "high" and 低 di "low" are both selected and there is no other in-between item on the gradable axis that has been selected. However, in terms of the dimension domain for 音, the selection is asymmetrical, for 中 zhong "middle" is also used besides the polar items 高 and 低. In this way, we can calculate the symmetry of modifiers selection for 聲 and 音 in each sub-domain, which is shown in Table 3. Thus, the whole symmetry ratio for 聲 is 50%, while that for 音 is only 38%.

Therefore, there is a noteworthy difference on selective constraints for the near synonyms on synaesthesia. Specifically speaking, 聲 receives more synaesthetic modifications than 音, and also employs higher symmetry on modifiers selection in each sub-domain.

3.2.2 Syntactic Function

Another difference on synaesthesia between 聲 and 音 is related to the whole syntactic function of the synaesthetic combinations. All the examples containing 音 refer to the entity, that is, a specific kind of sound, such as 長音 chang-yin "prolonged sound". However, most examples containing 聲 is concerned with the event, such as 大聲 da-sheng "loudly", for 大聲 can only be used to modify a predicate (e.g., 大聲唱歌 da-sheng-chang-ge "sing loudly") or express a state (e.g., 他說話很大聲 ta-shuo-hua-hen-da-sheng "his talking is loud"), whereas it cannot denote an entity (e.g., *一個大聲 yi-ge-da-sheng "a loud sound").

Sub-domains	聲 sheng1 "sound"	音 yin1 "sound"
size	+	NA
dimension	+	-
light	+	NA
shape	-	-
evaluation	-	-
length	+	+
color	-	-
transparency	-	+
weight	+	+
texture	+	-
temperature	-	NA
taste	-	NA

Table 3: The Synaesthetic Symmetry of 聲 and 音 in Mandarin Chinese.

As Table 1 and Table 2 shows, only 4 adjective morphemes exclusively form a noun when combining with 聲. In terms of these 4 exceptional examples, we can see that two of them are terminological words in some specific areas, namely 美聲 mei-sheng "bel canto" and 平聲 ping-sheng "level tone". In addition, the other two are used in a very low frequency, and 短聲 duan-sheng "short sound" as well as 雜聲 za-sheng "noise" neither occur in Sinica Corpus, with the calculated frequencies of only 0.013 and 0.014 respectively in the journal corpus of BCC. Therefore, the synaesthetic combinations of 聲 and 音 have different syntactic functions, of which combinations with 聲 are normally related to an event, whereas combinations with 音 always refer to an entity.

In conclusion, although 聲 and 音 are near synonyms and both can denote the sound; there are some noteworthy differences on synaesthesia. 聲 is much easier to be described through synaesthesia than 音, and also employs higher symmetry on synaesthetic selection of modifiers. Moreover, the combinations of 聲 or 音 have different syntactic functions, of which combinations with 聲 are normally related to an event, while combinations with 音 always refer to an entity.

4 Production and Perception in Sound

As a pair of near synonyms, 聲 and 音 have both similar properties and different characteristics on synaesthesia in Mandarin Chinese, which can be explained by combining the framework of Generative Lexicon (Pustejovsky, 1995) and the semantic/cognitive dichotomy of production and perception in the sound (Hong and Huang, 2004).

As Pustejovsky (1995) proposed that lexical items can be represented in Lexical Inheritance Structure and some semantic information encoded in lexical items are inherited from upper concepts, which determines their performances in languages. Both 聲 and 音 are in the auditory domain, which can denote the sound, thus, both of them can inherit common semantic information from the upper concept, namely sound. Therefore, we think that the similarities on synaesthesia between 聲 and 音 are determined by the whole synaesthetic characteristics for hearing, that is, hearing is a productive recipient of synaesthetic transfers and is much easier to be the target domain of vision than touch. [12]

In terms of synaesthetic differences between 聲 and 音, the semantic/cognitive dichotomy of production and perception really play a role. Hong and Huang (2004) suggested that in the whole transmission process of sounds it should include the starting point, the process and the ending point, of which some concepts focus on the starting point, namely the production of the sound, such as 聲, and some concepts concentrate on the ending point, namely perception and evaluation of the sound, such as 音. According to this proposal, the selective differences on synaesthesia between 聲 and 音 can be reasonably explained. From the cognitive point of view (Gibbs, 2006), embodied action can influence conceptualization in languages. Compared with the ending point of the sound, humans can impose much more active actions on the starting point, whereas the perception and evaluation can be received much more passively. Therefore, the production of the sound is conceptualized and characterized more frequently than the perception through synaesthesia. Also, we speculate that the volition may result in the higher symmetry on sound production for 聲, which needs further research.

The difference on syntactic functions of synaesthetic combinations for 聲 and 音 can be explained by the combination of Generative Lexicon and the distinction between production and perception. In Generative Lexicon, qualia structure of a lexical item, including formal role, constitutive role, telic role and agentive role, can predict their performances in languages (Pustejovsky, 1995). As 聲 focuses on the production of the sound, the salient qualia role in its semantic information is the agentive role, which is usually related to an event or predicate that brings something into being. Conversely, synaesthetic modifiers always contribute to the formal role of 音, for 音 focuses on perception and evaluation of the sound.

5 Conclusion

This paper is devoted to a fine-grained study on the interaction between synaesthesia and the near synonyms 聲 and 音 of the auditory domain in Mandarin Chinese. We take a corpus-based approach and at the same time employ a combination method of qualitative and quantitative analyses. Eventually, some interesting findings are obtained.

In particular, 聲 and 音, as a pair of near synonyms in the auditory domain, have both similar properties and different characteristics on synaesthesia. In terms of similarities, both 聲 and 音 can be productive recipients of synaesthetic transfers and both can be described by vision and touch. Moreover, vision is observed to act as the most predominant source domain for these near synonyms. In addition, the differences on synaesthesia between 聲 and 音 are also apparent. 聲 receives much more synaesthetic modifications than 音, and also has a higher symmetry on synaesthetic modifiers selection. On the other hand, the combinations of synaesthetic modifications with 聲 are normally related to an event (i.e., production of the sound), while those with 音 always refer to an entity (namely the perception or evaluation of the sound).

[12] Frankly speaking, we have not figure out the reason why vision transfers more easily into hearing than touch. However, we think that this issue will not influence the hypothesis proposed in this paper, and should be involved in our future work.

The similarities and differences mentioned above can be explained by semantic information and cognitive motivations. Both 聲 and 音 can denote the sound, so they can inherit common semantic information from the sound, which result in the similarity on synaesthesia. However, the different cognitive focuses on the sound, namely the distinction between production and perception, make 聲 and 音 have different synaesthetic performances.

In general, we can conclude that auditory synaesthesia is sensitive to the cognitive dichotomy of production/perception in Mandarin Chinese. In other words, synaesthesia can be predicted and determined by the cognitive modelling. Therefore, besides the transfer tendency recognized by previous studies, linguistic synaesthesia exhibit another regularity, that is, it can be determined by cognitive motivations. Therefore, linguistic synaesthesia is not a kind of random associations of different sensations, but of many principles and regularities, which deserves much more attention and deeper studies.

In the following study, we will expand the research scope and test more interactions between synaesthesia and the cognitive modelling, through which we hope that our studies could contribute to bridging the research on synaesthesia in linguistics and that in neuroscience eventually.

Acknowledgments

We would like to give thanks to Dennis Tay from the Hong Kong Polytechnic University for his insightful comments on this work.

References

Chu-Ren Huang. 2015. Towards a Lexical Semantic Theory of Synaesthesia in Chinese. *Keynote Speech in the 16th Chinese Lexical Semantics Workshop (CLSW-16).* Beijing.

Dirk Geeraerts. 2010. *Theories of Lexical Semantics.* Oxford University Press, New York.

Francesca Strik Lievers. 2015. Synaesthesia: A Corpus-Based Study of Cross-Modal Directionality. *Sensory Perceptions in Language and Cognition: 69-95*

Jia-Fei Hong and Chu-Ren Huang. 洪嘉馡, 黃居仁. 2004. A Comparative Analysis on the Near Synonyms sheng1 and yin1: the Relation between Lexical Semantics and Concepts「聲」與「音」的近義辨析: 詞義與概念的關係. *In the International Conference on the Situations and Trends about Chinese Lexical Semantics* 漢語詞彙語意研究的現狀與發展趨勢國際學術研討會. Peking University 北京大學.

Jia-Fei Hong and Chu-Ren Huang. 洪嘉馡, 黃居仁. 2005. A Comparative Analysis on Perceptual Verbs with Near Synonyms: the Relation between Lexical Semantics and Concepts, 感官動詞的近義辨析：詞義與概念的關係. *In the 6th Chinese Lexical Semantics Workshop (CLSW-6): 20-24.* Xiamen.

Jia-Fei Hong and Chu-Ren Huang. 2006. Using Chinese GigaWord Corpus and Chinese Sketch Engine in Linguistic Research. *In the Proceeding of the 20th Pacific Asia Conference on Language, Information and Computation (PACLIC-20): 183-190.* Wuhan.

John Lyons. 1977. *Semantics (1).* Cambridge University Press, New York.

James Pustejovsky. 1995. *The Generative Lexicon.* The MIT Press, Cambridge.

Joseph M. Williams. 1976. Synaesthetic Adjectives: A Possible Law of Semantic Change. *Language 52(2): 461 – 478.*

Keh-jiann Chen, Chu-Ren Huang, Li-ping Chang, and Hui-Li Hsu. 1996. Sinica Corpus: Design Methodology for Balanced Corpora. *In the Proceeding of the 11th Pacific Asia Conference on Language, Information and Computation (PACLIC-11):167-176.* Seoul.

Lian-Cheng Chief, Chu-Ren Huang, Keh-Jian Chen, Mei-Chih Tsai and Li-li Chang. 2000. What Can Near Synonyms Tell Us. *Computational Linguistics and Chinese Language Processing 5(1): 47-60.*

Qingqing Zhao and Chu-Ren Huang. 2015. A Corpus-Based Study on Synaesthetic Adjectives in Modern Chinese. *In the 16th Chinese Lexical Semantics Workshop (CLSW-16).* Beijing.

Richard E. Cytowic. 1993. *The Man Who Tasted Shapes.* MIT Press, Massachusetts.

Raymond W. Gibbs. 2006. *Embodiment and Cognitive Science.* Cambridge University Press, New York.

Stephen Ullmann. 1957. *The Principles of Semantics.* Basil Blackwell, Oxford.

System Utterance Generation by Label Propagation over Association Graph of Words and Utterance Patterns for Open-Domain Dialogue Systems

Hiroshi Tsukahara **Kei Uchiumi**
Denso IT Laboratory, Inc.
Shibuya Cross Tower 28F, 2-15-1 Shibuya, Shibuya-ku, Tokyo, Japan

Abstract

A novel graph-based utterance generation method for open-domain dialogue systems is proposed in this paper. After an association graph of words and utterance patterns from a dialogue corpus is constructed, a label propagation algorithm is used for generating system utterances from the words and utterance patterns in the association graph that are found to strongly correlate with the words and utterance patterns that appeared in previous user utterances. We also propose a crowdsourcing framework for collecting annotated chat data so that we can implement our method in a cost effective manner. Crowdsourcing is also used for conducting subjective evaluations and the results will show that the proposed method can not only provide interesting and informative responses but it also can appropriately expand the topics by comparing them to a well-known chat system in Japanese.

1 Introduction

Chatting plays a lot of important roles in human communications for naturally exchanging diverse information, facilitating collaborative tasks, or even enhancing the quality of the conversations themselves. For dialogue systems as well, the functionality of being able to create chats is considered to have a significant importance regardless of whether task-oriented or non-task-oriented. There are currently many types of smart devices in our daily life and most of them have spoken dialogue interfaces, although they are basically limited to question-answering. However, there are cases where people do not always have the clear intent on searching for something but they just want to know whether there is anything interesting they should know. In such cases, if the systems could offer a chats function instead, people may be able to make such unconscious or potential intentions clear by themselves through chats with these systems.

However, it is quite challenging for dialogue systems to automatically generate chat responses because of the wide variety of topics in user utterances. In ordinary dialogue systems, i.e., rule-based systems, a very large number of hand-crafted rules and utterance patterns, or templates, would need to be prepared for extending the coverage of topics they can handle. However, this would be a very formidable task both to create them and to maintain them while keeping them up to date. Thus, a data-driven approach that makes use of the huge amount of conversational resources currently on the web, such as microblogs or social network media, as corpora have been recently investigated (Shibata et al., 2009; Sugiyama et al., 2013). These corpora contain a large number of sentences that cover a wide range of topics, but there are many noisy sentences that do not contain meaningful content themselves. Another issue with this approach is that it basically selects sentences that are similar to the user utterances on the surface-level. Thus, the generated responses tend to be monotonous and the topic of conversation is not naturally changed by these systems.

We propose a graph-based approach to address these issues. It is based on a dialogue corpus with a considerably large number of utterances. Out of a corpus, we construct an association graph, which

29th Pacific Asia Conference on Language, Information and Computation pages 323 - 331
Shanghai, China, October 30 - November 1, 2015

is a bipartite graph with word and utterance pattern nodes, where a word represents a named entity and an utterance pattern represents a template of utterances reduced by replacing their named entities with slots holding the type of named entities that are originally placed there. The association graph is used for finding words and utterance patterns that belong to the same semantic category, or topic of conversation, and formed dynamically using label propagation over the association graph with the words and utterance patterns of previous utterances. The system utterances are synthesized out of those words and utterance patterns.

This paper is organized as follows. First, we explore the use of crowdsourcing for efficiently constructing a dialogue corpus in Sec. 2. The details of the proposed method are described in Sec. 3. We discuss the results from a subjective evaluation in Sec. 4. These results support the concept that the proposed method can create responses with significant and interesting information and that it can appropriately expand the topics. We introduce the related works in Sec. 5. Finally, we give a summary and present some future prospects for the present study in Sec. 6

2 Framework for Constructing a Dialogue Corpus with Crowdsourcing

We describe our framework for constructing a dialogue corpus in text chats by making use of crowdsourcing. The utilization of crowdsourcing is now getting popular for collecting data and conducting user assessments. (Eskenazi et al., 2013; Lasecki et al., 2013; Mitchell et al., 2014). The merits for using crowdsourcing are that many workers can work simultaneously at low cost.

In addition, we can now find many kinds of online collaboration platforms like slack[1]. We can create a number of rooms, which are called channels in slack for example, where a number of workers can simultaneously create chats on those platforms. They also support highly interactive customizable browser interfaces and many APIs for connecting to other services provided outside themselves. Therefore, we can define our own markers that can be used for annotation, or we can send utterances to bot servers outside the system for watching the progress of a conversation or violations of the guidelines in real-time. The notification to workers can be sent from the bot server to the channels as well. The chat logs can also be exported using those APIs. Thus, we found these are ideal environments for collecting chat data, annotating them online, and remotely managing them.

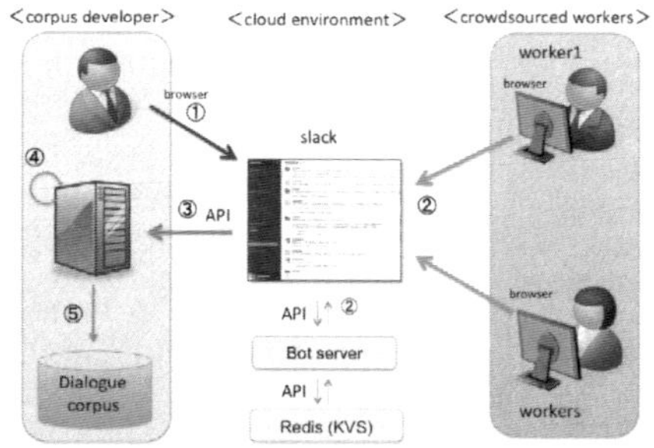

Figure 1: Framework for collecting chat data, annotating them, and exporting into a structured database as a corpus

We show our framework for collecting text chats, annotating them, and exporting the annotated chat logs into a structured database as a corpus in Fig. 1. We selected Slack as our online platform for this paper. The numbers in Fig. 1 show the procedural flow.

In the first procedure, the corpus developer creates a team in Slack and customizes the markers for quickly and correctly inputting annotations. Emoticons are used to represent these markers in a chat stream on the browser. We can create plural channels so that several pairs of workers are able to simultaneously input their chats. The connection to a bot server is also created so that the system can automatically watch the inputs by each worker. We use Hubot[2] for creating a bot server and Redis[3] for storing the working data of each worker. The bot server is placed on a cloud server hosted by Heroku[4]. In fact, all these components are open platforms and open source software. Thus, anyone can create such an environment without incurring any costs, so you can at least try this framework if you want.

In the second procedure, workers access the URL of a channel introduced by the corpus developer at a scheduled time. Once both of the workers arranged

[1]https://slack.com

[2]https://hubot.github.com/

[3]http://redis.io/

[4]https://www.heroku.com/

as a conversation pair come online, they start inputting utterances according to the prescribed guidelines. They begin with greetings and introducing themselves and expand the topics by selecting them from the specified genres. In our case, the workers are required to chat by choosing from news on current affairs, sports, entertainment, or gourmet information. The utterances input by the workers are sent to the bot server and the number of utterances are then counted. The check as to whether or not the utterances are in accord with the guidelines may also be checked here or presenting suggestions for annotation may also be sent on the fly to the workers in a working channel. A notification is sent to the channel directly if the number of utterances reaches a required amount so that the workers can notice the completion of a dialogue session. An example of the annotations for utterances are presented in Fig. 2. We designed the way of annotating so that the workers can easily input in the message format of the browser. We define only three kinds of annotations: (a) the location and type of named entities, (b) the dialogue acts of the utterances, and (c) the topics of the utterances. The types of dialogue acts is also limited to the following eight types so that even workers without a good knowledge of natural language processing can understand: (1) greetings, (2) yes-no questions, (3) yes-no answers, (4) provision of information/self-disclosure, (5) presentation of new topics, (6) questions, (7) answers, and (8) feedback/opinions. We found that it is useful to define some of the special annotations for smoothly managing the dialogue input tasks. For example, we define the annotation string "rem", which can be put at the beginning of the utterance, for indicating this utterance is in fact a comment. This annotation can be used to exchange messages between workers, corpus developers, and proofreaders directly on a channel. We also define the annotation string "NewDial", which is used by itself, to indicate the beginning of a new dialogue session.

In the third and fourth procedures, the chat logs are exported by the corpus developers in charge of proofreading the annotations. The annotations for each utterance are checked by two proofreaders in the present study. Thus, including a dialogue input worker, the annotations are checked by at least three people. We explain the proofreading procedures in

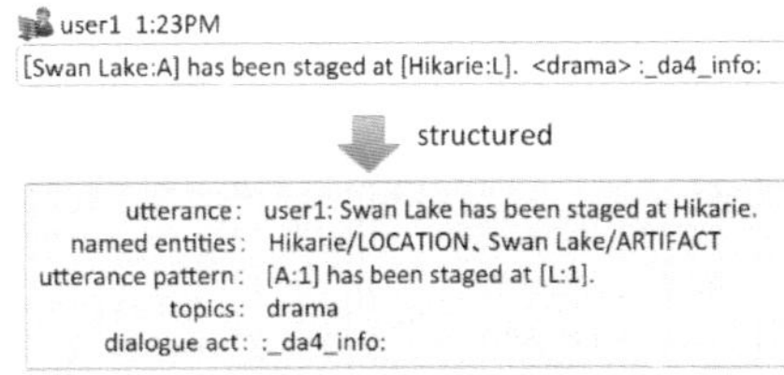

Figure 2: Example of annotations for an utterance. The square brackets ([and]) annotate the position of a named entity and its entity type is also supplied after a colon. The words enclosed in angle brackets ($<$ and $>$) annotate the topics of the utterance. A string enclosed by colons (e.g., :_da_info:) annotates the dialogue act of the utterance.

detail in the following paragraphs. After finishing proofreading the annotations, the fifth procedure is performed for exporting the annotated chat logs into a relational database to store the structured data of a dialogue corpus.

We recruited native Japanese-speaking crowd workers and collected twenty thousand annotated utterances over a period of about three months. The workers were distributed all over Japan from the north to the south and their ages ranged from 20 to 49. Only two workers were male. This size of the corpus was quite moderate compared to a web-scaled corpus, but it is still large enough for our proposed method to work. The speed of collecting annotated utterances depends on how many proofreaders are used. Proofreaders familiar with the work can check about six hundred utterances a day and two proofreaders were used in the present study.

We show the detailed procedures for proofreading annotations in Fig. 3. The numbers represent the flow of the proofreading procedures. The annotated utterances are exported for the first time in procedure (2). Then, two proofreaders check it in procedure (3), and the requests for revision are dispatched to each crowd worker from procedure (4) to (6), where the requests for revision are copied as a backup. Then, the workers revise the annotations by accessing the channel on Slack in procedure (7). The results of the revisions by the workers are checked by comparing them with the backup in procedure (8). If there are any differences, then new requests for revision are created in procedure (9). Procedures (4) to (9) are repeated until the differences are eliminated.

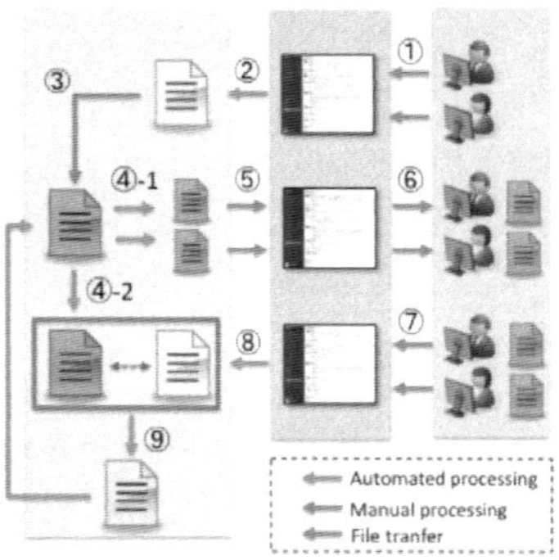

Figure 3: Procedures for proofreading annotations

The characteristic of our framework for collecting a corpus using crowdsourcing is that the workers are not independent but they collaborate with each other in one task. We can collect the utterances of the workers by using a dialogue system as a conversation partner. It might be reasonable to collect the user interaction behaviors using dialogue systems and make use of them to construct a dialogue corpus (Mitchell et al., 2014). We are interested in collecting worker dialogues to learn how people develop their conversations and how topics are naturally explored by them.

3 Graph-based Method for Generating Utterances

In this section, we describe our proposed method for generating utterances. It relies on an algorithm in semi-supervised learning called label propagation over graphs, and we apply it to the association graph of words and utterance patterns, and Fig. 4 depicts an example. We can see in the figure that the label propagation with the regularized Laplacian can successfully extract semantic categories depending on the structure of a bipartite graph of instances and patterns, i.e. words and utterance patterns in the present paper (Zhou et al., 2004; Komachi et al., 2009). Roughly speaking, the words and utterance patterns that are linked to each other are considered to share the same semantic relevance to some extent. This semantic relevance is called a semantic category and can be regarded as a topic talked about in the conversations. By making use of the label propagation over the association graph, we can extract words and utterance patterns that share the same semantic category with words and utterance patterns that appeared in previous utterances. It is expected that synthesizing those words and utterance patterns can help to generate utterances that expand the topics while maintaining the relevance to the current topic in a conversation.

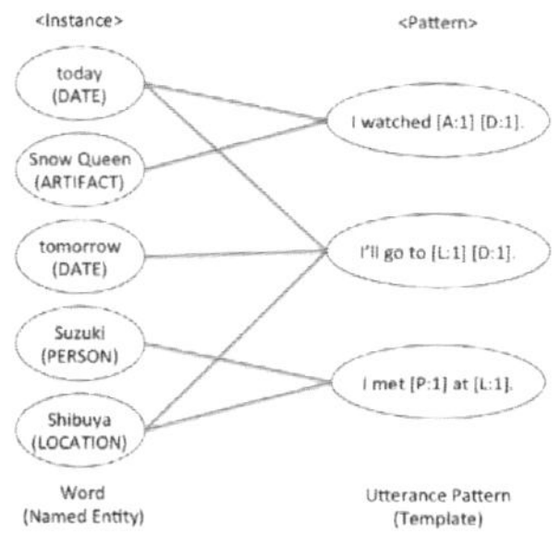

Figure 4: Association graph of words and utterance patterns.

We depict the architecture of our dialogue system in Fig. 5. Procedures (2) to (4) should be performed in advance to obtain the graph Laplacian data out of a corpus of procedure (1), which is necessary in the label propagation procedure. Procedure (2) extracts the named entities and utterance patterns making use of the annotations. The utterance patterns are obtained by replacing the named entities with slots that specify the type of named entities that can be applied. Then, an association graph of words and utterance patterns is constructed by linking the word and utterance pattern nodes if they co-occur in an utterance in the corpus. We introduce an instance-pattern matrix W, which represents the frequency of the co-occurrence of instances and patterns. Let us denote a word as w_i and a utterance pattern as p_j, and then, the instance-pattern matrix W is defined by

$$W_{ij} = \frac{|w_i, p_j|}{\sum_k |w_i, p_k|}, \quad (1)$$

where $|w, p|$ represents the frequency of the co-occurrence of a word w and an utterance pattern p.

In Laplacian label propagation, the similarity matrix A between instances is measured using a regularized Laplacian

$$L = I - D^{-1/2}(A)AD^{-1/2}(A), \quad (2)$$

in-stead of the naive product $A = W^TW$ of the instance-pattern matrix W, where $D(A)$ is a diagonal degree matrix defined as $D(A)_{ii} = \sum_j A_{ij}$.

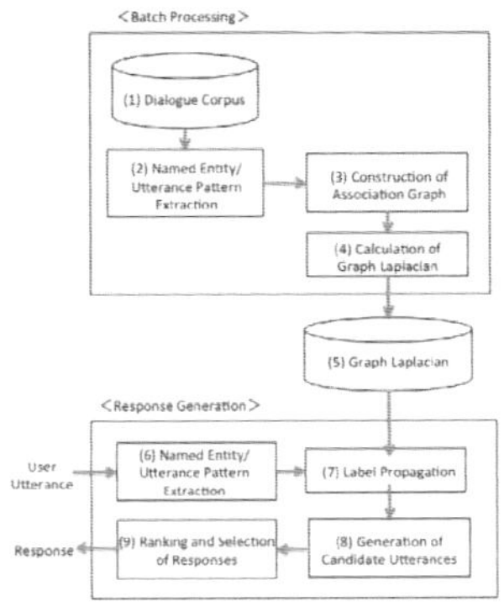

Figure 5: System architecture for utterance generation.

The regularized Laplacian has the effect of reducing the self-reinforcement by removing the contribution from the self-loops.

The procedure for generating responses to user utterances goes as follows. First, the named entities and an utterance pattern are extracted from the last utterance and the word and utterance pattern nodes in the association graph are matched to them if there are some that have the same word or utterance pattern. If these nodes are found, we assign a 1 as their initial score. For the other nodes that do not match, we assign a 0 as their initial score. We may take into consideration the history of the utterances before the last utterance as well. Let τ be the length of the turns that an utterance appeared in the past, i.e., $\tau = 1$ for the last utterance. Then, we extract the words and utterance patterns from those past utterances and search the association graph for word nodes or utterance patterns that match them. If some nodes are found, we assign $\lambda^{\tau-1}$ as their initial scores, where $\lambda \in (0, 1]$ is the decay rate. In practice, we limit τ to some extent T, such as $\tau \leq T$. By denoting the initial scores on the association graph as F_0, it is recursively spread using the following equation,

$$F_{t+1} = \alpha(-L)F_t + (1 - \alpha)F_0, \quad (3)$$

where a parameter $\alpha \in [0, 1)$ controls the contribution from the seeds and the graph structure. The contribution from the graph structure becomes dominant as the value of α approaches 1. The recursion is continued until the F_t score converges to F. In practice, this procedure is truncated within a finite number of recursions.

Let the resulting scores for each word w and utterance pattern p be $F(w)$ and $F(p)$. We define the score for an utterance s generated from an utterance pattern p and words $\{w_i | i = i_1, i_2, \ldots, i_n\}$ as

$$F(s) = \frac{1}{n} \sum_{k=1}^{n} F(w_{i_k})F(p). \quad (4)$$

We output the utterance s^*, which has the highest score among the generated utterances. There are cases where the utterance with the highest score already appeared in the current context of the dialogue, so we choose the utterance with the next highest score, and this is repeated until a new utterance is found.

4 Evaluation

We evaluated the performance of the proposed method by conducting a subjective assessment using crowdsourced workers. As the baseline for the evaluation, we adopted a well-known chat system in Japanese provided by NTT DoCoMo, Inc. The system is available through the Web API[5]. We call this chat system the baseline dialogue system in the paragraphs that follow.

We recruited twelve native Japanese-speaking crowd-workers in their 20's to 40's (seven females and five males). Each subject was presented five types of dialogues made for the same given seed utterance. We prepared 26 seed utterances as explained in the following paragraphs.

We selected topics from the top ten rankings of query keywords in Japan in 2014 provided by Google [6]. There were 55 different Japanese keywords among them. We limited them to 27 keywords from the genres of current affairs news, sports, entertainment, and TV programs which were covered by the corpus we constructed. However, our dialogue system failed to generate a response for one of them, so we omitted that keyword. Thus, we selected 26 keywords, among which 6 were from the field of current affairs, 6 from sports, 6 from entertainment, 2 from TV animations, and 6 from TV dramas (Tab. 1). As a seed utterance for each keyword, we picked the first sentence from the Wikipedia page with the given keyword as its title.

Starting from a seed utterance, we produced a dialogue using a pair of participants taking turns.

[5]https://dev.smt.docomo.ne.jp/

[6]http://googlejapan.blogspot.jp/2014/12/jp-year-in-search.html

Current affairs news	Nobel prize, Mt. Ontake, Haruko Obokata, Mamoru Samuragochi, Academy Awards, iPhone6
Sports	Asian Games, Yuzuru Hanyu, Kei Nishikori, Seiko Yamamoto, 2014 Winter Olympics, Mao Asada
Entertain-ment	Zawachin, May J., Takako Matsu, Sota Fukushi, Kanna Hashimoto, Japan Electric Union
Animations	Yokai Watch, Frozen
Dramas	Hanako to Anne, Massan, Sorry youth!, Gochisousan, Ken Takakura, First class

Table 1: List of keywords used for evaluation.

We produced five types of dialogues as indicated in Tab. 2. Each dialogue contained ten utterances including the seed utterance. In the cases of dialogues produced by human and system participants, the seed utterance was regarded as created by the human participant. For the cases of dialogues between two human participants, males in 30's and 40's were used separately from workers in charge of the assessment. One participant in their 30's was involved in all the type (a), (b) and (c) dialogues to avoid any fluctuation caused by the difference in participants. The type (a) dialogues were prepared to check whether the workers honestly assessed the dialogues. In the case where the evaluation of a worker for the type (a) dialogues was unnaturally bad, we could detect that the worker was cheating. We also added the type (d) and (e) dialogues to exclude the influence of the choice of human participant for creating the dialogues. These five types of dialogues were produced for all 26 keywords, respectively.

a	human vs. human
b	human vs. proposed dialogue system
c	human vs. baseline dialogue system
d	proposed dialogue system vs. proposed dialogue system
e	baseline dialogue system vs. baseline dialogue system

Table 2: Types of produced dialogues

We specify an example of a dialogue produced in the type (b) dialogues in Tab. 3. The initial topic keyword is Kei Nishikori in this example. The system successfully extracted the keyword Kei Nishikori from the seed utterance and generated the utterance to inform what organization he is endorsed by. A new keyword Cup Noodle was presented by a human participant, then the system expanded the topic by informing there is a series of interesting Cup Noodle's TV commercials that the comedian trio Dacho Club appeared.

U	Kei Nishikori is a male Japanese professional tennis player from Shimane Prefecture.
S	Kei Nishikori is endorsed by Nissin Food, so Nissin Food is benefiting from a worldwide advertising effect.
U	You mean Nissin's Cup Noodles could become hot sellers?
S	The Cup Noodle's TV commercial "Real intention and stated reason" in which the comedian trio Dacho Club appeared in is better known, isn't it?
U	Is there such a TV commercial? I didn't know.
S	I've seen the Cup Noodle's TV commercial "Real intention and stated reason" in which Dacho Club appeared only once.
U	What kind of story was it?
S	If you get to know the stories background, you could better enjoy watching the Cup Noodle's TV commercial "Real intention and stated reason" in which Dacho Club appeared.
U	Recently there are many commercials that continue in a series like dramas.
S	It was interesting watching the Cup Noodle's TV commercial "Real intention and stated reason" in which Dacho Club appeared.

Table 3: Example of dialogue in type (b) dialogues. U represents the turns by a human participant and S represents the turns by the proposed dialogue system.

We present these prepared dialogues to the workers in charge of the assessment by randomly shuffling the order of the dialogues for each keyword. We set up nine criteria to collect the workers' judgments on the dialogues as classified in Tab. 4. For the question concerning criterion C1, the workers answered in the order of their preference for the dialogues. The order was 1 for the best one and 5 for the worst. While for the question concerning criterion C2, the workers answered using a 4-point Likert scale: 4 for strongly agree, 3 for agree, 2 for disagree, 1 for strongly disagree. For the rest of the criteria, the workers answered using 6-point Likert scale: 6 for excellent, 5 for good, 4 for rather good, 3 for rather poor, 2 for poor, and 1 for terrible. It must be noted that criteria C2 and C7 are related and they are also used for checking the reliability of the judgments by the workers.

A Kruskal-Wallis test was performed on the results of the judgments by the workers to see whether there were statistically significant differences in the distributions of the scores selected by the workers for the five types of dialogues. The results are indicated in the notched box plots for each criterion in Fig. 6 – 14. It must be noted that we divided the workers into two groups with six workers to check the influence of the selection of workers. The boxes for dialogue types (a) to (e) are placed from the left to right in each plot. Although slight deviations are seen, the plots for the two worker groups basically agree with each other, which confirms the reliability of the results of the judgments by the workers. In addition, we found the type (a) dialogues have the best assessment for all the criteria with only slight deviations; there are cases where the boxes even collapse as seen in Figs. 6, 7, and 14. The plots in Figs. 7 and 12 do not qualitatively contradict each other as well. Thus, we can confirm all the workers earnestly conducted their evaluations.

C1	Personal preference for dialogues (like or dislike)
C2	Quality of expanding topics as a chat
C3	Quality of naturalness of utterances as a chat
C4	Quality of interest of content in utterances
C5	Quality of usefulness of information in utterances
C6	Quality of naturalness of continuity in two consecutive utterances
C7	Quality of continuity from topic to topic
C8	Grammatical appropriateness of utterances in Japanese
C9	Semantic appropriateness of utterances

Table 4: Criteria for assessment

The type (b) dialogues were judged as the highest next to the type (a) dialogues, outperforming other types of dialogues in most of the plots. The widths and shifts of the notches of the boxes indicate that the type (b) dialogues were statistically significantly superior to the other types of dialogues from (c) to (e), showing the effectiveness of our proposed method. Qualitatively the same plots were observed for other criteria as well. Surprisingly, in criteria C4 and C5, the type (d) dialogues gained a better assessment than the type (c) dialogues; nevertheless the type (d) dialogues were made only by the systems and the type (c) dialogues involved the human participant. This shows our method is especially superior in generating interesting and informative utterances compared to the baseline dialogue system.

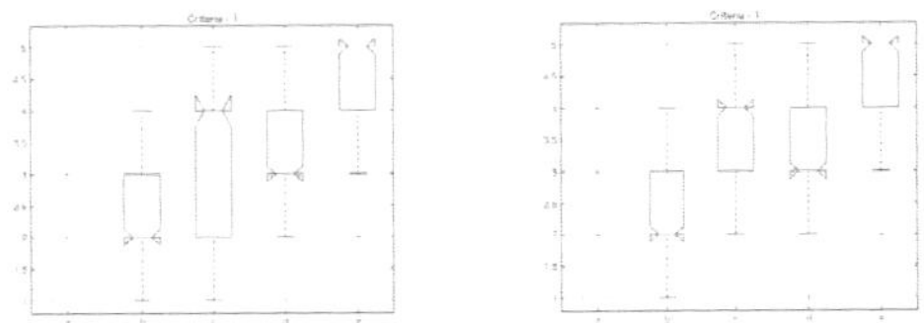

group-1 group-2

Figure 6: Plots of Kruskal-Wallis test for criterion C1.

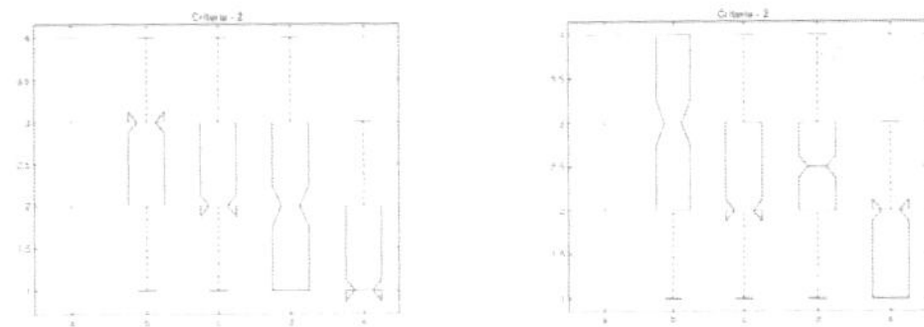

group-1 group-2

Figure 7: Plots of Kruskal-Wallis test for criterion C2.

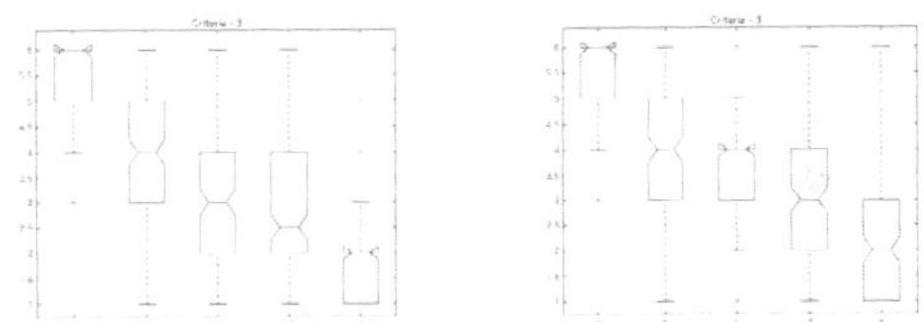

group-1 group-2

Figure 8: Plots of Kruskal-Wallis test for criterion C3.

5 Related Works

There are several modeling in the data driven approach. There is a statistical machine translation modeling for generating chat responses to the user utterances (Ritter et al., 2011). In this approach, generating a response to an input utterance is regarded as a mapping in translation. Collaborative filter modeling was also investigated, where responses are selected in terms of the user preference (Jafarpour and Burges, 2010). Making use of

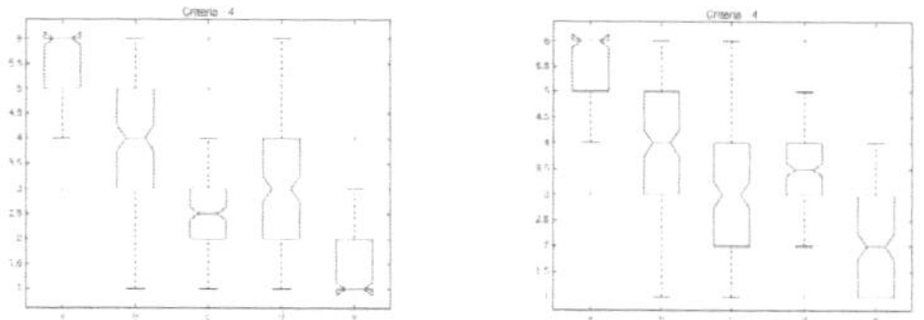

group-1 group-2

Figure 9: Plots of Kruskal-Wallis test for criterion C4.

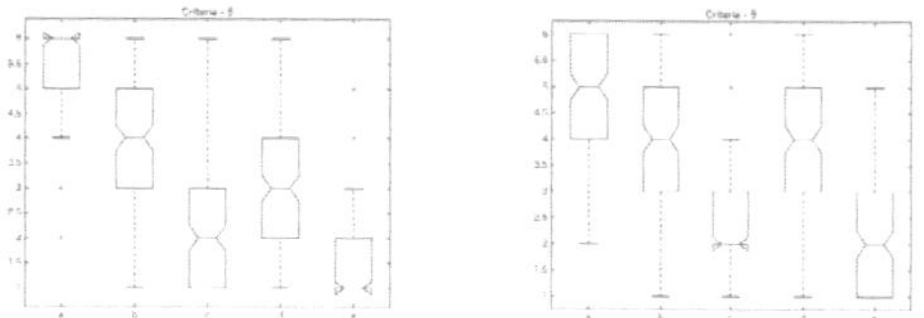

group-1 group-2

Figure 10: Plots of Kruskal-Wallis test for criterion C5.

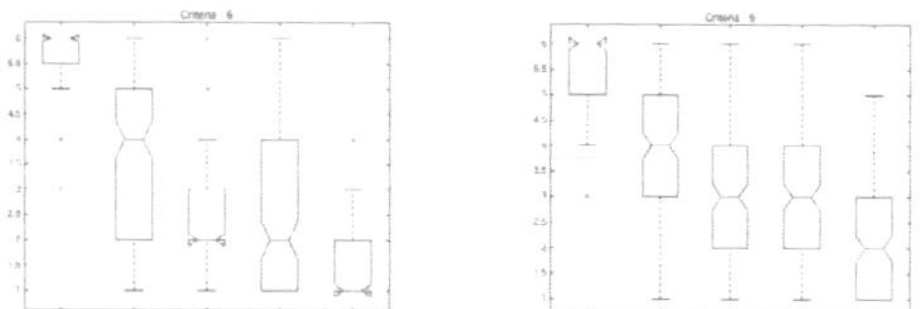

group-1 group-2

Figure 11: Plots of Kruskal-Wallis test for criterion C6.

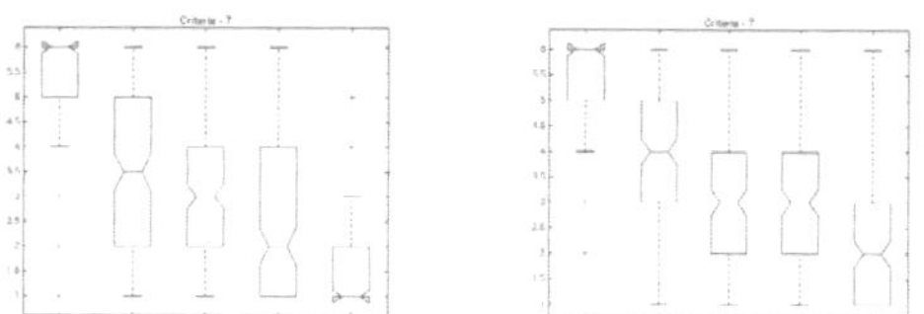

group-1 group-2

Figure 12: Plots of Kruskal-Wallis test for criterion C7.

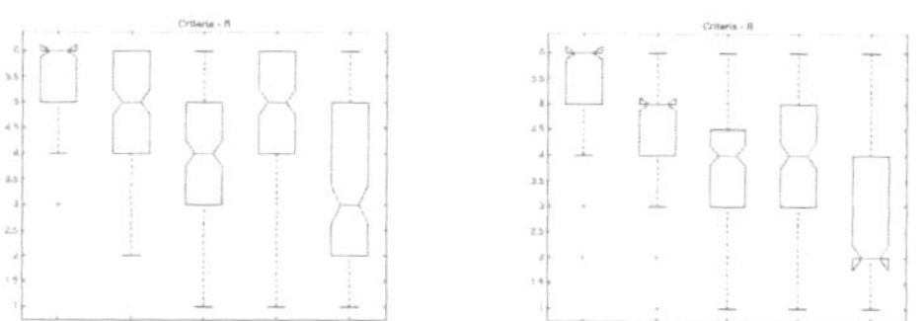

group-1 group-2

Figure 13: Plots of Kruskal-Wallis test for criterion C8.

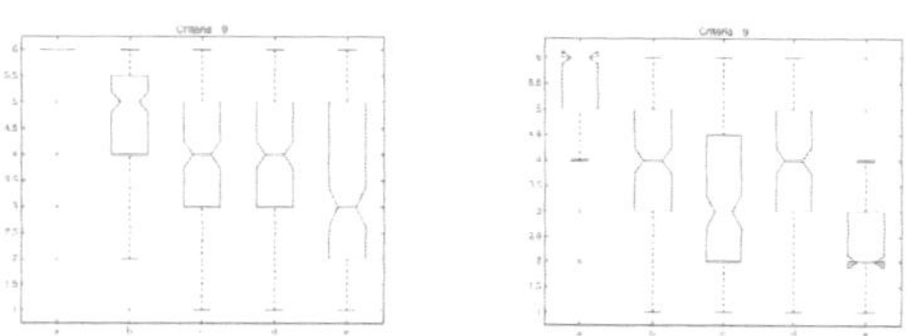

group-1 group-2

Figure 14: Plots of Kruskal-Wallis test for criterion C9.

recently raising crowdsourcing as a novel dynamical resource has also been proposed (Bessho et al., 2012).

6 Conclusion

We proposed a novel graph-based approach in this paper for the generation of system utterances in open-domain dialogue systems. Being different from ordinary statistical approaches, which basically select system responses from the utterances in a dialogue corpus that match an input utterance in surface-level similarity, utterances that semantically match an input utterance are generated by making use of the label propagation algorithm over an association graph of words and utterance patterns extracted from a dialogue corpus in the proposed approach. Thus, it is possible to generate non-trivial utterances that do not match the input utterances in surface-level and the topics of a dialogue can be expanded naturally.

We also proposed a framework for effectively collecting utterances and denoting the annotations simultaneously by making use of crowdsourcing and cloud open collaboration platforms. This framework is considered to have an advantage over the frameworks that make use of microblogs or Wikipedia in that we can control the quality of the contents of a dialogue corpus.

We implemented the proposed algorithm by constructing a considerably large dialogue corpus. The subjective evaluation was performed by using crowdsourcing workers and the effectiveness of the proposed approach was confirmed.

Our future work will focus on creating a dialogue act classifier making use of the annotations of the constructed dialogue corpus and integrating the filtering of responses so that they are in accordance with the recognized dialogue act of a previous utterance. Then it is expected that we can generate more natural responses than the current system can.

The framework of the label propagation can also be extended by adding more layers to the association graph, such as adding a layer of topic nodes. Then, the expansion of topics can be controlled by specifying the target topics that a system wants to move to.

References

Fumihiro Bessho, Tatsuya Harada, and Yasuo Kuniyoshi. 2012. Dialog system using real-time crowdsourcing and twitter large-scale corpus. In *SIGDIAL '12*, pages 227–231.

Maxine Eskenazi, Gina-Anne Levow, Helen Meng, Gabriel Parent, and David Suendermann. 2013. *Crowdsourcing for Speech Processing: Applications to Data Collection, Transcription and Assessment*. Wiley Publishing, 1st edition.

Sina Jafarpour and Christopher J.C. Burges. 2010. Filter, rank, and transfer the knowledge: Learning to chat. Technical Report MSR-TR-2010-93, July.

Mamoru Komachi, Shimpei Makimoto, Kei Uchiumi, and Manabu Sassano. 2009. Learning semantic categories from clickthrough logs. In *Proceedings of the ACL-IJCNLP 2009 Conference Short Papers*, pages 189–192, Suntec, Singapore, August. Association for Computational Linguistics.

Walter S. Lasecki, Ece Kamar, Dan Bohusa, and Eric Horvitz. 2013. Conversations in the crowd: Collecting data for task-oriented dialog learning. In *Workshop at Conference on Human Computation and Crowdsourcing 2013*.

Margaret Mitchell, Dan Bohus, and Ece Kamar, 2014. *Proceedings of the INLG and SIGDIAL 2014 Joint Session*, chapter Crowdsourcing Language Generation Templates for Dialogue Systems, pages 172–180.

Alan Ritter, Colin Cherry, and William B. Dolan. 2011. Data-driven response generation in social media. In *Proceedings of the Conference on Empirical Methods in Natural Language Processing*, EMNLP '11, pages 583–593, Stroudsburg, PA, USA. Association for Computational Linguistics.

Masahiro Shibata, Tomomi Nishiguchi, and Yoichi Tomiura. 2009. Dialog system for open-ended conversation using web documents. *Informatica*, 33(3):277–284.

Hiroaki Sugiyama, Toyomi Meguro, Ryuichiro Higashinaka, and Yasuhiro Minami, 2013. *Proceedings of the SIGDIAL 2013 Conference*, chapter Open-domain Utterance Generation for Conversational Dialogue Systems using Web-scale Dependency Structures, pages 334–338. Association for Computational Linguistics.

Dengyong Zhou, Olivier Bousquet, Thomas N. Lal, Jason Weston, and Bernhard Schölkopf. 2004. Learning with local and global consistency. In S. Thrun, L.K. Saul, and B. Schölkopf, editors, *Advances in Neural Information Processing Systems 16*, pages 321–328. MIT Press.

The Cross-modal Representation of Metaphors

Yu-tung Chang
Department of English
National Chengchi University
ytchang@nccu.edu.tw

Kawai Chui
Department of English
National Chengchi University
kawai@nccu.edu.tw

Abstract

This study investigates the habitual expressions of metaphors in language and gesture and the collaboration of these two modalities in conveying metaphors. This study examined 247 metaphoric expressions in Mandarin conversations. The data includes 110 (44.5%) metaphors being conveyed concurrently by speech and gesture as well as 137 (55.5%) metaphors being conveyed in gesture exclusively. Results show that Entity metaphor is the most frequent one expressed in daily conversations. The cooperation of language and gesture enables us to evaluate the various hypotheses of speech-gesture production. Results from this study tend to support the Interface Hypothesis, which suggests that gestures are generated from an interface representation between speaking and spatio-motoric thought.

1 Introduction

The thought that metaphor is not restricted to the realm of literature has been widely accepted since Lakoff and Johnson's study of conceptual metaphor in 1980. In Lakoff and Johnson's framework, the word *metaphor* refers to the "metaphorical concept" in thought and is presented in a form with small capital letters, for example, LOVE IS A JOURNEY (Lakoff & Johnson, 1980: 6). Metaphor can be conceived as a conceptual mapping from one domain to another domain (Lakoff, 1993). The Conceptual Metaphor Theory maintains four significant views about metaphors: metaphor is in thoughts; metaphor is based on the correlations or the structural similarity between two domains; metaphor helps to structure our ordinary conceptual system; and metaphor can be grounded in the body or socio-cultural experiences.

According to Lakoff and Johnson (1980), language is an essential modality for us to understand the metaphors. Although we are not usually aware of our conceptual system, we can explore the system by studying language, since communication shares the same system we use in thinking (Lakoff & Johnson, 1980). Because metaphors are conceptual, language is not the exclusive realization of metaphors. In the past studies (Cienki, 2008; Cienki & Müller, 2008; Müller, 2008; Gibbs, 2008), gesture is regarded as an independent non-verbal modality where we may find the metaphorical expressions. McNeill (1992: 14) states that metaphoric gestures are "like iconic gestures in that they are pictorial, but the pictorial content presents an abstract idea rather than a concrete object or event...[and] presents an image of the invisible—an image of an abstraction". A gestural study may also help to enhance the cognitive reality of metaphors. Therefore, the present study collects metaphoric expressions from conversational data, which allow us to see the cross-modal manifestations of metaphors.

Previous research on metaphors in language (Lakoff & Johnson, 1980; Lakoff, 1993; Kövecses, 2002) and gesture (McNeill, 1992; Cienki, 2008; Müller, 2008; Chui, 2011, 2013) have offered insightful thoughts and visible evidence about conceptual metaphor, such as the common source-domain and target-domain concepts, the correspondences between two domains, the profiles of metaphors, and the embodiment of metaphors. Nevertheless, most of them only take

29th Pacific Asia Conference on Language, Information and Computation pages 332 - 340
Shanghai, China, October 30 - November 1, 2015

account of qualitative analysis. This study would like to explore the metaphoric expressions from a quantitative perspective so that we can have reliable information about the habitual expressions of metaphors as well as the synchronization and collaboration of linguistic and gestural modality.

In addition, there are three hypotheses about the production process of speech and gesture: the Free Imagery Hypothesis (Krauss et al., 1996, 2000; de Ruiter, 2000), the Lexical Semantic Hypothesis (Schegloff, 1984; Butterworth & Hadar, 1989), and the Interface Hypothesis (Kita & Öyzürek, 2003). The first hypothesis maintains that gestures are independent from the content of speech and that gestures are produced before the formulation of speech. The second one suggests that gestures are generated from the semantics of lexical items. The third one sustains that the information in gesture originates from the representations based on the on-line interaction of spatial thinking and speaking. Kita and Öyzürek (2003) have conducted research on the cross-linguistic expressions of motion events to look at the three hypotheses. They focused on the informational coordination between iconic gestures and their corresponding lexical affiliates. Likewise, the present study investigates the relationship between language and gesture, but we will discuss the hypotheses from the perspective of metaphorical expressions.

To discuss (i) people's habitual expressions of metaphors to conceptualize concepts in daily communication, and (ii) the collaboration of language and gesture in expressing metaphors with regard to the hypothesis of speech-gesture production, this study address the following questions. What are the metaphor types people usually convey in daily communication? What is the temporal patterning of speech and gesture in presenting metaphors? What is the relevant linguistic unit accompanying the metaphoric gesture?

2 Data

The linguistic data used in this study is taken from the NCCU Corpus of Spoken Chinese[1] (Chui & Lai 2008). Its sub-corpus of spoken Mandarin includes daily face-to-face conversations collected since 2006. The participants in the conversations were familiar with each other and felt free to talk about any topics in front of a visible camera. From each conversation, a stretch (about twenty to forty minutes) was selected for transcription. The linguistic data used in this study come from twenty-six conversations in the sub-corpus of spoken Mandarin, and these conversations totally take about nine hours and fifty seconds. The gestural data relevant for this study are obtained from the gesture analysis of the twenty-six transcribed conversations.

Since this study has interest in the collaboration of language and gesture in expressing metaphorical concepts, metaphors occurring alone in speech were excluded. This study focuses on the metaphors concurrently manifested in speech and gesture ('language-gesture' or 'L-G') as well as the metaphors merely realized in gesture ('gesture-only' or 'G-only', i.e., a concept is metaphorically expressed in gesture but literally conveyed in speech). There are totally 247 metaphors examined in this study. These metaphors are divided into two main groups: the L-G group and the G-only group. The L-G group contains 110 (44.5%) metaphoric expressions; the G-only group involves 137 (55.5%) metaphors.

3 The Habitual Expressions of Metaphors

This study sorts the metaphoric expressions by different metaphor types to discuss people's habitual expression of metaphor in daily conversation. Several metaphor types have been proposed in the past studies (Reddy, 1979; Lakoff & Johnson, 1980, 1999; McNeill, 1992; Lakoff, 1993; Talmy, 1996; Gibbs, 2005, 2006). Based on the past research, this study recognizes nine kinds of metaphors to analyze both the linguistic and gestural data: body-part metaphor, causation metaphor, conduit metaphor, container metaphor, entity metaphor, fictive-motion metaphor, orientation metaphor, personification metaphor, and complex metaphor.

3.1 Classification of Metaphor Types

Except for the body-part metaphor and the personification metaphor, the other kinds of metaphors are produced from the current data. The following shows the definitions of these metaphors

[1] The website of the NCCU Corpus of Spoken Chinese is http://spokenchinesecorpus.nccu.edu.tw/

and the representative instances obtained from the data examined.

The *causation metaphor* treats causes as forces and causations/changes as movements (Lakoff, 1993). The concept of causation is metaphorically understood as a physical force resulting in motion or change of something. Lakoff and Johnson (1999: 184) proposed that *bring*, *drive*, *pull*, *push*, *throw* are all verbs of forced movement and they can be used to indicate abstract causation. This study finds an instance of the causation metaphor PSYCHOLOGICAL COMPELLING IS PUSHING in the G-only group as shown in Example 1. The speaker literally expresses the psychological operation with the verb *bī* 'compel'. Simultaneously, her hands forcefully push forward (Figure 1). The speaker does not physically push her boyfriend, yet a physical force is utilized to conceptualize a psychological force to cause someone to carry out a certain action.

(1) F1: *..nà wǒ jiù yìzhí* ***bī*** *tā*
'Then I keep compelling him.'

Figure 1. PSYCHOLOGICAL COMPELLING IS PUSHING in gesture

The *conduit metaphor* conceptualizes human communication as a conduit which can physically transfer our thoughts or feelings (Reddy, 1979). This kind of metaphor involves an important mechanism in which communication is seen as the action of sending. Example 2 is an instance of the conduit metaphor PROVIDING KNOWLEDGE IS TRANSFERRING OBJECTS which conveyed in both language and gesture. The speaker uses the verb *guànshū* 'transport' which indicates that the process of providing knowledge is metaphorically conceived as sending discrete entities. She also depicts the imagery of transferring something toward herself twice by her hand movement (Figure 2). This gesture does not refer to the physical action of sending but the abstract concept of offering knowledge.

(2) F: *..jiù jiāo de yǐjīng* ***guànshū*** *wǒmen hěn duō le*
'(They) teach and give us much knowledge.'

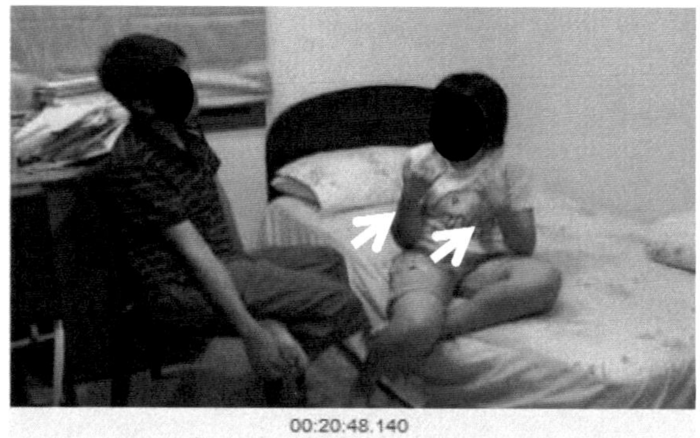

Figure 2. PROVIDING KNOWLEDGE IS TRANSFERRING OBJECTS in gesture

The *container metaphor* is the metaphor in which its target domain is conceived in terms of a container with a bounded surface and in-out orientation. In Example 3, the container metaphor A BASIN IS A CONTAINER is realized by both language and gesture.

(3) F: *..táiběi dìshì dīwā ..péndì* ***zuāng shuǐ***
'Taipei is in the low-lying area..the basin is filled with water.'

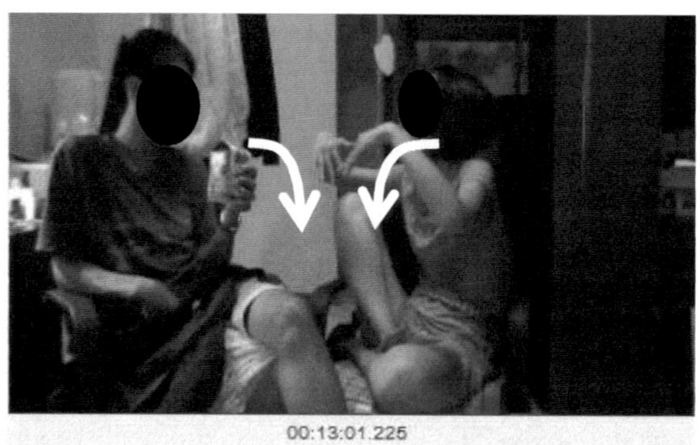

Figure 3. A BASIN IS A CONTAINER in gesture

A bounded surface is imposed to a land area without a physical or delineated boundary. The utterance *péndì zuāng shuǐ* 'basin is filled with water' shows that a basin is seen as a container. The physical land area is provided with artificial boundary which enables the land to have the function of a container to keep liquid in its interior. The metaphor is also expressed by the downward movement of the speaker's hands which depicts the image of pouring water into a container (Figure 3) and shows the in-out orientation about the concept of CONTAINER.

The *entity metaphor* conceptualizes a target domain in terms of discrete object or substances. In Example 4, the entity metaphor SPEECH CONTENT IS AN OBJECT is manifested in both language and gesture. The term *yìxiē* 'some' quantify the speech content, showing that SPEECH CONTENT is verbally conveyed as an object. In gesture, the speaker's right open palm turns up with slightly curled fingers to represent SPEECH CONTENT as a discrete object held in her hand (Figure 4).

(4) F1: *..jiù nǐ kěnéng jiǎng* ***yìxiē*** *shémo dōngxī*
'You may say something.'

Figure 4. SPEECH CONTENT IS AN OBJECT in gesture

The *fictive-motion metaphor* refers to the metaphor in which static things or abstract concepts are conceived in terms of dynamic motions. Such motion is called "fictive motion" (Talmy, 1996), since it does not have physical occurrences. Example 5 presents the fictive-motion metaphor THE SHIFT OF SPEECH CONTENT IS A MOTION in both language and gesture. The speaker states that a teacher's speech content always changes abruptly. The speech content of a talk does not really move; it is conceptualized in terms of fictive motion when the speaker utters the verb *tiào* 'jump'. Simultaneously, the speaker's one hand moves to upper left or upper right position as the other hand moves to the center position for three times (Figure 5). The gestural imagery of the movement to different spaces metaphorically represents the abstract concept SHIFT OF THE SPEECH CONTENT via MOTION.

(5) F: *..zhèbiān jiǎng yòu* ***tiào nàbiān***
..tiào nàbiān ..tiào nàbiān
'(He) talked about this and (the speech content) shifts to there, shifts to there, and shifts to there.'

Figure 5. THE SHIFT OF SPEECH CONTENT IS A MOTION in gesture

The *orientation metaphor* is the metaphor in which a target domain concept is conceptualized in terms of spatial concepts, including spatial orientations, path, location, etc. Example 6 shows the orientation metaphor AFTERNOON IS DOWN in both language and gesture. The speaker utters *xiàwǔ* 'afternoon' in speech, and the spatial term *xià* 'down' show that up-down orientation is used to refer to the abstract concept TIME. Simultaneously, the speaker's left fingers points down to metaphorically present the concept of AFTERNOON (Figure 6).

(6) F1: ***..xiàwǔ*** *dōushì ...déduó nà yíge mā*
'Are the classes in the afternoon taught by that German?'

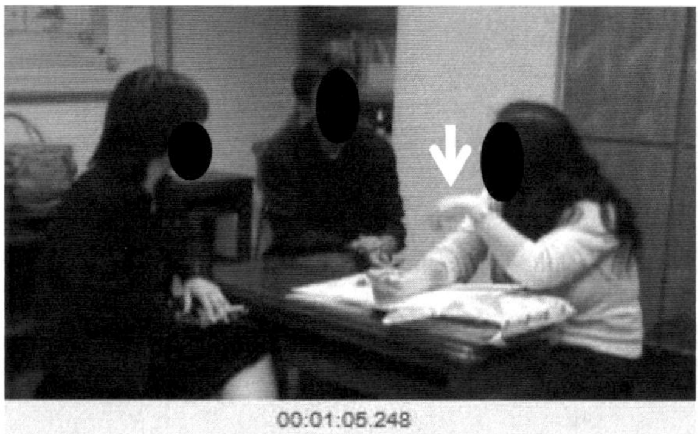

Figure 6. AFTERNOON IS DOWN in gesture

The *complex metaphor* refers to the metaphor which has no direct and independent correlation to our sensory-motor experiences. However, we still need the knowledge of our bodily experience or socio-cultural practices to comprehend such metaphor. Example 7 includes the expression of the complex metaphor CHOOSING PASSENGERS IS PICKING OBJECTS in both speech and gesture.

(7) F: *..dāng jìchéngchē ..**jiǎn** sānge **kèrén***
'(We are) the taxi driver and choose three passengers'

Figure 7. CHOOSING PASSENGERS IS PICKING OBJECTS in gesture

The speaker and her friend plan to attend a conference by car and mention that they can choose three slender girls to go with them. She utters *jiǎn sānge kèrén* 'pick three passengers' to describe the mental process of choosing people to go with them. At the same time, the speaker's right index finger and thumb make a pinch and move from the rather right position to her left hand at the center position twice (Figure 7). Such a gesture represents the idea of CHOOSING PASSENGERS as the imagery of picking objects. The physical activity of picking objects is the socio-cultural practice we perform in ordinary life, and it provides the basis for the complex metaphor in this case.

3.2 The Cross-Model Manifestation of Metaphors

Distribution of the metaphor types in Mandarin conversations is presented in Table 1. In the L-G group, six metaphor types are found. A large number of the expressions belong to entity metaphor (71.9%). Orientation metaphor accounts for 21.8%. Fictive-motion metaphor, container metaphor, conduit metaphor, and complex metaphor comprise less than 10% of the metaphors in language and gesture. Within the G-only group, four metaphor types are found. Entity metaphor is the overwhelming majority (82.5%), and orientation metaphor takes the second place (13.9%). Causation metaphor and complex metaphor just account for a small portion of metaphors in G-only.

Metaphor type	Group				Total	
	L-G		G-Only			
Entity metaphor	79	71.9%	113	82.5%	192	77.8%
Orientation metaphor	24	21.8%	19	13.9%	43	17.4%
Fictive-motion metaphor	3	2.7%	0	0.0%	3	1.2%
Container metaphor	2	1.8%	0	0.0%	2	0.8%
Conduit metaphor	1	0.9%	0	0.0%	1	0.4%
Causation metaphor	0	0.0%	1	0.7%	1	0.4%
Complex metaphor	1	0.9%	4	2.9%	5	2.0%
Total	110	100%	137	100%	247	100 %

Table 1. Types of metaphors in Mandarin conversations

In both the L-G and the G-only groups, entity metaphor is the one that people use more commonly to conceptualize metaphoric thoughts. When we conceive concepts in terms of entity metaphor, we are able to "refer to them, categorize them, group them, and quantify them—and, by this means, reason about them" (Lakoff & Johnson, 1980: 25). Entity metaphors serve various purposes, so they are widely used in everyday life. The Chi-square test shows that the difference between the L-G and the G-only groups is statistically significant regarding the metaphor types (χ^2 = 12.601, df = 6, p = 0.049) . Entity metaphors are prone to occur in the G-only group rather than the L-G group.[2] No causation metaphor is realized by the metaphor in the L-G group.

Results from current data agree with one of McNeill's (1992) claims in his study on metaphoric gestures in narratives. He asserted that entity metaphor and orientation metaphor are "instantly available" (McNeill, 1992: 163).[3] He also stated that Chinese lacks the gestures in which abstract ideas are represented as bounded and supported objects. Nevertheless, this study denies such a view. The gestural imagery to represent ideas as the bounded objects held in hand(s) is not rare in the current data. This kind of gestural expression is classified as the entity metaphor in this study. Within the entity metaphors, 73.4% (141 out of the total of 192 entity metaphors) of them involve the gestural representation of a bounded object supported in hand(s). The finding based on the current data then opposes McNeill's assertion that the image of a bounded and supported object is not a major source of metaphoric expressions in Chinese culture.

4 The Collaboration of Language and Gesture in Metaphoric Expressions

Different theoretical hypotheses about the production of speech and gesture—the Free Imagery Hypothesis, the Lexical Semantic Hypothesis, and the Interface Hypothesis—are proposed in previous studies. According to the Free Imagery Hypothesis, the content of speech will not affect what is encoded in gesture. All the data examined in this study, however, involve the gestures that are affiliated with corresponding lexicons. The referent of a metaphoric gesture is not the concrete imagery but the abstract concept that is also conveyed in the accompanying speech. While the Free Imagery Hypothesis provides a view about the production process of speech and gesture, this hypothesis is not suitable for discussing the findings based on the analysis taken in this study. Therefore, the present study put emphasis on the Lexical Semantic Hypothesis and the Interface Hypothesis.

To begin with, the temporal patterning of speech and gesture in conveying metaphors is discussed to evaluate the theoretical hypotheses. The Lexical Semantic Hypothesis suggests gestures are generated from the semantics of the lexical items. If a person has difficulty to produce a word for a concept in language, the production of gesture may help he/she to search a lexical item for such a concept. Hence, it is claimed that a gesture usually precedes the lexical component it depicts. The Interface Hypothesis, on the other hand, suggests that gestures are generated from the interactions between speaking and spatial thinking. In McNeill's (1985; 1992) framework, he proposed that a gesture lines up in time with the equivalent linguistic unit in speech. The temporal synchronization shows that speech and gesture belong to the same psychological structure and share a computational stage.

In order to examine the temporal relationship between speech and gesture in expressing metaphor, this study focuses on the stroke phase which is the relevant part to conveying information in a gesture.[4] There are three kinds of temporal patterning of speech and gestures: the *synchronizing gesture* (i.e., the stroke synchronizes with the associated words), the *preceding gesture* (i.e., the stroke comes before the associated words), and the *following gesture* (i.e., the stroke comes after the associated words). The distribution of each kind of gesture is shown in Table 2. In each group, synchronizing gestures comprise the majority (84.5% in the L-G group and 84.7% in the G-only group). The current data also contains several instances of preceding gestures (12.7% in

[2] The standardized residuals for entity metaphor are -2.0 in the L-G group and 2.0 in the G-only group.

[3] McNeill's (1992: 163) original words are "[c]onduit and spatial metaphors are instantly available." The conduit metaphor defined by McNeill is parallel to the entity metaphor in this study, since his definition did not involve the important feature of the conduit metaphor—the process of sending. His spatial metaphor is called orientation metaphor in this paper.

[4] According to McNeill (1992: 83), there are three phases of gesture: (i) the preparation phase in which the limb moves from its rest position to gesture space, (ii) the stroke phase which express the meaning of the gesture, and (iii) the retraction phase in which the limb returns to a rest position. Both the preparation and the retraction phases are optional, but the stroke phase is obligatory.

the L-G group and 15.3% in the G-only group). The following gestures are not common in each group of metaphoric expressions (2.7% in the L-G group and 0.0% in the G-only group). The Chi-square test shows that the differences between the L-G group and the G-only group are statistically insignificant ($\chi^2 = 4.028$, $df = 2$, $p = 0.133$), and results from the two groups of metaphors are combined and discussed together.

Temporal patterning	Group				Total	
	L-G		G-Only			
Synchronizing gesture	93	84.5%	116	84.7%	209	84.6%
Preceding gesture	14	12.7%	21	15.3%	35	14.2%
Following gesture	3	2.7%	0	0.0%	3	1.2%
Total	110	100%	137	100%	247	100 %

Table 2. Temporal patterning of speech and gestures

The temporal patterning that speech accompanies synchronizing gestures is quite common in conveying metaphors. Since speech plays an important role in interpreting idiosyncratic gestures, speech and gesture should be in close temporal synchrony. Among the 247 metaphoric expressions, 84.6% of them include metaphoric gestures synchronized with their linguistic referent. Only 14.2 % of them comprise metaphoric gestures produced before their associated speech. A small proportion (1.2%) of metaphoric gestures is even performed after the related speech. Results show that gestures commonly synchronize with their associated speech in expressing metaphors, and support the Interface Hypothesis more.

Next, the relevant linguistic unit accompanying the metaphoric gesture is examined. The Lexical Semantic Hypothesis stands for the view that the relevant linguistic unit to affect the content of a gesture is a single word, because gesture can help lexical search. If a person has difficulty to find a lexical item for a concept, he/she may produce a gesture to represent the idea. The production of such a gesture then helps the person utter the word for that concept in language. Thus, gestures are thought to be dominated by the computational stage in which a lexical item is selected from a semantically organized lexicon (Butterworth & Hadar, 1989). In contrast, the Interface Hypothesis proposes the relevant linguistic unit to affect the content of a gesture can be a unit larger than a single word. This hypothesis suggests that gestures are involved in the process of arranging the spatio-motoric imagery into informational units suitable for speech production (Kita & Öyzürek 2003). The informational unit suitable for speech formulation is what can be encoded in a clause in language.

The present study sorts the relating speech of the metaphoric gestures into words or phrases. A word refers to the realization of a lexeme (Katamba & Stonham, 2006), such as *xiàwŭ* 'afternoon' in Example 6. A phrase is a group of words, such as *tiào nàbiān* 'jump there' in Example 5. Table 3 shows the linguistic unit of the corresponding lexical affiliates of the metaphoric gestures examined in the present study.

Linguistic unit	Group				Total	
	L-G		G-Only			
Word	99	90.0%	105	76.7%	204	82.6%
Phrase	11	10.0%	32	23.3%	43	17.4%
Total	110	100%	137	100%	247	100 %

Table 3. Linguistic units of the lexical affiliates

Results concerning the two groups of metaphors are discussed together. Within the 247 metaphoric expressions, the majority of the lexical affiliates associated with the gestures are single words (82.6%). Phrases comprise 17.4 % of the lexical affiliates accompanying the gestures. A substantial portion of the lexical affiliates are phrases. This finding is in opposition to the claim of Lexical Semantic Hypothesis but supports the Interface Hypothesis. Example 5 is an instance where the grammatical unit of the lexical affiliate is a phrase. The speaker manifests SHIFT OF THE SPEECH CONTENT in terms of fictive motion when he utters *tiào nàbiān*. Accompanying the phrase *tiào nàbiān* 'jump there', his gesture depicts the imagery of the motion to different places. The gesture not only depicts the manner verb *tiào* but also the trajectories to the different places which are expressed by *nàbiān* in language. In this case, the information encoded in the gesture corresponds to the unit lager than a single word. Contrasting to the prediction of the Lexical Semantic Hypothesis, the relevant unit to influence the content of a gesture is not obligatory to be a lexical item (a word).

Furthermore, the informational coordination between language and gesture allow us to discuss the theoretical hypotheses as well. In the Lexical Semantic Hypothesis, gestures are generated from the semantics of the lexical items in the corresponding speech (Schegloff, 1984; Butterworth & Hadar, 1989). Thus, this hypothesis predicts that gestures do not convey the information which is not encoded in the accompanying speech. The Interface Hypothesis suggests that gestures are generated from the imagery representations which interact on-line with the linguistic representations (Kita & Öyzürek, 2003). The Interface Hypothesis then predicts that gesture may encode the information conveyed in speech or the information which is not included in speech. This study examined two groups of metaphors: metaphors realized in both language and gesture, and metaphors realized in gesture exclusively. In the G-only group, a concept is metaphorically expressed in gesture but literally conveyed in speech. Language merely conveys the target-domain concept; on the other hand, the source-domain concept is conveyed in gesture even though this information is not included in speech. In such kind of expressions, linguistic and gestural modalities encode different semantic contents which are relevant for realizing the metaphorical thought. Concerning the current data, the gesture-only metaphors comprise over a half of all the metaphoric expressions (55.5%) and provide considerable amount of evidence for the Interface Hypothesis, which suggests language and gesture can convey different information.

5 Conclusion

This study examined the linguistic and gestural manifestations of conceptual metaphors in conversational discourse. Different metaphor types were classified and their frequency was count to discuss the habitual use of metaphoric expressions. In both the L-G and G-only groups, entity metaphor is the common metaphor types to be expressed in daily communication. Understanding abstract concepts in terms of objects then allow us to project various experiences of object to the concepts. Thus, it is likely that entity metaphor is frequently used to conceive abstract concepts. Also, this study based on cross-modal data discusses the collaboration of speech and gesture, which enables us to look at the hypotheses of speech-gesture productions. The findings from the present study support the view of the Interface Hypothesis—gestures are produced from an interface between linguistic and spatio-motoric information.

The investigation of the cross-modal expressions of metaphors can be extended in future study to explore issues which are not discussed in this study. The first issue is how metaphors are embodied in daily experiences. In the past studies, the notion of image schema have been introduced to the research on metaphors (c.f., Johnson 1987; Lakoff 1987). Image schemas, the recurring dynamic patterns of our sensory-motor experience, are seen as the primary sources of metaphors. To see the common experiential bases of metaphors, the source-domain concepts can be analyzed on the basis of different image schemas. The second issue is associated with the semantic coordination of speech and gesture. This study does not put emphasis on the details about what information is profiled in the metaphoric expressions across modalities. When language and gesture manifest the same type of metaphors, the two modalities may profile different aspects of the same concept. In the current data, we can find the instances of such an expression. A speaker utters *néngliàng nàmo dài* 'the power is so big' to represent POWER with the entity metaphor POWER IS OBJECT. The size of an object (i.e. the strength of the power) is profiled in language. On the other hand, the speaker's left palm faces up as if he held an object. The speaker's manual representation merely focuses on the boundary of an object without referring to the size. In this case, the information encoded in speech is not equivalent to the information encoded in gesture. To explore how language and gesture cooperate to convey metaphors, we need to consider not only the metaphor types but also the profiled aspect in the two modalities in the future.

References

Butterworth, Brain & Hadar, U. 1989. Gesture, speech, and computational stages: A reply to McNeill. Psychological Review, 96(1): 168-174.

Chui, Kawai. 2011. Conceptual metaphors in gesture. Cognitive Linguistics, 22(3): 437-458.

Chui, Kawai. 2013. Gesture and embodiment in Chinese discourse. Journal of Chinese Linguistics, 41(1): 52-63.

Chui, Kawai & Huei-ling Lai. 2008. The NCCU corpus of spoken Chinese: Mandarin, Hakka, and Southern Min. Taiwan Journal of Linguistics, 6(2): 119-144.

Cienki, Alan. 2008. Why study metaphor and gesture. In Alan Cienki & Cornelia Müller (eds.), *Metaphor and Gesture*, 5-25. Amsterdam/Philadelphia: John Benjamins.

Cienki, Alan. & Cornelia Müller. 2008. Metaphor, gesture, and thought. In Raymond W. Gibbs, Jr. (ed.), *The Cambridge Handbook of Metaphor and Thought*, 483-501. New York: Cambridge University Press.

de Ruiter, Jan Peter. 2000. The production of gesture and speech. In David McNeill (ed.), *Language and gesture*, 284-311. Cambridge: Cambridge University Press.

Gibbs, Jr. Raymond W. 2005. Embodiment in metaphorical imagination. In Diane Pecher & Rolf A. Zwaan (eds.), *Grounding Cognition: The Role of Perception and Action in Memory, Language, and Thinking*, 65-92. Cambridge: Cambridge University Press.

Gibbs, Jr. Raymond W. 2006. *Embodiment and Cognitive Science*. New York: Cambridge University Press.

Gibbs, Jr. Raymond W. 2008. Metaphor and thought: the state of the art. In Raymond W. Gibbs, Jr. (ed.), *The Cambridge Handbook of Metaphor and Thought*, 3-13. New York: Cambridge University Press.

Johnson, Mark. 1987. *The Body in the Mind: The Bodily Basis of Meaning, Imagination, and Reason*. Chicago; London: The University of Chicago Press.

Katamba, Francis & John Stonham. 2006. *Morphology*. New York: Palgrave Macmillan.

Kita, Sotaro and Asli Özyürekb. 2003. What does cross-linguistic variation in semantic coordination of speech and gesture reveal?: Evidence for an interface representation of spatial thinking and speaking. *Journal of Memory and Language*, 48(1): 16-32.

Kövecses, Zoltán. 2002. Metaphor: A Practical Introduction. New York : Oxford University Press.

Krauss, Robert M., Yihsiu Chen, & Purnima Chawla. 1996. Nonverbal behavior and nonverbal communication: What do conversational hand gestures tell us? In Mark P. Zanna (ed.), Advances in Experimental Social Psychology, 389-450. San Diego: Academic Press.

Krauss, Robert M., Yihsiu Chen, & Rebecca F. Gottesman. 2000. Lexical gestures and lexical access: A process model. In David McNeill (ed.), Language and Gesture, 261-283. Cambridge: Cambridge University Press.

Lakoff, George. 1987. *Women, Fire, and Dangerous Things: What Categories Reveal About the Mind*. Chicago: University of Chicago Press.

Lakoff, George. 1993. The contemporary theory of metaphor. In Andrew. Ortony (ed.), *Metaphor and Thought* (2nd ed.), 202-251. Cambridge: Cambridge University Press.

Lakoff, George & Mark Johnson. 1980. *Metaphors We Live By*. Chicago: University of Chicago Press.

Lakoff, George & Mark Johnson. 1999. *Philosophy in the Flesh: The Embodied Mind and its Challenge to Western Thought*. New York: Basic Books.

McNeill, David. 1985. So you think gestures are nonverbal? *Psychological Review*, 92(3): 350-371.

McNeill, David. 1992. *Hand and Mind: What Gesture Reveal About Thought*. Chicago: University of Chicago Press.

Müller, Cornelia. 2008. What gestures reveal about nature of metaphor. In Alan Cienki & Cornelia Müller (eds.), *Metaphor and Gesture*, 219-245. Amsterdam/Philadelphia: John Benjamins.

Reddy, Michael J. 1979. The conduit metaphor: A case of frame conflict in our language about language. In Andrew Ortony (ed.), *Metaphor and Thought*, 164-189. Cambridge: Cambridge University Press.

Schegloff, Emanuel A. 1984. On some gestures' relation to speech. In J. Maxwell Atkinson & John Heritage (eds.), Structures of Social Action: Studies in Conversational Analysis, 266-296. Cambridge: Cambridge University Press.

Talmy, Leonard. 1996. Fictive motion and change in language and perception. In Paul Bloom, Mary A. Peterson, Lynn Nadel, & Merrill F. Garrett (eds.), *Language and Space*, 211-276. Cambridge: MIT Press.

Writing to read: the case of Chinese

Qi Zhang
School of Applied Languages and Intercultural Studies, Dublin City University
qi.zhang@dcu.ie

Ronan G. Reilly
Department of Computer Science
Maynooth University
ronan.reilly@nuim.ie

Abstract

This paper describes two experiments that explore the potential role of Chinese character writing on their visual recognition. Taken together, the results suggest that drawing Chinese characters privileges them in memory in a way that facilitates their subsequent visual recognition. This is true even when the congruency of the recognition response and other potential confounds are controlled for.

1 Introduction

With China's rapid economic rise, the Chinese language is becoming more of a practical and attractive subject for university students across the world. There has, consequently, been an increase in the popularity of learning Chinese as a foreign language (henceforth, CFL). According to a report in the Financial Times (Pignal, 2011), only one in 300 elementary schools include Chinese in their curriculum, while one in every 30 was teaching Chinese language by 2008 in the US. In the UK, the number of CFL learners in higher education institutions increased by 125% between 1996 and 2007 (Hu, 2010).

Despite the growing demand to learn Chinese, there have been general concerns regarding the difficulties of studying the language. Since the Chinese writing system is logographic in nature, it is significantly different from any European languages that use Roman-derived alphabets. For this reason, one of the main challenges for CFL learners is to learn Chinese characters (Shen, 2004: 168; Wang et al., 2003; Everson, 1998: 196).

2 A brief introduction to Chinese orthography

Before we look into the relationship between writing and reading, it is necessary to provide a brief overview of Chinese orthography. There are three tiers in the orthographic structure of a Chinese character: stroke, radical, and character (Shen and Ke, 2007). Usually, several strokes function as building blocks to construct a radical, and one or more radicals are used to form a character.

There are generally two kinds of Chinese characters: integral and compound (Shen and Ke, 2007; Wang et al., 2003). The former are composed using one radical only, while the latter consist of two or more radicals. For example, 女 (nǚ) means female and 马 (mǎ) denotes the meaning of a horse. When these two integral characters serve as left and the right radicals, their combination becomes a compound character 妈 (mā) meaning mother. A compound character usually has a semantic radical (i.e., 女 meaning female in the character of 妈) that denotes the meaning of that character and a phonetic radical (马 pronounced as mǎ) that provides insights into the pronunciation of the compound character.

Although the Chinese writing system has a pictographic origin, it also has a Romanised form – pinyin – to represent its phonology (Shen and Ke, 2007; Bassetti, 2005; Wang et al., 2003). Each Chinese character can be transcribed into pinyin including onset, rime and tone (Wang et al., 2004). As shown in Table 1 below, 女is represented by pinyin nǚ. 'n' is the onset, 'ǚ' is the rime and the symbol above it indicates the tone of this character.

29th Pacific Asia Conference on Language, Information and Computation pages 341 - 350
Shanghai, China, October 30 - November 1, 2015

	integral character /semantic radical	integral character /phonetic radical	compound character
	女	马	妈
Pinyin	nǚ	mǎ	mā
English	female	horse	mother

Table 1. An example of a Chinese compound character

The sharply contrasting differences between the phonology and orthography of Chinese present a challenge to adult CFL learners who have an alphabetic first language. Due to familiarity with alphabetic-like phonological representation of Chinese, they tend to develop an unbalanced acquisition of phonology and orthography. Typically, this involves a faster acquisition of phonology than orthography (Everson, 1998). Indeed, it is very common for CFL beginners to go through a mapping exercise in their mind between the logographic characters and alphabet-like phonology, as well as semantics, in reading. In other words, they attempt to associate form with sound and meaning when learning to read (Cao et al., 2013a; Xu et al., 2013; Shen, 2004).

Despite the complexity of orthographic representation in Chinese reading, CFL language classroom traditionally pays little attention to supporting adult learners facing difficulties arising with Chinese reading (Chang et al., 2014). There have been three different curricula used in CFL classrooms in general (Zhang and Lu, 2014; He and Jiao, 2010).

The 'unity type' encourages CFL beginning learners to develop all four language skills (i.e., listening, speaking, reading and writing) at the same time. In order to achieve the same proficiency in four skills, far more lecture hours have to be spent on learning to write. The second one is the 'delay' type, which simply delays learning to read and write. This curriculum disadvantages CFL ab initio learners in a way that they are unable to read or write Chinese after a certain period of studying. The 'lag' curriculum emphasises listening and speaking while some Chinese writing – but not everything that CFL beginners have acquired in oral/aural skills – is taught at the early stage. However, this may lead to a discrepancy between listening/speaking and reading/writing skills at a later stage. Therefore, the choice of curriculum depends on when it may be best to introduce reading and writing skills to adult CFL beginners.

The current study investigated whether orthographic knowledge acquired through writing significantly contributed to reading development in a group of Irish adult beginning CFL learners all of whom had an alphabetic-first language background.

3 Writing-on-reading in Chinese

As pointed out by Guan et al. (2011), the phonological representations of words are usually strengthened when learning to read an alphabetic writing system. This is based on the assumption that 'orthographic knowledge is intimately tied to the phonological constituent of a word' (Guan et al., 2011; see also Cao et al., 2013b). Since alphabetic writing is based on a number of orthographic units (i.e. letters) that can be mapped onto phonemes and recombined to form written words, reading proficiency depends on success in establishing the phonological connections to orthography (Cao et al., 2013b; Tan et al., 2005). In this case, alphabetic reading can be helped by learning orthographic representations, which in turn contribute to the development of writing skills. On the other hand, the contribution of writing to reading development may be moderate in English or any alphabetic languages compared to Chinese (Cao et al., 2013b; Guan et al., 2011).

Orthographic knowledge of Chinese does not correspond to systematic phonological representations, since the language uses a logographic writing system. There is little or no systematic grapheme-phoneme correspondence in Chinese script (Xu et al., 2013). Specifically, the basic Chinese writing units (i.e., strokes) are not mapped to phonemes (Guan et al., 2011). Although a phonetic radical of a compound character can be connected to the phonological awareness of this character in Chinese, the connection is much less intimate than in alphabetic languages (Cao et al. 2013b). As can be seen in the example of the character '妈', the connection of the phonetic radical '马' (mǎ) is associated with the phonological representation of '妈' (mā) at the syllabic level rather than the phoneme level. The same can be applied to '吗' (ma, being used at the end of a sentence functioned as a question mark), '骂' (mà, meaning to scold), but not to a number of other characters such as '驾' (jià, meaning to drive a horse), '驴' (lǘ, meaning donkeys). Therefore, the grapheme-phoneme correspondences are not reliable in Chinese (Shu, et al. 2003).

In addition, Chinese consists of a large number of homophones, which allows a syllable to correspond to many different characters with various meanings. Therefore, phonological information is unlikely to be as reliable as the orthographic form of a character in reading comprehension (Cao et al. 2013a; Tan et al. 2005).

For this reason, in comparison to alphabetic representations, orthographic rather than phonological awareness might be a more effective factor in Chinese reading achievement. Consequently, writing characters could be a more critical component of learning to read. In a study of Chinese children's reading, Tan et al. (2005) found that the writing performance of beginning readers is strongly associated with their reading skills. In other words, for native speakers who are exposed to Chinese in daily life and so have developed phonology-to-semantics link before formal schooling, their development in writing serves as a more significant contributing factor to their reading fluency than phonological awareness. Another study of Chinese children (Li et al., 2002) found that a significant contributing factor in reading proficiency was morphological awareness. At the character level, a single character usually represents a single morpheme and a character usually needs to combine with another one to form a word. Therefore, it is essential for Chinese learners to be able to recognise a character and activate the morphological knowledge from the visual input in order to go from comprehension of a word, to a phrase, and then to sentences and texts. For this reason, writing a character, rather than pronouncing it, is more likely to play an effective role in developing learners' morphological knowledge and consequently in learning to read Chinese (Packard et al., 2006). Apart from research on native Chinese speakers, Guan et al. (2011) conducted a study of adult CFL learners and found that handwriting characters, instead of pinyin-typing or reading-only conditions, produced greater accuracy in subsequent lexical decision and semantic tasks.

In addition, Chinese writing is different from alphabetic writing since the Chinese characters 'are packed into a square configuration, possessing a high, nonlinear visual complexity' (Tan et al., 2005). Guan et al. (2011) pointed out that Chinese orthography 'involves the coupling of writing related visual and motor systems'. This coupling may help establish the spatial configuration of strokes and radicals, which along with a temporal sequence of motor movements associated with stroke composition, completely defines the shape of the character (Cao et al., 2013b; Guan et al., 2011). Therefore, significant spatial analysis is intrinsic and highly organised motor activity is involved in writing a Chinese character (Tan et al., 2005).

Cao et al. (2013b) state that writing Chinese characters might facilitate the development of a visual-spatial memory, which also has a motor memory trace. Since motor memories can last for a very long period of time (Shadmehr and Holcomb, 1997), this writing-related motor information can be additional assistance for the activation of visual information in the process of Chinese character recognition. In other words, handwriting may pair the movement patterns, usually stroke sequencing through well-practiced writing (Parkinson et al., 2010), with the language stimuli, namely characters. This pairing-up can help establish long-lasting motor memories of Chinese characters which are exploited in the orthographic recognition process. This language-specific proposal is based on the concept of 'embodied cognition'. That is to say, a person must 'internally "run" or "simulate" the corresponding production process' when understanding a physical stimulus (Bi et al., 2009). In the case of writing-on-reading in Chinese, learners might automatically activate the corresponding motor programs for writing characters, which in turn in reading them.

The study by Tan et al. (2005) gives supporting evidence that motor programming contributes to the formation of long-term motor memory of characters amongst Chinese children. Most relevant to the current study, Cao et al. (2013b) has shown that character-writing training plays a crucial role in learning the visual-spatial aspects of characters among adult CFL learners. That is to say, handwriting can establish more precise visual-orthographic representations and therefore contribute to orthographic recognition in adult CFL beginners (Cao et al., 2013b; Guan et al., 2011).

The positive effect of writing on reading appears to be supported by results from native Chinese speakers and CFL adult learners. Nevertheless, the results from studies showing this effect have tended to be inconsistent. For example, Cao et al. (2013a) demonstrated that both handwriting and visual chunking can produce orthographic enhancement among adult CFL learners. While training on writing is effective for early visual attention, visual chunking, the decomposition of a character into orthographic 'chunks' such as radicals, can also be useful for recognition. The findings from Bi et al. (2009) challenged the writing-on-reading hypothesis in Chinese. A brain-damaged Chinese patient, who was impaired in accessing orthographic representations and had poor orthographic awareness and little graphic/stroke motor programs knowledge, was able to match characters to meaning-related pictures and reading them aloud. Writing, therefore, although important, may not be an essential factor in Chinese reading. Chang et al. (2014) suggested that handwriting was only mildly effective in reading by adopting certain types of teaching methods in a real classroom. The experiment on a group of Chinese children (Tan et al., 2005) also suggests a complex role played by phonological information in Chinese children's reading performance. Instead of no effect, there is a minor contribution of phonological awareness to Chinese reading ability.

Moreover, concerns have been raised about the usefulness of handwriting characters in an era of increasing reliance on electronic communication (Zhang and Lu, 2014; Allen, 2008). It might be an inefficient use of learners' time to practice handwriting as it is common to type the pinyin of a character and subsequently select the intended character from a list of computer-generated possibilities. Furthermore, with regard to theories of embodied cognition, typing can also be considered as a process of associating a pointing movement on keyboards to form a character, though this 'visuomotor association involved in typewriting should [...] have little contribution to its visual recognition' (Longcamp et al., 2008: 803). Tan et al. (2013) examined Chinese children's reading development by comparing the reading performance of frequent users of pinyin-typing on e-devices with those spending more time on handwriting. Interestingly, they discovered that children's reading scores were negatively correlated with the use of the pinyin input method, while the reading performance was significantly positively correlated with handwriting. As a result, their study suggests that heavy utilisation of the pinyin input method and e-tools may interfere with the learning of visual-spatial properties of characters, at least among Chinese children.

4 Present study

The current study investigated the performance of a group of CFL beginners to examine the effectiveness of training in character writing on subsequent character recognition. Apart from character handwriting, participants' training also incorporated a pinyin writing task. The point of this task was to act as a control; both pinyin and character drawing involve motor movements, both are effortful in rather similar ways. So if there were an effect due character drawing as opposed to pinyin transcription, it should be related to the inherent features of character writing.

5 Experiment 1: Method

5.1 Participants

Eighteen CFL learners, students from the first author's university, took part in this experiment. They were all speakers of English as a first language and none had received any instruction in Chinese. Heritage learners were excluded from the experiment.

5.2 Materials and Procedure

The training session consisted in learning 30 integral characters. Their frequency of occurrence in a modern Chinese corpus comprising over 193 million words ranged from 29,968 to 3,083,707 with an average of 645,355 (Jun Da, 2004). The stroke count for the characters ranged from 1 through 7 with a median of 4.

During the experiment, participants were seated in front of a desktop computer. The PsychoPy presentation software system (Pierce, 2007) was used to display the materials and to record participant responses. Following an initial presentation of a prompt character ("+"), there was a 5-second exposure of both a character's form and its sound (a female native speaker spoke the character). The screen then displayed either a large C, instructing the participant to draw the displayed character, or a large P, instructing them to write the pinyin representation of the sound. Fifty percent of the time, the training response was to write pinyin and 50% of the time the participant had to draw the character. Choice of response mode and sequencing of the characters was random and the usual counterbalancing measures were taken. Each participant was required to make three passes through the training set of characters.

After training, participants were asked to do a recognition test. In this task, participants were presented with a single character and had to decide whether or not they had encountered it during training. The 30 training characters were randomly combined with 30 distractors matched on frequency and stroke complexity. The participant pressed a key to indicate whether or not they had seen the character during training. See Figure 1 for a schematic representation of the procedure in Experiment 1.

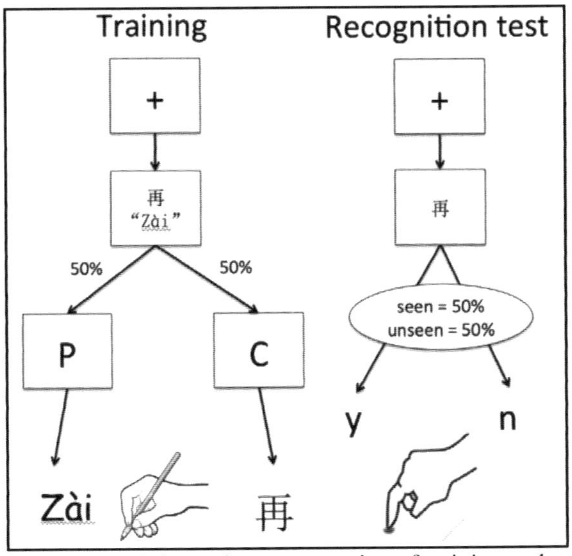

Figure 1: Schematic representation of training and testing modes in Experiment 1.

6 Experiment 1: Results and Discussion

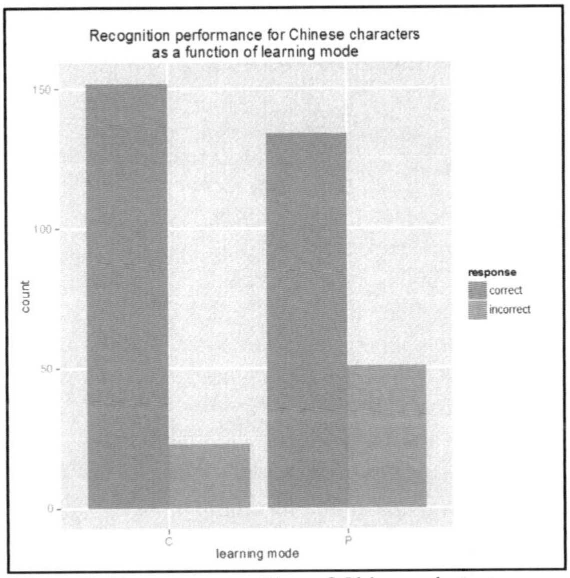

Figure 2: Correct recognition of Chinese characters as a function of learning mode: character drawing vs. pinyin transcription.

Participants responded correctly to the recognition task 81% of the time. Recognition data was analysed using a linear mixed model logistic regression (Jaeger, 2008). The dependent measure was the correctness of the recognition decision, the fixed factor was mode of training, and the random factors were participant and character. The probability of correctly responding was significantly affected by the mode of learning of the character (see Figure 2). If participants had been trained to draw it as opposed to transcribe its pinyin, there was a significant improvement in correct recognition ($|z|=3.21$; $p < 0.001$).

Now, it is possible that this character-drawing advantage may have been due simply to the character training mode causing participants to pay more attention overall to the character's orthography. It could be that the drawing task involved a greater depth of processing (Craik and Tulving, 1977) or a more elaborate encoding (Bransford et al., 1979). Moreover, the response task in Experiment 1 could be considered congruent to the character drawing training mode, since both training and testing focused on the orthography of the character. This congruency could have potentially biased the results to favour character drawing as a learning mode. Experiment

2 was designed to control for this and other potential confounds.

7 Experiment 2: Method

7.1 Participants

An additional 22 participants were recruited from a pool of CFL students who had completed seven weeks (approximately 45 hours) of previous instruction in Chinese in the first-year Chinese language course at both authors' universities. Heritage learners and learners whose native language was other than English were excluded from the experiment. The 22 participants reported having no substantial experience learning Chinese prior to enrolling in their current language programme. They were all taught from a similar curriculum employing the same textbook and instruction. Listening and speaking skills were developed simultaneously with reading and writing skills. Copying characters was regularly assigned as homework. Writing characters or pinyin from memory was also required for dictation quizzes. Before taking part in this experiment, the participants had prior knowledge of pinyin, general rules of stroke order, and knowledge of approximately 200 characters. Consequently, the effect of prior exposure to certain characters used in the current experiment was controlled for statistically in the data analyses.

7.2 Materials and Procedure

The training phase of the second experiment was identical to that of Experiment 1. Thirty-two integral characters were used in the training session. Among these characters, half were novel and half had been taught to the participants in class. The stroke count for the characters ranged from 1 through 7, with a median of 4. Based on the participants' existing knowledge of Chinese characters, none of the characters presented had more than one possible pronunciation. In addition, no two characters were selected which had the same possible pronunciation.

During the testing phase of Experiment 2, the stimuli were presented to the participants either as a character or as a sound. Participants had to decide whether a stimulus shown on a screen or played to them as audio was one of those taught to them in the training session. They were asked to make a decision quickly and accurately by pressing one of the keys on the keyboard to indicate their decision. The structure of the presentation of the materials was designed such that for half of the test items, the mode of presentation was congruent with the mode in which the item had been learned. By manipulating the congruency of training and testing modes it was hoped to control for any biases that might have affected the interpretation of the results from Experiment 1.

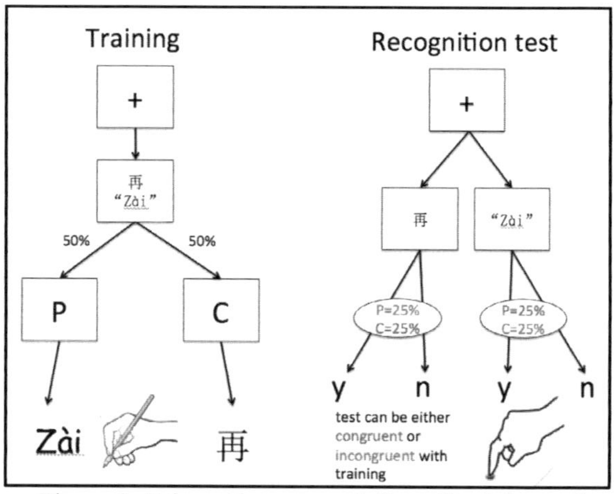

Figure 3: Schematic representation of training and testing in Experiment 2. Note that the training phase was identical to that of Experiment 1.

Recognition data was again analysed using linear mixed model logistic regression (Jaeger, 2008). The dependent measure was the correctness of the recognition decision, the fixed factors were mode of training (character drawing vs. pinyin transcription), congruency of recognition, and whether the participant had learned the character in class. A congruent recognition item involved the presentation of the character during training and the soliciting of a response during testing in the same modality (e.g., character drawing in training followed by character recognition as the test). The number of strokes comprising each character was entered into the model as a covariate to determine if the stroke count had an effect on correct responding.

Table 2 presents the results of the regression analysis. Note that the fixed factors (learn, train, and test) are coded as contrasts that test the difference in probability of responding for the two levels of each factor. The direction of the contrast is indicated by the labels: y-n, p-c, and ic-c. These represent, respectively, "yes - no", "pinyin - character", and "incongruent - congruent".

	estimate	SE	z	pr(>|z|)
intercept	-2.260	0.165	-13.69	< 0.001
strokes	-0.004	0.060	-0.063	0.950
learn:y-n	-0.882	0.255	-3.460	**< 0.001**
train:p-c	-0.277	0.246	-1.125	0.261
test:ic-c	0.533	0.273	1.954	**0.051**
learn x train	-0.562	0.496	-1.134	0.257
learn x test	0.162	0.507	0.320	0.749
train x test	-1.539	0.493	-3.125	**0.002**
learn x train x test	1.755	0.992	1.770	0.078

Table 2: Estimates from the logistic LMM predicting correct responses on the basis of stroke count, learning mode, testing congruency, prior learning in class, and the interactions between the last three terms.

The overall correct recognition rate was just over 85%. The results presented in Table 2 indicate that stroke count and training mode had no significant effect on correct responding. However, having already encountered a character in class had, as one would hope, a significant effect on recognition ($|z| = 3.46$; $p < 0.001$). The overall effect of congruency marginally improved recognition ($|z| = 1.954$; $p = 0.05$). There was, however, a significant interaction between congruency and training mode ($|z| = 6.7$; $p < 0.001$). This interaction is graphed in Figure 2 and suggests that congruency plays a greater role in improving performance when participants had to draw the character during training rather than transcribe its pinyin form. In fact, planned comparisons reveal that the source of the significant training-by-testing interaction is the difference between congruent and incongruent conditions in the character drawing condition ($|z| = 3.822$; $p < 0.001$). This can also be seen in the relative differences in the congruency effect between training modes in Figure 4. Another effect of note is the marginally significant three-way interaction between prior learning, training mode, and testing mode ($|z| = 1.77$; $p = 0.08$). The source of this effect is that the training-by-testing interaction just discussed is eliminated for those items to which participants had some prior exposure in class. Effectively, the participants respond significantly more accurately to the learned characters, giving rise to a ceiling effect in performance.

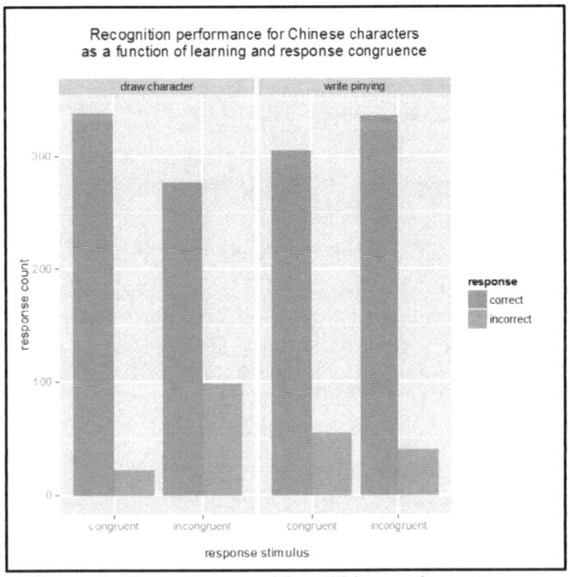

Figure 4: Correct recognition Chinese characters as a function of congruency of learning and testing modes.

8 General discussion

While the overall effect of congruency is close to significance, with congruent training and responding providing a recognition advantage, congruency alone cannot account for the significant advantage that training in character writing has for character recognition. The congruency-by-training interaction in Experiment 2 suggests that even when one controls for different response modes, learning to write the character rather than its pinyin has an overall stronger positive effect on visual recognition. Moreover, aural recognition appears to be less sensitive to congruency than visual recognition. If anything, we see a trend towards an inverted congruency effect in the case of pinyin training and aural recognition.

The basis for this interaction is not entirely clear. However, within a neuronal embodiment account (e.g., Pulvermueller, 2013), we could argue that it is due to differences in the neural encoding of the two modes of training. In the case of the character training mode, the participant goes straight from the visual representation to a motor encoding of the character. There is, therefore, potential for reciprocal connections to be reinforced between motor and visual representations, allowing visual representations to evoke motor ones, and vice versa (e.g., Garagnani et al., 2008). However, in the case of the pinyin encoding, there is an intermediate step involved – the sound has to be converted to the abstract pinyin code, which in turn is mapped to a motor programme involved in writing the pinyin. This affords the establishment of reciprocal connections between pinyin and its motor encoding, but NOT between the perceived sound and these motor encodings. This lack of direct support from the motor level in the case of the aural test may disadvantage recognition of the spoken character. A schematic representation of this account is given in Figure 5.

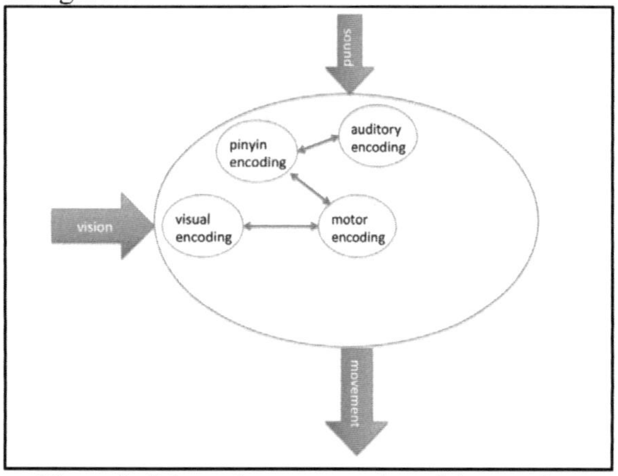

Figure 5: Schematic representation of the putative neural encoding processes underlying the two training modes in both experiments.

Returning to the initial motivation for carrying out this series of experiments, which was to understand what impact character drawing has on recognition in Chinese, the results of the two experiments described here support the hypothesis that character drawing is helpful in the visual recognition of Chinese characters. It is argued here that the reason for this is that the motor programs entrained during the learning phase of the experiments act to enhance recognition memory. This form of memory support, however, is not available for the pinyin learning phase (see Figure 5). Generalising this finding beyond the experimental paradigm to the broader topic of reading, we can argue that readers who draw characters as opposed to pinyin build a memory reserve for characters that can be used to augment their subsequent retrieval and recognition. On the other hand, readers who rely more extensively on pinyin input will not have this memory support to draw upon.

9 Conclusion

The result of the current study contributes to the debate regarding the optimum curriculum design for the CFL classroom. For example, it suggests that 'delay' or 'lag' curricula, which strongly focus on listening and speaking in the early stages of learning may not be optimal for CFL learners in helping them develop their knowledge of the relationship between character and sound. However, to definitively address this issue there would need to be a "lag" condition incorporated into the training regime.

Although the study may be interpreted as showing support for curricula that prioritise writing over other language skills, the results actually show that learning both the character and its pinyin simultaneously does not negatively affect character recognition. Therefore, some sort of combination of sound and character training, as exemplified in the training paradigm used here (see Figure 5), may turn out to be best.

The current study has several limitations that would need to be addressed in future research. For example, the corpus of Chinese characters we used consisted only of integral characters and was focused on their short-term recall rather than the acquisition of their meaning or long-term retention in context. Nonetheless, we hope our study will motivate future research to further investigate the effect of character writing on reading comprehension in Chinese language amongst CFL learners.

Acknowledgements

The research was supported by the Quality Improvement & Development Fund of Dublin City University. The authors thank Zhouxiang Lu for his help with data collection and three reviewers for their comments on an earlier draft of the paper.

References

Aho, Alfred V., & Ullman, Jeffrey D. (1972). *The Theory of Parsing, Translation and Compiling, volume 1*. Prentice-Hall, Englewood Cliffs, NJ.

Bassetti, Benedetta. (2005). Effects of writing systems on second language awareness: Word awareness in English learners of Chinese as a foreign language. In Vivian Cook & Benedetta Bassetti (Eds.), *Second Language Writing Systems: Second Language Acquisition* (Vol. 11), 335–356. Clevedon, UK: Multilingual Matters Ltd.

Bi, Yanchao, Han, Zaihua, & Zhang, Yumei. (2009). Reading does not depend on writing, even in Chinese. *Neuropsychologia*, *47*, 1193–1199.

Bransford, John D., Franks, J. J., Morris, C.D., & Stein, B.S. (1979). Some general constraints on learning and memory research. In L. S. Cermak & F. I. M. Craik (Eds.), *Levels of processing in human memory* (pp.331–354). Hillsdale, NJ: Lawrence Erlbaum Associates.

Cao, Fan, Rickles, Ben, Vu, Marianne, Zhu, Ziheng, Chan, Dereck Ho Lung, Harris, Lindsay N., Stafura, Joseph, Xu, Yi & Perfetti, Charles A. 2013a. Early stage visual-orthographic processes predict long-term retention of word form and meaning: a visual encoding training study. *Journal of Neurolinguistics*, *26*, 440–461.

Cao, Fan, Vu, Marianne, Ho, Dereck, Chan, Lung, Lawrence, Jason M., Harris, Lindsay N., Guan, Qun, Xu, Yi, & Perfetti, Charles A. (2013b). Writing affects the brain network of reading in Chinese: a functional magnetic resonance imaging study. *Human Brain Mapping, 34(7)*, 1670–1684.

Chan, Carol K. K., & Siegel, Linda S. (2001). Phonological processing in reading Chinese among normally achieving and poor readers. *Journal of Experimental Child Psychology, 80*, 23–43.

Chang, Li-Yun, Xu, Yi, Perfetti, Charles A., Zhang, Juan, & Chen Hsueh-Chih. (2014). Supporting orthographic learning at the beginning stage of learning to read Chinese as a second language. *International Journal of Disability, Development and Education, 61(3)*, 288–305.

Craik, Fergus I. M., & Tulving, Endel. (1975). Depth of processing and the retention of words in episodic memory. *Journal of Experimental Psychology: General, 104*, 268–294.

Everson, Michael E. (1998). Word recognition among learners of Chinese as a foreign language: Investigating the relationship between naming and knowing. *The Modern Language Journal, 82(ii)*, 194–204.

Garagnani, Max, Wennekers, Thomas, & Pulvermueller, Friedemann. (2008). A neuroanatomically grounded Hebbian-learning model of attention-language interactions in the human brain. *European Journal of Neuroscience, 27*, 492–513.

Guan, Connie Qun, Ying Liu, Derek Ho Leung Chan, Feifei Ye, & Charles A. Perfetti. (2011). Writing strengthens orthography and alphabetic-coding strengthens phonology in learning to read Chinese. *Journal of Educational Psychology, 103(3)*, 509–522.

Hu, Bo. (2010). The challenges of Chinese: a preliminary study of UK learners' perceptions of difficulty. *Language Learning Journal, 38(1)*, 99–118.

Ho, Connie Suk-Han, & Bryant, Peter. (1997). Learning to read Chinese beyond the logographic phase. *Reading Research Quarterly, 32*, 276–289.

Jaeger, T. Florian. (2008). Categorical data analysis: away from ANOVAs (transformation or not) and towards logit mixed models. *Journal of Memory and Language, 59*, 434–446.

Jun, Da. (2004). Chinese Text Computing. Accessed July 28 2015: http://lingua.mtsu.edu/chinese-computing/statistics/char/search.php

Li, Wenling., Anderson, Richard C., Nagy, William, & Zhang, Houcan. (2002). Facets of metalinguistic awareness that contribute to Chinese literacy. In W. L. Li, J. S. Gaffney, & J. L. Packard (Eds.), *Chinese Children's Reading Acquisition* (pp. 87–106). Dordreeht, The Netherlands: Kluwer Academic Publishers.

Longcamp, Marieke, Boucard, Celine, Gilhodes, Jean-Claude, Anton, Jean-Luc, Roth, Muriel, Nazarian, Bruno, & Velay, Jean-Luc. (2008). Learning through hand- or typewriting influences visual recognition of new graphic shapes: behavioural and functional imaging evidence. *Journal of Cognitive Neuroscience, 20(5)*, 802–815.

Packard, Jerome L., Chen, Xi, Li, Wenling, Wu, Xinchun, Gaffney, Janet S., Li, Hong, & Anderson,

Richard C. (2006). Explicit instruction in orthographic structure and word morphology helps Chinese children learn to write characters. *Reading and Writing, 19*, 457–487.

Parkinson, Jim, Dyson, Benjamin J., & Khurana, Beena. (2010). Line by line: the ERP correlates of stroke order priming in letters. *Experimental Brain Research, 201*, 575–586.

Peirce, Jonathan W. (2007) PsychoPy - Psychophysics software in Python. *J Neurosci Methods, 162(1-2)*, 8–13.

Pignal, Stanley. (2011). Mandarin has the edge in Europe's classrooms. Financial Times 16 October. Accessed November 13 2014: http://www.ft.com/intl/cms/s/0/73c7e4c8-e527-11e0-bdb8-00144feabdc0.html#axzz3Iy4gVvob

Pulvermueller, F. (2013). How neurons make meaning: brain mechanisms for embodied and abstract-symbolic semantics. *Trends in Cognitive Sciences, 17,* 458-470.

Shadmehr, Reza, & Holcomb, Henry H. (1997). Neural correlates of motor memory consolidation. *Science, 277*, 821–825.

Shen, Helen H. (2004). Level of cognitive processing: Effects on character learning among non-native learners of Chinese as a foreign language. *Language and Education, 18(2)*, 167–182.

Shen, Helen H., & Ke, Chuanren. (2007). Radical awareness and word acquisition among non-native learners of Chinese. *The Modern Language Journal, 91(i),* 97–111.

Shu, Hua, Anderson, Richard C., & Wu, Ningning. (2000). Phonetic awareness: knowledge on orthography-phonology relationships in character acquisition of Chinese children. *Journal of Educational Psychology, 92*, 56–62.

Shu, Hua, Meng, Xiangzhi, & Lai, Alice Cheng. (2003). Lexical representation and processing in Chinese-speaking poor readers. In C. McBride-Chang, & Hsuan-Chih Chen (Eds.), *Reading Development in Chinese Children* (pp. 199–214). Westport, CT: Greenwood Publishing Group.

Tan, Li Hai, Spinks, John A., Eden, Guinevere F., Perfetti, Charles A., & Siok, Wai Ting. (2005). Reading depends on writing, in Chinese. *Proceedings of the National Academy of Sciences USA, 102*, 8781–8785.

Tan, Li Hai, Xu, Min, Chang, Chun Qi, & Siok, Wai Ting. (2013). China's language input system in the digital age affects children's reading development. *Psychological Cognitive Sciences, 110(3),* 1119–1123.

Wang, Min, Perfetti, Charles A., & Liu, Ying. (2003). Alphabetic readers quickly acquire orthographic structure in learning to read Chinese. *Scientific Studies of Reading, 7(2)*, 183–208.

Wang, Min, Liu, Ying, & Perfetti, Charles A. (2004). The implicit and explicit learning of orthographic structure and function of a new writing system. *Scientific Studies of Reading, 8(4),* 357–379.

Xu, Yi, Chang, Li-Yun, Zhang, Juan, & Perfetti, Charles A. (2013). Reading, writing, and animation in character learning in Chinese as a foreign language. *Foreign Language Annals, 46(3),* 423–444.

Zhang, Qi, & Lu, Zhouxiang. (2014). The writing of Chinese characters by CFL learners: can writing on Facebook and using machine translation help? *Language Learning in Higher Education, 4(2),* 441–467.

Design of a Learner Corpus for Listening and Speaking Performance

Katsunori Kotani
Kansai Gaidai University
16-1 Nakamiyahigashino-cho, Hirakata,
Osaka, Japan 573-1001
kkotani@kansaigaidai.ac.jp

Takehiko Yoshimi
Ryukoku University
1-5 Yokotani, Seta, Otsu,
Shiga, Japan 520-7729

Abstract

A learner corpus is a useful resource for developing automatic assessment techniques for implementation in a computer-assisted language learning system. However, presently, learner corpora are only helpful in terms of evaluating the accuracy of learner output (speaking and writing). Therefore, the present study proposes a learner corpus annotated with evaluation results regarding the accuracy and fluency of performance in speaking (output) and listening (input).

1 Introduction

The linguistic properties of learners of English as a foreign language (EFL), which are different from those of native speakers, have been identified through the analysis of output compiled in learner corpora (Sugiura et al. 2007, Friginal et al. 2013, Barron and Black 2014). These properties have been used to statistically classify learners' output into a range of proficiency levels (Thewissen 2013). Thus, a learner corpus is a useful linguistic resource for developing assessment techniques that are implementable in a computer-assisted language learning (CALL) system.

Although the contribution of learner corpora is well acknowledged (Granger 2009), previous learner corpora are limited in that learners' outputs have only been examined in terms of linguistic accuracy. As noted by Housen et al. (2012), learners' performance should be analyzed in terms of both accuracy and fluency. On the one hand, it is true that a proficient learner uses a target language accurately; however, on the other hand, a trade-off is often observed, as a learner speaks grammatically correct sentences (high accuracy), but does so at an unnaturally slow speech rate (low fluency) (Brand and Götz 2011, Chang 2012).

Another limitation is typically seen in the target skill. Most previous learner corpora cover output skills in spoken or written language. From the viewpoint of communicative competence in spoken language, learners need to be proficient not only in speaking (output), but also in listening (input). Although speaking proficiency is well correlated with listening proficiency, a gap between these proficiencies is also known to exist (Liao et al. 2010, Liu and Costanzo 2013), as a learner may comprehend some sentences containing lexical and syntactic items that are difficult for them to actually articulate.

Because previous learner corpora have been limited in terms of speaking, a spoken learner corpus that demonstrates accuracy and fluency in speaking and listening is needed. The present study proposes to build a spoken learner corpus by annotating relevant information on sentences that learners spoke and listened to, respectively.

Another limitation is seen in the scope of corpus data analysis. Although the learner corpus of Kotani et al. (2015) addressed listening, it was only capable of providing listening comprehension data for analysis at the text level, because that was the level at which comprehension was examined. However, identifying which linguistic properties affect listening comprehension through text-level analysis is difficult. To identify learners' linguistic

29th Pacific Asia Conference on Language, Information and Computation pages 351 - 358
Shanghai, China, October 30 - November 1, 2015

problem areas, language use in local domains such as sentences needs to be analyzed, similar to machine translation evaluation at the sentence level (Gamon et al. 2005, Stanojević and Sima'an 2014). Therefore, the present study proposes to annotate listening comprehension data for individual sentences, which is expected to offer a finer-grained analysis for the identification of learners' linguistic problem areas.

2 Related Learner Corpora

According to Izumi et al. (2004), most learner corpora have covered written but not spoken language; therefore, they proposed a speaking corpus for EFL learners. However, their corpus did not cover listening. As Prince (2014) suggested, the lack of a listening corpus for EFL learners might be due to the difficulty of compiling data that demonstrate how learners listen to sentences. However, Luo et al. (2010) and Kotani et al. (2015) identified several issues regarding listening corpora for EFL learners.

The objective of Izumi et al. (2004) was to construct a model of the developmental stages of speaking ability among EFL learners that could also be used to develop techniques for automatically identifying errors. Their learner corpus was compiled using interviews with 1,200 EFL learners classified into nine levels according to the Standard Speaking Test, which evaluates oral proficiency. In their study, learners performed an interview-response exercise in which learners started and finished with an informal discussion on general topics, such as the interviewees' job and hobbies; between these informal chats, they performed three task-based activities: picture description, role-playing, and storytelling. Their corpus was then annotated with errors in relation to sentence generation, but not listening comprehension.

The objective of Luo et al. (2010) was to develop an automatic assessment technique for phonetic recognition. Their learner corpus was composed of data from 32 EFL learners classified into three levels according to Test of English for International Communication (TOEIC) scores. In their study, learners performed an exercise in which they repeated 14 sentences articulated by a native-speaking English teacher. In addition to phonetic recognition, listening comprehension was also examined at the text level. Comprehension questions were provided twice: once when learners finished listening to the material for the first time, and again after they listened to the material repeatedly until they felt they had reached full phonetic recognition.

The objective of Kotani et al. (2015) was to create a linguistic resource for analysis of pronunciation at the sentence level and listening comprehension at the text level. Their learner corpus was composed of data from 30 native English speakers and 90 EFL learners classified into three levels according to TOEIC scores. In their study, native speakers and learners performed reading aloud and listening comprehension exercises. In the former, native speakers and learners read 80 sentences from a set of four texts aloud. In the latter, they listened to 80 sentences from another set of four texts and answered five comprehension questions for each one.

3 Listening and Speaking Corpus

3.1 Objective

The objective of our learner corpus is to serve as linguistic resource for the development of techniques that can automatically assess performance, as well as material for listening and speaking exercises; this is described in greater detail in Section 4.

The target skills and exercises for compiling corpus data are summarized in Table 1. Our learner corpus demonstrates learners' performance in relation to listening and speaking skills. Listening is divided into phonetic recognition and comprehension, while speaking is divided into pronunciation and sentence generation. Listening data (phonetic recognition and comprehension) are compiled in a dictation exercise, while those of pronunciation and sentence generation are compiled in reading aloud and question-response exercises, respectively.

Compared with previous learner corpora (Izumi et al. 2004, Luo et al. 2010, Kotani et al. 2015), our corpus covers more skills, as shown in Table 2. The letter "X" indicates the presence of relevant data in a learner corpus.

Skill	Sub-skill	Exercise
Listening	Phonetic recognition	Dictation
	Comprehension	
Speaking	Pronunciation	Reading aloud
	Sentence generation	Question-response

Table 1: Target performance for EFL learners

	Izumi	Luo	Kotani	Ours
Phonetic recognition	---	X	---	X
Sentence comprehension	---	---	---	X
Text comprehension	---	X	X	X
Pronunciation	X	X	X	X
Sentence generation	X	---	---	X

Table 2: Comparison with existing corpora

Whereas the previous corpora were only capable of providing comprehension data for analysis at the text level, our corpus provides data for analysis at the sentence level, which offers a finer-grained analysis for the identification of learners' linguistic problem areas.

3.2 Data to be Compiled

Our corpus consists of three-layer annotation data and phonetic data for speech sounds. The first layer consists of text data (txt) in the form of transcribed speech sounds, and visual representation data (prapic) such as spectrograms produced by the Praat phonetic analysis program (Boersma and Weenink 2013). The second layer consists of text analysis involving tagging and dependency relation by the Stanford parser (de Marneffe et al. 2006), as well as analysis of descriptive information such as word length, syntactic pattern density, word information and readability provided by a computer tool called Coh-Metrix (McNamara et al. 2014). This layer also consists of phonetic analysis regarding pitch, intensity, and formant contour, as well as visible pulses (Boersma and Weeink 2013). The third layer consists of evaluation results of learners' performance.

Corpus data should cover accuracy and fluency in phonetic recognition, comprehension, pronunciation, and sentence generation, as shown in Table 3. Accuracy is represented in terms of a manual evaluation score, while fluency is represented in terms of speech rate and ease of processing.

	Accuracy	Fluency
Phonetic recognition	Evaluator's evaluation	Material speech rate & Ease of processing
Comprehension	Learner's evaluation	Material speech rate & Ease of processing
Pronunciation	Evaluator's evaluation	Learner speech rate & Ease of processing
Sentence generation	Evaluator's evaluation	Learner speech rate & Ease of processing

Table 3: Corpus data regarding accuracy and fluency data

The accuracy of phonetic recognition is evaluated using phonetic recognition scores. These scores are calculated as the rate of correctly repeated words per total number of words in a sentence/chunk. The success/failure of phonetic recognition for each word is manually evaluated by native-speaking English teachers on a binary scale (correct or incorrect).

The accuracy of comprehension is self-evaluated by learners on a binary scale (comprehensible or incomprehensible). The validity of this method, which makes the evaluation of sentence-by-sentence comprehension possible, has been acknowledged (Ross 1998).

The accuracy of both pronunciation and sentence generation are evaluated in terms of linguistic properties by native-speaking English teachers. Accuracy regarding linguistic properties is evaluated based on a 5-point Likert scale (Poor, Fair, Average, Good, Excellent). Linguistic properties reported as common errors made by EFL learners (Bryant 1984) are summarized in Table 4.

The fluencies of phonetic recognition and comprehension are also subjectively evaluated on a 5-point scale for ease of processing. These fluencies are also evaluated in consideration of the speech rate that learners actually hear. The speech rate is calculated as the number of words articulated in a minute of speech time. As learners continue listening until they fully understand the material, listening fluency is also evaluated in consideration of the number of repetitions.

The fluencies of pronunciation and sentence generation are evaluated based on speech rate and ease of processing among learners. The speech rate is calculated based on the speech time required for articulation. However, the speech time for sentence generation also includes the time during which questions are asked to learners, because learners start to consider their response at this time. Ease of processing among learners is subjectively evaluated on a 5-point scale.

Domain	Class	Instance
Pronunciation	Consonant	*/ð/ for /t/ in *Thames*
	Vowel	*/I/ for /ai/ in *bite*
	Silent consonant	*/saig/ for /sai/ in *sigh*
	Unstressed by schwa	*/me-mo-ry/ for /mem-(o)ry/
	Stress in word	*/tikét/ for /tíket/ in *ticket*
	Stress in sentence	*"**the** project" for "the **project**"
	Vowel-elision	*/cho-co-late/ for /choc-late/
	Consonant-elision	*/un-known/ for /u-known/
Sentence generation	Word-form	**chock* for *check*
	Inflection-form	**runned* for *ran*
	Agreement in pronoun	**he* for *she*
	Agreement with a modifier	**each cars* for *each car*
	Agreement between subject and verb	**he study* for *he studies*
	Inflectional agreement	**has study* for *has studied*
	Case form	**him* for *he*
	Determiner	**boy* for *a boy*
	Preposition	**look him* for *look at him*
	Verbal object	**saw* for *saw it*
	Determiner-choice	**a boy* for *the boy*
	Tense	**is* for *was*
	Aspect	**is having* for *has*
	Negation	**think that ...not* for *don't think...*
	Word-choice	**see* for *watch*

Table 4: Linguistic properties

3.3 Learners

We plan to compile our learner corpus using data from 120 university EFL learners classified into four levels according to TOEIC listening scores (range: 5-495) on the following scale (Liao 2010): beginner level (150-245); intermediate level (250-345); advanced level (350-425); and advanced-high level (430-495). EFL learners are divided equally among each level with respect to the number of learners (N = 30).

3.4 Tasks

In the experiment, EFL learners are first asked to perform a dictation exercise in which they listen to materials unit-by-unit and then write down what they hear. After completing each unit, learners subjectively evaluate the ease of phonetic recognition and comprehension on 5-point and binary scales, respectively. After learners listen to the material the first time, they listen again repeatedly until they are confident they have achieved full comprehension.

The second exercise is a reading aloud exercise in which they read the same texts from the listening materials aloud, sentence-by-sentence. After reading each sentence, they subjectively evaluate the ease of pronunciation on a 5-point scale.

The third exercise is a question-response exercise in which they answer five general questions regarding the listening material. After providing their answers, they evaluate the ease of sentence generation on a 5-point scale.

3.5 Materials

Since the target of this project includes beginner-level learners, the listening task should be fairly easy to complete. Therefore, listening material is obtained from the VOA (Voice of America) Learning English site (http://learningenglish.voa news.com).

This online resource was chosen due to the limited vocabulary (1,500 words), short sentences, and slower than natural speech rate in the material (VOA Special English 2009).

Four reports are chosen from the Level 1 (the easiest among the three levels) in order for learners at the beginner level to complete the tasks. The topic of the reports is education, which is a familiar topic for university students. This allows differences in learners' background knowledge on speaking and listening to be minimized, in contrast to specific news events. Both male and female voices are used for the reports. Two reports each are recorded in a male and female voice in order to minimize any influence from gender.

Each report is composed of less than 400 words. The linguistic properties of the material, including the length of each audio clip (sec), the number of sentences, the number of token (words), the number of word types, and the speech rate, are summarized in Table 5.

Report	A	B	C	D
Time	237	234	232	220
Sentence	25	25	15	15
Token	363	349	348	353
Type	196	182	195	187
Speech rate	91.9	89.5	90.0	96.3

Table 5: Linguistic properties of VOA texts

4 Reliability of the task

Whether learners could complete the exercises, especially the dictation exercises, remained unclear; therefore, we confirmed the validity of the listening material before compiling corpus data. Even though learners do not have to dictate all sentences correctly, they do need to make an attempt. If the chosen material is too difficult, learners dictate nothing, thereby resulting in corpus data that fail to demonstrate how English sounds are recognized by learners.

Therefore, a preliminary experiment examining whether learners were able to write down some words in a sentence was conducted to confirm the appropriateness of VOA Learning English as a resource. In addition, in order to evaluate learners' listening ability, the corpus data should include both recognizable and unrecognizable words; therefore, this experiment examined the accuracy of the dictation results.

Participants were 21 university EFL learners with beginner- to intermediate-level English proficiency (Test of English as a Foreign Language Institutional Testing Program scores: 383-463; average score = 431.3 (standard deviation = 25.0). The dictation exercise carried out was that in Report A, as shown in Table 5. They listened to and transcribed the report sentence-by-sentence. They were allowed to listen to the report three times. Although 21 learners participated, data from one learner were excluded because that learner did not complete the latter half of the exercise. Henceforth, the data analyzed in this paper were compiled from 20 learners.

The success/failure of the dictation was evaluated for each word, as shown in Table 6. The word ID shows both the sentence and the word number, and thus <s1.1> refers to the first word in the first sentence. The spoken words illustrate what learners listened to. Here, all the words, even proper nouns such as "VOA," are lowercase, because capitalization was not taken into consideration during evaluation.

The response rate shows the proportion of learners who wrote down something for a spoken word. When a learner wrote something down for a spoken word, a response score of 1 was assigned. On the other hand, when a learner wrote nothing, a response score of 0 was assigned.

The correct rate shows the proportion of learners who correctly dictated a spoken word. When the dictation of a spoken word was correct, a correct score of 1 was assigned. On the other hand, when dictation of a spoken word was incorrect, a correct score of 0 was assigned.

Word ID	Spoken word	Response rate	Correct rate
s1.1	from	1.00	1.00
s1.2	voa	1.00	0.15
s1.3	learning	1.00	1.00
s1.4	english	0.95	0.95
s1.5	this	1.00	1.00
s1.6	is	1.00	1.00
s1.7	the	0.80	0.65
s1.8	education	1.00	1.00
s19.1	for	1.00	0.80
s19.2	voa	0.95	0.15
s19.3	learning	1.00	0.80
s19.4	english	0.95	0.95
s19.5	i'm	1.00	0.75
s19.6	mario	0.75	0.55
s19.7	ritter	0.70	0.00

Table 6: Response and correct rates for the dictation exercise

The descriptive statistics show that the response rate ranged from 0.05 to 1.00 (Table 7). That is, every word received a response by at least one learner. In addition, approximately 80% of the words ((68 + 35 + 24 + 25 + 21 + 11 + 17) / 267) achieved high response rates (<0.70), and the greatest frequency (N = 68) was found for a response rate of 1.00 (Figure 1). These results suggest that the use of listening material from VOA Learning English is appropriate and allows adequate collection of learners' dictation data.

	Response rate	Correct rate
Total number of words	267	267
Minimum	0.05	0.00
Maximum	1.00	1.00
Mean	0.78	0.54
Standard Deviation	0.24	0.31

Table 7: Descriptive statics for response and correct rates

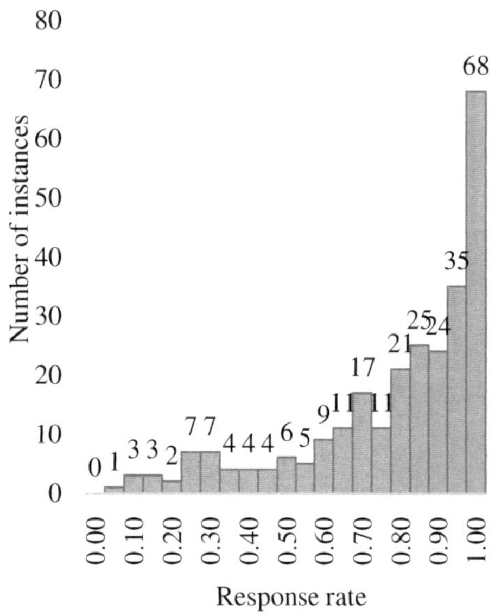

Figure 1: Frequency of the response rate

The descriptive statistics also show that the correct rate ranged from 0.00 to 1.00. In addition, as shown in Figure 2, the correct rate was evenly distributed. That is, no word was shown to be too easy or too difficult for dictation. Hence, listening material from VOA Learning English allows the collection of both correct and incorrect dictation data, thereby suggesting the appropriateness of using VOA Learning English as listening material in compiling corpus data.

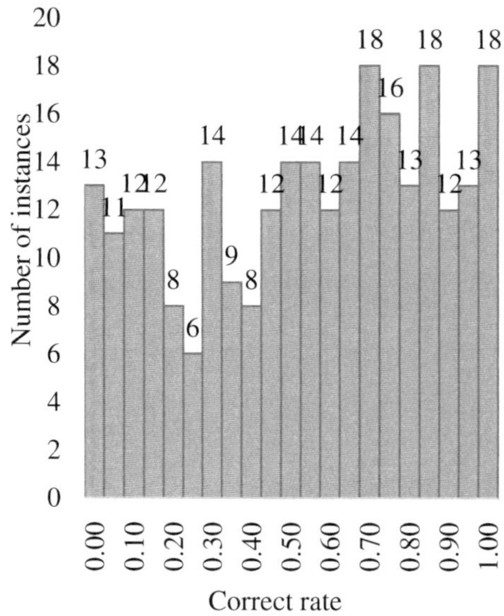

Figure 2: Frequency of the correct rate

Regarding minimum and maximum values in the response and correct rates, the minimum response rate of 0.05 was only found for the word <s15.6>, which is bolded here: "Georgetown University labor economist Anthony **Carnevale** says..." This word is a proper noun, and thus it seems unfamiliar to the learners. This unfamiliarity seems to decrease its associated response rate.

The minimum correct rate of 0.0 was found for 13 words. Among these incorrectly recognized words, an interesting example is the word <s7.1>, which is bolded here: "**Universities** say decreasing financial support..." This word should be frequently used by learners, and particularly familiar with the university learners in this experiment. This suggests that word familiarity is not related to a low correct rate. Upon further analysis, we found that most learners dictated the plural noun "universities" as a singular noun ("university"). The plural morpheme is pronounced unclearly, as illustrated by the dotted line in Figure

3. Hence, the presence of this morpheme should be made apparent due to the fact that the subsequent verb "say" would not follow the singular noun "university," or that a singular noun needs a determiner such as "a" or "the." Hence, learners fail to recognize this word due to a lack of syntactic knowledge or the failure to determine syntactic manipulation.

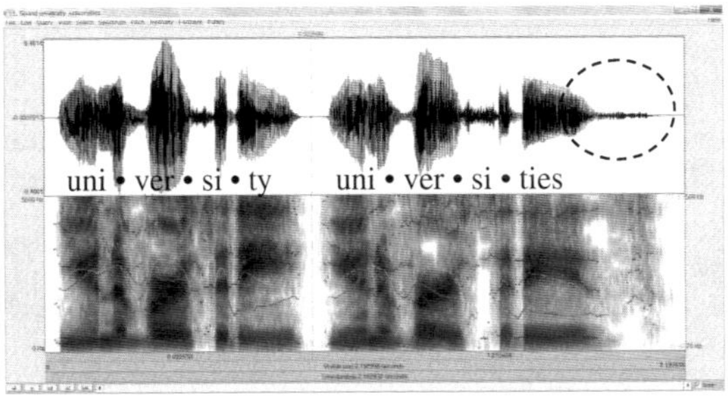

Figure 3: Spectrogram of "university" and "universities"

5 Application

An advantage of CALL-based learning is the use of "authentic" online materials such as news reports produced for native English speakers, but not designed for language learners. It is widely acknowledged that the use of authentic materials improves learners' performance, particularly regarding practical communicative competence; however, the use of authentic materials can cause several problems.

One such problem concerns the assessment of performance among learners, because unlike textbooks, authentic materials are not designed to assess whether a learner's language use is successful. Although CALL-based learning using authentic materials might be effective without it, assessment of performance certainly provides more effective learning because it enables the identification of linguistic problem areas among learners in daily communication.

Another problem concerns the difficulty of authentic materials, which, unlike textbooks, is uncontrolled, and thus increases the chance that a learner may lose motivation due to materials that are inappropriate or too difficult for their proficiency level. Hence, it is necessary to first assess the difficulty of authentic materials, and then to provide materials that are appropriate for the individual learner's proficiency, which is a rather burdensome task for language teachers. Therefore, automatic assessment of the materials' difficulty supports both effective learning and effective teaching.

Such automatic assessment techniques result in a by-product that also improves CALL-based learning. In developing these assessment techniques, statistical models will be constructed for calculating proficiency-based optimal performance. If a CALL system demonstrated performance in listening and speaking exercises as well as what would be considered optimal performance, learners would then be able to assess their performance in terms of how it compares with optimal performance. This type of self-evaluation would allow learners to recognize gaps in their performance, and then to address these gaps by doing relevant practice exercises until their performance reaches or outperforms optimal performance; therefore, this type of system would promote autonomy among learners.

6 Conclusion

The present paper introduced the design of a new learner corpus for analyzing the accuracy and fluency of listening and speaking. This design differs from existing designs with respect to performance targets for learners. In addition, unlike the previous corpora, our learner corpus offers spoken language analysis at the sentence-level. This proposed learner corpus is expected to serve as a linguistic resource for the development of assessment techniques for both listening and speaking exercises in a CALL system.

Acknowledgement

This work was supported by JSPS KAKENHI Grant Numbers, 22300299, 15H02940

References

Anne Barron and Emily Black. 2014. Constructing small talk in learner-native speaker voice-based telecollaboration: A focus on topic management and backchanneling. System, 48: 112–128.

Paul Boersma and David Weenink. 2013. Praat: Doing Phonetics by Computer. Version 5.3.51, retrieved 2 June 2013 from http://www.praat.org/

Christiane Brand and Sandra Götz. 2011. Fluency versus accuracy in advanced spoken learner language: A multi-method approach. Errors and Disfluencies in Spoken Corpora. Special Issue of International Journal of Corpus Linguistics, 16(2): 255–275.

William H. Bryant. 1984. Typical errors in English made by Japanese ESL students. JALT (Japan Association of Language Teachers) Journal, 6(1): 1–18.

Anna C.-S. Chang. 2012. Improving reading rate activities for EFL students: Timed reading and repeated oral reading. Reading in a Foreign Language, 24(1): 56–83.

Eric Friginal, Man Li, and Sara C. Weigle. 2013. Revisiting multiple profiles of learner compositions: A comparison of highly rated NS and NNS essays. Journal of Second Language Writing, .23: 1–16.

Michael Gamon , Anthony Aue , and Martine Smets. 2005. Sentence-level MT evaluation without reference translations: Beyond language modeling. In European Association for Machine Translation (EAMT) 2005 Conference Proceedings, pages 103–111.

Sylviane Granger. 2009. The contribution of learner corpora to second language acquisition and foreign language teaching: A critical evaluation. In K. Aijmer. (ed.) Corpora and Language Teaching, pages 13–32, John Benjamins, Amsterdam and Philadelphia.

Alex Housen, Folkert Kuiken, and Ineke Vedder. 2012. Complexity, accuracy and fluency: Definitions, measurement and research. In A. Housen, F. Kuiken, and I. Vedder. (eds.) Dimensions of L2 Performance and Proficiency: Complexity, Accuracy and Fluency in SLA, pages 1–20, John Benjamins, Amsterdam and Philadelphia.

Emi Izumi, Kiyotaka Uchimoto, and Hitoshi Isahara. 2004. The overview of the SST speech corpus of Japanese learner English and evaluation through the experiment on automatic detection of learners' errors. In Proceedings of the Fourth International Conference on Language Resources and Evaluation (LREC-2004), pages 1435–1438.

Katsunori Kotani and Takehiko Yoshimi. 2015 (to appear). Application of a corpus to identify gaps between English learners and native speakers. In Proceedings of Eighth Workshop on Building and Using Comparable Corpora (BUCC).

Chi-Wen Liao. 2010. TOEIC listening and reading test scale anchoring study. TOEIC Compendium, 5: 1–9.

Chi-Wen Liao, Yanxuan Qu, and Rick Morgan. 2010. The relationships of test scores measured by the TOEIC listening and reading test and TOEIC speaking and writing tests. TOEIC Compendium Study, 10(13): 1–15.

Jinghua Liu and Kate Costanzo. 2013. The relationship among TOEIC listening, reading, speaking, and writing skills. In D. E. Powers. (ed.) The Research Foundation for the TOEIC Tests: A Compendium of Studies, Volume II, pages 1–25, Educational Testing Service, Princeton, NJ.

Dean Luo, Yutaka Yamauchi, and Nobuaki Minematsu. 2010. Speech analysis for automatic evaluation of shadowing. In Proceedings of Speech and Language Technology in Education (SLaTE).

Danielle S. McNamara, Arthur C. Graesser, Philip M. McCarthy, and Zhigang Cai. 2014. Automated Evaluation of Text and Discourse with Coh-Metrix. Cambridge University Press, Cambridge, M.A.

Marie-Catherine de Marneffe, Bill MacCartney and Christopher D. Manning. 2006. Generating typed dependency parses from phrase structure parses. In Proceedings of the Sixth International Conference on Language Resources and Evaluation (LREC-2006), pages 449–454.

Peter Prince. 2014. Listening comprehension: Processing demands and assessment issues. In P. Leclercq, A. Edmonds, and H. Hilton. (eds.) Measuring L2 Proficiency: Perspectives from SLA, pages 93–108, Multilingual Matters, Clevedon.

Steven Ross. 1998. Self-assessment in second language testing: A meta-analysis and analysis of experiential factors. Language Testing, 15(1): 1–20.

Miloš Stanojević and Khalil Sima'an. 2014. Fitting sentence level translation evaluation with many dense features. In Proceedings of the 2014 Conference on Empirical Methods in Natural Language Processing (EMNLP), pages 202–206.

Masatoshi Sugiura, Masumi Narita, Tomomi Ishida, Tatsuya Sakaue, Remi Murao, and Kyoko Muraki. 2007. A discriminant analysis of non-native speakers and native speakers of English. In Proceedings of the 2007 Corpus Linguistics Conference.

Jennifer Thewissen. 2013. Capturing L2 accuracy developmental patterns: Insights from an error-tagged EFL learner corpus. The Modern Language Journal, 97(1): 77–101.

VOA Special English. 2009. Word Book. Voice of America, Washington, DC.

Understanding Infants' Language Development in Relation to Levels of Consciousness: An Approach in Building up an Agent-based Model

Helena Hong Gao
Bilingual Development Lab, School of Humanities and Social Sciences and Complexity Institute,
Nanyang Technological University
Singapore
helenagao@ntu.edu.sg

Can Guo
Bilingual Development Lab, School of Humanities and Social Sciences,
Nanyang Technological University
Singapore
kfcankf@gmail.com

Abstract

Language development in infants is a dynamic process that involves the emergence and increase of consciousness, with which built-in learning mechanisms make infants' imitation and interaction with their surroundings become socially meaningful. Taking Gao & Holland's (2008, 2013) statements of levels of consciousness for language development as the theoretical guideline, this study proposes a *rule-based, signal-processing* agent-based model to explore the dynamics of language development in early infants. In this model, we assume that an infant's rule-based learning behaviors can be featured by different levels of consciousness and that its adaptation processes can be explained in relation to levels of consciousness. In this paper we will discuss properties of consciousness at different levels and identify the influencing factors for reaching them. Our ultimate goal in building up the model is to understand the processes of language development with an approach that can better reflect reality.

1 Introduction

Understanding how language is acquired by infants has remained to be a challenging task. Previous attempts, such as the behavioral approach (e.g. Skinner, 1957; Roediger, 2004; Ramscar & Yarlett, 2007), relational frame theory (e.g. Hayes et al., 2001), nativist theories (Chomsky, 1967, 1975), social interactionist theories (Bruner, 1983; Carpenter et al., 1998; Tomasello, 2003), etc. all have achieved remarkable results that have shed light on future directions in research in child language acquisition.

More recent views emphasize that child language emerges through imitation and social interaction with the support of built-in learning mechanisms (Tomasello & Bates, 2001; Tomasello, 2003; Snow, 1999; MacWhinney, 2004; Bates & Goodman, 1999). For example, emergentist theories, represented by MacWhinney's competition model (1986), argue that language acquisition emerges from the interaction of biological pressures and the environment through a cognitive process. These theories emphasize that nature and nurture need to be jointly involved to trigger the language learning process.

In psychology, Jean Piaget's experimental studies on cognitive development revealed stage-development in children. Children's speech was discussed in terms of thought and reasoning (Piaget, 1926). Following Piaget, psychologists and linguists (e.g. Bowerman, 1990, 2004; Bates, 1975, 1999; Bates & Goodman, 1997, 1999; Mandler, 2004, 1998) made data-based assumptions that there could be many learning processes involved in language acquisition. Evolutionarily, some wired-in help supplied by a long evolutionary history is assumed to exist in supporting this task. For example, infants can imitate facial gestures between 12 and 21 days of age, an age much earlier than predicted by stage development theory (e.g. Piaget). Such imitation implies that human neonates equate their own behaviors with gestures they see others perform (Gopnik & Meltzoff, 1997; Meltzoff & Borton, 1979; Meltzoff & Moore, 1977). But how

29th Pacific Asia Conference on Language, Information and Computation pages 359 - 368
Shanghai, China, October 30 - November 1, 2015

does the newborn go on from there to make sense of the torrent of novel input? In particular, how does the newborn travel the long distance from very limited initial abilities to full language acquisition? Although we have large collections of relevant data, we have little theory of the dynamics of this process. These questions remain to be answered (Gao & Holland, 2013).

Our objective of this study is to apply the agent-based model (Holland, 1995) to explore language development in early infants. Our approach has substantial differences from the previous attempts. We will take Gao & Holland's (2008, 2013) statements of levels of consciousness (LoC) for language development as the theoretical guideline to build up a model that can reveal the dynamics of language development in early infants. By incorporate development observations into a theoretical framework, we will illustrate the mechanisms underlying LoC transitions and introduce an interdisciplinary approach to new experiments.

2 Level of Consciousness

Consciousness is often implicitly discussed as thought expressed in language (Carruthers, 1996, 2000). Even further back, in Plato's time, there was a general agreement that one can only speak of what one is consciously aware of. Therefore, it is reasonable to view infant language acquisition process from the perspective of consciousness. However, linguistic theories rarely touch upon consciousness.

Personal Construct theory (Kelly, 1955/1991) defines human consciousness as undergoing both conscious and unconscious processes. It postulates that human cognition starts from unconscious processes, or "low levels of cognitive awareness". According to Zelazo (2004), children's development of consciousness undergoes several dissociable levels before they reach full cognitive capability. His Viewing developmental and information-processing as the key features, Zelazo (2004) developed a hierarchically arranged LoCs and provided a metric for measuring the level at which consciousness is operating in specific situations. This is very different from models that are mainly based on adult data that distinguish between consciousness and a meta-level of consciousness (e.g., Moscovitch, 1989; Schacter, 1989; Schooler, 2002).

Based on Zelazo (2004) and Zelazo et al (2008)' work on the development of consciousness in children, Gao & Holland (2008, 2013) assumed that language development in a newborn depends upon expanding consciousness and that levels of consciousness can also be identified. Following Gao & Holland, we attempt to examine mechanisms (behavioral traits) that generate the behaviors at different levels of consciousness and their relations to well-known transitions as the newborn develops. In our model, infant's behavior is regarded not only simply as the output of the interaction between the infant and its surroundings, but also as the product of infant's understanding which is confined to age-related levels of consciousness.

In this paper, our focus is on the preverbal period (0-12 months). Although children during this period cannot express themselves by formal language that we can fully understand, they are obviously able to show their understanding and desires by non-verbal means together with simple but repeated trials of articulation of pre-linguistic sounds. To take a detailed look at these features, we follow Gao & Holland's (2008, 2013) definitions of the "level of consciousness" and make further divisions of these levels into more detailed sub-stages. Table 1 shows the "level of consciousness" sub-stages and their corresponding features in language development during a child's first year of life.

Level of Consciousnes s	**LoC Stage**	**Features relating to age**
LoC 0 Unconscious	**Stage 0** Reflective	Reflexive crying 0; Throaty noises 0
LoC 1 Minimal consciousness	**Stage 1.1** Intentionality	Sound localization 0; Distinguish consonant 1; Distinguish vowel 3
	Stage 1.2 Voluntary Action	Voluntary crying 2; Coos & laugh 2
	Stage 1.3 Repeated Action	Babbling & vocal play 4; Canonical babbling 6;
LoC 2 Recursive consciousness	**Stage 2.1** Differential Labels	Respond to name 5; Respond to "No" 6; Native preference 7; Segment speech 7;
	Stage 2.2	Patterned speech 10;

	Aware of Relationships	Adept to speech perception 11
	Stage 2.3 Functional Reactions	First words 12

Table 1: The "Level of Consciousness" Stages and main language development features within a child's first year of life

From birth to the end of the first year, an infant goes through three levels of consciousness (See Table 1). The first level of consciousness development is LoC 0 – Unconscious, at which babies can only respond to stimuli unconsciously, without awareness of even their own actions. The main character of infant's behaviours at this stage is reflective. Take "throaty noises" for example, they are the earliest vocalizations produced by infants, such as breathing, coughing, burping, sucking or sneezing. Babies make these sounds involuntarily. They are mainly physiological reactions that are partly characters of a living being in general.

LoC 1 starts with the feature of growth that is labeled as the "Intentionality stage", which is the first stage (stage 1.1) of LoC 2. At this stage, babies begin to respond to environmental stimulations. As the examples shown in Table 1, infants are gradually aware of what they hear, where the sounds come from (sound localization) and what are the differences between them (consonant and vowel distinctions). "Voluntary action stage" is the second stage, at which infants initiate to direct their actions according to their desire. Therefore, the crying (voluntary crying) and cooing sound (coos & laugh) at this stage may be more related to infants' desires and emotions. That is, they start to use their abilities as communication tools to communicate with their caregivers. At the third stage – "Repeated action stage", babies begin to show their preference of repetition. This is seen as the fact that upon their responses to their caregivers the feedback that babies receive from the caregivers generates pleasure. This is possibly why we see 4-month-old babies play with vocalizations (babbling & vocal play) and produce repetitive syllables.

However, all the actions under LoC 1 are restricted to present intero- and exteroreceptor stimulation (Now), which are only triggered by present stimuli.

When babies start to be able to relate certain signals to a certain kind of meanings, they arrive at LoC 2 – "Recursive consciousness". At the "Differential Labels" stage they are able to maintain the previous consciousness level and recall what they have acquired before. A typical observation is a baby's reaction when she hears a certain syllable or a voice pattern. For example, when a 5-month-old baby hears someone calls her name, which she must have heard for many times before, she will look toward the sound source (response to name), though she does not know yet that it is her name. When a baby begins to be aware of relationships, she is at stage 2.2. A 10-month-old infant's use of protowords (patterned speech) and an 11-month-old infant's understanding of others' expressions (adept at speech perception) are typical developmental features at this stage. When a baby is around 1 year old, she can use words comparatively accurately alike adults (first words). This is the feature named as "Functional Reactions" shown at stage 2.3, the last stage of LoC 2.

3 Agent-based Model of LoC

The theoretical framework of *agent-based model* (ABM) proposed by Holland (1995) creates a flexible abstraction of the real world and provides an approach in the general study of complex adaptive systems (*cas*).

ABMs consist of basic computer algorithm units, so-called agents, which are the central modeling focus points. Agents are modular or self-contained. An agent is an identifiable, discrete individual with a set of characteristics or attributes, behaviors, and decision-making capability. Figure 1 shows the structure of an individual agent in our model. We name it "baby-agent". First, we will give our modeling assumptions with the four typical elements of ABMs: environment, interactions, behavior rules, and adaptation. Then, in the next section, we will describe the model in detail.

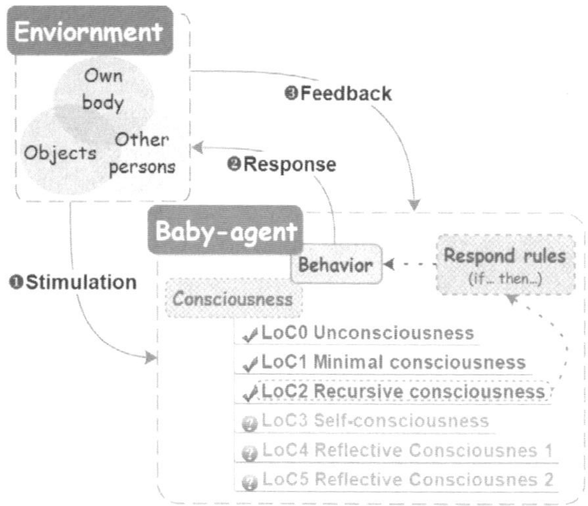

Figure 1: The structure of an individual baby-agent interacting with its environment confined to its LoC.

a) Environment

For a newborn, all the things including its own body are unfamiliar. Trevarthen and Aitken (2001) distinguished three type of engagement of a human subject with his body and the outside world: in his own body, to objects, and to other persons. These three aspects comprise a baby-agent's personal growth environment within which a baby-agent experiences three dimensional consciousness developments. The consequent accumulated consciousness forms a baby-agent's thought of the world and serves as fodder that muses for language expression.

b) Interactions

Baby-agents continuously interact with their environment as well as with other agents. A baby-agent is situated, or situationally dependent, in the sense that its behavior is based on the current state of its interactions with other agents and with its environment.

"Other agents" is a special part of the baby-agents' environment. Along with the increase of LoC, the interaction and relationship between a baby-agent and other agents will be greatly changed. For a baby-agent with the lowest LoC, it has no distinctive features from other agents within the entire environment. It can only receive and respond to signals, with no awareness of their existence and attributes. However, a baby-agent with a higher LoC can realize that some agents or signals are special for it. As a result, it will become conscious of other agents' identities as well as its personal connections with them, and thus begins to build up new protocols or mechanisms that channel its interactions with other agents.

c) Behavior rules

During the interaction and building up the relationship, a baby-agent is autonomous and self-directed. It can function independently in its environment and in its interactions with other agents. It seems as if its individual behavior processes are controlled by a combination of heuristic and stochastic rules. In our model, we define the behavior rules by a set of IF/THEN rules that respond to external and internal signals. A baby-agent interacts with its environment and other agents through an exchange of the signals. It should be noted that, baby-agent's behavior rules cannot be separated from its underlying level of consciousness. Providing the same scenario, baby-agents at different levels of consciousness are expected to show different behavior rules. The term "level" immediately suggests a progression from one level to another and a type of corresponding dynamics. The adaptation is the power that makes these progressions happens.

d) Adaptation

Being adaptive is the most important character of the agents. That is, the agents in the model can learn from their environment and dynamically change their behaviors in response to their experience. Casti (1997) argues that agents should contain both base-level rules for behavior as well as a higher-level set of "rules to change the rules." The base-level rules provide responses to the environment, while the "rules to change the rules" provide adaptation. A baby-agent has the ability to learn and adapt its behaviors based on its experience, which requires not only memory, but also feedback and recirculation. Suitable feedback is very important in the adaptation process, which points out the right direction for the cultivation of a new behavior pattern.

The behavior principle of the baby-agents with the lowest level of consciousness is quite simple. If a certain behavior pattern can make them feel happy directly, they will persevere in it and vice versa. This is the basis of the discovery of new rules and the modification of extant rules. However, as they reach a higher level of consciousness, they may consider more about the rules. Therefore, for different levels of consciousness, we may have different behavior principles according to the characters of each level. In addition, the kinds of signals processed determine the level of performance under a certain rule, and thus certain kinds of rule conditions can be typically associated with the LoC involved.

4 Model Description

4.1 IF/THEN rules and feature database

In our model, we will use *rule-based, signal-processing* agents (Holland et al., 1986), with rules of the form

IF (signal x is present)
THEN (send signal y).

Signals x and y could be utterances, gestures, or visual input.

In the following examples, T ("teacher", e.g. the mother) stands for a competent adult that regularly interacts with the infant L ("learner"). For example, a simple rule for L might be,

IF (T lifts a milk bottle)
THEN (L says "milk").

Signals can also serve to coordinate internal process, in which case they have no intrinsic meaning, serving much like the un-interpreted bit strings that coordinate instructions in a computer program. Each agent has many rules and, indeed, many rules can be active simultaneously (Gao & Holland, 2013). This simultaneous activity is roughly the counterpart of the simultaneous firing of assemblies of neurons in the central nervous system (Hebb, 1949).

By collecting data from literatures in the fields of linguistics, cognitive science, neuroscience, and psychology, we have built up an age-related development feature database. Beside the features of language development, we have identified other features. We believe that language acquisition is a complex process. Supports from various capabilities' development are needed (Gesell, 1928). The features arranged in different categories reflect the multiple dimensions of their interactions while the capacities of the baby-agent are being developed. Figure 2 shows main development features of the infants' first year of life and their associations with each other.

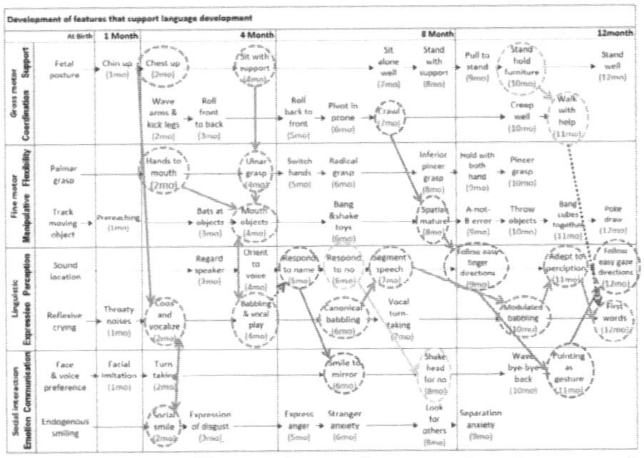

Figure 2: An illustration of some developmental features and their associations during infants' first year of life

To focus on the growth of the baby-agent, our model pays more attention to children's behavior transitions by applying IF/THEN rules referring to the development feature database. Based on the development features, we are able to determine a set of IF/THEN rules. The following are some examples:

[In the rules that follow, <action> denotes an overt action caused by a particular signal.]

Typical rule at LoC 0 [Unconscious activities].
At LoC 0, baby just has inherited ('wired in') cognitive abilities.

Stage 0 [Reflective – *action without awareness*]:
IF (T makes a tongue protrusion)
THEN (<L imitates the tongue protrusion >)

Typical rule at LoC 1 [Minimal consciousness].
At LoC 1, baby gradually shows innate reinforcement of repeatable activities.

Stage 1.1 [Intentionality – *begin to have some consciousness to environmental stimulations*]:
IF (T makes a sound)
THEN (<L turns his head towards the sound>)

Stage 1.2 [Voluntary action – *direct actions according to one's willing]*:
IF (L wants to be hugged by caregiver)
THEN (<L cries voluntarily>)

Stage 1.3 [Repeated action – *action repetitively and feel happy when doing it*]:
IF (a hand is in a vision cone)
THEN (<L waves his hand repetitively >)

Typical rule at LoC 2 [Recursive consciousness]. *At LoC 2, baby begins to awareness of the connections between object and its label.*

Stage 2.1 [Differential labels – *begin to aware that some signals have special means*]:
IF (T calls L's name)
THEN (<L pays attention to T>)

Stage 2.2 [Aware of relationships – *be conscious of the links between signals and objects]*:
IF (T say "milk")
THEN (<L looks to the milk bottle>)

Stage 2.3 [Action functionally – *be able to use related signals to indicate some objects*]:
IF (a milk bottle is present)
THEN (<L utters "milk">)

4.2 Learning Processes and Meta-Rules for Learning

According to Gao & Holland (2013), to *learn* in this rule-based context, the agent must have the ability to modify its signal-processing rules. Such rule-modifying, learning abilities are innate capacities supplied by evolution. Learning abilities can also be expressed as rules, functioning in a similar way as Hebb's (1949) learning rule in neuro-psychology. Therefore, these meta-rules for learning are clearly distinguished from the signal-processing rules. In agent-based models, the meta-rules are unchanging and common to all agents.

Our agent-based models described here are based on meta-rules that are demonstrably available to pre-primates. There are two general learning tasks that a baby-agent must be able to carry out:

a) Credit-assignment

As an agent interacts with other agents within a certain environment, it must be aware of the existence of rules and also able to decide which of the rules are helpful and which are detrimental. A mature agent must even be able to determine which early-acting, stage-setting rules make possible later beneficial outcomes. (As an example given by Holland (1998), consider the sacrifice of a piece in a game like checkers in order to make a triple jump later.) The credit-assignment learning process assigns strengths to the rules. A rule's strength reflects its usefulness to the system, useful rules having high strengths. Rules then compete to control the agent. The stronger rules have a better chance of winning the competition. In effect, the rules in this system are treated as hypotheses to be progressively confirmed or disconfirmed. (See Holland, 1998, chapter 4).

Obviously, during the credit-assignment procedure, recirculation and feedback are indispensable. The random variation and imitation provide a random sampling that helps uncover the most primitive behavior rules. When a behavior rule is repeatedly associated with rewarding feedback, such as food or a mother's smile, it becomes a sampled regularity that is associated with valuable experience. From the sampling point of view, the behavior rule's reliability is continually tested under the credit assignment procedure.

b) Rule discovery

Once rules have been rated by credit-assignment, it makes sense to replace rules that have little or no strength by generating new rules (hypotheses). Random generation of new rules is not an option here; that would be like trying to improve a computer program by inserting random instructions. Instead, newly generated rules must somehow be plausible hypotheses in terms of experience already accumulated. (See Holland, 1995, chapter 2).

For the baby-agent with a higher level of consciousness, random variation of rules from the very beginning is not the best way to get the beneficial behavior rules. A mature baby-agent may have the abilities to discover new rules by combining *building blocks* (Holland, 1995, chapter 1 ff) which are extracted from rules already established. An important advantage of building blocks is that they occur as repeated patterns in the ever-changing torrent of sensory input, which provide repeatable experiences in a perpetually novel environment.

4.3 Building blocks

According to Holland (1998), building blocks (*generators* in mathematics) have a familiar role in the sciences, best exemplified by the building block hierarchy of the physical sciences – the quark / nucleon / atom / molecule / membrane /... hierarchy. Selected combinations of building blocks at one level form the building blocks of the next level. For a spoken language there is a similar phoneme / word / sentence hierarchy. A grammar specifies the laws that determine how words can be combined to yield sentences. Actually, in viewing the levels of consciousness, we find a similar hierarchy. Higher levels of consciousness in the LoC theory are brought about by the iterative reprocessing of the contents of lower levels of consciousness. (Zelazo et al., 2007)

After a period of development process, a baby-agent has acquired a certain number of behavior rules, which can be seen as the building blocks for discovering new rules. Plausible new conditions and rules can be generated by *recombining* these building blocks that already confirmed. A confirmed building block becomes a plausible hypothesis when combined with other similarly distilled building blocks. The procedure is much like the crossbreeding of good plants (or animals) to get better plants. There is a substantial literature, centering on *genetic algorithms* (Holland, 1995), that discuss the production of new rules in agent-based models via the crossing of extant rules. There is not space here to discuss genetic algorithms in detail, but it is a well-established procedure.

The building blocks amount to hypotheses at different levels of precision, with the rules being confirmed (or disconfirmed) as the agent gains experience. These different levels of precision may be related to the levels of consciousness.

According to Gao & Holland (2013), the meta-rules for credit assignment and rule discovery allow the neonate to achieve a gradual increase in control, corresponding to increasing LoC. The process begins with the acquisition of repeatable sound and gestures. Sounds and gestures reinforced by T become the building blocks that can be used when the baby-agent is mature. For example, producing various combinations of utterances at LoC 1 can be simply a kind of play, while they are the necessary building block to form meaningful utterances at LoC 2. Connecting optional utterances with specific meanings greatly reduce behavior's ambiguity. In mathematical terms we refine a broad equivalence class into a set of smaller, more informative sub-classes.

In this way, selected combinations of building blocks at one LoC become the building blocks for the next level. Building blocks offer combinatoric possibilities: a large variety of useful or meaningful structures can be constructed from a small number of building blocks. Moving up the LoC hierarchy thus becomes a much more efficient process than trying to "establish" a monolithic rule for each possibility at the highest LoC.

4.4 A Baby-agent's consciousness properties

By now, almost every part of the agent-based model has been introduced, and we come to the final topic of this section – the properties of consciousness. Actually, there are three concepts of consciousness involved in our model: the level of consciousness, the consciousness capabilities, and consciousness status.

The level of consciousness and its impact on a baby-agent's behavior rules have already been emphasized. However, consciousness development is a continuous process, and the increase in LoC is a quantum leap from the accumulation of drip growth. Therefore, before determining at which level of consciousness a baby-agent is situated, we must know the factors that influence the development of a baby's *consciousness capability*. As an example, we focus on illustrating two main factors: time and training. Hereby, we give the measurement of *consciousness capability* as follows:

$$Consciousness_t = f(t) + h(N)$$

Where, $Consciousness_t$ is the measurement of a baby's *consciousness capability* at time $\boldsymbol{t}$ when a baby-agent has been consciously trained for N times; $f(t)$ and $h(N)$ are the consciousness increments gained from the time factor and the training factor separately.

There is no doubt that the increase of consciousness needs time. Ever since a baby was born, the internal and external environments provide it abundant stimulations, which promote the increase of its consciousness naturally. For convenience, we regard the natural increase rate (*rate*) of consciousness in our model as being constant, and thus the consciousness increment gained from the time factor can be defined as follows:

$$f(t) = rate \times t$$

As for the training factor, it should be much more complex. By denoting Δ as the consciousness increment of the i-th training, the consciousness increment gained from the training factor can be expressed as follows:

$$h(N) = \sum_{i=1}^{N} \Delta(feedback_i, status_i)$$

Where, i stands for the i-th training; N is the total training times by time t; $feedback_i$ and $status_i$ respectively indicate the feedback that the baby-agent receives and the *consciousness status* that baby-agent is situated in the i-th training.

The impact of the feedback on the learning process has been described. We now come to take a look at the *consciousness status*. It should be noted that, for a baby-agent whose consciousness capability can reach LoC 3, it doesn't mean that it remains situated at LoC 3. Actually, it will normally stay at a lower level of consciousness, and will elevate its own consciousness status to deal with specific requirement when needed. Just as we will achieve different scores if we bear different attitudes in exams, a baby-agent with a different consciousness status will have different amount of consciousness increase as well.

Given different parameters, we can model various development paths of baby-agents. By calibrating age-related development features according to the consciousness capabilities' increased integrally in a baby-agent, we can determine the consciousness condition of each behavior rule. This kind of treatment makes sense. Gao & Holland's (2013) framework makes it possible to observe an infant's language development in relation to the increase of levels of consciousness in specific situations. In principle, this approach takes the development of language as well as the growth of consciousness capabilities in an infant as being supported by diversified factors in reasonable environments.

5 Summary

This study proposes a *rule-based, signal-processing* agent-based model to reveal the dynamics of language development in early infants. This model shows how a newborn discovers behavior rules and improves its autonomy. With the establishment of such a model, we are able to explore the mechanisms that support language development and understand how language is acquired, used, and changes over time.

By building up the model, we are able to see that the influence of consciousness on language development is manifold. During the learning processes, it is very important to identify a role for interaction, without which it will be impossible for infants to develop a sense of learning. However, the impact of interaction on language development is limited by levels of consciousness. Infants cannot acquire the contents beyond the limit of LoC at a given age. That is, when consciousness does not exist or does not reach a certain level, a learning process cannot be activated in an infant. In addition, different learning procedures occur at different levels of consciousness. What infants acquire at a lower LoC will become the building blocks for a higher LoC, which is the reason why an infant at a higher LoC can acquire more complex rules for learning more quickly.

What is presented in this paper is only the description of a step toward building up experimentally executable versions of models. The present model setting described is seemingly simple. In the future work, such models will be further established to allow multiple agents to interact with each other at different levels of consciousness, suggesting that each agent will develop its own idiolect and that the agents that interact regularly with each other will have many common constructions in their idiolects.

Acknowledgements:

Academic Research Fund (AcRF) Tier 1 Complexity Seed Funding awarded to Helena Gao by the Ministry of Education of Singapore and Nanyang Technological University, Singapore. Experiment trials conducted by Can Guo.

Reference

Bates, E. (1975). Peer relations and the acquisition of language. *Friendship and peer relations*, 259-292.

Bates, E. (1999). Nativism versus development: comments on Baillargeon and Smith, MA, USA: Wiley-Blackwell.

Bates, E., & Goodman, J. C. (1997). On the inseparability of grammar and the lexicon: Evidence from acquisition, aphasia and real-time processing. *Language and cognitive Processes, 12*(5-6), 507-584.

Bates, E., & Goodman, J. C. (1999). On the emergence of grammar from the lexicon. *The emergence of language*, 29.

Bruner, J. (1983). *Child's talk: Learning to use language*. Oxford: Oxford University Press.

Bowerman, M. (1990). Mapping thematic roles onto syntactic functions: Are children helped by innate linking rules? *Linguistics, 28*(6), 1253-1290.

Bowerman, M. (2004). From universal to language-specific in early grammatical development [Reprint] *The child language reader* (pp. 131-146): Routledge.

Carpenter, M., Nagell, K., Tomasello, M., Butterworth, G., & Moore, C. (1998). Social cognition, joint attention, and communicative competence from 9 to 15 months of age. *Monographs of the Society for Research in Child Development, 63*(4), i+iii+v-vi+1-174.

Carruthers, P. (1996). *Language, Thought, and Consciousness: An Essay in Philosophical Psychology*: Cambridge University Press.

Carruthers, P. (2000). *Phenomenal Consciousness: A Naturalistic Theory*: Cambridge University Press.

Casti, J. L. (1997). *Would-be worlds: How simulation is changing the frontiers of science*. New York, NY: John Wiley and Sons.

Chomsky, N. (1967). Review of Skinner's Verbal Behavior. In L. A. Jakobovits & M. S. Miron (Eds.), *Readings in the Psychology of Language*: Prentice-Hall.

Chomsky, N. (1975). The logical structure of linguistic theory.

Gao, H. H., & Holland, J. H. (2008). *Agent-based Models of Levels of Consciousness*. SFI Working Papers. doi: SFI-WP 08-12-048. Santa Fe Institute. U.S. A.

Gao, H. H., & Holland, J. H. (2013). The Language Niche. *Eastward Flows the Great River: Festschrift in Honor of Professor William SY. WANG on his 80th Birthday*, 141.

Gesell, A. (1928). *Infancy and human growth*. New York: The Macmillan Company.

Gopnik, A., & Meltzoff, A. N. (1997). *Words, thoughts, and theories* (Vol. 1): Mit Press Cambridge, MA.

Hayes, S. C., Barnes-Holmes, D., & Roche, B. (2001). *Relational frame theory: A post-Skinnerian account of human language and cognition*: Springer Science & Business Media.

Hebb, D. O. (1949). *The organization of behavior: A neuropsychological approach*: John Wiley & Sons.

Holland, J. H. (1995). *Hidden Order: How Adaptation Builds Complexity*: Perseus Books.

Holland, J. H. (1998). *Emergence: From chaos to order*. Redwood City, California: AddisonWesley.

Holland, J. H., Holyoak, K. J., Nisbett, R. E., & Thagard, P. R. (1986). *Induction: Processes of inference, learning, and discovery*. Cambridge, MA: Bradford Books/ MIT Press.

Kelly, G. A. (1955/1991). *The psychology of personal constructs. Volume 1: A theory of personality*. New York, US: Norton. 2nd printing: 1991, London, New York: Routledge.

MacWhinney, B. (1986). *Toward a psycholinguistically plausible parser.* Paper presented at the Proceedings of the Eastern States Conference on Linguistics (ESCOL 1986), Columbus, OH.

MacWhinney, B. (2004). A multiple process solution to the logical problem of language acquisition. *J Child Lang, 31*(04), 883-914.

Mandler, J. M. (1998). Babies think before they speak. *Human Development, 41*(2), 116-126.

Mandler, J. M. (2004). *The foundations of mind: Origins of conceptual thought*: Oxford University Press.

Meltzoff, A. N., & Borton, R. W. (1979). Intermodal matching by human neonates.

Meltzoff, A. N., & Moore, M. K. (1977). Imitation of facial and manual gestures by human neonates. *Science, 198*(4312), 75-78.

Moscovitch, M. (1989). Confabulation and the Frontal Systems: Strategic versus Associative retrieval in Neuropsychological Theories of Memory. *Varieties of Memory and Consciousness: Essays in Honour of Endel Tulving*, 133.

Piaget, J. (1926). *The Language and Thought of the Child*. London: Routledge & Kegan Paul.

Piaget, J. (1959). *The Language and Thought of the Child*. London: Routledge & Kegan Paul.

Piaget, J. (2013). *The construction of reality in the child* (Vol. 82): Routledge.

Ramscar, M., & Yarlett, D. (2007). Linguistic Self-Correction in the Absence of Feedback: A New Approach to the Logical Problem of Language Acquisition. *Cogn Sci, 31*(6), 927-960.

Roediger, R. (2004). What happened to behaviorism. *APS Observer*.

Schacter, D. L. (1989). On the relation between memory and consciousness: Dissociable interactions and conscious experience. In H. L. I. Roediger & F. I. M. Craik (Eds.), *Varieties of Memory and Consciousness*.

Schooler, J. W. (2002). Re-representing consciousness: Dissociations between experience and meta-consciousness. *Trends in cognitive sciences, 6*(8), 339-344.

Skinner, B. F. (1957). *Verbal Behavior*. Acton, MA: Copley Publishing Group.

Snow, C. E. (1999). Social perspectives on the emergence of language. *The emergence of language*, 257-276.

Tomasello, M. (2003). Constructing a language: A usage-based theory of language acquisition.

Tomasello, M., & Bates, E. (2001). *Language development: The essential readings*, Blackwell.

Trevarthen, C., & Aitken, K. J. (2001). Infant intersubjectivity: Research, theory, and clinical applications. *Journal of Child Psychology and Psychiatry, 42*(1), 3-48.

Zelazo, P. D. (2004). The development of conscious control in childhood. *Trends in cognitive sciences, 8*(1), 12-17.

Zelazo, P. D., Gao, H. H., & Todd, R. (2007). The Development of Consciousness. In P. D. Zelazo, M. Moscovitch, & E. Thompson (Eds.), *The Cambridge Handbook of Consciousness* (pp. 405-432).

Pivot-Based Topic Models for Low-Resource Lexicon Extraction

John Richardson[†] Toshiaki Nakazawa[‡] Sadao Kurohashi[†]
[†]Graduate School of Informatics, Kyoto University, Kyoto 606-8501
[‡]Japan Science and Technology Agency, Kawaguchi-shi, Saitama 332-0012
john@nlp.ist.i.kyoto-u.ac.jp, nakazawa@pa.jst.jp, kuro@i.kyoto-u.ac.jp

Abstract

This paper proposes a range of solutions to the challenges of extracting large and high-quality bilingual lexicons for low-resource language pairs. In such scenarios there is often no parallel or even comparable data available. We design three effective pivot-based approaches inspired by the state-of-the-art technique of bilingual topic modelling, extending previous work to take advantage of trilingual data. The proposed models are shown to outperform traditional methods significantly and can be adapted based upon the nature of available training data. We demonstrate the accuracy of these pivot-based approaches in a realistic scenario generating an Icelandic-Korean lexicon from Wikipedia.

1 Introduction

Data-driven approaches to natural language processing have been shown to be greatly effective, and the case of bilingual lexicon extraction is no exception. Recent advances in this area have enabled the construction of large, high-quality bilingual lexicons, requiring less parallel data by making use of comparable corpora.

While such comparable corpora are readily available for many language pairs, particularly when one of those languages is English, previous direct approaches fail when there is no such data available. For many language pairs there simply does not exist comparable (and even less so parallel) data. Even for languages with a large volume of available parallel data, most corpora cover only limited domains.

There are two natural methods to deal with this problem: constructing or mining new data for the direct approach, and finding new ways to make better use of what data is already available. For an example of the construction of comparable corpora, see Zhu et al. (2013). We take the second approach and design pivot-based models for bilingual lexicon extraction. The major advantage of using a pivot language is that it is possible to take advantage of the large volume of comparable data sharing a common language such as English.

In this paper we develop pivot-based approaches to make use of modern bilingual lexicon extraction methods that can be trained on comparable corpora. We present a selection of efficient algorithms using the framework of topic modelling (Blei et al., 2003). Topic modelling has been a popular approach for bilingual lexicon extraction, however its use as a pivot model has yet to be explored. The use of topic models as a semantic similarity measure is a scalable method for low-resource languages because document-aligned comparable pivot training data (such as for English and a low-resource language) is growing ever more widely available. Examples of such sources are Wikipedia, multilingual newspaper articles and mined Web data.

While there have been many studies on bilingual lexicon extraction, there has been little focus on the important problem of resource construction for low-resource language pairs. We

29th Pacific Asia Conference on Language, Information and Computation pages 369 - 377
Shanghai, China, October 30 - November 1, 2015

present a variety of solutions to this problem, demonstrating their application to a practical scenario, and compare their effectiveness to mainstream approaches.

2 Related Work

The use of pivot models has been a common theme in the development of Natural Language Processing systems that deal with low-resource languages. In the field of Machine Translation, pivot models can be used in both decoding and the construction of parallel training data. Utiyama and Isahara (2007) give a comparison of possible methods for integrating a pivot language into phrase-based SMT systems.

Bilingual lexicon extraction has had a long history of using pivot languages. Tanaka and Umemura (1994) build a pivot lexicon by combining bilingual dictionaries, and more recently there have been attempts to extract lexicons or paraphrase patterns (Zhao et al., 2008) from bilingual corpora. A common problem with the use of a pivot language is associated noise, leading to a number of studies aiming to improve pivot lexicons, such as by using cross-lingual cooccurrences (Tanaka and Iwasaki, 1996) and 'non-aligned signatures' (Shezaf and Rappoport, 2010), a form of word context similarity.

Bilingual lexicon mining from non-parallel data has seen much popularity in recent years. Studies have considered a variety of methods such as canonical correlation analysis (Haghighi et al., 2008) and label propagation (Tamura et al., 2012). We use the method of bilingual topic modelling (Vulić et al., 2011), which has been recently applied to a variety of fields such as transliteration mining (Richardson et al., 2013).

3 Model Details

We consider the task of translating a source word s from language S to a target word t from language T. The baseline model is a direct approach using S-T training data. After describing the baseline model (bilingual LDA), we introduce three novel methods of taking advantage of data including a pivot language P, such as S-P + P-T and S-P-T data.

3.1 Baseline: Bilingual LDA

We begin with a baseline non-pivot lexicon extraction model $M_{ST} : S \times T \rightarrow \mathbb{R}$ that gives a similarity score to a source-target word pair (using S-T training data).

The non-pivot lexicon extraction model M_{ST} makes use of a bilingual topic similarity measure. We elected to use bilingual topic models rather than the more intuitive method of comparing monolingual context vectors (Rapp, 1995) as we believe topic modelling is more suitable for processing uncommon language pairs. This is because a bilingual seed lexicon is required for methods that learn a mapping between source and target vector spaces, such as Haghighi et al. (2008), in order to match cross-language word pairs. This data is unlikely to be available in sufficient quantity for low-resource language pairs, however comparable documents can be found from sources such as Wikipedia.

We base our implementation on the state-of-the-art system of Vulić et al. (2011) for comparison. This method uses the bilingual Latent Dirichlet Allocation (BiLDA) algorithm (Mimno et al., 2009), an extension of monolingual LDA (Blei et al., 2003). Monolingual LDA takes as its input a set of monolingual documents and generates a word-topic distribution ϕ classifying words appearing in these documents into semantically similar topics. Bilingual LDA extends this by considering pairs of comparable documents in each of two languages, and outputs a pair of word-topic distributions ϕ and ψ, one for each input language. The graphical model for polylingual LDA is illustrated in Figure 1.

In order to apply bilingual topic models to a lexicon extraction task, we must construct an effective word similarity measure for translation candidates. This can be achieved by a variety of methods comparing the similarity of K-dimensional word-topic vectors. We use the simple and well-studied cosine similarity measure (as defined below) to measure the similarity between topic distribution vectors ψ_{k,w_e} and ϕ_{k,w_f} for translation candidates w_e and w_f.

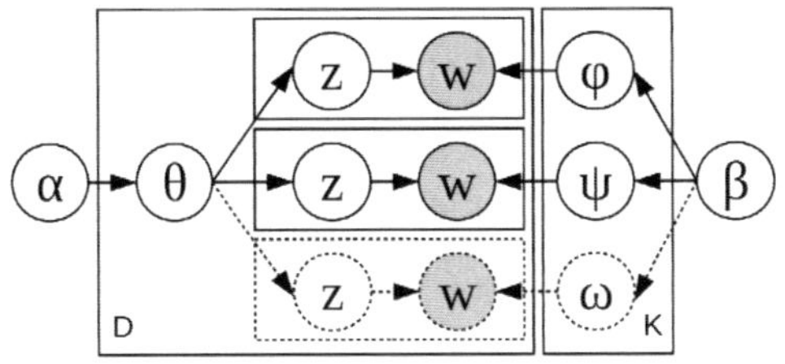

Figure 1: Graphical model for polylingual LDA with K topics, D document pairs and hyper-parameters α and β. Bilingual LDA is shown with solid lines and trilingual LDA adds the dotted lines. Topics for each document are sampled from the common distribution θ, and the two (three) languages have word-topic distributions ϕ, ψ (and ω). For further details of the LDA formulation see Blei et al. (2003).

$$Cos(w_e, w_f) = \frac{\sum_{k=1}^{K} \psi_{k,w_e} \phi_{k,w_f}}{\sqrt{\sum_{k=1}^{K} \psi_{k,w_e}^2} \sqrt{\sum_{k=1}^{K} \phi_{k,w_f}^2}} \quad (1)$$

3.2 Trilingual LDA Model

A simple yet interesting extension to applying bilingual LDA to source-target data is training trilingual LDA on a set of source-pivot-target language documents. Although in practice there may not exist such a large quantity of available trilingual data, we show in our experiments that this method is able to outperform the bilingual case even when there is a smaller volume of available trilingual data.

An advantage of this approach is that we can expect the additional (pivot) language to provide an additional point of reference, stabilizing the topic-document distribution. We show that this leads to a considerable reduction in noise, improving the translation accuracy.

The mathematical formulation is a natural extension of the bilingual case. We generate a triple of word-topic distributions ϕ, ψ and ω and a shared document-topic distribution θ using the same method as described above for bilingual LDA. The model is trained on triples of aligned comparable documents.

3.3 Pivot Model

In this section we consider an efficient method to construct a pivot model $M_{SP,PT} : S \times T \to \mathbb{R}$ (using S-P and P-T training data) that builds upon the non-pivot models M_{SP} and M_{PT}, which are built with the baseline (bilingual LDA) approach. The generation of a target word $t \in T$ is modelled as the two-step translation of a source word $s \in S$ to a pivot word $p \in P$ and then this p into T. We assume that for any translation candidate pair s, t:

$$M_{SP,PT}(s,t) = \max_{p \in P} M_{SP}(s,p) M_{PT}(p,t) \quad (2)$$

We would now like to generate the n-best distinct translations, however the size of the search space has increased to $|P||T|$ compared to $|T|$ for the non-pivot model.

The natural method for searching this space is to score every pivot translation $s \to p_i$ with M_{SP} ($|P|$ scoring operations) and then for each p_i to score every target translation $p_i \to t_j$ with M_{PT} ($|P||T|$ scoring operations). These scores are then multiplied together and sorted to generate an n-best list. As we have no further information about M it is not possible to reduce the complexity of this search without making some approximations.

We use a faster, approximate algorithm that greatly reduces the number of scoring operations required by using a beam search. The scoring operation, i.e. calculating $M(s,t)$, is the most time consuming step and therefore the most important to be avoided. Using a beam width b, the top-b pivot candidates $p_1, ..., p_b \in P$ for s are first generated, requiring $|P|$ scoring operations as we have no way to sort the p in advance. Then for each p_i, we generate the top-b target candidates $t_{i,1}, ..., t_{i,b}$ for the translation of p_i into T. This step requires only $b|T|$ scoring operations.[1]

There will be some search errors with this method and therefore b should be increased if a very accurate n-best list is required. The

[1]This can be further reduced to $b'|T|$ where $b' \leq b$ by keeping track of the final top-n list of translations t^*. This allows us to discard p_i for which $M_{SP}(s, p_i) \leq M_{SP,PT}(s, t_n^*)$, as we have $M_{PT}(p_i, t) \leq 1$.

approximate algorithm collapses into the exact method as b increases. If there are many s to translate, it would be possible to cache the M_{PT}, further improving the performance.

See Figure 2 for an illustration of our search algorithm.

3.4 'Box' Model

For many low-resource language pairs there does not exist source-target or trilingual data and therefore the pivot model is the only available option. However this is not always the case. For comparison we create one further model, the 'box' model, using all available data.

The 'box' model uses source-pivot, pivot-target, source-target and source-pivot-target data. The data is combined by creating (source, pivot, target) triples for each document. For each language L, if there is a version of the document written in L, we add it to the triple, otherwise we insert an empty string. We liken this method to packing boxes, one per document for each language, with whatever data is available. These triples are then used to train a trilingual topic model as in Section 3.2.

This approach has the advantages of avoiding noise and search errors that can be introduced by the pivot model in Section 3.3, however it relies on the availability of sufficient training data. When such data is not available we are still able to use the pivot model.

4 Experiments

In this section we consider a task where we wish to extract a Korean-Icelandic (KO-IS) and Icelandic-Korean (IS-KO) lexicon from comparable Wikipedia documents using English (EN) as a pivot language. This is a realistic scenario in which we have a sufficient quantity of aligned pivot-source and pivot-target document pairs but considerably less source-target data. We chose this language pair to demonstrate the effectiveness of our model on both low-resource and distant language pairs. English was the most natural pivot language for this task, however in some cases it might be preferable to use a different language.

The topic models were all trained on document-aligned Wikipedia data. We extracted these documents from mid-2013 Wikipedia XML dumps and they were aligned using Wikipedia 'langlinks'. The distribution of aligned document pairs including combinations of these three languages is shown in Table 1.

EN	IS	KO	Documents
✓	✓	?	22K
✓	?	✓	140K
?	✓	✓	14K
✓	✓	✓	14K
2+ languages			190K

Table 1: Number of aligned documents for each language combination. ✓ means 'included', ? means 'possibly included'. The last row shows the number of documents containing at least 2 languages.

Note that there is considerably less IS-KO data than for either EN-IS or EN-KO (only 60% of EN-IS, 10% of EN-KO). In fact the majority of trilingual data covers the same documents as the IS-KO subset, as the documents with IS and KO data very commonly also have an English version.

While it is true that there does exist some IS-KO data in Wikipedia that could be used directly to build an IS-KO lexicon, we show that there is not enough to extract translation pairs with high accuracy. Furthermore, we also show that the proposed pivot model in Section 3.3 functions well without requiring any of this data.

4.1 Settings

We used an in-house English lemmatizer and tokenizer to prepare the English data. Icelandic data was processed with IceNLP (Loftsson and Rögnvaldsson, 2007) and Korean analyzed with HanNanum (Park et al., 2010). For each language we extracted the most frequent 100K nouns for our experiments, a vocabulary size over 10 times larger than in previous work (Vulić et al., 2011).

The test data consisted of $N = 200$ (EN, KO, IS) translation triples. These were created by randomly selecting 200 nouns from our English

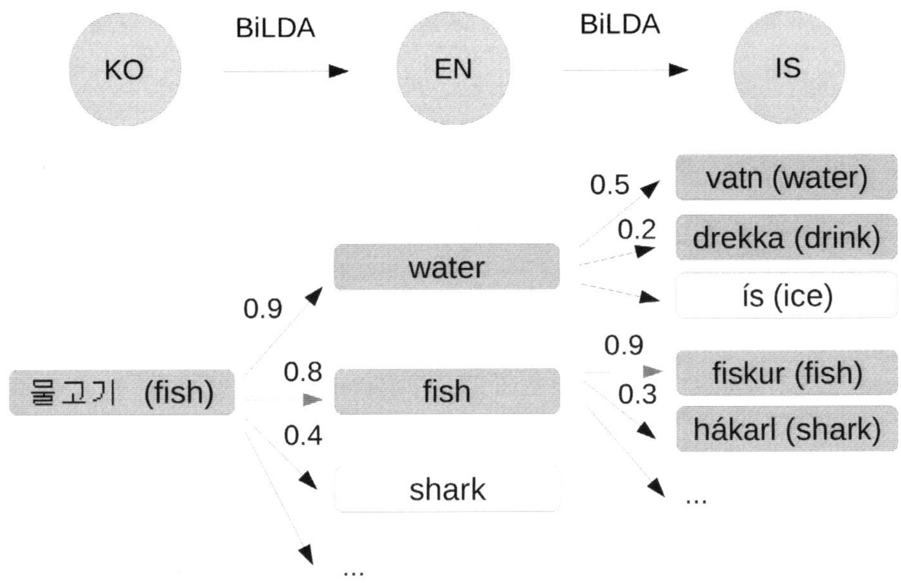

Figure 2: An illustration of the beam search algorithm using $b = 2$. The numbers shown are example similarity scores and the red arrows show the optimal path.

Wikipedia vocabulary and translating these by hand into Korean and Icelandic. For comparison the same test data was used for all experiments.

We used the PolyLDA++ tool (Richardson et al., 2013) to generate multilingual topic models. The training was run over 1000 iterations using $K = 2000$ topics. We set the LDA hyperparameters as $\alpha = 50/K$ and $\beta = 0.01$, which are the settings used most commonly in previous work on topic modelling.

The models were evaluated by generating an n-best list of translations for each word in the test set. The following statistics were then measured for the extracted lexicon, where $rank_i$ was the rank given to the correct translation in the n-best list (∞ if not in n-best list). We used $n = 10$. We also used $b = 10$ for the search beam width.

- Top-1 accuracy:

$$\frac{1}{N}\sum_{i=1}^{N}\delta_{rank_i,1} \tag{3}$$

- Mean Reciprocal Rank (MRR):

$$\frac{1}{N}\sum_{i=1}^{N}\frac{1}{rank_i} \tag{4}$$

Lang Pair	Method	Top-1	MRR
IS-KO	baseline	0.265	0.334
	pivot	**0.310**	**0.365**
KO-IS	baseline	0.220	0.286
	pivot	**0.240**	**0.321**

Table 2: Results of direct/pivot comparison experiment.

4.2 Comparison between Direct and Pivot Model

Before applying the proposed pivot-based approaches to a realistic lexicon extraction scenario, we first verified the effectiveness of the pivot model in Section 3.3 using a controlled data set.

We consider a task where we have a corpus of aligned triples of (EN, KO, IS) documents. Our data contained 14K triples (see Table 1) with a combined vocabulary size of 30K nouns. The experiment is to test the effectiveness of using the KO-IS data directly (baseline) with the non-pivot model M_{ST} against using the pivot model $M_{SP,PT}$ with only KO-EN and EN-IS data.

This is designed to be a fair comparison as we have the same number of documents in the pivot

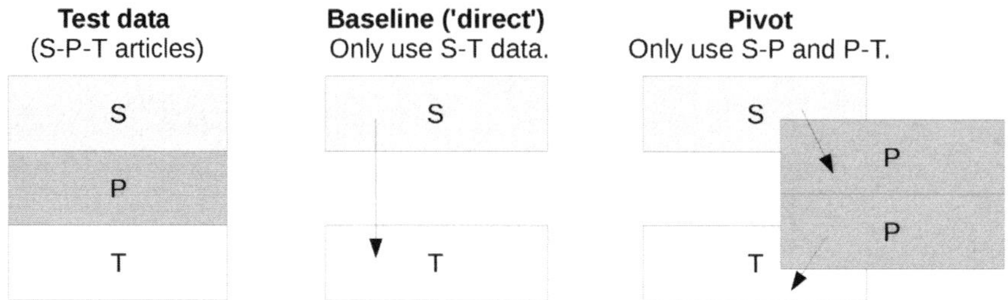

Figure 3: Training data used for direct/pivot comparison experiment.

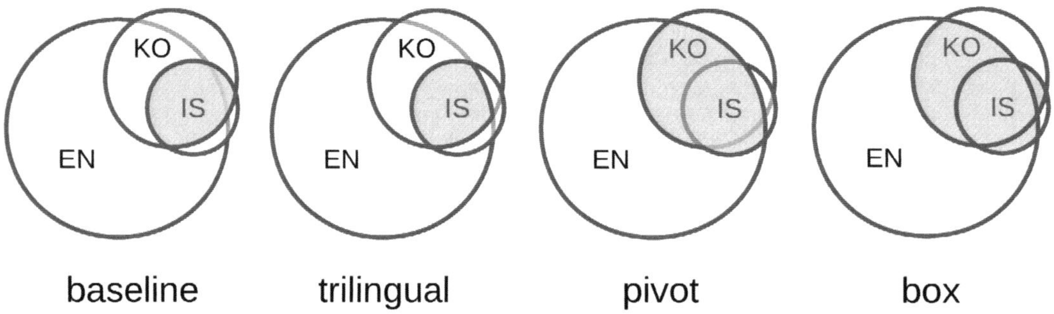

Figure 4: Subsets of Wikipedia data required for each method.

and non-pivot training sets. The organization of the training data is shown in Figure 3.

Table 2 shows the experimental results. These results show that when the same amount of data is available the pivot model is even more effective than using the source-target data directly.

In fact the scores are higher for the pivot model and we believe there could be two reasons for this. Despite the same number of documents being used, the English articles are on average longer than their Icelandic and Korean counterparts and this could improve the effectiveness of training.

It is also possible that many of the Icelandic and Korean articles were produced by partially or fully translating their corresponding English pages. This would lead to a tighter similarity in the models containing the pivot language.

4.3 Lexicon Extraction Experiment

We now turn to the main experiment, in which we consider the task of extracting a bilingual lexicon from Wikipedia for a low-resource language pair (IS-KO and KO-IS). In order to demonstrate the practical application of the proposed model, we use all the available data in Wikipedia, combining pivot and non-pivot models.

- The baseline score ('baseline') is calculated for the non-pivot model M_{ST} using only KO-IS data. This emulates the current state-of-the-art non-pivot lexicon extraction algorithm, which is only able to use the KO-IS data and model for direct translation. See Section 3.1.
- The trilingual score ('trilingual') is the accuracy of our model trained using a trilingual topic model on trilingual (KO-EN-IS)

data, which in practice is the most difficult to obtain. See Section 3.2.

- The pivot score ('pivot') is evaluated for the proposed pivot model $M_{SP,PT}$, able to make use of the KO-EN and EN-IS data. See Section 3.3.

- The score ('box'), using all possible data, is constructed by combining baseline (KO-IS), pivot (EN-KO, EN-IS) and trilingual (EN-KO-IS) data. See Section 3.4.

Figure 4 shows the data that is required (and was used) for each method. The results of the experiment are shown in Table 3.

Lang Pair	Method	Top-1	MRR
IS-KO	baseline	0.255	0.324
	trilingual	0.350	0.428
	pivot	0.380	0.459
	box	**0.420**	**0.495**
KO-IS	baseline	0.230	0.296
	trilingual	0.315	0.392
	pivot	0.305	0.398
	box	**0.390**	**0.475**

Table 3: Results of lexicon extraction experiment.

5 Analysis and Discussion

It can be seen from the results that all three proposed models considerably outperform the baseline. This demonstrates that these approaches are able to improve the quality of extracted lexicons for low-resource language pairs by making use of pivot language data, giving a large accuracy improvement over previous work.

An interesting observation is that the trilingual model is able to greatly improve upon the baseline even though it uses less training data. It is probable that the addition of the additional language (English) has helped to reduce the noise in the Korean-Icelandic model by stabilizing the document-topic distribution.

The pivot approach further improves on this by making use of the relatively large volume of EN-KO and EN-IS data. Furthermore, the

Candidate	Meaning	Score
결혼	marriage	0.875
남편	husband	0.796
아내	wife	0.756
약혼	engagement	0.732
결혼식	wedding	0.726

Table 4: An example of a good translation: 'hjónaband' (marriage).

Candidate	Meaning	Score
스튜어트	Stewart	0.355
주장	claim	0.327
반증	disproof	0.301
논란	controversy	0.296
증언	testimony	0.289

Table 5: An example of a bad translation: 'tilgangur' (purpose).

pivot model score is not far from the most effective method 'box', which requires all the data, some of which is difficult in general to obtain (trilingual and KO-IS data). This shows that the pivot model is still able to compete with a model trained directly on source-target data.

The most effective method was the 'box' approach and this is perhaps to be expected as it was able to make use of the largest volume of data. For relatively high-resource language pairs this method is likely to be the most effective as more data is available, however the pivot model becomes the only available option as the source-target data becomes sparse. When the necessary data is available, the 'box' approach can improve upon the pivot model.

Tables 4 and 5 give examples of successful and incorrect translations using the pivot model. The model can be seen to perform more effectively on words with a concrete meaning (Table 4) and less so on abstract concepts (Table 5), which often have more variation in their represention across languages. Analysis of the n-best lists revealed a tendency for clumping of pivot words. As in the example in Table 6, the same pivot word was often used to generate groups of consecutive target language words. This how-

Rank	Pivot p	Target t	$M_{SP}(s,p)$	$M_{PT}(p,t)$	Score
1	feminism	나혜석 (Na Hyeseok)	0.902	0.969	0.873
2	feminism	여자 (woman)	0.902	0.967	0.871
3	feminism	여성 (female)	0.902	0.907	0.818
...	...	...	...	...	...
9	feminism	여학교 (girls' school)	0.902	0.517	0.466
10	wife	아내 (wife)	0.315	0.914	0.288

Table 6: Analysis of translation for 'kona' (woman), showing high clumping.

Rank	Pivot p	Target t	$M_{SP}(s,p)$	$M_{PT}(p,t)$	Score
1	world	세계 (world)	0.712	0.851	0.606
2	world	월드 (world)	0.712	0.619	0.441
3	cosmos	창조 (creation)	0.278	0.965	0.268
4	cosmos	만물 (all things)	0.278	0.928	0.258
5	universe	우주론 (cosmology)	0.225	0.973	0.219
6	universe	빅뱅 (big bang)	0.225	0.965	0.217

Table 7: Analysis of translation for 'heimur' (world), showing less clumping.

ever seems not to reduce the quality of the output, as we did not notice any significant change in the MRR scores when adding the restriction that only one target word could be generated from any pivot word. An example with less clumping is shown in Table 7.

6 Conclusion and Future Work

In this paper we have presented three novel pivot-based approaches for bilingual lexicon extraction with low-resource language pairs. The proposed models are able to generate a high-quality lexicon for language pairs with no direct source-target training data, and we have shown that each model considerably outperforms a state-of-the-art non-pivot baseline. With a variety of approaches it is possible to select an appropriate method based on the size and nature of available training data.

There is much still to explore in the area of the construction of lexicons for low-resource language pairs. A possible extension to the proposed model is to use a larger pivot base, of not just one but of multiple pivot languages acting as a form of interlingua, similar to the idea in Dabre et al. (2014). This could improve the quality of the model in cases where there is not such a clear choice for an appropriate pivot language.

Another possibility for improvement is removing the assumption that there is an appropriate pivot word, using instead a direct mapping between the word-topic vector spaces for source-pivot and pivot-target topic models.

In the future we would like to use the proposed method to improve machine translation by extracting a large lexicon and applying it to a low-resource translation task.

Acknowledgments

We would like to thank the reviewers for their instructive comments. The first author is supported by a Japanese Government Scholarship (MEXT).

References

David Blei, Andrew Ng and Michael Jordan. 2003. Latent Dirichlet Allocation. In *The Journal of Machine Learning Research*, Volume 3.

Raj Dabre, Fabien Cromieres, Sadao Kurohashi and Pushpak Bhattacharyya. 2014. Leveraging Small Multilingual Corpora for SMT Using Many Pivot Languages. In *NAACL 2014*.

Aria Haghighi, Percy Liang, Taylor Berg-Kirkpatrick and Dan Klein. 2008. Learning Bilingual Lexicons from Monolingual Corpora. In *ACL 2008*.

Hrafn Loftsson and Eiríkur Rögnvaldsson. 2007. IceNLP: A Natural Language Processing Toolkit for Icelandic. In *Interspeech 2007*.

David Mimno, Hanna Wallach, Jason Naradowsky, David Smith and Andrew McCallum. 2009. Polylingual topic models. In *EMNLP 2009*.

Park, S., Choi, D., Kim, E., and Choi, K.-S. 2010. A plug-in component-based Korean morphological analyzer. In *HCLT 2010*.

Reinhard Rapp. 1995. Identifying Word Translations in Non-Parallel Texts. In *ACL 1995*.

John Richardson, Toshiaki Nakazawa and Sadao Kurohashi. 2013. Robust Transliteration Mining from Comparable Corpora with Bilingual Topic Models. In *IJCNLP 2013*.

Daphna Shezaf and Ari Rappoport. 2010. Bilingual Lexicon Generation Using Non-Aligned Signatures. In *ACL 2010*.

Akihiro Tamura, Taro Watanabe and Eiichiro Sumita. 2012. Bilingual Lexicon Extraction from Comparable Corpora Using Label Propagation. In *EMNLP-CoNLL 2012*.

Kumiko Tanaka and Hideya Iwasaki. 1996. Extraction of lexical translations from non-aligned corpora. In *Conference on Computational Linguistics 1996*.

Kumiko Tanaka and Kyoji Umemura. 1994. Construction of a bilingual dictionary intermediated by a third language. In *Conference on Computational Linguistics 1994*.

Masao Utiyama and Hitoshi Isahara. 2007. Comparison of Pivot Methods for Phrase-based Statistical Machine Translation. In *NAACL 2007*.

Ivan Vulić, Wim De Smet and Marie-Francine Moens. 2011. Identifying Word Translations from Comparable Corpora Using Latent Topic Models. In *ACL 2011*.

Shiqi Zhao, Haifeng Wang, Ting Liu and Sheng Li. 2008. Pivot Approach for Extracting Paraphrase Patterns from Bilingual Corpora. In *ACL 2008*.

Zede Zhu, Miao Li, Lei Chen, Zhenxin Yang. 2013. Building Comparable Corpora Based on Bilingual LDA Model. In *ACL 2013*.

A Corpus-Based Study of *zunshou* and Its English Equivalents

Ying Liu

Department of Linguistics and Translation
City University of Hong Kong
Tat Chee Avenue, Kowloon, Hong Kong
yliu227-c@my.cityu.edu.hk

Abstract

This paper describes a corpus-based contrastive study of collocation in English and Chinese. In light of the corpus-based approach to identify functionally equivalent units, the present paper attempts to identify the collocational translation equivalents of *zunshou* by using a parallel corpus and two comparable corpora. This study shows that more often than not, we can find in English more than one translation equivalents. By taking collocates into consideration, we are able to establish bilingual equivalence with more accuracy. The present study indicates that semantic preference and semantic prosody play a vital role in establishing equivalence between corresponding lexical sequences in English and Chinese. The studies of collocation across languages have potentially useful implications for foreign language teaching and learning, contrastive linguistic and translation studies, as well as bilingual lexicography.

1 Introduction

The importance of the concept of collocation has long been recognized in theoretical linguistics. It was first put forward as an academic terminology by Firth (1957). Since then, there have been three major approaches to the study of collocation, which can be referred to as the semantic approach, the lexical approach (Halliday, 1966; Sinclair, 1966) and the integrated approach (Mitchell, 1971). Since the 1980s, the notion of collocation has been at the center of much corpus-linguistic work. The corpus-based and corpus-driven approaches have been widely adopted in the study of collocation. Although numerous studies of collocation based on corpus data have been conducted, the features of collocation have mainly been explored in monolingual context and there are comparatively fewer attempts to investigate collocation across different languages. The use of parallel corpora has greatly facilitated cross-linguistic research in recent decades and indeed, "they have been a principal reason for the revival of contrastive linguistics" (Salkie, 1999).

As a tentative attempt, the present study focuses on investigating the cross-linguistic collocational equivalents of one verb – 遵守 *zunshou* using a bi-directional English-Chinese parallel corpus and two comparable corpora. A close observation of the right collocates of 遵守 *zunshou* and its English equivalents in terms of semantic preference and semantic prosody (Louw, 1993; Sinclair, 1996) have been made, with a view to determining the collocational translation equivalents in English and Chinese.

In what follows, we will first describe the research method of the present study in Section 2, which includes the corpora to be used, the procedure for the identification of translation equivalents, the approaches and analytical concepts of collocation. Section 3 will present our corpus findings, followed by some discussions in Section 4. Section 5 will conclude this research with various implications and prospects for future work.

2 Research Method

2.1 Corpora

The data analyzed in this study were obtained from one parallel corpus and two general corpora. The parallel corpus is the *Shanghai Jiao Tong University Parallel Corpus* (henceforth JDPC) (Wei and Lu, 2014). It is a 9-million bi-directional English-Chinese parallel corpus consisting of 3,626,890 English tokens and 5,362,748 Chinese characters. The three major categories in JDPC are politics, science and technology, and humanities.

29th Pacific Asia Conference on Language, Information and Computation pages 378 - 386
Shanghai, China, October 30 - November 1, 2015

In addition, JDPC has an associated database which contains 590,799 pairs of translation equivalents of varying lengths and grammatical ranks. JDPC serves as the point of departure from which the possible translation equivalents are extracted for further data analysis. The advantage of using a parallel corpus in this contrastive study of collocation is that "it gives the benefit of such input in a more reliable manner; it offers a range of possible translation pairs that have already been identified and used by translators, in other words, verified by actual translation usage" (Tognini-Bonelli, 2001).

The English general corpus is the *British National Corpus* (henceforth BNC) which consists of approximately 100 million words of British English, 90% from written texts, 10% from spoken texts. The written part of BNC was used in this study. The Chinese general corpus is the *Modern Chinese Corpus* (henceforth MCC). We use its core version, commonly known as the Main Corpus of MCC, which contains 20 million Chinese characters proportionally sampled from the whole corpus.

2.2 The Procedure for the Identification of Translation Equivalents

The procedure for identifying the collocational translation equivalents in English and Chinese involves three steps. The first step is to extract prima facie translation equivalents (Tognini-Bonelli, 2002: 81) from the parallel corpus. We searched 遵守 *zunshou* in JDPC and found that there are three prima facie translation equivalents of 遵守 *zunshou*, namely, *abide by*, *adhere to* and *observe*.

However, what a parallel corpus can do is only to offer a set of possible translation pairs. It is more important to base our observation on the comparable corpora to establish correspondence between the form and function of the lexical items or sequences under study. Therefore, the second step is to observe the formal and functional features of the node words in the two monolingual corpora. So we turn to MCC and BNC. The right collocates of 遵守 *zunshou*, *abide by*, *adhere to* and *observe* were extracted from MCC and BNC respectively.

Then we come to the last step – to identify de facto translation equivalents. Based on the data extracted in the previous steps, we analyzed the four node words in terms of their collocates, semantic preference and semantic prosody, which will reveal the key patterning of the node words and help to establish equivalence across the two languages.

2.3 The Approaches to the Study of Collocation and Analytical Concepts

Generally, there are two approaches to the study of collocation using corpora, namely, the corpus-based approach and the corpus-driven approach. Although there is no clear-cut demarcation between them, the major difference is whether corpus data is analyzed in the pre-constructed grammatical framework. The corpus-based approach generalizes collocational patterns on the basis of colligation and lexical co-occurrences (Wei, 2002), whilst the corpus-driven approach proceeds with data and uses purely statistical method to extract collocation. The present study adopts the former approach. The study to be presented in the remainder of this paper will be qualitative in nature and statistical test will not be applied due to the low frequency of many collocates of the node words. Through observing the concordance lines (the KWIC Format), we first generalized the colligation and then analyzed the right collocates of the node words in the colligational framework.

The study involves two key analytical concepts: semantic preference and semantic prosody. As with Sinclair, semantic preference refers to "the restriction of regular co-occurrence to items which share a semantic feature" (Sinclair, 2004: 142), and semantic prosody refers to the attitudinal meaning a node word and its co-selections convey, which essentially indicates the communicative purpose of the speaker (Sinclair, 1996: 87). The four node words will be compared in terms of these two analytical concepts in order to establish the de facto cross-linguistic equivalence.

3 Corpus Evidence

3.1 Evidence from the Parallel Corpus

An initial check of *zunshou* in JDPC yielded 30 occurrences which were translated by *abide by* in 10 times, by *adhere to* in 3 times, and by *observe* in 17 times of all cases. The profiles of the 30 prima facie collocational translation equivalents are presented in Table 1, Table 2 and Table 3 respectively.

Chinese collocations	*English collocations*	*Freq.*
遵守宪法和法律 *zunshou xianfa he falv*	abiding by the Constitution and laws	2
遵守党章 *zunshou dangzhang*	abide by the Party Constitution	2
遵守国家的法律法规 *zunshou guojia de falv fagui*	abide by the laws and decrees of the State	2
遵守人民政府法律 *zunshou renmin zhengfu falv*	abiding by its laws	1
遵守…法规和制度 *zunshou … fagui he zhidu*	abide by the rules and regulations	1
遵守约法八章 *zunshou yuefa bazhang*	abide by the following eight-point covenant	1
遵守中英联合声明 *zunshou zhongying lianhe shengming*	abide by the Sino-British Joint Declaration	1
TOTAL		10

Table 1. 遵守 *zunshou* and *abide by* with their right collocates in JDPC

Chinese collocations	*English collocations*	*Freq.*
遵守着"不干涉中国内政的政策" *zunshou zhe "bu ganshe zhongguo neizheng de zhengce"*	adhered to a policy of non-interference in China's internal affairs	1
遵守…宗旨和原则 *zunshou … zongzhi he yuanze*	adhere to the purpose and principles	1
遵守…各项重要文件 *zunshou … gexiang zhongyao wenjian*	adhere to the important documents	1
TOTAL		3

Table 2. 遵守 *zunshou* and *adhere to* with their right collocates in JDPC

Chinese collocations	*English collocations*	*Freq.*
遵守纪律 *zunshou jilv*	observe discipline	5
遵守党的指示 *zunshou dang de zhishi*	observe the directives of the party	2
遵守宪法和法律 *zunshou xianfa he falv*	observing the Constitution and laws	2
遵守正确的原则 *zunshou zhengque de yuanze*	observe the correct principles	2
遵守…法律法规 *zunshou … falv fagui*	observe…laws and regulations	1
遵守党纪国法 *zunshou dangji guofa*	observe party discipline and state laws	1
遵守党的章程 *zunshou dang de zhangcheng*	observe the provisions of the party constitution	1
遵守…原则 *zunshou … yuanze*	observing principles	1
遵守社会公德 *zunshou shehui gongde*	be polite and observe common courtesy	1
遵守基本行为准则 *zunshou jiben xingwei zhunze*	observing the basic code of conduct	1
TOTAL		17

Table 3. 遵守 *zunshou* and *observe* with their right collocates in JDPC

3.2 Evidence from the Chinese Corpus

Adopting the method as defined in Section 2.2, the present study obtained 497 instances of 遵守 *zunshou* from the core part of MCC. In order to show its patterning, we present 10 concordance lines randomly selected from the overall data as shown in Table 4 below.

1.	用生命换来的。我们一定要珍惜宪法	**遵守**	宪法，维护宪法。我国现行宪法是第五届全国人
2.	只有统治阶级的所有成员毫无例外地	**遵守**	法律，并制裁其中的违法犯罪分子，才能维护统
3.	犯罪，解决民事纠纷，教育公民自觉	**遵守**	法律，积极同违法犯罪行为作斗争，维护社会主
4.	鄙人完全拥护共产党的政策，一定	**遵守**	人民政府的法令，同意把分行改为代办行！朱德

5.	决要求回归祖国，希望美方管理当局	**遵守**	日内瓦战俘公约，尊重我们的个人意愿；为了我
6.	欢迎与中国合作。美国将坚定不渝地	**遵守**	中美之间的三个联合公报。美国的政策"是以只
7.	我们要把它记在心里，让它化为力量	**遵守**	党的政策，兢兢业业，为伟佤人民做好工作。象
8.	条令，我们抓管理的如果自身不自觉	**遵守**	规定，就不能正人。"他没为亲友办过一个后门
9.	自觉地保卫祖国啊！那就应该自觉地	**遵守**	纪律，革命军队需要铁的纪律，比不得在农村干
10.	一样，根据马克思列宁主义的精神，	**遵守**	马克思列宁主义的原则，同时又不机械抄袭现成

Table 4. Concordance lines of 遵守 *zunshou*

A close observation of the data reveals that over 90% of all the instances of 遵守 *zunshou* are followed by a noun phrase. In a few cases, it is used to end a clause or sentence. Since the present study focuses on collocates in the right co-text and examination of the usage of 遵守 *zunshou* in the sentence-final position does not reveal many new collocates, we only focus on analyzing the data in the first colligational framework.

It has been observed that most of the right collocates of 遵守 *zunshou* can be categorized into different groups according to two criteria: whether they are authoritative or compulsory. By being authoritative is meant that they are documented and enforced by a country's government or government organs (e.g. *laws* and *regulations*), or agreed between governments of different countries (e.g. *treaty* or *declaration*); by being compulsory is meant that they must be obeyed and if not, the related party should suffer the consequences. In terms of these two criteria, the right collocates of 遵守 *zunshou* can be put in a hierarchy scale with differing degrees of authoritativeness and compulsoriness. For reasons of space, we only present those right collocates of 遵守 *zunshou* with a frequency higher than five (including five) in Table 5. Note that the raw frequencies of the collocates are listed in the brackets.

Criteria	*Right collocates of 遵守 zunshou*
Most authoritative & compulsory	法律 *falv* (39), 宪法和法律 *xianfa he falv* (17), 宪法 *xianfa* (12), 法规 *fagui* (7), 法令 *faling* (5)
Authoritative & compulsory	规则 *guize* (20), 规定 *guiding* (8), 政策 *zhengce* (7), 条约 *tiaoyue* (5)
Non-compulsory	纪律 *jilv* (32), 原则 *yuanze* (15), 劳动纪律 *laodong jilv* (11), 规范 *guifan* (11), 道德 *daode* (11), 党的纪律 *dang de jilv* (9), 公共秩序 *gonggong zhixu* (7), 标准 *biaozhun* (5)
Non-authoritative	命令 *mingling* (6), 要求 *yaoqiu* (5), 指示 *zhishi* (5)

Table 5. Right collocates of 遵守 *zunshou*

It needs to be noted that the demarcation between these collocates of 遵守 *zunshou* is, in fact, not so clear-cut as Table 5 shows and the aim to present such a hierarchy scale is mainly for the sake of classification. As shown in Table 5, at the top of the hierarchy scale are the most authoritative and compulsory collocates such as 宪法 *xianfa*, 法律 *falv*, 法规 *fagui*, etc. Down the scale, we can find words such as 规则 *guize* and 政策 *zhengce* which are less authoritative and compulsory than words in the first layer. Words in the third layer include the non-compulsory 纪律 *jilv*, 道德 *daode*, 公共秩序 *gonggong zhixu*, etc. Although they might be authoritative, but people still can be free to choose to follow it or not. At the bottom of the hierarchy scale, we can find words such as 命令 *mingling* and 要求 *yaoqiu* which are usually non-authoritative but still might be compulsory. In the following sections, the right collocates of the three node words (i.e. *abide by*, *adhere to* and *observe*) are also classified according to the same criteria.

3.3 Evidence from the English Corpus

For the collocates of *abide by*, *adhere to* and *observe*, this study uses a span of up to five words to the right of the node. This is in line with Sinclair's (1991: 106) suggestion that beyond four words from the node there were no statistical indication of the attractive power of the node. It needs to be noted that the lists of the right collocates of these three node words in the following Table 7, Table 9 and Table 11 are not exhaustive and we also have removed a few collocates which seem to be of little relevance and importance. In addition, those collocates which are relevant to our study but difficult to categorize in terms of the two criteria defined above have been classified as "others".

3.3.1 *Abide by* with Its Right Collocates

We have extracted in total 193 instances of *abide by* from BNC. In Table 6, we report ten randomly selected concordance lines from the overall data to show the patterning of *abide by*.

1.	united States, who accepted them and agreed to	**abide by**	the new constitution. Our constitutional
2.	comes illegal which will I'm sure all people will	**abide by**	the law. I'm sorry about the turning a blind
3.	troops in the area until the factions agreed to	**abide by**	a ceasefire. The SOC government issued a
4.	achieve such aims, an advertiser usually has to	**abide by**	a number of laws and codes of practice.
5.	demanded that the Efta states agree in advance to	**abide by**	a common defence policy which is as yet
6.	Hussein was under pressure on the one hand to	**abide by**	the UN resolution to impose sanctions on
7.	The government stated its willingness to	**abide by**	the UN sanctions policy, but sought to
8.	Indian tradition with the obedience required to	**abide by**	the rules governing non-violent action.
9.	do its utmost to achieve reconciliation and to	**abide by**	the peace accord. Qian announced that
10.	practice. Companies wishing to join will have to	**abide by**	a code of conduct. Not all have welcome

Table 6. Concordance lines of *abide by*

As indicated in Table 6, in terms of colligation, it has been observed that *abide by* is often followed by a noun phrase. Then we categorize the right collocates of *abide by* according to the two criteria mentioned in Section 3.2. Note that the raw frequencies of the collocates are listed in the brackets in Table 7. For some words, we also give one example of a wider context (e.g. *the federation's code of practice*) to justify our classification.

Criteria	*Right collocates of abide by*
Authoritative & compulsory	rule(s) (30), law(s) (7), terms (5), Code (4), regulations (3), treaty (3), policies (3), conditions (3), provisions (2), proviso (2), accord (2), contract (2), constitution (1), convention (1), declaration (1), resolution (1), ceasefire (1), settlement (1), sanctions (1), etc
Compulsory (either from institutions or person in authority or as a must)	code of practice (5) (e.g. the federation's code of practice), order (5) (e.g. the court order), directive (4) (e.g. the directive of the government), plan (4) (e.g. a peace plan), standards (3) (e.g. government-imposed standards), principle(s) (2) (e.g. principle of non-interference in the internal affairs), injunctions (1) (e.g. the injunction of official leaders), etc
Others	decision(s) (12), restrictions (2), words (2), maxim (2), oath (1), intention (1), etc.

Table 7. Right collocates of *abide by*

3.3.2 *Adhere to* with Its Right Collocates

In BNC, there are 274 occurrences of *adhere to* in total. In Table 8 below, we also present ten randomly selected concordance lines from the overall data to show the collocational patterning of *adhere to.*

1.	h leadership. Many people had struggled to	**adhere to**	a strict moral code for years (while others
2.	selves, fellow workers or client employees,	**adhere to**	the rules relating to health and safety
3.	in which it was reared, did not necessarily	**adhere to**	the principles of predictability, even had
4.	the Charter, to settle disputes peacefully, to	**adhere to**	the principles of equal rights and self-deter
5.	onarchies, as well as with those that claimed to	**adhere to**	Marxism-Leninism. How far this reorienta
6.	nstrative staff. Departmental employees must	**adhere to**	the following guidelines to reduce the

7.	not know how many agencies and courts still	**adhere to**	this policy and practice. The purpose of
8.	responsibility of the employees concerned to	**adhere to**	these guidelines and procedures. No matter
9.	plicature. So Grice's point is not that we always	**adhere to**	these maxims on a superficial level but
10.	feature for more details). All members must	**adhere to**	a national Code of Practice, and a common

Table 8. Concordance lines of *adhere to*

As can be seen from Table 8, similar to 遵守 *zunshou* and *abide by*, *adhere to* is also frequently followed by a noun phrase at the colligational level. Table 9 below presents the categorization of the right collocates of *adhere to* in terms of the two criteria stated above. Note that the raw frequencies of the collocates are listed in the brackets in Table 9 and we also give one example of a wider context (e.g. *ethical standards*) for some words to justify our classification.

Criteria	*Right collocates of adhere to*
Authoritative & compulsory (but not so authoritative as *laws*)	policy (9), rule(s) (7), regulations (5), treaty (4), sanctions (2), resolution(s) (2), protocol (1), etc
Non-compulsory	standards (9) (e.g. ethical standards), principle (7), code (5) (e.g. moral code), doctrine(s) (3), guidelines (2), norm(s) (2) (e.g. cultural norms), disciplines (2) (eg. the economic and financial disciplines), school of thought (1), Marxism (1), Marxism-leninism (1), Pluralism (1), structuralism (1), ethic (1), code of practice (1), sect (1), ideals (1), scheme (1), etc
Non-authoritative	requirements (4), specification (2), demands (1), instructions (1), restrictions (1), etc
Personal	idea (2), position (2), convictions (1), arrangements (1), opinion (1), schedule(s) (2), timetable (1), lifestyle (1), etc
Others	practice(s) (6), procedure (5), programme (5), interpretations (2), values (1), etc

Table 9. Right collocates of *adhere to*

As can be seen from Table 7 in Section 3.3.1 and Table 9 above, *abide by* and *adhere to* share a few right collocates. However, a closer look at the modifiers of these shared collocates reveals marked differences between these two node words. Let us take *standards* for example. There are three cases of co-occurrences of *abide by* with *standards* in BNC. Let us look at a wider context as follows.

1. The American Mining Congress has lambasted the report as "a gross distortion of the truth", arguing that its members at least **abide by** government-imposed standards.
2. Ramprakash is a lad who could be a superb player, but there are standards you have to **abide by**. If you are an England player you have to behave in a certain way.
3. At the same time, the integrity of the profession was maintained by offering membership only to those who were willing to **abide by** prescribed standards.

In Example 1, *standards* is premodified by *government-imposed* which indicates that the standards in question must be obeyed. In Example 2, *abide by* follows *have to* which shows that the standards are compulsory. In Example 3, abiding by *prescribed standards* is required as a must for offering membership.

In contrast, with regard to *adhere to*, we can find a set of collocation such as *proper standards of behavior*, *general standards of decency*, *ethical standards*, etc. It can be seen that *adhere to* typically co-occurs with non-authoritative and non-compulsory standards. In addition to *standards*, we also find marked differences in other shared collocates such as *code*, *rule*, *principles*, etc. Here the point is that the shared collocates of *abide by* and *adhere to* co-occur with different modifiers whose meaning is in harmony with the whole environment, especially in harmony with the meaning indicated by the node words.

3.3.3 *Observe* with Its Right Collocates

The usage of *observe* is more complicated than that

of *abide by* and *adhere to* due to the reason that *observe* is a polysemous word. It has five senses in *Collins COBUILD Advanced Dictionary of English* (2009), but only one meaning – "If you observe something such as a law or custom, you obey it or follow it" is relevant for the present study. In BNC, there are 1,623 instances of *observe* in total. Manually removing those concordances lines carrying the irrelevant senses, we got 248 instances for *observe*. Table 10 below presents ten randomly selected instances from the overall data to show the patterning of *observe*.

1.	ion qua members of the Commission had to	**observe**	the rules in performance of the treaty. The
2.	then, although, as in the former case, they	**observe**	the law, the government is a pure
3.	again, can the citizens of a city properly	**observe**	the laws by habit only, and without
4.	ssion or assembly and knowingly failing to	**observe**	the conditions, and knowingly taking part
5.	then, that it would be far more advisable to	**observe**	the treaty, which their sagacious
6.	principle, which provides that a firm should	**observe**	high standards of integrity and fair dealing
7.	necessity. The wardens of the agora shall	**observe**	the order appointed by law for the
8.	instructions, labels or markings. You shall	**observe**	the requirements of UK legislation and any
9.	nanted with the landlord to pay the rent and	**observe**	the covenants during the residue of the term
10.	the question "What causes the peasant to	**observe**	this ethic?"; a question that can not really

Table 10. Concordance lines of *observe*

As shown in Table 10, similar to *abide by* and *adhere to*, at the colligational level, *observe* is also typically followed by a noun phrase. In Table 11 below, we present the categorization of the right collocates of *observe* in terms of the two criteria defined in Section 3.2. Note that the raw frequencies of the collocates are listed in the brackets in Table 11.

Criteria	*Right collocates of observe*
Authoritative & compulsory	rule(s) (70), law(s) (12), covenants (12), conditions (12), terms (3), treaty (2), truce (2), articles (2), provisions (2), stipulation (1), code (1), regulations (1), contract (1), etc
Non-compulsory	principle(s) (5), procedures (3), conventions (2), standards (2), ethic (1), methods (1), custom (1), routine (1), etc
Non-authoritative	order(s) (5), directions (4), requirements (3), instructions (2), commands (1), injunctions (1), request (1), etc
Others	restrictions (3), limitations (1), constraint (1), proprieties (1), faith (1), maxim (1), etc

Table 11. Right collocates of *observe*

4 Discussion

This section proposes an analysis of the four node words (i.e. 遵守 *zunshou*, *abide by*, *adhere to* and *observe*) in terms of their semantic preference and semantic prosody. Semantic preference and semantic prosody are crucial in establishing collocational translation equivalents; only when they are equivalent will a collocation be available as a possible choice to a translator. Semantic preference refers to the semantic sets into which the collocates fall. The corpus evidence presented in Section 3 shows that 遵守 *zunshou*, *abide by*, *adhere to* and *observe* allow collocates that fall into different semantic sets:

1. 遵守 *zunshou* usually collocates with things that must be or need to be obeyed or done.
2. *Abide by* allows collocates which are things that must be obeyed or done.
3. *Adhere to* is typically followed by things that need to be obeyed or done but not all of them are compulsory.
4. *Observe* allows collocates with a wider meaning. They are things that must be or need to be obeyed or done, either compulsory or non-compulsory.

In addition to the comparison of semantic preference, the matching of equivalents has to be verified when all the components that are necessary for the unit to function have been identified (Tognini-Bonelli, 2001). That is, equivalence also needs to be achieved at the level of the ultimate pragmatic function – the semantic prosody. In terms of semantic prosody, we can see that *abide by* is used to impose an obligation in various forms such as *laws*, *regulations* and *rules*. The function associated with *adhere to* is to ask people to obey something but still leaving some freedom for people to choose to follow it or not. *Observe* has an integrated function, incorporating the function of both *abide by* and *adhere to*. The semantic prosody of 遵守 *zunshou* is, in fact, the combination of that of its three English equivalents.

5 Conclusion and Implications

Taking account of the right collocates, the semantic preference and semantic prosody of the four node words, we can finally establish the following sets of de facto collocational translation equivalents in English and Chinese (see Table 12 below), the matching of which is not only at the formal and semantic level but also at the functional level.

Chinese collocations	*English collocations*
遵守宪法 *zunshou xianfa*	abide by the Constitution
遵守法律 *zunshou falv*	abide by/observe the law(s)
遵守法规 *zunshou fagui*	abide by/observe the code(s)
遵守政策 *zunshou zhengce*	abide by /adhere to the policy
遵守条例 *zunshou tiaoli*	abide by/adhere to/observe the regulation(s)
遵守条约 *zunshou tiaoyue*	abide by/ adhere to /observe the treaty
遵守条款 *zunshou tiaokuan*	abide by/observe the provisions/term(s)
遵守规则 *zunshou guize*	abide by/adhere to/observe the rule(s)
遵守原则 *zunshou yuanze*	abide by/adhere to/observe the principle(s)
遵守纪律 *zunshou jilv*	adhere to/observe the discipline(s)
遵守道德 *zunshou daode*	adhere to/observe a moral code
遵守命令 *zunshou mingling*	abide by/observe the order(s)
遵守要求 *zunshou yaoqiu*	adhere to/observe the requirement(s)

Table 12. De facto translation equivalents

Obviously, in some cases, English offers more than one possible equivalents for Chinese. It has been shown that *abide by*, *adhere to* and *observe* are used together with a specific set of words and encoded with an inherent semantic prosody. By taking into collocation into consideration, we are able to establish bilingual equivalence with more accuracy. Also, semantic preference and semantic prosody is found to play a vital role in establishing cross-linguistic equivalence.

The present contrastive study of collocation has potentially useful implications for foreign language teaching and learning. It can enhance learners' awareness that the correspondence across different languages needs to be identified not only at the formal and semantic level but also at the functional level. There is certainly danger if learners are totally ignorant of the semantic preference and semantic prosody of the lexical items or sequences. With parallel and monolingual corpora at hand, contrastive studies of collocation can also shed new light on contrastive linguistic and translation studies, as well as bilingual lexicography. However, the study of collocation across languages from a contrastive angle is still in its infancy. The present study is only a small-scaled tentative attempt and it is desirable that further explorations in this direction can be done in the future.

References

Collins COBUILD Advanced Dictionary of English. (2009). Beijing: Higher Education Press.

Firth, J. R. (1957). *Papers in Linguistics*. London: Oxford University Press.

Halliday, M. A.K. (1966). Lexis as a linguistic level. In C. E. Bazell, J. C. Catford, M. A. K. Halliday & R. H. Robins (Eds.). *In memory of J. R. Firth*, pp. 148-162. London: Longman.

Louw, B. (1993). Irony in the text or insincerity in the writer? The diagnostic potential of semantic prosodies. In M. Baker, G. Francis & E. Tognini-Bonelli (Eds.). *Text and Technology: In Honour of John Sinclair*, pp. 157-176. Amsterdam: John Benjamins.

Mitchell, T. F. (1971). *Linguistics 'Going On': Collocations and other Lexical Matters Arising on the Syntagmatic / Linguistics Record*. ARCHIVUM LINGUISTICUM, 2 (new series, 35-69).

Salkie, Raphael. (1999). *How can linguists profit from parallel corpora*? Paper given at the symposium on parallel corpora, 22-23 April 1999, University of Uppsala.

Sinclair, J. (1966). Beginning the study of lexis. In C. E. Bazell, J. C. Catford, M. A. K. Halliday & R. H. Robins (Eds.). *In memory of J. R. Firth*, pp. 148-162. London: Longman.

Sinclair, J. (1991). *Corpus, Concordance, Collocation*. Oxford: Oxford University Press.

Sinclair, J. (1996). The search for the units of meaning. *Textus*, 9(1): 75-106.

Sinclair, J. (2004). *Trust the Text*. London: Routledge.

The British National Corpus, version 3 (BNC XML Edition). (2007). Distributed by Oxford University Computing Services on behalf of the BNC Consortium.

Tognini-Bonelli, Elena. (2001). *Corpus Linguistics at Work*. Amsterdam: John Benjamins.

Tognini-Bonelli, Elena. (2002). Functionally complete units of meaning across English and Italian: Towards a corpus-driven approach. In B. Alenberg & S. Granger (Eds.). *Lexis in Contrast*, pp. 73-95. Amsterdam: John Benjamins.

Wei, Naixing. (2002). *The Definition and Research System of the Word Collocation*. Shanghai: Shanghai Jiao Tong University Press.

Wei, Naixing and Lu, Jun. (Eds.). (2014). *Phraseology in Contrast: Evidence from English-Chinese Corpora*. Beijing: Foreign Language Teaching and Research Press.

Self Syntactico-Semantic Enrichment of LMF Normalized Dictionaries

Elleuch Imen
MIRACL Laboratory
B.P. 1088
3018 Sfax, Tunisia
imen.elleuch@fsegs.rnu.tn

Gargouri Bilel
MIRACL Laboratory
B.P. 1088
3018 Sfax, Tunisia
bilel.gargouri@fsegs.rnu.tn

Ben Hamadou Abdelmajid
MIRACL Laboratory
B.P. 242
3021 Sakiet-Ezzit Sfax, Tunisia
abdelmajid.benhamadou@isimsf.rnu.tn

Abstract

The main challenge of this paper is the syntactico-semantic enrichment of LMF normalized dictionaries. To meet this challenge, we propose an approach based on the content of these dictionaries, namely the "Context" fields and the syntactic and semantic knowledge. The proposed approach is composed of three phases. The first one deals with the data set concerning the syntactic arguments of the "Context" fields. The second consists in connect semantic arguments to the syntactic ones. The last phase links syntactic and semantic arguments. In order to evaluate the proposed approach, we have applied it to an available Arabic normalized dictionary. The results are encouraging with respect to the measurement evaluation.

1 Introduction

Natural Language Processing (NLP) tasks require reliable linguistic resources such as lexicons. The latter represent lexical resources that should define for each lemma a highly valuable knowledge such as morphological features, syntactic behaviors and semantic knowledge like meanings, contexts, semantic classes and thematic roles. The availability of such knowledge favors the efficiency of NLP tools. For example, (Briscoe and Carroll, 2002) estimate that about half of the errors of parsers are based on the insufficient amount of knowledge concerning the syntactic argument structure in the used lexicons; on the other hand, (Carroll and Fang, 2004) show that the use of syntactic lexicons by a syntactic parser improves its performance. Furthermore, the lexicon is the core component for machine translation and information extraction (Surdeanu et al., 2011). Unfortunately, we find that the lexicons that combine syntactic and semantic knowledge (i.e., representing semantic predicates) are shallow for some languages and unavailable for many others. Among the first lexicons dealing with the syntactico-semantic knowledge, we note the framework of (Gross, 1975), which was a revelation in this field. However, the enrichment of the proposed structure and even that of the lexicons proposed thereafter was such a hard task that it could not be accomplished due to the varied and abundant knowledge to be represented and requiring a high linguistic expertise. Thus, this enrichment task is an expensive and time-consuming process. Some other researchers like (Medelyan et al., 2013) have proposed to enrich such lexicons automatically using statistical methods. Nevertheless, the obtained content of such lexicons lacks reliability compared to the expert enrichment work.

We feel that the enrichment issue of syntactico-semantic lexicons cannot be dealt with independently of their models. In this context, the International Organization of Standardization (ISO) has published the LMF-ISO 24613 (Lexical Markup Framework) standard (Francopoulo and George, 2008). LMF provides a unified model for constructing lexical resources covering all linguistic levels and dealing with the majority of languages. It offers a finely-structured model including the syntactico-semantic part. Many compliant lexicons to the LMF standard have been developed such as Wordnet-LMF (Henrich and Hinrichs, 2010), LG-LMF (Laporte and Matthieu-

29th Pacific Asia Conference on Language, Information and Computation pages 387 - 395
Shanghai, China, October 30 - November 1, 2015

Constant, 2013) and the El-Madar Arabic dictionary (Khemakhem et al., 2013).
Considering the richness and the fine structure of LMF lexicons, we propose in this paper an automatic approach for enriching LMF lexicons with syntactico-semantic links. This approach uses the available syntactic and semantic knowledge (already enriched) and operates the "Context" fields that explain each meaning with reference sentences. The proposed approach was experimented on an available Arabic dictionary named El-Madar (Khemakhem et al., 2013). This dictionary offered us a good framework for experimentation because it covers, among others, syntactic, semantic and syntactico-semantic levels. The content of this dictionary has been enriched regarding syntactic behaviors (Elleuch et al., 2015). Also, it contains the semantic classes of each meaning of a given lexical entry (Elleuch et al, 2014).

The remainder of this paper is devoted primarily to the presentation of some related works. Secondly, the proposed approach to enrich LMF normalized dictionaries with syntactico-semantic links is detailed. Then, the experimentation carried out on an available Arabic normalized dictionary is described and the obtained results are commented upon. Finally, some future works and perspectives are announced in the conclusion.

2 Related Works

Several lexical resources combining syntactic and semantic knowledge for numerous languages have been developed. In this section, we provide an overview of such lexical resources for the French, English and Arabic languages.

Regarding the French language, we quote the Lexicon-Grammar ((Gross, 1975), (Tolone, 2011)) that includes empirical knowledge that is quite extensive and detailed on the syntax and the semantics of verbs, nouns, adjectives and adverbs represented as tables. Each table represents a class which includes lexical items sharing some syntactic and semantic properties. This resource suffers from some gaps. Indeed, common properties of verbs are not encoded in the same tables but only described in the literature. In addition, this resource cannot be directly used in NLP applications due to its complex structure. Another lexicon for the French language is the Lefff (Lexicon of French inflected forms) (Sagot, 2010), which is widely-used and freely available. This lexicon is based on the Alexina (Architecture pour les LEXiques INformatiques et leur Acquisition) model. Thanks to this framework, Lefff can be directly used in NLP applications. However, this lexicon needs to be improved regarding its precision and its coverage.

Concerning the English language, we can mention VerbNet (Kipper et al., 2008), which is a lexical resource organizing verbs into classes based on the Levin (1993) verbal classification. Each class is described by thematic roles, semantic restrictions on the arguments, and frames consisting of a syntactic description and semantic predicates. This resource doesn't use any standard for its implementation. Moreover, certain verb uses are not covered by frames; besides, syntactic restrictions are not well-defined and difficult to operate. FrameNet (Baker et al., 2010) is another resource for English. It is based on semantic frames and confirmed by attestations in the corpus. It aims to document the syntactic and semantic combinatorial for each lexical entry through a manual annotation of examples selected from the corpus. Nonetheless, the main limitation of this resource is its poor coverage. Indeed, the lexical units are described only with a lexicographic definition, without any example sentences.

As regards the Arabic language, we note the Arabic VerbNet (Mousser, 2010), which is a lexicon for Arabic verbs using the same process as that of the English VerbNet. This Arabic version of VerbNet does not represent the native characteristics and features of Arabic verbs because it is a simple translation of the classes used in the English VerbNet with some adaptations. Another resource for Arabic is the Lexicon semantic verb classes (Snider et al., 2006), which is a lexicon classifying Arabic verbs into semantic classes. The semantic class puts in the same group verbs having similar syntactic behavior and sharing the same semantic elements of meaning, with reference to Levin's verb classes (Levin, 1993). For the arguments of verbs, only the Subject-animacy feature is used to describe the semantic construction of active verbs. This study is based on an unsupervised clustering technique to construct semantic classes of verbs exploiting the Arabic Treebank and the Arabic Gigaword resources. The major insufficient point of this lexicon is its primordial dependence on the most frequent verbs in the Arabic Treebank.

All the approaches presented in the above-mentioned related works suggest some interesting ideas, but each one of them represents some gaps related to their structure and content.

3 General Presentation of the Proposed Approach

The Context field is widely available, semantically well-guided, controlled and syntactically described. It includes reference sentences explaining the use of a meaning and containing the dealt with lexical entry. Thus, the analysis of such sentences provides enough knowledge on the syntactic and semantic arguments related to a given meaning.

The proposed approach is composed of three phases as shown in Figure 1 in below. The first phase, "Identifying syntactic arguments of Contexts", aims to find out the syntactic arguments for each Context. As for the second phase, "Identifying semantic arguments of Contexts", it consists in the identification of semantic classes for each syntactic argument from the LMF normalized dictionary. The third phase, "Establishing syntactico-semantic links", associates syntactic and semantic arguments in order to obtain syntactico-semantic links. In the following sections, we will detail these three phases.

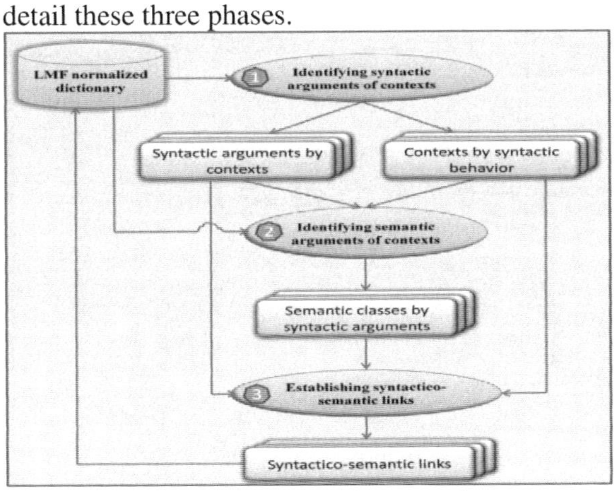

Figure 1: Proposed approach

4 Identifying the syntactic arguments of Contexts

According to the LMF representation, each lexical entry is linked to the concerned Syntactic Behaviors (SBs) and, in a fine representation, each meaning of an entry is linked to the syntactic behaviors that match with it.

As mentioned in Figure2, the purpose of this phase is to search all the SB instances attached to a processed lexical entry from the LMF normalized dictionary and to determine the related SBs for each meaning or Context. We point out that the contexts are associated to meanings. The Contexts will be segmented in order to identify their syntactic arguments (SAs).

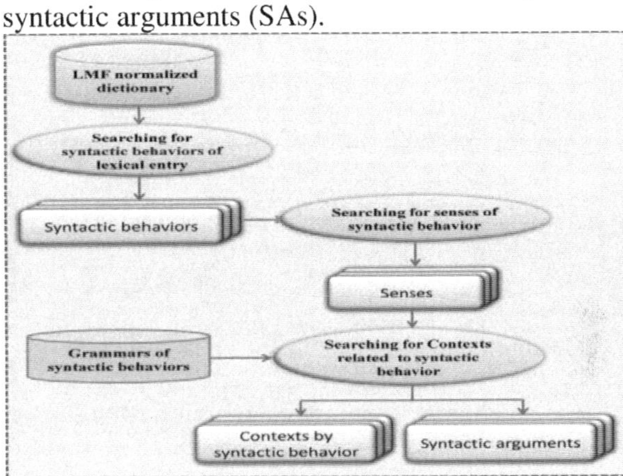

Figure 2: The "Identifying SA of Contexts" phase

4.1 Searching for the SBs of a Lexical Entry

It consists in finding out the SBs of a given lexical entry. For example, Figure 3, given below, represents the verb "eat", which has three SBs. The first SB describes the "SVC" (Subject (S) followed by a Verb (V) followed by a Complement (C)) syntactic construction. The second SB represents the "SVupC" syntactic construction ((S) followed by (V) followed by the "up" preposition followed by a (C)). The third SB characterizes the intransitive syntactic construction "SV" ((S) followed by a (V)). This step searches for those three SBs.

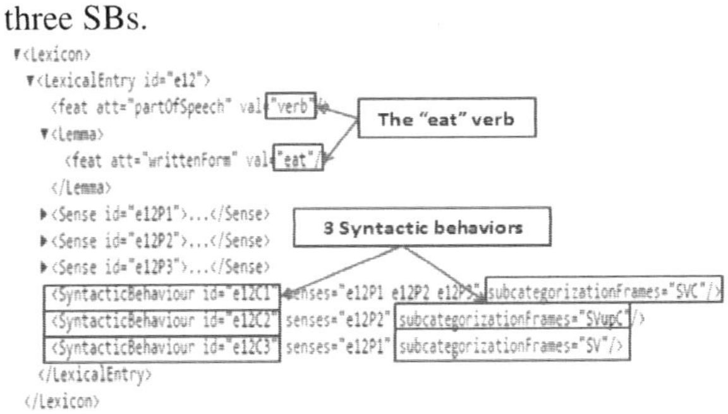

Figure 3: Application of the "Search for the SBs of the verb 'eat'"

4.2 Searching for Senses of SBs

As mentioned previously, an SB can be attached in the LMF dictionary to the Sense class. Indeed, an SB can have zero to many attached senses. The aim of this step is to search for each meaning of a lexical related SB.

The application of the "Search for senses of SBs" to the verb "eat", as shown in Figure 4, can reveals that senses "e12P1", "e12P2", and "e12P3" respect the "VSC" SB. Sense "e12P2" can use the "VSupC" SB. Also, Sense "e12P1" can use the "SV" SB.

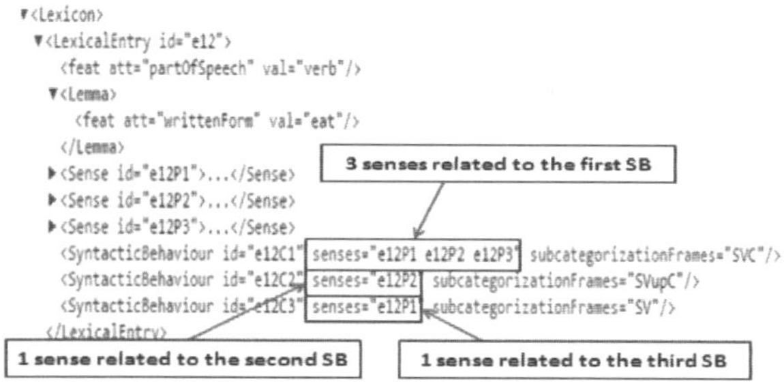

Figure 4: Application of the "Search for the senses of the SBs of the verb 'eat'"

4.3 Searching for Contexts Related to SBs

We point out here that in the LMF dictionary, the MRD extension contains the Context class that represents a text string which provides an authentic context for the use of the Lemma. This context is related to a sense of a given lexical entry. It represents an example of use by a simple sentence. Thus, a meaning of a lexical entry in the LMF dictionary can be attached to different SBs and it is described by Contexts of text strings. This step aims to associate Contexts to SBs. This search is performed by the application of the Grammars of syntactic behaviors -constructed in our previous work (Elleuch et al,. 2013)- to these Contexts. Thus, the application of the Grammars of syntactic behaviors on a sentence can out puts the corresponding syntactic behavior and all SAs composing the SB. At this stage, for each SB we know the related meanings. This step aims to detail the related contexts for each meaning attached to an SB.

Figure 5 illustrates the search for contexts of SBs with a concrete example. In this figure, the "SVC" SB is related to senses "e12P1", "e12P2" and "e12P3". The application of the Grammar of the "SVC" SB to the contexts of those senses reveals that only the first Context "The little boys eat green apples" of the first sense respects the rules of this Grammar. The latter segments this context into SA: "the little boys": the (S), "eat": the (V) and "green apples": the (C). For the "e12P2" sense, only the context "John is late for the meeting because the photocopier ate his report" respects the "SVC" SB. Regarding the "e12P3" sense, the only existing context "What's eating you" fulfills the "SVC" SB. To conclude, the contexts related to the "SVC" SB are: "The little boys eat green apples", "John is late for the meeting because the photocopier ate his report" and "What's eating you". The same treatment is performed on other SBs as described in Figure 5.

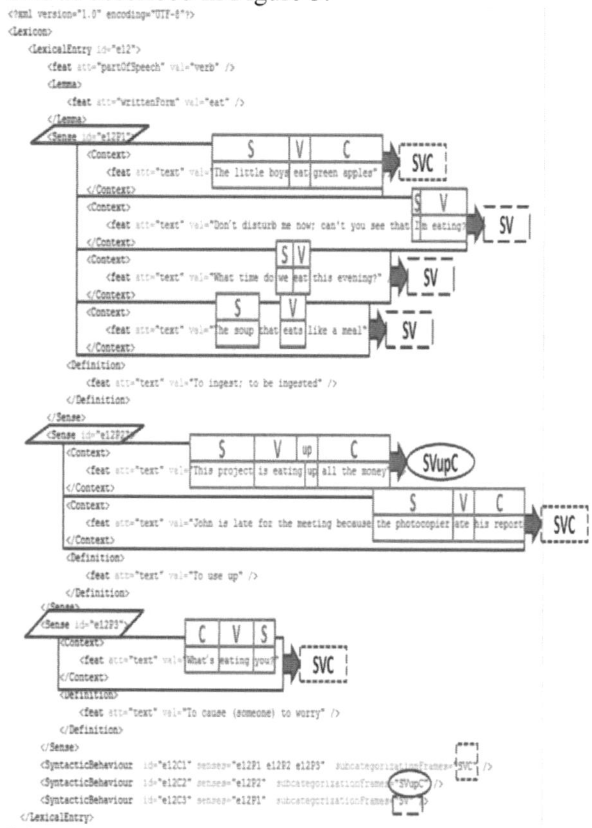

Figure 5: Application of the "Search for the contexts of the verb 'eat'"

5 "Identifying the Syntactic Arguments of Contexts" Phase

At this stage, for a given SB we know the related Senses and more precisely the Contexts. Furthermore, for each Context, the SAs are identified. The purpose of the second phase of the proposed approach is to determine the semantic argument corresponding to each context. As shown in Figure 6, this phase is composed of the "Segmentation of syntactic arguments", the "Lemmatization of tokens" and the "Search for semantic classes by syntactic arguments" steps.

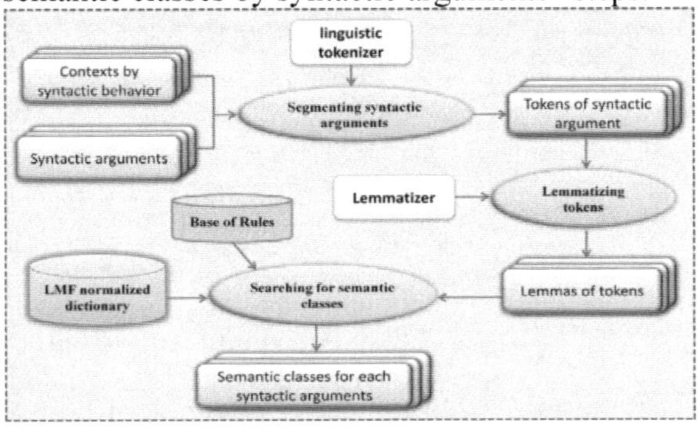

Figure 6: The "Identifying semantic arguments of contexts" phase

5.1 Segmenting Syntactic Arguments

An SA can be composed of one or many tokens. Indeed, the purpose of this step is to segment each SA into tokens. This segmentation is performed with a linguistic tokenizer.

In order to demonstrate the application of the "Segmenting syntactic arguments" step, we take "The little boys eat green apples" context of the first sense of the verb "eat" as illustrated in the following Figure 7. This context is associated to the "SVC" SB. In the last step, the SAs are: "The little boys" is the (S) of the sentence, "eat" is the treated lexical entry and "green apples" is the (C). The purpose of this step is to segment each SA into tokens. Thus, a linguistic tokenizer is used to parse the (S) into 3 tokens: "the", "little" and "boys". Regarding the (C), it is segmented into 2 elements: "green" and "apples".

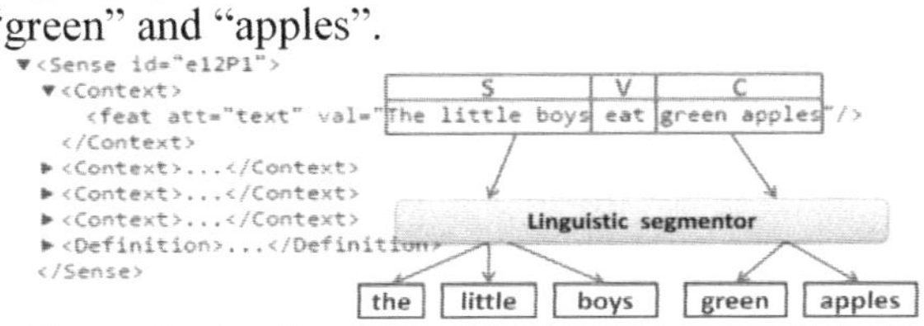

Figure 7: Application of the "Segmenting SAs" step

5.2 Lemmatizing Tokens

The step of "Lemmatizing tokens" of SAs puts the tokens of the SAs -recognized in the previous step- in input and uses a Lemmatizer in order to find their lemmas (gross forms). The Lemmas of tokens are necessary to find the corresponding Semantic Classes (SC) from the LMF dictionary.

Figure 8 details the "Lemmatizing tokens" step. Indeed, the corresponding lemmas for the (S) "the little boys" are: "the", "little" and "boy". The Lemmas of the (C) "green apples" are: "green" and "apple".

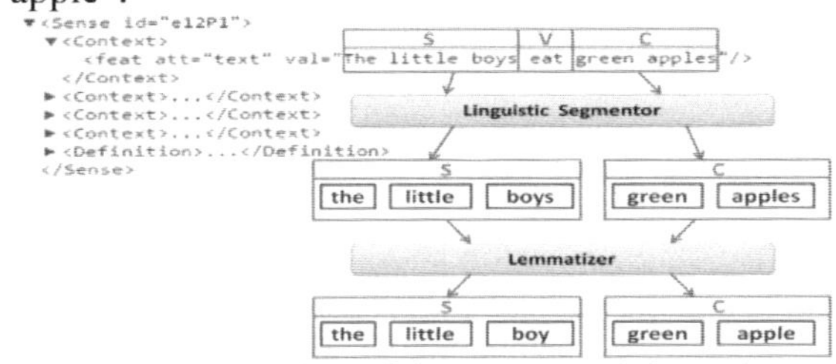

Figure 8: Application of the "Lemmatizing tokens" to the verb "eat"

5.3 Searching for Semantic Classes

As mentioned previously, the syntactico-semantic link is composed by the combination of the syntactic and semantic features. Since the syntactic content is already defined by the SBs, we have to find the SCs for each argument of the SB's Context. To search for the SCs, we need all the lemmas of each token of the LMF normalized dictionary. As the SC is attached to the sense of the lexical entry in the LMF dictionary, this step must find the relevant SCs consistent to the meaning of the treated Context. For this purpose, a base of rules is used to find the relevant one among the SCs of the SA.

Figure 9 searches for SCs for each lemma of SA. Indeed, for the (S) "the little boy", this step searches in the LMF normalized dictionary for the lexical entry "little", which has one sense. This sense can be applied to the "human/animal/abstract/concrete" SC. Furthermore, the search for the second token, "boy, of the (S) SA in the dictionary can identify two senses; both of them are applied to the "human" SC. So, the Rule R1: if the SA is composed of more than one token and a common SC is shared between tokens, then the relevant SC is the shared one. Thus, based on this rule, the corresponding SC of the (S) is "Human". Regarding the "green apple" (C), the search for the lexical item "green" in the dictionary identifies five senses. Sense1 and Sense2 have the "plants" SC; Sense4 and 5 have the "human" SC and Sense3 has the "plants:aliments:fruit" SC. Also, the search for the second token of the (C) "apple" in the dictionary finds two SCs: "plants:tree" and "plants:aliment:fruit". Thus, the base of rules identifies the "aliment:fruit" SC for the (C).

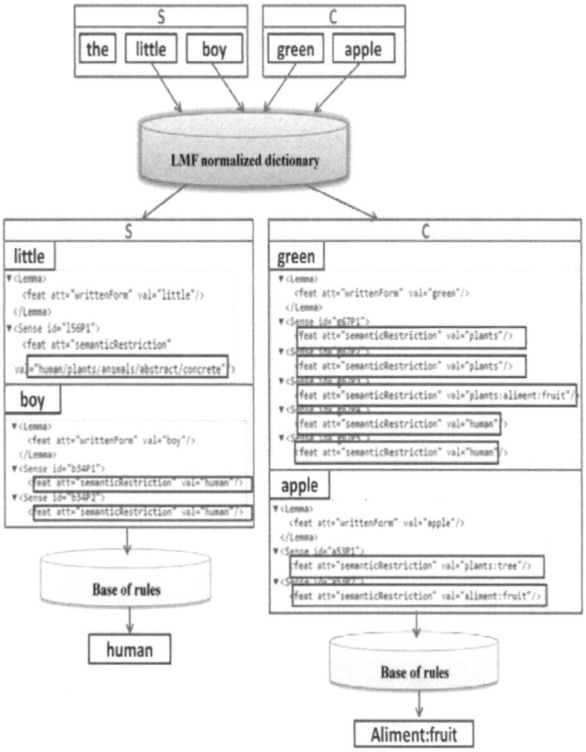

Figure 9: Application of the "search for the SCs" to the "the little boys eat green apples" context

6 The Establishment of Syntactico-Semantic Links Step

At this stage, for a given SB we know the related The last phase of the proposed approach is the Establishment of syntactico-semantic links. At this stage, for a given SB, we know the related Senses and more precisely the Contexts. Furthermore, for each Context, the syntactic and semantic arguments are identified. The purpose of the third phase is to associate syntactic and semantic arguments through a syntcatico-semantic links. As shown in Figure 10, two steps mark this phase: the "Construction of Semantic Predicates" and the "Association of syntactico-semantic links" steps. The details of each of the steps are given, with examples, in the following sections.

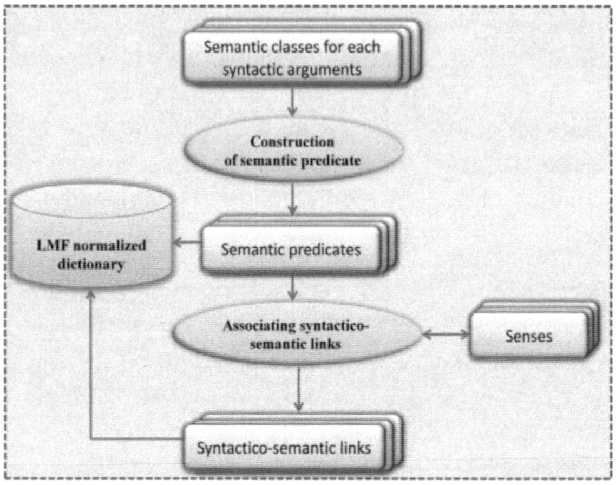

Figure10: the "Establishment of syntactico-semantic links" phase

6.1 Construction of Semantic Predicates

The LMF standard reserves Semantic Predicate (SP) class that represents the common meaning between different senses. A SP instance may be used to represent the common meaning between different senses. The purpose of this step is the construction of the SP class identified by the recognition of SCs of semantic arguments. Thus, the combination of those classes composes the SP.

The construction of the corresponding SP to the treated Context is given in Figure 11. Indeed, the SP is identified by the "humfru" identifier that is composed of two SAs; the first has the "human" "restriction" and the second has the "fruit" "restriction".

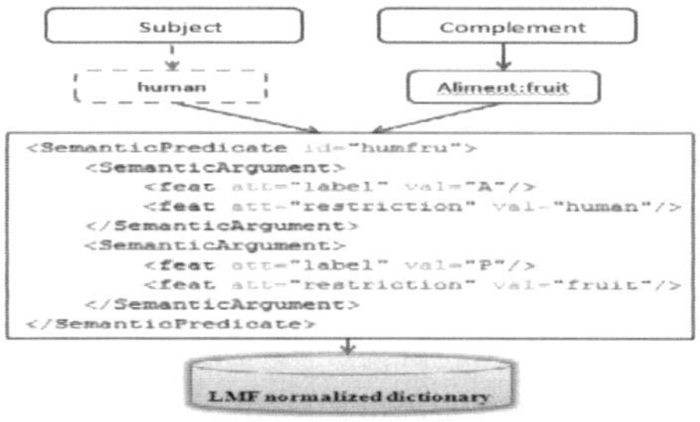

Figure 11: Application of the "Construction of SPs" step

6.2 Associating Syntactico-Semantic Links

At this stage, for one Sense, we have the corresponding SB, the compliant Context and the suitable SP. The last step aims to establish the syntactico-semantic link. It consists of two parts. The first part aims to construct the SynSemCorrespondence (SSC) class, which represents a set of SynSemArgMap (SSAM) instances representing the links between a semantic argument and an SA. The second part intends to introduce the PredicativeRepresentation (PR) class, which represents the link between the Sense and the SP classes.

Figure 12 demonstrates the unwinding of the last step of the proposed approach. This step constructs the SSC class identified by the id="SVC_humfru". It consists of two SSAMs that associate the (S) SA to the "A" semantic argument and the (C) SA to the "P" semantic argument. After that, the addition of the SP class to the treated first sense, "e12P1", takes place. The latter includes two elements: the SP "humfru" and the Correspondences "SVC_humfru".

Figure 12: Syntactico-semantic links of the context: "the little boys ate a green apple"

7 Experimentation

In spite of the generically of our proposed approach, we chose to experiment it on the Arabic language through an available LMF normalized dictionary named El-Madar. In this section, we will present the El-Madar Arabic LMF dictionary and we will detail the obtained results.

7.1 The LMF Normalized Arabic Dictionary

An Arabic LMF dictionary named El-Madar was developed by (Khemakhem et al, 2015). This dictionary takes into account the specificities of the Arabic language and covers the morphological, syntactic, semantic and syntactico-semantic levels. The current version of this dictionary contains about 37,000 lexical entries: 10,800 verbs, 3,800 roots and 22,400 nouns. These lexical entries comprise syntactic knowledge. Indeed, it includes 155 syntactic behaviors (Elleuch et al, 2013) of Arabic verbs and 9,800 verbs are linked to those syntactic behaviors (Elleuch et al, 2015). Concerning semantic features, this dictionary is expanded by semantic classes assigned to the Senses of lexical entries (Elleuch et al, 2014). This study is limited to assigning the following semantic classes: "Animal", "Insect", "Plant", "Aliment", "Furniture" and "Clothes" object classes.

7.2 Evaluation and Results

The experimentation that we carried out could not be applied to all semantic classes. Indeed, we have chosen to treat the "Clothes", "Aliment" and "Furniture" semantic classes (Elleuch et al, 2014) in the El-Madar dictionary because it is the most coverage and finest classes regarding the semantic content. In this experimentation, we have dealt with 406 verbs. For these verbs, syntactico-semantic links have been implemented and synthesis conclusions about SBs have been detected. A human linguistic expert evaluated the resulting assignments concerning the syntactico-semantic links.

Concerning the semantic predicative classes that represent effectively the syntactico-semantic links added to Senses of processed lexical verbal entries, the number of assignments made is equal to 790. Human linguistic experts evaluate the resulting assignments approves that 90 missed assignments were detected and 180 incorrect ones were discovered.

The resulting Recall and Precision measurement evaluation is presented in the following Table 1.

	Semantic classes		
	"Clothes"	"Aliment"	"Furniture"
Assigned syntactico-semantic links	360	280	150
Incorrect assignments	96	40	44
Missed assignments	30	24	36
Recall	0.89	0.90	0.74
Precision	0.73	0.85	0.70

Table 1: The obtained results

The erroneous assignments can be owed to the following reasons:

- Some syntactic behaviors – already existing and assigned to some Senses of the lexical entries in the Arabic dictionary are incorrect and don't reflect the exact meaning.
- The base of rules that makes the decision concerning the relevant SC related to the processed meaning generates more than one SC.

8 Conclusion

We proposed in this paper an approach to enrich LMF normalized dictionaries with syntactico-semantic links. This approach consists of three phases based on the analysis of the Context content presented in the LMF normalized dictionary. The first phase aims to determine the syntactic arguments of Contexts related to a specific syntactic behavior of a lexical entry by using Grammars of syntactic behaviors. The second phase intends to define the semantic arguments of these Contexts by means of the semantic classes of the lexical entries featured in the LMF dictionary. Concerning the third phase, it associates the syntactic and semantic arguments in order to establish the corresponding syntactico-semantic links.

We performed an experiment using an available Arabic LMF dictionary. The obtained results are satisfying concerning the verbal predicates of the "Clothes", "Aliment" and "Furniture" semantic classes .

In the future, we plan to complete the experimentation on the other domains of Arabic verbal predicates. Finally, we foresee that the resulting enrichments of the LMF dictionary can be incorporated in different NLP applications.

References

Baker, Kathryn, Bloodgood, Michael, Callison-Burch, Chris, J., Dorr, Bonnie, W., Filardo, Nathaniel, Levin, Lori, Miller, Scott & Piatko, Christine, (2010), Semantically-Informed Machine Translation: A Tree-Grafting Approach. Biennial Conference of the Association for Machine Translation in the Americas. Denver, Colorado, pp.411-438.

Carroll, John & Fang, Alex C. (2004). The automatic acquisition of verb subcategorisations and their impact on the performance of an HPSG parser. In Proceedings of the 1st International Conference on Natural Language Processing, Sanya City, China. pp. 107– 114.

Carroll, John & Fang, Alex C. (2004). The automatic acquisition of verb subcategorisations and their impact on the performance of an HPSG parser. In Proceedings of the 1st International Conference on Natural Language Processing, Sanya City, China. pp. 107– 114.

Elleuch, Imen, Gargouri, Bilel, & Ben-Hamadou, Abdelmajid, (2013), Syntactic enrichment of Arabic dictionaries normalized LMF using corpora. Language & Technology Conference (LTC). Poznan, Poland. pp.314-318.

Elleuch, Imen, Gargouri, Bilel, Ben-Hamadou, Abdelmajid, (2014), Towards automatic enrichment of standardized electronic dictionaries by semantic classes, In proceeding of the 26th International Conference on Computational Linguistics and Speech Processing (ROCLING), 25-26 September 2014, Zhongli, Taiwan. pp. 96-109.

Elleuch, Imen, Gargouri, Bilel, Ben-Hamadou, Abdelmajid, (2015), Self-Enrichment of Normalized LMF Dictionaries through Syntactic-Behaviours-to-Meanings Links, In proceeding of the 18th International Conference Text Speech and Dialogue (TSD), 14-17 September 2015, Plzen, Czech Republic. pp. 603-610.

Francopoulo, Gil & George, Monte (2008), Language resource management-Lexical markup framework (LMF). Technical Report, ISO/TC 37/SC 4 (N330 Rev.16).

Gross, Maurice, (1975), Méthodes en syntaxe : Régimes des constructions complétives. Hermann, Paris, France.

Khemakhem, A., Gargouri, B. and Ben-Hamadou, A. 2015. 'ISO standard modeling of a large Arabic dictionary'. Natural Language Engineering, Available on CJO 2015 doi:10.1017/S1351324915000224.

Kipper, Karin, Korhonen, Anna, Ryant , Neville & Palmer, Martha (2008). A large-scale classification of English verbs. Language Resources and Evaluation Journal. Volume 40. pp. 42-21.

Levin, Beth (1993), English Verb Classes and Alternations a Preliminary investigation, University of Chicago Press, Chicago and London.

Medelyan, Olena, Witten, Ian H., Divoli, Anna & Broeksra, Jeen. (2013). Automatic construction of lexicons, taxonomies, ontologies, and other knowledge structures. Wiley Interdisciplinary

Reviews: Data Mining and Knowledge Discovery. Volume 3, Issue 4, pp. 257–279.

Mousser, Jaoud (2010), A large Coverage Verb Taxonomy For Arabic. International Conference on Language Resources and Evaluation (LREC), Italy, Malte. pp.2675- 2681.

Sagot, Benoît (2010), The Lefff, a freely available and large-coverage morphological and syntactic lexicon for French. Proceedings of the International Conference on Language Resources and Evaluation, LREC 2010, 17-23 May 2010, Valletta, Malta. European Language Resources Association 2010, ISBN 2-9517408-6-7.

Snider, Neal & Diab, Mouna (2006), Unsupervized Induction of Modern Standard Arabic Verb Classes using syntactic Frames and LSA. International Conference on Computational Linguistics COLING/ACL, Sydney. pp.795-802.

Surdeanu, Mihai, McClosky, David, Smith, Mason R., Gusev, Andrey & Manning, Christopher D. (2011). Customizing an Information Extraction System to a New Domain. In Proceedings of the ACL 2011 Workshop on Relational Models of Semantics (RELMS 2011), Portland, Oregon, USA, June 23, 2011. pp. 2–10.

Tolone, Elsa & Sagot, Benoit, (2011), Using Lexicon-Grammar tables for French verbs in a large-coverage parser. Human Language Technology. Challenges for Computer Science and Linguistics LNCS Volume 6562, 2011, pp.183-191.

When Embodiment Meets Generative Lexicon: The Human Body Part Metaphors in Sinica Corpus

Ren-feng Duann
Department of Chinese and Bilingual Studies
The Hong Kong Polytechnic University
11 Yuk Choi Road, Hong Kong
renfeng.duann@polyu.edu.hk

Chu-Ren Huang
Department of Chinese and Bilingual Studies
The Hong Kong Polytechnic University
11 Yuk Choi Road, Hong Kong
churen.huang@polyu.edu.hk

Abstract

This research aims to integrate embodiment with generative lexicon. By analyzing the metaphorically used human body part terms in Sinica Corpus, the first balanced modern Chinese corpus, we reveal how these two theories complement each other. Embodiment strengthens generative lexicon by spelling out the cognitive reasons which underlies the production of meaning, and generative lexicon, specifically the qualia structure, complements embodiment by accounting for the reason underlying the selection of a particular body part for metaphorization. Discussing how the four body part terms—血 xie "blood", 肉 rou "flesh", 骨 gu "bone", 脈 mai "meridian"—behave metaphorically, this research argues that the visibility and the telic role of the qualia structure are the major reasons motivating the choice of a body part to represent a comparatively abstract notion. The finding accounts for what constrains the selection of body parts for metaphorical uses. It also facilitates the prediction of the behavior of the four body part terms in these uses, which can function as the starting point to examine whether the two factors—visibility and telicity—also motivate the metaphorization of the rest human body parts.

1 Introduction

Human body is an important medium through which people understand the world. It is through the interaction between the human body and the environment that people make sense of what they perceive, with which they conceive. Body part terminology, therefore, is used extensively to represent a variety of things, ranging from the physical surroundings, time, situations, to a person's emotion, temperament, behavior, etc. (e.g. Gibbs, 2006; Kovecses, 2002; Li, 2015). This is embodiment, which demonstrates how body part terms are used metaphorically. While embodiment provides cognitive reasons which underlies meaning production (e.g. Yu, 2003, 2007) and serves as the foundation of conceptual metaphor understanding and interpretation (e.g. Lakoff and Johnson, 1980, 1999; Johnson, 2008), it does not account for exactly what triggers the metaphorical use of a corporeal term, or what constrains the selection of a body part term to represent a comparatively abstract concept.

In order to answer this question, this research integrates the theory of embodiment, a key concept in cognitive linguistics, with the theory of Generative Lexicon (Pustejovsky, 1991, 1995), of which we focus on the qualia structure, by analyzing the lexical items containing body part terms in Sinica Corpus (Chen et al., 1996). Embodiment tackles how and where meaning arises, but it falls short in explaining what triggers the selection of a body part to represent an abstract notion. Generative lexicon functions as a way to study the representations and relations of meanings, but it lacks the explanation for the source of meanings. The integration of both, which has not been found in previ-

29th Pacific Asia Conference on Language, Information and Computation pages 396 - 403
Shanghai, China, October 30 - November 1, 2015

ous research, in the analysis of the corporeal metaphors in corpus data allows us to account for the cognitive motivation of body metaphors and to represent these metaphors by the qualia structure. More importantly, the combination of the two theories enables us to find out the motivation underlying the choice of certain human body parts for metaphorical uses.

2 Theoretical Background, Research Questions and Hypotheses

2.1 Embodiment

Embodiment, or the embodied theory of meaning by Johnson (2008), is proposed as a counterargument against mind-body dualism, a key concept of the Western philosophy and epistemology (Lakoff and Johnson, 1999). The Western tradition has regarded mind and body as distinct entities, which are independent of each other and cannot be integrated. The proposal of embodiment, arguing against the dualist view of knowledge in the West, claims that body and mind should be regarded as continuity (e.g. Johnson, 1987, 2008). Its central tenet is how people make sense of their experiences in the world lies in their interaction between their bodies and the environment. The meaning emerging from the corporeal experiences furthermore form the basis for people to understand abstract concepts. The human body and body parts, during the process of people's acquisition of knowledge and meaning, are involved and function as indispensable media. What the physical side goes through describe what the mental side conceives, and the mental states are instantiated by the physical states/actions. In a word, embodiment is to map the concrete body and/or body part(s) onto abstract concepts that are difficult to understand/convey so as to facilitate communication.

Previous studies on embodiment (e.g. Yu, 2009, 2011) focus on the identification of the human body and body parts used in the mappings, explaining how human body (parts) is/are activated for the conceptualization of abstract ideas. Despite the explanation of how the corporeal level influences the conceptual level, embodiment suffers a limitation it: it does not explain why the human body and/or body parts are chosen to represent abstract notions? To answer this question, we think visibility of the body part is consequential. Moreover, the supplementation of the qualia structure within the generative lexicon also helps us find out the answer.

2.2 Generative Lexicon

The generative lexicon (Pustejovsky, 1991, 1995) addresses the richness of word meanings. Tackling the creative use of words and the issues of compositionality of lexical items, it proposes four levels of representation connected by mechanisms of selection. Among the four levels—argument structure, event structure, qualia structure, and lexical inheritance structure (Pustejovsky, 1995: 61)—qualia structure accounts for the semantic richness of a lexical item in a construction, based on which. Based on the qualia structure, concepts in the world are composed of at least the following four roles:

(1) The constitutive role, which concerns the relation between an object and its constituents or parts;
(2) The formal role, which distinguishes the object within a larger domain;
(3) The telic role, which reveals the purpose and function of the object;
(4) The agentive role, which explains the factors bringing about an object.

The constitutive and formal roles provide the descriptive information of an object. The telic and agentive roles, not directly referring to the object, present the embodiment information of the object at issue, as they represent eventive dimensions which indicate the interaction between the object and human beings, i.e. how it functions to people and how it is brought into being.

The application of the qualia structure facilitates us to extrapolate why the human body or a specific body part is activated in the representation of an abstract notion. The quales, specifically the telic and agentive roles, help us find out the reason motivating the mappings, and furthermore make prediction about what body part(s) is/are to be chosen in other mappings. Combining embodiment with the generative lexicon, this research aims to enrich the embodiment and conceptual metaphor theory with a more sophisticated view brought about by the generative lexicon. Analyzing the metaphorical use of body parts, we will testify that human body parts are not treated as equal in embodiment. Instead, specific body parts are chosen, and the rationale behind the choices can be explained and predicted with the application of the qualia structure within the generative lexicon.

2.3 Research Questions and Hypotheses

This research aims to find the answers to the following two questions:

(1) How do embodiment and the generative lexicon interact? Does the qualia role influence the metaphorical use of the body part terms? Or does the metaphorical use of the body part terms facilitate the retrieval of the qualia role?

(2) What is the significance of the qualia structure in constraining the selection of a body part for metaphorical use?

This research is built on the following hypotheses:

(1) We hypothesize that the generative lexicon and embodiment complement each other: the generative lexicon strengthens embodiment by providing a way to explain the selection of a particular body part for metaphorization. Embodiment enhances the generative lexicon by providing the cognitive reasons which underlies the production of meaning (Huang et al., 2013; Huang and Hsieh, forthcoming).

(2) Among the five faculties employed by human beings to interact with the world—vision, hearing, smell, taste and touch—we hypothesize vision is consequential. That is, the visibility of human body parts is important for the selection of a body part to be used metaphorically.

(3) Among the four roles of the qualia structure, the telic role, referring to the purpose and function of body parts, is predicted to be the most productive in the representations of body metaphors.

3 Data and Method

3.1 Data

The corpus data under analysis come from Sinica Corpus, short for Academia Sinica Balanced Corpus of Modern Chinese used in Taiwan (Chen et al., 1996). It is the first balanced modern Chinese corpus with part of speech tagging and has been employed for a variety of research ranging from the core fields such as morphology, syntax, semantics (e.g. Liu, 2002; Myers et al., 2006; Tseng, 2001), to applied fields such as discourse analysis, computational linguistics, and cognitive linguistics (e.g. Huang, 2000; Huang et al., 2002). The corpus data are culled from different topics/themes: philosophy (8%), science (8%), society (38%), art (5%), life (28%), and literature (13%) (http://rocling.iis.sinica.edu.tw/CKIP/engversion/20corpus.htm).

3.2 Method

We choose to analyze the four atypical body parts: 血, 肉, 骨, 脈, each of which is defined by the online dictionary compiled by the Ministry of Education, Taiwan (MOE Dictionary) as[1]

血 xie "blood": "The red fluid in the veins/vessels of higher organisms, which starts from the heart and circulates throughout the body. It functions to carry nutrients and wastes so as to conduct metabolism."

肉 rou "flesh": "The soft part of an animal's body which encloses bones. E.g., flesh."

骨 gu "bone": "The frame inside the body of an animal which supports the body."

脈 mai "meridian": "The blood vessels, distributed all over the human body and animal body, carry blood everywhere." However, following the traditional Chinese medicine, we think the concept of 脈 should be regarded as part of the body in which life-sustaining substances are held through, rather than merely the blood vessels in anatomy. The substances circulating through the meridians are both visible and invisible, the former of which is blood and the latter 氣 qi "energy"

These four atypical body parts are chosen for the following reasons:

(1) They are not typical body parts. Unlike e.g. 手 shou "hand", 腳 jiao "foot", 肝 gan "liver", 肺 fei "lung", of which the boundaries are defined more clearly, these four parts of the body have no clear boundaries. Instead, they are "extensive" and compose a large proportion of the human body.

(2) They are intertwined with each other. One

[1] The definitions of the four body parts are translated by the authors.

functions to form another, e.g. flesh forms blood vessels, the tangible part of the meridian; one carries another, e.g. blood vessels, part of meridian, carry blood; one manufactures another, e.g. bone (marrow) manufactures blood. These four parts of the body are so intertwined, which we assume will be reflected in their metaphor uses.

(3) According to the definition, 血 xie "blood", 骨 gu "bone", and 肉 rou "flesh" are more embodied, while 脈 mai "meridian" is less so, as it involves an imagined part, i.e. the conduit circulating 氣 qi "energy". Comparing these four body parts reveals that the more embodied a body part is, the more easily we can predict its behavior, and vice versa.

Identifying metaphorically used word

We examine whether the lexical items consisting of body part terms are used metaphorically in the corpus. At this step, we modify the metaphor identification procedure (MIP) proposed by the Pragglejaz Group (2007) so that it better works for Chinese texts. The modification mainly involves

(1) The determination of the basic contemporary meaning of a lexical unit, and
(2) The analysis of the body part terminology in compounds of differing morphological structures.

The reason for the modification lies in the fact that the lexical items containing corporeal words in Sinica Corpus are mostly compounds, which are composed of a body part term with another/other word(s). The basic contemporary meaning thus cannot be determined based on a compound as a whole. Instead, the body part terms need to be extracted and examined on their own so as to reveal how these terms behave in the compound. The rationale behind this modified step is, when a word forms part of a compound, it usually undergoes metaphorical/metonymical extensions, except that it is part of a coordination structured compound.

Take the lexical item 血緣 xieyuan, which is a compound containing the body part 血 xie "blood". In the MOE dictionary, 血緣 is defined as 血統上的關係 xietong shang de guanxi "relations by blood". If the definition is taken as the basic contemporary meaning, this lexical item is considered literal. In our modified MIP, we take the unit or morpheme 血 xie "blood" out of the compound 血緣 xieyuan "relations by blood" and examine the semantic change occurring to the body part in the compound. In other words, considering 血, and other body part terms, as a lexical unit in compounds, we examine the basic contemporary meaning of these body part terms and their behavior in compounds.

The basic contemporary meaning of the unit 血 xie "blood" found in the MOE dictionary is "The red fluid in the veins/vessels of higher organisms, which starts from the heart and circulates throughout the body. It functions to carry nutrients and wastes so as to conduct metabolism". In the compound 血緣 xieyuan "relations by blood", 血 xie "blood" does not simply refer to the body fluid which sustains life. Instead, it has undergone semantic extension. The unit 血 xie "blood" refers to the genetic traits or ancestral tie carried by this fluid. It is the genetic/ancestral tie embedded in blood which forms the relations of a group of people. 血 xie "blood" in 血緣 xieyuan "relations by blood" is thus treated as a metaphorical expression.

Once we identify a metaphorically used lexical unit, we need to formulate how it behaves in the metaphor. We propose to incorporate the qualia structure, which provides more information for the metaphorically used word and helps us formulate metaphors, as elaborated below.

Retrieving qualia roles

In order to find out the constraints underlying the selection of a body part term in a metaphor, we incorporate the qualia structure, through which we retrieve the qualia role(s) of the body part(s) in the corpus data. We expand the method proposed by Song and Zhao (2013a, 2013b), as we focus on two levels: the qualia role of a body part term at the lexical and clausal levels. In brief,

(1) We first examine whether there is more than one sense of the body part at issue. E.g. in the corpus data, two senses are found in 血 xie "blood":
Sense 1 refers to the liquid circulating naturally inside human body, and sense 2 to the liquid flowing inside/out of human body due to injury or effort making.
(2) We spell out the qualia structure, i.e. the four

roles, of the body part at issue according to the sense(s) found in step (1). For example, the qualia structures of the two senses of 血 xie "blood" is shown below:

Sense 1

Constitutive=...
Formal= liquid, red
Telic= sustain life, carry ancestral features, carry emotion and personal traits, etc.
Agentive: Natural kind

Sense 2

Constitutive=...
Formal=liquid, red, smell, coagulation
Telic=...
Agentive=X which causes blood to flow out of body/body parts

(3) We examine the behavior of the body part term in a lexical form and see whether a specific role is highlighted.
(4) We then go beyond the lexical level into the clausal level to find out the role(s) of the body part which is/are specified at the clausal level.

We compare the role(s) specified at the lexical and clausal levels, and derive three kinds of meaning representations:

(1) The lexical item with a specified role at the lexical level and the word's metaphorical meaning is lexically accessed.
(2) The lexical item with a specified role at the lexical level but the word's metaphorical meaning is NOT lexically accessed.
(3) The lexical item with NO specified role at the lexical level and the word's metaphorical meaning is NOT lexically accessed.

We argue that the three representations of the words consisting of a body part term reveal a point not addressed in previous research on embodiment: the layeredness and inter-connectedness of the meaning extensions of body parts, which strengthens the human body as a whole in the embodiment process.

The hierarchy of visibility

We propose a hierarchy of visibility of the four body parts. We think 血 xie "blood" is the most visible, because it is the only body part among the four that most speakers have the experience of visualizing, as bleeding of small amounts of blood is a common human experience. On the other hand, seeing (human) bone or flesh requires traumatic unusual events, and meridian is comparatively abstract among the four, as it consists of not only the tangible but also the imagined parts.

We believe visibility is linguistically significant; i.e. the visibility of a body part is reflected in its collocation with visual verbs, the number of compounds and compounds indicating visibility. We thus examine (1) the construction of 見 jian "see" X (e.g. 見骨 jiangu "see the bone") and看 kan "see" and/or 見 jian "see"...X (e.g. *看 kan "see"...骨 gu "bone"; 看見 kanjian "see"...骨 gu "bone") in the corpus,[2] (2) all the types of compounds with the four body parts as components, regardless of the metaphoricity and morphological structure. These compounds may come into the form comprising the body part term followed/preceded by one, two, or three characters.

4 Results

Table 1 shows the four body parts in the constructions of 見 jian "see" X, and 看 kan "see" and/or 見 jian "see"...X. There are 15 tokens of 見血 jianxie "see blood", all of which occur as part of the fixed idiom 一針見血 yizhenjianxie, which metaphorically means "hit the nail (right) on the head; right on target", but none of 見骨 jiangu "see the bone", *見肉 jianrou "see flesh", and *見脈 jianmai "see meridians" can be found. We then examine the construction 看 kan "see" and/or 見 jian "see"...X. The token numbers of the 看 kan "see" and/or 見 jian "see"...血 xie "blood" still tops, followed by 看 kan "see" and/or 見 jian "see"...肉 rou "flesh", 看 kan "see" and/or 見 jian "see"...骨 gu "bone", and no token is found in 看 kan "see" and/or 見 jian "see"...脈 mai "meridian". Calculating the percentage of these two constructions against the total token numbers of 見 jian "see" X and X as a morpheme word, we have found the constructions with 血 xie "blood" presents the highest percentage (9.22%), followed by those with 骨 gu "bone" (2.27%), 肉 rou "flesh" (0.94%), and 脈 mai "meridian" (0%), upon which the hierarchy of visibility of the four body parts is

[2] 看 kan "see" and 見 jian "see" are chosen because they represent the most common visual verbs.

built: 血 xie "blood" > 骨 gu "bone" > 肉 rou "flesh" > 脈 mai "meridian".

Constructions	血	骨	肉	脈
見 X	15	0	0	0
看 and/or 見…X	5	1	2	0
Total token of 見 X	15	0	0	0
Total token of X (morpheme word)	202	44	213	24
Percentage	9.22%	2.27%	0.94%	0%

Table1. Constructions with the body parts as the object of verbs indicating vision

When it comes to the compound with the body part terms as a component, we investigate compounds comprising the body part term followed by one, two, or three characters (e.g. 血漬 xiezi "stain of blood", 血淋淋 xielinlin "bleeding", 血流如注 xieliuruzhu "blood streaming down"), or the other way around (e.g. 白骨 baigu "white bone", 皮包骨 pibaogu "skinny", 粉身碎骨 fenshensuigu "at the cost of one's life"). We then calculate the ratio between the number of the types indicating the visual perceptibility against those of all the compounds and make Table 2.

Body part	Number of types of all compounds (A)	Number of types of compounds indicating visibility (B)	Ratio (B/A)
血 compounds	152	65	42.76%
骨 compounds	124	15	12.10%
肉 compounds	130	8	6.15%
脈 compounds	47	1	2.13%

Table 2. Compounds with the body parts as components and their visibility

According to Table 2, 血 xie "blood" tops in terms of its visibility, with 152 types of all the compounds and 42.76% of compounds indicating visibility. 骨 gu "bone" ranks the second highest, with 124 types of all the compounds and 12.10% of the compounds conveying visibility. The third highest is the compounds composed of 肉 rou "flesh" preceded/followed by other characters, with 130 types of compounds and 6.15% of compounds denoting visibility. 脈 mai "meridian" demonstrate the lowest visibility, with only 47 types of all the compounds and 2.13% of compounds specifying visual perceptibility.

The analysis of these compounds basically supports the hierarchy of visibility we have formulated previously based on the analysis of the constructions 見 jian "see" X, and 看 kan "see" and/or 見 jian "see"…X, with 血 xie "blood" as the most visible body part, followed by 骨 gu "bone", 肉 rou "flesh", and 脈 mai "meridian" is the lest visible.

Regarding how the qualia structure works, we draw out all the two-character compounds with the four body parts positioned in front of and behind the other characters respectively. That is, we examine how each of the four body parts behaves in the compounds of the following patterns:

X 血 xie "blood", 血 xie "blood" X
X 肉 rou "flesh", 肉 rou "flesh" X
X 骨 gu "bone", 骨 gu "bone"X
X 脈 mai "meridian", 脈 mai "meridian"X

We go through all the clauses/sentences with these eight patterns of compounds, and check whether they are metaphorically used. To clearly present the interplay between the compounds and the metaphorically used body part terms, when a compound is assigned different types of metaphoricity, the compound is numbered according to number of types. Example 1 indicates the three types of metaphoricity of 血 xie "blood" in the coordinated compound 血脈 xiemai "blood (and) meridians", with the corresponding metaphors enclosed in the brackets.

Example 1

(1) 彷彿__根本__不__是__與__我們__**血脈**__相連__的__孩子 (FAMILY IS BLOOD)
As-if__fundamental__NEG__SHI__and__we__blood-meridian__connect__DE__children
…as if they were not our children.

(2) 不期然而然__地，我__立刻__**血脈**__賁張，坐立難安。(EMOTION IS BLOOD)
Unexpectedly__DE, I__immediately__blood-meridian__expand, cannot-sit-or-stand
Unexpectedly, I got hot immediately and restless.

	血 X (69 types)		X 血 (43 types)		骨 X (27 types)	X 骨 (57 types)		肉 X (53 types)	X 肉 (43 types)	脈 X (11 types)	X 脈 (26 types)
Sense	1	2	1	2	1	1	2	1	1	1	1
Modifier-modified	T*: 18	A: 8 F: 3	T: 3	A: 1 F: 1	T: 5	T: 6	A: 1	T: 2 F: 1 A: 1	0	T: 1 F: 1	T: 4 F: 2
Coordination	T: 4	0	T: 1 A: 1	0	T: 2	C: 1	0	0	T: 5	0	T: 1
Subject-predicate	0	0	0	0	0	0	0	0	0	T: 4	0
Verb-object	0	0	T: 2	A: 10 F: 6	0	0	0	0	0	0	0
Noun-particle	0	0	0	0	T: 1 C: 1	0	0	0	0	0	0
Total	T: 22	A: 8 F: 3	T: 6 A: 1	A: 11 F: 7	T: 8 C: 1	T: 6 C: 1	A: 1	T; 2 F: 1 A: 1	T: 5	T: 5 F: 1	T: 5 F: 2

*C=Constitutive; F=Formal; T=Telic; A=Agentive

Table 3. Compounding patterns, number of types in total, senses, the morphological structures, and number of the qualia roles

(3) 不得不__當__空中飛人，回頭__依靠__臺灣__的__「經濟__**血脈**」。(LIFE IS BLOOD)
Cannot-but__be__flying-trapeze (frequent flyer), look-back__rely-on__Taiwan__DE__“economy__blood-meridian”.
[They] cannot but become frequent flyers, coming back to rely on the economy of Taiwan.

Table 3 demonstrates the qualia roles correlated to the types of metaphorical uses. This is not a one-on-one correlation, as a type of metaphorical use may be encoded in more than one qualia role. It is thus not feasible to show the percentage of each qualia role. Instead, we compare the number of each qualia role in each compounding pattern. E.g. for Sense 2 of 血 xie “blood” X, the agentive role is more dominant than the formal role, as there are 8 occurrences of the former but only 3 hits of the latter. The inspection of the qualia roles across all the compound types shows that the telic role predominates in motivating the metaphors with the body parts as the source concept, except Sense 2 of 血 xie “blood” X, Sense 2 of X 血 xie “blood”, and Sense 2 of X 骨 gu “bone”, in which the agentive role predominates.

5 Conclusion

By incorporating embodiment with the generative lexicon, specifically the qualia structure, in the analysis of metaphors involving four atypical body parts in a balanced corpus, we have demonstrated that the visibility and the telic role of the body part are two major reasons constraining the selection of body parts for metaphorical uses. The finding not only accounts for the constraints which underlie the selection, but also facilitates the prediction of the behavior of the four body part terms in these uses. That is, the higher the visibility a body part is, the more possible it is to be employed metaphorically. Moreover, the telic role of a body part predominantly motivates the use of a body part as the source concept in a metaphor. With our finding as the starting point, for the future study, we will examine whether the two factors—visibility and telicity—also motivate the metaphorization of the rest human body parts in corpus data.

Acknowledgement

This research is supported by Project No. G-UB68, The Hong Kong Polytechnic University. We are indebted to the three anonymous reviewers for their insightful comments and suggestions.

References

Chen, Keh-Jiann, Chu-Ren Huang, Li-ping Chang, and Hui-Li Hsu. 1996. Sinica Corpus: Design methodology for balanced corpora. In *Proceedings of the 11th Pacific Asia Conference on Language, Information, and Computation (PACLIC 11)*, pages 167-176, Seoul.

Gibbs, Raymond W. 2006. *Embodiment and Cognitive Science*. Cambridge University Press, Cambridge and New York.

Huang, Chu-Ren, Chao-Jan Chen, and Claude C.C. Shen. 2002. The nature of categorical ambiguity and its implications for language processing: A corpus-based study of Mandarin Chinese. In Mineharu Nakayama, editor, *Sentence Processing in East Asian Languages. CSLI Lecture Notes*. CSLI Publications, Stanford.

Huang, Chu-Ren. 2000. From quantitative to qualitative studies: Developments in Chinese computational and corpus linguistics. *Special Issue of Chinese Studies,* 18: 473-509.

Huang, Chu-Ren and Shu-Kai Hsieh. Forthcoming. Chinese lexical semantics: From radicals to event structure. In William S.-Y. Wang and Caofen Sun, editors, *The Oxford Handbook on Chinese Linguistics*. Oxford University Press, Oxford, pages to be arranged.

Huang, Chu-ren, Jia-Fei Hong, Sheng-Yi Chen, and Ya Ming Chou. 2013. Exploring event structures in Hanzi radicals: An ontology-based approach. *Contemporary Linguistics*, 15(3): 294-311.

Johnson, Mark. 1987. *The Body in the Mind: The Bodily Basis of Meaning, Imagination, and Reason*. University of Chicago Press, Chicago.

Johnson, Mark. 2008. *The Meaning of the Body. Aesthetics of Human Understanding*. University of Chicago Press, Chicago and London.

Kovecses, Zoltan. 2002. *Metaphor: A Practical Introduction*. Oxford University Press, Oxford.

Lakoff, George and Mark Johnson. 1980. *Metaphors we live by*. University of Chicago Press, Chicago.

Lakoff, George and Mark Johnson. 1999. *Philosophy in the Flesh: The Embodied Mind and its Challenge to Western Though*. Basic Books, New York.

Li, Paul J. 2015. Metaphorical usage of body part terminology. Speech delivered at Chinese University of Hong Kong.

Liu, Mei-chun. 2002. Corpus-based lexical semantic study of verbs of doubt: Huaiyi 懷疑 and cai 猜 in Mandarin. *Concentric: Studies in English Literature and Linguistics,* 28(2): 43-55.

Myers, James, Yu-chi Huang, and Wenling Wang. 2006. Frequency effects in the processing of Chinese inflection. *Journal of Memory and Language,* 54(3): 300-323.

Pragglejaz Group. 2007. MIP: A mhod for identifying metaphorically used words in discourse. *Metaphor and Symbol, 22*(1): 1–39.

Pustejovsky, James. 1991. The generative lexicon. *Computational Linguistics,* 17(4): 409-441.

Pustejovsky, James. 1995. *The Generative Lexicon*. The MIT Press, Cambridge, MA and London.

Song, Zuoyan and Qingqing Zhao. 2013a. Annotating qualia relations and types in Chinese compound nouns. *International Journal of Knowledge and Language Processing,* 4(3): 39-47.

Song, Zuoyan and Qingqing Zhao. 2013b. Qualia relations in metaphorical noun-noun compounds. In *Proceedings of the 6th International Conference on Generative Approaches to the Lexicon. Generative Lexicon and Distributional Semantics*, pages 29-36, Pisa, Italy.

Tseng, Shu-Chuang. 2001. Highlighting utterances in Chinese spoken discourse. In *Language, Information and Computation: Proceedings of The 15th Pacific Asia Conference (PACLIC 15),* pages 163-174. Hong Kong.

Yu, Ning. 2003. Metaphor, body and culture: The Chinese understanding of gallbladder and courage. *Metaphor and Symbol,* 18(1): 13-31.

Yu, Ning. 2007. The Chinese conceptualization of the heart and its cultural context. Implications for second language learning. In Farzad Sharifian and Gary B. Palmer, editors, *Applied Cultural Linguistics: Implication for Second Language Learning and Intercultural Communication*. John Benjamins Publishing Company, pages 65-85.

Yu, Ning. 2009. *From Body to Meaning in Culture*. John Benjamins Publishing Company, Amsterdam and Philadelphia.

Yu, Ning. 2011. Speech organs and linguistic activity/function in Chinese. In Zouheir A. Maalej and Ning Yu, editors, *Embodiment via Body Parts. Studies from Various Languages and Cultures.* John Benjamins Publishing Company, Amsterdam and Philadelphia, pages 117-148.

Degree Variables by *Choose Degree* in *Izyooni* 'Than'-Clauses

Toshiko Oda
Tokyo Keizai University
1-7-34 Minami-Cho, Kokubuji,
Tokyo, Japan
University of International Business and Economics
Huixin East Street No.10, Chaoyang District,
Beijing, China
toda@tku.ac.jp

Abstract

Clausal *izyooni* 'than'-comparatives in Japanese allow *izyooni* 'than'-clauses with their degree positons filled. I consider them a degree version of Internally Headed Relative Clauses (IHRCs). In this preliminary study, I adopt Gross and Landman's (2012) *Choose Role* analysis of IHRCs in Japanese and propose a similar functional category *Choose Degree*, which "re-opens" a degree variable position for "closed" *izyooni*-clauses. This makes it possible for once closed *izyooni*-clauses to denote a set of degrees.

1 Introduction

Japanese comparatives have recently attracted wide attention in syntax and semantics. Most of the previous works are concerned with *yorimo* 'than'-comparatives. However, there is another 'than'-comparative in Japanese, as illustrated in (1). Comparatives of this type are called *izyooni* 'than'-comparatives.

Interestingly, *izyooni*-comparatives have the implication that the given degrees in the embedded clauses are "large" (Hayashishita 2007). For instance, (1) implies that Mary is smart. Consequently, Susan in the matrix clause is considered to be smart as well.

(1) Suusan wa [Mary ga kasikoi]
Susan Top Mary Nom smart
-izyooni kasikoi.
than smart
'Susan is smarter than Mary is.'
(Implication: Mary is smart.)

Such implication is not observed in the *yorimo* counterpart nor in the English equivalent. (2) with *yorimo* is even ungrammatical.[1]

(2) *Suusan wa [Mary ga kasikoi]
Susan Top Mary Nom smart
-yorimo kasikoi.
than smart
'Susan is smarter than Mary is.'

(3) Susan is smarter than Mary is.
(Not implied: Mary is smart.)

For the purpose of our discussion, I will call the degree implication of *izyooni*-comparatives a "positive implication." This is because the implication in (1) is intuitively the same as the interpretation of its corresponding positive sentence given in (4), where the null POS operator induces the interpretation that Mary's degree of smartness is large. The truth conditions of (4) are given in (6).

[1] As for why (2) is ungrammatical, the arguments are not settled yet. See Snyder et al. (1995), Beck et al. (2004), Kennedy (2009), and Sudo (2014), among others.

29th Pacific Asia Conference on Language, Information and Computation pages 404 - 412
Shanghai, China, October 30 - November 1, 2015

(4) Mary ga ∅$_{POS}$ kasikoi.
Mary Nom smart
'Mary is smart.'

(5) $[\![\varnothing_{POS}]\!]^{g} = \lambda P \in D_{<d,t>} \exists d[P(d) \wedge d > d_{\text{standard in c}}]$

(6) $\exists d[\text{Mary is d-smart} \wedge d > d_{\text{standard in c}}]$

I assume that the positive implication in (1) comes from the POS operator that occupies the degree variable position of *kasikoi* 'smart' in the *izyooni*-clause.

This may sound odd. Normally, such degree positions are abstracted over and occupied by a degree variable *d*. Therefore, the position cannot be filled by POS. (7) is the LF structure of the English example in (3). The degree variable position of the *than*-clause is occupied by $\boldsymbol{d_2}$, which is bound by an operator. Note that I assume *than* in this case is semantically null and indicate it with ∅.

(7) Clausal *than*-comparatives in English

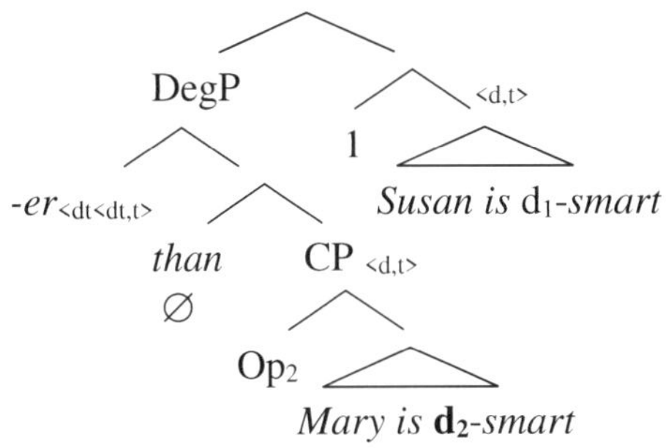

However, notice that Japanese is known to have "closed" relative clauses, namely, Internally Headed Relative Clauses (IHRCs). Consider the example in (8). It intuitively means that Taro brought cookies that Yoko put in the refrigerator. However, the object position of *ireteoita* 'put' in the embedded clause is overtly filled by *kukkii* 'cookies.'

(8) Taroo wa [$_{CP}$ Yoko ga reezooko ni
Taroo Top Yoko Nom refrigerator in
kukkii$_i$ o sukunakutomo mittu
cookie Acc at.least three.CL
ireteoia] no$_i$ o paatii ni mottekita.
put NM Acc party to brought

lit.'Taro brought [Yoko put at least three **cookies** in the refrigerator]-NM to the party.'
(Yoko put at least three **cookies** in the refrigerator, and Taro brought them to the party.)
(Grosu and Landman 2012)

Then, *izyooni*-clauses with filled degree positions can be captured as a degree version of IHRCs. If so, some analyses of IHRC can apply to closed *izyooni*-comparatives.

The IHRC construction is a popular topic in syntax/semantics studies of Japanese. One such study is Grosu and Landman (2012). They propose a functional category *Choose Role (ChR)*, which "re-opens" an individual variable position for a closed proposition. I propose a similar functional category *Choose Degree (ChD)*, which re-opens a degree variable position for a closed *izyooni*-clause. This straightforwardly explains how (1) is made possible with the positive implication: The original degree position of *kasikoi* 'smart' is occupied by the POS operator, and abstraction over degree takes place due to the newly created degree variable position by *ChD*. The LF of (1) is roughly schematized as (9), where d_3 is the degree variable position created by *ChD*.

(9) Clausal *izyooni*-comparatives in Japanese with "closed" *izyooni*-clauses

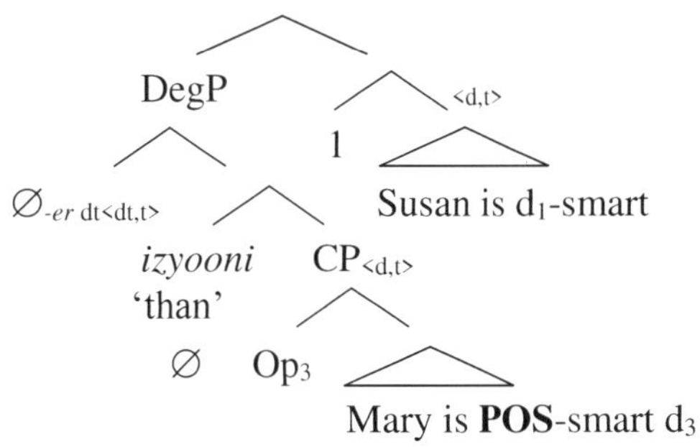

The organization of this paper is as follows. Section 2 introduces another example of *izyooni*-comparatives, in which the degree argument position of the *izyooni*-clause is filled with an overt degree item. In Section 3, I review Grosu and Landman's (2012) *ChR* analysis of IHRCs in Japanese. Then, I propose a similar functional category *ChD* and show how it accounts for *izyooni*-comparatives with filled degree positions.

Section 4 discusses how our analysis of *ChD* differs from previous studies of *izyooni*-comparatives.

2 *Izyooni*-Clauses with Filled Degree Positions

As already mentioned, I assume that the positive implication of (1), repeated below in (10), comes from an invisible POS operator that occupies the degree position of *kasikoi* 'smart' in the *izyooni*-clause.

(10) Suusan wa [Mary ga $\varnothing_{POS}$ kasikoi]
Susan Top Mary Nom smart
-izyooni kasikoi.
than smart
'Susan is smarter than Mary is.'
(Implication: Mary is smart.)

If this assumption is correct, it is predicted that the degree position can be filled by items other than the POS operator, including overt ones. This prediction is borne out. In order to show the relevant data, I will take several steps. It is known that some dimensional adjectives take overt measure phrases. For instance, in the English sentence in (11), ***10 pages*** occupies the degree position of *long*, and it represents the whole length of the paper.

(11) This paper is **10 pages** long.

Japanese *nagai* 'long' also takes a measure phrase, e.g., *2 peeji* 'two pages,' as shown in (12). (12) is what will appear in the complement of *izyooni* shortly.

(12) Ano peepaa wa **2 peeji** nagai.
that paper Top **2 page** long
'That paper is **2 pages** long**er**.'
Not: 'That paper is 2 pages long.'

However, (12) does NOT mean 'That paper is 2 pages long.' It rather has the comparative interpretation 'That paper is 2 pages longer (than a given standard).' It is known that measure phrases for Japanese dimensional adjectives always represent differential degrees. (Snyder et al. 1995, Beck et al. 2007, a.o.) The comparative semantics of (12) can be hard to see because Japanese does not employ overt comparative morphemes like *–er* in English. I assume there is a null comparative operator in Japanese. The point of (12) is that the length of 'that paper' is overtly shown as '**2 pages more** (than a given standard).' To my knowledge, this the best example of overt degree item in Japanese.

Now consider (13). Its *izyooni*-clause is identical to (12). (13) means that 'this paper' in the matrix clause is longer than 'that paper' in the embedded clause, which is '**2 pages more**' than a contextually given standard.

(13) Kono peepaa wa [ano peepaa ga
this paper Top that paper Nom
2 peeji nagai]-izyooni nagai.
2 page longer than long
lit. 'This paper is longer than [that paper is **2 pages** long**er** (than a given page limit).]'

In (13), the standard of comparison for the embedded comparative sentence is implicit, as indicated in parentheses in the translation. If one does not mind a more complex sentence, it is possible to have it overtly. (14) has the extra *than* phrase 'than the page limit' within the *izyooni*-clause. The length of 'that paper' is overtly shown as '**2 pages more than the page limit**.'

(14) Kono peepaa wa [ano peepaa ga
this paper Top that paper Nom
maisuu [seigenn yorimo] 2 peeji nagai]
page limit than 2 page long
-izyooni nagai.
than long
lit. 'This paper is longer than [that paper is **2 pages** long**er than the page limit**.]'

It should be noted that (13) and (14) are complicated, and not every speaker is comfortable with them. There are variations in acceptability among speakers. The language consultants in this study judged the sentences acceptable or at least marginally acceptable. The reason for the variation in acceptability is not clear at this point. However, the difference between such *izyooni*-comparatives and the corresponding English sentences is very clear. In English, *than*-clauses with filled degree positions are never acceptable.

The problem of (1) and (13) is their meanings should not be calculable due to type mismatch, contrary to our intuitions. In both (1) and (13), the degree position in the *izyooni*-clause is filled. To be more precise, it is filled in different ways in LF. In (15), the null POS operator occupies the degree argument position. In (16), the embedded *izyooni*-clause itself is a comparative sentence. Thus, the degree argument position of *nagai* 'long' is bound by DegP within the *izyooni*-clause. The point is that in both cases, the *izyooni*-clauses are closed and they denote type <t>.

(15) LF of (1): Type mismatch

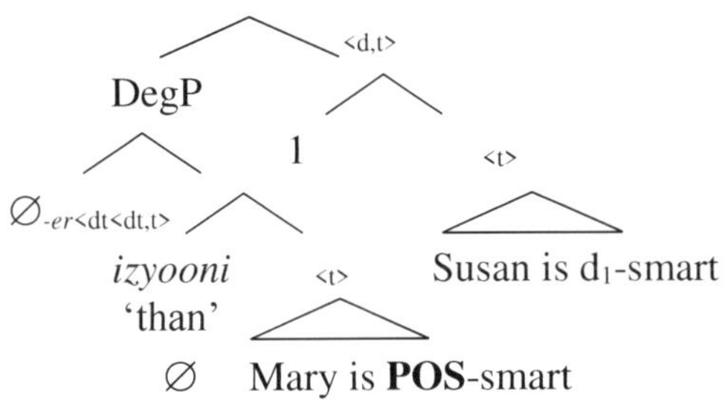

(16) LF of (13): Type mismatch

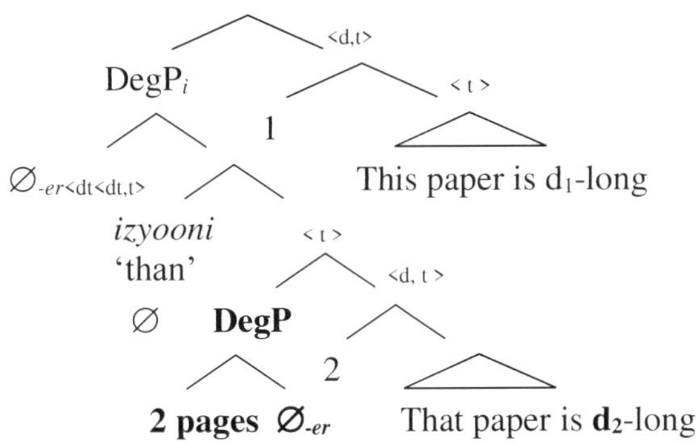

Type mismatch is already obvious in (15) and (16). Following the standard assumption of comparative operator (von Stechow 1984 a.o.), I assume that the Japanese null comparative operator $\varnothing_{-er}$ is type <dt<dt,t>>, as shown in (17).[2]

(17) $[\![\varnothing_{-er}]\!]^{g} = \lambda D_{1<d,t>} \lambda D_{2<d,t>}.\max(D_2) > \max(D_1)$

It requires the first argument to be type <d,t>. However the complement of *izyooni* denotes <t> in (15) and (16).

Despite this type mismatch, (1) and (13) are intuitively well formed. How does this happen? In the next section, I will propose a functional category of *ChD* that creates an additional degree variable position of type <d>.

3 Choose Degree

The problem we saw in the previous section is that the *izyooni*-clauses are "closed" and appear to be type <t>. This is a rare phenomenon for clausal *than*-comparatives. However, it is rather a familiar phenomenon in IHRC constructions in Japanese and other languages.

Relative clauses are normally a set of individuals. However, in the IHRC construction in (18), repeated from (8), all the argument positions are filled, including the object position. In other words, the sentence is "closed" and appears to be type <t>.

(18) Taroo wa [$_{CP}$ Yoko ga reezooko ni
Taroo Top Yoko Nom refrigerator in
kukkii$_i$ o sukunakutomo mittu
cookie Acc at.least three.CL
ireteoia] no$_i$ o paatii ni mottekita.
put NM Acc party to brought
lit. 'Taro brought [Yoko put at least three **cookies** in the refrigerator] to the party.'
(Yoko put at least three cookies in the refrigerator, and Taro brought them to the party.)
(Grosu and Landman 2012)

There has been a proposal to solve the problem. Then, let us apply it to *izyooni*-comparatives.

In this section, I will review how Grosu and Landman (2012) analyze (18). They propose a functional category *ChR* that re-opens an individual degree variable position for the closed IHRC. Then, I propose a similar functional category *ChD*, which creates a degree variable position for a closed *izyooni*-clause.

3.1 Gross and Landman (2012)

Grosu and Landman's (2012) definition of *ChR* is given in (19). *ChR* is a functional category that

[2] I also assume that *izyooni* is semantically null, and represent it with ∅ in LF structures.

takes E, a set of events that is provided by the VP as its sister. The role of *ChR* is to create an additional individual variable position for a closed sentence. C_E is the *Role Choice* function that chooses an argument of event e and gives an individual variable position x for the chosen argument. Then, operator movement takes place from the newly created positon of x.

(19) $[\![\text{ChR}]\!]^g = \lambda E \lambda x \lambda e.\ E(e) \wedge C_E(e) = x$
(Grosu and Landman 2012: 169)

The derivation a hypothetic IHRC proceeds as follows. Suppose α is a denotation of E.

(20) a. *ChR* takes α:
$\lambda x \lambda e.\ \alpha(e) \wedge C_\alpha(e) = x$
b. (20a) takes a degree variable created by operator movement:
$\lambda e.\ \alpha(e) \wedge C_\alpha(e) = x$
c. Existential closure of event:
$\exists e[\alpha(e) \wedge C_\alpha(e) = x]$
d. Lambda abstraction over x by the operator movement:
$\lambda x.\exists e[\alpha(e) \wedge C_\alpha(e) = x]$
(Grosu and Landman 2012: 169–170)

For example, the IHRC of (13) is analyzed as follows. C_E picks the theme of the putting event, i.e., cookies, and gives an extra variable position x. When operator movement takes place from the position of x to SpecCP, the clause denotes a set of x. This is simply put as in (21), and the denotation of (21) is in (22).

(21) $[_{CP}\ Op_i\ [_{TP}$ Yoko put at least three cookies $x_i]]$

(22) $\lambda x.\exists e[\text{PUT}(e) \wedge \text{Ag}(e)=\text{Yoko} \wedge \text{Th}(e)\in{}^*\text{COOKIE} \wedge |\text{Th}(e)|\geq 3 \wedge \text{Into}(e)=\sigma(\text{FR}) \wedge \mathbf{Th(e)=x}]$
(Grosu and Landman 2012: 180)

Gross and Landman's (2012) event-based analysis is meant to capture their observation that possible internal heads are limited to "a participant in an eventuality associated with the entire relative clause and does not permit an account of data in which the internal head is more deeply embedded nor of the sensitivity of such embedding to island constraints" (p. 164). For instance, it correctly rules out (23), where the intended internal head 'new hypothesis' does not participate in the praising event of the IHRC. Also, the newly created variable position x is in an island, as shown in the scheme in (24), which causes an island violation.

(23) *Mary ga [John ga [**atarasii kasetu**$_i$
Mary Nom John Nom new hypothesis
o teiansita gakusee] o homete ita no$_i$]
Acc proposed student Acc praise had NM
no kekkan o sitekisita.
Gen defective Acc pointed.out
'John praised the student who proposed **a new hypothesis**, and Mary pointed out a defect in **it**.'

(24) $[_{CP}\ Op_i\ [_{TP}$ John praised $[_{DP}$ the student who proposed a new hypothesis $x_i]]]$

In the next subsection, I will propose a degree version of *ChR*.

3.2 Creating a Degree Variable Position

We will alter *ChR* in order to account for *izyooni*-comparatives. Our goal is to propose a functional category that re-opens a degree variable position. In doing so, we need to come up with non-event semantics, because many *izyooni*-comparatives, including (1) and (13), are not eventive.

I propose the functional category *Choose Degree* or *ChD* in (25) that plays a similar role to that of *ChR*. *ChD* takes S, a set of situations, as its sister and creates an additional degree variable position. C_S is the *Predicate Choice* function that chooses a degree predicate in situation s and gives a degree variable position d for the chosen degree predicate.

(25) $[\![\text{ChD}]\!]^g = \lambda S \lambda d \lambda s.\ S(s) \wedge C_S(s) = d$

The derivation of a hypothetical *izyooni*-clause is given in (26). The process is essentially the same as we saw in (20). Suppose β is a denotation of S.

(26) a. *ChD* takes *β*:

$\lambda d \lambda s.\ \beta\ (s) \wedge C_\beta\ (s) = d$

b. (26a) takes a degree variable created by operator movement:

$\lambda s.\ \beta\ (s) \wedge C_\beta\ (s) = d$

c. Existential closure of situation:

$\exists s[\ \beta\ (s) \wedge C_\beta\ (s) = d]$

d. Lambda abstraction over *d* by the operator movement:

$\lambda d.\exists s[\ \beta\ (s) \wedge C_\beta\ (s) = d]$

Let us consider how to analyze (1) and (13). Their LF structures are given in (27) and (28), respectively. Unfortunately, it is not clear at this point exactly where *ChD* is located. I tentatively place it above the embedded clauses.[3] Note that the proposition is now type <s,t> due to the situation semantics. Accordingly, the semantic type of the null comparative operator is <<d,st>,<<d,st>, <s,t>>>. The point is that the complement of each *izyooni* denotes a set of degrees of type <d,st>. There is no type mismatch any more.

(27) LF of (1)

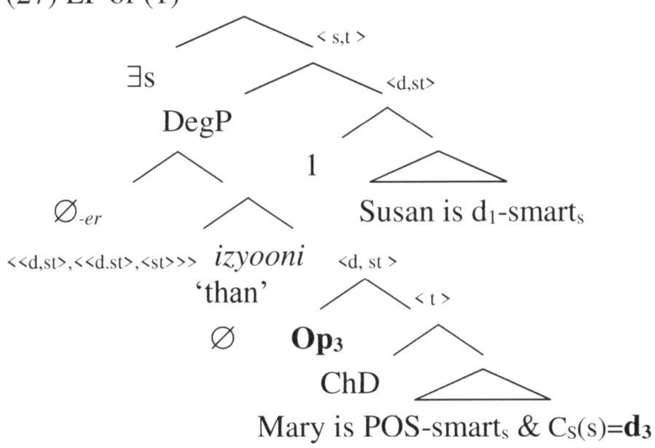

(28) LF of (13)

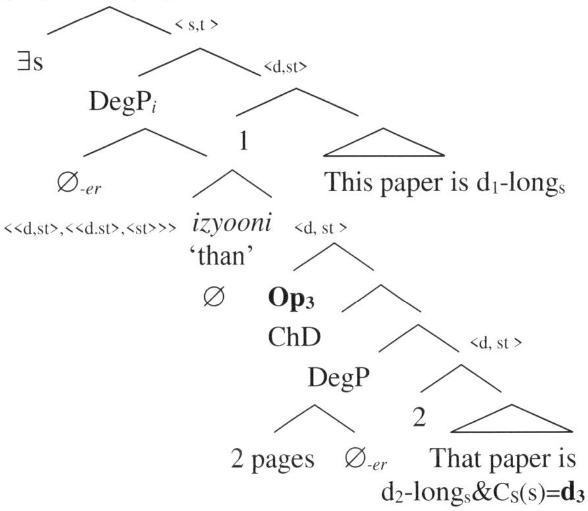

The truth conditions of the sentences are expected to be roughly as follows in (29) and (30).

(29) $\exists s[\max(\lambda d_1.$ Susan is d_1-smart in s) > $\max(\lambda d_3.\ \exists d[$Mary is d-smart in s $\wedge$ $d > d_{\text{standard in c}}] \wedge$ Mary's smartness in s = $d_3)]$

(30) $\exists s[\max(\lambda d_1.$ This paper is d_1-long in s) > $\max(\lambda d_3.$ That paper is 2 pages longer than a given page limit in s $\wedge$ The length of that paper in s = $d_3)]$

In summary, *ChD* somehow accounts for the two examples with filled *izyooni*-clauses. However, the analysis above is still preliminary, and there are many gaps left between the LFs and the truth conditions. Especially, it is not clear at this point exactly how $C_S(s)$ provides the degree we want. I will leave these details for further research.

4 In Relation to Other Analyses

What are the advantages of *ChD* compared to other analyses of *izyooni*-comparatives? To my knowledge, there are three previous studies of *izyooni*-comparatives. In this section, I briefly review them and discuss how our analysis of *ChD* is different from them.

The parallelism between *izyooni*-comparatives and IHRC constructions has already been pointed out by Oda (2014). Oda attempts to capture the parallelism by applying Shimoyama's (1999) E-

[3] Also, it is not clear exactly where the newly created variables are located in the LF structures. The same question arises for variables created by *ChR*.

type analysis of IHRC constructions to *izyooni*-comparatives. [4] The E-type analysis heavily depends on discourse. Without having much syntactic constraints, it is very flexible and it accounts for many peculiar behaviors of *izyooni*-comparatives. At the same time, it suffers from the same problem that Shimoyama (2012) does, namely, overgeneration.

A big advantage of our *ChD* analysis over that of Oda (2014) is that it captures island effects in *izyooni*-clauses observed by Hayashishita (2007). However, the judgments about island effects in *izyooni*-clauses are not settled yet (Kubota 2012). More careful observation is needed before we reach any conclusion. [5] Another advantage is that our *ChD* analysis less discourse dependent than the E-type analysis, because the situation variable *s* serves as an anchor and prevent some overgeneration. However, *ChD* analysis still depend on discourse. For instance, in (25) C_S chooses a degree predicate in situation *s*. The choice depends on the discourse. At this moment it is not clear how C_S behaves when there are more than one degree predicates in its scope.

Hayashishita (2007) and Kubota (2012) are based on more traditional semantics of *than*-comparatives. The parallelism between *izyooni*-comparatives and IHRCs discussed in this paper is not the scope of their analyses. Their primary goal is to account for the positive implication of *izyooni*-comparatives.

Hayashishita (2007) assumes that the positive implication comes from the null POS operator in *izyooni*-clauses. This is the same as we assume for (1). Instead of creating an additional variable position, however, Hayashishita assumes that Japanese POS accommodates a differential degree position, from which operator movement takes place. The same thing happens in the matrix clause. Thus, *izyooni*-comparatives are a comparison of two differential degrees. Based on Hayashishita's framework, the LF of (1) would be as in (31). Note that Hayashishita assumes that *izyooni* plays the role of *–er* in English.

(31) LF of (1) by Hayashishita

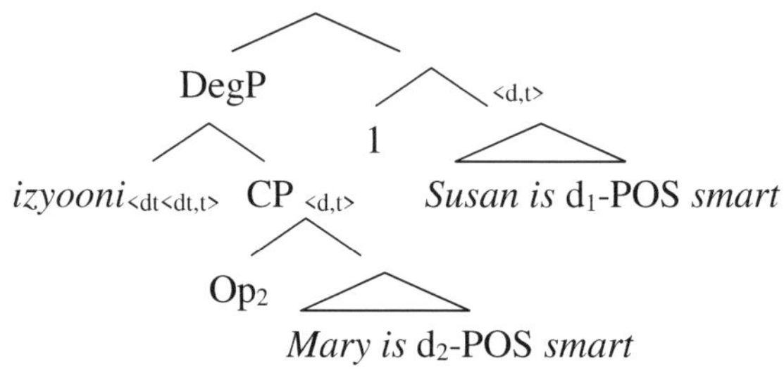

The truth conditions of (1) would be roughly as in (32). POS is translated as 'd-degree larger than the contextually given standard in context c.' Put simply, the positive implication is entailed as part of the truth conditions.

(32) $\max(\lambda d_1.\ \text{Susan is } d_1\text{-smarter than } d_{\text{stanard in c}}) > \max(\lambda d_2.\ \text{Mary is } d_2\text{- smarter than } d_{\text{stanard in c}})$

At least two major issues arise. First, it is not clear how this analysis accounts for cases like (13), where the relevant degree position is filled by an overt item, not by the POS operator. Second, POS normally represents a "vague" degree cross-linguistically (Kennedy 2007). However, Hayashishita's POS is not vague as it provides a measurable differential degree. This can be quite controversial.

Kubota (2012) argues that the positive implication in *izyooni*-clauses is a presupposition rather than an entailment. He proposes the lexical entry of *izyooni* for clausal *izyooni*-comparatives as in (33). *Izyooni* serves as a comparative operator, and also it requires degree presupposition for *izyooni*-comparatives. Here, w_0 represents the actual world. Therefore, the degree in the embedded clause needs to be larger than a given standard in the real world. If not, it would be a presupposition failure. This brings the effect of the positive implication. Note that he adopts the function-based analysis of gradable adjectives proposed by Kennedy (1999), which treats adjectives as denoting functions from individuals to degrees. (1) would be analyzed as in (34).

[4] Shimoyama's (1999) E-type analysis is developed from Hoshi (1995). Shimoyama argues against the raising analysis of IHRCs advocated by Ito (1986) and others.

[5] Interestingly, there is similar variation in acceptability about the island effect on IHRC constructions in Japanese (Watanabe 1992, Grosu and Landman 2012). This is another parallelism between *izyooni*-comparatives and IHRC constructions in Japanese.

(33) $[\![izyooni]\!]^{g} = \lambda x \lambda \delta \lambda y \lambda w.\ \delta(y)(w) > \delta(x)(w_0)$
(defined only if $\delta(x)(w_0) \geq stnd(\delta)$)
(Kubota 2012: 42)

(34) $\delta_{smart}(Susan)(w) > \delta_{smart}(Mary)(w_0)$
(defined only if $\delta_{smart}(Mary)(w_0) \geq stnd(\delta_{smart})$)

A major challenge for Kuroda is how to deal with the data with overtly filled degree positions, like (13).

Another challenge comes from Kubota's assumption that the positive implication is encoded in *izyooni*-comparatives *per se*. There is an interesting fact that suggests that the positive implication is closely related to gradable predicates rather than the whole *izyooni*-construction. Consider the contrast between (35) and (36). (35) does not employ a gradable adjective or exhibit positive implication. However, the positive implication appears once *takusanno* 'many' is added in the matrix clause, as shown in (36). Note that I assume that there is an elided *takusanno* 'many' in the *izyooni*-clause in (36).

(35) Suusan wa [Mary ga tabeta]-izyooni
Susan Top Mary Nom ate than
orenji o tabeta.
orange Acc ate
'Susan ate more oranges than Mary did.'
(Not implied: Mary ate many oranges.)

(36) Suusan wa [Mary ga __ tabeta]-izyooni
Susan Top Mary Nom ate than
takusanno aorenji o tabeta.
many orange Acc ate
'Susan ate more oranges than Mary did.'
(Implication: Mary ate many oranges.)

Kubota's (34) would predict (35) to have degree presupposition, or he would need to provide a different *izyooni* without degree presupposition.

In contrast, other analyses are somewhat compatible with the lack of positive implication in (35). For Hayashishita (2007), there is no gradable predicate that would host his non-vague POS-operator in *izyooni*-clauses. For Oda (2014), E-type anaphora pragmatically picks degrees without implication. Our *ChD* simply does not apply to (35) because its *izyooni*-clause is not closed.

5 Conclusion and Issues for Further Research

I proposed a lexical category *ChD* that re-opens a variable degree position for a closed *izyooni*-clause. This approach successfully captures the parallelism between *izyooni*-comparatives and IHRCs, namely, closed embedded clauses.[6] However, many details remain to be worked out.

A question for the bigger picture is the distribution of *ChD*. It remains to be seen whether or not *ChD* applies to other degree constructions in Japanese. Grosu and Landman also raise questions regarding cross- and intra-linguistic distribution of *ChR*. Further comparison between *ChR* and *ChD* may give us some insights.

Eventually, we may want to integrate *ChD* into *ChR* if it is at all possible. *ChD* is a degree version of *ChR*; thus, the common threads between *ChD* and *ChR* are obvious.

Acknowledgments

I thank the anonymous reviewers of PACLIC29 for their helpful comments. I also thank the anonymous reviewers of JK23 in 2013. They are the ones who recommended me to adopt Grosu and Landman (2012). All remaining errors are my own.

References

Beck, Sigrid, Toshiko Oda, and Koji Sugisaki. 2004. Parametric Variation in the Semantics of Comparison: Japanese vs. English. *Journal of East Asian Linguistics* 13:289–344.

Grosu, Alexander and Fred Landman. 2012. A Quantificational Discourse approach to Japanese and Korean Internally Headed Relatives. *Journal of East Asian Linguistics* 21:159–196.

Hayashishita, J.-R. 2007. *Izyoo(ni)*- and *Gurai*-Comparatives: Comparison of Deviation in Japanese. *Gengo Kenkyu* 132:77–109.

Heim, Irene and Angelika Kratzer. 1999. *Semantics in Generative Grammar*. Oxford: Blackwell.

Hoshi, Koji. 1995. Structural and Interpretive Aspects of Head-Internal and Head-External Relative

[6] An anonymous reviewer of PACLIC 29 pointed out that IHRCs are relatively rare in modern Japanese. (S)he also pointed out that correlative *–ni turete* may undergo a similar analysis. Thus it might be better to treat comparative and correlative sentences in Japanese within the same and independent framework.

Clauses. Doctoral dissertation, University of Rochester.

Ito, Junko. 1986. Head-Movement at LF and PF. *University of Massachusetts Occasional Papers in Linguistics* 11:109–138.

Kennedy, Christopher. 1999. *Projecting the adjective: The syntax and semantics of gradability and comparison*. New York: Garland Press.

Kennedy, Christopher. 2007. Vagueness and grammar: the semantics of relative and absolute gradable adjectives. *Linguistics and Philosophy* 30:1–45.

Kennedy, Christopher. 2009. Modes of comparison. *Papers from the 43rd Annual Meeting of the Chicago Linguistic Society* : 141–165.

Kubota, Yusuke. 2012. The Presuppositional Nature of Izyoo(-ni) and Gurai Comparatives: A Note on Hayashishita 2007. *Gengo Kenkyu* 141:33–46.

Oda, Toshiko. 2014. E-type Anaphora in *Izyooni* (than)-comparatives. *Paper presented at the JK* 23.

Shimoyama, Junko. 1999. Internally Headed Relative Clauses in Japanese and E-Type Anaphora. *Journal of East Asian Linguistics* 8:147–182.

Snyder, William, Kenneth Wexler, and Dolon Das. 1995. The syntactic representation of degree and quantity: Perspectives from Japanese and child English. *Proceedings of 31st West Coast Conference on Formal Linguistics*: 581–596.

Sudo, Yasutada. 2014. Hidden Degree Nominals in Japanese Clausal Comparatives. *Journal of East Asian Linguistics* 24:1–51.

von Stechow, Arnim. 1984. Comparing Semantic Theories of Comparison. *Journal of Semantics* 3:1–77.

Watanabe, Akira. 1992. Subjacency and S-structure movement of *wh*-in-situ. *Journal of East Asian Linguistics* 1: 255–291.

Not Voice but Case Identity in VP Ellipsis of English

Myung-Kwan Park
Department of English
College of Humanities
Dongguk University
Seoul, Korea
parkmk@dgu.edu

Sunjoo Choi
Department of English
College of Humanities
Dongguk University
Seoul, Korea
Sunjoo3008@gmail.com

Abstract

This paper develops a Case/case-theoretic account for what Merchant (2008) calls voice mismatch in ellipsis constructions of English. Merchant (ibid.) reports that VP ellipsis as an elision of smaller size VP allows voice mismatch, but Pseudogapping and Sluicing as an elision of bigger size vP/TP do not. However, Tanaka (2011) argues against Merchant's dichotomy in voice mismatch between VP ellipsis and Pseudogapping, reporting that voice mismatch in both types of ellipsis is permissible or not while interacting with what Kehler (2000) calls discourse coherence relations between ellipsis and antecedent clauses. Departing from Kehler's (2000) insight, we suggest that vP undergoes ellipsis in a resemblance discourse relation, but VP does so in a cause/effect discourse relation. Given the asymmetry in the size of ellipsis in tandem with discourse relations, we argue that since Accusative as well as Nominative Case is checked outside VP, the VP to be elided can meet the identity condition on ellipsis with its antecedent VP as the object element in the former and the subject one in the latter or vice versa have not been Case-checked yet, thus being identical in terms of Case-feature at the point of derivation building a VP.

1 Introduction

According to Merchant (2008), VP ellipsis (VPE) in English allows mismatch between the voice of an elided constituent and that of its antecedent, whereas Sluicing and Pseudogapping do not. This holds for either direction of voice alternation between an elided constituent and its antecedent. This is illustrated in (1) through (3) ((1) and (3), taken from Merchant (2008: 169-170); (2), taken from Merchant (2013: 81)).

(1) *Active antecedent, passive ellipsis (VPE)*

a. The janitor must <remove the trash$_1$> whenever it is apparent that [it]$_1$ should be [$_{VP}$ ~~removed t$_1$~~].

Passive antecedent, active ellipsis (VPE)

b. [The system]$_1$ can be <used t$_1$> by anyone who wants to [$_{VP}$ ~~use it$_1$~~].

(2) *Sluicing (TPE)*

*<Joe was murdered t>, but we don't know [who]$_1$ [$_{TP}$ ~~t$_1$ murdered Joe~~].

(3) *Pseudogapping*

*Roses were brought by some, and others did ~~bring~~ lilies.

This paper examines the very issue of voice mismatch in the above three types of ellipsis in English. The next section reviews Merchant's (2007, 2008) analysis of voice mismatch in ellipsis by postulating the functional category of Voice in the syntactic structure of a clause, and the subsequent rebuttal of Merchant's analysis by Tanaka (2011). Departing from the empirical generalization made by Tanaka, section 3 proposes a not Voice- but Case/case-theoretic account for apparent voice mismatch in VP ellipsis and

29th Pacific Asia Conference on Language, Information and Computation pages 413 - 421
Shanghai, China, October 30 - November 1, 2015

Pseudogapping. Section 4 investigates argument structure mismatch and its interaction with Pseudogapping. Section 5 explores a Case/case-theoretic account for voice mismatch in Sluicing. Section 6 wraps up with a conclusion.

2 No asymmetry in voice match between VP ellipsis and Pseudogapping

Consider the examples in (4) and (5). It seems clear that voice mismatch is disallowed only in some of elliptical structures like VP ellipsis, Pseudogapping and Sluicing. Unlike in the ellipsis structure of (4), voice mismatch is permissible in the non-elliptical structure of (5).

(4) *Roses were brought by some, and others did ~~bring roses~~, too.
(5) Roses were brought by some, and others brought roses, too.

Merchant's (2008) explanation for the contrast in voice mismatch between VP ellipsis and Pseudogapping in (1) and (2) hinges on the following assumptions:

(6) Syntactic isomorphism is required for ellipsis.
(7) The v head hosts the feature [voi(ce)] responsible for active versus passive voice.
(8) VP ellipsis deletes a VP, but Pseudogapping deletes a vP.

Like most previous studies on ellipsis, Merchant first takes ellipsis to be subject to a syntactic identity condition demanding that an elided constituent be identical syntactically to its antecedent. Given syntactic isomorphism for ellipsis, the uneven distribution in voice mismatch between VP ellipsis and Pseudogapping in (1) and (2) follows from the two specific components in (7) and (8). Merchant (2008) argues that Pseudogapping elides a vP rather than a VP. The elided constituent in Pseudogapping then includes the little v that has the value of the feature [voi] determined either as active or passive. When the ellipsis and the antecedent clauses are not identical in voice, Pseudogapping won't meet identity in ellipsis, hence being ruled out. In VPE, however, the little v hosting the feature [voi] is not included in the VPE site. In other words, the head v is external to the VPE site. Thus, voice mismatch does not matter for VP ellipsis, not being able to exert its effects on identity in ellipsis.

Though Merchant (2008) provides an effective account for the distributional generalization in voice mismatch between VP ellipsis and Pseudogapping, his account confronts several problems. The first problem concerns the size of ellipsis for Pseudogapping. The previous works on Pseudogapping such as Jayaseelan (1990), Lansnik (1999: chap 3), Levin (1978), and Takahashi (2004) argue that Pseudogapping is an operation of VP ellipsis rather than vP ellipsis, as typical examples of Pseudogapping in (9) and (10) show.

(9) *Roses were brought by some, and others did ~~bring~~ lilies.
(10) *Some brought roses, and lilies were ~~brought~~ by others.

Merchant (2008) in fact brings forth the examples in (11) and (12) to support his thesis that Pseudogapping applies to a larger category than VP ellipsis. The judgements reported in (11) and (12) are Merchant's.

(11) Many of them have turned in their assignment already, but they haven't yet all.
(12) Many of them have turned in their assignment already, but they haven't yet (*all) their paper (*all).

Merchant assumes with Sportiche (1988) that a floating quantifier like all can be dropped off in the specifier position of any functional category it has moved through. All in (11) presumably moves through [spec, vP]. Since the constituent elided in VP ellipsis, by assumption, is smaller than vP and all is external to ellipsis site, the sentence in (11) is received as acceptable. By contrast, the sentence in (12) involving Pseudogapping, according to Merchant, is ruled out because Pseudogapping elides a vP that includes the position all moves through; thus, the floating quantifier all should have been included in the portion elided by Pseudogapping.

Tanaka (2011), however, consulted three native speakers to verify the acceptability of (13) and (14), which are identical to (11) and (12), but except for one modification by placing the aspectual adverb yet not before but after the floating quantifier all:

(13) Many of them have turned in their assignment already, but they haven't all yet.
(14) ?Many of them have turned in their assignment already, but they haven't all yet their paper

None of the native speakers that Tanaka consulted ruled out these two sentences. Tanaka (2011) takes the acceptability of these examples to indicate that both VP ellipsis and Pseudogapping may delete a VP. It may also be the case that all in (13) and (14) occupies a position outside a vP, in which case the entire vP can be deleted (See Tanaka (2011: 473)).

Second, Merchant (2008: 170) notes that such Pseudogapping examples with voice mismatch as (15)-(16) are unacceptable.

(15) *Roses were brought by some, and others did ~~bring~~ lilies.
(16) *Some brought roses, and lilies were ~~brought~~ by others.

Importantly, however, Tanaka (2011: 475) reports that their VP ellipsis counterparts in (17)-(18) are also unacceptable:

(17) *Roses were brought by some boys, and some girls did ~~bring roses~~, too.
(18) *Some brought roses, and lilies were ~~brought by some~~, too.

Since ungrammatical Pseudogapping examples remain to be ungrammatical even under VP ellipsis, it may safely be concluded that there is no asymmetry between the two constructions in terms of the size of ellipsis.

Tanaka (2011: 476) also notes that the opposite situation also holds: If voice mismatch in VP ellipsis is acceptable in a certain structure, that in Pseudogapping is so, too. The following pair of examples shows that Pseudogapping behaves in a parallel fashion to VP ellipsis in terms of voice mismatch. Unlike the preceding two sets of Pseudogapping and VP ellipsis examples, however, both (19) and (20) are acceptable.

(19) This problem was to have been looked into, but obviously nobody did ~~look into this problem~~.
(20) ?My problem will be looked into by Tom, but he won't ~~look into~~ yours.

The additional pairs in (21)-(22), which are taken from Tanaka (2011: 476), do not display asymmetry in voice mismatch between Pseudogapping and VP ellipsis:

(21) Actually, I have implemented a computer system with a manager, but it doesn't ~~have to be implemented with a manager~~.
(22) ?Actually, I have implemented a computer system with a manager, but it should have been ~~implemented~~ by a computer technician.

Third, the additional rebuttal of Merchant's (2008) analysis comes from the experimental work by SanPietro et al. (2012: 309), who uses the following set of examples:

(23) Jean was trying to sell her car. I know that someone bought it,
a. and Lisa knows who. (big, resemblance, matched)
b. and Lisa knows by who. (big, resemblance, mismatched)
c. because she told me who. (big, cause/effect, matched)
d. because she told me by who. (big, cause/effect, mismatched)
e. and Lisa also knows that someone did. (small, resemblance, matched)
f. and Lisa also knows that it was. (small, resemblance, mismatched)
g. because she told me that someone did. (small, cause/effect, matched)
h. because she told me that it was. (small, cause/effect, mismatched)

The results of the experiment (cited from SanPietro et al. (2012: 310)) are: first, the interaction between ellipsis size (small VP vs. big TP) and discourse relations (resemblance vs. cause/effect relations, which we will turn to shortly in the next section) shows that in the small elliptical conditions only, cause/effect conditions (conditions (g) and (h) of (23); mean rating of 4.94 out of the highest score 7) were rated higher than resemblance conditions (conditions (e) and (f) above; mean rating of 4.32). Second, most critically, pairwise comparisons show a significant difference ($p < .001$) between the mismatched cause/effect condition (condition (h) above; mean rating of 4.42) and the mismatched resemblance condition (condition (f) above; mean rating of 3.69), but only in the VP ellipsis conditions. No effect of coherence (i.e., discourse relation) is found in the big elliptical conditions (conditions (a-d) above).

These results of the experiment show that voice mismatch in VP ellipsis is not always permissible, unlike what Merchant (2008) argues. Instead, discourse relations are a determining factor in ruling in or out voice mismatch in VP ellipsis.

The conclusion drawn from the review of Merchant (2007, 2008) and Tanaka (2011) is that the former analysis based on the different sizes of ellipsis for VP ellipsis and Pseudogapping over-generates and under-generates. It over-predicts that all the examples involving voice mismatch in VP are acceptable, and at the same time it cannot predict that some of those involving voice mismatch in VP ellipsis are unacceptable. In the next section, building on Kehler's (2000) insight into discourse relations between ellipsis and antecedent clauses, we argue that sizes of ellipsis for both VP ellipsis and Pseudogapping interact with such discourse relations.

3 Towards an analysis

Kehler (2000) argues that sentences/clauses in a discourse are linked together by (discourse) coherence relations. Coherence refers to the ways in which the hearer attempts to link together the sentences/clauses that form a discourse (Kehler (2000: 539)). For example, in a discourse, the hearer does not interpret the two sentences in (24a) to be unrelated, but he/she infers that Mary is upset at Bill because Bill forgot her birthday. Because it is more difficult to infer how the two sentences in (24b) could be linked together, the discourse is less coherent.

(24) a. Mary is upset with Bill. Bill forgot her birthday.
  b. Mary is upset with Bill. #Jupiter has 63 moons.

Kehler (2000) discusses two types of coherence relations relevant to ellipsis: resemblance and cause/effect. When a resemblance relation holds, the entities or properties in the elided material are interpreted as in some way parallel to those in its antecedent. For example, in (25), John and Bill are the entities, and they are parallel in that they both went to the store.

(25) John went to the store because Bill did <~~go to the store~~>.

There is a class of connectives and adverbs which serve as markers for the resemblance coherence relation, including *and, also, as well, too, likewise, etc.*

When a cause/effect relation holds, by contrast, the proposition expressed by the elided material has some sort of causal relationship to the proposition in the antecedent. For example, in (26), the fact that Bill went to the store is the cause for John to do so.

(26) John went to the store because Bill did <~~go to the store~~>.

As with the resemblance relations, certain adverbs and connectives regularly occur in cause/effect sentences which can serve as markers of this coherence relation, including *but, even though, because, as a result, therefore, so, consequently, etc.*

Kehler (2000) argues that when there is a voice mismatch in ellipsis, sentences where there is a cause/effect relation between antecedent and ellipsis sites are licit, while sentences where there is a resemblance relation are illicit. The contrast can be found in (27a) and (27b) below, where the acceptable (27a) contains a cause/effect relation, and the unacceptable (27b) contains a resemblance relation.

(27) a. In March, four fireworks manufacturers asked that the decision be reversed, and on Monday, the ICC did <~~reverse the decision~~>.
(Dalrymple et al. 1991)
  b. * This problem was looked into by John, and Bob did <~~look into the problem~~>, too.
(Kehler 2000: 551, example 34)

Kehler (2000: 543-46) ascribes this contrast to the fact that cause/effect relations require only semantic identity, which tolerates voice mismatch, while resemblance relations require syntactic identity in addition to semantic identity.

We depart from Kehler (2000), suggesting that a cause/effect relation as well as a resemblance relation requires syntactic identity in ellipsis, but that they are distinguished in terms of the category that undergoes ellipsis. In particular, when a resemblance relation holds, the bigger category vP is a target of ellipsis. By contrast, when a cause-effect relation holds, the smaller category VP can be elided, as schematized below:

(28) a. vP ellipsis in "parallel resemblance (or contrast) relations"

$[_{TP} <_{vP} [_{VP} \quad] >] \ldots [_{TP} [_{vP} [_{VP} \quad]]]$ (with the vP in the second clause struck through)

b. VP ellipsis in "non-parallel cause-effect relations"

$[_{TP} [_{vP} <_{VP} \quad >]] \ldots [_{TP} [_{vP} [_{VP} \quad]]]$ (with the VP in the second clause struck through)

The difference between the two types of relations in terms of the category of ellipsis is justified on the basis of the following reasoning. First, a parallel resemblance relation relates two clauses/sentences; the ellipsis clause and its antecedent clause. The proposition of the former clause holds true, in a parallel fashion as that of the latter clause does. Now the wisdom we has about the syntax of a clause is that a small clause vP, as a proxy of a full clause CP/TP, may have a parallel relation with another small clause vP. This is exactly what happens in the case of vP ellipsis when a resemblance relation holds. The ellipsis of a vP is the only option to respect the full clause-to-small clause correspondence in the case of a resemblance relation between the ellipsis and the corresponding antecedent clauses.

When a cause/effect relation holds, it also relates two clauses. However, the two clauses involved are non-parallel. Thus, no full clause-to-small clause correspondence is called for. Since the two clauses involved are non-parallel, one clause may relate not to another clause but to a constituent inside it. In other words, it is possible that one clause may, for example, modify the constituent inside another clause. This is the reason that VP ellipsis instead of vP ellipsis is permissible when a cause/effect relation holds, even though two clauses are related. The cause/effect, non-parallel relation gets away with not respecting the full clause-to-small clause correspondence.

Given the asymmetry between resemblance and cause/effect relations in terms of the size of ellipsis, we are now in a position to account for their contrast in voice mismatch when a verbal domain (VP or vP) undergoes ellipsis. The ideas we rely on are summarized below:

(29) **Identity condition on VP or vP ellipsis:**

a. Case/case mismatch (between the copy of the survivor/remnant and its correlate) is not allowed for ellipsis (as part of syntactic isomorphism in ellipsis).

b. Nominative and Accusative Case are checked outside VP, whereas inherent case is checked inside VP.

c. vP undergoes 'VP ellipsis' in a resemblance relation.

The key ingredient we rely on in this analysis is Case/case (mis)match in ellipsis. Simply stated, Case/case mismatch is not allowed between a survivor/remnant and its antecedent constituent (or correlate). This means that in the following structure one argument element A inside the ellipsis constituent and its correlate A' inside the antecedent constituent are required to be identical in terms of Case/case feature.

(30) ..$[_{\text{antecedent constituent}}$ A'] ...$[_{\text{ellipsis constituent}}$ A]

Now a question is what happens when A and A' are base-generated inside the ellipsis and antecedent constituents, but they participate in Case-checking relation outside them. We suppose that this situation holds exactly in such examples as (19) and (20), repeated below (31) and (32):

(31) ?My problem will be looked into by Tom, but he won't ~~look into~~ yours. PG

(32) This problem was to have been looked into, but obviously nobody did ~~look into this problem~~. VPE

As stated in (29b), in English either Nominative or Accusative Case is checked outside VP (cf. Chomsky (1995)). Thus, if in (31) and (32) the ellipsis clause has a cause/effect relation with its antecedent clause and what is elided is VP (as stated in (29c)), the apparent Case mismatch between the object element in the ellipsis clause and its correlate subject element in the antecedent clause is not harmful at all. This is because at the point of derivation where VP is elided, the former and the latter have not yet have its Case feature valued, thus being not distinct in form.

Now, we turn to the examples of Pseudogapping and VP ellipsis in a resemblance relation. (15) and (17), repeated below as (33) and (34), represent those examples:

(33) *Roses were brought by some, and others did ~~bring~~ lilies. PG

(34) *Roses were brought by some boys, and some girls did ~~bring roses~~, too. VPE

As argued above, both Pseudogapping and VP ellipsis in a resemblance relation involve an elision of vP rather than VP. Since vP is a domain where Accusative Case is checked, the object in the ellipsis clause is bound to relate to its correlate object in the antecedent clause. The unacceptability of (33) and (34) follows from the fact that in the examples, the object element in the ellipsis clause which is Case-checked in Spec of vP relates to its correlate in the antecedent clause, which is the subject element that cannot be Case-checked in Spec of vP. Therefore, there is bound to arise a Case mismatch in both Pseudogapping and VP ellipsis in a resemblance relation that holds for (33) and (34). In other words, voice mismatch for vP ellipsis in a resemblance relation is not permissible, because it always invites Case mismatch between an object element and its corresponding subject or vice versus, ultimately infringing on the syntactic isomorphism on ellipsis.

We now turn to the examples where a VP-internal element is assigned not structural Case but inherent case.

(35) a. *She embroiders peace signs on jackets more often than she does <~~embroider jackets~~> with swastikas.

b. ?She embroiders peace signs on jackets more often than she does <~~embroider peace signs on~~> shirt sleeves.

(36) a. *He'd give Yale money more readily than he would <~~give money~~> to charity.

b. ?He'd give money more readily to Yale than he would <~~give money to~~> charity.

(37) a. *Abby flirted more often in general than Beth did <~~flirt with~~> Max.

b. ?Abby flirted with Ben more often than she did <~~flirt with~~> Ryan.

Note that unlike structural Accusative Case that is checked outside VP but inside vP, inherent case is presumably determined by a verbal head inside VP and realized with an appropriate preposition. All the examples in (35)-(37) involve Pseudogapping because we cannot test out case forms of VP-internal argument elements inside the portion elided by VP ellipsis. The (b)-examples of (35)-(37) are a little bit degraded (we conjecture that, as noted by Levin (1979/1986) and Lasnik (1995), the degradedness of these examples are due to the general degradedness of Pseudogapping), but they are still acceptable. This is because in these examples, the VP in the ellipsis clause is identical to that in the antecedent clause in terms of inherent case realization of the argument elements inside them. Unlike these (b)-examples of (35)-(37), however, their (a)-examples are ruled out owing to case mismatch between a VP-internal argument element in the ellipsis clause and its correlate in the antecedent clause. For example, in (35a) neither jackets nor with swastikas inside the VP of the ellipsis clause matches with on jackets and signs in terms of case/Case feature, thereby inviting a violation of the syntactic isomorphism on ellipsis.

In leaving this section, let us note that Takita (2015: 14) proposed the revised Case condition on ellipsis, which states that a DP must be Case-licensed in the ellipsis site by a head identical to the corresponding head that Case-licenses the correlating DP in the antecedent. Simply speaking, Takita (ibid.) argues that a Case-licensing head rather than the Case/case form of a DP determined by it is critical in meeting the syntactic isomorphism on ellipsis. Takita's analysis works fine for (37b). Since in (37b) the same verb flirt Case-licenses Ryan and its correlate Ben with the realization of the preposition with, it meets the revised Case condition on ellipsis. To rule out (37a), however, Takita has to say that the verb flirt in the ellipsis clause is different from the verb flirt in the antecedent clause. Unlike Takita's analysis, we have argued that the Case/case form of a DP matters for ellipsis.

4 Consequences

If causative and unaccusatives also differ in their v (cf. Chomsky (1995)), it is surprising that the following examples are always unacceptable where VP ellipsis applies to the causative-unaccusative alternating verbs in an antecedent and ellipsis pair:

(38) *Causative-Unaccusative Alternations*:
a. This can freeze. *Please do.
(Johnson 2004: 7)
b. *Bill melted the copper vase, and the magnesium vase did, too.
(Sag 1976: 160)
c. *Maria still tried to break the vase even though it wouldn't.
(Houser et al. 2007)

(39) a. This can freeze. Please freeze this.
b. Bill melted the copper vase, and the magnesium vase melted, too.
c. Maria still tried to break the vase even though it wouldn't break.

Note that (38b) involves a resemblance relation, but (38a) and (38c) involve a cause/effect relation. The prediction is that if the subject element in (38) derived from an object position, just like subject elements of passives, and if the VP of (38c) in a cause-effect relation underwent ellipsis, (38c) would be acceptable, contrary to fact.

Transitive-middle alternating verbs behave in a parallel fashion as causative-unaccusative alternating verbs. The following two sets of examples show transitive/middle alternations.

(40) *Transitive-Middle Alternations:*
a. They market ethanol well in the Midwest.
b. They sell Hyundais in Greece.
c. Studios generally release action films in the summer.

(41) a. Ethanol markets well in the Midwest.
b. Hyundais don't sell in Greece.
c. This kind of movie generally releases in the summer.

No such alternations are found between antecedent and ellipsis pairs, as follows:

(42) a. *They market ethanol well in the Midwest, but regular gas doesn't.
b. *They sell Hyundais in Greece because Hondas don't.
c. *Studios generally release action films in the summer, and big-name comedies generally do as well.

(43) a. *Ethanol markets well in the Midwest, though they don't in the South.
b. *Hyundais don't sell in Greece because dealers don't.
c. *This kind of movie generally releases in the summer, though a studio might in the winter if it's Christmas-themed.

Why is there a contrast between passives, on the one hand, and unaccusatives and middles, on the other hand? We saw that passive-active alternation (i.e., voice mismatch) in the antecedent and ellipsis pair is permissible in a cause/effect relation. However, neither causative-unaccusative nor transitive-middle alternation in the antecedent and ellipsis pair is allowed. We suggest on the basis of the following do so replacement that in English, passives involve syntactic movement, but neither unaccusatives nor middles do so.

(44) *Passive*:
a. *This cat was adopted, but that one was not **done so**.
(from Thompson (2012))
b. *The vase was broken by the children, and the jar was **done so**, too.
(from Houser (2010))

(45) *Unaccusative and Middle:*
a. %John told Steve to hang the horseshoe over the door, and it **does so** now.
b. %I was told that this new peanut butter spreads very easily, and I am very excited to **do so**.
((12a-d) from Thompson (2012))
c. %Mary claimed that I closed the door, but it actually **did so** on its own.
(from Thompson (2012))

The contrast between (44) and (45) can be accounted for by the assumption that the VP-replacing anaphor so (while the light verb do of do so occupies the little v position (cf. Stroik (2001), among others) cannot replace a VP that contains a gap left behind by A or A'-movement. This account implies that passive verbs are potentially transitive verbs, thus being able to meet the identity condition on ellipsis with transitive verbs.

However, unaccusative and middle verbs are in fact intransitive verbs, thus not being able to meet the identity condition on ellipsis with causative or transitive verbs. This is how we account for the unacceptability of (38), (42), and (43). All these examples are ruled out independently of Case/case mismatch but because of verb-type mismatch between intransitive and causative/transitive verbs.

There is an additional alternation between an implicit argument-taking verb and its passive variant in an antecedent and ellipsis pair. This mismatch is not allowed, as follows:

(46) a. *I heard John ate in the cafeteria. But I don't know what was [~~eaten by John in the cafeteria~~].
b. *I watched John win in the last Olympics. But I don't know which medal was [~~won by John in the last Olympics~~].
c. *I saw John read in the library. But I don't know what book was [~~read by John in the library~~].

However, their Sluicing counterparts are acceptable, as in (47):

(47) a. I heard John ate in the cafeteria. But I don't know what.
b. I watched John win in the last Olympics. But I don't know which medal.
c. I saw John read in the library. But I don't know what book.

We assume that the implicit argument selected by verbs such as eat, win, and read implicitly carries Accusative-like inherent case. This inherent case is lexically assigned by such verbs to the implicit argument in-situ within VP without moving to [Spec, vP]. This assumption accounts for the contrast in acceptability between (46) and (47). In (46), the lexical-case-carrying implicit argument within the VP of the antecedent clause cannot meet a Case/case match with the complement of the passive verb within that of the ellipsis clause. In (47), by contrast, the wh-survivor/remnant in the ellipsis clause and its correlate implicit argument in the antecedent clause are understood to carry the same feature of Case/case, meeting syntactic isomorphism on ellipsis.

6 Conclusion

In this paper, we first started with reviewing Merchant's (2008) analysis of voice mismatch in ellipsis constructions and Tanaka's (2011) reply to this analysis. We took Tanaka's rebuttal of Merchant's dichotomy in voice mismatch between VP and Pseudogapping to be valid. Departing from Kehler's (2000) insight that the distinction between resemblance vs. cause/effect discourse coherence relations rather than between VP and Pseudogapping come into place in apparent voice mismatch, we argued that VP undergoes ellipsis in a resemblance relation, whereas vP does so in a cause/effect relation. Given the different sizes of ellipsis interacting with discourse relations, we went further to argue that apparent voice mismatch in VP ellipsis is attributed to the fact that structural Accusative Case is checked not within the VP domain that undergoes ellipsis. Thus, the object element in the ellipsis clause and the subject element in the antecedent clause, or vice versus, count as identical within a VP in terms of Case feature, meeting the identity condition on ellipsis. Unlike structural Case, however, a difference in case feature or argument structure (or verb type) within a VP always invites a violation of identity in ellipsis. In addition, Case/case mismatch in the case of an elision of a larger constituent such as TP under Sluicing was shown to induce fatal effects on the acceptability of sentences involving such a type of ellipsis.

Acknowledgement

We are grateful to the three anonymous reviewers for their comments and suggestions on the earlier version of the paper. All the remaining errors are, of course, ours. This work was supported by the National Research Foundation of Korea Grant funded by the Korean Government (NRF-2013S1A5A2A03044783).

References

Chomsky, Noam. 1995. The Minimalist Program. MIT Press , Cambridge, MA.

Dalrymple, Marry, Stuart M. Shieber, and Fernando CN Pereira. 1991. Ellipsis and Higher-order Unification. Linguistics and Philosophy, 14, 399-452.

Houser, Michael J, Line Mikkelsen, and Maziar Toosarvandani. 2007. Verb Phrase Pronominalization in Danish: Deep or Surface Anaphora? Ms., University of California, Berkeley.

Houser, Michael J. 2010. On the Anaphoric Status of Do So. URL http://linguistics.berkeley.edu/~mhouser/Papers/do_so_status.pdf.

Jayaseelan, Karattuparambil A. 1990. Incomplete VP Deletion and Gapping. Linguistic Analysis, 20, 64-81.

Johnson, Kyle. 2004. How to Be Quiet. In Papers from the Annual Meeting of the Chicago Linguistic Society, 40, 1-20. Chicago Linguistic Society.

Kehler, Andrew. 2000. Coherence and the Resolution of Ellipsis, Linguistics and Philosophy 23, 533-575.

Kehler, Andrew. 2002. Coherence, Reference, and the Theory of Grammar. CSLI Publications, Stanford.

Lasnik, Howard. 1995. A Note on Pseudogapping. MIT working papers in linguistics, 27, 143-163.

Lasnik, Howard. 1999. Minimalist Analysis. Blackwell, Oxford.

Levin, Nancy. 1978. Some Identity-of-sense Deletions Puzzle Me. Do They You?. In Papers from the Regional Meeting of the Chicago Linguistic Society, 14, 229-240. Chicago, Ill.

Levin, Nancy. 1979/1986. Main Verb Ellipsis in Spoken English (Doctoral dissertation, Ohio State University, Columbus. [Published in 1986 by Garland, New York]).

Merchant, Jason. 2007. Voice and Ellipsis. Ms., University of Chicago, Chicago.

Merchant, Jason. 2008. An Asymmetry in Voice Mismatches in VP-ellipsis and Pseudogapping. Linguistic Inquiry, 39(1), 169-179.

Merchant, Jason. 2013. Voice and Ellipsis. Linguistic Inquiry, 44, 77-108.

Sag, Ivan. 1976. Deletion and Logical Form. Doctoral dissertation, MIT, Cambridge, MA.

SanPietro, Steve, Jason Merchant, and Ming Xiang. 2012. Accounting for Voice Mismatch in Ellipsis. In Proceedings of the 30th West Coast Conference on Formal Linguistics, ed. by Nathan Arnett and Ryan Bennett, 303-312.

Sportiche, Dminique. 1988. A Theory of Floating Quantifiers and its Corollaries for Constituent Structure. Linguistic inquiry, 19, 425-451.

Stroik, Thomas. 2001. On the Light Verb Hypothesis. Linguistic Inquiry 32, 362-369.

Takahashi, Shoichi. 2004. Pseudogapping and Cyclic Linearization. In Proceedings of NELS, 34(2), 571-586.

Takita, Kensuke. 2015. Strengthening the Role of Case in Ellipsis. Ms., Mie University.

Tanaka, Hidekazu. 2011. Voice Mismatch and Syntactic Identity. Linguistic Inquiry, 42, 470-490.

Thompson, Anie. 2012. Categorizing Surface Proforms in the Typology of Anaphora. A talk given at Ellipsis 2012, Universidade de Vigo.

A Statistical Modeling of the Correlation between Island Effects and Working-memory Capacity for L2 Learners

Euhee Kim
Computer Science & Engineering
School of IT Convergence Engineering
Shinhan University
Dongducheon City, Korea
euhkim@shihan.ac.kr

Myung-Kwan Park
Department of English
College of Humanities
Dongguk University
Seoul, Korea
parkmk@dgu.edu

Abstract

The cause of island effects has evoked considerable debate within syntax and other fields of linguistics. The two competing approaches stand out: the grammatical analysis; and the working-memory (WM)-based processing analysis. In this paper we report three experiments designed to test one of the premises of the WM-based processing analysis: that the strength of island effects should vary as a function of individual differences in WM capacity. The results show that island effects present even for L2 learners are more likely attributed to grammatical constraints than to limited processing resources.

1 Introduction

The role of memory in language learning has long received ample attention from researchers in first and second language acquisition (SLA) (Baddeley (1999), Ellis (2001), Juffs (2006)). At an intuitive level, it seems right to reason that individual differences among adult learners in their successful attainment of a second language (L2) are attributable to individual differences in memory capacity. In SLA, researchers have focused on short-term or working rather than long-term memory differences because they think short-term or working-memory (WM) plays a more instrumental role for individual differences in language development. The rationale for this belief is that WM is an on-line capacity for processing and analyzing new information (words, grammatical structures and so on). As a consequence, the bigger the on-line capacity an individual has for new information, the more information will settle into off-line, long-term memory.

In this paper we concentrate on Korean leaners of English (KLEs) to examine the correlation between their individual WM capacity and their knowledge of island constraints on *wh*-dependencies in English. To this end we adopt the methodology that Sprouse, Wagers, and Phillips (SWP) (2012a, b) use for L1 speakers.

2 Hypothesis Testing

The main focus of this paper is to examine the question of whether there is a correlation between KLEs' WM capacity and their knowledge of island constraints on *wh*-dependencies in English. In order to investigate this question, we need (i) a measure of WM capacity, and (ii) a measure of knowledge of *wh*-island constraints. The second measure is often termed a measure of 'island effects', which refer to the relatively low acceptability ratings given to sentences with a *wh*-dependency between a *wh*-phrase and its gap position inside select syntactic environments (cf. Ross (1967), Rizzi (1990), and Chomsky (1995) among many others). Given the foremost interest in the role of such variables as GAP-POSITION (i.e. where a gap is) and STRUCTURE (i.e.

29th Pacific Asia Conference on Language, Information and Computation pages 422 - 430
Shanghai, China, October 30 - November 1, 2015

whether island structure is involved or not) in the instantiation of island effects, we want to bring forth the following two hypotheses.

Table 1: Proposed hypotheses

(i) KLEs recognize the island effects of GAP-POSITION and STRUCTURE for each island type.
(ii) KLEs' recognition of the island strength for each island type correlates with their WM capacity.

3 Materials and Methods

To investigate the correlation between KLEs' perception of the strength of island effects and their WM capacity, we employed the participants and tasks described below.

3.1 Participants

Forty KLEs participated in this experiment for 10,000 Korean Won. The experiment was carried out during a single visit to the lab during which the participants completed the reading span task, the n-back task, and the acceptability-rating task (in that order).

3.2 The Acceptability-rating Task

The materials we used were adopted from SWP (2012a, b). They contained four island types: *Whether*, Complex NP, Subject, and Adjunct islands. For each type of island, gap/extraction site and structural environment were manipulated in a 2×2 factorial design. For example, the *Whether* island type/condition has the four levels/subtypes of the following kind:

(1) a. Non-island/Matrix
Who __ thinks that John bought a car?
b. Non-island/Embedded
What do you think that John bought __?
c. Island/Matrix
Who __ wonders whether John bought a car?
d. Island/Embedded
What do you wonder whether John bought __?

The 2×2 factorial design of each island effect as in (1) controls for the two syntactic properties of island-violating sentences: (i) they contain a long-distance *wh*-dependency, and (ii) they contain an island structure. By converting these two properties into the two main factors such as GAP-POSITION and STRUCTURE, each with two levels (for the first factor: Matrix and Embedded; for the second factor: Non-island and Island), SWP (2012a, b) defined island effects as a superadditive interaction effects that exist between two factors. Recall that the island effects are understood as the effects on acceptability of processing both long-distance *wh*-dependency and island structure contained in a single sentence like (1d) above (see Fodor (1983), Stowe (1986), Kluender (1998, 2004), and more recently Hofmeister & Sag (2010) for the studies on L1 processing of *wh*-dependencies; Juffs & Harrington (1995; 1996), White & Juffs (1998), Williams et al (2001), and Juffs (2005) for the studies on their L2 processing). In other words, the combined effects of the two factors are greater (i.e. superadditive) than the linear sum of the individual factors; that is, ((1a) - (1b)) + ((1a) - (1c)) < ((1a) - (1d)).

The acceptability-rating task using the materials was administered as a paper survey. The surveys were one hundred and twenty-eight token sentences long (8 token sentences for each level of an island type). The task was a 4-point scale acceptability-rating one where 1 represents 'least acceptable' and 4 represents 'most acceptable'. The 4-point scale acceptability-rating task thus employs a continuous scale (the positive number line) for acceptability ratings (cf. Bard, Robertson, & Sorace (1996)). Participants were under no time constraints during the survey.

3.3 The Reading Span Task

The reading span (RS) task which was originally developed by Conway et al. (2005) was designed to assess participants' WM capacity and was run using E-prime (Psychology software tools Inc.). In the version of the RS task we used, participants were tested on sets of sentences ranging from two to five sentences per set. There were three trials for each set size, totaling forty-two sentences for the entire task (3×(2+3+4+5)=42). Each item was composed of a complete sentence followed by a question mark and then a capital alphabet letter.

Participants read each sentence aloud, paused at the question mark, and answered 'yes' or 'no,' depending on the semantic plausibility of the sentence. After the answer, they were to read the capital letter aloud also. By pressing the space bar, they proceeded to the next item. After they reached the last sentence in a set, they were to see three question marks ('???') on the screen. They stopped at this point and wrote down each of the letters in the order in which they had appeared in the set. A sample set of three items is shown in (2).

(2) a. No matter how much we talk to him, he is never going to change.? J
b. The prosecutor's dish was lost because it was not based on fact.? M
c. Every now and then I catch myself swimming blankly at the wall.? F ???

The correct responses to the semantic plausibility questions are 'yes, no, no,' and one point was given for every letter correctly written in the correct order on the answer sheet (J, M, F).

3.4 The N-back Task

To get a more reliable measure of WM capacity, the version of n-back (NB) task developed by Ragland et al. (2002) was administered on top of the RS task. In this task, participants were shown a sequence of visual stimuli and they had to respond each time the current stimulus was identical to the one presented n positions back in the sequence. The stimulus material consisted of 20 different consonants in English. The upper case consonants were all shown in white and presented centrally on a black background for 500 ms each, followed by a 2000 ms interstimulus interval. Participants were required to press a pre-defined key ("ENTER") for targets, and their response window lasted from the onset of the stimulus until the presentation of the next stimulus (2500 ms); no response was required for non-targets. Participants were tested on 0-, 1-, 2- and 3-back levels in a pseudo-randomized order, with each level presented for 3 blocks, resulting in a total of 12 blocks. A block consisted of 15 + n stimuli and contained 5 targets and 10 + n non-targets each. The dependent measure was the proportion of hits minus false alarms averaged over all n-back levels.

In short, the results of data in our experiments are reported in Table 2.

Table 2: The descriptive statistics of the experimental data

	READING SPAN	N-BACK	ACCEPT ABILITY
Min	.4800	3.083	1.00
1st Qu.	.5700	3.917	2.00
Median	.6400	4.167	3.00
Mean	.6645	4.171	2.89
3rd Qu.	.7450	4.500	4.00
Max.	.9300	4.917	4.00

4 Experiments and Results

4.1 The Syntactic Island Effects

In this section we report the formal acceptability-rating experiment that was used to quantitatively measure the target state for L2 learners' knowledge of island constraints on *wh*-dependencies in English. The acceptability ratings from each participant were z-score transformed. The z-score transformation was intended to eliminate the influence of scale bias on the size of the differences-in-differences (DD) scores (which are used to measure the strength of island effects) and therefore validate its comparison with the measure of WM capacity, which is the main focus in this paper.

The means and standard deviations for each condition (i.e. each of the island types) are presented in Table 3.

Table 3: The means and standard deviations for each condition (N = 40)

		Adjunct	Complex NP	Subject	Whether
Embedded	Island	-.61(.89)	-.70(.81)	-.86(.88)	-.85(.82)
	Non-island	-.72(.88)	-.27(.92)	-.46(.90)	.08(.92)
Matrix	Island	.30(.84)	.65(.64)	.39(.81)	.64(.61)
	Non-island	.51(.67)	.62(.66)	.52(.77)	.74(.56)

To test the first hypothesis (i) of Table 1, the question we examine with this set of data is whether the island effects for each condition are statistically present in the acceptability RATING. To answer this question, we constructed the linear mixed-effects regression models with GP (i.e. GAP-POSITION) and ST (i.e. STRUCTURE) as two fixed factors and with PA (i.e. participants) and ITEM (i.e. items) included as two random factors.

We assumed that fixed effects vary for all participants and items for each island type. In other words, we accounted for by-participant and by-item variations in overall acceptability ratings. So, what we need was random slope models, where participants and items have different intercepts, and where they also have different slopes for the fixed effects of the two factors.

4.1.1 The Interaction Plots for Each Island Type

We now turn to plots of the interaction (GP : ST; island effects) for each island type. The four panels in Figure 1 plotted the acceptability ratings for the four island types. Note that a superadditive effect is reflected statistically as an interaction, since the response to each level of one factor depends upon the level of the other. While linear additivity is visually identified by parallel lines, superadditivity is visually identified by nonparallel ones.

In the "cross-over" graph of the Adjunct island type in Figure 1, we see that the Island/Embedded group does better than the NonIsland/Embedded group. It is evident that ((1a) - (1b)) + ((1a) - (1c)) > ((1a) - (1d)). There is thus no superadditive interaction effect with Adjunct *wh*-dependencies in English when tested for KLEs.

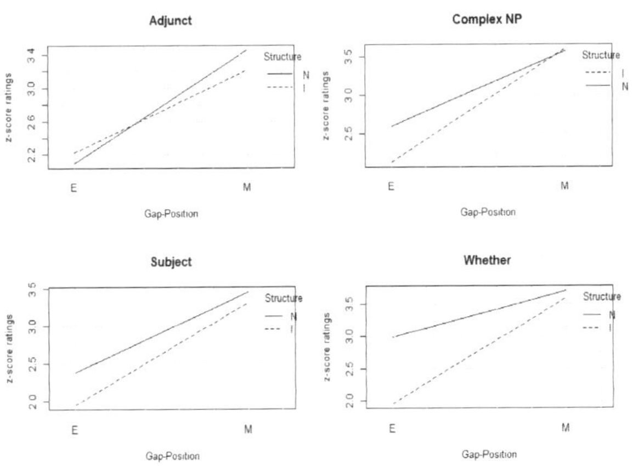

Figure 1: The interaction plots

In the "almost paralleling" graph of the Subject island type we see that ((1a) - (1b)) + ((1a) - (1c)) ≅((1a) - (1d)). So we cannot spot a superadditive interaction in the graph, either.

In the "almost intersecting at the level Matrix" graphs of the Complex NP and *Whether* island types, by contrast, we can spot superadditive interaction effects -- whenever there are no parallel lines there is an superadditive interaction present; in other words, ((1a) - (1b)) + ((1a) - (1c)) < ((1a) - (1d)). All in all, based on KLEs' acceptabiity ratings for the four island types, the graphs show that the island effects on acceptability are present for Complex NP and *Whether* islands, and absent for Adjunct and Subject islands.

4.1.2 The Selection of the Best Fit Regression Model on Island Types

To select a better fit regression model among simulated models, we used the lmerTest package for the statistical programming language R to perform a linear mixed effects analysis of the relationship between overall acceptability ratings and island effects.

What we need was a random slope model, where participants and items are allowed to have both different intercepts and slopes for the fixed effects. As fixed effects, we entered GAP-POSITION and STRUCTURE with an interaction term into the model. As random effects, we had intercepts for participants and items as well as by-participant and by-item random slopes for the fixed effects. The *p*-values were obtained by the likelihood ratio tests of the full model with the effects in question against the model without the effects in question.

With the 2x2 full factorial models for the island types, we constructed linear mixed-effects regressions, but, for lack of space, we won't describe them. Here's what we selected as the best fit model for the four island types:

$$Formula_1{:}Rating\sim GP+ST+GP{:}ST+(1+GP+ST+GP{:}ST\,|ITEM)+(1+GP+ST+GP{:}ST\,|\,PA).$$

4.1.3 The 2x2 Factorial Design Analysis

Using the lmer() method implemented in the lmerTest package, we estimated all *p*-values via the formula$_1$. Table 4 reports the *p*-values for main effects and the interaction effects of the formula$_1$.

The *p*-values for the coefficients of the interaction factor (GP_M : ST_N)[1] for the Adjunct and Subject island types are greater than the significance level (i.e. $p > 0.05$). Crucially, there

[1] In the description here and below, E and M refer to Embedded and Matrix (as two levels of GAP-POSITION), and I and N to Island and Non-island (as two levels of STRUCTURE), respectively.

are no significant interaction effects of GAP-POSITION and STRUCTURE for the Adjunct and Subject island types. Besides, the *p*-values for the coefficient of the interaction effects for the Complex NP and *Whether* island types are less than the significance level (p = .01581*; p =1.07e-07***). This experiment showed statistically significant interaction effects for the Complex NP and *Whether* island types.

Table 4: The fitted linear mixed-effects regression for the formula$_1$

Fixed Effects:

Type	effects	Estimate	SE	df	t-value	p-value
Adjunct	GP_M	.9149	.1540	36.74	5.940	7.76e-07***
	ST_N	-.1144	.1515	34.94	-.755	.455
	GP_M : ST_N	.3317	.2094	32.70	1.584	.123
Complex NP	GP_M	1.3609	.1369	44.11	9.941	7.80e-13***
	ST_N	.4289	.1310	40.11	3.273	.00219**
	GP_M : ST_N	-.4546	.1798	37.54	-2.528	.01581*
Subject	GP_M	1.2580	.1645	43.58	7.648	1.38e-09***
	ST_N	.3946	.1518	35.35	2.599	.0135*
	GP_M : ST_N	-.2688	.2119	34.04	-1.268	.2133
Whether	GP_M	1.4981	.1231	44.78	12.167	8.88e-16***
	ST_N	.9406	.1234	44.77	7.620	1.28e-09***
	GP_M : ST_N	-.8405	.1310	41.37	-6.414	1.07e-07***

As predicted in the plots of interactions for each island type in Figure 1, the 2x2 factorial design analysis with a linear mixed-effects regression model reveals that KLEs recognize the island effects of GAP-POSITION and STRUCTURE for both Complex NP and *Whether* island types.

4.1.4 Pairwise Comparisons of Main Factors

However, because the interaction effects are present in the island STRUCTURE within the embedded GAP-POSITION, it is possible that the embedded island condition is driving these main effects. Therefore we performed the two pairwise comparisons on the embedded GAP-POSITION condition and the non-island STRUCTURE condition to test for each independent effect of STRUCTURE and GAP-POSITION.

Below, Table 5 shows the coefficients of linear mixed-effects regression models of the pairwise comparisons on STRUCTURE at the two island/embedded and non-island/embedded conditions for each island type when the lmer() method applied to the linear mixed-effects regression model with ST random slope:

$$Formula_2{:}Rating{\sim}ST+(1+ST|ITEM)+(1+ST|PA)$$

Likewise, Table 5 shows the *p*-values of the pairwise comparisons on the GAP-POSITION at the two matrix/non-island and embedded/non-island conditions when the lmer() method applied to the model with GP random slope:

$$Formula_3{:}Rating{\sim}\ GP+(1+GP|ITEM)+(1+GP|PA)$$

Table 5: The pairwise comparisons: STRUCTURE and GAP-POSITION

Pairwise Comparison

Condition	Factor	Type	Estimate	SE	df	t-value	p-value
GP=E (formula$_2$)	ST_N	Adjunct	.1144	.1779	16.515	.643	.529
		Complex NP	-.4289	.1413	18.909	-3.035	.0068**
		Subject	-.3946	.1445	17.938	-2.731	.0137*
		Whether	-.9406	.1246	36.330	-7.548	.0000***
ST=N (formula$_3$)	GP_M	Adjunct	-1.2465	.1293	31.69	-9.637	.0000***
		Complex NP	-.9063	.1526	18.468	-5.940	.0000***
		Subject	-.9892	.1436	21.313	-6.888	.0000***
		Whether	-.6575	.1094	30.872	-6.007	.0000**

As the above table indicates, the pairwise comparison on GAP-POSITION for each island type with embedded/non-island and matrix/non-island conditions shows that it reaches a statistical significance for each island type ($p < .005$). As expected, the length cost of gap position was isolated from the structure of non-island condition.

4.2 The Strength of Island Effects and Working-Memory Capacity

Now that we have seen that for L2 learners, island effects are robust in both Complex NP and *Whether* island types, the question is whether their awareness of the effects is attributed to constraints on the amount of WM capacity that any language user can have. This question gains more significance, as one account of *wh*-islands predicts that there is inverse relationship across language users between the strength of island effects and WM capacity (see Hofmeister and Sag (2010) among many others). We indeed tested this prediction for L2 learners.

We measured the strength of island effects by adopting the idea of a differences-in-differences (DD) score (Maxwell & Delaney (2003); SWP (2012a, b)). Intuitively, the DD score measures how much greater the effects of an island structure are in a long-distance dependency sentence than in a sentence with a local dependency. As it is calculated for each individual tested by using the acceptability-rating experiment, it serves as a measure of the superadditive component of the interaction for each individual and for each island type. Thus the score is thought of as the strength of island effects for that individual. More concretely, the DD score is calculated for a two-way interaction as follows. First, calculate the difference (D1) between the scores for two of the four levels. More specifically, we define D1 as the difference between the Non-island/Embedded and the Island/Embedded levels. Second, calculate the difference (D2) between the scores for the other two levels. For our purposes, D2 is the difference between the Non-island/Matrix and the Island/Matrix levels. Finally, calculate the difference between these two difference scores (i.e. D1 and D2) to produce a DD score.

We constructed a set of three linear regressions for each island type using DD scores and the WM capacity (i.e. reading span (RS) and n-back (NB) scores, which will be reported in the next subsections), as follows:

$Formula_4 : DD \sim RS$
$Formula_5 : DD \sim NB$
$Formula_6 : DD \sim RS + NB$

The first set of linear regressions was run on the set of all DD scores for each island type. The second set of linear regressions was run on only the DD scores that were greater than or equal to zero for each island type. The logic behind the second analysis is that DD scores below 0 are indicative of a sub-additive interaction. No theory predicts the existence of sub-additive interactions, which raises questions about how to interpret participants who produce sub-additive island effects. One possibility is that DD scores below 0 may reflect a type of noise that we may not want to influence the linear regression. If they are indeed noise, then eliminating these scores from the analysis should increase the likelihood of finding a significant correlation in the data. On the other hand, it is possible that these DD scores represent participants who truly do not perceive a classic superadditive island effect. In this case, including these scores should increase the likelihood of finding a significant correlation in the data. We report both analyses for these two possibilities

4.2.1 The Reading Span Task

Table 6 reports the results of the simple linear regressions: line-of-best-fit (intercept and slope), goodness-of-fit (R^2), and significance of the slope (t-statistic and p-value).

Table 6: $Formula_4$ for all DDs (DD≥0) (N = 40)

scores	Type	line-of-best-fit		goodness-of-fit	significance test	
		intercept	Slope	R^2	*t*-statistic	*p*-value
all DDs (DDs >=0)	Adjunct	-.4969 (.6607)	-.1495 (-.0024)	-.0022 (-.0294)	-.909 (-.014)	.3661 (.989)
	Complex NP	.4444 (.9500)	.2001 (.0747)	.0129 (-.0097)	1.439 (.632)	.1539 (.53)
	Subject	.4378 (.9524)	.0487 (-.1133)	-.0104 (-.0016)	.335 (-.947)	.7385 (.347)
	Whether	.8095 (1.1065)	.0475 (-.0418)	-.0115 (-.0135)	.333 (-.324)	.74 (.747)

The results in Table 6 concern the two sets of all DD scores and non-negative DD scores (i.e. values in parentheses) for each island type. On the first set of all DDs, three out of four slopes of the line-of-best-fit have positive slopes, but the slope for Adjunct island type has a negative slope. On the other hand, after removing negative DDs scores from the first set DDs, we see that the line-of-best-fit has three negative slopes and one positive slope for Complex NP island type.

The goodness of fit of the line-of-best-fit captured 0-2% of the variance in the data set, which is explained by the line for the four island types, as all the R^2 statistic absolute values were between 0 and 0.02.

Even after removing the potentially noisy DD scores, the four regressions for non-negative DD scores returned the lines with slopes that were not significantly different from 0 at the significance level ($p > 0.05$), thereby failing to reject the null hypothesis. In short, the results above indicate that there is no correlation between the all DD scores and the RS scores.

Figure 2 plots the relationship between the two sets of DD scores for each island type and the RS scores. The solid line represents the line of best fit for all of the DD scores. The dashed line represents the line of best fit when DD scores below zero are removed from the analysis. As predicted in Table 6, the solid and dashed lines for each island type behave like horizontal lines.

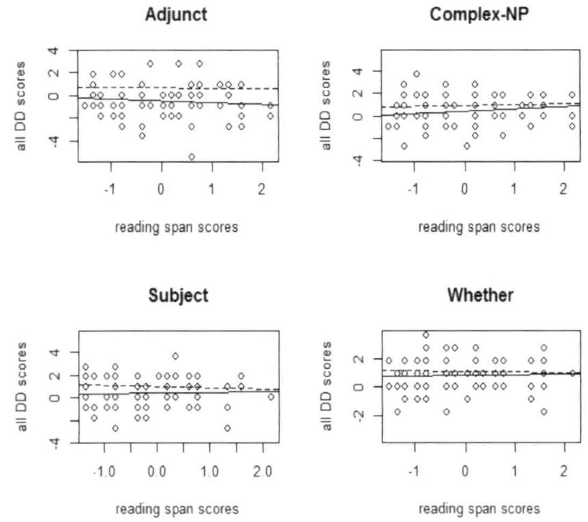

Figure 2: Plots for all DDs & RSs (N = 40)

4.2.2 The N-back Task

Table 7 shows that in the first set of all DDs, two out of four slopes of the line-of-best-fit have positive slopes, but the slopes for Complex NP and Subject island type are negative. On the other hand, after removing noisy scores from the first set DDs, we see that the line-of-best-fit has two negative slopes for Subject and *Whether* island type.

Table 7 shows that three of the four linear regressions of the set of all DD scores for Adjunct, Subject and *Whether* island types on the NB yielded R^2 statistic values that were approximately at 0, and the one for the Complex NP island type did so at .0167. Even after removing the noisy scores from the complete set of all DD scores, three island types such as Adjunct, Complex NP, and Subject have approximately zero R^2 statistic values, and *Whether* island type has it at -.0153. Because the goodness-of-fit of the lines was so extremely low, these results were not particularly meaningful for all DD scores.

The linear regression for four island types each returned the line-of-best-fit with a slope that was not significantly different from 0 at the significance level ($p > 0.1$) at the two sets of DD scores, thereby failing to reject the null hypothesis.

Table 7: $Formula_5$ for all DDs(DDs≥0) (N = 40)

scores	Islands	line-of-best-fit		goodness-of-fit	significance test	
		intercept	slope	R^2	*t*-statistic	*p*-value
all DDs (DDs >=0)	Adjunct	-.0938 (8797)	.1576 (.1173)	.0038 (-.0035)	1.138 (.925)	.259 (.36)
	Complex NP	.3342 (1.0282)	-.2391 (.1106)	.0167 (-.0051)	-1.549 (.848)	.1252 (.4)
	Subject	.1916 (1.2111)	-.1685 (-.1277)	-.0008 (-.0070)	-.962 (-.794)	.339 (.431)
	Whether	.7530 (1.1485)	.1534 (-.0094)	.0011 (-.0153)	1.044 (-.067)	.299 (.947)

Figure 3 plots the correlation between the set of DD scores for each island type and the NB scores. Each solid line and dashed line for each island type represents the line-of-best-fit with the intercept and slope. As predicted in Table 7, the solid line and dashed line for each island type behave like horizontal lines. Based on Figure 3, we can make a conclusion that there is no correlation between the NB scores and the DD scores for each island type.

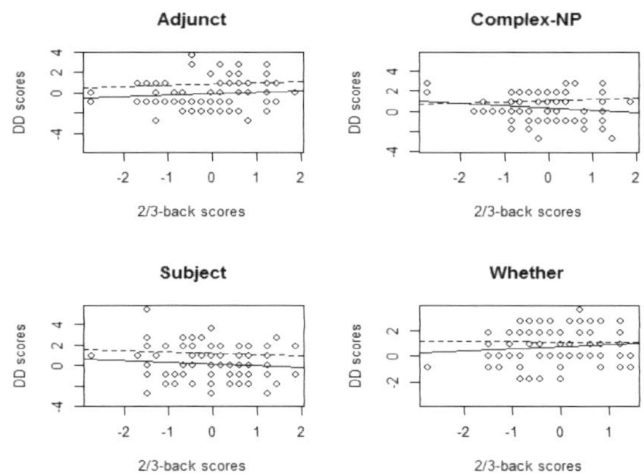

Figure 3: Plots for all DDs & NBs (N = 40)

4.2.3 Combining both RS and NB Scores

As a final analysis, we ran the multiple linear regression model for each island type, namely the $formula_6$, for the combined scores from both RS and NB tasks to ascertain if combining both scores of WM affects their relationship with the strength of island effects.

As Table 8 shows, even when doing the multiple regression analysis for the combined scores from both RS and NB tasks, there is no evidence of a significant correlation between WM and island effects. The four adjusted R^2 values of the regressions for all island types are at 0. After removing the noisy DD scores, the four adjusted R^2 values were improved and greater than 0. Although the regressions for all island types had the adjusted R^2 values that were slightly higher close to zero, their *p*-values for slope of NB and RS scores are not statistically significant ($p>0.05$), thus do not explain variation of the DD scores. Note that the *p*-value for slope of RS scores at the Complex NP type is statistically significant ($p<0.05$) after removing the noisy set of DD scores.

We draw the same conclusion as we did before, confirming that there is no correlation between WM scores and the DD scores for each island type even after combining the scores of both RS and NB.

Table 8: $Formula_6$ for all DDs(DDs≥0) (N = 40)

scores	islands	line-of-best-fit			goodness-of- fit	significance test	
		Intercept	slope (NB)	slope (RS)	R^2	*p*-value(NB)	*p*-value(RS)
	Adjunct	-.2556 (.6316)	-.2533 (-.3411)	-.1262 (-.1385)	.0064 (.0804)	.212 (.0544)	.545 (.4448)
ll DDs (DDs>=0)	Complex NP	.5264 (.5437)	-.1333 (-.3205)	.2028 (.3132)	.0032 (.0643)	.3388 (.0668)	.1788 (.0493*)
	Subject	.1745 (.7791)	.1285 (-.0513)	-.2544 (-.0325)	.0055 (-.0368)	.479 (.747)	.132 (.816)
	Whether	.9955 (1.5277)	-.2302 (-.0216)	.167 (.0539)	-.0035 (-.0300)	.238 (.89)	.328 (.715)

5 Discussion and Conclusion

In the previous literature on island effects in English and other languages there have been two diverging analyses for them: (i) the grammatical theory; (ii) the WM or processing resource capacity-based theory. The former grammatical theory predicts that the statistical GAP-POSITION : STRUCTURE interaction should not correlate with WM capacity measures, whereas the latter WM-based processing theory predicts that the interaction should correlate with such measures.

In this paper we reported three experiments that were designed to test for a correlation between the strength of the interaction and WM capacity. We used the acceptability-judgment task for the response scales, and two different types of WM measures (reading span and n-back), but found no evidence of a correlation between the statistical interaction and WM capacity. In fact, though Korean learners of English registered the GAP-POSITION : STRUCTURE interaction for the Complex NP and *Whether* islands, we didn't find evidence of their correlation with WM scores, refuting the main thesis of the WM-based processing theory. But this lack of the evidence is what is predicted by the grammatical theory of island effects. In short, the results of the experiments in this paper render strong support for a grammatical theory of island effects because we find no evidence of their correlation with WM or processing resource capacity.

Acknowledgement

We are grateful to the three anonymous reviewers for their comments and suggestions on the earlier version of the paper. This work was supported by the National Research Foundation of Korea Grant funded by the Korean Government (NRF- 2015S1A5A2A01010233).

References

Agresti, A. 2012. An introduction to Categorical Data Analysis (2nd ed.). Wiley & Sons, Inc, Hoboken, NJ.

Baayena, R. H., D. J. Davidsonb & D. M. Bates. 2008. Mixed-effects Modeling with Crossed Random Effects for Subjects and Items. Journal of Memory and Language, 59(4), 390-412.

Bard, E. G., D. Robertson & A. Sorace. 1996. Magnitude Estimation of Linguistic Acceptability. Language, 72, 32-68.

Chomsky, N. 1995. The Minimalist Program. MIT Press, Cambridge, MA.

Conway, A. R. A., M. J. Kane., M. F. Bunting., D. Z. Hambrick., O. Wilhelm., and R. W. Engle. 2005. Working Memory Span Tasks: A Methodological Review and User's Guide. Psychonomic Bulletin & Review, 12(5), 769-786.

Fodor, J. D. 1983. Phrase Structure Parsing and Island Constraints. Linguistics and Philosophy, 6, 163-223.

Hofmeister, P. and I. A. Sag. 2010. Cognitive Constraints and Island Effects. Language, 86, 366-415.

Juffs, A. 2005. The Influence of First Language on the Processing of Wh-movement in English as a Second Language. Second Language Research, 21(2), 121-151.

Juffs, A. 2006. Working-memory, Second Language Acquisition and Low-educated Second Language and Literacy Learners. LOT Occasional Papers: Netherlands Graduate School of Linguistics, 89-104.

Juffs, A. & M. Harrington. 1995. Parsing Effects in Second Language Sentence Processing: Subject and Object Asymmetries in Wh-extraction. Studies in Second Language Acquisition, 17, 483-516.

Juffs, A. & M. Harrington. 1996. Garden Path Sentences and Error Data in Second Language Processing Research. Language Learning, 46(2), 283-326.

Kluender, R. 1998. On the Distinction between Strong and Weak Islands: A Processing Perspective. In Culicover, P. and L. McNally (eds), Syntax and Semantics, vol. 29: The Limits of Syntax, 241-79. Academic Press, New York.

Kluender, R. 2004. Are Subject Islands Subject to a Processing Account? In West Coast Conference on Formal Linguistics (WCCFL) 23, 101-125.

Ragland, J.D., Turetsky, B.I., Gur, R.C, Gunning-Dixon, F., Turner, T, Schroeder, L., Chan, R., & Gur, R.E. 2002. Working Memory for Complex Figures: An fMRI Comparison of Letter and Fractal n-Back Tasks, Neuropsychology, 16, 370-379.

Rizzi, L. 1990. Relativized Minimality. MIT Press, Cambridge, MA.

Ross, J. 1967. Constraints on Variables in Syntax. Doctoral Dissertation, Massachusetts Institute of Technology.

Sprouse, J., M. Wagers & C. Phillips. 2012a. A Test of the Relation between Working-memory Capacity and Syntactic Island Effects. Language, 88, 82-123.

Sprouse, J., M. Wagers & C. Phillips. 2012b. Working-memory Capacity and Island Effects: A Reminder of the Issues and the Facts. Language 88, 401-407.

Stowe, L. A. 1986. Parsing Wh-constructions: Evidence for On-line Gap Location. Language and Cognitive Processes, 227-45.

White, L. and A. Juffs. 1998. Constraints on Wh-movement in Two Different Contexts of Non-native Language Acquisition: Competence and Processing. In Flynn, S., G. Martohardjono & W. O'Neil (eds), The Generative Study of Second Language Acquisition, 111-129. Erlbaum, Hillsdale, NJ.

Williams, J. N., P. Mobius & C. Kim. 2001. Native and Non-native Processing of English Wh-questions: Parsing strategies and Plausibility Constraints. Applied Psycholinguistics, 22, 509-540.

De-verbalization and Nominal Categories in Mandarin Chinese:

A corpus-driven study in both Mainland Mandarin and Taiwan Mandarin

Jiajuan Xiong
Department of Chinese and Bilingual Studies
The Hong Kong Polytechnic University
Hong Kong
jiajuanx@gmail.com

Chu-Ren Huang
Department of Chinese and Bilingual Studies
The Hong Kong Polytechnic University
Hong Kong
churen.huang@polyu.edu.hk

Abstract

This paper probes into the issue of de-verbalization in Chinese by starting from two potential and innovative uses of de-verbalization in Mainland Mandarin and Taiwan Mandarin, respectively. Then, we move to the exploration of various nominal categories in Chinese, with regard to their grammatical behaviors as well as their ontological differences. Crucially, we find that nominal categories in Chinese diverge upon individualization, which can be realized along either spatial or temporal dimension, as evidenced by the application of different types of classifiers. Specifically, event nouns and deverbal nouns allow temporal individualization only, while *xingwei*-marked nouns are exclusively compatible with spatial individualization. By contrast, entity nouns and *dongzuo*-marked nouns allow both spatial and temporal individualization. Hence, individualization is the key to our understanding of nominal categories in Chinese.

1 Introduction

This paper starts from examining two newly-emergent uses in Mainland Mandarin (MM) and Taiwan Mandarin (TM) and moves to the investigation of de-verbalization in Mandarin Chinese in section 2. In section 3 and 4, we probe into the grammatical behaviors and the ontological foundations of various nominal categories, respectively.

1.1 [*gezhong* 'all kinds of' + VP/AP] in MM

The function of classifiers is to modify nouns. However, it is found that the generic kind classifier *zhong* 'kind' (Huang 2015), in the form of *gezhong* 'each-kind; all kinds of', is frequently utilized to modify a verb phrase or an adjectival phrase in the social media. This use is noted as [*gezhong* 'all kinds of' + VP/AP]. The following examples (1) – (3) are extracted from *baidu* website for the sake of illustration.[1]

(1) Meng bao men bei wangyou **ge**
adorable child PL BEI cyber-pals each
zhong chengzan.
CL-kind praise
'The adorable children are praised so much by the cyber pals.'

(2) Xinwen wa wa wa, zhe yi ji haokan,
news PN the one CL interesting
ge zhong ma women.
each CL-kind abuse us
'This episode of News Wawawa is especially interesting. It abuses us in various ways.'

(3) Dang ma de dou zheyang, dui haizi
be mother DE all this_way to child
ge zhong xihuan.
each CL-kind like
'Mothers are always like this. They like their children in various ways/so much.'

1.2 [(*yi* 'one' + CL) + VP + (*de*) +

[1] Most of the examples in this paper are corpora data, of which the sources are indicated at the end of the sentences. Specifically, SC refers to Sinica Corpus and CCL the corpus constructed by the Chinese Center of Linguistics of Peking University.

29th Pacific Asia Conference on Language, Information and Computation pages 431 - 438
Shanghai, China, October 30 - November 1, 2015

***dongzuo* 'action'] in TM**

In Taiwan Mandarin, a verb phrase can be suffixed with the light noun *dongzuo* 'action', which allows the optional application of classifiers. This usage is exemplified in (4) - (6).

(4) Dan you zuo **yi ge yongbao de**
but have do one CL hug DE
dongzuo. (news)
action
'But I've conducted an action of hugging.'

(5) Bu jianyi touziren cishi, zai zuo
NEG recommend investor now again do
renhe jiama de dongzuo. (SC)
any raise_the_investment DE action
'It is not recommendable for investors to increase their investment in any forms.'

(6) Wu xu zuo **shanchu zhi dongzuo**. (SC)
NEG need do delete DE action
'There is no need to do any deleting action.'

1.3 The commonality between the two patterns

Those usages reported in 1.1 and 1.2 are parallel in the sense that de-verbalization is arguably involved in both cases. This is realized either by the application of a classifier *zhong* and/or the addition of a light noun *dongzuo* 'action'. Despite of being de-verbalized, they still serve as predicates in the above examples. This first case instantiates nominal predicates (Tang 1979; Zhu 1982; Tang 2001, 2002; Wei 2007, Zhang 2009), while the second case features the use of a light verb, such as *zuo* 'do' in (4) – (6).

These two innovative uses motivate us to explore de-verbalization, in particular, the mechanisms through which de-verbalization is realized.

2 De-verbalization

2.1 Zero-marked de-verbalization

De-verbalization needs not to be morphologically marked in Chinese (Huang 2015; Huang and Shi 2016), as evidenced by the free use of deverbal nouns. For examples, the verb *youyong* 'swim' can also be used as a deverbal noun in the following examples:

(7) a. Wo xihuan **youyong**.
1SG like swim
'I like swimming.'

b. **Youyong** hen youqu.
swim very interesting
'Swimming is interesting.'

2.2 Coercion-induced de-verbalization

The second attested mechanism of de-verbalization is coercion, by which a nominal feature is imposed on a verbal category. This can be illustrated by the application of classifiers to a verbal category, as in the case of [*gezhong* 'all kinds of' + VP/AP] presented in 1.1.

2.3 De-verbalization by means of the addition of a light noun

2.3.1 *dongzuo* 'action' as a light noun

The third attested mechanism of de-verbalization is the addition of a light noun to a verb or a verb phrase, with the possible assistance of *de*. What we presented in 1.2 in Taiwan Mandarin can instantiate this mechanism. In fact, a similar usage, albeit being rare, is also attested in Mainland Mandarin, as shown in (8).

(8) <u>*dongzuo* 'action' in MM (CCL)</u>
a. puying de dongzuo
catch_firefly DE action
'the action of catching fireflies'
b. fa fu de dongzuo
pronounce [f] DE action
'the action of pronouncing [f]'

It is noteworthy that the *dongzuo*-induced de-verbalization differs between Mainland Mandarin and Taiwan Mandarin in that the addition of *dongzuo* in MM is basically restricted to verbs and verb phrases denoting bodily actions, whereas the same mechanism in TM is applicable to various kinds of actions, be they concrete or abstract.

2.3.2 *xingwei* 'behavior' as a light noun

In fact, *dongzuo* 'action' is not the only light noun that can convert a verbal category into a nominal one. The light noun *xingwei* 'behavior' can serve the similar function in both MM and TM. This is illustrated in (9) and (10) below.

(9) <u>*xingwei* 'behavior' in MM (CCL)</u>
a. caichan rangdu xingwei
property transfer behavior
'the behavior of transferring property'
b. mofang mingxing de xingwei
mimic celebrity DE behavior
'the behavior of mimicking celebrities'

(10) <u>*xingwei* 'behavior' in TM (SC)</u>
a. jiechu xingwei
lend bebavior
'the behavior of lending'
b. liandan fuer de
do_alchemy consume_product DE

xingwei
behavior
'the behavior of doing alchemy and consuming alchemy products'

2.3.3 *dongzuo* 'action' versus *xingwei* 'behavior'

Even though both *dongzuo* 'action' and *xingwei* 'behavior' can be attached to a verbal category to produce a nominal category, they differ in at least two major points:

Firstly, *dongzuo* 'action' and *xingwei* 'behavior' are modified by different types of classifiers. We follow Huang & Ahrens (2003) and Ahrens & Huang (2016) to identify three subtypes of classifiers, viz. individual, kind and event classifiers, as exemplified by *ge* 'piece', *lei* 'kind', and *lun* 'round', respectively. The corpus data show that *dongzuo*-marked nominal can collocate with both individual and event classifiers, while *xingwei*-marked nominal is compatible with individual and kind classifiers. This is exemplified in (11) and (12).

(11) <u>the collocation between *dongzuo* and classifiers</u>
a. yi **ge** yongbao de dongzuo
one CL hug DE action
'a hugging action' (individual classifier)
b. ling yi **bo** caiche de dongzuo
another one CL lay_off DE action
'another turn of laying off action'
(event classifier)

(12) <u>the collocation between *xingwei* and classifiers</u>
a. yi **xiang** jiaoyi xingwei
one CL trade behavior
'one trading behavior'
(individual classifier)
b. zhe **zhong** pohuai xingwei
this CL destroy behavior
'this destroying behavior' (kind classifier)

Further consultation work with our informants shows that *xingwei*-marked nouns are incompatible with event classifiers, while *dongzuo*-marked nouns are compatible with kind classifiers, even though the latter is unattested in the corpus examined.

Secondly, unlike *dongzuo* 'action', *xingwei* 'behavior' barely collaborates with a light verb. In fact, only two instances (out of 801) of the collocation between *xingwei* 'behavior' and a light verb are attested, as cited in (13) and (14).

(13) huo zai haishang **congshi** haidao
or at sea_on do pirate
xingwei de maoxian shangren. (SC)
behavior DE adventure merchant
'those merchants who conduct the behavior of being pirates'

(14) ruo zhongjie danwei fei shu yiliao
if agency unit not belong medical
jigou, er **jinxing** yiliao
institution but do medical_treatment
xingwei... (SC)
behavior
'If an agent is not affiliated to any medical institution but conducts medical treatment...'

Based on the above two differences, we conclude that *dongzuo*-marked nominal and *xingwei*-marked nominal are of different types. Specifically, *dongzuo*-marked nominal is an event noun while *xingwei*-marked nominal tends to be an entity noun. This distinction becomes clearer in section 3 and 4.

To sum up, we have examined three mechanisms of de-verbalization in Mandarin Chinese, viz. zero-marked de-verbalization, coercion-induced de-verbalization and light-noun-motivated de-verbalization. These mechanisms help to enrich the nominal category in Mandarin Chinese. In the next section, we will explore various types of nouns, from both grammatical and ontological perspectives. Moreover, we will study how the endurant/perduant dichotomy (Huang 2015) is embodied in various Chinese nominal categories.

3 Various Nominal Categories: how heterogeneous are they?

3.1 Five nominal categories

The nominal category is usually defined as opposed to the verbal category. The former is basically referential while the latter indicates events or states along the dimension of time. However, as far as both grammatical behaviors and conceptual bases are concerned, the distinction is usually unclear. As Huang (2015: 6) points out, the nominal/verbal distinction can be easily blurred with many categorical change devices in language as well as with atypical members of each PoS: such as event nouns, deverbal nominal, denominal verbs etc. Relevant to this current study are various types of nominal categories, such as entity nouns, event nouns, deverbal nouns, *dongzuo*-marked nouns and *xingwei*-marked nouns. They are exemplified in (15) – (19).

(15) The entity nouns:
shu; ren
'book' 'person'

(16) The event nouns:
huiyi, bisai
'meeting' 'contest'

(17) The deverbal nouns:
youyong, kanshu
'swimming' 'reading'

(18) The *dongzuo*-marked nouns:
xiadun dongzuo;
squat action
'the action of squatting';
shanchu zhi dongzuo
delete DE action
'the action of deleting'

(19) The *xingwei*-marked nouns:
yiliao xingwei,
medical_treat behavior
'the behavior of medical treatment'
pohuai xingwei
destroy behavior
'the behavior of destroying'

In what follows, we will scrutinize the different types of nouns, with special regard to their collocation with classifiers, which reflect different conceptual saliency. Grammatically speaking, nouns in Chinese require the presence of classifiers for enumeration. Conceptually, classifiers form an ontological system (Huang 2015). In addition, Chinese is unique among classifier languages in the world to have classifiers for events and kinds in addition to individual objects (Huang and Ahrens 2003; Huang, 2015; Ahrens and Huang 2016). Based on the properties of classifiers, we will examine how different types of nouns interact with different types of classifiers in order to understand the conceptual differences among different nominal categories.

3.2 The interaction between nominal categories and classifiers

Prior to getting into the interaction issue, let us briefly review the three types of classifiers (Huang and Ahrens 2003; Huang 2015; Ahrens and Huang 2016), as in (20) – (22).

(20) Individual classifiers:
zhe **ben** shu
this CL book
'this book'

(21) Kind classifiers:
shier **zhong** dongwu
twelve CL animal
'twelve kinds of animals'

(22) Event classifiers:
yi **ban** che
one CL vehicle
'a scheduled run of transportation'

These three types of classifiers interact with nouns in different patterns.

Firstly, entity nouns are versatile in that they can co-occur with three types of classifiers. However, not all the entity nouns can collocate with event classifiers, as exemplified by the contrast (23b) and (24b).

(23) The entity noun *che* 'vehicle':
a. yi **liang** che (individual classifier)
one CL vehicle
'one vehicle'
b. yi **ban** che (event classifier)
one CL vehicle
'one scheduled run of vehicle'

(24) The entity noun *shu* 'book':
a. yi **ben** shu (individual classifier)
one CL book
'one book'
b. *yi **ci** shu (event classifier)
one CL book

The entity noun *che* 'vehicle' collocates with an individual classifier *liang* to refer to an identifiable entity, whereas it goes with an event classifier *ban* to indicate a scheduled run of vehicle. As already shown in the translation, the event classifier *ban* imposes an event meaning, i.e., running of vehicles, on the entity noun *che* 'vehicle'. These two classifiers embody two different types of individualization of nouns, viz. individualization along the spatial dimension and individualization along the temporal dimension. In other words, when an individual classifier is applied to an entity noun, the individualized entities can be said to exist simultaneously in the world and their individual-hood is obtained through their spatial differences. On the other hand, when an event noun modifies an entity noun, the individualized entities occupy different positions along the temporal dimension. However, such a difference may not be applicable to all the entity nouns. For instance, the entity noun *shu* 'book' defies individualization along the temporal dimension, even though *shu* 'book' can be naturally connected to actions like *kan-shu* 'read-book' and *xie-shu* 'write-book'. This might be due to the fact that the actions of reading and writing, albeit being conceptually important, are not salient enough to be encoded in the noun by means of the application of an event classifier. It seems that the saliency of an eventive element in an entity noun is determined, to a large extent, by the (scheduled) repeatability of an action with a large group of participants. This is corroborated by the uses of *yi* ***ban*** *che* 'one-CL-vehicle; a scheduled run of vehicle' and *yi* ***chang*** *dianying* 'one-CL-film; a scheduled show of a film'.

Secondly, we examine event nouns, as exemplified by *bisai* 'competition' and *huiyi* 'meeting', with regard to their compatibility with classifiers. An event noun usually requires the presence of an event classifier but not an individual classifier, as exemplified in the contrast between (25a) and (25c). When the meaning of "kind" is encoded, it requires the presence of a kind classifier, as shown in (25b).

(25) The event noun *bisai* 'competition':
  a. */??zhe **ge** bisai (individual classifier)
     this CL competition
     Intended: 'this competition'
  b. zhe **zhong** bisai (kind classifier)
     this CL competition
     'this kind of competition'
  c. zhe **chang** bisai (event classifier)
     this CL competition
     'this competition'

Thirdly, let us move to the zero-marked deverbal nouns, such as *youyong* 'swimming' and *kanshu* 'reading'. As illustrated in (26), a deverbal noun is most naturally compatible with an event classifier to refer to one instance of an action. An individual classifier is generally inapplicable, as an action is hardly individualized along a spatial dimension. A kind classifier is conditionally applicable to an event noun, when it is interpreted as a manner of conducting an action. However, it seems to us that the addition of a light manner noun, e.g., *fangshi* 'manner', is preferred in this case of a kind classifier.

(26) The deverbal noun *youyong* 'swimming':
  a. *zhe **ge** youyong (individual classifier)
     this CL swimming
  b. ?zhe **zhong** youyong (kind classifier)
     this CL swimming
     intended: 'this manner of swimming'
  c. zhe **ci** youyong (event classifier)
     this CL swimming
     'this (instance of) swimming'

Note that the application of a kind classifier to deverbal nouns differs between MM and TM. It is MM, but not TM, that allows the modification of a kind classifier *zhong*, on the condition that this kind classifier carries an all-around meaning in the form of *gezhong* 'all kinds of'. (Please refer to 1.1 for examples.)

Fourthly, we look at the grammatical behavior of *dongzuo*-marked nouns, which seem to be compatible with three types of classifiers, as shown in (27a-c).

(27) The *dongzuo*-marked noun: (TM)
  a. yi **ge** jiangjia de dongzuo
     one CL reduce_price DE action
     'an action of price-reduction'
     (individual classifier)
  b. zhe **zhong** jiangjia de dongzuo
     this CL reduce-price DE action
     'this action of price-reduction'
     (kind classifier)
  c. zhe **bo** jiangjia de dongzuo
     this CL reduce_price DE action
     'this turn of price-reduction action'
     (event classifier)

Recall that those uses in (27) are exclusive to TM (see section 2.3.1) and similar uses in MM are restricted to bodily actions. This restriction leads to a scarcity of *dongzuo*-marked nouns in MM.

Fifthly, we take a look at *xingwei*-marked nouns. The corpus data show that the most frequently-used classifier for *xingwei*-marked nouns is *zhong*, which is a generic kind classifier (Huang 2015), in addition to the rare cases of individual classifiers. However, neither the corpus data nor our consultation work testifies any compatibility between *xingwei*-marked nouns and event classifiers. They are illustrated in (28).

(28) The *xingwei*-marked noun:
  a. yi **xiang** jiaoyi xingwei
     one CL trade behavior
     'one trading behavior'
     (individual classifier)
  b. zhe **zhong** qipian ziji de xingwei
     this CL cheat oneself DE behavior
     'the behavior of cheating oneself'
     (kind classifier)
  c. *yi **ci** qipian ziji de xingwei

one CL cheat oneself DE behavior
(event classifier)

We summarize the above discussions in the following two tables. Table 1 shows how the five nominal categories in MM interact with different types of classifiers. Table 2 is illustrative of the same interactive patterns in TM.

	entity noun	event noun	deverbal noun	V-*dongzuo*	V-*xing*
individual classifier	√	X	X	√	√
kind classifier	√	√	√ (*gezhong*)	√	
event classifier	√ (occasional)	√	√	?	

Table 1: Nominal Categories in MM

	entity noun	event noun	deverbal noun	V-*dongzuo*
individual classifier	√	X	X	√
kind classifier	√	√	X	√
event classifier	√ (occasional)	√	√	√

Table 2: Nominal Categories in TM

(The yellow areas indicate the uses which involve semantic coercion; whereas the purple areas refer to those novel uses which are enforced by coercion.)

3.3 The differences between MM and TM

Basically, the interactive patterns between nominal categories and classifiers are very similar, except in the case of deverbal nouns and *dongzuo*-marked nouns. In fact, the differences are mainly confined to those innovative uses, as reported in section 1. A verb category in MM can undergo de-verbalization through the mechanism of classifier-induced coercion. While in TM, de-verbalization resorts to another mechanism, viz. the addition of a light noun *dongzuo* 'action' to a verbal category.

3.4 The differences between *dongzuo* 'action' and *xingwei* 'behavior'

Another crucial point that is worth pointing out is the differences between *dongzuo*- and *xingwei*-marked nominal categories. In fact, *dongzuo* 'action' and *xingwei* 'behavior' are synonymous and can co-occur to refer to one's behaviors in the general sense, as exemplified in (31).

(29) Dalu cengjing fasheng guo
mainland before happen PERF
wenhua da geming, ta suoyou de
culture big revolution it all DE
dongzuo he **xingwei**, he rujia shi
action and behavior with Confucian be
nayang de bu xianghe…(SC)
so DE NEG consistent
'The cultural revolution once happened in Mainland China. Therefore, the actions and behaviors there are not consistent with Confucian (culture)…'

Despite the semantic similarity, *dongzuo* and *xingwei*, which are nominal markers in this study, crucially differ in terms of their interaction with classifiers. We find that *dongzuo*-marked nouns pattern with event nouns whereas *xingwei*-marked nouns on a par with entity nouns. Two pieces of evidence can help to support this claim. First, *xingwei*-marked nouns defy modification by any event classifiers, while *dongzuo*-marked nouns do not have this restriction. Recall that many entity nouns are basically compatible with individual and kind classifiers, and only a small portion of entity nouns can be compatible with event classifiers under the coercion mechanism. Regarding *dongzuo*- and *xingwei*-marked nouns, it is the former, but not the latter, that can be compatible with event classifiers. Given this, *xingwei*-marked nouns should fall into the category of entity nouns. Second, *xingwei*-marked nouns cannot collocate with a light verb to serve as a predicate. By contrast, *dongzuo*-marked nouns can easily collocate with a light verb to function as a predicate.[2] This is indeed characteristic of event nouns.

---

[2] This usage is much more frequently used in TM than in MM. This contrast should be ascribed to the fact that *dongzuo* in MM is mostly restricted to bodily actions. This restriction, however, does not apply in TM. Despite of this semantic restriction in MM, when it comes to a bodily action, *dongzuo* can still co-occur with a light verb, as exemplified below:

(i) zuo yi ge dunxia de dongzuo (CCL)
do one CL squat DE action
'conduct an action of squatting'

Therefore, the scarcity of this usage in MM cannot undermine our analysis of *dongzuo*–marked nouns as event nouns. Crucially, the replacement of *dongzuo* with *xingwei* will lead to unacceptability, which holds true in both MM and TM, as shown in (ii).

(ii) *zuo yi ge dunxia de xingwei
do one CL squat DE behavior
intended: 'conduct an action of squatting'

4. Various Nominal Categories: their ontological differences

In section 3, our study revolves around the grammatical behaviors of the different nominal categories. In this section, we will explore their ontological or conceptual differences.

All of the afore-mentioned nouns exhibit the endurant property (Huang 2015).[3] The semantic denominator of various types of nominal categories lies in their referentiality. However, they differ in how they are individualized for enumeration. In particular, we identify two types of conceptually different individualization, i.e. separation into countable objects which exist simultaneously as separable individuals; and separation into countable objects which exist along the temporal dimension. Put differently, there are both spatial and temporal ways for individualization. In fact, the application of individual classifiers and event classifiers exactly reflects these two individualization mechanisms. Let us now examine how the five nominal categories execute their respective individualization.

At this point, the use of classifiers, in particular, individual and event classifiers, can be revealing with regard to the ontological differences of nominal categories, given that Chinese classifier system itself forms an ontological system (Huang 2015). Our approach is to place nominal categories into a matrix with both spatial (horizontal) and temporal (vertical) dimensions and see how individualization is realized. Our analyses show that some nominal categories allow individualization to be executed along one single dimension, either spatial or temporal. In fact, event nouns and deverbal nouns can only be individualized along the temporal dimension, while *xingwei*-marked nouns along the spatial dimension. Some other nominal categories, such as entity nouns and *dongzuo*-marked nouns, allow individualization in two different dimensions. For example, when entity nouns collocate with event classifiers, the entity nouns are individualized into sequentially different objects/events, by means of coercion. In the similar vein, *dongzuo*-marked nouns, albeit being originally verbal, can be wrapped into nominal objects along the spatial dimension through conceptual conversion.

All these mechanisms for individualization are exemplified from (32) to (36).[4]

(32) The entity noun *feiji* 'plane':
a. yi **jia** feiji (individual classifier)
one CL plane
'one plane'
b. yi **ban** feiji (event classifier)
one CL plane
'one scheduled flight'

(33) The event noun *bisai* 'competition':
yi **chang** bisai (event classifier)
one CL competition
'one competition'

(34) The deverbal noun *youyong* 'swimming':
Yi **ci** youyong (event classifier)
one CL swimming
'one instance of swimming'

(35) The *dongzuo*-marked noun:
a. yi ge jiangjia de dongzuo
one CL reduce_price DE action
'one action of price-reduction'
(individual classifier)
b. yi **bo** jiangjia de dongzuo
one CL reduce_price DE action
'a round of price-reduction'
(event classifier)

(36) The *xingwei*-marked noun:
yi **xiang** jiaoyi xingwei
one CL trade behavior
'one trading behavior'
(individual classifier)

For the sake of explanation, we place the five nominal categories into their respective two-dimensional matrix to illustrate how individualization is realized in each case. They are shown in Figure 1 to 5.

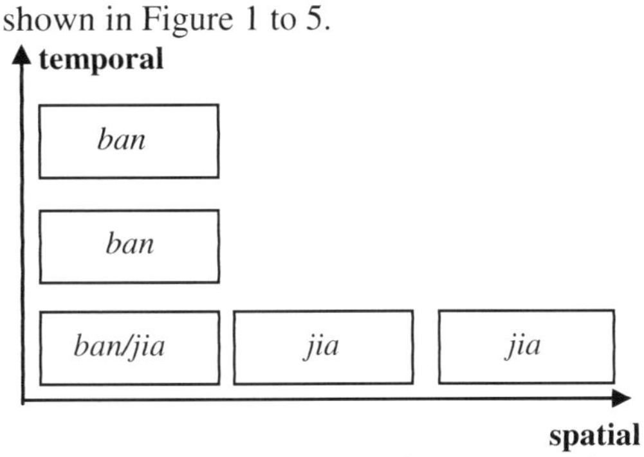

Figure 1: The individualization of *feiji* 'plane'

[3] Please see Huang (2015) for the detailed discussions on the dichotomy between endurant and perduant.

[4] We do not consider kind classifiers here, as they are conceptually in line with individual classifiers in that both of them realize individualization on the spatial dimension.

(an entity noun)

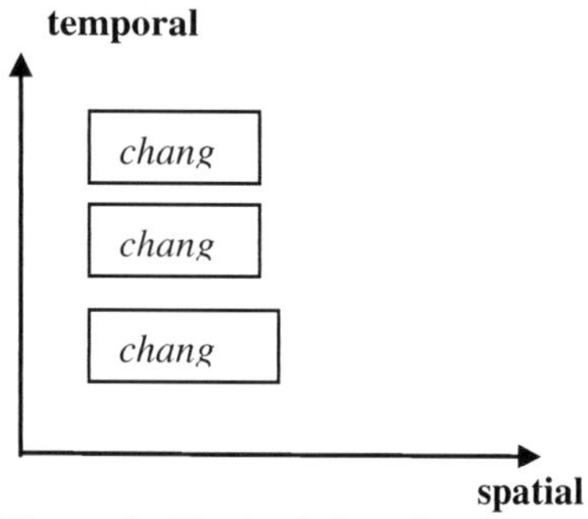

Figure 2: The individualization of *bisai* 'competition' (an event noun)

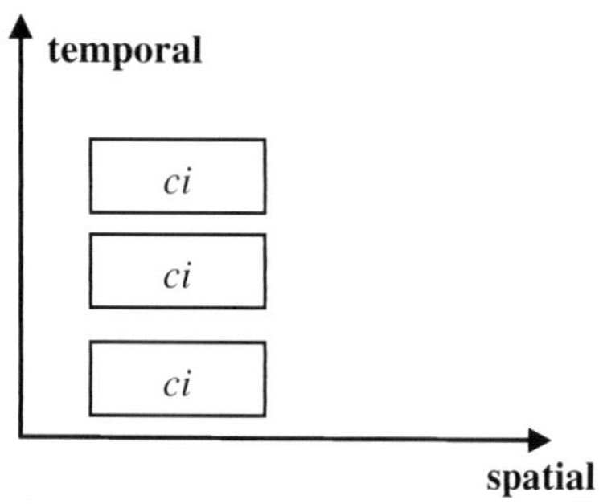

Figure 3: The individualization of *youyong* 'swimming' (a deverbal noun)

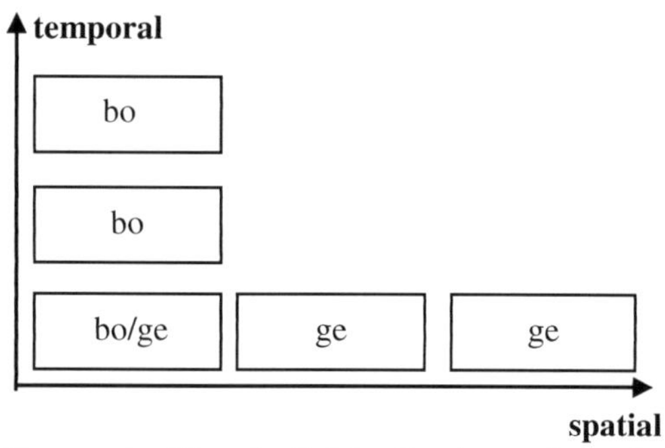

Figure 4: The individualization of a *dongzuo*-marked noun

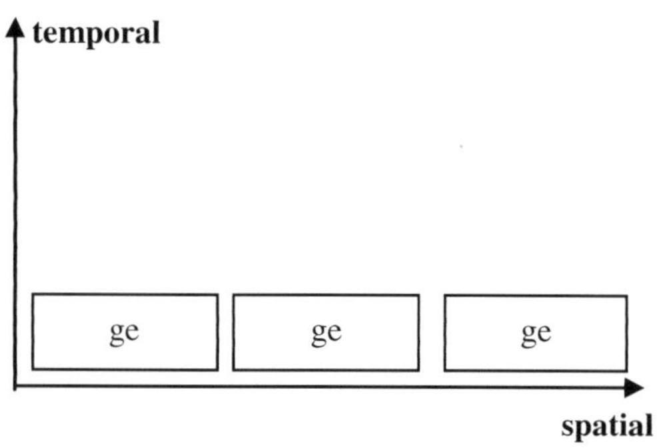

Figure 5: The individualization of a *xingwei*-marked noun

It is noteworthy that the temporal standard for individualization, in particular, in the case of event classifiers, does not undermine Huang's (2015) statement that a classifier serves as a linguistic device to express a defining property of a type of time-invariant entities. In fact, our proposal that individualization can be temporal is in the sense of comparison among various instances of the same nominal (e.g., this instance of meeting; that instance of meeting). If we place our vantage point onto one and the same nominal phrase, this nominal phrase must be time-independent, as in the case of *zhe ci bisai* 'this competition'.

References

Ahrens Kathleen and Chu-Ren Huang. 2016. Classifiers. In *A Reference Grammar of Chinese*, eds. Chu-Ren Huang and Dingxu Shi. Cambridge: Cambridge University Press.

Huang Chu-Ren and Kathleen Ahrens. 2003. Individuals, Kinds and Events: Classifier Coercion of Nouns. *Language Sciences* 25 (4). 2003: 353-373.

Huang Chu-Ren. 2015. Notes on Chinese Grammar and Ontology: the endurant/perduant dichotomy and Mandarin D-M compounds. *Lingua Sinica*.

Huang Chu-Ren and Shi Dingxu. 2016. *A Reference Grammar of Chinese*. Cambridge: Cambridge University Press.

Huang, C. R., Lin, J., Jiang, M., & Xu, H. (2014). Corpus-based Study and Identification of Mandarin Chinese Light Verb Variations. *COLING 2014*, 1.

Lin, Jingxia, Xu, Hongzhi, Jiang, Menghan and Huang, Chu-Ren. 2014. Annotation and Classification of Light Verbs and Light Verb Variations in Mandarin Chinese. In *Workshop on Lexical and Grammatical Resources for Language Processing* (p. 75)

Tang, Sze-Wing. 2001. Nominal predication and focus anchoring. In Gerhard Ja_ger, Anatoli Strigin, Chris Wilder, and Niina Zhang, eds., ZAS Papers in Linguistics 22: 159-172.

Tang, Sze-Wing. 2002. Economy principles and Chinese verbless sentence. Modern Foreign Languages 95: 1-13.

Tang, Ting-Chi. 1979. Studies in Chinese syntax. Taipei: Student Book Company.

Wei, Ting-Chi. 2004. Predication and sluicing in Mandarin Chinese. Ph.D. Dissertation, National Kaohsiung Normal University.

Wei, Ting-Chi. 2007. Nominal Predicates in Mandarin Chinese. *Taiwan Journal of Linguistics*. Vol. 5.2, 85-130.

Zhang Qingwen. 2009. On the syntax of non-verbal predication in Mandarin Chinese. Ph.D. dissertation at The Hong Kong Polytechnic University.

Zhu, Dexi. 1982. Yufa jiangyi (Lectures on grammar). Beijing: Commercial Press.

Zero Object Resolution in Korean

Arum Park
Dept. of German Linguistics & Literature, Sungkyunkwan University /
25-2, Sungkyunkwan-Ro, Jongno-Gu,
Seoul, Korea
remin2@skku.edu

Seunghee Lim
Dept. of German Linguistics & Literature, Sungkyunkwan University /
25-2, Sungkyunkwan-Ro, Jongno-Gu,
Seoul, Korea
rusilen21@skku.edu

Munpyo Hong*
Dept. of German Linguistics & Literature, Sungkyunkwan University /
25-2, Sungkyunkwan-Ro, Jongno-Gu,
Seoul, Korea
skkhmp@skku.edu

Abstract

Korean is one of the well-known 'pro-drop' languages. When translating Korean zero object into languages in which objects have to be overtly expressed, the resolution of zero object is crucial. This paper proposes a machine learning method to resolve Korean zero object. We proposed 8 linguistically motivated features for ML (Machine Learning). Our approach has been implemented with WEKA 3.6.10 and evaluated by using 10-fold cross validation method. The accuracy of the proposed method reached 73.37%.

1 Introduction

Korean is one of the so-called pro-drop languages. Certain pronouns may be omitted and the omitted pronouns are often called zero pronouns. This kind of pronoun also occurs in other languages, such as Japanese or Spanish. The omitted pronouns in Korean can appear in subject and object position, whereas in Spanish or Italian, they can appear only in subject position. A zero subject is the most frequent type of anaphoric expressions in Korean. Hong (2000) reported that about 57% of the pronouns are a zero subject pronoun in pronoun occurrences in Korean spoken text.

* Corresponding author

Zero object is the second most frequent zero pronoun type in Korean spoken text. Despite of the frequent use of zero objects, most of the previous works do not deal with the zero objects in Korean. In this work, we focus on Korean spoken texts, since zero pronouns occur more frequently than in a written text. Ryu (2001) showed that a zero pronoun rarely appears in written texts when it is compared with spoken texts in Korean. For this reason, we conduct a study for Korean zero object in Korean spoken text and try to find the linguistic clues for the zero object resolution.

In the context of machine translation, the resolution of Korean zero objects could be one of the most important issues in order to translate them into the target language like English and German. One of the reasons that zero objects in Korean is a problem in MT is that the omitted objects in Korean have to be translated into overt objects in target languages. Unfortunately, the majority of MT systems do not deal with this problem, because most of the current commercial MT systems do not treat the linguistic phenomena that go beyond a sentence level. To illustrate this issue, let's take a look at the following example (1).

(1) MT results from Korean(a) to German(b)

(a) Korean

A: 여권$_i$을 분실했습니다.

29th Pacific Asia Conference on Language, Information and Computation pages 439 - 448
Shanghai, China, October 30 - November 1, 2015

a passport-OBJ lost
(yekwenul punsilhaysssupnita.)

"I lost a passport."

B: øi 다시 발급받으셔야 합니다.
again have to issue
(tasi palkuppatusyeya hapnita.)

"You have to issue a passport again."

(b1) German - Systran translator

A: Verlor den Pass.
B: Fragen wiederholt.

(b2) German - Google translator

A: Ich habe meinen Pass verloren.
B: Wir müssen neu aufgelegt zu werden.

The omitted object is represented by the symbol ø. In this example, the Korean object is not overtly expressed in the sentence B and it refers to '여권'(yekwen, "Passport") in sentence A. To translate the omitted object into German correctly, the gender and number of the antecedent 'yekwen' has to be considered. Since the morphological information of 'yekwen' is 'masculine' and 'singular' in German, the omitted object has to be translated as 'ihn' considering its case. However, the object of the sentence B is not translated in German in either MT system. Then, the results would be ungrammatical in German. Therefore, the resolution of Korean zero objects is crucial in MT systems with Korean as a source language, when translating them into languages in which objects have to be overtly expressed.

In section 2 we present the related works about anaphora resolution and their limitation. Section 3 explains zero objects phenomenon in Korean. We suggest the machine learning (ML) method for Korean zero object resolution and propose 8 features for ML method in section 4. In addition, the effect of using ML is evaluated. Finally, the conclusion is presented in section 5.

2 Related Works

Zero pronouns have already been studied in other languages, such as Japanese (e.g. Nakaiwa and Shirai, 1996; Okumura and Tamura, 1996) and Spanish (Park and Hong, 2014; Palomar et al., 2001; Ferrández and Peral, 2000). These studies are based on the researches about anaphora resolution. It has been a wide-open research field since 1970 focusing on English. Regardless of languages, similar strategies for anaphora resolution have been applied. Using linguistic information is the most representative technique; constraints and preferences methods are distinguished in the related works (Baldwin, 1997; Lappin and Leass, 1994; Carbonell and Brown, 1988).

Constraints discard possible antecedents and are considered as absolute criteria. Preferences being proposed as heuristic rules tend to be relative. After applying constraints, if there are still unresolved candidate antecedents, preferences set priorities among candidate antecedents. Nakaiwa and Shirai (1996) focus on semantic and pragmatic constraints such as cases, modal expressions, verbal semantic attributes and conjunctions in order to determine the reference of Japanese zero pronouns. However, they proposed constraints focusing on zero subjects mainly. Therefore, it is hard to apply their approach on zero object resolution.

Centering theory (Grosz et al., 1995) is one of the approaches using heuristic rules. It is claimed that certain entities mentioned in an utterance are more central than others, and this property has been applied to determine the antecedent of the anaphor. Walker et al. (1994) applied the centering model on zero pronoun resolution in Japanese. Roh and Lee (2003) proposed a generation algorithm of zero pronouns using a Cost-based Centering Model which considers the inference cost. It is known that the most salient element of the given discourse is likely to be realized as a zero pronoun. We take this into account in selecting the features for ML.

Current anaphora resolution methods rely mainly on constraint and preference heuristics, which employ morpho-syntactic information or shallow semantic analysis. These methods are a deterministic algorithm which always produces the same output in a given particular condition. However, even if the condition is applied, the output can be wrong. ML methods which are a non-deterministic algorithm have been studied on anaphora resolution (Connolly et al., 1994; Paul et al., 1999). Since ML learns from data and makes predictions of the most likely candidate on the data, it can overcome the limitation of the deterministic method.

Park and Hong (2014) proposed a hybrid approach to resolve Spanish zero subjects that integrates heuristic rules and ML in the context of Spanish to Korean MT. Since Spanish zero subjects can be restored from the verb ending, they use morphological flections for verbs. After that, ML is utilized for some ambiguous cases. Unlike this work, our work deals with Korean zero object. Morphological information cannot be utilized for Korean because of the difference of the two languages. For this reason, we use ML method alone to determine the antecedent of the zero objects in spoken Korean.

3 Zero object phenomenon in Korean

A prominent phenomenon in Korean is the prevalence of zero pronouns. Unlike English, zero pronouns occur very frequently in Korean. In Korean, a zero subject is the most frequent type of anaphoric expression. The second most frequent type is zero objects, especially when the direct object is omitted. According to Hong (2000), when the direct object does not occur in spoken Korean, the rate becomes 19.1%.

To resolve zero object, centering theory can be utilized. The centering theory endeavors to identify the antecedent of a (zero) pronoun using the idea of the most central entity that a sentence concerns which tends to be expressed by a (zero) pronoun. There are some studies attempting to apply the centering theory to anaphora resolution (Choi and Lee, 1999; Hong, 2000; Hong, 2011). The forward looking center rankings for Korean are defined differently in the studies. Following Hong (2011)'s discussion, we accept the forward looking center ranking for Korean as follows:

· *Forward looking center ranking for Korean (Hong, 2011)*

TOPIC > SUBJECT > OBJECT > ADVERB > OTHERS

Given the hierarchy of the forward looking center ranking, a zero object can be interpreted as the topic which is the most salient discourse entity. The topic of the sentence contributes to discourse salience and maintains discourse coherence by preferring the CONTINUE transition state. The topic of the sentence can be detected easily in Korean using the topic markers '은'(eun), '는'(nun) and delimiters such as '도'(to), '만'(man). Therefore, it is likely a candidate antecedent is the antecedent of the zero object if the candidate has one of the topic markers or delimiters. We can see some examples in the following table.

Speaker	Korean dialogue
A	음식 주문$_1$을 ordering a food-OBJ (umsik cumunul 어떻게 하는 거죠? how can ettehkey hanun kecyo?) "How can I order a food?"
B	저 기계$_2$에서 메뉴$_3$를 that machine-ADV menu-OBJ (ce kikyeyeyse menyulul 선택한 후 식권$_4$을 after selecting a meal ticket-OBJ senthaykhan hu sikkwenul 뽑으세요. buy ppopuseyyo.) "You can buy a meal ticket after selecting menu from that vending machine."
A	아침 식사$_5$는 11 시까지만 breakfast-TOP until 11 o'clock (achim siksanun 11sikkaciman 되는 건가요? is possible to toynun kenkayo?) "Is it possible to have breakfast until 11 o'clock?"
B	네, 지금 Yes, right now (ney, cikum 정확히 11 시니까

	because it's 11 o'clock cenghwakhi 11sinikka ø 원하신다면 ø 해 드릴게요. if you want can serve wenhasintamyen hay tulilkeyyo.) "Yes, if you want, I can serve you a breakfast because it's 11 o'clock right now."
A	감사합니다. thank you (kamsahapnita.) "Thank you."

Table 1 dialogue example including topic markers

In table 1, the dialogue's omitted object is represented by the symbol ø. There are 5 candidate antecedents: 1. '음식 주문' (umsik cumun, "order"), 2. '기계' (kikyey, "machine"), 3. '메뉴' (menyu, "menu"), 4. '식권' (sikkwen, "meal ticket"), 5. '아침 식사' (achim siksa, "breakfast"). The first, third and fourth candidates occur in the object position, the second candidate is in the adverb position, and the last candidate has a topic marker 'nun'. Since the topic is the highest position of the forward looking center ranking, the last candidate is likely to be the antecedent of the zero object.

Speaker	Korean dialogue
A	무슨 일 있으신가요? what happened (musun il issusinkayo?) "What happened?"
B	화장실 $_1$ 에 휴지 $_2$ 가 in toilet-ADV toilet tissue-TOP (hwacangsiley hucika 없어서요. is not eppseseyo.) "There is no toilet paper in the restroom."
A	잠시만요. wait a minute (camsimanyo.) "Wait a minute."
A	제가 ø 꺼내 드릴게요. I-SUBJ will give (ceyka kkenay tulilkeyo.) "I'll give it to you."
B	알겠습니다. all right (alkeysssupnita.) "All right."

Table 2 dialogue example of syntactic function

In this case, there are 2 candidate antecedents for the zero object which are '화장실' (hwacangsil, "restroom") and '휴지' (huci, "toilet tissue"). Since the second candidate has the higher raking in the forward looking center ranking than the first one, it can be the antecedent of the zero object, and this is actually the case. As the syntactic function of the candidate antecedents is important to resolve Korean zero object, we utilize this information.

Property-sharing constraint can also be the clue to resolve Korean zero object. Kameyama (1986) suggested property-sharing constraint of zero pronouns in Japanese. She claimed that if a zero pronoun is the subject of a verb, the antecedent is perhaps a subject in the antecedent's sentence. In addition, if a zero pronoun is an object, the antecedent is highly likely an object. Since Japanese and Korean share many of their linguistic properties, we can apply this constraint to resolve Korean zero object. The following table shows an example of property-sharing constraint.

Speaker	Korean dialogue
A	제 애완동물 $_1$ 을 my pet-OBJ (cey aywantongmulul 잃어버렸습니다. have lost ilhepelyesssupnita.) "I have lost my pet."
B	$ø_1$ 어디서 잃어버리셨나요? where have lost (etise ilhepelisyessnayo?)

	"Where have you lost her?"	
A	객실 $_2$ 에서 나오면서 room-ADV when come out of (kayksileyse naomyense 사라졌습니다. disappeared salacyesssupnita.) "She disappeared when I came out of the room."	
B	모두 찾아보셨나요? everywhere have been looking for (motu chacaposyessnayo?) "Have you been looking for her everywhere?"	
A	관리실 $_3$ 빼고는 except management office-ADV (kwanlisil ppaykonun 다 찾아봤습니다. all have been looking for ta chacapwasssupnita.) "I have been looking for her everywhere except for the management office."	
B	그럼 저희 직원들 $_4$ 이 then our staff-SUBJ (kulem cehuy cikwentuli $ø_2$ 찾아보겠습니다. will look for chacapokeyssupnita.) "Then our staff will look for her there."	

Table 3 dialogue example of property-sharing constraint

In the above examples, there are 4 candidate antecedents for the second zero object. From the candidate antecedents, the first candidate '애완동물' (aywantongmul, "pet") is the antecedent of the zero object. Even if there is an entity which has ranked higher in the forward looking center ranking, the farthest candidate which is in the object position as the zero object is the antecedent of the second zero object. This is one of examples showing the property-sharing constraint. Therefore, the parallelism of syntactic function between a zero object and a candidate antecedent can be utilized.

The semantic relation between the predicate of a zero object and a candidate antecedent is another property of Korean zero object. When the semantic of the predicates correlates between a zero object and a candidate antecedent, the candidate preferred to be the antecedent of the zero object.

Speaker	Korean dialogue
A	어디 가시나요? where are you going (eti kasinayo?) "Where are you going?"
B	콘서트 $_1$ 를 관람하러 갑니다. concert-OBJ go to watch (khonsethulul kwanlamhale kapnita.) "I go to (watch) the concert."
A	이미 콘서트 광장 $_2$ 은 already the concert hall-TOP (imi khonsethu kwangcangun 사람 $_3$ 이 많아서 people-SUBJ many salami manhase 들어가실 수 없습니다. can't enter to tulekasil su epssupnita.) "You can't enter the concert hall because there are already too many people."
B	저도 좀 $ø_1$ 관람하고 싶습니다. I-SUBJ want to watch (ceto com kwanlamhako sipsupnita.) "I want to watch the concert, too."
A	좀 일찍 오셨더라면 $ø_2$ earliy if you have come (com ilccik osyesstelamyen 볼 수 있었을 겁니다. could see pol su issessul kepnita.) "If you had come earlier, then you could have seen the concert."

Table 4 dialogue example (1) including semantic relation of predicates

Table 4 shows the importance of utilizing semantic between the predicate of the candidate antecedents and the zero objects. In this case, there are three candidate antecedents: 1. '콘서트' (khonsethu, "concert"), 2. '콘서트 광장' (khonsethu kwangcang, "concert hall"), 3. '사람' (salam, "people"). Even though the last two candidates have the higher syntactic function than the first one, the first candidate 'khonsethu' is the antecedent of the zero objects, because the first candidate and the first zero object have the same predicate '관람하다' (kwanlamhata, "watch").

The antecedent of the second zero object is the first candidate antecedent. The meaning of predicates 'kwanlamhata' and '보다' (pota, "see") is similar. Therefore, we consider the semantic of predicates between a candidate antecedent and a zero object as one of the important indicators to resolve Korean zero object. The opposite meaning of predicates can also be the clue in the following table example.

Speaker	Korean dialogue
A	죄송합니다, 기내$_{1}$에서는 sorry, in flight-ADV (coysonghapnita, kinayeysenun 휴대전화$_{2}$를 the phone-OBJ hyutaycen-hwalul 꺼 주셔야 합니다. have to turn off kke cusyeya hapnita.) "Sorry, you have to turn off the cell-phone during the flight."
B	그런가요, 알겠습니다. all right (kulenkayo, alkeysssupnita.) "All right."
A	비행기$_{3}$가 완전히 flight-SUBJ completely (pihayngkika wancenhi 이륙한 후에는 ø takes off after ilyukhan hueynun 키셔도 됩니다. can turn on kisyeto toypnita.) "After the machine completely takes off, you can turn on the cell-phone."

Table 5 dialogue example (2) including semantic relation of predicates

The above table dialogue has 3 candidate antecedents. From these candidates, the second candidate is the antecedent of the zero object. The antecedent and the zero object have predicates '끄다' (kkuta, "turn off") and '켜다' (khyeta, "turn on"), respectively. The predicates are in an antonym relation which is much more important than the syntactic function. This is one of the reasons why we consider the semantic of predicates between the candidate antecedents and the zero object as a clue for Korean zero object resolution.

Like WordNet in English, Korean dictionary can give information whether predicates are identical or different or opposite in meaning. Sejong electronic dictionary[1] and KorLex[2] are one of the Korean dictionaries which are available to extract information. Sejong electronic dictionary includes information about word meaning relation such as synonyms and antonyms. KorLex is another dictionary based on WordNet. This dictionary is constructed by translating WordNet and then modifying for Korean. Using these dictionaries, meaning relation of predicates between the candidate antecedent and the zero object can be automatically compared.

4 Experiments

4.1 Feature sets

In this paper, we employ a machine learning method to deal with the zero objects phenomenon. In order to apply a machine learning method, 8 features are proposed as presented in table 6. The following table explains the functions of each feature with their value.

	Feature	Value
f1	Syntactic function of candidate antecedent	*top*, *sub*, *obj*, *adv*, *comp*,

[1] https://ithub.korean.go.kr/
[2] http://klpl.re.pusan.ac.kr/

		poss
f2	Parallelism of syntactic function	*para, diff*
f3	Semantic relation between predicates	*sim, same, oppo, diff, loc*[3]
f4	Sentence distance	*loc, 0, . . . n*
f5	Sentence distance based on Speaker of zero object	*-n . . . 0 . . . n*
f6	Headedness of candidate antecedent	*head, not*
f7	The most salient candidate antecedent	*1, 0*
f8	Gold referential relation	*yes, no*

Table 6 Features for ML

In this paragraph we explain feature 1 and 2 in detail. Among feature 1 values, if the value *top* is assigned to an entity, it has given preferential treatment to make them antecedent. In Korean, the markers 'eun', 'nun', 'to', 'man' show which entity is a topic or delimiter.

Feature 2 encodes whether the syntactic function of the candidate antecedent and the zero object are equal. When the syntactic functions are different, the value is *diff*. When a candidate antecedent has the same syntactic function as the zero object, it is more likely to be an antecedent. This is one of the reasons why we introduce feature 2.

Feature 3 represents the semantic relation of predicates between the candidate antecedent and the zero object. In Korean, it tends to be correlated for meaning between the predicate of the candidate antecedent and the zero object. The values of feature 3 encode this tendency.

Feature 4 is about the sentence distance between the zero object and the candidate antecedent. The value *loc* indicates that the pronoun and the potential antecedent are in the same local clause. When the pronoun and the potential antecedent occur in the same sentence but not in the same clause, the value becomes *0*. Higher values indicate larger distances. Candidates, which appear on the first sentence from the complex sentence or the sentence before the current sentence, are more preferred to be the antecedent than the other candidates.

[3] If the candidate antecedent and the zero object occur in the same clause, the value *loc* is assigned.

Since we deal with spoken text form, there is a chance to have some difficulties in applying the methods in the previous studies focusing on written sentences. Because of this reason, we introduce feature 5 which reflect the properties of spoken texts. Feature 5 encodes the sentence distance between the zero object and the candidate antecedent based on the speaker of the zero object. We assumed that considering the sentence distance based on the speaker of the zero object can reflect the original aim to introduce sentence distance for one of the features for ML. Unlike feature 4, the value of feature 5 can be negative according to the consistency of the speaker between the zero object and the candidate antecedent. If the speaker of them is not the same, then the value of this feature will be negative.

Feature 6 represents the headedness of the candidate antecedent. When a candidate antecedent NP occurs in the head of the NP, then it can be considered as the likeliest antecedent than the candidates which are not the head of the NP.

Feature 7 is based on the framework of centering theory. In the previous literature, it is argued that a salient entity recoverable by inference from the context is frequently omitted (Walker et al., 1994; Iida, 1998; Hong, 2000). Therefore, we utilize the forward looking center ranking for Korean, assuming the most salient candidate antecedent which is marked as a value *1* is likely to be the antecedent of the zero object.

Feature 8 encodes the gold referential relation between the candidate antecedent and the zero object. It takes the value *yes* if the noun phrase is in fact an antecedent of the zero object, and *no* if it is not.

4.2 Experiment

To evaluate the effect of machine learning method, we use 'WEKA' system (3.6.10 version). Since SVM (Support Vector Machine) algorithm has shown good performance in various tasks in NLP (Kudo and Matsumoto, 2001; Isozaki and Kazawa, 2002), SVM algorithm is selected for evaluation. We collect spoken texts about tourism containing Korean zero objects. 1123 coreferential pairs are extracted from the corpus; 308 pairs are positive, and 824 pairs are negative.

The experiment result was obtained by splitting the data set in ten parts equally for 10-fold cross validation. Each training set contains 90% of the total number of pairs, and the remaining 10% are assigned to the test sets. Using 8 features, we have found 73.37% of accuracy. It may not be quite fair comparison if we compare our result with the results of other studies on Korean written texts. Therefore, we set a baseline by choosing the most salient candidate in the discourse according to the forward looking center ranking in Hong (2011) for comparison. As shown in Table 7, the proposed method can improve the accuracy up to 62% which is above the baseline.

	Baseline	Experiment	remark
Accuracy	11.66%	73.37%	61.71% improved

Table 7 The result of experiment

Ranking	Feature	
1	f4	Sentence distance
2	f3	Semantic relation between predicates
3	f7	The most salient candidate antecedent
4	f5	Sentence distance based on Speaker of zero object
5	f1	Syntactic function of candidate antecedent
6	f2	Parallelism of syntactic function
7	f6	Headedness of candidate antecedent

Table 8 The ranking of features

Table 8 shows the ranking of the features selected by 'InfoGainAttribute Evaluator'. As table 8 shows, feature 5 has ranked top. Sentence distance is commonly utilized in other works on anaphora resolution, because candidate antecedents from the previous clause or sentence are preferred. McEnery et al. (1997) examined the distance of pronouns and their antecedent, and concluded that the antecedents of pronouns do exhibit clear patterns of distribution. The result of the feature ranking reflects the importance of the role of sentence distance.

As the table 8 shows, feature 3 ranked second. In the previous works, subcategorization information is utilized for semantic constraints. For example, if a zero is the subject of 'eat,' the antecedent is probably a person or an animal, and so on. However, feature 3, which is different from the semantic constraints from the other studies, is first introduced in this work for zero object resolution. From the result, we can assume that this feature plays very important role to zero object resolution in Korean.

We can also verify that the centering theory is crucial to resolve Korean zero object. According to the theory, there is a tendency that the most salient candidate antecedent is realized as a zero pronoun. Since feature 7 reflects this property and this feature ranked third among the features we proposed, the tendency is proven to be significant for zero object resolution.

5 Conclusion

In this paper, we proposed a ML method to resolve Korean zero object in spoken texts. Determining an antecedent of a zero object is crucial in developing MT systems with Korean as a source language. In case of translating Korean into target languages like English and German, the omitted object has to be resolved in order to generate overt objects in target languages. In order to utilize ML, 8 features were suggested for Korean zero object resolution. An experiment was conducted to test the feasibility for our method. The accuracy was 73.37% which was higher than the baseline, when 8 features were used for the ML. Currently, we are increasing the size of the training corpus, and are planning to validate our model in depth with the new training corpus.

Acknowledgments

This work was supported by the IT R&D program of MSIP/KEIT. [10041807, Development of Original Software Technology for Automatic Speech Translation with Performance 90% for Tour/International Event focused on Multilingual Expansibility and based on Knowledge Learning]

References

Baldwin, B. 1997. CogNAC: high precision coreference with limited knowledge and linguistic resources. In Proceedings of a Workshop on Operational Factors in Practical, Robust Anaphora Resolution for Unrestricted Texts. Association for Computational Linguistics, pp. 38-45.

Carbonell, J. G., & Brown, R. D. 1988. Anaphora resolution: a multi-strategy approach. In Proceedings of the 12th conference on Computational linguistics, Volume 1. Association for Computational Linguistics, pp. 96-101.

Choi, J. & Lee, M. 1999. Focus – Formal Semantics and description of Korean. Seoul: Hanshin publishing company. (in Korean)

Connolly, D., Burger, J. D., & Day, D. S. 1997. A machine learning approach to anaphoric reference. In New Methods in Language Processing. pp. 133-144.

Ferrández, A., & Peral, J. 2000. A computational approach to zero-pronouns in Spanish. In Proceedings of the 38th Annual Meeting on Association for Computational Linguistics. Association for Computational Linguistics. pp. 166-172.

Grosz, B. J., Weinstein, S., & Joshi, A. K. 1995. Centering: A framework for modeling the local coherence of discourse. Computational linguistics, 21(2), pp. 203-225.

Hong, M. 2000. Centering Theory and Argument Deletion in Spoken Korean. The Korean Journal Cognitive Science. Vol. 11(1). pp. 9-24. (in Korean)

Hong, M. 2002. A review on zero anaphora resolution theories in Korean. Studies in Modern Grammar, 29, pp. 167-186.

Hong, M. 2011. Zero subject Resolution in Korean for machine translation into German. German linguistics, 24, pp. 417-439. (in Korean)

Iida, M. 1998. Discourse coherence and shifting centers in Japanese texts. Centering theory in discourse, pp. 161-180.

Isozaki, H., & Kazawa, H. 2002. Efficient support vector classifiers for named entity recognition. In Proceedings of the 19th international conference on Computational linguistics, Volume 1. Association for Computational Linguistics. pp. 168-184.

Kameyama, M. 1986. A property-sharing constraint in centering. In Proceedings of the 24th annual meeting on Association for Computational Linguistics. Association for Computational Linguistics, pp. 200-206.

Kim, L. K. 2010. Korean Honorific Agreement too Guides Null Argument Resolution: Evidence from an Offline Study. University of Pennsylvania Working Papers in Linguistics, 16(1), 12. pp. 101-108.

Kudo, T., & Matsumoto, Y. 2001. Chunking with support vector machines. In Proceedings of the second meeting of the North American Chapter of the Association for Computational Linguistics on Language technologies. Association for Computational Linguistics, pp. 1-8.

Lappin, S., & Leass, H. J. 1994. An algorithm for pronominal anaphora resolution. Computational linguistics, 20(4), pp. 535-561.

Lee, D. 2002. Discourse Representation Methods and Korean Dialogue. In Proceedings of the 2002 Winter Linguistic Society of Korea Conference. Seoul National University, pp. 88-104.

Okumura, M., & Tamura, K. 1996. Zero pronoun resolution in Japanese discourse based on centering theory. In Proceedings of the 16th conference on Computational linguistics, Volume 2. Association for Computational Linguistics. pp. 871-876.

McEnery et al. 1997. Corpus annotation and reference resolution. In Proceedings of the ACL Workshop on Operational Factors in Practical, Robust Anaphora Resolution for Unrestricted Texts, pp. 67-74.

Nakaiwa, H., & Shirai, S. 1996. Anaphora resolution of Japanese zero pronouns with deictic reference. In Proceedings of the 16th conference on Computational linguistics, Volume 2. Association for Computational Linguistics. pp. 812-817.

Palomar, M., Ferrández, A., Moreno, L., Martínez-Barco, P., Peral, J., Saiz-Noeda, M., & Muñoz, R. 2001. An algorithm for anaphora resolution in Spanish texts. Computational Linguistics, 27(4), pp. 545-567.

Park, A., & Hong, M. 2014. Hybrid Approach to Zero Subject Resolution for multilingual MT-Spanish-to-Korean Cases. In Proceedings of the 28th Pacific Asia Conference On Language Information and Computing. pp.254-261.

Paul, M., Yamamoto, K., & Sumita, E. 1999. Corpus-based anaphora resolution towards antecedent preference. In Proceedings of the Workshop on Coreference and its Applications. Association for Computational Linguistics. pp. 47-52.

Roh, J. E., & Lee, J. H. 2003. An empirical study for generating zero pronoun in Korean based on Cost-based Centering Model. In Proceedings of Australasian Language Technology Association, pp. 90-97.

Ryu, B. R. 2001. Centering and zero anaphora in the Korean discourse. Seoul National University, MS Thesis.

Walker, M., Cote, S., & Iida, M. 1994. Japanese discourse and the process of centering. In Proceedings of Computational linguistics, 20(2), pp. 193-232.

An Improved Hierarchical Word Sequence Language Model Using Directional Information

Xiaoyi Wu
Nara Institute of Science and Technology
Computational Linguistics Laboratory
8916-5 Takayama, Ikoma, Nara Japan
xiaoyi-w@is.naist.jp

Yuji Matsumoto
Nara Institute of Science and Technology
Computational Linguistics Laboratory
8916-5 Takayama, Ikoma, Nara Japan
matsu@is.naist.jp

Abstract

For relieving data sparsity problem, Hierarchical Word Sequence (abbreviated as HWS) language model, which uses word frequency information to convert raw sentences into special n-gram sequences, can be viewed as an effective alternative to normal n-gram method. In this paper, we use directional information to make HWS models more syntactically appropriate so that higher performance can be achieved. For evaluation, we perform intrinsic and extrinsic experiments, both verify the effectiveness of our improved model.

1 Introduction

Probabilistic Language Modeling is a fundamental research direction of Natural Language Processing. It is widely used in many applications such as machine translation (Brown et al., 1990), spelling correction (Mays et al., 1991), speech recognition (Rabiner and Juang, 1993), word prediction (Bickel et al., 2005) and so on.

Most research about Probabilistic Language Modeling, such as back-off (Katz,1987), Kneser-Ney (Kneser and Ney, 1995), and modified Kneser-Ney (Chen and Goodman, 1999), only focus on smoothing methods because they all take n-gram approach (Shannon, 1948) as a default setting for extracting word sequences from a sentence. Yet even with 30 years worth of newswire text, more than one third of all trigrams are still unseen (Allison et al., 2005), which cannot be distinguished accurately even using a high-performance smoothing method such as modified Kneser-Ney (abbreviated as MKN). It is better to make these unseen sequences actually be observed rather than to leave them to smoothing method directly.

For the purpose of extracting more valid word sequences and relieving data sparsity problem, Wu and Matsumoto (2014) proposed a heuristic approach to convert a sentence into a hierarchical word sequence (abbreviated as HWS) structure, by which special n-grams can be achieved. In this paper, we improve HWS models by adding directional information for achieving higher performance.

This paper is organized as follows. In Section 2, we give a complete review of the HWS language model. We present our improved HWS model in Section 3. In Section 4, we show the effectiveness of our model by several experiments. Finally, we summarize our findings in Section 5.

2 Review of HWS Language Model

The HWS language model is defined as follows.

Suppose that we have a frequency-sorted vocabulary list $V = \{v_1, v_2, ..., v_m\}$, where $C(v_1) \geq C(v_2) \geq ... \geq C(v_m)$[1].

According to V, given any sentence $S = w_1, w_2, ..., w_n$, the most frequently used word $w_i \in S (1 \leq i \leq n)$ can be selected[2] for splitting S into two substrings $S_L = w_1, ..., w_{i-1}$ and $S_R = w_{i+1}, ..., w_n$. Similarly, for S_L and S_R, $w_j \in S_L (1 \leq j \leq i-1)$ and $w_k \in S_R (i+1 \leq k \leq n)$ can also be selected, by which S_L and S_R can be splitted

[1] $C(v)$ represents the frequency of v in a certain corpus.

[2] If w_i appears multiple times in S, then select the first one.

29th Pacific Asia Conference on Language, Information and Computation pages 449 - 454
Shanghai, China, October 30 - November 1, 2015

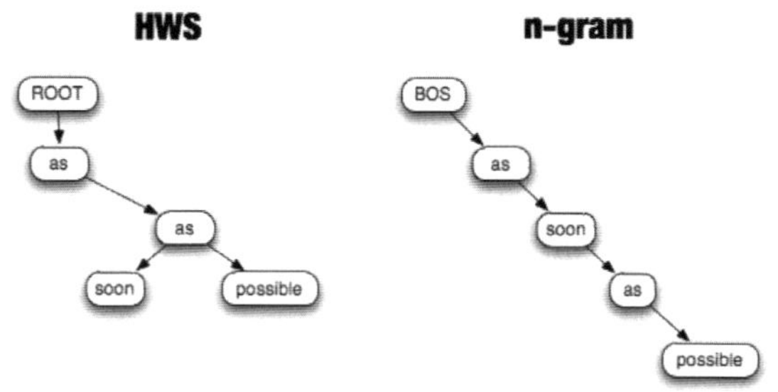

Figure 1: A comparison of structures between HWS and n-gram

into two smaller substrings separately. Executing this process recursively until all the substrings become empty strings, then a tree $T = (\{w_i, w_j, w_k, ...\}, \{(w_i, w_j), (w_i, w_k), ...\})$ can be generated, which is defined as an *HWS structure*.

In an HWS structure T, assuming that each node depends on its preceding n-1 parent nodes, then special n-grams can be trained. Such kind of n-grams are defined as *HWS-n-grams*.

The advantage of HWS models can be considered as *discontinuity*. Taking Figure 1 as an example, since n-gram model is a continuous language model, in its structure, the second 'as' depends on 'soon', while in the HWS structure, the second 'as' depends on the first 'as', forming a discontinuous pattern to generate the word 'soon', which is closer to our linguistic intuition. Rather than 'as soon ...', taking 'as ... as' as a pattern is more reasonable because 'soon' is quite easy to be replaced by other words, such as 'fast', 'high', 'much' and so on. Consequently, even using 4-gram or 5-gram, sequences consisting of 'soon' and its nearby words tend to be low-frequency because the connection of 'as...as' is still interrupted. On the contrary, the HWS model extracts sequences in a discontinuous way, even 'soon' is replaced by another word, the expression 'as...as' won't be affected. This is how the HWS models relieve the data sparseness problem.

It unsupervisedly construct a hierarchical structure to adjust the word sequence so that irrelevant words can be filtered out from contexts and long distance information can be used for predicting the next word. On this point, it has something in common with structured language model (Chelba, 1997), which firstly introduced parsing into language modeling. The significant difference is, structured language model is based on CFG parsing structures, while HWS model is based on pattern-oriented structures.

The experimental results reported by Wu and Matsumoto (2014) indicated that HWS model keeps better balance between coverage and usage than normal n-gram and skip-gram models (Guthrie, 2006), which means that more valid sequence patterns can be extracted in this approach.

However, the *discontinuity* of HWS models also brings a disadvantage. In normal n-gram models, since the generation of words is one-sided (from left to right), given any left-hand context, words generated from it can be considered as linguistically appropriate. In contrast, HWS structures are essentially binary trees, which also generate words on the left side. However, according to the definition of HWS-n-grams, the directional information are not taken into account, which causes a syntactical problem.

Taking Figure 1 as an example. According to the structure of HWS, HWS-3-grams are trained as {(ROOT, as, as), (as, as, soon), (as, as, possible)}, where 'soon' and 'possible' are generated from context (as, as) without any distinction, which means, an illegal sentence such like 'as possible as soon' can be also generated from this HWS-3-gram model.

3 Directional HWS Models

To solve this problem, we propose to use directional information. As mentioned previously, since HWS structures are essentially binary trees, directional information has already been encoded when HWS structures are established.

Thus, after an HWS structure being constructed, directional information can be easily attached to this tree as shown in Figure 2. Then, assuming that each node depends on its n-1 preceding parent nodes with their directional information, we can train a special n-gram from this binary tree. For instance, 3-grams trained from this tree are {(ROOT-R, as-R, as), (as-R, as-L, soon), (as-R, as-R, possible)}, where syntactical information can be encoded more precisely than original HWS-3-grams. For the purpose of distinguishing our models from the original HWS mod-

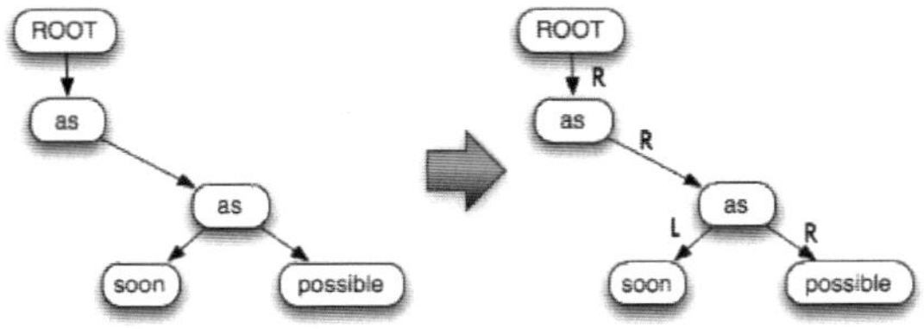

Figure 2: An example of HWS structure with directional information

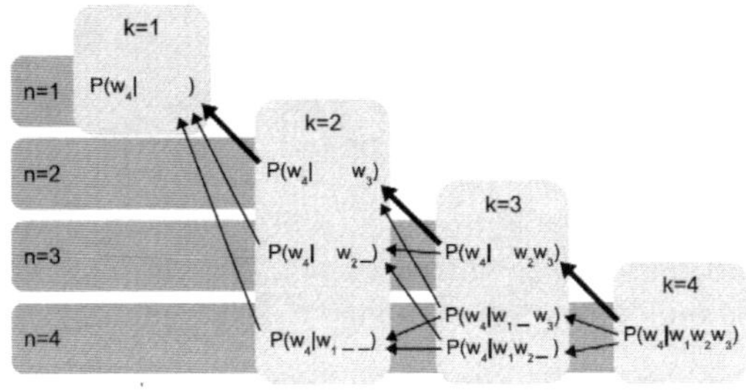

Figure 3: The interpolation of GLM model

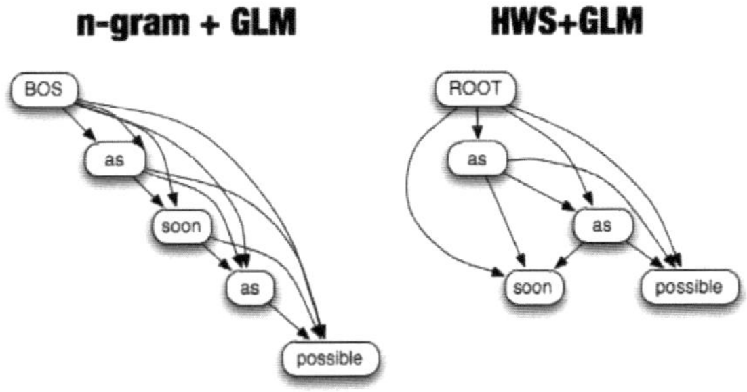

Figure 4: A demonstration for applying GLM smoothing to HWS structure

els, we call n-grams trained in our way as *DHWS-n-grams*.

In the above example of DHWS-3-grams, (as-R, as-L, soon) indicates that 'soon' is located between two 'as's, while (as-R, as-R, possible) indicates that 'possible' is located on the right side of the second 'as'. Similarly, if we use DHWS-4-grams or higher order ones, the relative position of each word will be more specific. In other words, according to a DHWS structure, for each word (node), its position (relative to the whole sentence) can be strictly determined by its preceding parent nodes. The bigger n is, the more syntactical information DHWS-n-grams can reflect.

As for smoothing methods for HWS models, Wu and Matsumoto (2014) only used an additive smoothing. Although HWS-n-grams are trained in a special way, they are essentially n-grams because each trained sequence is reserved as a $(n-1\ length\ context,\ word)$ tuple as normal n-grams, which makes it possible to apply MKN smoothing to HWS models. The main difference is that HWS models are trained by tree structures while n-gram models in a continuous way, which affects the counting of contexts $C(w_{i-n+1}^{i-1})$.

Taking Figure 1 as an example. According to the structure of HWS, HWS-3-grams are trained as {(ROOT, as, as), (as, as, soon), (as, as, possible)}, while the HWS-2-grams are trained as {(ROOT, as), (as, as), (as, soon), (as, possible)}. In the HWS-3-gram model, as the context of 'soon' and 'possible', 'as ... as' appears twice, however, in the HWS-2-gram model, $C(as, as)$ is counted only once. In normal n-gram models, $C(w_{i-n+1}^{i-1})$ can be directly achieved from its lower model because they are continuous, but in HWS models, $C(w_{i-n+1}^{i-1})$ should be counted as $\sum_{w_j \in \{w_i : C(w_{i-n+1}^{i})>0\}} C(w_{i-n+1}^{i-1}, w_j)$, which means that the frequencies of contexts should be counted in the model with the same order. Taking this into account, MKN smoothing method can be also applied to HWS models and DHWS models.

As an alternative of MKN smoothing method, we can also use GLM (Pickhardt et. al., 2014). GLM (Generalized Language Model) is a combination of skipped n-grams and MKN, which performs well on overcoming data sparseness. GLM smoothing considers all possible combinations of gaps in a local context and interpolates the higher order model with all possible lower order models derived from adding gaps in all different ways. As shown in Figure 3, n stands for the length of normal n-grams for calculation, k indicates the number of words actually be used, and the wildcard '_' represents the skipped words in a n-gram.

Since GLM is a generalized version of MKN smoothing, it can also be applied to HWS models (as shown in Figure 4). In the following experiments, we will use MKN and GLM as smoothing methods. To ensure the openness of our research, the source code used for following experiments can be downloaded.[3]

[3]https://github.com/aisophie/HWS

4 Evaluation

4.1 Intrinsic Evaluation

To test the performance on out-of-domain data, we use two different corpus: **British National Corpus** and **English Gigaword Corpus**.

British National Corpus (BNC) [4] is a 100 million word collection of samples of written and spoken language from a wide range of sources, designed to represent a wide cross-section of British English from the later part of the 20th century, both spoken and written. In our experiments, we randomly choose 449,755 sentences (10 million words) as training data.

English Gigaword Corpus [5] consists of over 1.7 billion words of English newswire from 4 distinct international sources. We randomly choose 44,702 sentences (1 million words) as test data.

As preprocessing of training data and test data, we use the tokenizer of NLTK (Natural Language Toolkit) [6] to split raw English sentences into words. We also converted all words to lowercase.

As intrinsic evaluation of Language Modeling, *perplexity* (Manning and Schütze, 1999) is the most common metric used for measuring the usefulness of a language model.

Wu and Matsumoto (2014) also proposed to use *coverage* and *usage* to evaluate efficiency of language models. The authors defined the sequences of training data as TR, and unique sequences of test data as TE, then the coverage is calculated by Equation 1.

$$coverage = \frac{|TR \bigcap TE|}{|TE|} \tag{1}$$

Usage (Equation 2) is used to estimate how much redundancy contained in a model and a balanced measure is calculated by Equation 3.

$$usage = \frac{|TR \bigcap TE|}{|TR|} \tag{2}$$

$$F\text{-}Score = \frac{2 \times coverage \times usage}{coverage + usage} \tag{3}$$

[4]http://www.natcorp.ox.ac.uk

[5]https://catalog.ldc.upenn.edu/LDC2011T07

[6]http://www.nltk.org

Models	PP(MKN)	PP(GLM)	C	U	F
2-gram	1244.535	-	**0.479**	**0.081**	**0.139**
HWS-2	1130.790	-	0.455	0.078	0.133
DHWS-2	**920.783**	-	0.447	0.075	0.129
3-gram	1107.430	925.666	0.229	0.028	0.051
HWS-3	1065.594	873.252	**0.316**	**0.045**	**0.079**
DHWS-3	**834.680**	**687.605**	0.298	0.041	0.072
4-gram	1093.799	861.930	0.086	0.009	0.016
HWS-4	1064.444	756.100	**0.240**	**0.030**	**0.054**
DHWS-4	**822.225**	**596.369**	0.216	0.027	0.048

Table 1: Performance of normal n-gram models, HWS models and DHWS models

Based on above measures, we compared our models with normal n-gram models and the original HWS models. The results are shown in Table 1.

According to this table, for each language model, higher order one brings lower perplexity. Besides, contrast to the result reported by Wu and Matsumoto (2014), after applied with MKN smoothing method, even for higher order models such as 3-grams and 4-grams, HWS models outperform normal n-gram models as well. Furthermore, after taking directional information into account, DHWS models perform even better than the original HWS models.

On the other hand, in DHWS models, since almost each word is distinguished as 'two words' ('-L' and '-R'), the coverage and usage tend to be relatively lower than the original HWS models. But it is worth because perplexity has been greatly decreased and syntactical information can be reflected better in this way.

We also noticed that for each model (n>2), perplexity is greatly reduced after applying GLM smoothing, which is consistent with the results reported by Pickhardt et. al.(2014).

4.2 Extrinsic Evaluation

Perplexity is not a definite way of determining the usefulness of a language model since a language model with low perplexity may not work equally well in a real world application. Thus, we also performed extrinsic experiments to evaluate our model. In this paper, we use the reranking of n-best translation candidates to examine how language models work in a statistical machine translation task.

We use the French-English part of TED talks parallel corpus as the experiment dataset. The training data contains 139761 sentence pairs, while the test data contains 1617 sentence pairs. For training language models, we set English as the target language.

As for statistical machine translation toolkit, we use Moses system[7] to train the translation model and output 50-best translation candidates for each french sentence of the test data. Then we use the 139761 English sentences to train language models. With these models, 50-best translation candidates can be reranked. According to these reranking results, the performance of machine translation system can be evaluated, which also means, the language models can be evaluated indirectly.

We use following two measures for evaluating reranking results.

BLEU (Papineni et al., 2002): BLEU score measures how many words overlap in a given candidate translation when compared to a reference translation, which provides some insight into how good the fluency of the output from an engine will be.

TER (Snover et al., 2006): TER score measures the number of edits required to change a system output into one of the references, which gives an indication as to how much post-editing will be required on the translated output of an engine.

As shown in Table 2, since the results performed by our implementation (3-gram+MKN) is almost the same as that performed by existing language model toolkits IRSTLM[8] and SRILM[9], we believe that our implementation is correct. Based on the results, considering both BLEU and TER score, DHWS-3-gram model using GLM smoothing outperforms other models.

Models(+Smoothing)	BLEU	TER
IRSTLM(+MKN)	31.2	49.1
SRILM(+MKN)	**31.3**	48.9
3-gram(+MKN)	**31.3**	49.1
3-gram(+GLM)	**31.3**	49.2
HWS-3-gram(+MKN)	31.2	**48.6**
HWS-3-gram(+GLM)	31.2	48.7
DHWS-3-gram(+MKN)	31.2	**48.6**
DHWS-3-gram(+GLM)	**31.3**	**48.6**

Table 2: Performance of SMT system using different language models. For the settings of IRSTLM and SRILM, we use default settings except for using modified Kneser-Ney as the smoothing method

5 Conclusion

We proposed an improved hierarchical word sequence language model using directional information. With this information, HWS models can be build more syntactically appropriate while remaining its original advances. Consequently, higher performance can be achieved, both intrinsic and extrinsic experiments confirmed our thoughts.

In this paper, we construct HWS structures (binary trees) based on its original heuristic rule. It is conceivable that more valid discontinuous patterns can be extracted if we use word association information to built HWS structures, which is a promising future study.

[7]http://www.statmt.org/moses/

[8]http://sourceforge.net/projects/irstlm/

[9]http://www.speech.sri.com/projects/srilm/

References

B. Allison, D. Guthrie, L. Guthrie, W. Liu, Y. Wilks. 2005. *Quantifying the Likelihood of Unseen Events: A further look at the data Sparsity problem.* Awaiting publication.

S. Bickel, P. Haider, and T. Scheffer. 2005. *Predicting sentences using n-gram language models. In Proceedings of the conference on Human Language Technology and Empirical Methods in Natural Language Processing*, HLT'05, pages 193-200, Stroudsburg, PA, USA. Association for Computational Linguistics.

P. F. Brown, J. Cocke, S. A. Pietra, V. J. Pietra, F. Jelinek, J. D. Lafferty, R. L. Mercer, and P. S. Roossin. 1990. *A statistical approach to machine translation. Computational linguistics*,16(2):79-85.

C. Chelba. 1997. *A Structured Language Model. Proceedings of ACL-EACL, Madrid, Spain*, 1997, 498-500.

S. F. Chen and J. Goodman. 1999. *An empirical study of smoothing techniques for language modeling. Computer Speech & Language*, 1999, 13(4): 359-393.

D. Guthrie, B. Allison, W. Liu, L. Guthrie. 2006. *A Closer Look at Skip-gram Modeling. Proceedings of the 5th international Conference on Language Resources and Evaluation*, 2006: 1-4.

S. Katz. 1987. *Estimation of probabilities from sparse data for the language model component of a speech recognizer. Acoustics, Speech and Signal Processing, IEEE Transactions on*, 1987, 35(3): 400-401.

R. Kneser and H. Ney. 1995. *Improved backing-off for m-gram language modeling. Acoustics, Speech, and Signal Processing, 1995. ICASSP-95., 1995 International Conference on. IEEE*, 1995, 1: 181-184.

C. D. Manning and H. Schütze. 1999. *Foundations of statistical natural language processing.* MIT Press, Cambridge, MA, USA.

E. Mays, F. J. Damerau, and R. L. Mercer. 1991. *Context based spelling correction. Information Processing & Management*, 27(5):517-522.

K. Papineni, S. Roukos, T. Ward, and W.J. Zhu. 2002. *BLEU: a method for automatic evaluation of machine translation. Proceedings of the 40th annual meeting on association for computational linguistics. Association for Computational Linguistics*, 2002: 311-318.

R. Pickhardt, T. Gottron, M. Körner, S. Staab. 2014. *A Generalized Language Model as the Combination of Skipped n-grams and Modified Kneser-Ney Smoothing. Proceedings of the 52nd Annual Meeting of the Association for Computational Linguistics*, 2014, 1145-1154.

L. Rabiner and B.H. Juang. 1993. *Fundamentals of Speech Recognition.* Prentice Hall.

C. E. Shannon. 1948. *A Mathematical Theory of Communication. The Bell System Technical Journal*, 27: 379-423.

M. Snover, B. Dorr, R. Schwartz, L. Micciulla, and J. Makhoul. 2006. *A study of translation edit rate with targeted human annotation. Proceedings of association for machine translation in the Americas*, 2006: 223-231.

X. Wu and Y. Matsumoto. 2014. *A Hierarchical Word Sequence Language Model. Proceedings of The 28th Pacific Asia Conference on Language, Information and Computation (PACLIC)*, 2014, 489-494.

Neural Network Language Model for Chinese Pinyin Input Method Engine

Shen-Yuan Chen[1,2], **Rui Wang**[1,2] **and Hai Zhao**[1,2*]
[1]Center for Brain-Like Computing and Machine Intelligence,
Department of Computer Science and Engineering,
Shanghai Jiao Tong University, Shanghai 200240, China
[2]Key Laboratory of Shanghai Education Commission for Intelligent Interaction
and Cognitive Engineering, Shanghai Jiao Tong University, Shanghai, 200240, China
chenshenyuan1992@sina.com, wangrui.nlp@gmail.com
and zhaohai@cs.sjtu.edu.cn

Abstract

Neural network language models (NNLMs) have been shown to outperform traditional n-gram language model. However, too high computational cost of NNLMs becomes the main obstacle of directly integrating it into pinyin IME that normally requires a real-time response. In this paper, an efficient solution is proposed by converting NNLMs into back-off n-gram language models, and we integrate the converted NNLM into pinyin IME. Our experimental results show that the proposed method gives better decoding predictive performance for pinyin IME with satisfied efficiency.

1 Introduction

Input method engine (IME) is the encoding method to input a variety of characters into computer or other information processing and communication devices, such as mobile phone. People working with computer cannot live without IMEs. With the development and improvement of IMEs, people are paying more and more attention to its efficiency and humanization. Since there are thousands of Chinese characters and only 26 English letters on standard keyboard, we cannot directly input the Chinese characters to the computer by simply hitting keys. A mapping or encoding from Chinese characters to English letters is required, and IME is such a system software to do the mapping (Chen and Lee, 2000; Wu et al., 2009; Zhao et al., 2006). Among various encoding schemes, most IMEs adopt Chinese pinyin, which is the phonetic representation of Chinese characters through Latin (English) letters. The advantage of pinyin IMEs is that it only requires for knowledge of pinyin rules, which are known by most educated Chinese users. Being easy to learn and use, pinyin IME is becoming the first choice of more and more Chinese users.

However, there are only under 500 pinyin syllables in standard Chinese, mandarin, but over 6,000 common Chinese characters, bringing huge ambiguities for pinyin-to-characters mapping (Jia and Zhao, 2014; Xu and Zhao, 2012; Zhang et al., 2014). Modern pinyin IMEs commonly use sentences-based decoding method (Chen and Lee, 2000; Zhang et al., 2012), that is, generating a Chinese sentence according to a pinyin sequence for disambiguation. The decoding method usually works with the help of statistic language model or other techniques.

Back-off N-gram language models (BNLMs) (Chen and Goodman, 1996; Chen and Goodman, 1999; Stolcke, 2002a) have been broadly used for pinyin IME because of their simplicity and efficiency. Recently, continuous-space language models (CLSMs), especially neural network language models (NNLMs) (Bengio et al., 2003; Schwenk, 2007; Le et al., 2010) are used in more and more natural language processing tasks, and practically outperform BNLMs in prediction accuracy. However, NNLMs are still out of consideration for IMEs according to our best knowledge. The main obstacle about using NNLMs in IME is that it is too time-consuming to meet the requirement from IME that needs a real-time response as human-computer interface.

*Corresponding author

29th Pacific Asia Conference on Language, Information and Computation pages 455 - 461
Shanghai, China, October 30 - November 1, 2015

Actually, too long computational time makes the direct integration of NNLMs infeasible for pinyin IMEs. We can hardly image that users have to wait for over 10 seconds to get the result after typing the pinyin sequence. So we have to find another way. Although some work have reduced the decoding time of NNLMs, such as (Arisoy et al., 2014), (Vaswani et al., 2013) and (Devlin et al., 2014), these methods are mainly designed for speech recognition or machine translation and can not be integrated into IME directly.

Instead of replacing BNLMs with NNLMs in IME, we propose to use NNLMs to enhance BNLMs, which means recalculating the probabilities of n-grams in the BNLMs with NNLMs. Thus we take advantage of the probabilities provided by NNLMs without increasing its on-site computational cost. Furthermore, we will also demonstrate that our method may indeed improve the prediction performance of pinyin IMEs.

In Section 2, we introduce the typical pinyin IME model and explain how language models work on the process of candidate sentence generation. In Section 3, we describe the basic concept of BNLMs and NNLMs, then we describe our approach of converting the NNLMs into BNLMs. In section 4 and 5, we do experiments and conclude.

2 Pinyin IME Model

Basically the core engine of IME is a pipeline of three parts: pinyin segmentation, candidate words fetching and candidate sentence generation.

Pinyin segmentation is a word segmentation task which may not be as typical as Chinese word segmentation. Since pinyin has a very small vocabulary that contains about 500 legal pinyin syllables, rule-based segmentation methods are widely used, i.e., backward maximum matching algorithm with additional rules (Goh et al., 2005). Carefully written rules can deal with most of the ambiguous conditions.

Pinyin segmentation breaks continuous user input into separated pinyin syllables and passes them on to the next stage, candidate words fetching. It is a table look-up task finding Chinese words corresponding to pinyin syllables. A table of candidate words is built according to pinyin syllables. Each column of the table is the words corresponding to the syllable and sorted by its probability of existing.

The most important part of pinyin IME is candidate sentence generation, into which we put much of our effort. Language model is commonly used for generating the most likely sentence through providing a conditional probability of words by its context (Chen and Lee, 2000; Zhao et al., 2013). So sentence generation is to find the sentence with the maximum probability, which is constructed by the candidate words fetched previously.

Candidate sentence generation can be regarded as a decoding problem. The goal is to find the most likely Chinese word sequence W^* with the highest joint probability that

$$\begin{aligned} W^* &= \arg\max_W P(W|S) \\ &= \arg\max_W \frac{P(W)P(S|W)}{P(S)} \\ &= \arg\max_W P(W)P(S|W) \\ &= \arg\max_{w_1,w_2,\dots,w_M} \prod_{w_i} P(w_i|w_{i-1}) \prod_{w_i} P(s_i|w_i) \end{aligned}$$

where $P(s_i|w_i)$ is the conditional probability mapping a word to its pinyin syllable, and $P(w_i|w_{i-1})$ is the transition probability. Here $P(s_i|w_i)$ is 1 while the word w_i is corresponding to the pinyin syllable w_i and 0 otherwise. Note that practically the transition probability is $P(w_i|w_{i-(n-1)}, ..., w_{i-1})$ provided by language model. We use Viterbi algorithm (Viterbi, 1967) to decode the character sentence. This problem is same as finding the shortest path on the candidate word lattice (Forney, 1973), which is shown in Figure 1, with all probabilities determined by the language models. Hence, we have reasons to believe that a better language model makes better candidate sentences.

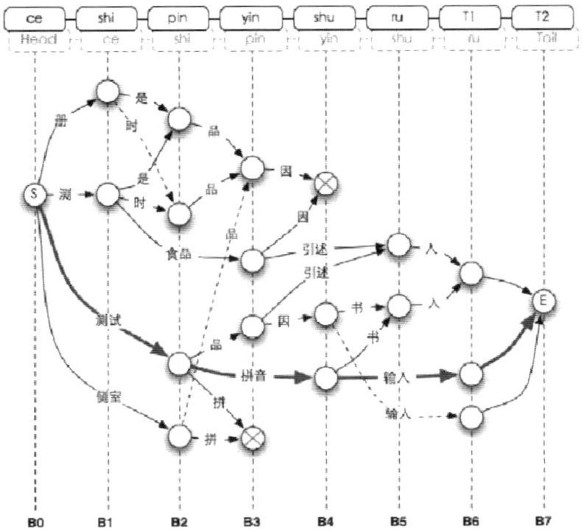

Figure 1: Candidate Sentence Generation

3.2 Neural network language model

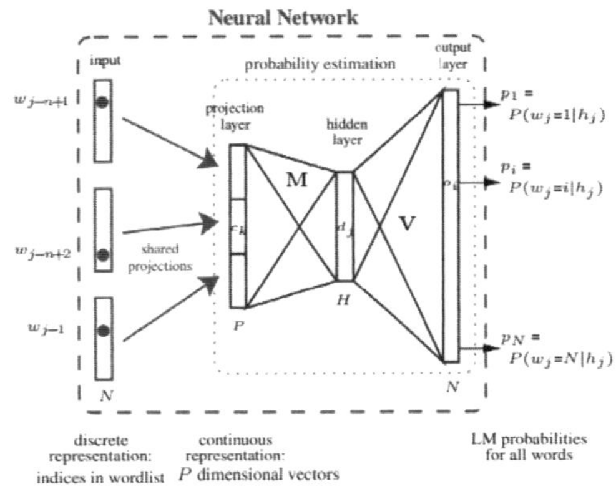

Figure 2: Neural Network Language Model

NNLM provides the condition probabilities $P(w_i|h_i)$ given the histories of the preceding words. , which is shown in Figure 2 (Schwenk, 2013) A typical NNLM consists of four layers: a input layer, a projection layer, a hidden layer and a output layer. The input layer represents the history of $n-1$ word-s, using one hot coding. Since this kind of coding makes the input layer very large and sparse, a shared matrix is used to project the high-dimensional input layer to the low dimensional projection layer. After that, the non-linear (commonly sigmoid or hyperbolic tangent) hidden layer, with usually hundreds of neurons, and the non-linear (commonly softmax) output layers, with the same size as the full vocabulary, jointly calculate the probability of each word in the vocabulary (Schwenk, 2007; Wang et al., 2013b; Wang et al., 2013c).

Since NNLMs calculate the probabilities of n-grams on the continuous space, it can estimate probabilities for any possible n-grams, without worrying about the zero-probability problem, in comparison with BNLM. Hence, there is no need for backing-off to smaller history. Experiments have shown that the NNLM has lower perplexity than the BNLM trained on the same corpus (Schwenk, 2010; Huang et al., 2013). However, the computational complexity of NNLMs is quite high. To reduce the computational costs, NNLMs are only used to compute the probabilities for the subset containing the most

3 Our Approach

This section will introduce the proposed method that uses NNLMs to enhance BNLMs.

3.1 Back-off n-gram language model

A BNLM is composed of the condition probabilities $P(w_i|h_i)$, which means the probability of word w_i given the previous history h_i of $n-1$ words. It-s advantage comes from its simplicity. However, it suffers from data sparseness, that is, the probability of the history h_i not appearing in the training will be zero. Therefore, we need smoothing technologies to alleviate this shortcoming. In the case of interpolated Kneser-Ney smoothing (Chen and Goodman, 1999), the probability under BNLM, $P_b(w_i|h_i)$, is:

$$P_b(w_i|h_i) = \hat{P}_b(w_i|h_i) + \gamma(h_i)P_b(w_i|w_{i-n+2}^{i-1})$$

where $\hat{P}_b(w_i|h_i)$ is a discounted probability and $\gamma(h_i)$ is the back-off weight.

frequent words in the vocabulary, called short-list (Schwenk, 2007; Schwenk, 2010); the probabilities of the rest words are given by BNLMs. The probability $P(w_i|h_i)$ using short-list is calculated as follows:

$$P(w_i|h_i) = \begin{cases} \frac{P_c(w_i|h_i)P_s(h_i)}{1-P_c(o|h_i)} & \text{if } w_i \in \text{short-list} \\ P_b(w_i|h_i) & \text{otherwise} \end{cases}$$

where $P_c(\cdot)$ is the probability calculated by NNLM, $P_c(o|h_i)$ is given by the neuron assigned for the words not in the short-list, $P_b(\cdot)$ is calculated by BNLM, and

$$P_s(h_i) = \sum_{v \in \text{short-list}} P_b(v|h_i)$$

In view of the pros and cons of NNLMs, we tried another way to use NNLMs in pinyin IME as the following section.

3.3 NNLM-enhanced BNLM

The main disadvantage of NNLMs is the large computational cost. During the process of pinyin IME, the language model needs to be frequently accessed, so simply replacing the BNLMs with NNLMs will make the process be very slow. This problem is especially serious to IMEs, which request for fast response. This is why it is infeasible to directly integrate the NNLMs into pinyin IME.

To solve this problem, we propose a method to efficiently apply NNLMs. In the case of a particular NNLM, it will provide the same probability distribution given the same input history. Thus, we can use NNLMs to calculate the probabilities of all the possible n-grams in advance and save the results, which is just like constructing the BNLMs from CSLMs. Our approach is as follow: First, a BNLM and a NNLM are respectively trained on the same corpus. Second, we extract all the n-gram from the BNLM and calculate the probability of them with the NNLM. Third, we re-write the BNLM with the probability computed by NNLM. Finally, we re-normalize the probabilities of BNLM. In this way, we convert the NNLM to the BNLM [1], which is a "conditional-probabilities-to-conditional-probabilities" adjustment. We may now use the NNLM-enhanced BNLM in the pinyin IME.

[1] Arsoy and Wang also proposed NNLM converting methods, however their methods are specially applied to speech recognition or machine translation.

4 Experiment

4.1 Commen Settings

We use the Chinese corpus from (Yang et al., 2012), which is extracted from the corpus of *People's Daily*. The sentences are already segmented into words and labeled with pinyin. The corpus is divided into training set, development set and testing set, which are shown in Table 1.

	Train	Dev	Test
Sentence	1M	2K	100K
Character	43,679,593	83,765	4,123,184

Table 1: Data set size.

In consideration of the model size and efficiency, most existing IMEs use a standard trigram setting for language model (Chen and Lee, 2000), therefore we evaluate the proposed method by following the setting. We first trained a trigram BNLM as the baseline with interpolated Kneser-Ney smoothing, using SRILM toolkit (Stolcke, 2002b). Note that SRILM is also used to re-normalize the re-written BNLMs. We then trained a trigram NNLM on the same training data, using CSLM toolkit (Schwenk, 2013). The vocabulary was extracted from (Wang et al., 2013a; Wang et al., 2014) with the size of 914,728 words, and were labeled with pinyin using the Pinyin-To-Chinese dictionary of *sunpinyin* [2], an open source pinyin IME. In addition, the re-written BNLM is interpolated with the baseline BNLM, using the interpolation weight 0.5, which is empirically tuned using development data.

4.2 Running Time

This subsection compares running time for different types of language models. First, we run the task of calculating the probabilities of 7 million trigrams using different language models to compare their time performance, each for 3 times, as shown in Table 2. The running time of CSLM is up to 100 times greater than our model, which is definitely unacceptable to pinyin IMEs. Besides, since our model has

[2] http://code.google.com/p/sunpinyin

the same structure as the BNLM, extra time cost is not requested. [3]

LMS	Run Time1	Run Time2	Run Time3
BNLM	17.9s	16.7s	16.9s
NNLM	1,684.5s	1,684.5s	1,683.9s
Our LM	17.0s	16.8s	16.5s

Table 2: Running Time of Language models.

4.3 Language Model Performance

We compare the perplexity of our model with the baseline BNLM. Table 3 show that our model outperforms the baseline BNLM in perplexity.

Language Model	perplexity
Baseline (trigram BNLM)	202.5
NNLM-enhanced trigram BNLM	196.4

Table 3: Perplexity of Language models.

However, the lower perplexity does not inevitably equal to the better performance in pinyin IME. We still need to integrate the our model into the pinyin IME to evaluate its actual effect.

4.4 Pinyin IME Performance

To evalue the performance of pinyin IME. We use hit rate of the first candidate sentence (HRF), hit rate of the first k (here $k = 10$) candidate sentences (HRF10) and character accuracy of the first candidate sentence (CA) as evaluation measures. The result is shown in Table 4:

Test	Models	HRF	HRF10	CA
10K	Baseline	74.72	89.92	96.80
10K	Our model	75.71	90.14	96.80
400K	Baseline	67.02	86.08	95.46
400K	Our model	67.68	86.45	95.59

Table 4: Pinyin IME performance(%).

[3]Here only language model computation cost is demonstrated. For decoding a sentence in IME, generally, thousands of language model accessing is usually required. Therefore, according to the above empirical results, integrating NNLM into IME without any modification will result in obvious response retardation, which gives a poor user experience.

The experimental results show that our method can effectively improve the performance of pinyin IME. Figures 3 and 4 indicate that the improvement of the pinyin IME with our model is particularly significant when the length of the input pinyin sequence is between 10-30 characters, meanwhile almost 69% of the sentences in the corpus are with the length of over 10 pinyin characters, which means our method perform better in most cases, especially for the long pinyin sequences. Note that since we only change the probabilities in the BNLM, the improvement does not call for extra time cost.

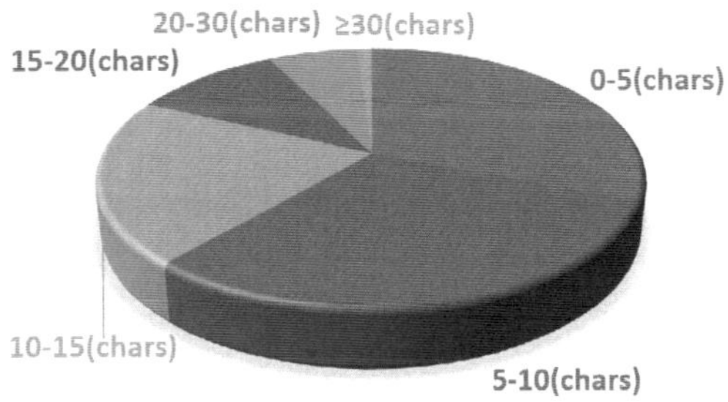

Figure 3: The length distribution of pinyin sequences in testing set

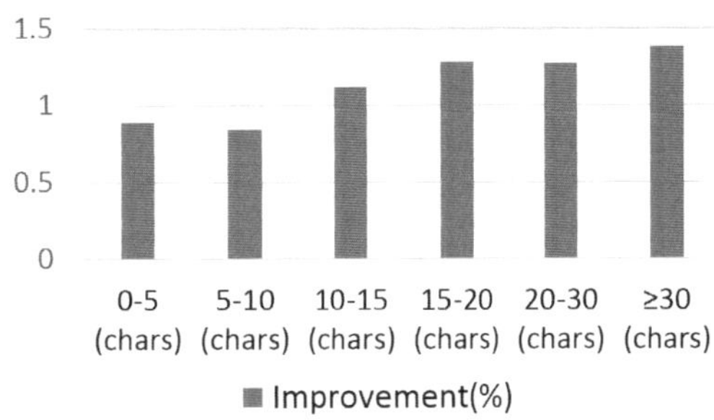

Figure 4: The improvement of HRF using our approach

5 Conclusion

In this paper, we propose an efficient way to apply NNLM to pinyin IME. The experiments demonstrate that our method can effectively improve the predictive performance of pinyin IME without extra time cost.

6 Acknowledge

We appreciate the anonymous reviewers for valuable comments and suggestions on our paper. Shen-yuan Chen, Rui Wang and Hai Zhao were partially supported by the National Natural Science Foundation of China (No. 60903119, No. 61170114, and No. 61272248), the National Basic Research Program of China (No. 2013CB329401), the Science and Technology Commission of Shanghai Municipality (No. 13511500200), the European Union Seventh Framework Program (No. 247619), the Cai Yuanpei Program (CSC fund 201304490199 and 201304490171), and the art and science interdiscipline funds of Shanghai Jiao Tong University(A study on mobilization mechanism and alerting threshold setting for online community, and media image and psychology evaluation: a computational intelligence approach).

References

Ebru Arisoy, Stanley F. Chen, Bhuvana Ramabhadran, and Abhinav Sethy. 2014. Converting neural network language models into back-off language models for efficient decoding in automatic speech recognition. *IEEE/ACM Transactions on, Audio, Speech, and Language Processing*, 22(1):184–192.

Yoshua Bengio, Réjean Ducharme, Pascal Vincent, and Christian Janvin. 2003. A neural probabilistic language model. *The Journal of Machine Learning Research*, 3:1137–1155.

Stanley F. Chen and Joshua Goodman. 1996. An empirical study of smoothing techniques for language modeling. In *Proceedings of the 34th annual meeting on Association for Computational Linguistics*, ACL '96, pages 310–318, Santa Cruz, California, June. Association for Computational Linguistics.

Stanley F. Chen and Joshua Goodman. 1999. An empirical study of smoothing techniques for language modeling. *Computer Speech & Language*, 13(4):359–393.

Zheng Chen and Kai-Fu Lee. 2000. A New Statistical Approach To Chinese Pinyin Input. In *Proceedings of the 38th Annual Meeting of the Association for Computational Linguistics, ACL*, pages 241–247, Hong Kong, October.

Jacob Devlin, Rabih Zbib, Zhongqiang Huang, Thomas Lamar, Richard Schwartz, and John Makhoul. 2014. Fast and robust neural network joint models for statistical machine translation. In *Proceedings of the 52nd Annual Meeting of the Association for Computational Linguistics, ACL, (Volume 1: Long Papers)*, pages 1370–1380, Baltimore, Maryland, June. Association for Computational Linguistics.

Jr George David Forney. 1973. The Viterbi Algorithm. *Proceedings of the IEEE*, 61(3):268–278.

Chooi-Ling Goh, Masayuki Asahara, and Yuji Matsumoto. 2005. Chinese word segmentation by classification of characters. *Computational Linguistics and Chinese Language Processing*, 10(3):381–396.

Zhongqiang Huang, Jacob Devlin, Spyros Matsoukas, and Rich Schwartz. 2013. BBN's systems for the chinese-english sub-task of the NTCIR-10 patentmt evaluation. *Proceedings of NII Testbeds and Community for Information access Research 10, NTCIR-10*, pages 287–293.

Zhongye Jia and Hai Zhao. 2014. A joint graph model for pinyin-to-chinese conversion with typo correction. In *Proceedings of Annual Meeting of the Association for Computational Linguistics, ACL*, pages 1512–1523, Baltimore, Maryland, June.

Hai-son Le, Alexandre Allauzen, Guillaume Wisniewski, and François Yvon. 2010. Training continuous space language models: some practical issues. In *Proceedings of the 2010 Conference on Empirical Methods in Natural Language Processing*, EMNLP '10, pages 778–788, Cambridge, Massachusetts, October. Association for Computational Linguistics.

Holger Schwenk. 2007. Continuous space language models. *Computer Speech & Language*, 21(3):492–518.

Holger Schwenk. 2010. Continuous-space language models for statistical machine translation. *The Prague Bulletin of Mathematical Linguistics*, 93:137–146.

Holger Schwenk. 2013. CSLM - a modular open-source continuous space language modeling toolkit. In *Interspeech*, pages 1198–1202.

Andreas Stolcke. 2002a. SRILM-An Extensible Language Modeling Toolkit. In *Proceedings of the international conference on spoken language processing*, volume 2, pages 901–904.

Andreas Stolcke. 2002b. Srilm-an extensible language modeling toolkit. In *Proceedings of International Conference on Spoken Language Processing, ICSLP*, pages 257–286, Seattle, USA, November.

Ashish Vaswani, Yinggong Zhao, Victoria Fossum, and David Chiang. 2013. Decoding with large-scale neural language models improves translation. In *Proceedings of the 2013 Conference on Empirical Methods in Natural Language Processing, EMNLP*, pages 1387–1392, Seattle, Washington, USA, October. Association for Computational Linguistics.

Andrew James Viterbi. 1967. Error bounds for convolutional codes and an asymptotically optimum decoding algorithm. *IEEE Transactions on Information Theory*, 13(2):260–269.

Peilu Wang, Ruihua Sun, Hai Zhao, and Kai Yu. 2013a. A New Word Language Model Evaluation Metric for Character Based Languages. In *Chinese Computational Linguistics and Natural Language Processing*

Based on Naturally Annotated Big Data, pages 315–324. Springer.

Rui Wang, Masao Utiyama, Isao Goto, Eiichro Sumita, Hai Zhao, and Bao-Liang Lu. 2013b. Converting Continuous-Space Language Models into N-Gram Language Models for Statistical Machine Translation. In *Proceedings of the 2013 Conference on Empirical Methods in Natural Language Processing, EMNLP*, pages 845–850, Seattle, Washington, USA, October. Association for Computational Linguistics.

Rui Wang, Hai Zhao, Bao-Liang Lu, Masao Utiyama, and Eiichiro Sumita. 2013c. Bilingual continuous-space language model growing for statistical machine translation.

Rui Wang, Hai Zhao, Bao-Liang Lu, Masao Utiyama, and Eiichro Sumita. 2014. Neural network based bilingual language model growing for statistical machine translation. In *Proceedings of the 2014 Conference on Empirical Methods in Natural Language Processing*, pages 189–195.

Jun Wu, Huican Zhu, and Hongjun Zhu. 2009. Systems and Methods for Translating Chinese Pinyin to Chinese Characters, January 13. US Patent 7,478,033.

Qiongkai Xu and Hai Zhao. 2012. Using deep linguistic features for finding deceptive opinion spam. In *COLING (Posters)*, pages 1341–1350. Citeseer.

Shaohua Yang, Hai Zhao, and Bao-liang Lu. 2012. A Machine Translation Approach for Chinese Whole-Sentence Pinyin-to-Character Conversion. In *Proceedings of the 26th Pacific Asia Conference on Language, Information, and Computation, PACLIC*, pages 333–342, Bali,Indonesia, November. Faculty of Computer Science, Universitas Indonesia.

Xiaotian Zhang, Hai Zhao, and Cong Hui. 2012. A machine learning approach to convert ccgbank to penn treebank. In *COLING (Demos)*, pages 535–542.

Jingyi Zhang, Masao Utiyama, Eiichro Sumita, and Hai Zhao. 2014. Learning hierarchical translation spans. In *Proceedings of the 2014 Conference on Empirical Methods in Natural Language Processing*, pages 183–188.

Hai Zhao, Chang-Ning Huang, and Mu Li. 2006. An improved chinese word segmentation system with conditional random field. In *Proceedings of the Fifth SIGHAN Workshop on Chinese Language Processing*, volume 1082117. Sydney: July.

Hai Zhao, Masao Utiyama, Eiichiro Sumita, and Bao-Liang Lu. 2013. An Empirical Study on Word Segmentation for Chinese Machine Translation. In *Computational Linguistics and Intelligent Text Processing*, pages 248–263. Springer.

Real-time Detection and Sorting of News on Microblogging Platforms

Wenting Tu **David W. Cheung** **Nikos Mamoulis** **Min Yang** **Ziyu Lu**
Department of Computer Science
The University of Hong Kong
Pokfulam, Hong Kong
{wttu,dcheung,nikos,myang,zylu}@cs.hku.hk

Abstract

Due to the increasing popularity of microblogging platforms (e.g., Twitter), detecting real-time news from microblogs (e.g., tweets) has recently drawn a lot of attention. Most of the previous work on this subject detect news by analyzing propagation patterns of microblogs. This approach has two limitations: (i) many non-news microblogs (e.g. marketing activities) have propagation patterns similar to news microblogs and therefore they can be falsely reported as news; (ii) using propagation patterns to identify news involves a time delay until the pattern is formed, therefore news are not detected in real time. We propose an alternative approach, which, motivated by the necessity of real-time detection of news, does not rely on propagation of posts. Moreover, we propose a real-time sorting strategy that orders the detected news microblogs using a translational approach. An experimental evaluation on a large-scale microblogging dataset demonstrates the effectiveness of our approach.

1 Introduction

Microblogging platforms (e.g., Twitter or SinaWeibo) have become very popular and their role as news media has been recognized. As people actively talk about what is happening, microblogs are the place where the first-hand news appear. Actually, over 85% of the leading topics on Twitter are news by nature (H. P et al, 2010).

Most of the recent works on news detection from microblogs rely on using temporal patterns of propagation (G. L. et al, 2010; R. G. and K. Lerman, 2010; J. L and J. Yang, 2011; F. Z. et al, 2012). As an instance, (F. Z. et al, 2012) assumes that bursty topics in microblogs correspond to events that have attracted the most online attention. To find such events, this work uses a model to detect busty topics, assuming that a global event is likely to follow a time-dependent global topic distribution. Although detection methods relying on the propagation characteristics of microblogs are based on reasonable assumptions, they have certain limitations. First, some microblogs not related to news have very similar propagation characteristics as news microblogs. For example, a microblog with a promotion or a gift may follow a similar propagation pattern as a popular news event. Second, propagation behavior can only be analyzed after a microblog has been posted for a certain amount of time. Previous work on news detection based on propagation knowledge cannot perform real-time detection, since propagation knowledge can only be obtained a period of time after microblogs are published. Some works explicitly mention that trying to detect microblogs using propagation knowledge in a short time reduces the effectiveness. For example, in (G. L. et al, 2010), experiments on Twitter data show that using 1-day propagation knowledge can mainly detect topics related to daily activities; only by using a 2-days history this method can detect some real emerging topics.

Therefore, using propagation characteristics is not a good idea if the objective is to detect news as soon as possible. An additional challenge is how to sort and present the newborn news microblogs according to their importance, Most of the current news detection platforms sort the microblogs by their pub-

29th Pacific Asia Conference on Language, Information and Computation pages 462 - 470
Shanghai, China, October 30 - November 1, 2015

lication time or their popularity. However, at any point in time, there can be lots of newborn news microblogs all of which have close publication time; thus, sorting them by the publication time may fail to show important news on the top. Besides, as we mentioned before, newborn news microblogs have limited prorogation information; thus, it is very difficult to access the popularity of newborn news microblogs. In this paper, we propose an alternative system for detecting and sorting microblogs with news in real time. Our framework does not rely on any propagation knowledge. Our system consists of three modules: news-microblog expert detection, news microblog detection, and news sorting. We observe that there exists a group of expert users, whose microblogs are all of a single type (e.g., news). In the first module, we apply a methodology for selecting *expert users* based on their *professionalism* and *activity*. By simulating the training corpus as the microblogs by the experts, the second module builds an ensemble classifier to detect news microblogs. The ensemble model combines weak classifiers trained from the corpora of different experts into a strong classifier. Moreover, it can be updated with low cost: once an expert posts some news microblogs, we only need to update the module corresponding to its corpus instead of the whole model. The third module defines a score for each detected news microblog, in order to rank these microblogs. In this module, we firstly propose a novel text representation called *Behavior-Actor-Venue bag of words* (BAVbow) for news microblogs which consolidates the most informative text from them. Then, we apply *value transfer with confidence* on the BAVbow representation, using the scores of the training corpus to rank the new microblogs whose scores are unknown.

We conduct experiments on data obtained from the microblogging service SinaWeibo, one of the most popular sites in China, used by well over 30% of Chinese Internet users, with a similar market penetration as Twitter. The effectiveness of each module is verified based on information collected by a group of users.

The remainder of this paper is organized as follows. In Section 2, we introduce our methodology by discussing in detail the news detection framework and the three sub-modules. Section 3 presents our experimental analysis. We conclude the paper and suggest directions for possible future work in Section 4.

2 Our methodology

Our system includes three modules. In a *training session*, the *News-microblog Expert Detection* module detects a set of microblogging users who actively post news microblogs. The posts by these experts forms the training corpus of news microblogs, used to train the other two modules: the *Expert-ensemble Classifier* and the *BAV Sorter*. The *Expert-ensemble Classifier* (Section 2.2) is used to classify newborn microblogs to news or non-news. It combines base classifiers constructed from the experts' corpus by considering the *professionalism* and *activity* degrees of experts. The *BAV Sorter* module (Section 2.3) provides a new representation method for news microblogs and employs a value transfer strategy to define an importance score for each new post classified as news by the *Expert-ensemble Classifier*. After the system has been trained, the newly posted microblogs can be classified as news/non-news by the *Expert-ensemble Classifier*, and those posts detected to be news can be ranked according to their importance by the *BAV Sorter* module. In the remainder of this section, we describe in detail the three modules.

2.1 News-microblog Expert Detection

Since microblogging data are large and they are updated at a high rate, it is not possible to manually label them. As an alternative, we propose an automatic corpus construction method, motivated by the observation that there exists a group of users whose microblogs are of a single type only. In the news domain, some real-world examples include: *@头条新闻 (#breaking news#)* from SinaWeibo and *@BBCWorld* from Twitter, which always post news microblogs. Next, we present our methodology for finding out these users which we call *news experts*. The selection strategy considers two characteristics of users: *professionalism* and *activity*.

2.1.1 Expert Candidates Retrieval via User Profile

Microblogging platforms have a very large number of users and it is impossible to analyze the microblogs written by all of them. Thus, it is necessary to select a subset of them, which is expected to include the news experts. Search for news experts will then be confined to this subset. There are two types of data that describe a user: his/her profile and the microblogs he/she posts. Profile information can be divided into three parts: (i), Description: This part includes usernames and other descriptive data given by the users themselves. (ii), Authority: Microblogging platforms provide verifications for some users, called *verified accounts*. Verification is currently used to establish authenticity in Twitter. The verified badge helps users toward discovering high-quality sources of information. (iii), Influence: A natural feature that indicates the influence of a microblogging user is the number of followers, since this number indicates how many people are reading the user's posts. After analyzing a certain amount of users whose microblogs focus on news, we found that some discriminative characteristics exist in their profiles. First, their descriptions always contain some keywords related to the type of microblogs they focus on ("新闻" and news, in the examples). Second, all of them have verified accounts. Third, they have high influence, i.e., they have at least a certain number of followers.

Therefore, to retrieve candidates of news experts, we can first define some news-related keywords $\mathcal{W} = \{w_1, w_2, \ldots, w_n\}$ and obtain candidate users to be news experts as follows. For each $w_i \in W$, we define a set $e^c(w_i)$ by selecting from the set of users those who (i) have w_i contained in their description, (ii) are verified, and (iii) have at least θ followers. Then, the set EC of *expert candidates* is defined by $\mathcal{E}^c = \bigcup_{i=1}^{n} e^c(w_i)$. Note that both of the keyword set W and θ can be seen as model parameters; they influence the number of retrieved expert candidates. For example, decreasing θ increases the number of candidates exponentially, therefore θ should be selected to be relatively large (e.g., we set θ =1,000 in our experiments). Still, as we will see next, since only the k most important candidates will be selected in the end as experts, the overall training cost of our system is not very sensitive to these parameters.

2.1.2 Selection of Professional and Active Experts among Candidates

After finding the set $\mathcal{E}^c$ of expert candidates, our method, as its second step, defines a score for each user in $\mathcal{E}^c$, which quantifies the candidate's appropriateness. The selection is based on the following rules: (i) microblogs posted by experts should focus on the type we are interested in (i.e., news), (ii) experts should be active, so that they provide time-relevant microblogs to be used in training our classification model. Thus, a candidate expert is more *professional* if a large percentage of his/her microblogs belong to the type. The more *active* the expert is, the more up-to-date his/her corpus is and the more adaptive it is to newborn microblogs.

Based on the above, we define the *professionalism* and *activity* degree of each candidate. To measure the professionalism of a candidate $e^c \in \mathcal{E}^C$, we need to use a classifier which indicates whether a post by e^c is a piece of news. However, when the system is firstly used, we do not have a training set for such a classifier. To tackle this problem, we define a special corpus called *exterior-professional corpus*, which is not taken from microblogging platforms but from professional news sources, e.g., news web sites. We use the content of these sites to train a classifier $\mathbb{C}$ to evaluate the professionalism degree of news-expert candidates. Note that the resulting classifier is not expected to be very accurate, since it is based on a corpus that does not consist of microblogs. However, here we only need $\mathbb{C}$ to *rank* the candidates based on their *professionalism* and this classifier does a good job in this direction: more professional experts typically get higher classification accuracy. Another problem is that the exterior-professional corpus only contains positive instances, while to train a classifier, we usually also need negative instances. This issue could be alleviated by the use of one-class classification methods (M. Y. and L.M. Manevitz, 2002). As an alternative, in our case (i.e., news detection), we construct a corpus of non-news microblogs as follows: we randomly extract microblogs from users not in the candidate set $\mathcal{E}^c$ and use microblogs by them with short content and limited forwarding. These microblogs have low probability to be news microblogs.

For each expert candidate $e_i^c \in \mathcal{E}^c$, we extract recent posts (e.g., posted during time interval $[T_b, T_e]$, where T_e is the extraction time) by e_i^c as $\mathcal{M}_i^T$. Then, we compute (i) ec_i's professionalism degree using classifier $\mathbb{C}$: $f^p(e_i^c) = \dfrac{n'}{n}$, where n is the number of posts in $\mathcal{M}_i^T$ and n' is the number of posts in

$\mathcal{M}_i^T$ classified as news by $\mathbb{C}$; (ii) e_i^c's activity degree as her posting frequency in a recent time interval (e.g., the last month): $f^a(e_i^c) = \frac{n}{T_e - max(T_b, T_u^i)}$, where T_u^i is the time when e_i^c registered at the microblogging platform. Then, the PA score $f^s(ec_i)$ is computed for the candidate as a weighted average of the user's normalized professionalism and activity (based on a weighing parameter α). Finally, the k users in $\mathcal{E}^c$ with the highest PA scores are selected as experts.

2.2 Expert-ensemble Classifier for Detecting News-Microblogs

After obtaining a set of news experts (denoted as $\mathcal{E}$) and their PA values, we utilize them to construct a classification model to identify whether a microblog is related to news. Considering this, we make use of the ensemble learning theory (Z. Zhou, 2012) to construct a classifier that detects news microblogs. First, given an expert $e_i \in \mathcal{E}$, we build a base classifier $\mathbb{C}_i$ corresponding to e_i's corpus (i.e., e_i's recent microblogs). To select an appropriate model for the base classifier in our experimental part, we first performed a comparison among the possible methods for training (not included in this paper, due to space constraints), and decided to use Multinomial Naive Bayes (MNB) (G. P. et al, 2006), owing to its good performance. Naive Bayes methods are a set of supervised learning algorithms based on applying Bayes' theorem with the "naive" assumption of independence between every pair of features. MNB is one of the two classic Naive Bayes variants used in text classification, where the data are typically represented as vectors of word counts and tf-idf vectors. Note that other classification methods also can be used for constructing base classifiers. Users of our methodology can select by comparing performance of different classification methods in their own data.

After k base classifiers $\mathbb{C}_1, \mathbb{C}_2, \cdots, \mathbb{C}_k$ are built (one for each of the k experts), when a newborn microblog m is posted, we can obtain a prediction from each $\mathbb{C}_i$ $(i = 1, \cdots, k)$ on whether m is a news microblog. We use a indication function $f_i^{\mathbb{C}}$ to "binarize" the output of $\mathbb{C}_i$: If $\mathbb{C}_i$ classifies input m as news, we set $f_i^{\mathbb{C}}(m) = 1$; otherwise $f_i^{\mathbb{C}}(m) = -1$.

Finally, by taking the PA values as weights, we aggregate the predictions of k base classifiers to a single prediction in the ensemble manner:

$$f^N(m) = \sum_{i=1}^{k} f^S(e_i) \times f_i^{\mathbb{C}}(m). \qquad (1)$$

A positive $f^N(m)$ value indicates that m is a news microblog.

We use ensemble theory to construct the classifier for the following reasons. First, it matches the structure of input data (news experts' microblogs and PA values). Moreover, PA values are proportional to the confidence of the prediction based on each expert's corpus, since a more processional and active corpus derives a more accurate prediction in principle. Last, the ensemble can be updated at a low cost: the final model (Equation 1) is a linear combination of the sub-models (i.e., $\mathbb{C}_i$'s); each $\mathbb{C}_i$ is based on the corpus of a single news expert ec_i. Therefore, if one expert's corpus is updated (e.g., e_i posts a number of new microblogs), only one sub-model (e.g., $\mathbb{C}_i$) needs to be updated.

2.3 BAV Sorting

The output of the ensemble classifier is just whether a newborn microblog is related to news. Therefore it is likely that a large number of newborn microblogs are classified as news. In order not to overwhelm the user of our system with a potentially huge number of news items, we can *rank* the items and present to the user only the most important ones. However, most of the research on ranking microblogs focus on subjective criteria (e.g., search-based (Y. Duan et al, 2010) or personalized ranking (W. C and I. Uysal, 2011)), which are not suitable for our problem (i.e., the detected newborn news are not based on search keywords or some user). Moreover, the ensemble prediction score (output of Equation 1) is proportional to the confidence of the predicted label, which may be independent to the importance of the classified news post. Therefore, we propose a novel ranking method for newborn news microblogs, called *Behavior-Actor-Venue based Sorting* (BAV sorting, for short). Firstly, for informatively representing news microblogs, we propose method called *Behavior-Actor-Venue BOW* (BAV_{bow}). Then, we apply a *value-transfer with confidence* method to transfer the knowledge of user-defined scores on a training set of microblogs, to the newborn microblogs, which can then be ranked based on their predicted scores.

2.3.1 Behavior-Actor-Venue Representation

Before text analysis, a common pre-processing approach *bag of words* (BOW)(J. L. et al, 2009) converts each document to a set of words, disregarding grammar and even word order. The BOW result is typically improved by eliminating uninformative or noisy terms. Recall that our work focuses on news microblogs; the most important components of a news item can be obtained by three questions: "Where it happened" (Venue),"Who did it" (Actor), and "Did what" (Behavior). Therefore, we design a representation model called *Behavior-Actor-Venue Bag-Of-Word* (BAV_{bow}) for analyzing news microblogs, which only keeps terms related to the information structure of news. These terms are extracted by making use of natural language processing (NLP) techniques, more specifically *Part-Of-Speech* (POS) tagging (S. J. DeRose, 1988) and *Named Entity Recognition* (NER) (F. Abedini et al, 2011). A common use of POS tagging is the identification of words as nouns, verbs, adjectives, adverbs, etc. NER locates and classifies atomic elements in text into predefined categories such as names of persons, organizations, locations, expressions of times, quantities, monetary values, percentages, etc. In news microblogs, verbs always indicate "Did what" (Behavior); persons and organizations recognized by NER always represent "Who did it" (Actors); "Where it happened" (Venues) can be found via Location terms (also recognized by NER). Therefore, in BAV_{bow}, only verbs and nouns related to people, organizations, or locations are kept. For example, a BAV_{bow} representation of "In this morning, Lee had a big parade in Beijing." is {Lee, had, parade, Beijing}.

2.3.2 Importance-Value Transfer with Confidence (VTC)

To assess the importance value $V^I(m)$ of a newborn microblog m in a BAV_{bow} representation, we make use of the concept of *knowledge transfer*; i.e., we transfer the knowledge about the importance values of old microblogs to the unknown values of newborn microblogs. There are several ways to define the importance values of old microblogs. One natural idea is employing the popularity (propagation characteristics) to calculate the importance value. For example, in the experimental part, we simulate the importance value of an old news microblog by how fast it spread among users of the platform. To model the *spread* of an item m, we use the number of reviews $n^r(m)$ and forwards $n^f(m)$ of m in a certain time window after m was published (e.g., one month):

$$V^I(m) = n^r(m) + \beta n^f(m), \quad (2)$$

β is a parameter to control the proportion of two terms.

An alternative way to implement this approach is to allow the users to rate the old news microblogs by themselves. Then the final order of news microblogs will conform to the subjective perception or interest of the users. For example, if they are more interested in news in some categories (e.g., technology), they would give higher values to the old microblogs in these categories; if they are more interested in some particular authors, they would value higher the old microblogs posted by or related to these authors.

Once we we have a *training* set of microblogs $\mathcal{M}_{tr}$ whose Val values are already known (i.e., computed based on spread values or defined by real experts), we can employ VTC to predict the Val-based ranking of news microblogs $\mathcal{M}_{te}$ whose Val values are unknown yet, i.e., $\mathcal{M}_{te}$ is a set of newborn microblogs classified as news by our ensemble classifier.

VTC compares the BAV_{bow} representation $BAV_{bow}(m_j)$ of each $m_j \in M_{te}$ to the BAV_{bow} representations of all $m_i \in M_{tr}$, in order to transfer the Val values of microblogs in $\mathcal{M}_{tr}$ to $V^I(m_j)$, based on the similarity of the representations. The intuition behind the transfer strategy is shown by the following example. Consider two posts m_1 and m_2 with different but overlapping BAV_{bow} representations:

$BAV_{bow}(m_1)$: Lee parade Beijing
$BAV_{bow}(m_2)$: Lee parade

Knowing that m_2 is important provides strong evidence that m_1 is at least somewhat important. However, knowing that m_1 is very important does not allow us to conclude that m_2 is, since the importance value of m_1 might also stem from Beijing. Thus, we can infer that, considering a microblog m_i of $\mathcal{M}_{tr}$ and a microblog m_j of $\mathcal{M}_{te}$, if the term set of m_j contains a large proportion of terms in m_i, then

$V^I(m_i)$ is transferred to $V^I(m_j)$ with high confidence. We define the confidence value of transferring the value of m_i to m_j as follows:

$$V^C(m_i \rightarrow m_j) = \frac{|BAV_{bow}(m_i) \cap BAV_{bow}(m_j)|}{|BAV_{bow}(m_i)|}, \quad (3)$$

where $|\cdot|$ denotes the cardinality of the enclosed set.

Specifically, for each document $m_j \in M_{te}$, we consider each document $m_i \in M_{tr}$, compute the corresponding confidence $V^C(m_i \rightarrow m_j)$, and then transfer the Val value of m_i, with $V^C(m_i \rightarrow m_j)$ as a weight, to m_j:

$$V^I(m_j) = \frac{\sum_i V^I(m_i) \times V^C(m_i \rightarrow m_j)}{|_{m_i \in \mathcal{M}_{tr}} V^C(m_i \rightarrow m_j) \neq 0|}; \quad (4)$$

The denominator of Equation 4 is the number of posts in $\mathcal{M}_{tr}$ for which the transfer confidence to m_j is non-zero. The objective of VTC is to sort the newborn microblogs $m_j \in M_{te}$ in increasing order of their predicted importance values $V^I(m_j)$.

3 Experimental Evaluation

In this section, we evaluate the effectiveness our proposed system. To test our method on news mining from microblogging platforms, we applied it on a collection of microblogs with no propagation knowledge from the SinaWeibo platform. To assess the accuracy of our results, we invited 10 experts to provide correct labels (news vs non-news) to the tested microblogs. All these experts have journalism and linguistics background and their help is acknowledged at the end of the paper. In our evaluation, we divide 1,000 test examples of microblogs in 10 folds. The real labels (i.e., news/non-news) of each fold (containing 100 cases) are evaluated by the experts.

3.1 Experiments on News-Expert Retrieval

As introduced in Section 2.1, our system constructs a microblogging training corpus by selecting news experts. We first define some news related keywords W ={新闻#news#,日报#dairly#, 时报#times#, 晨报, 晚报, 周报, #newspaper#} and then use them as queries to obtain news expert candidates with the threshold θ of minimum number of followers set to 1,000. For constructing the exterior professional corpus, we extracted 70,000 news titles for the period 2008/01/01-2012/12/31 from a news website[1]. Besides, as negative samples for our professionalism classifier $\mathbb{C}$ (see Section 2.1.2), we selected a non-news microblogging corpus of nrealtime 300,000 microblogs. Each has less than 30 Chinese characters and less than 50 forwards.

Finally, we obtained 486 expert candidates and their PA values. The parameter α, which is used in combining professionalism and activity was set to 0.6, giving slightly higher weight to professionalism. Cross-validation (R.Kohavi et al, 2012) could be used to fine-tune this value. Table 1 indicatively shows the expert candidates with the top 3 and bottom 3 PA values. By analyzing their profiles and the microblogs posted by these candidates, we observed that most of these candidates have potential to be news experts since, compared to other users, their microblogs are more focused on news.[2] In order to verify the suitability of our ranking over these candidates (i.e., the suitability of the PA values obtained by our method), we estimated their real professionalism and activity as follows. For each candidate, we extracted the 10 most recently posted microblogs. The number of real news microblogs (as labeled by our invited evaluators) in the fragment (denoted as News_in_10) and the timespan of the microblog sequence (denoted as Time_for_10) are shown in the last two columns of Table 1. By looking at these results, we can see that the PA order indeed reflects the professionalism (i.e., high News_in_10 value) and activity (i.e., low Time_for_10 value) of the users.

After obtaining the expert candidates and their PA values, we select the k candidates with the highest PA values to be the news experts. In order to determine k, we examine the PA values of the 467 candidates in our experiment in decreasing order. By looking closely at this sequence at the area around the 100th expert, we observe that there are several relatively sharp drops. In order to select the best k, we compute the moving average (the window size equals to 20) and compare it with the individual PA values. We select the PA value having the largest difference from the moving average value at that point. This value corresponds to the 109-th rank, thus we select k =108.

[1] http://news.sina.com.cn/media.html

[2] This observation is verified by the invited evaluators familiar with Chinese media.

Table 1: Top-5 and Bottom-5 candidates of news experts

Username	News_in_10 (number)	Time_for_10 (hours)
Top 5		
头条新闻#Breaking News#	10	5
法制日报#Legal Daily#	10	33
新闻晨报#Morning Post#	8	3
西安新闻网#Xi'an Web News#	9	26
宁波日报#Ningbo Daily#	8	16
Bottom 5		
每日甘肃网#Gansu Web Daily#	8	71
江西五套#Jiangxi Channel5#	8	330
晨报周刊#Morning Post Weekly#	5	31
光明日报#Guangming Daily#	7	7
辽沈晚报大活动#LiaoShen Evening Activities#	3	188

3.2 Experiments on News-microblog Classification

To perform detection of news microblogs, we used the posted microblogs (scale: 1,335,884 microblogs) of the k=108 news experts in the period 01/01/2012 to 31/12/2012. The test set (scale: 610,000 microblogs) was collected during January 2013 from about 32,000 users, randomly selected from the whole set of SinaWeibo users. We trained our model (denoted as *Expert-ensemble_pa*) to classify the test microblogs. Here, we compare our method with a natural method as the baseline (denoted as *Single*), which is used in TwitterStand (J. Sankaranarayanan et al, 2009): combine the microblogs from all news experts into a single corpus and train a single classifier. Moreover, to evaluate the fitness of using PA values to be ensemble weights, we also compared our method with Majority Voting (T. G. Dietterich, 2000) (denoted as *Expert-ensemble_mv*) which is a popular method in ensemble learning.

Since the scale of test microblogs is too large, we randomly selected 1,000 of them (including 400 predicted news results and 600 predicted non-news results) and asked our evaluators to label them. Based on the labeling and the prediction by the classifiers, we derived the average performance of the classifiers as shown in Table 2. As Table 2 indicates, our method outperforms the *Single* classifier in all evaluation terms, especially in the precision of news category. This indicates that although the *Single* method can extract most of the news microblogs (i.e. not a bad recall on news), the predicted news microblogs are mixed with a significant number of non-news microblogs. On the other hand, our method uses the PA values of experts as confidences of the individual classifiers in the ensemble and this gives a large improvement in the accuracy of news microblogs classification. Another observation is that the accuracy in predicting non-news is higher than that of predicting news. In other words, the probability of mistaking a news item as a non-news microblog is lower than taking a non-news item as news microblog. Since the cost of mistaking news as non-news microblogs is higher, this result can be considered good for real-world applications.

3.3 Experiments on BAV Sorting

Our method is independent of the definition of importance value Val for news, which may vary in different applications. In this experiment, we use as Val the spread range (as defined by Eq. 2 with $\beta = 4$ and a one-month time window) of microblogs written by news experts during 01/01/2012 to 31/12/2012. The test microblogs are taken from detected news microblogs from the classification experiment (Section 3.2).

Our sorting method is based on (i) the BAVbow representation and (ii) the Value Transfer with Confidence (VTC) approach. To evaluate the effectiveness of using both BAVbow and VTC (BAVbow + VTC) and using BOW and VTC (BOW + VTC), with a random ordering of news (Random). The comparison between BAVbow + VTC and BOW + VTC shows the effectiveness of our proposed BAVbow representation. The comparison between

Table 2: Classification performance

Evaluation terms	Single	Expert-ensemble_mv	Expert-ensemble_pa
Precsion on News	72.6%	86.3%	92.3%
Precsion on Non-news	95.1%	85.8%	96.6%
Recall on News	88.9%	95.1%	93.8%
Recall on Non-news	86.6%	94.2%	95.9%
Overall Precsion	87.2%	92.1%	95.1%

BAVbow (or BOW) + VTC and Random shows the effectiveness of VTC on predicting the importance values of news. For reducing the contingency of Random, we perform the comparison on 10 folds (each fold has 100 test microblogs) and average the results. For exploring the relationship between the real order and the order predicted by our method, in Figure 1, we show the average predicted rank sequences (BAVbow (or BOW) + VTC rank) as a function of the real ranked sequence (1 − 100). To assess the relationship between the real order[3] and the predicted order, we also plot the smoothed lines (by minimizing the least squares error) for BAVbow (or BOW) + VTC. Besides, we include lines corresponding to a Random order and the perfect order prediction.

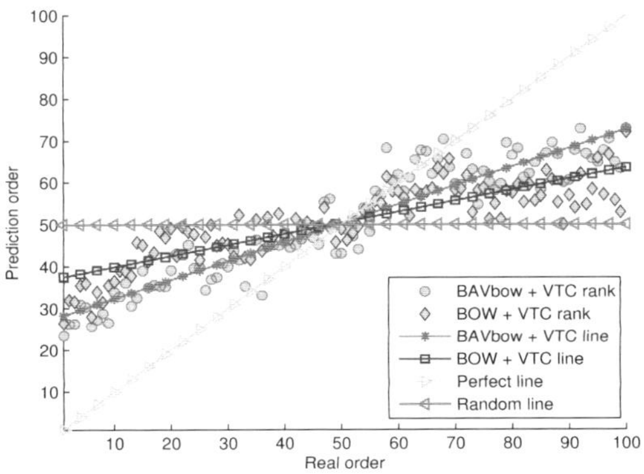

Figure 1: Comparison among BAVbow + VTC, BOW + VTC, perfect and random predictions.

As shown in the Figure 1, BAVbow + VTC is better than BOW + VTC, and the BAVbow + VTC line is closer to the perfect line, which indicates a good performance of our proposed BAVbow on representing news microblogs for knowledge transfer. Moreover, both of BAVbow + VTC and BOW + VTC are positively correlated with the correct ranking, as opposed to the Random line. We note that we also tested a method, which ranks the news posts according to the output of Equation 1 (i.e., confidence of the ensemble classifier) and found that its effectiveness is similar to that of the Random ordering.

[3]We compute the real values of formulation (2) of the test microblogs and then rank them to obtain the real order.

4 Conclusion

We have proposed a methodology for real-time news detection and sorting from microblogging platforms. Our approach automatically selects a set of users who are microblogging news experts. Based on the microblogs already posted by these expert users, together with the professionalism and activity knowledge of experts, we build an expert-ensemble classifier for detecting news microblogs. Then, newborn microblogs, which do not have any prorogation knowledge, will be classified as news or non-news ones. Going one step further, we propose a BAVbow + VTC sorting approach, which orders the detected news microblogs based on their expected value.

References

F. Abedini, F. Mahmoudi, and A. Jadidinejad. From text to knowledge: Semantic entity extraction using yago ontology. *International Journal of Machine Learning and Computing*, 1(2),2011.

F. Z., E. L., Q. Diao, and J. Jiang. Finding bursty topics from microblogs. In *Proceedings of the 50th Annual Meeting of the Association for Computational Linguistics*, pages 536–544. Association for Computational Linguistics, 2012.

G. L., C. S., M. Cataldi, and C. Di. Emerging topic detection on twitter based on temporal and social terms evaluation. In *Proceedings of the 10th International Workshop on Multimedia Data Mining*, page 4. ACM, 2010.

G. P., V. Metsis, and I. Androutsopoulos. Spam filtering with naive bayes-which naive bayes. In *Proceedings of the 3rd Conference on Email and Anti-spam*, volume 17, pages 28–69, 2006.

H. P., S. M., H. Kwak, and C. Lee. What is twitter, a social network or a news media? In *Proceedings of the 19th international conference on World wide web*, pages 591–600. ACM, 2010.

J. L., K. Weinberger, A. Dasgupta et al. Feature hashing for large scale multitask learning. In *Proceedings of the 26th Annual International Conference on Machine Learning*, pages 1113–1120. ACM, 2009.

J. L. and J. Yang. Patterns of temporal variation in online media. In *Proceedings of the 4th ACM international conference on Web search and data mining*, pages 177–186. ACM, 2011.

J. Sankaranarayanan, H. Samet, B. E. Teitler, M. D. Lieberman, and J. Sperling. Twitterstand: news in tweets. In *Proceedings of the 17th ACM SIGSPATIAL International Conference on Advances in Geographic Information Systems*, pages 42–51. ACM, 2009.

M. Y. and L.M. Manevitz. One-class svms for document classification. *The Journal of Machine Learning Research*, 2:139–154, 2002.

R. G. and K. Lerman. Information contagion: An empirical study of the spread of news on digg and twitter social networks. In *Proceedings of 4th International Conference on Weblogs and Social Media*, 2010.

R.Kohavi et al. A study of cross-validation and bootstrap for accuracy estimation and model selection. In *Proceedings of the 14th International Joint Conference on Articial Intelligence*, volume 14, pages 1137–1145, 1995.

S. J. DeRose. Grammatical category disambiguation by statistical optimization. *Computational Linguistics*, 14(1):31–39, 1988.

T. G. Dietterich. Ensemble methods in machine learning. In *Multiple Classifier Systems*, 2000.

W. C. and I. Uysal. User oriented tweet ranking: a filtering approach to microblogs. In *Proceedings of the 20th ACM international conference on Information and knowledge management*, pages 2261–2264. ACM, 2011.

Y. Duan, L. Jiang, T. Qin, M. Zhou, and H.-Y. Shum. An empirical study on learning to rank of tweets. In *Proceedings of the 23rd International Conference on Computational Linguistics*, 2010.

Z. Zhou. *Ensemble Methods: Foundations and Algorithms*. Chapman & Hall, 2012.

Trouble information extraction based on a bootstrap approach from Twitter

Kohei Kurihara **Kazutaka Shimada**
Department of Artificial Intelligence
Kyushu Institute of Technology
680-4 Kawazu Iizuka Fukuoka Japan
shimada@pluto.ai.kyutech.ac.jp

Abstract

In this paper, we propose a method for extracting trouble information from Twitter. One useful approach is based on machine learning techniques such as SVMs. However, trouble information is a fraction of a percent of all tweets on Twitter. In general, imbalanced distribution is not suitable for machine learning techniques to generate a classifier. Another approach is to extract trouble information by using handwritten rules. However, constructing high coverage rules by handwork is costly. First, we verify these problems in a preliminary experiment. Then, to solve these problems, we apply a bootstrapping method to our trouble information extraction task. We introduce three characteristics and a scoring method to the bootstrapping. As a result, the iteration process on the bootstrapping increased the number of tweets and patterns for trouble information dramatically.

1 Introduction

The World Wide Web contains a huge number of online documents that are easily accessible. Analysis of the documents has an important role for natural language processing. One of the important information for business companies is trouble information of a product as the risk management. If they can monitor the information about products and the troubles from the Web automatically, they might be able to avoid critical damages by realizing the risk in advance. Therefore trouble information extraction is a significant task in business. There are many studies which handled news articles (Sakai et al., 2006), review documents (Ivanov and Tutubalina, 2014), financial documents (Leider and Schilder, 2010), daily reports (Kakimoto and Yamamoto, 2008), a failure database on the Web (Awano et al., 2012) and so on, as the target data. However, these information sources are not usually instantaneous and exhaustive. To solve this problem, we focus on Twitter. It is one of the most famous microblogging services and text-based posts of up to 140 characters. The posted sentences are described as "tweets." We suppose users on Twitter often post tweets with trouble information because they tend to post tweets as lifelog data in real time. Some researchers focused on the characteristic (Aramaki et al., 2011; Sakaki et al., 2010; Shimada et al., 2012).

In this paper, we propose a method to extract trouble information from Twitter. One of the most common approaches is to classify an input into trouble information and non-trouble information by using a machine learning technique. However, most of the tweets do not relate to trouble information. In other word, the ratio of trouble tweets and non-trouble tweets is biased. Such biased data generally generate a unsuitable classifier. Another approach is to extract trouble information by using handwritten rules. However, constructing high coverage rules by handwork is usually a difficult task. In this paper, we investigate these problems through a preliminary experiment. On the basis of the result, we introduce a bootstrapping approach to our trouble information extraction task. Methods based on bootstrapping techniques are one of the effective approaches to extract information (Riloff and Jones, 1999; Etzioni et al., 2004). Riloff et al. (2013) have pro-

29th Pacific Asia Conference on Language, Information and Computation pages 471 - 479
Shanghai, China, October 30 - November 1, 2015

posed a method to identify sarcastic tweets by using a bootstrapping algorithm. Ohmori and Mori (2010) have proposed a method based on a bootstrapping approach with words and phrases for searching for failure cases among products. We focus on trouble expressions which indicate the malfunction and failure of products. We apply the trouble expressions as seeds into a bootstrapping approach. By the iteration process, our method obtains more trouble expressions, and then extracts tweets with trouble information.

2 Related work

Trouble identification is one category in sentiment analysis (Pang and Lee, 2008). The classification into trouble or non-trouble is similar to the classification into positive or negative (Pang et al., 2002; Turney, 2002). However, negative opinions are not always equal to trouble information. For example, "I don't like this product" is a negative opinion, but not trouble information. Therefore, they should be distinguished.

Saeger et al. (2008) have proposed a method to extract object-trouble relations from the Web. They acquired trouble expressions by an unsupervised method, and then classify them by using SVMs. Gupta (2011) has proposed a method to extract problem information using a machine learning technique from Twitter. As the two papers mentioned, the trouble descriptions in the training data were rare, less than 10%. In other words, the ratio of positive and negative instances for this task tends to be biased. Therefore, machine learning approaches are not always suitable for this task.

Solovyev and Ivanov (2014) have proposed a dictionary-based problem phrase extraction from product reviews. It was based on a simple pattern matching with their dictionaries. In (Ivanov and Tutubalina, 2014), they incorporated a clause feature, but-conjunction, with the dictionary-based method. Kakimoto and Yamamoto (2008) have proposed a method based on syntactic pieces for extracting troubles. The basic idea in these studies is similar to our method. However, these approaches did not contain an iteration process like bootstrapping. Although bootstrapping methods often generate noise seeds for the next process and the wrong seeds lead to the decrease of the precision rate, namely semantic drift, the iteration process is vital to obtain the high recall rate.

Although there are studies based on a bootstrapping approach such as (Leider and Schilder, 2010; Ohmori and Mori, 2010), the targets are not Twitter. Riloff et al. (2013) have handled tweets and used a bootstrapping approach for their task. However, the purpose is to generate a sarcasm recognizer.

3 Trouble information

In this section, we explain the target trouble information in this paper. Here we introduce two words; trouble sentences (TS) and trouble expressions (TE). The TSs are our target in the extraction process. They are tweets with trouble information about a product[1]. The TEs are phrases which indicate trouble situation, failure and so on.

TS : Why? My smartphone isn't powered on....
TE : not powered on

In this paper, a TS needs to contain a product name/information and TE(s). In other words, we do not handle any tweets without a product name/information. In the above instance, "smartphone" is the product name/information. For TEs, we admit figurative phrases, emoticons and Internet slangs. For example, "My phone is dead" and "The home button on iPhone is wroooooong (ToT)."

4 Preliminary experiment

In this section, we describe some problems of a simple machine learning approach and a rule-based approach through an experiment.

4.1 Machine learning based

We constructed a classification model based on SVM (Vapnik, 1995). We used SVM^{light} (Joachims, 1998) for the implementation. Although we utilized some features about emoticons, Internet slang dictionaries and so on, they were not effective. Therefore, we used only the bag-of-words features for SVM.

We prepared 900 tweets for the training data; 450 positive and 450 negative instances. We evaluated

[1]The actual tweets in the experiment are written in Japanese.

Recall	Precision	F
0.88	0.98	0.93

Table 1: The experimental result on the leave-one-out cross-validation.

# of EXT	# of COR	Precision
3,742	720	0.19

Table 2: The experimental result for a realistic situation.

the machine learning based method with the leave-one-out cross-validation. Table 1 shows the experimental result. The method produced high recall and precision rates for the cross-validation. However, most of real tweets are non-trouble information. In other words, this situation is not on the real world. Therefore, we also evaluated our method trained by 900 tweets with 30,000 tweets that extracted from Twitter randomly, as an opened test set. This is an real situation, namely unbalance data. We judged the correctness of the outputs of SVM. Table 2 shows the experimental result for the unbalance data. The EXT and COR in the table denote the number of tweets extracted by SVM and the number of tweets extracted correctly, respectively. From the table, the machine learning based method was not suitable for this task because the precision rate on the realistic data set dramatically decreased.

4.2 Rule-based

We also constructed a rule-based method with a simple matching approach. We prepared trouble expressions (TEs) by handwork. Although trouble sentences (TSs) always contain TE(s), all sentences with TEs are not always TSs. Therefore, we also prepared NG phrases for the rule-based method. For example, "can't charge" is a TE for mobile phones. However, "I can't charge my phone because I don't have a charger now" is not a TS because it is not trouble information about a product. To solve this problem, we need to add a NG phrase "because I don't have a charger."

We evaluated our rule-based method with 30,000 tweets in Section 4.1. Table 3 shows the experimental result. We obtained high precision rate by using the rule-based method, as compared with the machine learning method (See Table 2.) On the other hand, the number of tweets extracted correctly was reduced almost by half (720 vs. 444). As a result, the simple rule-based method faced with another problem for this task.

# of EXT	# of COR	Precision
474	444	0.94

Table 3: The experimental result of the rule-based method on the same situation with SVM.

4.3 Discussion

The problem of the machine learning method is caused by the number of tweets and the ratio of positive and negative instances in the training data. The training data with 900 instances was insufficient in terms of the size for machine learning, especially the coverage of non-trouble information. Besides, a classifier in this situation often generates a poor result because the distribution of the training data differs from that of the real data. One intuitive solution is to add new tweets as positive/negative instances. However, collecting tweets with positive/negative by handwork is costly. Moreover, the concrete definition of non-trouble tweets is essentially difficult. Since the realistic situation contains many non-trouble tweets as compared with trouble tweets, the training data should contain many non-trouble tweets. However, combined with the difficulty of the concrete definition of non-trouble tweets, collecting non-trouble tweets with high coverage is also a difficult task. Therefore, machine learning approaches are not appropriate for our task.

The rule-based method obtained the high precision rate. The reason was that we could focus on the trouble expressions in the method as compared with the machine learning method. Although we naturally needed to prepare NG phrases, the effort for the rule-based method was less than that for the machine learning method. Therefore, rule-based methods are essentially appropriate for our task. However, the recall rate was a critical problem for the method. One solution is to increase the number of TEs for the extraction process. On the other hand, constructing TEs with high coverage by handwork is costly. Therefore, we need to extract TEs from tweets automatically.

5 Proposed method

On the basis of the discussion in the previous section, we expand our rule-base method with a bootstrapping approach. The bootstrapping approach leads to the improvement of the coverage of the original rule-based method.

5.1 Outline

For extracting various types of trouble sentences, TSs, it is necessary to acquire new trouble expressions, TEs, automatically. In general, some TEs often appear in one TS. We focus on this characteristic. Figure 1 shows an example. Here, "broken" is a TE, a seed for a bootstrapping approach. Assume that the TE and the phrase "not make a call" often cooccur in tweets. From this observation, our method obtains the phrase "not make a call" as a new TE, and then extract a new TS by the new TE.

The outline of our method is shown in Figure 2. First, we create seed words with strong trouble meanings for a target product by hand. By using the initial seeds, namely TEs, our method extracts TSs from a tweet corpus. For the TS extraction process, we judge the presence of TEs in each sentence. As exceptional treatment, we prepare some non-extraction rules. The non-extraction rules contain hearsay expressions such as "someone told me that" and non-factual expressions such as "feel like." We do not extract sentences matching with the non extraction rules as TSs. Next, our method extracts TE candidates from the extracted TSs. For the candidates, we apply a scoring method for computing a confidence measure as new TEs. We acquire only TEs with high confidence values as new TEs. Finally, we add the new TEs to the previous seeds. Our method iterates these processes until it fulfills certain conditions. In this paper, we set two conditions; (1) if the iteration is repeated at 5 times or (2) if the method does not acquire new TEs.

5.2 TE acquisition

TE extraction is based on surface and part-of-speech tags patterns. We focus on the following characteristics for the extraction.

Specific adverbs Adverbs are closely related to trouble information. Murakami and Nasukawa (2011) have proposed a method to detect potential problems from documents. They focused on adverbs, such as "suddenly" and "arbitrarily", to detect the nouns and verbs that described the actual problems. This is a language-independent characteristic. We also extract phrases with the specific adverbs as TEs.

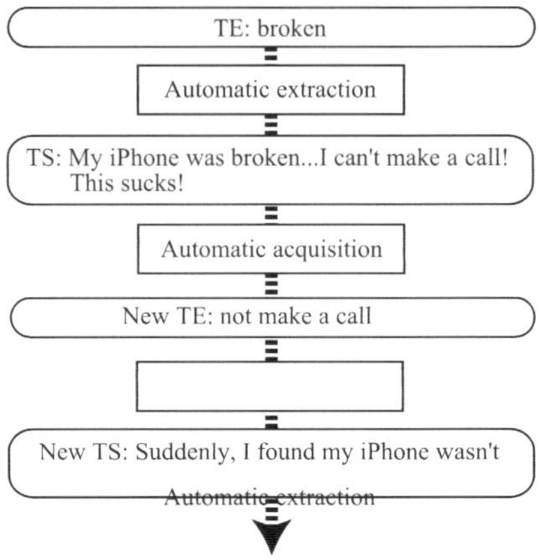

Figure 1: An example of the extraction process.

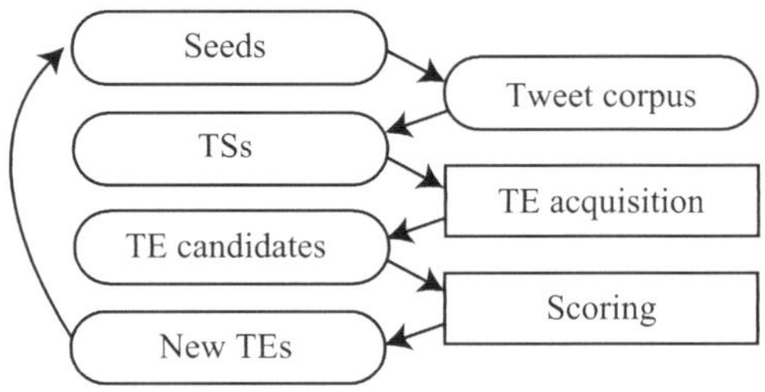

Figure 2: The outline of our method.

Imperfective forms The target tweets in this paper are written in Japanese. As one Japanese characteristic, TSs often contain the imperfective form of a verb with negation[2]. We extract phrases with this pattern as TEs.

Negative words As we mentioned in Section 2, negative opinions are closely related to trouble information. Tweets with negative expressions have high potentiality for TEs and TSs. On the other hand, as we also mentioned in Section 2, negative opinions are not always equal

[2]E.g., "動か ない (not work)" and "起動し ない (not start)."

to trouble information. Utilizing general sentiment dictionaries is not always suitable for this task because they contain many negative words not related to trouble information. In this paper, we prepare negative words related to trouble information about a target product, such as "bad", "wrong" and "failure", as a negative word set. We extract phrases with the negative words.

5.3 Scoring

A bootstrapping approach uses the previous outputs from the system as the inputs for the system in the next step. If the precision of the outputs is low, it leads to the decrease of the precision of the next outputs. The accuracy deterioration by the change of the meaning of seeds is well-known as "Semantic drift" (Curran et al., 2007). To solve this problem, we need to keep high precision in the iteration process. In other words, we need to reject noise TEs in candidate TEs. Therefore, we need to estimate a confidence measure of each candidate TE.

One of the most successful approaches is the Espresso algorithm (Komachi et al., 2008; Pantel and Pennacchiotti, 2006). The algorithm was based on recursive definition of pattern-instance scoring metrics. It computed the pointwise mutual information between each pattern and instance recursively. The method in this paper does not handle any patterns for the bootstrapping process. Therefore, we cannot incorporate this algorithm into our method directly.

We introduce another scoring method for a confidence measure in the bootstrapping process. First, we compute confidence values of nouns, verbs and adjectives in TSs. Then, we estimate the confidence value of each TE on the basis of the confidence values. The confidence measure is based on the following hypothesis:

- if a word frequently appears in TSs, the TE likelihood of the word is high.
- words appearing near a product name[3] contain high TE likelihood.

[3]It denotes not only concrete product names, such as "iPhone", but also product categories, such as "smartphone."

The value of a word w is computed as follows:

$$WS_w = \sum_{i \in I} \frac{1}{dist_i(w)} \tag{1}$$

where i and I are a sentence and sentences including a product name, respectively. $dist_i(w)$ is the distance between a product name and w in i. The confidence measure of a TE_t is the average value of WS_w in the TE.

$$TEscore_t = \frac{1}{N_w} \sum_{w \in TE_t} WS_w \tag{2}$$

where N_w is the number of words in TE_t. If a TE contains frequent words with the high WS_w, it obtains high $TEscore$.

After computation of $TEscore$, we extract phrases in the top $N\%$ as the new seeds for the next iteration. If the phrases in the current top $N\%$ are the same as the phrases in the previous step, the iteration is terminated.

6 Experiment

In this section, we evaluate our method with real tweets, and then discuss the results.

6.1 Result

The target product was cellphones. We collected 100,000 tweets about cellphones as the data set. These tweets contained words that related to cellphones. As initial seeds, we set the following seven words; 壊れる (broken), おかしい (wrong), 異常 (defect), 故障 (defect), フリーズ (freeze) and バグ (bug). We applied the seeds to the data set, and then obtained TEs and TSs by using the proposed bootstrapping method. In this experiment, the total number of iterations was 5. More properly speaking, when the number of iteration was 5, our method did not obtain new TEs. In other words, both of the two conditions in Section 5.1 were fortuitously fulfilled in this iteration.

Figure 3 shows the result of the precision rate and the number of extracted TSs on the iteration. Our method increased the number of TSs in the second step by using new TEs extracted in the first step. Despite the increase of TSs, our method maintained a high precision rate in the second step. After the third step, our method obtained a small increase in

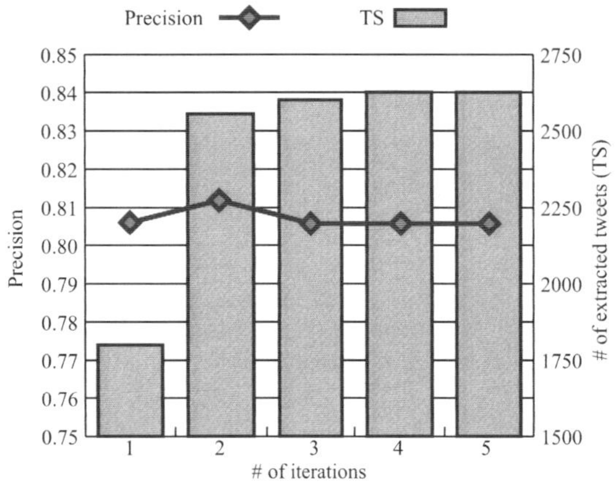

Figure 3: The precision and the number of TSs in each iteration.

勝手に電源がつく
(turn on arbitrarily)
電源がつかない
(not turn on)
急に電源が落ちる
(power off suddenly)
電源が落ちない
(not power off)
ボタンが押せない
(not push the button)
勝手にスピーカーがミュートになる
(put the speaker on mute arbitrarily)

Table 4: Extracted TEs.

# of tweets	# of TSs
10,000	121
50,000	623
100,000	2,623
500,000	9,088

Table 5: The number of extracted TSs on several data sets. The third row is the same as Section 6.1.

terms of the number of TSs and also held the high precision rate. This result denotes that the scoring method in Section 5.3 was effective for the bootstrapping in terms of the noise reduction from candidate TEs. The experimental result shows the effectiveness of our method, as compared with a non-bootstrapping method, because the result in the second step, namely bootstrapping, outperformed that in the first step, non-bootstrapping.

6.2 Analysis and discussion

Our method extracted TSs with a high precision rate through the iteration in the bootstrapping. Table 4 shows instances of TEs extracted by the method. These TEs related to the category "cellphones" and were suitable for the extraction of TSs. Our method correctly extracted some phrases with the opposite meaning, such as "turn on automatically" and "not turn on." These TEs were distinguished by adverbs; "arbitrarily" and "suddenly." It is difficult to extract these TEs by using only general sentiment dictionaries. We also obtained domain specific TEs, such as "put the speaker on mute arbitrarily." Our method extracted various types of TEs by using the bootstrapping method.

Next, we discuss the size of the target data and the accuracy. If the data size is small, our method might not extract sufficient TEs. As a result, it leads to the decrease of the number of TSs. If the data size is large, our method might extract many inappropriate TEs. It probably leads to the increase of the number of TSs with non-trouble information and the decrease of the precision. We investigated our method with the different size of data sets. Table 5 shows the result. For smaller data set, namely 10,000 and 50,000 tweets, the number of extracted TSs decreased dramatically. In these data sets, the number of outputs in the first iteration was insufficient. As a result, our method could not obtain TSs and new TEs in the next process. Thus, our method needs an adequate amount of tweets for the TE acquisition process. For a larger data set, 500,000 tweets, the predicted number of TSs was approximately 13,000[4]. The actual number of extracted TSs in the larger data set was 9,088. The result indicates that our method controlled noise TEs appropriately in the bootstrapping process. In addition, our method extracted different types of TEs from the larger data set, such as 勝手にアプリが起動する（an app starts arbitrarily） カードを読み込まない (not recognize a card) and 時計進まない (clock not work). Our method was robust to the increase

[4]It was $13,115 = 2,623 \times 5$ by simple arithmetic.

of target data and could extract new TEs and TSs efficiently.

Finally, we explain the results of TSs. The following sentences are tweets extracted from our method:

- 充電切れるわケータイ熱くなっちゃって充電できないわ勝手に電源切れるわ最悪です (My cellphone ran out of charge, too hot to charge the battery and power off automatically .... This sucks!)
- てか携帯画面真っ黒になって電池パック抜いて電源入れようとしても電源つかないんだけど (The display of my cellphone blacked out, I removed the battery, and then I powered on it, but it isn't turned on.)

Although these tweets did not contain direct expressions to trouble information, such as 壊れた (broken), our method correctly extracted them with acquired TEs, such as 勝手に電源が落ちる (power off automatically) and 電源がつかない (not turn on). The following sentence is an incorrect output TS from our method.

- iPhone の充電ケーブル壊れた (;´Д｀) 充電できない (;´Д｀) (The charging cable of my iPhone was broken ... I can't charge the battery.)

This tweet is trouble information about accessories, but not a TS for a cellphone itself. In this experiment, we regarded this kind of outputs as negative results. This is a difficult problem in trouble information extraction. One solution is to add NG rules to the extraction process. However, we cannot solve a problem of the following sentence, which is also a negative result, by addition of NG rules.

- どしたんやろーなんかあったんかな (･ω･｀) iPhone 壊れたんかな (An accident had happened (to him/her)? ... (his/her) iPhone might be broken[5].)

This tweet contained a trouble expression, but it is not a TS for a cellphone. It implied that a user was worried about someone. This problem is more difficult because we need deep analysis including semantics to solve it. Handling metaphor and Internet slangs appropriately is also important future work.

In the experiment, we evaluated our method in terms of the precision rate because it is difficult to measure the recall rate. Although we obtained more TSs by using our method, the number of TSs might be insufficient, namely the low recall rate. To improve this problem is the most important issue for our method.

We judged the correctness of the extracted TSs in Figure 3 with one annotator. We prepared a manual for the annotation, such as the definition of trouble information, in advance. However, for more correct and reliable annotation, we need to annotate TSs with several annotators and compute the agreement among them. This is also important future work.

7 Conclusions

In this paper, we proposed a bootstrapping method to extract trouble information from Twitter. As a preliminary experiment, we evaluated a simple machine learning method based on SVM and a simple rule-based method. Although the SVM-based method worked well for the cross-validation about a small data set, the precision rate dramatically decreased for a real and unknown tweet data set. The rule-based method obtained a high precision rate as compared with SVM. However, TSs extracted correctly were reduced almost by half. The main problems of these methods were (1) biased data, (2) coverage about non-trouble information and (3) a limited number of trouble expressions (TEs).

To solve the problems, we applied a bootstrapping approach to the trouble information extraction. By using a small seed set and the bootstrapping approach, our method increased the number of extracted trouble sentences (TSs) by 50% with a high precision rate. We used three characteristics in the TE acquisition; specific adverbs, imperfective forms and negative words. In addition, we introduced a scoring method to avoid the semantic drift problem. The scoring was based on the distance between product information and each word. We verified the effectiveness of our method with different size of data sets. Our method was robust to the increase

[5] Note that the question mark and the word "might" in the English translation don't appear explicitly in the original Japanese sentence.

of target data and could extract new TEs and TSs efficiently.

In the discussion part of this paper, we explained some problems through the extracted TSs. A simple solution to improve the accuracy is to expand rules for the TE acquisition. In addition, we need to introduce more deep analysis, such as semantic analysis, for the difficult problem described in Section 6.2. We have obtained many tweets with trouble information by our method. Deeper trouble mining from the tweets, such as risk-prone analysis, and visualization of the trouble information are our important future work. Torisawa et al. (2008) have reported a system based on graph drawing as a web search directory. It mapped a topic that a user inputted and the related keywords. This approach is useful to find and understand potential troubles from the extracted TSs. Another useful visualization approach is TreeMap styles (Johnson and Shneiderman, 1991). Carenini et al. (2006) have proposed an interactive multimedia summarization system based on a text summary and a visual summary. Shimada et al. (2010) have reported an interactive multimedia summarization method with the Tree-Map and fisheye-like styles for clustered sentences. The summarization and visualization of the extracted TSs are interesting future work.

References

Eiji Aramaki, Sachiko Maskawa, and Mizuki Morita. 2011. Twitter catches the flu: Detecting influenza epidemics using twitter. In *Proceedings of Conference on Empirical Methods in Natural Language Processing*, pages 1568–1576.

Yuki Awano, Qiang Ma, and Masatoshi Yoshikawa. 2012. Cause analysis of new incidents by using failure knowledge database. In *Proceedings of the 23rd International Conference on Database and Expert Systems Applications (DEXA 2012)*, pages 88–102.

Giuseppe Carenini, Raymond T. Ng, and Adam Pauls. 2006. Interactive multimedia summaries of evaluative text. In *Proceedings of Intelligent User Interfaces (IUI)*, pages 124–131.

James R. Curran, Tara Murphy, and Bernhard Scholz. 2007. Minimising semantic drift with mutual exclusion bootstrapping. In *Proceedings of the 10th Conference of the Pacific Association for Computational Linguistics (2007)*, pages 172–180.

Oren Etzioni, Michael Cafarella, Doug Downey, Stanley Kok, Ana-Maria Popescu, Tal Shaked, Stephen Soderland, Daniel S. Weld, and Alexander Yates. 2004. Web-scale information extraction in knowitall (preliminary results). In *Proceedings of the 13th international conference on World Wide Web (WWW2004)*, pages 100–110.

Narendra K. Gupta. 2011. Extracting descriptions of problems with product and service from twitter data. In *Proceedings of the 3rd Workshop on Social Web Search and Mining (SWSM2011)*.

Vladimir Ivanov and Elena Tutubalina. 2014. Clause-based approach to extracting problem phrases from user reviews of products. In *Analysis of Images, Social Networks and Texts, AIST 2014*, pages 229–236.

Thorsten Joachims. 1998. Text categorization with support vector machines: Learning with many relevant features. In *European Conference on Machine Learning (ECML)*, pages 137–142.

Brian Johnson and Ben Shneiderman. 1991. Treemaps: A space-filling approach to the visualization of hierarchical information structures. In *Proceedings of the 2nd International IEEE Visualization Conference*, pages 284–291.

Yoshifumi Kakimoto and Kazuhide Yamamoto. 2008. Extracting troubles from daily reports based on syntactic pieces. In *Proceedings of PACLIC 22*, pages 411–417.

Mamoru Komachi, Taku Kudo, Masashi Shimbo, and Yuji Matsumoto. 2008. Graph-based analysis of semantic drift in espresso-like bootstrapping algorithms. In *Proceedings of EMNLP 2008*, pages 1011–1020.

Jochen L. Leider and Frank Schilder. 2010. Hunting for the black swan: Risk mining from text. In *Proceedings of ACL2010 System Demonstration*, pages 54–59.

Takuma Murakami and Tetsuya Nasukawa. 2011. Detecting potential issues based on typical problem description (in Japanese). In *IEICE, SIG-NLC, 111*, pages 31–35.

Nobuyuki Ohmori and Tatsunori Mori. 2010. Novel approach for test methods automatic selection in product reliability — improved method for acquiring part-whole relation —. In *Proceedings of International Conference on Machine Learning and Application (ICMLA 2010)*, pages 834–839.

Bo Pang and Lillian Lee. 2008. Opinion mining and sentiment analysis. *Foundations and TrendsR in Information Retrieval*, 2.

Bo Pang, Lillian Lee, and Shivakumar Vaithyanathan. 2002. Thumbs up? sentiment classification using machine learning techniques. In *Proceedings of the Conference on Empirical Methods in Natural Language Processing (EMNLP)*, pages 79–86.

Patrick Pantel and Marco Pennacchiotti. 2006. Espresso: leveraging generic patterns for automatically harvesting semantic relations. In *Proceedings of the 44th annual meeting of the Association for Computational Linguistics*, pages 113–120.

Ellen Riloff and Rosie Jones. 1999. Learning dictionaries for information extraction by multi-level bootstrapping. In *Proceeding of AAAI 99*, pages 474–479.

Ellen Riloff, Ashequl Qadir, Prafulla Surve, Lalindra De Silva, Nathan Gilbert, and Ruihong Huang. 2013. Sarcasm as contrast between a positive sentiment and negative situation. In *Proceedings of EMNLP 2013*, pages 704–714.

Stijn De Saeger, Kentaro Torisawa, and Jun'ichi Kazama. 2008. Looking for trouble. In *Proceedings of COLING 08*, pages 185–192.

Hiroyuki Sakai, Shouji Umemura, and Shigeru Masuyama. 2006. Extraction of expressions concerning accident cause contained in articles on traffic accidents (in Japanese). *Journal of Natural Language Processing*, 13(2):99–123.

Takeshi Sakaki, Makoto Okazaki, and Yutaka Matsuo. 2010. Earthquake shakes twitter users: real-time event detection by social sensors. In *Proceedings of the 19th international conference on World Wide Web (WWW2010)*, pages 851–860.

Kazutaka Shimada, Masahi Yamaumi, Ryosuke Tadano, Masashi Hadano, and Tsutomu Endo. 2010. Interactive aspect summarization using word-aspect relations for review documents. In *Proceedings of the 5th International Conference on Soft Computing and Intelligent Systems and 11th International Symposium on Advanced Intelligent Systems (SCIS & ISIS 2010)*, pages 183–188.

Kazutaka Shimada, Shunsuke Inoue, and Tsutomu Endo. 2012. On-site likelihood identification of tweets for tourism information analysis. In *Proceedings of 3rd IIAI International Conference on e-Services and Knowledge Management (IIAI ESKM 2012)*, pages 117–122.

Valery Solovyev and Vladimir Ivanov. 2014. Dictionary-based problem phrase extraction from user reviews. In *Proceedings of TSD 2014, LNAI 8655*, pages 225–232.

Kentaro Torisawa, Stijn De Saeger, Yasunori Kakizawa, Jun'ichi Kazama, Masaki Murata, Daisuke Noguchi, and Asuka Sumida. 2008. Torishiki-kai, an autogenerated web search directory. In *Proceedings of the Second International Symposium on Universal Communication (ISUC 2008)*, pages 179–186.

Peter D. Turney. 2002. Thumbs up or thumbs down?: Semantic orientation applied to unsupervised classification of reviews. In *Proceedings of the 40th Annual Meeting on Association for Computational Linguistics*, ACL '02, pages 417–424.

Vladimir N. Vapnik. 1995. *The Nature of Statistical Learning Theory*. Springer-Verlag New York, Inc.

Using Twitter Data to Infer Personal Values of Japanese Consumers

Yinjun Hu
Synergy Marketing, Inc.
Dojima-Avanza 21F, 1-6-20 Dojima,
Kita-ku, Osaka 530-0003, Japan.
ko.inshun@syngery101.jp

Yasuo Tanida
Synergy Marketing, Inc.
Dojima-Avanza 21F, 1-6-20 Dojima,
Kita-ku, Osaka 530-0003, Japan.
tanida.yasuo@synergy101.jp

Abstract

Our purpose is to use Twitter data to infer personal values in marketing for Japanese consumers. In this paper, we reintroduce our personal value system and apply the model for inferring personal values with tweets. To adapt the model to the rapid change of wording in tweets, we propose a dynamic model based on time-weighted frequency in this research. We evaluated the prediction results from our previous approach, newly proposed approach (the dynamic model), and other methods with 10-fold cross-validation. Our experiment results show that personal values can be inferred from Twitter data, and our approach based on Bayesian network performs well with skewed training data.

1 Introduction

In marketing science, personal values have been considered the central determinants of consumer behavior. They are widely used for market segmentation and behavioral prediction. VALS (Values And Lifestyles) is a personal value system for market segmentation,[1] and (Wu, 2005) reconstructed it for Chinese consumers as China-Vals. Similarly, we developed a value system for Japanese consumers based on the *AIO (Activities, Interests, and Opinions)* (Plummer, 1974) rating statement during last two years. We gathered about 20,000 Japanese consumers' personal values data via questionnaires, and filled the value system database with this data.

Although we can "talk to" consumers directly with a questionnaire approach, subjective biases may appear in answers, such as a response-bias (Peer and Gamliel, 2011) and a choice-supportive bias (Mather et al., 2000). On the other hand, a data mining approach like microblog analysis, which is considered to have a sampling bias problem, as checked by (Mislove et al., 2011), can get objective "answers" for the "questions" without subjective biases. Hence, a microblog mining approach, like mining tweets, may be a complement to the questionnaire approach. Moreover, (Chen et al., 2014) pointed out that word use may be influenced by values, and made an effort to analyze the associations between personal values and their word uses in social media. In our research, we use Twitter for a data mining approach to infer personal values, because we consider that users on Twitter tend to tweet their real intentions with limited impersonation.

In our previous work, we proposed a model for extracting personal values from tweets with text mining technologies. This model demonstrated that we were able to predict consumer behavior with tweets and our value system. As a result, we applied it to marketing consulting and social contribution for trial-and-error. However, the wording on Twitter changes frequently, and the keywords used for inference in this model may be out of date. Hence, in this research, we propose a dynamic model which can update itself automatically. In addition, a detailed methodological comparison between our proposed model and other methods is discussed from the experiment results.

[1] VALS is developed by Mitchell, Arnold (May 1984) in the book *Nine American Lifestyles: Who We Are and Where We're Going*.

29th Pacific Asia Conference on Language, Information and Computation pages 480 - 487
Shanghai, China, October 30 - November 1, 2015

2 Methodology

2.1 A Value System for Japanese Consumers

To determine the latent benefits and interests of Japanese consumers, we proposed a value system for Japanese people during previous two years. The system contains 61 components *(value component, VC)* covering 8 frames of personal values extracted from 20,000 questionnaires with principal component analysis (PCA). However, an abbreviated and more flexible version of this system with 22 components (mini version) was preferred to use, because the questionnaire of mini version has only 60 questions as opposed to 303 questions for the full version. Table 1 shows details of the 22 components above. The instance of each component can be a binary value (i.e., 0 or 1). In addition, we defined 12 social types named *Societas* from full version with Ward's method, and trained the Societas Model with the Bayesian network (Pearl, 1985). We also take the word *Societas* in the wide sense of the value system we proposed.

Frame Name	Component Name
Character	Curiosity, Delicacy, Laxity, Cooperativeness
Positive	Narcissism, Self-realization
Negative	Sensitivity to criticism, Sensitivity to lack of common sense, Sensitivity to disappointment
Human relationship	Stress, Friendship emphasizing
Family relationship	Marriage aspiration, Spousal responsibility as housewife, Family discord
Sense of job	Satisfaction, Stress
Sense of money	Lack of money, Savings, Sufficiency
Sense of time	Priority to family, Sufficiency, Lack of time

Table 1: The detail of 22 value components in the mini version of Societas.

2.2 Societas Inference with Twitter Data

Model Our previous work proposed a model called *TwitterSocietas* for inferring Societas values from Twitter data. We made an effort to construct a TwitterSocietas Model with Bayesian network and the training data is extracted as follows.

1. Obtain Societas values (mini version) and Twitter id via questionnaires. Then, make a unique word set W from tweets of all users, and refine W with a DF(document frequency, we treat each Twitter user's tweets as a document) between 10% and 90%.

2. Calculate importance scores for each <word, VC> paired with the following formula.

   $$|P(w \in W_i|V_j = 1) - P(w \in W_i|V_j = 0)|$$

   Where, W_i represents the unique word set extracted from Twitter user i, V_j represents the binary set of value component j for all users calculated from the questionnaires, and w is the word in W.

3. For each value component, sort the importance score pairs decreasingly, and extract the top 30 words as the feature keywords *(speech keyword)* of the value component.

4. For each <speech keyword, VC> pair, calculate the relevant coefficients by Algorithm 1.

5. Calculate the binary data *(speech component, SC)* of speech keywords for each value component with the relevant coefficients as:

   $$f(SC) = \begin{cases} 1 & \text{if } \vec{kw} \cdot \vec{pca} - \bar{pca} > 0 \\ 0 & \text{otherwise} \end{cases} \quad (1)$$

   Where $\vec{kw}$ represents the vector of speech keyword appearance in Twitter user's vocabulary W_i, $\vec{pca}$ represents the relevant coefficient(i.e., $pca1$ or $pca2$ in Algorithm 1), and $\bar{pca}$ is the mean for all Twitter users.

6. Merge speech components and values components into the training data of TwitterSocietas Model IN the format of <SC1 for VC1, SC2 for VC1, SC1 for VC2, ..., VC1, VC2>

Notice that only the approach of inferring 22 value components is mentioned here because these components can be seen as the characteristics of 12 social types.

Algorithm 1 Relevant coefficients generation.

Input: speech keywords KW for value component j, word set $\{WC\}$ for all tweets, and the binary set V_j of value component j.

Output: Relevant coefficients data.

```
1: WT ⇐ matrix of length(Twitter users) * 30
   elements and initialize all elements to 0
2: for i = 1 to length(Twitter users) do
3:    for each kw in KW do
4:       if KW[k] in WC[i] then
5:          WT[i][kw] ⇐ 1
6:       end if
7:    end for
8: end for
9: pca ⇐ PCA(WT, V_j)
10: return 30 pairs of <pca1, pca2>, where pca1
    and pca2 represents the weights of the first prin-
    ciple component and the second one from pca
    for each speech keyword.
```

Inference We use the same approach of step 5 above to generate the evidence from object Twitter data, and the evidence contains 44 speech components (i.e., each value component has 2 speech components) in binary. To infer the personal values with 44 speech components, we employ the Loopy Belief Propagation algorithm in (Weiss, 2000) . As a result, the inferred data of value components are probabilities so that they can be used more flexibly than binary ones.

2.3 A Dynamic TwitterSocietas Model

As Twitter data is updated frequently, the words used in TwitterSocietas have an *aged problem* as soon as the tendency of wording in tweets changes. Furthermore, we assume that wording changes more frequently than personal values, so that recent tweets may be related to users' personal values more deeply than older ones. Hence, we propose an auto-updating TwitterSocietas Model in which recent tweets are weighted.

- Firstly, we define a weight of the words in each tweet as:

$$W1(w,t) = \sum_{i=1}^{N} \frac{C-i+1}{C} \times f(w,i) \quad (2)$$

$W1(w,t)$ is a function to calculate the weight of word w for Twitter user t. Where i represents the newness of tweet, i.e., $f(w,i)$ in (2) is related to the latest tweet of user t when i equals to 1. $f(w,i)$ is the relative frequency of word w in user t's ith newest tweet, and can be calculated as follows.

$$\frac{\text{frequency of word } w \text{ in user } t \text{ 's } i\text{th newest tweet}}{\text{total frequency of word } w \text{ in user } t \text{ 's all tweets}}$$

In equation (2), C is a constant and N is the amount of tweets for user t. Let C be 2,000 and $N \leq C$, i.e., N will be set to 2,000 when the amount of user t's tweets is more than 2,000. This is because 2,000 tweets are adequate for inferring personal values according to our preliminary experiment.

- Refine the weighting as follows.

$$W2(w,t) = \begin{cases} 1 + w_1 & \text{if } w_1 > 0 \\ 0 & \text{otherwise} \end{cases} \quad (3)$$

Here, w_1 is an enumeration of $W1(w,t)$ in equation (2).

- Take the weight $W2(w,t)$ calculated by equation (3) instead of word appearance at the formula of Step 2 in §2.2 and "1" at line 5 in Algorithm 1.

- Similarly, we let vector $\vec{kw}$ in equation (1) initialize with the weights calculated by (3) instead of the binary data.

3 Experiment

3.1 Preliminary

Morphology Unlike English, Japanese sentences are written in Chinese characters and kana (Japanese alphabet) without delimiters (i.e., space) between words. We used *MeCab* [2] to tokenize the tweets into words. Moreover, we included *List of all page titles* in the Japanese Wikipedia[3] as an additional dictionary into MeCab, in order to solve new named entities (i.e., book name, software name, etc.).

[2] MeCab is an open-source morphological analyzer software. http://taku910.github.io/mecab/

[3] http://dumps.wikimedia.org/jawiki/

	Curiosity				Cooperativeness				Savings			
Method	A(%)	P	R	F	A(%)	P	R	F	A(%)	P	R	F
SVM	61.5	0.63	0.85	0.72	61.9	0.56	0.36	0.44	82.3	0.00	0.00	0.00
NB	60.0	0.60	0.97	0.74	63.4	0.66	0.24	0.35	82.3	0.00	0.00	0.00
DTS	57.3	0.66	0.58	0.62	55.0	0.46	0.63	0.53	55.9	0.20	0.50	0.28

Table 2: The evaluation. The average of ten 10-fold cross-validation of inferred Societas values.

TF-IDF and LSA To give weight to words without ignoring zero idf terms, we used TF-IDF as:

$$tfidf(w) = tf \times (idf + 1)$$

Where tf represents the term frequency of word w, and idf is the inverse document frequency of word w. In addition, we applied LSA (latent semantic analysis) (Deerwester et al., 1990) to the TF-IDF values from Twitter corpus, and reduce the data to 1,000 dimension.

Baseline We employed a support vector machine (SVM) approach as the baseline in our experiment.[4] Moreover, Naive bayes classifier was employed as an alternative choice for classifying Twitter data.[4] According to (McCallum and Nigam, 1998), multinomial Naive Bayes (NB) is more suitable for context with large vocabulary size, and we considered that our training data (vocabulary size $> 10k$) fits this condition.

Bayesian Network As interpreted in §2, the Bayesian network is employed for our proposed method.[5] We experimented the Dynamic Twitter-Societas Model mentioned in §2.3 (DTS). From the preliminary experiment, it was expected that performance of TwitterSocietas Model would be similar to DTS, however, a DTS method solved the aged problem as mentioned in §2.3. To compare with other methods, we used the means of training data (training means) for discretization. For example, even if a probability of $vc = 1$ (vc is a value component) is close to 0.0 such as 0.02, its binary discretization can also be 1 when the training means of this component is smaller (i.e., 0.01).

[4]We used Machine learning toolkit *scikit-learn* in our experiment. http://scikit-learn.org/stable/

[5]We used "Bayonet", a Bayesian network software, to make the Societas and TwitterSocietas models. https://staff.aist.go.jp/y.motomura/bayonet/

Component	VC = 0	VC = 1
Curiosity	0.40	0.60
Cooperativeness	0.59	0.41
Savings	0.82	0.18

Table 3: Means of the value components for 1,147 Twitter users.

Dataset The dataset used in our experiment consisted of two subsets: Societas data and tweets, both related to 1,147 Twitter users.

Evaluation Metric We used accuracy (A), precision (P), recall (R), and F-measure (F) with 10-fold cross-validation to evaluate the performance of our proposed method and other methods. We treated the prediction result as the retrieved documents, the training data as the relevant documents, and "1" was the appearance of personal value.

3.2 Evaluation

Results Three representative personal values (*Curiosity*, *Cooperativeness*, *Savings*) were selected for discussion and the evaluation is shown in Table 2. Notice that the results of SVM and NB in Table 2 only involved the words between the DF of 10% and 90% when constructing feature vectors from the words in tweets. This is because keywords used in our proposed method were also extracted in this way as mentioned in §2.2. In addition, we normalized the feature vectors with TF-IDF and LSA for SVM and NB.

Comparison From Table 2 we can see that both SVM and NB performed better in terms of accuracy than DTS. However, DTS had better scores of recall and F-measure in cooperativeness and especially in *Savings*. This is due to the skewed distribution of the value components (i.e., $P(VC = 0) >> P(VC = 1)$) in our training data as shown in Table 3. DTS

Component	VC = 1	SVM: A(%) / F	NB: A(%) / F	DTS: A(%) / F
Delicacy	0.54	55.7 / 0.63	57.9 / 0.67	56.5 / 0.60
Laxity	0.61	64.2 / 0.74	62.8 / 0.76	54.5 / 0.59
Narcissism	0.46	66.3 / 0.61	66.4 / 0.68	62.9 / 0.62
Self-realization	0.56	53.9 / 0.64	55.8 / 0.71	53.9 / 0.58
Sensitivity to criticism	0.39	60.7 / 0.31	60.1 / 0.02	**50.4** / 0.42
Sensitivity to lack of common sense	0.61	58.9 / 0.73	60.0 / 0.75	52.7 / 0.60
Sensitivity to disappointment	0.39	59.8 / 0.22	61.6 / 0.08	**49.3** / 0.42
Stress(Human relationship)	0.50	52.7 / 0.51	53.3 / 0.52	**49.7** / 0.47
Friendship emphasizing	0.56	52.5 / 0.63	54.7 / 0.68	55.5 / 0.61
Marriage aspiration	0.57	65.5 / 0.72	62.1 / 0.72	59.5 / 0.63
Spousal responsibility as housewife	0.41	61.9 / 0.44	60.6 / 0.37	54.2 / 0.48
Family discord	0.41	58.8 / 0.35	58.7 / 0.03	**49.5** / 0.50
Satisfaction	0.47	60.3 / 0.53	57.5 / 0.43	58.0 / 0.58
Stress(Sense of job)	0.47	52.9 / 0.43	52.2 / 0.23	53.6 / 0.51
Lack of money	0.63	62.7 / 0.75	63.0 / 0.77	55.1 / 0.61
Sufficiency(Sense of money)	0.28	71.6 / 0.00	71.8 / 0.00	54.0 / 0.36
Priority to family	0.28	75.2 / 0.24	72.1 / 0.02	60.4 / 0.44
Sufficiency(Sense of time)	0.44	56.8 / 0.37	56.4 / 0.14	**50.8** / 0.45
Lack of time	0.32	68.6 / 0.11	68.2 / 0.00	56.2 / 0.39

Table 4: Evaluation results for other personal values with accuracy(A) and F-measure(F) metrics.

generates a posterior probability of the value component allowing conversion to binary with the most suitable threshold. Table 4 shows the evaluation results for other personal values that were not shown in Table 2, and we find that a Bayesian Network approach may be not appropriate for inferring the personal values corresponding to accuracy scores in bold font because they are as poor as random guessing.

4 Discussion

4.1 Speech keywords

We believe that every morphological element represents an aspect of the user's personal value on Twitter. Hence, dictionary form words without normalization are preferred in our research. For example, to infer personal values, *tsumetai* is different from a variation word use with *kaomoji* (the Japanese emoticon) like *tsumetatt(°∀° ⊂)⊂*, and this is similar to the relation between *cool* and *Cooooooooooooooolllllllllllll!!!!!!!!!!!!!!* in (Brody and Diakopoulos, 2011). This is another interesting characteristic of the TwitterSocietas Model, and was also used for sentiment analysis in (Barbosa and Feng, 2010).

4.2 Application of TwitterSocietas Model

In past years, we have succeeded to apply TwitterSocietas Model to infer personal values for marketing researches. For example, we explained TV viewers' characteristics with personal values inferred by TwitterSocietas Model to a TV program which has no demographic distribution data about it but has many Twitter followers (Fujii et al., 2013).

In addition, we succeeded to find the sudden change of personal value "Narcissism" (from a higher probability a lower one) for a blogger, during the period of her mother's death from Alzheimer's Disease (Tanida and Tokumi, 2014). For a text mining interest, we found that TwitterSocietas Model can also be applied to blog data. And we hope that in the future, we can acquire knowledge from online text data with text mining technologies, such as Twitter data or blog data, for giving some mental support to the people with dementia family members.

4.3 Multilinguistic Societas

In our recent work, we started a project on finding out the relations between text data in "Weibo" (A kind of Chinese microblogs) and personal values. Up to now, we have gathered 1,002 pieces of ef-

Component	Weibo N=1,002	Twitter N=1,147
Curiosity	0.76	0.60
Delicacy	0.49	0.54
Laxity	0.38	0.61
Cooperativeness	0.43	0.41
Narcissism	0.69	0.46
Self-realization	0.70	0.56
Sensitivity to criticism	0.63	0.39
Sensitivity to lack of common sense	0.47	0.61
Sensitivity to disappointment	0.28	0.39
Stress(Human)	0.36	0.50
Friendship emphasizing	0.71	0.56
Marriage aspiration	0.63	0.57
Spousal responsibility as housewife	0.64	0.41
Family discord	0.30	0.41
Satisfaction	0.69	0.47
Stress(Job)	0.53	0.47
Priority to family	0.46	0.28
Sufficiency(Time)	0.52	0.44
Lack of time	0.34	0.32
Lack of money	0.56	0.63
Sufficiency(Money)	0.36	0.28
Savings	0.35	0.18

Table 5: Societas personal values (arithmetic mean) of Weibo users and Japanese Twitter users.

fective data for our "Weibo-Societas" Model. However, we found that for Chinese people (especially who use Weibo), some personal values are very different from Japanese Twitter users' ones. Table 5 shows the arithmetic mean of Societas personal values about Weibo users and Japanese Twitter users. As shown in Table 5, Weibo users tend to have the value "Curiosity" than Japanese Twitter users. However, Japanese Twitter users may be more delicate than Weibo users.

5 Related Work

5.1 Demographic Inference for Twitter users

The earlier work by (Zamal et al., 2012) proposed an approach of Twitter users' latent attributes inference including gender, age, and political affiliation with Twitter. Similarly, (Ciot et al., 2013) made an effort to infer gender with non-English-based content and users, and (Bergsma and Durme, 2013) enabled substantial improvements on the task of Twitter gender classification. Moreover, (Beller et al., 2014) proposed a method to predict social roles such as doctor, teacher, etc. These attributes are considered as demographic attributes, and they are very important to market segmentation. In our research, we contributed to the inference of Twitter user's personal values which are also essential factors to marketing science and consumer behavior prediction.

5.2 Personal values Inference for Twitter users

For personal value inference, (Quercia et al., 2011) contributed to personality prediction with Twitter profiles based on Big Five. (Golbeck et al., 2011) provided a method to infer Twitter users' personality of Big Five with the statistics about their accounts and tweets. To infer the personality of Chinese people, (Bai et al., 2013) developed a method to infer the Big Five personality from "Weibo" data with a multivariate regression approach. In our research, we use the words in tweets to calculate the speech components (as mentioned in §2.2 Step 5) for each user, and these speech components can be used for inferring Societas personal values with TwitterSocietas Model. Moreover, we think that personal values are interactive to each other. As a result, we constructed our TwitterSocietas Model with a Bayesian Network approach.

(Sumner et al., 2012) attempted predicting personality traits from the lexicon features extracted tweets. Moreover, (Plank and Hovy, 2015) made an effort on inferring MBTI[6] personality type from tweets, gender and some meta-features (i.e., counts of tweets, followers, etc), and showed that social media can provide sufficient linguistic evidence to reliably predict some dimensions of personality. However, they suggested that it is hard to predict the personality dimensions of Judging/Perceiving with the linguistic evidence from tweets. Similarly, as shown in Table 4, we find that some Societas personal values, i.e., "Stress(Human)", are hard to predict from tweets no matter which classifier is employed.

In (Plank and Hovy, 2015), the words in tweets used as lexicon features were transformed into binary word n-grams. In our previous work, we also used the words in binary (whether the words appeared in users' tweets or not), and counted the co-occurrence between Societas personal values and these words, so that we can select sensitive words for each personal value to construct our TwitterSocietas Model. However, in this paper, we incorporated the

[6]MyersBriggs Type Indicator (MBTI) is a way to measure how people perceive the word and make decisions.

relative frequency of words in each tweet as mentioned in §2.3.

6 Conclusion and Future work

In this paper, we introduced our personal value system and its extension *TwitterSocietas*. Furthermore, we proposed a dynamic way to update the TwitterSocietas Model automatically based on Twitter data. We evaluated the performance of the model and compared it with SVM and NB. As a result, we found that our approach accurately inferred personal values with skewed training data.

In the future work, we will first check whether the Weibo-Societas Model, a derivation of Twitter-Societas, can be applied to predict personal values of Chinese people. Furthermore, we will try to implement the source of Societas personal values inference with other features, such as whether a link or a picture is contained in a tweet, the importance of a mentioned event (i.e., a word after "#" mark).

Acknowledgments

We wish to thank the anonymous reviewers for their valuable comments and suggestions.

References

Shuotian Bai, Bibo Hao, Ang Li, Sha Yuan, Rui Gao, and Tingshao Zhu. 2013. Predicting Big Five personality traits of microblog users. In *Proceedings of Web Intelligence (WI) and Intelligent Agent Technologies(IAT), 2013 IEEE/WIC/ACM International Joint Conferences*, 1:501–508.

Luciano Barbosa and Junlan Feng. 2010. Robust sentiment detection on Twitter from biased and noisy data. In *Proceedings of the International Conference on Computational Linguistics*, pages 36–44.

Charley Beller, Rebecca Knowles, Craig Harman, Shane Bergsma, Margaret Mitchell, and Benjamin Van Durme. 2014. I'm a belieber: social roles via Self-identification and conceptual attributes. In *Proceedings of the 52nd Annual Meeting of the Association for Computational Linguistics*, pages 181–186.

Shane Bergsma and Benjamin Van Durme. 2013. Using Conceptual Class Attributes to Characterize Social Media Users. In *Proceedings of the 51st Annual Meeting of the Association for Computational Linguistics*, pages 710–720.

Samuel Brody and Nicholas Diakopoulos. 2011. CooooooooooooooollllllllllllII!!!!!!!!!!!!!!: using word lengthening to detect sentiment in microblogs. In *Proceedings of the Conference on Empirical Methods in Natural Language Processing, EMNLP'11*, pages 562–570.

Jilin Chen, Gary Hsieh, Jalal Mahmud and Jeffrey Nichols. 2014. Understanding individuals' personal values from social media word use. In *Proceedings of the 17th ACM Conference on Computer-Supported Cooperative Work*, pages 405–414.

Morgane Ciot, Morgan Sonderegger, and Derek Ruths. 2013. Gender inference of Twitter users in non-English contexts. In *Proceedings of the 2013 Conference on Empirical Methods in Natural Language Processing*, pages 1136–1145.

Scott Deerwester, Susan T. Dumais, George W. Furnas, Thomas K. Landauer, and Richard Harshman. 1990. Indexing by Latent Semantic Analysis. *Journal of the American Society for Information Science*, 41(6):391–407.

Emiko Fujii, Yinjun Hu, Mathieu Bertin, Yasuo Tanida. 2013. Understanding the audience of TV program from microblog with Social type model. *IEICE Transactions on Information and Systems*, 83:25–29.

Jennifer Golbeck, Cristina Robles, Michon Edmondson, and Karen Turner. 2011. Predicting personality from Twitter. In *Proceedings of the 3rd IEEE International Conference on Social Computing*, pages 149–156.

Mara Mather, Eldar Shafir, and Marcia K. Johnson. 2000. Misremembrance of options past: Source monitoring and choice. *Psychological Science*, 11(2):132–138.

Andrew McCallum and Kamal Nigam. 1998. A comparison of event models for Naive Bayes text classification. In *Proceedings of the AAAI-98 Workshop on Learning for Text Categorization*, pages 41–48.

Alan Mislove, Sune Lehmann, Yong-Yeol Ahn, Jukka-Pekka Onnela, and J. Niels Rosenquist. 2011. Understanding the Demographics of Twitter Users. In *Proceedings of the 3rd International Conference on Weblogs and Social Media.*

Judea Pearl. 1985. Bayesian networks: A model of self-activated memory for evidential reasoning. In *Proceedings of the Cognitive Science Society.*

Eyal Peer and Eyal Gamliel. 2011. Too reliable to be true? Response bias as a potential source of inflation in paper-and-pencil questionnaire reliability. *Practical Assessment, Research and Evaluation*, 16(9):1–8.

Barbara Plank and Dirk Hovy. 2015. Personality Traits on Twitter -or- How to Get 1,500 Personality Tests in aWeek. In *Proceedings of the 6th Workshop on Computational Approaches to Subjectivity, Sentiment and Social Media Analysis*, pages 92–98.

Joseph T. Plummer. 1974. The concept and application of life style segmentation. *Journal of Marketing*, 38:33–37.

Daniele Quercia, Michal Kosinski, David Stillwell, and Jon Crowcrof. 2011. Our Twitter Profiles, Our Selves: Predicting Personality with Twitter. In *Proceedings of the 3rd IEEE International Conference on Social Computing*.

Chris Sumner, Alison Byers, Rachel Boochever and Gregory. J. Park. 2012. Predicting Dark Triad Personality Traits from Twitter usage and a linguistic analysis of Tweets. In *IEEE International Conference on Machine Learning and Applications*, pages 386–393.

Yasuo Tanida, Rie Tokumi. 2014. Measuring a change of mind of dementia family caregivers. In *Proceedings of the 28th Annual Conference of the Japanese Society for Artificial Intelligence.*

Yair Weiss. 2000. Correctness of local probability propagation in graphical models with loops. *Neural Computation*, 12:1–41.

Yin Wu. 2005. The Research towards Model of China-Vals. *NanKai Business Review*, 8(2):9–15.

Faiyaz Al Zamal, Wendy Liu, and Derek Ruths. 2012. Homophily and latent attribute inference: Inferring latent attributes of Twitter users from neighbors. In *Proceedings of the 6th International AAAI Conference on Weblogs and Social Media*, pages 387–390.

Distant-supervised Language Model for Detecting Emotional Upsurge on Twitter

Yoshinari Fujinuma[†,‡,*] **Hikaru Yokono**[‡] **Pascual Martínez-Gómez**[§,‡] **Akiko Aizawa**[†,‡]
[†]University of Tokyo [‡]National Institute of Informatics [§]Ochanomizu University
fujinumay@gmail.com {yokono, pascual, aizawa}@nii.ac.jp

Abstract

Event-specific twitter streams often reveal sudden spikes triggered by users' upsurge of emotions to crucial moments in the real world. Although upsurge of emotion is usually identified by a sudden rise in the number of tweets, the detection for diverse event streams is not a trivial task. In this paper, we propose a new method to extract spiking tweets with upsurge of emotions based on characteristic expressions used in tweets. The core part of our method is to use a distant-supervised language model (Spike LM) built from tweets in spikes to capture such expressions. We investigate the performance of detecting emotional spiking tweets using language models including Spike LM. Our experimental results show that the natural language expressions used in emotional upsurge fit specifically well to Spike LM.

1 Introduction

Twitter is one of the most popular micro-blogging platforms in recent days. There are over 500 million tweets posted per day[1] including real-world events described on Twitter which range from short and daily life events (e.g. falling to the ground) to long and widely-broadcasted events (e.g. a match in World Cup). Such tweets are good sources to detect users' reactions toward real-world events.

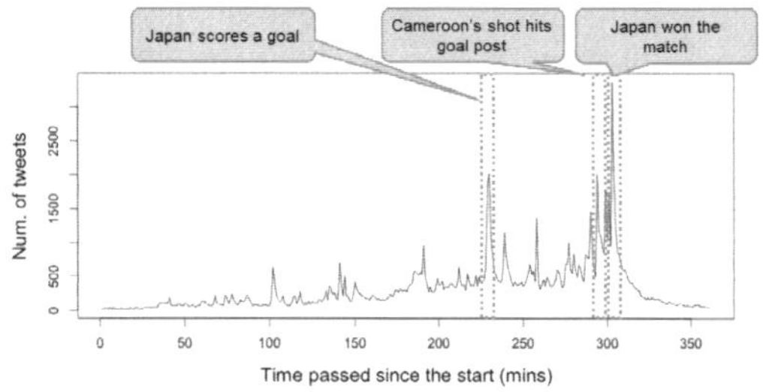

Figure 1: The number of tweets per minute (TPM) during Japan vs. Cameroon for hashtags related to World Cup 2010.

People behave unusually when they encounter exciting moments in an event, for example, yell out or dance with each other after their favorite soccer team scores a goal. On Twitter, this action is often reflected by a large number of posts within a short time period. When Japan scored a goal against Cameroon in World Cup 2010, there were a maximum of $2,940$ tweets per second (TPS), which marked the record TPS for goals at that time.[2] It is significantly larger than the average of 750 TPS.[2] In this paper, we call such bursty traffic as "numerical spikes". Figure 1 shows the number of tweets per minute during the match of Cameroon vs. Japan, and Table 1 shows the examples of tweets sampled from both numerical spikes and other parts.

Detecting emotional upsurge is important for both extracting emerging important real-world events and important moments of them. We call an upsurge that are caused by Twitter users' emotional spike as

[*]This work was done while the first author was at the University of Tokyo and National Institute of Informatics. The first author is currently at Amazon Japan K.K.

[1]https://blog.twitter.com/2013/new-tweets-per-second-record-and-how

[2]https://blog.twitter.com/2010/big-goals-big-game-big-records

29th Pacific Asia Conference on Language, Information and Computation pages 488 - 495
Shanghai, China, October 30 - November 1, 2015

	Moment	Example of a Tweet	English Translation
Emotional Upsurge	Japan won the match	やったああああああああああああああああああああ #jpn #worldcup #2010wc	Huraaaaaaaaaaaaay
	Japan scored a goal	ゴーーーーーーーーーーーーーーーーーーーール !!!!!!!! #2010wc	Gooooooooooooooal!!!!!!!!
Non-emotional Upsurge	50 mins after the match	興奮してると見せかけて感動しすぎてずっと泣いてました。いや興奮はしてるけど信じてたから割と冷静でいられる #2010wc	I look excited but actually I have been crying from being moved. Well, I have been excited but I believed that Japan will win so I am quite calm.

Table 1: Example of tweets from spikes and non-spikes.

"emotional upsurge". Emotional upsurge do overlap with numerical spikes, but it does include moments that are not numerical spikes. For example, Lanagan and Smeaton (2011) reported that emotional upsurge overlaps with numerical spikes and those are useful for tagging key moments in sports matches. However, detecting numerical spikes on Twitter becomes difficult when a target event is not pre-defined or rarely tweeted by Twitter users because the number event-related tweets per unit time is not directly computable. In such cases, detecting upsurge of emotions becomes crucial.

One characteristics of tweets is that expressions used in tweets entail many linguistic phenomena. For example, Brody and Diakopoulos (2011) analyzed occurrences of character repetitions in words from a sentiment dictionary. In this paper, we assume that such variations of language expressions are caused by real-world events. Table 1 shows that a character repetition ('Goooal', 'Huraaay') occurs in tweets during emotional upsurge rather than their canonical form ('Goal', 'Hurray'). In contrast, a character repetition does not frequently occur in tweets during non-emotional upsurge. However, to our knowledge, there has not been an attempt to capture emotional upsurge using the linguistic characteristics of tweets.

In this paper, we specifically investigate a method to detect emotional upsurge in real-world events using characteristic expressions in a Japanese tweet. Our contribution is that a *spiking tweet language model*, which we constructed automatically from existing tweet dataset, captures characteristic expressions well and it is an effective approach for detecting emotional upsurge.

2 Related Work

Our idea is related to many previous works on Twitter including the investigation toward non-standard languages used on Twitter, and various applications tackled using language models.

The nature of using non-standard languages including word lengthening in tweets largely differ from other corpus (Eisenstein, 2013). As further mentioned by Eisenstein (2013), these languages are affected by many factors including the 140 characters length limit of tweets, social factors (e.g. age (Rosenthal and McKeown, 2011)), location (Wing and Baldridge, 2011), input devices (Gouws et al., 2011) of an author of a tweet. Word lengthening is known to be useful for sentiment analysis (Brody and Diakopoulos, 2011). One way to model these expressions is to use language models and many studies successfully captured various characteristics of tweets using language model.

There are lots of applications for language models built from tweets or web texts. According to Liu et al. (2012), distant-supervised language models are useful for sentiment analysis of tweets. Neubig and Duh (2013) showed that for 26 languages used on Twitter, entropy of content in a retweet, the Twitter version of e-mail forward, is significantly higher than non-retweeted tweets. Danescu-Niculescu-Mizil et al. (2013) reported that users' career in an online community correlates with the cross entropy between each user's posts and the language used in the whole community. Lin et al. (2011) used multiple language models built from each hashtag to track broad topics. These researches show that language model is a powerful method to use on various applications.

To our knowledge, there is no prior research focused on languages used in emotional spiking tweets. Many tasks on Twitter including burst detection (Kleinberg, 2003; Diao et al., 2012), first story detection (Petrović et al., 2010), and topic tracking (Lau et al., 2012) failed to effectively incorporate the textual characteristics of tweets and regard it is out of their scope. Being able to characterize tweets from emotional upsurge would open a window to the identification of real-world events that emotionally influence Twitter users.

3 Language Model-based Detection of Emotional Upsurge

3.1 Outline of the Proposed Method

The motivation of using characteristic expressions used in tweets to detect emotional upsurge is there are various ways to express users' feelings. In the past investigations (for example (Schröder, 2001)), the emotion of a human speaker reflected by the tone or the pitch of speaker's voice. On Twitter, Brody and Diakopoulos (2011) reported that word lengthening in written words is used to express the difference in such user's voice, which is affected from user's sentiments. As shown earlier in Table 1, we assume that the language used in tweets can express difference in pitch or tone of voice as a written text in tweets. Therefore, we aim to capture such difference in voice-reflected tweets using language models.

In our approach, we further apply a distant supervision framework where the perplexity is calculated using a language model obtained from tweets in numerical spikes with some heuristic filtering strategy. If the perplexity of target tweets is small, we could then assert that they are likely to have come from the emotional tweet model.

3.2 Building Language Models

Since we can obtain a large number of tweets, we build tweet language models such that the language model is not biased by a particular topic. Given a tweet t with l characters, let t_i be a character in a tweet. The probability of t in an n-gram language model is calculated by the following formula:

$$P(t) = \prod_{i=1}^{l} P(t_i|t_{i-1}, ..., t_{i-n+1}). \quad (1)$$

We use SRILM (Stolcke, 2002) with Katz back-off smoothing (Katz, 1987) to build language models.

We build a character n-gram language model following Neubig and Duh (2013). To build a word n-gram language model, word segmentation is necessary to build a word n-gram language model since Japanese is an unsegmented language. However, various studies reported that tokenization in unsegmented languages on Twitter is not reliable enough due to the spelling variations and unknown words (Wang and Kan, 2013; Kaji and Kitsuregawa, 2014). We set the value of n for a character n-gram language model to 7. This is because when we consider n-grams with $n > 5$, the number of n-grams decreases which shows that the language model suffers from the sparsity problem. However, as reported by Brody and Diakopoulos (2011), word lengthening (e.g. coool) is a common phenomenon on Twitter. To accurately capture those phenomenon, we tried to use as long n-gram as possible and make it to 7-gram.

3.3 Perplexity

To quantify the difference between tweets during emotional upsurge and non-emotional upsurge, we used perplexity, a measurement of information-theoretic distance between a language model and a document. In this method, it is used as the similarity between a language model and a set of tweets. Perplexity PP of a tweet set T which consists of N number of 7-grams T_i is defined as the following:

$$PP(T) = \left(\frac{1}{\prod_{t \in T} P(t)}\right)^{\frac{1}{N}}. \quad (2)$$

Hashtag	Details	Date and Time	Num. of Tweets	Num. of EUT
#aibou	Name of a TV drama	2012-03-21T10:31 - 14:06	20,681	42
#hanshin	Name of a baseball team	2012-04-20T08:39 - 12:54	6,176	44
#ACV	Name of an online game	2012-02-13T12:08 - 15:41	1,562	9
#agqr	Name of a radio show	2012-02-15T11:39 - 14:08	13,434	86
#figureskate	Figure skating	2012-04-20T10:00 - 12:20	1,410	37
#momoclo	Name of a music artist	2012-02-11T15:36 - 17:21	1,823	63

Table 2: Statistics of six hashtags, its respective target intervals and with the number of manually annotated emotionally upsurging timestamps (EUT). All time are UTC +0.

We follow Danescu-Niculescu-Mizil et al. (2013) and use perplexity, which is equivalent to the cross-entropy of two empirical distributions, as similarity measure between a set of tweets and a language model. A set of tweets having low perplexity means tweets are close to the language model. Moreover, we assume that the minimum duration of an event is a minute. Therefore, we aggregate stream of tweets from the same minute into one set of tweets and compute the perplexity of it.

4 Tweet Dataset Construction

The dataset we use in this paper is extracted from Japanese tweets gathered by Gnip[3] during 5 consecutive periods such as 1) 2012-02-09 to 2012-02-17, 2) 2012-03-21 to 2012-03-22, 3) 2012-04-20 to 2012-04-21, 4) 2012-05-18 to 2012-05-19 and 5) 2012-05-25 to 2012-05-26. The dataset has a total of $413,008,939$ tweets with $527,661$ unique hashtags.

We construct four separate sub-datasets each of which is used for different purpose: evaluating the performance of detecting upsurge of emotion, building a language model. Since our research focuses on users' reactions to events, we filtered out tweets from bots[4] (Twitter accounts that automatically produce tweets according to a program) and tweets that include the characters 'RT', which indicates a retweet. For constructing the language models and the evaluation data, we regarded the Twitter specific elements such as hashtags, users (e.g. @Obama), hyperlinks as one character.

Dataset Used for Evaluating Language Models

To build a golden dataset of emotionally upsurging timestamps, we first extract hashtags which consist of both emotional upsurge and non-emotional upsurge from various genres. First, we selected six hashtags and we set a target interval for each hashtag as consecutive periods with the number of tweets ≥ 10 together with 20 minutes before and after the periods.

Next, we randomly sample 90 minutes from the target interval of each hashtag and aggregated tweets from the same minute as one tweet set. An annotator looks at all of the tweets from the same minute and annotate whether each timestamp is an emotional upsurge or not. As a result, 42 timestamps in #aibou, 44 timestamps in #hanshin, 9 timestamps in #ACV, 37 timestamps in #figureskate, 86 timestamps in #agqr and 63 timestamps in #momoclo are annotated as emotionally upsurging timestamps. Table 2 shows the details of the six hashtags and the target respective interval we used.

Dataset used for Building Spike LM

In order to construct a spiking tweet language model (Spike LM), we gather $1,197,935$ tweets

[3]http://gnip.com/

[4]Bots typically tweet from particular Twitter clients; thus, by looking at sampled data, we chose to use tweets from the top 43 Twitter clients in terms of frequency. These are not bots and covered over 90% of the tweets that we sampled for 3 days.

from all hashtags which exceed 50 TPM. We filter out hashtags including the word "follow" or "Follow" due to the large number of Twitter-specific hashtags. Moreover, we also exclude the six hashtags described in Table 2.

Dataset used for Building Surpervised LM

The limitation of the Spike LM is that we cannot avoid including tweets not from emotional upsurge. We build a fully supervised spike language model (Supervised LM) to observe whether clean but much low number of tweets will perform better than the language model built from less cleaned but more number of tweets. In order to filter out hashtags that include non-emotional numerical spikes, we used manually annotated emotionally upsurging timestamps (EUT) shown in Table 2, and constructed Supervised LM excluding the hashtags used for testing.

Dataset used to Evaluate Detecting Numerical Spikes using Spike LM

Since numerical spikes has some overlaps with emotional upsurge, we analyze if Spike LM can also detect numerical spikes. To analyze the detection of numerical spikes using Spike LM, we construct a tweet set containing 300 tweets from each hashtag in Table 2. The tweet set consist of one tweet set of 150 tweets sampled from numerical spikes and another tweet set of 150 tweets sampled from non-numerical spikes.[5] We compute the perplexity of a tweet set rather than to individual tweets to get a reliable perplexity.

5 Evaluation of Language Models

We evaluate how well does Spike LM detect numerical spikes and then compare the performance of detecting emotional upsurge against Supervised LM and Kleinberg's algorithm.

[5]To avoid test sets being biased from one incident, we constructed the test sets as the following steps: 1) Split the target interval into 3 sub-intervals. 2) For each sub-interval, gather the tweets from the most tweeted minutes until the total of number of tweets reaches 50. 3) If the number of tweets during the minutes exceeds 50, randomly sample 50.

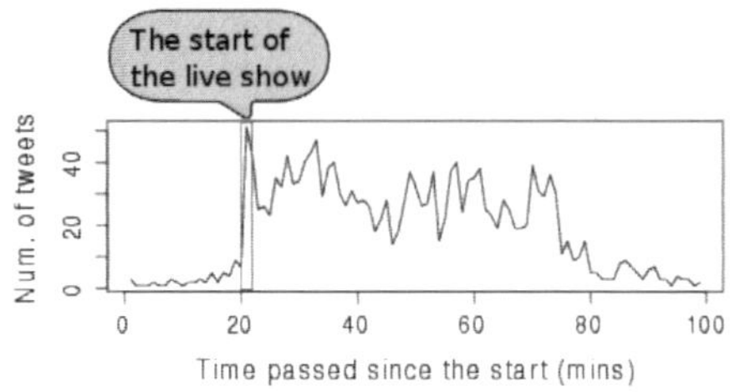

(a) Num. of TPM

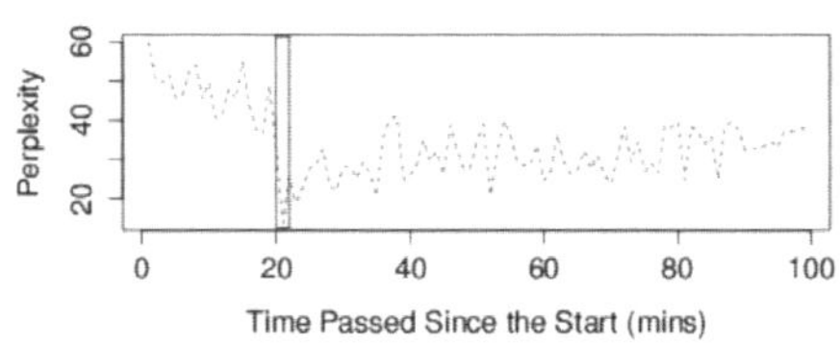

(b) Spike LM

Figure 2: Number of tweets in #momoclo hashtag shown together with the perplexity between the three language models. The blue box represents an example of a spike.

5.1 Evaluation of Detecting Numerical Spikes using Spike LM

We first evaluate the effectiveness of capturing numerical spikes on Spike LM. Figure 2 shows the perplexity of spiking timestamps are actually low compared to other timestamps. As a quantitative comparison, we sampled 300 tweets from each hashtag and calculate the perplexity of both numerical spiking and non-numerical spiking tweet sets using Spike LM as mentioned earlier in Section 4. Table 3 shows that for all the six hashtags, there is a significant difference between the perplexity of numerical spiking and non-numerical spiking tweets according to the Wilcoxon signed-rank test ($p < 0.02$). Therefore, Spike LM is useful for detecting tweets from numerical spikes.

Next, we evaluate the performance of detecting emotional upsurge from tweet sets aggregated by its timestamps using language models. We use the manually annotated ground truth emotional upsurge for evaluation.

5.2 Evaluation of Detecting Emotional Upsurge

To evaluate which language model best detect emotional upsurge, we derive precision, recall and F1-score for each language model by incrementing the perplexity decision threshold one by one. Specifi-

Hashtag	PP(S)	PP(NS)	PP(NS)-PP(S)
#aibou	22.027	27.735	5.708
#hanshin	30.705	63.416	32.711
#ACV	43.116	52.647	9.531
#agqr	9.938	23.134	13.196
#figureskate	27.505	39.176	11.671
#momoclo	23.261	39.283	16.022

Table 3: Perplexity of sampled set of tweets constructed from numerical spikes (S) and non-numerical spikes (NS) computed using Spike LM.

Hashtag	Spike LM	Sup LM	Kleinberg
#aibou	.656	.655	**.667**
#hanshin	**.707**	.642	.508
#ACV	**.571**	.500	.400
#agqr	**1.00**	**1.00**	.491
#figureskate	**.643**	.595	.500
#momoclo	.527	**.817**	.615

Table 4: The best F1-score of detecting annotated emotional upsurge for Spike LM, Supervised LM (Sup LM) and Kleinberg's algorithm.

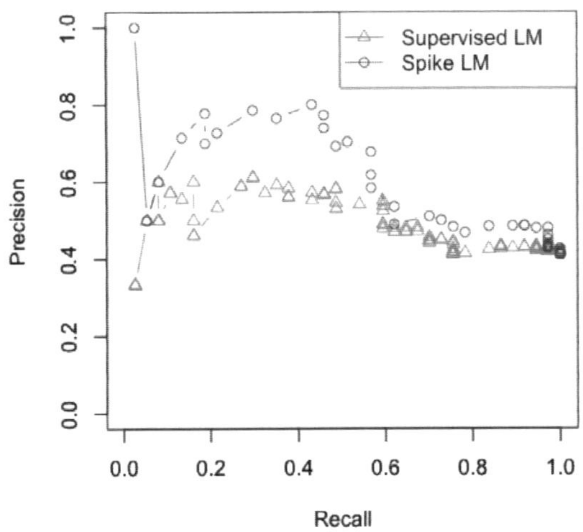

Figure 3: Precision-Recall curve for #figureskate data.

cally, if the perplexity of a set of tweets from one timestamp is lower than a decision threshold, we predict as a timestamp of emotional upsurge and vice versa. We eventually use the best F1-score among the various decision thresholds to evaluate which language model best fits to modeling emotional upsurge.

Baseline System

We employ Kleinberg's burst detection algorithm (Kleinberg, 2003) as a baseline method. This method assumes that all numerical spikes or bursts are emotional upsurge and all non-numerical spikes or non-bursts are not emotional upsurge. Kleinberg's burst detection algorithm modeled a burst of a stream of documents as a two-state finite state automata $B_{s,\gamma}$ with the scaling parameter s and the transition cost parameter γ. The states are assumed to be in either the burst state or the non-burst state. We further choose the optimal state sequence that requires minimum cost among all possible state sequences. As a result, we detect which timestamps are in a burst states and which timestamps are not. The two parameters of the algorithm is set according to the result from the preliminary experiment to detect numerical spikes based on mean and standard deviation with sufficiently high F1-scores. Specifically, the parameters γ and s are set to $\gamma = 1$ and $s = 2$.

Evaluation Result

Table 4 shows the result of detecting emotional upsurge for the two language models and Kleinberg's algorithm. Figure 3 shows the precision-recall curve for the two language models we built. According to this figure, Spike LM performs well among the majority of the test hashtags when compared to Supervised LM. Furthermore, the figure shows that the precision of Spike LM does not drop when we increase the decision threshold.

We observe that if a language model contains hashtags with similar emotional upsurge to the test hashtags, the performance of detecting emotional upsurge tend to get better. This is obvious for Supervised LM performing well on #momoclo hashtag because when testing on this hashtag, Supervised LM is built from the rest of five target hashtags including #agar and the suffix of the emotionally upsurging tweets from #momoclo are similar to that of #agqr. Specifically, those tweets include lots of "w"s which is an Internet slang meaning "lol (laugh out loud)" in English. Note that the effect of #agqr is magnified on Supervised LM since most of the annotated timestamps are annotated as emotional upsurge in #agqr.[6] This also explains why Spike LM performs better than Supervised LM on five hashtags because Spike LM is more likely to include emotional upsurge from hashtags similar to the six hashtags.

One of the challenges is to detect emotional upsurge with relatively low number of tweets because of the existence of noisy tweets. Example of noisy tweets are the tweets from Twitter accounts that only post about news. Table 5 shows an emotional spike including such noisy tweets, which scored 42.095 as the perplexity. This spike includes 7 tweets from #figureskate hashtag. This is relatively low since the number of tweets per timestamp in sampled #figureskate tweets range from 2 to 50. Among the 7 tweets, 2 tweets are from a Twitter account which only tweets about news, which does not reflect emotional upsurge of a Twitter user. Spike LM is robust to such noisy 2 tweets from the account which only tweets about news when computing the perplexity of that timestamp. However, Supervised LM is largely affected by such noisy tweets because Supervised LM is built from less noisy tweets compared to Spike LM and it end up with high perplexity. Spike LM detects such emotional upsurge which can be used to extract emotional upsurge from various domains on Twitter.

6 Discussion

We further investigate the impact of the tweet set size on the reliability of the perplexity estimation using language models. Perplexity is known to be affected by the amount of text used for the calculation (Brown et al., 1992). We analyzed the impact using the most tweeted minute in the hashtag #aibou. Figure 4 shows the transition of perplexity according to the number tweets used to calculate the perplexity in the hashtag #aibou. As a result, after the number of tweets from the same minute exceeds 11, the difference between the minimum and the maximum perplexity became less than 3. This result shows that the perplexity does not largely rely on the number of tweets from the same timestamp and implies that

[6]Therefore, both language models score 1.0 on #agqr.

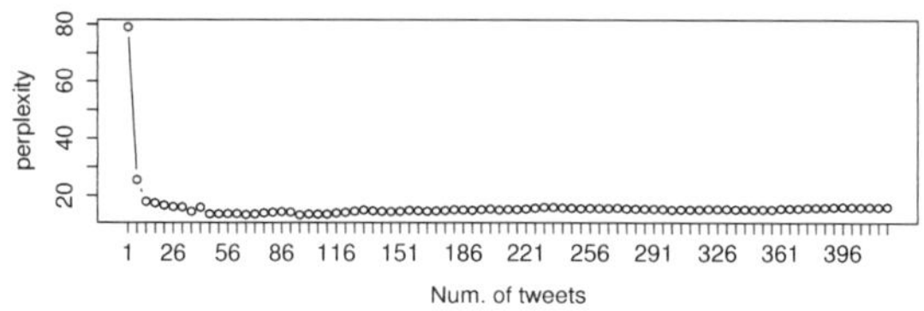

Figure 4: Perplexity computed with various number of tweets from the most tweeted minute in #aibou.

Spike LM can be used to detect emotional upsurge with low number of tweets.

7 Conclusion

In this paper, we showed that sequences of tweet characters in emotional spiking tweets are more similar to that of tweets modeled by Spike LM. By calculating the perplexity between Spike LM and sampled tweets from numerical spikes and non-numerical spikes among multiple hashtags, tweets from numerical spikes had lower perplexity than tweets from non-numerical spikes. Furthermore, Spike LM scored the highest F1-scores for detecting emotional upsurge in over half of the hashtags we examined. In conclusion, our method detects tweets that include Twitter users' upsurge of emotions, without largely depending on the number of tweets per minute by seeking for tweets modeled by Spike LM.

As a future task, we plan to investigate three further points: 1) Applying our method to other events tweeted on Twitter, 2) classification of emotional upsurge and non-emotional upsurge on the tweet level since we only investigated on a tweet set level, and 3) Test it on languages other than Japanese. Further studies are necessary to capture emotional spiking tweets on Twitter.

Acknowledgments

This work was supported by JSPS KAKENHI Grant Number 22240007. The authors would like to thank the anonymous reviewers for their constructive comments.

Tweets	English Translation
ジュベ様ジュベ様!! うわあああん大好きいい！衣装しっかりいいい #figureskate	Joubert! Joubert! Ahhhhhhh, I love him! His outfitsssss
ジュベール様のマトリックス (Happy Emoticon) #figureskate	Joubert's Matrix (Happy Emoticon)
男子シングルの結果です。→ URL #figureskate 高橋大輔選手が圧巻の演技を見せ、世界王者・チャンを破り 1 位に。日本チームとしてもトップのまま、最終日を迎えます。 #figureskate	This is the result of the mens' figure skating competition. → URL Daisuke Takashi showed an amazing performance and he became the number one after beating the world champion Chan. He is also the number one as part of the Japan team and reach the final day.

Table 5: An example of detected emotional upsurge with low number of tweets per minute.

References

Samuel Brody and Nicholas Diakopoulos. 2011. Cooooooooooooooollllllllllllll!!!!!!!!!!!!!! using word lengthening to detect sentiment in microblogs. In *EMNLP*, pages 562–570.

Peter F Brown, Peter V Desouza, Robert L Mercer, Vincent J Della Pietra, and Jenifer C Lai. 1992. Class-based n-gram models of natural language. *Computational linguistics*, 18(4):467–479.

Cristian Danescu-Niculescu-Mizil, Robert West, Dan Jurafsky, Jure Leskovec, and Christopher Potts. 2013. No country for old members: User lifecycle and linguistic change in online communities. In *WWW*, pages 307–318.

Qiming Diao, Jing Jiang, Feida Zhu, and Ee-Peng Lim. 2012. Finding bursty topics from microblogs. In *ACL*, pages 536–544.

Jacob Eisenstein. 2013. What to do about bad language on the internet. In *NAACL-HLT*, pages 359–369.

Stephan Gouws, Donald Metzler, Congxing Cai, and Eduard Hovy. 2011. Contextual bearing on linguistic variation in social media. In *Proc. of the Workshop on Language in Social Media (LSM 2011)*, pages 20–29.

Nobuhiro Kaji and Masaru Kitsuregawa. 2014. Accurate word segmentation and pos tagging for japanese microblogs: Corpus annotation and joint modeling with lexical normalization. In *EMNLP*, pages 99–109.

Slava M. Katz. 1987. Estimation of probabilities from sparse data for the language model component of a speech recognizer. In *IEEE Transactions on Acoustics, Speech and Signal Processing*, pages 400–401.

Jon Kleinberg. 2003. Bursty and hierarchical structure in streams. *Data Mining and Knowledge Discovery*, 7(4):373–397.

James Lanagan and Alan F Smeaton. 2011. Using twitter to detect and tag important events in live sports. *Artificial Intelligence*, pages 542–545.

Jey Han Lau, Nigel Collier, and Timothy Baldwin. 2012. On-line trend analysis with topic models: #twitter trends detection topic model online. In *COLING*, pages 1519–1534.

Jimmy Lin, Rion Snow, and William Morgan. 2011. Smoothing techniques for adaptive online language models: Topic tracking in tweet streams. In *KDD*, pages 422–429. ACM.

Kun-Lin Liu, Wu-Jun Li, and Minyi Guo. 2012. Emoticon smoothed language models for twitter sentiment analysis. In *AAAI*, pages 1678–1684.

Graham Neubig and Kevin Duh. 2013. How much is said in a tweet? a multilingual, information-theoretic perspective. In *AAAI Spring Symposium on Analyzing Microtext*, pages 32–39.

Saša Petrović, Miles Osborne, and Victor Lavrenko. 2010. Streaming first story detection with application to twitter. In *HLT-NAACL*, pages 181–189.

Sara Rosenthal and Kathleen McKeown. 2011. Age prediction in blogs: A study of style, content, and online behavior in pre- and post-social media generations. In *ACL-HLT*, pages 763–772.

Marc Schröder. 2001. Emotional speech synthesis: a review. In Paul Dalsgaard, Brge Lindberg, Henrik Benner, and Zheng-Hua Tan, editors, *INTERSPEECH*, pages 561–564.

Andreas Stolcke. 2002. SRILM-an extensible language modeling toolkit. In *Proc. of International Conference on Spoken Language Processing*, pages 901–904.

Aobo Wang and Min-Yen Kan. 2013. Mining informal language from chinese microtext: Joint word recognition and segmentation. In *ACL*, pages 731–741.

Benjamin Wing and Jason Baldridge. 2011. Simple supervised document geolocation with geodesic grids. In *ACL-HLT*, pages 955–964.

Hybrid Method of Semi-supervised Learning and Feature Weighted Learning for Domain Adaptation of Document Classification

Hiroyuki Shinnou, Liying Xiao, Minoru Sasaki, Kanako Komiya
Ibaraki University, Department of Computer and Information Sciences
4-12-1 Nakanarusawa, Hitachi, Ibaraki JAPAN 316-8511
hiroyuki.shinnou.0828@vc.ibaraki.ac.jp,
{14nm721x, minoru.sasaki.01, kanako.komiya.nlp}
@vc.ibaraki.ac.jp

Abstract

In regard to document classification, semi-supervised learning using the Naive Bayes method and EM algorithm was a great success, and we refer to this method as NBEM in this paper. Although NBEM is also effective for domain adaption of document classification, there is still room for improvement because NBEM does not employ valuable information for this task, that is the difference between source domain and target domain. Here, according to the similarity between the label distribution of the feature on source domain and the estimated label distribution of the feature on target domain, we set the weight on the features to reconstruct the training data. We use this reconstructed training data to perform document classification by NBEM. As a result of experiment by using a part of 20 Newsgroups, the effect of this method was confirmed.

1 Introduction

In this paper, for the domain adaption problems of document classification, we propose a hybrid method of semi-supervised learning and feature weighted learning. In many of the tasks of natural language processing, supervised learning has been a great success. However, if we want to use a supervised learning for real problems, there is often problems in domain adaptation. In general, the supervised learning is used to create a classifier which is usually using a learning algorithm such as support vector machine (SVM) by labeled training data, then it is possible to identify the label of the test data using this classifier. In this case, the problem is that the domain of training data and test data is different, so it is a problem of domain adaptation (Søgaard, 2013).

As a typical example, there is a sentiment analysis task to judge whether a review article for a commodity is positive or not (Blitzer et al., 2007). For example, if we use review articles for "book" as the training data to make a classifier, the classifier can not correctly identify the review articles for "movie" which is in another domain. In addition to the emotion analysis, supervised learning such as morphological analysis (Mori, 2012), parsing (Sagae and Tsujii, 2007), word sense disambiguation (Shinnou et al., 2015) (Komiya and Okumura, 2012) (Komiya and Okumura, 2011) is utilized in all tasks, it is possible that the domain adaptation problems come into being.

In general, the method of the domain adaptation can be divided into instance-based method and feature-based method (Pan and Yang, 2010). Instance-based method is a method of learning using weighted training data. Learning under covariate shift (Sugiyama and Kawanabe, 2011) is typical in this method. The covariate shift means the assumption that $P_S(\boldsymbol{x}) \neq P_T(\boldsymbol{x})$, $P_S(y|\boldsymbol{x}) = P_T(y|\boldsymbol{x})$. Learning under covariate shift is regarded as weighted learning, where the weight is set to the probability density ratio $P_T(\boldsymbol{x})/P_S(\boldsymbol{x})$. The feature-based method is a method that maps the source and target features spaces to a common features space to maintain important characteristics of both domains by reducing the difference between

29th Pacific Asia Conference on Language, Information and Computation pages 496 - 503
Shanghai, China, October 30 - November 1, 2015

domains. The paper (Blitzer et al., 2006) proposed the dimension reduction method called structural correspondence learning (SCL).

The paper (Daumé III, Hal, 2007) offered a weighting system for features . In this study, vector $\boldsymbol{x}_s$ of the training data in the source domain is mapped to an augmented input space $(\boldsymbol{x}_s, \boldsymbol{x}_s, \mathbf{0})$, and vector $\boldsymbol{x}_t$ of the training data in the target domain is mapped to an augmented input space $(\mathbf{0}, \boldsymbol{x}_t, \boldsymbol{x}_t)$. The classifier learned from the augmented vectors solves the classification problem. Daumé's method assumes that an effect can be determined by overlapping the characteristics that are common to the source and target domains.

Although these methods for domain adaption often work well, while the differences between the domains is small, there may be counterproductive by such an method. When the difference between the domains is small, it is realistic that the problem of domain adaption is simply regarded as data sparseness problem. In that case, the method of conventional semi-supervised learning (Chapelle et al., 2006) and active learning (Settles, 2010) (Rai et al., 2010) is better.

In this paper, we are dealing with problems of the domain adaption in document classification. Here, as described above, semi-supervised learning is available for dealing with domain adaption that difference between domains is small. Especially as semi-supervised learning of document classification, the method using the EM algorithm based on Naive Bayes method is very famous (Nigam et al., 2000). In this paper, we refer to this method as NBEM. Here, we also use the NBEM. However, there is still room for improvement because NBEM does not employ valuable information for this task, that is the difference between source domain and target domain. Here, we use the method shown by Chen (Chen et al., 2011) which has improved the learning of weighting feature. This method is named as Self-Training Feature Weight, called STFW for short. STFW uses self-learning to estimate the label distribution of features on target domain, but we use NBEM to do it in STFW. The original STFW can be applied to only a binary classification task. For the multi-class classification, we improve STFW. Finally, we use the combination of NBEM and STFW. The domain adaption of document classification can perform more accurately by this. As for the experiment we used the 20 Newsgroups data[1] to construct the domain A and the domain B, and then domain adaption experiments were conducted from domain A to domain B and from domain B to domain A. As a result, NBEM was effective for our task. And the proposed method was able to improve NBEM.

2 Related works

There are some researches using NBEM for domain adaptation of document classification. The Naive Bayes Transfer Classifier (NBTC) modifies EM parts in NBEM to adapt to a target domain (Dai et al., 2007). NBTC needs the probability that a test document appears in the source domain. NBTC estimates this probability by using KL divergence between the source domain and the target domain, and empirical parameters. The Adapting Naive Bayes (ANB) also modifies EM parts in NBEM like NBEM (Tan et al., 2009). AMB uses the mixture distribution of the source domain and the target domain as the document generative model. The weight of the source domain is reduced according to EM iterations. As a result, both of NBEM and ANB gives weight to a feature through the class distribution of target domain. On the other hand, our method is based on the idea that the feature must be weighted if the class distribution of a feature in the target domain are similar.

3 Hybrid method of NBEM and STFW

3.1 NBEM

NBEM is one of the semi-supervised learning for learning a classifier from a little labeled training data and much unlabeled data. Generally speaking, it is an method that learn the classifier of Naive Bayes from labeled training data, and use a large amount of unlabeled data and EM algorithm to improve this classifier.

In a classification problem, let $C = \{c_1, c_2, \cdots, c_m\}$ be a set of classes. An instance x is represented as a feature list

$$\boldsymbol{x} = (f_1, f_2, \cdots, f_n). \tag{1}$$

We can solve the classification problem by estimating the probability $P(c|x)$. Actually, the class

[1] tt http://qwone.com/~jason/20Newsgroups/

c_x of $\boldsymbol{x}$, is given by

$$c_x = \arg\max_{c \in C} P(c|\boldsymbol{x}). \tag{2}$$

Bayes theorem shows that

$$P(c|\boldsymbol{x}) = \frac{P(c)P(\boldsymbol{x}|c)}{P(\boldsymbol{x})}. \tag{3}$$

As a result, we get

$$c_x = \arg\max_{c \in C} P(c)P(\boldsymbol{x}|c). \tag{4}$$

In the above equation, $P(c)$ is estimated easily; the question is how to estimate $P(\boldsymbol{x}|c)$. Naive Bayes models assume the following:

$$P(\boldsymbol{x}|c) = \prod_{i=1}^{n} P(f_i|c). \tag{5}$$

The estimation of $P(f_i|c)$ is easy, so we can estimate $P(\boldsymbol{x}|c)$.

We can use the EM method if we use Naive Bayes for classification problems. In this paper, we show only key equations and the key algorithm of this method (Nigam et al., 2000).

Basically the method computes $P(f_i|c_j)$ where f_i is a feature and c_j is a class. This probability is given by[2]

$$P(f_i|c_j) = \frac{1 + \sum_{k=1}^{|D|} N(f_i, d_k)P(c_j|d_k)}{|F| + \sum_{m=1}^{|F|}\sum_{k=1}^{|D|} N(f_m, d_k)P(c_j|d_k)}. \tag{6}$$

- D: all data consisting of labeled data and unlabeled data
- d_k: an element in D
- F: the set of all features
- f_m: an element in F
- $N(f_i, d_k)$: the number of f_i in the instance d_k.

In our problem, $N(f_i, d_k)$ is 0 or 1, and almost all of them are 0. If d_k is labeled, $P(c_j|d_k)$ is 0 or 1. If d_k is unlabeled, $P(c_j|d_k)$ is initially 0, and is updated to an appropriate value step by step in proportion to the iteration of the EM algorithm.

[2]This equation is smoothed by taking into account the frequency 0.

By using equation 6, the following classifier is constructed:

$$P(c_j|d_i) = \frac{P(c_j)\prod_{f_n \in K_{d_i}} P(f_n|c_j)}{\sum_{r=1}^{|C|} P(c_r)\prod_{f_n \in K_{d_i}} P(f_n|c_r)}. \tag{7}$$

In this equation, K_{d_i} is the set of features in the instance d_i.

$P(c_j)$ is computed by

$$P(c_j) = \frac{1 + \sum_{k=1}^{|D|} P(c_j|d_k)}{|C| + |D|}. \tag{8}$$

The EM algorithm computes $P(c_j|d_i)$ by using equation 7 (E-step). Next, by using equation 6, $P(f_i|c_j)$ is computed (M-step). By iterating E-step and M-step, $P(f_i|c_j)$ and $P(c_j|d_i)$ converge. In our experiment, when the difference between the current $P(f_i|c_j)$ and the updated $P(f_i|c_j)$ comes to less than $8 \cdot 10^{-6}$ or the iteration number reaches 10 times, we judge that the algorithm has converged.

3.2 STFW

In this paper, we improved STFW proposed by Chen. STFW is a feature-based method which is effective in domain adaption. In essence, feature-based method can be regarded as a method which maps the common space of feature between the space of target domain and the source domain. As for the operation, we corresponds to weighting the feature, so intuitively, it is also considered as an method that set a weight to feature that is effective to identification in both domains of the source domain and the target domain. Chen set weight to the feature in the following ways. First, we set the value of feature f of data $\boldsymbol{x}$ to x_f, set the class of data $\boldsymbol{x}$ to y_x. We regard the correlation coefficient of x_f and y_x as $\rho_S(x_f, y_x)$ for labeled data in source domain. About the data $\boldsymbol{x}$ in target domain, its class is substituted for the class which estimated by self-learning y'_x, and we obtain the correlation coefficient $\rho_T(x_f, y'_x)$ of x_f and y'_x. Then the weight $w(f)$ of feature f is defined as the following.

$$w(f) = \frac{1 + \rho_S(x_f, y_x)\rho_T(x_f, y'_x)}{2} \tag{9}$$

A new value v_{new} of the feature come to be obtained by multiplying the weight:

$$v_{new} = w(f) \cdot v_{old} \tag{10}$$

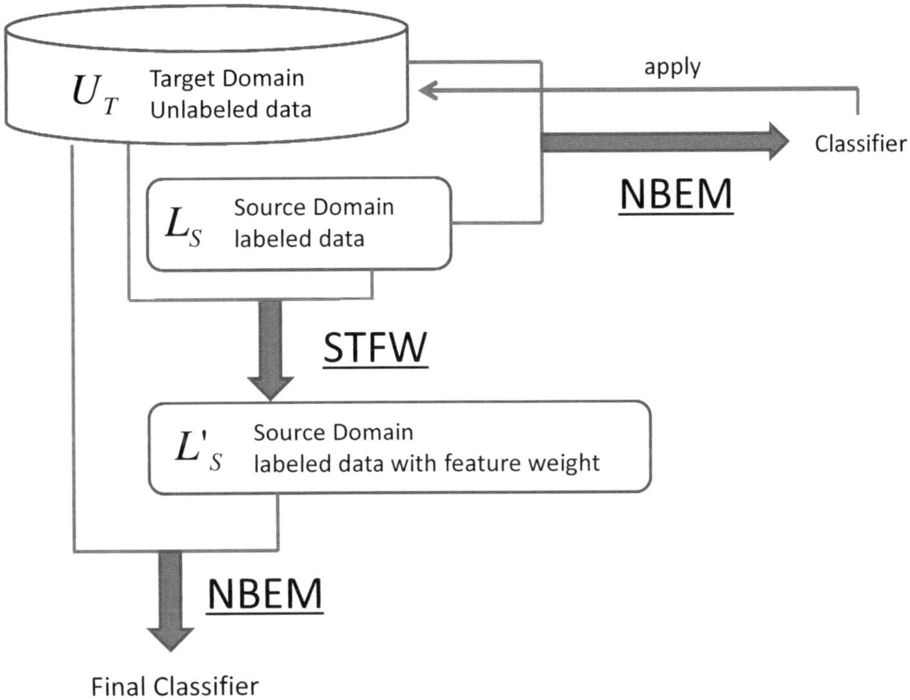

Figure 1: Hybrid method of NBEM and STFW

Note $v_{new} = 0$ if $v_{old} = 0$ in the equation 10.

Chen's method uses a correlation coefficient $\rho_S(x_f, y_x)$ と $\rho_T(x_f, y'_x)$ to define the weight. Because the label is a categorical value, in fact, only binary classification can be targeted. Based on Chen's method here, it is defined of weighting that it also can be used in the multi-class classification. The weight Chen defined can be regarded that measured the similarity of the label distribution P_s of feature f in source domain and label distribution P_t of feature f in target domain. The P_s is the distribution of the following set:

$$\{y_x | x \ in \ Source \ data \ set, x_f > 0\}. \quad (11)$$

The P_t can be defined by the same way.

Therefore, in this paper, first, define the distance $d(f)$ between P_s and P_t as following:

$$d(f) = |P_s - P_t|. \quad (12)$$

Then set the weight by using $d(f)$. However, our task is document classification. We use Naive Bayes as a learning algorithm, so the value of feature becomes frequency. Therefore, the value of feature (i.e. the weight) is desirably an integer of 0 or more. As a result, we define the new value v_{new} of the feature as follows:

$$v_{new} = \begin{cases} v_{old} + 1 & if \quad d(f) < \theta_1, v_{old} > 0 \\ v_{old} - 1 & if \quad d(f) > \theta_2, v_{old} > 0 \\ v_{old} & if \quad others \end{cases}$$

However, if v_{new} is a negative number after minus 1, $v_{new} = 0$. In the experiments of this paper, the parameter θ_1 and θ_2 was set to 0.2 and 1.5 respectively. These values were obtained through some experiments [3].

Also because there is no label of the data in target domain, P_t can not simply obtained. Chen labeled the data in target domain by self-learning, and

[3]The parameter θ_1 and θ_2 depend on the number of classes. In the experiments of this paper, all of the number of classes are three.

seeking P_t only on reliable data. In this paper, we do not use self-learning, but the classifier learned by NBEM. And it is not only limited to those reliable data, all of the data will be used to estimate P_t.

3.3 Combination of NBEM and STFW

In this paper we propose an method that uses a combination of NBEM and STFW, referring to Figure 1.

First, we learn a classifier by using the NBEM against labeled training data L_S of the source domain and unlabeled data U_T of the target domain. Use this classifier to estimate the label of U_T.

Using this label estimated, we set a weight to the feature of L_s by STFW, and construct new training data L'_S.

4 Experiment

It took out a 20 Newsgroups data set [4] from the document group of following six categories in our experiment. Symbols in parentheses refer to the class name.

```
A: comp.sys.ibm.pc.hardware (comp)
B: rec.sport.baseball  (rec)
C: sci.electronics (sci)
D: comp.sys.mac.hardware  (comp)
E: rec.sport.hockey  (rec)
F: sci.med  (sci)
```

We suppose the dataset of `(A,B,C)` to domain X, and the dataset of `(D,E,F)` to domain Y. Each domain has become a dataset of the document classification that `L = {comp, rec, sci}` is the class label set.

The document number (the number of data) of each document group is shown in Table 2. Although the class distribution of labeled training data is uniform in each domain, Class distribution of the test data which can fit the problem of reality was set to be different in each domain.

On the one hand, in domain adaption which is from domain X to domain Y, labeled data of A, B, C becomes training data (a total of 300 documents), and the unlabeled data of D, E, F is unlabeled data(a total of 900 documents) which can be used. Then the test data of D,E,F is used as test data (a total of 600 documents). On the other hand, in domain adaption which is from domain Y to domain X, labeled data of D, E, F becomes training data (a total of 300 documents), and the unlabeled data of A, B, C is unlabeled data(a total of 900 documents) which can be used. Then the test data of A, B, C is used as test data (a total of 600 documents).

[4] http://qwone.com/~jason/20Newsgroups/

Table 2: Number of data of each document group

	Labeled data	Unlabeled data	Test data
A	100	400	300
B	100	300	200
C	100	200	100
D	100	200	100
E	100	400	300
F	100	300	200

The results of the experiment is shown in table1.

The column of NB (S-Only) learns the classifier only from the training data of the source domain by Naive Bayes, has been written of the accuracy rate of test data identified. The column of NBEM is the accuracy rate using the training data and unlabeled data by NBEM, the column of NBEM+STFW is accuracy rate by hybrid method of NBEM and STFW proposed in this paper. The effect of the method proposed in Table1 can be confirmed. Also as reference accuracy rate that it learn the classifier from training data of target domain by Naive Bayes is shown in NB (T-Only). These values have shown the accuracy rate of supervised learning in the case of the usual problems of domain adaption have not occurred.

5 Discussion

5.1 Comparison with transductive method

Like semi-supervised learning, transductive learning is another method using unlabeled data in order to improve the classifier learned through labeled data. And then as a representative method of transductive learning, there is Transductive-SVM (TSVM) (Joachims, 1999).

In this paper, although we use NBEM of semi-supervised learning, it is also possible to use the TSVM instead of NBEM.

Table 1: Experimental results (%)

	NB (S-only)	NBEM	NBEM+STFW	NB (T-only)
X → Y	72.83	90.00	**92.33**	94.67
Y → X	81.17	82.67	**82.83**	90.00

Table 3: Another method using unlabeled data

	NB	NBEM	SVM	TSVM
X → Y	72.83	90.00	75.83	66.50
Y → X	81.17	82.67	71.16	70.83

Generally SVM has a higher accuracy than NB. However, NB sometimes has high accuracy in the case of document classification. In fact, in domain adaption of Y → X, NB is better than SVM. When using NB for document classification, it is better that documents simply represent by a bag of words. Thus, using SVM, it becomes necessary to make some processing. In the experiment using SVM above, we set the vector value by TF*IDF, and finally normalize the size of the vector to 1.

TSVM does not improve the accuracy of the SVM, conversely the accuracy become lower. It is because that TSVM assumes that the class distribution of test data and training data is the same, but this assumption is not satisfied in our experiments.

5.2 Comparison with other methods of domain adaption

The method of domain adaption can be classified to feature-based method and instance-based method. In this section we apply a feature-based method and an instance-based method, and compare them with our proposed method.

As a feature-based method, we use the structural correspondence learning (SCL) (Blitzer et al., 2006). This is the representative feature-base method. On the other hand, the typical instance-based method is learning by covariate shift. In learning by covariate shift, the calculation of the probability density ratio become the key point. Here we use a density calculation method named Unconstrained Least Squares Importance Fitting (uLSIF) (Kanamori et al., 2009).

The result of experiment is shown in Table 4. NBEM+STFW in the table is the our proposed method.

Table 4: Other domain adaptation methods

	NBEM+STFW	SVM	SCL	uLSIF
X → Y	**92.33**	75.83	74.33	73.67
Y → X	**82.83**	71.16	71.83	72.17

As a result of SCL and uLSIF has not changed a lot that both of them is based of SVM, there is a high overwhelmingly accuracy toward NBEM+STFW. Here we can see the great difference of the results is because that whether the base of the learning algorithm is SVM or NB. NB made a higher accuracy than SVM just in our task. Both of SCL and uLSIF are transductive method, although the test data in target domain is used in the process of learning, the unlabeled data are not used. On the other hand, NBEM+STFW does not use test data, but unlabeled data. Test data is also unlabeled data, but the former is smaller than the latter. In this experiment, the amount of unlabeled data is 1.5 times of the amount of test data. Therefore it can be considered one reason that NBEM+STFW is better than SCL and uLSIF.

5.3 Weighting to feature

In this paper we give a weight to the feature likely to be valid for identification in domain adaption, subtract the weight of the feature likely to make an adverse effect on identification.

Here we examined the points following:

- Weighting to Test Data
- Size of the Added Weight
- Negative Weights

We show results of the experiment in turn below.

Weighting to Test Data

In this paper we set the weight to features of training data only, but it is also conceivable to the test data. The result of the experiment is shown in Table 5.

Table 5: Weighting to Test Data (TW)

	NBEM+STFW (without TW) - our method -	NBEM+STFW (with TW)
X → Y	**92.33**	91.17
Y → X	82.83	**83.00**

Weighting to the test data is effective to domain adaption of Y → X, but it is not effective of X → Y.

Size of the Added Weight

In this paper, giving a weight means to plus 1, here we change it to plus 2, and the result of the experiment is shown in Table 6.

Table 6: Change the Size of the Added Weight

	NBEM+STFW (+1) - our method -	NBEM+STFW (+2)
X → Y	92.33	**93.33**
Y → X	82.83	82.83

While we make the twice of the weight, it is effective in domain adaption of X → Y, but it is not effective in Y → X.

Negative Weights

In domain adaption, there may be some labeled data which creates an adverse result in learning. This is called 'negative transfer' (Rosenstein et al., 2005). Our method is designed on the based on 'negative transfer.' That is, if the difference between class distributions of feature on the source domain and the target domain is quite big, we assign the feature negative weight (-1), In order to investigate the effect of negative weights here, we make an experiment which did not assign negative weight. And its result is shown in Table7.

Table 7: The Effect of Negative Weight (NW)

	NBEM+STFW (with NW) - our method -	NBEM+STFW (without NW)
X → Y	92.33	**93.00**
Y → X	**82.83**	82.67

Without negative weight, although it is effective in domain adaption of X → Y, it is not effective of Y → X.

It can be confirmed that the accuracy is subtly changed by the way of setting weight and its value.

6 Conclusion

In this paper, for the domain adaption problems of document classification, we proposed a hybrid method of semi-supervised learning and feature weighted learning. NBEM is used to learn a classifier, and then the learned classifier and SFTW reconstruct training data, and then the final classifier is learned by using the reconstruct training data and NBEM again. As a result of experiment by using a part of 20 Newsgroups, the effect of our method was confirmed. As for challenges in the future, we need to discover an more appropriate setting way and a better size of weight.

References

John Blitzer, Ryan McDonald, and Fernando Pereira. 2006. Domain adaptation with structural correspondence learning. In *EMNLP-2006*, pages 120–128.

John Blitzer, Mark Dredze, Fernando Pereira, et al. 2007. Biographies, bollywood, boom-boxes and blenders: Domain adaptation for sentiment classification. In *ACL*, volume 7, pages 440–447.

Olivier Chapelle, Bernhard Schölkopf, Alexander Zien, et al. 2006. *Semi-supervised learning*, volume 2. MIT press Cambridge.

Minmin Chen, Kilian Q Weinberger, and John Blitzer. 2011. Co-training for domain adaptation. In *NIPS-2014*, pages 2456–2464.

Wenyuan Dai, Gui-Rong Xue, Qiang Yang, and Yong Yu. 2007. Transferring Naive Bayes Classifiers for Text Classification. In *AAAI-2007*.

Daumé III, Hal. 2007. Frustratingly Easy Domain Adaptation. In *ACL-2007*, pages 256–263.

Thorsten Joachims. 1999. Transductive inference for text classification using support vector machines. In *ICML*, volume 99, pages 200–209.

Takafumi Kanamori, Shohei Hido, and Masashi Sugiyama. 2009. A least-squares approach to direct importance estimation. *The Journal of Machine Learning Research*, 10:1391–1445.

Kanako Komiya and Manabu Okumura. 2011. Automatic Determination of a Domain Adaptation Method for Word Sense Disambiguation using Decision Tree Learning. In *IJCNLP-2011*, pages 1107–1115.

Kanako Komiya and Manabu Okumura. 2012. Automatic Domain Adaptation for Word Sense Disambiguation Based on Comparison of Multiple Classifiers. In *PACLIC-2012*, pages 75–85.

Shinsuke Mori. 2012. Domain adaptation in natural language processing (in japanese). *The Japanese Society for Artificial Intelligence*, 27(4):365–372.

Kamal Nigam, Andrew McCallum, Sebastian Thrun, and Tom Mitchell. 2000. Text Classification from Labeled and Unlabeled Documents using EM. *Machine Learning*, 39(2/3):103–134.

Sinno Jialin Pan and Qiang Yang. 2010. A survey on transfer learning. *Knowledge and Data Engineering, IEEE Transactions on*, 22(10):1345–1359.

Piyush Rai, Avishek Saha, Hal Daumé III, and Suresh Venkatasubramanian. 2010. Domain adaptation meets active learning. In *NAACL HLT 2010 Workshop on Active Learning for Natural Language Processing*, pages 27–32.

Michael T Rosenstein, Zvika Marx, Leslie Pack Kaelbling, and Thomas G Dietterich. 2005. To transfer or not to transfer. In *NIPS 2005 Workshop on Transfer Learning*, volume 898.

Kenji Sagae and Jun'ichi Tsujii. 2007. Dependency parsing and domain adaptation with lr models and parser ensembles. In *EMNLP-CoNLL-2007*, pages 1044–1050.

Burr Settles. 2010. Active learning literature survey. *University of Wisconsin, Madison*.

Hiroyuki Shinnou, Yoshiyuki Onodera, Minoru Sasaki, and Kanako Komiya. 2015. Active Learning to Remove Source Instances for Domain Adaptation for Word Sense Disambiguation. In *PACLING-2015*, pages 156–162.

Anders Søgaard. 2013. *Semi-Supervised Learning and Domain Adaptation in Natural Language Processing*. Morgan & Claypool.

Masashi Sugiyama and Motoaki Kawanabe. 2011. *Machine Learning in Non-Stationary Environments: Introduction to Covariate Shift Adaptation* . MIT Press.

Songbo Tan, Xueqi Cheng, Yuefen Wang, and Hongbo Xu. 2009. Adapting Naive Bayes to Domain Adaptation for Sentiment Analysis. In *Advances in Information Retrieval*, pages 337–349.

Paraphrase Detection Based on Identical Phrase and Similar Word Matching

Hoang-Quoc Nguyen-Son[1], Yusuke Miyao[2], and Isao Echizen[2]
[1]University of Science, VNU-HCM, Hochiminh, Vietnam
nshquoc@fit.hcmus.edu.vn
[2]National Institute of Informatics, Tokyo, Japan
{yusuke,iechizen}@nii.ac.jp

Abstract

Paraphrase detection has numerous important applications in natural language processing (such as clustering, summarizing, and detecting plagiarism). One approach to detecting paraphrases is to use predicate argument tuples. Although this approach achieves high paraphrase recall, its accuracy is generally low. Other approaches focus on matching similar words, but word meaning is often contextual (e.g., 'get along with,' 'look forward to'). An effective approach to detecting plagiarism would take into account the fact that plagiarists frequently cut and paste whole phrases and/or replace several words with similar words. This generally results in the paraphrased text containing identical phrases and similar words. Moreover, plagiarists usually insert and/or remove various minor words (prepositions, conjunctions, etc.) to both improve the naturalness and disguise the paraphrasing. We have developed a similarity matching ($SimMat$) metric for detecting paraphrases that is based on matching identical phrases and similar words and quantifying the minor words. The metric achieved the highest paraphrase detection accuracy (77.6%) when it was combined with eight standard machine translation metrics. This accuracy is better than the 77.4% rate achieved with the state-of-the-art approach for paraphrase detection.

1 Introduction

Paraphrase detection is used to determine whether two texts (phrases, sentences, paragraphs, documents, etc.) of arbitrary lengths have the same meaning. Such detection is widely used to remove the tremendous amount of duplicate information on the Internet. It is also used to handle the overlap of semantic components in texts. Such components are used in various natural language applications such as word sense discrimination, summarization, automatic thesaurus extraction, question-and-answer generation, machine translation, and plagiarist or analogical relation identification.

Some researchers in the field of paraphrase detection have used vector-based similarity to identify the differences between two sentences (Mihalcea et al., 2006; Blacoe and Lapata, 2012). The two sentences are represented by two vectors based on the frequency of their words in text corpora. The vectors are compared to estimate sentence similarity. Plagiarists attempt to thwart this comparison by modifying the copied sentence by inserting or removing a few minor words, replacing words with similar words that have different usage frequencies, etc. Such modification reduces the effectiveness of vector-based similarity analysis.

Other researchers have analyzed the difference in meaning between two sentences on the basis of their syntactic parsing trees (Socher et al., 2011; Qiu et al., 2006; Das and Smith, 2009). The structure of the trees is a major factor used various sophisticated algorithms such as recursive autoencoders (Socher et al., 2011), heuristic similarity (Qiu et al., 2006), and probabilistic inference (Das and Smith, 2009). However, these algorithms are affected by manipulation (deleting, inserting, reordering, etc.) of the words in the sentences. Such manipulations can significantly change the structures of the parsing trees.

29th Pacific Asia Conference on Language, Information and Computation pages 504 - 512
Shanghai, China, October 30 - November 1, 2015

Other researchers (Mihalcea et al., 2006; Chan and Ng, 2008) have used matching algorithms to determine the similarity of two sentences. Mihalcea et al. (2006), for example, proposed a method for finding the best matching of a word in a sentence with the nearest word in the other sentence. However, word meaning is often contextual (e.g., 'make sure of,' 'take care of').

Machine translation (MT) metrics, which are generally used to evaluate the quality of translated text, can also be used to judge two texts in the same language. Due to the similarity of machine translation and paraphrase detection, many MT metrics have been applied to paraphrase detection (Finch et al., 2005; Madnani et al., 2012). For example, eight standard MT metrics have been combined to create a state-of-the-art paraphrase detection approach (Madnani et al., 2012). However, the objectives of machine translation and paraphrase detection differ: machine translation tries to effectively translate text from one language to another while paraphrase detection tries to identify paraphrased text. This difference affects the application of MT metrics to paraphrase detection.

A paraphrase is a restatement of the meaning of a text using other words. It is a specific type of plagiarisms. We identify common practices plagiarizers who try to paraphrase a text. The Microsoft Research Paraphrase (MSRP) corpus (Dolan et al., 2004) is commonly used to identify the common practices. An example paraphrase pair extracted from this corpus is shown in Figure 1.

Plagiarists frequently cut and paste several phrases of different lengths. This can result in a sentence pair containing *identical phrases*. The two sentences in Figure 1 have two identical phrases: "Intelligence officials" and "a week ago to expect a terrorist attack in Saudi Arabia." Plagiarists also add and delete *minor words* to improve the naturalness of the text. In the example pair, the preposition "in" (in bold) in the second sentence is considered a minor word.

Moreover, plagiarists can replace several words with *similar words* without changing the sentence meaning to avoid paraphrase detection. The words connected by dashed lines with arrows in the example are most likely such replacements. The remaining words are probably the combination of a few manipulations (reorganization, deletion, insertion, replacement, etc.). Such *modifications* are typically intended to ensure that the paraphrased sentence has the same meaning as the original sentence.

We make several contributions based on an analysis of related work and the common practices of plagiarists in this paper.

- We present a heuristic algorithm for finding an optimal matching of *identical phrases* with maximum lengths.

- We suggest removing the *minor words* from the words remaining in the sentences. These minor words include prepositions, subordinating conjunctions ('at,' 'in,' etc.), modal verbs, possessive pronouns ('its,' 'their,' etc.), and periods ('.').

- We present an algorithm for determining the perfect matching of *similar words* by using the matching algorithm proposed by Kuhn and Munkres (Kuhn, 1955; Munkres, 1957). The degree of similarity between two similar words is identified using WordNet (Pedersen et al., 2004). These similarities are used as weights for the matching algorithm.

- We present a related matching ($RelMat$) metric for quantifying the relationship between two sentences on the basis of matching identical phrases and similar words.

- We present a brevity penalty metric to reduce the effect of paraphrased sentence *modification*. This metric is combined with the $RelMat$ metric into a similarity matching $SimMat$ metric for effectively detecting paraphrases.

We used the MSRP corpus to evaluate the $SimMat$ metric. Our method using the $SimMat$ metric outperformed many previous methods. The $SimMat$ metric had the highest accuracy (77.6%) when used in combination with eight standard MT metrics (MAXSIM, SEPIA, TER, TERp, METEOR, BADGER, BLEU, and NIST). The accuracy was higher than with the state-of-the-art approach (accuracy=77.4%). The result shows that our method effectively uses the paraphrasing practices commonly used by plagiarists to detect them.

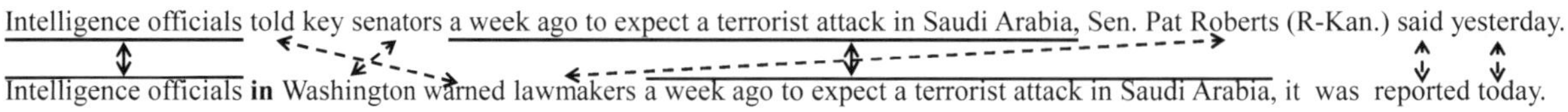

Figure 1: Example paraphrase pair taken from MSRP corpus.

2 Related work

2.1 Paraphrase detection

The baseline for paraphrase detection is based on vector-based similarity. Each source message and target message is represented as a vector using the frequencies of its words (such as term frequency (Mihalcea et al., 2006) and co-occurrence (Blacoe and Lapata, 2012)). The similarity of the two vectors is quantified using various measures (e.g., cosine (Mihalcea et al., 2006), addition and point-wise multiplication (Blacoe and Lapata, 2012)). The problem with vector-based methods is to focus on the frequency of separate words or phrases. However, plagiarists can paraphrase by replacing words with similar words that have a very different frequency. Moreover, they can delete and/or insert minor words that do not change the meaning of the original sentences. Such manipulations change the quality of the representation vector, which reduces paraphrase detection performance.

Several methods have been proposed for overcoming the manipulation problem that use syntactic parsing trees of messages. The replacement of similar words and the use of minor words do not change the basic structure of the trees. Qiu et al. (2006) reported a method that detects the similarity of two sentences by heuristically comparing their predicate argument tuples, which are a type of syntactic parsing tree. The high paraphrase recall (93%) it attained shows that most paraphrases have the same predicate argument tuples. However, the accuracy was very low (72%). Parsing trees were used for probabilistic inference of paraphrases by Das and Smith (2009).

Another method considers these trees as input for a paraphrase detection system based on recursive autoencoders (Socher et al., 2011). The drawback of the parsing tree approach is that parsing trees are affected by the reordering words in a sentence such as the conversion of a sentence from passive voice to active voice. Another method finds the maximum matching for each word in two sentences (Mihalcea et al., 2006). The similarity of matching two words is based on WordNet. However, the weakness of this method is that a word in a first sentence is probably matched to more than one word in the second sentence. This means that a very short sentence can be detected as a paraphrase of a long sentence in some cases. Another problem with word matching is that the meaning of some words depends on the context. For example, the basic meaning of 'get' changes when used in the phrasal verb 'get along with.'

Commonly used techniques for detecting paraphrases are based on MT metrics. This is because the translation task is very similar to the paraphrase detection task for text in the same language. For example, Finch et al. (2005) extended a MT metric (PER) and combined it with three other standard metrics (BLEU, NIST, and WER) into a method for detecting paraphrases. Another method developed by Madnani et al. (2012) is based on the integration of eight metrics (TER, TERp, BADGER, SEPIA, BLEU, NIST, METEOR, and MAXSIM). However, the main purpose of these metrics is for translating, and their integration is unsuitable for detecting paraphrases. To overcome these weaknesses, we developed a similarity metric and combined it with eight standard metrics, as described below.

2.2 Standard MT metrics

Two basic MT metrics for measuring the similarity of two text segments are based on finding the minimum number of operators needed to change one segment so that it matches the other one. The translation edit rate (TER) metric (Snover et al., 2006) supports standard operators, including shift, substitution, deletion, and insertion. The TER-Plus (TERp) metric (Snover et al., 2009) supports even more operators, including stemming and synonymizing.

The BADGER MT metric (Parker, 2008) uses compression and information theory. It is used to calculate the compression distance of two text segments by using Burrows-Wheeler transformation.

This distance represents for probability that one segment is a paraphrase of the other.

The SEPIA MT metric (Habash and Elkholy, 2008) is based on the dependence tree and is used to calculate the similarity of two text segments. It extends the tree to obtain the surface span, which is used as the main component of the similarity score. After the components of the tree are matched, a brevity penalty factor is suggested for deciding the difference in tree lengths for the two text segments.

Two other MT metrics commonly used in machine translation are the bilingual evaluation understudy (BLEU) metric (Papineni et al., 2002) and the NIST metric (Doddington, 2002) (an extension of the BLEU metric). Both also quantify similarity on the basis of matching words in the original text segment with words in the translated segment. Whereas the BLEU metric simply calculates the number of matching words, the NIST metric takes into account the importance of matching with different levels. The main drawback of these word matching metrics is that a word in a segment can match more than one word in the other segment.

Two MT metrics based on non-duplicate matching have been devised to overcome this problem. The METEOR metric (Denkowski and Lavie, 2010) uses explicit ordering to identify matching tuples with minimized cross edges. However, it simply performs word-by-word matching. The maximum similarity (MAXSIM) metric (Chan and Ng, 2008) finds the maximum matching of unigram, bigram, and trigram words by using the Kuhn-Munkres algorithm. However, the maximum length of the phrase is a trigram. Moreover, the similarities of the phrases (unigram, bigram, and trigram) are disjointly combined. To overcome these drawbacks with the standard MT metrics, we have developed a heuristic method for finding the maximum of matching tuples up to the length of the text segments being compared. We also developed a metric for sophisticatedly quantifying the similarity on the basis of the matching tuples.

3 Similarity matching ($SimMat$) metric

Our proposed similarity metric ($SimMat$) for quantifying the similarity of input text comprises four steps, as illustrated in Figure 2. The following is a step-by-step description of our method using two

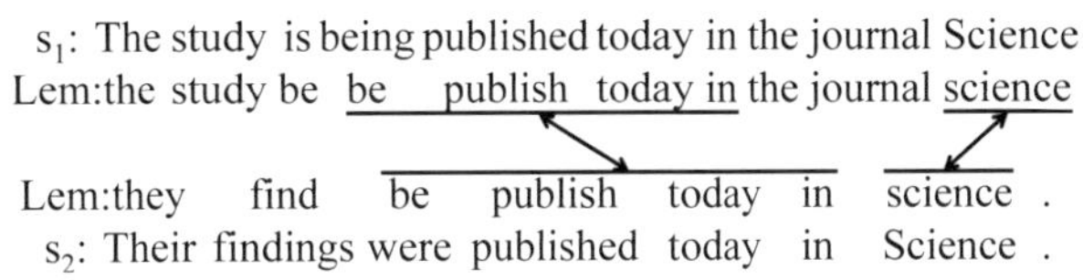

Figure 3: Matching identical phrases with their maximum lengths (Step 1).

sentences, which is an actual paraphrase pair from the MSRP corpus.

s_1: *"The study is being published today in the journal Science"*

s_2: *"Their findings were published today in Science."*

3.1 Match identical phrases (Step 1)

The individual words in the two input sentences are normalized using lemmas. The Natural Language Processing (NLP) library of Stanford University (Manning et al., 2014) is used to identify the lemmas. The lemmas for the two example sentences are shown in Figure 3.

The heuristic algorithm we developed for matching the lemmas in the two sentences repeatedly finds a new matching pair in each round. In each round, a new pair with the maximum phrase length is established. The pseudo code of the algorithm is illustrated in Algorithm 1. The stop condition is when there is no new matching pair. For example, two identical lemma of phrases, "be publish today in" and "science," are matched (as shown as Figure 3).

In algorithm 1, the function $getLemmas(s)$ extracts the lemmas of sentence s using the NLP library. The function len_L gets the number of elements in set L. The function $match(L_1[i], L_2[j])$ finds the maximum length matching of phrase L_1, which starts at the i-th position in the first sentence, and that of phrase L_2, which starts at the j-th position in the second sentence.

3.2 Remove minor words (Step 2)

The words remaining after phrase matching in Step 1 are used for removing minor words. First, the part of speech (POS) for each word is identified. The Stanford library tool (Manning et al., 2014) is used for this purpose. The POSs for the words in two the example sentences are shown in Figure 4.

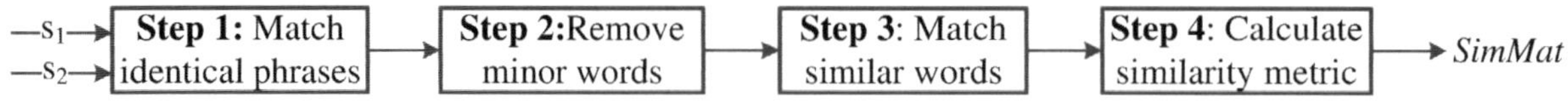

Figure 2: Four steps in calculation of similarity matching ($SimMat$) metric.

Algorithm 1 Match identical phrases.

```
function MATCHIDENTICALPHRASES(s1, s2)
    L1 ← getLemmas(s1);
    L2 ← getLemmas(s2);
    P ← ∅;
    repeat
        new ← ∅;
        for i = 0 to len_L1 − 1 do
            for j = 0 to len_L2 − 1 do
                if {L1[i], L2[j]} ∉ P then
                    tmp ← match(L1[i],L2[j]);
                    if len_tmp > len_new then
                        new ← tmp;
                    end if
                end if
            end for
        end for
        if new is not null then
            P = P ⋃ new;
        end if
    until (new = ∅);
    return P;
end function
```

Our analysis of the common practices of plagiarists showed that four types of minor words should be removed: prepositions and subordinating conjunctions (IN), modal verbs (MD), possessive pronouns (PRP$), and periods ("."). These minor POSs generally do not change the meaning of the paraphrased text as they are often used to simply improve the naturalness of the paraphrased text. For example, the two minor POSs (PRP$ and ".") were deleted from sentence s_2 in Figure 4. An example of preposition deletion is illustrated in Figure 1. Detection of remaining type of minor words (modal verbs) is illustrated for an actual paraphrase pair in Figure 5.

3.3 Match similar words (Step 3)

After minor word deletion in Step 2, the perfect matching of similar words is done using the al-

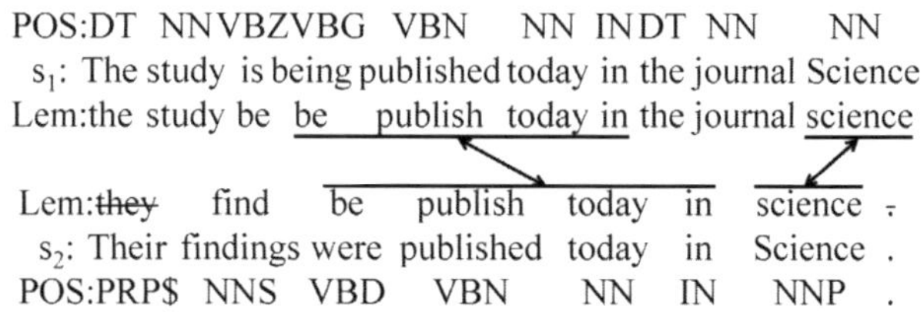

Figure 4: Remove minor words (Step 2).

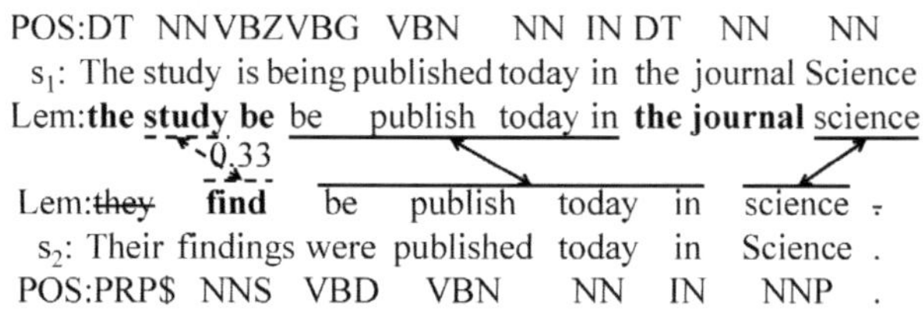

Figure 6: Find perfect matching of similar words using Kuhn-Munkres algorithm (Kuhn, 1955; Munkres, 1957) (Step 3).

gorithm we developed on the basis of the Kuhn-Munkres algorithm (Kuhn, 1955; Munkres, 1957). The weights of each pair in the algorithm are calculated from the similarity of the two lemmas of the words using the $path$ metric (Pedersen et al., 2004). The $path(w_1, w_2)$ metric computes the shortest path ($pathLength$) between two words w_1 and w_2 in the 'is-a' hierarchies of WordNet, as shown in Eq. 1. The $pathLength$ is constrained to be a positive integer to ensure that $0 <= path <= 1$. For example, the $path$ metric for the "study" and "find" pair is 0.33. The perfect matching found for the two example sentences is shown in Figure 6. The word "study" in sentence s_1 is matched with a similar word, "findings," in sentence s_2.

$$path(w_1, w_2) = \frac{1}{pathLength(w_1, w_2)} \quad (1)$$

3.4 Calculate similarity metric (Step 4)

Finally, the $RelMat$ metric is calculated using the results of identical phrase matching in Step 1 and similar word matching in Step 3:

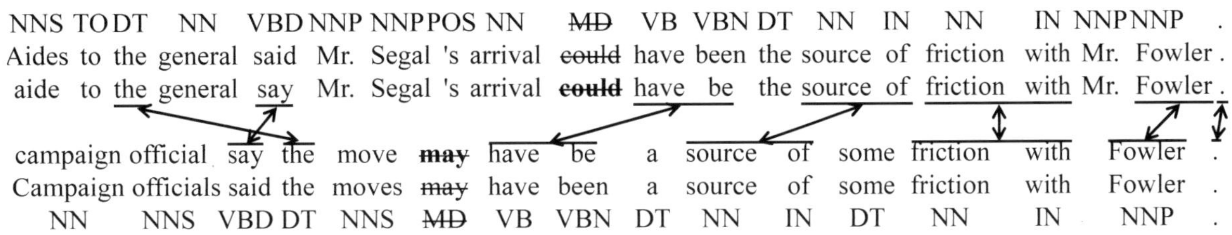

Figure 5: Example of removing minor words (modal verbs).

$$RelMat(s_1, s_2) = \\ = \frac{\#Np + \sum_{i=0}^{N-1} len(p_i)^\alpha + \sum_{j=0}^{M-1} path(w_j)^\alpha}{\#Np + \#Nw + \sum_{i=0}^{N-1} len(p_i)^\alpha + \sum_{j=0}^{M-1} 1^\alpha}, \quad (2)$$

where $\#Np$ is the total number of words in the matched identical phrases, $\#Nw$ is the number of matched similar words, N and M are the corresponding numbers of matched identical phrases and similar words, p_i is the i-th matched phrase in Step 1, $len(p_i)$ is the number of words in the phrase p_i, and $path(w_j)$ is the $path$ metric of the j-th matched word in Step 3.

Eq. 2 ensures that $0 <= RelMat <= 1$. The $RelMat$ metric equals 1 only if the two sentences are identical. Using $\#Np$ only in the numerator means that the matching of identical phrases is more important than the matching of similar words. The $len(p_i)^\alpha$ and $path(w_j)^\alpha$ with $\alpha >= 0$ indicate the respective contributions of matched phrase p_i and matched word w_j to the $RelMat$ metric. The greater the value of α, the greater the contribution of the identical phrases and the lesser the contribution of the similar words. Because $0 <= path(w_j) <= 1$, we use 1^α to normalize the contributions of the matched words.

Threshold α is set to an optimal value of 0.2, as described in more detail in Section 5. The $RelMat$ metric for the two example sentences is calculated using

$$RelMat = \frac{5 + (4^{0.2} + 1^{0.2}) + 0.33^{0.2}}{5 + 1 + (4^{0.2} + 1^{0.2}) + 1^{0.2}} = 0.87.$$

The remaining words are probably modified by few manipulations (e.g., insertion, deletion). Such modification is typically intended to improve the naturalness of text. Therefore, the two sentences being compared frequently have different lengths. To reduce this effect, we developed a brevity penalty metric p based on the METEOR metric (Denkowski and Lavie, 2010). It is calculated as shown in Eq. 3, where $\#ReW(s)$ is the number of words remaining in sentence s after phrase matching and minor word removal. Penalty p is combined with $RelMat$ into the similarity matching $SimMat$ metric, as shown in Eq. 4.

$$p(s_1, s_2) = \\ = 0.5 \times (\frac{|\#ReW(s_1) - \#ReW(s_2)|}{max(\#ReW(s_1), \#ReW(s_2))})^3 \quad (3)$$

$$SimMat = RelMat \times (1 - p) \quad (4)$$

Penalty metric p and the $SimMat$ metric are respectively calculated for the example sentences using Eq. 5 and Eq. 6. To calculate the $\#ReW$, the remaining words (in bold) are shown in Figure 6.

$$p(s_1, s_2) = 0.5 \times (\frac{|5 - 1|}{max(5, 1)})^3 = 0.26 \quad (5)$$

$$SimMat = 0.87 \times (1 - 0.26) = 0.64 \quad (6)$$

4 Combination of $SimMat$ metric and MT metrics

We proposed paraphrase detection method by combining the $SimMat$ metric with the eight standard MT metrics described above, as shown in Figure 7. The last two steps are described in detail below.

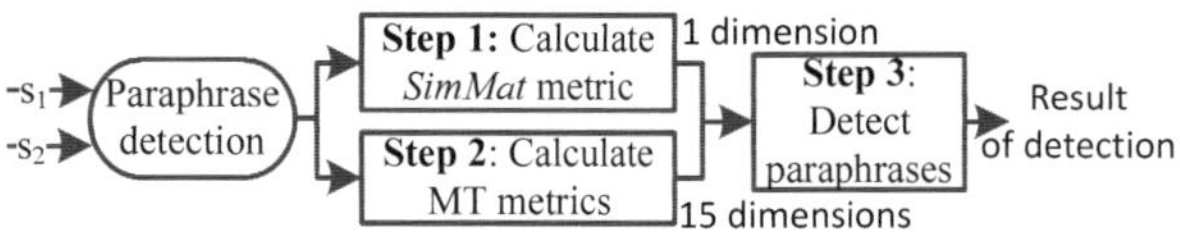

Figure 7: Combination of $SimMat$ metric with eight MT metrics.

4.1 Calculate MT metrics (Step 2)

The eight standard MT metrics are calculated for the two sentences. Eight libraries are used to quantify them. These libraries are suggested by NIST and the state-of-the-art approach for paraphrase detection (Madnani et al., 2012). The libraries are described in more detail in the evaluation section. The first six MT metrics (MAXSIM, SEPIA, TER, TERp, METEOR, and BADGER) create six dimensions in total. The two remaining metrics (BLEU and NIST) using the n-gram model create four (n=1..4) and five (n=1..5) dimensions, respectively. These 15 dimensions metrics are combined with that of our proposed metric ($SimMat$) for detecting paraphrases in the last step.

4.2 Detecting paraphrases (Step 3)

The 16 dimensions, 15 from the MT metrics and 1 from our proposed metric ($SimMat$) are combined for detecting paraphrases using a machine learning approach. Several commonly used machine learning algorithms (including support vector machine, logistic regression, etc.) were evaluated with these dimensions. Such algorithms are run with 10-fold cross validation in the training set of the MRPS corpus for choosing the best classifier. Logistic regression had the best performance and was used for detection.

5 Evaluation

5.1 MSRP corpus

We used the MSRP corpus to evaluate our method. It contains 5801 sentences pairs including 4076 for training and the remaining 1705 for testing.

The corpus has 2753 (67.5%) and 1147 (66.5%) paraphrase cases corresponding to training and testing datasets. The corpus was annotated by two native speakers. Disagreements in annotation were resolved by a third native speaker. Agreement between the two annotators was moderate to high (averaging 83%). This means that a perfect algorithm for detecting paraphrases would have 83% accuracy.

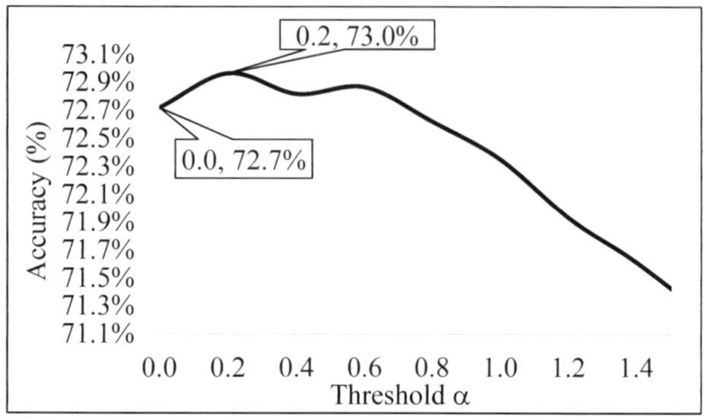

Figure 8: Estimated threshold α.

5.2 Estimating threshold α for $SimMat$ metric

A threshold α is used to adjust the contributions of matched identical phrases and matched similar words. It was estimated using Eq. 2 and the training dataset of the MRPS corpus. The $SimMat$ metric was used as the single dimension for the logistic regression algorithm with 10-fold cross validation, as shown in Figure 8. Using only the training dataset ensured that the results did not overfit the test data.

The higher the threshold α, the greater the contribution of the matched identical phrases and the lesser the contribution of the matched similar words. If α is small, the contributions of identical phrases are low and the contributions of similar words are high, resulting in lower accuracy. However, the $SimMat$ metric is over-estimated if the value of α is too large, resulting in lower accuracy. The highest accuracy (73.0%) was achieved for $\alpha = 0.2$. Therefore, α was set to 0.2 for the subsequent experiments.

5.3 MT metrics result

In our approach, the proposed metric ($SimMat$) is combined with eight MT metrics (MAXSIM, SEPIA, TER, TERp, METEOR, BADGER, BLEU, and NIST). These metrics are integrated to create what we call the MTMETRICS algorithm, which is state of the art for paraphrase detection. The eight metrics are re-implemented on the basis of standard libraries suggested by both of the state of the art and a well-known organization – NIST. The details of

MT metric	Re-implementation			MTMETRICS	
	Ver.	Acc.	F1	Acc.	F1
MAXSIM	1.01	67.5%	79.4%	67.2%	79.4%
SEPIA	0.2	68.3%	79.8%	68.1%	79.8%
TER	1.01	70.1%	81.0%	69.9%	80.9%
TERP	1.0	70.7%	81.0%	74.3%	81.8%
BADGER	2.0	67.2%	79.9%	67.6%	79.9%
METEOR	1.5	71.7%	80.0%	73.1%	81.0%
BLEU	13a	72.1%	80.8%	72.3%	80.9%
NIST	13a	71.8%	80.4%	72.8%	81.2%
Integration		76.6%	83.1%	77.4%	84.1%

Table 1: Results for re-implemented MT metrics and MTMETRICS algorithm (Madnani et al., 2012).

Method	Accuracy	F-score
Vector Based Similarity (baseline)	65.4%	75.3%
Mihalcea et al. (2006)	70.3%	81.3%
Qiu et al. (2006)	72.0%	81.6%
$SimMat$	72.7%	81.3%
Blacoe and Lapata (2012)	73.0%	82.3%
Finch et al. (2005)	75.0%	82.7%
Das and Smith (2009)	76.1%	82.7%
Madnani et al. (2012) (re-implemented)	76.6%	83.1%
Socher et al. (2011)	76.8%	83.6%
Madnani et al. (2012)	77.4%	**84.1%**
Combination	**77.6%**	83.9%

Table 2: Accuracy and F-score of our method ($SimMat$), previous methods, and combination of $SimMat$ with eight MT metrics.

the re-implementation are shown in Table 1.

The versions of the eight libraries for the re-implemented metrics are shown in column 2. They were the latest for each library, for which we used the default settings. Since the versions and settings are not shown for MTMETRICS, there is little difference between the re-implemented metric results and the MTMETRICS results. The results for the integration of the eight re-implemented metrics (accuracy=76.6%, F1=83.1%) also differ from the MTMETRICS results (accuracy=77.4%, F1=84.1%).

5.4 Comparison with previous methods

The results of our comparison with previous methods are summarized in Table 2. These methods were also evaluated using the MRPS corpus. Our proposed metric ($SimMat$) was evaluated using a threshold α of 0.2. This single metric outperformed many previous methods. The combination of $SimMat$ with the eight MT metrics had the highest accuracy (77.6%).

6 Conclusion

Our proposed similarity matching ($SimMat$) metric quantifies the similarity between two sentences and can be used to detect whether one is a paraphrase of the other. It is calculated using the matching of identical phrases and similar words. Phrase-by-phrase matching is done using a heuristic algorithm that determines the longest duplicate phrase in each iteration. Word matching is done using the Kuhn-Munkres algorithm. WordNet is used for determining the similarity of two words. This similarity is used as the weights for the word-matching algorithm. Minor words, which are often added or removed from paraphrased text to improve naturalness, can create noise when detecting paraphrases. They are thus removed as doing so generally does not change the meaning. A brevity penalty metric is combined with the $SimMat$ metric to quantify the effect of inserting and/or deleting words.

Evaluation using the MSRP corpus showed that the $SimMat$ metric detects paraphrases more effectively than previous methods. The $SimMat$ metric was combined with eight machine translation metrics. Although the accuracy of the eight re-implemented metrics (accuracy=76.6%, F-score=83.1%) was lower than the published result (accuracy=77.4%, F-score=84.1%), their combination with the $SimMat$ metric achieved the best accuracy (77.6%), which was higher than with the state-of-the-art approach (77.4%). Moreover, the F-score of the combination (83.9%) is nearly similar with the-state-of-the-art approach (84.1%). These results show that our method is promising approach to detecting paraphrasing.

Future work includes quantifying the weights of words in matched phrases, determining the effect of a word's position in a sentence, and analyzing misclassified pairs to improve performance.

References

William Blacoe and Mirella Lapata. 2012. A comparison of vector-based representations for semantic composition. In *EMNLP*, pages 546–556.

Yee Seng Chan and Hwee Tou Ng. 2008. Maxsim: A maximum similarity metric for machine translation evaluation. In *ACL*, pages 55–62.

Dipanjan Das and Noah A. Smith. 2009. Paraphrase identification as probabilistic quasi-synchronous recognition. In *ACL*, pages 468–476.

Michael Denkowski and Alon Lavie. 2010. Extending the meteor machine translation evaluation metric to the phrase level. In *NAACL*, pages 250–253.

George Doddington. 2002. Automatic evaluation of machine translation quality using n-gram co-occurrence statistics. In *Proc. of the 2nd International Conference on Human Language Technology Research*, pages 138–145.

Bill Dolan, Chris Quirk, and Chris Brockett. 2004. Unsupervised construction of large paraphrase corpora: Exploiting massively parallel news sources. In *COLING*, pages 350–356.

Andrew Finch, Young-Sook Hwang, and Eiichiro Sumita. 2005. Using machine translation evaluation techniques to determine sentence-level semantic equivalence. In *Proc. of the 3rd International Workshop on Paraphrasing*, pages 17–24.

Nizar Habash and Ahmed Elkholy. 2008. Sepia: surface span extension to syntactic dependency precision-based mt evaluation. In *Proc. of Association for Machine Translation in the Americas*.

Harold W. Kuhn. 1955. The hungarian method for the assignment problem. *Naval research logistics quarterly*, 2(1):83–97.

Nitin Madnani, Joel Tetreault, and Martin Chodorow. 2012. Re-examining machine translation metrics for paraphrase identification. In *NAACL*, pages 182–190.

Christopher D. Manning, Mihai Surdeanu, John Bauer, Jenny Finkel, Steven J. Bethard, and David McClosky. 2014. The Stanford CoreNLP natural language processing toolkit. In *ACL*, pages 55–60.

Rada Mihalcea, Courtney Corley, and Carlo Strapparava. 2006. Corpus-based and knowledge-based measures of text semantic similarity. In *AAAI*, volume 6, pages 775–780.

James Munkres. 1957. Algorithms for the assignment and transportation problems. *Journal of the Society for Industrial & Applied Mathematics*, 5(1):32–38.

Kishore Papineni, Salim Roukos, Todd Ward, and Wei-Jing Zhu. 2002. Bleu: a method for automatic evaluation of machine translation. In *ACL*, pages 311–318.

Steven Parker. 2008. Badger: A new machine translation metric. In *Proc. of Association for Machine Translation in the Americas*.

Ted Pedersen, Siddharth Patwardhan, and Jason Michelizzi. 2004. Wordnet:: Similarity: measuring the relatedness of concepts. In *NAACL: Demonstration*, pages 38–41.

Long Qiu, Min-Yen Kan, and Tat-Seng Chua. 2006. Paraphrase recognition via dissimilarity significance classification. In *EMNLP*, pages 18–26.

Matthew Snover, Bonnie Dorr, Richard Schwartz, Linnea Micciulla, and John Makhoul. 2006. A study of translation edit rate with targeted human annotation. In *Proc. of Association for Machine Translation in the Americas*, pages 223–231.

Matthew G. Snover, Nitin Madnani, Bonnie Dorr, and Richard Schwartz. 2009. Ter-plus: paraphrase, semantic, and alignment enhancements to translation edit rate. *Machine Translation*, 23(2-3):117–127.

Richard Socher, Eric H. Huang, Jeffrey Pennin, Christopher D. Manning, and Andrew Y. Ng. 2011. Dynamic pooling and unfolding recursive autoencoders for paraphrase detection. In *NIPS*, pages 801–809.

Multi-aspects Rating Prediction Using Aspect Words and Sentences

Takuto Nakamuta **Kazutaka Shimada**
Department of Artificial Intelligence
Kyushu Institute of Technology
680-4 Kawazu Iizuka Fukuoka 820-8502 Japan
shimada@pluto.ai.kyutech.ac.jp

Abstract

In this paper we propose a method for a rating prediction task. Each review consists of several ratings for a product, namely aspects. To predict the ratings of the aspects, we utilize not only aspect words, but also aspect sentences. First, our method detects aspect sentences by using a machine learning technique. Then, it incorporates words extracted from aspect sentences with aspect word features. For estimating aspect likelihood of each word, we utilize the variance of words among aspects. Finally, it generates classifiers for each aspect by using the extracted features based on the aspect likelihood. Experimental result shows the effectiveness of features from aspect sentences.

1 Introduction

As the World Wide Web rapidly grows, a huge number of online documents are easily accessible on the Web. Finding information relevant to user needs has become increasingly important. The most important information on the Web is usually contained in the text. We obtain a huge number of review documents that include user's opinions for products. Buying products, users usually survey the product reviews. More precise and effective methods for evaluating the products are useful for users. Many researchers have recently studied extraction and classification of opinions, namely sentiment analysis (Pang and Lee, 2008).

For sentiment analysis, one of the most primitive studies is to classify a document into two classes; positive and negative opinions (Pang et al., 2002; Turney, 2002). One simple extension of p/n classification is a rating prediction task. It is a finer-grained task, as compared with the p/n classification. Several researchers have challenged rating prediction tasks in reviews (Goldberg and Zhu, 2006; Li et al., 2011; Okanohara and Tsujii, 2005; Pang and Lee, 2005). They are called "seeing stars." These tasks handled an overall rating in the prediction. However, each review contains many descriptions about several aspects of a product. For example, they are "performance", "user-friendliness" and "portability" for laptop PCs and "script", "casting" and "music" for movies. Since reviewers judge not only the overall polarity for a product but also details for it, predicting stars of several aspects in a review is also one of the most important tasks in sentiment analysis, instead of a single overall rating. There are several studies to predict some stars in a review, namely "seeing several stars" or "aspect ratings" (Gupta et al., 2010; Pappas and Popescu-Belis, 2014; Shimada and Endo, 2008; Snyder and Barzilay, 2007).

In this paper we propose a method for a rating prediction task with some aspects. In other words, we focus on multi-scale and multi-aspects rating prediction for reviews. We handle video game reviews with seven aspects and zero to five stars. Here we also focus on feature extraction for the prediction. The most common approach is usually based on feature extraction from all sentences in each review. However, all sentences in a review do not always contribute to the prediction of a specific aspect in the review. In other words, the methods handling a review globally are not always suitable to gener-

29th Pacific Asia Conference on Language, Information and Computation pages 513 - 521
Shanghai, China, October 30 - November 1, 2015

ate a model for rating prediction. In addition, Pang and Lee (2004) mentioned that classifying sentences in documents into subjective or objective was effective for p/n classification. In a similar way, for the aspect rating tasks, aspect identification of each sentence and use of aspect sentences for feature extraction might contribute to the improvement for rating prediction. Therefore, the proposed method identifies the aspect of each sentence in each review first. Then, it extracts features for prediction models of seven aspects from all sentences and aspect sentences, on the basis of the variance of words. Finally, it generates prediction models based on Support Vector Regression (SVR) for seven aspects.

2 Related work

Snyder and Barzilay (2007) have proposed a method for multiple aspect ranking using the good grief algorithm. The method utilized the dependencies among aspect ratings to improve the accuracy. Gupta et al. (2010) also have reported methods for rating prediction. They discussed several features and methods for a restaurant review task. They also modified the method based on rating predictors and different predictors for joint assignment of ratings. These methods did not always focus on aspects of each word in reviews.

Shimada and Endo (2008) have proposed a method based on word variance for seeing several stars. They focused on aspect likelihood of each word. The basic idea of our method in this paper is also based on the variance of words in each aspect. However, they computed the variance from all sentences in reviews. On the other hand, our method also focuses on aspect sentences for the computation of the word variance. Pappas and Popescu-Belis (2014) have proposed a method using multiple-instance learning for aspect rating prediction. Their method estimated the weight of each sentences for the prediction. The weights led to the explanation of each aspect. They estimated the aspect weights of each sentence directly in their model. On the other hand, our method identifies the aspect of each sentence by using a machine learning method separately.

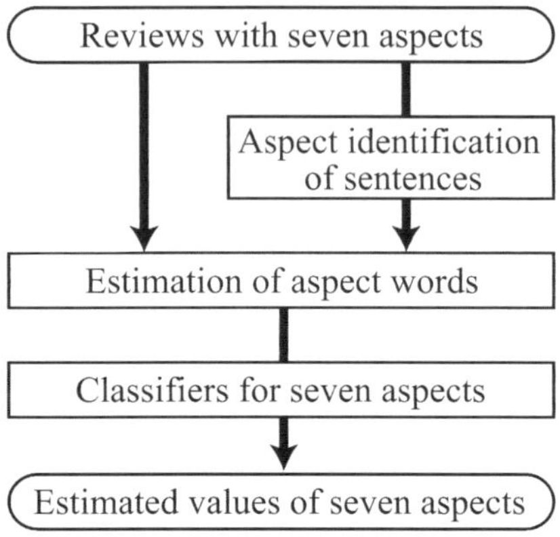

Figure 1: The outline of our method.

3 The proposed method

In this section, we explain the proposed method. Figure 1 shows the outline of our method. It consists of two parts; aspect identification of sentences and estimation of aspect likelihood of words. First, our method identifies the aspects of each sentence in reviews. Then, it estimates aspect likelihood of each word for each aspect, namely aspect words and the weight for each aspect, from aspect sentences and all sentences in reviews. Finally, it generates classifiers for each aspect by using the extracted features based on the aspect likelihood.

3.1 Target data

There are many review documents of various products on the Web. In this paper we handle review documents about video games. Figure 2 shows an example of a review document. The review documents consist of evaluation criteria, their ratings, positive opinions (pros text), negative opinions (cons text) and comments (free text) for a video game. The number of aspects, namely evaluation criteria, is seven: “Originality (o)”, “Graphics (g)”, “Music (m)”, “Addiction (a)”, “Satisfaction (s)”, “Comfort (c)”, and “Difficulty (d)”. The range of the ratings, namely stars, is zero to five points.

We extract review documents from a Web site[1]. The site establishes a guideline for contributions of reviews and the reviews are checked on the basis of the guideline. As a result, the reviews unfitting for

[1]http://ndsmk2.net

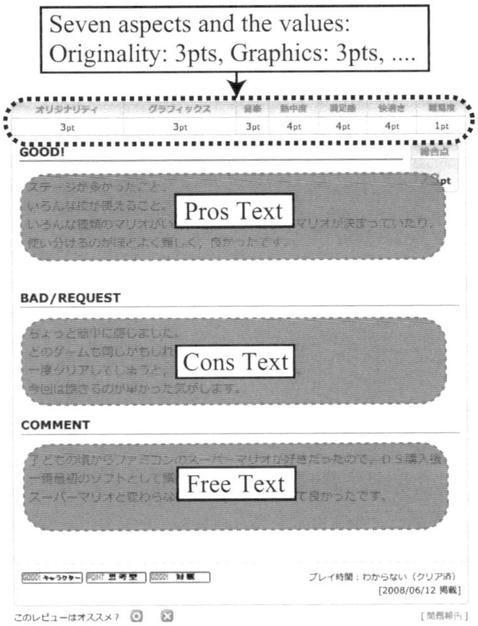

Figure 2: An example of a review document.

the guideline are rejected. Therefore the documents on the site are good quality reviews.

3.2 Aspect identification

First, we identify the aspects of sentences in reviews. For the purpose, we need to construct a aspect-sentence corpus. One annotator detects an evaluative expression from reviews. Then, the annotator selects not only sentences but also short phrases as the evaluative expression. Next, the annotator gives the annotation tags to the detected expression. The annotation tag consists of the polarity and the aspect. Some sentences contain multiple aspect tags. Figure 3 shows examples of the annotation.

We apply a simple machine learning approach with BOW features for the identification process. We employ Support Vector Machine (SVM) as the machine learning approach (Vapnik, 1995). We use nouns, adjectives and adverbs as features for SVM. The feature vector is as follows:

$$f = \{w_1^a, w_2^a, ..., w_{na}^a, w_1^c, ...w_{nc}^c, ..., w_1^s, ..w_{ns}^s\}$$

where w^x denotes a word w in an aspect x, and $x \in \{a, c, d, g, m, o, s\}$ (See Section 3.1). n_x denotes the number of words appearing in an aspect x.

<m p>The music is incredibly powerful sound!</>
Positive (p) about the aspect "Music (m)"

<s n>It lacks a feeling of accomplishment after finishing.</>
Negative (n) about the aspect "Satisfaction (s)"

<g,s p,p>Since the graphics was beautiful, we got the satisfaction from just watching them.</>
Combined tags are acceptable:
Positive (p) about the aspects "Graphics (g)" and "Satisfaction (s)"

Figure 3: Examples of aspect annotation of sentences.

The vector value of a word is computed as follows:

$$val(asp_i, w_j) = \frac{num_{ij}}{sent(asp_i)} \quad (1)$$

where num_{ij} and $sent(asp_i)$ denote the frequency of a word w_j in an aspect asp_i and the number of sentences belonging to an aspect asp_i, respectively. This is a normalization process because the numbers of sentences belonging to each aspect are non-uniform. We generate seven classifiers for seven aspects using the features and values; the classifier for the aspect "Addiction (a)" or not, the classifier for the aspect "Comfort (c)" or not, and so on. Figure 4 shows the aspect identification process[2]. We use the SVM^{light} package[3] with all parameters set to their default values (Joachims, 1998).

3.3 Rating prediction

Removing non-informative text from training data leads to the improvement of the accuracy (Fang et al., 2010). In this task, a word does not always contribute to all aspects. A word usually relates to one or two aspects. Therefore, estimating a relation between a word and each aspect is the most important task for the rating prediction. It improves the performance.

We introduce a variance-based feature selection proposed by (Shimada and Endo, 2008) into this process. They obtained small improvement in terms of an error rate by using the variance-based feature selection. The basic idea is to extract words appearing frequently with the same point (stars) regarding

[2]Note that the method does not estimate the polarity, namely positive or negative, in this process.

[3]http://svmlight.joachims.org

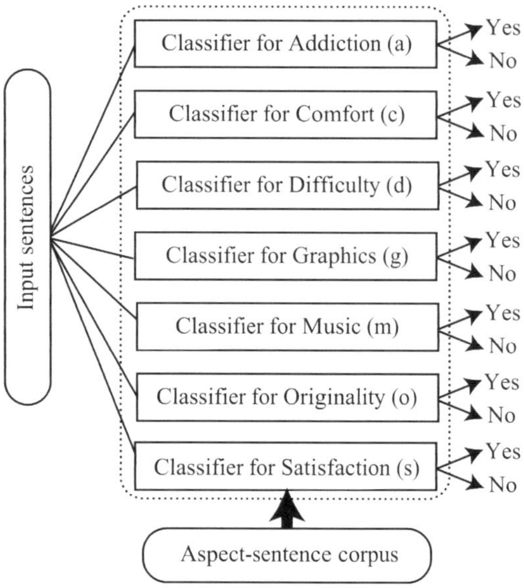

Figure 4: The sentence-aspect identification.

an evaluation criterion (aspect). It is computed as follows:

$$var(w_{a_j}) = \frac{1}{m} \sum_{i=0, w \in r_i}^{n} (real(r_i, a_j) - ave(w_{a_j}))^2 \quad (2)$$

where a_j is an aspect. m and n are the document frequency (*df*) of a word w and the number of documents respectively. $real(r_i, a_j)$ and $ave(w_{a_j})$ are the actual rating of a_j in r_i and the average score of w for a_j. We use w of which the var is a threshold or less.

We apply the variance-based feature selection to aspect sentences extracted in Section 3.2 and all sentences in pros and cons text areas[4]. We use MeCab for the morphological analysis[5]. We select words belonging to "noun", "adjective" and "adverb". Finally, we extract words as features on the basis of the word frequency ($freq$) and the value var. In addition, we distinguish words in the pros text areas and the cons text areas. In other words, for a word w_i, a word in the pros text areas is w_i^p and a word in the cons text areas is w_i^c. Besides, we distinguish words from all sentences ($w_i^{x^{al}}$) and aspect-sentences ($w_j^{x^{ap}}$). i and j are the numbers of words from all sentences and aspect-sentences, respectively. A vector of an aspect y for a review x is as follows:

$$r_{xy} = \{w_1^{p^{al}}, w_2^{p^{al}}, ..., w_i^{p^{al}}, w_1^{c^{al}}, w_2^{c^{al}}, ..., w_i^{c^{al}}, \\ w_1^{p^{ap}}, w_2^{p^{ap}}, ..., w_j^{p^{ap}}, w_1^{c^{ap}}, w_2^{c^{ap}}, ..., w_j^{c^{ap}}\}$$

We apply the vector into a machine learning approach. In this paper, we employ a linear support vector regression (SVR). This is one of straightforward methods for this task. Related studies also used SVR for the rating inference task (Okanohara and Tsujii, 2005; Pang and Lee, 2005; Shimada and Endo, 2008). We generate seven classifiers for seven aspects using the selected features. We also use the SVM^{light} for SVR.

4 Experiment

In this section, we describe two experiments about the aspect identification of sentences and the rating prediction. For the rating prediction, we evaluate the effectiveness of the aspect-sentences.

4.1 Aspect identification

The annotated corpus for the aspect identification consisted of 4719 sentences. Table 1 shows the distribution of aspects[6]. The table shows that there were large differences among aspects. Machine learning with unbalanced data usually leads to generation of a wrong classifier. Therefore, we adjusted the number of sentences in the training data (use_s) for each classifier by using the following equation.

$$use_s(asp_i, asp_j) = real_s(asp_j) \times \frac{real_s(asp_i)}{all_s - real_s(asp_i)} \quad (3)$$

where asp_i and asp_j denote the target aspect and the others, respectively. $real_s(asp_j)$ denotes the number of sentences of an aspect asp_j and all_s is the number of sentences in the corpus, 4719 in this experiment. The instance about Addiction (a) is shown in Table 2. Since the number of sentences in the Addiction (a), asp_i, was 429, the sum of the others was 427.

We evaluated our method with 10-fold cross validation. The criteria are the precision, recall and F-value. Table 3 shows the experimental result. The

[4] We ignore sentences in the free text area in Fig. 2.

[5] http://mecab.googlecode.com/svn/trunk/mecab/doc/index.html

[6] Note that more than half of sentences in the corpus contained two or three aspects.

Aspect	# of sentences
Addiction (a)	429
Comfort (c)	354
Difficulty (d)	353
Graphics (g)	230
Music (m)	258
Originality (o)	2339
Satisfaction (s)	2252

Table 1: The aspects and the number of sentences.

Aspect	Original	Training	
Addiction (a)	429	429	
Comfort (c)	354	26	427
Difficulty (d)	353	26	
Graphics (g)	230	17	
Music (m)	258	19	
Originality (o)	2339	173	
Satisfaction (s)	2252	166	

Table 2: Downsized and adjusted training data for Addiction (a)

aspects "Originality" and "Satisfaction" obtained comparatively higher accuracy rates because they consisted of sufficient training data. Sentences of the aspect "Graphics" tended to contain direct expressions related to graphics, such as "beautiful." In addition, they were usually simple sentences; "The graphics are ... ." The aspect identification about the aspects "Addiction", "Comfort" and "Difficulty" were difficult tasks. In comparison with the aspect "Graphics", sentences of these aspects did not always contain direct expressions; e.g., "I play this game every day" for "Addiction", "There are many situations about pressing A when I need to push B" for "Comfort", and "The enemy in the water area is too clever" for "Difficulty." This was one reason that the recall rates of them were extremely low, as compared with others. It is difficult to identify these aspects correctly, especially with a small dataset.

4.2 Rating prediction

Next, we evaluated our method for the rating prediction. We prepared three different sizes of training data; (ds1) 933 reviews about 7 games, (ds2) 2629 reviews about 37 games and (ds3) 3464 reviews about 44 games. They were balanced data sets. In other word, each data set contained reviews about products with high and low scores uniformly. These data sets did not contain any reviews that were used in the aspect identification of sentences in Section 4.1. For the determination of the thresholds about the aspect likelihood var and the word frequency ($freq$) in Section 3.3, we also prepared the development data set consisting of 76 reviews. If we set high thresholds for them, we might obtain features with high confidence about each aspect. However, too thigh thresholds usually generate a zero-vector, which does not contain any features. We estimated these thresholds, which did not generate a zero-vector, from the development data. In this experiment, var and $freq$ for all sentences were less than 1.5 and more then 3, and var and $freq$ for aspect-sentences were less than 0.5 and more than 4, respectively.

Aspect	Precision	Recall	F-value
Addiction (a)	0.941	0.186	0.310
Comfort (c)	0.772	0.249	0.377
Difficulty (d)	0.738	0.272	0.398
Graphics (g)	0.890	0.630	0.738
Music (m)	0.404	0.353	0.377
Originality (o)	0.805	0.559	0.660
Satisfaction (s)	0.746	0.562	0.641
Average	0.756	0.402	0.525

Table 3: The experimental result of aspect identification.

We evaluated our method with the leave-one-out cross-validation for the three data sets. The criterion for the evaluation was the mean squared error (MSE).

$$MSE_j = \frac{1}{n}\sum_{i=1}^{n}(out(d_{ij}) - real(d_{ij}))^2 \quad (4)$$

where i and j denote a review and an aspect in the review respectively. out and $real$ are the output of a method and the actual rating in a review respectively. We converted the outputs of the SVR into integral value with half adjust because it was continuous. The MSE is one of important criteria for the rating inference task because not all mistakes of estimation with the methods are equal. For example, assume that the actual rating of a criterion is 4.

Aspect	data (ds1)		data (ds2)		data (ds2)	
	Baseline	Proposed	Baseline	Proposed	Baseline	Proposed
Addiction (a)	1.146	**1.047**	1.203	**1.054**	1.288	**1.068**
Comfort (c)	0.887	**0.881**	0.975	**0.944**	0.980	**0.901**
Difficulty (d)	**0.855**	0.856	0.888	**0.872**	**0.864**	0.866
Graphics (g)	0.704	**0.674**	0.693	**0.644**	0.711	**0.677**
Music (m)	0.665	**0.654**	0.719	**0.666**	0.715	**0.671**
Originality (o)	**0.770**	0.772	**0.757**	0.766	0.789	**0.759**
Satisfaction (s)	1.296	**1.110**	1.210	**1.036**	1.266	**1.055**
Average	0.903	**0.856**	0.921	**0.854**	0.944	**0.857**

Table 4: The experimental result of the rating prediction.

In this situation, the mistake of estimating it as 3 is better than the mistake of estimating it as 1.

We compared our method[7] with a baseline. The baseline did not use any aspect-sentence information. In other words, it was based on (Shimada and Endo, 2008). Table 4 shows the experimental result. Our method outperformed the baseline for all data sets. The improvements were 0.047 (approximately 5% on the error rate) for the data (ds1), 0.066 (approximately 7% on the error rate) for the data (ds2) and 0.087 (approximately 9% on the error rate) for the data (ds3). For the data (ds2) and (ds3), our method yielded significant differences at $p < 0.05$ by t-test. The results show the effectiveness of the aspect identification of sentences and the feature extraction based on the aspect-sentences. In addition, the MSE values on the proposed method were stable although those on the baseline decreased when the size of the data set was changed. This result show the proposed method is robust in the case that noise in training data increases.

4.3 Discussion

A review does not always consist of sentences related to all aspects. Reviews often do not contain any sentences related to an aspect. Gupta et al. (2010) reported that only 62% of user given ratings have supporting text for ratings of the aspects in their review data. In (Shimada and Endo, 2008), it was approximately 75% in their dataset, which was similar to our dataset. Therefore, we computed the content rate of aspect-sentences in each data set. The rate is computed by

$$CR = \frac{NumAspRev}{NumRev} \tag{5}$$

where $NumAspRev$ denotes the number of reviews which contain identified aspect-sentences. $NumRev$ is the number of reviews about an aspect in the data set.

We computed the CR values for the three data sets and the development data. Table 5 shows the CR values of all aspects on each data set. The CR values on the development data was a kind of oracle situation because the sentences in the data were annotated by human. From the CR on the development in Table 5, approximately 30% of reviews in our data set were missing the textual support for some aspects in the reviews. This is one reason that the MSE values in Section 4.2 were not sufficient. In other words, owing to lack of textual information, the aspect rating prediction is essentially a difficult task.

The CR values of the aspects "Addiction", "Comfort" and "Difficulty" on the three test data set were lower than the development data. The accuracy of the aspect identification in Table 3 shows a similar trend. On the other hand, the CR of the aspect "Music" was too high, as compared with the development data. This was caused by the low precision rate of the aspect identification (also see Table 3). To improve the accuracy of the aspect identification leads to the improvement of the rating prediction. The improvement of these recall and precision rates for these aspects is one of the important tasks.

As you can see from Table 5, the rating prediction

[7] Note that the method used the aspect-sentences identified automatically in the previous section. They were not oracle data.

Aspect	development	data (ds1)	data (ds2)	data (ds3)
Addiction (a)	0.750	0.330	0.340	0.337
Comfort (c)	0.934	0.229	0.307	0.287
Difficulty (d)	0.631	0.227	0.231	0.232
Graphics (g)	0.408	0.410	0.426	0.424
Music (m)	0.237	0.478	0.477	0.479
Originality (o)	0.961	0.927	0.961	0.968
Satisfaction (s)	0.961	0.912	0.954	0.958
Average	0.697	0.502	0.528	0.526

Table 5: The content rate of aspect-sentences.

in the proposed method used only approximately 50% of the identified aspect-utterances. Moreover, 25% of sentences in the aspect identification were wrong (see the average precision rate in Table 3). Despite the fact that the input data of the rating prediction contained many mistakes, the proposed method with aspect-sentences outperformed the baseline without aspect-sentences. The result shows that the aspect-sentences are essentially effective to predict aspect ratings even if they contain misrecognized data. If the accuracy of the aspect identification is improved, the accuracy of the rating prediction is also improved. Therefore, the improvement of the aspect identification is the most important future work. The identification task in our study is a multi-label classification problem. Applying multi-label learning such as (Zhang and Zhou, 2007) to the task is one of the most interesting approaches although we used a binary classifier based on SVMs. Another problem in the identification task was the unbalance data. As we mentioned in Section 4.1, we handled this problem by adjusting the number of sentences in the training data. Under such circumstances, Complement Naive Bayes (CNB) (Rennie et al., 2003) is often effective. Applying this method to the task is interesting. Besides, we applied a classification method in the identification task. The recall rate was not sufficient. An extraction approach based on bootstrapping (Etzioni et al., 2004; Riloff and Jones, 1999), which uses the extracted aspect-sentences as seeds, is also an interesting approach to obtain more aspect sentences in the data.

In this experiment, we used SVR to estimate the ratings in a document. The SVR is often utilized in rating inference tasks. However, Pang and Lee (2005) have proposed a method based on a metric labeling formulation for a rating inference problem. The results of these studies denote that SVR is not always the best classifier for this task. Koppel and Schler (2006) have discussed a problem of use of regression for multi-class classification tasks and proposed a method based on optimal stacks of binary classifiers. Tsutsumi et al. (2007) have proposed a method based on the combination of several methods for sentiment analysis. We need to consider other methods for the improvement of the accuracy.

We estimated aspect likelihood based on a variance of each word. Kobayashi et al. (2004) have proposed a method to extract attribute-value pairs from reviews. The attributes relate to aspects in our work. Wilson et al. (2004) have proposed a method to classify the strength of opinions. Sentiment word dictionaries with aspects and strength are useful for the rating prediction. Besides, Kobayashi et al. (2005) have expanded their work with an anaphora resolution technique. To identify the aspect of a sentence more correctly, context information in reviews is also important.

In this paper, the aspects for the rating prediction are given. Yu et al. (2011) have proposed an aspect ranking method for reviews. They identified important product aspects automatically from reviews. Aspect mining is also interesting future work.

5 Conclusion

In this paper we proposed a multi-scale and multi-aspects rating prediction method based on aspect-sentences. The target reviews contained seven aspects with six rating points. Despite the fact that the input data of the rating prediction contained many mistakes, namely lack of 50% and misrecognition of 25%, the proposed method with aspect-sentences outperformed the baseline without aspect-sentences. The experimental results show the effectiveness of the aspect identification of sentences in reviews for the rating prediction. Therefore, the improvement of the aspect identification of sentences is the most important future work.

In this paper, we dealt with only predicting ratings in reviews. However, estimating relations between aspects and words is beneficial for many sentiment analysis tasks. Yu et al. (2011) reported that the extracted aspects improved the performance of a document-level sentiment classification. Applying the result and knowledge from the rating prediction in this paper to other tasks, such as summarization (Gerani et al., 2014; Shimada et al., 2011), is also interesting future work.

References

Oren Etzioni, Michael Cafarella, Doug Downey, Stanley Kok, Ana-Maria Popescu, Tal Shaked, Stephen Soderland, Daniel S. Weld, and Alexander Yates. 2004. Web-scale information extraction in knowitall (preliminary results). In *Proceedings of the 13th international conference on World Wide Web (WWW2004)*, pages 100–110.

Ji Fang, Bob Price, and Lotti Price. 2010. Pruning non-informative text through non-expert annotations to improve sentiment classification. In *Coling 2010 Workshop: The People's Web Meets NLP: Collaboratively Constructed Semantic Resources*.

Shima Gerani, Yashar Mehdad, Giuseppe Carenini, Raymond Ng, and Bita Nejat. 2014. Abstractive summarization of product reviews using discourse structure. In *Proceedings of the Conference on Empirical Methods in Natural Language Processing (EMNLP)*, pages 1602–1613.

Andrew B. Goldberg and Xiaojin Zhu. 2006. Seeing stars when there aren't many stars: Graph-based semi-supervised learning for sentiment categorization. In *Proceedings of the First Workshop on Graph Based Methods for Natural Language Processing*, pages 45–52.

Narendra Gupta, Giuseppe Di Fabbrizio, and Patrick Haffner. 2010. Capturing the stars: Predicting ratings for service and product reviews. In *Proceedings of the NAACL HLT 2010 Workshop on Semantic Search*, pages 36–43.

Thorsten Joachims. 1998. Text categorization with support vector machines: Learning with many relevant features. In *European Conference on Machine Learning (ECML)*, pages 137–142.

Nozomi Kobayashi, Kentaro Inui, Yuji Matsumoto, Kenji Tateishi, and Toshikazu Fukushima. 2004. Collecting evaluative expressions for opinion extraction. In *Proceedings of the First International Joint Conference on Natural Language Processing*, IJCNLP'04, pages 596–605.

Nozomi Kobayashi, Ryu Iida, Kentaro Inui, and Yuji Matsumoto. 2005. Opinion extraction using a learning-based anaphora resolution technique. In *In The Second International Joint Conference on Natural Language Processing (IJCNLP)*, pages 175–180.

Moshe Koppel and Jonathan Schler. 2006. The importance of neutral examples in learning sentiment. *Computational Intelligence*, 22(2):100–109.

Fangtao Li, Nathan Liu, Hongwei Jin, Kai Zhao, Qiang Yang, and Xiaoyan Zhu. 2011. Incorporating reviewer and product information for review rating prediction. In *Proceedings of the Twenty-Second International Joint Conference on Artificial Intelligence - Volume Volume Three*, IJCAI'11, pages 1820–1825.

Daisuke Okanohara and Jun'ichi Tsujii. 2005. Assigning polarity scores to reviews using machine learning techniques. In *Proceedings of the Second International Joint Conference on Natural Language Processing*, pages 314–325.

Bo Pang and Lillian Lee. 2004. A sentimental education: Sentiment analysis using subjectivity summarization based on minimum cuts. In *Proceedings of the 42Nd Annual Meeting on Association for Computational Linguistics*, ACL '04, pages 271–278.

Bo Pang and Lillian Lee. 2005. Seeing stars: Exploiting class relationships for sentiment categorization with respect to rating scales. In *Proceedings of the 43rd Annual Meeting on Association for Computational Linguistics*, ACL '05, pages 115–124.

Bo Pang and Lillian Lee. 2008. Opinion mining and sentiment analysis. *Foundations and TrendsR in Information Retrieval*, 2.

Bo Pang, Lillian Lee, and Shivakumar Vaithyanathan. 2002. Thumbs up? sentiment classification using machine learning techniques. In *Proceedings of the Conference on Empirical Methods in Natural Language Processing (EMNLP)*, pages 79–86.

Nikolaos Pappas and Andrei Popescu-Belis. 2014. Explaining the stars: Weighted multiple-instance learning for aspect-based sentiment analysis. In *Proceedings of the 2014 Conference on Empirical Methods In Natural Language Processing (EMNLP)*, pages 455–466.

Jason D. M. Rennie, Lawrence Shih, Jaime Teevan, and David R. Karger. 2003. Tackling the poor assumptions of naive bayes text classifiers. In *In Proceedings of the Twentieth International Conference on Machine Learning (ICML)*, pages 616–623.

Ellen Riloff and Rosie Jones. 1999. Learning dictionaries for information extraction by multi-level bootstrapping. In *Proceeding of AAAI 99*, pages 474–479.

Kazutaka Shimada and Tsutomu Endo. 2008. Seeing several stars: A rating inference task for a document containing several evaluation criteria. In *Advances in Knowledge Discovery and Data Mining, 12th Pacific-Asia Conference, PAKDD 2008*, pages 1006–1014.

Kazutaka Shimada, Ryosuke Tadano, and Tsutomu Endo. 2011. Multi-aspects review summarization with objective information. *Procedia - Social and Behavioral Sciences: Computational Linguistics and Related Fields*, 27:140–149.

Benjamin Snyder and Regina Barzilay. 2007. Multiple aspect ranking using the good grief algorithm. In *In Proceedings of the Human Language Technology Conference of the North American Chapter of the Association of Computational Linguistics (HLT-NAACL*, pages 300–307.

Kimitaka Tsutsumi, Kazutaka Shimada, and Tsutomu Endo. 2007. Movie review classification based on a multiple classifier. In *Proceedings of the 21st Pacific Asia Conference on Language, Information and Computation (PACLIC)*, pages 481–488.

Peter D. Turney. 2002. Thumbs up or thumbs down?: Semantic orientation applied to unsupervised classification of reviews. In *Proceedings of the 40th Annual Meeting on Association for Computational Linguistics*, ACL '02, pages 417–424.

Vladimir N. Vapnik. 1995. *The Nature of Statistical Learning Theory*. Springer-Verlag New York, Inc.

Theresa Wilson, Janyce Wiebe, and Rebecca Hwa. 2004. Just how mad are you? finding strong and weak opinion clauses. In *Proceedings of the 19th National Conference on Artifical Intelligence*, AAAI'04, pages 761–767.

Jianxing Yu, Zheng-Jun Zha, Meng Wang, and Tat-Seng Chua. 2011. Aspect ranking: Identifying important product aspects from online consumer reviews. In *Proceedings of the 49th Annual Meeting of the Association for Computational Linguistics: Human Language Technologies - Volume 1*, HLT '11, pages 1496–1505.

Min-Ling Zhang and Zhi-Hua Zhou. 2007. Ml-knn: A lazy learning approach to multi-label learning. *Pattern Recognition*, 40(7):2038–2048.

Understanding Rating Behaviour and Predicting Ratings by Identifying Representative Users

Rahul Kamath
University of Tokyo
7-3-1 Hongo, Bunkyo-ku
Tokyo, Japan

Masanao Ochi
University of Tokyo
7-3-1 Hongo, Bunkyo-ku
Tokyo, Japan

Yutaka Matsuo
University of Tokyo
7-3-1 Hongo, Bunkyo-ku
Tokyo, Japan

Abstract

Online user reviews describing various products and services are now abundant on the web. While the information conveyed through review texts and ratings is easily comprehensible, there is a wealth of hidden information in them that is not immediately obvious. In this study, we unlock this hidden value behind user reviews to understand the various dimensions along which users rate products. We learn a set of users that represent each of these dimensions and use their ratings to predict product ratings. Specifically, we work with restaurant reviews to identify users whose ratings are influenced by dimensions like 'Service', 'Atmosphere' etc. in order to predict restaurant ratings and understand the variation in rating behaviour across different cuisines. While previous approaches to obtaining product ratings require either a large number of user ratings or a few review texts, we show that it is possible to predict ratings with few user ratings and no review text. Our experiments show that our approach outperforms other conventional methods by 16-27% in terms of RMSE.

1 Introduction

With the advent of Web 2.0, a large number of platforms including e-commerce sites, discussion forums, blogs etc. have emerged that allow users to express their opinions regarding various businesses, products and services. These opinions are usually in the form of reviews, each consisting of text feedback describing various aspects of the product along with a single numeric rating representing the users' overall sentiment about the same (McAuley et al., 2012). Such user review ratings are normally aggregated to provide an overall product rating, which help other people form their own opinion and help them make an informed decision during purchase. However, in case of new products, there is a time delay till a sufficient number of ratings that give a 'complete picture' of the product can be obtained. In such a scenario, the seller of the product may find it useful to identify a few people whose ratings, when combined together, reflect this 'complete picture'. The seller may then invite these people to review the product and, as a result, reduce the time delay involved in getting the 'true' product rating.

Review text is unstructured and inherently noisy. But it can be a valuable source of information since users justify their ratings through such text (McAuley and Leskovec, 2013). Users tend to express their sentiments about different aspects of a product in the review text and provide a rating based on some combination of these sentiments (Ganu et al., 2009). However, some users are influenced heavily by one particular aspect of the product and this is reflected in their ratings. For example: While reviewing smartphones, the ratings provided by a user may be influenced heavily by just the battery-life, irrespective of the quality of other aspects of the phone. Similarly, while reviewing restaurants, some users' ratings may correlate with the ambience of the restaurant or the level of service provided. We call such users as 'representative users' since their ratings tend to 'represent' one particular dimension of the product.

Although latent factors obtained from ratings data have been used extensively for rating prediction,

29th Pacific Asia Conference on Language, Information and Computation pages 522 - 528
Shanghai, China, October 30 - November 1, 2015

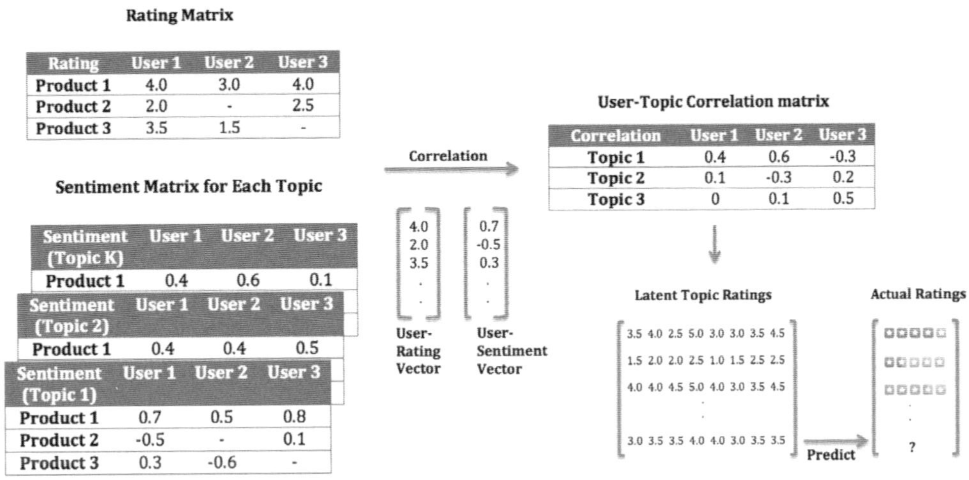

Figure 1: An overview of our proposed method

very few previous works have attempted to combine both review text and ratings. Our approach combines latent topics obtained from review text with users' rating data to learn representative users for each product. This enables us to predict ratings for new products by just looking at the ratings of a small set of users, even when no review text is available. In traditional methods, product ratings are obtained by modelling the product factors from ratings data. However, (McAuley and Leskovec, 2013) suggest that this approach is not accurate in case of new products due to the lack of sufficient number of ratings. They, in turn, propose a model which fits product factors from a few review texts. Our approach is free from both these constraints.

In this study, we use the topic model Multi-Grain Latent Dirchlet Allocation (MG-LDA) described in (Titov and McDonald, 2008a) on restaurant reviews obtained from Yelp[1] to obtain latent topics that correspond to ratable aspects of the restaurants. Since we segregate the reviews on the basis of restaurant category, we notice some interesting variations across different cuisines. The words associated with the extracted topics are then used to perform review segmentation where we identify the sentences that describe each topic. This also enables us to analyse the sentiment expressed regarding each topic in a review. We then capture the intuition of representative users to learn a set of users who best represent each topic. Latent topic ratings for restaurants are then obtained by aggregating the ratings of those users who represent that topic. The overall ratings of new restaurants are then predicted using a regression model. An overview of the proposed method is shown in Figure 1.

We also show how this concept could be used to better understand rating behaviour across different cuisines. For example: What do people who visit French restaurants care most about - food, service or value for money? How is this different from people who visit Italian restaurants?

The rest of the paper is structured as follows. Section 2 provides a review of related work. Section 3 describes our proposed method. In Section 4, we describe the experiments performed and report the results of our evaluation. Section 5 concludes the paper with a summary of the work and the scope for future work.

2 Related Work

One of the earliest attempts at rating prediction that combines both review text and ratings is (Ganu et al., 2009). However, their review segmentation method differs from ours in that their work depends on manual annotation of each review sentence into predetermined domain-specific aspects and the training of separate classifiers for each aspect. Furthermore,

[1] http://www.yelp.com

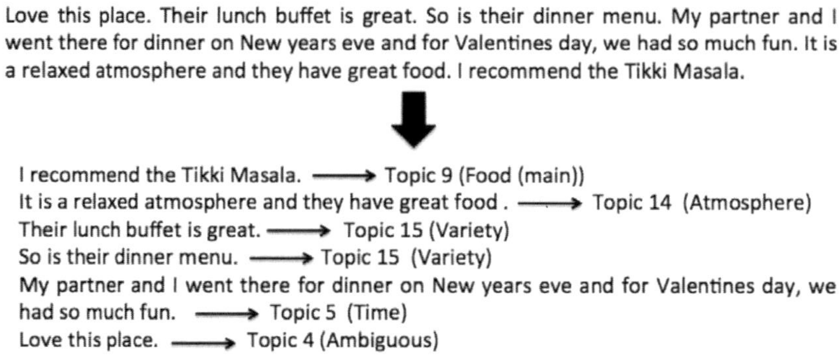

Figure 2: Review Segmentation

it does not capture the variation that may exist within the domain. For example: The aspects that affect ratings for French restaurants (e.g. 'Drinks (wine)', 'Deserts' etc.) may be different from those of Indian restaurants (e.g. 'Flavour (spiciness)', 'Variety' etc.). (Wang et al., 2010) approach the problem of segmentation by measuring the overlap between each sentence of the review and the seed words describing each aspect. However, these aspect seed words are chosen manually which are, again, domain-specific.

Topic models are normally used to make the segmentation task transferable across different domains. The problem of mapping such topics into aspects is studied in (Titov and McDonald, 2008b; Lu et al., 2011; Brody and Elhadad, 2010; McAuley et al., 2012; Jo and Oh, 2011). (Titov and McDonald, 2008b; McAuley et al., 2012) use explicit aspect ratings as a form of weak supervision to identify rated aspects while (Lu et al., 2011) use manually selected aspect seed words as a form of weak supervision. To remove the dependence on aspect ratings and aspect seed words, (Jo and Oh, 2011) develop a model that captures aspects using a set of sentiment seed words while (Brody and Elhadad, 2010) present an unsupervised method for extracting aspects by automatically deriving the sentiment seed words from review text. It is important to note that we do not map the latent topics we obtain into explicit aspects since it is not necessary for our final goal.

Rating prediction is also studied in (Gupta et al., 2010; Moghaddam and Ester, 2011; Baccianella et al., 2009) where the authors focus on multi-aspect rating prediction and in (McAuley and Leskovec, 2013) where the authors build a recommendation system using a combination of latent dimensions obtained from rating data and latent topics obtained from review text.

3 Methodology

3.1 Dataset and Preprocessing

We use the Yelp Challenge Dataset[2] consisting of around 1.12 million reviews of more than 42000 restaurants across 4 countries. These reviews are provided by more than 250000 users. Reviews contain a single star rating, text, author etc. Details of restaurants like average star rating, categories (cuisine) etc. are also available. We segment the restaurants according to its category since we would like to better understand the variation that exists across different cuisines. Note that we ignore the fact that certain restaurants may have multiple categories. For example: Some Indian restaurants may also serve Thai food.

We tokenize the review text along whitespaces, remove all punctuation and stop-words, and lemmatize the words using the NLTK Wordnet lemmatizer described in (Bird et al., 2009).

3.2 Topic Extraction

We run the topic model multi-grain LDA described in (Titov and McDonald, 2008a) on a corpus of restaurant reviews obtained from a single cuisine to extract K latent topics. Unlike standard topic

[2] http://www.yelp.com/dataset_challenge

Cuisine	Interpreted Topic	Top Words
Indian	Variety	buffet,lunch,dish,vegetarian,menu,selection,option,good,item,great
	Food	chicken,masala,tikka,curry,naan,lamb,dish,paneer,tandoori,ordered
	Flavour	spicy,spice,flavour,dish,hot,curry,food,like,sauce,taste
	Value	price,portion,food,meal,get,two,small,little,rice,bit
	Atmosphere	restaurant,place,nice,decor,inside,strip,little,clean,like,table,look
Italian	Food (Pizza)	pizza,crust,good,cheese,sauce,slice,thin,like,wing,great,topping
	Food (Salad)	salad,bread,cheese,garlic,tomato,fresh,sauce,olive,delicious,oil
	Service	service,staff,friendly,server,owner,customer,waiter,always,attentive
	Location	place,restaurant,location,strip,little,find,italian,away,parking,right
	Value	food,good,price,better,much,pretty,like,quality,portion,worth,nothing
French	Drinks	menu,wine,course,tasting,glass,bottle,ordered,selection,meal,two
	Dessert	dessert,chocolate,cream,cake,ice,coffee,sweet,creme,tart,also,good,souffle
	Food (Bread)	bread,egg,french,butter,good,toast,delicious,fry,cheese,fresh,croque
	Food	cheese,salad,soup,onion,ordered,good,french,delicious,appetizer,lobster
	Service Time	table,minute,time,wait,reservation,waiter,get,seated,server,took,order,got

Table 1: Local topics for Indian, Italian and French restaurants obtained using MG-LDA

modeling methods such as LDA and PLSA, which extract topics that correspond to global properties of a product, MG-LDA extracts much finer topics that correspond to ratable aspects of the product. To extract topics at such granular level, the model generates terms which are either chosen at the document level or chosen from a sliding window[3]. The terms chosen from the sliding window correspond to the fine topics.

3.3 Review Segmentation and Sentiment Analysis

Once cuisine-specific latent topics are obtained, the review segmentation task is performed where each review sentence s_i is assigned to one of the latent topics t_k. The purpose of this task is to understand which sentences of the review discuss which of the topics. The topic assignment is made as follows:

$$Topic(s_i) = \arg\max_k \sum_{w \in t_k} count(w, s_i) * P(w|t_k) \quad (1)$$

where w is the word associated with each topic, count(w, s_i) is the count of word w in sentence s_i and $P(w|t_k)$ is the probability as determined from the word distributions obtained using the MG-LDA model.

[3]A sliding window is a set of fixed number of adjacent sentences.

For every review, the sentences that discuss each topic are identified as shown in Figure 2. It is therefore possible to determine the sentiment expressed by the review author regarding each latent topic by averaging over the sentiments of its constituent sentences. We use the implementation TextBlob[4], which is based on the Pattern[5] library, to determine the polarity of each sentence. The polarity is obtained in the range of [-1, 1].

3.4 User Segmentation

We then proceed to learn the representative users for each latent topic. First, the feature vector $\theta_u^{overall}$ is obtained for each user u where each feature represents the users' review rating for a restaurant. We assume that each user writes only one review per restaurant. Similarly, $\theta_u^{t_k}$ is obtained where each feature represents the users' sentiment regarding topic t_k.

The influence of a topic on a users' rating is determined by calculating the Pearson's correlation between $\theta_u^{overall}$ and $\theta_u^{t_k}$. Only users who have provided a minimum of 5 reviews are considered. A user-topic correlation matrix C is thus obtained which indicates the dimensions along which each

[4]http://www.textblob.readthedocs.org/en/dev/

[5]http://www.clips.ua.ac.be/pattern

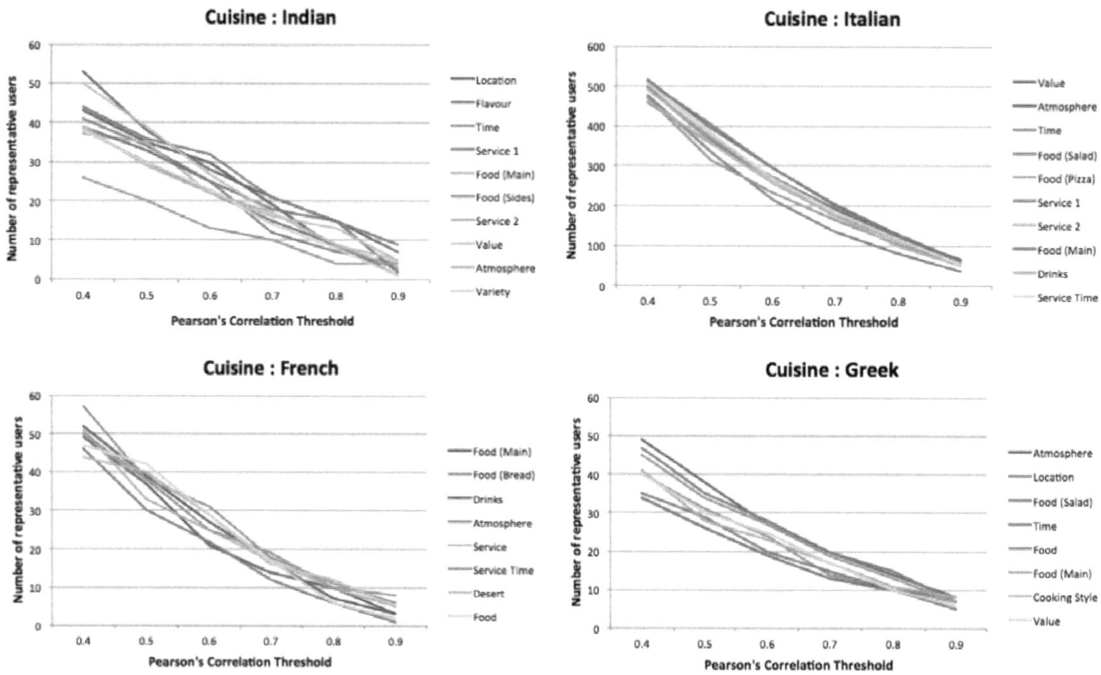

Figure 3: Number of Representative Users for various cuisines

user tends to rate restaurants. Simply put,

$$C(u, t_k) = PearsonCorr(\theta_u^{overall}, \theta_u^{t_k}) \quad (2)$$

The representative users for a topic are those users whose $C(u, t_k)$ value is above a certain threshold T for that particular topic. It is important to note that $C(u, t_k)$ value may not be available for all user-topic pairs since every user may not express sentiments regarding every topic.

3.5 Rating Prediction

We calculate the topic ratings of restaurants once we obtain a list of representative users for each latent topic. This rating is calculated as the average of the review ratings that are provided by the representative users of that particular topic. In case there are no representative users for a particular topic for that particular restaurant, this rating is calculated as the average of the other latent topic ratings. Such topic ratings provide some indication of the quality of various aspects of the restaurant (like food, service etc.), although we do not explicitly calculate the aspect ratings or map the topics to aspects.

Since the overall restaurant rating can be thought of as some combination of the ratings for food, service, atmosphere etc., we try to combine the latent topic ratings in some way. For this purpose, we fit a Support Vector Regression (SVR) model with radial basis function kernel on the latent topic ratings and use it to predict the overall rating of restaurants. During test time, just the ratings provided by a few representative users would be enough to obtain the overall restaurant rating. Such a rating takes into account the different dimensions of the restaurant and provides a 'complete picture' of the restaurant.

4 Experiments and Analysis

We use the topic model MG-LDA on a set of 8000 reviews each of Indian, Italian, French and Greek restaurants. The number of global topics is set at $K_{glo} = 40$ and local topics at $K_{loc} = 15$ (After trying various combinations, we found that this combination provides the best results. Previous works have also used a similar number of topics). The length of the sliding window is set at 2 and all the other parameters for the model is set at 0.1. We run the chain for 1000 iterations. While the global topics are ignored, some select local topics as determined by the model are shown in Table 1. We try to interpret the topics manually by looking at the constituent words. Usually, around 5-6 local topics are ambiguous and difficult to interpret.

A quick look at the topics obtained shows us the variation that exists among different cuisines. For example: While Indian restaurants have 'Flavour' and 'Variety' as topics; Italian restaurants have 'Drinks'; French restaurants have 'Drinks' and 'Dessert' as topics. Greek restaurants have 'Cooking Style' as a topic with words like dry, fry, fresh, cooked, soft, tender etc. Also, certain words like table, minute, time, wait, hour, bar, seated etc. appear together in case of French and Italian restaurants signaling, perhaps, a long wait to get seated at such restaurants.

Review segmentation is then performed on around 8500 reviews of Indian restaurants, 61000 reviews of Italian restaurants and 17000 reviews of French restaurants, where each sentence is assigned to one of the 15 latent topics. Sentiment analysis is conducted and the user-topic correlation matrix is obtained for each restaurant category.

Using the user-topic correlation matrix, we segment the users according to each latent topic. Figure 3 shows the number of representative users for each topic for different correlation thresholds T. For the sake of clarity, we only show those latent topics that could be interpreted by us. It is interesting to observe that people who visit Indian restaurants tend to care the most about 'Location' and 'Value (Pricing)' and the least about 'Service' and 'Atmosphere'. On the other hand, people who visit French restaurants care the most about 'Food (Bread)' and 'Food (Main)' and the least about 'Atmosphere'. Similarly, while providing ratings, more number of users are influenced by the 'Atmosphere' at Greek restaurants than 'Food'. We then proceed to obtain the latent topic ratings for each restaurant. For this purpose, we only select those users whose correlation threshold, $T >= 0.4$ as representative users. For each latent topic, we average over the ratings provided by such users to obtain the topic ratings (out of 5). It is therefore possible to obtain crude ratings for aspects like 'Food', 'Service' etc. which give an indication of the quality of the aspects. We then fit an SVR model, the performance of which is described below.

4.1 Evaluation

To evaluate the performance of rating prediction, we determine the RMSE between the actual and predicted ratings for Italian restaurants. We compare the RMSE for MG-LDA and online LDA described in (Hoffman et al., 2010). In case of LDA, we detect $K = 50$ topics as in previous works. We use the latent topic ratings of 640 restaurants for training and 215 restaurants for test. The results are shown in Table 2.

Models	RMSE
(a) MG-LDA, SVR with rbf kernel (Proposed Model)	0.4909
(b) MG-LDA, SVR with linear kernel	0.5377
(c) LDA, SVR with rbf kernel	0.5812
(d) LDA, SVR with linear kernel	0.6277
(e) Baseline 1	0.6737
(f) Baseline 2	0.5831
Improvement	
(a) vs. (e)	27%
(a) vs. (f)	16%

Table 2: Evaluation (Italian Restaurants)

An RMSE of 0.4909 is obtained when using MG-LDA and SVR with rbf kernel. Each restaurant has an average of 22 representative users. Inviting these users to rate new restaurants would help in predicting the 'true' restaurant rating (which is the rating obtained once a considerable number of users have rated the restaurant over a period of time). However, conventional methods just average over their ratings, without taking into account the different topics that they represent. Such an approach gives an RMSE of 0.6737 (Baseline 1). Our approach outperforms this method by 27%. Also, since most people provide a rating of 3, 3.5 or 4 when rating restaurants, predicting a constant rating every time may also give a reasonable result. We find that predicting a rating of 3.64 (average over the test set) every time results in an RMSE of 0.5831 (Baseline 2). Our approach outperforms such a constant classifier by 16%.

We repeat the same procedure for Indian restaurants by using the latent topic ratings of 120 restaurants for training and 40 restaurants for test. The results are shown in Table 3.

Models	RMSE
MG-LDA, SVR with rbf kernel	0.4635
MG-LDA, SVR with linear kernel	0.5795
LDA, SVR with rbf kernel	0.5734
LDA, SVR with linear kernel	0.6997

Table 3: Evaluation (Indian Restaurants)

5 Conclusion and Future Work

In summary, we show how latent topics in review text could be used to unlock hidden value in user reviews. We utilise the intuition that, while rating products, certain users are influenced heavily by one particular aspect of the product. We learn such users by detecting the sentiments expressed by them with regard to each latent topic and then by comparing these sentiments with the actual ratings provided. We also use this to draw some interesting insights regarding users' rating behaviour across different cuisines and obtain latent topic ratings for restaurants. Overall ratings, which take into account the different dimensions of the restaurant, are then obtained using a regression model.

In the future, we would like to show that this approach is transferable to other domains like e-commerce. Also, it would be interesting to segregate the reviews by star ratings as this would help us understand the factors that a restaurant is getting right and those they are getting wrong. For example: The dimensions corresponding to review text having 5-star ratings would be different from those having 1-star ratings.

References

Stefano Baccianella, Andrea Esuli, and Fabrizio Sebastiani. 2009. Multi-facet rating of product reviews. In *Advances in Information Retrieval*, pages 461–472. Springer.

Steven Bird, Ewan Klein, and Edward Loper. 2009. *Natural language processing with Python*. " O'Reilly Media, Inc.".

Samuel Brody and Noemie Elhadad. 2010. An unsupervised aspect-sentiment model for online reviews. In *Human Language Technologies: The 2010 Annual Conference of the North American Chapter of the Association for Computational Linguistics*, pages 804–812. Association for Computational Linguistics.

Gayatree Ganu, Noemie Elhadad, and Amélie Marian. 2009. Beyond the stars: Improving rating predictions using review text content. In *WebDB*, volume 9, pages 1–6.

Narendra Gupta, Giuseppe Di Fabbrizio, and Patrick Haffner. 2010. Capturing the stars: predicting ratings for service and product reviews. In *Proceedings of the NAACL HLT 2010 Workshop on Semantic Search*, pages 36–43. Association for Computational Linguistics.

Matthew Hoffman, Francis R Bach, and David M Blei. 2010. Online learning for latent dirichlet allocation. In *advances in neural information processing systems*, pages 856–864.

Yohan Jo and Alice H Oh. 2011. Aspect and sentiment unification model for online review analysis. In *Proceedings of the fourth ACM international conference on Web search and data mining*, pages 815–824. ACM.

Bin Lu, Myle Ott, Claire Cardie, and Benjamin K Tsou. 2011. Multi-aspect sentiment analysis with topic models. In *Data Mining Workshops (ICDMW), 2011 IEEE 11th International Conference on*, pages 81–88. IEEE.

Julian McAuley and Jure Leskovec. 2013. Hidden factors and hidden topics: understanding rating dimensions with review text. In *Proceedings of the 7th ACM conference on Recommender systems*, pages 165–172. ACM.

Julian McAuley, Jure Leskovec, and Dan Jurafsky. 2012. Learning attitudes and attributes from multi-aspect reviews. In *Data Mining (ICDM), 2012 IEEE 12th International Conference on*, pages 1020–1025. IEEE.

Samaneh Moghaddam and Martin Ester. 2011. Ilda: interdependent lda model for learning latent aspects and their ratings from online product reviews. In *Proceedings of the 34th international ACM SIGIR conference on Research and development in Information Retrieval*, pages 665–674. ACM.

Ivan Titov and Ryan McDonald. 2008a. Modeling online reviews with multi-grain topic models. In *Proceedings of the 17th international conference on World Wide Web*, pages 111–120. ACM.

Ivan Titov and Ryan T McDonald. 2008b. A joint model of text and aspect ratings for sentiment summarization. In *ACL*, volume 8, pages 308–316. Citeseer.

Hongning Wang, Yue Lu, and Chengxiang Zhai. 2010. Latent aspect rating analysis on review text data: a rating regression approach. In *Proceedings of the 16th ACM SIGKDD international conference on Knowledge discovery and data mining*, pages 783–792. ACM.

Cross-lingual Pseudo Relevance Feedback Based on Weak Relevant Topic Alignment

WANG Xu-wen
Institute of Medical Information & Library,
Chinese Academy of Medical Sciences,
Beijing 100020
wang.xuwen@imicams.ac.cn

ZHANG Qiang
State Grid Electric Power Research Institute,
Beijing 102200
zhangqiang7@sgepri.sgcc.com.cn

WANG Xiao-jie
Beijing University of Posts and Telecommunications,
Beijing, 100876
xjwang@bupt.edu.cn

LI Jun-lian
Institute of Medical Information & Library,
Chinese Academy of Medical Sciences,
Beijing 100020
li.junlian@imicams.ac.cn

Abstract

In this paper, a cross-lingual pseudo relevance feedback (PRF) model based on weak relevant topic alignment (WRTA) is proposed for cross language query expansion on unparallel web pages. Topics in different languages are aligned on the basis of translation. Useful expansion terms are extracted from weak relevant topics according to the bilingual term similarity. Experiment results on web-derived unparalell data show the contribution of the WRTA-based PRF model to cross language information retrieval.

1 Introduction

The problem of word mismatch between queries and retrieved documents is particularly serious in cross language information retrieval (CLIR). The integration of query expansion techniques and translation knowledge is considered as an effective way to improve the CLIR performance (Ballesteros and Croft, 1998; Qu et al., 2000).

Pseudo relevance feedback (PRF) is one of the useful query optimizing technologies for monolingual retrieval tasks (Rocchio, 1971; Ruthven and Lalmas, 2003). As to the CLIR task, researchers laid more efforts on establishing an effective cross-lingual PRF mechanism on the basis of the relevance and complementary of bilingual web pages (Ballesteros and Croft, 1997; Lavrenko et al., 2002). One of the key problems is how to choose useful or relevant bilingual expansion terms.

Typical cross-lingual PRF methods assume the top retrieved documents are relevant and perform feedback calculations on the whole pseudo-relevant document level. High-frequency words are often used for expanding original queries.

In recent years, topic models were applied to more and more multilingual tasks (Wang et al., 2009; Vulic et al., 2013). Ganguly (2012) proposed an improved cross-lingual topical relevance model based on the latent topics of top ranked documents. Wang (2013) proposed a cross-lingual PRF model based on bilingual topics and showed better results on parallel or comparable corpus. However, the hypothesis of common shared bilingual topics is not always suitable for unparallel documents, since they are often poor in content relevance.

In most cases, web pages retrieved from different language fields for a specific query may lack of parallelism. There may be some common topics shared by the retrieved documents in both languages, but there are also some specific topics for source language retrieval results or target language retrieval results respectively. Only the former common shared topics would be helpful to cross-lingual PRF.

29th Pacific Asia Conference on Language, Information and Computation pages 529 - 534
Shanghai, China, October 30 - November 1, 2015

In this paper, we assume that retrieved results in different languages have independent topical distribution, but there may be some overlapping topics that describe similar or relevant content. The overlapping content is defined as weak relevant topics.

A cross-lingual PRF model based on weak relevant topic alignment (WRTA) is proposed for modeling the weak correlation between unparallel documents. Relevant topics in different languages are aligned based on translation equivalent. Then useful expansion terms are extracted from relevant topics according to their bilingual similarity.

The structure of this paper is organized as follows: section 2 introduces the structure of the WTRA-based cross-lingual PRF model; section 3 presents the comparison experiment of different PRF methods on web-derived data; the final section shows our conclusion.

2 Method

It is assumed that cross-lingual retrieval results of a specific query, although lack of parallelism or comparability, may contain some relevant content.

Firstly, we perform monolingual topic modeling for source language documents D_S and target language documents D_T respectively. A widely used topic modeling method is the Latent Dirichlet Allocation (LDA) model, which is proposed by Blei (2003). So the LDA model is employed to generate candidate topic sets. Secondly, topics in different languages are aligned based on translation equivalence. Thirdly, useful expansion terms in aligned topics are selected on the basis of translation as well as web co-occurrence features. Figure 1 shows the process of weak relevant topic alignment and expansion terms extraction.

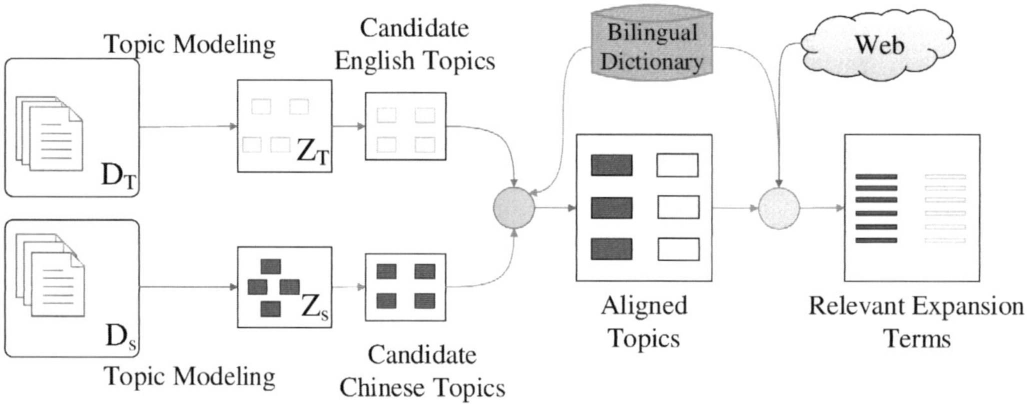

Figure. 1. Weak relevant topic alignment and extraction of relevant expansion terms

2.1 Weak Relevant Topic Alignment

For a specific query and its retrieved bilingual documents, we use the Gibbs sampling method for LDA inference (Han and Stibor, 2010) and generate two topic sets in different languages.

We need some clue for selecting candidate topics from the two topic sets. Topics that have close relation with the query or top-ranked documents are adopted as our candidate topics. Then relevant bilingual topic pairs with better translation equivalence are collected as the aligned topics.

1. Collecting candidate topics

Query related candidate topics: Topics including source language query terms Q_S or query translation terms Q_T are assumed to have directly correlation with users' query intention, namely query related topics Z_Q, see formula (1) and (2).

$$Z_Q^S = \bigcup_{z_S} \left(p(Q_S \mid Z_S) > 0\right) = \bigcup_{z_S} \sum_{i=1}^{n} p(q_i^S \mid z_S) > 0 \quad (1)$$

$$Z_Q^T = \bigcup_{z_T} \left(p(Q_T \mid Z_T) > 0\right) = \bigcup_{z_T} \sum_{i=1}^{n} p(q_i^T \mid z_T) > 0 \quad (2)$$

Alternative related candidate topics: The top M retrieved documents are supposed to be more relevant with users' query intention. So the top k topics with higher probability in the topic distribution $\theta(z)$ of the top M documents are adopted as the alternative related topics Z_E, see as formula (3) and (4).

Both of the query related topics Z_Q and the alternative related topics Z_E are collected as the candidate bilingual topic set Z_C, see as formula (5).

$$Z_E^S = \bigcup_{d \in D_M^S} k - \arg\max_{z} \theta_d(z) \quad (3)$$

$$Z_E^T = \bigcup_{d \in D_M^T} k - \arg\max_z \theta_d(z) \quad (4)$$

$$Z_C = Z_Q \cup Z_E \quad (5)$$

2. Topic alignment

Candidate topics in different languages are aligned according to their translation equivalence based on the machine-readable dictionary (MRD).

For a source language topic z_s and a target language topic z_t, which contain N_s terms or N_t terms respectively, the topical alignment rate is computed as formula (6). The *m* in numerator is the amount of terms in the source language topic z_s that have translation in the target language topic z_t, the *n* is the amount of terms in target language topic z_t that have translation in source language topic z_s.

$$f(z_s, z_t) = \frac{m + n}{N_s + N_t} \quad (6)$$

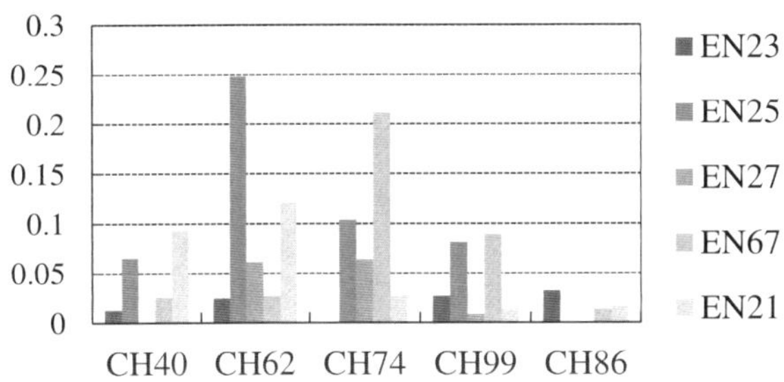

Figure. 2. The alignment rate between the candidate bilingual topics of "Information retrieval"

Figure 2 shows the alignment rate between candidate bilingual topics of the query "Information retrieval". The bi-directional translation process can be regard as a mutual multi-voting game between topics in different languages. The higher rate implies more latent relevance.

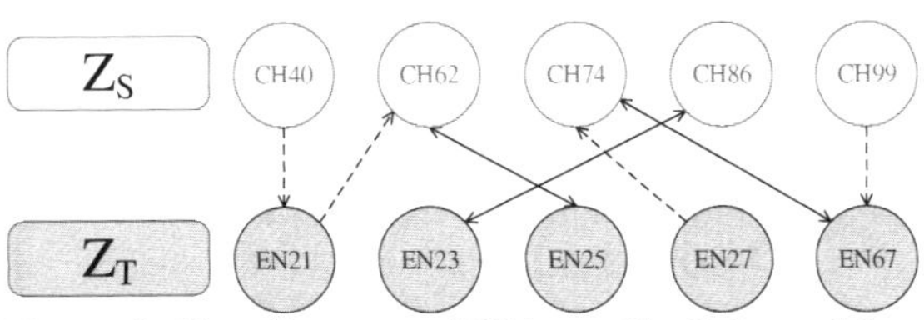

Figure. 3. The alignment of Chinese-English candidate topics of the query "Information retrieval"

Figure 3 shows the alignment relationship between candidate bilingual topics of the query. The solid arrow with two directions represents a mutual alignment between two topics, since they vote each other with the highest rate. In this case, three couples of topics are aligned successfully.

2.2 Selecting Relevant Expansion Terms

Cao et al. (2008) analyzed the potential influence of different terms to the performance of information retrieval tasks, and concluded that useful terms for query expansion in pseudo relevant documents only account for 18% in high frequency terms. Too many expansion terms may reduce the efficiency of retrieval systems (White and Marchionini, 2007).

In our work, terms from candidate topics are sorted into three categories. The first category contains semantically relevant terms that have translation or synonymy with original queries. Terms in the second category have no direct relationship with queries, but they are essential content in describing identical themes in bilingual context. The last category contains irrelevant noisy terms that should be filtered out.

To select useful expansion terms effectively, a bilingual term similarity score is computed based on web-derived data. For each pair of aligned topics, a source language term and a target language term are organized as a conjunctive query "$w_s + w_t$" for the real time web searching. In the real web searching, terms in different languages often co-occur in the title, snippet or URL of a retrieved multilingual webpage. So, the web co-occurrence of each pair of terms from aligned topics would be counted, see formula (7). The binary function in formula (8) represents the translation relationship between the term w_s and wt. The bilingual similarity score of the term pair is the linear combination of web co-occurrence and the translation feature, see as formula (9). The parameter λ is the weighting coefficient.

In each target language topic, terms are ranked according to the similarity score with the source language query terms, namely $\mathrm{Sim}(q_i^s, w_j^t)$. Terms with similarity score lower than the threshold μ will be filtered out.

$$f_C(w_i^S, w_j^t) = p(w_i^S, w_j^t) = \frac{\#\text{ retrieval records including } (w_i^S, w_j^t)}{\#\text{ retrieval records from IR system}} \propto \frac{N_c}{N} \quad (7)$$

$$f_T\left(w_i^S, w_j^t\right) = \mathrm{Trans}\left(w_i^S, w_j^t\right) = \begin{cases} 1, & \text{only if } \left(w_i^S, w_j^t\right) \text{are mutual translation} \\ 0, & \text{other} \end{cases} \tag{8}$$

$$\mathrm{Sim}\left(w_i^S, w_j^t\right) = \lambda\, f_T\left(w_i^S, w_j^t\right) + (1-\lambda)\, f_C\left(w_i^S, w_j^t\right), \quad (0 \le \lambda \le 1) \tag{9}$$

2.3 Cross Language Pseudo Relevance Feedback Based on WRTA

Based on the above algorithm, relevant terms are obtained for cross-lingual query expansion. Figure 4 shows the CLIR process with WRTA-based PRF mechanism.

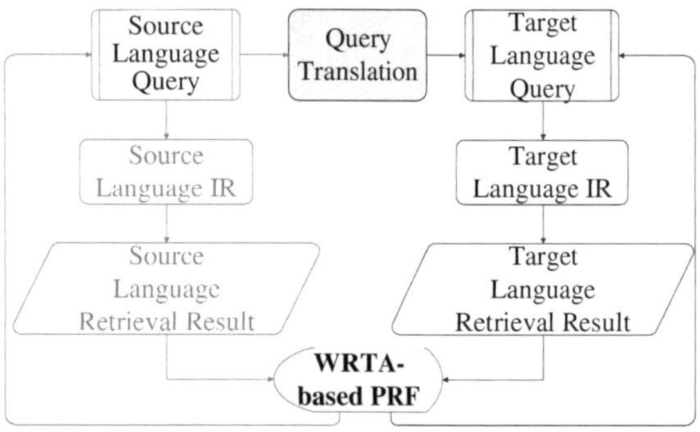

Figure. 4. CLIR process with cross language pseudo relevance feedback based on WRTA.

3 Experiments

3.1 Experimental setting and Data

We perform cross-lingual PRF experiments on a self-constructed CLIR system, namely CTP-CLIR system (Wang et al., 2013). As a prototype system, it contains a text pre-processing module, a query translation module, a retrieval model (Indri 5.2) and the pseudo relevance feedback module, which integrated various PRF mechanisms. The CTP-CLIR system could access web pages on line and retrieve local multilingual database automatically.

A Web-derived Chinese-English corpus was collected to simulate the real cross language web search task. The source language query set was selected from the Chinese science and technology concepts on CNKI. Each query contains 1 to 3 word tokens, totally 54 queries. The target language queries were the English translation of the Chinese queries, obtained from the query translation module.

The bilingual retrieval documents were collected from Google's real time retrieval results. Top 10 source language pages were crawled for each Chinese query, since most web users pay more attention to the top-ranked results in the retrieval list. The target language pages were retrieved via Google's cross-lingual retrieval. Totally 1080 web pages were collected.

Then 20 queries with poor comparable retrieval results were selected as our test set, totally 400 web pages. Other queries were saved as our training set, totally 34 queries and 680 web pages. All of the collected web pages were cleaned by the text preprocessing module and then be indexed by Indri 5.2.

Since the typical assessment criteria, such as precision or recall, shows no significant difference on the relatively small dataset, we take nDCG (Discounted Cumulative Gain) to evaluate the ranking effect of retrieval results. 27 volunteers were invited to judge the relevance of bilingual documents.

3.2 Parameters

All the parameters were tuned on the basis of our training set.

It was observed that topics from the top 1 document as well as the query related topic Z_Q contributed most to the best ranking results. So the parameters of topic alignment were configured as follows, the alternative document number M=1, the alternative topic number k=2. Each query has 1.5 pair of weak relevant topics on average. The filtering threshold of term probability in each topic σ=0.005.

The weighting coefficient of the bilingual term similarity score was set as λ=0.05, and its threshold for filtering terms μ=0.85.

The hyper parameters of the LDA model were optimized based on the training set, as follows, $\alpha = 0.1$, $\beta_s = 0.01$, $\beta_t = 0.02$. The number of training iterations was 10000.

3.3 Comparative Experiments

To examine the feedback effect of proposed method, we chose the normal CLIR results without PRF modulation as our baseline.

Various PRF methods, such as VSM-based PRF framework, LDA-based PRF model, bilingual LDA-based PRF model, etc., are also conducted before or after the query translation stage of CLIR, namely comparative experiments.

3.4 Results

Figure 5 shows the CLIR results employing different PRF methods on unparallel documents.

The first column is the result of CLIR without PRF mechanism. The second to the forth column show the results of PRF based on the Vector Space Model (VSM), namely pre-translation VSM-based PRF, post-translation VSM-based PRF and combined VSM-based PRF. The fifth to the seventh column show the results of PRF based on monolingual topic model, namely pre-translation LDA-based PRF, post-translation LDA-based PRF and combined LDA-based PRF. The eighth column is the result of bilingual LDA-based PRF, which performs integrated feedback on the basis of the bilingual LDA model. The last column shows the result of proposed WRTA-based cross-lingual PRF.

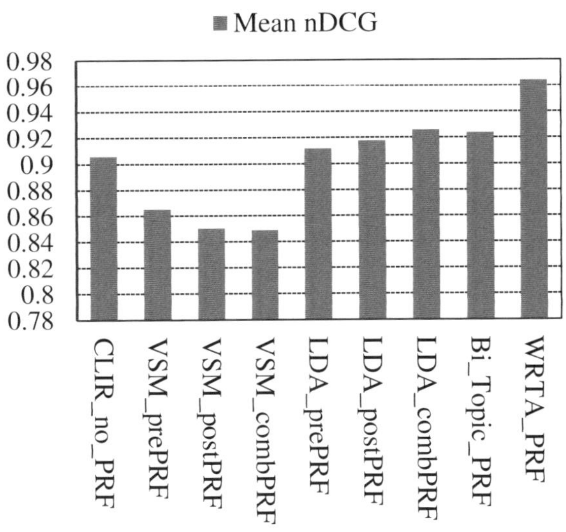

Figure. 5. Comparison of cross-lingual PRF based on WRTA and other PRF methods.

It can be observed that the VSM-based PRF methods introduced too much noise, since the feedback calculation was performed on the entire document level. The LDA-based PRF methods showed a slightly better performance than former methods, verifying the fact that a fine-grained topic may introduce more relevant terms into query expansion.

However, the PRF method based on bilingual LDA model, which used to achieve better performance than monolingual models on parallel documents, showed no advantage here, since the poor quality of the unparallel feedback documents limited the effectiveness of topical PRF methods.

In spite of the interference from the unparalleled documents, the WRTA-based PRF model achieved the highest improvement for CLIR. Expansion terms from aligned topics, which were selected based on the translation and web co-occurrence features, showed clear relevance with original queries. On one hand, noisy terms were filtered out effectively and the amount of expansion terms was reduced sharply. On the other hand, the remained expansion terms showed positive impact on the performance of CLIR on unparallel documents.

4 Conclusion

This paper describes a way to discover useful information from unparallel retrieval results for cross-lingual pseudo relevance feedback. A cross language PRF model based on weak-relevant topic alignment is proposed.

In comparison with various PRF methods, WRTA-based PRF model showed better performance and robustness in the CLIR task on less comparable documents. So it is proved to be more suitable for web oriented tasks.

It is worth noting that the effect of expansion terms for cross-lingual PRF is very complicated. The quality and quantity of expansion terms, which are influenced by the quality of translation as well as feedback documents, should be controlled carefully. Too many expansion terms may drown out valuable information, so the quantity of expansion terms is reduced sharply in our work. Noise terms are removed from candidate expansion terms effectively, so that useful terms may achieve positive feedback performance.

As to the further work, it will be necessary to introduce more multilingual knowledge resources into the cross-lingual PRF mechanism, such as Wikipedia, multilingual ontology, as well as semantic web knowledge, etc. Rich knowledge resources will be a helpful supplement for choosing relevant expansion terms, and furthermore, improving the performance of PRF model in CLIR tasks.

References

Andrzejewski D, Buttler D. Latent topic feedback for information retrieval [J]. Proceedings of the 17th Acm Sigkdd International Conference on Knowledge Discovery and Data Mining San Diego Ca Usa August 21 24 2011, 2011: 600-608.

Ballesteros L, Croft W. Statistical Methods for Cross-language Information Retrieval [J]. 1998.

Ballesteros L, Croft W. Phrasal translation and query expansion techniques for cross-language information retrieval [J]. Proceedings of the 20th Annual International Acm Sigir Conference on Research and Development in Information Retrieval, 1997, 31(SI): 84-91.

Blei D M, Ng A Y, Jordan M I. Latent dirichlet allocation [J]. The Journal of machine learning research, 2003, 3: 993-1022.

Cao G, Nie J Y, Gao J, et al. Selecting good expansion terms for pseudo-relevance feedback[C]//Proceedings of the 31st annual international ACM SIGIR conference on Research and development in information retrieval. ACM, 2008: 243-250.

Ganguly Debasis and Leveling Johannes and Jones Gareth J F Cross-lingual topical relevance models [C]. 24th International Conference on Computational Linguistics, 2012.

Han X, Stibor T. Efficient Collapsed Gibbs Sampling for Latent Dirichlet Allocation[J]. Jmlr, 2010.

Http://www.cnki.net/

J. J. Rocchio. Relevance feedback in information retrieval. [J]. In the SMART Retrieval System: Experiments in Automatic Document Processing, 1971:313-323

Lavrenko V, Choquette M, Croft W. Cross-lingual relevance models[J]. Proceedings of the 25th Annual International Acm Sigir Conference on Research and Development in Information Retrieval, 2002.

Orengo V, Huyck C. Relevance feedback and cross-language information retrieval[J]. Information Processing and Management an International Journal, 2006, 42(5): 1203-1217.

Qu Y, Eilerman A, Jin H. The Effect of Pseudo Relevance Feedback on MT-Based CLIR[J]. Riao 2000 Content Based Multi Media Information Access Csais, 2000.

Ruthven I, Lalmas M. A survey on the use of relevance feedback for information access systems[J]. The Knowledge Engineering Review, 2003.

Vulic I, De Smet W, Moens M. Cross-language information retrieval models based on latent topic models trained with document-aligned comparable corpora[J]. Information Retrieval, 2013.

Wang A, Li Y, Wei W. Cross language information retrieval based on LDA [J]. Intelligent Computing and Intelligent Systems. ICIS 2009.

Wang Xu-wen, Wang Xiao-jie, Sun Yue-ping, Cross-lingual pseudo relevance feedback based on bilingual topics, Journal of Beijing University of Posts and Telecommunications, Volume: 36; Issue 4; (JA) Pages: 81-84, August 2013.

Wang X, Zhang Q, Wang X, et al. LDA based PSEUDO relevance feedback for cross language information retrieval[C]// Cloud Computing and Intelligent Systems (CCIS), 2012 IEEE 2nd International Conference on-IEEE, 2012:1511-1516.

Wang X, Wang X, Zhang Q. A Web-Based CLIR System with Cross-Lingual Topical Pseudo Relevance Feedback [J]. Lecture Notes in Computer Science, Volume 8138 LNCS, 2013.

White, R.W., & Marchionini, G. (2007). Examining the effectiveness of real-time query expansion. Information Processing &Management, 43(3), 685–704.

Corpus annotation with a linguistic analysis of the associations between event mentions and spatial expressions

Jin-Woo Chung **Jinseon You** **Jong C. Park***

School of Computing
Korea Advanced Institute of Science and Technology
291 Daehak-ro, Daejeon, Republic of Korea
{jwchung, jsyou, park}@nlp.kaist.ac.kr

Abstract

Recognizing spatial information associated with events expressed in natural language text is essential for the proper interpretation of such events. However, the associations between events and spatial information found throughout the text have been much less studied than other types of spatial association as looked into in SpatialML and ISO-Space. In this paper, we present an annotation framework for the linguistic analysis of the associations between event mentions and spatial expressions in broadcast news articles. Based on the corpus annotation and analysis, we discuss which information should be included in the guidelines and what makes it difficult to achieve a high inter-annotator agreement. We also discuss possible improvements on the current corpus and annotation framework for insights into developing an automated system.

1 Introduction

Every event is situated within some real-world space and textual descriptions that refer to events in documents also convey such spatial information. Such information is important not only for the interpretation of single events but also for the understanding of the relations among them. Spatial information can be used for various applications such as information extraction, textual entailment, and question answering. For instance, if we want to answer the question "*Where did traffic accidents happen most frequently in 2014?*," we would need a method to access and collect spatial information associated with all traffic accidents from the relevant textual descriptions. However, such information is usually not provided explicitly in text since humans can intuitively understand from the context where each event occurs.

In general, two factors make it difficult to automatically recognize the location of events in text. First, there are usually more event mentions in text than expressions containing information about the location of events. A system must thus choose the most appropriate spatial expression for a given event mention. Second, such expressions are not always syntactically close to event mentions, which may make it less obvious to recognize their semantic association. The following three sentences exemplify different levels of difficulties in determining whether particular event mentions and spatial expressions are associated, i.e., whether a spatial expression refers to the space where an event occurred.

(1) A fire [broke out]$_{\text{EVENT}}$ at [a refrigerated warehouse]$_{\text{SPACE}}$ yesterday.
(2) A North Korean fishing vessel intruded 10 miles across [the Northern Limit Line]$_{\text{SPACE}}$ and South Korea's Navy [fired]$_{\text{EVENT}}$ 6 warning shots.
(3) He searched all over [the room]$_{\text{SPACE}}$ for his [missing]$_{\text{EVENT}}$ ring.

Sentence (1) shows that the event mention and the spatial expression are syntactically connected in a single clause, which can probably be identified in a straightforward manner with a conventional semantic role labeler. Sentence (2) shows that they exist in the same sentence but not in the same clause, and that there must be some inference in order to

* Corresponding author

29th Pacific Asia Conference on Language, Information and Computation pages 535 - 543
Shanghai, China, October 30 - November 1, 2015

find out that *fired* is likely to occur around *the Northern Limit Line*; for example, *intruded* and *fired* can occur in a similar place and the time interval between them may not be too long. Sentence (3) shows that, even though an event mention and a strong candidate for its spatial expression exist in the same sentence, their association may or may not hold depending on the context; there may be another place where the *missing* event actually happened. In this case, the system may have to search the text backwards to find out where *missing* or other relevant events are mentioned. Such information may, however, not have been stated at all in the available text.

In this paper, we present a linguistic analysis of how event mentions and spatial expressions are associated in text with respect to a corpus annotation process. More specifically, we discuss the following four issues:

- which information should be included in the guidelines in order to recognize spatial information about events in text,
- what kind of difficulties and issues arise during the annotation process,
- what trends are found in the corpus, and
- which factors could be of help to achieve a high inter-annotator agreement and to build an automated system.

The rest of this paper is organized as follows. Section 2 presents previous work on analyzing properties of events in text. Section 3 shows the proposed annotation framework for creating a corpus. Section 4 gives an analysis of the corpus and disagreements between annotators. Section 5 discusses issues on improving the proposed annotation framework, with concluding remarks.

2 Related Work

Research on analyzing aspects of events or relations among them has dealt mainly with temporal aspects and temporal relations. Much effort has been made to establish a specification for describing temporal properties of events in text and to create the labeled data, especially through the TimeML annotation standard and the TimeBank corpus (Pustejovsky et al., 2003a; Pustejovsky et al., 2003b). The availability of the standard and corpus has promoted further studies on extracting temporal information associated with events from text (Lapata and Lascarides, 2006; Mani et al., 2006; Yoshikawa et al., 2009; Mirza and Tonelli, 2014), including the TempEval challenges (Verhagen et al., 2009; Verhagen et al., 2010; UzZaman et al., 2013).

In contrast, analyzing spatial properties of events has received less attention than temporal analysis, though in recent years a few studies attempt to tackle relevant problems. SpatialML (Mani et al., 2008) presents an annotation specification for describing expressions that refer to geographic regions in a way similar to TimeML, but it deals only with spatial relations between non-event entities that are explicitly expressed in a single sentence. In a similar line, Spatiotemporal Markup Language (STML, Pustejovsky and Moszkowicz, 2008) was designed to annotate both the temporal and spatial properties of entities. While it includes the specification for spatial entities associated with events, it focuses primarily on associating motion events with motion-specific arguments, and does not deal with other types of event and other non-argument spatial entities found throughout the text. ISO-Space (Pustejovsky et al., 2011a; Pustejovsky et al., 2011b) addresses the integration of SpatialML and STML to establish the annotation standard. It considers events as a type of spatial entity and allows them to participate in spatial relations. However, these events are annotated only when the spatial relationship is explicitly stated in a single sentence. In particular, it does not consider *implicit* associations between general events and their spatial entities that are found across the text.

Another line of work would be spatial role labeling (Kordjamshidi et al., 2010), which addresses the task of identifying the location of objects and their spatial relations triggered by spatial indicators such as *on*, *at*, and *in*. However, it does not cover the location of general types of event, though a recent series of the SemEval challenges on this task (Kordjamshidi et al., 2012; Kolomiyets et al., 2013) discuss annotating motions.

Blanco and Vempala (2015) propose a method to infer temporally-anchored spatial knowledge from semantic roles. Their goal is to determine whether a certain argument of the verb is located in one of the locative arguments found in the same sentence and to temporally anchor their spatial relationship with respect to the duration of the target event. For example, given the sentence "*John was incarcerated at Shawshank prison*" and its PropBank-style semantic role annotation, they attempt to find out that *John* has been located at *Shawshank prison* **during** event *incarcerated*, but neither before nor after that event. This work makes use of properties of events to infer spatial knowledge, but does not handle the spatial relationship between events and locations outside the sentence.

Unlike the work mentioned above, work on analyzing event-centric spatial relations has not received much attention. The most relevant existing work would be the annotation and recognition of spatial containment relations between event mentions (Roberts et al., 2012; Roberts et al., 2013). They aim at inferring that the spatial boundary of a particular event contains that of another event. For instance, given the sentence "*The bombing victim died immediately,*" they infer that the *bombing* event is likely to spatially contain the *died* event. Their work is closely related to ours since it attempts to analyze the spatial aspects of events. However, it does not deal with directly linking event mentions to spatial expressions in a document although they utilize spatial expressions as one of the features for recognizing spatial relations between event mentions. Instead, they put more emphasis on what they call "implicit relation features", suggesting that the spatial containment relations could be recognized based on event semantic properties without relying heavily on contextual clues; we can see, for example, from the example above that the *bombing* and *died* events have some degree of semantic correlation. Their task does not necessarily aim at the recognition of such spatial expressions for events.

To the best of our knowledge, none of the previous studies address the associations between event mentions and spatial expressions found across the entire text.

3 Annotation Framework

In this section, we introduce our framework for annotating spatial expressions for given event mentions. We first describe the data we used for annotation and then present the definition of event mentions and spatial expressions to be annotated in a given document, together with the guidelines for selecting and labeling spatial expressions for given event mentions. We then present the overall annotation process and the corpus statistics.

3.1 Data

We chose to use texts in the broadcast news domain for our corpus as they contain various spatially bound events that happen in the real world as compared to texts in the newswire domain which usually include many editorials and opinions.

We used the data from the OntoNotes project (Hovy et al., 2006) in order to access diverse layers of linguistic annotations during our annotation process, such as part-of-speech tags, parse trees, named entities, and coreferences. We selected 48 documents from the collection of CNN broadcast news in OntoNotes Release 5.0 and used them as our corpus. Table 1 shows the statistics of the selected document collection. The figures in the table suggest that the corpus contains a varying number of words and sentences across the documents.

Measure	Figure
Total number of documents	48
Total number of sentences	416
Total number of words	7,810
Average number of words per sentence	18.8 (std. dev. 10.6)
Average number of sentences per document	8.7 (std. dev. 7.6)
Average number of words per document	162.7 (std. dev. 153.6)

Table 1: Statistics of the data in our corpus

The corpus also includes documents from various topics such as social issues, accidents, politics, finance, sports, and international news. We annotated the associations between event mentions and spatial expressions on top of these documents.

3.2 Annotation guidelines

Event mentions

There is no *de facto* standard definition of event mentions, and researchers usually adopt their own definition that fits into the goal of their work. One of the most widely used definitions would be the one in the TimeML schema. It regards an event mention as "a cover term for situations that happen or occur" (Pustejovsky et al., 2003a). A range of verbs that exhibit changes in the state of the world usually belong to this category. However, we do not restrict event mentions to a certain category of verbs. Instead, we regard almost all verbs as event mentions whether or not they refer to a situation that actually happened or that can be clearly anchored in a timeline. This is because we assume that any situations referred to by verbs including actions and states can be situated within a particular scope of space in the real world where it happens or takes effect. One of the goals of this work is to see if it is possible to pick out expressions that refer to such space for an event mention arbitrarily chosen within a given document.

We consider as event mentions all single word tokens labeled with part-of-speech tags that correspond to base verbs, inflicted verbs, gerunds, and participles in the Penn Treebank parse tree of the OntoNotes annotations. These tags include VB, VBD, VBG, VBN, VBP, and VBZ. When gerunds and participles were found, we excluded *be*-verbs and auxiliary verbs used with them and annotated only those gerunds and participles. We also excluded verbs in some patterns that act as auxiliary verbs such as *be going to* and *have to*. For example, given the sentence "*It has not been undertaken but will have to be considered,*" we annotated only *undertaken* and *considered* as event mentions to be associated with spatial expressions. Unlike TimeML, we did not consider noun phases as candidate event mentions since it is not clear which type of noun phrase can refer to spatially bound situations. Analyzing spatial aspects of noun phrases would be another interesting line of future work.

Spatial expressions

A spatial expression is either a single word or a sequence of words that refer to a particular space in which the situation or the state referred to by a given event mention happens or takes effect. More specifically, spatial expression S is said to be associated with event mention E if S refers to the space that encloses the spatial bounds of the event referred to by E while it happens or takes effect.

We did not restrict spatial expressions to certain semantic classes as in other studies, such as geographic and geopolitical places (Pustejovsky et al., 2011a; Roberts et al., 2012), locative arguments (Blanco and Vempala, 2015), and entities with spatial indicators (Kolomiyets et al., 2013). We instead asked our annotators to choose any word or phrase that they think provides some information about the spatial bounds of events even though they are not clearly grounded in physical and geographic space, such as *meeting*, *parliament*, *clashes*, *scene*, *demonstration*, *interview*, *network television*, and *political life*.

The annotation of spatial expressions relies largely on annotators' intuitive understanding of the text. In order to enable consistent annotation, we asked the annotators to stick to the following rules which are central to our annotation process, among others.

Rule 1: A spatial expression is either a noun phrase or an adverbial phrase. Our pilot annotation suggests that noun or adverbial phrases are sufficient enough to represent the space associated with events in text. However, we acknowledge one exception to this: adjectival forms of place names and their demonymic equivalents such as *Canadian*, *South American*, and *Northern Irish* can be annotated separately as a spatial expression even though they exist within a longer noun phrase, as shown in the example below.

(4) The [Yugoslav]$_{\text{SPACE}}$ Election Commission claims he did not [win]$_{\text{EVENT}}$ more than 50 % of the vote.

The annotators can choose *Yugoslav* as a spatial expression for event *win* if they consider it to be spatially bound in Yugoslavia. We found that the broadcast news exhibits this pattern frequently; such adjectival and demonymic forms themselves suggest a particular place for events when its nominal forms are not mentioned at all.

Rule 2: If the annotators choose a certain word to be included in a spatial expression for a given event mention, they must annotate the longest noun phrase or adverbial phrase that contains it as a head word. These phrases can contain any kind of modifier such as a relative clause and another nested adverbial phrase, as shown the example below.

(5) Students at a middle school in Calaveras County, California, are [getting]$_{\text{EVENT}}$ an unwanted lesson in entomology.

Here, if the annotators choose *school* as a head noun of a spatial expression for event *getting*, they must annotate "*at a middle school in Calaveras County, California*" as its spatial expression, which is the longest adverbial phrase containing *school* as a head noun, according to Rule 2. However, if they choose *County* as a head noun, they must annotate "*in Calaveras County, California*" as a spatial expression. Our intention behind this is to include as much information as possible in spatial expressions by annotating the longest span of expressions.

Rule 3: If there is more than one expression that refers to the space enclosing the spatial bounds of a given event, the annotators choose the one that refers to the narrowest space. For example, for event *getting* in example (5), we choose "*at a middle school in Calaveras County, California*" as its spatial expression instead of "*in Calaveras County, California*" since the former refers to narrower space than the latter.

The intuition is that narrow space conveys more information than broad space; knowing in example (5) that *getting* is associated with *a middle school* would be more informative than knowing that it is associated with *Calaveras County* because the former is less vague than the latter.

Rule 4: If there is still more than one expression that is not distinguished by Rules 1-3 above, the annotators choose the one that is closest to the event mention. The distance here is measured by the number of sentences between the event mention and its candidate spatial expression. If two equally qualified candidate expressions are found before and after the event mention, respectively, at an equal distance, then the annotators choose the one that appears before the event mention. If two such expressions are found in the same sentence, the annotators choose the one that is syntactically closer to the event mention.

Rule 5: For event mentions referring to a motion that creates a path, the annotators choose three distinct spatial expressions that refer to the beginning, intermediate, and end of the path, respectively, if they exist. When choosing a spatial expression for each of these components of the path, the annotators follow Rules 1-4 above. Such motion event mentions include *arrive*, *leave*, *travel*, and *return*. The following example shows that two motion event mentions appear in a single sentence.

(6) Finally, U.S. Marines [arrived]$_{E1}$ [at the hospital]$_{S1}$ to [take]$_{E2}$ him [to Kuwait and to a specialist burns unit]$_{S2}$.

Here, for event mention E1 (*arrive*), spatial expression S1 (*at the hospital*) can be chosen as the end of its path. For event mention E2 (*take*), spatial expressions S2 (*to Kuwait and to a specialist burns unit*) and S1 (*at the hospital*) can be chosen as the end and the beginning of the path, respectively. Note that associating E2 (*take*) and S1 (*at the hospital*) may require some inference; for instance, E2 may happen shortly after E1 happens.

Possible world analysis: As in the case of example (6), we always interpret the spatial bounds of events under the *possible worlds* assumption; even though they had not occurred or their occurrence is not clear, we estimate their spatial boundary by assuming the situation where they had already occurred. In this way, we can infer that event E2 (*take*) in example (6) has occurred in the space referred to by S1 (*at the hospital*). This type of interpretation can be applied to other similar constructions such as negation, condition, opinion, supposition, and conjecture.

Distinction between definite and plausible associations: Since the spatial information about events is highly implicit in text as discussed in Roberts et al. (2012), in most cases, it would not be possible to annotate spatial expressions with 100% confidence. Certain types of association may be more difficult to justify than others. For this reason, we introduce an additional label to distinguish between definite and plausible associations.

We consider associations to be *definite* if they can be reasonably inferred with common knowledge of the real world. In contrast, if the association cannot be inferred in such a way but is still presumed to exist in certain circumstances, we consider them to be *plausible*. The following example shows a sentence that contains both types of association.

(7) For the second day in a row, Lieutenant General Jay Garner was [mobbed]$_{E1}$ by friendly crowds after [touring]$_{E2}$ [a Kurdish school in the northern [Iraqi]$_{S1}$ city of Irbil]$_{S2}$.

Here, the association between event mention E2 (*touring*) and spatial expression S2 (*a Kurdish school in the northern Iraqi city of Irbil*) is considered to be definite since they are syntactically connected. On the other hand, it would be difficult to be fully confident that event mention E1 (*mobbed*) can be associated with S2. This is probably due to the existence of temporal relation indicator *after*. It suggests that there might be some time interval between E2 and E1, leading the annotators to believe that their locations might be different. In this case, their association is considered to be plausible. If *when* is used instead of *after* in this example, the association could be considered definite. The annotators are allowed to choose only one spatial expression for each of the two types of association for a given event mention; in other words, for general event mentions, the annotators choose at most two spatial expressions: one for the definite association and the other for the plausible association.

3.3 Annotation process

The process of annotating event mentions was fully automated because identifying them relies only on part-of-speech tags which are already provided by the OntoNotes annotations. Spatial expressions are annotated by our annotators, but only when at least one event mention is associated with it; in other words, we did not allow 'dangling' spatial expressions to be included in our corpus, as explained in the annotation guidelines. If the annotators fail to find a spatial expression for a given event mention, they just left it unassociated.

Two annotators participated in the annotation process. They were first provided with the documents that have been pre-annotated with event mentions. They then went over each document and for each event mention chose the text span of spatial expressions that are best associated with the event mention based on the guidelines. After that, they put a labeled link between the event mention and the spatial expression. One of the six labels can be attached to a single link: three labels for the definite associations and three labels for the plausible associations. We also provided the annotators with the web-based annotation tool to facilitate this process. The annotators are also allowed to consult information in the OntoNotes annotation files if necessary for more informed decisions.

Multi-phase annotation: In order to resolve disagreements and to improve the quality of the annotated data, we divided the entire annotation process into four phases and held a meeting whenever the annotation in each phase was completed. In each meeting, the annotators measured the inter-annotator agreement (IAA), analyzed and resolved disagreements, and revised the guidelines if necessary.

4 Corpus Analysis

4.1 Statistics

Table 2 shows the statistics of the annotated data in each annotation phase. On average, 85% (721/846) of the event mentions are associated with at least one spatial expression. This means that for most of the events it is possible to find descriptions of spatial information within a single document. Each spatial expression is associated with 2.5 (337/846) event mentions on average. Each document contains an average of 7.0 spatial expressions with a standard deviation of 5.4 and an average of 15.0 associations with a standard deviation of 14.5.

Statistics \ Phase	1	2	3	4	Total
# documents	5	15	10	18	48
# sentences	45	139	72	160	416
# words	898	2694	1554	2664	7810
# event mentions	95	319	160	272	846
# spatial expressions	31	121	69	116	337
# associations	85	270	140	226	721

Table 2: Statistics of the annotated data

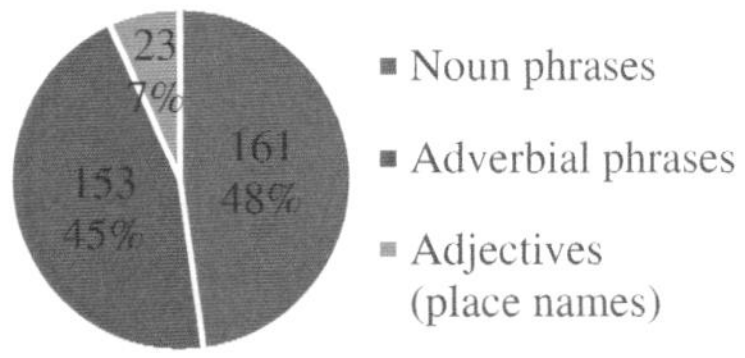

Figure 1. Distribution of phrase types of the annotated spatial expressions

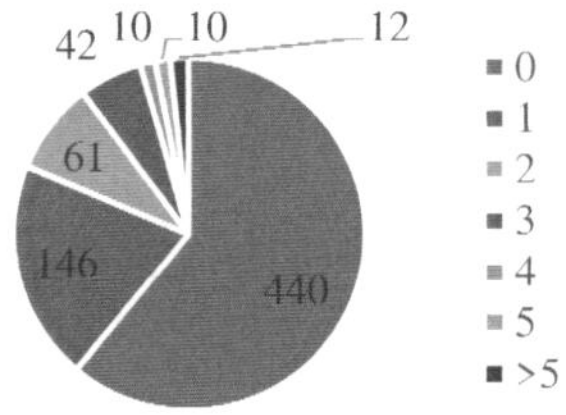

Figure 2. Distribution of the distances between event mentions and spatial expressions

Figure 1 shows the distribution of phrase types of the annotated spatial expressions. The phrase types are obtained from corresponding phrase tags in the OntoNotes parse tree annotations. The figure suggests that adverbial phrases such as locative prepositional phrases take up only less than half the whole spatial expressions and that it is also important to consider noun phrases as candidate spatial expressions.

Figure 2 shows the distribution of distances between event mentions and spatial expressions in the corpus. The distance here is the number of sentences between them. If the distance is zero, it means that they exist in the same sentence. The figure suggests that in many cases, spatial information about events can be found in local context; 61% (440/721) of them are found in the same sentence. The other associations, however, would require some degree of inference.

4.2 Disagreement analysis

Inter-annotator agreement: Conventional IAA measures such as Cohen's Kappa are not applicable to our task because we are not dealing with the data from a fixed set of categories; for each event mention, the annotators must choose the text span of spatial expressions from the entire text. In this work, we address IAAs by calculating the ratio of event mentions for which the two annotators agree. In order to make comparisons for different levels of strictness, we consider the following four cases of agreements for each event mention in documents.

(a) SIMPLE MATCHING: The two annotators both agree or disagree that the given event mention is associated with some spatial expression.

(b) SPAN OVERLAPPING: One of the spatial expressions annotated by one annotator overlaps one of the spatial expressions annotated by the other annotator. This corresponds to a loose measure for comparing two associations.

(c) SPAN MATCHING: *Each* spatial expression annotated by one annotator exactly matches with one of the spatial expression annotated by the other annotator, and vice versa.

(d) SPAN AND LABEL MATCHING: The text span and label of *each* spatial expression annotated by one annotator matches with those of one of the spatial expressions annotated by the other annotator, and vice versa. This corresponds to a strict measure for comparing two associations.

Measure \ Phase	1	2	3	4	Avg.
SIMPLE MATCHING	0.79	0.78	0.80	0.86	0.81
SPAN OVERLAPPING	0.58	0.63	0.49	0.63	0.60
SPAN MATCHING	0.48	0.53	0.39	0.44	0.47
SPAN AND LABEL MATCHING	0.48	0.49	0.36	0.42	0.44

Table 3: Inter-annotator agreements

Table 3 shows inter-annotator agreements for each phase and the entire corpus. Although the overall agreements are not very high, we believe that this is due to the highly implicit nature of spatial information in discourse as discussed in Roberts et al. (2012). The task requires the combination of contextual clues and the world knowledge, and relies heavily on the annotators' intuition and interpretation of implicit information. The annotators sometimes have different interpretations of definite and plausible associations, though they reached an agreement in the discussion after each annotation phase. Near-perfect agreement would thus not be a practical goal in this task.

Simple mistakes: Aside from the disagreements caused by the implicit nature of the task, the annotation within the current framework also produced a number of mismatches in choosing the exact span of spatial expressions even though the annotators correctly chose their head word. They also sometimes made a mistake in choosing the longest phrase by dropping modifiers. Another type of mistake is not to choose the closest one. This case happens when different expressions that refer to the same place are mentioned in a single document. The annotators often missed a closer expression and chose the distant one that refers to the same place, which are not actually genuine errors. We found that more than 40% of the disagreements in phases 3 and 4 are due to these types of mistake.

Although it is difficult to clearly classify the type of disagreements other than the mistakes above, we found that there are some frequent cases of disagreements as shown below.

Remote agents: In some cases, it is not clear whether the agent is remotely involved in a given event. This may cause disagreements between the annotators, as shown below

(8) Kostunica says he won't [turn]$_{\text{EVENT}}$ Milosevic over to a tribunal [in The Netherlands]$_{\text{SPACE}}$ where he was indicted as a war criminal.

One of the annotators was confused whether event *turn* can be associated with spatial expression *in The Netherlands*. The discussion led them to agree that event *turn* does not necessarily imply its agent being located in the remote place if there is no further contextual information that supports it.

Abstract events: It is often difficult to identify the spatial bounds of events because of their vague interpretation.

(9) After today's air strikes, 13 Iraqi soldiers [abandoned]$_{\text{EVENT}}$ [their posts]$_{\text{SPACE}}$ and [surrendered]$_{\text{EVENT}}$ to Kurdish fighters.

Here, while it is clear that event *abandoned* and spatial expression *their posts* are associated, it might not be so clear whether *surrendered* and *their posts* can be associated with each other. One annotator considered *surrendered* as a kind of declaration and associated it with *their posts*, but the other annotator considered that *surrendered* involves the location change of its agents into the place where the entities to which they surrender are located, i.e., the location of *Kurdish fighters*. For this disagreement, the annotators agree that there is a plausible association between *their posts* and *surrendered*.

Containment relations among spatial entities: Some documents contain several expressions that refer to geographic regions in spatial containment relations. For example, one of the documents in our corpus has seven candidate expressions that spatially contain one another, as shown in Figure 3. This made it difficult for the annotators to determine which must be chosen as a spatial expression for a given event mention, especially when its spatial boundary is not clear.

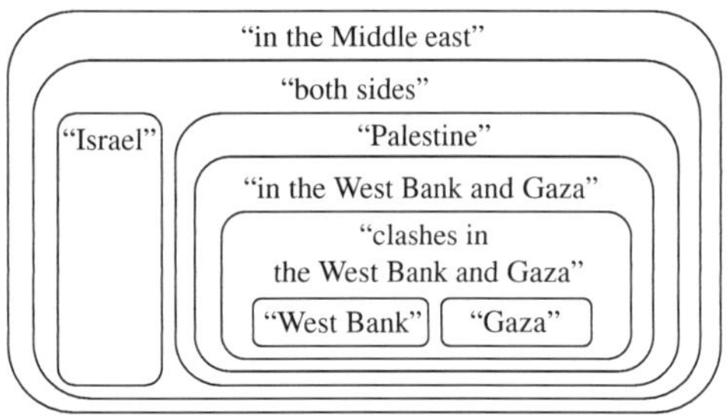

Figure 3. Relative containment relations among seven spatial expressions

Cascading disagreement: Disagreement that arises in a particular event mention often propagates through other neighboring mentions, especially when a set of related events that occur in a short time is mentioned in consecutive sentences. This is because the annotators usually try to cluster similar events first, and then associate them with a particular special expression at the same time.

5 Discussion and Concluding Remarks

In this work, we proposed our framework for annotating associations between event mentions and spatial expressions to analyze spatial information about events in text. Although the highly implicit nature of spatial information makes it difficult to achieve consistent annotation, we see that further improvements can be made on our current framework.

One of them is to restrict event mentions and spatial expressions to a certain category of words in order to remove cases where their spatial boundaries are too implicit. For instance, we could annotate only the event mentions referring to the situation that can be temporally anchored as in TimeML, or could restrict spatial expressions to geographical entities as in SpatialML and ISO-Space.

In order to avoid disagreements raised by mistakes in choosing an exact text span of spatial expressions, we may allow for annotating only head words and let the annotation tool automatically choose the longest phrases using the parse tree of the OntoNotes annotation because our goal is not to identify the exact boundary of such phrases.

Another possible improvement is to augment the current annotation to incorporate further linguistic information in order to facilitate the annotation process and to enable more practical evaluation. The most important one would be to annotate the spatial containment and coreference relations among spatial expressions. As discussed in our disagreement analysis, the annotators often make mistakes or disagree when choosing among spatial expressions that refer to highly overlapping regions, as in Figure 3. It may not be practical to make a sharp distinction among them. The current IAA measures in our framework do not consider the possibility of 'partial matches': for example, "*in the West Bank and Gaza*" and "*clashes in the West Bank and Gaza*". In order to assess the performance of an automated recognition system, there should also be a proper evaluation metric that compensates for these cases, such as CEAF in coreference resolution (Luo, 2005).

Future work also includes increasing the size of the present corpus and augmenting it with other layers of linguistic information such as event coreference. We also plan to build an automated system to recognize the associations with various linguistically motivated features. Our corpus is publicly available at http://nlp.kaist.ac.kr/resources.

Acknowledgements

This work was supported by the National Research Foundation of Korea (NRF) grant funded by the Korea government (MSIP) (No. NRF-2014R1A2A1A11052310).

References

Blanco, Eduardo and Alakananda Vempala, 2015. Inferring Temporally-Anchored Spatial Knowledge from Semantic Roles. Proceedings of the 2015 Annual Conference of the North American Chapter of the ACL, 452-461.

Hovy, Eduard, Mitchell Marcus, Martha Palmer, Lance Ramshaw, and Ralph Weischedel. 2006. OntoNotes: the 90% Solution. Proceedings of the Human Language Technology Conference of the NAACL, 57–60.

Kolomiyets, Oleksandr, Parisa Kordjamshidi, Steven Bethard, and Marie-Francine Moens. 2013. SemEval-2013 Task 3: Spatial role labeling, 7th International Workshop on Semantic Evaluation.

Kordjamshidi, Parisa, Steven Bethard, and Marie-Francine Moens. 2012. SemEval-2012 Task 3: Spatial role labeling. 6th International Workshop on Semantic Evaluation.

Kordjamshidi, Parisa, Martijn van Otterlo, and Marie-Francine Moens. 2010. Spatial role labeling: Task definition and annotation scheme. 7th International Conference on Language Resources and Evaluation.

Lapata, Mirella and Alex Lascarides. 2006. Learning sentence-internal temporal relations. Journal of Artificial Intelligence Research, 27:85-117.

Luo, Xiaoqiang. 2005. On coreference resolution performance metrics. Proceedings of the conference on Human Language Technology and Empirical Methods in Natural Language Processing, 25-32.

Mani, Inderjeet, Janet Hitzeman, Justin Richer, Dave Harris, Rob Quimby, and Ben Wellner. 2008. SpatialML: Annotation scheme, corpora, and tools. 6th International Conference on Language Resources and Evaluation.

Mani, Inderjeet, Marc Verhagen, Ben Wellner, Chong Min Lee, and James Pustejovsky. 2006. Machine learning of temporal relations. Proceedings of the 21st International Conference on Computational Linguistics and the 44th annual meeting of the Association for Computational Linguistics, 753-760.

Mirza, Paramita and Sara Tonelli. 2014. An analysis of causality between events and its relation to temporal information. Proceedings of the 25th International Conference on Computational Linguistics, 2097-2106.

Pustejovsky, James, José Castaño, Robert Ingria, Roser Saurí, Robert Gaizauskas, Andrea Setzer, and Graham Katz. 2003a. TimeML: Robust specification of event and temporal expressions in text. 5th International Workshop on Computational Semantics.

Pustejovsky, James, Patrick Hanks, Roser Saurí, Andrew See, Robert Gaizauskas, Andrea Setzer, Dragomir Radev, Beth Sundheim, David Day, Lisa Ferro, and Marcia Lazo. 2003b. The TIMEBANK corpus. Proceedings of the Corpus Linguistics 2003 conference, 647-656.

Pustejovsky, James and Jessica Moszkowicz. 2008. Integrating motion predicate classes with spatial and temporal annotations. Proceedings of the 22nd International Conference on Computational Linguistics, 95-98.

Pustejovsky, James, Jessica Moszkowicz, and Marc Verhagen. 2011a. ISO-Space: The annotation of spatial information in language. Proceedings of the 6th Joint ISO-ACL SIGSEM Workshop on Interoperable Semantic Annotation, 1-9.

Pustejovsky, James, Jessica Moszkowicz, and Marc Verhagen. 2011b. Using ISO-Space for annotating spatial information, 10th International Conference on Spatial Information Theory.

Roberts, Kirk, Travis Goodwin, and Sanda Harabagiu. 2012. Annotating spatial containment relations between events. 8th International Conference on Language Resources and Evaluation.

Roberts, Kirk, Michael A. Skinner, and Sanda M. Harabagiu. 2013. Recognizing spatial containment relations between event mentions. 10th International Conference on Computational Semantics.

UzZaman, Naushad, Hector Llorens, Leon Derczynski, Marc Verhagen, James Allen, and James Pustejovsky. 2013. SemEval-2013 Task 1: TempEval-3: Evaluating events, time expressions, and temporal relations. 7th International Workshop on Semantic Evaluation.

Verhagen, Marc, Robert Gaizauskas, Frank Schilder, Mark Hepple, Jessica Moszkowicz, and James Pustejovsky. 2009. The TempEval challenge: Identifying temporal relations in text. Language Resources and Evaluation, 43(2):161–179.

Verhagen, Marc, Roser Saurí, Tommaso Caselli, and James Pustejovsky. 2010. SemEval-2010 Task 13: TempEval-2. 5th International Workshop on Semantic Evaluation.

Yoshikawa, Katsumasa, Sebastian Riedel, Masayuki Asahara, and Yuji Matsumoto. 2009. Jointly identifying temporal relations with markov logic. Proceedings of the Joint Conference of the 47th Annual Meeting of the ACL and the 4th International Joint Conference on Natural Language Processing of the AFNLP, 405-413.

Recognizing Complex Negation on Twitter

Junta Mizuno **Canasai Kruengkrai** **Kiyonori Ohtake**
Chikara Hashimoto **Kentaro Torisawa** **Julien Kloetzer**
National Institute of Information and Communications Technology
Kyoto 619-0289, Japan
{junta-m,canasai,kiyonori.ohtake,ch,torisawa,julien}@nict.go.jp
Kentaro Inui
Graduate School of Information Sceinces, Tohoku University
Miyagi 980-8579, Japan
inui@ecei.tohoku.ac.jp

Abstract

After the Great East Japan Earthquake in 2011, an abundance of false rumors were disseminated on Twitter that actually hindered rescue activities. This work presents a method for recognizing the *negation* of predicates on Twitter to find Japanese tweets that refute false rumors. We assume that the predicate "occur" is *negated* in the sentence "The guy who tweeted that a nuclear explosion occurred has watched too many SF movies." The challenge is in the treatment of such *complex negation*. We have to recognize a wide range of complex negation expressions such as "it is theoretically impossible that..." and "The guy who... watched too many SF movies." We tackle this problem using a combination of a supervised classifier and clusters of n-grams derived from large un-annotated corpora. The n-gram clusters give us a gain of about 22% in F-score for complex negations.

1 Introduction

After the Great East Japan Earthquake in 2011, hundreds of false rumors were disseminated on Twitter. At the same time, many experts and other knowledgeable people posted tweets to refute such false rumors as "There is no truth to the rumor that a nuclear explosion has occurred in Fukushima." However, since many people did not notice such refutations, they retweeted the false rumors, inadvertently fueling the confusion and creating serious obstacles to rescue activities.

This paper presents a method that recognizes the *negation* of predicates on Twitter to identify the tweets that refute false rumors[1]. Our proposed method uses a supervised learning method to judge whether a given predicate in a tweet is negated.. An important point here is that we have to deal with *complex* forms of *negations* to achieve our final goal; the detection of false rumors. Note that although our target data are Japanese tweets, we provide examples in English for readability.

S1 It is theoretically impossible that a nuclear explosion *occurred* in Fukushima.

S2 The guy who tweeted that a nuclear explosion *occurred* has watched too many SF movies.

Both S1 and S2 refute that a nuclear explosion occurred. In other words, the predicate "occur" is negated, even though no negation words (e.g., "not") are explicitly written in the sentences. Many sentences similar to the above examples were actually posted on Twitter to refute false rumors after the earthquake.

In this paper, we categorize negation into two types: simple and complex. Given a predicate that is annotated as negation by a human annotator, its categorization is done based on the following criteria.

Simple negation If at least one of the words in the same phrase of the negated predicate ends with "ない nai, わけない wakenai, ぬ nu (all of which mean not)" we define this form as simple negation. These three words are called *simple negation suffixes (SNW)* hereafter (Table 1) and roughly correspond to such simple forms of negations in English as "do not" and "has not."

[1] Even though other linguistic expressions might also be useful to detect false rumors, we focus on negation.

29th Pacific Asia Conference on Language, Information and Computation pages 544 - 552
Shanghai, China, October 30 - November 1, 2015

Complex negation If a human annotator annotates a predicate as negated even without words that end with SNW in the same phrase of the negated predicate, we define this form as complex negation. For instance, the literal Japanese translations of S1 and S2 do not have any words that end with SNW.

We only focus on complex negation in this paper, since simple negation can be recognized by matching SNW against the words in the same phrase of the predicate with a high accuracy.

Thus, we have to recognize a wide range of expressions that indicate negation, including "it is theoretically impossible that..." and "The guy who... has watched too many SF movies." To tackle this problem, we use, as features for our supervised classifier, n-gram clusters derived from large unannotated corpora and generalize specific words or n-grams for them. Consider this sentence: "It is *untrue* that Kyoto has been heavily contaminated by radiation." If such a sentence exists in the training data for our classifier and the predicate "contaminated" is annotated as "negated," by the generalization of the word "*untrue*" to a cluster that includes "theoretically impossible," our method might successfully recognize that "occur" in S1 is negated. It also might even be possible to recognize the negation in S2 if several n-grams such as "guy," "too many," and "SF movies" are generalized to certain clusters and training samples can be found like "The people who claim that Tokyo was completely destroyed have watched too many Godzilla movies."

Through a series of experiments, we show that n-gram clusters give a 22% improvement in F-score for complex negations over the rule-based baseline. Our method successfully recognizes the complex forms of such negations as "An urban legend that..." and "Did dome idiot really say that...?".

To the best of our knowledge, this work is the first attempt to introduce n-gram clusters for recognizing complex forms of negation. Saurí (2008) developed a rule-based method to recognize the factuality of events, whose negation recognition can be regarded as a subtask. However, it seems quite difficult to write rules that cover the complex negation forms exemplified above. We expect that n-gram clusters play the role of the condition parts of the rules for complex negation forms.

Also note that we evaluate the performance of our method using the cross-validation on tweet data posted during one month immediately after the Great East Japan Earthquake. There is a possibility that this evaluation scheme may provide a high accuracy that cannot be achieved on real situation since the test data and training data were taken from the tweets concerning the same disaster. Nonetheless, it is difficult to provide test and training data concerning distinct large scale disasters. Therefore, we tried another setting in which the tweets posted during the two days immediately after the Great East Japan Earthquake were used as training data and the tweets posted after the first two days were used as test data. This evaluation scheme simulates the situation where new large scale disaster occurs and we have to prepare our system using the data available during first few days. We expect that the results give a lower bound of the performance of our method.

2 Related Work

Previous studies addressed negation recognition as part of modality/factuality analysis. Saurí and Pustejovsky (2009) annotated factuality for each event in TimeBank (Pustejovsky et al., 2003). Saurí and Pustejovsky (2007) defined three markers: polarity particles such as "not" or "no," modal particles such as "may" or "likely," and situation selecting predicates such as "prevent" or "suggest." They used these cue words to detect polarity (positive, negative, or unknown) and epistemic modality (certain, probable, possible, or unknown) and combined these two values to indicate an event's factuality.

de Marneffe et al. (2012) annotated the veridicality which roughly corresponds to the factuality for each event by ten annotators to the FactBank corpus (Saurí and Pustejovsky, 2009) and trained a classifier to predict the probabilistic distribution of event veridicality using a maximum entropy method (Berger et al., 1996). They compared the distributions predicted by the classifier and the distributions annotated by human annotators.

Soni et al. (2014) examined the factuality of quoted statements in tweets. They used the cue words defined in Saurí (2008) that introduced the quoted event negation or speculation and the tweet's author. They reported that conducting factuality analysis for quoted statements is quite difficult due to the error rate.

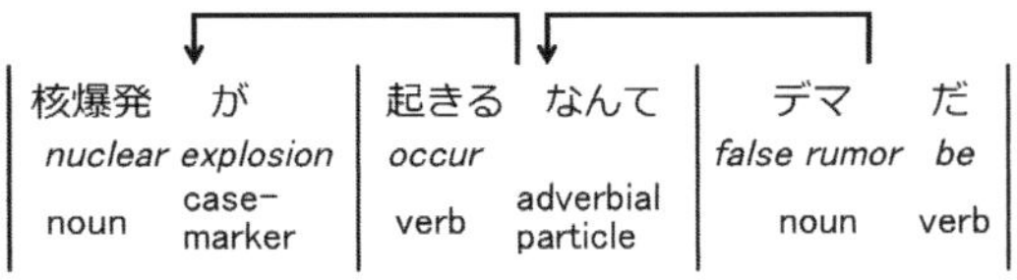

Figure 1: Japanese *bunsetsu* example

3 Approach

Our negation recognition algorithm takes an input sentence and classifies each predicate in it as "negated" or "non-negated." We train our classifier using support vector machines (SVMs) (Vapnik, 2000).

We use the notion of a *bunsetsu* which roughly corresponds to a *minimum* phrase in English and consists of a content words (basically nouns or verbs) and the functional words surrounding them. Figure 1 shows an example of a Japanese sentence, which means "That a nuclear explosion occurred is a false rumor." The vertical bars indicate the bunsetsu boundaries. A Japanese dependency tree is defined as a tree of the dependencies among the bunsetsus. In the above example, the first bunsetsu "核爆発_が kakubakuhatsu_ga (nuclear explosion)" depends on another bunsetsu "起きる_なんて okiru_nante (occur)," which in turn depends on "デマ_だ dema_da (be_false rumor)". The final bunsetsu is an exceptional case in which both a verb and a noun are included unlike the other bunsetsus that contain either a noun or a verb. Note that in this paper, bunsetsu boundaries and a dependency tree are given by J.DepP (Yoshinaga and Kitsuregawa, 2009).

3.1 Baseline Features

Basic Uni-, bi-, and tri-grams of words (surface, base form, and part of speech) in the bunsetsu include the target predicate and its head bunsetsu are used as basic features. The words in the two *bunsetsus* are distinguished in the feature set. If a *bunsetsu* includes a target predicate, n-grams are taken only from the strings following it. In the above example sentence, bi-gram "デマ_だ dema_da (be_false rumor)" and uni-gram "デマ dema (false rumor)" are included in this feature set when the target predicate is "起きる okiru (occur)."

Negation Words We manually created a short list of 33 words (CNW), such as "デマ dema (false rumor)" and "チェーンメール chainmail (chain letter)" shown in Table 2 that indicate complex forms of negations. These are often used to refute the information. Consider this tweet: "I have a chain letter that warns the occurrence of the explosion." The author of this tweet expresses his opinion that the explosion does not occur. For each word in the list, the features indicate the existence/non-existence of the word in the target sentence and its position ("before" or "after" the target predicate). They also include the distance of the negation words in the CNW from the target predicate. We encode the distance using 11-bit binary features (i.e., 1, 2, . . . , 10, or more). In the above example, the feature set encodes the information that the word "デマ dema (false rumor)" in the list is located after the target predicate "起きる okiru (occur)" along with the distance between "デマ dema (false rumor)" and "起きる okiru (occur)."

Sentiment We also consider the sentiment polarity of the words (positive or negative) in the *bunsetsus* from which the n-grams in the Basic feature set are taken. This feature set is useful because some words with negative polarities can express negation, like the word "ignorant" in "An *ignorant* person claimed a nuclear explosion actually occurred." We ignore words having neutral sentiment polarity. The words themselves with sentiment polarities are also encoded in this feature set. We use a list of words with manually annotated sentiment polarities (Oh et al., 2012).

Following Words In this feature set, we capture at most seven words (surface) that follow the target predicate, not including the target predicate. This feature is simple bag-of-words of uni-grams.

One crucial point is that we excluded from the feature set such *propositional contents* as "A nuclear explosion occurred," which is judged as "negated" in the S1 and S2 based on our criteria. This decision avoids the possibility that the classifier biases the negation of popular false rumors like the above nuclear explosion example. We assumed that propositional content which might be negated, is represented by a predicate and its argument and modifiers (and their descendants). Since Japanese is a head-final language, where a predicate appears at the right-hand side of its arguments and modifiers, we did not include the information concerning the left-hand side of a target predicate in the features and the target predicate itself[2]. In Figure 1, the predicate "起きる okiru (occur)" and its argument "核爆発 kakubakuhatsu (nuclear explosion)" are excluded.

[2]Except for the Sentiment Polarity features.

Synonyms of "not"	ない nai, ぬ nu, わけない wakenai

Table 1: List of simple negation suffixes (**SNW**)

Synonyms of "false rumor," "lie," "forgery" and "mistake"	デマ dema, でま dema, ガセ gase, ガセネタ gaseneta, がせ gase, ネタ neta, 風説 fusetsu, 流言 ryugen, 流言飛語 ryugenhigo, 流言蜚語 ryugenhigo, 誤報 goho, 誤情報 gojoho, 誤解 gokai, 嘘 uso, うそ uso, ウソ uso, 偽る itsuwaru, 偽り itsuwari, 捏造 netsuzo, ねつ造 netsuzo, 虚偽 kyogi, 間違う machigau, 間違い machigai, 出任せ demakase, でまかせ demakase, 誤る ayamaru, 誤り ayamari, 虚構 kyoko, 違う chigau, 違い chigai
Synonyms of "chain letter"	チェーンメール chainmail, チェンメ chenme, ちぇんめ chenme

Table 2: List of complex negation words (**CNW**)

3.2 N-Gram Cluster Features

A primary motivation behind the introduction of the n-gram cluster features is to *generalize* our CNW, which includes only 33 words. For instance, "デマ dema (false rumor)" has many synonymous expressions such as "偽_情報 nise_joho (false information)", and "不確かな_情報 futashikana_joho, 不正確な_情報 fuseikakuna_joho, 不確定な_情報 fukakuteina_joho, 真偽_不明な_情報 shingi_humeina_joho (all of which mean uncertain information)", which are not covered by CNW.

We used an implementation of a neural network-based algorithm (i.e., word2vec[3] (Mikolov et al., 2013)) to construct the synonym clusters. To get larger units of words (i.e. n-grams), we ran the word2phrase tool on these corpora twice and generated n-gram clusters by performing the k-means clustering algorithm on the top of the word (and phrase) vectors. This feature set encodes the semantic cluster IDs of the words and the n-grams ($n \leq 4$) found in the seven words that follow a target predicate. Note that we modified the k-means clustering of the word2vec tool so that the word vectors are normalized to the length of the vector.

Three distinct corpora were given to the word2vec tool:

1. All of the articles from Japanese Wikipedia (revision of 18 Jan. 2015),
2. Web pages crawled in 2007, i.e., about four years before the earthquake,
3. Twitter data posted from Feb. 14 to 28, 2015, i.e., about four years after the earthquake.

We randomly sampled sentences for corpora 2 (4.5 GB) and 3 (4.3 GB) to match Wikipedia's size (4.2 GB). We tokenized each document with a morphological analyzer MeCab (Kudo et al., 2004) and the Juman PoS tag set (Kurohashi et al., 1994) and applied the word2vec tool and k-means clustering. We needed to choose several parameters, including the numbers of vector dimensions and clusters, whose values were based on 5-fold cross-validation on our annotated training data, as described in Section 4.1. We tried eight dimensions (50, 100, 150, 200, 250, 300, 350, and 500) of vectors and six numbers of clusters (100, 500, 1,000, 2,000 5,000, and 10,000) for each corpus. For the optimal parameters, which worked best in our preliminary experiments, we finally chose 250 as the dimension and 10,000 as the number of clusters for Wikipedia, 350 dimensions and 10,000 clusters for the Web, and 300 dimensions and 10,000 number of clusters for Twitter. The tuning for the word2vec parameters was done by using a classifier with the word2vec features and the Basic, Negation Words, and Sentiment features for our classifiers.

In our experiments, many synonymous expressions such as "偽_情報 nise_joho (false information)" and "不確かな_情報 futashikana_joho, 不正確な_情報 fuseikakuna_joho, 不確定な_情報 fukakuteina_joho, 真偽_不明な_情報 shingi_fumeina_joho (all of which mean uncertain information)" were assigned vectors close to that of "デマ dema (false rumor)" in terms of cosine similarity. We assume that the clusters obtained by k-means might capture such synonyms, i.e., the cluster including "デマ dema (false rumor)" also includes its synonyms. CNW also includes only single words, while performing k-means clusters on word/phrase vectors can assign cluster IDs to n-grams. Actually, in the above examples the expression "不確かな_情報 futashikana_joho (uncertain information)" consists of two words. Furthermore, we assume that the combination of a supervised classifier and n-gram clusters can capture, to a certain degree, extremely complex negation forms, such as the negations of "occur" in the sentence, "The guy who tweeted that a nuclear explosion occurred has watched too many SF movies" by such clusters including n-grams as "guy," "too many," and "SF movies."

[3]https://code.google.com/p/word2vec/

Usage	Source	#predicates	#nps	#cns
training	tweets	96,824	11,842	1,541
	artificial	4,048	1,638	849
	total	100,872	13,480	2,390
test	tweets	14,253	2,250	393

Table 3: The training and test sets. **#nps** indicates number of negation instances and **#cns** indicates number of complex negated instances.

4 Experiments

4.1 Experimental Settings

We first asked human annotators to judge whether 115,125 predicate instances sampled from tweets were negated. Table 3 shows the number of instances in the training and test sets. Instances whose source is tweets in the table were extracted from tweets posted during within one month after the Great East Japan Earthquake (from March 11 2011 to April 11 2011) and instances whose source is artificial in the table were manually composed of tweet-like texts that included typical examples of complex forms of negations to expand the number of complex negations. Note that we also used the training set as the development set for parameter tuning by 5-fold cross-validation. All of the test set instances were extracted from tweets and there was no overlap between the training and test sets.

In both sets, each predicate was annotated by a single annotator by the following steps:

1. We annotated predicates based on Iida et al. (2007). All of the verbs and adjectives were annotated as predicates, and some nouns were annotated as nominal predicates.
2. We annotated negation by the negation cues surrounding the predicate. Both such functional expressions as "ない nai (not)" and such content words as "嘘_だ uso_da (it is doubtful that)" are used as negation cues.
3. The predicates (interpreted by the annotator as negated by the cues) are annotated as negated predicates and used as positive instances for SVM, and the others are used as negative instances.

Note that recognizing negated instances as either simple or complex is done automatically based on the definitions described in Section 1.

In all the experiments, we used LIBSVM (Chang and Lin, 2011) with a degree 2 polynomial kernel, where gamma = 1 and cost = 0.001, which worked best in our preliminary experiments. We set the remaining parameters to the tool's default values.

4.2 Baseline Methods

We conducted experiments using three baselines and created two baseline systems built on rule- and machine learning-based methods. We also adapted a method (de Marneffe et al., 2012) that recognizes veridicality and negation.

Rule is a simple rule-based method that regards a predicate as "negated" only when any of the negation words in Tables 1 and 2 are found in a window of seven words on each side of the target predicate as well as the target predicate itself.

ML uses the SVM classifier with the four features described in Section 3: basic, negation words, sentiment, and following words.

Marneffe12 predicts the veridicality of the propositions written in a sentence as well as the negation recognition. We replicated their features, except the "world knowledge" feature that captures the subject of the target predicate. In the following, we describe how to apply these features to Japanese.

Predicate classes Some words are often used to introduce the factuality of events. For instance, given "He confirmed that she will come," "confirmed" indicates that the factuality of "come" is certainty. We translated 779 words with 38 classes (Saurí, 2008) into 4,110 words in Japanese. We used the class name and the original form of the word as binary features to detect whether the target predicate is led by one of these words.

General features We used the original forms of the predicate and the sentence's root.

Modality features We identified such modal expressions as "かも kamo (might)" in two *bunsetsus* in a dependency, where the head *bunsetsu* contains the target predicate. The other modal expressions found elsewhere in the sentence are marked as different features.

Negation We used both SNW and CNW to find negation words.

Conditional We examined whether the predicates are in an *if*-clause and checked whether they end with "たら tara (if)" or "れば reba (if)" and words indicating *if*-clauses such as "もし moshi (if)" and "仮に karini (if)."

Quotation We also checked whether the sentence opened and ended with quotation marks.

Originally, de Marneffe et al. (2012) used the maximum entropy classifier (Berger et al., 1996).

Method	Precision (%)		Recall (%)		F-score (%)
Rule	8.01	(1071 / 13377)	44.81	(1071 / 2390)	13.59
Marneffe12	14.62	(371 / 2538)	15.52	(371 / 2390)	15.06
ML	77.43	(621 / 802)	25.98	(621 / 2390)	38.91
ML + web-d350	76.84	(617 / 803)	25.82	(617 / 2390)	38.65
ML + wikipedia-d250	76.89	(632 / 822)	26.44	(632 / 2390)	39.35
ML + twitter-d300	77.28	(643 / 832)	26.90	(643 / 2390)	39.91
ML + all	71.40	(839 / 1175)	35.10	(839 / 2390)	47.07
Proposed	69.81	(867 / 1242)	36.28	(867 / 2390)	**47.74**

Table 4: Results on the training set by 5-fold cross-validation

Method	Precision (%)		Recall (%)		F-score (%)
web d300 n2000	78.09	(613 / 785)	25.65	(613 / 2390)	38.61
wikipedia d500 n2000	77.42	(617 / 797)	25.82	(617 / 2390)	38.72
twitter d200 n2000	77.56	(622 / 802)	26.03	(622 / 2390)	38.97
noun-cls n2000	77.12	(691 / 896)	28.91	(691 / 2390)	42.06

Table 5: Comparison to other clustering methods on the training set by 5-fold cross-validation

We used SVM as a classifier with the same parameters as our proposed method described in Section 3.

4.3 Proposed Methods

In our proposed method, we used all of the features described in Section 3 along with all of the cluster IDs obtained using the Wikipedia, Tweets, and Web sets. Table 4 shows the results of our proposed methods, some baselines, and our method without certain types of features on the training set by 5-fold cross-validation. Although both simple and complex negations are used as positive instances for SVM, we evaluated only complex negations.

The comparison between "Rule" and "ML" suggests that a predicate is not always negated even if it is surrounded by negation words. There are two reasons for poor performance of "Rule." The first is false matching of simple negation words for idiomatic expressions. For instance, "思いがけ_ない omoigake_nai (unexpected)" contains the negation word "ない nai (not)" at the end of the word but it does not express negation in Japanese. The second is a double negative. For instance, "間違い_ない machigai_nai (it is not incorrect)" contains two negation words "間違う machigau (incorrect)" and "ない nai (not)" but it does not express negation and roughly corresponds to "it is correct." The comparison between "Marneffe12" and "ML" suggests that it is infeasible to cover various negation words and their n-grams using word lists organized manually.

The "ML+web-d350," "ML+wikipedia-d250," and "ML+twitter-d300" columns indicate the performance of using the n-gram cluster features with three types of corpora. The n-gram cluster feature generated from Twitter outperforms the other two corpora. The "ML+all" column indicates using three corpora at once. These features are distinguished by their sources. It outperforms the other settings of using each corpora. The comparisons between the "ML" and "ML+all" and "Marneffe12" and "ML+all" suggest that n-gram clusters successfully generalize complex negations forms by their cluster IDs.

We compare our n-gram clustering method with "noun-cls," another clustering method that was proposed by Kazama and Torisawa (2008). We applied their clustering algorithm to nouns extracted from roughly six hundred million Web documents. The Web documents that we used for our clustering are a subset of these documents. The variation of words in the noun-cluster is wider than in other clusters. We set the clustering number to 2,000 in our n-gram clustering method and "noun-cls." Table 5 compares the clustering method and the corpora that we used. We tried eight dimensions (50, 100, 150, 200, 250, 300, 350, and 500), and the number of dimensions in Table 5 achieved the best performance for each corpus. The "noun-cls" column outperformed the other clusters. This suggests that generalization by noun-cluster is more effective than n-gram clusters for complex negation recognition because the noun-cluster has more various words than the others. In future work, we will generate n-gram clusters from large-scale documents.

4.4 Results on the Test Set

We trained a classifier using the whole training set as training data and applied it to our test set. Table 6 shows the performance of the following seven methods. Here, "Proposed" indicates the performance of our proposed method, and "Rule" is the perfor-

Method	Precision (%)		Recall (%)		F-score (%)
Proposed	64.04	(114 / 178)	29.01	(114 / 393)	**39.93**
Rule	10.43	(220 / 2109)	55.98	(220 / 393)	17.59
ablation test					
$-n$-gram-cls	71.57	(73 / 102)	18.58	(73 / 393)	29.49
−noun-cls	62.96	(102 / 162)	25.95	(102 / 393)	36.76
−basic	73.04	(84 / 115)	21.37	(84 / 393)	33.07
−following	66.23	(100 / 151)	25.45	(100 / 393)	36.76
−negation	63.25	(105 / 166)	26.72	(105 / 393)	37.57
−sentiment	61.59	(101 / 164)	25.70	(101 / 393)	36.27
$-n$-gram-cls+uni-gram-cls	63.75	(102 / 160)	25.95	(102 / 393)	36.89

Table 6: Results on the test set

納豆が放射能に効くという都市伝説があったりも There's also this urban legend saying that natto (Japanese food made from fermented soybeans) **is effective** against radiation.
避難所で物資横流しが起きてるってツイートしてる奴、北斗の拳の見すぎ〜 The guy who tweeted that there **is some supplies black market** at the shelters, (I'm sure) he watched too much of "Fist of the North Star" (Japanese dystopic SF animation)
国会議事堂が破壊されたなんてほざいてるバカいるの Is there really an idiot who said that the National Diet (building) **was destroyed**?

Table 7: Examples of output

mance of a rule-based baseline method, which regards a predicate as "negated" only when any words of SNW and CNW in Tables 1 and 2 are found in a 14-word window centered on the predicate. The proposed method achieved more than 20% improvement in F-score over the rule-based method for complex negations.

Our ablation test on the test set is shown in "ablation test." For each result, one of the features is ablated. The "$-n$gram-cls+uni-gram-cls" column indicates that we only generalized a uni-gram (i.e., single word). This setting confirms the effect of n-gram generalization. In the ablation test, the results indicate that every feature was effective. In other words, lower performance was observed after removing each feature. The comparison between the proposed method and the method without cluster IDs "-n-gram-cls" suggests that cluster IDs are useful for recognizing complex types of negations. The comparison between the proposed method and the method without 2,3,4-gram generalization "$-n$-gram-cls+uni-gram-cls" suggests that n-gram generalization is effective for complex negation recognition. For instance, an n-gram cluster of Wikipedia has such uni-grams as "不正確である fuseikakudearu (incorrect)" and "不完全である fukanzendearu (incomplete)" as synonyms of bi-gram "正しく_ない tadashiku_nai (not correct)."

We also show in Table 7 three negated predicates extracted from real tweets that were not properly recognized by either the rule-based method or the machine learning method without the n-gram clusters, but they were correctly classified by our method.

5 Simulation of Disaster Situation

We constructed our data set from tweets in the month following the Great East Japan Earthquake. Since that the purpose of negation recognition is to detect false rumors during a disaster, taking one month to annotate the data and to train classifiers is too long. Therefore, we simulated the situation as in Figure 2.

Before 3/10	We do not have any annotated corpus.
14:46 at 3/11	The earthquake occurred. Start annotation.
14:00 at 3/13	Stop annotation. Now we have annotated the data extracted from tweets posted two days just after the earthquake.
After 14:00 at 3/13	Start negation recognition using the trained classifier with the annotated data.

Figure 2: Simulation settings

We re-organized the composition of the training and the test sets as follows:

- Training set 2 contains 626 complex negation instances extracted from tweets posted from 14:00 3/11 to 14:00 3/13,
- Test set 2 contains 1,269 complex negation instances extracted from tweets posted after 14:00 3/13.

Note that some tweets have been posted before 14:00 3/11 and they are not used in this experiments.

In this case, we should make the classifier more specific to the disaster that actually occurred; the previous experiments considered a general situation. We experimented with two approaches.

Method	Precision (%)		Recall (%)		F-score (%)
Proposed	48.96	(212 / 433)	16.71	(212 / 1269)	24.91
+twitter2days	46.41	(220 / 474)	17.34	(220 / 1269)	25.24
+content	52.49	(253 / 482)	19.94	(253 / 1269)	28.90
+twitter2days+content	51.64	(268 / 519)	21.12	(268 / 1269)	**29.98**

Table 8: Results of disaster situation simulation

The first approach obtained another set of n-gram clusters using all the tweets posted in the two days (4.8GB) denoted by twitter2days. We set the number of vector dimensions to 300 and the number of clusters to 10,000. This set of clusters has more specific synonymous words than the other clusters obtained for tweets not in the disaster. For instance, "雨 ame (rain)" has many expressions that are synonyms only in this disaster, such as "汚染_さ_れた_雨 osen_sa_reta_ame, 黒い_雨 kuroi_ame, 有害な_雨 yugaina_ame, 有毒な雨 yudokuna_ame (all of which mean toxic rain)," while in other clusters "雨 ame (rain)" has general synonyms, such as "小雨 kosame (light rain)," "冷たい_雨 tsumetai_ame (cold rain)," and "大雨 ohame (heavy rain)." These specific synonyms were obtained because the following false rumor was disseminated and repeated for a long period: "There may be toxic rain due to an explosion at Cosmo Oil."

The second approach uses target predicates and their arguments for feature generation. Some false rumors were disseminated and repeated for a long periods, such as "Drinking iodine protects against radiation." There were also many tweets to negate such false rumors. Therefore, we used the content of the false rumors for training to recognize other negated predicates whose content is the same as the trained ones. We modified the "following words" and "n-gram clusters" features to use not only the seven words that follow the target predicate but also the target predicate itself.

We had to choose two parameters: the number of vector dimensions and the number of clusters for four corpora: web, wikipedia, twitter, and twitter2days. We chose the same numbers of the previous experiment for the three former corpora and chose 300 as the dimension and 10,000 as the number of clusters for the last one that is identical to twitter in the general situation.

Table 8 shows the results. The "+twitter2days d300 n10000" column indicates that we used the extra n-gram cluster and outperformed "Proposed," which had the best setting in the previous experiments. Even if we have a limited amount of annotated data in the disaster, large un-annotated corpora can improve the performance of complex negation recognition. Note that the performance of complex negation recognition is lower than the previous experiments since we used a smaller annotated corpus in this simulation.

The "+content" column indicates that we modified the features to capture the content of the predicate, and the "+twitter2days+content" column indicates that we used the extra n-gram cluster with the content features. The comparisons between "Proposed" and "+content" and "+twitter2days" and "+twitter2days+content" suggest that when many tweets are disseminated and repeated for a long periods about particular topics, we must use content words.

6 Conclusion

We presented a method for recognizing negations on Twitter and showed that n-gram clusters derived from large un-annotated corpora obtained by word2vec are effective for capturing complex types of negations, like the negations of "occur" in the sentence "The guy who tweeted that a nuclear explosion occurred has watched too many SF movies." We also simulated the situation of the Great East Japan Earthquake in 2011. We used annotated data posted within two days after the earthquake for training, and we also recognized negation for tweets posted on other days. We found that using un-annotated data for the "n-gram clusters" feature and the capturing contents are effective for negation recognition. We are going to implement a false rumor detection system by integrating our proposed method with the rule-based method. We expect our system to be useful in future disaster situations.

Acknowledgments

This work was partially supported by the Council for Science, Technology and Innovation (CSTI) through the Cross-ministerial Strategic Innovation Promotion Program (SIP), titled "Enhancement of societal resiliency against natural disasters" (Funding agency: JST).

References

Adam L Berger, Vincent J Della Pietra, and Stephen A Della Pietra. 1996. A maximum entropy approach to natural language processing. *Computational linguistics*, 22(1):39–71.

Chih-Chung Chang and Chih-Jen Lin. 2011. LIBSVM: A library for support vector machines. *ACM Transactions on Intelligent Systems and Technology*, 2:27:1–27:27. Software available at `http://www.csie.ntu.edu.tw/~cjlin/libsvm`.

Marie-Catherine de Marneffe, Christopher D. Manning, and Christopher Potts. 2012. Did it happen? The pragmatic complexity of veridicality assessment. *Computational Linguistics*, 38(2):301–333.

Ryu Iida, Mamoru Komachi, Kentaro Inui, and Yuji Matsumoto. 2007. Annotating a Japanese text corpus with predicate-argument and coreference relations. In *Proceedings of the Linguistic Annotation Workshop*, pages 132–139.

Jun'ichi Kazama and Kentaro Torisawa. 2008. Inducing gazetteers for named entity recognition by large-scale clustering of dependency relations. In *Proceedings of ACL-08: HLT*, pages 407–415, Columbus, Ohio, June. Association for Computational Linguistics.

Taku Kudo, Kaoru Yamamoto, and Yuji Matsumoto. 2004. Applying conditional random fields to Japanese morphological analysis. In *EMNLP*, volume 4, pages 230–237.

Sadao Kurohashi, Toshihisa Nakamura, Yuji Matsumoto, and Makoto Nagao. 1994. Improvements of Japanese morphological analyzer JUMAN. In *Proceedings of The International Workshop on Sharable Natural Language*, pages 22–28.

Tomas Mikolov, Ilya Sutskever, Kai Chen, Greg S Corrado, and Jeff Dean. 2013. Distributed representations of words and phrases and their compositionality. In C.J.C. Burges, L. Bottou, M. Welling, Z. Ghahramani, and K.Q. Weinberger, editors, *Advances in Neural Information Processing Systems 26*, pages 3111–3119. Curran Associates, Inc.

Jong-Hoon Oh, Kentaro Torisawa, Chikara Hashimoto, Takuya Kawada, Stijn De Saeger, Jun'ichi Kazama, and Yiou Wang. 2012. Why question answering using sentiment analysis and word classes. In *Proceedings of the 2012 Joint Conference on Empirical Methods in Natural Language Processing and Computational Natural Language Learning*, pages 368–378. Association for Computational Linguistics.

James Pustejovsky, Patrick Hanks, Roser Sauri, Andrew See, Robert Gaizauskas, Andrea Setzer, Dragomir Radev, Beth Sundheim, David Day, Lisa Ferro, et al. 2003. The timebank corpus. In *Corpus linguistics*, volume 2003, page 40.

Roser Saurí and James Pustejovsky. 2007. Determining modality and factuality for text entailment. In *First IEEE International Conference on Semantic Computing*, pages 509–516. IEEE.

Roser Saurí and James Pustejovsky. 2009. FactBank: A corpus annotated with event factuality. *Language resources and evaluation*, 43(3):227–268.

Roser Saurí. 2008. *A factuality profiler for eventualities in text*. Ph.D. thesis, Brandeis University.

Sandeep Soni, Tanushree Mitra, Eric Gilbert, and Jacob Eisenstein. 2014. Modeling factuality judgments in social media text. In *Proceedings of the 52nd Annual Meeting of the Association for Computational Linguistics (Volume 2: Short Papers)*, pages 415–420, Baltimore, Maryland, June. Association for Computational Linguistics.

Vladimir Vapnik. 2000. *The nature of statistical learning theory*. Springer Science & Business Media.

Naoki Yoshinaga and Masaru Kitsuregawa. 2009. Polynomial to linear: Efficient classification with conjunctive features. In *Proceedings of the 2009 Conference on Empirical Methods in Natural Language Processing*, pages 1542–1551.

Topic Model for Identifying Suicidal Ideation in Chinese Microblog

Xiaolei Huang[1], **Xin Li**[1], **Lei Zhang**[2], **Tianli Liu**[3], **David Chiu**[4], **Tingshao Zhu***[5,6]
[1]Computer Network Information Center, Chinese Academy of Sciences (CAS), China,
{xlhuang, lixin}@cashq.ac.cn
[2]Jinan University, China, zl.ramiel@gmail.com
[3]Inst. of Population Research, Peking University, China, tianli.liu@pku.edu.cn
[4]Dept. of Math and Computer Science, University of Puget Sound, USA,
dchiu@pugetsound.edu
[5]Inst. of Psychology, CAS China, tszhu@psych.ac.cn
[6]Inst. of Computing Technology, CAS China

Abstract

Suicide is one of major public health problems worldwide. Traditionally, suicidal ideation is assessed by surveys or interviews, which lacks of a real-time assessment of personal mental state. Online social networks, with large amount of user-generated data, offer opportunities to gain insights of suicide assessment and prevention. In this paper, we explore potentiality to identify and monitor suicide expressed in microblog on social networks. First, we identify users who have committed suicide and collect millions of microblogs from social networks. Second, we build suicide psychological lexicon by psychological standards and word embedding technique. Third, by leveraging both language styles and online behaviors, we employ Topic Model and other machine learning algorithms to identify suicidal ideation. Our approach achieves the best results on topic-500, yielding $F_1-measure$ of 80.0%, Precision of 87.1%, Recall of 73.9%, and Accuracy of 93.2%. Furthermore, a prototype system for monitoring suicidal ideation on several social networks is deployed.

1 Introduction

Suicide is a severe health problem worldwide, which is one of leading causes of youth death in the world, especially in China. In the latest report (Organization and others, 2014) from World Health Organization (*WHO*), over 800,000 people committed suicide in 2012, including 120,730 Chinese; and it is very likely that the data is underestimated. Indeed, there are many more people who attempt suicide every year. Instead of calling health services or seeking for help in-person, choosing social networks is a preferable choice for some suicide because of privacy and facilitating sharing similar experiences among peers (Luxton et al., 2011).

Social network sites (*SNS*), such as Twitter, Sina Weibo, have become popular platforms for people to express themselves. Sina Weibo is a Chinese leading social network akin to Twitter. According to the latest Sina Weibo User Activity Report (http://data.weibo.com/report/reportDetail?id=215), Weibo now has more than 70 million active users per day, and over 160 million active users per month. It becomes a great platform for sharing opinions, emotions, and even to breaking news or public events. Recent work (Fu et al., 2013) showed that *SNS* not only enhanced our connections with others, but also facilitated selective self-presentation of undesirable behaviors, such as suicide.

The association between social media and suicide has drawn public attention recently, since several actual suicidal cases were reported in Sina Weibo, e.g., (http://news.sina.com.cn/zl/zatan/2014-12-02/18032759.shtml). However, new approaches towards online suicide ideation monitoring and prevention are still under development. (Fu et al., 2013) suggested that diffusion of microblogs about one's suicidal ideation or behaviors on social networks might serve as an early indication of a person's mental state. These indicators include one's writing through style, format, selection of specific words, and general

29th Pacific Asia Conference on Language, Information and Computation pages 553 - 562
Shanghai, China, October 30 - November 1, 2015

structure. It would therefore be desirable to build an appropriate suicide-monitoring system, to identify people who gave expressed suicidal ideation on *SNS* and provide follow-up support and services.

In this paper, we propose to detect suicide ideation in Chinese *SNS* and explore the possibility of using Topic Model (Blei et al., 2003). In particular, we first collect and evaluate suicidal microblogs by psychological standards. Second, we construct our psychological lexicons using word embedding techniques and explore the differences of online behaviors between suicide and none-suicide Weibo users. Then, in order to avoid the adverse outcomes that high dimensions of lexicon feature, which could weaken both efficiency and accuracy of classifiers, we model features of microblog in social networks and utilize the popular unsupervised model, Topic Model. Finally we design, develop, and test a model that can effectively identify suicidal ideation in *SNS*.

To summarize, our research has three main contributions: first, we use word embedding technique to construct psychological lexicons to enable utilization of suicide online behaviours; second, we employ Topic Model with lexicon knowledge and hybrid approaches for suicidal ideation identification on real-world datasets; third, a real-time application of suicide ideation prototype monitoring system is deployed online.

2 Related Work

Psychologists' researches on suicide cases in social networks started in recent years. Research (Fu et al., 2013) found that social media not only can spread suicidal ideation very quickly, but it also can be used to identify suicidal ideation in its early stages. Psychologists (Jashinsky et al., 2013) implied that evaluating suicidal risk factors in Twitter can be used to prevent suicide. Undoubtedly, previous research (Li et al., 2014b; Guan et al., 2014; Li et al., 2014b) also have dug interesting patterns for suicide prevention, however, these patterns can not be deployed on large population to provide timely service.

"Sentiment Analysis"(Pang and Lee, 2008) has been researched on various corpus for years, such as product reviews (Wang et al., 2010), movie reviews (Whitelaw et al., 2005). The core method in most of previous works (Pestian et al., 2010; Pestian et al., 2012) in this field is using $N-Gram$ (Brown et al., 1992) to model clinical suicide note. Another promising approach to learn sentiment from microblogs is *LDA* (Blei et al., 2003), a unsupervised algorithm that takes documents as a mixture of topics. It can discover latent semantics in documents and compute documents into a low-dimensional topic distributions. The potentiality of using topic models also has been applied in sentiment analysis (Mei et al., 2007; Lin and He, 2009).

Mental Health problems have been attracted much attention from researchers all over the world. Wu *et al.* (Wu et al., 2005) mined depressive symptoms from psychiatric consultation records. Researches on depression in *SNS* have been studied in single depression case (Wang et al., 2013), multimedia content of depressive microblogs (Lin et al., 2014), depression research in Twitter (De Choudhury et al., 2013) or mining emotion labels from social texts (Yu and Ho, 2014). Researchers (Resnik et al., 2013) applied *LDA* on essay's depression judgement among college students and compared its effectiveness with *LIWC*.

Given much research have been done on suicide ideation and sentiment analysis, and they have produced much promising results, which inspire us to investigate efficient methods to better understand and identify suicidal ideation on *SNS*.

3 Data Collection

We trained model on data collected through our Java-based crawler from Sina Weibo. We collected publicly reported suicide cases from 2011 to 2014, and spent another 6 months collecting and tagging their data. Based on evaluation criteria (Rudd et al., 2006), six experts first summarized and evaluated 12 warning signs of suicide, such as threatening to hurt or kill themselves. Those experts were trained to ensure the lowest biased tagging. They spent significant time in assessment and diagnosis of suicide risk. Before tagging data, the experts were tested by tagging 50 microblogs independently; and the test's interrater agreement coefficient[1] is 0.819.

[1]Kendall's W: a statistic, ranged from 0 to 1, can be used for assessing agreement among raters. The higher score, more agreements among raters are reached.

For each piece of microblog, only if it was voted by more than half of the experts, it would be tagged as suicidal microblog. During tagging process, each suicidal microblog has three levels: there is suicide warning sign, but no suicide plan; microblog indicates suicide plan, but author is not going to commit it; microblog indicates the author is going to commit suicide. Since we only focus on binary classification in this study, all three levels will be consider as suicide. Finally, 664 suicidal microblogs were obtained from over 30,000 microblogs.

Table 1: The composition of experiment data

All	Suicide	Non-suicide
7,314	664	6,650

To perform 10-fold cross validation, we randomly sampled 6,650 microblogs from a Weibo User Pool (WUP) (Li et al., 2014a) with 1.06 million active users' microblogs, which share the same time interval. Statistics of the data is illustrated in Table 1.

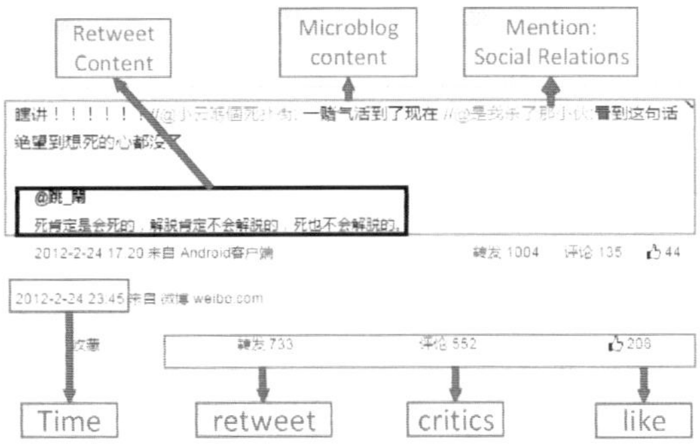

Figure 1: Detail Descriptions of One Microblog

Microblogs were segmented and tokenized using *Ansj* (Sun, 2014), a Chinese segmentation tool. *URLs* were removed by regular expression rules. In Fig. 1, we present an example of microblog. For each microblog, we extracted both content related features and meta features (i.e., time, like, *etc*).

3.1 Traditional & Simplified Chinese Conversion

Currently, there are two types of Chinese encoding: Simplified Chinese and Traditional Chinese. Words have the same meaning but different encodings, so computer program treats them differently. We converted Traditional Chinese into Simplified Chinese in our research.

4 Lexicons Construction

Primarily, we took advantage of existing sentiment dictionary, the latest version of *HowNet* (Dong and Dong, 2003), which is a Chinese-based emotional-words resource for sentiment analysis. *HowNet* is designed for general sentiment analysis.

Intuitively, words with similar contexts or co-occurrence may share similar meanings (Turney and Pantel, 2010). In order to extended our existing suicide lexicons and take advantage of words contextual information, we run word2vec (Mikolov et al., 2013) over 100 millions microblogs from WUP by the following steps: first, we segmented and tokenized corpus, and trained vector features for each word; top 5 semantic synonyms were chosen empirically for each word in our existing lexicons (each synonym was chosen if at least half of our experts reached agreement); we elaborately collected words into our extended suicide dictionary. Examples of suicide dictionary are shown in Table 2.

Table 2: Suicide Lexicon Table

Type	Number	Example
Suicide Words	3453	insomnia, stilnox
Suicide Phrases	3763	disapear+myself

We categorized suicide words and phrases according to 12 suicide warning signs, which differs from categories in previous work (Gao et al., 2013). Details of 12 potential suicide warning signs can be found in (Rudd et al., 2006), such as "Acting reckless" . Because when we associate each word or phrase with one or more warning signs, words or phrases become more interpretable and might describe more details of suicide.

We also extended our suicide lexicons by adding references such as I, me, mom and so on. (Li et al., 2014b) found that self-reference was used more common among suicide than none suicide's microblog. We found that suicidal ideation words (*i.e.* death, depression or estazolam) always co-occur with some particular words, such as "I", "psychologist", or "medicine". Furthermore, suicide prefer to mention their families or other suicidal victims. The statistics of reference comparison between suicide and none suicide is shown in Table 3.

Table 3: Statistics of Reference Comparison

Type	Self-reference	Other-reference
Suicide	71%	29%
None Suicide	26%	22%
Example	I, myself	Dad, mother

5 Modeling

5.1 Knowledge-based Modeling

In order to take advantage of domain knowledge from psychology, the extended suicide lexicons was also used. These features are based on its subjectivity, sentiments or categories. It contains both positive and negative words. In addition, we added reference including both self-reference and other-reference as an independent category in the modeling process. For any input sentence, we count the numbers of positive, negative, suicide words, reference words according to our lexicon resources.

5.2 Syntactic Features

Syntactic features contains dependency relation, Part of Speech (POS) tagging, *etc*. Considering that some types of words or their POS(e.g., adverbs, adjectives, *etc*) are likely to convey sentiments, we obtained POS features by counting the numbers of words with the following POS tags: adjective (VA), adverb (AD), noun (NN/NR/NT), verb (VV/VE/VC), pronoun (PN) and preposition (P). Those tagging signs are from Chinese Penn Treebank Tag Set[2].

Table 4: Syntactic Features Comparison Table

Type	Suicide POS	None Suicide POS
Adjective	2.10%	1.63%
Adverb	18.50%	11.52%
Noun	20.56%	37.21%
Verb	29.95%	26.75%
Pronoun	10.36%	4.21%
Preposition	2.77%	2.98%
Total	84.24%	84.30%

[2]http://www.cis.upenn.edu/\~chinese/posguide.3rd.ch.pdf

We applied Stanford Parser (Toutanova et al., 2003) to acquire the statistics of POS. The statistics of data is illustrated in Table 4. Two observations were derived from the Table 4: in suicide microblogs, the users prefer to mention self-reference or other people than in none suicidal microblogs; more adverb, more verb and adjective appear in suicidal microblogs may suggest people with suicidal ideation would like to express more about their emotions or behaviors in their microblogs.

5.3 Topic Modeling

Another approach we used in our experiment is Latent Dirichlet Allocation (*LDA*) (Blei et al., 2003). It can generate predefined topics over the "bag of words" and infer topic distributions in new documents. We are interested in incorporating sentiment dictionary with topic models to make topics more interpretable. Part of LDA-induced topics are shown in Table 5.

Table 5: Part of LDA-induced topics related to suicide

Themes	Topic Words
Depression	me, depression, leave, bye
Stress & Negative	death, I won't love fear of death, to die
Anxiety	long, desperate, take medicine
Family	Mother, Father
Sadness & Hopeless	dead, don't, one day pain, past, wrong
Reference	me, we, myself, you

5.4 Topic Model with More Layers

In this paper, we hypothesize that non-sentiment words around implicit sentiment words could be affected, which may be interpreted as sentiment-propagation from word-to-word. Derived from *LDA*, sentiment associated the topic will also be reflected by its associated sentiment words. Motivated by these observations, we implemented a new approach, which adopts sentiment dictionaries into the topic model.

As illustrated in Fig. 2, the basic idea is that each suicide microblog may contain multiple topics, and each topic may associate with one or several suicide keywords. From the topic perspective, a topic associating with sentiment words could be identified as sentiment topic. Thus, words, associated with sentiment words within the same topic, convey some sort of sentiment, which could be viewed as the process of sentiment propagation. Each microblog has several topics labeled by sentiment words following different multinomial distributions. Therefore, a suicidal-sentiment layer can be extracted from annotating each sentiment word and computing the sentiment polarity that is associated with words and topics in documents.

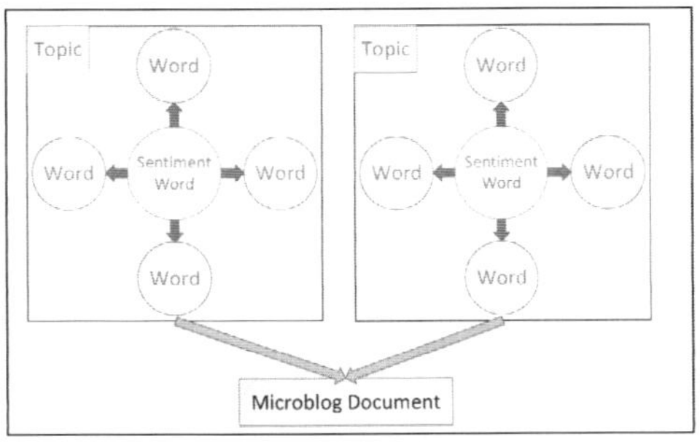

Figure 2: Basic Idea of Sentiment Propagation

While training model, psychological dictionaries are incorporated into topic modeling. The sentiment layer in our approach associates with both topic and word. Each topic associates with more sentiment words. From this perspective, the process of computing the sentiment layer could be viewed as mining for sentiments from documents and labeling suicidal words to topics on behalf of psychologists. For example, as illustrated in Fig. 3, if one microblog is about "Insomnia" and "Dysthymia", then intuitively, the topics within that microblog could be annotated by keywords, which are associated with psychological dictionaries. In general, the sentiment layer can be viewed as describing a group of words that represent a psychological mental state.

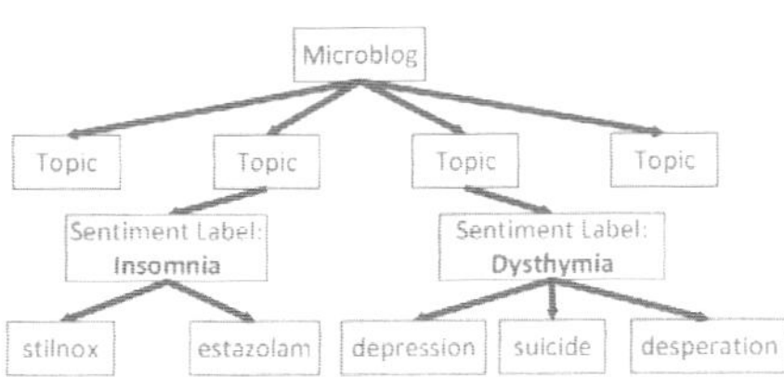

Figure 3: Extend sentiment words with dictionary

Our proposed algorithm is presented in Algorithm 1. We first load the map of sentiment words with their initial polarity, $Lexicon_p$, from lexicons. We scan each microblog and annotate sentiment words within microblog. Then the labeled word will be enriched with more sentiment words, which is measured by initial sentiment polarity. Next a matrix of the data's topic multinomial probabilities, $TopicProb$, and the map of topic alphabet, $Topic_{alphabet}$, are inferenced. K is the number of topics.

Algorithm 1 Process of recomputing Topic Model

Ensure:
  Matrix of Topic Distributions, $TopicProb$;
1: Build and load $Lexicon_p$;
2: Scan each microblog and label sentiment words;
3: Label word with psychological lexicons;
4: Recompute Topic Probabilities, $TopicProb$;
5: Recompute Topic alphabets, $Topic_{alphabet}$;
6: Iterate $Topic_{alphabet}$, calculate $Polarity_k$ for each topic
7: Normalize $Polarity_k$ matrix;
8: **for** each topic multinomial probability in $TopicProb$ **do**
9:   Recompute probability using $Polarity_k$;
10:   Update topic probability in $TopicProb$;
11: **end for**
12: **return** $TopicProb$;

$$Polarity_k = \log\left(e^{\left(\sum_{k,w} P_{wk}\right) e^{\frac{N_{ws}}{N_w}} - \frac{\sum_{k,w} \tilde{P}_{wk}}{e^{\frac{N_{ws}}{N_w}}}} \right) \quad (1)$$

The $Polarity_k$ encodes the sentiment-topic polarity for the kth topic of the microblog. P_{wk} is the initial weight of negative word w appears in k^{th} topic, and $\tilde{P}_{wk}$ refers to initial weight of the positive word, respectively. According to (Kay et al., 1987), positive information would reduce the influence of negative emotion. However, researchers (Martin et al., 1993) found that negative effects bring longer and deeper impacts than positive effects. We thus use $e^{\frac{N_{ws}}{N_w}}$ to simulate the cumulative impact of negative sentiment impact, where N_{ws} refers to the frequency of the word w appearing in the kth topic, and

N_w refers to the number of words associated with k^{th} topic.

Given the normalized sentiment matrix at step 7, we incorporate it with original topic multinomial distribution in step 8. We recompute the topic multinomial distribution to simulate the sentiment-diffusion process as shown back in Fig. 2.

5.5 Meta Features within Microblogs

Although previous work (Lin et al., 2014) reported detecting depression from pictures in microblog, in our dataset, microblogs rarely contain pictures, thus we mainly focused on text content. We also observed that the number of critics, like, retweet surged after the suicide was reported publicly. Thus, we took three meta features into consideration: *posting type*, *posting time* and *social relationship*. Detail descriptions can be found in Fig. 1.

5.5.1 Posting Type

The posting type refers to one microblog's origin, either *original creation* or *retweet*. In our research, it appears that suicidal users prefer to post original suicide notes instead of retweeting. The comparisons in experimental data are shown in Fig. 4.

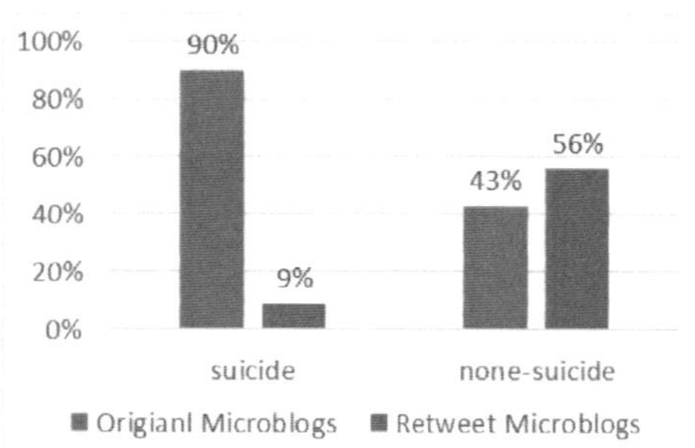

Figure 4: Comparisons in Microblog's Type

5.5.2 Posting Time

We also found that temporal features matter. Empirically, we separated 24 hours into four periods: 23:00 to 06:00, 07:00 to 13:00, 14:00 to 18:00, and 18:00 to 23:00. The result shows that suicidal microblogs are posted more frequently during 23:00 to 06:00 and less in the morning, which is in contrast to none suicidal microblogs. Specific details can be gleaned from Fig. 5. A plausible explanation might be that some suicidal users suffer from insomnia, which hypnotic pills appear in their microblogs, such as tranquillizers or stilnox.

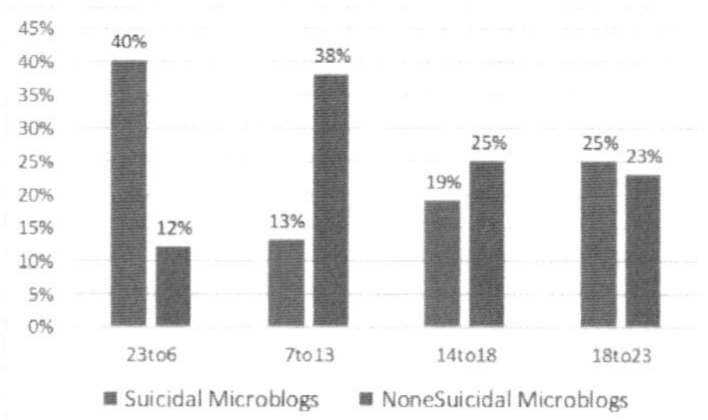

Figure 5: Comparisons in Microblogs' Time

5.5.3 Social Relationships

Microblogs also contain much useful information like social relationships, which connect microblogs to microblogs, or microblogs to users, as shown in Figure 6.

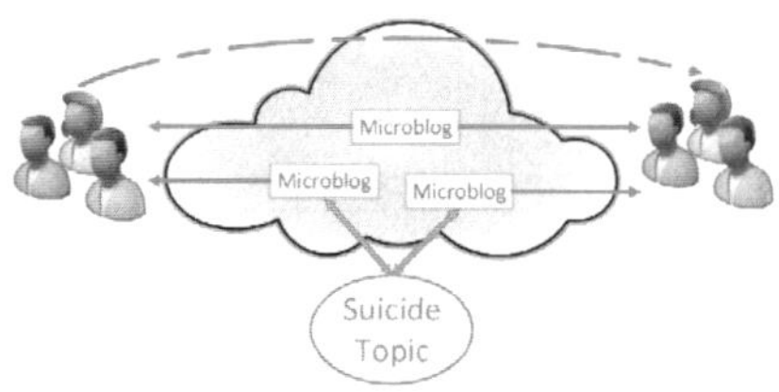

Figure 6: Social Relations within Microblogs

There is one major social relationship existed in microblog: mention. People use "@" to mention individuals or group of individuals. In addition, retweeting microblogs also generate mention behavior. According to our study, we found that several users mentioned other suicide before committing suicide. From this perspective, it could be explained by part of suicidal ideation diffusion and suicide mimic engagement among social networks (Fu et al., 2013). We employed binary value to indicate whether the microblogs have relationship with other suicide or suicide related subjects.

6 Experiment and Discussion

6.1 Experiment Approach

In the experiment, we run *LDA* (implemented by Mallet (McCallum, 2002)) to infer *k*-topic probabilities and alphabet associated with each topic. Mallet's parameters were set with default values, and stoplist was extended by Chinese punctuations. We trained *SVM* classifier by using *LibSVM* (Chang and Lin, 2011) package. The *SVM* classifier in our experiments used a *RBF* kernel and was trained by default parameter values. Weka (Hall et al., 2009), an useful machine learning tools, was also employed in our experiment for training and testing.

We run 10-fold cross validation to avoid evaluation bias. In Table 6, we list all features that were selected for training classification models in our experiment.

Table 6: Summarization of Features in Experiment

Feature	Compute Method
Knowledge-based Features	Count * Lexicon polarity
Syntactic Features	Count
Topic Model	Topic Distributions
Advanced Topic Model	Topic Distributions
Posting Type	Binary Value
Posting Time	Intervals
Social Relationships	Binary Value
N-gram	Count

The performance of classification are measured by "Precision", "Recall", "$F_1 - measure$", "Accuracy". "Precision" refers to the ratio of true suicidal microblogs against all microblogs predicted as suicidal. "Recall" refers to the fraction of suicidal instances retrieved by trained models. "Accuracy" refers to all predictions match their labels regardless whether they are suicidal microblogs or not. "$F_1 - measure$" is defined as follows 2.

$$F_1 - measure = 2 * \frac{precision * recall}{precision + recall} \quad (2)$$

6.2 Comparison between Lexicons and *LDA*

The Lexicon approach uses psychological lexicons, described in Section 3, to extract lexicon features and train the classifiers. We run *LDA* with number of topics from 100 to 1000 topics with increment of 100 (*i.e.* 100, 200, ..., 1000). Comparison of classification performance is presented in Table 7.

Table 7: Comparison between Prior-knowledge-based Features and *LDA* approach

Topics	F_1	Precision	Recall	Accuracy
100	31.2%	74.9%	19.7%	92.1%
200	47.4%	**86.5%**	32.7%	93.4%
300	53.1%	82.5%	39.2%	93.7%
400	48.8%	78.3%	35.4%	93.2%
500	56.8%	68.7%	40.4%	93.6%
600	52.1%	79.6%	38.7%	93.5%
700	59.0%	80.7%	46.5%	94.1%
800	59.5%	80.7%	47.1%	94.2%
900	**60.3%**	80.2%	**48.3%**	**94.3%**
1000	58.1%	79.9%	45.6%	94.0%
Lexicon	54.2%	85.4%	39.6%	93.9%

Table 7 shows that more topic features can improve the performance of classification. The highest $F_1 - measure$ is 60.3% with 900 topics in *LDA*. Although in the low topic dimensions *LDA* performs poorer than Lexicon approach, *LDA* could perform better than Lexicons when assigned a high topic value.

6.3 Experiment with advanced Topic Model

To test our proposed method in Section 5.4, we also conducted experiments with the same topic number and default parameter settings as in Section 6.2, and the results are shown in Table 8. Table 8 shows that compared with *LDA* in Table 7, our approach works better.

Table 8: Cross-validation performance on Topic Model after adding psychological lexicons

Topics	F_1	Precision	Recall	Accuracy
100	44.1%	95.9%	28.6%	93.4%
200	62.4%	89.6%	47.9%	94.8%
300	67.9%	93.2%	53.4%	95.4%
400	74.2%	96.8%	60.1%	96.2%
500	**76.2%**	94.6%	**63.9%**	**96.4%**
600	75.1%	**98.8%**	60.5%	96.3%
700	74.0%	95.0%	60.5%	96.1%
800	67.3%	84.0%	56.2%	95.1%
900	64.6%	76.1%	56.2%	94.4%
1000	61.8%	72.3%	53.9%	93.9%

The best performance is on 500 topics, with $F_1 - measure$ at 76.2%, Recall at 63.9%, Accuracy over 96%. The results indicate that it is feasible to predict and even prevent the suicides through analyzing microblogs.

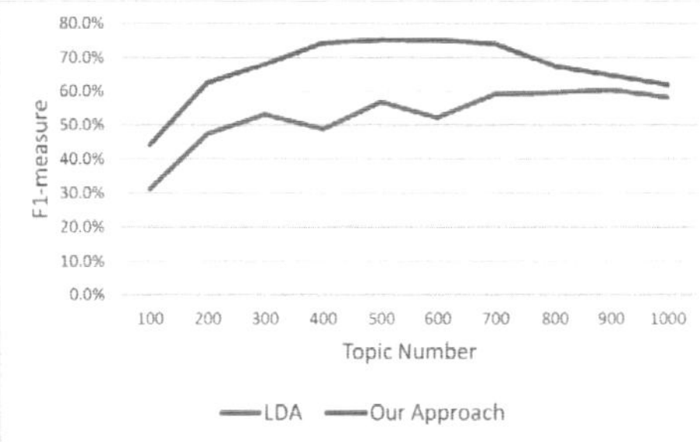

Figure 7: Comparisons in $F_1 - measure$ between *LDA* and Advanced Topic Model

Compared with previous approaches both in lexicons and *LDA*, we obtained around 25% improvement in F1-measure. Fig. 7 presents a more detailed comparison between *LDA* (in blue) and our approach (in red) on $F_1 - measure$.

6.4 Results with Meta Features

To further improve the performance, we add meta features described in Section 5.5 with topic 500. We run *SVM* and several classifiers in Weka (Hall et al., 2009): Logistic, J48 classifier, Random Forest(*RF*), Random Tree(*RT*), Decision Table(*DT*). All classifiers are trained and tested with default parameters, and performances are presented in Table 9.

Table 9: Cross-validation performance of Different classifiers

	F_1	Precision	Recall	Accuracy
SVM	76.8%	**96.8%**	63.7%	**96.5%**
Logistic	53.0%	59.2%	48.0%	92.3%
J48	**80.0%**	87.1%	**73.9%**	93.2%
RF	71.3%	98.2%	56.0%	93.6%
RT	67.7%	71.0%	64.6%	94.4%
DT	74.6%	92.0%	62.7%	96.1%

Clearly, *J48* attains the best $F_1 - measure$ (80.0%) and Recall (73.9%). Compared with Table 8, we acquired a better performance after integrating meta features.

We found that there are still about nearly one fourth suicidal microblogs that were not identified correctly. There might be several reasons: first, the complexity and ambiguity of language on the Internet, especially the *SNS*; second, the psychological lexicon is quite limited.

This research has a number of potential applications. The trained model can be used to build a suicide monitoring system to help professionals execute suicide intervention in time. If this system was effective in detecting suicide ideation in microblogs from *SNS*, it might also help psychologists investigate how linguistic and behavioral patterns are correlated with suicide thoughts and provide them with advanced decision support.

7 Conclusion

In this paper, for the purpose of identifying suicidal ideation of microblogs on social networks, first, we build a suicidal domain lexicons and develop hybrid approaches combined both contextual and meta information for suicidal ideation identification; second, we run Topic Model for feature selection with less than 1,000 dimensions left, and achieve more than 38% accuracy increased over lexicon approach; furthermore, we deploy a real-time engine to detect suicide ideation in microblogs for monitoring suicide, which might be helpful for professional organizations to assess people's suicide ideation; finally, from psychological perspective, we found that writing styles and time variations are highly correlated with suicidal ideation. A prototype system[3] has been deployed online to detect suicide ideation of *SNS* in real-time.

The performance of model is limited by several issues as follows: first the model has been trained and tested on small size data sample; second, we need to try more advanced machine learning algorithms. Our future work is undertaken in two directions: improving performance and mining latent social relationships.

8 Acknowledge

We would like to thank Google Summer of Code 2014 and Portland State University for sponsoring the open-source development of this project. The authors acknowledge the support from National High-tech R&D Program of China (2013AA01A606), National Basic Research Program of China (2014CB744600), and Key Research Program of Chinese Academy of Sciences (KJZD-EWL04). Thank anonymous reviewers for their valuable comments to improve quality of the paper.

[3]It can be visited at `http://ccpl.psych.ac.cn/suicide/`.

References

David M Blei, Andrew Y Ng, and Michael I Jordan. 2003. Latent dirichlet allocation. *the Journal of machine Learning research*, 3:993–1022.

Peter F Brown, Peter V Desouza, Robert L Mercer, Vincent J Della Pietra, and Jenifer C Lai. 1992. Class-based n-gram models of natural language. *Computational linguistics*, 18(4):467–479.

Chih-Chung Chang and Chih-Jen Lin. 2011. Libsvm: a library for support vector machines. *ACM Transactions on Intelligent Systems and Technology (TIST)*, 2(3):27.

Munmun De Choudhury, Michael Gamon, Scott Counts, and Eric Horvitz. 2013. Predicting depression via social media. In *ICWSM*.

Zhendong Dong and Qiang Dong. 2003. Hownet-a hybrid language and knowledge resource. In *Natural Language Processing and Knowledge Engineering, 2003. Proceedings. 2003 International Conference on*, pages 820–824. IEEE.

King-wa Fu, Qijin Cheng, Paul WC Wong, and Paul SF Yip. 2013. Responses to a self-presented suicide attempt in social media: A social network analysis. *Crisis: The Journal of Crisis Intervention and Suicide Prevention*, 34(6):406.

Rui Gao, Bibo Hao, He Li, Yusong Gao, and Tingshao Zhu. 2013. Developing simplified chinese psychological linguistic analysis dictionary for microblog. In *Brain and Health Informatics*, pages 359–368. Springer.

Li Guan, Bibo Hao, and Tingshao Zhu. 2014. How did the suicide act and speak differently online? behavioral and linguistic features of china's suicide microblog users. *arXiv preprint arXiv:1407.0466*.

Mark Hall, Eibe Frank, Geoffrey Holmes, Bernhard Pfahringer, Peter Reutemann, and Ian H Witten. 2009. The weka data mining software: an update. *ACM SIGKDD explorations newsletter*, 11(1):10–18.

Jared Jashinsky, Scott H Burton, Carl L Hanson, Josh West, Christophe Giraud-Carrier, Michael D Barnes, and Trenton Argyle. 2013. Tracking suicide risk factors through twitter in the us.

Stanley R Kay, Abraham Flszbein, and Lewis A Opfer. 1987. The positive and negative syndrome scale (panss) for schizophrenia. *Schizophrenia bulletin*, 13(2):261.

Lin Li, Ang Li, Bibo Hao, Zengda Guan, and Tingshao Zhu. 2014a. Predicting active users' personality based on micro-blogging behaviors. *PLoS ONE*, 9(e84997).

Tim MH Li, Michael Chau, Paul SF Yip, and Paul WC Wong. 2014b. Temporal and computerized psycholinguistic analysis of the blog of a chinese adolescent suicide.

Chenghua Lin and Yulan He. 2009. Joint sentiment/topic model for sentiment analysis. In *Proceedings of the 18th ACM conference on Information and knowledge management*, pages 375–384. ACM.

Huijie Lin, Jia Jia, Quan Guo, Yuanyuan Xue, Jie Huang, Lianhong Cai, and Ling Feng. 2014. Psychological stress detection from cross-media microblog data using deep sparse neural network.

David D Luxton, Jennifer D June, and Julie T Kinn. 2011. Technology-based suicide prevention: current applications and future directions. *Telemedicine and e-Health*, 17(1):50–54.

Leonard L Martin, David W Ward, John W Achee, and Robert S Wyer. 1993. Mood as input: People have to interpret the motivational implications of their moods. *Journal of Personality and Social Psychology*, 64(3):317.

Andrew Kachites McCallum. 2002. Mallet: A machine learning for language toolkit.

Qiaozhu Mei, Xu Ling, Matthew Wondra, Hang Su, and ChengXiang Zhai. 2007. Topic sentiment mixture: modeling facets and opinions in weblogs. In *Proceedings of the 16th international conference on World Wide Web*, pages 171–180. ACM.

Tomas Mikolov, Ilya Sutskever, Kai Chen, Greg S Corrado, and Jeff Dean. 2013. Distributed representations of words and phrases and their compositionality. In *Advances in Neural Information Processing Systems*, pages 3111–3119.

World Health Organization et al. 2014. *Preventing suicide: A global imperative*. World Health Organization.

Bo Pang and Lillian Lee. 2008. Opinion mining and sentiment analysis. *Foundations and trends in information retrieval*, 2(1-2):1–135.

John Pestian, Henry Nasrallah, Pawel Matykiewicz, Aurora Bennett, and Antoon Leenaars. 2010. Suicide note classification using natural language processing: A content analysis. *Biomedical informatics insights*, 2010(3):19.

John P Pestian, Pawel Matykiewicz, Michelle Linn-Gust, Brett South, Ozlem Uzuner, Jan Wiebe, K Bretonnel Cohen, John Hurdle, and Christopher Brew. 2012. Sentiment analysis of suicide notes: A shared task. *Biomedical informatics insights*, 5(Suppl 1):3.

Philip Resnik, Anderson Garron, and Rebecca Resnik. 2013. Using topic modeling to improve prediction of neuroticism and depression. In *Proceedings of the 2013 Conference on Empirical Methods in Natural*, pages 1348–1353. Association for Computational Linguistics.

M David Rudd, Alan L Berman, Thomas E Joiner, Matthew K Nock, Morton M Silverman, Michael

Mandrusiak, Kimberly Van Orden, and Tracy Witte. 2006. Warning signs for suicide: Theory, research, and clinical applications. *Suicide and Life-Threatening Behavior*, 36(3):255–262.

Jian Sun. 2014. Ansj Chinese Lexical Analysis System. Website. `http://ansj.org/`.

Kristina Toutanova, Dan Klein, Christopher D. Manning, and Yoram Singer. 2003. Feature-Rich Part-of-Speech Tagging with a Cyclic Dependency Network. In *North American Chapter of the Association for Computational Linguistics*.

Peter D. Turney and Patrick Pantel. 2010. From Frequency to Meaning: Vector Space Models of Semantics. *Computing Research Repository*, abs/1003.1.

Hongning Wang, Yue Lu, and Chengxiang Zhai. 2010. Latent aspect rating analysis on review text data: a rating regression approach. In *Proceedings of the 16th ACM SIGKDD international conference on Knowledge discovery and data mining*, pages 783–792. ACM.

Xinyu Wang, Chunhong Zhang, Yang Ji, Li Sun, Leijia Wu, and Zhana Bao. 2013. A depression detection model based on sentiment analysis in microblog social network. In *Trends and Applications in Knowledge Discovery and Data Mining*, pages 201–213. Springer.

Casey Whitelaw, Navendu Garg, and Shlomo Argamon. 2005. Using appraisal groups for sentiment analysis. In *Proceedings of the 14th ACM international conference on Information and knowledge management*, pages 625–631. ACM.

Chung-Hsien Wu, Liang-Chih Yu, and Fong-Lin Jang. 2005. Using semantic dependencies to mine depressive symptoms from consultation records. *Intelligent Systems, IEEE*, 20(6):50–58.

Liang-Chih Yu and Chun-Yuan Ho. 2014. Identifying emotion labels from psychiatric social texts using independent component analysis. In *Proceedings of COLING 2014, the 25th International Conference on Computational Linguistics: Technical Papers*, pages 837–847, Dublin, Ireland, August. Dublin City University and Association for Computational Linguistics.

Predicting Sector Index Movement with Microblogging Public Mood Time Series on Social Issues

Yujie Lu[1] **Jinlong Guo**[2] **Sakamoto Kotaro**[1] **Shibuki Hideyuki**[1] **Tatsunori Mori**[1]
[1]Graduate School of Environment and Information Science,
Yokohama National University, Yokohama, 2408501, JAPAN
[2]Graduate School of Library and Information Science,
University of Illinois at Urban-Champaign, Champaign, IL 61820, USA
{luyujie,sakamoto,shib,mori}@forest.eis.ynu.ac.jp,
jguo24@illinois.edu

Abstract

This paper develops a technique that unfolds public mood on social issues from real-time social media for sector index prediction. We first propose a low-dimensional support vector machine (SVM) classifier using surrounding information for twitter sentiment classification. Then, we generate public mood time series by aggregating message-level weighted daily mood (WDM) based on the sentiment classification results. Lastly, we evaluate our method against the real stock index in two kinds of time periods (fluctuating and monotonous) separately using static cross-correlation coefficient (CCF) and dynamic vector auto-regression (VAR). The experiments on "food safety" issue show that the proposed WDM method outperforms the word-level baseline method in predicting stock movement, especially during fluctuating period.

1 Introduction

Social media websites, such as Twitter and Facebook, have generated a great amount of public opinions on a variety of issues, especially hot events and emergencies. As a result, user-generated content has become a significant resource for exploring useful knowledge. In the use of public mood entailed in the real-time message streaming, researchers have proposed a wide range of applications, for example, election prediction (Andranik et al., 2009), anti-terrorism assistance (Cheong and Lee, 2009) and consumer confidence poll (O'Connor et al., 2010). In this paper, we use it for stock prediction.

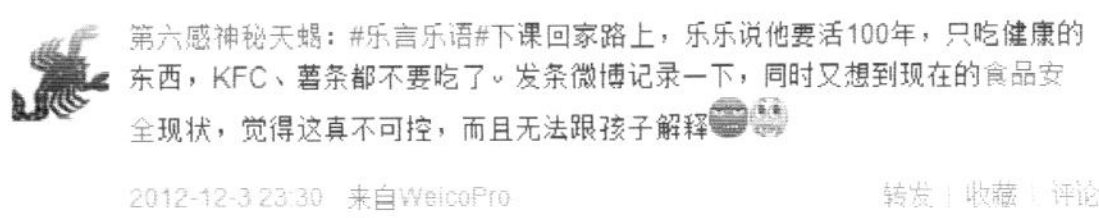

Figure 1: An example tweet from Sina Weibo

Sina Weibo is a Twitter-like microblogging service in China. Launched in 2009, it now has near 200 million monthly active users[1], which makes it the most dominant social networking service in China. Users discuss all kinds of social topics and express their opinions on the platform. As an example, food safety issue has become a prominent social problem and caused much concern in recent years in China. Figure 1 is an example tweet talking about food safety from Sina Weibo, in which the author expresses his dissatisfaction to the situation of food safety in China. Note that besides the text part, there is auxiliary information around the text (called surrounding information in this paper).

Previous work shows that indicators from real-time media can conceivably be used to predict changes for many economic indexes (Bollen et al. 2011), and behavioral finance theory suggests that public mood can drive stock market (Nofsinger, 2005).Hence, we construct public mood time series by analyzing millions of tweets in a time span to predict stock movement in the corresponding period.

Our main contributions are summarized as follows:

- We investigate how microblogging public mood on certain social issues relates to the stock movement of the relevant sector. In this study, we conduct an experiment on the topic of "food safety" using tweets from Sina Weibo and Shenzhen Stock Exchange (SZSE) Food & Beverage Index.

[1] According to 2015 first quarter financial results released by Weibo Corp.

29th Pacific Asia Conference on Language, Information and Computation pages 563 - 571
Shanghai, China, October 30 - November 1, 2015

- We utilize not only the text part of the tweet, but also the non-text part, namely surrounding information and user information, and show that both sentiment classification and public mood time series can be improved in use of it.
- We study how the methods perform for different types of periods of stock index. Both CCF and VAR evaluation show that public mood time series has better predictive power during fluctuating period than monotonous period.

To the best of our knowledge, this work is the first to predict sector stock index by public mood time series on social issues in Chinese microblogging.

2 Related Work

2.1 Stock Prediction with Social Media

With the popularity of real-time social media, stock market prediction based on microblog has attracted more and more attention. Past work can be roughly categorized into two classes depending on whether sentiment is used or not.

One class is sentiment-based methodology using general tweets. Bollen et al. (2011) generated seven different public mood time series using Opinion-Finder and Google-Profile of Mood States. Both Granger causality analysis with Dow Jones Industrial Average and a Self-Organizing Fuzzy Neural Network predictor showed that "Calm" dimension had the best predictive effect. Vu et al. (2012) experimented a Decision Tree classifier with different combinations of features to predict daily up and down movement of the stock price of tech companies. They proved that positive/negative sentiment, bullish/bearish orientation, and stock price change of three previous days are effective features. Si et al. (2013) proposed a topic-based method called continuous Dirichlet Process Mixture to learn subtopics, drew sentiment time series by aggregating opinion words over the topic chains. The VAR analysis with Standard & Poor's 100 showed its effectiveness.

The other class is non-sentiment-based methodology using financial tweets. Bar-Haim et al. (2011) distinguished expert users from non-experts according to the correctness of stock rise prediction against one's bullish posts. The precision of predicting stock rise showed that Per-User Model after expert classification performed better than other pattern methods. Ruiz et al. (2012) represented financial tweet sets as graphs, and extracted activity features and graph features. The correlation analysis with stock market activities showed that the number of connected components is the best feature, and the correlation with traded volume is stronger than stock price.

Our method belongs to the former. The main deference from previous work is that our public mood time series is based on message-level sentiment analysis on general tweets, and we creatively involve non-text information. Besides, unlike Bollen et al. (2011) predicting composite index value or Vu et al. (2012) forecasting individual company stock price, we observe how public mood on social issues affects stock movement at sector level.

2.2 Sentiment Analysis in Social Media

Pang et al. (2002) and Turney et al. (2002) are generally regarded as the start of the research area of sentiment analysis. These two works represent the two main methodologies of sentiment analysis — supervised method and unsupervised method. Pang fed machine learning methods, including support vector machine, maximum entropy, and Naïve Bayes, with features such as n-gram, part of speech to classify the polarity of texts. On the other hand, Turney calculated the comprehensive polarity of a text by aggregating the similarity between the keywords in the text and the seed words, which is known as SO-PMI algorithm. Broader overviews on traditional sentiment analysis are presented in Pang and Lee (2008) and Liu (2012).

Recent studies on sentiment analysis focus on social media. As an early attempt, Go et al. (2009) annotated a noisy training set based on emoticons in tweets, carried out analogous experiments as Pang et al. (2002), and showed that SVM classier achieved the best precision. Pak and Paroublek (2010) proposed a Naïve Bayes classifier using n-gram (embedded in POS distribution), and concluded that 2-gram worked the best. The SemEval Task reports (Nakov et al., 2013; Rosenthal et al., 2014) pointed out that participants leveraged various features, depended heavily on sentiment lexicons, and obtained the best accuracy around 70%. Xiang and Zhou (2014) proposed a topic-based sentiment mixture model, and achieved higher precision than the top systems in SemEval 2013.

Despite some special characteristics of Sina Weibo, sentiment analysis of Sina Weibo is similar to Twitter. Wang and Li (2014) proposed a SVM classifier with three-layered features which aggregate syno-

nyms and highly-related words to help reduce feature dimension, and indicated that it was better than SVM classifiers using n-gram and POS tags. Xie et al. (2012) proposed a set of weibo-specific features, such as the number of emoticon, for SVM classifier, and achieved an accuracy around 67%.
Concerning word-based features unavoidably cause data sparseness problem, similar to Xie et al. (2012), we use a SVM classifier with microblog-specific low-dimensional features due to its flexibility and efficiency. However, unlike previous work that only employs the text part of a tweet, we also make use of non-text information, such as the number of retweet and the number of reply.

3 Approach Outline

The overall framework of our research is shown in Figure 2.The core of our method is to build a sound public mood time series curve from tweets. This includes two main steps — bullish/bearish orientation representation and daily mood indicator design. Regarding the manifestation of bullish/bearish orientation, instead of using lexicon-based word sentiment of general tweets (Bollen et al., 2011; Si et al., 2013) or explicit buy/sell transaction of stock tweets (Bar-Haim et al., 2011), we utilize global polarity of general tweets, since global polarity contains more accurate emotion about its related object and general tweets allow us to have a wider base (Vu et al., 2012).In our study, tweets are divided into three categories: “positive”, “negative” and “neutral”. A positive tweet can be a potential “bullish” signal and a negative message can be a potential “bearish” signal for stock price.
To have a better message-level sentiment classification, we train a customized classifier for our selected topic instead of using existing general tools (e.g. OpinionFinder). We first extract text features and non-text features from tweets and feed the classier with different combination of them to find the best classifier. Using the customized classifier, we then obtain the global polarity of each tweet. Rather than using simple sentiment ratio as daily mood, we take non-text information into account to design a weighted daily mood indicator. The public mood time series curve can be easily drawn once we had weighted daily mood values of each day. We adopt two different perspectives to evaluate the prediction ability of mood curves — CCF and VAR. Moreover, as shown at the bottom of Figure 2, the stock index is divided into fluctuating period and two monotonous periods according to the degree of volatility. We will compare how differently mood curves perform during the two kinds of time periods.

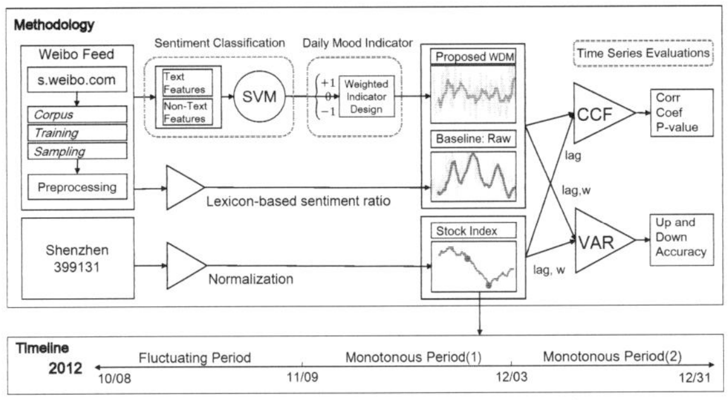

Figure 2: Overview of the research

4 Customized Sentiment Classification

Both Pang et al. (2002) and Go et al. (2009) reported that SVM outperformed other classifiers where n-gram and POS features are used and unigram feature worked the best for traditional and twitter sentiment analysis respectively. Therefore, we choose SVM as our classier. Given the limited length of microblogging (only 140 characters), word-based n-gram and POS features lead to severe sparseness problem, so we design our microblog-specific features for SVM classifier.

4.1 SVM Classifier

Support Vector Machine (SVM) has proved to be an efficient classification model. The basic idea of it is to find a hyperplane represented by its normal vector **w** which maximizes the margin (the distance from the closest instances).This search then becomes a constrained optimization problem and the solution can be written as:

$$\mathbf{w} = \sum_{i=1}^{n} \alpha_i y_i x_i, \alpha_i \geq 0 \tag{1}$$

where α_i can be obtained by standard quadratic programming, x_i are support vectors lying on the margin and $y_i \in \{1, -1\}$[2]. SVM can solve non-linear tasks using kernel trick as well. In this work, our SVM classifier is trained with LibSVM toolkit using RBF kernel (Chang and Lin, 2011).

[2] Multiclass classification problem can be turned into multiple binary classification.

4.2 Text Features

Besides traditional text features like n-gram, POS tags and simple lexicon-based emotional word number, there are many microblogging-specific features in the text part of the tweet.

Entity Tag Count Entities are special elements in microblog. We exploit four kinds of often-used entities: hashtag, @tag, URL and seed. The former three are the same as Twitter, while the last one is a weibo-specific entity which allows users to subscribe RSS news about tagged words. The number of the four kinds of entities are used as features. These features were also used in previous work.

Set-count Neutral Signals Based on observation of many tweets, we collect heuristic neutral signals for identifying objective tweets. The more neutral signals a tweet contains, the more possible it is objective. The neutral signals consist of two subsets. One subset includes: bracket pair (【】), book title mark (《》), time patterns(e.g. *月*日) and numbers(e.g. 35%), and the other contains 5 types of words: news vocabulary (e.g. 宣传日), Q&A words (e.g. 科普), stock terms (e.g. 沪指), sharing words (e.g. 下载), and irrelevant words (e.g. 抽奖). Neutral signals are set-count features[3], so there are two features in total.

Sentence Count Unlike English tweet, Chinese tweet can easily have 3 or more sentences, so sentence information is important for weibo. We count the number of sentences, the number of exclamatory sentence indicated by exclamation marks, and the number of questions indicated by question marks.

The sum of emotional words is the basic element to measure the sentiment of a sentence or a message. We compute sentiment scores at both sentence and message level. They are defined as:

$$\text{Score}(U) = \sum_{i=1}^{|U|} \text{polarity}(i) \qquad (2)$$

where U denotes a unit of text and i denotes a word or an emoticon whose polarity is in {1, 0,-1}.

Sentence Sentiment Score The first sentence and the last sentence are always more important than others. Thus we compute sentiment scores of them respectively. Firstly, we clear up tags (entities, emoticon etc.) in the raw tweet, normalize the abnormal full stops, tokenize the cleaned text using NLPIR/ICTCLAS and segment it into sentences by punctuation (period, semicolon, exclamation mark, question mark, and suspension points).Then we turn sentences into word polarity vectors and gain the sentence score by summing up all the values in the vector. For example, "各种|食品安全|问题|集中|爆发|，|有些|是|问题|，|有些|是|误解|。" is transformed to [0,0,-1,1,-1,0,0,0,-1,0,0,0,-1,0].This calculation relies heavily on the quality of polarity dictionaries. There are three open-source sentiment lexicons for Chinese: How-net dictionary, DTU ontology dictionary and NTU dictionary. By comparing the effectiveness of these lexicons and their combinations on a small test set, we use the integration of all of them.

Message Sentiment Score We compute two global sentiment scores by emoticons and emotional words respectively. Emoticon is such a special reference for noisy labeling (Pak and Paroubek, 2010) and a strong indicator of global polarity (Kouloumpis et al., 2011) that we consider it separately. Unlike the emoticons in English that are combinations of ASCII characters, Sina Weibo emoticons are stipulated icons. Thus, we first classified 72 often-used emoticons in Sina Weibo into 3 categories (positive, negative and neutral), then sum up their polarities as the global sentiment score. There are two emoticons at the end of the example tweet (see Figure 1). Global sentiment score by emotional words is computed the same as the sentence sentiment score but on a larger scale.

4.3 Non-Text Features

Apart from text features, there are many metadata of the tweet (surrounding information) and the author (user information). Previous studies have not made full use of these data. Since raw data is stored in HTML pages, basic fields enclosed by HTML tags can be extracted by HTML parser. We extract message ID, user ID, user badge, user nickname, sending date, sending source, the number of retweet, the number of replies, the state of embedded picture and video. Some of these fields are just identificati-

[3] A set-count feature is a count of the number of instances from a set of terms.

on with little meaning such as message ID and user ID, while other fields can potentially be useful features.

Surrounding Information Surrounding information refers to the fields surrounding the text part of the tweet (see Figure 1). In our study, user badge, the number of retweet, the number of replies, the state of embedded picture and video are selected as features.

User Information We can access the user information using Sina Weibo user interface by user ID. Many fields such as gender, city, badge, and brief introduction about the user can be returned. We only make use of three numeric fields: the number of follower, following and posted tweets.

5 Daily Mood Indicator Design

Bollen et al. (2011) has shown that daily #positive/ #negative ratio (happiness) time series can represent public mood and emotionally responded to hot social events. Different from Bollen's curves based on word polarity aggregation, our time series are built on message-level sentiment analysis.
Considering the sentiment distribution of our experiment topic is skewed at the message level (very few positive tweets on food safety problem), we use Eq.3 as our basic daily mood indicator instead. It also means the degree of happiness and is monotonically decreasing (the more there are negative tweets, the less it will be).The public mood of day t (denoted as Daily Mood, DM) is defined as:

$$\mathrm{DM}(t) = \frac{\#_t(\mathrm{tweet})}{\#_t(\mathrm{tweet}_-)} \quad (3)$$

where $\#_t(\mathrm{tweet})$ denotes the number of tweets in date t and $\#_t(\mathrm{tweet}_-)$ denotes the number of negative tweets in date t.
Different tweets have different weights. A tweet that has many retweets or posted by famous people will have stronger impact on public mood and then on stock market. So we need to take these useful non-text fields into account. The weighted daily mood (WDM) and Weight(t) are represented as:

$$\mathrm{WDM}(t) = \mathrm{DM}(t) * \mathrm{Weight}(t) \quad (4)$$

$$\mathrm{Weight}(t) = \log_2\left(\frac{\sum_t(\mathrm{retweet})}{\sum_{t,-}(\mathrm{retweet})} * \frac{\lg(\sum_t(\mathrm{follower}))}{\lg\left(\sum_{t,-}(\mathrm{follower})\right)}\right) \quad (5)$$

where retweet means the number of the retweets of a tweet and follower means the number of the followers of the author of the tweet. We compute the total number of them in day t. Since follower is much greater than retweet, it is log transformed. The product is also log transformed for order reduction.

6 Experiment on Sentiment Classification

6.1 Text Data

Given that Sina Weibo API does not provide search interface freely as Twitter does, we scrape tweets discussing food safety with the keyword — "食品安全" (food safety in Chinese) from its search service platform[4]. Unlike Twitter API, Sina Weibo search platform allows to backtrack until 2009.The collecting interval is the fourth season of 2012(Oct. 1st 2012- Dec.31st 2012) when food safety problem was the most concerned problem for Chinese people. To sidestep undesired repetition, the original option is ticked. Totally we fetched 51,611 pieces of tweets (denoted as *Corpus*).
A training dataset is annotated for SVM classifier (denoted as *Training*). In accordance with Go et al. (2009), the definition of our polarity is "a personal positive or negative feeling". The polarity is presented as "+1(positive), 0(neutral), and -1(negative)". In addition, irrelevant tweets and objective tweets (e.g. news, commercial) are regarded as 0(as strict neutral ones consisting of both positive and negative are rare). All the tweets were tagged with one of {+1, 0,-1} by annotators. *Training* consists of 901 pieces of labelled messages coming from a randomly selected date.

6.2 Sector Index

In order to evaluate our public mood time series, a sector stock index for food industry is needed. We select SZSE Food & Beverage Index 399131(denoted as *Index*) as our stock index. *Index* consists of 56 main companies in food sector of China. The pe-

[4] http://s.weibo.com/

riod of *Index* corresponds to *Corpus* collecting period (Oct. 1st 2012- Dec.31st 2012)[5].To make it continuous, the values at weekends is computed by linear interpolation[6].

Figure 3 shows the *Index* curve (in order to compare with mood curves, the curve is Z-score normalized). As we can see, there are continuous decline and increase periods in the curve. On one hand, these long-term (soft) monotonous movement will render prediction more difficult since public mood changes drastically. On the other hand, prediction in long-term monotonous periods in less meaningful than it is in fluctuating periods for stock investors. So we discuss prediction in two types of periods: fluctuating period (Oct.8th - Nov.9th) and monotonous periods (Nov.10th - Dec.3rd, and Dec 4th - Dec.31st).

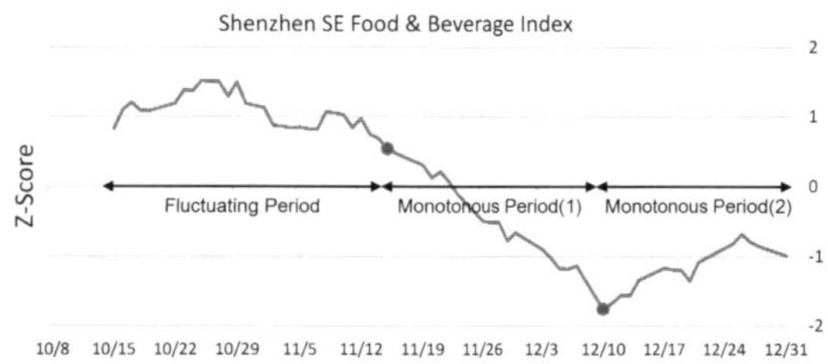

Figure 3: SZSE Food & Beverage closing values (Oct. 8th- Dec.31st)

6.3 Classification Result

The unigram method for sentiment classification described in Go et al. (2009) is used as a baseline. We employ WEKA[7] to construct the unigram model and classify tweets by its embedded LibSVM. We tried three combinations of our features. The evaluation method is five-fold cross-validation. Table 2 show the precision of each method.

Features	#Dim	Precision
baseline: unigram	2517	79.69%
C1:text features only	13	89.79%
C2:C1 + surrounding info	17	92.23%
C3:C2 + user info	20	87.35%

Table 1: The results of different classifiers

From Table 2 we can see:

1. C* classifiers perform better than the baseline by 10.1% on average. In addition, the number of the dimension of C* classifiers is far way less than baseline, which saves learning time. The result also implies that the traditional classification methods based on words have limitation for sentiment analysis, because word alone is not necessarily the carrier of emotion. Hence, although the dimension is very high, each of them does not contribute much. In contrast, each of our features has its underlying influence on the global polarity.

2. C2 is higher than C1 by 2.44%, and C3 decreased by 4.88%.This suggests surrounding information improves the classification, while user information does not. This makes sense because we know controversial tweets on social issues having many retweets or replies are more likely to be emotional. On the contrary, user information is not only different from other features in magnitude, but also incompatible with them in quality so that it disturbs the learning. This indicates that message sentiment is mainly decided by tweet text and its surrounding information.

As a result, we utilize C2 as our model. Now we look into the precision of different categories. The precision for neutral class reaches an impressive 98%, for negative class (majority) reaches 72.3%, both of which are higher than Xie et al. (2012)[8]. However, public mood on social events always goes to extremes. The majority of subjective class in *Corpus* is negative, because public mood for food safety in China is irritated at the collecting period. There are only 8 positive samples in *Training* and only 1 of them are classified correctly. Consequently, the prediction for positive tweets is unreliable. In fact, according to manual check, the positive tweets account for less than 1% of *Corpus*. This is why we changed the definition of daily mood in Section 5.

6.4 SVM Mood Curve & Sample Mood Curve

In theory, we simulate the real mood curve based on the result of SVM classier, but what if the real mood curve itself has no predictive power at the first place? In order to make sure whether there is a relationship between the real mood curve and the stock index curve, we annotated another larger dataset (denoted as *Sample*). *Sample* is sampled from tweets in *Corpus* during fluctuating period (Oct.8th-Nov.9th) at the

[5] Unfortunately 399131 *Index* has been delisted from Mar 1st, 2013.

[6] Since Oct 1st – Oct 7th is national holiday in China, we ignore these days.

[7] http://www.cs.waikato.ac.nz/ml/weka/

[8] This is a loose comparison because the training dataset is different.

rate of 20% (4106 tweets in total)[9]. Each tweet has been tagged by two independent annotators, and the agreement rate between annotators is 88%. The organizer double-check the left inconsistent 12%, and decide the final polarity.
First, we see how close SVM-based curve is to *Sample*-based curve. Figure 4 shows the two curves. The vertical axis is WDM value. Figure 4 suggests that the two curves are correlated significantly (p-value of correlation analysis < 0.01), which means that the C2 classifier is reliable for building WDM time series. The prediction performance of *Sample*-based curve is shown in the next section.

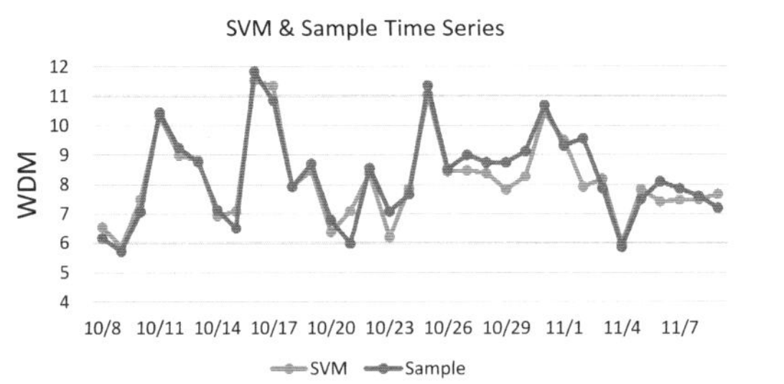

Figure 4: SVM & Sample WDM Time Series (Oct.8th - Nov.9th)

7 Experiment on Mood Time Series

Stock prediction is an extremely complex process. To better verify the prediction effect of proposed mood time series, we evaluate it in two ways (CCF and VAR). CCF observes the static similarity between mood time series and stock index, while VAR assesses the dynamic one-day-ahead prediction ability of mood time series. Besides, we evaluate the proposed method separately during fluctuating period and monotonous periods.

7.1 Public Mood Time Series

We apply the best C2 model to predict the polarity for each tweet in *Corpus*. Since there is not yet similar work on message-level sentiment time series, we use Bollen's method as our baseline (denoted as **Raw**).
Based on WDM, we can draw our proposed time series (denoted as **WDM**). For comparison, we also draw the DM time series ((denoted as **DM**)) and *Sample*-based mood time series (denoted as **Sample**) [10]. However, concerning that original public mood is highly vibrant (O'Connor et al. 2010), we smooth the mood curves by moving average over a window of the past 7 days. Smoothed time series of **Raw**, **DM**, and **WDM** are shown in Figure 5(Z-score normalized).

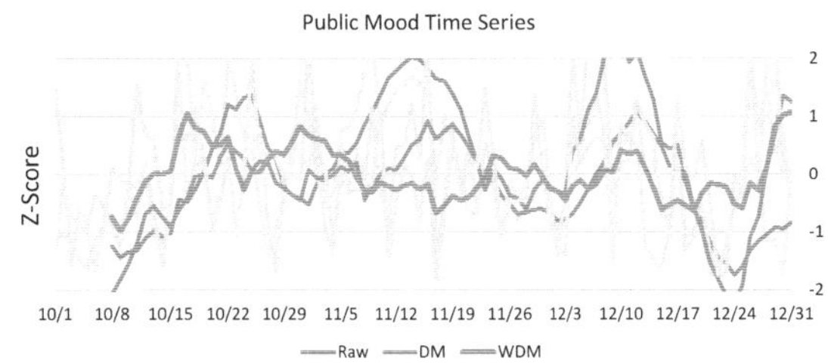

Figure 5: Public mood time series (Oct.8t -Dec.31st)

7.2 Cross-Correlation Coefficient

Cross-correlation coefficient shifts one curve back and forth to estimate correlation between two series at different time lag (Eduardo et al. 2012). We shift *Index* curve, so the right part where lag is greater than 0 means the ability to predict.
Figure 6 shows correlation coefficients between mood curves[t] and *Index* [t + lag]. We can see that the **WDM** curve has the best similarity with *Index* in prediction part in all the time spans. The average correlation value for **WDM** is 0.31 at predicting stage in entire period[11]. As expected, **WDM** has a similar trend with **Sample**, and what surprised us is that **WDM** is even higher than **Sample** curve. This may be because that **Sample** only contains 20% of *Corpus*, while **WDM** observes the whole *Corpus*. Moreover, It is obvious that **WDM** works better than simple **DM**， which verifies our idea that non-text information helps. Besides, we can see that **WDM** works much better in fluctuating period than monotonous periods and achieves the best value when lag is 2 in fluctuating period. On the other hand, both **DM** and **Raw** have little predictive ability in fluctuating period.

7.3 Vector Auto Regression

To access dynamic prediction ability, we use the vector auto-regression evaluation proposed in Si et al. (2013). The first order (lag=1) VAR model is defined as:

[9] The best way to obtain the real curve is to tag all the tweets in *Corpus*, but that is too large for manual annotation.
[10] To compare with **Sample**, the first 6 days of fluctuating period are cut off because of smoothing.
[11] Eduardo et al. (2012) reported 0.1 averagely on their time series.

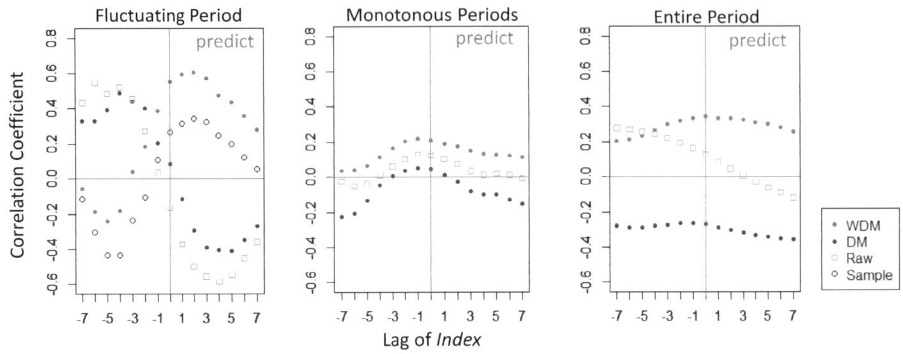

Figure 6: Correlation coefficient for different lags in different periods

$$x_t = \vartheta_{11}x_{t-1} + \vartheta_{12}y_{t-1} + \varepsilon_{x,t}$$
$$y_t = \vartheta_{21}x_{t-1} + \vartheta_{22}y_{t-1} + \varepsilon_{y,t} \quad (6)$$

The training data is a sliding window of the past w days. VAR uses the training data to predict the one-day-ahead up and down of *Index*. In our study, lag is in {1, 2, 3} and w is in {5, 10, 15}.Apart from mood curves, we test *Index* itself by univariate autoregression model for reference. All curves are normalized to [0, 1].

Table 3 shows the average accuracy of the prediction in different lags. We can see from Table 3 that **WDM** performs best on average in fluctuating period, and achieves the highest accuracy 72.9% on lag 2, which is in accordance with the CCF result. Since the curve fluctuates much in this period, accuracy of *Index* itself is only 51.4%, which is nearly guess. However, if we look at the monotonous periods, all the three mood curves are worse than the *Index* itself. This is because the tendency in monotonous periods is very clear, *Index* itself can be a very strong predictor. Besides, **DM** performs the best among the mood curves. In the entire period, we combine a **W&D** curve using **WDM** in fluctuating period and **DM** in monotonous periods and achieves an accuracy of 65.3% averagely, performs better than **DM** or **WDM** alone. Since the monotonous periods is nearly twice the length as the fluctuating period, the overall accuracy does not win *Index*.

Fluctuating Period					
Lag	*Index*	Raw	DM	WDM	Hand
1	0.579	0.592	0.592	0.601	0.592
2	0.454	0.617	0.626	0.729	0.647
3	0.510	0.626	0.550	0.610	0.626
avg	0.514	0.612	0.589	**0.647**	0.622
Monotonous Periods					
Lag	*Index*	Raw	DM	WDM	
1	0.755	0.735	0.769	0.683	
2	0.757	0.688	0.717	0.738	
3	0.797	0.695	0.683	0.667	
avg	0.769	0.706	**0.723**	0.696	
Entire Period					
Lag	*Index*	Raw	DM	WDM	W&D
1	0.694	0.653	0.658	0.636	0.673
2	0.677	0.668	0.659	0.683	0.678
3	0.685	0.600	0.634	0.591	0.606
avg	0.685	0.640	0.650	0.637	**0.653**

Table 2: Average accuracies over all training windows size and different lags in different periods (Boldface: best performance)

8 Conclusion and Future Work

In this paper, we presented a framework using public mood on social issues to predict sector index movement. We developed a low-dimensional supervised sentiment classifier and designed a weighted daily mood indicator.

We found non-text information of tweet was useful for both sentiment classification and daily mood design. Experiment results showed that our proposed method worked best in terms of static CCF. For predicting one-day-ahead up and down by VAR, mood curves perform better during fluctuating period.

Although we presented an experiment on the topic of "food safety", the described technique can be extended to any other social topics. In the future, we plan to experiment controversial topics, such as "genetically modified food". In addition, since the prediction power depends on period type, it's meaningful to judge where the boundary of the period types is. These will be part of our future work.

References

Alec Go, Richa Bhayani, and Lei Huang.2009. Twitter sentiment classification using distant supervision. CS224N Project Report, Stanford, pages 1–6.

Alexander Pak and Patrick Paroubek. 2010. Twitter as a corpus for sentiment analysis and opinion mining. In Proceedings of the Seventh International Conference on Language Resources and Evaluation (LREC'10), pages 1320–1326.

Bing Liu. 2012. Sentiment analysis and opinion mining. Synthesis Lectures on Human Language Technologies, 5(1):1–167.

Bing Xiang and Liang Zhou.2014. Improving twitter sentiment analysis with topic-based mixture modeling and semi-supervised training. In Proceedings of the 52nd Annual Meeting of the Association for Computational Linguistics (ACL'14), pages 434–439.

Bo Pang and Lillian Lee. 2008. Opinion mining and sentiment analysis. Foundations and trends in information retrieval, 2(1-2):1–135.

Bo Pang, Lillian Lee, and Shivakumar Vaithyanathan. 2002. Thumbs up? Sentiment classification using machine learning techniques. In Proceedings of the Conference on Empirical Methods in Natural Language Processing (EMNLP'02), pages 79–86.

Brendan O'Connor, Ramnath Balasubramanyan, Bryan R. Routledge, and Noah A. Smith. 2010. From Tweets to Polls: Linking Text Sentiment to Public Opinion Time Series. In Proceedings of the International AAAI Conference on Weblogs and Social Media (ICWSM'10), pages 122–129.

Chih-Chung Chang and Chih-Jen Lin. 2011. LIBSVM: A library for support vector machines. In ACM Transactions on Intelligent Systems and Technology, 2(3):27.

Eduardo J. Ruiz, Vagelis Hristidis, Carlos Castillo, Aristides Gionis, Alejandro Jaimes. 2012. Correlating financial time series with micro-blogging activity. In Proceedings of the fifth ACM international conference on Web search and data mining (WSDM'12), pages 513–522.

Efthymios Kouloumpis, Theresa Wilson, and Johanna Moore .2011.Twitter sentiment analysis: the good the bad and the OMG!. In Proceedings of the Fifth International AAAI Conference on Weblogs and Social Media (ICWSM'11), pages 538–541.

Jianfeng Si, Arjun Mukherjee, Bing Liu, Qing Li, Huayi Li, and Xiaotie Deng. 2013. Exploiting topic based twitter sentiment for stock prediction. In Proceedings of the 51st Annual Meeting of the Association for Computational Linguistics (ACL'13), pages 24–29.

Johan Bollen, Huina Mao, and Xiaojun Zeng. 2011. Twitter mood predicts the stock market. Journal of Computational Science, 2(1):1–8.

John R. Nofsinger. 2005. Social Mood and Financial Economics. Journal of Behavioral Finance, 6(3):144–160.

Marc Cheong and Vincent C. S. Lee. 2011. A microblogging-based approach to terrorism informatics: Exploration and chronicling civilian sentiment and response to terrorism events via Twitter. Information Systems Frontiers, 13 (1):45–59.

Peter D. Turney.2002.Thumbs up or thumbs down? Semantic orientation applied to unsupervised classification of reviews. In Proceedings of the Association for Computational Linguistics (ACL'02), pages 417-424.

Preslav Nakov, Sara Rosenthal, Zornitsa Kozareva, Veselin Stoyanov, Alan Ritter, and Theresa Wilson .2013.SemEval-2013 Task 2: Sentiment Analysis in Twitter. In Proceedings of the 7th International Workshop on Semantic Evaluation (SemEval'13), pages 312–320.

Roy Bar-Haim, Elad Dinur, Ronen Feldman, Moshe Fresko, and Guy Goldstein.2011.Identifying and Following Expert Investors in Stock Microblogs. In Proceedings of the 2011 Conference on Empirical Methods in Natural Language Processing (EMNLP'11), pages 1310–1319.

Sara Rosenthal, Alan Ritter, Preslav Nakov, and Veselin Stoyanov. 2014. SemEval-2014 Task 9: Sentiment Analysis in Twitter. In Proceedings of the 8th International Workshop on Semantic Evaluation (SemEval'14), pages 73–80.

Tien Thanh Vu, Shu Chang, Quang Thuy Ha, and Ni gel Collier. 2012. An Experiment in Integrating Sentiment Features for Tech Stock Prediction in Twitter. In Proceedings of the Workshop on Information Extraction and Entity Analytics on Social Media Data (COLING'12), pages 23–38.

Tumasjan Andranik, Sprenger Timm O, Sandner Philipp G, Welpe, and Isabell M. 2011. Election Forecasts with Twitter: How 140 Characters Reflect the Political Landscape. Social Science Computer Review, 29(4):402–418.

Xie Lixing, Zhou Ming, and Sun Maosong. 2012. Hierarchical structure based hybrid approach to sentiment analysis of Chinese microblog and its feature extraction. Journal of Chinese Information Processing, 26(1):73–83.

Association for Computational Linguistics
209 N. Eighth Street
Stroudsburg, Pennsylvania 18360

ISBN 978-1-5108-1756-2

CURRAN ASSOCIATES INC.
proceedings.com